THE WESTERN TRADITION

THE
WESTERN
TRADITION

VOLUME TWO

From the Renaissance to the Present

FIFTH EDITION

EUGEN WEBER

University of California, Los Angeles

D. C. Heath and Company
Lexington, Massachusetts   Toronto

Address editorial correspondence to:
D. C. Heath and Company
125 Spring Street
Lexington, MA 02173

Acquisitions Editor: James Miller
Developmental Editor: Pat Wakeley
Production Editor: Rachel D'Angelo Wimberly
Designer: Henry Rachlin
Photo Researcher: Linda Finigan
Production Coordinator: Richard Tonachel
Permissions Editor: Margaret Roll

PREFACE

My father, who died not long ago, was born in 1893: four years before Queen Victoria's Diamond Jubilee, which everybody at the time recognized as the climax to a glorious age; and four years after the birth of Hitler, who was going to provide another climax, much less glorious, to *his* age.

The world into which my father came was much larger than the world we know today. There has always been only one real way of judging distance: how long it takes to get from one place to another. Measured by that standard, the Moscow of my father's day was nearly a week from London, Australia was two or three months away from Europe, South Africa about six weeks from Europe. If you wanted to communicate with someone abroad, you wrote a letter and waited for the answer, which would come in three months from Africa, in six months from the South Pacific.

The four inventions that have done the most to make the world smaller—the airplane, the telephone, the television, and the computer—were developed after my father was born. He was ten when the Wright brothers first flew at Kitty Hawk; when he learned to fly in 1917, during the First World War, "aeroplanes" were only fourteen years old. The telephone had been around since the 1870s, but my father never lived in a house with a telephone until he was thirty years old. Broadcasting began in the 1920s, but he was past thirty when he acquired a radio set.

It is not just that my father's world seemed broader and distant places less accessible, mobility was severely limited. In my father's youth, British law required every automobile on the road to be preceded by a man with a red flag. My father never saw a car during his childhood. There were horse-drawn vehicles, of course, and oxcarts, and trains had been around since his father's time. But the fastest self-propelled machine was the bicycle; and traveling any distance was arduous, expensive, and exceptional. That may be why, when people went abroad, they did not need a passport: just the fare, a purse with whatever coins it held, and a visiting card (if they had one) to identify themselves. Before the First World War my father roamed all over Europe, from Paris to Constantinople, without a passport. The kind of passports we know now, complete with photographs, were introduced only after the First World War. They struck him as a demeaning novelty.

Novelties, both cheering and distressing, were the hallmark of the modern age. The world has always changed, it is always in transition: every age is an age of transition. But the sort of changes that alter the way men and women actually live and think— making fire, forging metals, printing, improving guns—are few and far between. From the later 1700s more of these radical changes appear, in the 1800s they come thick and fast, and in the 1900s they become the norm. The world alters its rhythm; the rate of change accelerates. Two-thirds of this volume is dedicated to this extraordinary epoch.

The Renaissance revived Protagoras's image, coined in the fifth century B.C. of man (and, in due course, woman) as the measure of all things. The question, as Disraeli quipped, was whether man was ape or angel. Many visionaries, in many centuries,

sought to turn brutes into virtuous, productive, law-abiding citizens. The results were uneven at best. The firmer the establishment of law and order, the sharper the outcry against their trammels; the greater the successes of free enterprise, the more plausible the pleas that the freedom of some restricted that of others. The more striking the technological triumphs, the more appalling the technological holocausts; the higher the productivity of capital and industry, the greater the revulsion against the exploitation of those who actually produced the goods and the keener the consciousness of injustices hitherto taken for granted.

All these and more find a place in the following pages, along with a host of recipes to improve the world: despotism and democracy, liberalism and socialism, science and sentiment, revolution and reform, fascism and communism. Even the best intentioned were responsible for blood and suffering; even the most destructive played a part in the advances of the West. The values and institutions that generation after generation have sought to share with other parts of Europe and the world—national sovereignty, parliamentary government, public education, manhood suffrage (women's suffrage came much later), equal rights and laws for all—were formulated in the seventeenth and eighteenth centuries, then gradually established around the Atlantic rim and beyond into the nineteenth century. The Western tradition has proved imperialistic, coercive, constricting; and sometimes it has changed the world for the better.

Perhaps "enlightened" reforms are not essential. The human race has managed without parliamentary government, or suffrage, or literacy, for an awfully long time; it has done without full employment, social security, or universal health care for even longer. These values represent the aspirations of our modern age. And it is worth finding out by what steps the West moved out of the oxcart era into the era of space travel, out of autocracy into bureaucracy, out of the despotism of unenlightened kings and enlightened despots into the despotism of more sinister rulers.

Curiously, while this went on, we have managed to realize many of the dreams dismissed as utopian in the day of my father: dreams of societies with less iniquity, less violence, less misery. And, just as curiously, it is the realization of our forefather's dreams that presents us with some of the most serious problems that we face today: better diet and medical care create overpopulation, democracy imposes conformity, exuberant consumption results in ecological deterioration, technological wonders spawn threats of annihilation. Nothing fails like success.

This is the second volume of a collection meant to illustrate major aspects of the past that helped to make our present: *The Western Tradition*. The first volume began by reviewing the roots of western tradition in the ancient world of the Mediterranean and the Middle East, and ended with Louis XIV in the age of absolute monarchies. This volume carries the tale up to the present day. To make the story more complete and to offer more flexibility for a variety of courses, Volume Two begins with the Renaissance. State systems and rivalries that have marked the West since the eighteenth century, as well as major political and philosophical issues that have fueled debate and strife for the past three hundred years, were formed and formulated in the age of the Renaissance and the Reformation, or during its seventeenth-century aftermath. Documents concerning those eventful times are relevant to our own age. Their inclusion here allows the reader to glance back at the modern world in the making.

The mass of this volume, however, illuminates the eighteenth century Enlightenment and the two centuries since then. It was in the 1700s, and ever more in the 1800s, that people and events began to crowd each other, that the tempo of life, information, and exchange became more urgent, that students of history find themselves in times and places with a familiar ring. After 1800, despite crinolines and stove-pipe hats, Western peoples' language, gestures, attitudes, and concerns become more recognizable—even more comprehensible. The journey on which *The Western Tradition* embarked on the shores of the Nile and Euphrates and which in this volume begins in Florence and Rome, now draws close to home. The documents reflect this. They are increasingly about revolution, whether in political structures, society, productivity, or ways of life; and about new kinds of claims and problems: social, racial, feminist. Problems of education, emancipation, overpopulation, bring us to the present day—or to what is the present day as I write these lines, but this too will soon recede into the past, eventually to be forgotten or taught as history.

The passages gathered in this second volume reflect the attitudes, ideas, or circumstances of the times that produced them. The choices have not been easy, because each period is a muddle of different attitudes, tendencies, problems, people. The best one can do is to select documents that will throw light on the most typical or significant circumstances of an age. Any selection must be somewhat arbitrary, likely to slant in the direction of the editor's interests. I can only hope that the following passages will put a little flesh on the bare bones of textbooks and give some body to those ghostly figures that flit through the pages of history books.

The Western Tradition generally finds its greatest use in introductory history courses as material for discussions to complement the lectures, and as a source for some of the works or documents to which the courses refer. It includes most of the classic texts that instructors might wish to use. These and other passages lend themselves to discussion, argument, and various interpretations. In this connection, I have avoided the copious introductions that, in some books, tend to furnish many ideas that discussion should elicit and elucidate. My introductions *try* to be fairly noncommittal. Great classic texts and traditional documents are interspersed with more deliberately illustrative material that throws an intimate light on the life and problems of a given time and place without necessarily lending itself to discussion. Thus, in assignments, the teacher can pick and choose among passages that are illustrative or controversial. I rather hope that passages not assigned may also catch the eye of the curious or browsing reader and lead to further exploration.

This fifth edition, while preserving the basic structure of earlier editions with selections from each era organized under dominant themes, differs from its predecessors in three significant ways. First, material by and about women has been integrated throughout the text, rather than grouped in a single section as before. New selections such as the "Declaration of the Rights of Women" and John Stuart Mill's views on the subjection of women have been added. Second, visual illustrations appear for the first time in this edition. Photo essays explore such topics as the disciplining of violence, the rebirth of urban life during the Renaissance, the new domestic intimacy, and modern technology. The revision has been lightened somewhat by cuts in earlier material and, I hope, enriched by the large number of illustrations and new texts ranging from

Malthus, Adam Smith, and Robespierre to Camille Paglia and Marshall McLuhan. Bringing a collection of readings up to date raises the question, What has been going on around us that really is important? Wise historians let time provide an answer. They need only bet on horses that have already won. Live issues, races still being run, pose a problem. My answer, in the third significant change from previous editions, lies in a complete revision of the last part of Volume Two. A new group of selections depicts personal reactions to the slaughter of World War I. Additionally, the last half century is represented more extensively by four entirely new sections: the Cold War and its collapse, overpopulation, education, and political correctness.

There is always some risk in collections of readings: their removal from context, their accumulation in a grab bag difficult to explore, the implication that complex activities and intricate concepts can be made simple. Nevertheless, as we trace the self-destructive progress of civilization, the passages in this volume reflect both their makers and their times. They are the bricks and straw that have built the world we live in.

E. W.

CONTENTS

Political and Economic Changes   94

The Seventeenth Century   133

Economic Revolution   348

But Life Goes On   382

Liberalism, Nationalism, and 1848   389

Crime   734

Epilogue   750

DOING HISTORY

A statesman once said that, if you have a taste for fiction, you might as well read history. Maybe he did not mean it: some statesmen have a sense of humor. But François Guizot had been a professor of history before he started to run France, which he did during the eight years before the Revolution of 1848. He knew that evidence could be interpreted, manipulated, ignored or falsified; that documents can be forged, manufactured, or made to disappear; that historians depend on evidence, and evidence is as debatable and uncertain when drawn from archives or from memory as it can be in a court of law. Even with the best will in the world, we mainly see what we want to see (I'm counting trees, I'm not interested in cattle), or see it as expected (torrents and mountain crags, picturesque to the nineteenth century eye, are horrid nuisances to the seventeenth century observer). We notice what our preconceptions or our imaginations permit us to notice. How many accounts of battle describe the footsoldiers? How many faceless servants stood around bed- or thronerooms where momentous doings took place? How many women has history left mute? The stories that history tells, even the best history, are only part of the story. The light that documents shed leaves a great deal in the shadows.

Nor is there only one way, one proper way, to read history. Stendhal, the great French novelist, once suggested that the relationship between books and readers is like that between the bow and the violin it plays. The book is the bow; the violin that makes the sounds is the reader's spirit or, if you prefer, the reader's personality. With certain reservations the same may be said about history and historical documents; and the most important of these reservations is bound to be the fact that while readers of a novel can make out pretty well with a bit of native intelligence and some imagination, readers of history, like the violinist, do better if they know how to wield the bow and read the notes. But even for those who come to it without preparation, without particular knowledge, with nothing but curiosity, history can offer both pleasure and form. True, it is we who endow it with the latter. Order and coherence are artificial creations of the human mind; we introduce them to make complicated subjects easier to grasp, easier to understand. If we really want more we must go beyond this into the realm of a reality which is never simple and try to perceive the underlying complexity of the whole. So, perhaps it is not history that suggests a pattern or form but we who endow it with one or with many. When we speak of pleasure, however, the issue is simpler. Though history has its uses, these are less important and more controversial than its pleasures. And these last, however intellectually valid they might be, rely in the final analysis on the fundamental nature of history, which is a vast, many-sided, sometimes passionate, often commonplace, diverse, monotonous, exciting, depressing, exhilarating, terrifying, inspiring, disillusioning, unending story.

From this follows the commonplace, but perhaps still necessary, reminder that while history as it happens is only partly connected with us, history as we write it—that is, the tale and interpretation of these happenings—is altogether of our making.

The study of history may be, indeed should be, as scientific and scrupulous as possible; its telling can never be more than a work of art and the fact that it is so often botched means only that we are clumsy. The study of history is, of course, discovery. It is also a matter of selection and interpretation for which facts, whatever they might be, are only the raw material. Above all, perhaps, it is part of our constant struggle to understand ourselves and what makes us tick. We are products, we are part, of our place, time, and class, all of which are themselves determined, affected—*committed,* so to speak—by previous and contemporary developments which they cannot escape any more than we can. If "know thyself" has any meaning, then history is analysis on a very vast scale.

In one sense the documents that follow are evidence in the case of a Western Tradition and how it developed. In another sense this evidence has been rigged—rigged by the editor's selection, of course; but, besides, by our natural inclination, when looking over the past, to pick only horses that have won and to read a pattern into what was in its own time unpredictable confusion. The events of a time very often seem chaotic at the time. Later they seem clear enough; their general lines appear evident and so do the principles of their development. And this may be because we, as it were, *invent* them and invest them with coherence. But it may be, too, because there really is such a thing as a general trend, a dominant tendency or climate of opinion at any one time, and that this only becomes apparent in the perspective lent by distance. Still, invented or perceived, history remains an artifact, the work of our minds and imaginations.

The best of history brings men and women to life. But in real life, as things happen and we live history in the making, our minds find it hard to imagine the historical context. Whatever they may think, few know where they are going or (death apart) where their particular circumstances lead. They do not know that the war to which they march will last a hundred years, or thirty, or seven days; that the barricade they build will help topple an empire; that the marriage they plan will start a dynasty—or end it. This should warn us to remember the unselfconscious character of so many historical developments, the remarkably unplanned, irrational fashion of human developments, the tremendous possibilities of alternative happenings, of things turning out differently. Naturally, we cannot stop again and again to consider what might have happened if Napoleon had failed to win the battle of Austerlitz, or if Luther had been burnt like Hus or allowed to die ineffectively like Wycliffe; our history is necessarily determined because it is the story of what has been, not of what might have been. And because the material with which we deal is so vast, we select what we know now are the significant development, the ones with a future, the acts and the writings that are on the winning side, and we put them end to end to show just how coherently everything happened, that it was simply bound to happen, to create the world and the society we know, to shape countries like France or Spain within practically foreordained borders, or illustrate the Manifest Destiny that turned much of a continent into the United States.

It is because such thoughts are so tempting that it is healthy to remember that nothing, so far as we know, was foreordained; that peoples, countries, and ideas fumbled for a long, long time against a background of reality that pointed to nowhere in particular, or perhaps in the wrong direction as seen from today. In the fifteenth century the princess Catherine of Castile might have married the heir to the throne of Portugal instead of Ferdinand of Aragon, and the destinies of Spain, perhaps the destinies of the world, might have been different. And it is possible to argue in the same vein that for a long time the union of England, Scotland, Wales, and Ireland in one kingdom seemed no more natural and necessary than the union of Denmark, Iceland, Norway, and England in one kingdom under King Knut—or Canute.

Thus, we ought to have some constant reminders of the unreality of deterministic history, in the same way as certain monastic Orders have constantly under their eyes the reminder that death lies at the end of life and to this purpose paint the words *Memento Mori*—Remember Death—on the walls of their refectories and on the doors of their cells. We ought to remember the infinite possibilities of what looks like sheer chance, or luck; and the fact that the patterns we see in history are conventions, artificially inserted like coat hangers, in what is really a shapeless garment—an otherwise shapeless mass of events. Such awareness is particularly important because we are forced to use these conventions—indeed, by the selective presentation of facts which we in particular consider significant, we have to *create* patterns in order to see our way through history at all. So there is nothing wrong with selective history, with deterministic history, with patterns of history like those that Toynbee, or Pirenne, or Marx, or the eschatology of Christian belief can present to us. They are, as a matter of fact, inescapable and necessary, and useful too, provided we remember that each offers one presentation of one aspect of a vaster truth which no one yet has managed to encompass and which it seems beyond the powers of a human being even to conceive.

Another thing worth bearing in mind is that documents of another age speak a language of their own, which may be understood at the price of great scholarship and self-exertion but which at the very least demands from us an effort of sympathy and imagination. A document, of course, does not have to be written on paper or parchment to serve the historian: a gravestone, a shield, a golden necklace, or a cathedral is as much a document as a twelfth-century charter or the text of the Treaty of Versailles. Each is the product of attitudes and preconceptions peculiar to its time; each can provide—not only in itself but through its position in place and time—information precious to the historian. But though, to take one example, we can gape at a Gothic cathedral, marvel at the strength of the sculpture or the embroidery of its ornament, enjoy or admire it, the cathedral no more speaks our language than a dogmatic Hindu does. It belongs to another world, with different conventions and different beliefs; the feelings it inspires in us are not necessarily, or even probably, the feelings it inspired in those who built it or worshiped in it at the time when it dominated the life as well as the architecture of its city. The cathedral and ourselves, today, carry on two monologues, what the French call a *dialogue de sourds* (dialog of the deaf); and however brilliant the interlocutors may be, there is nothing they can do about this unless one crosses into the opposite camp and learns, indeed accepts, the language of the other.

The same thing is true about written documents. Like the artifacts we survey, the poets, the philosophers, and the politicians whose writings we may study speak to a world that is not our world, that is very far from us, and very difficult to imagine, let alone comprehend. The kinds of motives they appeal to, the kinds of values they refer to, are at times so strange that they can become irritating or incomprehensible. The *Song of Roland* or the political philosophy of Bossuet are only two instances in which our acceptance of the values and the motives of an age, the cause-and-effect relationships which these people took for granted, may prove grudging and ill-natured.

And it is no good saying that a particular pattern of culture is that of a minority. Or, rather, it is important to know this, but also to know what it implies. Culture, after all, like all social influence, like political power in all ages, like belief, is the creation and often the preserve of a minority. Modern sociologists like to emphasize the obvious fact that the mass of people tends to follow and imitate certain "cultural" or "fashionable" leaders, whether individuals or groups. But one might say further that the character and climate of a society are set by the significant few, whether these are followed or not by the insignificant many. There is, after all, no need to actually share in the highest achievements of a form of art or thought in order to feel its influence. We can enjoy the works of Michelangelo or Beethoven even if we cannot perhaps soar as high as they, even if we cannot fully understand the conception behind them. More than that, the work of the men who pitched cathedral spires up into the skies just as much as that of those who split the atom can be treated as a reflection—symbol or caricature—of certain important tendencies, moods, characteristics of a period, facets of it in which all people of that time must share even though they may be far from understanding, or appreciating, these works—sometimes even from knowing them. Many of the documents in this volume represent the ideas and the doings of a single figure or a very few; such activities probably did not touch the great majority of people and perhaps still do not today. And yet quantitatively feeble, statistically unimpressive, they cast their influence like a great shadow far, far from the solid mass.

Too little, also, has been said about the extremely important fact that a work of the mind is naturally allusive. Even if the author wants to give a complete account of the subject, it is never possible to tell absolutely everything. We always know more than we tell; we take certain things for granted as we assume that our readers will know them already. To people of the same period, to the members of the same society, there is no need to write everything. They share certain key ideas, you might say key words, which automatically evoke other ideas, emotions, reactions, if they are used to the right audience. Ali Baba found this out when his magic "Open sesame!" proved useless except in a given circumstance, in front of the particular cave where it got results. In the same way, an appeal to Christianity, Democracy, National Feeling, Class, or Race would be effective only upon minds and societies familiar with these concepts and ready to react to them. Thus every work of the mind carries within itself the image of the public for which it is meant. This is what makes it a historical document for us, but it is also what demands the effort of understanding needed to consider it in its proper context.

The use of documents, like the use of statistics, is full of hazards. The greatest of these is that words or phrases, when taken out of context, can convey almost anything you want, but not necessarily the meaning or intentions of their authors. Take Henry Ford's oft-quoted statement: "History is bunk." Did Ford really say that? A small effort reveals that what he really said was, "History is more or less bunk," which trips less lightly off the tongue but amounts to the same thing. Yet there is more to it. What

Ford actually said in an interview with the *Chicago Tribune* in 1916 was: "History is more or less bunk. It is tradition. We want to live in the present, and the only history that's worth a tinker's dam is the history we make today. That's the trouble with the world. We're living in books and history and tradition. We want to get away from that and take care of today. We've done too much looking back. What we want to do, and do it quick, is to make *just* history, right now. The men who are responsible for the present war in Europe knew all about history. Yet they brought on the worst war in the world's history."

That is more specific. Ford says that reference to the past can keep us from grappling with the present. He appeals from a past filled with injustice to a present that creates a greater justice; in other words, he rejects the politics of 1916. He asks, in effect, "What use is traditional history, if it does not help us avoid past traps?" He suggests that too many people who read history may learn from the mistakes of the past—but only how to make new mistakes. History, says Ford, does not keep people from doing terrible things, from doing the same terrible things all over again. Look, he says, at the present war in Europe: the men who brought it on knew all about history. . . .

Here, then, is the context. We are in 1916, and Europe welters in war. Ford is a pacifist, and he dismisses arguments that American interventionists drew from history to suggest that war was unavoidable, and that the United States, still at peace, must arm and prepare for war. "Do not repeat the mistakes of past history," he says. Make *just* history, here and now.

So, not all history is bunk for Ford, only the kind of history he did not like. As a matter of fact, the great entrepreneur was very interested in studying the past, but he felt strongly that battles and wars, the comings and goings of kings, court intrigues, and diplomatic negotiations, represented only a partial record of human events, and a biased one. He even offered a large prize for a history of war that would not glorify it, that would show war in all its horror, that would discourage war by showing how great the lives of men and women can be in times of peace. Talking about history to a friend, he said: "When I went to our American history books to learn how our forefathers harrowed the land, I discovered that historians knew nothing about harrows. Yet our country had depended more on harrows than on guns and speeches. I thought that a history which excludes harrows, and all the rest of daily life, was bunk." Harrows are large rakes that break up the soil, pull up weeds, and cover up seeds that have been sown. Maybe Ford felt strongly about harrows because he manufactured them, but his views make sense. It doesn't seem that he underrated the force of history, but he wanted it to teach the lessons that he wanted taught. We may agree or disagree with his point of view, or even with the propaganda value that he attributed to historical writing. The point is that a full quotation and its context are crucial before we make up our minds.

Time is part of context. Dates may be sterile in themselves, but it is significant that Ford was speaking in 1916, that Caesar lived before Augustus, Charlemagne before Columbus, Marx after Adam Smith.

Context may be a text, like Ford's interview, or it may be a situation. If someone breaks into your house to steal, that is a burglary. If someone breaks into your house to put out a fire, it is a heroic act. Putting people in the stocks or branding them seem cruel and unusual punishments today. They might have seemed less so when the alternative was the gallows, because there were few prisons, scant taxes to build prisons, and primitive machinery to collect taxes.

Rejecting the past is as pointless as rejecting the weather. History is not bunk. Most of us want to know who our parents were, where we came from, what made us what we are, what made the world around us. But it is not pointless to reject a certain way of looking at the past, a certain kind of history, because you think a different perspective is more worthwhile. Although the history of kings and queens and battles may make sense for ages when kings, queens, and battles mattered more and left more records than did ordinary people, the sort of history that Ford wanted is pretty much the history that we do today.

The story outlined in these pages is manifold and, of course, unfinished as history itself. It does, however, possess a certain internal coherence, for it reflects the gradual progress of Western folk to greater self-consciousness and self-control, their repeated attempts to master not only themselves but the world around them—aims in the pursuit of which they were never more than partially successful. The forty centuries on which we touch in these two volumes led our forebears through a wide gamut of experience and experimentation. Several times—as in Egypt, Greece, or Rome—they achieved types of civilization that seemed supremely satisfactory, and several times these collapsed or were destroyed, though leaving behind them a fund of techniques and thought and values that were eventually incorporated into subsequent societies in the way in which the stones and the statues of ancient Rome were incorporated into the buildings of the Renaissance.

The latest of these cultural structures began to rise after the disintegration of the Roman Empire in the West, and upon its ruins. The notion of a middle age seems to be the invention of certain fifteenth-century humanists who felt that only two historical periods really counted: the long-lost golden age of classical antiquity and their own, modern, Renaissance. The intervening period, across which these people saw themselves continuing a great tradition, was dark and useless, a time of chaos and terror better forgotten now that it was past and deserving no name, unless to describe its character—dark or Gothic (i.e., barbarous)—or its position in the middle. Yet, neither the bubbling buoyancy of the humanists nor their intellectual snobbery would have been possible without the foundations—economic, political, and scholarly—laid by their predecessors' long struggle against chaos and unreason—enemies of man and of civilization as much in their spirit as in the world around them. Hence, much of this book concerns the slow and self-conscious efforts of Europeans, like fallen angels, trying to recover the heights of order, knowledge, and sophistication upon which humans were thought to have stood in Augustan days. By the time of Louis XIV many believed that this had been achieved, that the ground lost during the "dark ages" had been regained, and that the Great Century, the seventeenth, had reached a cultural level no whit inferior to that of the ancients. It had been a long haul, but modern man had made it: the latest times had nothing to envy the past.

While Louis XIV and many of his contemporaries viewed history—and particularly modern history—as a long campaign to recapture lost and ancient glories, we can see that it was much more than that. On our trek, back to past heights as a humanist might have it, forward to new heights as others were soon to claim, we had picked up, invented, developed many things the ancients had not known. The court of Louis XIV was not the court of Titus or Trajan, still less that of Darius or Alexander. For one thing, it was Christian. For another, it rested on a social and economic structure the ancients had not known. And then, quite simply, it was not the court of an ancient prince because such princes and such courts had had their day and existed no more except in tales. It was different because it came later, because the intervening times had taught and untaught a great deal, had discovered vast unsuspected realms and changed the face of Europe and also of the world. In other words, whatever they thought, these people had not come back to a coveted golden-age starting point, but had gone on to something which, better or worse, was altogether different. Though Louis the Great might look backward to Cyrus and Apollo, his regime pointed forward to the enlightened Despot and the modern state.

Yet what seemed to matter at the time were the new confidence and the slowly dawning feeling in some quarters that, now that they had made up the lost ground, nothing would stop Westerners from going forward. Here was the feeling that foreshadowed the great hopes of the eighteenth century:

> Go, wondrous creature! mount where science guides!
> Go, measure earth, weigh air, and state the tides;
> Instruct the planets in what orbs to run,
> Correct old Time and regulate the sun!

And behind it, ever present, was man himself, Homer's *Odysseus* or Swift's *Gulliver*, sly, enterprising, conceited, too clever by half and sometimes twice as foolhardy, taunting the Cyclops and sometimes the gods; feeling their wrath and surviving. Men and women, hoisting themselves on the shoulders of their fellows and too often at their expense, towards greater wisdom though never enough, towards higher goals, though never attained.

First the eighteenth century, then the nineteenth, mark the high point of this optimism and the beginning of its decline. The nineteenth century opens with the echoes of 1789 still ringing in people's ears. To some they sound ominous; to others they carry promises of a better future. The twentieth century justifies both views, though terror and trepidation overshadow triumph. It closes with the hopes of 1989 betrayed in a welter of political feud and economic chaos, Eastern Europe a slough of despond, Western Europe a minefield of resentments.

The latest moods and ideas always take time to percolate before they seriously affect public opinion. Long after scientists and scholars had begun to change their minds, ordinary men and women continued to believe that progress was inevitable—a law of nature and of history no less apparent in the long run than that of gravity. Thus the discovery that evil is part of the world order, that we could not, apparently, by the mere use of our reason and will, build the good life uncorrupted—came as a shock to many in the twentieth century.

Once upon a time evil had seemed an integral part of creation. Though they feared and, at least theoretically, abhorred it, people took it into account. But the eighteenth and still more the nineteenth century had exorcised the Devil together, only too often, with God and encouraged the belief that in time evil and corruption could and would be eradicated from the world and from human nature. More and more things could be explained, adjusted, and improved. Utopia grew less utopian and more like the pattern of the better life that awaited us or our near descendants—the forward projection of improvements already implicit in present techniques and present thought. And yet it was seen that, as the twentieth century advanced, human reason seemed unable to prevent wars and revolutions, while improved techniques served to make such conflicts vaster and bloodier than ever. Nor was the new order that followed upon them, at least in the eyes of many, an improvement on the old.

Even apparent successes were fraught with disillusion. One after another the panaceas from which so much had been expected in the past were tried or mistried, and found wanting: education and democracy, freedom of thought and of the press, parliamentary government, national self-determination, socialism and communism. All had been tried, and none had worked the miracles expected of them. Perhaps our ancestors had been mistaken in trusting to any formula to find perfection. At any rate, folk felt increasingly nonplussed, disillusioned, disoriented. They had proved themselves capable of harnessing wind and water but not their own passions, and now they realized with horror not only that their improved techniques enabled them to inflict suffering and destruction upon themselves greater than ever before, but also that they lacked the standards or firm beliefs which might show how and to what purpose these vast and new-found powers should be used. They could not, indeed, decide whether tolerant indifference should be preferred to harsh, exclusive dogmas, or whether firm standards were better than none at all.

Most people, of course, live as they have always lived: from day to day, accepting without particular comment or examination whatever ideas happen to be entertained around them. Some can settle for this lowest common denominator and some cannot. They must investigate, question, criticize and, perhaps, hope. Between echoes of the past and echoes of the future, a future which is really the shadow which the present casts before it, the men and women of these centuries have lived and still live in very interesting times. But the Chinese have a saying that it were better if one's enemies alone lived in interesting times; for interesting times have a way of being uncomfortable times.

Few, of course, appreciate that they live in interesting times, though few in any age ignore their discomforts. Most people in all ages have lived lives that were insecure, troubled, often scary. Many of the documents in this collection bear evidence of that. Putting our own discomforts in historical perspective brings little consolation. But it may provide enlightenment, and that would be some help.

The Making of
the Modern World

Fresh Fields and Pastures New
Reformation and Counter Reformation
Political and Economic Changes
The Seventeenth Century
The Political Debate

THERE HAS BEEN A GREAT DEAL OF DEBATE ABOUT THE period to which the term *Renaissance* may legitimately be applied. Eminent historians have pressed the claims of the twelfth century; others equally as eminent put forward those of the seventeenth. The case for each is strong; decision is difficult. A compromise between the two would bring us back to the period favored by most, that is, to the fifteenth century. One point in favor of such an old-fashioned view is that the people of the fifteenth century thought of themselves as living through a renaissance, a time of renewal that they contrasted with the dark and "gothic" barbarism of the past. They might well have written, as did Shelley, that

> The world's great age begins anew,
> The golden years return,
> The earth doth like a snake renew
> Her winter weeds outworn:
> Heaven smiles, and faiths and empires gleam
> Like wrecks of a dissolving dream.

Certainly much that was new or, at least, refurbished, appeared during this busy, bubbling period when in retrospect Heaven does seem to have smiled briefly upon Europe, even if the smile was only wryly ironical.

Fresh Fields and Pastures New

THE documents that follow originated in the confused and busy period we like to call the Renaissance. No period has only one aspect or mood, but in the long run every period can be defined in terms of its dominant or most historically significant trends. Thus we can see these years as a time of questioning and reaffirmation, a rediscovery of forms and values that had been submerged since the barbarian invasions, a sense of emerging from the dark "gothic" ages into the sunlight of a new world—broadened by new discoveries, enriched by new enterprises, invested with a new significance. We may or may not agree, but to many intellectuals of the time—and to many nonintellectuals, too—this seemed a better world to live in, a forward-looking world in which human society, which had already accomplished so much, might be expected to accomplish yet more.

The New Man

Giovanni Pico della Mirandola (1463–1494) distinguished himself during his brief career by the precocity of his learning and the boldness of his ideas in philosophy and theology. His motto, De omni re scibili ("Of all things that one can know"), asserted that he knew all there was to be known. Though a doubt is permissible on that score, the claim itself seems to reflect a characteristic attitude of his time in which the borders between confidence and foolhardiness were very ill defined.

Pico della Mirandola: from Oration on the Dignity of Man

In the writings of the Arabs I have read, oh reverend Fathers [of the Church], that when someone asked the Saracen Abdalah what seemed to him the most wonderful thing in this theater of the world, he replied that nothing seemed more wonderful than man. The opinion of Mercury agrees with this: "What a miracle, oh Asclepius, is man!" As I was pondering the meaning of these words, the opinions which many had advanced about the greatness of human nature did not satisfy me—that man is the mediator of all creatures, the servant of superior beings, the lord of inferior ones, that he is the interpreter of nature by the keenness of his senses, by rational inquiry, by the light of his intellect; the intermediary between time and eternity, and, as the Persians say,

From Pico della Mirandola, *Oration on the Dignity of Man* (1486), tr. from the original by Donald Weinstein; reprinted by courtesy of the translator.

the nexus of the world, its very wedding song; according to David a little lower than the angels. These are great reasons, to be sure, but they are not the most important. It is not those which give man the privilege of unlimited admiration to men. Indeed, why not, therefore admire the angels and the blessed heavenly choirs even more?

But at last it seems that I have understood why man is the most fortunate of creatures and therefore worthy of all admiration, and what is the position which has been granted him in the universal order, so that not only the beasts but even the stars and the other worldly intelligences envy him. Incredible and marvelous! And why not, if it is indeed for that that he is considered to be a great miracle and a wonderful creature? But what this position is, listen, oh Fathers, if you please, to my discourse and grant it a favorable hearing.

The most high Father, God the Creator, had wrought this worldly home which we see, this august temple of divinity, according to the laws of his secret wisdom. He furnished the supercelestial region with intelligences, the celestial sphere he provided with eternal souls, the filthy and disgusting parts of the lower world he populated with a great assortment of creatures of every species. But, when the work was finished, the Creator wanted some one to reflect upon the reason behind such a great creation, who might love its beauty and marvel over its grandeur. And therefore, when everything was finished, as Moses and Timaeus attest, he thought at last of creating man. However, there was not one model left by which he might fashion a new offspring; there was nothing left in the treasury with which he could endow this new son. There was no station in all the world where this contemplator of the universe could sit. All were full; everything had been distributed to the highest, the middle and the lowest orders. But it was not fitting of the paternal power to have been worn out in the last act of creation. It was not worthy of his wisdom to have been left perplexed over an important problem. Nor was it fitting to his provident love that the creature who was to have praised his divine liberality to others was compelled to complain of the lack of it to himself. At last that excellent creator decided that he to whom he was to give nothing for his own could share everything which had been given individually to the others. Thus he took man as the product of an undetermined nature and placed him in the middle of the world and said to him: "I have not given you, oh Adam, a definite seat or a special appearance, or any function of your own. The seat or the appearance or the function which you want, you may have and keep by your own desire and your own counsel.

"The other creatures have a defined nature which is fixed within limits prescribed by me. You, unhampered, may determine your own limits according to your own will, into whose power I have placed you. I have set you in the center of the world; from there you can better see whatever is in the world. I have made you neither heavenly nor terrestrial, neither mortal nor immortal, in order that, like a free and sovereign artificer, you can fashion your own form out of your own substance. You can degenerate to the lower orders of the brutes; you can, according to your own will, recreate yourself in those higher creatures which are divine."

Oh supreme generosity of God the Father! Oh supreme and wonderful felicity of man, to whom it is granted to have what he desires, to be what he wishes! The brutes receive all that they have from their mother's womb when they are born, as Lucullus says. The supreme spirits become either immediately or soon afterward that which they were destined to be for all eternity. At the time of man's birth the Father plants every kind of seed and the germs of every kind of existence; and the ones which each man cultivates are the ones which will grow, and they will bear their fruit in him. If they are vegetative, he will be a plant; if animal, he will be a brute; if they are rational, he will become a celestial creature; if intellectual, he will be an angel and the son of God. But if, not content with the lot of any kind of creature, he draws into the center of his own unity, his spirit will become one with God. In the solitary darkness of the Father he who has been set above all things will stand above all things. Who will not admire our chameleon? Or rather, who will admire anything more? Of him Asclepius the Athenian said, with justice, that, in religious rites, because of his versatility and his changeable nature, he symbolized Proteus. Hence those famous metamorphoses among the Hebrews and the Pythagoreans. In fact, the esoteric theology of the Jews at one moment transforms St. Enoch into an angel of divinity. Then, others into other divine spirits. The Pythagoreans changed wicked men into beasts and (if Empedocles is to be believed) even into plants. In imitation of that Mahomet frequently repeated, and rightly, that he who retreated from the sacred law became a brute. For it is not the bark which makes the tree but the stupid and insensitive nature; not the hide which makes the mule but the brutish and sensual soul. It is not separation from the body that makes an angel, but spiritual intelligence. If you see someone who is a slave of his stomach, crawling on the ground, it is a plant that you see, not a man. If you see someone blinded like Callypso by vain illusions of fantasy and emprisoned by dark allurements, the slave of his senses, he is a brute, not a man. If he is a philosopher who looks at everything with reason, you will revere him: he is a heavenly creature, not an earthbound one. If he is a pure contemplative, unaware of his body, given over to mental perceptions, he is not an earthly nor a celestial creature, he is a more exalted spirit, surrounded by human flesh. And who would not admire the man who in the Old and New Testament is called, and rightly, first with the name of all flesh, then with the name of every creature, because he shapes, creates, and transforms himself into the appearance of every kind of flesh and into the nature of every kind of creature. So the Persian, Evantes writes, where he explains Chaldaean theology, that man does not have any image of his very own but many exterior and foreign ones. Hence the saying of the Chaldeans that man is an animal of varying nature, multiform and inconstant. What of all this? It is that we may understand that from the time that we are born in this condition we are what we wish to be. We should take care that it be not said of us that, being honored, we did not realize we have become similar to brutes and foolish jackasses. Let rather the words of Asaph be repeated: "You are Gods, and you are all children of heaven," lest, abusing the indulgent generosity of the Father, we render harmful rather than salutary that choice liberty which he has given us. Let a sacred ambition enter our souls so that we do not satisfy ourselves with mediocre things, but aspire to the highest things, and strive with all our strength to reach them. From the moment that we wish it, we can. Let us despise earthly objects, let us disdain celestial ones, and leaving aside whatever is worldly, let us soar to that supramundane court which is close to the most high divinity. There, according to the sacred mysteries, the Seraphim, Cherubim, and Thrones have the primacy. Unable to give up, and impatient of second place, let us emulate their dignity and glory and, if we desire it, we shall be in no way inferior to them.

The New Woman?

"The whole world was made for man; but the twelfth part of man for woman; man is the whole world, and the breath of God; woman the rib and cooked piece of man." Thus wrote Sir Thomas Browne, an English physician, in Religio Medici, *a book published in 1642. There he expounded his attitudes as a Christian and a doctor toward God, church, and life in general.*

Most male authors (who produced the mass of documents in those days) diminished women's character or denied that women had any character at all. Almost all agreed that women are foolish, neglecting to add, as George Eliot (Mary Ann Cross) did in Adam Bede *(1859), that "God Almighty made 'em to match the men." Except in gentle, maternal, or loving roles, positive female figures continued to be rare; when they did appear, they were classed as manly: viragos. One exception to this rule was provided by a Renaissance Italian woman writing in late medieval Paris. Christine de Pisan's (1364–1430) father was physician and astrologer to the king of France, Charles V, whose biography Christine would later write. Widowed at twenty-five, the highly educated Christine became a poet and professional writer to support herself and her three young children. In 1405 she published* The Book of the City of Ladies, *a history of women famous for their heroism, virtue, or wisdom. In it de Pisan intended to vindicate a much-misused sex by chronicling its accomplishments.*

Christine de Pisan: from The Book of the City of Ladies

Book I

Christine, who aspires to knowledge, encounters only contempt for the female sex. Three ladies—Reason, Uprightness, and Justice—appear before her to refute the calumnies of men. Speaking first, Reason advises Christine to take the pick of her intelligence and dig beneath the ruling stereotypes.

VIII. How Christine, with the help of Reason, began to dig underground

Lady Reason explains that some men who blame women do it with good intentions, though good intentions are no excuse for error. Others blame them because of their own vices, others because of the infirmity of their own bodies, others by pure jealousy,

---

From Christine de Pisan, *The Book of the City of Ladies.* Translated by Eugen Weber.

others still because they like to slander. Some, finally, eager to show that they have read a lot, take their stand on what they find in books and simply quote familiar authors, repeating what has been said before.

By those who do it because of their own vices I mean those men who dissipated their youth in debauchery and dedicated themselves to promiscuity. The great number of their adventures has made them rogues. Grown old in sin, they spend their time regretting the transgressions of their youth—the more so since Nature prevents them from slaking their impotent desires. They purge their bile by denigrating women, thinking thus to disgust others from enjoying what they cannot enjoy.

Those motivated by the infirmity of their bodies are cripples with misshapen bodies and crooked limbs. Their minds are malicious and sharp, and they have no other means of vengeance for the misery of their impotence than to blame those [women] who bring gladness to others. . . .

Those who blame women by jealousy are unworthy men who, having known or met many women of greater intelligence or nobler heart than theirs, have conceived bitterness and rancor. . . .

As for those who are scandal-mongers by nature, it is not surprising that they slander women, when they speak ill of everyone. Yet I assure you that every man who takes pleasure in vilifying women has an abject heart, for he acts against Reason and against Nature: against Reason because he is ungrateful and belittles the blessings that women bring him, against Nature because there is no bird or beast that does not naturally seek out its other half, that is to say the female. It is thus unnatural for a reasonable man to do the contrary.

XI. WHERE CHRISTINE ASKS REASON WHY WOMEN ARE EXCLUDED FROM THE JUDICIARY

Lady Reason points out how wrong it would be to assume that women are not sufficiently intelligent to learn the law, experience having clearly shown the contrary.

One has seen many women—they can still be found today—who were great philosophers and who mastered disciplines more difficult and noble than the written laws and statutes of mankind. On the other hand, if anyone affirmed that women have no natural disposition for politics and power, I could name you many famous women who reigned in the past. And so that you may grasp this truth more firmly, let me remind you of some contemporaries who, in widowhood, managed their affairs so well after their husband's death that they provide irrefutable proof that no task is too difficult for an intelligent woman. . . .

There is a multitude of women of high, middling, or humble condition who, if only we bothered to notice, have maintained and maintain their fiefs in widowhood in as good a state as their husbands did, and who are as loved by their subjects as their husbands were, if not more. And whatever men like to think, there is no doubt that such women are numerous. Of course, there are stupid women; but many have more intelligent, livelier and shrewder minds than a lot of men—you know it well. And if their husbands trusted them or had as much sense as they have, that would be to their advantage.

However, if women do not normally judge or pass sentence, that should not vex them, for they thus avoid physical and moral dangers. Though it is necessary to punish the wicked and render justice to all, there are many men who, carrying out such duties, must wish that they were as ignorant as their mothers! . . .

XXVII. WHERE CHRISTINE ASKS REASON WHETHER GOD EVER PERMITTED A WOMAN'S INTELLIGENCE ACCESS TO THE NOBLEST SCIENCES

Is their mind capable of it? I very much want to know the answer, for men affirm that women have only slight intellectual capacity.

She answered: My child, everything I told you shows that this opinion is quite contrary to the truth. . . . I say it again and do not fear contradiction: if little girls were sent to school and methodically taught the sciences as little boys are, they would learn and understand the difficulties of all the arts and sciences as well as boys do. And this is in effect what happens for . . . women having more delicate bodies than men, weaker and less suited to certain tasks, have a keener and a livelier intellect when they take the trouble to use it.

What are you saying, My Lady? I beg you, explain if you please. Certainly men would never accept such an affirmation if it was not presented more clearly, for they would say that it is evident to all that men know more than women.

She answered: Do you know why [women] know less?

No, My Lady, you must tell me.

It is doubtless because they lack experience of many different things for, restricted to housekeeping, they stay home, when nothing is as stimulating for a being endowed with reason as a rich and varied experience. . . . As for their intelligence being slighter because normally they know less than men, think of those who live in isolated parts of the countryside or on high plateaux; you will admit that in many such places the people are so simple that one could take them for animals. Yet Nature has given them all the physical and intellectual gifts that it offers to the wisest and most learned men that one can find in our capitals and towns. For all this [the appearance of ignorance] comes from not learning, which does not exclude the fact that, with women as with men, some are more intelligent than others. . . .

XXXIII–XXXVI.

Where Reason provides examples of women who created new sciences or revealed new knowledge and techniques: Greek letters, the Latin alphabet, numbers, the arts of shearing, spinning, carding, weaving, pressing olives for oil, making musical instruments and their music, harnessing horses, forging armor, mustering armies, ploughing, sowing, harvesting and grinding corn, building dwellings, living in towns, and many others.

XXXVII. OF ALL THE BLESSINGS THAT WOMEN BROUGHT THE WORLD

My Lady, I marvel at what you tell me: so many benefits due to the intelligence of women! For men generally affirm that feminine knowledge has no value and one often hears, when some foolishness is mentioned, that it is surely a woman's notion. In sum, men think that women were never any use and have no social utility beyond bearing children and spinning wool.

She answered: See the ingratitude of those who talk that way! They are like those who live off the largesse of others and, not knowing the source of their comforts, never think to thank anyone. But you can understand now that God, who does nothing without reason, wanted to show men that he does not esteem the female sex any less than theirs. It pleased him to grant so much light to female intellects that they can not only learn and assimilate the sciences but invent new ones, and moreover sciences so useful and profitable to humanity that it would be difficult to find more essential ones. Carmenta . . . who invented the Latin alphabet, illustrates my point. Almost all of Europe uses it, an infinity of books in all disciplines is printed in those characters, where the exploits of men, the splendor of divine power, the sciences and arts all shine for ever . . . We may conclude that the good this woman did is infinite for, thanks to her, men, even if they do not admit it, were drawn out of their state of ignorance and brought to culture. They can record and communicate their thoughts and their will; can know each other without having ever seen each other; can know the past, the present, and sometimes the future. One could not describe all the blessings that we owe to writing. . . . Was there ever a man, I ask you, to whom we owe more?

XXXVIII. WHERE WE PURSUE THE SAME SUBJECT

And was there ever a man who did more for humanity than the noble queen Ceres . . . who brought the barbarian nomads who dwelt in forests, without faith or law, like savage beasts to come fill towns and cities where now they live respectful of the law? She provided them with better food than the acorns and crab apples that they used to eat: wheat, corn, foods that make the body more beautiful, the complexion more radiant, the limbs stronger and more agile, for they are more substantial and better suited to the needs of the human race. What is more worthy than to develop a land filled with thistles, thorn bushes and wild trees, to till it and sow it and turn wild heath to cultivated fields? Human nature was thus enriched by this woman who carried it from barbarous wildness to orderly society, rescuing these lazy nomads from gloomy ignorance and opening access to the highest forms of thought and the noblest occupations.

Isis did the same for crops. Who can detail the good she brought humanity by teaching it to graft fine fruit trees and to husband the good plants appropriate to human sustenance?

And then Minerva! . . . People went clad in skins and she provided woolen garments; people carried their goods in their arms and she invented the art of building carts and chariots, relieving humanity of that burden; she taught noble knights how to manufacture coats of mail, so that their bodies should be better protected in war— a handsomer, nobler, more solid armor than the leather jerkins they had before that!

Then I said to her: Ah! My Lady! To hear you, I realize more than ever how great is the ignorance and the ingratitude of all those men who speak so much ill of women! I already believed that having had a mother and having experienced the services that women normally provide to men would be sufficient to still their mischievious tongues.

But I see now that women have overwhelmed them with gifts, and continue bounteous with their blessings. Let them shut up! Let them henceforth be silent, those clerks who speak ill of women! Let all their accomplices and allies who speak ill of women in their writings or poems hold their tongues. Let them lower their eyes in shame to have dared lie so much in their books, when one sees that the truth goes counter to what they say . . .

And let noble knights, many of whom speak ill of women, hold their tongues, knowing that it is to a woman that they owe armor, the art of war and of marshalling armies, that profession of arms of which they are so proud. And generally, when one sees men living on bread and dwelling in civilized towns subject to civil law, when they work their fields, how can one in view of so many good turns condemn and despise women the way so many do? For it was women—Minerva, Ceres, Isis—who brought them all those useful things that they enjoy all their lives and that they will always enjoy. Are these things insignificant? Not at all, My Lady, and it seems to me that not the philosophy of Aristotle—so useful and so highly praised, and rightly too!— nor all other philosophies that ever existed, ever brought or ever will bring so many advantages to humanity as the inventions that we owe to the spirit of these women.

The New State

Niccolò Machiavelli (1469–1527) is one of the most interesting writers of the Italian Renaissance and one of the most controversial. Born in Florence, he engaged in the politics and the diplomacy of the powerful republic, wrote its history, and then found himself in exile when his opponents, the Medici, returned to power. The Prince (1513) is not a work of advice so much as of observation. Machiavelli does not offer his ideas of what is good, but his impressions or conclusions of what seems to work. It is just this essay's amoral quality that has shocked so many of his readers and fascinated others. Catherine de Médicis, Francis Bacon, Richelieu, Spinoza, and Napoleon counted among his admirers. Machiavelli's writings have continued to provide a textbook of practical politics to this day.

Niccolò Machiavelli: from The Prince

OF NEW PRINCEDOMS ACQUIRED BY THE AID OF OTHERS
AND BY GOOD FORTUNE

They who from a private station become Princes by mere good fortune, do so with little trouble, but have much trouble to maintain themselves. They meet with no hindrance on their way, being carried as it were on wings, but all their difficulties arise when they arrive. Of this class are those on whom territories are conferred either in return for money or through the favour of him who confers them; as it happened to many who were made Princes by Darius in the Greek cities of Ionia and the Hellespont, so that they might hold them for his security and glory; and as happened in the case

---

From Machiavelli, *The Prince,* adapted by editor from the London edition of 1674.

of those Emperors who, from private station, attained the Imperial dignity by corrupting the army. Such Princes are wholly dependent on the favour and fortunes of those who have made them great, though no supports could be less stable or less secure than these; and they lack both the knowledge and the power that would enable them to maintain their position. They lack the knowledge, because unless they have great talent and force of character, it is not to be expected that having always lived in a private station they should have learned how to command. They lack the power, since they cannot look for support from attached and faithful troops. Moreover, realms suddenly acquired, like all else that is produced and grows up rapidly, can never have such root or hold as that the first storm that strikes them shall not overthrow them; unless, indeed, as I have said already, they who thus suddenly become Princes have a capacity for learning quickly how to defend what Fortune has placed in their lap, and can lay those foundations after their rise which by others are laid before.

Of each of these methods of becoming a Prince, namely by valour and by good fortune, I shall give you an example from times we can remember: the cases of Francesco Sforza and Cesare Borgia. By suitable measures and a great deal of ability, Francesco Sforza rose from privacy to be Duke of Milan, preserving with little trouble what it cost him infinite efforts to gain. On the other hand, Cesare Borgia, vulgarly spoken of as Duke Valentino, obtained his Princedom through the favourable fortunes of his father, and with these lost it, although, so far as in him lay, he used every effort and practised every expedient that a prudent and able man should, who desires to strike root in a realm given him by the arms and fortune of another. For, as I have already said, he who does not lay his foundations at first, may if he be very talented, succeed in laying them afterwards, though with inconvenience to the builder and risk to the building. And if we consider the various measures taken by Duke Valentino, we shall perceive how broad were the foundations he had laid whereon to rest his future power.

I do not think it superfluous to examine these, since I know not what lessons I could teach a new Prince more useful than the example of his actions. And if the measures taken by him did not profit him in the end, it was through no fault of his, but from the extraordinary and extreme malignity of Fortune.

In his efforts to aggrandize the Duke his son, [Pope] Alexander VI[1] had to face many difficulties, both immediate and remote. In the first place, he saw no way to make him Lord of any State which was not a State of the Church, while, if he sought to take for him a State belonging to the Church, he knew that the Duke of Milan and the Venetians would not consent: Faenza and Rimini being already under the protection of the latter. Further, he saw that the arms of Italy, and those especially he could have used, were in the hands of men who had reason to fear his aggrandizement, that is, of the Orsini, the Colonnesi, and their followers. These, therefore, he could not trust. So, it was necessary that the existing order of things should be changed, and the States of Italy embroiled in trouble, in order that he might safely make himself master of some part of them. This became easy for him when he found that the Venetians, moved by other causes, were plotting to bring the French once more into Italy. This design

---

[1]For the Borgias, see pp. 48–52.

he accordingly did not oppose, but furthered by annulling the first marriage of the French King.

King Louis, therefore, came into Italy invited by the Venetians and with the consent of Pope Alexander. No sooner was he in Milan than the Pope got troops from him to aid him in his enterprise against Romagna, which Province, moved by the reputation of French arms, at once submitted. After thus obtaining possession of Romagna, and defeating the Colonnesi, Duke Valentino wanted to follow up and extend his conquests. Two causes, however, held him back, namely, the doubtful fidelity of his own forces, and the waywardness of France. For he feared that the Orsini, of whose arms he had made use, might let him down, and not merely prove a hindrance to further acquisitions, but take from him what he had gained, and that the King might do him the same turn. How little he could count on the Orsini was made plain when, after the capture of Faenza, he directed his arms against Bologna, and saw how reluctantly they took part in that enterprise. The King's mind he understood, when, after seizing on the Dukedom of Urbino, he was about to attack Tuscany; from which attempt Louis made him desist. Whereupon the Duke resolved to depend no longer on the arms or fortune of others. His first step, therefore, was to weaken the factions of the Orsini and Colonnesi in Rome. Those of their following who were of good birth, he gained over by making them his own gentlemen, assigning them a liberal provision, and conferring upon them commands and appointments suited to their quality; so that in a few months their old partisan attachments died out, and the hopes of all rested on the Duke alone.

He then waited for a chance to crush the chiefs of the Orsini, for those of the house of Colonna he had already scattered, and a good opportunity presenting itself, he turned it to the best account. For when the Orsini came at last to see that the greatness of the Duke and the Church involved their ruin, they assembled a council at Magione in the Perugian territory, from which resulted the revolt of Urbino, commotions in Romagna, and an infinity of dangers to the Duke, all of which he overcame with the help of France. His credit thus restored, the Duke, trusting no longer to the French or to other foreign aid, that he might not have to confront them openly, resorted to stratagem, and was so well able to dissemble his designs, that the Orsini, through the mediation of Signor Paolo (whom he attracted by every friendly attention, furnishing him with clothes, money, and horses) were so won over as to be drawn in their simplicity into his hands at Sinigaglia.[2] The leaders thus disposed of, and their followers made his friends, the Duke had laid sufficiently good foundations for his future power, since he held all Romagna together with the Dukedom of Urbino, and had ingratiated himself with the entire population of these States, more especially of Romagna, who now began to see that they were well off.

And since this part of his conduct merits both attention and imitation, I shall not pass it over in silence. After the Duke had taken Romagna, finding that it had been ruled by feeble Lords, who thought more of plundering than correcting their subjects, and gave them more cause for division than for union, so that the country was overrun

---

[2]Where they were murdered.

with robbery, riot, and every kind of outrage, he judged it necessary, with a view to render it peaceful and obedient to his authority, to provide it with a good government. Accordingly he set over it Messer Remiro d'Orca, a stern and prompt ruler, who being entrusted with the fullest powers, in a very short time, and with much credit to himself, restored it to tranquillity and order. But afterwards apprehending that such unlimited authority might become odious, the Duke decided that it was no longer needed, and established in the centre of the Province a civil Tribunal, with an excellent President, in which every town was represented by its advocate. And knowing that past severities had created ill-feeling against himself, in order to purge the minds of the people and gain their goodwill, he tried to show them that any cruelty which had been done had not originated with him, but in the harsh character of his minister. Availing himself of the pretext this afforded, he one morning caused Remiro to be beheaded and exposed in the market place of Cesena with a block and bloody axe by his side—a savage spectacle which at once astounded and satisfied the populace.

But, returning to the point from which we diverged, I say that the Duke, finding himself fairly strong and in a measure secured against present dangers, being furnished with arms of his own choosing and having to a great extent got rid of those which, if left near him, might have caused him trouble, had to consider, if he desired to follow up his conquests, how he was to deal with France, since he saw he could expect no further support from King Louis, whose eyes were at last opened to his mistake. He therefore began to look about for new alliances, and to waver in his adherence to the French, then engaged in an expedition into the kingdom of Naples against the Spaniards, who were besieging Gaeta; his object being to secure himself against France; and in this he would soon have succeeded had Alexander lived.

Such was the line he took to meet present needs. As regards the future, he had to fear that a new Head of the Church might not be his friend, and might even seek to deprive him of what Alexander had given. This he thought to provide against in four ways. First, by exterminating all who were related to those Lords whom he had despoiled of their possessions, thereby leaving the new Pope no occasion for interference. Second, by gaining over all the Romans of good birth, so as to be able, as has been said, with their aid to hold the Pope in check. Third, by bringing the College of Cardinals, so far as possible, under his control. And fourth, by establishing his authority so firmly before his father's death, that he could by himself withstand the shock of a first onset.

Of these four objects, at the time when Alexander died, he had already effected three, and had almost carried out the fourth. For, of the Lords whose possessions he had usurped, he had put to death all whom he could reach, and very few had escaped. He had gained over the Roman nobility, and had the majority in the College of Cardinals on his side.

As to further acquisitions, his plan was to make himself master of Tuscany. He was already in possession of Perugia and Piombino, and had assumed the protectorate of Pisa, on which city he was about to spring, taking no heed of France, as indeed he no longer had occasion, since the French had been deprived of the kingdom of Naples by the Spaniards under conditions which made it necessary for both powers to buy his friendship. Pisa taken, Lucca and Siena must at once have yielded, partly through jealousy of Florence, partly through fear, and the position of the Florentines would then have been desperate.

If he had succeeded in these designs, as he was succeeding in that very year in which Alexander died, he would have won such power and reputation that he might afterwards have stood alone, relying on his own strength and resources, without being beholden to the forces and fortune of others. But Alexander died five years from the time he first unsheathed the sword, leaving his son with the State of Romagna alone consolidated, with all the rest unsettled, between two most powerful hostile armies, and sick almost to death. And yet such were the fire and courage of the Duke, he knew so well how men must either be conciliated or crushed, and so solid were the foundations he had laid in that brief period, that had these armies not been upon his back, or had he been in sound health, he must have surmounted every difficulty.

How strong his foundations were may be seen from this, that Romagna waited for him more than a month; and that although half dead, he remained in safety in Rome, where though the Baglioni, the Vitelli, and the Orsini came to attack him, they found no support. Moreover, since he was able if not to make whom he would Pope, at least to prevent the election of any whom he disliked, had he been in health at the time when Alexander died, all would have been easy for him. But he told me himself at the time when Julius II was created, that he had foreseen and provided for all else that could happen on his father's death, but had never anticipated that when his father died he too should be at death's door.

Taking all these actions of the Duke together, I can find no fault with him. It seems to me reasonable to put him forward, as I have done, as a pattern for all such as rise to power by good fortune and the help of others. For with his great spirit and high ambition he could not act otherwise than he did, and nothing but the shortness of his father's life and his own illness prevented the success of his designs. Whoever, therefore, on entering a new Princedom, judges it necessary to rid himself of enemies, to conciliate friends, to prevail by force or fraud, to make himself feared yet loved by his subjects, followed and revered by his soldiers, to crush those who can or ought to injure him, to introduce changes in the old order of things, to be at once severe and affable, magnanimous and liberal, to do away with a mutinous army and create a new one, to maintain relations with Kings and Princes on such a footing that they must see it is in their interest to aid him, and dangerous to offend, can find no brighter examples than in the actions of this Prince.

The one thing for which he may be blamed was the creation of Pope Julius II, in respect of whom he chose badly. Because, as I have said already, though he could not secure the election he desired, he could have prevented any other; and he ought never to have consented to the creation of any one of those Cardinals whom he had injured, or who on becoming Pope would have reason to fear him; for fear is as dangerous an enemy as resentment. Those whom he had offended were, among others, San Pietro ad Vincula, Colonna, San Giorgio, and Ascanio; all the rest, excepting d'Amboise and the Spanish Cardinals (the latter from their being connected and under obligations, the former from the power he derived through his relations with the French Court), would on assuming the Pontificate have had reason to fear him. The Duke, therefore, ought, in the first place, to have laboured for the creation of a Spanish Pope; failing wherein, he should have agreed to the election of d'Amboise, but never to that of San Pietro ad Vincula. It is a bad mistake to think that, when dealing with the powerful, recent benefits cause old wrongs to be forgotten.

The Duke, therefore, erred in the part he took in this election; and his error was the cause of his ultimate downfall.

OF THOSE WHO BY CRIME COME TO BE PRINCES

But since from a private station a man may also rise to be a Prince in one or other of two ways, neither of which can be ascribed wholly either to valour or to fortune, it is fit that I note them here, though one of them may fail to be discussed more fully in treating of Republics.

The ways I speak of are, first, when the ascent to power is made by paths of wickedness and crime; and second, when a private person becomes ruler of his country by the favour of his fellow-citizens. The former method I shall make clear by two examples, one ancient the other modern, without entering further into the merits of the matter, for these, I think, should be enough for anyone who is constrained to follow them.

Agathocles the Sicilian came, not merely from a private station, but from the very dregs of the people, to be King of Syracuse. Son of a potter, through all the stages of his career he led an evil life. His vices, however, were conjoined with so much vigour both of mind and body, that enlisting as a common soldier, he rose through the various grades of the service to be Praetor of Syracuse. Established in that post, he resolved to make himself Prince, and to hold by violence and without obligation to others the authority which had been by consent entrusted to him. Accordingly, after imparting his design to Hamilcar, who with the Carthaginian armies was at that time waging war in Sicily, he one morning assembled the people and senate of Syracuse as though to consult with them on matters of public moment, and on a preconcerted signal caused his soldiers to put to death all the senators, and the wealthiest of the commons. These being thus disposed of, he seized and kept the sovereignty of the city without opposition from the people; and though twice defeated by the Carthaginians, and afterwards besieged, he was able not only to defend his city, but leaving a part of his forces for its protection, to invade Africa with the remainder, and so in a short time to raise the siege of Syracuse, reducing the Carthaginians to the utmost extremities, and forcing them to make terms whereby they resigned Sicily to him and confined themselves to Africa.

Whoever examines this man's actions and achievements will discover little or nothing in them that can be ascribed to chance, seeing, as has already been said, that it was not through the favour of any one but by the regular steps of the military service, gained at the cost of a thousand hardships and hazards, he reached the Princedom which he afterwards maintained by so many daring and dangerous exploits. Still, to slaughter fellow-citizens, to betray friends, to be devoid of honour, pity, and religion, cannot be counted as merits, for these are means that may lead to power, but confer no glory. Wherefore, if in respect of the valour with which he encountered and extricated himself from dangers, and the constancy of his spirit in supporting and conquering adverse fortune, there seems no reason to judge him inferior to the greatest captains that have ever lived, his unbridled cruelty and inhumanity, together with his countless other crimes, forbid us to number him with the greatest men; but, at any rate, we cannot attribute to luck or to merit what he accomplished without either.

In our own times, during the papacy of Alexander VI, Oliverotto of Fermo, who, left an orphan some years before, had been brought up by his maternal uncle Giovanni Fogliani, was sent while still a lad to serve under Paolo Vitelli, in order that a thorough training under that commander might qualify him for high rank as a soldier. After the death of Paolo, he served under his brother, Vitellozzo, and in a very short time, being quick-witted, hardy, and resolute, he became one of the first soldiers of his company. But he thought it beneath him to serve under others; so, with the support of the Vitelleschi and the connivance of certain citizens of Fermo who preferred the slavery to the freedom of their country, he planned to seize on that town.

He accordingly wrote to Giovanni Fogliani that after many years of absence from home, he desired to see him and his native city once more and to look a little into the condition of his patrimony; and as his one endeavour had been to make himself a name, in order that his fellow-citizens might see his time had not been wasted, he proposed to return honourably attended by a hundred horsemen from among his own friends and followers; and he begged Giovanni graciously to arrange for his reception by the citizens of Fermo with corresponding marks of distinction, as this would be creditable not only to himself, but also to the uncle who had brought him up.

Giovanni, accordingly, did not fail in any proper attention to his nephew, but caused him to be splendidly received by his fellow-citizens, and lodged him in his house; where Oliverotto having passed some days, and made the necessary arrangements for carrying out his wickedness, gave a sumptuous banquet, to which he invited his uncle and all the first men of Fermo. When the repast and the other entertainment proper to such an occasion had come to an end, Oliverotto artfully turned the conversation to matters of grave interest, by speaking of the greatness of Pope Alexander and Cesare his son, and of their enterprises; and when Giovanni and the others were replying to what he said, he suddenly rose, observing that these were matters to be discussed in a more private place, and so moved to another room; whither his uncle and the other citizens followed him, and where they had no sooner seated themselves, than soldiers rushing out from places of concealment slew Giovanni and all the others.

After this butchery, Oliverotto mounting his horse, rode through the streets, and besieged the chief magistrate in the place, so that all were forced by fear to submit and accept a government of which he made himself the head. And all who from being disaffected, were likely to stand in his way, he put to death, while he strengthened himself with new ordinances, civil and military, to such effect, that for the space of a year during which he retained the Princedom, he not merely remained safe in Fermo, but grew formidable to all his neighbours. And it would have been as difficult to unseat him as to unseat Agathocles, had he not let himself be overreached by Cesare Borgia on the occasion when, as has already been told, the Orsini and Vitelli were entrapped at Sinigaglia; where he too being taken, one year after the commission of his parricidal crime, was strangled along with Vitellozzo, who had been his master in villainy as in valour.

It may be asked how it came that Agathocles and some like him, after numberless acts of treachery and cruelty, were able to live long in their own country in safety, and defend themselves from foreign enemies, without being conspired against by their fellow-citizens, whereas, many others, by reason of their cruelty, have failed to maintain their position even in peaceful times, not to speak of the perilous times of war. I believe that this results from cruelty being well or ill used. Those cruelties we may say are well used, if we may speak well of things evil, which are done once for all as necessary for your security, and are not afterwards persisted in, but so far as possible adapted to the advantage of the governed. Ill-used cruelties, on the other hand, are those which from small beginnings increase rather than diminish with time. Those who follow the first of these methods, may, by the grace of God and man, find, as Agathocles did, that their condition is not desperate; but by no possibility can the others maintain themselves.

Hence we may learn the lesson that on seizing a State, the usurper should plan ahead all the injuries he must inflict, and inflict them all at one stroke, that he may not have to renew them daily, but be enabled by their discontinuance to reassure men's minds and win them by benefits. Whosoever, either through timidity or from following bad counsels, acts otherwise, must keep the sword always drawn, and can put no trust in his subjects, who suffering from continued and constantly renewed severities can never feel sure of him. Injuries, therefore, should be inflicted all at once, that their ill savour being less lasting may less offend; whereas, benefits should be conferred little by little, that so they may be more fully relished.

But, before all things, a Prince should so live with his subjects that no vicissitude for better or worse shall cause him to alter his behaviour; for if the need to change come through adversity, it is too late to resort to severity; and any leniency you may then use will be wasted, since it will be seen to be compulsory and bring you no thanks.

OF THE QUALITIES FOR WHICH MEN, AND MOST OF ALL PRINCES, ARE PRAISED OR BLAMED

It now remains for us to consider what ought to be the conduct and bearing of a Prince in relation to his subjects and friends. And since I know that many have written on this subject, I fear it may be thought presumptuous in me to write of it also; the more so, because in my treatment of it, I depart widely from the views that others have taken.

But since it is my object to write what shall be useful to whosoever understands it, it seems to me better to follow the real truth of things than an imaginary view of them. For many Republics and Principalities have been imagined that were never seen or known to really exist. And the way in which we live, and that in which we ought to live, are things so wide apart, that he who leaves the one for the other is more likely to destroy than to save himself; since any one who would act up to a perfect standard of goodness in everything, must be ruined among so many who are not good. It is essential, therefore, for a Prince who would maintain his position, to have learned how to be other than good, and to use or not to use his goodness as necessity requires.

Laying aside, therefore, all fanciful notions concerning a Prince, and considering those only that are true, I say that all men when they are spoken of, and Princes more than others from their being set so high, are noted for certain of those qualities which attach either praise or blame. Thus one is accounted liberal, another miserly; one is generous, another greedy; one cruel, another tenderhearted; one is faithless, another true to his word; one effeminate and cowardly, another high-spirited and courageous; one is courteous, another haughty; one lewd, another chaste; one upright, another crafty; one firm, another facile; one grave, another frivolous; one devout, another unbelieving; and the like. Everyone, I know, will admit that it would be praiseworthy for a Prince to be endowed with all of the above qualities that are reckoned good; but since it is impossible for him to possess or constantly practise them all, the conditions of human nature not allowing it, he must be discreet enough to know how to avoid the reproach of those vices that would deprive him of his government, and, if possible, be on his guard also against those which might not deprive him of it. Though if he cannot wholly restrain himself, he may with less scruple indulge in the latter. But he need never hesitate to incur the reproach of those vices without which his authority can hardly be preserved; for if he well considers the whole matter, he will find that there may be a line of conduct that looks like virtue, but which would ruin him; and that there may be another course that looks like vice on which his safety and well-being may depend.

OF LIBERALITY AND MISERLINESS

Beginning, then, with the first of the qualities above noticed, I say that it may be well to be reputed liberal[3] but that liberality without a reputation for it is bad; since, though it be worthily and rightly used, still if it be not known, you escape not the reproach of its opposite vice. Thus, to have credit for liberality with the world at large, you must neglect no circumstance of sumptuous display; the result being that a Prince who would be thought liberal will consume his whole substance in things of this sort and after all be obliged, if he would maintain his reputation for liberality, to burden his subjects with extraordinary taxes and resort to confiscations and all the other shifts whereby money is raised. But in this way he becomes hateful to his subjects, and growing impoverished is held in little esteem by any. So that in the end, having by his liberality offended many and obliged few, he is no better off than when be began, and exposed to all his original dangers. Recognizing this, and trying to retrace his steps, he at once incurs the reproach of miserliness.

A Prince, therefore, since he cannot without injury to himself practise this virtue of liberality so that it may be known, will not, if he is wise, greatly concern himself though he be called miserly. Because in time he will come to be regarded as more and more liberal, when it is seen that through his parsimony his revenues are sufficient; that he is able to defend himself against any who make war on him; that he can engage in enterprises against others without burdening his subjects; and thus exercise liberality towards all from whom he does not take, whose number is infinite, while he is miserly in respect of those only to whom he does not give, whose number is small.

---

[3] Meaning generous. In this sense, liberality is generosity.

In our own days we have seen no Princes accomplish great results save those who have been accounted miserly. All others have been ruined. Pope Julius II, after using his reputation for liberality to arrive at the Papacy, made no effort to preserve that reputation when making war on the King of France but carried on all his many campaigns without levying from his subjects a single extraordinary tax, providing for the increased expenditure out of his long-continued savings. Had the present King of Spain been accounted liberal, he never could have engaged or succeeded in so many enterprises.

A Prince, therefore, if he is enabled thereby to avoid plundering his subjects, to defend himself, to escape poverty and contempt and the necessity of becoming rapacious, ought to care little about the reproach of miserliness, for this is one of those vices which enable him to reign.

And should any object that Caesar by his liberality rose to power and that many others have been advanced to the highest dignities from their having been liberal and so reputed, I reply, Either you are already a Prince or you seek to become one; in the former case liberality is hurtful, in the latter it is very necessary that you be thought liberal; Caesar was one of those who sought the sovereignty of Rome; but if after obtaining it he had lived on without retrenching his expenditure, he must have ruined the Empire. And if it be further urged that many Princes reputed to have been most liberal have achieved great things with their armies, I answer that a Prince spends either what belongs to himself and his subjects, or what belongs to others; and that in the former case he ought to be sparing but in the latter ought not to refrain from any kind of liberality. Because for a Prince who leads his armies in person and maintains them by plunder, pillage, and forced contributions, dealing as he does with the property of others, this liberality is necessary, since otherwise he would not be followed by his soldiers. Of what does not belong to you or to your subjects you may, therefore, be a lavish giver, as were Cyrus, Caesar, and Alexander, for to be liberal with the property of others does not take from your reputation, but adds to it. What injures you is to give away what is your own. And there is no quality so self-destructive as liberality; for while you practise it you lose the means whereby it can be practised, and become poor and despised, or else, to avoid poverty, you become rapacious and hated. For liberality leads to one or other of these two results, against which, beyond all others, a Prince should guard.

And hence it is wiser to put up with the name of being miserly, which breeds ignominy, but without hate, than be obliged, from the desire to be reckoned liberal, to incur the reproach of rapacity, which breeds both hate and ignominy.

OF CRUELTY AND CLEMENCY, AND WHETHER
IT IS BETTER TO BE LOVED OR FEARED

Passing to the other qualities above mentioned, I say that every Prince should desire to be accounted merciful and not cruel. Nevertheless, he should be careful not to abuse this quality of mercy. Cesare Borgia was reputed cruel, yet his cruelty restored Romagna, united it, and brought it to order and obedience; so that if we look at things in their true light, it will be seen that he was in reality far more merciful than the people of Florence, who, to avoid the imputation of cruelty, suffered Pistoia to be destroyed by factions.

A Prince should therefore disregard the reproach of cruelty where it enables him to keep his subjects united and faithful. For he who puts down disorder by a minimum of striking examples, will in the end be more merciful than he who from excessive leniency suffers things to take their course and so result in rapine and bloodshed; for these hurt the entire State, whereas the severities of the Prince injure individuals only.

And for a new Prince, above all others, it is impossible to escape a name for cruelty, since new States are full of dangers. . . .

Nevertheless, the new Prince should not be too ready of belief, nor too easily influenced. Nor should he himself be the first to raise alarms; but should so temper prudence with kindliness that too great confidence in others shall not throw him off his guard, nor groundless distrust render him insupportable.

This brings up the question whether it is better to be loved rather than feared, or feared rather than loved. It might be answered that we should wish to be both; but since love and fear can hardly exist together, if we must choose between them, it is far safer to be feared than loved. For of men it may generally be said that they are thankless, fickle, false, eager to avoid danger, greedy of gain, devoted to you while you confer benefits upon them, and ready, as I said before, while the need is remote, to shed their blood and sacrifice their property, their lives, and their children for you; but when it comes near they turn against you. The Prince, therefore, who without otherwise securing himself builds wholly on what men say or promise is undone. For the friendships we buy with a price and not gain by greatness and nobility of character, though fairly earned, are not made good but fail us when we need them most.

Moreover, men are less careful how they offend him who makes himself loved than him who makes himself feared. For love is held by the tie of obligation, which, because men are a poor lot, is broken on every prompting of self-interest; but fear is bound by the apprehension of punishment which never loosens its grasp.

Nevertheless a Prince should inspire fear so that if he do not win love he may escape hate. For a man may very well be feared and yet not hated, as will always be the case so long as he does not intermeddle with the property or with the women of his citizens and subjects. And if forced to put any one to death, he should do so only when there is manifest cause or reasonable justification. But, above all, he must keep his hands off the property of others. For men will sooner forget the death of their father than the loss of their patrimony. Moreover, excuses for confiscation are never hard to find, and he who has once started to live by rapine always finds reasons for taking what is not his; whereas reasons for shedding blood are fewer and sooner exhausted.

But when a Prince is with his army, and has many soldiers under his command, he must wholly disregard the reproach of cruelty, for without such a reputation in its Captain, you cannot hold an army together, ready for every emergency. Among other things remarkable in Hannibal this has been noted, that having a very great army, made up of men of many different nations and brought to serve in a foreign country, no dissension ever arose among the soldiers themselves, nor any mutiny against their leader, either in his good or in his evil fortunes. This we can only ascribe to the tremendous cruelty, which, joined with numberless great qualities, rendered him at once wonderful and terrible in the eyes of his soldiers; for without this reputation for cruelty his other virtues would not have had the results they did.

Unreflecting writers, indeed, while praising his achievements, have condemned the chief cause of them; but that his other merits would not by themselves have been so useful we may see from the case of Scipio, one of the greatest Captains of all times, whose armies rose against him in Spain from no other cause than his excessive leniency in allowing them freedoms inconsistent with military discipline. With which weakness Fabius Maximus taxed him in the Senate House, calling him the corrupter of the Roman soldiery. Again, when the Locrians were shamefully outraged by one of his lieutenants, he neither avenged them nor punished the insolence of his officer; and this because he was so easy-going. So that it was said in the Senate by one who tried to excuse him, that there were many who knew better how to refrain from doing wrong themselves than how to correct the wrong-doing of others. This temper, however, would in time have spoiled the name and fame even of Scipio, if he had continued in it, and retained his command. But living as he did under the control of the Senate, this hurtful quality was not merely veiled but came to be regarded as a glory.

Returning to the question of being loved or feared, I sum up by saying, that since his being loved depends upon his subjects, while his being feared depends upon himself, a wise Prince should build on what is his own and not on what rests with others. Only, as I have said, he must do his best to escape hatred.

HOW PRINCES SHOULD KEEP FAITH

Every one recognises how praiseworthy it is in a Prince to keep faith, and to act uprightly and not craftily. Nevertheless, we see from what has happened in our own days that Princes who have set little store by their word but have known how to overreach others by their cunning, have accomplished great things and in the end had the better of those who trusted to honest dealing.

It should be known, then, that there are two ways of acting, one in accordance with the laws, the other by force; the first of which is proper to men, the second to beasts. But since the first method is often ineffectual, it becomes necessary to resort to the second. A Prince should, therefore, understand how to use well both the man and the beast. And this lesson has been discreetly taught by the ancient writers, who relate how Achilles and many others of these old Princes were given over to be brought up and trained by Chiron the Centaur; since the only meaning of their having for teacher one who was half man and half beast is, that it is necessary for a Prince to know how to use both natures and that the one without the other has no stability.

But since a Prince should know how to use the beast's nature wisely, he ought of beasts to choose both the lion and the fox; for the lion cannot guard himself from traps, nor the fox from wolves. He must therefore be a fox to discern traps, and a lion to drive off wolves.

To rely wholly on the lion is unwise; and for this reason a prudent Prince neither can nor ought to keep his word, when to keep it is hurtful to him and the causes which led him to give it are removed. If all men were good, this would not be good advice, but since they are dishonest and do not keep faith with you, you in return need not keep faith with them; and no Prince was ever at a loss for plausible reasons to cover a breach of faith. Of this infiniteness recent instances could be given, and it might be shown how many solemn treaties and engagements have been made empty and idle through want of faith in Princes and that he who has best known to play the fox has had the best success.

It is necessary, indeed, to put a good colour on this nature, and to be skillful in feigning and dissembling. But men are so simple and governed so absolutely by their present needs, that he who wishes to deceive will never fail in finding willing dupes. One recent example I will not omit. Pope Alexander VI had no care or thought but how to deceive, and always found material to work on. No man ever had a more effective manner of affirming things, or made promises with more solemn protestations, or observed them less. And yet, because he understood this side of human nature, his frauds always succeeded.

It is not essential, then, that a Prince should have all the good qualities I have enumerated above, but it is most essential that he should seem to have them. As a matter of fact I will venture to affirm that if he has and invariably practises them all, they are hurtful, whereas the appearance of having them is useful. Thus, it is well to seem merciful, faithful, humane, religious, and upright, and also to be so; but the mind should remain so balanced that were it needful not to be so, you should be able and know how to change to the contrary.

And you are to understand that a Prince, and most of all a new Prince, cannot observe all those rules of conduct in respect of which men are considered good; since he is often forced to act in opposition to good faith, charity, humanity, and religion in order to preserve his Princedom, he must therefore keep his mind ready to shift as the winds and tides of Fortune turn, and, as I have already said, ought not to leave good courses if he can help it but should know how to follow evil if he must.

A Prince should therefore be very careful that nothing ever escapes his lips which is not full of the five qualities above named, so that to see and hear him, one would think him the embodiment of mercy, good faith, integrity, kindliness, and religion. And there is no virtue which it is more necessary for him to seem to possess than this last; because men in general judge rather by the eye than by the hand, for all can see but few can touch. Every one sees what you seem, but few know what you are, and these few dare not oppose themselves to the opinion of the many who have the majesty of the State to back them up.

Moreover, in the actions of all men, and most of all of Princes, where there is no tribunal to which we can appeal, we look to results. Wherefore if a Prince succeeds in establishing and maintaining his authority, the means will always be judged honourable and be approved by every one. For the vulgar are always taken by appearances and by results, and the world is made up of the vulgar, the few only finding room when the many have no longer ground to stand on.

A certain Prince of our own days, whom it is as well not to name,[4] is always

---

[4] Ferdinand of Aragon.

preaching peace and good faith, although he is the mortal enemy of both; and both, had he practised as he preaches, would, oftener than once, have lost him his kingdom and authority.

The New Education

François Rabelais (1494–1553)—Franciscan friar, Benedictine monk, doctor, professor of anatomy—had a learned and inquisitive mind, representative of the best in French humanism. Quite a traveler, he was responsible for introducing Roman lettuce to western Europe, but his surviving fame depends less on his medical studies or his culinary exploits than on the enduring popularity of the happy and lunatic world of giants and heroes he created in Gargantua and Pantagruel. *The books describing their adventures have been banned repeatedly since the Sorbonne first placed* Pantagruel *on its* Index *in 1533. They are supposed to be coarse; they are certainly robust and rambunctious. But fundamentally Rabelais is a serious man and a critic of society, and the fun he makes of the pretensions of his day often applies just as well to ours. The selections that follow reflect the contemporary debate between the old-fashioned techniques of education and the new ideas of the humanists.*

François Rabelais: from Gargantua and Pantagruel

GARGANTUA'S EDUCATION AND SOCIAL LIFE UNDER THE DIRECTION
OF HIS PRECEPTORS AT THE SORBONNE

The first few days having been spent thus and the bells put back in place, the citizens of Paris, in acknowledgment of Gargantua's civility, offered to feed and maintain his mare as long as he wished. Gargantua accepted this courtesy, so the Parisians sent the beast to graze in the Forest of Bière or Fontainebleau. (I do not believe she is still there.)

This accomplished, Gargantua resolved with all his heart to study under the direction of Ponocrates. But the latter, wishing to learn how the lad's former teachers had wasted so much time making a crack-brained, addlepated dunce of him, decided he should do exactly as he had in the past.

Gargantua therefore arranged his schedule so as to awake usually between eight and nine o'clock, rain or shine, dark or daylight, simply because his preceptors had decided this on the strength of the Psalmist's saw: "*Vanum est vobis ante lucem surgere.*"[1]

Then he wriggled and writhed, wallowing in his bed and tossing about like a parched pea, the better to stimulate his vital spirits. Next, he would dress, according

From *The Complete Works of Rabelais* (Chaps. XXI, XXIII), tr. by Jacques LeClercq (New York: Random House, 1936).

[1] "It is foolish to rise before the light."

to the season, but he was always happy to don a long, hanging gown of heavy wool lined with fox. Next, he combed out his hair with the comb of Jacques Almain, the Sorbonne theologian, known in English as John Handy—a comb consisting of four fingers and a thumb—for his mentors maintained that to brush one's hair, wash one's face and make oneself clean were, in this world, a pure waste of time.

Next Gargantua dunged, piddled, vomited, belched, broke wind, yawned, spat, coughed, hiccoughed, sneezed and snotted himself as majestically and bountifully as an archdeacon. Next he proceeded to breakfast in order to fortify himself against the morning mist and cold. His menu consisted of splendid fried tripe, choice meats grilled on charcoal, rich hams, succulent roast venison and numerous soups and brews, with toast, cheese, parsley and chopped meat floating on the surface.

Ponocrates objected that he should not eat so soon after rising without having taken any exercise. To which he replied:

"Exercise? Good God, didn't I tumble and jounce in bed six or seven times before I got up? Surely, that is exercise enough? Pope Alexander VI did this on the advice of his Jew physician, Bonnet de Lates, and lived till the day of his death in spite of his enemies. My first masters taught me this habit, for breakfast, they said, gave man a good mind. So they started the day by drinking. It suits me perfectly and I manage to dine the better for it. Master Tubal Holofernes, who was graduated Licentiate in Paris at the head of his class, used to tell me that to hasten was not enough, one must set out early. By the same token, the total health of mankind does not consist in drinking down and lapping up, *glub, glub, glub,* like so many ducks, but rather in falling to, early in the morning. *Unde versus;* so runs the verse:

To rise betimes is not enough,
To drink at morning, that's the stuff!"

After an abundant breakfast, Gargantua repaired to church, with, in his train, a varlet bearing a basket. The latter contained a huge breviary swaddled in velvet and weighing about twelve hundred and six pounds including the filth of thumbmarks, dogeared corners, golden clasps and nonpareil parchment. Twenty-six, if not thirty, masses ensued for the benefit of Gargantua and his chaplain. Under his tall hood, this chaplain looked for all the world like a peewit . . . and had very thoroughly antidoted his breath against possible poisons with much syrup of the vine! Chaplain and pupil babbled the mumbo jumbo of the litany, thumbing their rosaries so carefully that not one single bead fell to the ground.

As he left the church, they brought him an oxcart laden with a huge heap of prayer books, chaplets and relics from St. Claude in the Jura, each bigger than a hatblock. Gargantua and his chaplain then strolled in the cloisters, galleries or garden, saying more aves than sixteen hermits.

After, Gargantua would study for a short half-hour, his eyes glued to his book but his mind, to quote Terence's *Eunuch,* woolgathering in the kitchen. Then he proceeded to make water, filling a large urinal to capacity, after which he sat down at table, and, being naturally phlegmatic, began his meal with a few dozen hams, smoked tongues of beef, caviar, sausages and other like forerunners of wine.

Then four servants in turn shovelled mustard into his mouth by the spadeful, thus preparing him to drain a horrific draught of white wine to relieve his kidneys. Then the meal proper began with viands to his liking, according to the season; Gargantua ceasing to eat only when his belly had reached bursting point.

When he came to drinking, he acknowledged neither end nor rule; for, he said, there were no limits and boundaries to swilling until the tosspot felt the cork soles of his shoes swell up a half-foot from the ground.

HOW PONOCRATES GAVE GARGANTUA SUCH INSTRUCTION THAT NOT AN HOUR OF THE DAY WAS WASTED

When Ponocrates saw Gargantua's vicious mode of life, he determined to bring him up otherwise. But for the first few days he bore with him, for he realized that nature cannot endure sudden and violent changes.

To begin his work the better, Ponocrates requested a learned physician of the times, Master Theodore—the name means "God-given"—to examine Gargantua thoroughly with a view to steering him on the right course. The scholar purged Gargantua canonically with Anticyrian hellebore,[2] an herb indicated for cerebral disorders and insanity, thus cleansing his brain of its unnatural, perverse condition. Ponocrates, by the same aperient means, made the lad forget all he had learned under his former teachers, just as Timotheus of old treated pupils who had already studied under other musicians. Timotheus, incidentally, used to charge this class of students double!

For Gargantua's further edification, Ponocrates made him mingle among learned men whose company fired him with a desire to emulate them, to study more profitably and to make his mark. Next, Ponocrates so arranged the lad's schedule that not a moment of the day was wasted; all his time was spent in the pursuit of learning and honest knowledge.

By this new dispensation, Gargantua awoke at about four in the morning. While the servants massaged him, he would listen to some page of Holy Scripture, read aloud in clear tones and pronounced with fitting respect for the text. A young page, a native of Basché, near Chinon, was appointed reader, as his name, Anagnostes, shows. According to the purpose and argument of this lesson, Gargantua frequently turned to worship, adore, pray and reverence Almighty God, Whose majesty and wondrous wisdom were made manifest in the reading.

Next, he would repair to secret places to make excretion of his natural digestions; here his tutor repeated what had been read, expounding its more obscure and difficult features. Returning to the house, they would study the heavens. Was it the same sky they had observed the night before? Into what signs was the sun entering that day? and the moon?

After this astronomical survey, Gargantua was dressed, combed, curled, trimmed and perfumed, and, while this was being done, he heard the lessons of the day before. Then, having recited them by heart, he would argue certain practical, human and utilitarian cases based upon the principles enunciated. This part of the program sometimes

---

[2] A kind of buttercup used as a stimulant or, in this case, a cathartic.

took two or three hours, though usually he had exhausted it by the time he was fully clad.

Then, for three good hours, he was read or lectured to, after which they went to the Tennis Court at the Grande Bracque in the Place de l'Estrapade or to the playing fields.

On the way, they discussed various aspects of the subject previously treated. Then they would play tennis, handball and three-cornered catch, exercising their bodies as vigorously as they had exercised their minds before.

All their play was free for they left off when they pleased, which was usually when they had sweated a good bit or were otherwise tired. They were thoroughly wiped and rubbed down, after which they changed their shirts and walked quietly home to see if dinner were ready. As they waited, they would go over certain points they had retained of the lectures.

Meanwhile My Lord Appetite put in an appearance and they sat down most opportunely to table.

At the beginning of the meal, they listened to the reading of some agreeable chronicle of chivalry in ancient times, until Gargantua gave the signal for wine to be served. Then, if they wished, the reading went on or they could talk merrily together. Often they discussed the virtues, property, efficacy and nature of what was served at table: bread, wine, water, salt, meat, fish, fruit, herbs, roots and their preparation. Thus Gargantua soon knew all the relevant passages in Pliny's *Natural History* . . . in the grammarian Athenæus' *Deipnosophistes* or *The Banquet of the Sages,* which treats of flowers, fruits and their various uses . . . in Dioscorides' famous medical treatise, the bible of apothecaries . . . in the *Vocabularium* by Julius Pollux, a grammarian and sophist of Marcus Aurelius' day, who wrote of hunting and fishing . . . in Galen's numerous dissertations upon alimentation . . . in the works of Porphyrius, the third-century Greek author of a *Treatise upon Abstinence from Meat* . . . in Oppian's two poems, *Cynegetica* which deals with venery and *Halieutica* with angling . . . in *Of Healthy Diet* by Polybius of Cos, disciple and son-in-law of Hippocrates . . . in Heliodorus of Emesa, Syrian Bishop of Tricca and a celebrated novelist of the fourth century . . . in Aristotle's essays on natural history . . . in the Greek works upon animals by Claudius Ælianus, a Roman contemporary of Heliogobalus . . . and in various other tomes. . . . Often for surer authority as they argued, they would have the book in question brought to the table. Gargantua so thoroughly and cogently learned and assimilated all he heard that no physician of his times knew one-half so much as he.

They discussed the lessons they had learned that morning and topped their meal off with quiddany, a sort of quince marmalade and an excellent digestive. After which Gargantua picked his teeth with a fragment of mastic, washed his hands and daubed his eyes with cool clear water, and, instead of saying grace, sang the glory of God in noble hymns, composed in praise of divine bounty and munificence.

Presently cards were brought them and they played, not for the sake of the pastime itself but to learn a thousand new tricks and inventions all based on arithmetic.

Thus Gargantua developed a keen enthusiasm for mathematics, spending his leisure after dinner and supper every evening as pleasantly as once he had, dicing and gaming. As a result, he knew so much about its theory and practice that Cuthbert

Tunstal, Bishop of Durham and secretary to King Henry VIII, a voluminous writer on the subject, confessed that, beside Gargantua, he knew no more about arithmetic than he did about Old High Gothic. Nor was it arithmetic alone our hero learned, but also such sister sciences as geometry, astronomy and music.

Now the digestion of foods is a most important matter. There is the first stage which occurs in the stomach, where the viands are changed into chyle; the second, in the liver, where the chyle is transformed into blood; the third, in the habit of the body, where the blood is finally converted into the substance of each part. So, whilst Gargantua awaited the first stage of digestion, they made a thousand delightful instruments, drew geometrical figures and even applied the principles of astronomy.

After, they amused themselves singing a five-part score or improvising on a theme chosen at random. As for musical instruments, Gargantua learned to play the lute, the spinet, the harp, the nine-holed transverse or German flute, the viol and the sackbut or trombone.

Having spent an hour thus and completed his digestion, he discharged his natural excrements and then settled down again to work three hours or more at his principal study. Either he revised the morning reading, or proceeded in the text at hand or practised penmanship in the most carefully formed characters of modern Roman and ancient Gothic script.

Next, they went out with a young gentleman of Touraine, the esquire Gymnastes, who instructed Gargantua in the art of horsemanship. Having changed his clothes, he proceeded to mount a fiery Italian charger, a Flemish dray horse, a Spanish jennet, an Arab thoroughbred and a hackney. These he would put vigorously through their paces, letting them "career" or gallop a short distance at full speed, making them leap high in the air, jump ditches, clear stiles, and turn short in a ring both to the right and to the left. Next he wielded but did not break his lance, for it is arrant stupidity to boast: "I have broken ten lances in a tilt or fight." A wretched carpenter can do the same. On the contrary, the whole glory of such combat lies in besting ten enemies with one and the same lance. So with strong, stiff, steel-tipped lance, Gargantua would force the outer door of some house, pierce an adversary's armor, beat down a tree, pick up a ring, carry off a cuirassier saddle, a hauberk or a gauntlet. And he performed these feats armed cap-à-pie.[3]

In the technique of parading his horse with prances and flourishes to a fanfare of trumpets—the ceremonial of knights as they enter the lists—he had no equal. As for the divers terms of the equine vocabulary from *giddy-up* and *cluck* to *whoa* and *grrr*, no horseman could hold a candle to him. Indeed Cesare Fieschi, the celebrated jockey of Ferrara, was a mere monkey in comparison.

He learned, too, to leap hastily and with singular dexterity from one horse to another without setting foot to the ground (the nags were circus horses or, to be technical, "desultories"). Further, lance in hand, he could leap on horseback from either side without stirrups and rule the beast at will without a bridle, for such accomplishments are highly useful in military engagements.

---

[3] Clad in armor from head to foot.

Another day he would practise wielding the battle-axe, which he managed so skilfully, in the nimblest thrusts, the most powerful lunges and the vast encircling sweeps of
the art, that he passed knight-at-arms in the field and at all tests. Sometimes unarmed,
sometimes carrying a buckler or a rolled cape of mail over his arm or a small shield
over his wrist, Gargantua brandished the pike, plied the double-edged, two-handed
sword, the bastard claymore used by archers, the Spanish rapier, the dagger and the
poniard.

He hunted, too: stag, roebuck, bear, fallow deer, wild boar, hare, partridge, pheas-
ant and otter . . . he played at ball, ever ready with well-aimed foot or powerful fist
to send the great sphere whizzing through the air . . . he learned to wrestle and to run.
. . . As for jumping, he did not go in for the various forms of running jumps, such
as the three-steps-and-a-leap, the hop-step-and-jump or the German high-jump. As
Gymnastes pointed out, these were quite useless in warfare. Instead, he practised the
standing jumps. Starting from scratch, he could in one leap top a hedge, clear a ditch,
mount six paces upon a wall and thus reach a windowledge one lance's height from
the ground.

Gargantua could swim in the deepest water, breaststroke, back and sidestroke,
using his whole body or his feet alone. He could cross the breadth of the Seine or the
Loire at Montsoreau, dragging his cloak along in his teeth and holding a book high
and dry over the waters—thus renewing the exploit with which Plutarch credits Julius
Cæsar during the Alexandrian War. Then, using one hand only, he could, with a single
great pull, climb into a boat, whence a moment later he would dive headlong into the
water again, sound its utmost depths, touch bottom, explore the hollows of rocks and
plunge into any pits and abysses he fancied. He would turn the boat about, managing
it perfectly, bringing it swiftly or slowly upstream or down and arresting its course at
a milldam. He could guide it with one hand while he plied hard about him with a
great oar; he could run up a sail, hoist himself up a mast by the shrouds, dance along
the yards, operate the compass, tackle the bowlines to sail close to the wind and steer
the helm.

His water sports done, he would dash full speed up a mountain, then down quite
as fast. He climbed trees like a cat, hopping from one to the next like a squirrel and
pulling down great boughs—like the celebrated Milo of Crotona who, Pausanias tells
us, met his death devoured by wolves, his hands caught in the cleft of an oak he had
sought to split. With two well-steeled daggers and a pair of well-tried mason's punches,
he could scurry up the side of a house like a rat, then leap down again, from roof to
ground, so expertly that he landed without hurt. Gargantua also cast the dart, threw
the iron bar, put the stone, tossed the boar-spear, hurled the javelin, shied the halberd.
He drew the bow to breaking point; he could shoulder a harquebuss—a great siege
piece weighing fifty pounds—and fire it off like a crossbow. He could set a huge cannon
on its carriage, hit buttmarks and other targets for horizontal shooting, or, point-blank,
bring down papgays (stuffed figures of parrots on poles), clay pigeons and other verticle
marks, facing them on a level or upwards, or downwards or sidewise. Like the ancient
Parthians, he could even hit them as he retreated.

They would tie a cable to a high tower and let it dangle to the ground. Gargantua
hoisted himself up with both hands, then slipped down again as evenly, surely and

plumb as a man running along a flat meadow. Or they would set a great pole across two trees for Gargantua to hang from by his hands. He moved along the pole from tree to tree so swiftly, without setting foot on *terra firma,* that a man, running on the ground below, could not have caught him. To expand his chest and exercise his lungs, he would roar like all the devils in hell. Once indeed, I heard him call Eudemon across all Paris, from the Porte St. Victor, the gate by the University, all the way to Montmartre, a village on a hill two miles beyond the walls of the city. Stentor, who cried louder than forty men, displayed no such vocal power, even at the siege of Troy.

To develop his sinews, they made him two great pigs of lead, each weighing eight hundred and five tons. These pigs (called salmons in France because the metal is shaped like this fish) Gargantua named *alteres,* an ancient Greek term for the weights used to give jumpers their initial spring—our modern dumb-bells. Taking one in each hand, Gargantua then performed an inimitable feat. He would raise them high above his head and, never turning a hair, stock-still as a statue, hold them aloft for three-quarters of an hour. He played at Barriers or Tug-of-War with the stoutest champions. When his turn came he took root so firmly as to defy the sturdiest to budge him. Nor was it thus alone he emulated Milo of Crotona. Like the ancient athlete, he could hold a pomegranate so fast in his hand that none could wrest it from him, yet so adroitly that he did not crush it.

Having spent his time in such manly sports, he had himself washed, rubbed down and given a change of clothes. Then he returned home at a leisurely pace, passing through some meadow or grassy space to examine the trees and plants. These he would compare with what the authorities wrote of them in their books: among the Ancients, Theophrastus, the successor of Aristotle and teacher of Menander . . . or Palladius, whose poem *De re rustica* was translated by Pietro Marini . . . or Dioscorides Pedanius, the Greek physician of the first century . . . or Pliny or Nicander or Aemilius Macer, the Roman, or Galen himself. . . . Gargantua and his companions picked specimens by the handful and took them home to a young page named Rhizotome or Rootcutter, who watched over them and the various small mattocks, pickaxes, hooks, hoes, pruning-knives, shears and other botanical instruments.

At home, whilst the servants prepared dinner, our young men repeated certain passages of what had been read. Then they sat down to table. Here I would have you note that their dinner was simple and frugal; they ate no more than necessary to quiet the baying of the belly. Supper, on the contrary, was a large and copious meal; they ate what they needed for their sustenance and nourishment. Such indeed is the true system prescribed by the art of sound, self-respecting physicians though a rabble of dunderhead quacks, wrangling eternally in the claptrap routine of the Arab nostrum shop of Avicenna, recommend the exact opposite. During supper, they continued the lesson given at dinner as long as they saw fit; the rest of the meal was spent in earnest and profitable discussion.

Having said grace, they applied their voices to sing tunefully or they played upon harmonious instruments. Or they amused themselves with such minor pastimes as cards, dice cups and dice afforded. Sometimes they tarried here enjoying themselves and making merry until bedtime; they would visit learned men or such as had travelled in foreign lands. Well into the night, before retiring, they would go to the most exposed spot in the house, whence they examined the face of the sky, noting the comets, if any were visible, and the various figures, positions, aspects, oppositions and conjunctions of the heavenly bodies.

According to the Pythagorean system, Gargantua would, with his tutor, recapitulate briefly all that he had read, seen, learned, done and assimilated in the course of the day.

Then they prayed to God the Creator, doing Him worship and confirming their faith in Him, glorifying Him for His immense goodness, vouchsafing thanks for all the mighty past and imploring His divine clemency for all the future.

And so they retired to rest.

The New Economics

Carolus Molineus, or Charles Dumoulin (1500–1566), was one of the greatest jurists of his time. His life was stormy, his character somewhat difficult, plentifully endowed with the self-satisfaction current among the men of the Renaissance, calculated to influence people but not to make too many friends. The views he expressed in his treatise On Contracts and Usury *(1546) met with a tempest of abuse from ecclesiastical quarters. Current doctrine, which was still that of Aquinas, held the simple act of lending money at interest, however low the rate, to be un-Christian. This rule had never prevented such financial transactions, but it had made business life more difficult. Dumoulin argued for more realistic attitudes better suited to the realities of the time.*

Charles Dumoulin: from On Contracts and Usury

Scholastic theologians, as well as canonists and jurists, considering the letter rather than the spirit or intent and purpose of the divine law, have believed there was something peculiarly and inherently vicious about usury or usurious gains, more than in unjust, deceitful sales, or other similar kinds of fraud. And this, not because one's neighbor is more harmed thereby; but because in a loan something more than the principal is received; as if usury *per se* were more detestable and more wicked, or *per se* more unlawful. Thus some hold that, although usury may sometimes not be contrary to charity, as if it were harmful, still there is always something rather dishonorable about it; or again, that the prohibition of usury is so strict according to divine law that it cannot be modified by legislation, even in cases where it is a question of public utility and the common good, and the civil amity which nature has established among men. Hence they have fallen into the infinite evasions and numerous errors and fallacies with which their very confused books are filled; all because they have not considered the purpose of the divine law, which is charity, as Christ himself testifies: *All things, therefore, whatsoever you would that men should do to you, do you also unto them. For this is the law and the prophets.* That is to say, this is its purpose. And St. Paul (I

Reprinted by permission of the publishers from Arthur E. Monroe, editor *Early Economic Thought: Selections from Economic Literature Prior to Adam Smith.* Cambridge, Mass.: Harvard University Press, 1924.

Timothy): *The end of the law is charity.* Also Romans 13 and Galatians 5: *He who loveth his neighbor hath fulfilled the law.* Therefore, usury is not forbidden and unlawful according to divine law, except insofar as it is contrary to charity. Since, however, usury is taken in many ways, that form alone is prohibited and condemned which offends against charity and love of one's neighbor. . . .

Suppose a merchant of means borrows money in order to make a profit from legitimate business, and promises to pay usury monthly or annually, instead of a portion of the expected profit: Should you say that the creditor, if unable to prove his claim to that much interest, or perhaps any interest at all, cannot lawfully contract for or receive such usury without injury to the debtor? Whatever all this crowd may have written, I see no harm in this, nothing contrary to divine or natural law; since nothing is done in it contrary to charity, but rather from mutual charity. It is plain that one grants the favor of a loan from his property; the other remunerates his benefactor with a part of the gain derived therefrom, without suffering any loss. Therefore the creditor lawfully receives more than his principal; and by the same reasoning, he may from the beginning covenant to this effect, within legitimate limits, however, and provided that the one who covenants does not plan any fraud against his neighbor, or demand usury unfairly. . . .

Just as the invention of money was necessary for the sake of exchange and the needs of men, so for a similar, though not so great, necessity, usury was invented and tolerated; for it is clear that people in business often need to use other people's money, nor is it expedient in all cases to arrange a partnership, a single man's industry being involved; and none are found who will lend for nothing. . . . Under these conditions [usury] is lawful, not only according to human law but also according to all law, divine and natural. . . .

THE NEW WORLD

Early in the fifteenth century the thought occurred to some of the traders, sailors, and princes of Europe that the Italo-Arab hold on the rich Eastern trade might be broken by the discovery of another route to the Indies. The need for new trade routes, which would permit western Europe to break the Italian monopoly on trade with Egypt and the Levant, went along with contemporary humanists' interest in the nature of the physical world. This interest led to better maps as cartographers took account of the works of the ancient Ptolemy and of travelers like Marco Polo and the experience of more recent explorers on land or sea.

Though some of the greatest sailors involved in the new adventures were Italians—Columbus, Cabot, and Amerigo Vespucci among them—their first patrons were the rulers of the rising Iberian kingdoms of Portugal, Aragon, and Castile. Although these rulers still were chiefly concerned through much of the fifteenth century with the reconquest of the Iberian peninsula from its remaining Moorish masters, the Portuguese had early started to send vessels along the coast of Africa and into the South Atlantic. Thus as Portuguese enterprises traveled mostly to the south and the east, they eventually reached India by rounding the Cape of Good Hope. This is partly why the later, Spanish, explorers sailed due west. On the heels of Spain came the vessels of other nations, eager to discover the vast possibilities of the new lands.

Paolo Toscanelli: Letter to Columbus

In the summer of 1474 the Florentine scientist and astronomer Paolo Toscanelli found his advice in great demand on the subject of the resources of the Indies and the best way of getting there. Here is a letter he wrote in July of that year.

Paul, the Physician, to Cristobal Colombo, greeting. I perceive your magnificent and great desire to find a way to where the spices grow, and in reply to your letter I send you the copy of another letter which I wrote some days ago to a friend and favorite of the most serene King of Portugal, in reply to another which, by direction of his Highness he wrote to me on the said subject, and I send you another sea chart like the one I sent him, by which you will be satisfied respecting your enquiries: which copy is as follows:

"Paul the Physician, to Fernan Martins, Canon at Lisbon, greeting. It was pleasant to me to understand that your health was good, and that you are in the favor and intimacy with the most generous and most magnificent Prince, your King. I have already spoken with you respecting a shorter way to the places of spices than that which you take by Guinea, by means of maritime navigation. The most serene King now seeks from me some statement, or rather a demonstration to the eye, by which the slightly learned may take in and understand that way. I know this can be shown from the spherical shape of the earth, yet to make the comprehension of it easier, and to facilitate the work, I have determined to show that way by means of a sailing chart. I, therefore, send his Majesty a chart made by my own hands, on which are delineated your coasts and islands, whence you must begin to make your journey always westward, and the places at which you should arrive, and how far from the pole or the equinoctial line you ought to keep, and through how much space or over how many miles you should arrive at those most fertile places full of all sorts of spices and jewels. You must not be surprised if I call the parts where the spices are west, when they usually call them east, because to those always sailing west, those parts are found by navigation on the under side of the earth. But if by land and by the upper side, they will always be found to the east. . . . It is asserted that none but merchants live on the islands. For there the number of navigators with merchandize is so great that in all the rest of the world there are not so many as in the most noble port called Zaitun. For they affirm that a hundred ships laden with pepper discharge their cargoes in that port in a single year, besides other ships bringing other spices. That country is very populous and very rich, with a multitude of provinces and kingdoms, and with cities without number, under one prince who is called the Great Kan, which name signifies King of Kings, whose seat and residence is generally in the province of Katay. His ancestors

From *The Journal of Christopher Columbus,* tr. Clement R. Markham (London, 1893).

RESTORATION OF THE TOSCANELLI MAP

From *The Journal of Christopher Columbus*, tr. Clement R. Markham (London, 1893).

desired intercourse with Christians now 200 years ago. They sent to the Pope [he refers to the journey of Nicolo and Maffeo Polo, who reached the court of Kublai Khan in 1260, returned as his envoys in 1269, and started east again in 1271, taking their nephew Marco with them] and asked for several persons learned in the faith that they might be enlightened, but those who were sent, being impeded in their journey, went back. Also in the time of Eugenius[1] one of them came, who affirmed their great kindness towards Christians, and I had a long conversation with him on many subjects, about the magnitude of their rivers in length and breadth, and on the multitude of cities on the banks of the rivers. He said that on one river there were near 200 cities with marble bridges great in length and breadth, and everywhere adorned with columns. This country is worth seeking by the Latins, not only because great wealth may be obtained from it, gold and silver, all sorts of gems and spices, which never reach us; but also on account of its learned men, philosophers and expert astrologers, and by what skill and art so powerful and magnificent a province is governed, as well as how their wars are conducted. This is for some satisfaction to his request, so far as the shortness of time and my occupations admitted: being ready in future more fully to satisfy his royal Majesty as far as he may wish. Given at Florence, June 24th, 1474."

From the city of Lisbon due west there are 26 spaces marked on the map, each of which has 250 miles, as far as the most noble and very great city of Quinsay [which Marco Polo calls the City of Heaven]. For it is a hundred miles in circumference and has ten bridges, and its name signifies the city of Heaven; many wonders being related concerning it, touching the multitude of its handicrafts and its resources. This space is almost a third part of the whole sphere. That city is . . . near the province of Katay, in which land is the royal residence. But from the island Antilia, known to you [a fabulous island, after which the West Indian islands were first named around 1500] to the most noble island of Cipango there are ten spaces. For that island is most fertile in gold, pearls, and precious stones, and they cover the temples and palaces with solid gold. Thus the spaces of the sea to be crossed in the unknown part are not great. Many things might perhaps have been declared more exactly, but a diligent thinker will be able to clear up the rest for himself. Farewell, most excellent one.

Christopher Columbus: from The Journal

Christopher Columbus (1451–1506) was born in Genoa, Italy. His beginnings are still obscure. The ideas that led to his great project of reaching China by sailing west were based on the belief, going back to the Middle Ages, that there were lands in the Atlantic— lands he presumed to be Cipango and Cathay. Rebuffed by the Portuguese, who had other fish to fry, he entered the service of Spain and eventually persuaded Queen Isabella of Castile to grant him command of the three ships with which he would discover the New World. Leaving Spain on August 2, 1492, he returned eight months later, having effected landings in San Salvador, Cuba, and Haiti. A second voyage brought him to Guadeloupe,

---

[1] Pope Eugenius IV, 1431–1447.

From *The Journal of Christopher Columbus*, tr. Clement R. Markham (London, 1893).

*Puerto Rico, and Jamaica; a third enabled him, after touching Trinidad, to reach the
continent and sail along the South American coast from the mouth of the Orinoco River
to Caracas. On his fourth—and last—trip he explored the coast of Central America from
Honduras to the Gulf of Darien. By then, however, he had lost his credit at court; after
his return in 1504 he was left to die in relative poverty and disgrace.*

In the name of our Lord Jesus Christ. Because, O most Christian, and very high, very
excellent and puissant Princes, King and Queen of the Spains and of the islands of the
Sea, our Lords, in this present year of 1492, after your Highnesses had given an end
to the war with the Moors who reigned in Europe, and had finished it in the very great
city of Granada, where in this present year, on the second day of the month of January,
by force of arms, I saw the royal banners of your Highnesses placed on the towers of
Alhambra, which is the fortess of that city, and I saw the Moorish King come forth
from the gates of the city and kiss the royal hands of your Highnesses, and of the
Prince my Lord, and presently in that same month, acting on the information that I
had given to your Highnesses touching the lands of India, and respecting a Prince who
is called Gran Can, which means in our language King of Kings, how he and his ancestors had sent to Rome many times to ask for learned men of our holy faith to teach him,
and how the Holy Father had never complied, insomuch that many people believing in
idolatries were lost by receiving doctrine of perdition: YOUR HIGHNESSES, as Catholic Christians and Princes who love the holy Christian faith, and the propagation of
it, and who are enemies to the sect of Mahomet and to all idolatries and heresies,
resolved to send me, Cristobal Colon, to the said parts of India to see the said princes,
and the cities and lands, and their disposition, with a view that they might be converted
to our holy faith; and ordered that I should not go by land to the eastward, as had
been customary, but that I should go by way of the west, whither up to this day we
do not know for certain that any one has gone.

Thus, after having turned out all the Jews from all your kingdoms and lordships,
in the same month of January, your Highnesses gave orders to me that with a sufficient
fleet I should go to the said parts of India. . . .

[The expedition left Palos on August 2, 1492; on October 12th,] at two hours after
midnight, the land was sighted at a distance of two leagues. They shortened sail, and
lay by under the mainsail without the bonnets. The vessels were hove to, waiting for
daylight; and on Friday they arrived at a small island of the Lucayos [Columbus named
it San Salvador; it is now Watling Island]. Presently they saw naked people. The Admiral
went on shore in the armed boat, and Martin Alonzo Pinzon and Vicente Yañez, his
brother, who was captain of the *Nina*. The Admiral took the royal standard, and the
captains went with two banners of the green cross, which the Admiral took in all the
ships as a sign, with an F and a Y and a crown over each letter, one on one side of
the cross and the other on the other. Having landed, they saw trees very green, and
much water, and fruits of diverse kinds. The Admiral called to the two captains and
to the others who leaped on shore . . . and said that they should bear faithful testimony
that he, in the presence of all, had taken, as he now took, possession of the said island
for the King and for the Queen, his Lords making the declarations that are required. . . .

Presently many inhabitants of the island assembled. . . . I saw and knew (says the Admiral) that these people are without any religion, not idolaters but very gentle, not knowing what is evil, nor the sins of murder and theft, being without arms, and so timid that a hundred would fly before one Spaniard, although they joke with them. They, however, believe and know that there is a God in heaven, and say that we have come from heaven. At any prayer that we say, they repeat, and make the sign of the cross. Thus your Highnesses should resolve to make them Christians, for I believe that if the work was begun, in a little time the multitude of nations would be converted to our faith, with the acquisition of great lordships, peoples, and riches for Spain. Without doubt there is in this land a vast quantity of gold, and the Indians . . . do not speak without reason when they say that in these islands there are places where they dig out gold, and wear it on their necks, ears, arms and legs, the rings being very large. There are also precious stones, pearls, and an infinity of spices. . . . Here also there is a great quantity of cotton, and I believe it would have a good sale here without sending it to Spain, but to the cities of the Gran Can, which will be discovered without doubt, and many others ruled over by other lords, who will be pleased to serve your Highnesses, and whither will be brought other commodities of Spain and of the Eastern lands; but these are to the West as regards us.

They were to the west all right; but Columbus was never to enter into the land of Canaan that he had dreamed of for so long. Cuba was not Cipango; Katay he never found; and though the New World he discovered soon revealed other riches, it did not bring his masters the trade of the Indies. This was soon to fall into the hands of travelers following another route.

Vasco da Gama: from A Journal of the First Voyage

The first half of the fifteenth century had seen the sailors of Portugal pushing south, along the African coast, in search of knowledge and gain. A series of expeditions, supported by the government, enabled Diego Cam to discover the Congo in 1484 and Bartholomeo Diaz to round the Cape of Good Hope in 1488. It was not for another ten years, however, that this discovery could be put to use by Vasco da Gama (c. 1469–1524), who set out in 1497 to reach India by rounding the Cape, and did actually reach Calecut, one of the chief trading ports of southern India, a year later. Vasco da Gama's voyage was the fount of Portugal's eastern empire, whose bases soon reached from Mozambique and the Persian Gulf to Canton. The great explorer himself was appointed first viceroy of the Indies.

In the year 1497 King Dom Manuel, the first of that name in Portugal, dispatched four vessels to make discoveries and go in search of spices. Vasco da Gama was the captain-major of these vessels.

[On May 20, 1498] we anchored two leagues from the city of Calecut [in India]. The city . . . is inhabited by Christians. They are of a tawny complexion. Some of them

From *A Journal of the First Voyage of Vasco da Gama* (London, 1898), E. J. Ravenstein, Ed.; from *The Three Voyages of Vasco da Gama and His Viceroyalty*, H. E. J. Stanley, Ed. 1869.

have big beards and long hair, whilst others clip their hair short or shave the head, merely allowing a tuft to remain on the crown as a sign that they are Christians. They also wear mustaches. They pierce the ears and wear much gold in them. . . . The women of this country, as a rule, are ugly and of small stature. They wear many jewels of gold round the neck, numerous bracelets on their arms, and rings set with precious stones on their toes. All these people are well disposed and apparently mild of temper. At first sight they seem covetous and ignorant. . . . On the following morning . . . the captain-major set out to speak to the king, and took with him thirteen men, of whom I was one. We put on our best attire, placed bombards in our boats, and took with us trumpets and many flags. On landing, the captain-major was received by the alcalde, with whom were many men, armed and unarmed. The reception was friendly, as if the people were pleased to see us. . . . [On first arriving in Calecut] they took us to a large church [obviously a pagoda or temple] and this is what we saw: The body of the church is as large as a monastery, all built of stone and covered with tiles. . . . In the centre of the body of the church rose a chapel, all built of hewn stone, with a bronze door sufficiently wide for a man to pass, and stone steps leading up to it. Within this sanctuary stood a small image which they said represented Our Lady. Along the walls, by the main entrance, hung seven small bells. In this church the captain-major said his prayers, and we with him. . . . Many other saints were painted on the walls of the church, wearing crowns. They were painted variously, with teeth protruding an inch from the mouth, and four or five arms. . . .

The further we advanced in the direction of the king's palace, the more did the crowd increase in number. And when we arrived there, men of much distinction and great lords came out to meet the captain, and joined those who were already in attendance upon him. It was then an hour before sunset. When we reached the palace, we passed through a gate into a courtyard of great size and, before we arrived at where the king was, we passed four doors, through which we had to force our way, giving many blows to the people. When at last we reached the door where the king was, there came forth from it a little old man who holds a position resembling that of a bishop, and upon whose advice the king acts in all affairs of the church. This man embraced the captain when he entered the door. Several men were wounded at this door, and we only got in by the use of much force.

The king was in a small court, reclining upon a couch covered with a cloth of green velvet, above which was a good mattress, and upon this again a sheet of cotton stuff, very white and fine, more so than any linen. The cushions were after the same fashion. In his left hand the king held a very large golden spittoon, having a capacity of eight pints. At its mouth this cup was 16 inches wide, and apparently it was massive. Into this cup the king threw the husks of a certain herb which is chewed by the people of this country for its soothing effects, and which they call betel nut. On the right side of the king stood a basin of gold, so large that a man might just encircle it with his arms: this contained the herbs. There were likewise many silver jugs. The canopy above the couch was all gilt. . . .

The king beckoned to the captain . . . to come nearer, but the captain did not approach him, for it is the custom of the country for no man to approach the king except only the servant who hands him the herbs, and when anyone addresses the king he holds his hand before his mouth, and remains at a distance. When the king beckoned to the captain he looked at us others, and ordered us to be seated on a stone bench near him, where he could see us. He ordered that water for our hands should be given us, also some fruit, one kind of which resembled a melon, except that its outside was rough and the inside sweet, whilst another kind of fruit resembled a fig and tasted very nice [apparently jack (a kind of breadfruit) and bananas].

And the captain told him he was the ambassador of a King of Portugal, who was Lord of many countries and the possessor of great wealth of every description, exceeding that of any king of these parts; that for a period of sixty years his ancestors had annually sent out vessels to make discoveries in the direction of India, as they knew that there were Christian kings like themselves. This, he said, was the reason which induced them to order this country to be discovered, not because they sought for gold or silver, for of this they had such an abundance that they needed not what was to be found in this country. . . . The captains sent out traveled for a year or two, until their provisions became exhausted, and then returned to Portugal, without having succeeded in making the desired discovery. There reigned a king now whose name was Dom Manuel, who had ordered him to build three vessels . . . and not to return to Portugal until he should have discovered this king of the Christians, on pain of having his head cut off. . . . And, finally, he had been instructed to say by word of mouth that the King of Portugal desired to be his friend and brother. . . .

On Tuesday [May 29, 1498] the captain got ready the following things to be sent to the king [of Calecut], viz., twelve pieces of striped cloth, four scarlet hoods, six hats, four strings of coral, a case containing six washstand basins, a case of sugar, two casks of oil and two of honey. And as it is the custom not to send anything to the king without the knowledge of the Moor, his factor, and of the *bale* [governor], the captain informed them of his intention. They came, and when they saw the present they laughed at it, saying that it was not a thing to offer to a king, that the poorest merchant from Mecca, or any other part of India, gave more, and that if he wanted to make a present it should be in gold, as the king would not accept such things. When the captain heard this he grew sad, and said that he had brought no gold; that, moreover, he was no merchant, but an ambassador; that he gave of that which he had, which was his own private gift, and not the king's; that if the king of Portugal ordered him to return he would intrust him with far richer presents. . . . Upon this they declared that they would not forward his presents, nor consent to his forwarding them himself. When they had gone, there came certain Moorish merchants and they all depreciated the present which the captain desired to be sent to the king. . . .

As a result of this and of other misunderstandings, relations between the Indians and the Portuguese got worse and worse. Nevertheless, the king of Calecut did let Vasco da Gama have a letter for his royal master, and the tenor of the letter was as follows:

Vasco de Gama, a gentleman of your household, came to my country, whereat I was pleased. My country is rich in cinnamon, cloves, ginger, pepper, and precious stones. That which I ask of you in exchange is gold, silver, corals, and scarlet cloth.

The survivors of the expedition reached Lisbon in July 1499, and their reports greatly cheered the king; that same month we find him writing to his neighbors, the King and Queen of Castile:

Most high and excellent Prince and Princess, most potent Lord and Lady!

Your Highnesses already know that we had ordered Vasco da Gama, a nobleman of our household, and his brother Paulo da Gama, with four vessels to make discoveries by sea, and that two years have now elapsed since their departure. And as the principal motive of this enterprise has been, with our predecessors, the service of God our Lord, and our own advantage, it pleased Him in His mercy to speed them on their route. From a message which has now been brought to this city by one of the captains, we learn that they did reach and discover India and other kingdoms and lordships bordering upon it; that they entered and navigated its sea, finding large cities, large edifices and rivers, and great populations, among whom is carried on all the trade in spices and precious stones, which are forwarded in ships . . . to Mecca, and thence to Cairo, whence they are dispersed throughout the world. Of these spices, etc., they have brought a quantity, including cinnamon, cloves, ginger, nutmeg, and pepper, as well as other kinds, together with the boughs and leaves of the same; also many fine stones of all sorts, such as rubies and others. And they also came to a country in which there are mines of gold, of which, as of the spices and precious stones, they did not bring as much as they could have done, for they took no merchandise with them.

As we are aware that your Highnesses will hear of these things with pleasure and satisfaction, we thought well to give this information. And your Highnesses may believe, in accordance with what we have learnt concerning the Christian people whom these explorers reached, that it will be possible, notwithstanding that they are not as yet strong in the faith nor possessed of a thorough knowledge of it, to do much in the service of God and the exaltation of the Holy Faith, once they shall have been converted and fully fortified in it. And when they shall thus have been fortified in the faith, there will be an opportunity for destroying the Moors of those parts. Moreover, we hope, with the help of God, that the great trade which now enriches the Moors of those parts, through whose hands it passes without the intervention of other persons or peoples, shall, in consequence of our regulations, be diverted to the natives and the ships of our own kingdom, so that henceforth all Christendom, in this part of Europe, shall be able, in a large measure, to provide itself with those spices and precious stones. This, with the help of God, who in his mercy thus ordained it, will cause our designs and intentions to be pushed with more ardor, especially as concerns the war upon the Moors of the territories conquered by us in these parts, which your Highnesses are so firmly resolved upon, and in which we are equally zealous.

And we pray your Highnesses, in consideration of this great favor, which, with much gratitude, we received from our Lord, to cause to be addressed to Him those praises which are His due.

But, although Manuel had reason to regard the discovery of India as a favor of God, and although Ferdinand and Isabella probably gnashed their teeth to see the Portuguese finding spices and jewels to the east, where their ships had found mostly "savages" to the west, the Indians themselves had no cause to praise the God of these arrogant interlopers. Back in India, we find da Gama up to his old tricks.

He then ordered the boats to go and plunder the small vessels, which were sixteen, and the two ships in which they found rice, and many jars of butter, and many bales of stuffs. They then gathered all this together into the ships, with the crews of the two large ships, and he ordered the boats to get as much rice as they wanted, and they took that of four of the small vessels, which they emptied, for they did not want more. Then the captain-major commanded them to cut off the hands and noses of all the crews, and put all that into one of the small vessels, into which he ordered them to put the friar [a Brahmin envoy, dressed as a friar, who had come aboard under safe conduct], also without ears or nose or hands, which he had ordered to be strung up round his neck, with a palm leaf for the king, on which he told him to have a curry made to eat of what his friar brought with him. When all the Indians had been thus executed, he ordered their feet to be tied together, as they had no hands with which to untie them, and in order that they should not untie them with their teeth, he ordered men to strike upon their teeth with staves until they knocked them down their throats; and they were thus put on board, heaped up on top of each other, mixed up with the blood which streamed from them, and he ordered mats and dry leaves to be spread over them, and the sails to be set for the shore, and the vessel set on fire and there were more than eight hundred Moors. And the small vessel with the friar, with all the hands and ears, was also sent on shore under sail, without being fired. These vessels went at once on shore, where many people flocked together to put out the fire, and draw out those whom they found alive, upon which they made great lamentations.

Richard Hakluyt: from Divers Voyages Touching the Discovery of America

As the sixteenth century drew to a close, England had made little serious effort to colonize the New World. The Elizabethans were interested in discovery, pillage, and war, but few showed any enthusiasm for the hard, sustained work that would be involved in founding new communities on the North American shore. Sir Walter Raleigh was one of these few. Another was Richard Hakluyt (1553–1616), an Oxford man and preacher, whose Principal Navigations, Voyages, Traffiques, and Discoveries of the English Nation *is, in H. A. L. Fisher's words, the prose epic of this age of adventurers, though one devoted largely to recommending colonies as means of promoting trade and of ridding the country of its unprofitable members.*

Hakluyt's propaganda led to the foundation in 1584 of a colony named, after the queen, Virginia; but the interest it generated was apparently insufficient to keep the new

From *Divers Voyages Touching the Discovery of America* (London, 1850).

settlement alive. The colony was allowed to fade away without adequate support, and it had to be founded anew in 1607, under the succeeding reign of James I.

I marvel not a little (right worshipful) that since the first discovery of America (which is now full forescore and ten years), after so great conquests and plantings of the Spaniards and Portuguese there, that we of England could never have the grace to set fast footing in such fertile and temperate places as are left as yet unpossessed of them. But again, when I consider that there is a time for all men, and see the Portuguese time to be out of date, and that the nakedness of the Spaniards and their long hidden secrets are now at length espied, whereby they went about to delude the world, I conceive great hope that the time approaches and now is, that we of England may share and participate (if we will ourselves) both with the Spaniard and the Portuguese, in part of America and other regions, as yet undiscovered. And surely if there were in us that desire to advance the honor of our country which ought to be in every good man, we would not all this while have forborne [neglected] the possessing of those lands, which of equity and right appertain unto us, as by the discourses that follow shall appear most plainly. Yea, if we would behold with the eye of pity how all our Prisons are pestered and filled with able men to serve their Country, which for small robberies are daily hanged up in great numbers, even twenty at a clap, out of one jail (as was seen at the last assizes at Rochester), we would hasten and further every man to his power the deducting of [conveying] to some Colonies of our superfluous people into those temperate and fertile parts of America, which, being within six weeks sailing of England, are yet unpossessed by any Christians: and seem to offer themselves unto us, stretching nearer unto her Majesty's Dominions than to any other part of Europe. We read that the Bees when they grow to be too many in their own hives at home, are wont to be led out by their Captains to swarm abroad and seek themselves a new dwelling place. If the examples of the Grecians and Carthaginians of old time and the practice of our age may not move us yet let us learn wisdom of these small weak and unreasonable creatures. It chanced very lately that upon occasion I had great conference in matters of Cosmography with an excellent learned man of Portugal most privy to all the discoveries of his nation, who wondered that those blessed countries from the point of Florida northward were all this while unplanted by Christians, protesting with great affection and zeal, that if he were now as young as I (for at present he is three score years of age) he would sell all he had, being a man of no small wealth and honor, to furnish a convenient number of ships to sea for the inhabiting of those countries, and reducing those gentle people to Christianity. . . .

IMAGES: DISCIPLINING VIOLENCE

Anarchy and violence that disorganized and terrorized could be put down only by still greater violence. A feudal world ruled by small and greater gangsters was gradually brought to heel by a central power that could bear the costs of modern armaments and maintain regular troops. The discipline slowly forced on unruly vassals would be imposed on other subjects, too. As with training soldiers to obey orders, training civilians to obey laws and behave in an orderly way was more a matter of intimidation than of persuasion.

Siege using longbows and crossbows.
(Photographie Bulloz, Paris)

Late Medieval Warfare. These fifteenth-century miniatures represent a formidable novelty: firearms. Medieval walls could not resist the stone or iron balls fired by increasingly mobile cannon. In the pictures shown here, one sees the great bows, which unhorsed so many knights, supplemented by arbalets, crossbows, and "firestaffs", the ancestors of muskets and of rifles.

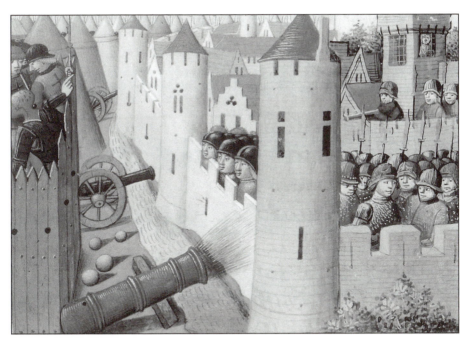

Siege of a town using artillery.
(Bibliothèque Nationale, Paris, Fr 5054, Folio 54V)

Siege using lances, bows, artillery, and firestaffs.
(Photographie Bulloz, Paris)

Military Execution by Firing Squad. Ill-trained, ill-paid, or not paid at all, most early modern armies behaved like pillaging hordes—robbing, raping, murdering, and burning no matter what side they were on. Discipline was cruel, as in this Jacques Callot engraving of an executioner. One blindfolded soldier waits to be shot and four corpses lie on the ground beside him, while in the right foreground, others wait their turn.

(Photographie Bulloz, Paris)

The Spectacle of Public Executions. Before civil behavior could take hold, uncivil violence had to be fought with counter-violence. Only fear of suffering and death could drive sin back. The theatre of torture taught that this was so, and the public flocked to the entertainment it provided. But punishment was no monopoly of the state. If you look closely at this Jacques Callot engraving, you will see a small boy being spanked and an apprentice being flogged by his master. Once society had begun to repress disorder, sensibility would be free to intervene and appeal for clemency and compassion.
(Photographie Bulloz, Paris)

The Battle of Fontenoy, 1745. The French and the English face each other in the slen-der rows designed to minimize losses from artillery fire and appropriate for firing and reloading their muskets. Armies were no longer rag-tag bands but highly disciplined troops, trained for sophisticated tactics. New and complex evolutions of warfare were designed to economize on the lives of soldiers whose training was too long and costly for waste. (Photographie Bulloz, Paris)

Reformation and
Counter Reformation

Movements for Church reform were nothing new in the Christian world. All through the Middle Ages the clergy were frequently attacked for failing to lead worthy lives; new doctrines were debated, though seldom accepted; and attempts were made to replace the Latin Bible—incomprehensible to the vast majority of the laity and to a surprising number of the clergy—with translations in the local tongue. A look at the Wycliffite conclusions condemned by the Church, and at John Wycliffe's letter to the pope, reveals defiance to be as rife in the fourteenth century as it would be in the sixteenth.

When Martin Luther tacked up his Ninety-Five Theses on the church door at Wittenberg, he did not think he was taking an original or revolutionary step. A feeling for Church reform was in the air, fostered by the studies and translations of Renaissance humanists such as Erasmus and by the growth of a self-confident public opinion more critical of its religious leaders than ever before. But there was no reason to think that reform would turn into revolt; nor would it have done so, perhaps, had German complaints been properly handled. However, once Luther and his supporters were driven into open revolt, they benefited from economic and political circumstances that linked religious ideas to political ones. After 1521 there seems to have been no turning back; there would have to be reform, whether within the Church or outside it. As it happened, there were both, with the "protestant" reform spurring the Church of Rome to put its house in order and reaffirm its doctrines. Thus, as the sixteenth century drew to a close, the unity of the Christian West had been shattered, but the divisions themselves created an intensity of religious concern and belief unknown in Europe for a long time.

Wycliffe and the Lollards

John Wycliffe (1324–1384) was born in Yorkshire, England; taught at Oxford; and, on being expelled from that university in 1382, returned to his Leicestershire vicarage of Lutterworth, where he lived quietly until his death. Wycliffe used his great knowledge and academic position at Oxford to attack the scandals and corruption in the Roman Catholic Church, protesting against much of its teaching and practice. He wanted preachers to preach in English, not Latin; to base their preaching on the Scriptures; and to use an English Bible that would make the Scriptures available to all. The English Bible that bears his name was translated by his disciples, and preachers inspired by him spread the message throughout England. His work also reached the University of Prague, where it led one of the professors there, John Hus (1369–1415), to spread Wycliffe's doctrine that the pope was to be obeyed only insofar as he acted in accordance with Scripture. The following writings are a sample of Wycliffite religious views and Wycliffe's reply to the authorities who condemned them.

John Wycliffe: Conclusions

WYCLIFFITE CONCLUSIONS, TEN CONDEMNED AS HERETICAL AND FOURTEEN AS ERRONEOUS

I. That the material substance of bread and of wine remains, after the consecration, in the sacrament of the altar.

II. That the accidents do not remain without the subject, after the consecration, in the same sacrament.[1]

III. That Christ is not in the sacrament of the altar identically, truly, and really in his proper corporal presence.

IV. That if a bishop or priest lives in mortal sin he does not ordain, or consecrate, or baptize.

V. That if a man has been truly repentant, all external confession is superfluous to him, or useless.

VI. Continually to assert that it is not founded in the gospel that Christ instituted the mass.

VII. That God ought to be obedient to the devil.

VIII. That if the Pope is foreordained to destruction and a wicked man, and therefore a member of the devil, no power has been given to him over the faithful of Christ by any one, unless perhaps by the Emperor.

IX. That since Urban the Sixth, no one is to be acknowledged as Pope; but all are to live, in the way of the Greeks, under their own laws.

X. To assert that it is against sacred scripture that men of the church should have temporal possessions.

XI. That no prelate ought to excommunicate any one unless he first knows that the man is excommunicated by God.

XII. That a person thus excommunicating is thereby a heretic or excommunicate.

---

[1] Which comes to saying that, consecrated or not, bread and wine remain just that: bread and wine. You can treat them *symbolically* as the flesh and blood of Christ but, as said in Conclusion III, Christ is not really, truly in them.

From *Translations and Reprints from the Original Sources of European History* (henceforth to be cited as *Translations and Reprints*), Vol. 2, No. 5, E. P. Cheyney, Ed.

XIII. That a prelate excommunicating a clerk who has appealed to the king, or to a council of the kingdom, on that very account is a traitor to God, the king, and the kingdom.

XIV. That those who neglect to preach, or to hear the word of God, or the gospel that is preached, because of the excommunication of men, are excommunicate, and in the day of judgment will be considered as traitors to God.

XV. To assert that it is allowed to any one, whether a deacon or a priest, to preach the word of God, without the authority of the apostolic see, or of a catholic bishop, or some other which is sufficiently acknowledged.

XVI. To assert that no one is a civil lord, no one is a bishop, no one is a prelate, so long as he is in mortal sin.

XVII. That temporal lords may, at their own judgment, take away temporal goods from churchmen who are habitually delinquent; or that the people may, at their own judgment, correct delinquent lords.

XVIII. That tithes are purely charity, and that parishioners may, on account of the sins of their curates, detain these and confer them on others at their will.

XIX. That special prayers applied to one person by prelates or religious persons, are of no more value to the same person than general prayers for others in a like position are to him.

XX. That the very fact that any one enters upon any private religion whatever, renders him more unfitted and more incapable of observing the commandments of God.

XXI. That saints who have instituted any private religions whatever, as well of those having possessions as of mendicants, have sinned in thus instituting them.

XXII. That religious persons living in private religions are not of the Christian religion.

XXIII. That friars should be required to gain their living by the labor of their hands and not by mendicancy [begging].

XXIV. That a person giving alms to friars, or to a preaching friar, is excommunicate; also the one receiving.

REPLY OF WYCLIFFE TO HIS SUMMONS BY THE POPE TO COME TO ROME, 1384

I have joyfully to tell what I hold, to all true men that believe and especially to the Pope; for I suppose that if my faith be rightful and given of God, the Pope will gladly confirm it; and if my faith be error, the Pope will wisely amend it.

I suppose over this that the gospel of Christ be heart of the body of God's law; for I believe that Jesus Christ, that gave in his own person this gospel, is very God and very man, and by his heart passes all other laws.

From *Translations and Reprints*, Vol. 2, No. 5, E. P. Cheyney, Ed.

I suppose over this that the Pope be most responsible for the keeping of the gospel among all men that live here; for the Pope is highest vicar that Christ has here in earth. For moreness of Christ's vicar is not measured by worldly moreness, but by this, that this vicar follows more Christ by virtuous living; for thus teaches the gospel, that this is the sentence of Christ.

And of this gospel I believe, that Christ for time that he walked here, was most poor man of all, both in spirit and in having; for Christ says that he had nought for to rest his head on. And Paul says that he was made needy for our love. And more poor might no man be, neither bodily nor in spirit. And thus Christ put from him all manner of worldly lordship. For the gospel of John tells that when they would have made Christ king, he fled and hid him from them, for he wanted no such worldly highness.

And over this I believe, that no man should follow the Pope, nor any saint that now is in heaven, but in as much as he follows Christ. For John and James erred when they coveted worldly highness; and Peter and Paul sinned also when they denied and blasphemed in Christ; but men should not follow them in this, for then they went from Jesus Christ. And this I take as wholesome counsel, that the Pope leave his worldly lordship to worldly lords, as Christ gave them,—and move speedily all his clerks to do so. For that is what Christ did, and what He taught his disciples, till the fiend blinded this world. And it seems to some men that clerks that dwell lastingly in this error against God's law, and fail to follow Christ in this, are open heretics, and those who led them into error are so too.

And if I err in this opinion, I will meekly be corrected, yea, by the death, if it be skilful,[2] for that I hope were good for me. And if I might travel in mine own person, I would willingly go to the Pope. But God has needed me to the contrary, and taught me more obedience to God than to men. And I suppose of our Pope that he will not be Antichrist, and reverse Christ in this working, to the contrary of Christ's will; for if he gives orders against reason, by him or by any of his, and pursues this unreasonable summoning [ordering], he is an open Antichrist. And merciful intent excused not Peter, that Christ should not call him Satan; so blind intent and wicked counsel excuses not the Pope here; but if he ask of true priests that they travel more than they may, he is not excused by reason of God, that he should not be Antichrist. For our belief teaches us that our blessed God suffers us not to be tempted more than we may; how should a man ask such service? And therefore pray we to God for our Pope Urban the Sixth, that his old holy intent be not quenched by his enemies. And Christ, who may not lie, says that the enemies of a man are especially his home family; and this is true of men and friends.

The Borgias

The increasing worldliness of the Church of Rome and of its leading representatives sapped respect for the institution and spurred demands for reform. Among the most outrageous

---

[2] If the basis for correcting me is reasonable and discerning.

figures of Renaissance Italy were two members of the Borgia family, Pope Alexander VI (1492–1503) and his son Caesar (1475–1507), energetic and ruthless men whose efforts to break the power of the great Roman lords of the Orsini and Colonna clans and establish their power all over central Italy failed only after much bloodshed. Caesar, of course, is almost the hero of Machiavelli's Prince; but his father was just as unscrupulous and perhaps even more scandalous. And if none of his successors on the throne of St. Peter ever equalled his egregious performance, their political and financial activities continued to worry those who found these popes too worldly for the service of God.

The Predecessors

Sixtus IV, Innocent VIII, and Alexander VI are [the Popes] filling the most degraded period in papal history, and providing to what a state Italy was then reduced. The first of these men was a Genoese friar, who immediately after his election (1471) exhibited himself as a violent despot, devoid of all scruples and all decency. He needed money, and therefore put up to sale offices, benefices, and indulgences. He showed a downright mania for the advancement of his nephews, some of whom were, according to the general verdict, his own sons. One of these, Pietro Riario, was made Cardinal, with an income of sixty thousand crowns, and plunged so desperately into luxury, dissipation, and debauchery of all kinds, that he soon died, worn out by his vices, and overwhelmed with debts. The other brother, Girolamo, as zealously patronized [supported], led the same sort of life. The Pope's whole policy was ruled by his greed of fresh acquisitions for his sons and nephews. It was solely because Lorenzo dei Medici had crossed these designs that the conspiracy of the Pazzi was hatched in the Vatican, and that on its failure the Pope made war upon Florence, and launched a sentence of excommunication against that city. Later, he joined the Venetians in their expedition against Ferrara, always with the same object of snatching some province for his family. A general war was the result, in which even the Neapolitans took part, by making an attack upon Rome, where fresh feuds among the nobility quickly broke out. . . .

The palaces of the Riario were being sacked, the Orsini and the Colonna in arms, when the Cardinals hurriedly assembling in conclave succeeded in patching up a truce. Then began a most scandalous traffic in votes for election to the Papal chair, which was sold to the highest bidder. The fortunate purchaser was Cardinal Cibo, who was proclaimed Pope on 29th August 1484, under the name of Innocent VIII. . . .

During all this confusion, anarchy had again broken loose in Rome, nor was any way found to restrain it: no morning passed without corpses being found in the streets. Malefactors who could pay, obtained safe conducts; those who could not were hung. Every crime had its price, and all sums over 150 ducats went to Franceschetto Cibo, the Pope's son; smaller amounts to the Chamber. Parricide, rape, any sort of crime, could obtain absolution for money. . . .

From Pasquale Villari, *The Life and Times of Niccolò Machiavelli*, trans. Mme. L. Villari (London, 1898), pp. 51–55.

Meanwhile, Innocent VIII passed his time in festivities. He was the first Pope who openly acknowledged his own children, and celebrated their wedding feasts. Franceschetto espoused Maddalena, daughter of Lorenzo dei Medici (1487), and by way of recompense her brother, Giovanni, was made a Cardinal at the age of fourteen. . . . The Pope's sons and nephews made the town ring with the scandal of their daily life. Franceschetto Cibo lost 14,000 florins in a single night at play with Cardinal Riario, whom he accused to the Pope of cheating at cards; the money, however, had already disappeared. The Eternal City had become a great market of offices and posts, often created only in order to be sold. And not only offices, but false bulls, indulgences to sinners, impunity for assassins could be had for money: a father, by payment of 800 ducats, obtained absolution for the murder of his two daughters. Every evening corpses found about the streets were thrown into the Tiber.

In the midst of these diabolical orgies, the Pope every now and then fell into a lethargy that was mistaken for death, and then his relations and his cardinals hurried to secure their treasures . . . and all Rome was in a tumult. The Pope would awake from his trance, and thereupon the merry-making went on as before, and assassination was once more the order of the day. At last a fresh attack of the Pope's malady left little room for hope. Anxious relations crowded round the bed of the dying man, who could take nothing but woman's milk; then, it was said, transfusion of blood was tried and three children sacrificed to the experiment.

But all was in vain and on the 25th of July, 1492—the same year in which Lorenzo dei Medici had died—Innocent VIII breathed his last at the age of sixty. At the death of Sixtus IV men had blessed the day that freed the world from so great a monster, and the following Pope was much worse than his predecessor. Nobody now believed that a worse than Innocent could be found, yet the infamy of the new Pope, Alexander VI, caused that of his predecessors to be totally forgotten.

The Son

Francesco Matarazzo, erudite philologist and secretary of the governor of Perugia, witnessed events which he later described in his Cronaca della Città di Perugia dal 1492 al 1503.

[Cesare Borgia] was then the first captain of Italy, not so much by his great military science, but by treason and the power of gold; he had turned the art of war into the art of deception, which everybody learnt from him. After having destroyed all the lordships, he had the best of fighters on his side, all the most famous *condottieri*. Besides, wherever his soldiers went, he had them quartered free; thus they gained more in time of war than in time of peace and, thus, he had a great number of soldiers with him.

He was also one of the happiest of men; he had picked up a greater quantity of treasure and objects than anyone else in Italy. And nowhere in Italy were the soldiers so well provided with horses and fine clothing. Captain and *Gonfaloniere* of the Church, he was esteemed by all the lords. . . . Astrologers and necromancers declared him to be the very son of Fortune.

The Father

The jubilee of 1500 and the crowds it brought to Rome helped spread abroad the rumors concerning the private lives, debaucheries, and crimes of the Borgia clan, not least of the pope himself, Alexander VI. In his Diaries *(Venice: 1871–1882), Mario Sanuto, a Venetian historiographer and a contemporary of the Borgias, notes that "daily one finds in Rome men murdered, four or five every night, even bishops, prelates and others; everyone in Rome trembles in fear of being murdered by the Duke."*

Among Machiavelli's many correspondents, Agostino Vespucci, the brother of the explorer Amerigo, reflected the general opinion concerning the death of a cardinal, one among many, whose inheritance fell to the pope.

Here everyone holds it to have been due to poison and to not having been on sufficiently good terms with the great *Gonfaloniere.* One hears often, very often in Rome of deaths of this sort. . . .

The Pope seems to me very worried by these rumors concerning the Great Turk, rumors that get ever stronger; he begins to say with many sighs, "Alas! in what land, on what seas shall I find a haven?" He doubles the guard at his palace, night and day, shows himself only with the greatest difficulty, and yet still plays Sylla with his proscriptions. In everybody's sight he deprives one of his property, another of his life, sends one into exile, another to forced labor, grabs the dwelling of another to install some rascal in it; and all this for the slightest motive, or for no motive at all. Besides, he lets his barons and his friends carry out every kind of outrage and crime, steal, ransack the shops and a thousand things of this sort. Here, benefices are for sale more readily than melons, waffles or drinking water in Florence. The courts of Rome are unemployed because all law rests in force and is in the hands of these rascals: to the point that the Turk seems necessary, since the Christians do not arise to extirpate this blackguard from the human conclave; such is the unanimous language of all decent men.

I have still to tell you that every night, between the Angelus and the first hour, one sees twenty-five women and more who are brought to the pontifical palace, behind a few riders—without speaking of the Pope who, for his part, keeps his illicit herd permanently on the premises—to the point that the whole palace has become the bawdy-house of every turpitude. . . .

Pope Alexander VI would live another three years, but the conditions of his death (on August 18, 1503) and the stories it evoked seemed to confirm his living reputation. In the papal palace, as in the Basilica of St. Peter, chaos prevailed. Lackeys and soldiers struggled with the clergy for pillows, vestments, and torches, all too precious to waste in burial. Soon Alexander's corpse began to turn black, decompose, and stink frightfully—developments to be expected in a Roman August but attributed to poison, the devil, or both. As the marquis of Mantua wrote to his wife, Isabella d'Este: "After the death of Pope Innocent VIII, [his predecessor] during the conclave, [Borgia] made a pact with the devil, to whom he sold his soul in exchange for the papacy. . . . There are persons who affirm having seen, at the moment of death, seven devils in his room. After death, his body began to boil and the mouth to bubble like a cauldron on the fire. . . . He swelled so much that he had nothing of human form, and had become as broad as he was long. His burial was carried out with little ceremony. As everybody refused to touch him, a man dragged him by a rope tied to his feet, from his bed to a place where he was burnt."

The Machinery of Indulgences

The idea that the pope could issue indulgences for the remission of sins was based on the theory that St. Peter and his successors had control of an inexhaustible treasury of merit that they could dispense to the faithful. This merit, due first to Christ and then to successive generations of good Christians, was seen as a store of spiritual wealth into which the popes could dip at will for the benefit of the living and the dead. The popes first began to use this power seriously as an inducement to pious activity, such as pilgrimages or crusades, but soon saw its pecuniary usefulness. As a rule, the administration of indulgences was accompanied by certain moral requirements—repentance, confession, and so on. This is apparent in the instructions issued by Albert, archbishop of Mainz, at the start of the great campaign of 1517, designed to raise money for the St. Peter's building fund. However, such scrupulous instructions were not always obeyed.

Instructions Issued by Albert of Mainz

The first grace is the complete remission of all sins; and nothing greater than this can be named, since sinful man, deprived of the grace of God, obtains complete remission by these means and once more enjoys God's grace; moreover, through this remission of sins the punishment which one is obliged to undergo in purgatory on account of the affront to the Divine Majesty is all remitted, and the pains of purgatory completely blotted out. And although nothing is precious enough to be given in exchange for such a grace—since it is a free gift of God and grace is beyond price—yet in order that Christian believers may be the more easily induced to procure the same, we establish the following rules, to wit:

In the first place, every one who is contrite in heart and has made oral confession, shall visit at least the seven churches indicated for this purpose, to wit, those in which the papal arms are displayed, and in each church shall say five Paternosters and five Ave Marias in honour of the five wounds of our Lord Jesus Christ, whereby our salvation is

From *Documents of the Christian Church*, ed. Henry Bettenson (Oxford, 1943), pp. 257–260. Reprinted by permission of Oxford University Press and Geoffrey Cumberlege.

won, or one Miserere, which psalm is particularly well adapted for obtaining forgiveness of sins. . . .

THE METHOD OF CONTRIBUTING TO THE CHEST, FOR THE CONSTRUCTION
OF THE SAID FABRIC OF THE CHIEF OF THE APOSTLES.

Firstly, the penitentiaries and confessors, after they have explained to those making confession the greatness of this kind of plenary remission and of these privileges, shall ask them for how large a contribution, in money or in other temporal goods, they would wish, in good conscience, to be spared this method of full remission and privileges; and this is to be done that they may be more easily induced to contribute. And because the conditions of men, and their occupations, are so various and manifold, and we cannot consider and assess them individually, we have therefore decided that the rates can be determined thus, according to recognized classifications. . . .

Then follows a graded schedule of rates: kings and their families, bishops, and the like, twenty-five Rhenish gold guilders, a good deal more than a skilled worker's annual income. Abbots, counts, barons, and such, were to pay ten guilders; lesser nobles and ecclesiastics and others with incomes of 500, six guilders; citizens with their own income, one guilder; those with less, half a guilder. Those with nothing were to supply their contribution with prayer and fasting, "for the kingdom of heaven should be open to the poor as much as the rich."

The second principal grace is a "confessional" [confessional letter] replete with the greatest, most important, and hitherto unheard of privileges. . . .

Firstly, the privilege of choosing a suitable confessor, even a regular of the mendicant orders. . . .

[The other privileges include the power given to this confessor to absolve in cases normally "reserved" for the Apostolic See.]

The third important grace is the participation in all the benefits of the Church universal; which consists in this, that contributors toward the said building, together with their deceased parents, who have departed this world in a state of grace, shall now and for eternity be partakers in all petitions, intercessions, alms, fastings, prayers, in each and every pilgrimage, even those to the Holy Land; furthermore, in the stations at Rome, in masses, canonical hours, mortifications, and all other spiritual benefits which have been, or shall be, brought forth by the universal, most holy Church militant or by any of its members. Believers who purchase confessional letters may also become participants in all these things. Preachers and confessors must insist with great perseverance upon these advantages, and persuade believers not to neglect to acquire these benefits along with their confessional letter.

We also declare that in order to obtain these two most important graces, it is not necessary to make confession, or to visit the churches and altars, but merely to procure the confessional letter. . . .

The fourth important grace is for those souls which are in purgatory, and is the complete remission of all sins, which remission the pope brings to pass through his intercession, to the advantage of said souls, in this wise: that the same contribution shall be placed in the chest by a living person as one would make for himself. It is our wish, however, that our subcommissioners should modify the regulations regarding contributions of this kind which are given for the dead, and that they should use their judgment in all other cases where, in their opinion, modifications are desirable.

It is, furthermore, not necessary that the persons who place their contributions in the chest for the dead should be contrite in heart and have orally confessed, since this grace is based simply on the state of grace in which the dead departed, and on the contribution of the living, as is evident from the text of the bull. Moreover preachers shall exert themselves to make this grace more widely known, since through the same, help will surely come to departed souls, and the construction of the church of St. Peter will be abundantly promoted at the same time. . . .

John Tetzel (c. 1465–1519) was a German Dominican friar blessed with the art of sales-manship and evident oratorical talents whose sermons on indulgences, when delivered not far from Wittenberg, were the cause of Luther's Ninety-Five Theses. In this way the sale of indulgences and Tetzel's exaggerations may have touched off the Reformation.

John Tetzel: A Sermon on Indulgences

Venerable Sir, I pray you that in your utterances you may be pleased to make use of such words as shall serve to open the eyes of the mind and cause your hearers to consider how great a grace and gift they have had and now have at their very doors. Blessed eyes indeed, which see what they see, because already they possess letters of safe conduct by which they are able to lead their souls through that valley of tears, through that sea of the mad world, where storms and tempests and dangers lie in wait, to the blessed land of Paradise. Know that the life of man upon earth is a constant struggle. We have to fight against the flesh, the world and the devil, who are always seeking to destroy the soul. In sin we are conceived,—alas! what bonds of sin encompass us, and how difficult and almost impossible it is to attain to the gate of salvation without divine aid; since He causes us to be saved, not by virtue of the good works which we accomplish, but through His divine mercy; it is necessary then to put on the armour of God.

You may obtain letters of safe conduct from the vicar of our Lord Jesus Christ, by means of which you are able to liberate your soul from the hands of the enemy, and convey it by means of contrition and confession, safe and secure from all pains of Purgatory, into the happy kingdom. For we know that in these letters are stamped and engraven all the merits of Christ's passion there laid bare. Consider, that for each

From *Translations and Reprints*, Vol. 2, No. 6, J. H. Robinson, Ed.

and every mortal sin it is necessary to undergo seven years of penitence after confession and contrition, either in this life or in Purgatory.

How many mortal sins are committed in a day, how many in a week, how many in a month, how many in a year, how many in the whole course of life! They are well-nigh numberless, and those that commit them must needs suffer endless punishment in the burning pains of Purgatory.

But with these confessional letters you will be able at any time in life to obtain full indulgence for all penalties imposed upon you, in all cases except the four reserved to the Apostolic See. Therefore throughout your whole life, whenever you wish to make confession, you may receive the same remission, except in cases reserved to the Pope, and afterwards, at the hour of death, a full indulgence as to all penalties and sins, and your share of all spiritual blessings that exist in the church militant and all its members.

Do you not know that when it is necessary for anyone to go to Rome, or undertake any other dangerous journey, he takes his money to a broker and gives a certain percent—five or six or ten—in order that at Rome or elsewhere he may receive again his funds intact, by means of the letter of this same broker? Are you not willing, then, for the fourth part of a florin, to obtain these letters, by virtue of which you may bring, not your money, but your divine and immortal soul safe and sound into the land of Paradise?

Wherefore I counsel, order, and by virtue of my authority as shepherd, I command that they shall receive together with me and other priests, this precious treasure, especially those who were not confessed at the time of the holy Jubilee, that they may be able to obtain the same forever. For the time may come when you may desire, but yet be unable to obtain the least portion of the grace.

Also on the part of S. D. N.[1] the Pope and of the most Holy Apostolic See and of the most reverend sir, my legate, to each and every one who shall have profited by the sacred Jubilee and made confession, and to all who may profit by this present brief opportunity, and who shall have lent a helping hand to the construction of the aforesaid house of the Prince of the Apostles, they shall all be participants and sharers in all prayers, suffrages, alms, fasts, supplications, masses, canonical hours, disciplines, pilgrimages, papal stations, benedictions, and all other spiritual goods which now exist or may exist forever in the church militant, and in all of these, not only they themselves, but their relatives, kindred and benefactors who have passed away; and as they were moved by charity, so God, and SS. Peter and Paul, and all the saints whose bodies rest in Rome, shall guard them in peace in this vale, and conduct them through it to the heavenly kingdom. Give everlasting thanks in the aforesaid names and in mine to the reverend secular priests and prelates, etc.

Martin Luther

Martin Luther (1483–1546) was the son of a successful Saxon peasant-entrepreneur. He joined the order of Augustine friars to seek peace of mind and assurance of salvation—

---

[1] His Holiness Our Lord (the Pope). Sanctus Dominus Noster.

some kind of bridge between the wickedness of man and the goodness of God. Unable to visualize this bridge in the corrupt Church of his time, he found it at last in the faith that had also effected St. Augustine's salvation. If man had faith, he could be saved; in comparison to this supreme truth, "works" were of no avail, a priest's unction of no importance. Every baptized Christian was a priest.

These conclusions appear in the pamphlets he published in 1520, all urging the laity to take a hand in reforming the Church. An excerpt of one is given here. But the success of such fighting works must be attributed in the first place to Luther's original attack, in 1517—the Ninety-Five Theses—upon those practical abuses of the Roman Catholic Church which most right-minded Germans regarded as shocking.

The Ninety-Five Theses

The theses were posted on the side door of the castle church in Wittenberg on Halloween, 1517. Posting theses in a public place was the usual way of giving notice of the disputations which were a regular feature of academic life. In this sense there was nothing peculiar or revolutionary in Luther's action. As a matter of fact, Luther thought the pope would support his exposure of the evils of the indulgence trade.

In the desire and with the purpose of elucidating the truth, a disputation will be held on the underwritten propositions at Wittenberg, under the presidency of the Reverend Father Martin Luther, Monk of the Order of St. Augustine, Master of Arts and of Sacred Theology, and ordinary Reader of the same in that place. He therefore asks those who cannot be present and discuss the subject with us orally, to do so by letter in their absence. In the name of our Lord Jesus Christ. Amen.

1. Our Lord and Master Jesus Christ in saying "Repent ye" (*poenitentiam agite*), etc., intended that the whole life of believers should be penitence (*poenitentia*).

2. This word cannot be understood as sacramental penance (*poenitentia*), that is, of the confession and satisfaction which are performed under the ministry of priests.

3. It does not, however, refer solely to inward penitence (*poenitentia*); nay, such inward penitence is naught, unless it outwardly produces various mortifications of the flesh.

4. The penalty (*poena*) thus continues as long as the hatred of self (that is, true inward penitence); namely, till our entrance into the Kingdom of Heaven.

5. The Pope has neither the will nor the power to remit any penalties except those which he has imposed by his own authority, or by that of the canons.

From *Translations and Reprints,* Vol. 2, No. 6, J. H. Robinson, Ed.

6. The Pope has no power to remit any guilt, except by declaring and warranting it to have been remitted by God; or at most by remitting cases reserved for himself; in which cases, if his power were despised, guilt would certainly remain.

7. Certainly God remits no man's guilt without at the same time subjecting him, humbled in all things, to the authority of his representative the priest.

8. The penitential canons are imposed only on the living, and no burden ought to be imposed on the dying, according to them.

9. Hence, the Holy Spirit acting in the Pope does well for us in that, in his decrees, he always makes exception of the article of death and of necessity.

10. Those priests act unlearnedly and wrongly who, in the case of the dying, reserve the canonical penances for Purgatory.

11. Those tares about changing the canonical penalty into the penalty of Purgatory seem surely to have been sown while the bishops were asleep.

12. Formerly the canonical penalties were imposed not after but before absolution, as tests of true contrition.

13. The dying pay all penalties by death, and are already dead to the canon laws, and are by right relieved from them.

14. The imperfect vigor or love of a dying person necessarily brings with it great fear, and the less it is, the greater the fear it brings.

15. This fear and horror is sufficient by itself, to say nothing of other things, to constitute the pains of Purgatory, since it is very near to the horror of despair.

16. Hell, Purgatory, and Heaven appear to differ as despair, almost despair, and peace of mind differ.

17. With souls in Purgatory it seems that it must needs be that as horror diminishes so love increases.

18. Nor does it seem to be proved by any reasoning or any Scriptures, that they are outside of the state of merit or of the increase of love.

19. Nor does this appear to be proved, that they are sure and confident of their own blessedness, at least all of them, though we may be very sure of it.

20. Therefore the Pope, when he speaks of the plenary remission of all penalties, does not mean really of all, but only of those imposed by himself.

21. Thus those preachers of indulgences are in error who say that by the indulgences of the Pope a man is freed and saved from all punishment.

22. For in fact he remits to souls in Purgatory no penalty which they would have had to pay in this life according to the canons.

23. If any entire remission of all penalties can be granted to any one it is certain that it is granted to none but the most perfect, that is to very few.

24. Hence, the greater part of the people must needs be deceived by this indiscriminate and high-sounding promise of release from penalties.

25. Such power over Purgatory as the Pope has in general, such has every bishop in his own diocese, and every parish priest in his own parish, in particular.

26. The Pope acts most rightly in granting remission to souls not by the power of the keys (which is of no avail in this case), but by the way of intercession.

27. They preach man who say that the soul flies out of Purgatory as soon as the money thrown into the chest rattles.

28. It is certain that, when the money rattles in the chest, avarice and gain may be increased, but the effect of the intercession of the Church depends on the will of God alone.

29. Who knows whether all the souls in Purgatory desire to be redeemed from it—witness the story told of Saints Severinus and Paschal?

30. No man is sure of the reality of his own contrition, much less of the attainment of plenary remission.

31. Rare as is a true penitent, so rare is one who truly buys indulgences—that is to say, most rare.

32. Those who believe that, through letters of pardon, they are made sure of their own salvation will be eternally damned along with their teachers.

33. We must especially beware of those who say that these pardons from the Pope are that inestimable gift of God by which man is reconciled to God.

34. For the grace conveyed by these pardons has respect only to the penalties of sacramental satisfaction, which are of human appointment.

35. They preach no Christian doctrine who teach that contrition is not necessary for those who buy souls (out of Purgatory) or buy confessional licenses.

36. Every Christian who feels true compunction has of right plenary remission of punishment and guilt even without letters of pardon.

37. Every true Christian, whether living or dead, has a share in all the benefits of Christ and of the Church, given by God, even without letters of pardon.

38. The remission, however, imparted by the Pope is by no means to be despised, since it is, as I have said, a declaration of the divine remission.

39. It is a most difficult thing, even for the most learned theologians, to exalt at the same time in the eyes of the people the ample effect of pardons and the necessity of true contrition.

40. True contrition seeks and loves punishment; while the ampleness of pardons relaxes it, and causes men to hate it, or at least gives occasion for them to do so.

41. Apostolic pardons ought to be proclaimed with caution, lest the people should falsely suppose that they are placed before other good works of charity.

42. Christians should be taught that it is not the wish of the Pope that the buying of pardons should be in any way compared to works of mercy.

43. Christians should be taught that he who gives to a poor man, or lends to a needy man, does better than if he bought pardons.

44. Because by works of charity, charity increases, and the man becomes better; while by means of pardons, he does not become better, but only freer from punishment.

45. Christians should be taught that he who sees any one in need, and, passing him by, gives money for pardons, is not purchasing for himself the indulgences of the Pope but the anger of God.

46. Christians should be taught that, unless they have superfluous wealth, they are bound to keep what is necessary for the use of their own households, and by no means to lavish it on pardons.

47. Christians should be taught that while they are free to buy pardons they are not commanded to do so.

48. Christians should be taught that the Pope, in granting pardons, has both more need and more desire that devout prayer should be made for him than that the money should be readily paid.

49. Christians should be taught that the Pope's pardons are useful if they do not put their trust in them, but most hurtful if through them they lose the fear of God.

50. Christians should be taught that, if the Pope were acquainted with the exactions of the Preachers of pardons, he would prefer that the Basilica of St. Peter should be burnt to ashes rather than that it should be built up with the skin, flesh, and bones of his sheep.

51. Christians should be taught that as it would be the duty so would it be the wish of the Pope even to sell, if necessary, the Basilica of St. Peter, and to give of his own money to very many of those from whom the Preachers of pardons extract money.

52. Vain is the hope of salvation through letters of pardon, even if a commissary— nay, the Pope himself—were to pledge his own soul for them.

53. They were enemies of Christ and of the Pope who, in order that the pardons may be preached, condemn the Word of God to utter silence in other churches.

54. Wrong is done to the Word of God when, in the same sermon, an equal or longer time is spent on pardons than on it.

55. The mind of the Pope necessarily is that, if pardons, which are a very small matter, are celebrated with single bells, single processions, and single ceremonies, the Gospel, which is a very great matter, should be preached with a hundred bells, a hundred processions, and a hundred ceremonies.

56. The treasures of the Church, whence the Pope grants indulgences, are neither sufficiently named nor known among the people of Christ.

57. It is clear that they are at least not temporal treasures, for these are not so readily lavished, but only accumulated, by means of the preachers.

58. Nor are they the merits of Christ and of the saints, for these, independently of the Pope, are always working grace to the inner man, and the cross, death, and hell to the outer man.

59. St. Lawrence said that the treasures of the Church are the poor of the Church, but he spoke according to the use of the term in his time.

60. We are not speaking rashly when we say that the keys of the Church, bestowed through the merits of Christ, are that treasure.

61. For it is clear that the power of the Pope is sufficient of itself for the remission of [canonical] penalties and of [reserved] cases.

62. The true treasure of the Church is the Holy Gospel of the glory and grace of God.

63. This treasure, however, is deservedly most hateful, because it makes the first to be last.

64. While the treasure of indulgences is deservedly most acceptable, because it makes the last to be first.

65. Hence the treasures of the Gospel are nets, wherewith of old they fished for the men of riches.

66. The treasures of indulgences are nets, wherewith they now fish for the riches of men.

67. Those indulgences, which the preachers loudly proclaim to be the greatest graces, are seen to be truly such as regards the promotion of gain.

68. Yet they are in reality most insignificant when compared to the grace of God and the piety of the cross.

69. Bishops and parish priests are bound to receive the commissaries of apostolical pardons with all reverence.

70. But they are still more bound to see to it with all their eyes, and take heed with all their ears, that these men do not preach their own dreams in place of the Pope's commission.

71. He who speaks against the truth of apostolical pardons, let him be anathema and accursed.

72. But he, on the other hand, who exerts himself against the wantonness and license of speech of the Preachers of pardons, let him be blessed.

73. As the Pope justly thunders against those who use any kind of contrivance to the injury of the traffic in pardons.

74. Much more is it his intention to thunder against those who, under the pretext of pardons, use contrivances to the injury of holy charity and of truth.

75. To think that the Papal pardons have such power that they could absolve a man even if—by an impossibility—he had violated the Mother of God, is madness.

76. We affirm on the contrary that Papal pardons cannot take away even the least of venial sins, as regards its guilt.

77. The saying that, even if St. Peter were now Pope, he could grant no greater graces, is blasphemy against St. Peter and the Pope.

78. We affirm on the contrary that both he and any other Pope has greater graces to grant, namely, the Gospel, powers, gifts of healing, etc. (I Cor. XII).

79. To say that the cross set up among the insignia of the Papal arms is of equal power with the cross of Christ, is blasphemy.

80. Those bishops, priests and theologians who allow such discourses to have currency among the people will have to render an account.

81. This license in the preaching of pardons makes it no easy thing, even for learned men, to protect the reverence due to the Pope against the calumnies, or at all events, the keen questioning of the laity.

82. As for instance: Why does not the Pope empty Purgatory for the sake of most holy charity and of the supreme necessity of souls—this being the most just of all reasons—if he redeems an infinite number of souls for the sake of that most fatal thing, money, to be spent on building a basilica—this being a very slight reason?

83. Again; why do funeral masses and anniversary masses for the deceased continue, and why does not the Pope return, or permit the withdrawal of, the funds bequeathed for this purpose, since it is a wrong to pray for those who are already redeemed?

84. Again; what is this new kindness of God and the Pope, in that, for money's sake, they permit an impious man and an enemy of God to redeem a pious soul which loves God, and yet do not redeem that same pious and beloved soul out of free charity on account of its own need?

85. Again; why is it that the penitential canons, long since abrogated and dead in themselves, in very fact and not only by usage, are yet still redeemed with money, through the granting of indulgences, as if they were full of life?

86. Again; why does not the Pope, whose riches are at this day more ample than those

of the wealthiest of the wealthy, build the single Basilica of St. Peter with his own money rather than with that of poor believers?

87. Again; what does the Pope remit or impart to those who through perfect contrition have a right to plenary remission and participation?

88. Again; what greater good could the Church receive than if the Pope, instead of once, as he does now, were to bestow these remissions and participations a hundred times a day on any one of the faithful?

89. Since it is the salvation of souls, rather than money, that the Pope seeks by his pardons, why does he suspend the letters and pardons granted long ago, since they are equally efficacious?

90. To repress these scruples and arguments of the laity by force alone, and not to resolve them by giving reasons, is to expose the Church and the Pope to the ridicule of their enemies, and to make Christian men unhappy.

91. If then pardons were preached according to the spirit and mind of the Pope, all these questions would be resolved with ease; nay, would not exist.

92. Away then with all those prophets who say to the people of Christ: "Peace, peace," and there is no peace.

93. Blessed be all those prophets who say to the people of Christ: "The cross, the cross," and there is no cross.

94. Christians should be exhorted to strive to follow Christ their head through pains, deaths, and hells.

95. And thus trust to enter Heaven through many tribulations, rather than in the security of peace.

On the Babylonish Captivity of the Church

OF ORDERS

Of this sacrament the Church of Christ knows nothing; it was invented by the church of the Pope. It not only has no promise of grace, anywhere declared, but not a word is said about it in the whole of the New Testament. Now it is ridiculous to set up as a sacrament of God that which can nowhere be proved to have been instituted by God. Not that I consider that a rite practised for so many ages is to be condemned; but I would not have human inventions established in sacred things, nor should it be allowed to bring in anything as divinely ordained, which has not been divinely ordained; lest we should be objects of ridicule to our adversaries. . . .

From *First Principles of the Reformation,* tr. H. Wace and C. A. Buchheim (Philadelphia: Lutheran Publication Society, 1885).

Which of the ancient Fathers has asserted that by these words priests were ordained? Whence then this new interpretation? It is because it has been sought by this device to set up a source of implacable discord, by which clergy and laity might be placed farther asunder than heaven and earth, to the incredible injury of baptismal grace and confusion of evangelical communion. Hence has originated that detestable tyranny of the clery over the laity, in which, trusting to the corporal unction by which their hands are consecrated, to their tonsure, and to their vestments, they not only set themselves above the body of lay Christians, who have been anointed with the Holy Spirit, but almost look upon them as dogs, unworthy to be numbered in the Church along with themselves. Hence it is that they dare to command, exact, threaten, drive, and oppress, at their will. *In fine,* the sacrament of orders has been and is a most admirable engine for the establishment of all those monstrous evils which have hitherto been wrought, and are yet being wrought, in the Church. In this way Christian brotherhood has perished; in this way shepherds have been turned into wolves, servants into tyrants, and ecclesiastics into more than earthly beings.

How if they were compelled to admit that we all, so many as have been baptized, are equally priests? We are so in fact, and it is only a ministry which has been entrusted to them, and that with our consent. They would then know that they have no right to exercise command over us, except so far as we voluntarily allow of it. Thus it is said: "Ye are a chosen generation, a royal priesthood, a holy nation." (I Pet. ii. 9.) Thus all we who are Christians are priests; those whom we call priests are ministers chosen from among us to do all things in our name; and the priesthood is nothing else than a ministry. . . .

As far then as we are taught from the Scriptures, since what we call the priesthood is a ministry, I do not see at all for what reason a man who has once been made priest cannot become a layman again, since he differs in no wise from a layman, except by his ministerial office. But it is so far from impossible for a man to be set aside from the ministry, that even now this punishment is constantly inflicted on offending priests, who are either suspended for a time, or deprived for ever of their office. For that fiction of an indelible character has long ago become an object of derision. I grant that the Pope may impress this character, though Christ knows nothing of it, and for this very reason the priest thus consecrated is the lifelong servant and bondsman, not of Christ, but of the Pope, as it is at this day. But, unless I deceive myself, if at some future time this sacrament and figment fall to the ground, the Papacy itself will scarcely hold its ground, and we shall recover that joyful liberty in which we shall understand that we are all equal in every right, and shall shake off the yoke of tyranny and know that he who is a Christian has Christ, and he who has Christ has all things that are Christ's, and can do all things—on which I will write more fully and more vigorously when I find that what I have here said displeases my friends the papists.

The Peasant Revolt, 1525

Once ordinary people had taken it upon themselves to interpret Scripture, it was only a matter of time before different interpretations would divide the reformers. Those who believed that ultimate sanction and authority were to be found in Scripture had no reason, other than their own judgment, to consider the authority of one interpreter superior to that of another. If Wittenberg was as good as Rome, then Zurich or Geneva, Münster, Canterbury, or Strasbourg need be no less. The ultimate appeal would always be to the Bible and to the believer's heart. But it is difficult to say in what proportion political motives mingled with religious ones in assuring the success of reformed ideas.

The serious peasant revolt which ravaged German lands in 1525 throws a lurid light on social and economic conditions in the area at the opening of the Reformation. The abuses against which the peasants rose were of long standing: local revolts had punctuated the history of the Middle Ages. But the concurrent religious crisis helped fire peasant discontent into an explosion that threatened the princes, the cities, the whole social order, and even the Lutheran reform itself. As they rose, the peasants drafted their demands, of which there were many versions. The articles that follow reflect the attitude of the least radical reformers. Luther, who at first had appealed for peace, soon turned against the rebels and published his notorious plea to the German nobility, in which he asked them to "take pity on us poor people, and so kill, destroy, exterminate, drown in blood without mercy" the dangerous radicals.

The Twelve Articles of the Peasants

Peace to the Christian reader, and the Grace of God through Christ.

There are many evil writings put forth of late which take occasion on account of the assembling of the peasants, to cast scorn upon the Gospel, saying: Is this the fruit of the new teaching, that no one should obey but all should everywhere rise in revolt, and rush together to reform, or perhaps destroy entirely, the authorities, both ecclesiastical and lay? The articles below shall answer these godless and criminal fault-finders, and serve in the first place to remove the reproach from the word of God and, in the second place, to give a Christian excuse for the disobedience or even the revolt of the entire Peasantry. In the first place the Gospel is not the cause of revolt and disorder, since it is the message of Christ, the promised Messiah, the Word of Life, teaching only love, peace, patience and concord. Thus, all who believe in Christ should learn to be loving, peaceful, long-suffering and harmonious. This is the foundation of all the articles of the peasants (as will be seen) who accept the gospel and live according to it. How then can the evil reports declare the Gospel to be a cause of revolt and disobedience? That the authors of the evil reports and the enemies of the Gospel oppose themselves to these demands is due not to the Gospel but to the Devil, the worst enemy of the Gospel, who causes this opposition by raising doubts in the minds of his followers; and thus the word of God, which teaches love, peace and concord, is overcome. In the second place, it is clear that the peasants demand that this Gospel be taught them as a guide in life, and they ought not to be called disobedient or disorderly.

From *Translations and Reprints*, Vol. II, No. 6, J. H. Robinson, Ed.

Whether God grant the peasants (earnestly wishing to live according to his word) their requests or no, who shall find fault with the will of the Most High? Who shall meddle in his judgments or oppose his majesty? Did he not hear the children of Israel when they called upon him and save them out of the hands of Pharaoh? Can he not save his own today? Yes, he will save them and that speedily. Therefore, Christian reader, read the following articles with care and then judge. Here follow the articles:

The First Article: First, it is our humble petition and desire, as also our will and resolution, that in the future we should have power and authority so that each community should choose and appoint a pastor, and that we should have the right to depose him should he conduct himself improperly. The pastor thus chosen should teach us the Gospel pure and simple, without any addition, doctrine or ordinance of man. For to teach us continually the true faith will lead us to pray God that through his grace this faith may increase within us and become a part of us. For if his grace work not within us we remain flesh and blood, which availeth nothing; since the Scripture clearly teaches that only through true faith can we come to God. Only through his mercy can we become holy. Hence such a guide and pastor is necessary, and in this fashion grounded upon the Scriptures.

The Second Article: According as the just tithe is established by the Old Testament and fulfilled in the New, we are ready and willing to pay the fair tithe of grain. The word of God plainly provides that in giving according to right to God and distributing to his people the services of a pastor are required. We will that for the future our church provost, whomsoever the community may appoint, shall gather and receive this tithe. From this he shall give to the pastor, elected by the whole community, a decent and sufficient maintenance for him and his [*im und den seynen*], as shall seem right to the whole community (or, with the knowledge of the community). What remains over shall be given to the poor of the place, as the circumstances and the general opinion demand. Should anything farther remain, let it be kept, lest anyone should have to leave the country from poverty. Provision should also be made from this surplus to avoid laying any land tax on the poor. In case one or more villages have themselves sold their tithes on account of want, and the village has taken action as a whole, the buyer should not suffer loss, but we will that some proper agreement be reached with him for the repayment of the sum by the village with due interest. But those who have tithes which they have not purchased from a village, but which were appropriated by their ancestors, should not, and ought not, to be paid anything farther by the village, which shall apply its tithes to the support of the pastors elected as above indicated, or to solace the poor, as is taught by the Scriptures. The small tithes, whether ecclesiastical or lay, we will not pay at all, for the Lord God created cattle for the free use of man. We will not, therefore, pay farther an unseemly tithe which is of man's invention.

The Third Article: It has been the custom hitherto for men to hold us as their own property, which is pitiable enough, considering that Christ has delivered and redeemed us all, without exception by the shedding of his precious blood, the lowly as well as the great. Accordingly, it is consistent with Scripture that we should be free and wish to be so. Not that we would wish to be absolutely free and under no authority. God does not teach us that we should lead a disorderly life in the lusts of the flesh, but that we should love the Lord our God and our neighbor. We would gladly observe all this as God has commanded us in the celebration of the communion. He has not commanded us not to obey the authorities, but rather that we should be humble, not only towards those in authority, but towards everyone. We are thus ready to yield obedience according to God's law to our elected and regular authorities in all proper things becoming to a Christian. We, therefore, take it for granted that you will release us from serfdom, as true Christians, unless it should be shown us from the Gospel that we are serfs.

The Fourth Article: In the fourth place it has been the custom heretofore, that no poor man should be allowed to touch venison or wild fowl, or fish in flowing water, which seems to us quite unseemly and unbrotherly, as well as selfish and not agreeable to the word of God. In some places the authorities preserve the game to our great annoyance and loss, recklessly permitting the unreasoning animals to destroy to no purpose our crops, which God suffers to grow for the use of man, and yet we must remain quiet. This is neither godly nor neighborly. For when God created man he gave him dominion over all the animals, over the birds of the air and over the fish in the water. Accordingly it is our desire if a man holds possession of waters that he should prove from satisfactory documents that his right has been unwittingly acquired by purchase. We do not wish to take it from him by force, but his rights should be exercised in a Christian and brotherly fashion. But whosoever cannot produce such evidence should surrender his claim with good grace.

The Fifth Article: In the fifth place we are aggrieved in the matter of woodcutting, for the noble folk have appropriated all the woods to themselves alone. If a poor man requires wood he must pay double for it, [or perhaps, two pieces of money]. It is our opinion in regard to a wood which has fallen into the hands of a lord, whether spiritual or temporal, that unless it was duly purchased it should revert again to the community. It should, moreover, be free to every member of the community to help himself to such firewood as he needs in his own home. Also, if a man requires wood for carpenter's purposes he should have it free, but with the knowledge of a person appointed by the community for that purpose. Should, however, no such forest be at the disposal of the community, let that which has been duly bought be administered in a brotherly and Christian manner. If the forest, although unfairly appropriated in the first instance, was later duly sold, let the matter be adjusted in a friendly spirit and according to the Scriptures.

The Sixth Article: Our sixth complaint is in regard to the excessive services demanded of us, which are increased from day to day. We ask that this matter be properly looked into so that we shall not continue to be oppressed in this way, and that some gracious consideration be given us, since our forefathers were required only to serve according to the word of God.

The Seventh Article: Seventh, we will not hereafter allow ourselves to be farther oppressed by our lords, but will let them demand only what is just and proper according to the word of the agreement between the lord and the peasant. The lord should no longer try to force more services or other dues from the peasant without payment, but permit the peasant to enjoy his holding in peace and quiet. The peasant should, however, help the lord when it is necessary, and at proper times, when it will not be disadvantageous to the peasant, and for a suitable payment.

The Eighth Article: In the eighth place, we are greatly burdened by holdings which cannot support the rent exacted from them. The peasants suffer loss in this way and are ruined; and we ask that the lords may appoint persons of honor to inspect these holdings, and fix a rent in accordance with justice, so that the peasant shall not work for nothing, since the laborer is worthy of his hire.

The Ninth Article: In the ninth place, we are burdened with a great evil in the constant making of new laws. We are not judged according to the offence, but sometimes with great ill will, and sometimes much too leniently. In our opinion we should be judged according to the old written law, so that the case shall be decided according to its merits, and not with partiality.

The Tenth Article: In the tenth place, we are aggrieved by the appropriation by individuals of meadows and fields which at one time belonged to a community. These we will take again into our own hands. It may, however, happen that the land was rightfully purchased, but when the land has unfortunately been purchased in this way, some brotherly arrangement should be made according to circumstances.

The Eleventh Article: In the eleventh place we will entirely abolish the due called *Todfall*,[1] and will no longer endure it, nor allow widows and orphans to be thus shamefully robbed against God's will, and in violation of justice and right, as has been done in many places, and by those who should shield and protect them. These have disgraced and despoiled us, and although they had little authority they assumed it. God will suffer this no more, but it shall be wholly done away with, and for the future no man shall be bound to give little or much.

Conclusion: In the twelfth place it is our conclusion and final resolution, that if one or more of the articles here set forth should not be in agreement with the word of God, as we think they are, such article we will willingly recede from, when it is proved really to be against the word of God by a clear explanation of the Scripture. Or if articles should now be conceded to us that are hereafter discovered to be unjust, from that hour they shall be dead and null and without force. Likewise, if more complaints should be discovered which are based upon truth and the Scriptures, and relate to offences against God and our neighbor, we have determined to reserve the right to present these also, and to exercise ourselves in all Christian teaching. For this we shall pray God, since he can grant this, and he alone. The peace of Christ abide with us all.

Martin Luther: Against the Robbing and Murdering Hordes of Peasants, 1525

The peasants have taken on themselves the burden of three terrible sins against God and man, by which they have abundantly merited death in body and soul. In the first place they have [sworn as part of the oath of homage] to be true and faithful, submissive and obedient to their rulers, as Christ commands when He says "Render unto Cesar the things that are Cesar's," and in Romans xiii, "Let everyone be subject unto the

---

[1] or *heriot*—a feudal duty or tribute due to a lord upon the death of a tenant.

higher powers." Because they are breaking this obedience, and are setting themselves against the higher powers, wilfully and with violence, they have forfeited body and soul, as faithless, perjured, lying, disobedient knaves and scoundrels are wont to do. St. Paul passed this judgment on them in Romans xiii, when he said that they who resist the power will bring a judgment upon themselves. This saying will smite the peasants sooner or later, for it is God's will that faith be kept and duty be done.

In the second place, they are starting a rebellion, and violently robbing and plundering monasteries and castles which are not theirs, by which they have a second time deserved death in body and soul, if only as highwaymen and murderers. Besides, any man against whom it can be proved that he is a maker of sedition is outside the law of God and Empire, so that the first who can slay him is doing right and well. For if a man is an open rebel every man is his judge and executioner, just as when a fire starts, the first to put it out is the best man. For rebellion is not simply murder, but is like a great fire, which attacks and lays waste a whole land. Thus rebellion brings with it a land full of murder and bloodshed, makes widows and orphans, and turns everything upside down like the greatest disaster. Therefore let everyone who can, smite, slay and stab, secretly or openly, remembering that nothing can be more poisonous, hurtful or devilish than a rebel. It is just as when one must kill a mad dog; if you do not strike him, he will strike you, and a whole land with you.

In the third place, they cloak this terrible and horrible sin with the Gospel, call themselves "Christian brethren," receive oaths and homage, and compel people to hold with them to these abominations. Thus they become the greatest blasphemers of God and slanderers of His holy Name, serving the devil under the outward appearance of the Gospel, thus earning death in body and soul ten times over. I have never heard of a more hideous sin. . . .

It does not help the peasants when they pretend that, according to Genesis i and ii, all things were created free and common, and that all of us alike have been baptized. For under the New Testament Moses does not count; for there stands our Master, Christ, and subjects us, with our bodies and our property, to the emperor and the law of this world, when He says "Render unto Cesar the things that are Cesar's". . . . By this doctrine of Christ we are bound to live. For baptism does not make men free in body and property, but in soul; and the Gospel does not make goods common. . . . [The Apostles] did not demand, as do our insane peasants in their raging, that the goods of others should be common, but only their own goods. Our peasants, however, would have other men's goods common, and keep their own goods for themselves. Fine Christians these! I think there is not a devil left in hell; they have all gone into the peasants. Their raving has gone beyond measure.

Since the peasants, then, have brought both God and man down upon them . . . a prince and lord must remember that he is God's minister and the servant of His wrath, to whom the sword is committed for use upon such fellows, and that he sins as greatly against God if he does not punish and protect and does not fulfil the duties of his office, as does one to whom the sword has not been committed when he commits a murder. If he can punish and does not . . . then he is guilty of all the murder and all the evil which these fellows commit, because by wilful neglect of the divine command he permits them to practice their wickedness, though he can prevent it, and is in duty bound to do so. Here, then, there is no time for sleeping; no place for patience or mercy. It is the time of the sword, not the day of grace. . . .

Finally, there is another thing that ought to move the rulers. The peasants are not content to be themselves the devil's own, but they force and compel many good people against their wills to join their devilish league, and so make them partakers of all of their own wickedness and damnation. . . . Therefore, dear lords, here is a place where you can release, rescue, help. Have mercy on these poor people. Stab, smite, slay, whoever can. If you die in doing it, well for you! A more blessed death can never be yours, for you die in obeying the divine Word . . . and in loving service of your neighbor whom you are rescuing from the bonds of hell and of the devil. And so I beg everyone who can to flee from the peasants as from the devil himself; those who do not flee I pray that God will enlighten and convert. As for those who are not to be converted, God grant that they may have neither fortune nor success. . . . If anyone thinks this too hard, let him remember that rebellion is intolerable and that the destruction of the world is to be expected every hour.

Calvinism

John Calvin, born at Noyon in Picardy, France, in 1509, died in 1564 at Geneva, where he had organized a Protestant republic. His religious system, known as Calvinism, has certain distinctive features: (1) its democratic origins, which he attributes to religious authority; (2) the elimination of religious ceremonies; (3) the denial of any authority to tradition; (4) the dogma of predestination; (5) the reduction of the sacraments to two—baptism and communion. In France, Calvin's disciples were also known as Huguenots, either after one of the Genevan leaders called Hughes or after the German word for fellows, Eidgenossen.

Built on very slender foundations, Calvin's authority grew rapidly. A letter from the Venetian ambassador in Paris, written in 1561, informs the Doge: "Your Serenity will hardly believe the influence and power which the principal minister of Geneva, by name Calvin . . . possesses in this kingdom. He is a man of extraordinary authority, who by his mode of life, his doctrines, and his writings rises superior to all the rest." The French philosopher Renan explains this influence by saying that Calvin succeeded in an age and in a country hungry for Christianity simply by being the most Christian man of his generation. If Renan's reasoning is debatable, the prestige of Calvin and that which he reflected upon Geneva are not.

John Calvin: The Institutes of the Christian Church, 1559

The first edition of the Institutio *was published in 1536, when Calvin was twenty-six. It was revised several times, but, as an English scholar noted, there was no development in*

From *Documents of the Christian Church*, ed. Henry Bettenson (London, 1950). Reprinted by permission of Oxford University Press and Geoffrey Cumberlege.

Calvin's thought after the first edition. Calvin's genius was for organization rather than theological speculation.

Book II. Chap. i. Therefore original sin is seen to be an hereditary depravity and corruption of our nature, diffused into all parts of the soul . . . wherefore those who have defined original sin as the lack of the original righteousness with which we should have been endowed, no doubt include, by implication, the whole fact of the matter, but they have not fully expressed the positive energy of this sin. For our nature is not merely bereft of good, but is so productive of every kind of evil that it cannot be inactive. Those who have called it concupiscence have used a word by no means wide of the mark, if it were added (and this is what many do not concede) that whatever is in man, from intellect to will, from the soul to the flesh, is all defiled and crammed with concupiscence; or, to sum it up briefly, that the whole man is in himself nothing but concupiscence. . . .

Chap. iv. The old writers often shrink from the straight-forward acknowledgement of the truth in this matter, from motives of piety. They are afraid of opening to the blasphemers a window for their slanders concerning the works of God. While I salute their restraint, I consider that there is very little danger of this if we simply hold to the teaching of Scripture. Even Augustine is not always emancipated from that superstitious fear; as when he says (Of Predestination and Grace ss 4, 5) that "hardening" and "blinding" refer not to the operation of God, but to His foreknowledge. But there are so many sayings of Scripture which will not admit of such fine distinctions; for they clearly indicate that God's intervention consists in something more than His foreknowledge. . . . In the same way their suggestions as to God's "permission" are too weak to stand. It is very often said that God blinded and hardened the reprobate, that he turned, inclined, or drove on their hearts. . . . And no explanation of such statements is given by taking refuge in "foreknowledge" or "permission." We therefore reply that this [process of hardening or blinding] comes about in two ways. When His light is removed, nothing remains but darkness and blindness; when His Spirit is taken away, our hearts harden into stone; when His guidance ceases, we are turned from the straight path. And so He is rightly said to blind, to harden, to turn, those from whom He takes away the ability to see, to obey, to keep on the straight path. But the second way is much nearer the proper meaning of the words; that to carry out his judgements he directs their councils and excites their wills, in the direction which he has decided upon, through the agency of Satan, the minister of his wrath. . . .

Book III. chap xxi. No one who wishes to be thought religious dares outright to deny predestination, by which God chooses some for the hope of life, and condemns others to eternal death. But men entangle it with captious quibbles; and especially those who make foreknowledge the ground of it. We indeed attribute to God both predestination and foreknowledge; but we call it absurd to subordinate one to the other. When we attribute foreknowledge to God we mean that all things have ever been, and eternally remain, before his eyes; so that to his knowledge nothing is future or past, but all things are present; and present not in the sense that they are reproduced in imagination (as we are aware of past events which are retained in our memory), but present in the sense that He really sees and observes them placed, as it were, before His eyes. And this foreknowledge extends over the whole universe and over every creature. By predestination we mean the eternal decree of God, by which He has decided in His own mind what He wishes to happen in the case of each individual. For all men are not created on an equal footing, but for some eternal life is pre-ordained, for others eternal damnation. . . .

Book IV. chap xiv. *Concerning Sacraments.* . . . It is convenient first of all to notice what a Sacrament is. Now the following seems to me to be a simple and proper definition of a Sacrament. An external symbol by which the Lord attests in our consciences his promises of good-will towards us to sustain the inferiority of our faith, and we on our part testify to our piety towards Him as well as in His presence and before the angels as in the sight of men. Another way of putting it, more condensed but equally valid, would be: A testimony of God's grace to us confirmed by an external sign, with our answering witness of piety towards Him. . . .

Chap. xvii. *Concerning the Sacred Supper of Christ.* That sacred communication of his own flesh and blood by which Christ pours his life into us, just as if he were to penetrate into the marrow of our bones, he witnesses and attests in the Supper. And that he does not by putting before us a vain or empty sign, but offering there the efficacy of his Spirit, by which he fulfils his promise. And in truth he offers and displays the thing there signified to all who share that spiritual feast; though only by the faithful is it perceived and its fruits enjoyed. . . . If it is true that the visible sign is offered to us to attest the granting of the invisible reality, then, on receiving the symbol of the body, we may be confident that the body itself is no less given to us.

The Counteroffensive

The Protestant Revolution was spreading over northwestern Europe: in 1534, the English church broke from Rome; in 1536, Calvin began his work in Geneva; then Denmark (1537), Saxony and Brandenburg (1539), and the Rhineland Palatinate (1541) turned toward reform. Meanwhile, in 1541, John Knox, an enthusiastic follower of Calvin, introduced reform in Scotland. During this time, however, the Roman Catholic Church had not remained inactive: it had founded new militant orders—Jesuits and Capuchins—to carry the fight into the enemy camp, and had reorganized the Inquisition on the Spanish model. For a few years after 1553, England had been reconciled to Rome. But above all, in the long-drawn-out Council of Trent (1545–1563), the Church puts its own house in order and reaffirmed the fundamentals of Catholic doctrine.

Ignatius Loyola: from Spiritual Exercises

The Society of Jesus, founded by Ignatius Loyola (1491–1556), was skillfully organized into a great force for the conservation and propagation of the Roman Catholic Church.

From *Documents of the Christian Church*, ed. Henry Bettenson (London, 1950). Reprinted by permission of Oxford University Press.

The society started with six friends, in 1534, but it was not until 1540 that Pope Paul III could be induced to give it his approval. The following extracts from the Jesuit Rule convey the spirit of obedience that served to make the society such a mighty propaganda tool.

A. RULES FOR THINKING WITH THE CHURCH

1. Always to be ready to obey with mind and heart, setting aside all judgment of one's own, the true spouse of Jesus Christ, our holy mother, our infallible and orthodox mistress, the Catholic Church, whose authority is exercised over us by the hierarchy.

2. To commend the confession of sins to a priest as it is practiced in the Church; the reception of the Holy Eucharist once a year, or better still every week, or at least every month, with the necessary preparation.

3. To commend to the faithful frequent and devout assistance at the holy sacrifice of the Mass, the ecclesiastical hymns, the divine office, and in general the prayers and devotions practiced at stated times, whether in public in the churches or in private.

4. To have a great esteem for the religious orders, and to give the preference to celibacy or virginity over the married state.

5. To approve of the religious vows of chastity, poverty, perpetual obedience, as well as the other works of perfection and supererogation. Let us remark in passing, that we must never engage by vow to take a state (such e.g. as marriage) that would be an impediment to one more perfect. . . .

6. To praise relics, the veneration and invocation of Saints: also the stations, and pious pilgrimages, indulgences, jubilees, the custom of lighting candles in the Churches, and other such aids to piety and devotion.

7. To praise the use of abstinence and fasts as those of Lent, of Ember Days, of Vigils, of Friday, of Saturday, and of others undertaken out of pure devotion: also voluntary mortifications, which we call penances, not merely interior, but exterior also.

8. To commend moreover the construction of Churches and ornaments; also images, to be venerated with the fullest right, for the sake of what they represent.

9. To uphold especially all the precepts of the Church, and not censure them in any manner; but, on the contrary, to defend them promptly, with reasons drawn from all sources, against those who criticize them.

10. To be eager to commend the decrees, mandates, traditions, rites and customs of the Fathers in the Faith or our superiors. As to their conduct; although there may not always be the uprightness of conduct that there ought to be, yet to attack or revile them in private or in public tends to scandal and disorder. Such attacks set the people against their princes and pastors; we must avoid such reproaches and

never attack superiors before inferiors. The best course is to make private approach to those who have power to remedy the evil.

11. To value most highly the sacred teaching, both the Positive and the scholastic, as they are commonly called. . . .

12. It is a thing to be blamed and avoided to compare men who are still living on the earth (however worthy of praise) with the Saints and Blessed, saying: This man is more learned than St. Augustine, etc. . . .

13. That we may be altogether of the same mind and in conformity with the Church herself, if she shall have defined anything to be black which to our eyes appears to be white, we ought in like manner to pronounce it to be black. For we must undoubtingly believe, that the spirit of our Lord Jesus Christ, and the Spirit of the Orthodox Church His Spouse, by which Spirit we are governed and directed to Salvation, is the same; . . .

14. It must also be borne in mind, that although it be most true, that no one is saved but he that is predestinated, yet we must speak with circumspection concerning this matter, lest perchance, stressing too much the grace or predestation of God, we should seem to wish to shut out the force of free will and the merits of good works; or on the other hand, attributing to these latter more than belongs to them, we derogate meanwhile from the power of grace.

15. For the like reason we should not speak on the subject of predestination frequently; if by chance we do so speak, we ought so to temper what we say as to give the people who hear no occasion of erring and saying, "If my salvation or damnation is already decreed, my good or evil actions are predetermined"; whence many are wont to neglect good works, and the means of salvation.

16. It also happens not unfrequently, that from immoderate preaching and praise of faith, without distinction or explanation added, the people seize a pretext for being lazy with regard to any good works, which precede faith, or follow it when it has been formed by the bond of charity.

17. Nor any more must we push to such a point the preaching and inculcating of the grace of God, as that there may creep thence into the minds of the hearers the deadly error of denying our faculty of free will. We must speak of it as the glory of God requires . . . that we may not raise doubts as to liberty and the efficacy of good works.

18. Although it is very praiseworthy and useful to serve God through the motive of pure charity, yet we must also recommend the fear of God; and not only filial fear, but servile fear, which is very useful and often even necessary to raise man from sin. . . . Once risen from the state, and free from the affection of mortal sin, we may then speak of that filial fear which is truly worthy of God, and which gives and preserves the union of pure love.

B. OBEDIENCE OF THE JESUITS

Let us with the utmost pains strain every nerve of our strength to exhibit this virtue of obedience, firstly to the Highest Pontiff, then to the Superiors of the Society; so that in all things, to which obedience can be extended with charity, we may be most ready to obey his voice, just as if it issued from Christ our Lord . . . , leaving any work, even a letter, that we have begun and have not yet finished; by directing to this goal all our strength and intention in the Lord, that holy obedience may be made perfect in us in every respect, in performance, in will, in intellect; by submitting to whatever may be enjoined on us with great readiness, with spiritual joy and perseverance; by persuading ourselves that all things (commanded) are just; by rejecting with a kind of blind obedience all opposing opinion or judgment of our own; and that in all things which are ordained by the Superior where it cannot be clearly held (*definiri*) that any kind of sin intervenes. And let each one persuade himself that they that live under obedience ought to allow themselves to be borne and ruled by divine providence working through their Superiors exactly as if they were a corpse which suffers itself to be borne and handled in any way whatsoever; or just as an old man's stick which serves him who holds it in his hand wherever and for whatever purpose he wish to use it.

The Council of Trent

The chief act of the Counter Reformation took place in the Alpine city of Trent, where in three meetings (1545–1549, 1551–1552, and 1562–1563) the Church tackled the problems of Protestantism, the need for a more precise definition of Catholic faith, and ultimately the need for a new internal discipline. Thus the council compensated for the loss of many Catholics, who had left Rome for rival churches, by raising the standards of religious life and by reorganizing and systematizing both doctrine and Church administration.

DECREE TOUCHING THE OPENING OF THE COUNCIL

Doth it please you,—unto the praise and glory of the holy and undivided Trinity, Father, and Son, and Holy Ghost; for the increase and exaltation of the Christian faith and religion; for the extirpation of heresies; for the peace and union of the Church; for the reformation of the Clergy and Christian people; for the depression and extinction of the enemies of the Christian name,—to decree and declare that the sacred and general council of Trent do begin, and hath begun?

   They answered: It pleaseth us.

From *The Canons and Decrees of the Sacred and Oecumenical Council of Trent,* tr. J. Waterworth (London, 1848).

DECREE CONCERNING THE EDITION, AND THE USE OF THE SACRED BOOKS

Moreover, the same sacred and holy Synod,—considering that no small utility may accrue to the Church of God, if it be made known which out of all the Latin editions, now in circulation, of the sacred books, is to be held as authentic,—ordains and declares, that the said old and vulgate edition, which, by the lengthened usage of so many ages, has been approved of in the Church, be, in public lectures, disputations, sermons and expositions, held as authentic; and that no one is to dare, or presume to reject it under any pretext whatever.

Furthermore, in order to restrain petulant spirits, it decrees, that no one, relying on his own skill, shall,—in matters of faith, and of morals pertaining to the edification of Christian doctrine,—wrestling the sacred Scripture to his own senses, presume to interpret the said sacred Scripture contrary to that sense which holy mother Church,—whose it is to judge of the true sense and interpretation of the holy Scriptures,—hath held and doth hold; or even contrary to the unanimous consent of the Fathers; even though such interpretations were never (intended) to be at any time published. Contraveners shall be made known by their Ordinaries, and be punished with the penalties by law established.

DECREE CONCERNING ORIGINAL SIN

That our Catholic *faith, without which it is impossible to please God,* may, errors being purged away, continue in its own perfect and spotless integrity, and that the Christian people may not *be carried about with every wind of doctrine;* whereas that old serpent, the perpetual enemy of mankind, amongst the very many evils with which the Church of God is in these our times troubled, has also stirred up not only new, but even old, dissensions touching original sin, and the remedy thereof; the sacred and holy, oecumenical and general Synod of Trent,—lawfully assembled in the Holy Ghost, the three same legates of the Apostolic See presiding therein,—wishing now to come to the reclaiming of the erring, and the confirming of the wavering,—following the testimonies of the sacred Scriptures, of the holy Fathers, of the most approved councils, and the judgment and consent of the Church itself, ordains, confesses, and declares these things touching the said original sin:

1. If any one does not confess that the first man, Adam, when he had transgressed the commandment of God in Paradise, immediately lost the holiness and justice wherein he had been constituted; and that he incurred, through the offense of that prevarication, the wrath and indignation of God, and consequently death, with which God had previously threatened him, and, together with death, captivity under his power who thenceforth *had the empire of death, that is to say, the devil,* and that the entire Adam, through that offense of prevarication, was changed, in body and soul, for the worse; let him be anathema.

2. If any one asserts, that the prevarication of Adam injured himself alone, and not his posterity; and that the holiness and justice, received of God, which he lost, he lost for himself alone, and not for us also; or that he, being defiled by the sin of

disobedience, has only transfused death, and pains of the body, into the whole human race, but not sin also, which is the death of the soul; let him be anathema:— whereas he contradicts the apostle who says: *By one man sin entered into the world, and by sin death, and so death passed upon all men, in whom all have sinned.*

3. If any one asserts, that this sin of Adam,—which in its origin is one, and being transfused into all by propagation, not by imitation, is in each one as his own,— is taken away either by the powers of human nature, or by any other remedy than the merit of the *one mediator, our Lord Jesus Christ, who hath reconciled us to God in his own blood, made unto us justice, sanctification, and redemption;* or if he denies that the said merit of Jesus Christ is applied, both to adults and to infants, by the sacrament of baptism rightly administered in the form of the Church; let him be anathema: *For there is no other name under heaven given to men, whereby we must be saved.* Whence that voice: *Behold the Lamb of God, behold him who taketh away the sins of the world;* and that other: *As many as have been baptized have put on Christ.*

DECREE ON JUSTIFICATION

. . . No one, moreover, so long as he is in this mortal life, ought so far to presume as regards the secret mystery of divine predestination, as to determine for certain that he is assuredly in the number of the predestinate; as if it were true, that he that is justified, either cannot sin any more, or, if he do sin, that he ought to promise himself an assured repentance; for except by special revelation, it cannot be known whom God hath chosen unto Himself. . . .

DECREE ON THE SACRAMENTS IN GENERAL

Canon I. If any one saith, that the sacraments of the New Law were not all instituted by Jesus Christ, our Lord; or, that they are more, or less, than seven, to wit, Baptism, Confirmation, the Eucharist, Penance, Extreme Unction, Holy Orders, and Matrimony; or even that any one of these seven is not truly and properly a sacrament; let him be anathema. . . .

Canon IV. If any one saith, that the sacraments of the New Law are not necessary unto salvation, but superfluous; and that, without them, or without the desire thereof, men obtain of God, through faith alone, the grace of justification;—though all (the sacraments) are not indeed necessary for every individual; let him be anathema.

Canon V. If any one saith that these sacraments were instituted for the sake of nourishing faith alone; let him be anathema.

Canon VI. If any one saith, that the sacraments of the New Law do not contain the grace which they signify; or, that they do not confer that grace on those who do not place an obstacle thereunto; as though they were merely outward signs of grace or justice received through faith, and certain marks of the Christian profession, whereby believers are distinguished amongst men from unbelievers; let him be anathema.

Canon VII. If any one saith, that grace, as far as God's part is concerned, is not given through the said sacraments, always, and to all men, even though they receive them rightly, but (only) sometimes, and to some persons; let him be anathema.

Canon VIII. If any one saith, that by the said sacraments of the New Law grace is not conferred through the act performed, but that faith alone in the divine promise suffices for the obtaining of grace; let him be anathema.

Canon IX. If any one saith, that, in the three sacraments, Baptism, to wit, Confirmation, and Order, there is not imprinted in the soul a character, that is, a certain spiritual and indelible sign, on account of which they cannot be repeated; let him be anathema.

Canon X. If any one saith, that all Christians have power to administer the word, and all the sacraments; let him be anathema.

Canon XI. If any one saith, that, in ministers, when they effect, and confer the sacraments, there is not required the intention at least of doing what the Church does; let him be anathema.

Canon XII. If any one saith, that a minister, being in mortal sin,—if so be that he observe all the essentials which belong to the effecting, or conferring of, the sacrament,—neither effects, nor confers the sacrament; let him be anathema. . . .

DECREE CONCERNING THE MOST HOLY SACRAMENT OF THE EUCHARIST

. . . And because that Christ, our Redeemer, declared that which He offered under the species of bread to be truly His own body, therefore has it ever been a firm belief in the Church of God, and this holy Synod doth now declare it anew, that, by the consecration of the bread and of the wine, a conversion is made of the whole substance of the body of Christ our Lord, and of the whole substance of the wine into the substance of His blood; which conversion is, by the holy Catholic Church, suitably and properly called Transubstantiation.

ON THE MOST HOLY SACRAMENT OF THE EUCHARIST

Canon I. If any one denieth, that, in the sacrament of the most holy Eucharist, are contained truly, really and substantially, the body and blood together with the soul and divinity of our Lord Jesus Christ, and consequently the whole Christ; but saith that He is only therein as in a sign, or in figure, or virtue; let him be anathema.

Canon II. If any one saith, that, in the sacred and holy sacrament of the Eucharist, the substance of the bread and wine remains conjointly with the body and blood of our Lord Jesus Christ, and denieth that wonderful and singular conversion of the whole substance of the bread into the Body, and of the whole substance of the wine into the Blood—the species only of the bread and wine remaining—which conversion indeed the Catholic Church most aptly calls Transubstantiation; let him be anathema.

Canon III. If any one denieth, that, in the venerable sacrament of the Eucharist, the whole Christ is contained under each species, and under every part of each species, when separated; let him be anathema.

Canon IV. If any one saith, that, after the consecration is completed, the body and blood of our Lord Jesus Christ are not in the admirable sacrament of the Eucharist, but (are there) only during the use, whilst it is being taken, and not either before or after; and that, in the hosts, or consecrated particles, which are reserved or which remain after communion, the true Body of the Lord remaineth not; let him be anathema.

Canon V. If any one saith, either that the principal fruit of the most holy Eucharist is the remission of sins, or, that other effects do not result therefrom; let him be anathema.

Canon VI. If any one saith, that, in the holy sacrament of the Eucharist, Christ, the only-begotten Son of God, is not to be adorned with the worship, even external of latria; and is, consequently, neither to be venerated with a special festive solemnity, nor to be solemnly borne about in processions, according to the laudable and universal rite and custom of holy church; or, is not to be proposed publicly to the people to be adored, and that the adorers thereof are idolators; let him be anathema.

Canon VII. If any one saith, that it is not lawful for the sacred Eucharist to be reserved in the *sacrarium,* but that, immediately after consecration, it must necessarily be distributed amongst those present; or, that it is not lawful that it be carried with honour to the sick; let him be anathema.

Canon VIII. If any one saith, that Christ, given in the Eucharist, is eaten spiritually only, and not also sacramentally and really; let him be anathema.

Canon IX. If any one denieth, that all and each of Christ's faithful of both sexes are bound, when they have attained to years of discretion, to communicate every year, at least at Easter, in accordance with the precept of holy Mother Church; let him be anathema.

Canon X. If any one saith, that it is not lawful for the celebrating priest to communicate himself; let him be anathema.

Canon XI. If any one saith, that faith alone is a sufficient preparation for receiving the sacrament of the most holy Eucharist; let him be anathema. And for fear lest so great a sacrament may be received unworthily, and so unto death and condemnation, this holy Synod ordains and declares, that sacramental confession, when a confessor may be had, is of necessity to be made beforehand, by those whose conscience is burdened with mortal sin, how contrite even soever they may think themselves. But if any one shall presume to teach, preach, or obstinately to assert, or even in public disputation to defend the contrary, he shall be thereupon excommunicated.

ON THE SACRIFICE OF THE MASS

... Canon I. If any one saith, that in the mass a true and proper sacrifice is not offered to God; or, that to be offered is nothing else but that Christ is given us to eat; let him be anathema.

Canon II. If any one saith, that by those words, *Do this for the commemoration of me* ... Christ did not institute the apostles priests, or, did not ordain that they, and other priests should offer His own body and blood; let him be anathema.

Canon III. If any one saith, that the sacrifice of the mass is only a sacrifice of praise and of thanksgiving; or, that it is a bare commemoration of the sacrifice consummated on the cross, but not a propitiatory sacrifice; or, that it profits him only who receives; and that it ought not to be offered for the living and the dead for sins, pains, satisfactions, and other necessities; let him be anathema.

DECREE ON REFORMATION

And forasmuch as, though the habit does not make the monk, it is nevertheless needful that clerics always wear a dress suitable to their proper order, that by the decency of their outward apparel they may show forth the inward correctness of their morals; but to such a pitch, in these days, have the contempt of religion and the rashness of some grown, as that, making but little account of their own dignity, and of the clerical honour, they even wear in public the dress of laymen—setting their feet in different paths, one of God, the other of the flesh;—for this cause, all ecclesiastical persons, howsoever exempted, who are either in sacred orders or in possession of any manner of dignities, personates, or other offices, or benefices ecclesiastical; if, after having been admonished by their own bishop, even by a public edict, they shall not wear a becoming clerical dress, suitable to their order and dignity, and in conformity with the ordinance and mandate of the said bishop, they may, and ought to be, compelled thereunto, by suspension from their orders, office, benefice, and from the fruits, revenues, and proceeds of the said benefices; and also, if, after having been once rebuked, they offend again herein [they are to be coerced] even by deprivation of the said offices and benefices. . . .

Whereas too, *he who has killed his neighbour on set purpose and by lying in wait for him, is to be taken away from the altar*, because he has voluntarily committed a homicide; even though that crime have neither been proved by ordinary process of law, nor be otherwise public, but is secret, such a one can never be promoted to sacred orders; nor shall it be lawful to confer upon him any ecclesiastical benefices, even though they have no cure of souls; but he shall be forever excluded from every ecclesiastical order, benefice, and office. . . .

There is nothing that continually *instructs others unto piety*, and the service of God, more than the life and example of those who have dedicated themselves to the divine ministry. For as they are seen to be raised to a higher position, above the things of this world, others fix their eyes upon them as upon a mirror, and derive from them what they are to imitate. Wherefore clerics called to have the Lord for their portion, ought by all means so to regulate their whole life and conversation, as that in their dress, comportment, gait, discourse, and all things else, nothing appear but what is grave, regulated, and replete with religiousness; avoiding even slight faults, which in them would be most grievous; that so their actions may impress all with veneration. Whereas, therefore, the more useful and decorous these things are for the Church of God, the more carefully also are they to be atttended to; the holy Synod ordains, that those things which have been heretofore copiously and wholesomely enacted by sovereign pontiffs and sacred councils,—relative to the life, propriety of conduct, dress, and learning of clerics, and also touching the luxuriousness, feastings, dances, gambling, sports, and all sorts of crime whatever, as also the secular employments, to be by them shunned,—the same shall be henceforth observed, under the same penalties, or greater, to be imposed at the discretion of the Ordinary; nor shall any appeal suspend the execution hereof, as relating to the correction of manners. But if anything of the above shall be found to have fallen into desuetude, they shall make it their care that it be brought again into use as soon as possible, and be accurately observed by all, any customs to the contrary notwithstanding; lest they themselves may have, God being the avenger, to pay the penalty deserved by their neglect of the correction of those subject to them . . .

ON REFORMATION

. . . How shameful a thing, and how unworthy it is of the name of clerics who have devoted themselves to the service of God, to live in the filth of impurity, and unclean bondage, the thing itself doth testify, in the common scandal of all the faithful, and the extreme disgrace entailed on the clerical order. To the end, therefore, that the ministers of the Church may be recalled to that continency and integrity of life which becomes them; and that the people may hence learn to reverence them the more, that they know them to be more pure of life: the holy Synod forbids all clerics whatsoever to dare to keep concubines, or any other woman of whom any suspicion can exist, either in their own houses, or elsewhere, or to presume to have any intercourse with them: otherwise they shall be punished with the penalties imposed by the sacred canons, or by the statutes of the (several) churches. But if, after being admonished by their superiors, they shall not abstain from these women, they shall be *ipso facto* deprived of the third part of the fruits, rents, and proceeds of all their benefices whatsoever, and pensions; which third part shall be applied to the fabric of the church, or to some other pious place, at the discretion of the bishop. If, however, persisting in the same crime, with the same or some other woman, they shall not even yet have obeyed upon a second admonition, not only shall they thereupon forfeit all the fruits and proceeds of their benefices and pensions, which shall be applied to the places aforesaid, but they shall also be suspended from the administration of the benefices themselves, for as long a period as shall seem fit to the Ordinary, even as the delegate of the Apostolic See. And if, having been thus suspended, they nevertheless shall not put away those women, or even if they shall have intercourse with them, then shall they be for ever deprived of their ecclesiastical benefices, portions, offices, and pensions of whatsoever kind, and be rendered thenceforth incapable and unworthy of any manner of honours, dignities, benefices and offices, until, after a manifest amendment of life, it shall seem good to their superiors, for a cause, to grant them a dispensation. But if, after having once put them away, they shall have dared to renew the interrupted connexion, or to take to themselves other scandalous women of this sort, they shall, in addition to the penalties aforesaid, be smitten with the sword of excommunication. Nor shall any appeal, or exemption, hinder or suspend the execution of the aforesaid; and the cognizance of all the matters above-named shall not belong to arch-deacons, or deans, *or* other inferiors, but to the bishops themselves, who may proceed without the noise and the formalities of justice, and by the sole investigation of the truth of the fact. . . .

ON THE SACRAMENT OF ORDER

Canon I. If any one saith, that there is not in the New Testament a visible and external priesthood; or that there is not any power of consecrating and offering the true body and blood of the Lord, and of forgiving and retaining sins; but only an office and bare ministry of preaching the Gospel; or, that those who do not preach are not priests at all; let him be anathema.

Canon II. If any one saith, that, besides the priesthood, there are not in the Catholic Church other orders, both greater and minor, by which, as by certain steps, advance is made unto the priesthood; let him be anathema.

Canon III. If any one saith, that order, or sacred ordination, is not truly and properly a sacrament instituted by Christ the Lord; or, that it is a kind of human figment devised by men unskilled in ecclesiastical matters; or, that it is only a kind of rite for choosing ministers of the word of God and of the sacraments; let him be anathema.

Canon IV. If any one saith, that, by sacred ordination, the Holy Ghost is not given; and that vainly therefore do the bishops say, *Receive ye the Holy Ghost;* or, that a character is not imprinted by that ordination; or, that he who has once been a priest, can again become a layman; let him be anathema.

Canon V. If any one saith, that the sacred unction which the Church uses in holy ordination, is not only not required, but is to be despised and is pernicious, as likewise are the other ceremonies of Order; let him be anathema.

Canon VI. If any one saith, that in the Catholic Church there is not a hierarchy by divine ordination instituted, consisting of bishops, priests, and ministers; let him be anathema.

Canon VII. If any one saith, that bishops are not superior to priests; or, that they have not the power of confirming and ordaining; or, that the power which they possess is common to them and to priests; or, that orders, conferred by them, without the consent, or vocation of the people, or of the secular power, are invalid; or, that those who have neither been rightly ordained, nor sent, by ecclesiastical and canonical power, but come from elsewhere, are lawful ministers of the word and of the sacraments; let him be anathema.

Canon VIII. If any one saith, that the bishops, who are assumed by authority of the Roman Pontiff, are not legitimate and true bishops, but are a human figment; let him be anathema.

ON THE SACRAMENT OF MATRIMONY

Canon IX. If any one saith, that clerics constituted in sacred orders, or Regulars, who have solemnly professed chastity, are able to contract marriage, and that being contracted it is valid, notwithstanding the ecclesiastical law or vow; and that the contrary is nothing else than to condemn marriage; and, that all who do not feel that they have the gift of chastity, even though they have made a vow thereof, may contract marriage; let him be anathema: seeing that God refuses not that gift to those who ask for it rightly, neither does *He suffer us to be tempted above that which we are able.*

ON THE INVOCATION, VENERATION, AND RELICS OF SAINTS
AND ON SACRED IMAGES

The holy Synod enjoins on all bishops, and others who sustain the office and charge of teaching, that, agreeably to the usage of the Catholic and Apostolic Church, received from the primitive times of the Christian religion, and agreeably to the consent of the holy Fathers, and to the decrees of sacred Councils, they especially instruct the faithful diligently concerning the intercession and invocation of saints; the honour (paid) to relics; and the legitimate use of images: teaching them, that the saints, who reign together with Christ, offer up their own prayers to God for men; that it is good and useful suppliantly to invoke them, and to have recourse to their prayers, aid, (and) help for obtaining benefits from God, through His Son, Jesus Christ our Lord, who is alone our Redeemer and Saviour; but that they think impiously, who deny that the saints, who enjoy eternal happiness in heaven, are to be invocated; or who assert either that they do not pray for men; or, that the invocation of them to pray for each of us even in particular, is idolatry; or, that it is repugnant to the word of God; and is opposed to the honour of the *one mediator of God and men, Christ Jesus;* or, that it is foolish to supplicate, vocally, or mentally, those who reign in heaven. Also, that the holy bodies of holy martyrs, and of others now living with Christ,—which bodies were the living members of Christ, and *the temple of the Holy Ghost,* and which are by Him to be raised unto eternal life, and to be glorified,—are to be venerated by the faithful; through which (bodies) many benefits are bestowed by God on men; so that they who affirm that veneration and honour are not due to the relics of saints; or, that these, and other sacred monuments, are uselessly honoured by the faithful; and that the places dedicated to the memories of the saints are in vain visited with the view of obtaining their aid; are wholly to be condemned, as the Church has already long since condemned, and now also condemns them.

Moreover, that the images of Christ, of the Virgin Mother of God, and of the other saints, are to be had and retained particularly in temples, and that due honour and veneration are to be given them; not that any divinity, or virtue, is believed to be in them, on account of which they are to be worshipped; or that anything is to be asked of them; or, that trust is to be reposed in images, as was of old done by the

Gentiles who placed their hope in idols; but because the honour which is shown them is referred to the prototypes which those images represent; in such wise that by the images which we kiss, and before which we uncover the head and prostrate ourselves, we adore Christ; and we venerate the saints, whose similitude they bear; as, by the decrees of Councils, and especially of the second Synod of Nicaea, has been defined against the opponents of images. . . .

DECREE CONCERNING INDULGENCES

Whereas the power of conferring Indulgences was granted by Christ to the Church; and she has, even in the most ancient times, used the said power, delivered unto her of God; the sacred holy Synod teaches, and enjoins, that the use of Indulgences, for the Christian people most salutary, and approved of by the authority of sacred Councils, is to be retained in the Church; and It condemns with anathema those who either assert, that they are useless; or who deny that there is in the Church the power of granting them. In granting them, however, It desires that, in accordance with the ancient and approved custom in the Church, moderation be observed; lest, by excessive facility, ecclesiastical discipline be enervated. And being desirous that the abuses which have crept therein, and by occasion of which this honourable name of Indulgences is blasphemed by heretics, be amended and corrected, It ordains generally by this decree, that all evil gains for the obtaining thereof,—whence a most prolific cause of abuses amongst the Christian people has been derived,—be wholly abolished. But as regards the other abuses which have proceeded from superstition, ignorance, irreverence, or from whatever other source, since by reason of the manifold corruptions in the places and provinces where the said abuses are committed, they cannot conveniently be specially prohibited; It commands all bishops, diligently to collect, each in his own church, all abuses of this nature, and to report them in the first provincial Synod; that, after having been reviewed by the opinions of the other bishops also, they may forthwith be referred to the Sovereign Roman Pontiff, by whose authority and prudence that which may be expedient for the universal Church will be ordained; that thus the gift of holy Indulgences may be dispensed to all the faithful, piously, holily, and incorruptly. . . .

Amen.

The Massacre of St. Bartholomew

The clash of two or more opposing views of truth, each claiming to be ultimate, each intolerant of every other view, would have been bitter enough. Matters were not improved when religious confession was enlisted in the service of rival political interests—as it was, for instance, in France, where Protestantism became identified with the struggle of a section of the nobility against the growing power of central government. Throughout the second half of the sixteenth century, France was ravaged by savage struggles known as the Wars of Religion—a long series of plots and counterplots, murders, massacres, and actual open warfare. The Catholic party was headed by the Lorraine family of Guise, and the Protestants by the Bourbons, supported by Admiral de Coligny. Both sides tried to secure control of the royal government, which was in the hands of a widow-queen, Catherine de Médicis, and her rather unimpressive sons. In 1572, the marriage of Henri de Bourbon, King of Navarre, a Protestant, to Catherine's daughter Margaret—a ceremony that brought the most important Protestant nobles to Paris—seemed to offer the Catholic party a chance to decapitate the enemy in one master stroke. The result was the massacre that began on St. Bartholomew's night and continued into the following day. Ordered by the king and enthusiastically carried out by the ultra-Catholic population of Paris, the massacre claimed some three thousand victims in the capital as well as a good many in the provinces.

Philip II of Spain and the Court of Rome rejoiced greatly. It is said that the news of the massacre made Philip laugh for the only time in his life. The pope, for his part, ordered a Te Deum, declaring that the news pleased him more than fifty victories of Lepanto (against the Turks). Such joy, however, proved somewhat premature, and the massacre became only one more bloody incident in a conflict that was to drag out for another twenty years. France would remain Catholic, though tolerant of Protestants, but Henri of Navarre became its king—the first of the Bourbons, who were to rule the country for two centuries. More important, far from declining, as its opponents had hoped, royal power grew, and the anarchy of half a century's civil war brought grist to the mill of central authority.

St. Bartholomew's feast falls on August 24. The letter that follows, written on August 26 by a Jesuit teaching in Paris to the abbot of the great Swiss monastery of Saint-Gall, tells a tale to delight and rejoice the Christian world.

Joachim Opser, S.J.: Letter to the Abbot of Saint-Gall

I think I shall not bore you if I mention in detail an event as unexpected as it is useful to our cause, and which not only delights the Christian world with admiration, but brings it to a peak of rejoicing. Concerning this you will hear what the Captain has to say [the Captain commanding the detachment of the King's Swiss Mercenaries that broke into the house of the Huguenot leader, Admiral Coligny, and murdered the Admiral]. Rejoice in advance, but do not for that disdain or reject as superfluous the lines I write with more satisfaction perhaps than seems quite proper, for I affirm nothing I have not got from authoritative sources.

The Admiral has perished miserably on August 24, with all the heretical French nobility. (One can say it without exaggeration.) What immense carnage! I shuddered at the sight of this river [the Seine] full of naked and horribly mutilated corpses. Up to the present, the King has spared none but the King of Navarre [the future Henry IV]. In effect, today August 26, towards one o'clock, the King of Navarre attended Mass with the King Charles, so that all conceive the greatest hopes of seeing him change his religion. . . . Everyone agrees in praising the prudence and magnanimity of the King who, after having by his kindness and indulgence fattened, as it were, the heretics like cattle, has suddenly had them slaughtered by his soldiers. . . . All heretical booksellers that one could find have been massacred and cast naked into the river. Ramus,

From *Bulletin de la Société de l'Histoire du Protestantisme français*, Vol. XIII (Paris, 1882), pp. 243–247.

who had jumped out of his bedroom, quite high up, still lies naked on the river bank, pierced by numerous dagger-blows. In a word, there is no one (even women not excepted) who has not been either killed or wounded.

One more thing as concerns the massacre of the Admiral; I hold these details from the man who gave him the third blow with his battle axe, from that Conrad Burg who used to be groom at Steward Joachim Waldemann's at Wyl. When the Swiss, under the orders of the Duc d'Anjou, had broken in the doors, Conrad, followed by Leonhard Grunenfelder of Glaris and Martin Koch of Fribourg, reached the Admiral's room which was the third in the house. The servant was killed first. The Admiral was in a dressing gown and none at first wanted to lay hands on him; but Martin Koch, more daring than the others, struck the wretch with his halberd; Conrad gave him the third blow, and at the seventh at last he fell dead against the chimney of his room. By order of the Duc de Guise his corpse was thrown out of the window and, after tying a rope round his neck as is the way with criminals, he was offered in display for all the people by dragging him to the Seine. Such was the end of that pernicious man, who not only brought a great many to the brink [of perdition] in his lifetime, but who, dying, swept a crowd of heretical nobles into hell with him.

Papire Masson: Histoire de Charles IX

Papire Masson, who was Charles IX's official historiographer, made these observations in 1572.

This carnage arrived in the sight of the King, who watched it from the Louvre with much pleasure. A few days later, he went himself to the gallows of Montfaucon to see the corpse of Coligny which was hanging by its feet; and as some of his suite feigned reluctance to step near because of the corpse's stink: "The smell of a dead foe," said he, "is sweet and pleasant."

The Roman Reaction: A Prayer of Thanks

On September 8, 1572, Rome celebrated the massacre's success with a Mass of Thanks in the Church of Saint-Louis-des-Français, "for the great grace received of God."

All-powerful God, who stands against the proud and grants grace to the humble, we offer you the tribute of our most fervent praise for that, caring for the faith of your servants, you have granted them a brilliant triumph over the perfidious opponents of the Catholic people and we humbly beseech you to continue in your mercy that which you have begun in your constancy, for the glory of your name which is invoked in our midst. In the name of Christ, grant us our prayer!

IMAGES: AN URBAN RENAISSANCE

Civilization, civility, urbanity, are urban products. City dwellers are not necessarily urbane, but the economic activity connected with city living spurs social and cultural activities. When Roman power decayed, so did Roman cities and civilization. Much later, as order was gradually restored in the West, production and trade benefitted. Money, goods, and people circulated more freely, as markets, ports, and towns were revived. Within these towns, men and women began to affirm themselves as individuals even if they happened not to be warriors or nobles. The Renaissance utopia was the urban dream of an ideal urban setting.

The Amphitheater at Arles. Close to the Rhone delta and to the Mediterranean, Arles was a leading city of Roman Gaul, preeminent in navigation, commerce, and law. In the sixth century it was sacked by Visigoths; in the eighth century by Saracens. When two centuries later Burgundians made it the capital of a kingdom, the ancient Arelate was only a shadow of its former self. The first century arena, once seating 20,000 people, had been turned into fortified shelter for what remained of a once thriving population.
(Culver Pictures, Inc.)

88

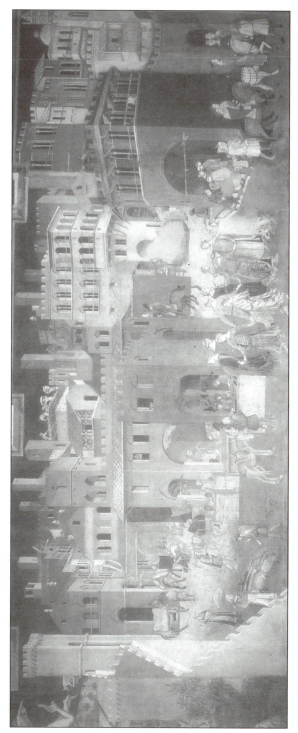

Family Strongholds in Siena. In Italy, where the Roman urban tradition persisted, nobles were as quarrelsome and violent as elsewhere. Yet many among the aristocracy chose to live in cities where they clashed with each other and with the hard-working, sober, cautious burgher-merchants. Living in feuding family groups or clans, like Shakespeare's Montagues and Capulets of Verona, they built fortified family towers that housed shops and workshops as well as retainers who could turn out to fight at need. This fourteenth-century depiction of "The Well-Governed City" shows everyday activities in a prosperous urban center still dominated by the towers of feudal gangs. It took centuries before the civil authorities managed to take control, raze the towers, and impose law. At Bologna, where 194 such family towers were documented during the twelfth century, only two survive today.

(*Good Government in the City* by Ambrogio Lorenzetti, courtesy of The Bridgeman Art Library)

Paris in the Sixteenth Century. Although it was the political centre of France, six-teenth-century Paris was still a walled city, crowded with spires that stood in close rela-tion to the surrounding countryside. The gentleman in the foreground is Paris of Troy, legendary founder of the city that bears his name.
(From Beauvais, Cathedrale Saint-Pierre/Giraudon, Paris)

Tournament at Nuremberg, 1561. Even at this rather late date, knighthood survived
in an urban environment. At this tournament in the center of Nuremberg in 1561, the public
watches jesters and clowns as eagerly as they watch the jousters.
(*The Last Gesellenstechen in Nuremberg* by Jost Ammann, courtesy of Bayerisches National Museum,
Munich)

Antwerp Harbor. In the early sixteenth century, Antwerp was the economic center of Europe. The high tower of the cathedral vies for attention with the busy shipping routes. The road in the foreground is a reminder that Antwerp was a terminus for the great land route that led from Italy across the Alps and through the Rhineland to the North Sea. (Antwerp, National Maritime Museum)

"Ideal City." An urbanist's dream: an unreal city inspired by memories of ancient monuments. It is an orderly and harmonious space for urban living, which is rigorously organized in geometrical perspective as it never was and never would be. (Walters Art Gallery, Baltimore)

Political and Economic Changes

CULTURAL developments take place against a political and economic background. The fifteenth and sixteenth centuries witnessed profound changes in the political and economic structure of the West. New worlds had been discovered, new powers had risen, old powers had waned, and the trickle of goods and bullion from overseas was growing into a stream. The Muslims, expelled from the Iberian peninsula, had made great strides at the other end of Europe, where Hungary had fallen in 1526 and Vienna itself for the first time was besieged in 1529.

Hard pressed by changing realities, the old feudal order of society had decayed but had not yet been replaced by a new order. Hence this was a period of transition, with all the suffering and the disorder that follow social changes as yet uncomprehended and, therefore, unmastered. The Reformation, too, had created political problems which princes and statesmen strove to handle as best they could: What should be the relationship between church and state? Whence comes the prince's right to rule? Can more than one religious belief be tolerated in the state? These issues were to be threshed out in the course of the sixteenth century, and the answers proposed would be very different in tenor from those that the pre-Reformation world might have found acceptable.

The Power and Revenues of the States of Europe in 1423

The document that follows is given to facilitate comparison with later developments. It appears in a fifteenth-century life of the Venetian doge, Mocenigo. The Venetian ambassadors, the best intelligence agents of their time, kept their government informed of the activities of foreign powers through a system of regular reports.

Report of a Venetian Ambassador

Income of all the Christian powers and what they are able to do. The king of France with all his force and the feudal services of princes, dukes, marquises, counts, barons, knights, bishops, abbots, canons, priests, and citizens, can in his own country raise 30,000 horsemen skilled in arms. If desiring to send them out of the country the said realm could not, since the costs would be doubled, send more than 15,000 horse. Before

---

From *Translations and Reprints,* Vol. 3, No. 2, R. P. Falkner, Ed.

the war with their own countrymen, it could have raised 100,000, for that war destroyed both Church and revenues. In the total therefore 15,000 horse. The king of England with the power of his revenues, and the feudal services of princes and others as above could, paying them every month, raise at home 30,000 horsemen skilled in arms. In making the test of war these powers are equal. They have always been powerful in their undertakings. And if one of these forces had been greater than the other, one would have been destroyed. The English were overcome, after the division occurred in England, and they could not make provision for their forces. This was before 1414. They had 40,000 horse. Wars have weakened these countries, their men and their revenues, so that now wishing to send a force out of the country it is agreed that they have the half, i.e., 15,000 horsemen. The king of Scotland is lord of a great country, and of a people of so great poverty that he would not be able to maintain with his revenues and the taxes and dues of the clergy and laity, 10,000 horsemen skilled in arms in his own country; outside of the country on account of the great cost, 5000 horse. The king of Norway who is lord of a great country, and a people equally poor could not maintain at home with his revenues and the taxes and dues of clergy and laity 10,000 horsemen skilled in arms, abroad 5000 horse. The king of Spain with all his revenues and feudal dues of clergy and laity, with all his forces 30,000 horsemen skilled in arms. In 1414 he paid for 20,000. Wishing to maintain them out of the country at double cost they would be 15,000 horsemen. The king of Portugal with all his revenues from clergy and laity, with all his force, would have, if he paid every month, at home 6000 horsemen skilled in arms, abroad 3000 horse. The king of Brittany with all his revenues and feudal dues of clergy and laity, paying every month could maintain at home 8000 horsemen skilled in arms, abroad 4000. The master of St. James with all his force of men skilled in arms, at home 4000 horsemen, abroad 2000. The duke of Burgundy with all his force as above at home 3000 cavalry. In 1414 he held 1000. But war has destroyed the country. Abroad 5000 men. The king René (of Provence) with all his revenues would be able to raise at home 6000 horse, abroad 3000. The duke of Savoy with all his revenues would be able to raise at home 8000 horse, abroad 4000. The marquis of Montferrat would be able to hold 2000 horse at home, 1000 abroad. The count Francesco Sforza, duke of Milan, with all his force could hold as mercenaries 10,000 horse at home and 5000 abroad. The signory of Venice can, with all its force pay for 10,000 horsemen skilled in arms at home, and 5000 abroad. The marquis of Ferrara at home 2000 horsemen, abroad 1000. The marquis of Mantua, at home 2000, abroad 1000. The signory of Bologna 2000 at home, 1000 abroad. The community of Siena at home 2000, abroad 1000. The signory of Florence with all its revenues of 1414 could place 1000. At present through the wars it can place 4000 horsemen at home and 2000 abroad.

The pope with all his revenues of his States of the Church, and with the profits of churches which he receives, was able in 1414 to raise 8000 horsemen; at present at home 6000 horsemen, abroad 3000. The king of Aragon in the Realm of Naples can raise with all his revenues 12,000 horsemen at home and 6000 abroad. The princes of the Realm are able with all their revenues to raise 4000 horsemen at home, 2000 abroad. The Community of Genoa were able in 1414 to maintain 5000 horsemen. But through their present dissension and the wars they are only able to maintain at present 2000.

The Barcelonians with all the community and the lord of Catalonia, counting citizens and knights, can at home every month maintain 12,000 horsemen, and abroad 6000. All Germany with the lords temporal and spiritual, the free and the other cities, north and south Germany, and the Emperor who is German, can raise with all their resources and revenues 60,000 horsemen at home and 30,000 abroad. The king of Hungary, with all the dukes, lords, princes, barons, prelates, clergy and laity, and with all his resources and revenues can raise at home 80,000 horsemen, abroad 40,000. The grand master of Prussia with all his revenues, 30,000 horsemen. In 1414 he had 50,000. But war has weakened him. Abroad 15,000 horsemen. The king of Poland with all his revenues, with dukes, marquises, barons, cities and boroughs can raise at home 50,000 horsemen, abroad 25,000. The Wallachians with all their revenues and feudal service, at home 20,000 horsemen, abroad 10,000. Morea with its resources of 1414 could raise 50,000 horsemen. War has weakened them. At present at home 20,000, abroad 10,000. All Albania, Croatia, Slavonia, Servia, Russia, and Bosnia with all their revenues at home 30,000, abroad 15,000. The king of Cyprus with all his revenues can raise in the Island 2000, abroad 1000. The duke of Nicea in the Archipelago with all his power can pay for 2000 horsemen at home, 1000 abroad. The grand master of Rhodes with all his revenues and feudal dues of his liegemen, clergy and laity of the island, would be able to raise 4000 horsemen at home, 2000 abroad. The lord of Mitylene 2000 horsemen, abroad 1000. The emperor of Trebizonde with all his power could raise at home 25,000 horsemen, abroad 15,000. The king of Georgia with his revenues of 1414 could raise 30,000 horsemen. At present he can raise at home 10,000 horsemen, abroad 5000.

Power of the Infidel Monarchs. The Turk can in all his dominions raise 40,000 horsemen, valiant men to defend him against the Christians. The Caraman with all his power can raise at home 60,000 horsemen, abroad 30,000. Ussun Cassan with all his power can raise at home 20,000 horsemen in the service of Mahomet, abroad 10,000. The Caraifan with all his resources at home 20,000, abroad 10,000. Tamerlane with all his Tartar power can raise at home 1,000,000 horsemen, abroad 500,000. The king of Tunis, of Granada and the other cities of Barbary who have galleys and boats to the injury of Christians, at home are 100,000 horsemen, abroad 50,000.

Revenues of some Christian princes in the year 1423. The king of France in the year 1414 had 2,000,000 ducats ordinary revenues. But the wars which have continued for forty years have reduced the ordinary revenues to 1,000,000 ducats. The king of England had 2,000,000 ducats ordinary revenue. The continued wars have desolated the island. At the present time he has 700,000 ducats revenue. The king of Spain had in 1410, 3,000,000 ducats ordinary revenue, but the continued wars have reduced it to 800,000 ducats. The king of Portugal had in 1410, 200,000 ducats revenue. By the wars it is reduced to 140,000 ducats. The king of Brittany in 1414 had 200,000 ducats revenue. By the wars it is reduced to 140,000 ducats. The duke of Burgundy had in 1400, 3,000,000 ducats. By the wars it is reduced to 900,000 ducats. The duke of Savoy as a free country has 150,000 ducats revenue. The marquis of Montferrat as a free country has 150,000 ducats revenue. Count Francesco, duke of Milan [in 1423 Duke Filippo Maria Visconti of Milan had 1,000,000 ducats revenue] Count Francesco has at present on account of the wars only 500,000 ducats. The signory of Venice had in 1423, 1,100,000 ducats ordinary revenue. By reason of great wars which have destroyed commerce it has 800,000 ducats ordinary revenue. The marquis of Ferrara had in 1423, 70,000 ducats ordinary revenue. Through the Italian wars he has by remaining at peace 150,000 ducats. The marquis of Montferrat had in 1423, 150,000 ducats, today 60,000 ducats. The Bolognese had in 1423, 400,000 ducats ordinary revenue. But by the wars it has come to 200,000 ducats. Florence in 1423 had a revenue of 400,000 ducats. But since then, through the great wars it is reduced to 200,000 ducats. The pope, though formerly he had none, has 400,000 ducats ordinary revenue. The Genoese through the great division among them are reduced to 130,000 ducats. The king of Aragon, in all his realm with Sicily, though at first he had considerably more, has a revenue of 310,000 ducats.

Henry VIII

In an age of forceful figures, Henry VIII stands out as one of the most conspicuous. His popular fame seems to rest primarily on half a dozen wives, but historians see him as the central figure and dominating force in England during the whole of his long reign (1509–1547)—fighting hard to establish a secure succession for the Tudor dynasty that his father, Henry VII, had founded on Bosworth Field (1485); beginning the English Reformation; and gathering in his hands powers and loyalties for which Church and Crown had vied a long time.

The Act of Supremacy (1534)

An Act concernynge the Kynges Highness to be supreme heed of the Churche of Englande and to have auctoryte to reforme and redresse all errours, heresyes and abuses yn the same.

Albeit the Kynges Majestie justely and rightfully is and oweth to be the supreme heed of the Churche of England, so is recognysed by the clery of this Realme in theyr convocacions; yet neverthelesse for corroboracion and confirmacion thereof, and for increase of vertue in Cristis Religion within this Realme of England, and to represse and extirpe all errours, heresies and other enormyties and abuses heretofore used in the same. Be it enacted by auctority of this present Parliament that the Kyng our Soveraign Lorde, his heires and successours Kynges of this Realme shall be takyn, acceptyd, and reputed the onely supreme heed in erthe of the Churche of England callyd Anglicana Ecclesia, and shall have and enjoye annexed and unyted to the Ymperyall Crowne of this Realme as well the title and style thereof, as all Honours Dignyties prehemynences jurisdiccions privileges auctorities ymunyties profitis and commodities to the said dignyties of supreme heed of the same Churche belongyng and apperteyning: And that our said Soveraigne Lorde his heires and successours Kynges of this Realme shall

From *Translations and Reprints*, Vol. 1, No. 1, E. P. Cheyney, Ed.

have full power and auctorite from tyme to tyme to visite represse redresse reforme order correct restrayne and amende all suche errours heresies abuses offences contemptes and enormyties whatsoever they be whiche by any maner spirituall auctoryte or juristiccion ought or maie lawfullye be reformyd repressyd ordred redressyd correctyd restrayned or amendyd, most to the pleasure of almyghtie God the increase of vertue yn Chrystis Religion and for the conservacy of the peace unyte and tranquylyte of this Realme: Any usage custome foreyne laws foreyne auctoryte prescripcion or anye other thinge or thinges to the contrarie hereof notwithstandinge.

The Act of the Six Articles (1539)

AN ACT ABOLISHING DIVERSITY IN OPYNIONS

Where the Kinges most excellent Majestie is by Gods lawe supreme head ymmediately under him of this hole churche and congregation of Englande intendinge the conservacion of the same Churche and congregation in a true syncere and unyforme doctrine of Christ's Religion.

Forasmuche as in the saide parliament synode and convacacion there were certen articles, matters and questions proponed and set forth touchinge Christen Religion.

The Kinges most Royal Majestie most prudently ponderinge and consideringe that by occasion of variable and sundrie opinions and judgements of the saide articles, greate discorde and variance hathe arisen as well amongest a great number of vulgar people his lovinge subjects of the same, and beinge in a full hope and truste that a full and perfect resolucion of the saide articles should make a perfecte concorde and unyte generally amonge all his lovinge and obedient subjects; of his most excellent goodness not only commanded that the saide articles shoulde deliberately and advisedly by his saide Archbisshops Bishopps and other lerned men of his clergie be debated argued and reasoned, and their opinions therein to be understood declared and knowne, but also most graciously vouchsaved in his owne princelie person to discend and come into his said highe Courte of Parliament and Counsaile and there like a Prince of most highe Prudence and noe lesse lernynge opened and declared many things of highe lerning and great knowledge touchinge the said articles matters and questions, for an unytye to be had in the same; whereupon, after a greate and longe deliberate and advised disputacion and consultacion had and made concerning the saide articles, as well by the consent of the Kinges Highness as by the assent of the Lordes spirituall and temporall and other lerned men of his clergie in their convacacion, and by the consent of the Commons in this present parliament assembled, it was and is fynally resolved accorded and agreed in manner and forme following, that is to say: First, that in the most blessed Sacrament of the aulter, by the strengthe and efficacy of Christs myghtie worde, it beinge spoken by the prest, is present really, under the forme of bread and wyne, the naturale bodye and bloode of our Saviour Jesu Crist, conceyved

From *Translations and Reprints*, Vol. 1, No. 1, E. P. Cheyney, Ed.

of the Virgin Marie, and after the consecracion there remayneth noe substance of bread or wyne, nor any other substance but the substance of Criste, God and man; secondly, that Communion in bothe kinds is not necessarie *ad salutem* [for salvation] by the lawe of God to all persons; and that it is to be believed and not doubted of, but that in the fleshe under forme of bread is the verie blode, and withe the blode under forme of wyne is the verie fleshe, as well aparte as thoughe they were bothe together; thirdly, that Priests after the order of Presthode receyved as afore may not marye by the law of God; fourthlye, that vowes of chastitye and wydowhood by man or woman made to God advisedly ought to be observed by the lawe of God, and that it exempteth them from other libertyes of Cristen people, which without that they myght enjoye; fyftly, that it is mete and necessarie that private masses be contynued and admytted in this the Kings English Churche and congregacion as whereby good Cristen people orderinge them selfes accordingly doe receyve bothe godly and goodly consolacions and benefyttes and it is agreable also to Gods lawe; sixtly, that auricular confession is expedient and necessarie to be retayned and contynued used and frequented in the Churche of God.

Charles V

Whereas Henry VIII appears as the new king of the new nation-state, his contemporary, Charles V (1500–1558), king of Spain, Holy Roman Emperor, and ruler of many realms besides, may almost be said to close the medieval tradition in which the prince's authority, derived from God, did not necessarily have local or national attachments. The emperor tried to be a "parfit, gentil," and, of course, Christian knight; but, though his revenues were very great and though his writ ran from Bohemia to the Indies, he met with disappointment. In the weariness of failure, Charles retired to the Spanish monastery of San Yuste to spend the rest of his life in relative peace. But perhaps it is the anachronism he represents that explains the frustration of his attempts to hold together his vast and disconnected realm—the failure Charles expressed in his abdication speech that follows.

The Abdication in Brussels (1555)

Although Philibert has fully explained to you, my friends, the causes which have determined me to surrender these states and leave them to my son Don Philip, in order that he may possess and rule them, yet I wish to say certain things with my own mouth. You will remember that upon the 5th of February of this year there had elapsed forty years since my grandfather the emperor Maximilian, in the same place and at the same hour declared my majority at the age of fifteen, withdrew me from the guardianship under which I had remained up to that time and made me master of myself. The

From *Translations and Reprints*, Vol. 3, No. 3, E. P. Cheyney, Ed.

following year, which was my sixteenth, king Ferdinand died, my mother's father and my grandfather, in the kingdom over which I then commenced to reign, because my beloved mother, who has but lately died, was left, after the death of my father, with disordered judgment and never sufficiently recovered her health to become mistress of herself.

At that time I went to Spain, by way of the sea. Soon came the death of my grandfather Maximilian, in my 19th year, and although I was still young they conferred upon me in his stead the imperial dignity. I had no inordinate ambition to rule a multitude of kingdoms, but merely sought to secure the welfare of Germany, to provide for the defence of Flanders, to consecrate my forces to the safety of Christianity against the Turk and to labor for the extension of the Christian religion. But although such zeal was mine, I was unable to show so much of it as I might have wished, on account of the troubles raised by the heresies of Luther and the other innovators of Germany, and on account of serious war into which the hostility and envy of neighboring princes had driven me, and from which I have safely emerged, thanks to the favor of God.

This is the fourth time that I go to Spain, there to bury myself. I wish to say to you that nothing I have ever experienced has given me so much pain or rested so heavily upon my soul as that which I experience in parting from you to-day, without leaving behind me that peace and quiet which I so much desired. My sister Mary, who in my absence has governed you so wisely and defended you so well, has explained to you, in the last assembly, the reasons for my determination. I am no longer able to attend to my affairs without great bodily fatigue and consequent detriment to the affairs of the state. The cares which so great a responsibility involves; the extreme dejection which it causes; my health already ruined; all these leave me no longer the strength sufficient for governing the states which God has confided to me. The little strength that remains to me is rapidly disappearing. So I should long ago have put down the burden, if my son's immaturity and my mother's incapacity had not forced both my spirit and my body to sustain its weight until this hour.

The last time that I went to Germany I had determined to do what you see me do to-day, but I could not bring myself to do it when I saw the wretched condition of the Christian state, a prey to such a multitude of disturbances, of innovations, of singular opinions as to faith, of worse than civil wars, and fallen finally into so many lamentable disorders. I was turned from my purpose because my ills were not yet so great, and I hoped to make an end of all these things and restore the peace. In order that I might not be wanting in my duty I risked my strength, my goods, my repose and my life for the safety of Christianity and the defence of my subjects. From this struggle I emerged with a portion of the things I desired. But the king of France and certain Germans, failing to preserve the peace and amity they had sworn, marched against me and were upon the point of seizing my person. The king of France took the city of Metz, and I, in the dead of winter, exposed to intense cold, in the midst of snow and blood, advanced with a powerful army raised at my own expense to retake the city and restore the Empire. The Germans saw that I had not yet laid aside the imperial crown and had no disposition to allow its majesty to be diminished.

I have carried out what God has permitted, since the outcome of our efforts depends upon the will of God. We human beings act according to our powers, our strength, our spirit, and God awards the victory and permits defeat. I have ever done as I was able, and God has aided me. I return to Him boundless thanks for having succored me in my greatest trials and in all my dangers.

To-day I feel so exhausted that I should not be of any aid to you, as you see yourselves. In my present state of dejection and weakness, I should have to render a great and serious account to God and man, if I did not lay aside authority, as I have resolved to do, since my son, king Philip, is of an age sufficiently advanced to be able to govern you, and he will be, I hope, a good prince to all my beloved subjects.

I am determined then to retire to Spain, to yield to my son Philip the possession of all my states, and to my brother, the king of the Romans, the Empire. I particularly commend to you my son, and I ask you only in remembrance of me, that you extend to him the love which you have always borne towards me; moreover I ask you to preserve among yourselves the same affection and harmony. Be obedient towards justice, zealous in the observance of the laws, preserve respect for all that merits it, and do not refuse to grant to authority the support of which it stands in need.

Above all, beware of infection from the sects of neighboring lands. Extirpate at once the germs, if they appear in your midst, for fear lest they may spread abroad and utterly overthrow your state, and lest you may fall into the direst calamities. As to the manner in which I have governed you I confess that I have been more than once deceived, led astray by the inexperience of youth, by the hasty conclusions of young manhood, or by some other fault of human weakness. Nevertheless I make bold to assert, that never of my knowledge or by my will has wrong or violence been done to any of my subjects. If any can complain of having suffered such, I aver that it is unknown to me and against my will: I declare before all the world that I regret it from the bottom of my heart, and I beseech all present, and those who are not here as well, to wish me well and to pardon me.

Philip II

Though after 1555 the imperial crown passed to the German branch of the Habsburg family, Philip II (1527–1598) was probably the most powerful prince of his time. For his policy and his almost continuous wars he could draw upon the resources of a vast realm upon which the sun never set. Not the least part of his wealth derived from Spain's American colonies, where important silver deposits were discovered in Mexico and Peru (the most famous, at Cerro de Potosi, was opened in 1545). Yet it would appear that, even so, the king lived well beyond his income. A great and growing amount of bullion found its way into Europe, to pay the king's debts to foreign bankers and the wages of his soldiers. War and mismanagement drained Spain of its wealth, decimated its manpower, and contributed to the inflation so characteristic of the period. In 1617 we shall find the Castilian Cortes complaining that the treasure from America "immediately goes to foreign kingdoms, leaving this one in extreme poverty."

The Gold of the Indies (1559)

From New Spain are obtained gold and silver, cochineal [little insects like flies], from which crimson dye is made, leather, cotton, sugar and other things; but from Peru nothing is obtained except minerals. The fifth part of all that is produced goes to the king, but since the gold and silver is brought to Spain and he has a tenth part of that which goes to the mint and is refined and coined, he eventually gets one-fourth of the whole sum, which fourth does not exceed in all four or five hundred thousand ducats, although it is reckoned not alone at millions, but at millions of pounds. Nor is it likely that it will long remain at this figure, because great quantities of gold and silver are no longer found upon the surface of the earth, as they have been in past years; and to penetrate into the bowels of the earth requires greater effort, skill and outlay, and the Spaniards are not willing to do the work themselves, and the natives cannot be forced to do so, because the Emperor has freed them from all obligation of service as soon as they accept the Christian religion. Wherefore it is necessary to acquire negro slaves, who are brought from the coasts of Africa, both within and without the Straits, and these are selling dearer every day, because on account of their natural lack of strength and the change of climate, added to the lack of discretion upon the part of their masters in making them work too hard and giving them too little to eat, they fall sick and the greater part of them die.

Revenues of the King of Spain (1559)

From these his realms his majesty receives every year an income of five millions of gold in times of peace: one and one-half millions from Spain; a half-million from the Indies; one from Naples and Sicily, and another from Flanders and the Low Countries. But his expenses are six millions, and this excess is covered by extraordinary taxes according to his pleasure, whence it appears that he could control only a small amount of money for special undertakings, since he consumes for his ordinary needs everything that he derives from his realms. But looked at from another point of view, the Emperor, his father, although he had the same burdens, was nevertheless able to carry on extensive wars and enterprises in Italy and outside of Italy, both by land and sea, and the same king was able in these later years to maintain great armies in Flanders, in Piedmont, in Lombardy and in the kingdom, and many soldiers in Africa against the Turk. So that we may calculate that he spent more than ten millions of gold; wherefore it may be put down as a fact that although expenses may exceed income, yet a way is not wanting to great princes, whereby they may find large sums of money in times of great need, particularly in the case of the king of Spain, not so much on account of the mines which are found in Spain and the Indies, of which the Spanish nation, according to its custom, makes no great account, as from the fact that he has so many

From *Translations and Reprints*, Vol. 3, No. 3, E. P. Cheyney, Ed.

states and so many subjects and nearly all are rich, and from them he has had so much aid, not through force or violence, but for the most part with common consent of the people, persuaded that public and private interest demanded such a policy.

It would appear that the great results which the Spaniards have accomplished are not to be ascribed to the financial strength derived from the mines, because you see on one side France and the Turk, extremely rich without mines, and on the other the Emperor, with more mines in his realms than all the rest of Europe possesses, always in need.

Henry VIII: Beggars Act of 1531

One of the first tasks the rulers of the new nation-states had to face was the establishment of order in their territories. Prosperity meant power, but order meant prosperity, and to that end new legislation was needed and had to be enforced. Throughout Europe the problem of beggars, rogues, and vagabonds was one of the first that princes had to tackle. Ignoring the economic causes of the evils that plagued these people, the princes did their best to cope with this population by means of laws and decrees that sought to cauterize ills they could neither prevent nor cure. Yet one law was never enough; law enforcement was difficult, and unemployment, even then, turned numbers of unsettled and often violent men and women into potential sources of trouble.

An Act Concerning Punishment of Beggars and Vagabonds (1531)

Where in all places throughout this realm of England vagabonds and beggars have of long time increased and daily do increase in great and excessive numbers, by the occasion of idleness, mother and root of all vices, whereby hath risen and sprung and daily rises and springs continual thefts, murders, and other heinous offences and great enormities, to the high displeasure of God, the disquiet and damage of the King's people, and to the marvellous disturbance of the common weal of this realm. And whereas many and sundry good laws, strait statutes and ordinances, have been before this time devised and made, as well by the King our Sovereign Lord as also by divers his most noble progenitors, kings of England, yet, notwithstanding, the number of vagabonds and beggars is not seen to be diminished, but rather daily augmented and increased into great gangs and companies; be it therefore enacted. . . . That the Justices of the Peace . . . shall make diligent search and enquiry of all aged, poor, and impotent[1] persons which live or of necessity be compelled to live by alms of the charity of the people that be or shall be hereafter abiding . . . within the limits of their division, and after and upon such search made the said Justices of Peace . . . shall have power and authority by their discretions to enable to beg, within such . . . limits as they shall

---

[1] disabled, infirm.

From *Statutes of the Realm*, III, 328.

appoint, such of the said impotent persons which they shall find and think most convenient within the limits of their division to live of the charity and alms of the people, and to give in commandment to every such aged and impotent beggar (by them enabled) that none of them shall beg outside the limits to them so appointed, and shall also register and write the names of every such impotent beggar in a list. . . . And that the said Justices of Peace . . . shall make and deliver to every such impotent person by them enabled to beg, a letter containing the name of such impotent person and witnessing that he is authorized to beg and the limits within which he is appointed to beg, [if they are found to beg beyond these limits] then the Justices of Peace . . . shall by their discretions punish all such persons by imprisonment in the stocks by the space of 2 days and 2 nights, giving them but only bread and water, and after that cause every such impotent person to be sworn to return again without delay to the (limits . . .) where they be authorized to beg in.

II. And be it enacted, that no such impotent person (as is above said) . . . shall beg within any part of this realm except he be authorized by writing under seal as is above said. And if any such impotent person . . . be vagrant and go a-begging having no such letter under seal as is above specified, that then the constables and all other inhabitants within such town or parish where such person shall beg shall cause every such beggar to be taken and brought to the next Justice of Peace or High Constable . . . they shall strip him naked from the middle upward and cause him to be whipped within the town where he was taken, or within some other town where the same Justice or High Constable shall appoint . . . ; And if not, then to command such beggar to be set in the stocks in the same town or parish where he was taken by the space of 3 days and 3 nights, there to have only bread and water; and thereupon the said Justice or High Constable afore whom such beggar shall be brought shall limit to him a place to beg in, and give to him a letter under seal in form above remembered, and swear him to depart and repair thither immediately after his punishment to him executed.

III. And be it further enacted . . . That if any person or persons being whole and mighty in body and able to labour, . . . or if any man or woman being whole and mighty in body and able to labour having no land, master, nor using any lawful merchandise, craft, or mystery, whereby he might get his living . . . be vagrant and can give none reckoning how he doth lawfully get his living, that then it shall be lawful to the constables and all other the King's officers, ministers, and subjects of every town, parish and hamlet to arrest the said vagabonds and idle persons and them to bring to any of the Justices of Peace . . . to be tied to the end of a cart naked and be beaten with whips throughout the same market town or other place till his body be bloody by reason of such whipping; and after such punishment and whipping had, the person so punished . . . shall be enjoined upon his oath to return forthwith without delay in the next and straight way to the place where he was born, or where he last dwelled before the same punishment by the space of 3 years, and there put himself to labour like as a true man oweth to do; and after that done, every such person so punished and ordered shall have a letter sealed with the seal of the city, borough, town, wherein he shall be punished, witnessing that he hath been punished according to this Statute, and containing the day and place of his punishment, and the place whereunto he is limited to go, and by what time he is limited to come thither, within which time he may lawfully beg by the way, shewing the same letter, and otherwise not; And if he do not accomplish the order to him appointed by the said letter, then to be at once taken and whipped till he returns where he was born or where he last dwelled by the space of three years, and there put his body to labour for his living or otherwise truly get his living without begging as long as he is able so to do; And if the person so whipped be an idle person and no common beggar, then after such whipping he shall be kept in the stocks till he hath found surety to go to service or else to labour after the discretion of the said Justice of Peace. . . . And if the constables and inhabitants within any town or parish . . . be negligent . . . that then the township or parish . . . shall lose and forfeit for every such impotent beggar . . . 3s. 4d., and for every strong beggar, . . . 6s. 8d. . . .

IV. And be it enacted . . . that scholars of the Universities of Oxford and Cambridge that go about begging, not being authorized under the seal of the said Universities by the Commissary, Chancellor, or Vice-Chancellor of the same, and all sailors pretending losses of their ships and goods of the sea going about the country begging without sufficient authority witnessing the same, shall be punished and ordered in manner and form as is above rehearsed of strong beggars; and that all proctors and pardoners going about in any country or countries or abiding in any city, borough, or town, some of them using diverse and subtile crafty and unlawful games and plays, and some of them feigning themselves to have knowledge of physic, faces, palmistry, or other crafty sciences, whereby they delude people that they can tell their destinies, deceases, and fortunes, and such other like fantastical imaginations, to the great deceit of the King's subjects, shall be punished by whipping at two days together after the manner above rehersed: And if he again offend in the said offence or any like offence, then to be scourged two days and the third day to be put upon the pillory from 9 of the clock till 11 before noon of the same day, and to have one of his ears cut off; and if he offend the third time, to have like punishment with whipping, standing on the pillory, and to have his other ear cut off.

Elizabeth I: Poor Relief Act of 1598

The first English statute specifically directed "for the provision and relief of the poor" dates back to 1552; this sort of legislation was strengthened in 1563 by introducing the principle of compulsion to the collection of funds for poor relief. The English Poor Law reached its final stages with the acts of 1598 and 1601, the second patterned on the first, whose main features endured until the nineteenth century. In the act of 1598, which follows, we find the principle of poor relief recognized as a public concern and put to the charge of the community.

An Act for the Relief of the Poor (1598)

Be it enacted by the authority of this present Parliament, That the Churchwardens of every parish, and four substantial householders there . . . who shall be nominated yearly in Easter week, under the hand and seal of two or more Justices of Peace in the same county, whereof one to be of the Quorum, dwelling in or near the same parish, shall be called Overseers of the Poor of the same parish; and they or the greater part of them shall take order from time to time by and with the consent of two or more Justices of Peace for setting to work of the children of all such whose parents shall not by the said persons be thought able to keep and maintain their children. And also all such persons married or unmarried as having no means to maintain them use no ordinary and daily trade of life to get their living by; and also to raise weekly or otherwise (by taxation of every inhabitant and every occupier of lands in the said parish in such competent sum and sums of money as they shall think fit) a convenient stock of flax, hemp, wool, thread, iron, and other necessary ware and stuff to set the poor on work, and also competent sums of money for and towards the necessary relief of the lame, impotent, old, blind, and such other among them being poor and not able to work, and also for the putting out of such children to be apprentices, to be gathered out of the same parish according to the ability of the said parish; and to do and execute all other things, as well for disposing of the said stock as otherwise concerning the premises, as to them shall seem convenient: . . .

II. And be it also enacted, That if the said Justices of Peace do perceive the inhabitants of any parish are not able to levy among themselves sufficient sums of money for the purposes aforesaid, That then the said Justices shall and may tax, rate, and assess as aforesaid any other of other parishes, or out of any parish within the hundred where the said parish is, to pay such sum and sums of money to the Churchwardens and Overseers of the said poor parish for the said purposes as the said Justices shall think fit, according to the intent of this law; And if the said hundred shall not be thought to the said Justices able and fit to relieve the said several parishes nor able to provide for themselves as aforesaid, then the Justices of Peace at their general Quarter Sessions, or the greater number of them, shall rate and assess as aforesaid, . . . other parishes . . . as in their discretion shall seem fit.

III. And that it shall be lawful for the said Churchwardens and Overseers or any of them, by warrant from any such two Justices of Peace, to levy as well the said sums of money of every one that shall refuse to contribute according as they shall be assessed, by forced seizure and sale of the offender's goods, as the sums of money or stock which shall be behind upon any account to be made as aforesaid, rendering to the party the overplus; and in defect of such seizure, it shall be lawful for any such two Justices of Peace to commit him to prison, there to remain without bail till payment of the said sum or stock; and the said Justices

---

From *Statutes of the Realm,* IV, 896.

of Peace or any one of them to send to the House of Correction such as shall not employ themselves to work being appointed thereunto as aforesaid; And also any two such Justices of Peace to commit to prison every one of the said Churchwardens and Overseers which shall refuse to account, there to remain without bail till he have made a true account and satisfied and paid so much as upon the said account shall be remaining in his hands.

IV. And be it further enacted, That it shall be lawful for the said Churchwardens and Overseers, to bind any such children as aforesaid to be apprentices where they shall see convenient, till such man-child shall come to the age of four and twenty years, and such woman-child to the age of one and twenty years; the same to be as effectual to all purposes as if such child were of full age and by indenture of covenenant bound him or herself.

V. And to the intent that necessary places of habitation may more conveniently be provided for such poor impotent people, Be it enacted, That it shall and may be lawful . . . to erect, build, and set up in fit and convenient places of habitation in such waste or common, at the general charges of the parish or otherwise of the hundred or county as aforesaid, to be taxed, rated, and gathered in manner before expressed, convenient Houses of Dwelling for the said impotent poor; And also to place inmates or more families than one in one cottage or house. . . .

VII. And be it further enacted, That the parents or children of every poor, old, blind, lame, and impotent person, or other poor person not able to work, being of sufficient ability, shall at their own charges relieve and maintain every such poor person in that manner and according to that rate as the Justices of Peace [shall assess] . . .

X. And be it further enacted by the authority aforesaid, That . . . no person or persons whatsoever shall go wandering abroad and beg in any place whatsoever, by license or without, upon pain to be esteemed, taken, and punished as a rogue: Provided always, That this present Act shall not extend to any poor people which shall ask relief of victuals only in the same parish where such poor people do dwell . . .

XVI. Provided always nevertheless, That every soldier being discharged of his service or otherwise lawfully licensed to pass into his country, and not having wherewith to relieve himself in his travel homewards, and every seafaring man landing from sea not having wherewith to relieve himself in his travel homewards, having a testimonial under the hand of some one Justice of Peace of or near the place where he was landed or was discharged, setting down therein the place and time where and when he landed or was discharged, and the place of the party's dwellingplace or birth unto which he is to pass, and a convenient time to be limited therein for his passage, shall and may, without incurring the danger or penalty of this Act, in the usual ways directly to the place unto which he is directed to pass and within the time in such his testimonial limited for his

passage, ask and receive such relief as shall be necessary in and for his passage;
This Act or anything therein contained to the contrary notwithstanding.

XVII. Provided always, That this Act shall endure no longer than to the end of the
next Session of Parliament.

Thomas More

*Sir Thomas More was born in London in 1478, the son of a justice of the King's Bench.
At sixteen, according to the custom of his time, he was placed in the household of the
archbishop of Canterbury, there to learn the ways of a gentleman by serving a gentleman.
The archbishop thought highly of the lad, for whom he predicted a great future; in turn,
More never lost his early respect for his first master, whom he brings into the passage that
follows. The young man's education was perfected at Oxford, where he became the friend
of men such as Erasmus and John Colet and drank deep of the new learning of the time.
Brilliant lawyer and parliament man, he was appointed—much against his will—lord
chancellor of England after Wolsey's fall. He disapproved of Henry VIII's ecclesiastical
policy and finally resigned his office in 1532. With his conscience forcing him to refuse the
Oath of Supremacy, he was imprisoned in the Tower of London and beheaded in 1535,
to the shock and indignation of all Catholic Europe. He had written a number of works
of controversy and two histories; but his reputation rests on the* Utopia, *two books written
in Latin—the first in 1515, the second in 1516—that were immediately popular and soon
translated (into German, 1524; French, 1530; Italian, 1548; English, 1551). In the following passage from Book I, More presents some views on the England of his day.*

From Utopia

"Please tell me," said I. "Did you visit us?" "Yes," he said, "and I stayed there several
months, not long after the western English rose in civil war [in 1497] against their
king and were crushed with pitiful slaughter. During that time I was much indebted
to the Right Reverend Father John Morton, Archbishop of Canterbury and Cardinal,
and at that time Chancellor of England too. What I am about to say is well known to
More, but believe me, Peter, he was a man worthy of the highest respect not more for
his authority than for his wisdom and goodness. He was of moderate height and belied
his advanced years. His face inspired reverence, not fear. In dealing with people he
was easy, yet serious and dignified. It was his pleasure on occasions to speak harshly
to those with requests to make of him, without any malice, just to find out what
readiness of mind and spirit each man had. As long as a man kept away from impudence, he was delighted by such readiness, as being congenial to his own nature, and
he welcomed it as a quality appropriate to a man of action. His conversation was

From *Utopia* by Thomas More, trans. by Peter K. Marshall. Copyright © 1965 by Simon & Schuster, Inc.
Reprinted by permission of Washington Square Press, a division of Simon & Schuster, Inc.

polished and to the point. He had great skill in law, an incomparable intellect and a prodigious memory. He had these virtues in great abundance from birth, but he advanced them still further by studying and practice.

"The King appeared to put great trust in his advice, and the state to rely upon it heavily when I was there. For practically from his early youth he was taken straight from school to court and was employed in important matters all his life. Constantly tossed by the varying tides of fortune, he had with many great dangers learned worldly wisdom. When it is won this way, it does not easily leave.

"It happened one day that I was at his table, and a certain layman was there, learned in your laws. On some pretext or other he began loudly to sing the praises of that stern justice which was then being used in England against thieves, who, he said, were strung up everywhere, sometimes twenty on one gallows. And so he said he was all the more puzzled, when so few escaped punishment, what evil fate produced so many robbers all over the country. Then, presuming to speak freely in front of the Cardinal, I said, 'There is no reason why you should be surprised. For this punishment inflicted upon thieves is beyond the bounds of justice and not to the public advantage. It is too severe for punishing robbery, but not sufficient to restrain it. For simple theft is not so great a crime as to deserve capital punishment, nor is there any penalty strong enough to keep from theft men who have no other means of gaining a livelihood. So in this matter not only you, but a good part of this world also, seem to copy bad teachers, who more readily beat their students than educate them. For harsh and terrible punishments are inflicted upon thieves, when it would be much better to see that they had a means to earn a living. In this way they would be freed from the awful necessity of stealing and then being put to death.'

" 'This has all been seen to well enough,' he said. 'There are manual crafts and there is farming: from these a man may support his life, unless by nature he prefers to be evil.' 'But you will not get out of it as easily as this,' I said. 'In the first place, let us forget those who often come home mutilated from foreign or civil wars, as recently happened among your people in the Cornish war, and not so long ago in France. These men give their limbs to their country or their king; their disability does not allow them to practice their former crafts, nor at such an age can they learn a new one. As I say, let us forget these, as wars come and go. Let us consider those cases that arise every day.

" 'Now, there is a large number of noblemen who live in idleness like drones by the labors of others—in other words, they skin the tenants on their farms by increasing the rents. For that is the only thrift they know, though in other spheres they are so lavish as to beggar themselves. But as well as this, they take around an immense crowd of idle attendants, who have never learned any means of making a living. As soon as their master dies, or they themselves fall sick, they are thrown out straightaway. For masters are readier to support idlers than invalids, and often an heir cannot immediately afford the number of servants his dead father kept. Meanwhile they have the choice of violent hunger or vilent robbery. For what are they to do? In wandering about, they wear out their clothes and health, and when they are unkempt with sickness and their clothes covered with patches, no gentleman deigns to receive them and no countryman dares. For they are well aware of the value of a man brought up softly in idleness and luxuries, who is used to sneering at the whole neighborhood with a braggart's look and despising everyone but himself, dressed up with his sword and shield. They know that he will be quite unsuited to be the faithful servant of a poor man, with a spade and a hoe, niggardly wages and scant food.'

" 'No,' he said, 'this is the kind of man we ought especially to cultivate. For these are men of higher and nobler spirit than craftsmen or farmers, and in them lies the power and strength of the army whenever a battle must be fought.'

" 'Of course,' I said, 'you might just as well say that we should cultivate thieves because of wars; for undoubtedly you will never be without wars as long as you have thieves. For neither are robbers faint-hearted soldiers, nor are soldiers cowardly robbers; so nice an agreement is there between these two arts. But this is frequent among you, but not confined to you. For it belongs to practically all nations. Another more pestilential plague infests France as well; the whole country is filled and besieged with mercenary soldiers in peacetime too (if that can be called peace). They were brought in under the same belief through which you English thought that idle servants ought to be supported here: because, that is, the wise fools decided that the public safety depended upon the constant presence of a strong and firm garrison, especially of veterans. For they have no confidence in inexperienced men. The result is that they even have to seek out a war so as not to have unskilled soldiers, and wantonly to kill men so that (as Sallust wittily puts it) their hands or spirits may not grow dull through lack of practice.

" 'But how dangerous it is to keep beasts of this kind France has learned to her cost, and the same lesson is shown by the Romans, the Carthaginians, the Syrians and many other people. For their standing armies on various pretexts have overthrown their empires, and ravaged their country and cities. But how unnecessary this is can be seen from the example of the French: their soldiers, though trained to the fingertips, yet, when matched with your levies, cannot often boast that they have come off superior—I say no more, so as not to seem to flatter you to your face. But neither those city craftsmen of yours nor the rough and uncouth farmers are believed to be very afraid of the idle attendants of the noblemen—except for those who do not happen to have a body to match their strength and boldness, or whose strength of spirit is broken by poverty. So there is no danger that these attendants might grow soft if they were trained in honest crafts for their livelihood and exercised in manly work; for as it is now, their strong and robust bodies (nobles choose to corrupt only picked men) grow feeble with idleness or soft with womanly tasks. Certainly, whatever is the truth of this matter, of one thing I am quite sure: that it is by no means to the interest of the state to keep, against the possibility of a war which you never have except when you wish, an immense crowd of the sort that destroys the peace—and we ought to have much more consideration for peace than war.

" 'But this is not the only reason which drives men to steal. There is another one more peculiar to you English in my opinion.' 'What is that?' said the Cardinal. 'Your sheep,' I said, 'which are normally so gentle and need so little food. Now (so they say) they have begun to be so ravenous and wild that they even eat up men. They devastate and destroy fields, houses and towns. For in whatever parts of the kingdom fine and therefore more precious wool is produced, there the nobles and gentlemen, and also some holy abbots, are not content with the rents and annual profits that their predecessors used to get from their farms. They are not satisfied to live in luxury and idleness and be of no use to the state; they even harm it. They leave nothing for arable land, enclose everything for pasture, destroy houses, tear down towns and leave only the church to house the sheep; and as if the forests and parks lost you too little ground, those good men turn all houses and cultivated land into a desert.

" 'Thus, so that one glutton, the insatiable and terrible plague of the country, may join together fields and enclose several thousand acres, some tenants are ejected. Others are stripped of their own land by trickery or violence, or, wearied by their wrongs, are driven to sell. And so, however it happens, the wretched people leave, men, women, husbands, wives, orphans, widows, parents with small children, and with their large, but impoverished, band of servants (as farming needs many hands); they leave, I say, the home they knew so well, nor can they find anywhere to go. All their furniture, which would not bring a high price even if it could wait for a buyer, they sell for a pittance, since it must go out. This money they soon spend on their wanderings. What is there left for them then except to steal and hang (justly, of course), or else roam and beg? Although even then they are thrown into prison as vagrants, because they are traveling around with nothing to do. For no one will hire their services, even though they offer them eagerly. For those accustomed to farming have nothing to do where no crops are sown. One shepherd or attendant is enough to graze the land with cattle, although formerly many hands were needed to cultivate it so as to ensure a good harvest.

" 'And this is the reason why in many places food is much dearer. The price of wool too has risen so high that it just cannot be bought by the poor, who usually make their cloth from it in England; and for that reason more people are driven from work to idleness. For after the institution of the enclosures, the rot destroyed a very large number of sheep. It was as if God punished the owners' greed by sending destruction to the sheep, although it would have been juster if it had fallen on their own heads. But even if the number of sheep increases enormously, yet the price does not come down. For although there cannot be said to be a monopoly on sheep, since more than one man is engaged in selling them, they are certainly in the control of a very small number. For they have almost all fallen into the hands of a few rich men who are under no necessity to sell before they want, and who do not want to until they may at their own price.' "

Richard Hooker

As the sixteenth century drew to a close, it became increasingly clear in western Europe that concern for the spiritual welfare and unity of a nation might well harm its political welfare and unity. Lengthy religious conflicts had torn France and had traced their bloody marks across the face of England. Statesmen and philosophers began to suggest that tolerance was not necessarily sin and that an uncompromising religious attitude might be more hindrance than help in the politics of this world. These men who put the visible welfare of the community above its spiritual salvation were known as the Politiques.

Richard Hooker (1554–1600) was an English theologian who undertook to show that religious extremism, either Catholic or Puritan, was undesirable. His fundamental idea was that law is the manifestation of the divine order of the universe, and the sovereign who administers the law must preserve and enforce this divine order.

From Preface to the Laws of Ecclesiastical Polity

One example herein may serve for many, to shew that false opinions, touching the will of God to have things done, are wont to bring forth mighty and violent practices against the hinderances of them; and those practices new opinions more pernicious than the first, yea most extremely sometimes opposite to that which the first did seem to intend. Where the people took upon them the reformation of the Church by casting out popish superstition, they having received from their pastors a general instruction "that whatsoever the heavenly Father hath not planted must be rooted out," proceeded in some foreign places so far that down went oratories and the very temples of God themselves. For as they chanced to take the compass of their commission stricter or larger, so their dealings were accordingly more or less moderate. Amongst others there sprang up presently one kind of men, with whose zeal and forwardness the rest being compared were thought to be marvellous cold and dull. These grounding themselves on rules more general; that whatsoever the law of Christ commandeth not, thereof Antichrist is the author: and that whatsoever Antichrist or his adherents did in the world, the true professors of Christ are to undo; found out many things more than others had done, the extirpation whereof was in their conceit as necessary as of any thing before removed. Hereupon they secretly made their doleful complaints every-where as they went, that albeit the world did begin to profess some dislike of that which was evil in the kingdom of darkness, yet fruits worthy of a true repentance were not seen; and that if men did repent as they ought, they must endeavor to purge the earth of all manner of evil, to the end there might follow a new world afterward, wherein righteousness only should dwell. Private repentance they said must appear by every man's fashioning his own life contrary unto the customs and orders of this present world, both in greater things and in less. To this purpose they had always in their mouths those greater things, charity, faith, the true fear of God, the cross, the mortification of the flesh. All their exhortations were to set light of the things in this world, to count riches and honours vanity, and in token thereof not only to seek neither, but if men were possessors of both, even to cast away the one and resign the other, that all men might see their unfeigned conversion unto Christ. They were solicitors of men to fasts, too often meditations of heavenly things, as it were conferences in secret with God by prayers, not framed according to the frozen manner of the world, but expressing such fervent desires as might even force God to hearken unto them. Where they

---

From R. Hooker, *Works*, 3 vols., 7th ed. (Oxford, 1888).

found men in diet, attire, furniture of house, or any other way, observers of civility and decent order, such they reproved as being carnally and earthly minded. Every word otherwise than severely and sadly uttered seemed to pierce like a sword through them. If any man were pleasant, their manner was presently with deep sighs to repeat those words of our Saviour Christ, "Woe be to you which now laugh, for ye shall lament." So great was their delight to be always in trouble, that such as did quietly lead their lives, they judged of all other men to be in most dangerous case. They so much affected to cross the ordinary custom in every thing, that when other men's use was to put on better attire, they would be sure to shew themselves openly abroad in worse: the ordinary names of the days in the week they thought it a kind of profaneness to use, and therefore accustomed themselves to make no other distinction than by numbers, the First, Second, Third day.

From this they proceeded unto public reformation, first ecclesiastical, and then civil. Touching the former, they boldly avouched that themselves only had the truth, which thing upon peril of their lives they would at all times defend; and that since the Apostles lived, the same was never before in all points sincerely taught. Wherefore that things might again be brought to that ancient integrity which Jesus Christ by his word requireth, they began to control the ministers of the gospel for attributing so much force and virtue unto the scriptures of God. . . . The Book of God they notwithstanding for the most part so admired, that other disputation against their opinions than only by allegation of Scripture they would not hear; besides it they thought no other writings in the world should be studied; insomuch as one of their great prophets exhorting them to cast away all respects unto human writings, so far to his motion they condescended, that as many as had any books save the Holy Bible in their custody, they brought and set them publicly on fire. When they and their Bibles were alone together, what strange fantastical opinion soever at any time entered into their heads, their use was to think the Spirit taught it them. Their phrenesies concerning our Saviour's incarnation, the state of souls departed, and such-like, are things needless to be rehersed. And forasmuch as they were of the same suite with those of whom the Apostle speaketh, saying, "They are still learning, but never attain to the knowledge of truth," it was no marvel to see them every day broach some new thing, not heard of before. Which restless levity they did interpret to be their growing to spiritual perfection, and a proceeding from faith to faith. The differences amongst them grew by this mean in a manner infinite, so that scarcely was there found any one of them, the forge of whose brain was not possessed with some special mystery. Whereupon, although their mutual contentions were most fiercely prosecuted amongst themselves, yet when they came to defend the cause common to them all against the adversaries of their faction, they had ways to lick one another whole; the sounder in his own persuasion excusing *the dear brethren*, which were not so far enlightened, and professing a charitable hope of the mercy of God towards them notwithstanding their swerving from him in some things. Their own ministers they highly magnified as men whose vocation was from God; the rest their manner was to term disdainfully Scribes and Pharisees, to account their calling a human creature, and to detain the people as much as might be from hearing them. . . .

The pretended end of their civil reformation was that Christ might have dominion over all; that all crowns and sceptres might be thrown down at his feet; that no other might reign over Christian men but he, no regiment keep them in awe but his discipline, amongst them no sword at all be carried besides his, the sword of spiritual excommunication. For this cause they laboured with all their might in overturning the seats of magistracy, because Christ hath said, "Kings of nations"; in abolishing the execution of justice, because Christ hath said, "Resist not evil"; in forbidding oaths, the necessary means of judicial trial, because Christ hath said, "Swear not at all": finally, in bringing in community of goods, because Christ by his Apostles hath given the world such example, to the end that men might excel one another not in wealth the pillar of secular authority, but in virtue.

These men at the first were only pitied in their error, and not much withstood by any; the great humility, zeal, and devotion, which appeared to be in them, was in all men's opinion a pledge of their harmless meaning. . . . Luther made request unto Frederick duke of Saxony, that within his dominion they might be favourably dealt with and spared, for that (their error exempted) they seemed otherwise right good men. By means of which merciful toleration they gathered strength, much more than was safe for the state of the commonwealth wherein they lived. They had their secret corner-meetings and assemblies in the night, the people flocked unto them by thousands. . . .

In all these things being fully persuaded, that what they did, it was obedience to the will of God, and that all men should do the like; there remained, after speculation, practice, whereby the whole world thereunto (if it were possible) might be framed. This they saw could not be done but with mighty opposition and resistance; against which to strengthen themselves, they secretly entered into league of association. And peradventure considering that, although they were many, yet long wars would in time waste them out; they began to think whether it might not be that God would have them do, for their speedy and mighty increase, the same which sometime God's own chosen people, the people of Israel, did. Glad and fain they were to have it so; which very desire was itself apt so to breed both an opinion of possibility, and a willingness to gather arguments of likelihood, that so God Himself would have it. Nothing more clear unto their seeming, than that a new Jerusalem being often spoken of in Scripture, they undoubtedly were themselves that new Jerusalem, and the old did by way of a certain figurative resemblance signify what they should both be and do. Here they drew in a sea of matter, by applying all things unto their own company, which are any where spoken concerning divine favours and benefits bestowed upon the old commonwealth of Israel: concluding that as Israel was delivered out of Egypt, so they spiritually out of the Egypt of this world's servile thraldom unto sin and superstition; as Israel was to root out the idolatrous nations, and to plant instead of them a people which feared God; so the same Lord's good will and pleasure was now, that these new Israelites should, under the conduct of other Joshuas, Samsons, and Gideons, perform a work no less miraculous in casting out violently the wicked from the earth, and establishing the kingdom of Christ with perfect liberty: and therefore, as the cause why the children of Israel took upon one man many wives, might be lest the casualties of war should any way hinder the promise of God concerning their multitude from taking effect in them; so it was not unlike that for the necessary propagation of Christ's kingdom under the Gospel the Lord was content to allow as much.

Now whatsoever they did in such sort collect out of Scripture, when they came to justify or persuade it unto others, all was the heavenly Father's appointment, his commandment, his will and charge. Which thing is the very point, in regard whereof I have gathered this declaration. For my purpose herein is to show, that when the minds of men are once erroneously persuaded that it is the will of God to have those things done which they fancy, their opinions are as thorns in their sides, never suffering them to take rest till they have brought their speculations into practice. The lets and impediments of which practice their restless desire and study to remove leadeth them every day forth by the hand into other more dangerous opinions, sometimes quite and clean contrary to their first pretended meanings; so what will grow out of such errors as go masked under the cloak of divine authority, impossible it is that ever the wit of man should imagine, till time have brought forth the fruits of them; for which cause it behoveth wisdom to fear the sequels thereof, even beyond all apparent cause of fear. These men, in whose mouths at the first sounded nothing but only mortification of the flesh, were come at the length to think they might lawfully have their six or seven wives apiece; they which at the first thought judgment and justice itself to be merciless cruelty, accounted at the length their own hands sanctified with being embrued in Christian blood; they who at the first were wont to beat down all dominion, and to urge against poor constables, "Kings of nations"; had at the length both consuls and kings of their own erection amongst themselves; finally, they which could not brook at the first that any man should see, no not by law, the recovery of goods injuriously taken or withheld from him, were grown at the last to think they could not offer unto God more acceptable sacrifice, than by turning their adversaries clean out of house and home, and by enriching themselves with all kinds of spoil and pillage; which thing being laid to their charge, they had in a readiness their answer, that now the time was come, when according to our Saviour's promise, "the meek ones must inherit the earth"; and that their title hereunto was the same which the righteous Israelites had unto the goods of the wicked Egyptians. . . .

Wherefore if we anything respect their error, who being persuaded even as you are have gone further upon that persuasion than you allow; if we regard the present state of the highest governor placed over us, if the quality and disposition of our nobles, if the orders and laws of our famous universities, if the profession of the civil or the practice of the common law amongst us, if the mischiefs whereinto even before our eyes so many others have fallen headlong from no less plausible and fair beginnings than yours are: there is in every of these considerations most just cause to fear lest our hastiness to embrace a thing of so perilous consequence should cause posterity to feel those evils, which as yet are more easy for us to prevent than they would be for them to remedy.

The best and safest way for you therefore, my dear brethren, is, to call your deeds past to a new reckoning, to reexamine the cause ye have taken in hand, and to try it even point by point, argument by argument, with all the diligent exactness ye can; to lay aside the gall of that bitterness wherein your minds have hitherto over-abounded, and with meekness to search the truth. Think ye are men, deem it not impossible for you to err; sift unpartially your own hearts, whether it be force of reason or vehemency of affection, which hath bred and still doth feed these opinions in you. If truth do anywhere manifest itself, seek not to smother it with glosing delusions, acknowledge the greatness thereof, and think it your best victory when the same doth prevail over you. . . .

Far more comfort it were for us (so small is the joy we take in these strifes) to labour under the same yoke, as men that look for the same eternal reward of their labours, to be joined with you in bands of indissoluble love and amity, to live as if our persons being many our souls were but one, rather than in such dismembered sort to spend our few and wretched days in a tedious prosecuting of wearisome contentions: the end whereof, if they have not some speedy end, will be heavy even on both sides. Brought already we are even to that estate . . . whereby all parts are entered into a deadly war amongst themselves, and that little remnant of love which was, is now consumed to nothing. The only godliness we glory in, is to find out somewhat whereby we may judge others to be ungodly. Each other's faults we observe as matter of exprobration and not of grief. . . . With the better sort of our own our fame and credit is clean lost. The less we are to marvel if they judge vilely of us, who although we did well would hardly allow thereof. On our backs they also build that are lewd, and what we object one against another, the same they use to the utter scorn and disgrace of us all. This we have gained by our mutual home-dissensions. This we are worthily rewarded with, which are more forward to strive than becometh men of virtuous and mild disposition.

But our trust in the Almighty is, that with us contentions are now at their highest float, and that the day will come (for what cause of despair is there?) when the passions of former enmity being allayed, we shall with ten times redoubled tokens of our unfeignedly reconciled love, shew ourselves each towards other the same which Joseph and the brethren of Joseph were at the time of their interview in Egypt. Our comfortable expectation and most thirsty desire whereof what man soever amongst you shall any way help to satisfy (as we truly hope there is no one amongst you but some way or other will) the blessings of the God of peace, both in this world and in the world to come, be upon him more than the stars of the firmament in number.

Jean Bodin

Jean Bodin (1530–1596) was a French magistrate and political writer. Concerned by the waste and destruction brought to France by the religious struggles between Huguenots and Catholics, he put his faith in a central power that would be a monarchy tempered by the popular will as expressed by the States-General. In 1576, only four years after the Massacre of St. Bartholomew, Bodin published his great book on the republic.[1] The book was meant to strengthen the position of the king as a source of national unity above rival sects and political parties. Its arguments achieved a great reputation in their day, especially in those moderate circles which, wanting to separate politics from theology, saw in the royal power a mainstay of peace and order.

---

[1] the Commonwealth.

From La République

Since an impetuous tempest has tormented the ship of our Republic with such violence that the captain himself and the pilots are engaged in continual labor, it is needful that the passengers themselves lend a hand with the sails, with the ropes, and with the anchor; as well as to those who have not enough strength. [It is needful] that they give some good advice or that they present their suggestions plainly to those who can command the weather and appease the tempests, because all together run the same danger, one which does not affect our enemies which are on certain ground and who take a singular pleasure at the wreck of our Republic; who run amongst the debris and who enrich themselves by the precious things which are constantly manufactured in order to save the kingdom. [The kingdom] which once upon a time possessed all the empires of Germany, of Hungary, of Spain and of Italy and all the possessions of the Gauls just until the Rhine and which were under the rule of its laws. . . .

That is why for myself, not being able to do anything better, I have undertaken to talk of the Republic in popular language because the sources of the Latin language have practically dried up . . . [since Plato] those who have written speak of the affairs of the world without any knowledge of the laws, and even of public law, which has been forgotten beneath conclusions which one has drawn especially out of the profound and sacred mysteries of political philosophy a thing which has given occasion of trouble and tribulation [for] good states. We have, for example, Machiavelli, who has been the vogue amongst tyrants, and whom Paul Iove, having put him among the outstanding men, nevertheless calls an atheist and ignorant of all literature. As to atheism, he has glorified it by his writings. As to knowledge, I think that those who are in the know [and] who talk softly and learnedly and resolve subtly the high affairs of state are in agreement that he has never gotten to the bottom of political science which does not lie in the tricks of tyrants which he has brought together from all the corners of Italy and which like a soft poison run through his book on the Prince. . . .

Sovereignty is the absolute and perpetual power of a republic which the Romans called *majestas* . . . the Republic is a legal government of several families and that which they have in common with sovereignty added. I have said that this [sovereign] power is perpetual. . . . It is possible to give sovereign power to one or to many for a limited time. . . . [Such men] are nothing better than subjects, and when they are in power they cannot call themselves sovereign princes because they are nothing but administrators and trustees of that power until it pleases the people or the prince to revoke it. . . . The People are continually invested of it [the power]. They can give power and authority to judge or to command for a certain time, or for so long and so much a time as pleases them. . . . That is why the law says that the governor of a province . . . after his time has expired, gives the power back to those depositories.

Let us perceive now another part of our definition and see what the words "absolute power" actually mean. The people are the rulers of a Republic. [They can] give pure and simple perpetual power to someone to dispose of their goods and persons,

From Bodin, *Les six livres de la république* (Lyon, 1593), tr. George L. Mosse in *Europe in Review* (New York, 1957), pp. 67–69; by permission of Rand McNally & Co.

or of all the state at his pleasure, and to let him do as he likes, just as the property owner can give his goods pure and simple without any other reason than his liberality. That is a true gift which has no strings attached once it has been made and accepted, in contrast with other gifts which have conditions and qualifications and which [therefore] are not true gifts. . . . So the sovereignty or absolute power. It must be that the conditions imposed in the creation of a prince conform, however, to the laws of God and of nature. . . .

In this we can recognize the power and majesty of a true sovereign prince: When the estates of the people are assembled, persons request and supplicate to their prince in all humility without [however] having any power to command, disclaim, or to deliberate, [or] to declare laws, edicts and ordinances [unless] it pleases the king to consent or to dissent, to command or to defend. And those . . . who have written of the duty of magistrates and others have gone out of their way to argue that the estates of the people are more illustrious than the prince; a thing which revolts true subjects in the obedience which they owe to their sovereign monarch. There is neither reason nor any foundation whatsoever for such an opinion. . . .

The prince is not held to ordinances and edicts unless these edicts and ordinances coincide with natural justice. . . . It is divine and natural law to obey the edicts and ordinances of him to whom God has given the power over us, if these edicts are not directly opposed to the rule of God who is above all princes. . . . The subject owes obedience to his sovereign prince against all, saving the majesty of God who is the absolute ruler of all the princes of the world. From this axiom we can draw a rule of state: that is to know that the sovereign prince is held to the contracts which he has made, be it with his subjects [or] be it with strangers, because he is the guardian for the subjects of [those] mutual conventions and obligations which they have made one with the other. . . .

There is no crime more detestable in a prince [than] perjury. . . . Also, it is badly spoken to say that the sovereign prince has the power to steal the goods of anyone and to do evil . . . because that connotes weakness, feebleness and laxness of heart. Moreover, the sovereign prince does not have the power to infringe the law of nature which God, of Whom it is the image, has instituted. He [the prince] cannot, therefore, take the goods of anyone without just and reasonable cause, be it by buying or exchange, or legitimate confiscation, or [by] making a treaty with the enemy which he cannot conclude otherwise than by taking the goods of particular or private persons for the preservation of the state. . . . For natural law decrees that the public good is above all individuals and that subjects surrender not only their injuries and vengeances, but also their goods for the well being of the republic. . . . Because there is nothing higher on earth after God than sovereign princes, and as they are established by Him as His lieutenants to command men, it is necessary to be aware of their station, to respect them and to revere their majesty in all obedience, to talk to them with all honor; because he who abuses his sovereign prince abuses God of Whom he is the image on earth. . . . In order that one can recognize him who is . . . the sovereign prince, one has to know his qualities which are not common to other subjects; because if they were common they could not be any part of a sovereign prince. . . .

He who has no [earthly] sovereign is he who gives law to all his subjects, who makes peace and war, who gives power to all the offices and magistrates of his country, who levies taxes, [who] enfranchises him who seems worthy, and who gives pardon to him who had deserved death: What more power could one desire in a sovereign prince? These are always the marks of sovereign power. . . . Just as the great sovereign God cannot create a god who is His equal because He is infinite, so we can say that the princes whom we have described as the image of God cannot elevate a subject to his station because then his [the prince's] power would no longer exist. . . .

Because this is so, it follows that the prime mark of sovereignty is not to give justice, because that is common to the prince and to the subjects, just as is [the power] to institute or to abolish offices, because the prince and the subject [both] may share that power—especially as respects the officers serving justice or the police, or war or finance . . . [nor] is it the prime mark of sovereignty to give rewards to them who have merited them, because that is common to the prince and the magistrates, because the magistrates may receive that power from the prince; also, it is not a prime mark of sovereignty to take counsel of the affairs of a state, because that may be the charge of the privy council or the senate of the Republic. . . . We might say the same thing as regards the law [which] the magistrates can give to them who are within the power of their jurisdiction, but he [the magistrate] can do nothing against the edicts and ordinances of his sovereign prince and to make this point clearer, we must presuppose that the word of the law signifies the right command of him, or of those who have power over all others without exception of person; and to go further, . . . there is no one but the sovereign prince who can give law to all his subjects without exception, be it in general or in particular.

Montaigne

"If you can keep your head, when all about you are losing theirs . . ." Michel Eyquem de Montaigne (1533–1592) was one of the few who did. Counselor in the Parlement (high court) of Bordeaux, near which his estate lay, and eventually mayor of the great port, he soon left the public life to which his rank had led him for the peace of his manor at Montaigne, where he read books and composed the essays whose publication, beginning in 1580, would make him famous. Unusual in trying to take no side in the religious wars that were tearing France apart, Montaigne was more unusual still in that he felt no hatred for his enemies—at least, no more than circumstances required. His humorous scepticism and his detachment would be recognized as subversive when his book was placed on the Index of prohibited books in 1676. In his own lifetime, though, he lived as a conformist and died as a Catholic, appreciated by his king (Henry IV), by his neighbors, and, even, by his (sometimes nagging) wife.

"We are great fools. 'He has spent his life in idleness,' we say. 'I have done nothing today.' What, have you not lived? That is not only the fundamental but the most illustrious of your occupations. 'If I had been placed in a position to manage great affairs, I would have shown what I could do.' Have you been able to think out and to manage your own life? You have done the greatest task of all. . . . Our great and glorious masterpiece is to

live appropriately. All other things—ruling, building, hoarding up treasure—are only little appendages and props, at most." We can consider this a fitting epitaph for the man whose tomb now stands in the hallway of what was once the University of Bordeaux.

The following essay, one of his most famous, reflects the wide reading of a Renaissance man, greedy like many of his contemporaries for the wisdom of the ancients, ready to quote them at the drop of a quill, but also ready to assimilate this wisdom into a stoic epicureanism of his own: moderate, good-humored, and philosophical in the best sense of the word.

Of Husbanding Your Will

In comparison with most men, few things touch me, or, to put it better, hold me; for it is right that things should touch us, provided they do not possess us. I take great care to augment by study and reasoning this privilege of insensibility, which is naturally well advanced in me. I espouse, and in consequence grow passionate about, few things. My sight is clear, but I fix it on few objects; my sensitivity is delicate and tender. But my perception and application are hard and deaf: I do not engage myself easily. As much as I can, I employ myself entirely upon myself; and even in that subject I would still fain bridle my affection and keep it from plunging in too entirely, since this is a subject that I possess at the mercy of others, and over which fortune has more right than I have. So that even in regard to health, which I so esteem, I ought not to desire it and give myself to it so frantically as to find illnesses therefore unbearable. One must moderate oneself between hatred of pain and love of pleasure; and Plato prescribes a middle way of life between the two.

But the passions that distract me from myself and attach me elsewhere, those in truth I oppose with all my strength. My opinion is that we must lend ourselves to others and give ourselves only to ourselves. . . . To engage in contested disputes only to see my opponent get the better of me, or to have to turn back red-faced after giving hot pursuit, might well vex me cruelly. If I were to bite off as much as others do, my soul would never have the strength to bear the alarms and emotions that afflict those who embrace so much; it would be put out of joint from the start by this inner agitation.

If people have sometimes pushed me into the management of other men's affairs, I have promised to take them in hand, not in lungs and liver; to take them on my shoulders, not incorporate them into me; to be concerned over them, yes; to be impassioned over them, never. I look to them, but I do not brood over them. I have enough to do to order and arrange the domestic pressures that oppress my entrails and veins, without giving myself the trouble of adding extraneous pressures to them; I am enough involved in my essential, proper, and natural affairs, without inviting in foreign ones.

Those who know how much they owe to themselves, and for how many duties they are obligated to themselves, find that nature has given them in this a commission full enough and not at all idle. You have quite enough to do at home; don't go away.

Men give themselves for hire. Their faculties are not for them, they are for those to whom they enslave themselves; their tenants are at home inside, not they. This common humor I do not like. We must husband the freedom of our soul and mortgage it only on the right occasions; which are in very small number, if we judge sanely. See the people who have been taught to let themselves be seized and carried away: they do so everywhere, in little things as in big, in what does not touch them as in what does; they push in indiscriminately wherever there is business and involvement, and are without life when they are without tumultuous agitation. *They are in business for business' sake* [Seneca]. They seek business only for busyness.

It is not that they want to be on the go, so much as that they cannot keep still; no more nor less than a stone that has started falling, and that does not stop until it comes to rest. Occupation is to a certain manner of people a mark of ability and dignity. Their mind seeks its repose in movement, like children in the cradle. They may be said to be as serviceable to their friends as they are importunate to themselves. No one distributes his money to others, everyone distributes his time and his life on them. There is nothing of which we are so prodigal as of the only things in which avarice would be useful to us and laudable.

I take a wholly different attitude. I keep myself to myself, and commonly desire mildly what I desire, and desire little; occupy and busy myself likewise: rarely and tranquilly. Whatever they desire and take in hand, they do with all their will and vehemence. There are so many bad spots that, for greatest safety, we must slide over this world a bit lightly and on the surface. We must glide over it, not break through into it. Even sensual pleasure is painful in its depth:

Treacherous ashes hide
The fires through which you stride.
HORACE

Messieurs of Bordeaux elected me mayor of their city when I was far from France and still farther from such a thought. I excused myself, but I was informed that I was wrong, since the king's command also figured in the matter. It is an office that must appear all the handsomer for this, that it has no remuneration or gain other than the honor of its execution. The term is two years; but it can be extended by a second election, which happens very rarely. This was done in my case, and had been done only twice before. . . .

On my arrival I deciphered myself to them faithfully and conscientiously, exactly such as I feel myself to be: without memory, without vigilance, without experience, and without vigor; also without hate, without ambition, without avarice, and without violence; so that they should be informed and instructed about what they were to expect of my service. And because their knowledge of my late father had alone incited them to this, and their honor for his memory, I added very clearly that I should be very sorry if anything whatsoever were to weigh so heavily on my will as their affairs and their city had formerly done on his, while he was administering it in this same spot to which they had called me.

I remembered in my boyhood having seen him old, his soul cruelly agitated by this public turmoil, forgetting the sweet air of his home, to which the weakness of years had attached him long since, and his household and his health; and, truly heedless of his life, which he nearly lost in this, engaged for them in long and painful journeys. He was like that; and this disposition in him sprang from a great goodness of nature: there was never a more kindly and public-spirited soul.

This course, which I commend in others, I do not love to follow, and I am not without excuse. He had heard it said that we must forget ourselves for our neighbor, that the individual was not to be considered at all in comparison with the general.

Most of the rules and precepts of the world take this course of pushing us out of ourselves and driving us into the market place, for the benefit of public society. They thought to achieve a fine result by diverting and distracting us from ourselves, assuming that we were attached to ourselves only too much and by too natural a bond; and they have spared no words to that end. For it is not new for the sages to preach things as they serve, not as they are. Truth has its inconveniences, disadvantages, and incompatibilities with us. We must often be deceived that we may not deceive ourselves, and our eyes sealed, our understanding stunned, in order to redress and amend them. *For it is the ignorant who judge, and they must frequently be deceived, lest they err* [Quintilian]. When they order us to love three, four, fifty degrees of things before ourselves, they imitate the technique of the archers who, to hit the mark, take aim a great distance above the target. To straighten a bent stick you bend it back the other way. . . .

The main responsibility of each of us is his own conduct; and that is what we are here for. Just as anyone who should forget to live a good and saintly life, and think he was quit of his duty by guiding and training others to do so, would be a fool; even so he who abandons healthy and gay living of his own to serve others thereby, takes, to my taste, a bad and unnatural course.

I do not want a man to refuse, to the charges he takes on, attention, steps, words, and sweat and blood if need be. . . . But this is by way of loan and accidentally, the mind holding itself ever in repose and in health, not without action, but without vexation, without passion. Simply to act costs it so little that it is acting even in sleep. But it must be set in motion with discretion. For the body receives the loads that are placed on it exactly according as they are; the mind often extends them and makes them heavier to its cost, giving them the measurements it sees fit. We do like things with different degrees of effort and tension of the will. The one goes very well without the other. For how many people risk themselves every day in the wars, which are no concern to them, and press forward to the dangers of battles, the loss of which will not trouble their next night's sleep! This man in his own house, outside of this danger which he would not have dared to face, is more passionate about the outcome of this war, and more worked up in his soul about it, than the soldier who is spending his blood and his life in it.

I have been able to take part in public office without departing one nail's breadth from myself, and to give myself to others without taking myself from myself. This fierceness and violence of desire hinders more than it serves the performance of what we undertake, fills us with impatience toward things that come out contrary or late, and with bitterness and suspicion toward the people we deal with. We never conduct well the thing that possesses and conducts us:

> Passion handles all things ill.
>
> STATIUS

He who employs in it only his judgment and skill proceeds more gaily. He feints, he bends, he postpones entirely at his ease according to the need of the occasions; he misses the target without torment or affliction, and remains intact and ready for a new undertaking; he always walks bridle in hand. In the man who is intoxicated with a violent and tyrannical intensity of purpose we see of necessity much imprudence and injustice; the impetuosity of his desire carries him away. These are reckless movements, and, unless fortune lends them a great hand, of little fruit.

Philosophy wills that in chastising injuries received we keep anger out of it, not so that the vengeance may be less, but on the contrary so that it may be all the better dealt out and heavier; which purposes, so philosophy thinks, this impetuosity hinders. Not only does anger confuse, but of itself it also tires, the arms of those who chastise. That fire benumbs and consumes their strength. As in precipitancy—*more haste, less speed* [Quintus Curtius]—haste trips itself up, hobbles and stops itself. *Speed gets itself tangled up* [Seneca]. For example, according to what I see by ordinary experience, avarice has no greater impediment than itself: the more tense and vigorous it is, the less fertile it is. Commonly it catches riches more promptly when masked with an image of liberality. . . .

Consider that even in actions which are vain and frivolous, in chess, tennis, and the like, this fierce and ardent involvement of an impetuous desire instantly casts the mind and limbs into thoughtlessness and disorder: we daze and hamper ourselves. He who bears himself more moderately toward winning and losing is always self-possessed. The less he becomes excited and impassioned about the game, the more advantageously and surely he plays it.

Moreover, we impede the mind's grasp and grip by giving it so many things to seize: Some must be simply presented to it, others attached to it, others incorporated into it. It can see and feel all things, but it should feed only on itself, and should be instructed about what properly concerns it and what is properly of its own possession and its own substance. The laws of Nature teach us what we rightly need. When the sages tell us that according to Nature no one is indigent and that everyone is so according to opinion, they distinguish subtly between the desires that come from her and those that come from the disorder of our imagination; in this way: those whose limits we can see are hers, those that flee before us and whose end we cannot reach are ours. Poverty of goods is easy to cure, poverty of soul impossible. . . .

Socrates, seeing a great quantity of riches, jewels, and costly articles carried in pomp through his city, said: "How many things I do not desire!" Metrodorus lived on twelve ounces a day, Epicurus on less; Metrocles slept in winter with the sheep, in summer in the cloisters of the churches. *Nature supplies what it demands* [Seneca]. Cleanthes lived by his hands and boasted that Cleanthes, if he wanted, could feed still another Cleanthes. . . .

I am no longer headed for any great change or inclined to plunge into a new and untried way of life, not even a better one. It is too late to become other than I am. And as I would be sorry about any great good fortune that might now fall into my hands, because it would not come at a time when I could enjoy it—

What good are Fortune's gifts if I'm denied their use?
                                                                        HORACE

—so likewise I would complain of any inward acquisition. It is almost better never to become a good man than so late, or an expert in living when one has no more life. I, who am on my way out, would readily resign to anyone who came along what wisdom I am learning for dealing with the world. Mustard after dinner. I have no use for a good thing of which I can make no use. What good is knowledge to a man who no longer has a head? It is an insult and unkindness of fortune to offer us presents which fill us with a just resentment that they failed us in their season. Guide me no more, I can go no more. Of all the parts that ability has, patience is enough for us. Give the capacity of an excellent treble to a singer who has rotten lungs, and eloquence to a hermit relegated to the deserts of Arabia! . . .

I want to mention this as an example: that the recent eclipsing of ten days by the Pope[1] has so taken me aback that I cannot feel comfortable with it. I belong to the years in which we reckoned differently. Such an ancient and long practice claims me and calls me back to it. I am constrained to be a bit of a heretic on that point, incapable of innovation, even when it is corrective. My imagination, in spite of me, is always casting itself ten days forward or back and muttering in my ears: "This rule concerns those who are yet to be."

If health itself, sweet as it is, happens to revisit me by fits and starts, it is rather in order to make me regret it than to return into my possession; I no longer have anywhere to harbor it. Time is forsaking me; without it nothing can be possessed. Oh, what little account I should make of those great elective dignities I see in the world which are given only to men ready to depart; in which people do not consider so much how well the duties will be discharged as how briefly they will be discharged. Right from their entry people look to their exit.

In short, here I am in the act of finishing up this man, not of making another out of him. By long usage this form of mine has turned into substance, and fortune into nature.

So I say that every one of us feeble creatures is excusable for considering as his own what is comprised under this measure. But it is also true that beyond these limits there is nothing left but confusion. This is the broadest extent that we can grant to our claims. The more we amplify our need and our possession, the more we involve ourselves in the blows of fortune and adversity. The range of our desires should be circumscribed and restrained to a narrow limit of the nearest and most contiguous good things; and moreover their course should be directed not in a straight line that ends up elsewhere, but in a circle whose two extremities by a short sweep meet and

---

[1]The introduction of the Gregorian calendar in 1582, which put the calendar forward by ten days.

terminate in ourselves. Actions that are performed without this reflexive movement, I mean a searching and genuine reflexive movement—the actions, for example, of the avaricious, the ambitious, and so many others who run in a straight line, whose course carries them ever forward—are erroneous and diseased actions.

Most of our occupations are low comedy. *The whole world plays a part* [Petronius]. We must play our part duly, but as the part of a borrowed character. Of the mask and appearance we must not make a real essence, nor of what is foreign what is our very own. We cannot distinguish the skin from the shirt. It is enough to make up our face, without making up our heart. I see some who transform and transubstantiate themselves into as many new shapes and new beings as they undertake jobs, who are prelates to their very liver and intestines, and drag their position with them even into their privy. I cannot teach them to distinguish the tips of the hat that are for them from those that are for their office, or their retinue, or their mule. *They give themselves up so much to their fortune that they even unlearn their natures* [Quintus Curtius]. They swell and inflate their soul and their natural speech to the height of their magisterial seat.

The mayor and Montaigne have always been two, with a very clear separation. For all of being a lawyer or a financier, we must not ignore the knavery there is in such callings. An honest man is not accountable for the vice or stupidity of his trade, and should not therefore refuse to practice it: it is the custom of his country, and there is profit in it. We must live in the world and make the most of it such as we find it. But the judgment of an emperor should be above his imperial power, and see and consider it as an extraneous accident; and he should know how to find pleasure in himself apart, and to reveal himself like any Jack or Peter, at least to himself.

I do not know how to involve myself so deeply and so entirely. When my will gives me over to one party, it is not with so violent an obligation that my understanding is infected by it. In the present broils of this state, my own interest has not made me blind to either the laudable qualities in our adversaries or those that are reproachable in the men I have followed. People adore everything that is on their side; as for me, I do not even excuse most of the things that I see on mine. A good work does not lose its grace for pleading against my cause.

Except for the knot of the controversy I have maintained my equanimity and pure indifference. *And beyond the necessities of war I bear no special hatred* [adapted from Livy]. For which I am pleased with myself, inasmuch as I see men commonly fail in the opposite direction. *Let him make use of passion who cannot make use of reason* [Cicero]. Those who prolong their anger and hatred beyond the affairs in question, as most men do, show that it comes from another part of them and from a personal cause; just as a man who, cured of an ulcer, still has his fever, shows that it had another, more hidden origin. The fact is that they have no hatred for the cause in general and in so far as it hurts the interest of all and of the state; they resent it only in that it galls them in private. That is why they are stung by it with a personal passion and beyond justice and public reason. *For they did not all blame the terms as a whole so much as they each blamed those that affected them individually* [Livy].

I want the advantage to be for us, but I do not fly into a frenzy if it is not. I adhere firmly to the healthiest of the parties, but I do not seek to be noted as especially hostile to the others and beyond the bounds of the general reason. I condemn extraordinarily this bad form of arguing: "He is of the League, for he admires the grace of Monsieur de Guise." "The activity of the king of Navarre amazes him: he is a Huguenot." "He finds this to criticize in the king's morals: he is seditious in his heart." And I did not concede even to the magistrate that he was right to condemn a book for having placed a heretic among the best poets of this century. Should we not dare say of a thief that he has a fine leg? And if she is a whore, must she also necessarily have bad breath? . . .

If they have formed a hatred for [a lawyer] the next day in their view he becomes ineloquent. I have elsewhere touched on the zeal that impels good men into similar faults. For my part, I can perfectly well say: "He does this wickedly and that virtuously." Likewise in predictions or in the unfavorable outcome of affairs, they want everyone to be blind and stupid in his own cause, and our conviction and judgment to serve, not the truth, but the aim of our desire. I should rather err toward the other extreme, so much do I fear being suborned by my desire. Besides, I am somewhat tenderly distrustful of the things I wish for.

I have in my time seen wonders in the undiscerning and prodigious ease with which peoples let their belief and hope be led and manipulated in whatever way has pleased and served their leaders, passing over a hundred mistakes one on top of the other, passing over phantasms and dreams. I am no longer amazed at those who are hoodwinked by the monkey tricks of Apollonius and Mohammed. Their sense and understanding is entirely smothered in their passion. Their discernment is left no other choice than the one that smiles upon them and comforts their cause.

I had observed this to a supreme degree in the first of our feverish factions. This other, which has been born since, in imitating it surpasses it. Wherefore I am led to believe that this is a characteristic inseparable from popular errors. After the first one that starts out, the others push each other forward, following the wind like waves. A man is not a part of the body if he can renounce it, if he does not wander along with the common movement. But truly we wrong the just sides when we want to assist them with fraud. I have always opposed that practice. It has effect only with sickly heads; with sane ones, there are ways that are surer, as well as more honest, for keeping up their courage and accounting for adverse events. . . .

We must not rush so frantically after our passions and interests. Just as when I was young I opposed the progress of love, which I felt advancing too far upon me, and took care that it should not be so pleasing to me as in the end to overpower me and hold me completely at its mercy, so I do the same on all other occasions where my will is seized with too strong an appetite. I lean in the opposite direction from its inclination, as I see it plunging in and getting drunk with its own wine. I avoid feeding its pleasure to such an extent that I can no longer regain control of it without cruel loss.

The souls that through stupidity see things only by half enjoy this good fortune, that harmful things hurt them less. It is a spiritual leprosy that has some appearance of health, and such health as philosophy does not scorn at all. But yet it is not right to call it wisdom, as we often do. . . .

But the souls that will have to see adversities and the injuries of fortune in all their depth and sharpness, that will have to weigh them and taste them according to their natural bitterness and their gravity, let them employ their art to keep from entering into their causes and let them turn aside from the approaches that lead to them. What did King Cotys do? He paid liberally for the beautiful rich vessel that had been offered to him; but because it was singularly fragile, he immediately broke it himself, to remove early such an easy occasion for anger against his servants. In like manner I have deliberately avoided having my affairs mixed up with others', and have not sought to have my property contiguous with that of my relations and of those with whom I am to be joined by close friendship: whence ordinarily arise grounds for estrangement and dissension.

I used to be fond of games of chance with cards and dice. I gave them up long ago for this reason only, that however good a face I put on my losses, I did not fail to feel stung by them within.

A man of honor, who must take the giving of the lie or an affront to heart, who is not one to take a silly excuse as payment and consolation for his loss, should avoid letting doubtful affairs and contentious altercations run their course.

I shun gloomy dispositions and surly men like those with the plague, and in subjects that I cannot discuss disinterestedly and dispassionately I do not meddle unless duty forces me to. *It is better for them not to begin than to desist* [Seneca]. The safest way, then, is to be prepared before the occasions.

I know well that some wise men have taken another way, and have not feared to grapple, and engage themselves to the quick, with many subjects. Those men are sure of their strength, under which they take cover in all kinds of adverse events, making their power of endurance wrestle with the misfortunes. . . . Let us not tackle these examples; we would not come up to them. These men obstinately determine to see resolutely and without perturbation the ruin of their country, which possessed and commanded their entire will. For our common souls there is too much effort and harshness in that. . . . We little men must flee the storm from further away; we must try to avoid feeling it, not try to endure it, and dodge the blows we cannot parry. . . .

He who desires the good of his country as I do, without getting ulcers and growing thin over it, will be unhappy, but not stunned, to see it threatened either with ruin or with conditions of survival no less ruinous. Poor vessel, which the waves, the winds, and the pilot pull about with such contrary purposes. . . . He who does not gape after the favor of princes as a thing he cannot do without is not much stung by the coolness of their reception and countenance or by the inconstancy of their will. He who does not brood over his children or his honors with a slavish fondness manages to live comfortably after their loss. He who does good chiefly for his own satisfaction is not much upset by seeing men judge his actions contrary to his merit. A quarter of an ounce of patience is remedy enough against such annoyances. I find myself well off with this recipe, buying myself off at the beginning as cheaply as I can, and I feel that by means of it I have escaped much travail and many difficulties. With very little effort I arrest this first movement of my emotions, and abandon the subject that is beginning to weigh on me before it carries me away. He who does not arrest the start has no chance to arrest the course. He who cannot close the door to emotions will not drive them out once they are in. He who cannot get the better of the beginning will not get the better of the end. Nor will he withstand their fall who has been unable to withstand their first stirring. . . .

How many times have I done myself a very evident injustice to avert the hazard of receiving an even worse one from the judges, after an age of vexations, of vile and dirty practices, more hostile to my nature than the rack and the flames! *It is proper to shun lawsuits as much as is permissible, and perhaps even a little more than is permissible. For it is not only generous, but sometimes even profitable, to come down a little from our rights* [Cicero]. If we were really wise, we should rejoice and boast, like the young man of a great family whom I heard one day informing everyone with naïve delight that his mother had just lost her lawsuit, as if it were her cough, her fever, or something else troublesome to keep. Even the favors that fortune might have given me by my kinship or acquaintance with those who have sovereign authority in those things, I have very conscientiously and insistently avoided using to the prejudice of others or to raise my rights above their right value.

In short, I have managed so well by my daily efforts—fortunately, may I say— that here I am still virgin of lawsuits, which have not failed to offer themselves to my service many times with a very just title, if I had wanted to listen to them, and virgin of quarrels. I shall soon have spent a long life without serious offense received or given, and without having heard anything worse than my name: a rare favor of Heaven.

Our greatest agitations have ridiculous springs and causes. And I have seen in my time the wisest heads in this kingdom assembled, with great ceremony and public expense, for treaties and accords of which the real decision meanwhile depended in all sovereignty on the talk in the ladies' boudoir and the inclination of some little woman. The poets understood this well who put Greece and Asia to fire and sword for an apple. See why that man goes off to risk his honor and his life with his sword and dagger; let him tell you whence comes the source of this quarrel; he cannot do so without blushing, so frivolous is the occasion of it.

At the beginning only a little reflection is needed; but once you are embarked, all the ropes start pulling. Then you need great resources, much more difficult and important. How much easier it is not to go into it than to get out of it! . . . We guide affairs at their beginnings and hold them at our mercy; but afterward, when they are under way, it is they that guide us and carry us away, and we have to follow them.

Yet this is not to say that this plan has relieved me of all difficulty, and that I have not often had trouble curbing and bridling my passions. They are not always to be governed according to the importance of the occasion, and even their beginnings are often sharp and violent. At all events, a fine saving and some profit may be derived from this plan, except for those who in well-doing are not content with any profit if no reputation is involved. For in truth, such an action is valued only by each man in himself. You are happier for it, but not more esteemed, if you have reformed before joining in the dance and before the matter was in view. At the same time, however, not only in this but in all other duties of life, the road of those who aim at honor is very different from the one followed by those whose goal is order and reason.

I find some who enter the lists heedlessly and furiously, and slow up in the charge. Plutarch says that those who through the vice of false shame are soft and easy in granting whatever they are asked, are afterward easy in failing their word and recanting; by the same token, he who enters a quarrel lightly is apt to get out of it just as lightly. This same difficulty that keeps me from cutting into it would spur me on when I was once stirred up and heated. It is a bad habit: once you are in it, you must go through with it or burst. "Undertake softly," said Bias, "but pursue hotly." For want of prudence men fall back into want of courage, which is still less tolerable.

Most of the settlements of our quarrels nowadays are shameful and dishonest: we seek only to save appearances, and meanwhile betray and disavow our true intentions. We plaster over the fact: we know how we have said it and in what sense, and those present know it, and our friends, whom we wanted to have feel our advantage. It is at the expense of our frankness and of the honor of our courage that we disown our thought, and seek rabbit-holes in falsehood in order to come to an agreement. We give ourselves the lie to save the lie we have given to someone else.

You must not consider whether your action or your word may have another interpretation; it is your true and sincere interpretation that you must henceforth maintain, whatever it costs you. Your virtue and your conscience are addressed; these are not parts to put behind a mask. Let us leave these vile means and expedients to the chicanery of the Palace of Justice.

The excuses and reparations that I see made every day to purge our indiscretion seem to me uglier than indiscretion itself. It would be better to offend your adversary once more than to offend yourself by making such amends to him. You have defied him when you were moved with anger, and you are going to appease and flatter him when you are in a more sober and affable mood; thus you are giving way further than you have advanced. I do not consider anything a gentleman can say as vicious as the unsaying of it seems to me shameful, when it is an unsaying that is wrenched from him by authority; inasmuch as stubbornness is more excusable in him than pusillanimity.

Passions are as easy for me to avoid as they are hard for me to moderate. *They are more easily torn from the mind than checked* [Seneca]. He who cannot attain that noble impassibility of the Stoics, let him take refuge in the bosom of this plebeian stupidity of mine. What those men did by virtue, I train myself to do by disposition. The middle region harbors the tempests; the two extremes, philosophers and rustics, concur in tranquility and happiness. . . .

All things are weak and tender at birth. Therefore we must have our eyes open to the beginnings; for as then, when a thing is little, we do not discover its danger, so when it is grown we no longer discover the remedy for it. I would have found it harder to digest the million frustrations that I would have encountered every day in an ambitious career, than I have found it to arrest the natural inclination that bore me to it:

> I shrank with rightful dread
> From raising my conspicuous head.
> HORACE

All public actions are subject to uncertain and diverse interpretations, for too many heads judge them. Some say about this municipal service of mine (and I am glad to say a word about it, not that it is worth it, but to serve as an example of my conduct in such things) that I went about it like a man who exerts himself too weakly and with a languishing zeal; and they are not at all far from having a case. I try to keep my soul and my thoughts in repose. *Always calm by nature, now even more so with age* [Q. Cicero]. And if they sometimes veer under some rough and penetrating attack, it is in truth without my consent. From this natural languor, however, one ought not to derive any proof of impotence (for lack of assiduity and lack of sense are two different things), and still less of insensibility and ingratitude toward the people of Bordeaux, who did everything in their power to gratify me, both before they knew me and after, and did much more for me by giving me my office again than by giving it to me in the first place. I wish them all possible good, and certainly, had an occasion arisen, there is nothing I would have spared for their service. I bestirred myself for them just as I do for myself. They are a good people, warlike and idealistic, yet capable of obedience and discipline and of serving some good purpose if they are well guided.

People also say that my administration passed without a mark or a trace. That's a good one! They accuse me of inactivity in a time when almost everyone was convicted of doing too much.

I have a lively way of acting, wherever my will carries me along. But this eagerness is an enemy to perseverance. If anyone wants to use me according to my nature, let him give me tasks in which vigor and freedom are needed, tasks that require direct, brief, and even hazardous conduct; in those I can do something. If it has to be long, subtle, laborious, artificial, and tortuous, he will do better to apply to someone else.

Not all important offices are difficult. I was prepared to work myself a bit more roughly if there had been any great need of it. For it is in my power to do something more than I do or than I like to do. I did not leave undone, as far as I know, any action that duty genuinely required of me. I easily forgot those that ambition mixes up with duty and covers with its name. Those are the ones that most often fill the eyes and ears, and satisfy men. Not the thing but the appearance pays them. If they hear no noise, it seems to them that we are asleep.

My humors are the opposite of noisy humors. I could easily check a disturbance without being disturbed, and punish a disorder without losing my temper. Do I need anger and inflammation? I borrow it and wear it as a mask. My behavior is mild, rather tame than fierce. I do not condemn a magistrate who sleeps, provided that those who are under his care are also asleep; the laws sleep too. For my part I commend a gliding, obscure, and quiet life, *neither groveling and abject nor overbearing* [Cicero]. My fortune so wills it. I was born of a family that from way back has flowed along without glamour and without tumult, a family ambitious above all for integrity.

Men of our time are so formed for agitation and ostentation that goodness, moderation, equability, constancy, and such quiet and obscure qualities are no longer felt. Rough bodies are felt, smooth ones are handled imperceptibly. Sickness is felt, health little or not at all; nor do we feel the things that charm us compared with those that harm us. It is acting for our private reputation and profit, not for the good, to put off and do in the public square what we can do in the council chamber, and at high noon what we could have done the night before, and to be jealous to do ourselves what our colleague does as well. Thus some surgeons of Greece used to perform the operations of their art on platforms in the sight of the passers-by in order to acquire a greater practice and clientele. They think that good rules can be heard only to the sound of trumpets.

Ambition is not a vice for little fellows and for undertakings such as ours. Someone said to Alexander: "Your father will leave you a great dominion, easy and peaceful." That boy was envious of his father's victories and of the justice of his government. He would not have wanted to enjoy the empire of the world softly and peacefully. Alcibiades, in Plato, prefers to die supremely young, handsome, rich, noble, learned, rather than to stand still in that condition.

This malady is perhaps excusable in so strong and full a soul. When these dwarfish and puny soullets behave like vain baboons and think to spread their name for having rightly judged an affair or continued the order of the guards at a city gate, the more they hope to raise their head, the more they show their tail. These minute good works have neither body nor life: they vanish at the first telling and travel only from one street corner to the next. Entertain your son and your valet with them boldly, like that ancient who, having no other auditor of his praises or witness of his valor, boasted to his chambermaid, exclaiming: "Oh, Perrette, what a gallant and capable man you have for a master!" Entertain yourself with them, if worst comes to worst, like a councillor of my acquaintance who, after disgorging a boatload of paragraphs with extreme effort and equal ineptitude, retired from the council chamber to the Palace urinal, where he was heard muttering very conscientiously between his teeth: *"Not unto us, O Lord, not unto us, but unto thy name give glory"* [Psalms]. If he cannot get it from anyone else, let him pay himself out of his own purse.

Renown does not prostitute itself at so cheap a rate. The rare and exemplary actions to which it is due would not endure the company of that innumerable crowd of petty everyday actions. Marble will exalt your titles as much as you please for having had a piece of wall patched up or a public gutter cleaned out; but men who have sense will not. Reputation does not follow every good deed if difficulty and strangeness are not joined to it. Nor indeed is even esteem due to every action that is born of virtue, according to the Stoics, and they do not want even recognition accorded to a man who through temperance abstains from a blear-eyed old woman. Those who have acknowledged the admirable qualities of Scipio Africanus refuse him the glory that Panaetius accords him for having abstained from taking gifts, as a glory belonging not so much to him as to his whole age.

We have the pleasures suitable to our lot; let us not usurp those of greatness. Ours are more natural and all the more solid and sure for being humbler. Since we will not do so out of conscience, at least out of ambition let us reject ambition. Let us disdain this base and beggarly hunger for renown and honor which makes us grovel for it before all sorts of people—*What is that praise that may be sought in the market place?* [Cicero]—abjectly and at no matter how vile a price. It is dishonor to be so honored. Let us learn to be no more avid of glory than we are capable of it. To be puffed up at every useful and harmless action is for people with whom these are extraordinary and rare; they want to put them at the price they cost them. In proportion as a good deed is more brilliant, I deduct from its goodness the suspicion I have that it was performed more to be brilliant than to be good: put on display, it is half sold. Those actions have much more grace which escape from the hand of the workman nonchalantly and noiselessly, and which some worthy man later picks out and lifts back out of obscurity to push them into the light for their own sake. *To me indeed all things seem more praiseworthy which are done without ostentation and without public witness* [Cicero], says the most vainglorious man in the world.

I had nothing to do but conserve and endure, which are noiseless and imperceptible acts. Innovation has great luster, but it is forbidden in these times, when we are hard pressed and have to defend ourselves mainly against innovations. Abstention from doing is often as noble as doing, but it is less open to the light; and the little that I am worth is almost all on that side.

In short, the occasions in my term of office were suited to my disposition, for which I am very grateful to them. Is there anyone who wants to be sick in order to see his doctor at work, and shouldn't we whip any doctor who would wish us the plague in order to put his art into practice? I have not had that iniquitous and rather common disposition of wanting the trouble and sickness of the affairs of this city to exalt and honor my government; I heartily lent a shoulder to make them easy and light. Anyone who will not be grateful to me for the order, the gentle and mute tranquility, that accompanied my administration, at least cannot deprive me of the share of it that belongs to me by right of my good fortune. And I am so made that I like as well to be lucky as wise, and to owe my successes purely to the grace of God as to the effect of my own action.

The Seventeenth Century

Wterized the seventeenth century. The economic activity ensured the rise of a
newly significant social class, one which owed its position to trade rather than to traditional rank or prowess and which left its mark on the political thought of the time by
introducing the notion of contract into the search for social authority. At the same
time, the new scientific activity stressed a rational approach that had been somewhat
ignored in centuries past. But just because the seventeenth century was a time of scientific revolution does not mean that superstition was dead. On the contrary, this was
the golden age of witches, when witch-hunters lit their pyres all over Europe and the
shadow of the Black Mass hung even over the court of Louis XIV.

The Thirty Years' War

*Hans Jacob Christopher von Grimmelshausen was a German writer (c. 1620–1676) who
spent part of his life soldiering on various sides during the Thirty Years' War. In the
picaresque novel that he published in 1668, he left us fascinating descriptions of German
life during this period and also a document concerning some of the directions taken during
these years by the speculations of some. For most of Germany these were difficult years,
in which towns and countryside were occupied successively by Catholics and Protestants,
Danes, Swedes, Frenchmen and Saxons, and mercenaries of Wallenstein or Tilly, and
devastated by men, famines, and epidemics, all seeming to vie with each other in their
destructiveness. This was the country over which the young Grimmelshausen marched—
now with the imperial soldiers, now with the Swedes—and over which he carries his hero.*

Hans Jacob Christopher von Grimmelshausen: from Simplicissimus

THE FATE OF A FARM

When these horsemen took over my father's smoky house, the first thing they did was
to bring in their horses; then each one started to destroy everything and tear everything
to pieces. Some were killing the cattle, and broiling or roasting the carcasses; others
were going through the house, determined not to miss any thing good there might be

---

Tr. by the editor from chaps. 4, 15, 16 of Simplicius *Simplicissimus* (1669).

for them to find; even the privy was not safe from their investigations, as if we had hidden there Jason's Golden Fleece. Others were making great bundles of linen and clothes and all sorts of stuff, as if they were going to open a flea market someplace, and what they weren't going to carry away with them they pulled to pieces. Some shoved their swords through the piles of straw or hay as if they hadn't had enough pigs to kill; others shook the feathers out of the mattresses and filled them with bacon and salt meat and other things as if they expected to sleep on them better that way. Others were breaking down the stoves and the window panes, as if they thought that summer was going to last forever. They were smashing the tableware and carrying away with them these useless pieces of copper or pottery or pewter. They burnt beds, and the tables, and the chairs, and the benches, when they could have found plenty of dry fire-wood in the yard. Of pots and of pans they shattered the lot; either because they didn't want to eat anything but roast meat any more, or because they only planned to stay with us for one single meal. Our maid underwent such treatment in the stables that she could hardly walk coming out. Is it not shameful to have such things happening? As for the groom, they laid him on the ground, they put a funnel into his mouth, and they poured in a whole tubful of foul matter. They called this "a little drink in the Swedish manner"; but he didn't find it at all to his taste. They also forced him to guide them on another raid, where they captured both people and cattle whom they brought into our yard. Among them they got my father, and my mother, and my sister Ursula.

Then they started to take the flints out of the cocks of the pistols in order to use them as thumbscrews, and to torture the poor beggars as if they were sorcerers who needed to be punished before being burnt. As a matter of fact, the soldiers had already shoved one of the captured peasants into the oven and they were trying to keep him warm in there (so he would tell them the hiding place of his little hoard). They had tied a cord around the head of another, and they were tightening the cord with a garrot, so that with every turn they gave it, the blood gushed out of his mouth, his nose and his ears. In short, each man was busy working out some new kind of torture for the peasants and so each victim had his own particular kind of torment.

However it seemed to me at the time that my father was the luckiest of them all, because he admitted with roars of laughter what the others were forced to reveal in the midst of sufferings and fearful plaints.

This kind of honor was his, no doubt, because he was the head of the family. The soldiers put him before a great fire, they tied him so that he couldn't move his arms or his legs, and they rubbed the soles of his feet with damp salt; then they had our old goat lick it off. He was so tickled by this that he nearly died of laughter. It all seemed to me so pleasant and so silly—I had never seen nor heard my father laugh so long—that, either because his laughter was contagious, or else because I couldn't understand what was going on, I had to laugh too. That is how my father told the raiders what they wanted to know, and revealed the hiding place of his treasure which consisted of gold and pearls and jewels; a much richer hoard than one would have expected a peasant to own.

I cannot say anything about the treatment of the women, the maids, and the young girls who had been captured, because the soldiers didn't let me see what they were doing to them. I know only that one heard sighs and groans in various corners, and I thought that my mother and my sister Ursula were probably no better off than the others.

Mercantilism and Other Novelties

With growing economic activity, the seventeenth century developed an intense and novel economic awareness. Trade was seen to play such an important part in the wealth—and hence the power—of all countries that statesmen and publicists considered it with more attention than ever before. Repeated attempts were made to attract bullion (that is, riches), to secure the greatest possible share of the profits of the carrying trade, and to attract craftsmen whose skills were expected to improve the country's industrial position. The economic ideal for a country was seen as self-sufficiency at home combined with a vigorous export trade that would bring in bullion; a great deal of legislation tried to implement this ideal. These mercantilistic ideas, as they are called, would alter and develop with time, but the economic activity with which they were connected also encouraged the growth of a numerous and increasingly self-confident bourgeoisie. This rising class would soon make its presence felt, and its down-to-earth rationalism would affect cultural attitudes in years to come.

Thomas Mun: from England's Treasure by Foreign Trade

The mercantilist theory of national wealth appears very clearly in the following passage from Thomas Mun's book, England's Treasure by Foreign Trade *(1664). Mun (1571–1641), who was a director of the English East India Company, was not interested in the crude mercantilism that concentrated only on getting as much gold and silver as possible with no idea of the real meaning of a country's import-export balance. He believed that England's real wealth lay in trade, in the volume and the profits of its exports, and he put his ideas in a little book, published some years after his death, that was essentially a plea for free trade.*

THE MEANS TO ENRICH THE KINGDOM, AND TO INCREASE OUR TREASURE

Although a Kingdom may be enriched by gifts received, or by purchase taken from some other Nations, yet these are things uncertain and of small consideration when they happen. The ordinary means therefore to increase our wealth and treasure is by Foreign Trade, wherein we must ever observe this rule: to sell more to strangers yearly than we consume of theirs in value. For suppose that when this Kingdom is plentifully served with the Cloth, Lead, Tin, Iron, Fish and other native commodities, we do yearly

---

From Thomas Mun, *England's Treasure by Foreign Trade* (New York, 1895), pp. 7–27.

export the overplus to foreign Countries to the value of twenty two hundred thousand pounds; by which means we are enabled beyond the Seas to buy and bring in foreign wares for our use and Consumptions, to the value of twenty hundred thousand pounds; by this order duly kept in our trading, we may rest assured that the Kingdom shall be enriched yearly two hundred thousand pounds, which must be brought to us in so much Treasure; because that part of our stock which is not returned to us in wares must necessarily be brought home in treasure.

For in this case it cometh to pass in the stock of a Kingdom, as in the estate of a private man; who is supposed to have one thousand pounds yearly revenue and two thousand pounds of ready money in his Chest: If such a man through excess shall spend one thousand five hundred pounds per annum, all his ready money will be gone in four years; and in the like time his said money will be doubled if he take a Frugal course to spend but five hundred pounds per annum; which rule never faileth likewise in the Commonwealth, but in some cases (of no great moment) which I will hereafter declare, when I shall shew by whom and in what manner this balance of the Kingdom's account ought to be drawn up yearly, or so often as it shall please the State to discover how much we gain or lose by trade with foreign Nations. But first I will say something concerning those ways and means which will increase our exportations and diminish our importations of wares; which being done, I will then set down some other arguments both affirmative and negative to strengthen that which is here declared, and thereby to shew that all the other means which are commonly supposed to enrich the Kingdom with Treasure are altogether insufficient and mere fallacies.

THE PARTICULAR WAYS AND MEANS TO INCREASE THE EXPORTATION OF OUR COMMODITIES, AND TO DECREASE OUR CONSUMPTION OF FOREIGN WARES

The revenue or stock of a Kingdom by which it is provided of foreign wares is either Natural or Artificial. The Natural wealth is so much only as can be spared from our own use and necessities to be exported unto strangers. The Artificial consists in our manufactures and industrious trading with foreign commodities, concerning which I will set down such particulars as may serve for the cause we have in hand.

1. First, although this Realm be already exceeding rich by nature, yet might it be much increased by laying the waste grounds (which are infinite) into such employments as should no way hinder the present revenues of other manured lands, but hereby to supply ourselves and prevent the importations of Hemp, Flax, Cordage, Tobacco, and divers other things which we fetch from strangers to our great impoverishing.

2. We may likewise diminish our importations, if we would soberly refrain from excessive consumption of foreign wares in our diet and rayment, with such often change of fashions as is used so much the more to increase the waste and charge; which vices at this present are more notorious amongst us than in former ages. Yet might they easily be amended by enforcing the observation of such good laws as are strictly practiced in other Countries against the said excesses; where likewise

by commanding their own manufactures to be used, they prevent the coming in of others, without prohibition, or offense to strangers in their mutual commerce.

3. In our exportations we must not only regard our own superfluities, but also we must consider our neighbors' necessities, that so upon the wares which they cannot want, nor yet be furnished thereof elsewhere, we may (besides the vent of the Materials) gain so much of manufacture as we can, and also endeavor to sell them dear, so far forth as the high price cause not a less vent in the quantity. But the superfluity of our commodities which strangers use, and may also have the same from other Nations, or may abate their vent by the use of some such like wares from other places, and with little inconvenience; we must in this case strive to sell as cheap as possible we can, rather than to lose the utterance of such wares. For we have found of late years by good experience, that being able to sell our Cloth cheap in Turkey, we have greatly increased the vent thereof, and the Venetians have lost as much in the utterance of theirs in those Countrys, because it is dearer. And on the other side a few years past, when by the excessive price of Wools our Cloth was exceeding dear, we lost at the least half our clothing for foreign parts, which since is no otherwise (well near) recovered again than by the great fall of price for Wools and Cloth. We find that twenty five in the Hundred less in the price of these and some other wares, to the loss of private mens revenues, may raise above fifty upon the hundred in the quantity vented to the benefit of the publique. For when Cloth is dear, other Nations do presently practice clothing, and we know they want neither art nor materials to this performance. But when by cheapness we drive them from this employment, and so in time obtain our dear price again, then do they also use their former remedy. So that by these alterations we learn, that it is in vain to expect a greater revenue of our wares than their condition will afford, but rather it concerns us to apply our endeavors to the times with care and diligence to help ourselves the best we may, by making our cloth and other manufactures without deceit, which will increase their estimation and use.

4. The value of our exportations likewise may be much advanced when we perform it ourselves in our own ships. For then we get not only the price of our wares as they are worth here, but also the Merchants gains, the charges of insurance, and freight to carry them beyond the seas. As for example, if the Italian Merchants should come hither in their own shipping to fetch our Corn, our red Herrings or the like, in this case the Kingdom should have ordinarily but 25 s. for a quarter of Wheat, and 20 s. for a barrel of red herrings, whereas if we carry there wares ourselves into Italy upon the said rates, it is likely that we shall obtain fifty shillings for the first, and forty shillings for the last, which is a great difference in the utterance or vent of the Kingdoms stock. And although it is true that the commerce ought to be free to strangers to bring in and carry out at their pleasure, yet nevertheless in many places the exportation of victuals and munition are either prohibited, or at least limited to be done only by the people and Shipping of those places where they abound.

5. The frugal expanding likewise of our own natural wealth might advance much yearly to be exported unto strangers; and if in our payment we will be prodigal, yet let this be done with our own materials and manufactures, as Cloth, Lace, Embroideries, Cutworks and the like, where the excess of the rich may be the employment of the poor, whose labours notwithstanding of this kind, would be more profitable for the Commonwealth, if they were done to the use of Strangers.

6. The Fishing in his Majesties seas of England, Scotland, and Ireland is our natural wealth, and would cost nothing but labour, which the Dutch bestow willingly and thereby draw yearly a very great profit to themselves by serving many places of Christendom with our Fish, for which they return and supply their wants both of foreign Wares and Money, besides the multitudes of Mariners and Shipping, which hereby are maintain'd, whereof a long discourse might be made to shew the particular management of this important business. Our Fishing plantation likewise in New England, Virginia, Greenland, the Summer Islands and the Newfoundland, are of the like nature, affording much wealth and employments to maintain a great number of poor, and to increase our decaying trade.

7. A Staple or Magazine for foreign Corn, Indigo, Spices, raw Silks, Cotton, Wool or any other commodity whatsoever, to be imported will increase Shipping, Trade, Treasure, and the Kings customs, by exporting them again where need shall require, which course of Trading hath been the chief means to raise Venice, Genoa, the low Countrys, with some others; and for such a purpose England stands most commodiously, wanting nothing to this performance but our own diligence and endeavor.

8. Also we ought to esteem and cherish those trades which we have in remote or far Countrys, for besides the increase of Shipping and Mariners thereby, the wares also sent thither and receiv'd from thence are far more profitable unto the kingdom than by our trades near at hand; As for example; suppose Pepper to be worth here two Shillings the pound constantly, if then it be brought from the Dutch at Amsterdam, the Merchant may give there twenty pence the pound and gain well by the bargain, but if he fetch this Pepper from the East Indies, he must not give above three pence the pound at the most, which is a mighty advantage, not only in that part which serveth for our own use, but also for the great quantity which (from hence) we transport yearly unto divers other Nations to be sold at a higher price: whereby it is plain, that we make a far greater stock by gain upon these Indian Commodities, than those Nations do where they grow, and to whom they properly appertain, being the natural wealth of their Countries. But for the better understanding of this particular, we must ever distinguish between the gain of the Kingdom, and the profit of the Merchant; for although the Kingdom payeth no more for this Pepper than is before supposed, nor for any other commodity bought in foreign parts more than the Stranger receiveth from us for the same, yet the Merchant payeth not only that price, but also the freight, insurance, customs, and other charges which are exceeding great in these long voyages; but yet all these in the Kingdoms accompt are but commutations among ourselves, and no privation

of the Kingdoms stock, which being duly considered, together with the support also of our other trades in our best Shipping to Italy, France, Turkey, the East Countries and other places, by transporting and venting the wares which we bring yearly from the East Indies. It may well stire up our utmost endeavors to maintain and enlarge this great and noble business, so much importing the Publique wealth, Strength, and Happiness. Neither is there less honour and judgment by growing rich (in this manner) upon the stock of other Nations, than by an industrious increase of our own means, especially when this later is advanced by the benefit of the former, as we have found in the East Indies by sale of much of our Tin, Cloth, Lead and other Commodities, the vent whereof doth daily increase in those Countries which formerly had no use of our wares.

9. It would be very beneficial to export money as well as wares, being done in trade only, it would increase our Treasure; but of this I write more largely in the next Chapter to prove it plainly.

10. It were policy and profit for the State to suffer manufactures made of foreign Materials to be exposed custom-free, as Velvets and all other wrought Silks, Fustians, thrown Silks and the like, it would employ very many poor people, and much increase the value of our stock yearly issued into other Countries, and it would (for this purpose) cause the more foreign Materials to be brought in, to the improvement of His Majesties Customes. I will here remember a notable increase in our manufacture of winding and twisting only of foreign raw Silk, which within 35 years to my knowledge did not employ more than 300 people in the City and suburbs of London, where at this present time it doth set on work above fourteen thousand souls, as upon diligent inquiry hath been credibly reported unto his Majesties Commissioners for Trade. And it is certain, that if the said foreign Commodities might be exported from hence, free of custome, this manufacture would yet increase very much, and decrease as fast in Italy and the Netherlands. But if any man allege the Dutch proverb, "Live and let others live"; I answer, that the Dutchmen notwithstanding their own Proverb, do not only in these Kingdoms, encroach upon our livings, but also in other foreign parts of our trade (where they have power) they do hinder and destroy us in our lawful course of living, hereby taking the bread out of our mouth, which we shall never prevent by plucking the pot from their nose, as of late years too many of us do practice to the great hurt and dishonour of this famous Nation; We ought rather to imitate former times in taking sober and worthy courses more pleasing to God and suitable to our ancient reputation.

11. It is needful also not to charge the native commodities with too great customes, lest by indearing them to the strangers use, it hinder their vent. And especially foreign wares brought in to be transported again should be favoured, for otherwise that manner of trading (so much importing the good of the Commonwealth) cannot prosper nor subsist. But the consumption of such foreign wares in the Realm may be the more charged, which will turn to the profit of the Kingdom in the Balance of the Trade, and thereby also enable the King to lay up the more Treasure

out of his yearly incomes. As of this particular I intend to write more fully in his proper place, where I shall shew how much money a Prince may conveniently lay up without the hurt of his subjects.

12. Lastly, in all things we must endeavor to make the most we can of our own, whether it be Natural or Artificial; And forasmuch as the people which live by the Arts are far more in number than they who are masters of the fruits, we ought the more carefully to maintain those endeavors of the multitude, in whom doth consist the greatest strength and riches both of King and Kingdom: for where the people are many, and the arts good, there the traffique must be great, and the Country rich. The Italians employ a greater number of people, and get more money by their industry and manufactures of the raw Silks of the Kingdom of Cicilia, than the King of Spain and his Subjects have by the revenue of this rich commodity. But what need we fetch the example so far, when we know that our own natural wares do not yield us so much profit as our industry? For Iron ore in the Mines is of no great worth, when it is compared with the employment and advantage it yields being digged, tried, transported, bought, sold, cast into Ordnance, Muskets, and many other instruments of war for offense and defense, wrought into Anchors, bolts, spikes, Hayles and the like, for the use of Ships, Houses, Carts, Coaches, Ploughs, and other instruments for Tillage. Compare our Fleece-wools with our Cloth, which requires shearing, washing, carding, spinning, weaving, fulling, dying, dressing and other trimmings, and we shall find these Arts more profitable than the natural wealth, whereof I might instance other examples, but I will not be more tedious, for if I would amplify upon this and the other particulars before written, I might find matter sufficient to make a large volume, but my desire in all is only to prove what I propound with brevity and plainness.

THE EXPORTATION OF OUR MONEYS IN TRADE OF MERCHANDISE IS A MEANS TO INCREASE OUR TREASURE

This Position is so contrary to the common opinion, that it will require many and strong arguments to prove it before it can be accepted of the Multitude, who bitterly exclaim when they see any moneys carried out of the Realm; affirming thereupon that we have absolutely lost so much Treasure, and that this is an act directly against the long continued laws made and confirmed by the wisdom of this Kingdom in the High Court of Parliament, and that many places, nay Spain itself which is the Fountain of Money, forbids the exportation thereof, some cases only excepted. To all which I might answer that Venice, Florence, Genoa, the Low Countries and divers other places permit it, their people applaud it, and find great benefit by it; but all this makes a noise and proves nothing, we must therefore come to those reasons which concern the business in question.

First, I will take for granted which no man of judgment will deny, that we have no other means to get Treasure but by foreign trade, for Mines we have none which do afford it, and how this money is gotten in the managing of our said Trade I have already shewed, that it is done by making our commodities which are exported yearly to over balance in value the foreign wares which we consume; so that it resteth only to shew how our moneys may be added to our commodities, and being jointly exported may so much the more increase our Treasure.

We have already supposed our yearly consumptions of foreign wares to be for the value of twenty hundred thousand pounds, and our exportations to exceed that by two hundred thousand pounds, which sum we have thereupon affirmed is brought to us in treasure to balance the accompt. But now if we add three hundred thousand pounds more in ready money unto our former exportations in wares, what profit can we have (will some men say) although by this means we should bring in so much ready money more than we did before, seeing that we have carried out the like value.

To this the answer is, that when we have prepared our exportations of wares, and sent out as much of everything as we can spare or vent abroad; it is not therefore said that then we should add our money thereunto to fetch in the more money immediately, but rather first to enlarge our trade by enabling us to bring in more foreign wares, which being sent out again will in due time much increase our Treasure.

For although in this manner we do yearly multiply our importations to the maintenance of more Shipping and Mariners, improvement of His Majesties Customs and other benefits; yet our consumption of those foreign wares is no more than it was before; so that all the said increase of commodities brought in by the means of our ready money sent out as afore written, doth in the end become an exportation unto us of far greater value than our said moneys were, which is proved by three several examples following.

1. For I suppose that 100,000 Pounds being sent in our Shipping to the East Countries, will buy there one hundred thousand quarters of wheat clear aboard the Ships, which after being brought into England and housed, to export the same at the best time for vent thereof in Spain or Italy, it cannot yield less in those parts than two hundred thousand pounds to make the Merchant but a saver, yet by this reckoning we see the Kingdom hath doubled that Treasure.

2. Again this profit will be far greater when we trade thus in remote Countries, as for example, if we send one hundred thousand pounds into the East Indies to buy Pepper there, and bring it hither, and from hence send it for Italy or Turkey, it must yield seven hundred thousand pounds at least in those places, in regard of the excessive charge which the Merchant disburseth in those long voyages in Shipping, Wages, Victuals, Insurance, Interest, Customes, Imposts, and the like, all which notwithstanding the King and the Kingdom gets.

3. But where the voyages are short and the wares rich, which therefore will not employ much Shipping, the profit will be far less. As when another hundred thousand pounds shall be employed in Turkey in raw Silks, and brought hither to be after transported from hence into France, the Low Countries, or Germany, the Merchant shall have good gain, although he sell it there but for one hundred and fifty thousand pounds: and thus take the voyages altogether in their Medium, the moneys exported will be returned unto us more than Trebled. But if any man will yet

object, that these returns come to us in wares, and not really in money as they were issued out.

The answer is (keeping our first ground) that if our consumption of foreign wares be no more yearly than is already supposed, and that our exportations be so mightily increased by this manner of Trading with ready money as is before declared: it is not then possible but that all the over-balance or difference should return either in money or in such wares as we must export again, which, as is already plainly shewed will be still a greater means to increase our Treasure.

For it is in the stock of the Kingdom as in the estates of private men, who having store of ware, do not therefore say that they will not venture out or trade with their money (for this were ridiculous) but do also turn that into wares, whereby they multiply their Money, and so by a continual and orderly change of one into the other grow rich, and when they please turn all their estates into Treasure; for they that have Wares cannot want money.

Neither is it said that Money is the Life of Trade, as if it could not subsist without the same; for we know that there was great trading by way of commutation or barter when there was little money stirring in the world. The Italians and some other Nations have such remedies against this want, that it can neither decay nor hinder their trade, for they transfer bills of debt, and have Banks both public and private, wherein they do assign their credits from one to another daily for very great sums with ease and satisfaction by writings only, whilst in the mean time the Mass of Treasure which gave foundation to these credits is employed in Foreign Trade as a Merchandise, and by the said means they have little other use of money in those countries more than for their ordinary expenses. It is not therefore the keeping of our money in the Kingdom; but the necessity and use of our wares in foreign Countries, and our want of their commodities which causeth the vent and consumption on all sides, which makes a quick and ample Trade. If we were once poor, and now having gained some store of money by trade with resolution to keep it still in the Realm; shall this cause other Nations to spend more on our commodities than formerly they have done, whereby we might say that our trade is Quickened and Enlarged? No verily it will produce no such good effect: but rather according to the alteration of times by their true causes we may expect the contrary; for all men do consent that plenty of money in a Kingdom doth make the native commodities dearer, which as it is to the profit of some private men in their revenues, so is it directly against the benefit of the Publique in the quantity of the trade; for as plenty of money makes wares dearer, so dear wares decline their use and consumption as hath been already plainly shewed in the last Chapter upon that particular of our cloth; And although this is a very hard lesson for some great landed men to learn, yet I am sure it is a true lesson for all the land to observe, lest when we have gained some store of money by trade, we lose it again by not trading with our money. I knew a Prince in Italy (of famous memory) Ferdinando the first, great Duke of Tuscanie, who being very rich in Treasure, endevoured therewith to enlarge his trade by issuing out to his Merchants great sums of money for very small profit; I myself had forty thousand crowns of him gratis for a whole year, although he knew that I would presently send it away in Specie for the parts of Turkey to be employed in wares for his Countries, he being well assured that in this course of trade it would return again (according to the old saying) with a Duck in the mouth. This noble and industrious Prince by his care and diligence to countenance and favour Merchants in their affairs, did so increase the practice thereof, that there is scarce a Nobleman or Gentleman in all his dominions that doth not Merchandise either by himself or in partnership with others, whereby within these thirty years the trade to his port of Leghorn is so much increased, that of a poor little town (as I myself knew it) it is now become a fair and strong City, being one of the most famous places for trade in all Christendom. And yet it is worthy of our observation, that the multitude of Ships and wares which come hither from England, the Low Countries, and other places, have little or no means to make their returns from thence but only in ready money, which they may and do carry away freely at all times, to the incredible advantage of the said great Duke of Tuscanie and his subjects, who are much enriched by the continual great concourse of Merchants from all the States of the neighbor Princes, bringing them plenty of money daily to supply their wants of the said wares. And thus we see that the current of Merchandise which carries away their Treasure, becomes a flowing stream to fill them again in a greater measure with money.

There is yet an objection or two as weak as all the rest: that is, if we trade with our Money we shall issue out the less wares; as if a man should say, those Countries which heretofore had occasion to consume our Cloth, Lead, Tin, Iron, Fish and the like, shall now make use of our moneys in the place of these necessaries, which were most absurd to affirm, or that the Merchant had not rather carry out wares by which there is ever some gains expected, than to export money which is still but the same without any increase.

But on the contrary there are many Countries which may yield us very profitable trade for our money, which otherwise afford us no trade at all, because they have no use of our wares, as namely the East Indies for one in the first beginning thereof, although since by industry in our commerce with those Nations we have brought them into the use of much of our Lead, Cloth, Tin, and other things, which is a good addition to the former vent of our commodities.

Again, some men have alleged that those Countries which permit money to be carried out, do it because they have few or no wares to trade withall: but we have great store of commodities, and therefore their action ought not to be our example.

To this the answer is briefly, that if we have such a quantity of wares as doth fully provide us of all things needful from beyond the seas: why should we then doubt that our moneys sent out in trade, must not necessarily come back again in treasure; together with the great gains which it may procure in such manner as is before set down? And on the other side, if those Nations which send out their moneys do it because they have but few wares of their own, how come they then have so much Treasure as we ever see in those places which suffer it freely to be exported at times and by whomsoever? I answer, even by trading with their Moneys; for by what other means can they get it, having no Mines of Gold or Silver?

Thus may we plainly see, that when this weighty business is duly considered in his end, as all our humane actions ought well to be weighed, it is found much contrary to that which most men esteem thereof, because they search no further than the beginning of the work, which mis-informs their judgments, and leads them into error: For if we only behold the actions of the husbandman in the seed-time when he casteth away much good corn into the ground, we will rather accompt him a mad man than a husbandman; but when we consider his labours in the harvest which is the end of his endeavors, we find the worth and plentiful increase of his actions. . . .

The Rise of the Bourgeoisie

Daniel Defoe (c. 1659–1731), novelist and political pamphleteer, has left us some excellent descriptions of the events of his time. In The Complete English Tradesman, *however, he wanted to show the respectability, indeed the prestige, of trade and its connection with England's strength and prosperity. Chapter 24 of the book gives a long list of intermarriages between nobles and bourgeois, purporting to show "how some families owe their rise to trade, and others their descent and fortunes to prudent alliances with the families of citizens." Chapter 25, which follows, is more down to earth.*

Daniel Defoe: from The Complete English Tradesman

The instances which we have given in the last chapter, abundantly make for the honour of the British traders; and we may venture to say, at the same time, are very far from doing dishonour to the nobility who have from time to time entered into alliance with them; for it is very well known, that besides the benefit which we reap by being a trading nation, which is our principal glory, trade is a very different thing in England than it is in many other countries, and is carried on by persons who, both in their education and descent, are far from being the dregs of the people.

King Charles II, who was perhaps the prince of all the kings that ever reigned in England, who best understood the country and the people he governed, used to say, that the tradesmen were the only gentry in England. His majesty spoke it merrily, but it had a happy signification in it, such as was peculiar to the bright genius of that prince, who, though he was not the best governor, was the best acquainted with the world of all the princes of his age, if not of all the men in it; and I make no scruple to advance these three points in honour of our country; viz.—

1. That we are the greatest trading country in the world, because we have the greatest exportation of the growth and product of our land, and of the manufacture and labour of our people; and the greatest importation and consumption of the growth, product, and manufactures of other countries from abroad, of any nation in the world.

2. That our climate is the best and most agreeable to live in, because a man can be more out of doors in England than in other countries.

From Daniel Defoe, *The Complete English Tradesman* (London, 1724), Chap. XXV.

3. That our men are the stoutest and best, because, strip them naked from the waist upwards, and give them no weapons at all but their hands and heels, and turn them into a room or stage, and lock them in with the like number of other men of any nation, man for man, and they shall beat the best men you shall find in the world.

As so many of our noble and wealthy families, as we have shown, are raised by and derived from trade, so it is true, and indeed it cannot well be otherwise, that many of the younger branches of our gentry, and even of the nobility itself, have descended again into the spring from whence they flowed, and have become tradesmen; and thence it is that, as I said above, our tradesmen in England are not, as it generally is in other countries, always of the meanest of our people. Nor is trade itself in England, as it generally is in other countries, the meanest thing the men can turn their hand to; but, on the contrary, trade is the readiest way for men to raise their fortunes and families; and therefore it is a field for men of figure and of good families to enter upon.

Having thus done a particular piece of justice to ourselves, in the value we put upon trade and tradesmen in England, it reflects very much upon the understandings of those refined heads who pretend to depreciate that part of the nation which is so infinitely superior in wealth to the families who call themselves gentry, and so infinitely more numerous.

As to the wealth of the nation, that undoubtedly lies chiefly among the trading part of the people; and though there are a great many families raised within few years, in the late war, by great employments and by great actions abroad, to the honour of the English gentry, yet how many more families among the tradesmen have been raised to immense estates, even during the same time, by the attending circumstances of the war; such as the clothing, the paying, the victualling and furnishing, &c., both army and navy. And by whom have the prodigious taxes been paid, the loans supplied, and money advanced upon all occasions? By whom are the banks and companies carried on, and on whom are the customs and excises levied? Have not the trade and tradesmen borne the burden of the war? And do they not still pay four millions a year interest for the public debts? On whom are the funds levied, and by whom the public credit supported? Is not trade the inexhausted fund of all funds, and upon which all the rest depend?

As is the trade, so in proportion are the tradesmen; and how wealthy are tradesmen in almost all the several parts of England, as well as in London? How common is it to see a tradesman go off the stage, even but from mere shopkeeping, with from ten to forty thousand pounds' estate to divide among his family! When, on the contrary, take the gentry in England, from one end to the other, except a few here and there, what with excessive high living, which is of late grown so much into a disease, and the other ordinary circumstances of families, we find few families of the lower gentry, that is to say from six or seven hundred a year downwards, but they are in debt, and in necessitous circumstances, and a great many of greater estates also.

On the other hand, let any one who is acquainted with England, look but abroad into the several counties, especially near London, or within fifty miles of it; how are the ancient families worn out by time and family misfortunes, and the estates possessed by a new race of tradesmen, grown up into families of gentry, and established by the immense wealth gained, as I may say, behind the counter; that is, in the shop, the warehouse, and the counting-house.

How many noble seats, superior to the palaces of sovereign princes, in some countries, do we see erected within few miles of this city by tradesmen, or the sons of tradesmen, while the seats and castles of the ancient gentry, like their families, look worn out and fallen into decay!

Again; in how superior a port do our tradesmen live, to what the middling gentry either do or can support! An ordinary tradesman now, not in the city only, but in the country, shall spend more money by the year, than a gentleman of four or five hundred pounds a year too; whereas the gentleman shall at the best stand stock still just where he began, nay, perhaps, decline: and as for the lower gentry, from a hundred pounds a year to three hundred, or thereabouts, though they are often as proud and high in their appearance as the other; as to them, I say, a shoemaker in London shall keep a better house, spend more money, clothe his family better, and yet grow rich too. It is evident where the difference lies; an estate's a pond, but trade's a spring: the first, if it keeps full, and the water wholesome, by the ordinary supplies and drains from the neighbouring grounds, it is well, and it is all that is expected; but the other is an inexhausted current, which not only fills the pond, and keeps it full, but is continually running over, and fills all the lower ponds and places about it.

This being the case in England, and our trade being so vastly great, it is no wonder that the tradesmen in England fill the lists of our nobility and gentry; no wonder that the gentlemen of the best families marry tradesmen's daughters, and put their younger sons apprentices to tradesmen; and how often do these younger sons come to buy the elder sons' estates, and restore the family, when the elder and head of the house, proving rakish and extravagant, has wasted his patrimony, and is obliged to make out the blessing of Israel's family, where the younger son bought the birthright, and the elder was doomed to serve him!

Trade is so far here from being inconsistent with a gentleman, that, in short, trade in England makes gentlemen, and has peopled this nation with gentlemen; for, after a generation or two, the tradesman's children, or at least their grandchildren, come to be as good gentlemen, statesmen, parliamentmen, privy-counsellors, judges, bishops, and noblemen, as those of the highest birth and the most ancient families; as we have shown. Nor do we find any defect either in the genius or capacities of the posterity of tradesmen, arising from any remains of mechanic blood, which, it is pretended, should influence them; but all the gallantry of spirit, greatness of soul, and all the generous principles that can be found in any of the ancient families, whose blood is the most untainted, as they call it, with the low mixtures of a mechanic race, are found in these; and, as is said before, they generally go beyond them in knowledge of the world, which is the best education.

We see the tradesmen of England, as they grow wealthy, coming every day to the herald's office to search for the coats of arms of their ancestors, in order to paint them upon their coaches, and grave them upon their plate, embroider them upon their furniture, or carve them upon the pediments of their new houses; and how often do we see them trace the registers of their families up to the prime nobility, or the most ancient gentry of the kingdom!

In this search we find them often qualified to raise new families, if they do not descend from old; as was said of a certain tradesman of London, that if he could not find the ancient race of gentlemen, from which he came, he would begin a new race, who should be as good gentlemen as any that went before him.

Thus, in the late wars between England and France, how was our army full of excellent officers, who went from the shop, and behind the counter, into the camp, and who distinguished themselves there by their merits and gallant behaviour! And several such came to command regiments, and even to be general officers, and to gain as much reputation in the service as any; as Colonel Pierce, Wood, Richards, and several others that may be named.

All this confirms what I have said before, viz., that trade in England neither is or ought to be compared with what it is in other countries; or the tradesman depreciated as they are abroad, and as some of our gentry would pretend to do in England; but that as many of our best families rose from trade, so many branches of the best families in England, under the nobility, have stooped so low as to be put apprentices to tradesmen in London, and to set up and follow those trades when they have come out of their times, and have thought it no dishonour to their blood.

To bring this once more home to the ladies, who are scandalized at that mean step, which they call it, of marrying a tradesman, it may be told them, for their humiliation, that, however they think fit to act, sometimes those tradesmen come of better families than their own; and oftentimes, when they have refused them to their loss, those very tradesmen have married ladies of superior fortune to them, and have raised families of their own, who, in one generation, have been superior to those nice ladies both in dignity and estate; and have, to their great mortification, been ranked above them upon all public occasions.

The word "tradesmen," in England, does not sound so harsh as it does in other countries; and to say a gentleman-tradesman, is not so much nonsense as some people would persuade us to reckon it; and, indeed, the very name of an English tradesman, will and does already obtain in the world; and as our soldiers, by the late war, gained the reputation of being some of the best troops in the world; and our seamen are at this day, and very justly too, esteemed the best sailors in the world; so the English tradesman may be allowed to rank with the best gentlemen in Europe.

And hence it is natural to ask, whence comes all this to be so? How is it produced? War has not done it; no, nor so much as helped or assisted to it; it is not by any martial exploits; we have made no conquests abroad, added no new kingdoms to the British empire, reduced no neighbouring nations, or extended the possession of our monarchs into the properties of others; we have gained nothing by war and encroachment; nay, we have lost all the dominions which our ancient kings for some hundreds of years held in France; and, instead of being enriched by war and victory, on the contrary, we have been torn in pieces by civil wars and rebellions, and that several times, to the ruin of our richest families, and the slaughter of our nobility and gentry.

These things prove abundantly that the greatness of the British nation is not owing to war and conquests, to enlarging its dominions by the sword, or subjecting the people of other countries to our power; but it is allowing to trade, to the increase of our commerce at home, and the extending it abroad.

It is owing to trade, that new discoveries have been made in lands unknown, and new settlements and plantations made, new colonies planted, and new governments formed, in the uninhabited islands, and the uncultivated continent of America; and those plantings and settlements have again enlarged and increased the trade, and thereby the wealth and power of the nation by whom they were discovered and planted; we have not increased our power, or the number of our subjects, by subduing the nations which possess those countries, and incorporating them into our own; but have entirely planted our colonies, and peopled the countries with our own subjects, natives of this island; and, excepting the negroes, which we transport from Africa to America as slaves to work in the sugar and tobacco plantations, all our colonies, as well in the islands as on the continent of America, are entirely peopled from Great Britain and Ireland, and chiefly the former; the natives having either removed further up into the country, or, by their own folly and treachery raising war against us, been destroyed and cut off.

As trade has thus extended our colonies abroad, so it has (except those colonies) kept our people at home, where they are multiplied to that prodigious degree, and do still continue to multiply in such a manner, that, if it goes on so, time may come that all the lands in England will do little more than serve for gardens for them and to feed their cows, and their corn and cattle be supplied from Scotland and Ireland.

What is the reason that we see numbers of French, and of Scots, and Germans, in all the foreign nations in Europe, and especially filling up their armies and courts, and that you see few or no English there?

What is the reason that, when we want to raise armies, or to man navies, in England, we are obliged to press the seamen, and to make laws, and empower the justices of peace and magistrates of towns, to force men to go for soldiers, and enter into the service, or allure them by giving bounty-money as an encouragement to men to list themselves; whereas the people of other nations, and even the Scots and Irish, travel abroad and run into all the neighbour-nations, to seek service and to be admitted into their pay?

What is it but trade, the increase of business at home, and the employment of the poor in the business and manufactures of this kingdom, by which the poor get so good wages, and live so well, that they will not list for soldiers; and have so good pay in the merchants' service, that they will not serve on board the ships of war, unless they are forced to do it?

What is the reason that, in order to supply our colonies and plantations with people, besides the encouragement given in those colonies to all people that will come hither to plant and to settle, we are obliged to send away thither all our petty offenders, and all the criminals that we think fit to spare from the gallows, besides that we formerly called the kidnapping trade, that is to say, the arts made use of to wheedle and draw away young, vagrant, and indigent people, and people of desperate fortunes, to sell themselves, that is, bind themselves for servants, the number of which are very great?

It is poverty fills armies, mans navies, and peoples colonies; in vain the drums beat for soldiers to serve in the armies for fivepence a day, and the king's captains invite seamen to serve in the royal navy for twenty-three shillings per month, in a country where the ordinary labourer can have nine shillings a week for his labour, and the manufacturers earn from twelve to sixteen shillings a week for their work, and while trade gives thirty shillings per month wages to the seamen on board merchant-ships, men will always stay or go, as the pay gives them encouragement; and this is the reason why it has been so much more difficult to raise and recruit armies in England, than it has been in Scotland and Ireland, France and Germany.

The same trade that keeps our people at home, is the cause of the well-living of the people here; for as frugality is not the national virtue of England, so the people that get much, spend much; and as they work hard, so they live well, eat and drink well, clothe warm, and lodge soft; in a word, the working manufacturing people of England, eat the fat, drink the sweet, live better, and fare better, than the working poor of any other nation in Europe; they make better wages of their work; and spend more of the money upon their backs and bellies than in any other country. This expense of the poor, as it causes a prodigious consumption both of the provisions and of the manufactures of our country at home, so two things are undeniably the consequence of that part.

1. The consumption of provisions increases the rent and value of the lands; and this raises the gentlemen's estates, and that again increases the employment of people, and consequently the numbers of them, as well those that are employed in the husbandry of land, breeding and feeding of cattle, &c., as of servants to the gentlemen's families, who as their estates increase in value, so they increase their families and equipages.

2. As the people get greater wages, so they, I mean the same poorer part of the people, clothe better, and furnish better; and this increases the consumption of the very manufactures they make; then that consumption increases the quantity made; and this creates what we call inland trade, by which innumerable families are employed, and the increase of the people maintained; and by which increase of trade and people the present growing prosperity of this nation is produced.

The whole glory and greatness of England then being thus raised by trade, it must be unaccountable folly and ignorance in us to lessen that one article in our own esteem, which is the only fountain from whence we all, take us as a nation, are raised, and by which we are enriched and maintained. The Scripture says, speaking of the riches and glory of the city of Tyre, which was indeed at that time the great port or emporium of the world for foreign commerce, from whence all the silks and fine manufactures of Persia and India were exported all over the western world, "that her merchants were princes," and in another place, "by thy traffic thou hast increased thy riches." Certain it is, that our traffic has increased our riches; and it is also certain, that the flourishing of our manufacture is the foundation of all our traffic, as well our merchandise as our inland trade.

THE NEW SCIENCE

The "scientific revolution" is usually associated with the sixteenth and seventeenth centuries, although, of course, its origins may be traced back further still. But for a technique or an idea to be historically significant, mere existence is not enough: acceptance and practice are needed, and success is, to some extent, measured quantitatively. This is why the seventeenth century seems crucial to that revolution which, in the words of Herbert Butterfield (The Origins of Modern Science, London, 1949), "overturned the authority in science not only of the middle ages but of the ancient world." To Professor Butterfield this change of techniques and attitudes is the most important event since the rise of Christianity, more important by far than the Renaissance or the Reformation: "Since it changed the character of men's habitual mental operations even in the conduct of the non-material sciences, while transforming the whole diagram of the physical universe and the very texture of human life itself, it looms so large as the real origin both of the modern world and of the modern mentality that our customary periodisation of European history has become an anachronism and an encumbrance."

Quite apart from the new interpretations and perspectives these words suggest, it is interesting to see that such tremendous changes came about in the first place and quite literally as changes of mind; *in other words, not as a result of new discoveries, new facts, new observations, but of new ways of looking at evidence that had been available for quite some time. What we find in the work of Descartes or Newton, as in that of William Harvey or Galileo, is "the art of handling the same bundle of data as before, but placing them in a new system of relations with one another by giving them a new framework." It was a system that would prepare people's minds for Darwin's* Origin of Species *two centuries later.*

Galileo: What Is Scientific Authority?

In the early sixteenth century, Nicolaus Copernicus (1473–1543) proposed the theory that, contrary to accepted views of a stable earth around which sun and other planets revolve, the earth was one of several planets that turn around a stationary sun. A hundred years after Copernicus, an Italian mathematician, astronomer, and physicist named Galileo Galilei (1564–1642), heard about a new invention—the telescope—that could be used to observe what went on in the skies. After building his own telescope, Galileo found that the surface of the moon was irregular, not smooth; discovered the satellites of Jupiter and the rings of Saturn; observed spots on the sun; and became convinced Copernicus was right. The implications of Galileo's discoveries, which challenged accepted philosophy and

Excerpts from *Discoveries and Opinions of Galileo*, tr. by Stillman Drake, © 1957 by Stillman Drake. Reprinted by permission of Bantam, Doubleday, Dell, pp. 175–183, 190.

beliefs, were soon denounced as blasphemous. To defend himself, Galileo wrote a number of public letters. Excerpts from one of these, written in 1615 and addressed to the grand duchess of Tuscany, wife of his patron, follow. Neither Galileo's arguments nor his scientific data prevented Copernicanism from being declared "false and erroneous" or Copernicus's works from being placed on the Index *of prohibited books. Galileo, who continued to discuss the world system as he saw it, was eventually brought to trial on suspicion of heresy in 1633 and was forced to recant his views. He spent the last years of his life under house arrest on his estate near Florence, busily corresponding with scientists all over Europe and developing views that even condemnation could not prevent from being right.*

Some years ago, as Your Serene Highness well knows, I discovered in the heavens many things that had not been seen before our own age. The novelty of these things, as well as some consequences which followed from them in contradiction to the physical notions commonly held among academic philosophers, stirred up against me no small number of professors—as if I had placed these things in the sky with my own hands in order to upset nature and overturn the sciences. They seemed to forget that the increase of known truths stimulates the investigation, establishment, and growth of the arts; not their diminution or destruction.

Showing a greater fondness for their own opinions than for truth, they sought to deny and disprove the new things which, if they had cared to look for themselves, their own senses would have demonstrated to them. To this end they hurled various charges and published numerous writings filled with vain arguments, and they made the grave mistake of sprinkling these with passages taken from places in the Bible which they had failed to understand properly, and which were ill suited to their purposes.

. . . Men who were well grounded in astronomical and physical science were persuaded as soon as they received my first message. There were others who denied them or remained in doubt only because of their novel and unexpected character, and because they had not yet had the opportunity to see for themselves. These men have by degrees come to be satisfied. But some, besides allegiance to their original error, possess I know not what fanciful interest in remaining hostile not so much toward the things in question as toward their discoverer. No longer being able to deny them, these men now take refuge in obstinate silence, but being more than ever exasperated by that which has pacified and quieted other men, they divert their thoughts to other fancies and seek new ways to damage me.

. . . Possibly because they are disturbed by the known truth of other propositions of mine which differ from those commonly held, and therefore mistrusting their defense so long as they confine themselves to the field of philosophy, these men have resolved to fabricate a shield for their fallacies out of the mantle of pretended religion and the authority of the Bible. These they apply, with little judgment, to the refutation of arguments that they do not understand and have not even listened to.

First they have endeavored to spread the opinion that such propositions in general are contrary to the Bible and are consequently damnable and heretical. . . . Hence they have had no trouble in finding men who would preach the damnability and heresy of the new doctrine from their very pulpits with unwonted confidence, thus doing impious and inconsiderate injury not only to that doctrine and its followers but to all mathematics and mathematicians in general.

. . . They go about invoking the Bible, which they would have minister to their deceitful purposes. Contrary to the sense of the Bible and the intention of the holy [Church] Fathers, if I am not mistaken, they would extend such authorities until even in purely physical matters—where faith is not involved—they would have us altogether abandon reason and the evidence of our senses in favor of some biblical passage, though under the surface meaning of its words this passage may contain a different sense.

I hope to show that I proceed with much greater piety than they do, when I argue not against condemning this book, but against condemning it in the way they suggest— that is, without understanding it, weighing it, or so much as reading it. For Copernicus never discusses matters of religion or faith, nor does he use arguments that depend in any way upon the authority of sacred writings which he might have interpreted erroneously. He stands always upon physical conclusions pertaining to the celestial motions, and deals with them by astronomical and geometrical demonstrations, founded primarily upon sense experiences and very exact observations. He did not ignore the Bible, but he knew very well that if his doctrine were proved, then it could not contradict the Scriptures when they were rightly understood.

. . . The reason produced for condemning the opinion that the earth moves and the sun stands still is that in many places in the Bible one may read that the sun moves and the earth stands still. Since the Bible cannot err, it follows as a necessary consequence that anyone takes an erroneous and heretical position who maintains that the sun is inherently motionless and the earth movable.

With regard to this argument, I think in the first place that it is very pious to say and prudent to affirm that the holy Bible can never speak untruth—whenever its true meaning is understood. But I believe nobody will deny that it is often very abstruse, and may say things which are quite different from what its bare words signify. Hence in expounding the Bible if one were always to confine oneself to the unadorned grammatical meaning, one might fall into error.

. . . Now the Bible, merely to condescend to popular capacity, has not hesitated to obscure some very important pronouncements, attributing to God himself some qualities extremely remote from (and even contrary to) His essence. Who, then, would positively declare that this principle has been set aside, and the Bible has confined itself rigorously to the bare and restricted sense of its words, when speaking but casually of the earth, of water, of the sun, or of any other created thing? Especially in view of the fact that these things in no way concern the primary purpose of the sacred writings, which is the service of God and the salvation of souls—matters infinitely beyond the comprehension of the common people.

This being granted, I think that in discussions of physical problems we ought to begin not from the authority of scriptural passages, but from sense-experiences and necessary demonstrations. . . . Nothing physical which sense-experience sets before our eyes, or which necessary demonstrations prove to us, ought to be called in question (much less condemned) upon the testimony of biblical passages which may have some different meaning beneath their words.

. . . I do not feel obliged to believe that that same God who has endowed us with senses, reason, and intellect has intended to forgo their use and by some other means to give us knowledge which we can attain by them. He would not require us to deny sense and reason in physical matters which are set before our eyes and minds by direct experience or necessary demonstrations.

. . . It is obvious that such [anti-Copernican] authors, not having penetrated the true sense of Scripture, would impose upon others an obligation to subscribe to conclusions that are repugnant to manifest reason and sense, if they had any authority to do so. God forbid that this sort of abuse should gain countenance and authority, for then in a short time it would be necessary to proscribe all the contemplative sciences. People who are unable to understand perfectly both the Bible and the sciences far outnumber those who do understand. The former, glancing superficially through the Bible, would arrogate to themselves the authority to decree upon every question of physics on the strength of some word which they have misunderstood, and which was employed by the sacred authors for some different purpose. And the smaller number of understanding men could not dam up the furious torrent of such people, who would gain the majority of followers simply because it is much more pleasant to gain a reputation for wisdom without effort or study than to consume oneself tirelessly in the most laborious disciplines.

René Descartes: from The Discourse upon Method

René Descartes (1596–1650) was a versatile French philosopher and mathematician. Not only did he criss-cross Europe as a soldier during some of the campaigns connected with the Thirty Years' War, he made several important scientific discoveries as well. His meditations ruined the medieval scholastic methods and laid the foundations for modern philosophy by suggesting a new principle for the use of reason in metaphysical matters. This method, generally known as Cartesianism, is summarized as follows: "In order to get at truth, we must at least once in a lifetime get rid of all received [accepted] opinions, and reconstruct completely afresh, from the ground up, all the systems of our knowledge."

Descartes's work reflects a newly critical attitude to evidence and to ideas. Doubt had existed before: a hundred years earlier, Montaigne had represented the amiable but unconstructive doubt of the worldly-wise skeptic. But now doubt was to be used rationally, according to critical rules of evidence which would serve as an instrument of knowledge. This was the time when scientific attitudes were born, with William Harvey in medicine, Richard Simon in biblical exegesis, and Mabillon in historical criticism presenting the typical attitudes of the future.

PART FIRST

. . . My design is not to point out the method which everyone must follow for the right direction of his understanding, but merely to show how I have attempted to

From *The Philosophy of Descartes*, tr. Henry A. P. Torrey (New York, 1892), pp. 37–49.

conduct my own. Those who take it upon themselves to give precepts to others must assume that they are themselves better instructed than those to whom they give them, and if they make the least error, they are answerable for it. But as I offer this production merely as a piece of personal history, or of fiction, if you please, in which, among some examples which may well be imitated, there will be found, perhaps, many others also which one might reasonably decline to follow, I hope that it may prove useful to some and harmful to none, and that all will take my frankness kindly.

I was brought up to letters from my childhood, and because I was led to believe that by means of them clear and certain knowledge of all that was useful in life might be acquired, I had an extreme desire for learning. But no sooner had I completed the whole course of studies at the end of which it is customary for one to be received into the circle of the learned, than I changed my opinion entirely. For I found myself involved in so many doubts and errors, that it seemed to me that I had derived no other advantage from my endeavors to instruct myself but only to find out more and more how ignorant I was. And yet I was in one of the most celebrated schools in Europe, where I thought there must be learned men if there were any such in the world. I had acquired all that others learned there, and more than that, not being content with the sciences which were taught us, I ran through all the books I could get hold of which treated of matters considered most curious and rare. Moreover, I knew what others thought about me, and I did not perceive that they considered me inferior to my fellow-students, albeit there were among them some who were destined to fill the places of our masters. And finally, our time appeared to me to be as flourishing and as prolific of good minds as any preceding time had been. Such considerations emboldened me to judge all others by myself, and served to convince me that there did not exist in the world any such wisdom as I had been led to hope for. However, I did not cease to think well of scholastic pursuits. I knew that the languages taught in the schools were indispensable for the understanding of the ancient books; that light and graceful stories stimulate the mind; that the memorable deeds of history exalt it, and that when read with discretion they help to form the judgment; that the reading of all good books is like conversation with the noble men of bygone times—a studied conversation, even, in which only their best thoughts are disclosed. . . . But I thought I had already given time enough to languages and to the literature of the ancients, to their histories and to their fables. To talk with men of other times is like traveling. It is well to know something of the manners of foreign peoples, in order that we may judge our own more wisely, and that we may not suppose that what is different from our own habits is ridiculous and contrary to reason, as those do who have not seen the world. But if one spends too much time in traveling in foreign countries, he becomes at last a stranger in his own; and when one is too curious to know what has been done in past ages, he is liable to remain ignorant of what is going on in his own time. Moreover, fiction represents many events as possible which are not so; and even the most faithful histories, if they do not deviate from truth nor dignify events to make them more impressive, at least they almost always omit the meaner and the less illustrious incidents, so that it comes about that the rest is not what it really was, and those who govern their conduct by the examples there furnished are liable to fall into the extravagances of the paladins of our romances, and to conceive designs which surpass their ability. . . .

Above all I was delighted with the mathematics, on account of the certainty and evidence of their demonstrations, but I had not as yet found out their true use, and although I supposed that they were of service only in the mechanic arts, I was surprised that upon foundations so solid and stable no loftier structure had been raised: while, on the other hand, I compared the writings of the ancient moralists to palaces very proud and very magnificent, but which are built on nothing but sand or mud. . . . I revered our theology, and, as much as anyone, I strove to gain heaven; but when I learned, as an assured fact, that the way is open no less to the most ignorant than to the most learned, and that the revealed truths which conduct us thither lie beyond the reach of our intelligence, I did not presume to submit them to the feebleness of my reasonings, and I thought that, to undertake the examination of them and succeed in the attempt, required extraordinary divine assistance and more than human gifts. I had nothing to say of philosophy, save that, seeing it had been cultivated by the best minds for many ages, and still there was nothing in it which might not be brought into dispute, and which was, therefore, not free from doubt, I had not the presumption to hope for better success therein than others; and considering how many diverse opinions may be held upon the same subject and defended by the learned, while not more than one of them can be true, I regarded as pretty nearly false all that was merely probable. Then, as to the other sciences which derive their principles from philosophy, I judged that nothing solid could be built upon foundations so unstable; and neither the fame nor the emolument they promised me were sufficient to induce me to acquire them; for, thanks to a kind Providence, I did not find myself in a condition of life which required me to make science a profession for the bettering of my estate; and although I did not profess to despise fame, like a cynic, still I thought very little of that which I could not hope to acquire except on false pretenses. And finally, as for the pseudo-sciences, I thought I was already sufficiently acquainted with their value to be proof against the promises of the alchemist, the predictions of the astrologer, the impostures of the magician, the artifices and vain boasting of those who profess to know more than they actually do know.

For these reasons, so soon as I was old enough to be no longer subject to the control of my teachers, I abandoned literary pursuits altogether, and, being resolved to seek no other knowledge than that which I was able to find within myself or in the great book of the world, I spent the remainder of my youth in traveling, in seeing courts and armies, in mingling with people of various dispositions and conditions in life, in collecting a variety of experiences, putting myself to the proof in the crises of fortune, and reflecting on all occasions on whatever might present itself, so as to derive from it what profit I might. For it appeared to me that I might find a great deal more of truth in reasonings such as everyone carries on with reference to the affairs which immediately concern himself, and where the issue will bring speedy punishment if he make a mistake, than in those which a man of letters conducts in his private study with regard to speculations, which have no other effect and are of no further consequence to him than to tickle his vanity the less they are understood by common people, and the more they require wit and skill to make them seem probable. And I always had an extreme desire to learn how to distinguish the true from the false, so that I might see clearly and proceed with assurance in the affairs of this present life.

It is true that while I employed myself only in observing the manners of foreigners, I found very little to establish my mind, and saw as much diversity here as I had seen before in the opinions of philosophers. So that the principal benefit I derived from it was that, observing many things which, although they appear to us to be very extravagant and ridiculous, are yet commonly received and approved by other great peoples, I gradually became emancipated from many errors which tend to obscure the natural light within us, and make us less capable of listening to reason. But after I had spent some years thus in studying in the book of the world, and trying to gain some experience, I formed one day the resolution to study within myself, and to devote all the powers of my mind to choosing the paths which I must thereafter follow; a project attended with much greater success, as I think, than it would have been had I never left my country nor my books.

PART SECOND

I was then in Germany, whither the wars, which were not yet ended there, had summoned me; and when I was returning to the army, from the coronation of the emperor, the coming on of the winter detained me in a quarter where, finding no one I wished to talk with, and fortunately having no cares nor passions to trouble me, I spent the whole day shut up in a room heated by a stove, where I had all the leisure I desired to hold converse with my own thoughts. One of the first thoughts to occur to me was that there is often less completeness in works made up of many parts and by the hands of different masters than in those upon which only one has labored. Thus we see that buildings which a single architect has undertaken and erected are usually much more beautiful and symmetrical than those which many have tried to reconstruct, using old walls which were built for other purposes.

... And so I thought that the sciences contained in books, at least those in which the proofs were merely probable and not demonstrations, being the gradual accumulation of opinions of many different persons, by no means come so near the truth as the plain reasoning of a man of good sense in regard to the matters which present themselves to him.

And I thought still further that, because we all have been children before we were men, and for a long time of necessity were under the control of our inclinations and our tutors, who were often of different minds, and none of whom perhaps gave us the best of counsels, it is almost impossible that our judgments should be as free from error and as solid as they would have been if we had had the entire use of our reason from the moment of our birth, and had always been guided by that alone. ...

As for all the opinions which I had accepted up to that time, I was persuaded that I could do no better than get rid of them at once, in order to replace them afterward with better ones, or perhaps with the same, if I should succeed in making them square with reason. And I firmly believed that in this way I should have much greater success in the conduct of my life than if I should build only on the old foundations, and should rely only on the principles which I had allowed myself to be persuaded of in my youth, without ever having examined whether they were true. ...

My design has never reached further than the attempt to reform my own opinions, and to build upon a foundation altogether my own. But although I am well enough pleased with my work to present you here a sketch of it, I would not on that account advise anyone to imitate me. . . . The simple resolution to strip one's self of all that he has hitherto believed is not an example for everyone to follow. . . .

But having discovered while at college that there is nothing whatever so strange or incredible that has not been said by some philosopher; and afterward, in my travels, having observed that not all those who cherish opinions quite contrary to our own are therefore barbarians or savages, but that many of these peoples use their reason as well or better than we do; and having considered how differently the same man, with the same mind, would turn out, if he were brought up from infancy among the French or the Germans, from what he would if he always lived among the Chinese or with cannibals; and observing how, even in fashions of dress, the same thing which pleased us ten years ago, and, it may be, will please us again ten years hence, appears to us now extravagant and ridiculous; so that it is rather custom and example than certain knowledge which persuades us; and yet a plurality of votes is no proof that a thing is true, especially where truths are difficult of discovery, in which case it is much more likely that a man left to himself will find them out sooner than people in general—taking all these things into consideration, and not being able to select anyone whose opinions seemed to me to be preferable to those of others, I found myself, as it were, compelled to take myself as my guide. But like a man who walks alone and in the dark, I resolved to go so slowly and to use so much caution in everything, that, even if I did not get on very far, I should at least keep from falling. Likewise I was unwilling at the start to reject summarily any opinion which might have insinuated itself into my belief without having been introduced there by reason, but I would first spend time enough to draw up a plan of the work I was undertaking and to discover the true method for arriving at the knowledge of whatever my mind was capable of.

I had studied, in earlier years, of the branches of philosophy, logic, and in mathematics, geometrical analysis and algebra, three arts or sciences which seemed likely to afford some assistance to my design. But on examination of them I observed, in respect to logic, that its syllogisms and the greater part of its processes are of service principally in explaining to another what one already knows himself, or, like the art of Lully, they enable him to talk without judgment on matters in which he is ignorant, rather than help him to acquire knowledge of them; and while it contains in reality many very true and very excellent precepts, there are nevertheless mixed with these many others which are either harmful or superfluous, and which are almost as difficult to separate from the rest as to draw forth a Diana or a Minerva from a block of marble which is not yet rough-hewn. . . . For this reason I thought that some other method should be sought out which, comprising the advantages of these three, should be exempt from their defects. And as a multiplicity of laws often furnishes excuses for vices, so that a state is best governed which has but few and those strictly obeyed; in like manner, in place of the multitude of precepts of which logic is composed, I believed I should find the four following rules quite sufficient, provided I should firmly and steadfastly resolve not to fail of observing them in a single instance.

The first rule was never to receive anything as a truth which I did not clearly know to be such; that is, to avoid haste and prejudice, and not to comprehend anything more in my judgments than that which should present itself so clearly and so distinctly to my mind that I should have no occasion to entertain a doubt of it.

The second rule was to divide every difficulty which I should examine into as many parts as possible, or as might be required for resolving it.

The third rule was to conduct my thoughts in an orderly manner, beginning with objects the most simple and the easiest to understand, in order to ascend as it were by steps to the knowledge of the most composite, assuming some order to exist even in things which did not appear to be naturally connected.

The last rule was to make enumerations so complete, and reviews so comprehensive, that I should be certain of omitting nothing.

Those long chains of reasoning, quite simple and easy, which geometers are wont to employ in the accomplishment of their most difficult demonstrations, led me to think that everything which might fall under the cognizance of the human mind might be connected together in a similar manner, and that, provided only one should take care not to receive anything as true which was not so, and if one were always careful to preserve the order necessary for deducing one truth from another, there would be none so remote at which he might not at last arrive, nor so concealed which he might not discover. . . .

And I am free to say that the exact observance of these few rules which I had laid down gave me such facility in solving all the questions to which these two sciences apply, that in the two or three months which I spent in examining them, having begun with the simplest and most general, and each truth that I discovered being a rule which was of service to me afterward in the discovery of others, not only did I arrive at many which formerly I had considered very difficult, but it seemed to me, toward the end, that I was able to determine even in those matters where I was ignorant by what means and how far it would be possible to resolve them. In this I shall not appear to you to be very vain, perhaps, if you will only consider that there is, in respect to each case, but one truth, and that he who finds it knows as much about it as anyone can know; as, for example, a child, who has learned arithmetic, when he has made an addition according to the rules, can be assured that he has found out, in respect to the sum that he has computed, all that it is possible for the human mind to discover. Because, in a word, the method which shows one how to follow the true order, and to take account exactly of all the circumstances of the subject under investigation, contains all that which gives certitude to the rules of arithmetic. But that which pleased me most in this method was the fact that by means of it I was using my reason in everything, if not perfectly, yet in a manner the very best in my power. . . .

PART FOURTH

I am in doubt as to the propriety of making my first meditations in the place above mentioned a matter of discourse; for these are so metaphysical, and so uncommon, as not, perhaps, to be acceptable to every one. And yet, that it may be determined whether the foundations that I have laid are sufficiently secure, I find myself in a measure constrained to advert to them. I had long before remarked that, in relation to practice, it is sometimes necessary to adopt, as if above doubt, opinions which we discern to be highly uncertain, as had been already said; but as I then desired to give my attention solely to the search after truth, I thought that a procedure exactly the opposite was called for, and that I ought to reject as absolutely false all opinions in regard to which I could suppose the least ground for doubt, in order to ascertain whether after that there remained aught in my belief that was wholly indubitable. Accordingly, seeing that our senses sometimes deceive us, I was willing to suppose that there existed nothing really such as they presented to us; and because some men err in reasoning, and fall into paralogisms, even on the simplest matters of Geometry, I, convinced that I was as open to error as any other, rejected as false all the reasonings I had hitherto taken for demonstrations; and finally, when I considered that the very same thoughts [presentations] which we experience when awake may also be experienced when we are asleep, while there is at that time not one of them true, I supposed that all the objects [presentations] that had ever entered into my mind when awake, had in them no more truth than the illusions of my dreams. But immediately upon this I observed that, whilst I thus wished to think that all was false, it was absolutely necessary that I, who thus thought, should be somewhat; and as I observed that this truth, *I think, hence I am,* was so certain and of such evidence, that no ground of doubt, however extravagant, could be alleged by the Sceptics capable of shaking it, I concluded that I might, without scruple, accept it as the first principle of the Philosophy of which I was in search.

In the next place, I attentively examined what I was, and as I observed that I could suppose that I had no body, and that there was no world nor any place in which I might be; but that I could not therefore suppose that I was not; and that, on the contrary, from the very circumstance that I thought no doubt of the truth of other things, it most clearly and certainly followed that I was; while, on the other hand, if I had only ceased to think, although all the other objects which I had ever imagined had been in reality existent, I would have had no reason to believe that I existed; I thence concluded that I was a substance whose whole essence or nature consists only in thinking, and which, that it may exist, has need of no place, nor is dependent on any material thing; so that "I," that is to say, the mind by which I am what I am, is wholly distinct from the body, and is even more easily known than the latter, and is such, that although the latter were not, it would still continue to be all that it is.

After this I inquired in general into what is essential to the truth and certainty of a proposition; for since I had discovered one which I knew to be true, I thought that I must likewise be able to discover the ground of this certitude. And as I observed that in the words *I think, hence I am,* there is nothing at all which gives me assurance of their truth beyond this, that I see very clearly that in order to think it is necessary to exist, I concluded that I might take, as a general rule, the principle, that all the things which we very clearly and distinctly conceive are true, only observing, however, that there is some difficulty in rightly determining the objects which we distinctly conceive.

In the next place, from reflecting on the circumstance that I doubted, and that consequently my being was not wholly perfect, (for I clearly saw that it was a greater perfection to know than to doubt,) I was led to inquire whence I had learned to think of something more perfect than myself; and I clearly recognised that I must hold this notion from some Nature which in reality was more perfect. As for the thoughts of many other objects external to me, as of the sky, the earth, light, heat, and a thousand more, I was less at a loss to know whence these came; for since I remarked in them nothing which seemed to render them superior to myself, I could believe that, if these were true, they were dependencies on my own nature, in so far as it possessed a certain perfection, and, if they were false, that I held them from nothing, that is to say, that they were in me because of a certain imperfection of my nature. But this could not be the case with the idea of a Nature more perfect than myself; for to receive it from nothing was a thing manifestly impossible; and, because it is not less repugnant that the more perfect should be an effect of, and dependence on the less perfect, than that something should proceed from nothing, it was equally impossible that I could hold it from myself: accordingly, it but remained that it had been placed in me by a Nature which was in reality more perfect than mine, and which even possessed within itself all the perfections of which I could form any idea; that is to say, in a single word, which was God. And to this I added that, since I knew some perfections which I did not possess, I was not the only being in existence, (I will here, with your permission, freely use the terms of the schools;) but, on the contrary, that there was of necessity some other more perfect Being upon whom I was dependent, and from whom I had received all that I possessed; for if I had existed alone, and independently of every other being, so as to have had from myself all the perfection, however little, which I actually possessed, I should have been able, for the same reason, to have had from myself the whole remainder of perfection, of the want of which I was conscious, and thus could of myself have become infinite, eternal, immutable, omniscient, all-powerful, and, in fine, have possessed all the perfections which I could recognise in God. For in order to know the nature of God, (whose existence has been established by the preceding reasonings,) as far as my own nature permitted, I had only to consider in reference to all the properties of which I found in my mind some idea, whether their possession was a mark of perfection; and I was assured that no one which indicated any imperfection was in him, and that none of the rest was wanting. Thus I perceived that doubt, inconstancy, sadness, and such like, could not be found in God, since I myself would have been happy to be free from them. Besides, I had ideas of many sensible and corporeal things; for although I might suppose that I was dreaming, and that all which I saw or imagined was false, I could not, nevertheless, deny that the ideas were in reality in my thoughts. But, because I had already very clearly recognised in myself that the intelligent nature is distinct from the corporeal, and as I observed that all composition is an evidence of dependency, and that a state of dependency is manifestly a state of imperfection, I therefore determined that it could not be a perfection in God to be compounded of these two natures, and that consequently he was not so compounded; but that if there were any bodies in the world, or even any intelligences, or other natures that were not wholly perfect, their existence depended on his power in such a way that they could not subsist without him for a single moment.

I was disposed straightway to search for other truths; and when I had represented to myself the object of the geometers, which I conceived to be a continuous body, or a space indefinitely extended in length, breadth, and height or depth, divisible into divers parts which admit of different figures and sizes, and of being moved or transposed in all manner of ways, (for all this the geometers suppose to be in the object they contemplate,) I went over some of their simplest demonstrations. And, in the first place, I observed, that the great certitude which by common consent is accorded to these demonstrations, is founded solely upon this, that they are clearly conceived in accordance with the rules I have already laid down. In the next place, I perceived that there was nothing at all in these demonstrations which could assure me of the existence of their object: thus, for example, supposing a triangle to be given, I distinctly perceived that its three angles were necessarily equal to two right angles, but I did not on that account perceive anything which could assure me that any triangle existed: while, on the contrary, recurring to the examination of the idea of a Perfect Being, I found that the existence of the Being was comprised in the idea in the same way that the equality of its three angles to two right angles is comprised in the idea of a triangle, or as in the idea of a sphere, the equidistance of all points on its surface from the centre, or even still more clearly; and that consequently it is at least as certain that God, who is this Perfect Being, is, or exists, as any demonstration of Geometry can be.

But the reason which leads many to persuade themselves that there is a difficulty in knowing this truth, and even also in knowing what their mind really is, is that they never raise their thoughts above sensible objects, and are so accustomed to consider nothing except by way of imagination, which is a mode of thinking limited to material objects, that all that is not imaginable seems to them not intelligible. The truth of this is sufficiently manifest from the single circumstance, that the philosophers of the Schools accept as a maxim that there is nothing in the Understanding which was not previously in the Senses, in which however it is certain that the ideas of God and of the soul have never been; and it appears to me that they who make use of their imagination to comprehend these ideas do exactly the same thing as if, in order to hear sounds or smell odours, they strove to avail themselves of their eyes; unless indeed that there is this difference, that the sense of sight does not afford us an inferior assurance to those of smell or hearing; in place of which, neither our imagination nor our senses can give us assurance of anything unless our Understanding intervene.

Finally, if there be still persons who are not sufficiently persuaded of the existence of God and of the soul, by the reasons I have adduced, I am desirous that they should know that all the other propositions, of the truth of which they deem themselves perhaps more assured, as that we have a body, and that there exist stars and an earth, and such like, are less certain; for, although we have a moral assurance of these things, which is so strong that there is an appearance of extravagance in doubting of their existence, yet at the same time no one, unless his intellect is impaired, can deny, when the question relates to a metaphysical certitude, that there is sufficient reason to exclude entire assurance, in the observation that when asleep we can in the same way imagine ourselves possessed of another body and that we see other stars and another earth, when there is nothing of the kind. For how do we know that the thoughts which occur in dreaming are false rather than those other which we experience when awake, since the former are often not less vivid and distinct than the latter? And though men of the highest genius study this question as long as they please, I do not believe that they will be able to give any reason which can be sufficient to remove this doubt, unless they presuppose the existence of God. For, in the first place, even the principle which I have already taken as a rule, viz., that all the things which we clearly and distinctly conceive are true, is certain only because God is or exists, and because he is a Perfect Being, and because all that we possess is derived from him: whence it follows that our ideas or notions, which to the extent of their clearness and distinctness are real, and proceed from God, must to that extent be true. Accordingly, whereas we not unfrequently have ideas or notions in which some falsity is contained, this can only be the case with such as are to some extent confused and obscure, and in this proceed from nothing, [participate of negation,] that is, exist in us thus confused because we are not wholly perfect. And it is evident that it is not less repugnant that falsity or imperfection, in so far as it is imperfection, should proceed from God, than that truth or perfection should proceed from nothing. But if we did not know that all which we possess of real and true proceeds from a Perfect and Infinite Being, however clear and distinct our ideas might be, we should have no ground on that account for the assurance that they possessed the perfection of being true.

But after the knowledge of God and of the soul has rendered us certain of this rule, we can easily understand that the truth of the thoughts we experience when awake, ought not in the slightest degree to be called in question on account of the illusions of our dreams. For if it happened that an individual, even when asleep, had some very distinct idea, as, for example, if a geometer should discover some new demonstration, the circumstance of his being asleep would not militate against its truth; and as for the most ordinary error of our dreams, which consists in their representing various objects in the same way as our external senses, this is not prejudicial, since it leads us very properly to suspect the truth of the ideas of sense; for we are not unfrequently deceived in the same manner when awake; as when persons in the jaundice see all objects yellow, or when the stars or bodies at a great distance appear to us much smaller than they are. For, in fine, whether awake or asleep, we ought never to allow ourselves to be persuaded of the truth of anything unless on the evidence of our Reason. And it must be noted that I say of our *Reason,* and not of our imagination or of our senses: thus, for example, although we very clearly see the sun, we ought not therefore to determine that it is only of the size which our sense of sight presents; and we may very distinctly imagine the head of a lion joined to the body of a goat, without being therefore shut up to the conclusion that a chimaera exists; for it is not a dictate of Reason that what we thus see or imagine is in reality existent; but it plainly tells us that all our ideas or notions contain in them some truth; for otherwise it could not be that God, who is wholly perfect and veracious, should have placed them in us. And because our reasonings are never so clear or so complete during sleep as when we are awake, although sometimes the acts of our imagination are then as lively and distinct, if not more so than in our waking moments, Reason further dictates that, since all our thoughts cannot be true because of our partial imperfection, those possessing truth must infallibly be found in the experience of our waking moments rather than in that of our dreams.

Isaac Newton: from The Mathematical Principles of Natural Philosophy

Isaac Newton (1642–1727) was perhaps the most illustrious, well-rounded man of the early eighteenth century. Mathematician, physicist, astronomer, philosopher, and amateur

From Isaac Newton, *The Mathematical Principles of Natural Philosophy,* 2 vols. (London, 1803), II, 160–162.

theologian, he discovered the laws of universal gravity and of the decomposition of light, and he disputed with Leibnitz the priority of the differential calculus. The prevailing veneration of the great scientist appears in Alexander Pope's couplet intended for Newton's tomb in Westminster Abbey:

Nature and Nature's laws lay hid in night;
God said, "Let Newton be" and all was light.

For our purpose, we can find no better brief expression of the new scientific approach than in the definition of scientific method that Newton laid down in the great Philosophiae Naturalis Principia Mathematica *of 1687.*

RULES OF REASONING IN PHILOSOPHY

Rule I. *We are to admit no more causes of natural things than such as are both true and sufficient to explain their appearances.*

To this purpose the philosophers say that Nature does nothing in vain, and more is in vain when less will serve; for Nature is pleased with simplicity, and affects not the pomp of superfluous causes.

Rule II. *Therefore to the same natural effects we must, as far as possible, assign the same causes.*

As to respiration in a man and in a beast; the descent of stones in Europe and in America; the light of our culinary fire and of the sun; the reflection of light on the earth, and in the planets.

Rule III. *The qualities of bodies, which admit neither intension nor remission of degrees, and which are found to belong to all bodies within the reach of our experiments, are to be esteemed the universal qualities of all bodies whatsoever.*

For since the qualities of bodies are only known to us by experiments, we are to hold for universal all such as universally agree with experiments and such as are not liable to diminution can never be quite taken away. We are certainly not to relinquish the evidence of experiments for the sake of dreams and vain fictions of our own devising; nor are we to recede from the analogy of Nature, which uses to be simple, and always consonant to itself. We no other way know the extension of bodies than by our senses, nor do these reach it in all bodies; but because we perceive extension in all that are sensible, therefore we ascribe it universally to all others also. That abundance of bodies are hard, we learn by experience; and because the hardness of the whole arises from the hardness of the parts, we therefore justly infer the hardness of the undivided particles not only of the bodies we feel but of all others. That all bodies are impenetrable, we gather not from reason, but from sensation. The bodies which we handle we find impenetrable, and thence conclude impenetrability to be an universal property of all bodies whatsoever. That all bodies are moveable, and endowed with certain powers (which we call the *vires inertiae*) of persevering in their motion, or in their rest, we only infer the like properties observed in the bodies which we have seen. The extension, hardness, impenetrability, mobility, and *vis inertiae* of the whole, result from the extension, hardness, impenetrability, mobility, and *vires inertiae* of the parts; and thence we conclude the least particles of all bodies to be also all extended, and hard, and impenetrable, and moveable, and endowed with their proper *vires inertiae*. And this is the foundation of all philosophy. Moreover, that the divided but contiguous particles of bodies may be separated from one another, is matter of observation; and, in the particles that remain undivided, our minds are able to distinguish yet lesser parts, as is mathematically demonstrated. But whether the parts so distinguished and not yet divided, may, by the powers of Nature, be actually divided and separated from one another, we cannot certainly determine. Yet had we the proof of but one experiment that any undivided particle, in breaking a hard and solid body, suffered a division, we might by virtue of this rule conclude that the undivided as well as the divided particles may be divided and actually separated to infinity.

Lastly, if it universally appears, by experiments and astronomical observations, that all bodies about the earth gravitate towards the earth, and that in proportion to the quantity of matter which they severally contain; that the moon likewise, according to the quantity of its matter, gravitates towards the earth; that, on the other hand, our sea gravitates towards the moon; and all the planets mutually one towards another; and the comets in like manner towards the sun; we must, in consequence of this rule, universally allow that all bodies whatsoever are endowed with a principle of mutual gravitation. For the argument from the appearances concludes with more force for the universal gravitation of all bodies than for their impenetrability; of which, among those in the celestial regions, we have no experiments, nor any manner of observation. Not that I affirm gravity to be essential to bodies: by their *vis infita* I mean nothing but their *vis inertiae*. This is immutable. Their gravity is diminished as they recede from the earth.

Rule IV. *In experimental philosophy we are to look upon propositions collected by general induction from phaenomena as accurately or very nearly true, notwithstanding any contrary hypotheses that may be imagined, till such time as other phaenomena occur, by which they may either be made more accurate, or liable to exceptions.*

This rule must follow, that the argument of induction may not be evaded by hypotheses.

John Locke: from An Essay Concerning Human Understanding

John Locke (1632–1704) was not only a scholar but also a doctor, civil servant, and amateur diplomat. Attached to the powerful Ashley family (the Lords of Shaftesbury) he met some of the greatest men in contemporary English politics (Buckingham, Halifax) and was tutor to the second and the third lords of Shaftesbury. At one time he produced a constitution for the newly founded American colony of Carolina. In exile with his patron in Holland from 1682 to 1688, he returned in the fleet of William of Orange and set himself to provide a philosophical explanation for the dispossession of James II. Two Treatises on Government *resulted; part of one makes up the following excerpt. Locke's fame, however, rests primarily on his philosophical writings, chief of which is the* Essay Concerning Human

From John Locke, *An Essay Concerning Human Understanding* (London, 1881), pp. 59–61; 424.

Understanding, *published in 1690. It is divided into four books: the first discusses innate ideas and concludes that they do not exist; the second deals with the origin of ideas; the third addresses language; and the fourth lays down the limit of human understanding. Only two brief passages from books one and four are given here.*

OF IDEAS IN GENERAL, AND THEIR ORIGIN

1. Idea is the object of thinking.—Every man being conscious to himself, that he thinks, and that which his mind is applied about, whilst thinking, being the ideas that are there, it is past doubt that men have in their mind several ideas, such as are those expressed by the words, "whiteness, hardness, sweetness, thinking, motion, man, elephant, army, drunkenness," and others. It is in the first place then to be inquired, How he comes by them? I know it is a received doctrine, that men have native ideas and original characters stamped upon their minds in their very first being. This opinion I have at large examined already; and, I suppose, what I have shown whence the understanding may get all the ideas it has, and by what ways and degrees they may come into the mind; for which I shall appeal to every one's own observation and experience.

2. All ideas come from sensation or reflection.—Let us then suppose the mind to be, as we say, white paper, void of all characters, without any ideas; how comes it to be furnished? Whence comes it by that vast store, which the busy and boundless fancy of man has painted on it with an almost endless variety? Whence has it all the materials of reason and knowledge? To this I answer, in one word, From experience: in that all our knowledge is founded, and from that it ultimately derives itself. Our observation, employed either about external sensible objects, or about the internal operations of our minds, perceived and reflected on by ourselves, is that which supplies our understandings with all the materials of thinking. These two are the fountains of knowledge, from whence all the ideas we have, or can naturally have, do spring.

3. The object of sensation one source of ideas.—First. Our senses, conversant about particular sensible objects, do convey into the mind several distinct perceptions of things, according to those various ways wherein those objects do affect them; and thus we come by those ideas we have of yellow, white heat, cold, soft, hard, bitter, sweet, and all those which we call sensible qualities; which when I say the senses convey into the mind, I mean they from external objects convey into the mind what produces there those perceptions. The great source of most of the ideas we have, depending wholly upon our senses, and derived by them to the understanding, I call "sensation."

4. The operations of our minds the other source of them.—Secondly. The other fountain, from which experience furnisheth the understanding with ideas, is the perception of the operations of our own minds within us, as it is employed about the ideas it has got; which operations, when the soul comes to reflect on and consider, do furnish the understanding with another set of ideas which could not be had

from things without; and such are perception, thinking, doubting, believing, reasoning, knowing, willing, and all the different actings of our own minds; which we, being conscious of, and observing in ourselves, do from these receive into our understanding as distinct ideas, as we do from bodies affecting our senses. This source of ideas every man has wholly in himself; and though it be not sense as having nothing to do with external objects, yet it is very like it, and might properly enough be called "internal sense." But as I call the other "sensation," so I call this "reflection," the ideas it affords being such only as the mind gets by reflecting on its own operations within itself. By reflection, then, in the following part of this discourse, I would be understood to mean that notice which the mind takes of its own operations, and the manner of them, by reason whereof there come to be ideas of these operations in the understanding. These two, I say, viz., external material things as the objects of sensation, and the operations of our own minds within as the objects of reflection, are, to me, the only originals from whence all our ideas take their beginnings. The term "operations" here, I use in a large sense, as comprehending not barely the actions of the mind about its ideas, but some sort of passions arising sometimes from them, such as is the satisfaction or uneasiness arising from any thought.

5. All our ideas are of the one or the other of these.—The understanding seems to me not to have the least glimmering of any ideas which it doth not receive from one of these two. External objects furnish the mind with the ideas of sensible qualities, which are all those different perceptions they produce in us; and the mind furnishes the understanding with ideas of its own operations.

These, when we have taken a full survey of them, and their several modes, combinations, and relations, we shall find to contain all our whole stock of ideas; and that we have nothing in our minds which did not come in one of these two ways. Let any one examine his own thoughts, and thoroughly search into his understanding, and then let him tell me, whether all the original ideas he has there, are any other than of the objects of his senses, or of the operations of his mind considered as objects of his reflection; and how great a mass of knowledge soever he imagines to be lodged there, he will, upon taking a strict view, see that he has not any idea in his mind but what one of these two hath imprinted, though perhaps with infinite variety compounded and enlarged by the understanding, as we shall see hereafter. . . .

OF KNOWLEDGE IN GENERAL

1. Our knowledge conversant about our ideas.—Since the mind, in all its thoughts and reasonings, hath no other immediate object but its own ideas, which it alone does or can contemplate, it is evident that our knowledge is only conversant about them.

2. Knowledge is the perception of the agreement or disagreement of two ideas.— Knowledge then seems to me to be nothing but the perception of the connection and agreement or disagreement and repugnancy, of any of our ideas. In this alone

it consists. Where this perception is, there is knowledge; and where it is not, there, though we may fancy, guess, or believe, yet we always come short of knowledge. For, when we know that white is not black, what do we else but perceive that these two ideas do not agree? When we possess ourselves with the utmost security of the demonstration that the three angles of a triangle are equal to two right ones, what do we more but perceive that equality to two right ones does necessarily agree to, and is inseparable from the three angles of a triangle?

3. This agreement fourfold.—But to understand a little more distinctly, wherein this agreement or disagreement consists, I think we may reduce it all to these four sorts: (1.) Identity, or diversity. (2.) Relation. (3.) Co-existence, or necessary connection. (4.) Real existence. . . .

Witch-Hunting

As mentioned earlier, the high intellectual caliber of the era did nothing to banish the prevalence of witches, something that seems to have troubled Europe since the high Middle Ages. Superstition was rife, but superstition went hand in hand with faith. As the eminent seventeenth-century minister Joseph Glanvill pointed out, if you do not believe in witches you do not believe in spirits; if you do not believe in spirits, you do not believe in angels; if you do not believe in angels, you do not believe in God. Since all believed in God, all believed in devils and their fellow traveling witches. The persecution of the devil's fifth column on earth culminated in a series of semihysterical panics that terrorized western Europe from Scotland to Bohemia and even impinged on the attention of Cardinal de Richelieu (see A. Huxley, The Devils of Loudun*) and Louis XIV, one of whose mistresses, Mme. de Montespan, was involved in a lurid and complicated scandal.*

Persecutions for witchcraft continued to take place through most of the eighteenth century. In England the last execution for this crime seems to have been carried out in 1684, but in Scotland a woman was burned as a witch as late as 1727. European countries were slower to lose the habit: in 1749, a high-born nun was executed for witchcraft at Würzburg; six years later, a young adventurer called Casanova was imprisoned by the Inquisition at Venice on a charge of magic, but escaped. He was luckier than the two witches burned in Glarus, Switzerland, in 1782 and the two who suffered a similar fate in Poland eleven years later, when the revolution had already triumphed in France. But these were the last, it would seem: witches and the fear of witches endured, but the growth of skepticism meant that the law and authorities no longer countenanced superstition. John Wesley had foreseen the dire consequences of such skeptical tolerance: "It is true," he noted in 1768 in his Journal *(Vol. V, p. 375), "that the English have given up all accounts of witches and apparitions as mere old wives' fables. I am sorry for it. . . . Infidels have hooted witchcraft out of the world. . . . They well know (whether Christians know it or not) that the giving up of witchcraft is in effect giving up the Bible." However, we know that such dangerous skepticism did not long endure; like the poor, witches of one sort or another are always with us.*

The first and briefest of the selections that follow relates to the witch-hunts that took place in the second half of the sixteenth century in the domains of the elector-archbishop of Trier in the Rhineland. The subsequent selections are self-explanatory.

The Witch-Persecution at Trier

Inasmuch as it was popularly believed that the continued sterility of many years was caused by witches through the malice of the Devil, the whole country rose to exterminate the witches. This movement was promoted by many in office, who hoped for wealth from the persecution. And so, from court to court throughout the towns and villages of all the diocese, scurried special accusers, inquisitors, notaries, jurors, judges, constables, dragging to trial and torture human beings of both sexes and burning them in great numbers. Scarcely any of those who were accused escaped punishment. Nor were there spared even the leading men in the city of Trier. For the Judge, with two Burgomasters, several Councilors and Associate Judges, canons of sundry collegiate churches, parish-priests, rural deans, were swept away in this ruin. So far, at length, did the madness of the furious populace and of the courts go in this thirst for blood and booty that there was scarcely anybody who was not smirched by some suspicion of this crime.

Meanwhile notaries, copyists, and inn-keepers grew rich. The executioner rode a blooded horse, like a noble of the court, and went clad in gold and silver; his wife vied with noble dames in the richness of her array. The children of those convicted and punished were sent into exile; their goods were confiscated; plowman and vintner failed—hence came sterility. A direr pestilence or a more ruthless invader could hardly have ravaged the territory of Trier than this inquisition and persecution without bounds: many were the reasons for doubting that all were really guilty. This persecution lasted for several years; and some of those who presided over the administration of justice gloried in the multitude of the stakes, at each of which a human being had been given to the flames.

At last, though the flames were still unsated, the people grew impoverished, rules were made and enforced restricting the fees and costs of examinations and examiners, and suddenly, as when in war funds fail, the zeal of the persecutors died out.

The Witch-Persecution at Bamberg

On Wednesday, June 28, 1628, was examined without torture, Johannes Junius, Burgomaster at Bamberg, on the charge of witchcraft: how and in what fashion he had fallen into that vice. Is fifty-five years old, and was born at Niederwaysich in the Wetterau. Says he is wholly innocent, knows nothing of the crime, has never in his life renounced

All witch-hunting documents are from *Translations and Reprints*, Vol. 3, No. 4, G. L. Burr, Ed.

God; says that he is wronged before God and the world, would like to hear of a single human being who has seen him at such gatherings [as the witches' Sabbath].

Confrontation of Dr. Georg Adam Haan. Tells him to his face he will stake his life on it [*er wolle darauf leben und sterben*], that he saw him, Junius, a year and a half ago at a witch-gathering in the electoral council-room, where they ate and drank. Accused denies the same wholly.

Confronted with Hopffens Elsse. Tells him likewise that he was on Haupts-moor at a witch-dance; but first the holy wafer was desecrated. Junius denies. Hereupon he was told that his accomplices had confessed against him and was given time for thought.

On Friday, June 30, 1628, the aforesaid Junius was again without torture exhorted to confess, but again confessed nothing, whereupon, . . . since he would confess nothing, he was put to the torture, and first the

Thumb-screws were applied. Says he has never denied God his Savior nor suffered himself to be otherwise baptized; will again stake his life on it; feels no pain in the thumb-screws.

Leg-screws. Will confess absolutely nothing; knows nothing about it. He has never renounced God; will never do such a thing; has never been guilty of this vice; feels likewise no pain.

Is stripped and examined; on his right side is found a bluish mark, like a clover leaf, is thrice pricked therein, but feels no pain and no blood flows out.

Strappado. He has never renounced God; God will not forsake him; if he were such a wretch he would not let himself be so tortured; God must show some token of his innocence. He knows nothing about witchcraft. . . .

On July 5, the above named Junius is without torture, but with urgent persuasions, exhorted to confess, and at last begins and confesses:

When in the year 1624 his law-suit at Rothweil cost him some six hundred florins, he had gone out, in the month of August, into his orchard at Friedrichsbronnen; and, as he sat there in thought, there had come to him a woman like a grass-maid, who had asked him why he sat there so sorrowful; he had answered that he was not despondent, but she had led him by seductive speeches to yield him to her will. . . . And thereafter this wench had changed into the form of a goat, which bleated and said, "Now you see with whom you have had to do. You must be mine or I will forthwith break your neck." Thereupon he had been frightened, and trembled all over for fear. Then the transformed spirit had seized him by the throat and demanded that he should renounce God Almighty, whereupon Junius said, "God forbid," and thereupon the spirit vanished through the power of these words. Yet it came straightway back, brought more people with it, and persistently demanded of him that he renounce God in Heaven and all the heavenly host, by which terrible threatening he was obliged to speak this formula: "I renounce God in Heaven and his host, and will henceforward recognize the Devil as my God."

After the renunciation he was so far persuaded by those present and by the evil spirit that he suffered himself to be otherwise baptized in the evil spirit's name. The Morhauptin had given him a ducat as dower-gold, which afterward became only a potsherd.

He was then named Krix. His paramour he had to call Vixen. Those present had congratulated him in Beelzebub's name and said that they were now all alike. At this baptism of his there were among others the aforesaid Christiana Morhauptin, the young Geiserlin, Paul Glaser, [and others]. After this they had dispersed.

At this time his paramour had promised to provide him with money, and from time to time to take him to other witchgatherings. . . . Whenever he wished to ride forth [to the witches' Sabbath] a black dog had come before his bed, which said to him that he must go with him, whereupon he had seated himself upon the dog and the dog had raised himself in the Devil's name and so had fared forth.

About two years ago he was taken to the electoral council-room, at the left hand as one goes in. Above at a table were seated the Chancellor, the Burgomaster Ney-dekher, Dr. Georg Haan, (and many others). Since his eyes were not good, he could not recognize more persons.

More time for consideration was now given him. On July 7, the aforesaid Junius was again examined, to know what further had occurred to him to confess. He confesses that about two months ago, on the day after an execution was held, he was at a witch-dance at the Black Cross, where Beelzebub had shown himself to them all and said expressly to their faces that they must all be burned together on this spot, and had ridiculed and taunted those present. . . .

Of crimes. His paramour had immediately after his seduction demanded that he should make away with his youngest son Hans Georg, and had given him for this purpose a gray powder; this, however, being too hard for him, he had made away with his horse, a brown, instead.

His paramour had also often spurred him on to kill his daughter . . . and because he would not do this he had been maltreated with blows by the evil spirit.

Once at the suggestion of his paramour he had taken the holy wafer out of his mouth and given it to her. . . .

A week before his arrest as he was going to St. Martin's church the Devil met him on the way in the form of a goat, and told him that he would soon be imprisoned, but that he should not trouble himself—he would soon set him free. Besides this, by his soul's salvation, he knew nothing further; but what he had spoken was the pure truth; on that he would stake his life. On August 6, 1628, there was read to the aforesaid Junius this his confession, which he then wholly ratified and confirmed, and was willing to stake his life upon it. And afterward he voluntarily confirmed the same before the court.

So ended the trial of Junius, and he was accordingly burned at the stake. But it so happens that there is also preserved in Bamberg—in Franconia, southwestern Germany—a letter, in quivering hand, secretly written by him to his daughter while in the midst of his trial (July 24, 1628):

Many hundred thousand good nights, dearly beloved daughter Veronica. Innocent have I come into prison, innocent have I been tortured, innocent must I die. For whoever comes into the witch prison must become a witch or be tortured until he invents something out of his head—and God pity him—bethinks him of something. I will tell you how it has gone with me. When I was the first time put to the torture, Dr. Baum, Dr. Kotzendorffer, and two strange doctors were there. Then Dr. Braun asks me, "Kinsman, how come you here?" I answer, "Through falsehood, through misfortune." "Hear, you," he says, "You are a witch; will you confess it voluntarily? If not, we'll bring in witnesses and the executioner for you." I said, "I am no witch. I have a pure conscience in the matter; if there are a thousand witnesses, I am not anxious, but I'll gladly hear the witnesses." Now the Chancellor's son was set before me . . . and afterward Hopffens Elsse. She had seen me dance on Haupts-moor. . . . I answered: "I have never renounced God, and will never do it—God graciously keep me from it. I'll rather bear whatever I must." And then came also—God in highest Heaven have mercy—the executioner, and put the thumb-screws on me, both hands bound together, so that the blood ran out at the nails and everywhere, so that for four weeks I could not use my hands, as you can see from the writing. . . . Thereafter they first stripped me, bound my hands behind me, and drew me up in the torture. Then I thought heaven and earth were at an end; eight times did they draw me up and let me fall again, so that I suffered terrible agony. . . .

And this happened on Friday, June 30, and with God's help I had to bear the torture. . . . When at last the executioner led me back into the prison, he said to me: "Sir, I beg you, for God's sake confess something, whether it be true or not. Invent something, for you cannot endure the torture which you will be put to; and, even if you bear it all, yet you will not escape, not even if you were an earl, but one torture will follow after another until you say you are a witch. Not before that," he said, "will they let you go, as you may see by all their trials, for one is just like another." . . .

And so I begged, since I was in wretched plight, to be given one day for thought and a priest. The priest was refused me, but the time for thought was given. Now, my dear child, see in what hazard I stood and still stand. I must say that I am a witch, though I am not,—must now renounce God, though I have never done it before. Day and night I was deeply troubled, but at last there came to me a new idea. I would not be anxious, but, since I had been given no priest with whom I could take counsel, I would myself think of something and say it. It were surely better that I just say it with mouth and words, even though I had not really done it; and afterwards I would confess it to the priest, and let those answer for it who compel me to do it. . . . And so I made my confession, as follows; but it was all a lie.

Now follows, dear child, what I confessed in order to escape the great anguish and bitter torture, which it was impossible for me longer to bear.

Here follows his confession, substantially as it is given in the minutes of his trial. But he adds:

Then I had to tell what people I had seen [at the witches' Sabbath]. I said that I had not recognized them. "You old rascal, I must set the executioner at you. Say—was not the Chancellor there?" So I said yes. "Who besides?" I had not recognized anybody. So he said: "Take one street after another; begin at the market, go out on one street and back on the next." I had to name several persons there. Then came the long street. I knew nobody. Had to name eight persons there. Then the Zinkenwert—one person more. Then over the upper bridge to the Georgthor, on both sides. Knew nobody again. Did I know nobody in the castle—whoever it might be, I should speak without fear. And thus continuously they asked me on all the streets, though I could not and would not say more. So they gave me to the executioner, told him to strip me, shave me all over, and put me to the torture. "The rascal knows one on the market-place, is with him daily, and yet won't name him." By that they meant Dietmeyer: so I had to name him too.

Then I had to tell what crimes I had committed. I said nothing. . . . "Draw the rascal up!" So I said that I was to kill my children, but I had killed a horse instead. It did not help. I had also taken a sacred wafer, and had desecrated it. When I had said this, they left me in peace.

Now, dear child, here you have all my confession, for which I must die. And they are sheer lies and made-up things, so help me God. For all this I was forced to say through fear of the torture which was threatened beyond what I had already endured. For they never leave off with the torture till one confesses something; be he never so good, he must be a witch. Nobody escapes, though he were an earl. . . .

Dear child, keep this letter secret so that people do not find it, else I shall be tortured most piteously and the jailers will be beheaded. So strictly is it forbidden. . . . Dear child, pay this man a dollar. . . . I have taken several days to write this: my hands are both lame. I am in a sad plight.

Good night, for your father Johannes Junius will never see you more. July 24, 1628.

And on the margin of the letter he added:

Dear child, six have confessed against me at once: the Chancellor, his son, Neudecker, Zaner, Hoffmaisters Ursel, and Hopffens Elsse—all false, through compulsion, as they have all told me, and begged my forgiveness in God's name before they were executed. . . . They know nothing but good of me. They were forced to say it, just as I myself was. . . .

The Methods of the Witch-Persecutions

It was in Franconia, during the persecutions just described, that the noble Jesuit poet Friedrich von Spee was made the confessor of those sentenced to death for witchcraft and thus was inspired to write (though anonymously) the book whose eloquent protest gave

From Friedrich von Spee, *Cantio criminalis* (Rintein, 1631), in *Translations and Reprints*, vol. 3, No. 4, G. L. Burr, Ed.

the persecution throughout Europe its first effective check. The following passage expresses some of the concerns that turned the Jesuit's hair white before its time.

WHAT, NOW, IS THE OUTLINE AND METHOD OF THE TRIALS AGAINST WITCHES
TO-DAY IN GENERAL USE?——A THING WORTHY OF GERMANY'S CONSIDERATION

I answer: . . .

1. Incredible among us Germans and especially (I blush to say it) among Catholics are the popular superstition, envy, calumnies, backbitings, insinuations, and the like, which, being neither punished by the magistrates nor refuted by the pulpit, first stir up suspicion of witchcraft. All the divine judgments which God has threatened in Holy Writ are now ascribed to witches. No longer do God or nature do aught, but witches everything.

2. Hence it comes that all at once everybody is clamoring that the magistrates proceed against the witches—those witches whom only their own clamor has made seem so many.

3. Princes, therefore, bid their judges and counselors to begin proceedings against the witches.

4. These at first do not know where to begin, since they have no testimony or proofs, and since their conscience clearly tells them that they ought not to proceed in this rashly.

5. Meanwhile they are a second time and a third admonished to proceed. The multitude clamors that there is something suspicious in this delay; and the same suspicion is, by one busybody or another, instilled into the ear of the princes.

6. To offend these, however, and not to defer at once to their wishes, is in Germany a serious matter: most men, and even clergymen, approve with zeal whatever is but pleasing to the princes, not heeding by whom these (however good by nature) are often instigated.

7. At last, therefore, the judges yield to their wishes, and in some way contrive at length a starting-point for the trials.

8. Or, if they still hold out and dread to touch the ticklish matter, there is sent to them a commissioner [inquisitor] especially deputed for this. And, even if he brings to his task something of inexperience or of ardor, as is wont to happen in things human, this takes on in this field another color and name, and is counted only zeal for justice. This zeal for justice is no whit diminished by the prospect of gain, especially in the case of a commissioner of slender means and avaricious, with a large family, when there is granted him as salary so many dollars per head for each witch burned, besides the fees and assessments which he is allowed to extort at will from the peasants.

9. If now some utterance of a demoniac or some malign and idle rumor then current

(for proof of the scandal is never asked) points especially to some poor and helpless Gaia, she is the first to suffer.

10. And yet, lest it appear that she is indicted on the basis of rumor alone, without other proofs, as the phrase goes, lo a certain presumption is at once obtained against her by posing the following dilemma: Either Gaia has led a bad and improper life, or she has led a good and proper one. If a bad one, then, say they, the proof is cogent against her; for from malice to malice the presumption is strong. If, however, she has led a good one, this also is none the less a proof; for thus, they say, are witches wont to cloak themselves and try to seem especially proper.

11. Therefore it is ordered that Gaia be haled away to prison. And lo now a new proof is gained against her by this other dilemma: Either she then shows fear or she does not show it. If she does show it (hearing forsooth of the grievous tortures wont to be used in this matter), this is of itself a proof; for conscience, they say accuses her. If she does not show it (trusting forsooth in her innocence), this too is a proof; for it is most characteristic of witches, they say, to pretend themselves peculiarly innocent and wear a bold front.

12. Lest, however, further proofs against her should be lacking, the commissioner has his own creatures, often depraved and notorious, who question into all her past life. This, of course, cannot be done without coming upon some saying or doing of hers which evil-minded men can easily twist or distort into ground for suspicion of witchcraft.

13. If, too, there are any who have borne her ill will, these, having now a fine opportunity to do her harm, bring against her such charges as it may please them to devise; and on every side there is a clamor that the evidence is heavy against her.

14. And so, as soon as possible, she is hurried to the torture, if indeed she be not subjected to it on the very day of her arrest, as often happens.

15. For in these trials there is granted to nobody an advocate or any means of fair defense, for the cry is that the crime is an expected one, and whoever ventures to defend the prisoner is brought into suspicion of the crime—as are all those who dare to utter a protest in these cases and to urge the judges to caution; for they are forthwith dubbed patrons of the witches. Thus all mouths are closed and all pens blunted, lest they speak or write.

16. In general, however, that it may not seem that no opportunity of defense has been given to Gaia, she is brought out and the proofs are first read before her and examined—if examination it can be called.

17. But, even though she then denies these and satisfactorily makes answer to each, this is neither paid attention to nor even noted down: all the proofs retain their force and value, however perfect her answer to them. She is only ordered back into prison, there to bethink herself more carefully whether she will persist in her obstinacy—for, since she has denied her guilt, she is obstinate.

18. When she has bethought herself, she is next day brought out again, and there is read to her the sentence of torture—just as if she had before answered nothing to the charges, and refuted nothing.

19. Before she is tortured, however, she is led aside by the executioner, and lest she may by magical means have fortified herself against pain, she is searched, her whole body being shaved, . . . although up to this time nothing of the sort was ever found. . . .

21. Then, when Gaia has thus been searched and shaved, she is tortured that she may confess the truth, that is to say, that she may simply declare herself guilty; for whatever else she may say will not be the truth and cannot be.

22. She is, however, tortured with the torture of the first degree, i.e., the less severe. This is to be understood thus: that, although in itself it is exceeding severe, yet, compared with others to follow, it is lighter. Wherefore, if she confesses, they say and noise it abroad that she has confessed without torture.

23. Now, what prince or other dignitary who hears this can doubt that she is most certainly guilty who thus voluntarily without torture confesses her guilt?

24. Without any scruples, therefore, after this confession she is executed. Yet she would have been executed, nevertheless, even though she had not confessed; for when once a beginning has been made with the torture, the die is already cast—she cannot escape, she must die.

25. So, whether she confesses or does not confess, the result is the same. If she confesses, the thing is clear, for, as I have said and as is self-evident, she is executed: all recantation is in vain, as I have shown above. If she does not confess, the torture is repeated—twice, thrice, four times: anything one pleases is permissible, for in an excepted crime there is no limit of duration or severity or repetition of the tortures. As to this, think the judges, no sin is possible which can be brought up before the tribunal of conscience.

26. If now Gaia, no matter how many times tortured, has not yet broken silence,— if she contorts her features under the pain, if she loses consciousness, or the like, then they cry that she is laughing or has bewitched herself into taciturnity, and hence deserves to be burned alive, as lately has been done to some who though several times tortured would not confess.

27. And then they say—even clergymen and confessors—that she died obstinate and impenitent, that she would not be converted or desert her paramour, but kept rather her faith with him.

28. If, however, it chances that under so many tortures one dies, they say that her neck has been broken by the Devil.

29. Wherefore justly, forsooth, the corpse is dragged out by the executioner and buried under the gallows.

30. But if, on the other hand, Gaia does not die and some exceptionally scrupulous judge hesitates to torture her further without fresh proofs or to burn her without a confession, she is kept in prison and more harshly fettered, and there lies for perhaps an entire year to rot until she is subdued.

31. For it is never possible to clear herself by withstanding and thus to wash away the aspersion of crime, as is the intention of the laws. It would be a disgrace to her examiners if when once arrested she should thus go free. Guilty must she be, by fair means or foul, whom they have once but thrown into bonds.

32. Meanwhile, both then and earlier, they send to her ignorant and headstrong priests, more importunate than the executioners themselves. It is the business of these to harass in every wise the wretched creature to such a degree that, whether truly or not, she will at last confess herself guilty; unless she does so, they declare, she simply cannot be saved, nor share in the sacraments.

33. The greatest care is taken lest there be admitted to her priests more thoughtful and learned, who have aught of insight or kindliness; as also that nobody visits her prison who might give her counsel or inform the ruling princes. For there is nothing so much dreaded by any of them as that in some way the innocence of any of the accused should be brought to light. . . .

34. In the meantime, while Gaia, as I have said, is still held in prison, and is tormented by those whom it least behooves, there are not wanting to her industrious judges clever devices by which they not only find new proofs against Gaia, but by which moreover they so convict her to her face (an't please the gods!) that by the advice of some university faculty she is then at last pronounced to deserve burning alive. . . .

35. Some, however, to leave no stone unturned, order Gaia to be exorcised and transferred to a new place, and then to be tortured again, in the hope that by this exorcism and change of place the bewitchment of taciturnity may perhaps be broken. But, if not even this succeeds, then at last they commit her alive to the flames. Now in Heaven's name, I would like to know, since both she who confesses and she who does not, perish alike, what way of escape there is for any, however innocent? O unhappy Gaia, why hast thou rashly hoped? why hast thou not, at first entering prison, declared thyself guilty? why, O foolish woman and mad, wilt thou die so many times when thou mightst die but once? Follow my counsel, and before all pain declare thyself guilty and die. Thou wilt not escape; for this were a disgrace to the zeal of Germany.

36. If, now, any under stress of pain has once falsely declared herself guilty, her wretched plight beggars description. For not only is there in general no door for her escape, but she is also compelled to accuse others, of whom she knows no ill, and whose names are not seldom suggested to her by her examiners or by the executioner, or of whom she has heard as suspected or accused or already once arrested and released. These in their turn are forced to accuse others, and these still others, and so it goes on: who can help seeing that it must go on without end?

37. Wherefore the judges themselves are obliged at last either to break off the trials and so condemn their own work or else to burn their own folk, aye themselves and everybody: for on all soon or late false accusations fall, and, if only followed by the torture, all are proved guilty.

38. And so at last those are brought in question who at the outset most loudly clamored for the constant feeding of the flames; for they rashly failed to foresee that their turn, too, must inevitably come—and by a just verdict of heaven, since with their pestilent tongues they created us so many witches and sent so many innocent to the flames.

39. But now gradually many of the wiser and more learned begin to take notice of it, and, as if aroused from deep sleep, to open their eyes and slowly and cautiously to bestir themselves. . . .

46. From all which there follows this corollary, worthy to be noted in red ink: that, if only the trials be steadily pushed on with, there is nobody in our day, of whatsoever sex, fortune, rank or dignity who is safe, if he have but an enemy and slanderer to bring him into suspicion of witchcraft. . . .

The Political Debate

IN the great orderly pattern of seventeenth-century thought, one thing still remained to be settled: the nature and justification of political authority. In the Middle Ages this had rested with God and had been shared equally between God's representatives on earth—the pope and the prince. With the Reformation, this ideal equilibrium had been broken: where once only one pope had reigned, now there were several, each claiming ultimate religious authority for his version of God's will and revelation. The result was a growth in the power of princes at the expense of the Church. Where, once upon a time, religious authority had provided the sanction of political power, under the new dispensation political authority guaranteed and reinforced this or that form of religion. By a natural evolution, it came to be argued that ultimately the prince was the significant representative of God on earth, ruling his country by divine right and dispensation. This was the thesis of Bossuet, but it was challenged by a rival theory based on a justification more immediate and worldly than the will of God: the contract.

The contract theory of government, which appealed to the common sense of an increasingly businesslike public, presented society as the result of an agreement between its members, and the political form of society—its system of government—as arising out of a similar agreement. The contract theory was not necessarily more liberal than that of divine right: the king of Hobbes is a less restrained and probably harsher ruler than Bossuet's. But, in the hands of Locke, the logical implications of contractual relationships were carried to revolutionary conclusions: a contract was seen for what it had always been: an undertaking with mutual obligations binding on both parties and with sanctions for failure to carry out its terms. This new view severely shook the firm, unquestioned basis of monarchical power.

Jacques Bénigne Bossuet

Jacques Bénigne Bossuet (1627–1704), bishop of Meaux, was one of the great orators and polemicists of the reign of Louis XIV. Appointed tutor to the dauphin (the king's heir), Bossuet wrote for his edification a series of works expounding the divine rights and God-appointed duties of kings. The following passages are taken from one of these, the Treatise on Politics, Based on the Very Words of Holy Writ, *most of which was composed in 1678.*

On the Nature and the Properties of Royal Authority

Firstly, royal authority is sacred; secondly, it is paternal; thirdly, it is absolute; fourthly, it is subject to reason. . . .

God establishes kings as his ministers, and reigns through them over the peoples. We have already seen that all power comes from God. The prince, adds Saint Paul, "is a minister of God to thee for good. But if thou do that which is evil, be afraid; for he beareth not the sword in vain: for he is a minister of God, an avenger for wrath to him that doeth evil." So princes act as ministers of God and his lieutenants on earth. It is through them that He rules His empire. This is why we have seen that the royal throne is not the throne of a man, but the throne of God Himself. Nor is it peculiar to the Jews alone to have kings appointed by God. . . . He governs all peoples, and gives kings to all. . . .

It appears from all this that the person of the king is sacred, and that it is a sacrilege to attack him. God has His prophets anoint them with a sacred unction, as He has His pontiffs and His altars anointed. But, even without the external application of this unction,[1] their charge renders them sacred, as being the representatives of the divine majesty, delegated by His providence to the execution of His designs. It is thus that God Himself speaks of Cyrus as His anointed—"his right hand I have holden to subdue nations before him." The title of Christ is given to kings; and everywhere we see them called the Christ, or the anointed of the Lord.

Kings must be guarded as being sacred; and he who neglects to guard them deserves to die. He who guards the life of the prince, places his own in the safe-keeping of God. . . .

Saint Paul, after having said that the prince is the minister of God, concludes thus: "Wherefore Ye must needs be in subjection, not only because of the wrath, but also for conscience's sake." . . . And again, "servants, obey in all things your temporal masters and whatsoever Ye do, do it heartily as to the Lord, and not as unto men." If the apostle speaks thus of servitude, which is an unnatural condition; what should we think of legitimate subjection to princes and to the magistrates who are the protectors of public liberty? This is why Saint Peter says, "submit yourselves to every ordinance of man for the Lord's sake: whether it be to the king as supreme, or unto governors, as unto them that are sent by him for the punishment of evil-doers and for the praise of them that do well." And, even if they did not carry out their duty, we must respect in them their charge and their ministry. "Servants, be subject to your masters with all fear; not only to the good and gentle, but also to the froward and unjust." There is thus a religious character about the respect we show to the prince. The service of God and the respect for kings are one; and Saint Peter puts these two duties together: "Fear God; honor the king." . . . Indeed, God has infused something of divinity into princes: "I have said Ye are Gods; and all of you are children of the Most High."

Translated by the editor.

[1] Anointment, or the act of anointment.

The kings must respect their own power and use it only to the public good. Their power coming from above, as we have said, they must not believe that it belongs to them to be used as they please; but they must use it with fear and restraint, as a thing which comes from God and for which God will call them to account. Kings should therefore tremble when using the power that God has given them, and think how horrible is the sacrilege of misusing a power which comes from God.

THE ROYAL AUTHORITY IS PATERNAL, AND ITS INHERENT CHARACTER IS GOODNESS

We have seen that kings take the place of God, who is the true father of all mankind. We have also seen that the first idea of power arrived at by men is that of paternal power; and that kings have been made on the model of fathers. Also, everybody agrees that the obedience which is due to the public power is to be found, in the Ten Commandments, in the commandment which obliges men to honor their parents. From all this, it follows that the title of king is the title of a father, and that goodness is the most natural characteristic of kings. . . .

Because God is great and sufficient unto Himself, He turns, so to speak, entirely towards doing good to men, according to the word: "As is His greatness, so is His compassion." He places an image of His greatness in kings in order to force them to imitate His goodness. He raises them to a level where they have nothing more to desire for themselves. We have heard David saying: "What can Your servant add to all the greatness with which You have clothed him?"

THE ROYAL AUTHORITY IS ABSOLUTE

In order to render this idea odious and unbearable, many pretend to confuse absolute government with arbitrary government. But there are no two more dissimilar things. . . . The prince need render no account to anyone for the orders he gives. "I counsel thee to keep the king's commandment and that in regard to the oath of God. Be not hasty to go out of his sight: stand not in an evil thing; for he does whatsoever pleases him. Where the word of a king is, there is power; and who may say unto him, What dost thou?" Without this absolute authority the king can do no good, nor punish evil; his power must be such that no one can hope to escape it. . . .

Men must therefore obey princes as they obey justice itself, without which there can be no order or purpose in things. They are Gods, and share in a fashion the divine independence: "I have said Ye are Gods. . . ." There is only God who can judge their judgements and their persons. "God standeth in the congregation of the mighty; He judgeth among the Gods."

THE ROYAL AUTHORITY MUST BE INVINCIBLE

If there is in a State any authority which can stand in the path of public power and embarrass it in its exercise, no one is safe. . . .

If the prince himself, who is the judge of judges, fears powerful men, what stability could there be in the State? It is therefore necessary that authority should be invincible, and that nothing should be able to breach the rampart behind which the public peace and private weal are safe.

OF MAJESTY

Majesty is the reflection of the greatness of God in the prince. God is infinite, God is all. The prince, as a prince, is not regarded as a private individual: he is a public figure, the whole State rests in him; the will of the whole people is comprehended in his. Just as all perfection and all virtue are concentrated in God, so all the power of private individuals is concentrated in the person of the prince. What greatness, that one man should carry so much! The power of God makes itself felt in an instant from one end of the world to the other: the royal power acts in the same way throughout the whole kingdom. It keeps the whole kingdom in being, as God keeps the whole world. If God were to withdraw His hand, the world would fall back into nothingness: if authority ceased in the kingdom, everything would be confusion. . . .

Now, put together all the great and august things that we have said on the subject of royal authority. See a great people united in one person: see this sacred, paternal, and absolute power: see the secret purpose which governs the whole body of the State comprehended in one head: you see the image of God in the kings; and you get an idea of royal majesty. . . . God is holiness itself, goodness itself, power itself, reason itself. The majesty of God is in these things. The majesty of the prince is in the image of these things. This majesty is so great that its source cannot be in the prince; it is borrowed from God who gives it to him for the good of the peoples, for whom it is salutary that they should be held in by a superior power. . . .

There is something divine about a prince, which inspires the peoples with fear. . . .

Therefore, use your power boldly, oh, kings! For it is divine and salutary to mankind; but use it with humility. You are endowed with it from outside. Fundamentally, it leaves you weak; it leaves you mortal; it leaves you sinners; and burdens you with greater responsibility towards God.

ON THE OBEDIENCE DUE TO THE PRINCE

The subjects owe unlimited obedience to the prince. If the prince is not punctually obeyed, the public order is overthrown and there is no more unity, and consequently no more cooperation or peace in a State. . . .

Open godlessness, and even persecution, do not absolve the subjects from the obedience they owe to princes. The character of royalty is holy and sacred, even in infidel princes; and we have seen that Isaiah calls Cyrus "the anointed of the Lord." Nebuchadnezzar was godless, and proud to the point of wanting to equal God and put to death those who refused him a sacrilegious worship; and nevertheless Daniel addresses him thus: "You are the king of kings: and the God of Heavens has given you the kingdom and the power and the empire and the glory." . . .

The subjects may oppose to the violence of princes only respectful remonstrances, without murmurs or rebellion, and prayers for their conversion.

If God does not hearken to the prayers of His faithful; if in order to try and chasten His children He permits their persecution to grow worse, they must then remember that Jesus Christ has "sent them as lambs in the midst of wolves." Here is a truly holy doctrine, truly worthy of Jesus Christ and of His disciples.

ON THE DUTIES OF THE PRINCE

The purpose of government is the welfare and conservation of the State. . . .

The good constitution of the body of the State consists in two things: religion and justice. These are the internal and constitutive principles of States. By the one we render to God what is owed to Him, and by the other we render to men that which they deserve. . . . The prince must employ his authority to destroy false religion in his State. . . .

The prince is the minister of God: "He beareth not the sword in vain: for he is a revenger to execute wrath upon him that doeth evil." He is the protector of the public peace which is based upon religion; and he must maintain his throne, of which, as we have seen, religion is the foundation. Those who will not suffer the prince to act strictly in religious matters, because religion should be free, make an impious error. Otherwise, one would have to tolerate in all the subjects and in all the country idolatry, mohammedanism, judaism, any false religions; blasphemy, even atheism, and the greatest crimes would be the least punished.

Thomas Hobbes

Thomas Hobbes (1588–1679) was born and brought up an Elizabethan and died at the age of ninety-one under the Restoration. As tutor to the noble Cavendish family and as a scholar in his own right, he traveled widely, meeting many of the greatest minds of his time. Friend of Ben Jonson, Francis Bacon, and Galileo, he also knew, and argued with, Descartes. The troubles of the English civil war drove him to Paris, where he lived from 1641 to 1652. In 1647 he was appointed tutor to the prince of Wales, but the future Charles II had to break off the relationship when the publication of Hobbes's Leviathan *in 1651 shocked too many people. It nevertheless remains one of the most thorough—and perhaps, therefore, thoroughly depressing—analyses of the motives and patterns of political behavior.*

The extreme authoritarianism of Hobbes has been attributed to the natural timidity of a man whose mother may have been frightened by the Spanish Armada and whom the civil war had persuaded that anything was better than disorder.

From The Leviathan

OF THE NATURAL CONDITION OF MANKIND AS CONCERNING THEIR FELICITY
AND MISERY

Nature has made men so equal, in the faculties of the body and mind; as that though there be found one man sometimes manifestly stronger in body, or of quicker mind than another, yet when all is reckoned together, the difference between man and man, is not so considerable, as that one man can thereupon claim to himself any benefit, to which another may not pretend, as well as he. For as to the strength of body, the weakest has strength enough to kill the strongest, either by secret machination, or by confederacy with others, that are in the same danger with himself.

And as to the faculties of the mind, setting aside the arts grounded upon words, and especially that skill of proceeding upon general and infallible rules, called science; which very few have, and but in few things; as being not a native faculty, born with us; nor attained, as prudence, while we look after somewhat else, I find yet a greater equality among men than that of strength. For prudence is but experience; which equal time equally bestows on all men, in those things they equally apply themselves unto. That which may perhaps make such equality incredible, is but a vain concept of one's own wisdom, which almost all men think they have in a greater degree than the vulgar; that is, than all men but themselves, and a few others, whom by fame or for concurring with themselves, they approve. For such is the nature of men, that howsoever they may acknowledge many others to be more witty, or more eloquent, or more learned; yet they will hardly believe there be many so wise as themselves; for they see their own wit at hand, and other men's at a distance. But this proves rather that men are in that point equal, than unequal. For there is not ordinarily a greater sign of the equal distribution of anything, than that every man is contented with his share.

From this equality of ability, arises equality of hope in the attaining of our ends. And therefore if any two men desire the same thing, which nevertheless they cannot both enjoy, they become enemies; and in the way to their end, which is principally their own conservation, and sometimes their delectation only, endeavour to destroy or subdue one another. And from hence it comes to pass, that where an invader has no more to fear than another man's single power; if one plant, sow, build, or possess a convenient seat, others may probably be expected to come prepared with forces united, to dispossess and deprive him, not only of the fruit of his labour, but also of his life or liberty. And the invader again is in the like danger of another.

And from this diffidence of one another, there is no way for any man to secure himself, so reasonable, as anticipation; that is, by force, or wiles, to master the persons of all men he can, so long, till he see no other power great enough to endanger him: and this is no more than his own conservation requires, and is generally allowed. Also because there be some, that taking pleasure in contemplating their own power in the

From Thomas Hobbes, *The Leviathan* (London, n. d.), pp. 63–65, 82–88.

acts of conquest, which they pursue farther than their security requires; if others, that otherwise would be glad to be at least within modest bounds, should not by invasion increase their power, they would not be able, long time, by standing only on their defence, to subsist. And by consequence, such augmentation of dominion over men being necessary to a man's conservation, it ought to be allowed him.

Again, men have no pleasure, but on the contrary, a great deal of grief, in keeping company, where there is no power able to overawe them all. For every man looks for his companion to value him, at the same rate he sets upon himself: and upon all signs of contempt, or undervaluing, naturally endeavours, as far as he dares (which among them that have no common power to keep them in quiet, is far enough to make them destroy each other), to extort a greater value from his contemners, by damage; and from others, by the example.

So that in the nature of man we find three principal causes of quarrel. First, competition; second, diffidence; thirdly, glory.

The first makes men invade for gain; the second, for safety; and the third, for reputation. The first use violence, to make themselves masters of other men's persons, wives, children, and cattle; the second, to defend them; the third, for trifles, as a word, a smile, a different opinion, and any other sign of undervalue, either direct in their persons, or by reflection in their kindred, their friends, their nation, their profession, or their name.

Hereby it is manifest, that during the time men live without a common power to keep them all in awe, they are in that condition which is called war; and such a war, as is of every man, against every man. For "war" consists not in battle only, or the act of fighting, but in a tract of time, wherein the will to contend by battle is sufficiently known; and therefore the notion of "time" is to be considered in the nature of war, as it is in the nature of weather. For as the nature of foul weather lies not in a shower or two of rain, but in an inclination thereto of many days together; so the nature of war consists not in actual fighting, but in the known disposition thereto during all the time there is no assurance to the contrary. All other time is "peace."

Whatsoever therefore is consequent to a time of war, where every man is enemy to every man, the same is consequent to the time wherein men live without other security than what their own strength and their own invention shall furnish them. In such condition there is no place for industry, because the fruit thereof is uncertain, and consequently no culture of the earth; no navigation, nor use of the commodities that may be imported by sea; not commodious building; no instruments of moving and removing such things as require much force; no knowledge of the face of the earth; no account of time; no arts; no letters; no society; and, which is worst of all, continual fear and danger of violent death; and the life of man, solitary, poor, nasty, brutish, and short.

It may seem strange to some man, that has not well weighed these things, that Nature should thus dissociate, and render men apt to invade, and destroy one another; and he may therefore, not trusting to this inference made from the passions, desire perhaps to have the same confirmed by experience. Let him therefore consider with himself, when taking a journey, he arms himself, and seeks to go well accompanied; when going to sleep, he locks his doors; when even in his house, he locks his chests;

and this when he knows there be laws, and public officers, armed, to revenge all injuries shall be done him; what opinion he has of his fellow-subjects, when he rides armed; of his fellow citizens, when he locks his doors; and of his children and servants, when he locks his chests. Does he not there as much accuse man's nature in it? The desires and other passions of man are in themselves no sin. No more are the actions that proceed from those passions, till they know a law that forbids them; which till laws be made they cannot know, nor can any law be made till they have agreed upon the person that shall make it.

It may peradventure be thought there was never such a time nor condition of war as this; and I believe it was never generally so, over all the world, but there are many places where they live so now. For the savage people in many places of America, except the government of small families, the concord whereof depends on natural lust, have no government at all, and live at this day in that brutish manner, as I said before. Howsoever, it may be perceived where there were no common power to fear, by the manner of life which men that have formerly lived under a peaceful government, use to degenerate into a civil war.

But though there had never been any time, wherein particular men were in a condition of war one against another; yet in all times, kings, and persons of sovereign authority, because of their independency, are in continual jealousies, and in the state and posture of gladiators; having their weapons pointing, and their eyes fixed on one another; that is, their forts, garrisons, and guns upon the frontiers of their kingdoms; and continual spies upon their neighbours; which is a posture of war. But because they uphold thereby the industry of their subjects; there does not follow from it that misery which accompanies the liberty of particular men.

To this war of every man, against every man, this also is consequent; that nothing can be unjust. The notions of right and wrong, justice and injustice, have there no place. Where there is no common power, there is no law: where no law, no injustice. Force and fraud are in war the two cardinal virtues. Justice and injustice are none of the faculties neither of the body nor mind. If they were, they might be in a man that were alone in the world, as well as his senses, and passions. They are qualities that relate to men in society, not in solitude. It is consequent also to the same condition, that there be no propriety, no dominion, no "mine" and "thine" distinct; but only that to be every man's, that he can get; and for so long, as he can keep it. And thus much for the ill condition, which man by mere nature is actually placed in; though with a possibility to come out of it, consisting partly in the passions, partly in his reason.

The passions that incline men to peace, are fear of death; desire of such things as are necessary to commodious living; and a hope by their industry to obtain them. And reason suggests convenient articles of peace, upon which men may be drawn to agreement. These articles are they which otherwise are called the Laws of Nature. . . .

OF THE CAUSES, GENERATION AND DEFINITION OF A COMMONWEALTH

The final cause, end, or design of men, who naturally love liberty, and dominion over others, in the introduction of that restraint upon themselves, in which we see them live in commonwealths, is the foresight of their own preservation, and of a more contented life thereby; that is to say, of getting themselves out from that miserable condition of war, which is necessarily consequent, as has been shown above to the natural passions of men, when there is no visible power to keep them in awe, and tie them by fear of punishment to the performance of their covenants, and observation of those laws of Nature. . . .

For the laws of Nature, as "justice," "equity," "modesty," "mercy," and in sum, "doing to others, as we would be done to," of themselves, without the terror of some power, to cause them to be observed are contrary to our natural passions, that carry us to partiality, pride, revenge, and the like. And covenants, without the sword, are but words, and of no strength to secure a man at all. Therefore notwithstanding the laws of Nature, which every one has then kept, when he has the will to keep them, when he can do it safely, if there be no power erected, or not great enough for our security; every man will, and may lawfully rely on his own strength and art, for caution against all other men. And in all places, where men have lived by small families, to rob and spoil one another, has been a trade, and so far from being reputed against the law of Nature, that the greater spoils they gained, the greater was their honour; and men observed no other laws therein, but the laws of honour; that is, to abstain from cruelty, leaving to men their lives, and instruments of husbandry. And as small families did then; so now do cities and kingdoms, which are but greater families, for their own security, enlarge their dominions, upon all pretences of danger, and fear of invasion, or assistance that may be given to invaders, and endeavour as much as they can, to subdue, or weaken their neighbours, by open force and secret arts, for want of other caution, justly; and are remembered for it in after ages with honour.

Nor is it the joining together of a small number of men, that gives them this security; because in small numbers, small additions on the one side or the other, make the advantage of strength so great, as is sufficient to carry the victory; and therefore gives encouragement to an invasion. The multitude sufficient to confide in for our security, is not determined by any certain number, but by comparison with the enemy we fear; and is then sufficient, when the odds of the enemy is not of so visible and conspicuous moment, to determine the event of war, as to move him to attempt.

And be there never so great a multitude; yet if their actions be directed according to their particular judgments and particular appetites, they can expect thereby no defence, nor protection, neither against a common enemy, nor against the injuries of one another. For being distracted in opinions concerning the best use and application of their strength, they do not help but hinder one another; and reduce their strength by mutual opposition to nothing; whereby they are easily, not only subdued by a very few that agree together; but also when there is no common enemy, they also make war upon each other, for their particular interests. For if we could suppose a great multitude of men to consent in the observation of justice, and other laws of Nature, without a common power to keep them all in awe, we might as well suppose all mankind to do the same; and then there neither would be, nor need to be any civil government or commonwealth at all; because there would be peace without subjection.

Nor is it enough for the security, which men desire should last all the time of their life, that they be governed and directed by one judgment, for a limited time: as in one battle, or one war. For though they obtain a victory by their unanimous endeavour against a foreign enemy; yet afterwards, when either they have no common enemy, or he that by one part is held for an enemy, is by another part held for a friend, they must needs by the difference of their interests dissolve, and fall again into a war among themselves.

It is true that certain living creatures, as bees and ants, live sociably one with another, which are therefore by Aristotle numbered amongst political creatures; and yet have no other direction than their particular judgments and appetites; nor speech, whereby one of them can signify to another, what he thinks expedient for the common benefit: and therefore some man may perhaps desire to know, why mankind cannot do the same. To which I answer,

First, that men are continually in competition for honour and dignity, which these creatures are not; and consequently among men there arises on that ground, envy and hatred, and finally war; but among these not so.

Secondly, that among these creatures, the common good differs not from the private, and being by nature inclined to their private, they procure thereby the common benefit. But man, whose joy consists in comparing himself with other men, can relish nothing but what is eminent.

Thirdly, that these creatures, having not, as man, the use of reason, do not see, nor think they see any fault in the administration of their common business; whereas among men, there are very many that think themselves wiser, and abler to govern the public, better than the rest; and these strive to reform and innovate, one this way, another that way; and thereby bring it into distraction and civil war.

Fourthly, that these creatures, though they have some use of voice, in making known to one another their desires and other affections; yet they want that art of words, by which some men can represent to others that which is good in the likeness of evil; and evil in the likeness of good; and augment or diminish the apparent greatness of good and evil; discontenting men, and troubling their peace at their pleasure.

Fifthly, irrational creatures cannot distinguish between "injury" and "damage"; and therefore as long as they be at ease, they are not offended with their fellows, whereas man is then most troublesome, when he is most at ease; for then it is that he loves to show his wisdom, and control the actions of them that govern the commonwealth.

Lastly, the agreement of these creatures is natural; that of men is by covenant only, which is artificial: and therefore it is no wonder if there be somewhat else required, besides covenant, to make their agreement constant and lasting; which is a common power, to keep them in awe, and to direct their actions to the common benefit.

The only way to erect such a common power, as may be able to defend them from the invasion of foreigners, and the injuries of one another, and thereby to secure them in such sort, as that by their own industry, and by the fruits of the earth, they may nourish themselves and live contentedly, is, to confer all their power and strength upon one man, or upon one assembly of men, that may reduce all their wills, by plurality of voices, unto one will: which is as much as to say, to appoint one man, or assembly of men, to bear their person; and every one to own, and acknowledge himself to be author of whatever he that bears their person, shall act, or cause to be acted, in those things which concern the common peace and safety; and therein to submit their wills, every one to his will, and their judgments, to his judgment. This is more than consent, or concord; it is a real unity of them all, in one and the same person, made by covenant of every man, in such manner, as if every man should say to every man, "I authorize and give up my right of governing myself, to this man, or to this assembly of men, on this condition, that thou give up thy right to him, and authorize all his actions in like manner." This done, the multitude so united in one person is called a "commonwealth," in Latin *civitas*. This is the generation of that great LEVIATHAN, or rather, to speak more reverently, of that "mortal god," to which we owe under the "immortal God," our peace and defence. For by this authority, given him by every particular man in the commonwealth, he has the use of so much power and strength conferred on him, that by terror thereof, he is enabled to perform the wills of them all, to peace at home, and mutual aid against their enemies abroad. And in him consists the essence of the commonwealth; which, to define it, is *one person of whose acts a great multitude, by mutual covenants one with another, have made themselves every one the author, to the end he may use the strength and means of them all, as he shall think expedient, for their peace and common defence.*

And he that carries this person is called "sovereign," and is said to have "sovereign power"; and every one besides, his "subject."

The attaining to this sovereign power is by two ways. One, by natural force; as when a man makes his children to submit themselves and their children to his government, as being able to destroy them if they refuse; or by war subdues his enemies to his will, giving them their lives on that condition. The other is, when men agree among themselves to submit to some man, or assembly of men, voluntarily, on confidence to be protected by him against all others. This latter may be called a political commonwealth, or commonwealth by "institution"; and the former, a commonwealth by "acquisition." And first, I shall speak of a commonwealth by institution.

OF THE RIGHTS OF SOVEREIGNS BY INSTITUTION

A "commonwealth" is said to be "instituted," when a "multitude" of men do agree, and "covenant, every one, with every one," that to whatsoever "man," or "assembly of men," shall be given by the major part, the "right" to "represent" the person of them all, that is to say, to be their "representative"; every one, as well he that "voted for it," as he that "voted against it," shall "authorize" all the actions and judgments, of that man, or assembly of men, in the same manner, as if they were his own, to the end, to live peaceably among themselves, and be protected against other men.

From this institution of a commonwealth are derived all the "rights" and "faculties" of him, or them, on whom sovereign power is conferred by the consent of the people assembled.

First, because they covenant, it is to be understood, they are not obliged by former covenant to anything repugnant hereunto. And consequently they that have already instituted a commonwealth, being thereby bound by covenant, to own the actions and judgments of one, cannot lawfully make a new covenant, among themselves, to be obedient to any other, in anything whatsoever, without his permission. And therefore, they that are subjects to a monarch, cannot without his leave cast off monarchy, and return to the confusion of a disunited multitude: nor transfer their person from him that bears it, to another man, or other assembly of men: for they are bound, every man to every man, to own, and be reputed author of all, that he that already is their sovereign, shall do, and judge fit to be done; so that one man dissenting, all the rest should break their covenant made to that man, which is injustice: and they have also every man given the sovereignty to him that bears their person; and therefore if they depose him, they take from him that which is his own, and so again it is injustice. Besides, if he that attempts to depose his sovereign, be killed, or punished by him for such attempt, he is author of his own punishment, as being by the institution, author of all his sovereign shall do: and because it is injustice for a man to do anything for which he may be punished by his own authority, he is also upon that title unjust. And whereas some men have pretended for their disobedience to their sovereign, a new covenant, made not with men, but with God; this also is unjust: for there is no covenant with God but by mediation of somebody that represents God's person; which none does but God's lieutenant, who has the sovereignty under God. But this pretence of covenant with God, is so evident a lie, even in the pretenders' own consciences, that it is not only an act of an unjust, but also of a vile and unmanly disposition.

Secondly, because the right of bearing the person of them all, is given to him they make sovereign, by covenant only of one to another, and not of him to any of them; there can happen no breach of covenant on the part of the sovereign: and consequently none of his subjects, by any pretence of forfeiture, can be freed from his subjection. That he which is made sovereign makes no covenant with his subjects before hand, is manifest; because either he must make it with the whole multitude, or one party to the covenant; or he must make a several covenant with every man. With the whole, as one party, it is impossible; because as yet they are not one person and if he make so many several covenant as there be men, those covenants after he has the sovereignty are void; because what act soever can be pretended by any one of them for breach thereof, is the act both of himself and of all the rest, because done in the person and by the right of every one of them in particular. Besides, if any one or more of them pretend a breach of the covenant made by the sovereign at his institution; and others, or one other of his subjects, or himself alone, pretend there was no such breach, there is in this case no judge to decide the controversy; it returns therefore to the sword again; and every man recovers the right of protecting himself by his own strength, contrary to the design they had in the institution. It is therefore in vain to grant sovereignty by way of precedent covenant. The opinion that any monarch receives his power by covenant, that is to say, on condition, proceeds from want of understanding this easy truth, that covenants being but words and breath, have no force to oblige, contain, constrain, or protect any man, but what it has from the public sword; that is, from the united hands of that man, or assembly of men that have the sovereignty, and whose actions are avouched by them all, and performed by the strength of them all, in him united. But when an assembly of men is made sovereign, then no man imagines any such covenant to have passed in the institution; for no man is so dull as to say, for example, the people of Rome made a covenant with the Romans, to hold the sovereignty on such or such conditions; which not performed, the Romans might lawfully depose the Roman people. That men see not the reason to be alike in a monarchy, and in a popular government, proceeds from the ambition of some, that are kinder to the government of an assembly, whereof they may hope to participate, than of monarchy, which they despair to enjoy.

Thirdly, because the major part has by consenting voices declared a sovereign; he that dissented must now consent with the rest; that is, be contented to avow all the actions he shall do, or else justly be destroyed by the rest. For if he voluntarily entered into the congregation of them that were assembled, he sufficiently declared thereby his will, and therefore tacitly covenanted to stand to what the major part should ordain: and therefore if he refuse to stand thereto, or make protestation against any of their decrees, he does contrary to his covenant, and therefore unjustly. And whether he be of the congregation or not; and whether his consent be asked or not, he must either submit to their decrees, or be left in the condition of war he was in before; wherein he might without injustice be destroyed by any man whatsoever.

Fourthly, because every subject is by this institution author of all the actions and judgments of the sovereign instituted, it follows, that whatsoever he does it can be no injury to any of his subjects, nor ought he to be by any of them accused of injustice. For he that does anything by authority from another does therein no injury to him by whose authority he acteth: but by this institution of a commonwealth every particular man is author of all the sovereign does; and consequently, he that complains of injury from his sovereign complains of that whereof he himself is author, and therefore ought not to accuse any man but himself; no, nor himself of injury; because to do injury to one's self is impossible. It is true that they that have sovereign power may commit iniquity, but not injustice or injury in the proper signification.

Fifthly, and consequently to that which was said last, no man that has sovereign power can justly be put to death, or otherwise in any manner by his subjects punished. For seeing every subject is author of the actions of his sovereign, he punishes another for the actions committed by himself.

And because the end of this institution is the peace and defence of them all; and whosoever has right to the end has right to the means; it belongs of right to whatsoever man or assembly that has the sovereignty to be judge both of the means of peace and defence, and also of the hindrances and disturbances of the same, and to do whatsoever he shall think necessary to be done, both beforehand, for the preserving of peace and security, by prevention of discord at home and hostility from abroad; and, when peace and security are lost, for the recovery of the same. And therefore,

Sixthly, it is annexed to the sovereignty to be judge of what opinions and doctrines are averse and what conducing to peace; and consequently, on what occasions, how far, and what men are to be trusted withal, in speaking to multitudes of people, and who shall examine the doctrines of all books before they be published. For the actions of men proceed from their opinions, and in the well-governing of opinions consists the well-governing of men's actions, in order to their peace and concord. And though in matter of doctrine nothing ought to be regarded but the truth; yet this is not repugnant to regulating the same by peace. For doctrine repugnant to peace can be no more true than peace and concord can be against the law of Nature. It is true that in a commonwealth, where, by the negligence or unskilfulness of governors and teachers, false doctrines are by time generally received; the contrary truths may be generally offensive. Yet the most sudden and rough bursting in of a new truth that can be, does never break the peace, but only sometimes awakes the war. For those men that are so remissly governed, that they dare take up arms to defend or introduce an opinion, are still in war; and their condition not peace, but only a cessation of arms for fear of one another; and they live, as it were, in the precincts of battle continually. It belongs therefore to him that has the sovereign power to be judge, or constitute all judges of opinions and doctrines, as a thing necessary to peace, thereby to prevent discord and civil war.

Seventhly, is annexed to the sovereignty, the whole power of prescribing the rules, whereby every man may know what goods he may enjoy, and what actions he may do, without being molested by any of his fellow subjects; and this it is men call "propriety." For before constitution of sovereign power, as has already been shown, all men had right to all things, which necessarily causes war: and therefore this propriety, being necessary to peace, and depending on sovereign power, is the act of that power, in order to the public peace. These rules of propriety, or *meum* and *tuum,* and of "good," "evil," "lawful," and "unlawful" in the actions of subjects, are the civil laws; that is to say, the laws of each commonwealth in particular; though the name of civil law be now restricted to the ancient civil laws of the city of Rome, which being the head of a great part of the world, her laws at that time were in these parts the civil law.

Eighthly, is annexed to the sovereignty, the right of judicature; that is to say, of hearing and deciding all controversies, which may arise concerning law, either civil or natural, or concerning fact. For without the decision of controversies, there is no protection of one subject against the injuries of another; the laws concerning *meum* and *tuum* are in vain, and to every man remains, from the natural and necessary appetite of his conservation, the right of protecting himself by his private strength, which is the condition of war, and contrary to the end of which every commonwealth is instituted.

Ninthly, is annexed to the sovereignty, the right of making war and peace with other nations and commonwealths; that is to say, of judging when it is for the public good, and how great forces are to be assembled, armed, and paid for that end; and to levy money upon the subjects to defray the expenses thereof. For the power by which the people are to be defended consists in their armies, and the strength of an army, in the union of their strength under one command, which command the sovereign instituted, therefore has; because the command of the "militia," without other institution, makes him that has it sovereign. And therefore whosoever is made general of an army, he that has the sovereign power is always generalissimo.

Tenthly, is annexed to the sovereignty, the choosing of all counsellors, ministers, magistrates, and officers, both in peace and war. For seeing the sovereign is charged with the end, which is the common peace and defence, he is understood to have power to use such means as he shall think most fit for his discharge.

Eleventhly, to the sovereign is committed the power of rewarding with riches or honour, and of punishing with corporal or pecuniary punishment, or with ignominy, every subject according to the law he has formerly made, or if there be no law made, according as he shall judge most to lead to the encouraging of men to serve the commonwealth, or deterring of them from doing disservice to the same.

Lastly, considering what value men are naturally apt to set upon themselves; what respect they look for from others; and how little they value other men; from which continually arise among them, emulation, quarrels, factions, and at last war, to the destroying of one another, and diminution of their strength against a common enemy; it is necessary that there be laws of honour, and a public rate of the worth of such men as have deserved, or are able to deserve well of the commonwealth; and that there be force in the hands of some or other, to put those laws in execution. But it has already been shown, that not only the whole "militia," or forces of the commonwealth, but also the judicature of all controversies, is annexed to the sovereignty. To the sovereign therefore it belongs also to give titles of honour; and to appoint what order of place and dignity each man shall hold; and what signs of respect, in public or private meetings, they shall give to one another. . . .

OF THE SEVERAL KINDS OF COMMONWEALTH BY INSTITUTION,
AND OF SUCCESSION TO THE SOVEREIGN POWER

The difference of commonwealths consists in the difference of the sovereign, or the person representative of all and every one of the multitude. And because the sovereignty is either in one man, or in an assembly of more than one; and into that assembly either every man has right to enter, or not every one, but certain men distinguished from the rest; it is manifest, there can be but three kinds of commonwealth. For the representative must needs be one man, or more: and if more, when it is the assembly of all that will come together, then it is a "democracy," or popular commonwealth: when an assembly of a part only, then it is called an "aristocracy." Other kind of commonwealth there can be none: for either one or more, or all, must have the sovereign power, which I have shown to be indivisible, entire.

There be other names of government in the histories and books of policy, as "tyranny," and "oligarchy": but they are not the names of other forms of government, but of the same forms misliked. For they that are discontented under "monarchy," call it "tyranny"; and they that are displeased with "aristocracy," call it "oligarchy": so also they which find themselves grieved under a "democracy," call it "anarchy," which signifies want of government; and yet I think no man believes that want of government is any new kind of government: nor by the same reason ought they to believe that the government is of one kind when they like it, and another when they dislike it, or are oppressed by the governors.

It is manifest, that men who are in absolute liberty may, if they please, give authority to one man to represent them every one; as well as give such authority to any assembly of men whatsoever; and consequently may subject themselves, if they think good, to a monarch as absolutely as to any other representative. Therefore, where there is already erected a sovereign power, there can be no other representative of the same people, but only to certain particular ends, by the sovereign limited. For that were to erect two sovereigns; and every man to have his person represented by two actors, that by opposing one another, must needs divide that power, which, if men will live in peace, is indivisible, and thereby reduce the multitude into the condition of war, contrary to the end for which all sovereignty is instituted. And therefore as it is absurd to think that a sovereign assembly, inviting the people of their dominion to send up their deputies, with power to make known their advice, or desires, should therefore hold such deputies rather than themselves, for the absolute representatives of the people; so it is absurd also to think the same in a monarchy. And I know not how this so manifest a truth should of late be so little observed; that in a monarchy, he that had the sovereignty from a descent of six hundred years, was alone called sovereign, had the title of Majesty from every one of his subjects, and was unquestionably taken by them for their king, was notwithstanding never considered as their representative; the name without contradiction passing for the title of those men, which at his command were sent up by the people to carry their petitions, and give him, if he permitted it, their advice. Which may serve as an admonition, for those that are the true and absolute representative of a people, to instruct men in the nature of that office, and to take heed how they admit of any other general representation upon any occasion whatsoever, if they mean to discharge the trust committed to them.

The difference between these three kinds of commonwealth, consists not in the difference of power; but in the difference of convenience, or aptitude to produce the peace and security of the people; for which end they were instituted. And to compare monarchy with the other two, we may observe; first, that whosoever bears the person of the people, or is one of that assembly that bears it, bears also his own natural person. And though he be careful in his politic person to procure the common interest; yet he is more or no less careful to procure the private good of himself, his family, kindred, and friends; and for the most part, if the public interest chance to cross the private, he prefers the private: for the passions of men are commonly more potent than their reason. From whence it follows, that where the public and private interest are most closely united, there is the public most advanced. Now in monarchy, the private interest is the same with the public. The riches, power, and honour of a monarch, arise only from the riches, strength, and reputation of his subjects. For no king can be rich, nor glorious, nor secure, whose subjects are either poor, or contemptible, or too weak through want or dissension, to maintain a war against their enemies: whereas in a democracy, or aristocracy, the public prosperity confers not so much to the private fortune of one that is corrupt, or ambitious, as do many times a perfidious advice, a treacherous action, or a civil war.

Secondly, that a monarch receives counsel of whom, when, and where he pleases; and consequently may hear the opinion of men versed in the matter about which he deliberates, of whatever rank or quality, and as long before the time of action, and with as much secrecy, as he will. But when a sovereign assembly has need of counsel, none are admitted but such as have a right thereto from the beginning; which for the most part are of those who have been versed more in the acquisition of wealth than of knowledge; and are to give their advice in long discourses, which may and do commonly excite men to action, but not govern them in it. For the "understanding" is by the flame of the passions, never enlightened, but dazzled. Nor is there any place, or time, wherein an assembly can receive counsel with secrecy, because of their own multitude.

Thirdly, that the resolutions of a monarch are subject to no other inconstancy, than that of human nature; but in assemblies, besides that of Nature, there arises an inconstancy from the number. For the absence of a few, that would have the resolution once taken, continued firm, which may happen by security, negligence, or private impediments, or the diligent appearance of a few of the contrary opinion, undoes to-day all that was concluded yesterday.

Fourthly, that a monarch cannot disagree with himself, out of envy or interest; but an assembly may; and that to such a height, as may produce a civil war.

Fifthly, that in monarchy there is this inconvenience; that any subject, by the power of one man, for the enriching of a favorite or flatterer, may be deprived of all he possesses; which I confess is a great and inevitable inconvenience.

But the same may as well happen, where the sovereign power is an assembly: for their power is the same; and they are as subject to evil counsel, and to be seduced by orators, as a monarch by flatterers; and becoming one another's flatterers, serve one another's covetousness and ambition by turns. And whereas the favorites of monarchs are few, and they have none else to advance but their own kindred; the favorites of an assembly are many; and the kindred much more numerous than of any monarch. Besides there is no favorite of a monarch, which cannot as well succour his friends as hurt his enemies; but orators, that is to say, favorites of sovereign assemblies, though they have great power to hurt, have little to save. For to accuse, requires less eloquence, such is man's nature, than to excuse; and condemnation, than absolution more resembles justice.

John Locke

Though probably written earlier, Locke's treatises on government have generally been considered as having been offered in justification of the English Revolution of 1688. Such justification is provided largely by arguing that government and society exist in order to preserve the individual's rights, and that a ruler's failure to abide by this fundamental stipulation calls for his removal. This theory explains society in terms of individual interests. Its assumptions were outlined in a description of the "state of nature" and in conclusions drawn from the way Locke envisioned the state of nature. Locke's views, which were quite different from those of Hobbes, proved far more influential.

From The Second Treatise on Government

OF THE STATE OF NATURE

To understand political power aright, and derive it from its original, we must consider what estate all men are naturally in, and that is, a state of perfect freedom to order their actions, and dispose of their possessions and persons as they think fit, within the bounds of the law of nature, without asking leave or depending upon the will of any other man.

From John Locke, *Treatise on Government* (London, 1690), Book 2.

A state also of equality, wherein all the power and jurisdiction is reciprocal, no one having more than another, there being nothing more evident than that creatures of the same species and rank, promiscuously born to all the same advantages of nature, and the use of the same faculties, should also be equal one among another without subordination or subjection, unless the lord and master of them all should, by any manifest declaration of his will, set one above another, and confer on him, by an evident and clear appointment, an undoubted right to dominion and sovereignty. . . .

But though this be a state of liberty, yet it is not a state of license; though man in that state have an uncontrollable liberty to dispose of his person or possessions, yet he has not liberty to destroy himself, or so much as any creature in his possession, but where some nobler use than its bare preservation calls for it. The state of nature has a law of nature to govern it, which obliges every one, and reason, which is that law, teaches all mankind who will but consult it, that being all equal and independent, no one ought to harm another in his life, health, liberty or possessions. For men being all the workmanship of one omnipotent and infinitely wise Maker—all the servants of one sovereign Master, sent into the world by his order and about his business— they are his property, whose workmanship they are, made to last during his, not one another's pleasure. And, being furnished with like faculties, sharing all in one community of nature, there cannot be supposed any such subordination among us that may authorize us to destroy one another, as if we were made for one another's uses, as the inferior ranks of creatures are for ours. Every one as he is bound to preserve himself, and not to quit his station willfully, so by the like reason, when his own preservation comes not in competition, ought he as much as he can, to preserve the rest of mankind, and not unless it be to do justice on an offender, take away, or impair the life or what tends to be the preservation of the life, the liberty, health, limb, or goods of another. . . .

OF THE BEGINNINGS OF POLITICAL SOCIETIES

Men, being, as has been said, by nature all free, equal, and independent, no one can be put out of this estate and subjected to the political power of another without his own consent. The only way whereby anyone divests himself of his natural liberty and puts on the bonds of civil society, is by agreeing with other men, to join and unite into a community for their comfortable, safe and peaceable living one among another, in a secure enjoyment of their properties, and a greater security against any that are not of it. This any number of men may do, because it injures not the freedom of the rest; they are left, as they were, in the liberty of the state of nature. When any number of men have so consented to make one community or government, they are thereby presently incorporated, and make one body politic, wherein the majority have a right to act and conclude the rest. . . .

And thus every man, by consenting with others to make one body politic under one government, puts himself under an obligation to every one of that society to submit to the determination of the majority, and to be concluded by it; or else this original compact whereby he with others incorporates into one society, would signify nothing. . . .

For if the consent of the majority shall not, in reason be received as the act of the whole, and conclude every individual; nothing but the consent of every individual can make anything to be the act of the whole; but such a consent is next to impossible ever to be had. . . .

OF THE ENDS OF POLITICAL SOCIETY AND GOVERNMENT

If man in the state of nature be so free as has been said, if he be absolute lord of his own person and possessions, equal to the greatest and subject to nobody, why will he part with his freedom? Why will he give up this empire, and subject himself to the dominion and control of any other power? To which it is obvious to answer, that though in the state of nature he has such a right, yet the enjoyment of it is very uncertain and constantly exposed to the invasion of others; for all being kings as much as he, every man his equal, and the greater part no strict observers of equity and justice, the enjoyment of the property he has in this state is very unsafe, very insecure. This makes him willing to quit this condition which, however free, is full of fears and continual dangers; and it is not without reason that he seeks out and is willing to join in society with others who are already united, or have a mind to unite for the mutual preservation of their lives, liberties and estates, which I call by the general name—property.

The great and chief end, therefore, of men uniting into commonwealths, and putting themselves under government, is the preservation of their property; to which in the state of nature there are many things wanting.

First, There wants an established, settled, known law, received and allowed by common consent to be the standard of right and wrong, and the common measure to decide all controversies between them. For though the law of nature be plain and intelligible to all rational creatures, yet men, being biased by their interest, as well as ignorant for want of study of it, are not apt to allow of it as a law binding to them in the application of it to their particular cases.

Secondly, In the state of nature there wants a known and indifferent judge, with authority to determine all differences according to the established law. For every one in that state, being both judge and executioner of the law of nature, men being partial to themselves, passion and revenge is very apt to carry them too far, and with too much heat in their own cases, as well as negligence and unconcernedness, make them too remiss in other men's.

Thirdly, In the state of nature there often wants power to back and support the sentence when right, and to give it due execution. They who by any injustice offend will seldom fail where they are able by force to make good their injustice. Such resistance many times makes the punishment dangerous, and frequently destructive to those who attempt it.

Thus mankind, notwithstanding all the privileges of the state of nature, being but in an ill condition while they remain in it, are quickly driven into society. Hence it comes to pass, that we seldom find any number of men live any time together in this state. The inconveniences that they are therein exposed to by the irregular and uncertain exercise of the power every man has of punishing the transgressions of others, make them take sanctuary under the established laws of government, and therein seek the preservation of their property. It is this makes them so willingly give up every one his single power of punishing to be exercised by such alone as shall be appointed to it among them, and by such rules as the community, or those authorized by them to that purpose, shall agree on. And in this we have the original right and rise of both the legislative and executive power as well as of the governments and societies themselves.

For in the state of nature, to omit the liberty he has of innocent delights, a man has two powers.

The first is to do whatsoever he thinks fit for the preservation of himself and others within the permission of the law of nature, by which law, common to them all, he and all the rest of mankind are of one community, make up one society, distinct from all other creatures. And were it not for the corruption and viciousness of degenerate men there would be no need of any other, no necessity that men should separate from this great and natural community, and associate into lesser combinations.

The other power a man has in the state of nature is the power to punish the crimes committed against that law. Both these he gives up when he joins in a private, if I may so call it, or particular political society, and incorporates into any commonwealth separate from the rest of mankind.

The first power—viz., of doing whatsoever he thought fit for the preservation of himself and the rest of mankind, he gives up to be regulated by laws made by the society, so far forth as the preservation of himself and the rest of that society shall require; which laws of the society in many things confine the liberty he had by the law of nature.

Secondly, the power of punishing he wholly gives up, and engages his natural force (which he might before employ in the execution of the law of nature, by his own single authority, as he thought fit), to assist the executive power of the society as the law thereof shall require. For being now in a new state, wherein he is to enjoy many conveniences from the labor, assistance, and society of others in the same community, as well as protection from its whole strength, he is to part also with as much of his natural liberty, in providing for himself, as the good, prosperity, and safety of the society shall require, which is not only necessary but just, since the other members of the society do the like.

But though men when they enter into society give up the equality, liberty, and executive power they had in the state of nature into the hands of the society, to be so far disposed of by the legislative as the good of the society shall require, yet it being only with an intention in every one the better to preserve himself, his liberty and property (for no rational creature can be supposed to change his condition with an intention to be worse), the power of the society or legislative constituted by them can never be supposed to extend farther than the common good, but is obliged to secure every one's property by providing against those three defects above mentioned that made the state of nature so unsafe and uneasy. And so, whoever has the legislative or supreme power of any commonwealth, is bound to govern by established standing laws, promulgated and known to the people, and not by extemporary decrees; by indifferent and upright judges, who are to decide controversies by those laws; and to employ the force of the community at home only in the execution of such laws, or abroad to prevent or redress foreign injuries and secure the community from inroads and invasion. And all this to be directed to no other end, but the peace, safety, and public good of the people.

OF THE EXTENT OF THE LEGISLATIVE POWER

The great end of men's entering into society being the enjoyment of their properties in peace and safety, and the great instrument and means of that being the laws established in that society, the first and fundamental positive law of all commonwealths is the establishing of the legislative power. . . . This legislative is not only the supreme power of the commonwealth, but sacred and unalterable in the hands where the community have once placed it. Nor can any edict of anybody else, in what form soever conceived, or by what power soever backed, have the force and obligation of a law which has not its sanction from that legislative which the public has chosen and appointed. . . .

Though the legislative . . . be the supreme power in every commonwealth; yet,

First, it is not, nor can possibly be, absolutely arbitrary over the lives and fortunes of the people. . . . For nobody can transfer to another more power than he has in himself, and nobody has an absolute arbitrary power over himself, or over any other, to destroy his own life, or take away the life or property of another. A man, as has been proved, cannot subject himself to the arbitrary power of another; and having, in the state of nature, no arbitrary power over the life, liberty, or possession of another, but only so much as the law of nature gave him for the preservation of himself and the rest of mankind, this is all he does, or can give up to the commonwealth, and by it to the legislative power, so that the legislative can have no more than this. Their power in the utmost bounds of it is limited to the public good of the society. It is a power that has no other end but preservation, and therefore can never have a right to destroy, enslave, or designedly to impoverish the subjects. The obligations of the law of nature cease not in society, but only in many cases are drawn closer, and have, by human laws, known penalties annexed to them to enforce their observation. Thus the law of nature stands as an external rule to all men, legislators as well as others. The rules that they make for other men's actions must, as well as their own and other men's actions, be conformable to the law of nature—i.e., to the will of God, of which that is a declaration, and the fundamental law of nature, being the preservation of mankind, no human sanction can be good or valid against it.

Secondly, the legislative or supreme authority cannot assume to itself a power to rule by extemporary arbitrary decrees, but is bound to dispense justice and decide the rights of the subject by promulgated standing laws, and known authorized judges. For the law of nature being unwritten, and so nowhere to be found but in the minds of men, they who, through passion or interest, shall miscite or misapply it, cannot so easily be convinced of their mistake where there is no established judge. To avoid these inconveniences which disorder men's properties in the state of nature, men unite into societies that they may have the united strength of the whole society to secure and defend their properties, and may have standing rules to bound it by which every one may know what is his. To this end, it is that men give up all their natural power to the society they enter into, and the community put the legislative power into such hands as they think fit, with this trust, that they shall be governed by declared laws, or else their peace, quiet, and property will still be at the same uncertainty as it was in the state of nature.

Absolute arbitrary power, or governing without settled standing laws, can neither of them consist with the ends of society and government. . . . And, therefore, whatever form the commonwealth is under, the ruling power ought to govern by declared and received laws, and not by extemporary dictates and undetermined resolutions. . . . For all the power the government has, being only for the good of the society, as it ought not to be arbitrary and at pleasure, so it ought to be exercised by established and promulgated laws, that both the people may know their duty, and be safe and secure within the limits of the law, and the rulers, too, kept within their due bounds, and not tempted by the power they have in their hands to employ it to purposes, and by such measures as they would not have known, and own not willingly.

Thirdly, the supreme power cannot take from any man any part of his property without his own consent. For the preservation of property being the end of government, and that for which men enter into society, it necessarily supposes and requires that the people should have property, without which they must be supposed to lose that by entering into society, which was the end for which they entered into it; too gross an absurdity for any man to own. Men, therefore, in society having property, they have such a right to the goods, which by the law of the community are theirs, that nobody has a right to take them, or any part of them, from them without their own consent; without this they have no property at all. For I have truly no property in that which another can by right take from me when he pleases against my consent. Hence it is a mistake to think that the supreme or legislative power of any commonwealth can do what it will, and dispose of the estates of the subject arbitrarily, or take any part of them at pleasure. This is not much to be feared in governments where the legislative consists wholly or in part in assemblies which are variable, whose members upon the dissolution of the assembly are subjects under the common laws of their country, equally with the rest. But in governments where the legislative is in one man as in absolute monarchies, there is danger still, that they will think themselves to have a distinct interest from the rest of the community, and so will be apt to increase their own riches and power by taking what they think fit from the people. For a man's property is not at all secure, though there be good and equitable laws to set the bounds of it between him and his fellow-subjects, if he who commands those subjects have power to take from any private man what part he pleases of his property, and use and dispose of it as he thinks good.

But government into whosesoever hands it is put, being as I have before showed, entrusted with this condition, and for this end, that men might have and secure their properties, the prince or senate, however it may have power to make laws for the regulating of property between the subjects one among another, yet can never have a power to take to themselves the whole, or any part of the subjects' property, without their own consent; for this would be in effect to leave them no property at all. And to let us see that even absolute power, where it is necessary, is not arbitrary by being absolute, but is still limited by that reason, and confined to those ends which required it in some cases to be absolute, we need look no farther than the common practice of martial discipline. For the preservation of the army, and in it of the whole common-wealth, requires an absolute obedience to the command of every superior officer, and it is justly death to disobey or dispute the most dangerous or unreasonable of them; but yet we see that neither the sergeant that could command a soldier to march up to the mouth of a cannon, or stand in a breach where he is almost sure to perish, can command that soldier to give him one penny of his money; nor the general that can condemn him to death for deserting his post, or not obeying the most desperate orders, cannot yet with all his absolute power of life and death dispose of one farthing of that soldier's estate, or seize one jot of his goods; whom yet he can command anything, and hang for the least disobedience. Because such a blind obedience is necessary to that end for which the commander has his power—viz., the preservation of the rest, but the disposing of his goods has nothing to do with it.

It is true governments cannot be supported without great charge, and it is fit every one who enjoys his share of the protection should pay out of his estate his proportion for the maintenance of it. But still it must be with his own consent—i.e., the consent of the majority, giving it either by themselves or their representatives chosen by them; for if any one shall claim a power to lay and levy taxes on the people by his own authority, and without such consent of the people, he thereby invades the fundamental law of property, and subverts the end of government. For what property have I in that which another may by right take when he pleases to himself?

Fourthly, the legislative cannot transfer the power of making laws to any other hands, for it being but a delegated power from the people, they who have it cannot pass it over to others. The people alone can appoint the form of the commonwealth, which is by constituting the legislative, and appointing in whose hands that shall be. And when the people have said, "We will submit, and be governed by laws made by such men, and in such forms," nobody else can say other men shall make laws for them; nor can they be bound by any laws but such as are enacted by those whom they have chosen and authorized to make laws for them. . . .

These are the bounds which the trust that is put in them by the society and the law of God and nature have set to the legislative power of every commonwealth, in all forms of government.

First: They are to govern by promulgated established laws, not to be varied in particular cases, nor to have one rule for rich and poor, for the favorite at court, and the countryman at plough.

Secondly: These laws also ought to be designed for no other end ultimately but the good of the people.

Thirdly: They must not raise taxes on the property of the people without the consent of the people given by themselves or their deputies. . . .

Fourthly: The legislative neither must nor can transfer the power of making laws to anybody else, or place it anywhere but where the people have.

OF THE SUBORDINATION OF THE POWERS OF THE COMMONWEALTH

Though in a constituted commonwealth . . . there can be but one supreme power, which is the legislative, to which all the rest are and must be subordinate, yet the legislative being only a fiduciary power to act for certain ends, there remains still in the people a supreme power to remove or alter the legislative, when they find the legislative act contrary to the trust reposed in them. For all power given with trust for the attaining of an end being limited by that end; whenever that end is manifestly neglected or opposed, the trust must necessarily be forfeited, and the power devolve into the hands of those that gave it, who may place it anew where they shall think best for their safety and security. And thus the community perpetually retains a supreme power of saving themselves from the attempts and designs of anybody, even of their legislators, whenever they shall be so foolish or so wicked as to lay and carry on designs against the liberties and properties of the subject. For no man or society of men having a power to deliver up their preservation, or consequently the means of it, to the absolute will and arbitrary dominion of another, whenever any one shall go about to bring them into such a slavish condition, they will always have a right to preserve what they have not a power to part with, and to rid themselves of those who invade this into society. And thus the community may be said in this respect to be always the supreme power, but not as considered under any form of government, because this power of the people can never take place till the government be dissolved.

In all cases whilst the government subsists, the legislative is the supreme power. For what can give laws to another must needs be superior to him. . . .

It may be demanded here, what if the executive power, being possessed of the force of the commonwealth, shall make use of that force to hinder the meeting and acting of the legislative, when the original constitution or the public exigencies require it? I say, using force upon the people, without authority, and contrary to the trust put in him that does so, is a state of war with the people, who have a right to reinstate their legislative in the exercise of their power. . . . In all states and conditions the true remedy of force without authority is to oppose force to it. The use of force without authority always puts him that uses it into a state of war as the aggressor, and renders him liable to be treated accordingly. . . .

OF TYRANNY

As usurpation is the exercise of power which another has a right to, so tyranny is the exercise of power beyond right, which nobody can have a right to; and this is making use of the power any one has in his hands, not for the good of those who are under it, but for his own private, separate advantage. When the governor, however entitled, makes not the law but his will the rule, and his commands and actions are not directed to the preservation of the properties of his people, but the satisfaction of his own ambition, revenge, covetousness, or any other irregular passion [that is, tyranny]. . . .

It is a mistake to think this fault is proper [that is, belongs] only to monarchies. Other forms of government are liable to it as well as that; for wherever the power that is put in any hands for the government of the people and the preservation of their properties is applied to other ends, and made use of to impoverish, harass, or subdue them to the arbitrary and irregular commands of those that have it, there it presently becomes tyranny, whether those that thus use it are one or many. Thus we read of the thirty tyrants at Athens, as well as one at Syracuse; and the intolerable dominion of the Decemviri at Rome was nothing better.

Wherever law ends, tyranny begins, if the law be transgressed to another's harm; and whosoever in authority exceeds the power given him by the law, and makes use of the force he has under his command to compass that upon the subject which the law allows not, ceases in that to be a magistrate, and acting without authority may be opposed, as any other man who by force invades the right of another. This is acknowledged in subordinate magistrates. He that has authority to seize my person in the street may be opposed as a thief and a robber if he endeavors to break into my house to execute a writ, notwithstanding that I know he has such a warrant and such a legal authority as will empower him to arrest me abroad. And why this should not hold in the highest, as well as in the most inferior magistrate, I would gladly be informed. Is it reasonable that the eldest brother, because he has the greatest part of his father's estate, should thereby have a right to take away any of his younger brothers' portions? Or, that a rich man, who possessed a whole country, should from thence have a right to seize, when he pleased, the cottage and garden of his poor neighbor? The being rightfully possessed of great power and riches, exceedingly beyond the greatest part of the sons of Adam, is so far from being an excuse, much less a reason for rapine and oppression, which the endamaging another without authority is, that it is a great aggravation of it. For the exceeding the bounds of authority is no more a right in a great than a petty officer, no more justifiable in a king than a constable.

May the commands, then, of a prince be opposed? May he be opposed? May he be resisted, as often as any one shall find himself aggrieved, and but imagine he has not right done him? This will unhinge and overturn all politics, and instead of government and order, leave nothing but anarchy and confusion.

To this I answer: That force is to be opposed to nothing but to unjust and unlawful force. Whoever makes any opposition in any other case draws on himself a just condemnation, both from God and man, and no such danger or confusion will follow, as is often suggested.

OF THE DISSOLUTION OF GOVERNMENT

He that will, with any clearness, speak of the dissolution of government, ought in the first place to distinguish between the dissolution of the society and the dissolution of the government. That which makes the community, and brings men out of the loose state of nature into one politic society, is the agreement which everyone has with the rest to incorporate and act as one body, and so be one distinct commonwealth. The usual, and almost only way whereby this union is dissolved, is the inroad of foreign force making a conquest upon them. . . . The world is too well instructed in, and too forward to allow of this way of dissolving of governments, to need any more to be said of it. . . .

There is, therefore, secondly, another way whereby governments are dissolved, and that is, when the legislative, or the prince, either of them act contrary to their trust.

First: the legislative acts against the trust reposed in them when they endeavor to invade the property of the subject, and to make themselves, or any part of the community, masters or arbitrary disposers of the lives, liberties, or fortunes of the people.

. . . Whensoever, therefore, the legislative shall transgress this fundamental rule of society, and either by ambition, fear, folly, or corruption, endeavor to grasp themselves, or put into the hands of any other, an absolute power over the lives, liberties, and estates of the people; by this breach of trust they forfeit the power the people had put into their hands for quite contrary ends; and it devolves to the people, who have a right to resume their original liberty, and by the establishment of a new legislative (such as they shall think fit), provide for their own safety and security, which is the end for which they are in society. What I have said here concerning the legislative in general holds true also concerning the supreme executor, who having a double trust put in him, both to have a part in the legislative and the supreme execution of the law, acts against both, when he goes about to set up his own arbitrary will as the law of the society. He acts also contrary to his trust when he employs the force, treasure, and offices of the society to corrupt the representatives, and gain them to his purposes, when he openly pre-engages the electors, and prescribes, to their choice, such whom he has, by solicitation, threats, promises, or otherwise, won to his designs, and employs them to bring in such who have promised beforehand what to vote and what to enact. Thus to regulate candidates and electors, and new model the ways of election, what is it but to cut up the government by the roots, and poison the very fountain of public security?

To this, perhaps it will be said that the people being ignorant and always discontented, to lay the foundation of government in the unsteady opinion and uncertain humor of the people, is to expose it to certain ruin; and no government will be able long to subsist if the people may set up a new legislative whenever they take offense at the old one. To this I answer, quite the contrary. People are not so easily got out of their old forms as some are apt to suggest. They are hardly to be prevailed with to amend the acknowledged faults in the frame they have been accustomed to. And if there be any original defects, or adventitious ones introduced by time or corruption, it is not an easy thing to get them changed, even when all the world sees there is an opportunity for it. This slowness and aversion in the people to quit their old constitutions has in the many revolutions that have been seen in this kingdom, in this and former ages, still kept us to, or after some interval of fruitless attempts, still brought us back again to, our old legislative of kings, lords, and commons; and whatever provocations have made the crown be taken from some of our princes' heads, they never carried the people so far as to place it in another line.

But it will be said this hypothesis lays a ferment for further rebellion. To which I answer:

First: no more than any other hypothesis. For when the people are made miserable, and find themselves exposed to the ill usage of arbitrary power, cry up their governors as much as you will for sons of Jupiter, let them be sacred and divine, descended or authorized from Heaven; give them out for whom or what you please, the same will happen. The people generally ill treated, and contrary to right, will be ready upon any occasion to ease themselves of a burden that sits heavy upon them. They will wish and seek for the opportunity, which in the change, weakness, and accidents of human affairs, seldom delays long to offer itself. He must have lived but a little while in the world, who has not seen examples of this in his time; and he must have read very little who cannot produce examples of it in all sorts of governments in the world.

Secondly: I answer, such revolutions happen not upon every little mismanagement in public affairs. Great mistakes in the ruling part, many wrong and inconvenient laws, and all the slips of human frailty will be borne by the people without mutiny or murmur. But if a long train of abuses, prevarications, and artifices, all tending the same way, make the design visible to the people, and they cannot but feel what they lie under, and see whither they are going, it is not to be wondered that they should then rouse themselves, and endeavor to put the rule into such hands which may secure to them the ends for which government was at first erected, and without which, ancient names and specious forms are so far from being better, that they are much worse than the state of nature or pure anarchy; the inconveniences being all as great and as near, but the remedy farther off and more difficult.

Thirdly: I answer, that this . . . power in the people of providing for their safety anew by a new legislative when their legislators have acted contrary to their trust by invading their property, is the best fence against rebellion, and the probablest means to hinder it. For rebellion being an opposition, not to persons, but authority, which is founded only in the constitutions and laws of the government; those, whoever they be, who by force break through, and by force justify their violations of them, are truly and properly rebels. For when men, by entering into society and civil government, have excluded force, and introduced laws for the preservation of property, peace, and unity amongst themselves, those who set up force again in opposition to the laws, do *rebellare*—that is, bring back again the state of war, and are properly rebels, which they who are in power (by the pretence they have to authority, the temptation of force they have in their hands, and the flattery of those about them), being likeliest to do, the properest way to prevent the evil is to show them the danger and injustice of it who are under the greatest temptation to run into it. . . .

But if they who say it lays a foundation for rebellion mean that it may occasion civil wars or intestine broils to tell the people they are absolved from obedience when illegal attempts are made upon their liberties or properties, and may oppose the unlawful violence of those who were their magistrates when they invade their properties, contrary to the trust put in them, and that, therefore, this doctrine is not to be allowed, being so destructive to the peace of the world; they may as well say, upon the same ground, that honest men may not oppose robbers or pirates, because this may occasion disorder or bloodshed. If any mischief come in such cases, it is not to be charged upon him who defends his own right, but on him that invades his neighbor's. If the innocent honest man must quietly quit all he has for peace's sake to him who will lay violent hands upon it, I desire it may be considered what a kind of peace there will be in the world which consists only in violence and rapine, and which is to be maintained only for the benefit of robbers and oppressors. Who would not think it an admirable peace betwixt the mighty and the mean, when the lamb, without resistance, yielded his throat to be torn by the imperious wolf?

The end of government is the good of mankind; and which is best for mankind, that the people should be always exposed to the boundless will of tyranny, or that the ruler should be sometimes liable to be opposed when they grow exorbitant in the use of their power, and employ it for the destruction, and not the preservation, of the properties of their people?

Nor let any one say that mischief can arise from hence as often as it shall please a busy head or turbulent spirit to desire the alteration of the government. It is true such men stir whenever they please, but it will be only to their own just ruin and perdition. For till the mischief be grown general, and the ill designs of the rulers become visible, or their attempts sensible to the greater part, the people who are more disposed to suffer than right themselves by resistance, are not apt to stir. The examples of particular injustice or oppression of here and there an unfortunate man moves them not. But if they universally have a persuasion grounded upon manifest evidence that designs are carrying on against their liberties, and the general course and tendency of things cannot but give them strong suspicions of the evil intention of their governors, who is to be blamed for it? Who can help it if they, who might avoid it, bring themselves into this suspicion? Are the people to be blamed if they have the sense of rational creatures, and can think of things no otherwise than as they find and feel them? And is it not rather their fault who put things in such a posture that they would not have them thought as they are? I grant that the pride, ambition, and turbulency of private men have sometimes caused great disorders in commonwealths, and factions have been fatal to states and kingdoms. But whether the mischief has oftener begun in the people's wantonness, and a desire to cast off the lawful authority of their rulers, or in the rulers' insolence and endeavors to get and exercise an arbitrary power over their people, whether oppression or disobedience gave the first rise to the disorder, I leave it to impartial history to determine. This I am sure, whoever, either ruler or subject, by force goes about to invade the rights of either prince or people, and lays the foundation for overturning the constitution and frame of any just government, he is guilty of the greatest crime I think a man is capable of, being to answer for all those mischiefs of blood, rapine, and desolation, which the breaking to pieces of governments brings on a country; and he who does it is justly to be esteemed the common enemy and pest of mankind; and is to be treated accordingly. . . .

Here it is like, the common question will be made, Who shall be judge whether the prince or legislative act contrary to their trust? . . . To this I reply, The people shall be judge; for who shall be judge whether his trustee or deputy acts well and according to the trust reposed in him, but he who deputes him and must, by having deputed him, have still a power to discard him when he fails in his trust? If this be reasonable in particular cases of private men, why should it be otherwise in that of the greatest moment, where the welfare of millions is concerned and also where the evil, if not prevented, is greater, and the redress very difficult, dear, and dangerous? . . .

If a controversy arise between a prince and some of the people in a matter where the law is silent or doubtful, and the thing be of great consequence, I should think the proper umpire in such a case should be the body of the people. For in cases where the prince has a trust reposed in him, and is dispensed from the common, ordinary rules of the law, there, if any men find themselves aggrieved, and think the prince acts contrary to, or beyond that trust, who so proper to judge as the body of the people (who at first lodged that trust in him) how far they meant it should extend? But if the prince, or whoever they be in the administration, decline that way of determination, the appeal then lies nowhere but to Heaven; force between either persons who have no known superior on earth, or which permits no appeal to a judge on earth, being properly a state of war, wherein the appeal lies only to Heaven; and in that state the injured party must judge for himself when he will think fit to make use of that appeal and put himself upon it.

To conclude: The power that every individual gave the society when he entered into it can never revert to the individuals again, as long as the society lasts, but will always remain in the community; because without this there can be no community—no commonwealth, which is contrary to the original agreement; so also when the society has placed the legislative in any assembly of men, to continue in them and their successors, with direction and authority for providing such successors, the legislative can never revert to the people while that government lasts; because, having provided a legislative with power to continue forever, they have given up their political power to the legislative and cannot resume it. But if they have set limits to the duration of their legislative, and made this supreme power in any person or assembly only temporary; or else, when, by the miscarriages of those in authority it is forfeited; upon the forfeiture of their rules, or at the determination of the time set, it reverts to the society, and the people have a right to act as supreme, and continue the legislative in themselves or place it in a new form, or new hands, as they think good.

A Time of Belief

The Eighteenth Century
Enlightened Despotism
A Dawn of Revolution
The Reaction
Romantics and Romanticism
Economic Revolution
But Life Goes On
Liberalism, Nationalism, and 1848

THE TEMPTATION TO SELECT ONE CHARACTERISTIC OF A period and arbitrarily proclaim its dominance over all others is always strong and always dangerous. But the temptation becomes a necessity when one seeks a principle of unity in a period as full of diversity as the one that runs from the death of Louis XIV to the revolutions of 1848: enlightened despotism, constitutional monarchy, revolution, Jacobin terror, liberalism and reaction, the dreams of the romantic poets and the no less exalted dreams of industrialists and economists—these make an ill-matched company. Yet they all have one thing in common: the same self-confidence, the same belief that by following their particular recipe the world could be made a better place—indeed, quite likely, a perfect place.

This is why the years between the birth of Frederick the Great and the death of the Second Republic in France were a time of belief, in which the failure of one panacea merely brought more grist to the mill of the others; belief that was shared by all the most typical representatives of the time . . . except for Metternich. And if Metternich had no particular faith in the future, he had a prodigious faith in himself, which makes him, too, a man of his time.

IMAGES: INTIMACY

In the twentieth century, an English gentlewoman, Virginia Woolf, voiced the yearning for a room of her own. Privacy, until recently, was a rare commodity, reserved for the fortunate few; but it was suggested by the individualism born with the Renaissance. For a long time, though, small chambers and studios that could provide privacy were exceptional, and so was access to intimate space. As more families acknowledged the desirability of space and comfort, opportunities for intimate intercourse began to match the growing appreciation of it. Family affection, intimate occasions, the opportunity to read, reflect, or talk undistracted, were some of the achievements of the modern age.

Federico da Montefeltro (1422–1482). The greatest general of his day, Montefeltro invested the profits of his wars in rebuilding the family castle of Urbino, where he built a library study and had himself portrayed on one of its walls reading one of his manuscripts. He wears armor and his helmet sits beside him, but what he shows off is his literary taste and his enjoyment of privacy, both of which were exceptional in his day. Federico's bookseller once asked him what was essential in ruling. "To be human," the duke replied. The court of Federico's son and heir, Guidobaldo (shown standing beside him), would later be the stage of Castiglione's celebration of gentlemanly manners, *The Courtier* (1528).
(Alinari/Art Resource, NY)

Arnolfini and His Wife (1434), by Jan van Eyck. The Arnolfinis were wool merchants and bankers, originally from Lucca, who had settled in Bruges. This wedding portrait celebrates the holiness of marriage. The spouses commit themselves to each other by clasping their hands in a room cluttered with symbols. The marriage bed appears, of course, and the single candle burning on the chandelier evokes Christ as witness to their vows. The rosary and the mirror stand for innocence and purity. The fruit on the windowsill recalls paradise lost. The little dog represents faithfulness. The pattens, used for walking through muddy city streets, have been cast off to honor God's presence. (Jan van Eyck, *The Arnolfini Marriage, 1434,* courtesy, National Gallery, London)

Le Déjeuner, by François Boucher. This family breakfast painted by Boucher (an artist we more readily associate with erotic sensuality) is about the simple joys of life. It portrays father, mother, governess, and two little children who may testify to the beginnings of family planning, or else to their parents' youth. Dress, furniture, decoration, and porcelain are expensive enough to suggest the comfort without which access to simple joys becomes difficult.

(*Le Déjeuner* by François Boucher, Cliché des Musées Nationaux, Paris)

The Young Schoolmistress, by Jean-Baptiste Chardin. The painting illustrates the advance of literacy in the 1700s: one child teaching another to recognize letters and spell them out in one of the primers that began spreading through the urban middle classes toward the end of the 1800s. The girl most likely learned her letters at home and the little boy will be sent to school in due course.
(*The Young Governess* by Jean-Baptiste Chardin, The National Gallery of Art, Washington, DC, Andrew Mellon Collection, 1937)

The Salon. Known in English as the withdrawing room, where one can withdraw to be with whom one chooses or to be alone, the salon represents the leisure class at its best: cultured, refined, and dominated by women, as in this Jean-François de Troy painting. Conversation, fashion, wit, and intellectual exploration among social equals in an intimate atmosphere was the essence of that "douceur de vivre," or sweetness of life, that Talleyrand claimed vanished with the Revolution of 1789.
(*Reading Molière* by Jean-François de Troy, Private Collection, courtesy The Bettmann Archive)

The Eighteenth Century

As the seventeenth century drew to a close, many of the lines for future development had been laid down. But they are much clearer to the historian, with the advantage of hindsight, than they were to the people of the time. It is in the eighteenth century that the decisive steps were taken toward establishing the institutions and the attitudes of our own age; and, although it is wrong to see these as disconnected from the trends and the thinking that had gone before, it would be even more difficult to gain an understanding of events after 1789 without knowing their eighteenth-century background.

More than any other century, perhaps, the thought of the eighteenth was preoccupied by order and by the use of reason, which can, if properly utilized, discover and establish order even in this apparently chaotic world. Educated people generally accepted the advice of that most passionately reasonable poet, Alexander Pope, who opened his *Essay on Man* (1733) with the admonition:

> Let us (since Life can little more supply
> Than just to look about us and to die)
> Expatiate free o'er all this scene of Man;
> A mighty maze! but not without a plan.

Certainly the educated public of the eighteenth century loved to expatiate—mostly in French—but for the benefit of all (including sometimes women), who would naturally be included in the universal plan—a plan, reasonable and accessible to reason, that would make sense of the mighty maze about them. This lust for a beneficial (re)ordering of the world was expressed on the international scene in the policies of the so-called enlightened despots, the most articulate of whom was Frederick (the Great) of Prussia. On the intellectual plane, rationalism's place is harder to determine; perhaps on reflection the age may as justly be called one of Faith as of Reason. It is, at any rate, tempting to compare the mood of the Enlightenment with that of Renaissance humanism: similarities and differences are both significant. But in the end the question remains: what exactly do we mean by "Enlightenment"? Just how enlightened, for instance, were the enlightened despots?

Samuel Johnson

Samuel Johnson (1709–1784)—moralist, essayist, lexicographer—dominated London literary society after 1755, when his great Dictionary *appeared. He has come down to us mainly in the account of James Boswell, who seems to have spent the years between 1763 and 1784 drinking in and noting down the great man's sayings. As a matter of fact, many of them were well worth noting, both for themselves and as illustrations of what an intelligent and articulate English conservative might think in the second half of the eighteenth century.*

James Boswell: from Life of Dr. Samuel Johnson

He talked in his usual style with a rough contempt for popular liberty. "They make a rout about universal liberty, without considering that all that is to be valued, or indeed can be enjoyed by individuals, is private liberty. Political liberty is good only so far as it produces private liberty. Now, Sir, there is the liberty of the press, which you know is a constant topic. Suppose you and I and two hundred more were restrained from printing our thought: what then? What proportion would that restraint upon us bear to the private happiness of the nation?"

This mode of representing the inconveniences of restraint as light and insignificant, was a kind of sophistry in which he delighted to indulge himself, in opposition to the extreme laxity for which it has been fashionable for too many to argue, when it is evident, upon reflection, that the very essence of government is restraint; and certain it is, that as government produces rational happiness, too much restraint is better than too little. But when restraint is unnecessary, and so close as to gall those who are subject to it, the people may and ought to demonstrate; and, if relief is not granted, to resist. Of this manly and spirited principle, no man was more convinced than Johnson himself. . . .

I told him that Mrs. Macaulay said, she wondered how he could reconcile his political principles with his moral; his notions of inequality and subordination with wishing well to the happiness of all mankind, who might live so agreeably, had they all their portions of land, and none to domineer over another. JOHNSON. "Why, Sir, I reconcile my principles very well, because mankind are happier in a state of inequality and subordination. Were they to be in this state of equality, they would soon degenerate into brutes;—they would become Monboddo's nation;—their tails would grow. Sir, all would be losers were all to work for all:—they would have no intellectual improvement. All intellectual improvement arises from leisure; all leisure arises from one working for another."

I introduced the subject of toleration. JOHNSON. "Every society has a right to preserve public peace and order, and therefore has a good right to prohibit the propagation of opinions which have a dangerous tendency. To say the magistrate has this right, is using an inadequate word; it is the society for which the magistrate is agent. He may be morally or theologically wrong in restraining the propagation of opinions which he thinks dangerous, but he is politically right." MAYO. "I am of opinion, Sir, that every man is entitled to liberty of conscience in religion; and that the magistrate cannot

---

From James Boswell, *Life of Dr. Samuel Johnson* (London, 1791).

restrain that right." JOHNSON. "Sir, I agree with you. Every man has a right to liberty of conscience, and with that the magistrate cannot interfere. People confound liberty of thinking with liberty of talking; nay, with liberty of preaching. Every man has a physical right to think as he pleases; for it cannot be discovered how he thinks. He has not a moral right, for he ought to inform himself, and think justly. But, Sir, no member of a society has a right to teach any doctrine contrary to what the society holds to be true. The magistrate, I say, may be wrong in what he thinks: but while he thinks himself right, he may and ought to enforce what he thinks." MAYO. "Then, Sir, we are to remain always in error, and truth never can prevail; and the magistrate was right in persecuting the first Christians." JOHNSON. "Sir, the only method by which religious truth can be established is by martyrdom. The magistrate has a right to enforce what he thinks; and he who is conscious of the truth has a right to suffer. I am afraid there is no other way of ascertaining the truth, but by persecution on the one hand and enduring it on the other." GOLDSMITH. "But how is a man to act, Sir? Though firmly convinced of the truth of his doctrine may he not think it wrong to expose himself to persecution? Has he a right to do so? Is it not, as it were, committing voluntary suicide?" JOHNSON. "Sir, as to voluntary suicide, as you call it, there are twenty thousand men in an army who will go without scruple to be shot at, and mount a breach for five-pence a day." GOLDSMITH. "But have they a moral right to do this?" JOHNSON. "Nay, Sir, if you will not take the universal opinion of mankind, I have nothing to say. If mankind cannot defend their own way of thinking, I cannot defend it. Sir, if a man is in doubt whether it would be better for him to expose himself to martyrdom or not, he should not do it. He must be convinced that he has a delegation from heaven." GOLDSMITH. "I would consider whether there is the greater chance of good or evil upon the whole. If I see a man who had fallen into a well, I would wish to help him out; but if there is greater probability that he shall pull me in; than that I shall pull him out, I would not attempt it. So were I to go to Turkey, I might wish to convert the Grand Signor to the Christian faith; but when I considered that I should probably be put to death without effectuating my purpose in any degree, I should keep myself quiet." JOHNSON. "Sir, you must consider that we have perfect and imperfect obligations. Perfect obligations, which are generally not to do something, are clear and positive; as, 'thou shalt not kill.' But charity, for instance, is not definable by limits. It is a duty to give to the poor; but no man can say how much another should give to the poor, or when a man has given too little to save his soul. In the same manner it is a duty to instruct the ignorant, and of consequence to convert infidels to Christianity; but no man in the common course of things is obliged to carry this to such a degree as to incur the danger of martyrdom, as no man is obliged to strip himself to the shirt in order to give charity. I have said, that a man must be persuaded that he has a particular delegation from heaven." GOLDSMITH. "How is this to be known? Our first reformers, who were burnt for not believing bread and wine to be Christ"— JOHNSON. (Interrupting him,) "Sir, they were not burnt for not believing bread and wine to be Christ, but for insulting those who did believe it. And Sir, when the first reformers began, they did not intend to be martyred: as many of them ran away as could." BOSWELL. "But, Sir, there was your countryman, Elwal, who you told me challenged King George with his blackguards, and his red-guards." JOHNSON. "My countryman, Elwal, Sir, should have been put in the stocks: a proper pulpit for him; and he'd have had a numerous audience. A man who preaches in the stocks will always have hearers enough." BOSWELL. "But Elwal thought himself in the right." JOHNSON. "We are not providing for mad people; there are places for them in the neighbourhood." (Meaning Moorfields.) MAYO. "But, Sir, is it not very hard that I should not be allowed to teach my children what I really believe to be the truth?" JOHNSON. "Why, Sir, you might contrive to teach your children *extra scandalum;* but, Sir, the magistrate, if he knows it, has a right to restrain you. Suppose you teach your children to be thieves?" MAYO. "This is making a joke of the subject." JOHNSON. "Nay, Sir, take it thus:—that you teach them the community of goods; for which there are as many plausible arguments as for most erroneous doctrines. You teach them that all things at first were in common, and that no man had a right to any thing but as he laid his hands upon it; and that this still is, or ought to be, the rule amongst mankind. Here, Sir, you sap a great principle in society,—property. And don't you think the magistrate would have a right to prevent you? Or, suppose you should teach your children the notion of the Adamites, and they should run naked into the streets, would not the magistrate have a right to flog 'em into their doublets?" MAYO. "I think the magistrate has no right to interfere till there is some overt act." BOSWELL. "So, Sir, though he sees an enemy to the state charging a blunderbuss, he is not to interfere till it is fired off?" MAYO. "He must be sure of its direction against the state." JOHNSON. "The magistrate is to judge of that.—He has no right to restrain your thinking, because the evil centers in yourself. If a man were sitting at this table, and chopping off his fingers, the magistrate, as guardian of the community, has no authority to restrain him; however he might do it from kindness as a parent.—Though, indeed, upon more consideration, I think he may; as it is probable, that he who is chopping off his own fingers, may soon proceed to chop off those of other people. If I think it right to steal Mr. Dilly's plate, I am a bad man; but he can say nothing to me. If I make an open declaration that I think so, he will keep me out of his house. If I put forth my hand, I shall be sent to Newgate. This is the gradation of thinking, preaching, and acting: if a man thinks erroneously, he may keep his thoughts to himself, and nobody will trouble him; if he preaches erroneous doctrine, society may expel him; if he acts in consequence of it, the law takes place, and he is hanged." MAYO. "But, Sir, ought not Christians to have liberty of conscience?" JOHNSON. "I have already told you so, Sir. You are coming back to where you were." BOSWELL. "Dr. Mayo, like other champions for unlimited toleration, has got a set of words. Sir, it is no matter, politically, whether the magistrate be right or wrong. Suppose a club were to be formed to drink confusion to King George the Third, and a happy restoration to Charles the Third, this would be very bad with respect to the State; but every member of that club must either conform to its rules, or be turned out of it. Old Baxter, I remember, maintains that the magistrate should 'tolerate all things that are tolerable.' This is no good definition of toleration upon any principle; but it shews that he thought some things were not tolerable." TOPLADY. "Sir, you have untwisted this difficult subject with great dexterity."

During this argument, Goldsmith sat in restless agitation, from a wish to get in and shine. Finding himself excluded, he had taken his hat to go away, but remained for some time with it in his hand, like a gamester, who at the close of a long night, lingers for a little while, to see if he can have a favourable opening to finish with success.

Once when he was beginning to speak, he found himself overpowered by the loud voice of Johnson, who was at the opposite end of the table, and did not perceive Goldsmith's attempt. Thus disappointed of his wish to obtain the attention of the company, Goldsmith in a passion threw down his hat, looking angrily at Johnson, and exclaiming in a bitter tone, "Take it." When Toplady was going to speak, Johnson uttered some sound, which led Goldsmith to think that he was beginning again, and taking the words from Toplady. Upon which, he seized this opportunity of venting his own envy and spleen, under the pretext of supporting another person: "Sir, (said he to Johnson,) the gentleman has heard you patiently for an hour; pray allow us now to hear him." JOHNSON. (Sternly,) "Sir, I was not interrupting the gentleman. I was only giving him a signal of my attention. Sir, you are impertinent." Goldsmith made no reply, but continued in the company for some time.

A gentleman present ventured to ask Dr. Johnson if there was not a material difference as to toleration of opinions which lead to action, and opinions merely speculative; for instance, would it be wrong in the magistrate to tolerate those who preach against the doctrine of the Trinity? Johnson was highly offended, and said, "I wonder, Sir, how a gentleman of your piety can introduce this subject in a mixed company." He told me afterwards that the impropriety was, that perhaps some of the company might have talked on the subject in such terms as might have shocked him; or he might have been forced to appear in their eyes a narrow-minded man. The gentleman, with submissive deference, said, he had only hinted at the question from a desire to hear Dr. Johnson's opinion upon it. JOHNSON. "Why then, Sir, I think that permitting men to preach any opinion contrary to the doctrine of the established church tends, in a certain degree, to lessen the authority of the church, and consequently, to lessen the influence of religion." "It may be considered, (said the gentleman,) whether it would not be politic to tolerate in such a case." JOHNSON. "Sir, we have been talking of right: this is another question. I think it is not politic to tolerate in such a case." . . .

Patriotism having become one of our topics, Johnson suddenly uttered, in a strong determined tone, an apophthegm, at which many will start: "Patriotism is the last refuge of a soundrel." But let it be considered, that he did not mean a real and generous love of our country, but that pretended patriotism which so many, in all ages and countries, have made a cloak for self-interest. I maintained, that certainly all patriots were not scoundrels. Being urged, (not by Johnson,) to name one exception, I mentioned an eminent person, whom we all greatly admired. JOHNSON. "Sir, I do not say that he is not honest; but we have no reason to conclude from his political conduct that he is honest. Were he to accept a place from this ministry, he would lose that character of firmness which he has, and might be turned out of his place in a year. This ministry is neither stable, nor grateful to their friends, as Sir Robert Walpole was, so that he may think it more for his interest to take his chance of his party coming in."

Montesquieu

Charles de Secondat, baron de Montesquieu (1689–1755), came from a good family of lawyers and judges, and himself presided over the Parliament Court of Bordeaux. He made his name by a brilliant satire, The Persian Letters, *containing descriptions of contemporary life and ways produced by a supposed Persian visitor to France. He then established this reputation in 1748 with* The Spirit of the Laws, *in which he discussed in detail, with great learning and sometimes also with great tediousness, the nature of the state, its laws, and the factors that affected them. Of all the forerunners of the revolutions that marked the last quarter of the eighteenth century, Montesquieu is probably the one with the broadest views and the one whose ideas were most fertile in practical results.*

From The Spirit of the Laws

OF THE LAWS IN GENERAL

Laws, in their most general signification, are the necessary relations arising from the nature of things. In this sense, all beings have their laws, the Deity his laws, the material world its laws, the intelligences superior to man their laws, the beasts their laws, man his laws. . . .

There is then a primitive reason; and laws are the relations subsisting between it and different beings, and the relations of these to one another.

God is related to the universe as creator and preserver: the laws by which he created all things are those by which he preserves them. He acts according to these rules, because he knows them; he knows them, because he made them; and he made them, because they are relative to his wisdom and power.

Since we observe that the world, though formed by the motion of matter, and void of understanding, subsists through so long a succession of ages, its motions must certainly be directed by invariable laws: and, could we imagine another, it must also have constant rules, or it would inevitably perish.

Thus the creation, which seems an arbitrary act, supposeth laws as invariable as those of the fatality of the atheists. It would be absurd to say, that the Creator might govern the world without those rules, since without them it could not subsist. . . .

Particular intelligent beings may have laws of their own making; but they have some likewise which they never made. Before there were intelligent beings, they were possible; they had therefore possible relations, and consequently possible laws. Before laws were made, there were relations of possible justice. To say that there is nothing just or unjust, but what is commanded or forbidden by positive laws, is the same as saying that, before the describing of a circle, all the radii were not equal.

We must therefore acknowledge relations of justice antecedent to the positive law by which they are established. . . .

Man, as a physical being, is, like other bodies, governed by invariable laws. . . . Such a being might every instant forget his Creator; God has therefore reminded him of his duty by the laws of religion. Such a being is liable every moment to forget himself; philosophy has provided against this by the laws of morality. Formed to live in society, he might forget his fellow-creatures; legislators have, therefore, by political and civil laws, confined him to his duty. . . .

From *The Complete Works of M. de Montesquieu* (London, 1777).

Law in general is human reason, inasmuch as it governs all the inhabitants of the earth; the political and civil laws of each nation ought to be only the particular cases in which human reason is applied.

They should be adapted in such a manner to the people for whom they are framed, that it is a great chance if those of one nation suit another.

They should be relative to the nature and principle of each government; whether they form it, as may be said of political laws; or whether they support it, as in the case of civil institutions.

They should be relative to the climate of each country, to the quality of its soil, to its situation and extent, to the principal occupation of the natives, whether husbandmen, huntsmen, or shepherds: they should have a relation to the degree of liberty which the constitution will bear, to the religion of the inhabitants, to their manners, and customs. In fine, they have inclinations, riches, numbers, commerce, relations to each other, as also to their origin, to the intent of the legislator, and to the order of things on which they are established; in all which different lights they ought to be considered.

This is what I have undertaken to perform in the following work. These relations I shall examine, since all these together constitute what I call the Spirit of Laws.

OF POLITICAL LIBERTY AND THE CONSTITUTION OF ENGLAND

Democratic and aristocratic states are not in their own nature free. Political liberty is to be found only in moderate governments; and even in these it is not always found. It is there only when there is no abuse of power: but constant experience shows us that every man invested with power is apt to abuse it, and to carry his authority as far as it will go. Is it not strange, though true, to say, that virtue itself has need of limits?

To prevent this abuse, it is necessary, from the very nature of things, power should be a check to power. A government may be so constituted as no man shall be compelled to do things to which the law does not oblige him, nor forced to abstain from things which the law permits. . . .

The political liberty of the subject is a tranquility of mind arising from the opinion each person has of his safety. In order to have this liberty, it is requisite the government be so constituted as one man need not be afraid of another.

When the legislative and executive powers are united in the same person, or in the same body of magistrates, there can be no liberty; because apprehensions may arise, lest the same monarch or senate should enact tyrannical laws, to execute them in a tyrannical manner.

Again, there is no liberty if the judiciary power be not separated from the legislative and executive. Were it joined with the legislative, the life and liberty of the subject would be exposed to arbitrary control; for the judge would be then the legislator. Were it joined to the executive power, the judge might behave with violence and oppression.

There would be an end of everything, were the same man, or the same body, whether of the nobles or of the people, to exercise those three powers, that of enacting laws, that of executing the public resolutions, and of trying the causes of individuals.

* * *

The judiciary power ought not to be given to a standing senate; it should be exercised by persons taken from the body of the people, at certain times of the year, and consistently with a form and manner prescribed by law, in order to erect a tribunal that should last only so long as necessity requires.

By this method, the judicial power, so terrible to mankind, not being annexed to any particular state or profession, becomes, as it were, invisible. People have not then the judges continually present to their view; they fear the office, but not the magistrate. . . .

But though the tribunals ought not to be fixed, the judgments ought; and to such a degree, as to be ever conformable to the letter of the law. Were they to be the private opinion of the judge, people would then live in society without exactly knowing the nature of their obligations.

As, in a country of liberty, every man who is supposed a free agent ought to be his own governor, the legislative power should reside in the whole body of the people. But, since this is impossible in large states, and in small ones is subject to many inconveniences, it is fit the people should transact by their representatives what they cannot transact by themselves.

The inhabitants of a particular town are much better acquainted with its wants and interests than with those of other places; and are better judges of the capacity of their neighbours than of that of the rest of their countrymen. The members, therefore, of the legislature should not be chosen from the general body of the nation; but it is proper, that in every considerable place, a representative should be elected by the inhabitants.

The great advantage of representatives is their capacity of discussing public affairs. For this, the people collectively are extremely unfit, which is one of the chief inconveniences of a democracy. . . .

All the inhabitants of the several districts ought to have a right of voting at the election of a representative, except such as are in so mean a situation as to be deemed to have no will of their own.

In such a state, there are always persons distinguished by their birth, riches, or honours; but, were they to be confounded with the common people, and to have only the weight of a single vote, like the rest, the common liberty would be their slavery, and they would have no interest in supporting it, as most of the popular resolutions would be against them. The share they have, therefore, in the legislature ought to be proportioned to their other advantages in the state; which happens only when they form a body that has a right to check the licentiousness of the people, as the people have a right to oppose any encroachment of theirs.

The legislative power is, therefore, committed to the body of the nobles, and to that which represents the people; each having their assemblies and deliberations apart, each their separate views and interests. . . .

The body of the nobility ought to be hereditary. In the first place, it is so in its own nature; and, in the next, there must be a considerable interest to preserve its privileges: privileges, that, in themselves, are obnoxious to popular envy, and of course, in a free state, are always in danger.

But, as an hereditary power might be attempted to pursue its own particular interests, and forget those of the people, it is proper, that, where a singular advantage may be gained by corrupting the nobility, as in the laws relating to supplies, they should have no other share in the legislation than the power of rejecting, and not that of resolving.

The executive power ought to be in the hands of a monarch, because this branch of government, having need of dispatch, is better administered by one than by many: on the other hand, whatever depends on the legislative power, is oftentimes better regulated by many than by a single person. . . .

Were the legislative body to be a considerable time without meeting, this would likewise put an end to liberty. For, of two things, one would naturally follow; either that there would be no longer any legislative resolutions, and then the state would fall into anarchy; or that these resolutions would be taken by the executive power, which would render it absolute. . . .

But, if the legislative power, in a free state, has no right to stay the executive, it has a right, and ought to have the means, of examining in what manner its laws have been executed; an advantage which this government has over that of Crete and Sparta, where the Cosmi and the Ephori gave no account of their administration.

But, whatever may be the issue of that examination, the legislative body ought not to have a power of arraigning the person, nor, of course, the conduct of him who is entrusted with the executive power. His person should be sacred, because, as it is necessary, for the good of the state, to prevent the legislative body from rendering themselves arbitrary, the moment he is accused or tried there is an end of liberty.

In this case, the state would be no longer a monarchy, but a kind of republic, though not a free government. But, as the person, entrusted with the executive power, cannot abuse it without bad counsellors, and such as hate the laws as ministers, though the laws protect them as subjects, these men may be examined and punished: an advantage which this government has over that of Gnidus, where the law allowed of no such thing as calling the Amymones to account, even after their administration; and therefore the people could never obtain any satisfaction for the injuries done to them. . . .

The executive power, pursuant to what has been already said, ought to have a share in the legislature by the power of rejecting; otherwise it would soon be stripped of its prerogative. But, should the legislative power usurp a share of the executive, the latter would be equally undone.

If the prince were to have a part in the legislature by the power of resolving, liberty would be lost. But, as it is necessary he should have a share in the legislature for the support of his own prerogative, this share must consist in the power of rejecting. . . .

Were the executive power to determine the raising of public money otherwise than by giving its consent, liberty would be at an end; because it would become legislative in the most important point of legislation. . . .

To prevent the executive power from being able to oppress, it is requisite that the armies with which it is entrusted should consist of the people, and have the same spirit as the people, as was the case at Rome till the time of Marius. To obtain this end, there are only two ways; either that the persons employed in the army should have sufficient property to answer for their conduct to their fellow-subjects, and be enlisted only for a year, as was customary at Rome; or, if there should be a standing-army composed chiefly of the most despicable part of the nation, the legislative power should have a right to disband them as soon as it pleased; the soldiers should live in common with the rest of the people; and no separate camp, barracks, or fortress, should be suffered.

In perusing the admirable treatise of Tacitus on the manners of the Germans, we find it is from that nation the English have borrowed the idea of their political government. This beautiful system was invented first in the woods. . . .

It is not my business to examine whether the English actually enjoy this liberty, or not. Sufficient it is for my purpose to observe, that it is established by their laws; and I inquire no farther.

Neither do I pretend by this to undervalue other governments, nor to say that this extreme political liberty ought to give uneasiness to those who have only a moderate share of it. How should I have any such design; I who think that even the highest refinement of reason is not always desirable, and that mankind generally find their account better in mediums than in extremes?

Voltaire

François Marie Arouet, better known as Voltaire (1694–1778), is probably the most characteristic, certainly the most brilliant, figure of the Enlightenment. Born in Paris, son of a notary, endowed with a daring, supple, and inquiring mind and a great gift for writing in prose or verse, Voltaire produced plays, poems, pamphlets, histories, novels, and encyclopedia and journalistic articles in tremendous profusion. He spent most of his life in a long but effective private war against prejudice, intolerance, superstition, and their embodiment in the Catholic Church and the ancien régime. His rationalism, however, did not lead him to share the optimism common to his time. In several satires he held up to scorn the idea that "Whatever is, is right." It would be a dull person who did not bother to read at least his Candide, *which is not included here because selection proved impossible: too much of it is too good to leave out.*

One of the best translations of his works is also the earliest, that of Tobias Smollett, dating back to the eighteenth century; the two excerpts that follow are from this translation.

On English Commerce

Carthage, Venice and Amsterdam were undoubtedly powerful; but their conduct has been exactly like that of merchants grown rich by traffic,[1] who afterwards purchase lands that carry with them the dignity of lordship. Neither Carthage, Venice, nor Holland have, from a warlike and even conquering beginning, ended in a commercial

---

From Voltaire, *Letters on England* (London, 1764), tr. T. Smollett.
[1] trading.

nation. The English are the only people in existence who have done this; they were for a long time warriors before they learned to cast accounts. They were entirely ignorant of numbers when they won the battles of Agincourt, Crécy, and Poitiers, and were also ignorant that it was in their power to become corn merchants and woollen drapers, two things that would certainly turn to much better account than winning battles. This science alone has rendered the nation at once populous, wealthy, and powerful. London was a poor country town when Edward III conquered one half of France; and it is wholly owing to this that the English have become merchants; that London exceeds Paris in extent and number of inhabitants; that they are able to equip and man two hundred sail of ships of war, and keep the kings who are their allies in pay. The Scots are born warriors, and, from the purity of their air, inherit good sense. Whence comes it then that Scotland, under the name of a Union, has become a province of England? It is because Scotland has scarcely any other commodity than coal, and that England has fine tin, excellent wool, and abounds in corn, manufactures, and trading companies.

Even the younger son of a peer of the realm is not above trading. Lord Townshend, secretary of state, has a brother who is satisfied with being a merchant in the city. At the time when Lord Oxford ruled all England, his younger brother was a trader at Aleppo, whence he could never be prevailed on to return, and where he died. This custom which is now unhappily dying out, appears monstrous to a German, whose head is full of the coats of arms and the pageants of his family. They can never conceive how it is possible that the son of an English peer should be no more than a rich and powerful citizen, when in Germany they are all princes. I have known more than thirty highnesses of the same name, whose whole fortune and estate put together amounted to a few coats of arms, and the starving pride they inherited from their ancestors.

In France everybody is a marquis; and a man just come from the obscurity of some remote province, with money in his pocket and a name that ends in "*ac*" or "*ille,*" may give himself airs, and usurp such phrases as "A man of my quality and rank"; and hold merchants in the most sovereign contempt. The merchant again, by dint of hearing his profession despised on all occasions, at last is fool enough to blush at his condition. I will not, however, take it upon me to say which is the most useful to his country, and which of the two ought to have the preference; whether the powdered lord, who knows to a minute when the king rises or goes to bed, perhaps to stool, and who gives himself airs of importance while playing the part of a slave in the antechamber of a minister; or the merchant, who enriches his country, and from his counting house sends his orders into Surat or Cairo, thereby contributing to the happiness and convenience of human nature.

Another interesting aspect of English institutions, not unconnected with the first and one which Voltaire obviously thought his compatriots might well imitate, was religious tolerance. He describes it here in characteristically striking terms.

On Presbyterians

To the Presbyterians is owing the sanctification of Sunday in the three kingdoms. People are forbidden to work or take any recreation on that day, which is being twice as severe as the Church of Rome. No operas, plays, or concerts are allowed in London on Sundays; and even cards are so expressly forbidden that none but persons of quality, and those we call genteel, play on that day; the rest of the nation go either to church, to the tavern, or to a kept mistress.

Though the Episcopal and Presbyterian sects are the two prevailing ones in Great Britain, yet all others are very welcome to come and settle in it, and they live very sociably together, though most of their preachers hate one another almost as cordially as a Jansenist damns a Jesuit.[1]

Take a view of the Royal Exchange in London, a place more venerable than many courts of justice, where the representatives of all nations meet for the benefit of mankind. There the Jew, the Mahometan, and the Christian transact business together, as though they were all of the same religion, and give the name of Infidels to none but the bankrupts; there the Presbyterian confides in the Anabaptist, and the Churchman depends upon the Quaker's word. At the breaking up of this pacific and free assembly, some withdraw to the synagogue, others go to drink. This man goes to be baptized in a great tub in the name of the Father, Son and Holy Ghost; that man has his son's foreskin cut off and has Hebrew words mumbled over him which he does not understand himself; others retire to their churches and there await the inspiration of heaven with their hats on their heads; and all are satisfied.

If one religion only were allowed in England, the government would very possibly become arbitrary; if there were but two, the people would cut one another's throats; but as there is such a multitude, they all live happy and in peace.

Jean Jacques Rousseau

Jean Jacques Rousseau (1712–1778) was born in Geneva/Switzerland, the odd and adventurous son of an odd and adventurous watchmaker/dancing master. Orphaned at an early age, he never ceased his wanderings. Something of a musician and literary jack-of-all-trades, he basked for a while in the searing glory of the Paris salons, contributed to the Encyclopedia,[2] *quarreled with the Encyclopedists, lived some time in England where he quarreled with the philosopher David Hume and in Germany where he quarreled with nearly everybody, and became more and more difficult and embittered until he died, a melancholy and rather mad old man, at Ermenonville, near Paris.*

He reacted to the excessive rationalism of his time by reemphasizing instinct against reason, unspoilt virtue against corrupt society, inspiration against discipline, nature against artifice. But he also reminded his readers that man is a member of society and, being a

---

[1] Jesuits were members of the Society of Jesus (founded 1534). Critics associated them and their followers with moral sophistry, doctrinal laxism, and opportunism in religion and politics. Jansenists were rigorous Catholics inspired by the doctrines of Cornelis Jansen (1585–1638), who believed in predestination, denied free will, and emphasized the depraved nature of fallen humankind. In seventeenth- and eighteenth-century France, Jesuits and Jansenists were at daggers drawn.

[2] The great dictionary published during the 1750s and 1760s under the direction of Denis Diderot, symbol and inspiration of the eighteenth-century search for reasonable understanding in all things.

social animal, should be concerned to reorganize society and life in it according to sensible, virtuous, and natural rules. Society is corrupt because it has moved too far from nature; hence man in society is corrupt, too. Hope, however, lies for man in education and for society in political reorganization. Rousseau tried to present his prescriptions for a healthier, saner approach in Emile *and in the essay* The Social Contract, *both of which appeared in 1762. His ideas not only made him the prophet of the romantic movement, which was going to dominate European literature during the early nineteenth century, but also the inspiration of terroristic democrats such as Robespierre.*

From The Social Contract

INTRODUCTORY NOTE

I wish to enquire whether, taking men as they are and laws as they can be made, it is possible to establish some just and certain rule of administration in civil affairs. In this investigation I shall always strive to reconcile what right permits with what interest prescribes, so that justice and utility may not be severed. . . .

CHAPTER I

Man is born free, and everywhere he is in chains. Many a one believes himself the master of others, and yet he is a greater slave than they. How has this change come about? I do not know. What can render it legitimate? I believe that I can settle this question.

If I considered only force and the results that proceed from it, I should say that so long as a people is compelled to obey and does obey, it does well; but that, so soon as it can shake off the yoke and does shake it off, it does better; for, if men recover their freedom by virtue of the same right by which it was taken away, either they are justified in resuming it, or there was no justification for depriving them of it. But the social order is a sacred right which serves as a foundation for all others. This right however, does not come from nature. It is therefore based on conventions. The question is to know what these conventions are. Before coming to that, I must establish what I have just laid down.

THE RIGHT OF THE STRONGEST

The strongest man is never strong enough to be always master, unless he transforms his power into right, and obedience into duty. Hence the right of the strongest—a right apparently assumed in irony, and really established in principle. But will this phrase never be explained to us? Force is a physical power; I do not see what morality

---

From Rousseau, *The Social Contract*, tr. Henry J. Tozer (London, 1895).

can result from its effects. To yield to force is an act of necessity, not of will; it is at most an act of prudence. In what sense can it be a duty?

Let us assume for a moment this pretended right. I say that nothing results from it but inexplicable nonsense; for if force constitutes right, the effect changes with the cause, and any force which overcomes the first succeeds to its rights. As soon as men can disobey with impunity, they may do so legitimately; and since the strongest is always in the right, the only thing is to act in such a way that one may be the strongest. But what sort of a right is it that perishes when force ceases? If it is necessary to obey by compulsion, there is no need to obey from duty; and if men are no longer forced to obey, obligation is at an end. We see, then, that this word "right" adds nothing to force; it here means nothing at all.

Obey the powers that be. If that means, Yield to force, the precept is good but superfluous; I reply that it will never be violated. All power comes from God, I admit; but every disease comes from him too; does it follow that we are prohibited from calling in a physician? If a brigand should surprise me in the recesses of a wood, am I bound not only to give up my purse when forced, but am I also morally bound to do so when I might conceal it? For, in effect, the pistol which he holds is a superior force.

Let us agree, then, that might does not make right, and that we are bound to obey none but lawful authorities. Thus my original question ever recurs.

THE SOCIAL PACT

I assume that men have reached a point at which the obstacles that endanger their preservation in the state of nature overcome by their resistance the forces which each individual can exert with a view to maintaining himself in that state. Then this primitive condition can no longer subsist, and the human race would perish unless it changed its mode of existence.

Now, as men cannot create any new forces, but only combine and direct those that exist, they have no other means of self-preservation than to form by aggregation a sum of forces which may overcome the resistance, to put them in action by a single motive power, and to make them work in concert.

This sum of forces can be produced only by the combination of many; but the strength and freedom of each man being the chief instruments of his preservation, how can he pledge them without injuring himself, and without neglecting the cares which he owes to himself? This difficulty, applied to my subject, may be expressed in these terms:

"To find a form of association which may defend and protect with the whole force of the community the person and property of every associate, and by means of which each, coalescing with all, may nevertheless obey only himself, and remain as free as before." Such is the fundamental problem of which the social contract furnishes the solution.

The clauses of this contract are so determined by the nature of the act that the slightest modification would render them vain and ineffectual; so that, although they have never perhaps been formally enunciated, they are everywhere the same, everywhere tacitly admitted and recognised, until, the social pact being violated, each man regains his original rights and recovers his natural liberty, whilst losing the conventional liberty for which he renounces it.

These clauses, rightly understood, are reducible to one only, viz. the total alienation to the whole community of each associate with all rights; for, in the first place, since each gives himself up entirely, the conditions are equal for all; and, the conditions being equal for all, no one has any interest in making them burdensome to others.

Further, the alienation being made without reserve, the union is as perfect as it can be, and an individual associate can no longer claim anything; for, if any rights were left to individuals, since there would be no common superior who could judge between them and the public, each being on some point his own judge, would soon claim to be so on all; the state of nature would still subsist, and the association would necessarily become tyrannical or useless.

In short, each giving himself to all, gives himself to nobody; and as there is not one associate over whom we do not acquire the same rights which we concede to him over ourselves, we gain the equivalent of all that we lose, and more power to preserve what we have.

If, then, we set aside what is not of the essence of the social contract, we shall find that it is reducible to the following terms: "Each of us puts in common his person and his whole power under the supreme direction of the general will; and in return we receive every member as an indivisible part of the whole."

Forthwith, instead of the individual personalities of all the contracting parties, this act of association produces a moral and collective body, which is composed of as many members as the assembly has voices, and which receives from this same act its unity, its common self, its life, and its will. This public person, which is thus formed by the union of all the individual members, formerly took the name of "city" and now takes that of "republic" or "body politic," which is called by its members "State" when it is passive, "sovereign" when it is active, "power" when it is compared to similar bodies. With regard to the associates, they take collectively the name of "people," and are called individually "citizens," as participating in the sovereign power, and "subjects," as subjected to the laws of the State. But these terms are often confused and are mistaken one for another; it is sufficient to know how to distinguish them when they are used with complete precision.

THE SOVEREIGN

We see from this formula that the act of association contains a reciprocal engagement between the public and individuals, and that every individual, contracting so to speak with himself, is engaged in a double relation, viz. as a member of the sovereign towards individuals, and as a member of the State towards the sovereign. But we cannot apply here the maxim of civil law that no one is bound by engagements made with himself: for there is a great difference between being bound to oneself and to a whole of which one forms part.

We must further observe that the public resolution which can bind all subjects to the sovereign in consequence of the two different relations under which each of them is regarded cannot, for a contrary reason, bind the sovereign to itself; and that accordingly it is contrary to the nature of the body politic for the sovereign to impose on itself a law which it cannot transgress. As it can only be considered under one and the same relation it is in the position of an individual contracting with himself; whence we see that there is not, nor can be, any kind of fundamental law binding upon the body of the people, not even the social contract. This does not imply that such a body cannot perfectly well enter into engagements with others in what does not derogate from this contract; for, with regard to foreigners, it becomes a simple being, an individual.

But the body politic or sovereign, deriving its existence only from the sanctity of the contract, can never bind itself, even to others, in anything that derogates from the original act, such as alienation of some portion of itself, or submission to another sovereign. To violate the act by which it exists would be to annihilate itself; and what is nothing produces nothing.

So soon as the multitude is thus united in one body, it is impossible to injure one of the members without attacking the body, still less to injure the body without the members feeling the effects. Thus duty and interest alike oblige the two contracting parties to give mutual assistance; and the men themselves should seek to combine in this twofold relationship all the advantages which are attendant on it.

Now, the sovereign, being formed only of the individuals that compose it, neither has nor can have any interest contrary to theirs; consequently the sovereign power needs no guarantee towards its subjects, because it is impossible that the body should wish to injure all its members; and we shall see hereafter that it can injure no one as an individual. The sovereign, for the simple reason that it is so, is always everything that it ought to be.

But this is not the case as regards the relation of subjects to the sovereign, which, notwithstanding the common interest, would have no security for the performance of their engagements, unless it found means to ensure their fidelity.

Indeed, every individual may, as a man, have a particular will contrary to, or divergent from, the general will which he has as a citizen; his private interest may prompt him quite differently from the common interest; his absolute and naturally independent existence may make him regard what he owes to the common cause as a gratuitous contribution, the loss of which will be less harmful to others than the payment of it will be burdensome to him; and, regarding the moral person that constitutes the State as an imaginary being because it is not a man, he would be willing to enjoy the rights of a citizen without being willing to fulfil the duties of a subject. The progress of such injustice would bring about the ruin of the body politic.

In order, then, that the social pact may not be a vain formulary, it tacitly includes this engagement, which can alone give force to the others,—that whoever refuses to obey the general will shall be constrained to do so by the whole body; which means nothing else than that he shall be forced to be free; for such is the condition which, uniting every citizen to his native land, guarantees him from all personal dependence, a condition that ensures the control and working of the political machine, and alone renders legitimate civil engagements, which, without it, would be absurd and tyrannical, and subject to the most enormous abuses.

THE CIVIL STATE

The passage from the state of nature to the civil state produces in man a very remarkable change, by substituting in his conduct justice for instinct, and by giving his actions the moral quality that they previously lacked. It is only when the voice of duty succeeds physical impulse, and law succeeds appetite, that man, who till then had regarded only himself, sees that he is obliged to act on other principles, and to consult his reason before listening to his inclinations. Although, in this state, he is deprived of many advantages that he derives from nature, he acquires equally great ones in return; his faculties are exercised and developed; his ideas are expanded; his feelings are ennobled; his whole soul is exalted to such a degree that, if the abuses of this new condition did not often degrade him below that from which he has emerged, he ought to bless without ceasing the happy moment that released him from it for ever, and transformed him from a stupid and ignorant animal into an intelligent being and a man.

Let us reduce this whole balance to terms easy to compare. What man loses by the social contract is his natural liberty and an unlimited right to anything which tempts him and which he is able to attain; what he gains is civil liberty and property in all that he possesses. In order that we may not be mistaken about these compensations, we must clearly distinguish natural liberty, which is limited by the general will; and possession, which is nothing but the result of force or the right of first occupancy, from property, which can be based only on a positive title.

Besides the preceding, we might add to the acquisitions of the civil state moral freedom, which alone renders man truly master of himself; for the impulse of mere appetite is slavery, while obedience to a self-prescribed law is liberty. But I have already said too much on this head, and the philosophical meaning of the term "liberty" does not belong to my present subject.

WHETHER THE GENERAL WILL CAN ERR

It follows from what precedes that the general will is always right and always tends to the public advantage; but it does not follow that the resolutions of the people have always the same rectitude. Men always desire their own good, but do not always discern it; the people are never corrupted, though often deceived, and it is only then that they seem to will what is evil.

There is often a great deal of difference between the will of all and the general will; the latter regards only the common interest, while the former has regard to private interests, and is merely a sum of particular wills; but take away from these same wills the pluses and minuses which cancel one another, and the general will remains as the sum of the differences.

If the people came to a resolution when adequately informed and without any communication among the citizens, the general will would always result from the great number of slight differences, and the resolution would always be good. But when factions, partial associations, are formed to the detriment of the whole society, the will of each of these associations becomes general with reference to its members, and particular with reference to the State; it may then be said that there are no longer as many voters as there are men, but only as many voters as there are associations. The differences become less numerous and yield a less general result. Lastly, when one of these associations becomes so great that it predominates over all the rest, you no longer have as the result a sum of small differences, but a single difference; there is then no longer a general will, and the opinion which prevails is only a particular opinion.

It is important, then, in order to have a clear declaration of the general will, that there should be no partial association in the State, and that every citizen should express only his own opinion. Such was the unique and sublime institution of the great Lycurgus. But if there are partial associations, it is necessary to multiply their number and prevent inequality, as Solon, Numa, and Servius did. These are the only proper precautions for ensuring that the general will may always be enlightened, and that the people may not be deceived.

THE LIMITS OF THE SOVEREIGN POWER

If the State or city is nothing but a moral person, the life of which consists in the union of its members, and if the most important of its cares is that of self-preservation, it needs a universal and compulsive force to move and dispose every part in the manner most expedient for the whole. As nature gives every man an absolute power over all his limbs, the social pact gives the body politic an absolute power over all its members; and it is this same power which, when directed by the general will, bears, as I said, the name of sovereignty.

But besides the public person, we have to consider the private persons who compose it, and whose life and liberty are naturally independent of it. The question, then, is to distinguish clearly between the respective rights of the citizens and of the sovereign, as well as between the duties which the former have to fulfil in their capacity as subjects and the natural rights which they ought to enjoy in their character as men.

It is admitted that whatever part of his power, property, and liberty each one alienates by the social compact is only that part of the whole of which the use is important to the community; but we must also admit that the sovereign alone is judge of what is important.

All the services that a citizen can render to the State he owes to it as soon as the sovereign demands them; but the sovereign, on its part, cannot impose on its subjects any burden which is useless to the community; it cannot even wish to do so, for, by the law of reason, just as by the law of nature, nothing is done without a cause.

The engagements which bind us to the social body are obligatory only because they are mutual; and their nature is such that in fulfilling them we cannot work for others without also working for ourselves. Why is the general will always right, and why do all invariably desire the prosperity of each, unless it is because there is no one but appropriates to himself this word "each" and thinks of himself in voting on behalf of all? This proves that equality of rights and the notion of justice that it produces are derived from the preference which each gives to himself, and consequently from man's nature; that the general will, to be truly such, should be so in its object as well as in its essence; that it ought to proceed from all in order to be applicable to all; and that it loses its natural rectitude when it tends to some individual and determinate object, because in that case, judging of what is unknown to us, we have no true principle of equity to guide us.

From this we must understand that what generalises the will is not so much the number of voices as the common interest which unites them; for, under this system, each necessarily submits to the conditions which he imposes on others—an admirable union of interest and justice, which gives to the deliberations of the community a spirit of equity that seems to disappear in the discussion of any private affair, for want of a common interest to unite and identify the ruling principle of the judge with that of the party.

By whatever path we return to our principle we always arrive at the same conclusion, viz. that the social compact establishes among the citizens such an equality that they all pledge themselves under the same conditions and ought all to enjoy the same rights. Thus, by the nature of the compact, every act of sovereignty, that is, every authentic act of the general will, binds or favours equally all the citizens; so that the sovereign knows only the body of the nation, and distinguishes none of those that compose it.

What, then, is an act of sovereignty properly so called? It is not an agreement between a superior and an inferior, but an agreement of the body with each of its members; a lawful agreement, because it has the social contract as its foundation; equitable, because it is common to all; useful, because it can have no other object than the general welfare; and stable, because it has the public force and the supreme power as a guarantee. So long as the subjects submit only to such conventions, they obey no one, but simply their own will; and to ask how far the respective rights of the sovereign and citizens extend is to ask up to what point the latter can make engagements among themselves, each with all and all with each.

Thus we see that the sovereign power, wholly absolute, wholly sacred, and wholly inviolable as it is, does not, and cannot, pass the limits of general conventions, and that every man can fully dispose of what is left to him of his property and liberty by these conventions; so that the sovereign never has a right to burden one subject more than another, because then the matter becomes particular and his power is no longer competent.

These distinctions once admitted, so untrue is it that in the social contract there is on the part of individuals any real renunciation, that their situation, as a result of this contract, is in reality preferable to what it was before, and that, instead of an alienation, they have only made an advantageous exchange of an uncertain and precarious mode of existence for a better and more assured one, of natural independence for liberty, of the power to injure others for their own safety, and of their strength, which others might overcome, for a right which the social union renders inviolable. Their lives, also, which they have devoted to the State, are continually protected by it; and in exposing their lives for its defence, what do they do but restore what they have received from it? What do they do but what they would do more frequently and with more risk in the state of nature, when, engaging in inevitable struggles, they would defend at the peril of their lives their means of preservation? All have to fight for their country in case of need, it is true; but then no one ever has to fight for himself. Do we not gain, moreover, by incurring, for what ensures our safety, a part of the risks that we should have to incur for ourselves individually, as soon as we were deprived of it?

From Emile

BOOK III

The man and the citizen, whichever he may be, has no other property to give to society except himself, all his other property being there without his will; and when a man is rich, either he does not enjoy his wealth, or the public enjoys it also. In the first case he steals from others that of which he deprives himself; and in the second case, he gives them nothing. Thus the whole indebtedness to society remains with him, so long as he pays only with his property. "But," you may say, "my father, in gaining this property, served society." Very well, then; he has paid his own debt, but not yours. You owe more to others than if you had been born without property; because you were favored at birth. It is not just that what one man has done for society should discharge the obligation of another; because each owing his entire self, can pay only for himself, and no father can transmit to his son the right of being useless to his kind; yet it is just that which he does, according to you, when he transmits to him his wealth, which is the evidence and the reward of labor. He who eats in idleness that which he himself has not earned, steals it; and a capitalist whom the state pays for doing nothing differs little in my eyes from a brigand, who lives at the expense of passers-by. Outside of society, an isolated man, owing nothing to any one, has a right to live as it pleases him: but in society, where he necessarily lives at the expense of others, he owes them in labor the price of his maintenance; there is no exception to this rule. To work is then an indispensable duty to the social man. Rich or poor, powerful or weak, every idle citizen is a rogue.

Now of all occupations which can furnish subsistence to man, that which most nearly approaches to the state of nature is manual labor; of all conditions the most independent of chance and of men is that of the artisan. The artisan depends only upon his labor; he is as free as the husbandman is enslaved; for the latter is dependent upon his field, whose crop is at the discretion of others. The enemy, the price, a powerful neighbor, a suit at law may take from him his field; through this field they may harass him in a thousand ways. But wherever they wish to harass the artisan, his luggage is soon packed; he goes, taking his strong arms with him. Nevertheless agriculture is the first of human employments; it is the most honest, the most useful, and consequently the noblest that he can practice. I do not say to Emile: "Learn agriculture";

From *Translations and Reprints*, VI, No. 1, M. Whitcomb, Ed.

he knows it. All forms of rustic labor are familiar to him; he began with them, and to them he is ever returning. I say to him then: "Cultivate the heritage of your fathers. But if you lose this heritage, or if you have none, what will you do? Learn a trade."

"A trade for my son! My son an artisan! My dear sir, are you serious?" More serious than you, madam, who would make it impossible for him to be other than a lord, a marquis, a prince, and perhaps some day less than nothing; as for me, I wish to give him a position that he cannot lose, a position that will honor him at all times. I wish to elevate him to man's estate, and whatever you may say, he will have fewer equals with this title than with all those which he may derive from you.

The letter kills and the spirit makes alive. It is a matter of learning a trade less for the purpose of knowing a trade than to overcome the prejudices which tend to treat it with contempt. You think that you will never be reduced to work for a living. Ah! so much the worse—so much the worse for you! But never mind, do not work from necessity, work for glory. Lower yourself to the splendor of the artisan in order to be above your own. In order to put fortune and things under your control, begin by making yourself independent of them. In order to rule by opinion, commence by ruling over it.

Remember that it is by no means an accomplishment that I ask of you; it is a trade, a true trade, a purely mechanical art, where the hands work more than the head, which does not lead to fortune, but with which one can be independent of it. In families far above the danger of wanting bread, I have seen fathers push foresight to the point of joining to the labor of instructing their children that of providing them with a knowledge with which, in any event, they might gain their living. These provident fathers believe they are accomplishing much; but they are doing nothing, because the resources which they believe they are providing for their children depend upon the very fortune which they desire to make themselves independent of. So that with all these fine accomplishments, unless he who possesses them finds himself in circumstances favorable for their employment, he will perish as if he had none of them.

Since it is a question of management and intrigue, it is as necessary to employ these means to maintain yourself in abundance as to regain, from the depths of misery the means of re-ascending to your former estate. If you cultivate the arts whose success depends upon the reputation of the artist, if you turn your attention to those employments which are obtained only by favor, of what use will it all be to you, when rightly disgusted with the world, you disdain the means without which you cannot hope to succeed? You have studied diplomacy and the interests of princes? Good; but what will you do with this knowledge, unless you know how to conciliate the ministers, the ladies of the court, the heads of the bureaus; unless you possess the secret of pleasing them; unless all find in you the rascal that suits their purposes? You are an architect or painter? Good; but it is necessary that you should make your talent known. Do you expect to go straightway and exhibit your work at the salon? Alas! that doesn't happen so easily! It is necessary to be in the Academy; it is necessary to be a favorite in order to obtain even a dark corner of the wall. Give up your model and your brush, take a cab and go from door to door; it is in this way that you will acquire celebrity. But you ought to know that all these illustrious doors have Swiss or porters who understand only motions, and whose ears are in their hands. Do you wish to impart what you have learned, and become a teacher of geography, or mathematics, or languages, or music, or drawing? For that it is necessary to find pupils, and consequently somebody to recommend you. Remember, it contributes more toward success to be plausible than to be able, and that, if you know no trade but your own, you will never be anything but a dunce.

See then how little solidity all these brilliant resources possess, and how many other resources are necessary in order to derive any advantage from them. And then, what will become of you in this cowardly abasement? Reverses, instead of instructing you, debase you. More than ever the creature of public opinion, how will you elevate yourself above those prejudices, arbiters of your lot? How will you despise baseness and the vices of which you have need for your subsistence? You were dependent only on wealth, and now you are dependent on wealth; you have only deepened your slavery and surcharged it with your poverty. You are poor without becoming free; it is the worst state into which a man can fall.

But instead of resorting for a livelihood to those high knowledges which are made for nourishing the soul and not the body, if you resort, in time of need, to your hands and the use which you know how to make of them, all difficulties vanish, all artifices become useless. Your resources are always ready at the moment their use is required; probity and honor are no longer an obstacle to living; you have no need to be a coward and a liar before the great, to bend and cringe before rascals, a vile pander to all the world, a borrower or a thief, which are almost the same thing when one has nothing. The opinion of others concerns you not; you have your court to make to no one, no fool to flatter, no Swiss to knuckle to, no courtier to fee, or what is worse, to worship. That rogues manage the affairs of the great is of no consequence to you. That does not prevent you in your obscure life from being an honest man and having bread. You enter the first shop whose trade you have learned: "Master, I need work." "Journeyman, go there and get to work." Before the dinner hour arrives you have earned your dinner. If you are diligent and sober, before eight hours have passed you will have wherewith to live eight hours more. You will have lived free, sound, true, industrious and just. To gain it thus is not to lose one's time.

Cesare Beccaria

Cesare Beccaria (1738–1794) was a Milanese aristocrat caught up in the intellectual ferment of the Enlightenment. He became interested in criminal reform, and in 1764 published An Essay on Crimes and Punishments, *which made him internationally famous when only twenty-six years old. Arguing that punishment should fit the crime and that excessive harshness was counterproductive, Beccaria's work was translated almost at once into half a dozen languages and affected legislative reforms in Russia, Sweden, and the Habsburg Empire (of which Milan was a part), as well as in several American states.*

From An Essay on Crimes and Punishments

If we look into history we shall find that laws, which are, or ought to be, conventions between men in a state of freedom, have been, for the most part the work of the passions of a few, or the consequences of a fortuitous or temporary necessity; not dictated by a cool examiner of human nature, who knew how to collect in one point the actions of a multitude, and had this only end in view, *the greatest happiness of the greatest number.*

Observe that by *justice* I understand nothing more than that bond which is necessary to keep the interest of individuals united, without which men would return to their original state of barbarity. All punishments which exceed the necessity of preserving this bond are in their nature unjust.

The end of punishment, therefore, is no other than to prevent the criminal from doing further injury to society, and to prevent others from committing the like offence. Such punishments, therefore, and such a mode of inflicting them, ought to be chosen, as will make the strongest and most lasting impressions on the minds of others, with the least torment to the body of the criminal.

The torture of a criminal during the course of his trial is a cruelty consecrated by custom in most nations. It is used with an intent either to make him confess his crime, or to explain some contradiction into which he had been led during his examination, or discover his accomplices, or for some kind of metaphysical and incomprehensible purgation of infamy, or, finally, in order to discover other crimes of which he is not accused, but of which he may be guilty.

No man can be judged a criminal until he be found guilty; nor can society take from him the public protection until it have been proved that he has violated the conditions on which it was granted. What right, then, but that of power, can authorise the punishment of a citizen so long as there remains any doubt of his guilt? This dilemma is frequent. Either he is guilty, or not guilty. If guilty, he should only suffer the punishment ordained by the laws, and torture becomes useless, as his confession is unnecessary. If he be not guilty, you torture the innocent; for, in the eye of the law, every man is innocent whose crime has not been proved.

Crimes are more effectually prevented by the *certainty* than the *severity* of punishment.

In proportion as punishments become more cruel, the minds of men, as a fluid rises to the same height with that which surrounds it, grow hardened and insensible; and the force of the passions still continuing, in the space on a hundred years the *wheel* terrifies no more than formerly the *prison*. That a punishment may produce the effect required, it is sufficient that the evil it occasions should exceed the *good* expected from the crime, including in the calculation the certainty of the punishment, and the privation of the expected advantage. All severity beyond this is superfluous, and therefore tyrannical.

From *An Essay on Crimes and Punishments*, tr. E. D. Ingraham (Philadelphia: H. Nicklin, 1819).

The punishment of death is pernicious to society, from the example of barbarity it affords. If the passions, or the necessity of war, have taught men to shed the blood of their fellow creatures, the laws, which are intended to moderate the ferocity of mankind, should not increase it by examples of barbarity, the more horrible as this punishment is usually attended with formal pageantry. Is it not absurd, that the laws, which detest and punish homicide, should, in order to prevent murder, publicly commit murder themselves?

It is better to prevent crimes than to punish them. This is the fundamental principle of good legislation, which is the art of conducting men to the *maximum* of happiness, and to the *minimum* of misery, if we may apply this mathematical expression to the good and evil of life. . . .

Would you prevent crimes? Let the laws be clear and simple, let the entire force of the nation be united to their defence, let them be intended rather to favour every individual than any particular classes of men; let the laws be feared, and the laws only. The fear of the laws is salutary, but the fear of men is a fruitful and fatal source of crimes.

Antoine Nicholas de Condorcet

Antoine Nicholas de Condorcet (1743–1794) was a philosopher and mathematician very typical of his "enlightened" generation, its dreams, and its fall. Perpetual secretary of the French Academy under the monarchy, member of the Convention during the French Revolution, he poisoned himself during the Terror in order to escape the guillotine.[1] A burning faith, which he thought scientific, supported his belief that great possibilities of infinite progress lay before humankind. Even when in hiding from his Jacobin enemies shortly before his death, Condorcet labored to finish his great historical survey, The Progress of the Human Mind.

From The Progress of the Human Mind

And now we arrive at the period when philosophy, the most general and obvious effects of which we have before remarked, obtained an influence on the thinking class of men, and these on the people and their governments, that, ceasing any longer to be gradual, produced a revolution in the entire mass of certain nations, and gave thereby a secure

---

[1] The term *Terror* describes the time from mid-1793 to mid-1794 when France, at war with most of Europe and embroiled in civil war, lived under the dictatorship of a radical minority of Jacobins (members of the Jacobin Club) who used spies, police, kangaroo courts, and intimidation to eliminate political opponents.
From Condorcet, *The Progress of the Human Mind* (Philadelphia, 1796).

pledge of the general revolution one day to follow that shall embrace the whole human species.

After ages of error, after wandering in all the mazes of vague and defective theories, writers upon politics and the law of nations at length arrived at the knowledge of the true rights of man, which they deduced from this simple principle: that he is a being endowed with sensation, capable of reasoning upon and understanding his interests, and of acquiring moral ideas.

They saw that the maintenance of his rights was the only object of political union, and that the perfection of the social art consisted in preserving them with the most entire equality, and in their fullest extent. They perceived that the means of securing the rights of the individual, consisting of general rules to be laid down in every community, the power of choosing these means, and determining these rules, could vest only in the majority of the community: and that for this reason, as it is impossible for any individual in this choice to follow the dictates of his own understanding without subjecting that of others, the will of the majority is the only principle which can be followed by all, without infringing upon the common equality.

Each individual may enter into a previous engagement to comply with the will of the majority, which by this engagement becomes unanimity; he can however bind nobody but himself, nor can he bind himself except so far as the majority shall not violate his individual rights, after having recognized them.

Such are at once the rights of the majority over individuals, and the limits of these rights; such is the origin of that unanimity, which renders the engagement of the majority binding upon all; a bond that ceases to operate when, by the change of individuals, this species of unanimity ceases to exist. There are objects, no doubt, upon which the majority would pronounce perhaps oftener in favour of error and mischief, than in favour of truth and happiness; still the majority and the majority only, can decide what are the objects which cannot properly be referred to its own decision; it can alone determine as to the individuals whose judgment it resolves to prefer to its own, and the method which these individuals are to pursue in the exercise of their judgment; in fine, it has also an indispensable authority of pronouncing whether the decisions of its officers have or have not wounded the rights of all.

From these simple principles men discovered the folly of former notions respecting the validity of contracts between a people and its magistrates, which it was supposed could only be annulled by mutual consent, or by a violation of the conditions by one of the parties; as well as of another opinion, less servile, but equally absurd, that would chain a people for ever to the provisions of a constitution when once established, as if the right of changing it were not the security of every other right, as if human institutions, necessarily defective, and capable of improvement as we become enlightened, were to be condemned to an eternal monotony. Accordingly the governors of nations saw themselves obliged to renounce that false and subtle policy, which, forgetting that all men derive from nature an equality of rights, would sometimes measure the extent of those which it might think proper to grant by the size of territory, the temperature of the climate, the national character, the wealth of the people, the state of commerce and industry; and sometimes cede them in unequal portions among the different classes of society, according to their birth, their fortune, or their profession, thereby creating contrary interests and jarring powers, in order afterwards to apply correctives, which, but for these institutions, would not be wanted, and which, after all, are inadequate to the end.

It was now no longer practicable to divide mankind into two species, one destined to govern, the other to obey, one to deceive, the other to be duped: the doctrine was obliged universally to be acknowledged, that all have an equal right to be enlightened respecting their interests, to share in the acquisition of truth, and that no political authorities appointed by the people for the benefit of the people, can be entitled to retain them in ignorance and darkness.

These principles, which were vindicated by the generous Sydney at the expense of his blood, and to which Locke gave the authority of his name, were afterwards developed with greater force, precision, and extent by Rousseau, whose glory it is to have placed them among those truths henceforth impossible to be forgotten or disputed. . . .

Hence it appears to be one of the rights of man that he should employ his faculties, dispose of his wealth, and provide for his wants in whatever manner he shall think best. The general interest of the society, so far from restraining him in this respect, forbids, on the contrary, every such attempt; and in this department of public administration, the care of securing to every man the rights which he derives from nature, is the only sound policy, the only control which the general will can exercise over the individuals of the community.

David Hume

The pursuit of critical thought to whatever realms it might lead proved a powerful dissolvent. Analytical tinkering with established beliefs, customs, and institutions was deeply subversive of the existing order, whose foundations it shook in the minds not only of the general public but of the very men who ruled, profited from, and preserved that order. Belief, said David Hume, must be proportioned to the evidence; reason must be the ultimate test—even of religion, as can be seen from the essay on miracles that this Scottish philosopher (1711–1776) included in his Inquiry into Human Understanding *(1748).*

But reason exercised upon itself, investigating its own processes, produced results even more subversive than at first suspected. Applied to reasoning itself, Hume's philosophical scepticism suggested that no belief could be rationally grounded. "All probable reasoning is nothing but a species of sensation. 'Tis not solely in poetry and music we must follow our taste and sentiment, but likewise in philosophy. When I am convinced of any principle, 'tis only an idea, which strikes more strongly upon me. When I give the preference to one set of arguments above another, I do nothing but decide from my feeling concerning the superiority of their influence." This disastrous suggestion of the impossibility of positive thought provoked the violent anger of Rousseau, as well as the reactions of a great many others, including Kant and Hegel, who never quite succeeded in refuting Hume's arguments. There was no way of doing so, except in the irrational terms of a later—much later—generation. Meanwhile, the skeptic himself indicated skepticism as to the effects his arguments might achieve: "This sceptical doubt, both with respect to reason and the senses, is a malady, which can never be radically cured, but must return upon us every moment, however we may chase it away, . . . Carelessness and inattention alone can afford us any remedy. For this reason I rely entirely upon them; and take it for granted, whatever may be the reader's opinion at this present moment, that an hour hence he will be persuaded [of whatever he wishes to believe]."

From The Essay on Miracles

A miracle is a violation of the laws of nature; and as a firm, an unalterable experience has established these laws, the proof against a miracle, from the very nature of the fact, is as entire as any argument from experience can possibly be imagined. Why is it more than probable, that all men must die; that lead cannot, of itself, remain suspended in the air; that fire consumes wood, and is extinguished by water; unless it be, that these events are found agreeable to the laws of nature, and there is required a violation of these laws, or in other words a miracle to prevent them? Nothing is esteemed a miracle, if it ever happened in the common course of nature. It is no miracle that a man, seemingly in good health, should die on a sudden: because such a kind of death, though more unusual than any other, has yet been frequently observed to happen. But it is a miracle, that a dead man should come to life; because that has never been observed in any age or country. There must, therefore, be a uniform experience against every miraculous event, otherwise the event would not merit that appellation. And as a uniform experience amounts to a proof, there is here a direct and full *proof*, from the nature of the fact, against the existence of any miracle; nor can such a proof be destroyed, or the miracle rendered credible, but by an opposite proof, which is superior.

The plain consequence is (and it is a general maxim worthy of our attention), "That no testimony is sufficient to establish a miracle, unless the testimony be of such a kind, that its falsehood would be more miraculous than the fact which it endeavours to establish; and even in that case there is a mutual destruction of arguments, and the superior only gives us an assurance suitable to that degree of force, which remains, after deducting the inferior." When anyone tells me, that he saw a dead man restored to life, I immediately consider with myself whether it be more probable, that this person should either deceive or be deceived, or that the fact, which he relates, should really have happened. I weigh the one miracle against the other; and according to the superiority, which I discover, I pronounce my decision, and always reject the greater miracle. If the falsehood of his testimony would be more miraculous than the event which he relates; then, and not till then, can he pretend to command my belief or opinion.

In the foregoing reasoning we have supposed, that the testimony, upon which a miracle is founded, may possibly amount to an entire proof, and that the falsehood of that testimony would be a real prodigy: But it is easy to show, that we have been a great deal too liberal in our concessions, and that there never was a miraculous event established on so full an evidence.

From *The Essay on Miracles* (1741).

For *first*, there is not to be found, in all history, any miracle attested by a sufficient number of men, of such unquestioned good sense, education, and learning, as to secure us against all delusion in themselves; of such undoubted integrity, as to place them beyond all suspicion of any design to deceive others; of such credit and reputation in the eyes of mankind, as to have a great deal to lose in case of their being detected in any falsehood; and at the same time, attesting facts performed in such a public manner and in so celebrated a part of the world, as to render the detection unavoidable: All which circumstances are requisite to give us a full assurance in the testimony of men.

Secondly. We may observe in human nature a principle which, if strictly examined, will be found to diminish extremely the assurance which we might, from human testimony, have in any kind of prodigy. The maxim, by which we commonly conduct ourselves in our reasonings, is, that the objects of which we have no experience, resemble those of which we have; that what we have found to be most usual is always most probable; and that where there is an opposition of arguments, we ought to give the preference to such as are founded on the greatest number of past observations. But though, in proceeding by this rule, we readily reject any fact which is unusual and incredible in an ordinary degree; yet in advancing further, the mind observes not always the same rule; but when anything is affirmed utterly absurd and miraculous, it rather the more readily admits of such a fact, upon account of that very circumstance, which ought to destroy all its authority. The passion of *surprise* and *wonder,* arising from miracles, being an agreeable emotion, gives a sensible tendency towards the belief of those events, from which it is derived. And this goes so far, that even those who cannot enjoy this pleasure immediately, nor can believe those miraculous events, of which they are informed, yet love to partake of the satisfaction at second hand or by rebound, and place a pride and delight in exciting the admiration of others.

With what greediness are the miraculous accounts of travellers received, their descriptions of sea and land monsters, their relations of wonderful adventures, strange men, and uncouth manners? But if the spirit of religion join itself to the love of wonder, there is an end of common sense; and human testimony, in these circumstances, loses all pretensions to authority. A religionist may be an enthusiast, and imagine he sees what has no reality: he may know his narrative to be false, and yet persevere in it, with the best intentions in the world, for the sake of promoting so holy a cause: or even where this delusion has not place, vanity, excited by so strong a temptation, operates on him more powerfully than on the rest of mankind in any other circumstances; and self-interest with equal force. His auditors may not have, and commonly have not, sufficient judgment to canvass his evidence: what judgment they have, they renounce by principle, in this sublime and mysterious subject: or if they were ever so willing to employ it, passion and a heated imagination disturb the regularity of its operations. Their credulity increases his impudence: and his impudence overpowers their credulity.

Eloquence, when at its highest pitch, leaves little room for reason or reflection; but addressing itself entirely to the fancy or the affections, captivates the willing hearers, and subdues their understanding. Happily, this pitch it seldom attains. But what a Tully or a Demosthenes could scarcely effect over a Roman or Athenian audience, every Capuchin, every itinerant or stationary teacher can perform over the generality of mankind, and in a higher degree, by touching such gross and vulgar passions.

The many instances of forged miracles, and prophecies, and supernatural events, which, in all ages, have either been detected by contrary evidence, or which detect themselves by their absurdity, prove sufficiently the strong propensity of mankind to the extraordinary and the marvellous, and ought reasonably to beget a suspicion against all relations of this kind. . . .

Thirdly. It forms a strong presumption against all supernatural and miraculous relations, that they are observed chiefly to abound among ignorant and barbarous nations; or if a civilized people has ever given admission to any of them, that people will be found to have received them from ignorant and barbarous ancestors, who transmitted them with that inviolable sanction and authority which always attend received opinions. When we peruse the first histories of all nations, we are apt to imagine ourselves transported into some new world; where the whole frame of nature is disjointed, and every element performs its operations in a different manner from what it does at present. Battles, revolutions, pestilence, famine and death, are never the effect of those natural causes, which we experience. Prodigies, omens, oracles, judgments, quite obscure the few natural events that are intermingled with them. But as the former grow thinner every page, in proportion as we advance nearer the enlightened ages, we soon learn, that there is nothing mysterious or supernatural in the case, but that all proceeds from the usual propensity of mankind towards the marvellous, and that, though this inclination may at intervals receive a check from sense and learning, it can never be thoroughly extirpated from human nature.

It is strange, a judicious reader is apt to say, upon the perusal of these wonderful historians, *that such prodigious events never happen in our days.* But it is nothing strange, I hope, that man should lie in all ages. You must surely have seen instances enough of that frailty. You have yourself heard many such marvellous relations started, which, being treated with scorn by all the wise and judicious, have at last been abandoned even by the vulgar. Be assured, that those renowned lies, which have spread and flourished to such a monstrous height, arose from like beginnings; but being sown in a more proper soil, shot up at last into prodigies almost equal to those which they relate. . . .

The advantages are so great, of starting an imposture among an ignorant people, that, even though the delusion should be too gross to impose on the generality of them (*which, though seldom, is sometimes the case*), it has a much better chance for succeeding in remote countries, than if the first scene had been laid in a city renowned for arts and knowledge. The most ignorant and barbarous of these barbarians carry the report abroad. None of their countrymen have a large correspondence, or sufficient credit and authority to contradict and beat down the delusion. Men's inclination to the marvellous has full opportunity to display itself. And thus a story, which is universally exploded in the place where it was first started, shall pass for certain at a thousand miles distance. . . .

I may add as a *fourth* reason, which diminishes the authority of prodigies, that there is no testimony for any, even those which have not been expressly detected, that is not opposed by an infinite number of witnesses; so that not only the miracle destroys the credit of testimony, but the testimony destroys itself. To make this the better understood, let us consider that, in matters of religion, whatever is different is contrary; and that it is impossible the religions of ancient Rome, of Turkey, of Siam, and of China, should, all of them, be established on any solid foundation. Every miracle, therefore, pretended to have been wrought in any of these religions (and all of them abound in miracles), as its direct scope is to establish the particular system to which it is attributed; so has it the same force, though more indirectly, to overthrow every other system. In destroying a rival system, it likewise destroys the credit of those miracles on which that system was established; so that all the prodigies of different religions are to be regarded as contrary facts, and the evidences of these prodigies, whether weak or strong, as opposite to each other. According to this method of reasoning, when we believe any miracle of Mahomet or his successors, we have for our warrant the testimony of a few barbarous Arabians. And on the other hand, we are to regard the authority of Titus Livius, Plutarch, Tacitus, and, in short, of all the authors and witnesses, Grecian, Chinese, and Roman-Catholic, who have related any miracle in their particular religion; I say, we are to regard their testimony in the same light as if they had mentioned that Mahometan miracle, and had in express terms contradicted it, with the same certainty as they have for the miracle they relate. This argument may appear oversubtle and refined; but it is not in reality different from the reasoning of a judge, who supposes, that the credit of two witnesses, maintaining a crime against anyone, is destroyed by the testimony of two others, who affirm him to have been two hundred leagues distant, at the same instant when the crime is said to have been committed. . . .

Upon the whole, then, it appears that no testimony for any kind of miracle has ever amounted to a probability, much less to a proof; and that, even supposing it amounted to a proof, it would be opposed by another proof, derived from the very nature of the fact which it would endeavor to establish. It is experience only which gives authority to human testimony; and it is the same experience which assures us of the laws of nature. When, therefore, these two kinds of experience are contrary, we have nothing to do but to subtract the one from the other, and embrace an opinion either on one side or the other, with that assurance which arises from the remainder. But according to the principle here explained, this subtraction with regard to all popular religions amounts to an entire annihilation; and therefore we may establish it as a maxim, that no human testimony can have such force as to prove a miracle, and make it a just foundation for any such system of religion.

A Farm Boy's Life

Jean-Roch Coignet was an eighteenth-century farmer's son who ran away from home after one beating too many, and worked around from the age of eight until he joined the armies of Napoleon. He soldiered from 1799, when he was twenty-three, until Waterloo, in 1815. During that time he fought in forty-eight battles, from Russia to Spain, and, though never wounded, was among the first to be decorated with the Legion of Honor. He had learned to read in 1809, at thirty-three, when promoted to the rank of sergeant. When he was retired as a captain on half-pay, in 1815, he began to write his memoirs. First published in 1851, they provide a fascinating firsthand account of the realities of a soldier's life. The story of his childhood, in the passage that follows, is taken from the first few pages of these memoirs. It reminds us that, in the age of high mortality that lasted from the beginnings of humanity into the nineteenth century, orphans were more the norm than the exception, and the problems faced by folk characters such as Cinderella, Snow White, or Hansel and Gretel were faced by many children in real life.

Jean-Roch Coignet: My Youth

I was born at Druyes-of-the-Fountains, in the department of the Yonne, in 1776, the 16th of August, of a father who had the means to bring up his children.

My father had three wives: the first left him two daughters; he remarried a second time. Of the second, he was left with four children: one daughter and four sons. The youngest was 6, my sister 7. I was 8, my brother who was eldest, was 9. We had the misfortune of losing our dear mother.

My father remarries a third time: he married his servant who gave him seven children.

I shall sketch the portrait of my father, the first poacher of France: amiable, sober, loving only hunting, fishing, and suing neighbors, who passed his life hunting and fishing. Finally, he was the cock of all the girls and women of all classes.

Of his three wives, he had 28 sons and four daughters, 32 in all. I think that's enough. I was born of the second wife. The third was our servant. She was 18 years old, they called her the pretty one, so after fifteen days she was pregnant and consequently mistress of the house, and you can imagine that this stepmother took over all authority in the household.

See these poor little orphans beaten night and day! She would squeeze our necks to make us look better. When we discovered some chick peas in a sack, we plundered it all. The blows didn't take long in coming. This life lasted for two months before my father finally married her. What followed was worse.

Every day, my father came home from hunting, "My Dearest," he would say, "what about the children?"

"They've gone to bed," the stepmother would answer; and every day the same thing. We never saw our father. She did everything to avoid our being able to complain. However, her vigilance was deceived when, one morning, my brother and myself found ourselves before our father, our faces full of tears: "What's the matter with you?", our father asked. "We are starving. She beats us every day."—"Go on, go back. I'll look into it."

But this complaint proved a terrible mistake. There were more blows and even less bread. Finally, when we were unable to stand it any longer, my eldest brother took me by the hand and said, "If you agree, we shall go away. Let's each take one shirt and we shall not say goodbye to anyone."

From *Les Cahiers du Capitaine Coignet* (Paris, Hachette, 1892), tr. Eugen Weber.

Well, we started out early and got to Etais, one league [about 3 miles] from our home. It was the day of our fair. My brother puts a bunch of oak leaves on my little hat, and here I am hired to guard the sheep. I earned 24 francs and a pair of clogs a year. Here is the first day of labor.

I arrived in a place called Charmoy, a village surrounded by forests. I served as dog to the shepherdess. "Go this way!" the girl would tell me, and as I went along the wood, turning the goats away from it, a big wolf comes out of the trees who charges my sheep and picks up one of the finest in the herd. I didn't know what that beast was, the shepherdess was lamenting and telling me to run after him. I get to the place where the wolf was. The wolf couldn't carry off the sheep; I have time to get there and take it by its hind legs, and the wolf pulls on his end and I on mine.

But providence comes to my aid; two big dogs come to help me; they had iron collars and they fall on the wolf like lightning and in a moment the wolf has been strangled. Imagine my joy to have my sheep, and this monster laying there on the ground!

So I acted as dog to the shepherdess for the whole year. I had to pick up the loaves for the week and take them out to the fields where we spent a night and day. I stayed a year in that job.

From there, I leave for the fair at Entrains. I hired myself out for 30 francs,[1] a smock and a pair of clogs in a nearby village, near Menou, working for two old land-owners who sold timber and who gained from 12 to 1500 francs by my two arms. There were twelve horned beasts, including six oxen. In winter I would flail the grain in the barn and sleep on the straw. I was covered with vermin and deep in misery.

Starting the first of May, I would leave with my three carts to take the ground grain to the [river] landings, and from there I would go to the pasture. Every evening my Master would bring my food for twenty-four hours: a bit of bread and an omelet of two eggs cooked with leeks and linseed oil. That was my every day food. This life lasted three years. I only went back to the Master's house on St. Martin's Day, when they would do me the honor of giving me a piece of salt pork. From there I would go back to my straw with my clothes full of vermin. Outside, I slept in the open, in the fine woods of Madame de Damas. I had my favorite, the friendliest of my six oxen. As soon as he lay down, I laid down beside him. I took off my clogs and stuck my feet between his back legs and my head on his neck. But around two in the morning my six oxen got up quietly and my comrade would rise without my feeling him go. So here's the poor herdsman left behind, not knowing where to find his oxen, especially in the pitch dark. I put my clogs back on and listened hard to hear my oxen. I would go towards the new plantings, through brambles and thorns that had the blood running into my clogs, and I cried. Finally, my ankles were torn to the sinews. And often I ran into wolves on my way, with eyes that burned like candles; but my courage never left me.

Finally, I would find my six oxen and I would cross myself [in relief]. How happy I was! I would bring my deserters back to my three carts, charged with milled grain,

---

[1] A skilled Paris workman would get five francs a day. A boy got his keep; child labor was cheap labor.

and there I waited for my Master, before I harnessed them and left first for the landing, then for the pasture. And the Master would leave me there in the evening. I got my loaf, and always the two eggs cooked with leeks and linseed oil. And the same every day for three years. But the worst thing for me was the vermin that never left me.

When I couldn't stand it any longer, I left. Despite their entreaties, I left that village. Several years had passed since I left [home]. I was unrecognizable, so I returned where I had come from to see if I would be recognized, but nobody thought any longer about the lost child. I arrive on a Sunday and go to see the fine springs that run beside my father's yard. I start to cry but already, being stronger than adversity, I make my decision, and I wash in this limpid water where once upon a time I would walk with my brothers and my sister.

Anyway, the bells ring for Mass, and I go towards the church, my little handkerchief in my hand, for my heart was very heavy, but I hold myself in. I go to Mass. I kneel down, I say my little prayer and glance around a bit. Nobody paid any attention to me. Yet I hear a woman who says "There's a little boy who prays to God with a good heart." I was so well disguised that nobody recognized me. But for me it wasn't the same thing. I don't say anything to anybody. The Mass finished, I come out of the church. I had seen my father singing in the choir; he had no idea that he had one of his children near him, whom he had abandoned.

Anyway I had walked three leagues and had great need to eat. When I came out of Mass, I went to my sister of the first marriage who kept an inn; I asked her for food.

"What do you want, my boy?"—"I want to dine, Madam. Half a bottle and a little meat and bread, please."

I am served a piece of stew. I eat like an ogre. I sat in a little corner to see everybody coming in from the countryside. At last, my little meal finished, I asked, "How much do I owe you?"—"Nineteen sous, my boy."—"Here they are, Madam."—"Are you from around here, little one?"—"Yes, Madam. I've come to look for work."

She calls her husband. "Granger," she says, "Here's a little boy who's asking for a place."—"How old are you?"—"Twelve, sir."—"From where do you come?"—"From Menou."—"Oh, you are a local?"—"Yes, sir."—"Do you know how to thresh grain?"—"Yes, Sir."—"Have you served already?"—"Four years."—"How much do you want to earn a year?"—"Sir, where I come from we are paid in grain and in money."—"Well, if you like you can stay here. You will be stable boy and all the tips will be yours. Are you used to sleeping on the straw?"—"Yes, sir."—"You'll thresh the grain in the barn?"—"Yes, sir."—"If I'm satisifed with you I will give you five dollars a year."—"That is enough. I will stay. So I don't have to pay for my meal?"—"No," he says, "I will put you to work."

He takes me into the yard that I knew before him, and where I had played as a child. I was the most turbulent child of the village, so my pals would run after me and throw stones at me. They would call me red-head. I was always the strongest, I wasn't afraid of blows, our stepmother had gotten us used to it.

I remember one day my nose was dirty. She took the fire tongs to wipe my nose with. She wanted to make me suffer. "I will tear your nose off." So the tongs were thrown into the well.

My brother-in-law takes me into the yard and gives me a spade. I work for a quarter of an hour and he says, "That is enough, it is well done. One doesn't work on Sunday."—"Well," says my sister, "what is he going to do?"—"He will serve at table. Come bring some wine from the cellar."

I take a basket of bottles and I serve everybody. I was running around like a partridge. In the evening they gave me bread and cheese. At ten my brother-in-law takes me to the barn, for me to rest, and he says, "You have to get up early to prepare the baking, and then to clean the stable properly."—"Don't worry, it will all be done," says I.

I say goodnight to my Master. I burrow into the straw, and think how much I cried. I can say that, if they had looked at me, they would see my eyes, red like a rabbit, to find myself at my sister's, and especially her servant, and at my father's door.

I had no trouble waking up. Since I had only to come out of the hole I made in the straw and shake my ears, I start to thresh the grain for the morning's baking. At eight, I start on the stables where I get everything in order, and at nine I see my Master appear.—"Well, Jean, how is the work?"—"Not bad, sir."—"Let's see the barn, what you have done." "Oh!" he says, "it is well done. These bundles of straw are well made, it's not bad at all."—"Sir, at Menou I threshed all winter long."—"Come on, boy, let's have something to eat."

Anyway, with a heavy heart I go to that sister that my mother had raised like her only child. I take off my hat. "Wife," said he, "here is a little boy who works well. Give him something to eat." They gave me bread, cheese and a glass of wine, but my brother-in-law says, "Make him some soup."—"I'll do it tomorrow, I got up too late."

Next day I went to work and at the proper hour went to eat. Ah! for once I found a cheese-and-onion soup, and my glass of wine. "Don't be timid, boy, go digging in the yard.—"Yes, sir." At nine with my spade on my shoulder, I go to work. What a surprise! I see my father watering his cabbages. He looks at me, I take off my hat, my heart is heavy, but I stay firm. He speaks to me and says, "So, you're at my son-in-law's?"—"Yes, sir. So he is your son-in-law?"—"Yes my boy, where do you come from?"—"From around here."—"From where?"—"I come from Menou. I was working in a hamlet nearby."—"I know that country. Do you know the village of Coignet?"—"Yes, sir."—"Well, it was built by my ancestors."—"That may be, sir."—"Have you seen the fine forests that belong to Madame de Damas?"—"I know them all because I guarded my Master's oxen for three years. I slept every night under its oak trees."—"Well, my boy, you will be better off with my daughter."—"That may be, sir."—"Jean, what about your father?"—"They call him the lover. I don't know if that is his real name."—"Any children?"—"Four."—"What does he do?"—"He goes into the woods, there is a lot of game there. All one sees is stags and deer and wolves; it is full of them. They have scared me more than once. I suffered too much and I left."—"That's fine, my boy. Work and you'll be all right at my son-in-law's."

Anyway, there came travellers, two carriages. I stabled the horses and, on the next day, I received a franc as tip. How happy I was! At last people were satisfied with me. Then I was sent down to the cellar to rinse out the bottles, and I did it properly, so they made me fill them afterwards. So the little stable boy was good for everything. And they made me work hard: "Jean, here." "Jean, there." I served the tables, I was in the cellar, in the stable, in the barn, in the yard. Ah! There I was content! I see my father: "Good day, Mr. Coignet." I couldn't forget that name. It was too well engraved in my heart. "Good day, Jean. You're not getting bored?"—"No, sir, not at all." Anyway, every day I made some money.

I ended up getting rid of my vermin. It took some time, but at end of two months I was clean. My Sundays brought money: including the tips from the stable, six francs a week. That life lasted three months. But that wasn't my greatest concern. It was to find my two youngest brother and sister.

Every day I saw two of my childhood friends, who lived just next door. We would greet each other. The youngest of the two came to see me in the garden. I was digging and my father was in his garden next door.—"Good day, Mr. Coignet," says the young boy.—"Ah, there you are," says my father, and he goes off. So we start talking.—"Are you from far away?", says he.—"No, I'm from the region."—"So, is it far away?"—"Oh, no, about five leagues; Mr. Coignet knows the area. Around where we live there is a village called Coignet."

"Ah," says my friend, "that wicked man has lost his four children. We have cried, my brother and I, over the loss of such good pals. We were always together. They lost their mother when they were pretty young. They had the bad luck to get a stepmother who beat them every day. They would come over to us every day and we would give them bread, for they were not fed and they cried. We were sorry for them. We would take bread in our pocket and carry it to them so they could share it, all four. They would devour it, it was a pity to see. One day, my brother says, 'Let's go see the little Coignets. We have to bring them bread.' But what is our surprise: the two eldest ones had left, and no one knew where to find them. The next day no news. We tell this to our father. 'The poor children, they were too unhappy and always beaten!' The next day I went to ask the little one and his sister where his brothers were. 'They're gone,' said they.—'And where?'—'I don't know.' So my father goes to ask Old Man Coignet. 'They say your boys have left'; and Coignet answers, 'I think they have gone to see relatives not far from here. I'll give them a good hiding when they return.'" But he didn't have that trouble, he never saw us again.

But that is not all. Little Alex and little Marianne were still left to embarrass that wicked woman. Not wanting to waste any time, one fine day when my father was out hunting, she takes out the poor little ones, takes them by the hand, in the evening as night was falling, and takes them into the forest, led them as deep into it as she can, and says "I am coming back." But not at all. She leaves them to the mercy of God. Imagine the poor little ones, in the middle of the forest, in absolute darkness, without bread, unable to find their way. They remain three days in that deplorable state, living only on wild fruit and crying, and calling for help. Finally God sends them a savior. That man, his name is Thibault, he is the miller at Beauvoir.

But I have gotten too far ahead of the story. I only found that out in 1804.

Anyway, I come back to my story. My pal just told me that the two youngsters were no longer in the house: "These poor little ones," he said, "nobody knows what became of them. And everybody blames old Coignet and his wife." Listening to his story, I couldn't keep the tears out of my eyes.

"But you are crying?" said the boy.—"It hurts too much to hear things like that."—"Oh, Lord, they were beaten every day. Their father didn't look for them at all."

It was time for this conversation to end, for I was at the end of my tether. I couldn't stand it any more. . . . I go into the barn to cry freely, not knowing what I should do, if I should go back to my house to reproach and accuse my father and meet that dreadful woman, my stepmother, who was the cause of our unhappiness. I decide to cause no scandal. I take my shovel and go to work in the yard. What was my surprise to see my stepmother appear, with a little child that she was holding by the hand. Oh! at that moment I simply couldn't hold myself in, seeing this dreadful woman appear before me! I would have done something awful, but I left the garden; when I see her come near me, I take off like a shot towards the stables to cry at my ease.

I had come to hate the garden. Every time I went there, I always found the father or the mother that I avoided as much as I could. How often was I tempted to pass across the fence between the two gardens to bash the mother and her child a good blow with my spade, but God held back my hand and I would take myself away.

Enlightened Despotism

THE spirit of the enlightenment and the influence of the *philosophes* were reflected in the policies of the second half of the eighteenth century—policies of reform designed to secure the more efficient administration of the state and the greater prosperity of its subjects. The chief protagonists of this "enlightened despotism" were not to be found in the more advanced West but among the rulers of less developed countries, princes, and their ministers who sought to increase their power by increasing the productivity and resources of their lands and the efficiency of the governmental machine: Emperor Joseph II of Austria (who reigned from 1765 to 1790), Empress Catherine II of Russia (1762–1796), and, above all, King Frederick II of Prussia (1740–1786).

Frederick the Great

Frederick II of Brandenburg-Prussia was born in Berlin in 1712, the son of a brute who was nicknamed the Sergeant King because of his delight in soldiers, beer, tobacco, and barrack-room manners. Father and son never got on and, in consequence, Frederick's youth was far from happy; but when in 1740 he succeeded to the throne, he found that his father had left him an excellent military establishment. This the young king proceeded to put to use in a series of wars which, combined with his skillful diplomacy and firm administrative policy, raised Prussia to the rank of a first-rate power.

But Frederick was not only a great soldier and statesman; he was also a friend of literature and the arts, a sensitive and not untalented dilettante in the field of music and letters. His long and temperamental flirtation with Voltaire is one of the more fascinating stories of the eighteenth century, and his palace at Sans Souci outside Berlin attracted a cosmopolitan crowd of scientists, philosophers, and artists.

From The Political Testament of Frederick II

Politics is the science of always using the most convenient means in accord with one's own interests. In order to act in conformity with one's interests one must know what

---

From *Die Politischen Testamente Friedrichs des Grossen* (Berlin, 1920), tr. Professor George L. Mosse, in *Europe in Review* (New York, 1957), pp. 110–112. By permission of Rand McNally and Co.

these interests are, and in order to gain this knowledge one must study their history and application. . . . One must attempt, above all, to know the special genius of the people which one wants to govern, in order to know if one must treat them leniently or severely, if they are inclined to revolt . . . to intrigue. . . .

[The Prussian nobility] has sacrificed its life and goods for the service of the state, its loyalty and merit have earned it the protection of all its rulers, and it is one of the duties [of the ruler] to aid those [noble] families which have become impoverished, in order to keep them in possession of their lands: for they are to be regarded as the pedestals and the pillars of the state. In such a state no factions or rebellions need be feared . . . it is one goal of the policy of this state to preserve the nobility.

A well conducted government must have an underlying concept so well integrated that it could be likened to a system of philosophy, all actions taken must be well reasoned, and all financial, political and military matters must flow towards one goal: which is the strengthening of the state and the furthering of its power. However, such a system can flow but from a single brain, and this must be that of the sovereign. Laxness, hedonism, and imbecility, these are the causes which restrain Princes in working at the noble task of bringing happiness to their subjects. . . . A sovereign is not elevated to his high position, supreme power has not been confided to him, in order that he may live in lazy luxury, enriching himself by the labour of the people, being happy while everyone else suffers. The sovereign is the first servant of the state. He is well paid in order that he may sustain the dignity of his office, but one demands that he work efficiently for the good of the state, and that he, at the very least, pay personal attention to the most important problems. . . .

You can see, without doubt, how important it is that the King of Prussia govern personally. Just as it would have been impossible for Newton to arrive at his system of attractions if he had worked in harness with Leibnitz and Descartes, so a system of politics cannot be arrived at and continued, if it has not sprung from a single brain. . . . All parts of the government are inexorably linked with each other. Finance, politics and military affairs are inseparable; it does not suffice that one be well administered; they must all be. . . . A Prince who governs personally, who has formed his [own] political system, will not be handicapped when occasions arise where he has to act swiftly: for he can guide all matters towards the end which he has set for himself.

Catholics, Lutherans, Reformed, Jews, and other Christian sects live in this state, and live together in peace: if the sovereign, actuated by a mistaken zeal, declares himself for one religion or another, parties will spring up, heated disputes ensue, little by little persecutions will commence and, in the end, the religion persecuted will leave the fatherland and thousands of subjects will enrich our neighbours by their skill and industry.

It is of no concern in politics whether the ruler has a religion or whether he has none. All religions, if one examines them, are founded on superstitious systems, more or less absurd. It is impossible for a man of good sense, who dissects their contents, not to see their error; but these prejudices, these errors and mysteries were made for men, and one must know enough to respect the public and not to outrage its faith, whatever religion be involved.

From Forms of Government

If we look back into the most remote antiquity, we shall find that the people whose history has descended to us led pastoral lives, and did not form social bodies. What the book of Genesis relates of the history of the Patriarchs is sufficient proof. . . .

The Gauls were forming into societies at the time they were conquered by Julius Cesar; but it appears Great Britain had not attained this point of perfection, when the conqueror first passed into that island with his Roman legions. In the age of this great man, the Germans could only be compared with what the Iroquois and Algonquins, or some equally savage people, are at present. . . .

We are astonished at imagining the human race so long existing in a brutal state, and without forming itself into societies. Reasons are accordingly suggested, such as might induce people like these to unite in bodies. It must have been the violence and pillage which existed, among neighboring hordes, that could have first inspired such savage families with the wish of uniting, that they might secure their possessions by mutual defence. Hence laws took birth, which taught those societies to prefer the general to individual good. From that time, no person durst seize on the effects of another, because of the dread of chastizement. The life, the wife, and the wealth of a neighbor were sacred; and, if the whole society were attacked, it was the duty of the whole to assemble for its defence. The grand truth "That we should do unto others as they should do unto us" became the principle of laws and of the social compact. Hence originated the love of our country, which was regarded as the asylum of happiness.

But, as these laws could neither be maintained nor executed unless some one should incessantly watch for their preservation, magistrates arose out of this necessity, whom the people elected, and to whom they subjected themselves. Let it be carefully remembered that the preservation of the laws was the sole reason which induced men to allow of, and to elect, a superior; because this is the true origin of sovereign power. The magistrate, thus appointed, was the first servant of the state. When rising states had anything to fear from their neighbors, the magistrate armed the people and flew to the defence of the citizens.

That general instinct in men which leads them to procure for themselves the greatest possible happiness, occasioned the creation of the various forms of government. . . .

But, however sage the legislators, and those who first assembled the people in bodies were, however good their intentions might be, not one of these governments is found to have maintained its perfect integrity. And why? Because men are imperfect, consequently so are their works: because the citizens, employed by the prince, were blinded by individual interest, which always overthrows the general good: and, in fine, because there is no stability on earth.

In aristocracies, the abuse which the principal members of the society make of their authority is the general cause of succeeding revolutions. The Roman democracy was destroyed by the people themselves. The blind multitude of the Plebeians suffered

From *The Posthumous Works of Frederick II, King of Prussia*, tr. Thomas Holcroft (London, 1789).

themselves to be corrupted by ambitious citizens, by whom they were afterward deprived of their liberty and enslaved. This is what England has to dread, if the lower house of parliament should not prefer the true interest of the nation to that infamous corruption by which it is degraded. . . .

With respect to the true monarchical government, it is the best or the worst of all others, according to how it is administered.

We have remarked that men granted preeminence to one of their equals, expecting that he should do them certain services. These services consisted in the maintenance of the laws; a strict execution of justice; and employment of his whole powers to prevent any corruption of manners; and defending the state against its enemies. It is the duty of this magistrate to pay attention to agriculture; it should be his care that provisions for the nation should be in abundance, and that commerce and industry should be encouraged. He is a perpetual sentinel, who must watch the acts and the conduct of the enemies of the state. His foresight and prudence should form timely alliances, which should be made with those who might most conduce to the interest of the association.

. . . To this must be added a profound study of the local situation of the country, which it is the magistrate's duty to govern, and a perfect knowledge of the genius of the nation; for the sovereign who sins through ignorance is as guilty as he who sins through malice: the first is guilty of idleness, the latter of a vicious heart; but the evil that results to society is the same.

Princes and monarchs, therefore, are not invested with supreme authority that they may, with impunity, riot in debauchery and voluptuousness. They are not raised by their fellow citizens in order that their pride may pompously display itself, and contemptuously insult simplicity of manners, poverty and wretchedness. Government is not intrusted to them so that they may be surrounded by a crowd of useless people, whose idleness engenders every vice.

The ill administration of monarchical government originates in various causes, the source of which is the character of the sovereign. Thus a prince addicted to women suffers himself to be governed by his mistresses, and his favourites, who abuse the ascendancy they have over his mind, commit injustice, protect the most vicious, sell places, and are guilty of other similar acts of infamy. If the prince, through debility, should abandon the helm of the state to mercenary hands, I mean to ministers, in that case, each having different views, no one proceeds on general plans: the new minister fritters away what he finds already established, however excellent that may be, to acquire the character of novelty, and execute his own schemes, generally to the detriment of the public good. His successors do the like; they destroy and overturn with equal want of understanding, so that they may be supposed to possess originality. Hence that succession of change and variation which allows no project time to take root; hence confusion, disorder, and every vice of a bad administration. Prevaricators have a ready excuse; they shelter their turpitude under these perpetual changes.

Men attach themselves to that which appertains to them, and the state does not appertain to these ministers, for which reason they have not its real good at heart; business is carelessly executed, and with a kind of stoic indifference; and hence results the decay of justice, and the ill administration of the finances and the military. From a monarchy, as it was, the government degenerates into a true aristocracy, in which ministers and generals conduct affairs according to their own fancies. There is no longer any comprehensive system; each pursues his own plans, and the central point, the point of unity, is lost. As all the wheels of a watch correspond to effect the same purpose, which is that of measuring time, so ought the springs of government to be regulated, that all the different branches of administration may equally concur to the greatest good of the state; an important object, of which we ought never to lose sight.

We may add, the personal interest of the ministers and generals usually occasions them to counteract each other without ceasing, and sometimes to impede the execution of the best plans because they have not been conceived by themselves. But the evil is at its utmost when perverse minds are able to persuade the sovereign that his welfare and the public good are two separate things. The monarch then becomes the enemy of his people, without knowing why; is severe, rigorous, inhuman, from mistake; for, the principle on which he acts being false, the consequences must necessarily be the same.

The sovereign is attached by indissoluble ties to the body of the state; hence it follows that he, by repercussion, is sensible to all the ills which afflict his subjects; and the people, in like manner, suffer from the misfortunes which affect their sovereign. There is but one general good, which is that of the state. If the monarch loses his provinces, he is no longer able to assist his subjects as before. If misfortune should oblige him to contract debts, they must be liquidated by the poor citizens; and, in return, if the people are not numerous, and if they are oppressed by poverty, the sovereign is destitute of all resource. These are truths so incontestable that there is no need to insist on them further.

I once more repeat, the sovereign represents the state; he and his people form but one body, which can only be happy as far as united by concord. The prince is to the nation he governs what the head is to the man; it is his duty to see, to think, and act for the whole community, so that he may procure it every advantage of which it is capable. . . . He must be active, possess integrity, and collect his whole powers, that he may be able to run the course he has commenced. Here follow my ideas concerning his duties.

He ought to procure exact and circumstantial information of the strength and weakness of his country, as well relative to pecuniary resources as to population, finance, trade, laws, and the genius of the nation whom he is appointed to govern. If the laws are good, they will be clear in their definitions; otherwise, chicanery will seek to elude their spirit to its advantage, and arbitrarily and irregularly determine on the fortunes of individuals. Law suits ought to be as short as possible, to prevent the ruin of the appellants who consume in useless expenses what is justly and duly their right. This branch of government cannot be too carefully watched, so that every possible barrier may be opposed to the avidity of judges and counsellors. Every person is kept within the limits of their duty, by occasional visits into the provinces. Whoever imagines himself to be injured will venture to make his complaints to the commission; and those who are found to be prevaricators ought to be severely punished. It is perhaps superfluous to add that the penalty ought never to exceed the crime; that violence never ought to supersede law; and that it were better that the sovereign should be too merciful than too severe.

As every person who does not proceed on principle is inconsistent in his conduct, it is still more necessary that the magistrate who watches over the public good should act from a determinate system of politics, war, finance, commerce and law. Thus, for example, a people of mild manners ought not to have severe laws, but such as are adapted to their character. The basis of such systems ought always to be correspondent to the greatest good society can receive. Their principles ought to be conformable to the situation of the country, to its ancient customs, if they are good, and to the genius of the nation.

As an instance, it is a known truth in politics that the most natural allies, and consequently the best, are those whose interests concur, and who are not such near neighbors as to be engaged in any contest respecting frontiers. It sometimes happens that strange accidents give place to extraordinary alliances. We have seen, in the present times, nations that had always been rivals and even enemies, united under the same banners. But these are events that rarely take birth, and which never can serve as examples. Such connections can be no more than momentary; whereas the other kind, which are contracted from a unity of interests, are alone capable of exertion. In the present situation of Europe, when all her princes are armed, and among whom preponderating powers rise up capable of crushing the feeble, prudence requires alliances should be formed with other powers, as well to secure aid in case of attack, as to repress the dangerous projects of enemies, and to sustain all just pretensions by the succour of such allies in opposition to those by whom they are controverted.

Nor is this sufficient. It is necessary to have among our neighbors, especially among our enemies, eyes and ears which shall be open to receive and report with fidelity what they have seen and heard. Men are wicked. Care must especially be taken not to suffer surprise, because whatever surprises intimidates and terrifies, which never happens when preparations are made, however vexatious the event may be which there is reason to expect. European politics are so fallacious, that the most sage may become dupes, if they are not always alert and on their guard.

The military system ought, in like manner, to rest on good principles, which from experience are known to be certain. The genius of the nation ought to be understood; of what it is capable, and how far its safety may be risked by leading it against the enemy. The warlike customs of the Greeks and Romans are interdicted in our times. The discovery of gunpowder has entirely changed the mode of making war. A superiority of fire at present decides the day. Discipline, rules and tactics have all been changed, in order that they may conform to the new custom; and the recent and enormous abuse of numerous trains of artillery, which incumber armies, obliges others in like manner to adopt this method; as well to maintain themselves in their posts as to attack the foe in those positions which they shall occupy. . . . So many new refinements have therefore so much changed the art of war that it would, at present, be unpardonable temerity in a general who, in imitation of Turenne, Condé, or Luxembourg, should risk a battle according to the dispositions made by those great commanders in the age in which they lived. Victory then was carried by valor and strength: it is at present decided by artillery; and the art of the general consists in his near approach to the army of the enemy, without suffering his own troops to be destroyed before the attack. To gain this advantage, it is necessary to silence the fire of the enemy by the superiority of that with which it is opposed. . . .

There are states which, from their situation and constitution, must be maritime powers: such are England, Holland, France, Spain and Denmark. They are surrounded by the sea, and the distant colonies which they possess oblige them to keep a navy, to maintain communication and trade between the mother country and these detached members. There are other states, such as Austria, Poland, Prussia, and even Russia, some of which may well do without shipping; and others that would commit an unpardonable fault in politics were they to divide their forces by employing a part of their troops at sea, of the services of which they indispensably stand in need on land.

The number of troops which a state maintains ought to be in proportion to the troops maintained by its enemies. Their force should be equal, or the weakest is in danger of being oppressed. It may perhaps be objected that a king ought to depend on the aid of his allies. The reasoning would be good were allies what they ought to be. But their zeal is only lukewarm; and he who shall depend upon another as on himself will most certainly be deceived. If frontiers can be defended by fortresses, there must be no neglect in building, nor any expense spared to bring them to perfection. Of this France has given an example, and she has found the advantage of it on different occasions.

But neither politics nor the army can prosper if the finances are not kept in the greatest order, and if the prince himself be not a prudent economist. Money is like the wand of the magician, for by its aid miracles are performed. Grand political views, the maintenance of soldiers, and the best conceived plans for the welfare of the people, will all remain in a lethargic state if not animated by money. The economy of the sovereign is the more useful to the public good, because if he have not sufficient funds in reserve, either to supply the expenses of war without loading his people with extraordinary taxes, or to succour citizens in times of public calamity, all these burdens will fall on the subjects, who will be without resource in such unhappy times, just when they need it most.

No government can exist without taxation, which is equally necessary to the republic and to the monarchy. The sovereign who labors in the public cause must be paid by the public; the judge the same, that he may have no need to prevaricate. The soldier must be supported so that he may commit no violence for lack of having whereon to subsist. In like manner, it is necessary that those persons who are employed in collecting the finances should receive such salaries as may not put them under any temptation to rob the public. These various expenses demand very considerable sums, and to these must still be added money that should be saved to serve only in the most extraordinary emergencies. This money must all be necessarily levied on the people; and the grand art consists in levying so as not to oppress. That taxes may be equally and not arbitrarily imposed, surveys and registers should be made by which, if the people are properly classified, the money will be proportionate to the income of the persons paying. This is a thing so necessary that it would be an unpardonable fault in finance if ill imposed taxes should disgust the husbandman of his labors. Having performed his duties, it is afterwards necessary that he and his family should live in a certain degree of ease. Far from oppressing the nursing fathers of the state, they ought to be encouraged in the cultivation of the lands; for in this cultivation the true wealth of a country is to be found. . . .

Excise is another species of tax, levied on cities, and this must be managed by able persons; otherwise, those provisions which are most necessary to life, such as bread, small beer, meat, etc., will be overtaxed; and the weight will fall on the soldier, the laborer, and the artisan. The result will be, unhappily for the people, that the price of labor will be raised; consequently merchandize will become so dear as not to be saleable in foreign markets. Such is at present the case in Holland and in England. These two nations, having contracted immensely heavy debts in the last wars, have imposed new taxes to pay the interest; but, having very unadvisedly taxed labor, they have almost ruined their manufacturers. Hence, all things having become dearer in Holland, the Dutch are obliged to purchase their cloths from Verviers and Liège [in the Austrian Netherlands]; and England has lost a very considerable sale of her woollens in Germany. To obviate such inconveniences, the sovereign ought frequently to remember the condition of the poor, to imagine himself in the place of the peasant or the manufacturer, and then to say "Were I born one among the class of citizens whose labors constitute the wealth of the state what should I require from the king?" The answer which, on such a supposition, good sense would suggest, it is his duty to put in practice.

In most of the kingdoms of Europe there are provinces in which the peasants are attached to the glebe, or are serfs to their lords. This, of all conditions, is the most unhappy, and that at which humanity most revolts. No man certainly was born to be the slave of his equal. We reasonably detest such an abuse; and it is supposed that nothing more than will is needed to abolish so barbarous a custom. But this is not true: it is held on ancient tenures, and contracts made between the landholders and colonists. Tillage is regulated according to the service performed by the peasantry; and whoever should suddenly desire to abolish this abominable administration would entirely overthrow the mode of managing estates, and would be obliged, in part, to indemnify the nobility for the losses which their rents must suffer.

The state of manufactures and of trade, an article no less important, next presents itself. For the country to be preserved in prosperity, it is indubitably necessary that the balance of trade should be in its favor. If it pay more for importation than it gains by exportation, the result will be that it will be annually impoverished. Let us suppose a purse in which there are a hundred ducats, from which let us daily take one, and put none in, and everybody will allow that in a hundred days the purse will be empty. The means to avoid incurring any such loss are to work up all the raw materials of which the country is in possession, and to manufacture foreign raw materials, so that the price of labor may be gained, in order to procure a foreign market.

Three things are to be considered in respect to commerce: first the surplus of native products which are exported; next the products of foreign states, which enrich those by whom they are carried; and thirdly foreign merchandize, which home consumption obliges the state to import. The trade of any kingdom must be regulated according to these three articles, for of these only is it susceptible, according to the nature of things. England, Holland, France, Spain and Portugal, have possessions in the two Indies, and more extensive resources for their merchant ships than other kingdoms. To profit by such advantages as we are in possession of, and to undertake nothing beyond our strength, is the advice of wisdom.

We have now to speak of what are the most proper means invariably to maintain those provinces in abundance, of which society stands in absolute need, that it may continue flourishing. The first is to be careful that the lands are well cultivated; to clear such grounds as are capable of tillage; to increase the breed of sheep and cattle, so that the more may be gained by milk, butter, cheese and manure; afterwards to obtain an exact statement of the quantity of the various species of corn, grown in good, indifferent, and bad seasons, and to subtract the quantity consumed, so that from the result information may be gained of the surplus, and the point at which exportation ought to stop; or of the deficiency in consumption, and of the consequently necessary importation. Every sovereign actuated by the public good is obliged to keep storehouses abundantly furnished, that supplies may be ready when the harvest is bad and famine prevented. During the scarcity of the years 1771 and 1772, Germany beheld the miseries with which Saxony and the provinces of the empire were afflicted, because this very useful precaution had not been taken. The people pounded oak bark, on which they fed, and this wretched food did but accelerate death. Numerous families perished unsuccoured, and the desolation was universal. The survivors were pale, livid, and lean, and fled from their country to seek food elsewhere. The sight of them excited compassion: they would have been pitied by a heart of iron. What were the reproaches with which their governors ought to have loaded themselves, spectators as they were of such calamities and unable to afford any relief!

We shall now speak of another article, which perhaps is equally interesting. There are few countries in which the people are all of one religious opinion; they often totally differ. There are some who are called sectaries. The question then is stated—Is it requisite that the people should all think alike, or may each one be allowed to think as he pleases? Gloomy politicians will tell us everybody ought to be of the same opinion, so that there may be no division among the citizens. The priest will add "whoever does not think like me is damned, and it is by no means proper that my king should be the king of the damned." The inevitable deduction is that they must be destroyed in this world, so that they may be the more prosperous in the next.

To this is answered that all the members of one society never thought alike; that, among Christian nations, the majority are anthropomorphites; that among the Catholics, most of the people are idolaters, for I shall never be persuaded that a clown is capable of distinguishing between *Latria* and *Hyperdulia*.[1] He firmly and really adores the image he invokes. Therefore there are a number of heretics in all Christian sects. What is more, each man believes that which appears to him to be the truth. A poor wretch may be forced to pronounce a certain form of prayer, although he inwardly refuses his consent. His persecutor consequently has gained nothing. But, if we revert to the origin of all society, it will be found evident that the sovereign has no right to interfere in the belief of the subject. Would it not be madness to imagine men who have said to another man, their equal, "We raise you to be our superior, because we are in love with slavery; and we bestow on you the power of directing our thoughts, according to your will"? On the contrary, they have said "We have need of you for the maintenance of those laws which we are willing to obey, and that we may be wisely

---

[1] Adoration of God alone, and adoration of the Virgin Mary.

governed and defended; but we also require that you should respect our freedom."
This is the sentence pronounced, and it is without appeal. Nay, tolerance is itself so
advantageous, to the people among whom it is established, that it constitutes the happiest of states. As soon as there is that perfect freedom of opinion, the people are all at
peace; whereas persecution has given birth to the most bloody civil wars, and such as
have been the most inveterate and the most destructive. The least evil that results from
persecution is to occasion the persecuted to emigrate. The population of France has
suffered in certain provinces, and those provinces still are sensible of the revocation
of the edict of Nantes.

Such are in general the duties imposed upon a prince, from which, in order that
he may never depart, he ought often to recollect that he himself is but a man like the
least of his subjects. If he be the first general, the first minister of the realm, it is not
so that he should shelter in the shadow of authority, but that he should fulfil the duties
of such titles. He is only the first servant of the state, who is obliged to act with probity
and prudence; and to remain as totally disinterested as if he were each moment liable
to render an account of his administration to his fellow citizens.

Thus is he culpable, if he be prodigal of the money of the people, dispersing the
produce of the taxes in luxury, pomp, or licentiousness. It is for him to watch over
morals, which are the guardians of the laws, and to improve the national education,
and not pervert it by ill examples. One of the most important objects is the preservation
of good morals, in all their purity; to which the sovereign may greatly contribute by
distinguishing and rewarding those citizens who have performed virtuous actions, and
testifying his contempt for such as are so depraved as not to blush at their own disorders. The prince ought highly to disapprove of every dishonest act, and refuse distinctions to men who are incorrigible.

There is another interesting object which ought not to be lost sight of, and which,
if neglected, would be of irreparable prejudice to good morality; which is that princes
are liable too highly to notice persons who are possessed of no other merit than that
of great wealth. Honours so undeservedly bestowed, confirm the people in the vulgar
prejudice that wealth only is necessary to gain respect. Interest and cupidity will then
break forth from the curb by which they are restrained. Each will wish to accumulate
riches; and, to acquire these, the most iniquitous means will be employed. Corruption
increases, takes root, and becomes general. Men of abilities and virtue are despised,
and the public honor none but the bastards of Midas, who dazzle by their excessive
dissipation and their pomp. To prevent national manners from being perverted to an
excess so horrible, the prince ought to be incessantly attentive to distinguish nothing
but personal merit, and to show his contempt for that opulence which is destitute of
morals and virtue.

As the sovereign is properly the head of a family of citizens, the father of his people,
he ought on all occasions to be the last refuge of the unfortunate; to be the parent of
the orphan, and the husband of the widow; to have as much pity for the lowest wretch
as for the greatest courtier; and to shed his benefactions over those who, deprived of
all other aid, can only find succour in his benevolence.

Such, according to the principles which we established at the beginning of this Essay,
is the most accurate conception we can form of the duties of a sovereign, and the only
manner which can render monarchical government good and advantageous. . . .

We ought however to add that the prince who should pursue the laborious route which we have indicated, would never attain absolute perfection; because, with all possible good will, he might be deceived in the choice of the persons whom he should employ in the administration. Incidents might be depicted under false colors; his orders might not be punctually executed; iniquitous acts might be so concealed as never to arrive at his knowledge; and his ministers, rigorous and consequential, might be too severe, too haughty in their exactions. In fine, it is impossible a monarch should be everywhere in an extensive kingdom. Such therefore is and must be the destiny of earthly affairs, that the degree of perfection which the happiness of the people requires, as far as it depends on government, never can be attained. Therefore, in this as in everything else, we must of necessity remain satisfied with that which is the least defective.

Joseph II

The French Revolution would emancipate Jews in France via decrees signed in 1790 and 1791. But enlightened despots preceded enlightened antidespots. In 1781, the Edict of Tolerance issued by the Holy Roman Emperor, Joseph II (1741–1790), sought to bring the emperor's territories into the modern world. The edict granted freedom of the press, established religious equality before the law, introduced civil marriage (including the possibility of divorce), and gave non-Catholics—including Jews—full rights as citizens. The emperor's mother, Maria Theresa, who died in 1780, had declared "the Jewish nation" to be "the worst pest of the state." Joseph's edict integrated Jews into civil society, extended tolerance to their religion, and granted them rights concerning domicile, education, and occupation. Note that the reform was based on a utilitarian argument.

From The Edict of Tolerance (1781)

In order to make the Jews more useful, the discrimination hitherto observed in relation to their clothing is abolished in its entirety. Consequently the obligation for the men to wear yellow armbands and for the women to wear yellow ribbons is abolished. If they behave quietly and decently, then no one has the right to dictate to them on matters of dress.

Within two years the Jews must abandon their own language. . . . Consequently, the Jews may use their own language only during religious services.

Those Jews who do not have the opportunity to send their children to Jewish schools are to be compelled to send them to Christian schools, to learn reading, writing, arithmetic and other subjects.

Jewish youths will also be allowed to attend the imperial universities.

To prevent the Jewish children and the Jews in general suffering as a result of the concessions granted to them, the authorities and the leaders of local communities must instruct the subjects in a rational manner that the Jews are to be regarded like any

From T. C. W. Blanning, *Joseph II and Enlightened Despotism* (London: Longman, 1970), pp. 142–144.

other fellow human beings and that there must be an end to the prejudice and contempt which some subjects, particularly the unintelligent, have shown towards the Jewish nation, and which several times in the past have led to deplorable behavior and even criminal excesses. On the other hand, the Jews must be warned to behave like decent citizens, and it must be emphasized in particular that they must not allow the beneficence of His Majesty to go to their heads and indulge in wanton and licentious excesses and swindling.

Catherine II

In 1768, Empress Catherine of Russia, good friend of the French philosophes, issued her "Grand Instructions to the Commissioners appointed to frame a new code of laws for the Russian Empire," a document typical of an age when good intentions often took precedence over practice. Though urged by the empress to spare no pains "in bringing this great Work to a Conclusion, that Our Age might soon enjoy the happy Fruits of those Seeds which are now planted," the commissioners seem to have made haste rather slowly. Meanwhile, however, the empress was interested in profiting from the propaganda value of her progressive gesture. Aware of the value of publicity, she had already bought Diderot's private library on condition that it continued in his possession until his death, thus securing the goodwill of a master publicist and his circle of friends. Now she had her "Grand Instructions" translated and published in all of Europe's major cities, another eloquent witness to her enlightened views. The Soviet Constitution of 1936, also the most progressive document of its time and the most unreal, proved equally impressive to those who were ready to be impressed.

From The Grand Instructions (1768)

O Lord my God, hearken unto me, and instruct me; that I may administer Judgment unto thy People; as thy sacred Laws direct to judge with Righteousness!

THE INSTRUCTIONS TO THE COMMISSIONERS
FOR COMPOSING A NEW CODE OF LAWS

1. The Christian Law teaches us to do mutual Good to one another, as much as possibly we can.

2. Laying this down as a fundamental Rule prescribed by that Religion, which has taken, or ought to take Root in the Hearts of the whole People; we cannot but

---

From *The Grand Instructions to the Commissioners Appointed to Frame a New Code of Laws for the Russian Empire: Composed by Her Imperial Majesty Catherine II, Empress of all the Russias* (London, 1768); tr. Michael Tatischeff.

suppose, that every honest Man in the Community is, or will be, desirous of seeing his native Country at the very Summit of Happiness, Glory, Safety, and Tranquility.

3. And that every Individual Citizen in particular must wish to see himself protected by Laws, which should not distress him in his Circumstances, but, on the Contrary, should defend him from all Attempts of others, that are repugnant to this fundamental Rule.

4. In order therefore to proceed to a speedy Execution of what *We* expect from such a general Wish, *We*, fixing the Foundation upon the above first-mentioned Rule, ought to begin with an Inquiry into the natural Situation of this Empire.

5. For those Laws have the greatest Conformity with Nature, whose particular Regulations are best adapted to the Situation and Circumstances of the People, for whom they are instituted.
   This natural Situation is described in the three following Chapters.

CHAPTER I

6. Russia is an European State.

7. This is clearly demonstrated by the following Observations: The Alterations which *Peter the Great* undertook in Russia succeeded with the greater Ease, because the Manners, which prevailed at that Time, and had been introduced amongst us by a Mixture of different Nations, and the Conquest of foreign Territories, were quite unsuitable to the Climate. *Peter the First,* by introducing the Manners and Customs of Europe among the European People in his Dominions, found at that Time such Means as even he himself was not sanguine enough to expect.

CHAPTER II

8. The Possessions of the Russian Empire extend upon the terrestrial Globe to 32 Degrees of Latitude, and to 165 of Longitude.

9. The Sovereign is absolute; for there is no other Authority but that which centers in his single Person, that can act with a Vigour proportionate to the Extent of such a vast Dominion.

10. The Extent of the Dominion requires an absolute Power to be vested in that Person who rules over it. It is expedient so to be, that the quick Dispatch of Affairs, sent from distant Parts, might make ample Amends for the Delay occasioned by the great Distance of the Places.

11. Every other Form of Government whatsoever would not only have been prejudicial to Russia, but would even have proved its entire Ruin.

12. Another Reason is: That it is better to be subject to the Laws under one Master, than to be subservient to many.

13. What is the true End of Monarchy? Not to deprive People of their natural Liberty; but to correct their Actions, in order to attain the *Supreme Good*.

14. The Form of Government, therefore, which best attains this End, and at the same Time sets less Bounds than others to natural Liberty, is that which coincides with the Views and Purposes of rational Creatures, and answers the End, upon which we ought to fix a stedfast Eye in the Regulations of civil Polity.

15. The Intention and the End of Monarchy, is the Glory of the Citizens, of the State, and of the Sovereign.

16. But, from this Glory, a Sense of Liberty arises in a People governed by a Monarch; which may produce in these States as much Energy in transacting the most important Affairs, and may contribute as much to the Happiness of the Subjects, as even Liberty itself.

CHAPTER III

17. *Of the Safety of the Institutions of Monarchy.*

18. The intermediate Powers, subordinate to, and depending upon the supreme Power, form the essential Part of monarchical Government.

19. *I* have said, that the intermediate Powers, subordinate and depending, proceed from the supreme Power; as in the very Nature of the Thing the Sovereign is the Source of all imperial and civil Power.

20. The Laws, which form the Foundation of the State, send out certain Courts of Judicature, through which, as through smaller Streams, the Power of the Government is poured out, and diffused.

21. The Laws allow these Courts of Judicature to remonstrate, that such or such an Injunction is unconstitutional, and prejudicial, obscure, and impossible to be carried into Execution; and direct, beforehand, to which Injunction one ought to pay Obedience, and in what Manner one ought to conform to it. These Laws undoubtedly constitute the firm and immoveable Basis of every State.

CHAPTER IV

22. There must be a political Body, to whom the Care and strict Execution of these Laws ought to be confided.

23. This Care, and strict Execution of the Laws, can be no where so properly fixed as in certain Courts of Judicature, which announce to the People the newly-made Laws, and revive those, which are forgotten, or obsolete.

24. And it is the Duty of these Courts of Judicature to examine carefully those Laws which they receive from the Sovereign, and to remonstrate, if they find any Thing in them repugnant to the fundamental Constitution of the State, &c. which has been already remarked above in the third Chapter, and twenty-first Article.

25. But if they find nothing in them of that Nature, they enter them in the Code of

Laws already established in the State, and publish them to the whole Body of the People.

26. In Russia the Senate is the political Body, to which the Care and due Execution of the Laws is confided.

27. All other Courts of Judicature may, and ought to remonstrate with the same Propriety, to the Senate, and even to the Sovereign himself, as was already mentioned above.

28. Should any One inquire, wherein the Care and due Execution of the Laws consists? I answer, That the Care, and due Execution of the Laws, produces particular Instructions; in consequence of which, the before-mentioned Courts of Judicature, instituted to the End that, by their Care, the Will of the Sovereign might be obeyed in a Manner comfortable to the fundamental Laws and Constitution of the State, are obliged to act, in the Discharge of their Duty, according to the Rules prescribed.

29. These Instructions will prevent the People from transgressing the Injunctions of the Sovereign with impunity; but, at the same Time, will protect them from the Insults, and ungovernable Passions of others.

30. For, on the one Hand, they justify the Penalties prepared for those who transgress the Laws; and, on the other, they confirm the Justice of that Refusal to enter Laws repugnant to the good Order of the State, amongst those which are already approved of, or to act by those Laws in the Administration of Justice, and the general Business of the whole Body of the People.

CHAPTER V

31. *Of the Situation of the People in general.*

32. It is the greatest Happiness for a Man to be so circumstanced, that, if his Passions should prompt him to be mischievous, he should still think it more for his Interest not to give Way to them.

33. The Laws ought to be so framed, as to secure the Safety of every Citizen as much as possible.

34. The Equality of the Citizens consists in this; that they should all be subject to the same Laws.

35. This Equality requires Institutions so well adapted, as to prevent the Rich from oppressing those who are not so wealthy as themselves, and converting all the Charges and Employments intrusted to them as Magistrates only, to their own private Emolument.

36. General or political Liberty does not consist in that licentious Notion, *That a Man may do whatever he pleases.*

37. In a State or Assemblage of People that live together in a Community, where there

are Laws, Liberty can only consist *in doing that which every One ought to do,* and *not to be constrained to do that which One ought not to do.*

38. A Man ought to form in his own Mind an exact and clear Idea of what Liberty is. *Liberty is the Right of doing whatsoever the Laws allow:* And if any one Citizen could do what the Laws forbid, there would be no more Liberty; because others would have an equal Power of doing the same.

39. The political Liberty of a Citizen is the Peace of Mind arising from the Consciousness, that every Individual enjoys his peculiar Safety; and in order that the People might attain this Liberty, the Laws ought to be so framed, that no one Citizen should stand in Fear of another; but that all of them should stand in Fear of the same Laws.

CHAPTER VI

40. *Of Laws in general.*

41. Nothing ought to be forbidden by the Laws, but what may be prejudicial, either to every Individual in particular, or to the whole Community in general.

42. All Actions, which comprehend nothing of this Nature, are in nowise cognizable by the Laws; which are made only with the View of procuring the greatest possible Advantage and Tranquillity to the People, who live under their Protection.

43. To preserve Laws from being violated, they ought to be so good, and so well furnished with all Expedients, tending to procure the greatest possible Good to the People; that every Individual might be fully convinced, that it was his Interest, as well as Duty, to preserve those Laws inviolable.

44. And this is the most exalted Pitch of Perfection which we ought to labour to attain to.

45. Many Things rule over Mankind. Religion, the Climate, Laws, the Maxims received from Government, the Example of past Ages, Manners, and Customs.

46. Hence results a general Sense in the People, similar to these Causes.

47. For Instance, Nature and Climate domineer almost alone over the savage People.

48. Customs govern the Chinese.

49. The Laws tyrannise with savage Ferocity over the Japonese.

50. Manners heretofore took the Lead amongst the Lacedemonians.

51. Maxims of Government, and their ancient Manners bore the Sway at Rome.

52. The different Characters of Nations are blended with Virtues and Vices, with good and bad Qualities.

53. That Composition, or Admixture, might be pronounced happy, from which many

and great Blessings spring; though, we frequently cannot even conjecture the Cause, from whence they should issue.

54. To prove this, I here produce in Evidence different Examples òf different Facts. The Spaniards were at all Times remarkably eminent for their Good Faith. History furnishes us with remarkable Instances of their Fidelity in keeping a Pledge intrusted to their Care: They frequently submitted to Death, rather than betray their Trust, and they still retain this Fidelity, for which they were formerly so renowned. All Nations, who trade in Cadiz intrust their Fortunes to the Spaniards; and, hitherto, have had no Reason to repent of their Confidence. But this amazing Quality, blended with their Laziness, forms such a strange Medly, as produces Effects prejudicial to themselves. The other European Nations carry on all that Trade, before their very Eyes, which belongs properly to their Monarchy only.

55. The Character of the Chinese is of a different Complexion, and forms a Contrast which is the very Reverse of that of the Spaniards. The Precariousness of their Lives (arising from the very Nature of their Soil and Climate) produces in them an Activity almost inconceivable; and so immoderate a Fondness for Gain, that no trading Nation can trust them. This known Perfidy of theirs, has preserved to them the sole Trade of Japon. Not one of the European Merchants durst ever venture to engage in the Japon Trade under their Names, though they might have done it with great Ease through their maritime Provinces.

56. By what *I* have here advanced, *I* meant not, in the least, to abridge that infinite Distance which must ever subsist between Vices and Virtues. God forbid! *My* Intention was only to shew, that all the *political* Vices are not *moral* Vices; and that all the *moral* Vices are not *political* Ones. This Distinction ought to be known and carefully attended to, that in making the Laws nothing may be introduced in them which is contrary to the general Sense of a Nation.

57. The Legislation ought to adapt its Laws to the general Sense of a Nation. We do nothing so well as what we do freely and uncontrouled, and following the natural Bent of our own Inclinations.

58. In order to introduce better Laws, it is essentially necessary to prepare the Minds of the People for their Reception. But that it may never be pleaded in Excuse, that it is impossible to carry even the most useful Affairs into Execution, because the Minds of the People are not yet prepared for it; you must, in that Case, take the Trouble upon yourselves to prepare them; and, by these Means, you will already have done a great Part of the Work.

59. Laws are the peculiar and distinct Institutions of the Legislator; but Manners and Customs are the Institutions of the whole Body of the People.

60. Consequently, if there should be a Necessity of making great Alterations amongst the People for their greater Benefit, that must be corrected by Laws, which has been instituted by Laws, and that must be amended by Custom, which has been

introduced by Custom; and it is extreme bad Policy to alter that by Law, which ought to be altered by Custom.

61. There are Means of preventing the Growth of Crimes, and these are the Punishments inflicted by the Laws. At the same Time there are Means for introducing an Alteration in Customs, and these are Examples.

62. Besides, the more a People have an Intercourse with one another, the more easy it is for them to introduce a Change in their Customs.

63. In a Word, every Punishment, which is not inflicted through Necessity, is tyrannical. The Law has not its Source merely from Power. Things indifferent in their Nature, do not come under the Cognizance of the Laws.

CHAPTER VII

64. *Of the Laws in particular.*

65. Laws carried to the Extremity of Right, are productive of the Extremity of Evil.

A Footnote from Alexander Herzen (1859)

The gesture was impressive; the reality less so. This is what Alexander Herzen, a Russian liberal, would write in 1859 in his preface to the Memoirs of Empress Catherine II:

In reading these memoirs one is surprised that one thing is constantly forgotten, to the point of being nowhere mentioned,—it is *Russia* and *the people*. And this is the characteristic trait of the period.

The Winter Palace, with its administrative and military machinery, was a world apart. Like a ship floating on the water's surface, the only intercourse it had with the inhabitants of the Ocean was to eat them. It was *the State for the State's sake*. Organized in the German fashion, it imposed itself upon the people as a victor would. In this monstrous barracks, in this enormous chancellery, there was a dry sort of rigidity, as in a camp. The ones gave or transmitted the orders, the others obeyed in silence. There was only one point where human passions reappeared, stormy and agitated, and this point was, in the Winter Palace, the domestic focus not of the nation but of the State. Behind the triple line of guards, in these heavily ornate *salons*, a feverish life fermented with its intrigues and its struggles, its drama and its tragedies. It was there that Russia's destinies were plotted in the obscurity of the alcove, in the midst of orgies, beyond the reach of police and spies.

From Alexander Herzen, *Memoirs of Empress Catherine II* (London, 1859), pp. xiv–xv.

A Dawn of Revolution

THE idea that natural laws existed that not even kings could transgress with impunity was one which the eighteenth century had learned from the seventeenth. This was now blended with the belief that society was perfectible. Dr. Johnson, pessimistically swimming against the contemporary tide, had reminded his age that

> Of all the ills that human hearts endure
> How few that kings or laws can cause or cure.

But this was not the accepted attitude; on the contrary, human beings were thought able to forge their fates, shape the societies in which they lived according to the laws of nature and reason, and cure a great many of the ills that human hearts endure. These hopes erupted in the last quarter of the century in two great revolutions, one in America and one in France. The documents that follow give some idea of the motives and results of the two, and of the reactions which they called forth.

The American Revolution

About a year after the Second Continental Congress began its work, Richard Henry Lee of Virginia introduced a resolution stating that "These united Colonies are and of right ought to be, free and independent States." In two other resolutions he called for confederation and foreign alliances. Thomas Jefferson, John Adams, Benjamin Franklin, Roger Sherman, and Robert R. Livingston were appointed a committee to draw up a declaration of independence. Thomas Jefferson was the principal author of the draft approved by the Second Continental Congress on July 4, 1776.

The Declaration of Independence (1776)

In Congress, July 4, 1776.
The Unanimous Declaration of the
Thirteen United States of America

When in the course of human events, it becomes necessary for one people to dissolve the political bands which have connected them with another, and to assume among the Powers of the earth, the separate and equal station to which the Laws of Nature and of Nature's God entitle them, a decent respect to the opinions of mankind requires that they should declare the causes which impel them to the separation.

We hold these truths to be self-evident, that all men are created equal, that they are endowed by their Creator with certain unalienable Rights, that among these are Life, Liberty and the pursuit of Happiness. That to secure these rights, Governments are instituted among Men, deriving their just powers from the consent of the governed. That whenever any Form of Government becomes destructive of these ends, it is the Right of the People to alter or to abolish it, and to institute a new Government, laying its foundation on such principles and organizing its powers in such form, as to them shall seem most likely to effect their Safety and Happiness. Prudence, indeed, will dictate that Governments long established should not be changed for light and transient causes; and accordingly all experience hath shown, that mankind are more disposed to suffer, while evils are sufferable, than to right themselves by abolishing the forms to which they are accustomed. But when a long train of abuses and usurpations, pursuing invariably the same Object, evinces a design to reduce them under absolute Despotism, it is their right, it is their duty, to throw off such Government, and to provide new Guards for their future security.—Such has been the patient sufferance of these Colonies; and such is now the necessity which constrains them to alter their former Systems of Government. The history of the present King of Great Britain is a history of repeated injuries and usurpation, all having in direct object the establishment of an absolute Tyranny over these States. To prove this, let Facts be submitted to a candid world.

He has refused his Assent to Laws, the most wholesome and necessary for the public good.

He has forbidden his Governors to pass Laws of immediate and pressing importance, unless suspended in their operation till his Assent should be obtained; and when so suspended, he has utterly neglected to attend to them.

He has refused to pass other Laws for the accommodation of large districts of people, unless those people would relinquish the right of Representation in the Legislature, a right inestimable to them and formidable to tyrants only.

He has called together legislative bodies at places unusual, uncomfortable, and distant from the depository of their Public Records, for the sole purpose of fatiguing them into compliance with his measures.

He has dissolved Representative Houses repeatedly, for opposing with manly firmness his invasions on the rights of the people.

He has refused for a long time, after such dissolutions, to cause others to be elected; whereby the Legislative Powers, incapable of Annihilation, have returned to the People at large for their exercise; the State remaining in the meantime exposed to all the dangers of invasion from without, and convulsions within.

He has endeavoured to prevent the population of these States; for that purpose obstructing the Laws for Naturalization of Foreigners; refusing to pass others to encourage their migration hither, and raising the conditions of new Appropriations of Lands.

He has obstructed the Administration of Justice, by refusing his Assent to Laws for establishing Judiciary Powers.

He has made Judges dependent on his Will alone, for the tenure of their offices, and the amount and payment of their salaries.

He has erected a multitude of New Offices, and sent hither swarms of Officers to harass our People, and eat out their substance.

He has kept among us, in time of peace, Standing Armies without the Consent of our legislature.

He has affected to render the Military independent of and superior to the Civil Power.

He has combined with others to subject us to a jurisdiction foreign to our constitution, and unacknowledged by our laws; giving his Assent to their acts of pretended Legislation:

For quartering large bodies of armed troops among us:

For protecting them, by a mock Trial, from Punishment for any Murders which they should commit on the Inhabitants of these States:

For cutting off our Trade with all parts of the world:

For imposing Taxes on us without our Consent:

For depriving us in many cases, of the benefits of Trial by Jury:

For transporting us beyond Seas to be tried for pretended offences:

For abolishing the free System of English Laws in a Neighbouring Province, establishing therein an Arbitrary government, and enlarging its boundaries so as to render it at once an example and fit instrument for introducing the same absolute rule into these Colonies:

For taking away our Charters, abolishing our most valuable Laws, and altering fundamentally the Forms of our Governments:

For suspending our own Legislatures, and declaring themselves invested with Power to legislate for us in all cases whatsoever.

He has abdicated Government here, by declaring us out of his Protection and waging War against us.

He has plundered our seas, ravaged our Coasts, burnt our towns, and destroyed the Lives of our people.

He is at this time transporting large Armies of foreign Mercenaries to complete the works of death, desolation and tyranny, already begun with circumstances of Cruelty & perfidy scarcely paralleled in the most barbarous ages, and totally unworthy of the Head of a civilized nation.

He has constrained our fellow Citizens taken Captive on the high Seas to bear Arms against their Country, to become the executioners of their friends and Brethren, or to fall themselves by their Hands. He has excited domestic insurrections amongst us, and has endeavoured to bring on the inhabitants of our frontiers the merciless Indian Savages, whose known rule of warfare is an undistinguished destruction of all ages, sexes, and conditions.

In every stage for these Oppressions we have Petitioned for Redress in the most humble terms: Our repeated petitions have been answered only by repeated injury. A Prince, whose character is thus marked by every act which may define a Tyrant, is unfit to be the ruler of a free People.

Nor have we been wanting in attention to our British brethren. We have warned them from time to time of attempts by their legislature to extend an unwarrantable jurisdiction over us. We have reminded them of the circumstances of our emigration and settlement here. We have appealed to their native justice and magnanimity, and we have conjured them by the ties of our common kindred to disavow these usurpations, which would inevitably interrupt our connections and correspondence. They too have been deaf to the voice of justice and of consanguinity. We must, therefore, acquiesce in the necessity, which denounces our Separation, and hold them, as we hold the rest of mankind, Enemies in War, in Peace Friends.

We, therefore, the Representatives of the United States of America, in General Congress Assembled, appealing to the Supreme Judge of the world for the rectitude of our intentions, do, in the Name, and by Authority of the good People of these Colonies, solemnly publish and declare, That these United Colonies are, and of Right ought to be Free and Independent States; that they are Absolved from all Allegiance to the British Crown, and that all political connection between them and the State of Great Britain, is and ought to be totally dissolved; and that as Free and Independent States, they have full power to levy War, conclude Peace, contract Alliances, establish Commerce, and to do all other Acts and Things which Independent States may of right do. And for the support of this Declaration, with a firm reliance on the protection of Divine Providence, we mutually pledge to each other our lives, our Fortunes and our sacred Honor.

James Madison: from The Federalist

The Federalist is the title given to a series of articles published in the New York press between October 1787 and August 1788 that expounded and defended the proposed new Constitution of the United States, which had just emerged out of the discussions of the Federal Convention in Philadelphia. The authors, Alexander Hamilton and John Jay of New York, and James Madison of Virginia, were trying to persuade the public, and especially the electors of New York State, to vote in favor of ratification. Incidentally to this purpose, they produced a very clear-sighted study of government and politics that is still worth our attention.

NUMBER 10 (MADISON)

Among the numerous advantages promised by a well constructed Union, none deserves to be more accurately developed than its tendency to break and control the violence of faction. The friend of popular governments, never finds himself so much alarmed for their character and fate, as when he contemplates their propensity to this dangerous vice. He will not fail, therefore, to set a due value on any plan which, without violating the principles to which he is attached, provides a proper cure for it. The instability, injustice, and confusion, introduced into the public councils have, in truth, been the mortal diseases under which popular governments have everywhere perished; as they continue to be the favourite and fruitful topics from which the adversaries to liberty derive their most specious declamations. The valuable improvements made by the American constitutions on the popular models, both ancient and modern, cannot certainly be too much admired; but it would be an unwarrantable partiality, to contend that they have as effectually obviated the danger on this side, as was wished and expected. Complaints are everywhere heard from our most considerate and virtuous citizens, equally the friends of public and private faith, and of public and personal liberty, that our governments are too unstable; the the public good is disregarded in the conflicts of rival parties; and that measures are too often decided, not according to the rules of justice, and the rights of the minor party, but by the superior force of an interested and overbearing majority. However anxiously we may wish that these complaints had no foundation, the evidence of known facts will not permit us to deny that they are in some degree true. It will be found, indeed, on a candid review of our situation, that some of the distresses under which we labour, have been erroneously charged on the operation of our governments; but it will be found, at the same time, that other causes will not alone account for many of our heaviest misfortunes; and, particularly, for that prevailing and increasing distrust of public engagements, and alarm for private rights, which are echoed from one end of the continent to the other. These must be chiefly, if not wholly, effects of the unsteadiness and injustice, with which a factious spirit has tainted our public administrations.

By a faction, I understand a number of citizens, whether amounting to a majority or minority of the whole, who are united and actuated by some common impulse of passion, or of interest, adverse to the rights of other citizens, or to the permanent and aggregate interests of the community.

There are two methods of curing the mischiefs of faction. The one, by removing its causes; the other, by controlling its effects.

There are again two methods of removing the causes of faction: The one, by destroying the liberty which is essential to its existence; the other, by giving to every citizen the same opinions, the same passions, and the same interests.

It could never be more truly said, than of the first remedy, that it was worse than the disease. Liberty is to faction what air is to fire, an aliment, without which it instantly expires. But it could not be a less folly to abolish liberty, which is essential to political life because it nourishes faction, than it would be to wish the annihilation of air, which is essential to animal life, because it imparts to fire its destructive agency.

The second expedient is as impracticable, as the first would be unwise. As long as the reason of man continues fallible, and he is at liberty to exercise it, different opinions will be formed. As long as the connection subsists between his reason and his self-love, his opinions and his passions will have a reciprocal influence on each other; and the former will be objects to which the latter will attach themselves. The diversity in the faculties of men, from which the rights of property originate, is no less an insuperable obstacle to an uniformity of interests. The protection of those faculties is the first object of government. From the protection of different and unequal faculties of acquiring property, the possession of different degrees and kinds of property immediately results; and from the influence of these on the sentiments and views of the respective proprietors, ensues a division of the society into different interests and parties.

The latent causes of faction are thus sown in the nature of man; and we see them everywhere brought into different degrees of activity, according to the different circumstances of civil society. A zeal for different opinions concerning religion, concerning government, and many other points, as well of speculation as of practice; an attachment to different leaders, ambitiously contending for pre-eminence and power; or to persons of other descriptions, whose fortunes have been interesting to the human passions, have, in turn, divided mankind into parties, inflamed them with mutual animosity, and rendered them much more disposed to vex and oppress each other, than to co-operate for their common good. So strong is this propensity of mankind, to fall into mutual animosities, that where no substantial occasion presents itself, the most frivolous and fanciful distinctions have been sufficient to kindle their unfriendly passions, and excite their most violent conflicts. But the most common and durable source of factions has been the various and unequal distribution of property. Those who hold, and those who are without property, have ever formed distinct interests in society. Those who are creditors, and those who are debtors, fall under a like discrimination. A landed interest, a manufacturing interest, a mercantile interest, a moneyed interest, with many lesser interests, grow up of necessity in civilized nations, and divide them into different classes, actuated by different sentiments and views. The regulation of these various and interfering interests forms the principal task of modern legislation, and involves the spirit of party and faction in the necessary and ordinary operations of government.

No man is allowed to be a judge in his own cause; because his interest will certainly bias his judgment, and, not improbably, corrupt his integrity. With equal, nay, with greater reason, a body of men are unfit to be both judges and parties at the same time; yet what are many of the most important acts of legislation, but so many judicial determinations, not indeed concerning the rights of single persons, but concerning the rights of large bodies of citizens? and what are the different classes of legislators, but advocates and parties to the causes which they determine? Is a law proposed concerning private debts? It is a question to which the creditors are parties on one side, and the debtors on the other. Justice ought to hold the balance between them. Yet the parties are, and must be, themselves the judges: and the most numerous party, or, in other words, the most powerful faction, must be expected to prevail. Shall domestic manufactures be encouraged, and in what degree, by restrictions on foreign manufactures? are questions which would be differently decided by the landed and the manufacturing classes; and probably by neither with a sole regard to justice and the public good. The apportionment of taxes, on the various descriptions of property, is an act which seems to require the most exact impartiality; yet there is, perhaps, no legislative act, in which greater opportunity and temptation are given to a predominant party, to trample on the rules of justice. Every shilling, with which they overburden the inferior number, is a shilling saved to their own pockets.

It is in vain to say, that enlightened statesmen will be able to adjust these clashing interests, and render them all subservient to the public good. Enlightened statesmen will not always be at the helm: nor, in many cases, can such an adjustment be made at all, without taking into view indirect and remote considerations, which will rarely prevail over the immediate interest which one party may find in disregarding the rights of another, or the good of the whole.

The inference to which we are brought is, that the *causes* of faction cannot be removed; and that the relief is only to be sought in the means of controlling its *effects*.

If a faction consists of less than a majority, relief is supplied by the republican principle, which enables the majority to defeat its sinister views, by regular vote. It may clog the administration, it may convulse the society; but it will be unable to execute and mask its violence under the forms of the constitution. When a majority is included in a faction, the form of popular government, on the other hand, enables it to sacrifice to its ruling passion or interest, both the public good and the rights of other citizens. To secure the public good, and private rights, against the danger of such a faction, and at the same time to preserve the spirit and the form of popular government, is then the great object to which our inquiries are directed.

The French Revolution

Arthur Young (1741–1820), the son of a Suffolk clergyman, was best known in his time as a practical farmer and a writer on agricultural subjects. To us, however, he is interesting as one of the most intelligent and readable diarists of his time. The notes he kept as he traveled through Europe in the 1780s contain clear-sighted descriptions of the circumstances and mood of the people he observed and mixed with. Here are excerpted some of his experiences in France between 1787 and 1789.

Arthur Young: from Travels in France

August 3, 1787 At Mirepoix they are building a most magnificent bridge of seven flat arches, each of 64 feet span, which will cost 1,800,000 livres (gold); it has been 12 years erecting, and will be finished in two more. The weather for several days has been as fine as possible, but very hot; . . . The myriads of flies were ready to devour me, and I could hardly support any light in the room. Riding fatigued me, and I inquired for a carriage of some sort to carry me, while these great heats should continue; I had done the same at Carcassonne; but nothing like a cabriolet of any sort was to be had. When it is recollected that that place is one of the most considerable manufacturing towns in France, containing 15,000 people, and that Mirepoix is far from being a mean place, and yet not a . . . vehicle of any kind to be had, how will an Englishman bless himself for the universal conveniences that are spread through his own country, in which I believe there is not a town of 1500 people in the kingdom where post chaises

---

From Arthur Young, *Travels in France* (London, 1890).

and able horses are not to be had at a moment's warning? What a contrast! This confirms the fact deducible from the little traffic on the roads even around Paris itself. Circulation is stagnant in France. . . . Many vines about Pamiers, which is situated in a beautiful vale, upon a fine river. The place itself is ugly, stinking, and ill built; with an inn! Adieu, Monsieur Gacit; if fate sends me to such another house as thine—be it an expiation for my sins!—28 miles.

August 4, 1787 . . . At St. Geronds go to the Croix Blanche Inn, the most execrable receptacle of filth, vermin, impudence, and imposition that ever exercised the patient, or wounded the feelings of a traveller. A withered hag, the daemon of beastliness, presides there. I laid, not rested, in a chamber over a stable, whose effluviae through the broken floor were the least offensive of the perfumes afforded by this hideous place.—It could give me nothing but two stale eggs, for which I paid, exclusive of all other charges, 20 francs. Spain brought nothing to my eyes that equalled this stink, from which an English hog would turn with disgust. But the inns all the way from Nismes are wretched, except at Lodève, Gange, Carcassonne, and Mirepoix. St. Geronds must have, from its appearance, four or five thousand people. Pamiers near twice that number. What can be the circulating connection between such masses of people and other towns and countries, that can be held together and supported by such inns? There have been writers who look upon such observations as rising merely from the petulance of travellers, but it shews their extreme ignorance. Such circumstances are political data. We cannot demand all the books of France to be opened in order to explain the amount of circulation in that kingdom: a politician must therefore collect it from such circumstances as he can ascertain; and among these, traffic on the great roads, and the convenience of the houses prepared for the reception of travellers, tell us both the number and the condition of those travellers; by which term I chiefly allude to the natives, who move on business or pleasure from place to place; for if they are not considerable enough to cause good inns, those who came from a distance will not, which is evident from the bad accommodations even in the high road from London to Rome. On the contrary, go in England to towns that contain 1500, 2000, or 3000 people, in situations absolutely cut off from all dependence on, or almost the expectation of, what are properly called travellers, yet you will meet with neat inns, well dressed and clean people keeping them, good furniture, and a refreshing civility; your senses may not be gratified, but they will not be offended; and if you demand a post chaise and a pair of horses, the cost of which is not less than 80 pounds in spite of a heavy tax, it will be ready to carry you whither you please. Are no political conclusions to be drawn from this amazing contrast? It proves that such a population in England have connections with other places to the amount of supporting such houses. The friendly clubs of the inhabitants, the visits of friends and relations, the parties of pleasure, the resort of farmers, the intercourse with the capital and with other towns, form the support of good inns; and in a country where they are not to be found, it is a proof that there is not the same quantity of motion; or that it moves by means of less wealth, less consumption, and less enjoyment. In this journey through Languedoc, I have passed an incredible number of splendid bridges, and many superb causeways. But this only proves the absurdity and oppression of government. Bridges that cost 70 or 80,000 pounds and immense causeways to connect towns, that have no better inns than such as I have described, appear to be gross absurdities. They cannot be made for the mere use of the inhabitants, because one-fourth of the expense would answer the purpose of the real utility. They are therefore objects of public magnificence, and consequently for the eye of travellers. But what traveller, with his person surrounded by the beggarly filth of an inn, and with all his senses offended, will not condemn such inconsistencies as folly, and will not wish for more comfort and less appearance of splendour?—30 miles.

August 23, 1787 Pass a rich and highly cultivated vale to Aguillon; much hemp, and every woman in the country employed on it. Many neat well built farmhouses on small properties, and all the country very populous. View the chateau of the Duc d'Aguillon, which, being in the town, is badly situated, according to all rural ideas; but a town is ever an accompanyment of a chateau in France, as it was formerly in most parts of Europe; it seems to have resulted from a feudal arrangement, that the Grand Seigneur might keep his slaves the nearer to his call, as a man builds his stables near his house. This edifice is a considerable one, built by the present duke; began about twenty years ago, when he was exiled here during eight years. And, thanks to that banishment, the building went on nobly; the body of the house done, and the detached wings almost finished. But as soon as the sentence was reversed, the duke went to Paris, and has not been here since, consequently all now stands still. It is thus that banishment alone will force the French nobility to execute what the English do for pleasure—reside upon and adorn their estates. There is one magnificent circumstance, namely, an elegant and spacious theatre; it fills one of the wings. The orchestra is for twenty-four musicians, the number kept, fed, and paid, by the duke when here. This elegant and agreeable luxury, which falls within the compass of a very large fortune, is known in every country in Europe except England: the possessors of great estates here preferring horses and dogs very much before any entertainment a theatre can yield. To Tonnance.—25 miles.

August 24, 1787 Many new and good country seats, of gentlemen, well built, and set off with gardens, plantations, etc. These are the effects of the wealth of Bordeaux. These people, like other Frenchmen, eat little meat; in the town of Levrac five oxen only are killed in a year; whereas an English town with the same population would consume two or three oxen a week.

October 13, 1787 There has been much rain to-day; and it is almost incredible to a person used to London, how dirty the streets of Paris are, and how horribly inconvenient and dangerous walking is without a footpavement. We had a large party at dinner, with politicians among them, and some interesting conversation on the present state of France. The feeling of every body seems to be that the King's minister, Loménie de Brienne, will not be able to do any thing towards exonerating the state from the burthen of its present situation; some think that he has not the inclination; others that he has not the ability. By some he is thought to be attentive only to his own interest; and by others, that the finances are too much deranged to be within the power of any system to recover, short of the states-general of the kingdom; and that it is impossible for such an assembly to meet without a revolution in the government ensuing. All seem to think that something extraordinary will happen; and a bankruptcy is an idea not at all uncommon. But who is there that will have the courage to make it?

October 14, 1787 To the benedictine abbey of St. Germain, to see pillars of African marble, etc. It is the richest abbey in France: the abbot has 300,000 liv. [livres] a year. I lose my patience at such revenues being thus bestowed; consistent with the spirit of the tenth century, but not with that of the eighteenth. What a noble farm would the fourth of this income establish! what turnips, what cabbages, what potatoes, what clover, what sheep, what wool!—Are not these things better than a fat ecclesiastic? If an active English farmer was mounted behind this abbot, I think he would do more good to France with half the income than half the abbots of the kingdom with the whole of theirs. Pass the Bastile; another pleasant object to make agreeable emotions vibrate in a man's bosom. I search for good farmers, and run my head at every turn against monks and state prisoners.

October 17, 1787 Dined to-day with a party, whose conversation was entirely political. Mons. de Calonne's "Request to the King" is come over, and all the world are reading and disputing on it. It seems, however, generally agreed that, without exonerating himself from the charge of the speculation, he has thrown no inconsiderable load on the shoulders of Loménie, the present premier, who will be puzzled to get rid of the attack. But both these ministers were condemned on all hands in the lump; as being absolutely unequal to the difficulties of so arduous a period. One opinion pervaded the whole company, that they are on the eve of some great revolution in the government: that every thing points to it: the confusion in the finances great; with a deficit impossible to provide for without the states-general of the kingdom, yet no ideas formed of what would be the consequence of their meeting: no minister existing, or to be looked to in or out of power, with such decisive talents as to promise any other remedy than palliative ones: a prince on the throne, with excellent dispositions, but without the resources of a mind that could govern in such a moment without ministers: a court buried in pleasure and dissipation; and adding to the distress, instead of endeavouring to be placed in a more independent situation: a great ferment amongst all ranks of men, who are eager for some change, without knowing what to look to, or to hope for: and a strong leaven of liberty, increasing every hour since the American revolution; altogether form a combination of circumstances that promise e'er long to ferment into motion, if some master hand, of very superior talents, and inflexible courage, is not found at the helm to guide events, instead of being driven by them. It is very remarkable, that such conversation never occurs, but a bankruptcy is a topic: the curious question on which is, would a bankruptcy occasion a civil war, and a total overthrow of the government? The answers that I have received to this question, appear to be just: such a measure, conducted by a man of abilities, vigour, and firmness, would certainly not occasion either one or the other. But the same measure, attempted by a man of a different character, might possibly do both. All agree, that the states of the kingdom cannot assemble without more liberty being the consequence; but I meet with so few men that have any just ideas of freedom, that I question much the species of this new liberty that is to arise. They know not how to value the privileges of THE PEOPLE: as to the nobility and the clergy, if a revolution added anything to their scale, I think it would do more mischief than good.

October 20, 1787 To the Ecole Militaire, established by Louis XV for the education of 140 youths, the sons of the nobility; such establishments are equally ridiculous and unjust. To educate the son of a man who cannot afford the education himself, is a gross injustice, if you do not secure a situation in life answerable to that education. If you do secure such a situation, you destroy the result of the education, because nothing but merit ought to give that security. You educate the children of men, who are well able to give the education themselves, you tax the people who cannot afford to educate their children, in order to ease those who can well afford the burthen; and in such institutions, this is sure to be the case. At night to l'Ambigu Comique, a pretty little theatre, with plenty of rubbish on it. Coffee-houses on the boulevards, music, noise, and whores without end; every thing but scavengers and lamps. The mud is a foot deep; and there are parts of the boulevards without a single light.

October 22, 1787 . . . Madame du Barry's residence, Lusienne, is . . . decorated with much elegance. There is a table of Sèvres porcelain, exquisitely done. I forget how many thousand louis d'ors it cost. The French, to whom I spoke of Lusienne, exclaimed against mistresses and extravagance, with more violence than reason in my opinion. Who, in common sense, would deny a king the amusement of a mistress, provided he did not make a business of his plaything? "Look at Frederic the Great!" they say. "Did he have a mistress? Did he build her mansions? Did he waste his money furnishing them with porcelain?" No: but he had that which was fifty times worse: a king had better make love to a handsome woman than to one of his neighbour's provinces. The king of Prussia's mistress cost an hundred millions sterling, and the lives of 500,000 men; and before the reign of that mistress is over, may yet cost as much more. The greatest genius and talents are lighter than a feather, weighed philosophically, if rapine, war, and conquest, are the effects of them.

October 25, 1787 This great city appears to be in many respects the most ineligible and inconvenient for the residence of a person of small fortune of any that I have seen; and vastly inferior to London. The streets are very narrow, and many of them crouded, nine tenths dirty, and all without foot-pavements. Walking, which in London is so pleasant and so clean, that ladies do it every day, is here a toil and a fatigue to a man, and an impossibility to a well dressed woman. The coaches are numerous and, what are much worse, there are an infinity of one-horse cabriolets, which are driven by young men of fashion and their imitators, alike fools, with such rapidity as to be real nuisances, and render the streets exceedingly dangerous, without an incessant caution. I saw a poor child run over and probably killed, and have been myself many times blackened with the mud of the kennels. This beggarly practice, of driving a one-horse booby hatch about the streets of a great capital, flows either from poverty or wretched and despicable economy; nor is it possible to speak of it with too much severity. If young noblemen at London were to drive their chaises in streets without foot-ways, as their brethren do at Paris, they would speedily and justly get very well threshed, or rolled in the kennel. This circumstance renders Paris an ineligible residence for persons, particularly families that cannot afford to keep a coach; a convenience which is as dear as at London. The fiacres, hackney-coaches, are much worse than at that city; and chairs there are none, for they would be driven down in the streets. To this circumstance also it is owing, that all persons of small or moderate fortune, are forced to dress in black, with black stockings; the dusky hue of this in company is not so disagreeable a circumstance as being too great a distinction; too clear a line drawn in company between a man that has a good fortune, and another that has not. With the pride, arrogance, and ill temper of English wealth this could not be borne; but the prevailing good humour of the French eases all such untoward circumstances. Lodgings are not half so good as at London, yet considerably dearer. If you do not hire a whole suite of rooms at an hotel, you must probably mount three, four, or five pair of stairs, and in general have nothing but a bed-chamber. After the horrid fatigue of the streets, such an elevation is a delectable circumstance. You must search with trouble before you will be lodged in a private family, as gentlemen usually are at London, and pay a higher price. Servants' wages are about the same as at that city. It is to be regretted that Paris should have these disadvantages, for in other respects I take it to be a most eligible residence for such as prefer a great city. The society for a man of letters, or who has any scientific pursuit, cannot be exceeded. The intercourse between such men and the great, which if it is not upon an equal footing, ought never to exist at all, is respectable. Persons of the highest rank pay an attention to science and literature, and emulate the character they confer. I should pity the man who expected, without other advantage of a very different nature, to be well received in a brilliant circle at London, because he was a fellow of the Royal Society. But this would not be the case with a member of the Academy of Sciences at Paris; he is sure of a good reception every where. Perhaps this contrast depends in a great measure on the difference of the governments of the two countries. Politics are too much attended to in England to allow a due respect to be paid to anything else; and should the French establish a freer government, academicians will not be held in such estimation, when rivalled in the public esteem by the orators who hold forth liberty and property in a free parliament.

August 13, 1788 Rouen is dearer than Paris, and therefore it is necessary for the pockets of the people that their bellies should be wholesomely pinched. At the table d'hôte, at the Pinecone Hotel we sat down, sixteen, to the following dinner, a soup, about 3 lb. of stew, one fowl, one duck, a small fricassee of chicken, roast of veal, of about 2 lb. and two other small plates with a sallad: the price 45 francs and 29 francs more for a pint of wine; at an ordinary of 20p. a head in England there would be a piece of meat which would, literally speaking, outweigh this whole dinner![1] The ducks were swept clean so quickly, that I moved from table without half a dinner. Such table d'hôtes are among the cheap things of France! Of all sombre and triste meetings a French table d'hôte is foremost; for eight minutes a dead silence, and as to the politeness of addressing a conversation to a foreigner, he will look for it in vain. Not a single word has any where been said to me unless to answer some question: Rouen not singular in this. The parliament-house here is shut up, and its members exiled a month past to their country seats, because they would not register the edict for a new land-tax. I inquired much into the common sentiments of the people, and found that the King personally from having been here, is more popular than the parliament, to whom they attribute the general dearness of everything.

September 2, 1788, Brittany Rennes is well built, and it has two good squares; that

---

[1] 20 pence equaled, in those days, about 30 U.S. cents. There are 20 shillings in one pound, 12 pence in one shilling. Five shillings were about one dollar; the franc was two for a penny.

particularly of Louis XV, where is his statue. The parliament being in exile, the house is not to be seen. The Benedictines garden, called the Tabour, is worth viewing. But the object at Rennes most remarkable at present is a camp, with a marshal of France (de Stainville), and four regiments of infantry, and two of dragoons, close to the gates. The discontents of the people have been double, first on account of the high price of bread and secondly for the banishment of the parliament. The former cause is natural enough, but why the people should love their parliament was what I could not understand, since the members, as well as of the states, are all noble, and the distinction between the nobles and commoners no where stronger, more offensive, or more abominable than in Bretagne. They assured me, however, that the populace have been blown up to violence by every art of deception, and even by money distributed for that purpose. The commotions rose to such a height before the camp was established, that the troops here were utterly unable to keep the peace. Mon. Argentaise, to whom I had brought letters, had the goodness, during the four days I was here, to shew and explain every thing to be seen. I find Rennes very cheap; and it appears the more so to me just come from Normandy, where every thing is extravagantly dear. The table d'hôte, at the *grand maison,* is well served; they give two courses, containing plenty of good things, and a very ample regular dessert: the supper one good course, with a large joint of mutton, and another good dessert; each meal, with the common wine, 40 francs and for 20 more you have very good wine, instead of the ordinary sort: 30 francs for the horse: thus, with good wine, it is no more than 6 liv. 10 francs a day, or 5s. 10p. Yet a camp which they complain has raised prices enormously.

September 5, 1788 To Montauban. The poor people seem poor indeed; the children terribly ragged, if possible worse clad than if with no cloaths at all; as to shoes and stockings they are luxuries. A beautiful girl of six or seven years playing with a stick, and smiling under such a bundle of rags as made my heart ache to see her: they did not beg, and when I gave them any thing seemed more surprised than obliged. One third of what I have seen of this province seems uncultivated, and nearly all of it in misery. What have kings, and ministers, and parliaments, and states, to answer for their prejudices, seeing millions of hands that would be industrious, idle and starving, through the execrable maxims of despotism, or the equally detestable prejudices of a feudal nobility. Sleep at the Lion d'or, at Montauban, an abominable hole.—20 miles.

September 6, 1788 . . . At the little town of Lamballe, there are above fifty families of noblesse that live in winter, who reside on their estates in the summer. There is probably as much foppery and nonsense in their circles, and for what I know as much happiness, as those of Paris. Both would be better employed in cultivating their lands, and rendering the poor industrious.

1789 My two preceding journeys had crossed the whole western half of France, in various directions; and the information I had received in making them, had made me as much a master of the general husbandry, the soil, management and productions, as could be expected, without penetrating in every corner, and residing long in various stations; a method of surveying such a kingdom as France, that would demand several lives instead of years. The eastern part of the kingdom remained. The great mass of country, formed by the triangle, whose three points are Paris, Strasbourg and Moulins, and the mountainous region S.E. of the last town, presented in the map an ample space, which it would be necessary to pass before I could have such an idea of the kingdom as I had planned the acquisition; I determined to make this third effort, in order to accomplish a design which appeared more and more important, the more I reflected on it; and less likely to be executed by those whose powers are better adapted to the undertaking than mine. The meeting of the States General of France also, who were now assembled, made it the more necessary to lose no time; for in all human probability, that assembly will be the epoch of a new constitution, which will have new effects, and, for what I know, attended with a new agriculture; and to have the regal sun in such a kingdom, both rise and set without the territory being known, must of necessity be regretted by every man solicitous for real political knowledge. The events of a century and half, including the brilliant reign of Louis XIV, will for ever render the sources of the French power interesting to mankind, and particularly that its state may be known previous to the establishment of an improved government, as the comparison of the effects of the old and new system will be not a little curious in future.

June 8, 1789, Paris To my friend Lazowski, to know where were the lodgings I had written him to hire me, but my good dutchess d'Estissac would not allow him to execute my commission. I found an apartment in her house prepared for me. Paris is at present in such a ferment about the States General, now holding at Versailles, that conversation is absolutely absorbed by them. Not a word of any thing else talked of. Every thing is considered, and justly so, as important in such a crisis of the fate of four-and-twenty millions of people. It is now a serious contention whether the representatives are to be called the Commoners or *Tiers Etat;* they call themselves steadily the former, while the court and the great lords reject the term with a species of apprehension, as if it involved a meaning not easily to be fathomed. But this point is of little consequence, compared with another, that has kept the states for sometime in inactivity, the verification of their power separately or in common. The nobility and the clergy demand the former, but the Commons steadily refuse it; the reason why a circumstance, apparently of no great consequence, is thus tenaciously regarded, is that it may decide their sitting for the future in separate houses or in one. Those who are warm for the interest of the people declare that it will be impossible to reform some of the grossest abuses in the state, if the nobility, by sitting in a separate chamber, shall have a negative on the wishes of the people: and that to give such a veto to the clergy would be still more preposterous; if therefore, by the verification of their powers in one chamber, they shall once come together, the popular party hope that there will remain no power afterwards to separate. The nobility and clergy foresee the same result, and will not therefore agree to it. In this dilemma it is curious to remark the feelings of the moment. It is not my business to write memoirs of what passes, but I am intent to catch, as well as I can, the opinions of the day most prevalent. While I remain at Paris, I shall see people of all descriptions, from the coffee-house politicians to the leaders in the estates; and the chief object of such rapid notes as I throw on paper, will be to catch the ideas of the moment; to compare them afterwards with the actual events that shall happen, will afford amusement at least. The most prominent feature that appears at present is, that an idea of common interest and common danger does not seem to unite those, who, if not united, may find themselves too weak to oppose the common danger that must arise from the people being sensible of a strength the result of their weakness. The king, court, nobility, clergy, army, and parliament, are nearly in the same situation. All these consider, with equal dread, the ideas of liberty, now afloat; except the first, who, for reasons obvious to those who know his character, troubles himself little, even with circumstances that concern his power the most intimately. Among the rest, the feeling of danger is common, and they would unite, were there a head to render it easy, in order to do without the states at all. That the commons themselves look for some such hostile union as more than probable, appears from an idea which gains ground, that they will find it necessary should the other two orders continue to refuse to unite with them in one chamber, to declare themselves boldly the representatives of the kingdom at large, calling on the nobility and clergy to take their places—and to enter upon deliberations of business without them, should they refuse it. All conversation at present is on this topic, but opinions are more divided than I should have expected. There seem to be many who hate the clergy so cordially, that rather than permit them to form a distinct chamber would venture on a new system, dangerous as it might prove.

June 9, 1789 The business going forward at present in the pamphlet shops of Paris is incredible. I went to the Palais Royal to see what new things were published, and to procure a catalogue of all. Every hour produces something new. Thirteen came out today, sixteen yesterday, and ninety-two last week. We think sometimes that book shops at London are crouded, but they are mere deserts, compared to Desein's, and some others here, in which one can scarcely squeeze from the door to the counter. The price of printing two years ago was from 27 liv. to 30 liv. per sheet, but now it is from 60 liv. to 80 liv. This spirit of reading political tracts, they say, spreads into the provinces, so that all the presses of France are equally employed. Nineteen-twentieths of these productions are in favour of liberty, and commonly violent against the clergy and nobility; I have to-day bespoke many of this description, that have reputation; but enquiring for such as had appeared on the other side of the question, to my astonishment I find there are but two or three that have merit enough to be known. Is it not wonderful, that while the press teems with the most levelling and even seditious principles, that if put in execution would overturn the monarchy, nothing in reply appears, and not the least step is taken by the court to restrain this extreme licentiousness of publication. It is easy to conceive the spirit that must thus be raised among the people. But the coffee-houses in the Palais Royal present yet more singular and astonishing spectacles; they are not only crouded within, but other expectant crouds are at the doors and windows, listening open-mouthed to certain orators, who from chairs or tables harangue each his little audience: the eagerness with which they are heard, and the thunder of applause they receive for every sentiment of more than common hardiness or violence against the present government, cannot easily be imagined. I am all amazement at the ministry permitting such nests and hotbeds of sedition and revolt, which disseminate amongst the people, every hour, principles that by and by must be opposed with vigour, and therefore it seems little short of madness to allow the propagation at present.

June 10, 1789 Every thing conspires to render the present period in France critical: the want of bread is terrible: accounts arrive every moment from the provinces of riots and disturbances, and calling in the military, to preserve the peace of the markets. The prices reported are the same as I found at Abbeville and Amiens: 5 francs (2½p.) a pound for white bread, and 3½ francs to 4 francs for the common sort, eaten by the poor: these rates are beyond their faculties, and occasion great misery. At Meudon, the police, that is to say the intendant, ordered that no wheat should be sold on the market without the person taking at the same time an equal quantity of barley. What a stupid and ridiculous regulation, to lay obstacles on the supply, in order to be better supplied; and to shew the people the fears and apprehensions of government, creating thereby an alarm, and raising the price at the very moment they wish to sink it. I have had some conversation on this topic with well informed persons, who have assured me that the price is, as usual, much higher than the proportion of the crop demanded, and there would have been no real scarcity if Mr. Necker would have let the corn-trade alone; but the edicts of restriction, which have been mere comments on his book on the legislation of corn, have operated more to raise the price than all other causes together. It appears plain to me, that the violent friends of the commons are not displeased at the high price of corn, which seconds their views greatly, and makes any appeal to the common feeling of the people more easy, and much more to their purpose than if the price was low. Three days past, the chamber of the clergy contrived a cunning proposition; it was to send a deputation to the commons, proposing to name a commission from the three orders to take into consideration the misery of the people, and to deliberate on the means of lowering the price of bread. This would have led to the deliberation by order, and not by heads, consequently must be rejected, but unpopularly so from the situation of the people: the commons were equally dextrous; in their reply, they prayed and conjured the clergy to join them in the common hall of the states to deliberate, which was no sooner reported at Paris than the clergy became doubly an object of hatred; and it became a question with the politicians of the Caffé de Foy, whether it was not lawful for the commons to decree the application of their estates towards easing the distress of the people.

June 11, 1789 I have been in much company all day, and cannot but remark, that there seem to be no settled ideas of the best means of forming a new constitution. Yesterday the Abbé Sieyès made a motion in the house of commons, to declare boldly to the privileged orders, that if they will not join the commons, the latter will proceed in the national business without them; and the house decreed it, with a small amendment. This causes much conversation on what will be the consequence of such a proceeding; and on the contrary, on what may flow from the nobility and clergy continuing steadily to refuse to join the commons, and should they so proceed, to protest against all they decree, and appeal to the King to dissolve the states, and recall them in such a form as may be practicable for business. In these most interesting discussions, I find a general ignorance of the principles of government; a strange and unaccountable appeal, on one side, to ideal and visionary rights of nature; and, on the other, no settled plan that shall give security to the people for being in future in a much better situation than hitherto; a security absolutely necessary. But the nobility, with the principles of great lords that I converse with, are most disgustingly tenacious of all old rights, however hard they may bear on the people; they will not hear of giving way in the least to the spirit of liberty, beyond the point of paying equal land-taxes, which they hold to be all that can with reason be demanded. The popular party, on the other hand, seem to consider all liberty as depending on the privileged classes being lost, and outvoted in the order of the commons, at least for making the new constitution; and when I urge the great probability, that should they once unite, there will remain no power of ever separating them; and that in such a case, they will have a very questionable constitution, perhaps a very bad one; I am always told, that the first object must be for the people to get the power of doing good; and that it is no argument against such a conduct to urge that an ill use may be made of it. But among such men, the common idea is, that anything tending towards a separate order, like our house of lords, is absolutely inconsistent with liberty; all which seems perfectly wild and unfounded.

June 15, 1789 This has been a rich day, and such an one as ten years ago none could believe would ever arrive in France; a very important debate being expected on what, in our house of commons, would be termed the state of the nation. My friend Mons. Lazowski and myself were at Versailles by eight in the morning. We went immediately to the hall of the states to secure good seats in the gallery; we found some deputies already there, and a pretty numerous audience collected. The room is too large; none but stentorian lungs, or the finest clearest voices can be heard; however, the very size of the apartment, which admits 2000 people, gave a dignity to the scene. It was indeed an interesting one. The spectacle of the representatives of twenty-five millions of people, just emerging from the evils of 200 years of arbitrary power, and rising to the blessings of a freer constitution, assembled with open doors under the eye of the public, was framed to call into animated feelings every latent spark, every emotion of a liberal bosom. To banish whatever ideas might intrude of their being a people too often hostile to my own country,—and to dwell with pleasure on the glorious idea of happiness to a great nation—of felicity to millions yet unborn.

In regard to their general method of proceeding, there are two circumstances in which they are very deficient: the spectators in the galleries are allowed to interfere in the debates by clapping their hands, and other noisy expressions of approbation: this is grossly indecent; it is also dangerous; for, if they are permitted to express approbation, they are, by parity of reason, allowed expressions of dissent; and they may hiss as well as clap; which it is said, they have sometimes done:—this would be, to overrule the debate and influence the deliberations. Another circumstance, is the want of order among themselves; more than once today there were a hundred members on their legs at a time, and the President, Monsieur Bailly absolutely without power to keep order.

July 9, 1789 To Châlons, through a poor country and poor crops. M. de Broussonet had given me a letter to Mons. Sabbatier, secretary to the academy of sciences, but he was absent. A regiment passing to Paris, an officer at the inn addressed me in English:—He had learned, he said, in America, damme!—He had taken lord Cornwallis, damme!—Maréchal Broglie was appointed to command an army of 50,000 men near Paris—it was necessary—the third estate were running mad—and wanted some wholesome correction;—they want to establish a republic—absurd! Pray, Sir, what did you fight for in America? To establish a republic. What was so good for the Americans, is it so bad for the French? Aye, damme! that is the way the English want to be revenged. It is, to be sure, no bad opportunity. Can the English follow a better example? He then made many inquiries about what we thought and said upon it in England: and I may remark, that almost every person I meet has the same idea.—The English must be very well contented at our confusion. They feel pretty pointedly what they deserve.—12½ miles.

July 14, 1789 They have a reading room at Metz, and they admit any person to read or go in and out for a day, on paying 4 francs. To this I eagerly resorted, and the news from Paris, both in the public prints, and by the information of a gentleman, I found to be interesting. Versailles and Paris are surrounded by troops: 35,000 men are assembled, and 20,000 more on the road, large trains of artillery collected, and all the preparations of war. The assembling of such a number of troops has added to the scarcity of bread; and the magazines that have been made for their support, are not easily by the people distinguished from those they suspect of being collected by monopolists. This has aggravated their evils almost to madness; so that the confusion and tumult of the capital are extreme. A gentleman of an excellent understanding, and apparently of consideration, from the attention paid him, with whom I had some conversation on the subject, lamented in the most pathetic terms, the situation of his country; he considers a civil war as impossible to be avoided. There is not, he added, a doubt but the court, finding it impossible to bring the National Assembly to terms, will get rid of them; a bankruptcy at the same moment is inevitable; the union of such confusion must be a civil war; and it is now only by torrents of blood that we have any hope of establishing a freer constitution: yet it must be established; for the old government is rivetted to abuses that are insupportable. He agreed with me entirely, that the propositions of the royal sitting, though certainly not sufficiently satisfactory, yet, were the ground for a negotiation, that would have secured by degrees all even that the sword can give us, let it be as successful as it will. The purse—the power of the purse is everything; skilfully managed, with so necessitous a government as ours, it would, one after another, have gained all we wished. As to a war, Heaven knows the event; and if we have success, success itself may ruin us; France may have a Cromwell in its bosom, as well as England.

July 20, 1789 To Strasbourg, through one of the richest scenes of soil and cultivation to be met with in France, and rivalled only by Flanders, which however, exceeds it. I arrived there at a critical moment, which I thought would have broken my neck; a detachment of horse, with their trumpets on one side, a party of infantry, with their drums beating on the other, and a great mob hallooing, frightened my French mare; and I could scarcely keep her from trampling on Messrs. the *tiers état*. On arriving at the inn, hear the interesting news of the revolt of Paris.—The French Guards joining the people; the little dependence on the rest of the troops; the taking the Bastile; and the institution of the bourgeois militia: in a word, of the absolute overthrow of the old government. Everything being now decided, and the kingdom absolutely in the hands of the assembly, they have the power to make a new constitution, such as they think proper; and it will be a great spectacle for the world to view, in this enlightened age, the representatives of twenty-five millions of people sitting on the construction of a new and better order and fabric of liberty, than Europe has yet offered. It will now be seen, whether they will copy the constitution of England, freed from its faults, or attempt, from theory, to frame something absolutely speculative: in the former case, they will prove a blessing to their country; in the latter they will probably involve it in inextricable confusions and civil wars, perhaps not in the present period, but certainly at some future one. I hear nothing of their removing from Versailles; if they stay there under the control of an armed mob, they must make a government that will please the mob; but they will, I suppose, be wise enough to move to some central town Tours, Blois, or Orléans, where their deliberations may be free. But the Parisian spirit of commotion spreads quickly; it is here; the troops that were near breaking my neck, are employed, to keep an eye on the people who show signs of an intended revolt. They have broken the windows of some magistrates that are no favourites; and a great mob of them is at this moment assembled demanding clamourously to have meat at 5 franc a pound. They have a cry among them that will conduct them to good lengths,—No taxes and long live the estates!

July 21, 1789 I have spent some time this morning at the reading room, reading the gazettes and journals that give an account of the transactions at Paris: and I have had some conversation with several sensible and intelligent men on the present revolution. The spirit of revolt is gone forth into various parts of the kingdom; the price of bread has prepared the populace every where for all sorts of violence; at Lyons there have been commotions as furious as at Paris, and the same at a great many other places: Dauphiné is in arms: and Bretagne in absolute rebellion. The idea is, that the people will, from hunger, be driven to revolt; and when once they find any other means of subsistence than that of honest labour, every thing will be to be feared. Of such consequence it is to a country, and indeed to every country, to have a good police of corn; a police that shall by securing a high price to the farmer, encourage his culture enough to secure the people at the same time from famine. . . . Night . . . I have been witness to a scene curious to a foreigner; but dreadful to Frenchmen that are considerate. Passing through the square of the city hall, the mob were breaking the windows with stones, notwithstanding an officer and a detachment of horse was in the square. Perceiving that their numbers not only increased, but that they grew bolder and bolder every moment, I thought it worth staying to see what it would end in, and clambered on to the roof of a row of low stalls opposite the building, against which their malice was directed. Here I beheld the whole commodiously. Perceiving that the troops would not attack them, except in words and menaces, they grew more violent, and furiously attempted to beat the door in pieces with iron crows; placing ladders to the windows. In about a quarter of an hour, which gave time for the assembled magistrates to escape by a back door, they burst all open, and entered like a torrent with a universal shout of the spectators. From that minute a shower of casements, sashes, shutters, chairs, tables, sophas, books, papers, pictures, etc., rained incessantly from all the windows of the house, which is seventy or eighty feet long, and which was then succeeded by tiles, skirting boards, bannisters, framework, and every part of the building that force could detach. The troops, both horse and foot, were quiet spectators. They were at first too few to interpose, and, when they became more numerous, the mischief was too far advanced to admit of any other conduct than guarding every avenue around, permitting none to go to the scene of action, but letting every one that pleased retire with his plunder; guards being at the same time placed at the doors of the churches, and all public buildings. I was for two hours a spectator at different places of the scene, secure myself from the falling furniture, but near enough to see a fine lad of about 14 crushed to death by something as he was handing plunder to a woman, I suppose his mother, from the horror pictured in her countenance. I remarked several common soldiers, with their white cockades, among the plunderers, and instigating the mob even in sight of the officers of the detachment. There were amongst them, people so decently dressed, that I regarded them with no small surprise:—they destroyed all the public archives; the streets for some way around strewed with papers; this has been a wanton mischief; for it will be the ruin of many families unconnected with the magistrates.

July 26, 1789 For twenty miles to Lisle sur Daube, the country nearly as before; but after that, to Baume les Dames. It is all mountainous and rock, much wood, and many pleasing scenes of the river flowing beneath. The whole country is in the greatest agitation; at one of the little towns I passed, I was questioned for not having a cockade of the Third Estate. They said it was ordained by the Third, and, if I was not a Seigneur, I ought to obey. But suppose I am a Seigneur, what then, my friends?—What then? they replied sternly, why, be hanged; for that most likely is what you deserve. It was plain this was no moment for joking, the boys and girls began to gather, whose assembling has every where been the preliminaries of mischief; and if I had not declared myself an Englishman, and ignorant of the ordinance, I had not escaped very well. I immediately bought a cockade, but the hussey pinned it into my hat so loosely, that before I got to Lisle it blew into the river, and I was again in the same danger. My assertion of being English would not do. I was a Seigneur, perhaps in disguise, and without a doubt a great rogue. At this moment a priest came into the street with a letter in his hand: the people immediately collected around him, and he then read aloud a detail from Belfort giving an account of M. Necker's passing, with some general features of news from Paris, and assurances that the condition of the people would be improved. When he had finished, he exhorted them to abstain from all violence; and assured them, they must not indulge themselves with any ideas of impositions being abolished; which he touched on as if he knew that they had got such notions. When he retired, they again surrounded me, who had attended to the letter like others; were very menacing in their manner; and expressed many suspicions: I did not like my situation at all, especially on hearing one of them say that I ought to be secured till somebody would give an account of me. I was on the steps of the inn, and begged they would permit me a few words; I assured them, that I was an English traveller, and to prove it, I desired to explain to them a circumstance in English taxation, which would be a satisfactory comment on what the priest had told them, to the purport of which I could not agree. He had asserted, that the impositions must be paid was certain, but not as heretofore, as they might be paid as they were in England. Gentlemen, we have a great number of taxes in England, which you know nothing of in France; but the Third Estate, the poor do not pay them; they are laid on the rich; every window in a man's house pays; but if he has no more than six windows, he pays nothing; the rich for their horses, their carriages, and their servants, and even for liberty to kill their own partridges, but the poor farmer nothing of all this: and what is more, we have in England a tax paid by the rich for the relief of the poor; hence the assertion of the priest, that because taxes existed before they must exist again, did not at all prove that they must be levied in the same manner; our English method seemed much better. There was not a word of this discourse, they did not approve of; they seemed to think that I might be an honest fellow, which I confirmed, by crying: "Long live the Third Estate and down with taxes," when they gave me a bit of a huzza, and I had no more interruption from them. My miserable French was pretty much on a par with their own patois. I got, however, another cockade, which I took care to have so fastened as to lose it no more. I do not half like travelling in such an unquiet and fermenting moment; one is not secure for a hour beforehand.—35 miles.

July 27, 1789 To Besançon; the country mountain, rock, and wood, above the river; some scenes are fine. I had not arrived an hour before I saw a peasant pass the inn on horseback, followed by an officer of the bourgeois militia, of which there are 1200 here, and 200 under arms, and his party-coloured detachment, and those by some infantry and cavalry. I asked, why the militia took the place of the King's troops. For a very good reason, they replied, the troops would be attacked and knocked on the head, but the populace will not resist the milice. This peasant, who is a rich proprietor, applied for a guard to protect his house, in a village where there is much plundering and burning. The mischiefs which have been perpetrated in the country, towards the mountains and Vesoul, are numerous and shocking. Many chateaus have been burnt, others plundered, the seigneurs hunted down like wild beasts, their wives and daughters ravished, their papers and titles burnt, and all their property destroyed: and these abominations not inflicted on marked persons, who were odious for their former conduct or principles, but an indiscriminating blind rage for the love of plunder. Robbers, galley-slaves, and villains of all denominations, have collected and instigated the peasants to commit all sorts of outrages. Some gentlemen at the table informed me, that letters were received from the Mâconois, the Lyonois, Auvergne, Dauphiné, etc. and that similar commotions and mischiefs were perpetrating every where; and that it was expected they would pervade the whole kingdom. The backwardness of France is beyond credibility in every thing that pertains to information. From Strasbourg hither, I have not been able to see a newspaper. Here I asked for the Reading Room. None. The gazettes? At the coffeehouse. Very easily replied; but not so easily found. Nothing but the *Gazette de France;* for which at this period, a man of common sense would not give one cent. To four other coffee-houses; at some no paper at all, not even the *Mercure;* at the *Caffé Militaire,* the *Courier de l'Europe* a fortnight old; and well dressed people are now talking of the news of two or three weeks past, and plainly by their discourse know nothing of what is passing. The whole town of Besançon has not been able to afford me a sight of the *Journal de Paris,* nor of any paper that gives a detail of the transactions of the states; yet it is the capital of a province, large as half a dozen English counties, and containing 25,000 souls,—with strange to say! the post coming in but three times a week. At this eventful moment, with no license, nor even the least restraint on the press, not one paper established at Paris for circulation in the provinces, with the necessary steps taken by poster, or placard, to inform the people in all the towns of its establishment. For what the country knows to the contrary, their deputies are in the Bastile, instead of the Bastile being razed: so the mob plunder, burn, and destroy, in complete ignorance: and yet, with all these shades of darkness, these clouds of tenebrity, this universal mass of ignorance, there are men every day in the states,

who are puffing themselves off for the FIRST NATION IN EUROPE! the GREATEST
PEOPLE IN THE UNIVERSE! as if the political juntos, or literary circles of a capital
constituted a people; instead of the universal illumination of knowledge, acting by
rapid intelligence on minds prepared by habitual energy of reasoning to receive, combine, and comprehend it. That this dreadful ignorance of the mass of the people, of
the events that most intimately concern them, is owing to the old government, no one
can doubt; it is however curious to remark, that if the nobility of other provinces are
hunted like those of Franche Comté, of which there is little reason to doubt, that whole
order of men undergo a proscription, suffer like sheep, without making the least effort
to resist the attack. This appears marvellous, with a body that have an army of 150,000
men in their hands; for though a part of those troops would certainly disobey their
leaders, yet let it be remembered, that out of the 40,000 or possibly 100,000 noblesse
of France, they might, if they had intelligence and union amongst themselves, fill half
the ranks of more than half the regiments of the kingdom, with men who have fellow-
feelings and fellow-sufferings with themselves; but no meetings, no associations among
them; no union with military men; no taking refuge in the ranks of regiments to defend
or avenge their cause; fortunately for France they fall without a struggle and die without
a blow. That universal circulation of information, which in England transmits the least
vibration of feeling or alarm, with electric sensibility, from one end of the kingdom
to another, and which unites in bands of connection men of similar interests and
situations, has no existence in France. Thus it may be said, perhaps with truth, that
the fall of the king, courts, lords, nobles, army, church, and parliaments is owing to
a want of information being quickly circulated, consequently is owing to the very effects
of that thraldom in which they held the people: it is therefore a retribution rather than
a punishment.—18 miles.

Emmanuel Joseph Sieyès: from What Is the Third Estate?

*Emmanuel Joseph Sieyès was born in Fréjus, France, on May 3, 1748. He was educated
at a Jesuit school, became a licentiate of canon law, and was appointed vicar-general by
the bishop of Chartres. He first came into prominence with the publication of his pamphlet,
"Qu'est-ce que le tiers état?" In 1789 he was elected delegate to the States-General from
Paris, and in the preliminary struggle for organization was made spokesman of the Third
Estate. The policy outlined in his pamphlet was that which was carried out in the conservative period of the revolution. As the revolution progressed, Sieyès dropped out of sight and
had the good fortune to escape destruction. When asked at a later period what he had
done during the Terror, he summed up his whole experience in the words "I survived."
In 1795 he again came forward and was appointed member of a commission to draft a*

From *Translations and Reprints*, VI, No. 1, M. Whitcomb, Ed.

new constitution. His views did not obtain prominence in the constitution of 1795, and he refused to accept a position in the Directoire.[1]

Sieyès took part with Napoleon in the coup d'état of 18th Brumaire and was made one of the provisional consulate with Napoleon and Ducos. Later on he was made a count of the empire and given extensive estates as a reward for his services to France; this marked Sieyès's final retirement from public life. He fled to Brussels on the second return of the Bourbons, returned after the revolution of 1830, and died in Paris on June 20, 1836.

What is necessary that a nation should subsist and prosper? Individual effort and public functions.

All individual efforts may be included in four classes: 1. Since the earth and the waters furnish crude products for the needs of man, the first class, in logical sequence, will be that of all families which devote themselves to agricultural labor. 2. Between the first sale of products and their consumption or use, a new manipulation, more or less repeated, adds to these products a second value more or less composite. In this manner human industry succeeds in perfecting the gifts of nature, and the crude product increases two-fold, ten-fold, one hundred-fold in value. Such are the efforts of the second class. 3. Between production and consumption, as well as between the various stages of production, a group of intermediary agents establish themselves, useful both to producers and consumers; these are the merchants and brokers: the brokers who, comparing incessantly the demands of time and place, speculate upon the profit of retention and transportation; merchants who are charged with distribution, in the last analysis, either at wholesale or at retail. This species of utility characterizes the third class. 4. Outside of these three classes of productive and useful citizens, who are occupied with real objects of consumption and use, there is also need in a society of a series of efforts and pains, whose objects are directly useful or agreeable to the individual. This fourth class embraces all those who stand between the most distinguished and liberal professions and the less esteemed services of domestics.

Such are the efforts which sustain society. Who puts them forth? The Third Estate.

Public functions may be classified equally well, in the present state of affairs, under four recognized heads; the sword, the robe, the church and the administration. It would be superfluous to take them up one by one, for the purpose of showing that everywhere the Third Estate attends to nineteen-twentieths of them, with this distinction; that it is laden with all that which is really painful, with all the burdens which the privileged classes refuse to carry. Do we give the Third Estate credit for this? That this might come about, it would be necessary that the Third Estate should refuse to fill these places, or that it should be less ready to exercise their functions. The facts are well known. Meanwhile they have dared to impose a prohibition upon the order of the

---

[1] The regime that governed France for several years following the Terror, from 1795 to the coup of 18th Brumaire (November 9, 1799), by which General Napoleon Bonaparte replaced the *Directoire* with a *Consulate*, with himself as first consul. In 1804 Napoleon proclaimed himself emperor.

Third Estate. They have said to it: "Whatever may be your services, whatever may be your abilities, you shall go thus far; you may not pass beyond!" Certain rare exceptions, properly regarded, are but a mockery, and the terms which are indulged in on such occasions, one insult the more.

If this exclusion is a social crime against the Third Estate; if it is a veritable act of hostility, could it perhaps be said that it is useful to the public weal? Alas! who is ignorant of the effects of monopoly? If it discourages those whom it rejects, is it not well known that it tends to render less able those whom it favors? Is it not understood that every employment from which free competition is removed, becomes dearer and less effective?

In setting aside any function whatsoever to serve as an appanage for a distinct class among citizens, is it not to be observed that it is no longer the man alone who does the work that it is necessary to reward, but all the unemployed members of that same caste, and also the entire families of those who are employed as well as those who are not? Is it not to be remarked that since the government has become the patrimony of a particular class, it has been distended beyond all measure; places have been created, not on account of the necessities of the governed, but in the interests of the governing, etc., etc.? Has not attention been called to the fact that this order of things, which is basely and—I even presume to say—beastly respectable with us, when we find it in reading the History of Ancient Egypt or the accounts of Voyages to the Indies, is despicable, monstrous, destructive of all industry, the enemy of social progress; above all degrading to the human race in general, and particularly intolerable to Europeans, etc., etc.? But I must leave these considerations, which, if they increase the importance of the subject and throw light upon it, perhaps, along with the new light, slacken our progress.

It suffices here to have made it clear that the pretended utility of a privileged order for the public service is nothing more than a chimera; that with it all that which is burdensome in this service is performed by the Third Estate; that without it the superior places would be infinitely better filled; that they naturally ought to be the lot and the recompense of ability and recognized services, and that if privileged persons have come to usurp all the lucrative and honorable posts, it is a hateful injustice to the rank and file of citizens and at the same time a treason to the public weal.

Who then shall dare to say that the Third Estate has not within itself all that is necessary for the formation of a complete nation? It is the strong and robust man who has one arm still shackled. If the privileged order should be abolished, the nation would be nothing less, but something more. Therefore, what is the Third Estate? Everything; but an everything shackled and oppressed. What would it be without the privileged order? Everything, but an everything free and flourishing. Nothing can succeed without it, everything would be infinitely better without the others.

It is not sufficient to show that privileged persons, far from being useful to the nation, cannot but enfeeble and injure it; it is necessary to prove further that the noble order does not enter at all into the social organization; that it may indeed be a burden upon the nation, but that it cannot of itself constitute a nation.

In the first place, it is not possible in the number of all the elementary parts of a nation to find a place for the caste of nobles. I know that there are individuals in great number whom infirmities, incapacity, incurable laziness, or the weight of bad habits render strangers to the labors of society. The exception and the abuse are everywhere found beside the rule. But it will be admitted that the less there are of these abuses, the better it will be for the State. The worst possible arrangement of all would be where not alone isolated individuals, but a whole class of citizens should take pride in remaining motionless in the midst of the general movement, and should consume the best part of the product without bearing any part in its production. Such a class is surely estranged to the nation by its indolence.

The noble order is not less estranged from the generality of us by its civil and political prerogatives.

What is a nation? A body of associates, living under a common law, and represented by the same legislature, etc.

Is it not evident that the noble order has privileges and expenditures which it dares to call its rights, but which are apart from the rights of the great body of citizens? It departs there from the common order, from the common law. So its civil rights make of it an isolated people in the midst of the great nation. This is truly *imperium in imperio.*

In regard to its political rights, these also it exercises apart. It has its special representatives, which are not charged with securing the interests of the people. The body of its deputies sit apart; and when it is assembled in the same hall with the deputies of simple citizens, it is none the less true that its representation is essentially distinct and separate: it is a stranger to the nation, in the first place, by its origin, since its commission is not derived from the people; then by its object, which consists of defending not the general, but the particular interest.

The Third Estate embraces then all that which belongs to the nation; and all that which is not the Third Estate, cannot be regarded as being of the nation. What is the Third Estate? It is the whole.

Decree of the French National Assembly Abolishing the Feudal System (1789)

The abolition of the feudal system, which took place during the famous night session of August 4 and 5, 1789, was caused by the reading of a report on the misery and disturbances in the provinces, and was carried out in a fervor of enthusiasm and excitement. The decree here given was drawn up during the following days.

I. The National Assembly hereby completely abolishes the feudal system. It decrees that, among the existing rights and dues, both feudal and censual (perpetual), all those originating in or representing real or personal serfdom

---

From *Translations and Reprints,* I, No. 5, J. H. Robinson, Ed.

(mainmorte) or personal servitude, shall be abolished without indemnification. All other dues are declared redeemable, the terms and mode of redemption to be fixed by the National Assembly. Those of the said dues which are not extinguished by this decree shall continue to be collected until indemnification shall take place.

II. The exclusive right to maintain pigeon-houses and dovecotes is abolished. The pigeons shall be confined during the seasons fixed by the community. During such periods they shall be looked upon as game, and every one shall have the right to kill them upon his own land.

III. The exclusive right to hunt and to maintain unenclosed warrens is likewise abolished, and every land owner shall have the right to kill or to have destroyed on his own land all kinds of game, observing, however, such police regulations as may be established with a view to the safety of the public.

All hunting captainries, including the royal forests, and all hunting rights under whatever denomination, are likewise abolished. Provision shall be made, however, in a manner compatible with the regard due to property and liberty, for maintaining the personal pleasures of the king.

The president of the assembly shall be commissioned to ask of the King the recall of those sent to the galleys or exiled, simply for violations of the hunting regulations, as well as for the release of those at present imprisoned for offences of this kind, and the dismissal of such cases as are now pending.

IV. All manorial courts are hereby suppressed without indemnification. But the magistrates of these courts shall continue to perform their functions until such time as the National Assembly shall provide for the establishment of a new judicial system.

V. Tithes of every description, as well as the dues which have been substituted for them, under whatever denomination they are known or collected (even when compounded for), possessed by secular or regular congregations, by holders of benefices, members of corporations (including the Order of Malta and other religious and military orders), as well as those devoted to the maintenance of churches, those impropriated to lay persons and those substituted for the portion congrue, are abolished, on condition, however, that some other method be devised to provide for the expenses of divine worship, the support of the officiating clergy, for the assistance of the poor, for repairs and rebuilding of churches and parsonages, and for the maintenance of all institutions, seminaries, schools, academies, asylums, and organizations to which the present funds are devoted. Until such provision shall be made and the former possessors shall enter upon the enjoyment of an income on the new system, the National Assembly decrees that the said tithes shall continue to be collected according to law and in the customary manner.

Other tithes, of whatever nature they may be, shall be redeemable in such manner as the Assembly shall determine. Until such regulation shall be issued, the National Assembly decrees that these, too, shall continue to be collected.

VI. All perpetual ground rents, payable either in money or in kind, of whatever nature they may be, whatever their origin and to whomsoever they may be due, as to members of corporations, holders of the domain or appanages or to the Order of Malta, shall be redeemable. No due shall in the future be created which is not redeemable.

VII. The sale of judicial and municipal offices shall be suppressed forthwith. Justice shall be dispensed gratis. Nevertheless, the magistrates at present holding such offices shall continue to exercise their functions and to receive their emoluments until the Assembly shall have made provision for indemnifying them.

VIII. The fees of the country priests are abolished, and shall be discontinued so soon as provision shall be made for increasing the minimum salary of the parish priests and the payment to the curates. A regulation shall be drawn up to determine the status of the priests in the towns.

IX. Pecuniary privileges, personal or real, in the payment of taxes are abolished forever. Taxes shall be collected from all the citizens, and from all property, in the same manner and in the same form. Plans shall be considered by which the taxes shall be paid proportionally by all, even for the last six months of the current year.

X. Inasmuch as a national constitution and public liberty are of more advantage to the provinces than the privileges which some of these enjoy, and inasmuch as the surrender of such privileges is essential to the intimate union of all parts of the realm, it is decreed that all the peculiar privileges, pecuniary or otherwise, of the provinces, principalities, districts, cantons, cities and communes, are once for all abolished and are absorbed into the law common to all Frenchmen.

XI. All citizens, without distinction of birth, are eligible to any office or dignity, whether ecclesiastical, civil or military; and no profession shall imply any derogation.

XII. Hereafter no remittances shall be made for annates or for any other purpose to the court of Rome, the vice-legation at Avignon, or to the nunciature at Lucerne. The clergy of the diocese shall apply to their bishops in regard to the filling of benefices and dispensations, the which shall be granted gratis without regard to reservations, expectancies and papal months, all the churches of France enjoying the same freedom.

XIII. The rights of Peter's pence, and other dues of the same kind, under whatever denomination, established in favor of bishops, archdeacons, archpresbyters, chapters, and regular congregations which formerly exercised priestly functions, are abolished, but appropriate provision shall be made for those benefices of archdeacons and archpresbyters which are not sufficiently endowed.

XIV. Pluralities shall not be permitted hereafter in cases where revenue from the benefice or benefices held shall exceed the sum of three thousand livres. Nor shall any individual be allowed to enjoy several pensions from benefices, or a pension and a benefice, if the revenue which he already enjoys from such sources exceeds the same sum of three thousand livres.

XV. The National Assembly shall consider, in conjunction with the King, the report which is to be submitted to it relating to pensions, favors and salaries, with a view to suppressing all such as are not deserved and reducing those which shall prove excessive; and the amount shall be fixed which the King may in the future disburse for this purpose.

XVI. The National Assembly decrees that a medal shall be struck in memory of the recent grave and important deliberations for the welfare of France, and that a Te Deum shall be chanted in gratitude in all the parishes and the churches of France.

XVII. The National Assembly solemnly proclaims the King, Louis XVI, the Restorer of French Liberty.

XVIII. The National Assembly shall present itself in a body before the King, in order to submit to him the decrees which have just been passed, to tender to him the tokens of its most respectful gratitude and to pray him to permit the Te Deum to be chanted in his chapel, and to be present himself at this service.

XIX. The National Assembly shall consider, immediately after the constitution, the drawing up of the laws necessary for the development of the principles which it has laid down in the present decree. The latter shall be transmitted without delay by the deputies to all the provinces, together with the decree of the tenth of this month, in order that it may be printed, published, announced from the parish pulpits, and posted up wherever it shall be deemed necessary.

The Declaration of the Rights of Man and Citizen (1789)

The resolutions passed on the night of August 4 had, in the words of the decree that made them final, "entirely destroyed the feudal regime." With the ground thus prepared, the National Assembly proceeded to lay down what it considered the fundamental rights of men and citizens. The final text, voted on August 26, 1789, proclaimed its belief in liberty, equality, and national sovereignty. It was appended to the Constitution of 1791. Though several times revised, the statement contains the basic principles of the revolution, inspired by English and American experience, and might well be considered the death certificate of the old regime, signed by the popular revolution.

From F. M. Anderson, *Constitutions and Other Select Documents Illustrative of the History of France* (Minneapolis, 1908).

The representatives of the French people, organized in National Assembly, considering that ignorance, forgetfulness, or contempt of the rights of man, are the sole causes of the public miseries and of the corruption of governments, have resolved to set forth in a solemn declaration the natural, inalienable and sacred rights of man, in order that this declaration, being ever present to all the members of the social body, may unceasingly remind them of their rights and duties; in order that the acts of the legislative power and those of the executive power may be each moment compared with the aim of every political institution and thereby may be more respected: and in order that the demands of the citizens, grounded henceforth upon simple and incontestable principles, may always take the direction of maintaining the constitution and the welfare of all.

In consequence, the National Assembly recognizes and declares, in the presence and under the auspices of the Supreme Being, the following rights of man and citizen.

1. Men are born and remain free and equal in rights. Social distinctions can be based only upon public utility.

2. The aim of every political association is the preservation of the natural and imprescriptible rights of man. These rights are liberty, property, security and resistance to oppression.

3. The source of all sovereignty is essentially in the nation; no body, no individual can exercise authority that does not proceed from it in plain terms.

4. Liberty consists in the power to do anything that does not injure others; accordingly, the exercise of the natural rights of each man has no limits except those that secure to the other members of society the enjoyment of these same rights. These limits can be determined only by law.

5. The law has the right to forbid only such actions as are injurious to society. Nothing can be forbidden that is not interdicted by the law, and no one can be constrained to do that which it does not order.

6. Law is the expression of the general will. All citizens have the right to take part personally, or by their representatives, in its formation. It must be the same for all whether it protects or punishes. All citizens, being equal in its eyes, are equally eligible to all public dignities, places, and employments, according to their capacities, and without other distinction than that of their virtues and their talents.

7. No man can be accused, arrested, or detained, except in the cases determined by the law and according to the forms that it has prescribed. Those who procure, expedite, execute, or cause to be executed arbitrary orders ought to be punished; but every citizen summoned or seized in virtue of the law ought to render instant obedience; he makes himself guilty by resistance.

8. The law ought to establish only penalties that are strictly and obviously necessary, and no one can be punished except in virtue of a law established and promulgated prior to the offence and legally applied.

9. Every man being presumed innocent until he has been pronounced guilty; if it is thought indispensable to arrest him, all severity that may not be necessary to secure his person ought to be strictly suppressed by law.

10. No one should be disturbed on account of his opinions, even religious, provided their manifestation does not derange the public order established by law.

11. The free communication of ideas and opinions is one of the most precious of the rights of man; every citizen then can freely speak, write and print, subject to responsibility for the abuse of this freedom in the cases determined by law.

12. The guarantee of the rights of man and citizen requires a public force; this force then is instituted for the advantage of all and not for the personal benefit of those to whom it is entrusted.

13. For the maintenance of the public force and for the expenses of administration a general tax is indispensable; it ought to be equally apportioned among all the citizens according to their means.

14. All the citizens have the right to ascertain by themselves or by their representatives, the necessity of the public tax, to consent to it freely, to follow the employment of it, and to determine the quota, the assessment, the collection, and the duration of it.

15. Society has the right to call for an account of his administration from every public agent.

16. Any society in which the guarantee of rights is not secured, or the separation of powers not determined, has no constitution at all.

17. Property being a sacred and inviolable right, no one can be deprived of it, unless a legally established public necessity evidently demands it, under the condition of a just and prior indemnity.

Olympe de Gouges: Declaration of the Rights of Woman and the Female Citizen (1791)

Women were active in the revolution—on all sides—but most revolutionaries saw the place of women as they had learnt it in the Latin classics: as housewives and mothers who spent their time nurturing heroes (all male) and inspiring civic virtue (a largely masculine trait). Women were not to be treated as full citizens, and they would not be given the right to vote. The rights of man had been affirmed in 1789. In 1791, a feminist, Olympe de Gouges (1755–1793), wrote a declaration of the rights of women. It came to nothing, and its author died under the guillotine two years later, not for her feminism but for her defense of King Louis XVI.

Man, are you capable of being just? It is a woman who poses the question; you will not deprive her of that right at least. Tell me, what gives you sovereign empire to oppress my sex? Your strength? Your talents? Observe the Creator in his wisdom; survey in all her grandeur that nature with whom you seem to want to be in harmony, and give me, if you dare, an example of this tyrannical empire. Go back to animals, consult the elements, study plants, finally glance at all the modifications of organic matter, and surrender to the evidence when I offer you the means; search, probe, and distinguish, if you can, the sexes in the administration of nature. Everywhere you will find them mingled; everywhere they cooperate in harmonious togetherness in this immortal masterpiece.

Man alone has raised his exceptional circumstances to a principle. Bizarre, blind, bloated with science and degenerated—in a century of enlightenment and wisdom— into the crassest ignorance, he wants to command as a despot a sex which is in full possession of its intellectual faculties; he pretends to enjoy the Revolution and to claim his rights to equality in order to say nothing more about it.

For the National Assembly to decree in its last sessions, or in those of the next legislature:

PREAMBLE

Mothers, daughters, sisters [and] representatives of the nation demand to be constituted into a national assembly. Believing that ignorance, omission, or scorn for the rights of woman are the only causes of public misfortunes and of the corruption of governments, [the women] have resolved to set forth in a solemn declaration the natural, inalienable, and sacred rights of woman in order that this declaration, constantly exposed before all the members of the society, will ceaselessly remind them of their rights and duties; in order that the authoritative acts of women and the authoritative acts of men may be at any moment compared with and respectful of the purpose of all political institutions; and in order that citizens' demands, henceforth based on simple and incontestable principles, will always support the constitution, good morals, and the happiness of all.

Consequently, the sex that is as superior in beauty as it is in courage during the sufferings of maternity recognizes and declares in the presence and under the auspices of the Supreme Being, the following Rights of Woman and of Female Citizens.

Article I Woman is born free and lives equal to man in her rights. Social distinctions can be based only on the common utility.

Article II The purpose of any political association is the conservation of the natural and imprescriptible rights of woman and man; these rights are liberty, property, security, and especially resistance to oppression.

Article III The principle of all sovereignty rests essentially with the nation, which is nothing but the union of woman and man; no body and no individual can exercise any authority which does not come expressly from it [the nation].

Article IV Liberty and justice consist of restoring all that belongs to others; thus, the only limits on the exercise of the natural rights of woman are perpetual male tyranny; these limits are to be reformed by the laws of nature and reason.

Article V Laws of nature and reason proscribe all acts harmful to society; everything which is not prohibited by these wise and divine laws cannot be prevented, and no one can be constrained to do what they do not command.

Article VI The law must be the expression of the general will; all female and male citizens must contribute either personally or through their representatives to its formation; it must be the same for all: male and female citizens, being equal in the eyes of the law, must be equally admitted to all honors, positions, and public employment according to their capacity and without other distinctions besides those of their virtues and talents.

Article VII No woman is an exception; she is accused, arrested, and detained in cases determined by law. Women, like men, obey this rigorous law.

Article VIII The law must establish only those penalties that are strictly and obviously necessary, and no one can be punished except by virtue of a law established and promulgated prior to the crime and legally applicable to women.

Article IX Once any woman is declared guilty, complete rigor is [to be] exercised by the law.

Article X No one is to be disquieted for his very basic opinions; woman has the right to mount the scaffold; she must equally have the right to mount the rostrum, provided that her demonstrations do not disturb the legally established public order.

Article XI The free communication of thoughts and opinions is one of the most precious rights of woman, since that liberty assures the recognition of children by their fathers. Any female citizen thus may say freely, I am the mother of a child which belongs to you, without being forced by a barbarous prejudice to hide the truth; [an exception may be made] to respond to the abuse of this liberty in cases determined by the law.

Article XII The guarantee of the rights of woman and the female citizen implies a major benefit; this guarantee must be instituted for the advantage of all, and not for the particular benefit of those to whom it is entrusted.

Article XIII For the support of the public force and the expenses of administration, the contributions of woman and man are equal; she shares all the duties [*corvées*] and all the painful tasks; therefore, she must have the same share in the distribution of positions, employment, offices, honors, and jobs [*industrie*].

Article XIV Female and male citizens have the right to verify, either by themselves or through their representatives, the necessity of the public contribution. This can only apply to women if they are granted an equal share, not only of wealth, but also of public administration, and in the determination of the proportion, the base, the collection, and the duration of the tax.

Article XV The collectivity of women, joined for tax purposes to the aggregate of men, has the right to demand an accounting of his administration from any public agent.

Article XVI No society has a constitution without the guarantee of rights and the separation of powers; the constitution is null if the majority of individuals comprising the nation have not cooperated in drafting it.

Article XVII Property belongs to both sexes whether united or separate; for each it is an inviolable and sacred right; no one can be deprived of it, since it is the true patrimony of nature, unless the legally determined public need obviously dictates it, and then only with a just and prior indemnity.

POSTSCRIPT

Woman, wake up; the tocsin of reason is being heard throughout the whole universe; discover your rights. The powerful empire of nature is no longer surrounded by prejudice, fanaticism, superstition, and lies. The flame of truth has dispersed all the clouds of folly and usurpation. Enslaved man has multiplied his strength and needs recourse to yours to break his chains. Having become free, he has become unjust to his companion. Oh, women, women! When will you cease to be blind? What advantages have you received from the Revolution? A more pronounced scorn, a more marked disdain. In the centuries of corruption you ruled only over the weakness of men. The reclamation of your patrimony, based on the wise decrees of nature—what have you to dread from such a fine undertaking? . . . Do you fear that our French legislators, correctors of that morality, long ensnared by political practices now out of date, will only say again to you: women, what is there in common between you and us? Everything, you will have to answer. If they persist in their weakness in putting this non sequitur in contradiction to their principles, courageously oppose the force of reason to the empty pretentions of superiority; unite yourselves beneath the standards of philosophy; deploy all the energy of your character, and you will soon see these haughty men, not groveling at your feet as servile adorers, but proud to share with you the treasures of the Supreme Being. Regardless of what barriers confront you, it is in your power to free yourselves; you have only to want to. . . .

Women in Paris Politics (May 1793)

The agitation for women's rights met with scant sympathy. An Englishwoman who was a keen sympathizer of the French Revolution mentioned in passing:

From Helen Maria Williams, *Letters Containing a Sketch of the Politics of France* (London, 1795), I, 139–140.

A certain class of the women of Paris, who gave themselves the title of revolutionary women, had been serviceable auxiliaries to the conspirators, and had taken the place of the fish wives, who not having all the energy which the present exigencies required, had yielded the palm to their revolutionary successors. These female politicians held deliberative assemblies, and afterwards presented their views to the convention, while they influenced its debates by their vociferations in the tribunes, which they now exclusively occupied. On the days of tumult which preceded the 31st of May they had mounted guard in person at the convention, and prevented the execution of certain orders which they disliked. They now presented themselves at the bar of the assembly, and demanded the exclusion of the former nobles from every function civil or military, the renewal of all the administrations throughout the republic, the examination of the conduct of the ministers, arrest of every suspected person, the raising of the whole nation in mass; and obliging the woman to wear red caps. The convention having shewn some disinclination to comply with these modest requisitions, these female politicians insulted some of the members, and the society was dissolved by a decree.

Clubs and Societies for Women

The records of the French National Assembly, called the Convention, describe the situation in greater detail here.

. . . (A Representative of the *Committee of General Security*): Citizens, your Committee has been working without respite on means of warding off the consequences of disorders which broke out the day before yesterday in Paris at the Marché des Innocents, near Saint-Eustache. It [the Committee] spent the night receiving deputations, listening to various reports which were made to it, and taking measures to maintain public order. Several women, calling themselves Jacobines, from an allegedly revolutionary society, were going about in the morning, . . . in pantaloons and red bonnets. They intended to force other *citoyennes* [citizens] to wear the same costume; several [of the latter] testified that they had been insulted by them. A mob of nearly six thousand women gathered. All the women were in agreement that violence and threats would not make them dress in a costume [which] they respected but which they believed was intended for men; they would obey laws passed by the legislators and acts of the people's magistrates, but they would not give in to the wishes and caprices of a hundred lazy and suspect women. They all cried out, "*Vive la République, une et indivisible!*"

Municipal officers and members of the Revolutionary Committee of the Section du Contrat Social quieted people down and dispersed the mobs. In the evening the same disturbance broke out with greater violence. A brawl started. Several self-proclaimed Revolutionary Women were roughed up. Some members of the crowd in-

From the Debates of the National Convention, quoted in Levy, Applewhite and Johnson, eds., *Women in Revolutionary Paris*, pp. 213–217.

dulged themselves in acts of violence towards them which decency ought to have pro-
scribed. Several remarks reported to your Committee show that this disturbance can
be attributed only to a plot by enemies of the state. Several of these self-proclaimed
Revolutionary Women may have been led astray by an excess of patriotism, but others,
doubtless, were motivated only by malevolence.

Right now, when Brissot and his accomplices are being judged, they want to work
up some disorders in Paris, as was the case whenever you [the Convention] were about
to consider some important matter and when it was a question of taking measures
useful for the Fatherland.

The Section des Marchés, informed of these events, drew up a resolution in which
it informs your Committee that it believes several malevolent persons have put on the
mask of an exaggerated patriotism to foment disturbances in the Section and a kind
of counterrevolution in Paris. This Section requests that it be illegal to hinder anyone's
freedom of dress and that popular societies of women be strictly prohibited, at least
during the revolution.

The committee thought it should carry its investigation further. It raised the following questions: (1) Is it permissible for citizens or for an individual society to force
other citizens to do what the law does not prescribe? (2) Should meetings of women
gathered together in popular societies in Paris be allowed? Don't the disorders already
occasioned by these societies argue against tolerating their existence any longer?

Naturally, these questions are complicated, and their resolution must be preceded
by two more general questions, which are: (1) Can women exercise political rights and
take an active part in affairs of government? (2) Can they deliberate together in political
associations or popular societies?

With respect to these two questions, the Committee decided in the negative. Time
does not allow for the full development to which these major questions—and the first,
above all—lend themselves. We are going to put forward a few ideas which may shed
light on them [these questions]. In your wisdom you will know how to submit them
to thorough examination.

1. Should women exercise political rights and meddle in affairs of government?
To govern is to rule the commonwealth by laws, the preparation of which demands
extensive knowledge, unlimited attention and devotion, a strict immovability, and self-
abnegation; again, to govern is to direct and ceaselessly to correct the action of constituted authorities. Are women capable of these cares and of the qualities they call for?
In general, we can answer, no. Very few examples would contradict this evaluation.

The citizen's political rights are to debate and to have resolutions drawn up, by
means of comparative deliberations, that relate to the interest of the state, and to resist
oppression. Do women have the moral and physical strength which the exercise of one
and the other of these rights calls for? Universal opinion rejects this idea.

2. Should women meet in political associations? The goal of popular associations
is this: to unveil the maneuvers of the enemies of the commonwealth; to exercise surveillance both over citizens as individuals and over public functionaries—even over
the legislative body; to excite the zeal of one and the other by the example of republican
virtues; to shed light by public and in-depth discussion concerning the lack or reform
of political laws. Can women devote themselves to these useful and difficult functions?

No, because they would be obliged to sacrifice the more important cares to which nature calls them. The private functions for which women are destined by their very nature are related to the general order of society; this social order results from the differences between man and woman. Each sex is called to the kind of occupation which is fitting for it; its action is circumscribed within this circle which it cannot break through, because nature, which has imposed these limits on man, commands imperiously and receives no law.

Man is strong, robust, born with great energy, audacity, and courage; he braves perils [and] the intemperance of seasons because of his constitution; he resists all the elements; he is fit for the arts, difficult labors; and as he is almost exclusively destined for agriculture, commerce, navigation, voyages, war—everything that calls for force, intelligence, capability, so in the same way, he alone seems to be equipped for profound and serious thinking which calls for great intellectual effort and long studies which it is not granted to women to pursue.

What character is suitable for woman? Morals and even nature have assigned her functions to her. To begin educating men, to prepare children's mind and hearts for public virtues, to direct them early in life towards the good, to elevate their souls, to educate them in the political cult of liberty: such are their functions, after household cares. Woman is naturally destined to make virtue loved. When they have fulfilled all these obligations, they will have deserved well of the Fatherland. Doubtless they must educate themselves in the principles of liberty in order to make their children cherish it; they can attend the deliberations of the Sections [and] discussions of the popular societies, but as they are made for softening the morals of man, should they take an active part in discussions the passion of which is incompatible with the softness and moderation which are the charm of their sex?

We must say that this question is related essentially to morals, and without morals, no republic. Does the honesty of woman allow her to display herself in public and to struggle against men? to argue in full view of a public about questions on which the salvation of the republic depends? In general, women are ill suited for elevated thoughts and serious meditations, and if, among ancient peoples, their natural timidity and modesty did not allow them to appear outside their families, then in the French Republic do you want them to be seen coming into the gallery to political assemblies as men do? abandoning both reserve—source of all the virtues of their sex—and care of their family?

They have more than one alternative way of rendering service to the Fatherland; they can enlighten their husbands, communicating precious reflections, the fruit of the quiet of a sedentary life, [and] work to fortify their love of country by means of everything which intimate love gives them in the way of empire. And the man, enlightened by peaceful family discussions in the midst of his household, will bring back into society the useful ideas imparted to him by an honest woman.

We believe, therefore, that a woman should not leave her family to meddle in affairs of government.

There is another sense in which women's associations seem dangerous. If we consider that the political education of men is at its beginning, that all its principles are not developed, and that we are still stammering the word liberty, then how much more reasonable is it for women, whose moral education is almost nil, to be less enlightened concerning principles? Their presence in popular societies, therefore, would give an active role in government to people more exposed to error and seduction. Let us add that women are disposed by their organization to an overexcitation which would be deadly in public affairs and that interests of state would soon be sacrificed to everything which ardor in passions can generate in the way of error and disorder. Delivered over to the heat of public debate, they would teach their children not love of country but hatreds and suspicions.

We believe, therefore, and without any doubt you will think as we do, that it is not possible for women to exercise political rights. You will destroy these alleged popular societies of women which the aristocracy would want to set up to put them [women] at odds with men, to divide the latter by forcing them to take sides in these quarrels, and to stir up disorder. . . .

The National Convention, after having heard the report of its Committee of General Security, decrees:

Article I: Clubs and popular societies of women, whatever name they are known under, are prohibited. . . .

In the homeland of revolution, French women would finally get the vote in 1944.

The Guillotine: Letter from the Public Executioner

The revolutionaries sought liberty and equality for all. Yet for equality to be established, liberty had to be restricted. And if citizens were to be educated to their new rights in a new world, misleading or corrupting influences had to be eliminated and obstacles to their forward march thrust out of the way. The French Revolution, made to assert the rights of man, therefore began by restraining these rights and by proscribing those whom it counted as its enemies. The monarchy was abolished in 1792, the king and queen executed in 1793. The strains of internal dissension, foreign war, and the struggle for power between rival revolutionary factions made the years between 1792 and 1794 a period of terror whose symbol remains less the tricolor flag than the guillotine—named after a medical member of the Constituent Assembly, the professor of anatomy at the University of Paris, Dr. Joseph Guillotin (1738–1814).

For the sake of greater humanity, Dr. Guillotin argued, an enlightened assembly should replace current methods of execution with the simple, expeditious, and far less messy process of decapitation. This could be carried out efficiently by means of a machine already employed in parts of Italy, but recently perfected by a Frenchman, Dr. Louis. Guillotin's proposition was adopted, and the machine, first called louisette, *was put into use on April 25, 1792. It was destined to a brilliant future.*

From Ernest Belfort Bax, *The Last Episode of the French Revolution* (London: Richards Press Ltd., 1911).

PUBLIC EXECUTIONER SANSON TO THE ATTORNEY GENERAL
OF THE DEPARTMENT OF THE SEINE.
AUGUST 6, 1792

Sir,

It is very respectfully that I have the honor to put before you the position in which I find myself. It is such that I beg you, Sir, to give it a moment of your attention.

The kind of execution practised today easily triples costs when compared to the old expenses, and this besides the rise in prices of all necessities of life.

The service and the number of criminal courts force me to keep a number of persons ready to carry out the orders I receive. I cannot personally be everywhere at once. I need dependable people. For the public still wants to see us do a decent job. I have to pay for that.

To have proper people for this work, they want twice the pay of previous years. And just last Saturday they have come to warn me that without at least a twenty-five per cent raise they could not do their work any longer. The present circumstances have forced me to promise.

The abolition of prejudices seemed to have eased my problem in finding help. On the contrary, I find it has merely made disappear all those in the class of which I could recruit, by the ease with which they now can find domestic service or some other job, or join the army.

It is therefore necessary, if one wishes to find help, to chain them by the hope of gain.

I have fourteen persons to feed every day, of whom eight are on salary, three horses, three carts, and accessories. . . .

An enormous rent, which should be paid by the state (the executioner has always been lodged by the King).

The extra expenses of execution, very common daily, other family responsibilities, like relatives and sick old servants who have sacrificed their lives in this service, and who have a right to humanity.

My present request, Sir, is that eight months have passed since I submitted an account of expenses and costs to the Office of Judicial Costs, which have always in the past paid me at the price of the tariff I provided, and now I cannot get my bills paid. Yet I have very carefully kept to the prices of the tariff; I have even personally made rebates on certain articles.

I had the honor, Sir, to present you a request concerning this matter last June 11, without receiving an answer. I am faced with financial embarrassment, even in debt, if I may say so, not knowing any more where to turn for funds. And unable to address myself to creditors whom I cannot repay if I am not paid.

I have no recourse but you, Sir, to order the payment of what is owed me, without which, after the sacrifice I have made to manage up to date to carry out my duties conscientiously, will cause the total subversion of my existence and inevitable ruin in forcing me to abandon my post and my family after forty-two years of faithful service.

Since my position is pressing, I beg you, Sir, to have the kindness to have a trustworthy person inform you of the facts I have the honor to submit.

I have the honor to be with the most profound respect, Sir, your very humble and obedient servant.

SANSON
Executor of Criminal Judgments in Paris

THE TERROR

Beset by internal rebellion and mounting disorder, the new rulers of France sought escape in a foreign war, which they declared in April 1792. By July things were going so badly that a decree declared the Fatherland in danger and mobilized all French citizens in its defense. The internal counterpart of foreign conflict was the Terror, designed to affirm and advance the achievements of 1789.

Decree for the Levy en Masse (1793)

1. From this moment until that in which the enemy shall have been driven from the territory of the Republic, all Frenchmen are in permanent requisition for the service of the armies.

    The young men shall go to battle; the married men shall forge arms and transport provisions; the women shall make tents and clothing and shall serve in the hospitals; the children shall make old linen into lint; the old men shall take themselves to the public places in order to arouse the courage of the warriors and preach the hatred of kings and the unity of the Republic.

2. The public buildings shall be converted into barracks, the public squares into workshops for arms, the soil of the cellars shall be washed in order to extract the saltpeter from them.

3. The arms of military calibre shall be reserved exclusively for those who shall march upon the enemy; the service of the interior shall be provided with hunting pieces and side arms.

4. The saddle horses shall be requisitioned to equip the cavalry corps; the workhorses, other than those employed in agriculture, shall haul the artillery and the provisions.

5. The Committee of Public Safety is charged with the taking of all the necessary measures without delay for the establishment of an extraordinary manufacture of arms of every kind which corresponds with the zeal and energy of the French people. It is authorized in consequence, to form all the establishments, factories, workshops and mills which shall be indeed necessary for the execution of these works, as well as to requisition for this objective within the entire extent of the Republic, the artisans and workingmen who can contribute to their success. To

---

From J. B. Duvergier, ed., *Collection complète des lois, décrets, ordonnances* (Paris, 1834), Vol. VI, tr. Henry Bertram Hill, *Europe in Review* (Chicago: Rand McNally, 1957), pp. 170–171.

this end there shall be put at the disposal of the Minister of War a sum of thirty millions, to be taken out of the four hundred ninety-eight million two hundred thousand livres in monies which are in reserve in the fund of the three keys. The central establishment of this extraordinary manufacture shall be at Paris.

6. The representatives of the people sent out for the execution of the present law shall have the same authority in their respective districts, and act in concert with the Committee of Public Safety; they are invested with the unlimited powers assigned to the representatives of the people to the armies.

7. Nobody can have a substitute for himself in the service for which he shall have been requisitioned. Civil service employees shall remain at their posts.

8. The levy shall be general. The unmarried citizens and widowers without children, from eighteen to twenty-five years of age shall march first; they shall assemble without delay at the head-towns of their districts, where they shall practice every day in the use of arms while awaiting the hour of departure.

Robespierre: Notes

We identify the name of Maximilien de Robespierre (1758–1794) with the Terror that imprisoned half a million "suspects" and "enemies of the people," put 16,000 of them to death, and ended with his own execution. In an age of ranting, this inflexible lawyer's chief weapon was speechifying that played on current obsessions of conspiracy to destroy his opponents and anyone suspected of opposition. As long as this strategy worked, the absolute sovereignty of militant fanatics would replace the less than absolute sovereignty of the deposed king.

The lines that follow are hasty notes that Robespierre scribbled in preparation for a speech delivered in the National Assembly late in 1793. Note the rhetorical devices employed to warn against counterrevolutionary wiles.

What is the aim? To apply the Constitution in favor of the people.

Who will be our enemies? The vicious and *the rich.*

What means will they use? Calumny and hypocrisy.

What can favor the use of such means? The ignorance of the people.

It follows that the people must be enlightened. But what are the obstacles to its education?

[They are] the money-hungry writers who daily lead it astray by shameless impostures.

What are we to conclude from this?

From Robespierre's manuscript notebooks, Archives nationales (Paris), tr. Eugen Weber.

1. That one has to outlaw writers as the most dangerous enemies of the fatherland.

2. That good [virtuous] writings have to be diffused in profusion.

What are the obstacles to the establishment of liberty?
Foreign war and civil war.
By what means can we bring foreign war to an end?
Place republican generals at the head of our armies, and punish generals who have betrayed us.
By what means can we end civil war?
Punish traitors and conspirators, *especially guilty legislators and administrators*; send patriotic troops with patriotic leaders to put down the aristocrats of Lyon, Marseille, Toulon, of the Vosges, of the Jura, and of all other regions where the flag of rebellion and of royalism has been raised, and to make terrible examples of all the villains who have outraged liberty and shed the blood of patriots.

1. *Outlaw perfidious and counter-revolutionary writers; spread the good word.*

2. Punish traitors and conspirators, especially guilty legislators and administrators.

3. Appoint patriotic generals; dismiss and punish the others.

4. Control wages and prices; pass *popular laws.*

Robespierre: Democracy and Terror

The Terror was less a matter of principle than of improvisation under pressure: what the French call a fuite en avant *("running away forward"). Yet principles provided the battle calls for practice—above all the principles of Rousseau (especially the concept that he termed the "General Will") and of Robespierre, who believed that the true people are virtuous and that democracy is the reign of virtue. The revolution had celebrated Liberty and Equality (Fraternity, always marginal, had long gone overboard). But Liberty and Equality are contradictory ideals, and Rousseau's ideal democracy chose equality over liberty, as this 1794 speech by Robespierre makes clear.*

Democracy is a state where the sovereign people, guided by the laws which it has made does itself all that it can do, and delegates to its representatives all that which it can not do itself. . . . As the essence of a Democracy is equality, it follows that love of fatherland includes necessarily love of equality. . . .

It has been said that the terror belongs to a despotic government. Does our terror have anything in common with despotism? Yes, just as the sword which glitters in the hands of the heroes of liberty resembles that with which the henchmen of Tyranny

---

Discours et Rapports de Robespierre, ed. Vellay (Paris, 1908), tr. George L. Mosse.

are armed. . . . The Government of the Revolution is the Despotism of Liberty against Tyranny. Nature imposes on all physical and moral beings the duty to preserve themselves. . . . If Tyranny rules a single day there will not be a patriot alive the next morning. . . . How much one is concerned for the oppressors and how little for the oppressed. . . . One or the other must perish. Indulgence for the Royalists, cry some men. Mercy for the scoundrels. No: mercy and compassion for the innocents . . . for humanity.

The protection of society is due only to peaceful Citizens, and in a Republic there are no other citizens than republicans. The Royalists, the Conspirators, are to them . . . enemies. This terrible war of Liberty against Tyranny is it not one and indivisible? Our internal enemies, are they not the allies of our foreign foes? . . .

Napoleon Bonaparte: Proclamation of 19th Brumaire, 11 O'clock P.M.

Although the Equals had been effectively dealt with, the relatively moderate Directorate (1795–1799), caught between the specter of a new Jacobin terror and the more concrete threat of a right-wing restoration, was unable to rule constitutionally. Perhaps it did not really want to do so. At any rate, having once called in the generals to eliminate their political opponents, it was only a matter of time before an enterprising general took it into his head to eliminate them. That time came on 18th Brumaire (November 9), 1799, when General Napoleon Bonaparte, who had returned in haste from his unsuccessful Egyptian expedition, dispersed the assemblies, liquidated the Directorate, and replaced it with a consular regime that was to be the prelude to his imperial rule.

To the People:

Frenchmen, on my return to France I found division reigning among all the authorities. They agreed only on this single point, that the constitution was half destroyed and was unable to protect liberty.

Each party in turn came to me, confided to me their designs, imparted their secrets, and requested my support. But I refused to be the man of any party.

The Council of Elders appealed to me. I answered their appeal. A plan of general restoration had been conspired at by men whom the nation has been accustomed to regard as the defenders of liberty, equality, and property. This plan required calm deliberation, free from all influence and all fear. The Elders therefore resolved upon the removal of the legislative bodies to St. Cloud. They placed at my disposal the force necessary to secure their independence. I was bound, in duty to my fellow-citizens, to the soldiers perishing in our armies, and to the national glory acquired at the cost of so much blood, to accept the command. The Council assembled at St. Cloud. Republican troops guaranteed their safety from without, but assassins created terror within.

From J. H. Robinson and C. A. Beard, *Readings in Modern European History*, 2 vol. (Boston, 1908), I, 322–323.

Many deputies in the Council of Five Hundred, armed with stilettos and pistols, spread the menace of death around them.

The plans which ought to have been developed were withheld. The majority of the Council was disorganized, the boldest orators were disconcerted, and the futility of submitting my salutary proposition was quite evident.

I proceeded, filled with indignation and chagrin, to the Council of the Elders. I besought them to carry their noble designs into execution. I directed their attention to the evils of the nation, which were their motives for conceiving those designs. They concurred in giving me new proofs of their unanimous good will.

I presented myself before the Council of the Five Hundred alone, unarmed, my head uncovered, just as the Elders had received and applauded me. My object was to restore to the majority the expression of its will and to secure to it its power.

The stilettos which had menaced the deputies were instantly raised against their deliverer. Twenty assassins rushed upon me and aimed at my breast. The grenadiers of the legislative body, whom I had left at the door of the hall, ran forward and placed themselves between me and the assassins. One of these brave grenadiers had his clothes pierced by a stiletto. They bore me out.

At the same moment cries of "Outlaw him!" were raised against the defender of the law. It was the horrid cry of assassins against the power destined to repress them. They crowded around the president, uttering threats. With arms in their hands, they commanded him to declare me outlawed. I was informed of this. I ordered him to be rescued from their fury, and six grenadiers of the legislative body charged the hall and cleared it.

The seditious, thus intimidated, dispersed and fled. The majority, freed from their assailants, returned freely and peaceably into the hall, listened to the propositions for the public safety, deliberated, and drew up the salutary resolution which will become the new provisional law of the republic.

Frenchmen, you will doubtless recognize in this conduct the zeal of a soldier of liberty, of a citizen devoted to the republic. Conservative, judicial, and liberal ideas resumed their sway upon the dispersion of those seditious persons who had domineered in the councils and who proved themselves the most odious and contemptible of men.

BONAPARTE

The Reaction

IT was inevitable that the subversive ideas and world-shattering events examined in the previous chapter should generate a reaction. One aspect of the reaction, when it came, was reflected in the profoundly romantic ideas of Edmund Burke, who felt that the good society was equivalent to the natural society—"natural" in so far as it is the product of organic development and growth. Rousseau and some of his followers had expressed such ideas by suggesting that the existing society and social order, which had deviated from a healthy, natural form, be pulled down and replaced by something better. Burke, on the contrary, saw in the very existence of social forms and institutions both proof of their healthy, organic nature and an argument against their being replaced by artificial products of the human mind—theories or systems that could never fit the needs of society as well as the traditional norms and forms it had evolved over the course of many years. A brilliant pamphleteer rather than a consistent political thinker, Burke's ideas are sometimes pragmatic but often also ambiguous; he had only himself to blame for being frequently misunderstood.

About Metternich's ideas, on the other hand, there was little ambiguity. The man knew what he wanted: to preserve the status quo. His difficulty was that he had to work with men who were far less single-minded than he. He preserved the old world, his world, for over thirty years after the Congress of Vienna, but only by fighting a continuous battle on two fronts—one against the rising powers of nationalism and liberalism, and the other against the masters and associates whom he had to persuade of the rightness of his views. Though he seemed to have lost his battles in 1848, his uncompromising brand of conservatism lived on for many years, and may be found today in the clubs and last ditches where it still holds out.

Edmund Burke

Edmund Burke (1729–1797)—statesman, orator, and political philosopher—was born in Dublin, the son of a Protestant father and a Catholic mother. Trained to be a lawyer like his father, he went into pamphleteering and politics instead. As a member of Parliament he took the side of the insurgent American colonists, but opposed the French revolutionaries in his Reflections on the French Revolution, *published in 1790. He felt that violent breaks with tradition could only harm men whose life and society were like part of a tree with roots in the past. Revolution, the cutting of the roots, can only kill or maim society. Reform and change, as natural developments on historical foundations, are the only healthy ways of bringing about growth in conformity with the real character and needs of a nation. Burke's ideas carried far, but their full effect was not to be felt until the nineteenth century.*

310

Reflections on the French Revolution

THE ROAD TO EMINENCE

I do not, my dear sir, conceive you to be of that sophistical, captious spirit, or of that uncandid dulness, as to require for every general observation or sentiment, an explicit detail of the correctives and exceptions, which reason will presume to be included in all the general propositions which come from reasonable men. You do not imagine, that I wish to confine power, authority, and distinction to blood, and names, and titles. No, sir. There is no qualification for government but virtue and wisdom, actual or presumptive. Wherever they are actually found, they have, in whatever state, condition, profession or trade, the passport of heaven to human place and honour. Woe to the country which would madly and impiously reject the service of the talents and virtues, civil, military or religious, that are given to grace and to serve it; and would condemn to obscurity everything formed to diffuse lustre and glory around a state. Woe to that country too, that, passing into the opposite extreme, considers a low education, a mean contracted view of things, a sordid, mercenary occupation, as a preferable title to command. Everything ought to be open; but not indifferently to every man. No rotation; no appointment by lot; no mode of election operating in the spirit of sortation, or rotation, can be generally good in a government conversant in extensive objects. Because they have no tendency, direct or indirect, to select the man with a view to the duty, or to accommodate the one to the other. I do not hesitate to say that the road to eminence and power, from obscure condition, ought not to be made too easy, nor a thing too much of course. If rare merit be the rarest of all rare things, it ought to pass through some sort of probation. The temple of honour ought to be seated on an eminence. If it be opened through virtue, let it be remembered too that virtue is never tried but by some difficulty and some struggle.

Nothing is a due and adequate representation of a state that does not represent its ability, as well as its property. But as ability is a vigorous and active principle, and as property is sluggish, inert and timid, it never can be safe from the invasions of ability, unless it be, out of all proportion, predominant in the representation. It must be represented too in great masses of accumulation, or it is not rightly protected. The characteristic essence of property, formed out of the combined principles of its acquisition and conservation, is to be unequal. The great masses therefore which excite envy, and tempt rapacity, must be put out of the possibility of danger. Then they form a natural rampart about the lesser properties in all their gradations. The same quantity of property, which is by the natural course of things divided among many, has not the same operation. Its defensive power is weakened as it is diffused. In this diffusion each man's portion is less than what, in the eagerness of his desires, he may flatter himself to obtain by dissipating the accumulations of others. The plunder of the few would indeed give but a share inconceivably small in the distribution to the many.

From *The Works of the Right Honourable Edmund Burke*, 2 vol. (London, 1834), I.

But the many are not capable of making this calculation; and those who lead them to rapine never intend this distribution.

The power of perpetuating our property in our families is one of the most valuable and interesting circumstances belonging to it, and that which tends the most to the perpetuation of society itself. It makes our weakness subservient to our virtue; it grafts benevolence even upon avarice. The possessors of family wealth, and of the distinction which attends hereditary possession, (as most concerned in it,) are the natural securities for this transmission. With us the House of Peers is formed upon this principle. It is wholly composed of hereditary property and hereditary distinction; and made therefore the third of the legislature; and in the last event, the sole judge of all property in all its subdivisions. The House of Commons too, though not necessarily, yet in fact, is always so composed, in the far greater part. Let those large proprietors be what they will, and they have their chance of being among the best, they are, at the very worst, the ballast in the vessel of the commonwealth. For though hereditary wealth, and the rank which goes with it, are too much idolized by creeping syncophants, and the blind, abject admirers of power, they are too rashly slighted in shallow speculations of the petulant, assuming, short-sighted coxcombs of philosophy. Some decent, regulated pre-eminence, some preference (not exclusive appropriation), given to birth, is neither unnatural, nor unjust, nor impolitic.

It is said, that twenty-four millions ought to prevail over two hundred thousand. True; if the constitution of a kingdom be a problem of arithmetic. This sort of discourse does well enough with the lamp-post for its second: to men who *may* reason calmly, it is ridiculous. The will of the many, and their interest, must very often differ; and great will be the difference when they make an evil choice. A government of five hundred country attorneys and obscure curates is not good for twenty-four millions of men, though it were chosen by eight and forty millions; nor is it the better for being guided by a dozen of persons of quality, who have betrayed their trust in order to obtain that power. At present, you seem in everything to have strayed out of the high road of nature. The property of France does not govern it. Of course property is destroyed, and rational liberty has no existence. All you have got for the present is a paper circulation, and a stock-jobbing constitution: and, as to the future, do you seriously think that the territory of France, upon the republican system of eighty-three independent municipalities (to say nothing of the parts that compose them), can ever be governed as one body, or can ever be set in motion by the impulse of one mind? When the National Assembly has completed its work, it will have accomplished its ruin.

THE RIGHTS OF MEN

Far am I from denying in theory, full as far is my heart from withholding in practice (if I were of power to give or to withhold) the *real* rights of men. In denying their false claims of right, I do not mean to injure those which are real, and are such as their pretended rights would totally destroy. If civil society be made for the advantage of man, all the advantages for which it is made become his right. It is an institution of beneficence; and law itself is only beneficence, acting by a rule. Men have a right to live by that rule; they have a right to do justice; as between their fellows, whether their fellows are in politic function or in ordinary occupation. They have a right to the fruits of their industry; and to the means of making their industry fruitful. They have a right to the acquisitions of their parents; to the nourishment and improvement of their offspring; to instruction in life, and to consolation in death. Whatever each man can separately do, without trespassing upon others, he has a right to do for himself; and he has a right to a fair portion of all which society, with all its combinations of skill and force, can do in his favour. In this partnership all men have equal rights: but not to equal things. He that has but five shillings in the partnership, has as good a right to it as he that has five hundred pounds has to his larger portion. But he has not a right to an equal dividend in the product of the joint stock; and as to the share of power, authority, and direction which each individual ought to have in the management of the state, that I must deny to be amongst the direct original rights of man in civil society; for I have in my contemplation the civil social man, and no other. It is a thing to be settled by convention.

If civil society be the offspring of convention, that convention must be its law. That convention must limit and modify all the descriptions of constitution which are formed under it. Every sort of legislature, judicial, or executory power, are its creatures. They can have no being in any other state of things; and how can any man claim, under the conventions of civil society, rights which do not so much as suppose its existence?—rights which are absolutely repugnant to it? One of the first motives to civil society, and which becomes one of its fundamental rules, is, *that no man should be judge in his own cause.* By this each person has at once divested himself of the first fundamental right of uncovenanted man, that is, to judge for himself and to assert his own cause. He abdicates all right to be his own governor. He inclusively, in a great measure abandons the right of self-defence, the first law of nature. Men cannot enjoy the rights of an uncivil and of a civil state together. That he may obtain justice, he gives up his right of determining what it is in points the most essential to him. That he may secure some liberty, he makes a surrender in trust of the whole of it.

Government is not made in virtue of natural rights, which may and do exist in total independence of it; and exist in much greater clearness, and in a much greater degree of abstract perfection; but their abstract perfection is their practical defect. By having a right to everything, they want everything. Government is a contrivance of human wisdom to provide for human *wants.* Men have a right that these wants should be provided for by this wisdom. Among these wants is to be reckoned the want, out of civil society, of a sufficient restraint upon their passions. Society requires not only that passions of individuals should be subjected, but that even in the mass and body, as well as in the individuals, the inclinations of men should frequently be thwarted, their will controlled, and their passions brought into subjection. This can only be done *by a power out of themselves;* and not, in the exercise of its function, subject to that will and to those passions which it is its office to bridle and subdue. In this sense the restraints on men, as well as their liberties, are to be reckoned among their rights. But as the liberties and the restrictions vary with times and circumstances, and admit of infinite modifications, they cannot be settled upon any abstract rule; and nothing is so foolish as to discuss them upon that principle.

The moment you abate anything from the full rights of men, each to govern himself, and suffer any artificial, positive, limitation upon those rights, from that moment the whole organization of government becomes a consideration of convenience. This it is which makes the constitution of a state, and the due distribution of its powers, a matter of the most delicate and complicated skill. It requires a deep knowledge of human nature and human necessities, and of the things which facilitate or obstruct the various ends, which are to be pursued by the mechanism of civil institutions. The state is to have recruits to its strength, and remedies to its distempers. What is the use of discussing a man's abstract right to food or medicine? The question is upon the method of procuring and administering them. In that deliberation I shall always advise to call in the aid of the farmer and the physician, rather than the professor of metaphysics.

The science of constructing a commonwealth, or renovating it, or reforming it, is, like every other experimental science, not to be taught *a priori*. Nor is it a short experience that can instruct us in that practical science; because the real effects of moral causes are not always immediate; but that which in the first instance is prejudicial may be excellent in its remoter operation; and its excellence may arise even from the ill effects it produces in the beginning. The reverse also happens; and very plausible schemes, with very pleasing commencements, have often shameful and lamentable conclusions. In states there are often some obscure and almost latent causes, things which appear at first view of little moment, on which a very great part of its prosperity or adversity may most essentially depend. The science of government being therefore so practical in itself, and intended for such practical purposes, a matter which requires experience, and even more experience than any person can gain in his whole life, however sagacious and observing he may be, it is with infinite caution that any man ought to venture upon pulling down an edifice, which has answered in any tolerable degree for ages the common purposes of society, or on building it up again, without having models and patterns of approved utility before his eyes.

These metaphysic rights entering into common life, like rays of light which pierce into a dense medium, are, by the laws of nature, refracted from their straight line. Indeed, in the gross and complicated mass of human passions and concerns, the primitive rights of men undergo such a variety of refractions and reflections, that it becomes absurd to talk of them as if they continued in the simplicity of their original direction. The nature of man is intricate; the objects of society are of the greatest possible complexity: and therefore no simple disposition or direction of power can be suitable either to man's nature, or to the quality of his affairs. When I hear the simplicity of contrivance aimed at and boasted of in any new political consitutions, I am at no loss to decide that the artificers are grossly ignorant of their trade, or totally negligent of their duty. The simple governments are fundamentally defective, to say no worse of them. . . . If you were to contemplate society in but one point of view, all these simple modes of polity are infinitely captivating. In effect each would answer its single end much more perfectly than the more complex is able to attain all its complex purposes. But it is better that the whole should be imperfectly and anomalously answered, than that, while some parts are provided for with great exactness, others might be totally neglected, or perhaps materially injured, by the overcare of a favourite member.

The pretended rights of these theorists are all extremes: and in proportion as they are metaphysically true, they are morally and politically false. The rights of men are in a sort of middle, incapable of definition, but not impossible to be discerned. The rights of men in governments are their advantages; and these are often in balances between differences of good; in compromises sometimes between good and evil, and sometimes between evil and evil. Political reason is a computing principle; adding, subtracting, multiplying, and dividing, morally and not metaphysically, or mathematically, true moral denominations.

By these theorists the right of the people is almost always sophistically confounded with their power. The body of the community, whenever it can come to act, can meet with no effectual resistance; but till power and right are the same, the whole body of them has no right inconsistent with virtue, and the first of all virtues, prudence. Men have no right to what is not reasonable, and to what is not for their benefit.

EFFECTS OF REVOLUTION

It is now sixteen or seventeen years since I saw the queen of France, then the dauphiness, at Versailles; and surely never lighted on this orb, which she hardly seemed to touch, a more delightful vision. I saw her just above the horizon, decorating and cheering the elevated sphere she just began to move in,—glittering like the morning-star, full of life, and splendour, and joy. Oh! what a revolution! and what a heart must I have to contemplate without emotion that elevation and that fall! Little did I dream when she added titles of veneration to those of enthusiastic, distant respectful love, that she should ever be obliged to carry the sharp antidote against disgrace concealed in that bosom; little did I dream that I should have lived to see such disasters fallen upon her in a nation of gallant men; in a nation of men of honour and of cavaliers. I thought ten thousand swords must have leaped from their scabbards to avenge even a look that threatened her with insult. But the age of chivalry is gone. That of sophisters, economists, and calculators, has succeeded; and the glory of Europe is extinguished for ever. Never, never more shall we behold that generous loyalty to rank and sex, that proud submission, that dignified obedience, that subordination of the heart, which kept alive, even in servitude itself, the spirit of an exalted freedom. The unbought grace of life, the cheap defense of nations, the nurse of manly sentiment and heroic enterprise, is gone. It is gone, that sensibility of principle, that chastity of honour, which felt a stain like a wound, which inspired courage whilst it mitigated ferocity, which ennobled whatever it touched, and under which vice itself lost half its evil, by losing all its grossness.

This mixed system of opinion and sentiment had its origin in the ancient chivalry; and the principle, though varied in its appearance by the varying state of human affairs, subsisted and influenced through a long succession of generations, even to the time we live in. If it should ever be totally extinguished, the loss I fear will be great. It is this which has given its character to modern Europe. It is this which has distinguished it under all its forms of government, and distinguished it to its advantage, from the states of Asia, and possibly from those states which flourished in the most brilliant periods of the antique world. It was this which, without confounding ranks, had produced a noble equality, and handed it down through all the gradations of social life. It was this opinion which mitigated kings into companions, and raised private men to be fellows with kings. Without force or opposition, it subdued the fierceness of pride and power; it obliged sovereigns to submit to elegance, and made a dominating vanquisher of laws to be subdued by manners.

But now all is to be changed. All the pleasing illusions, which made power gentle and obedience liberal, which harmonized the different shades of life, and which, by a bland assimilation, incorporated into politics the sentiments which beautify and soften private society, are to be dissolved by this new conquering empire of light and reason. All the decent drapery of life is to be rudely torn off. All the superadded ideas, furnished from the wardrobe of a moral imagination, which the heart owns, and the understanding ratifies, as necessary to cover the defects of our naked, shivering nature, and to raise it to dignity in our own estimation, are to be exploded as a ridiculous, absurd, and antiquated fashion.

On this scheme of things, a king is but a man, a queen is but a woman; a woman is but an animal, and an animal not of the highest order. All homage paid to the sex in general as such, and without distinct view, is to be regarded as romance and folly. Regicide, and parricide, and sacrilege, are but fictions of superstition, corrupting jurisprudence by destroying its simplicity. The murder of a king, or a queen, or a bishop, or a father, are only common homicide; and if the people are by any chance, or in any way, gainers of it, a sort of homicide much the most pardonable, and into which we ought not to make too severe a scrutiny.

On the scheme of this barbarous philosophy, which is the offspring of cold hearts and muddy understandings, and which is as void of solid wisdom as it is destitute of all taste and elegance, laws are to be supported only by their own terrors, and by the concern which each individual may find in them from his own private speculations, or can spare to them from his own private interests. In the groves of *their* academy, at the end of every vista, you see nothing but the gallows. Nothing is left which engages the affections on the part of the commonwealth. On the principles of this mechanic philosophy, our institutions can never be embodied, if I may use the expression, in persons; so as to create in us love, veneration, admiration, or attachment. But that sort of reason which banishes the affections is incapable of filling their place. These public affections, combined with manners, are required sometimes as supplements, sometimes as correctives, always as aids to law. . . .

But power, of some kind or other, will survive the shock in which manners and opinions perish; and it will find other and worse means for its support. The usurpation which, in order to subvert ancient institutions, has destroyed ancient principles, will hold power by arts similar to those by which it has acquired it. When the old feudal and chivalrous spirit of *fealty,* which, by freeing kings from fear, freed both kings and subjects from the precautions of tyranny, shall be extinct in the minds of men, plots and assassinations will be anticipated by preventive murder and preventive confiscation, and that long roll of grim and bloody maxims, which form the political code of all power, not standing on its own honour, and the honour of those who are to obey it. Kings will be tyrants from policy, when subjects are rebels from principle.

When ancient opinions and rules of life are taken away, the loss cannot possibly be estimated. From that moment we have no compass to govern us; nor can we know distinctly to what port we steer. Europe, undoubtedly, taken in a mass, was in a flourishing condition the day on which your revolution was completed. How much of that prosperous state was owing to the spirit of our old manners and opinions is not easy to say; but as such causes cannot be indifferent in their operation, we must presume, that, on the whole, their operation was beneficial.

We are but too apt to consider things in the state in which we find them, without sufficiently adverting to the causes by which they have been produced, and possibly may be upheld. Nothing is more certain, than that our manners, our civilization, and all the good things which are connected with manners and with civilization, have, in this European world of ours, depended for ages upon two principles; and were indeed the result of both combined; I mean the spirit of a gentleman, and the spirit of religion. The nobility and the clergy, the one by profession, the other by patronage, kept learning in existence, even in the midst of arms and confusions, and whilst governments were rather in their causes, than formed. Learning paid back what it received to nobility and to priesthood; and paid it with usury by enlarging their ideas, and by furnishing their minds. Happy if they had all continued to know their indissoluble union, and their proper place! Happy if learning, not debauched by ambition, had been satisfied to continue, the instructor, and not aspired to be the master! Along with its natural protectors and guardians, learning will be cast into the mire, and trodden down under the hoofs of a swinish multitude.

If, as I suspect, modern letters owe more than they are always willing to own to ancient manners, so do other interests which we value full as much as they are worth. Even commerce, and trade, and manufacture, the gods of our economical politicians, are themselves perhaps but creatures; are themselves but effects, which, as first causes, we choose to worship. They certainly grew under the same shade in which learning flourished. They too may decay with their natural protecting principles. With you, for the present at least, they will threaten to disappear together. Where trade and manufactures are wanting to a people, and the spirit of nobility and religion remains, sentiment supplies, and not always ill supplies, their place; but if commerce and the arts should be lost in an experiment to try how well a state may stand without these old fundamental principles, what sort of a thing must be a nation of gross, stupid, ferocious, and, at the same time, poor and sordid, barbarians, destitute of religion, honour, or manly pride, possessing nothing at present, and hoping for nothing hereafter?

I wish you may not be going fast, and by the shortest cut, to that horrible and disgustful situation. Already there appears a poverty of conception, a coarseness and vulgarity, in all the proceedings of the Assembly and of all their instructors. Their liberty is not liberal. Their science is presumptuous ignorance. Their humanity is savage and brutal. . . .

THE ENGLISH SCENE

We are not the converts of Rousseau; we are not the disciples of Voltaire; Helvetius has made no progress amongst us. Atheists are not our preachers; madmen are not our lawgivers. We know that *we* have made no discoveries; and we think that no discoveries are to be made, in morality; nor many in the great principles of government, nor in the ideas of liberty, which were understood long before we were born, altogether as well as they will be after the grave has heaped its mould over our presumption, and the silent tomb shall have imposed its law on our pert loquacity. In England we have not yet been completely embowelled of our natural entrails: we still feel within us, and we cherish and cultivate, those inbred sentiments which are the faithful guardians, the active monitors of our duty, the true supporters of all liberal and manly morals. We have not been drawn and trussed, in order that we may be filled, like stuffed birds in a museum, with chaff and rags and paltry blurred sheets of paper about the rights of man. We preserve the whole of our feelings still native and entire, unsophisticated by pedantry and infidelity. We have real hearts of flesh and blood beating in our bosoms. We fear God; we look up with awe to kings; with affection to parliaments; with duty to magistrates; with reverence to priests; and with respect to nobility. Why? Because when such ideas are brought before our minds, it is *natural* to be so affected; because all other feelings are false and spurious, and tend to corrupt our minds, to vitiate our primary morals, to render us unfit for rational liberty; and by teaching us a servile, licentious, and abandoned insolence, to be our low sport for a few holidays, to make us perfectly fit for, and justly deserving of, slavery, through the whole course of our lives.

You see, Sir, that in this enlightened age I am bold enough to confess that we are generally men of untaught feelings; that instead of casting away all our old prejudices, we cherish them to a very considerable degree; and, to take more shame to ourselves, we cherish them because they are prejudices; and the longer they have lasted and the more generally they have prevailed, the more we cherish them. We are afraid to put men to live and trade each of his own private stock of reason; because we suspect that this stock in each man is small, and that the individuals would do better to avail themselves of the general bank and capital of nations and of ages. Many of our men of speculation, instead of exploding general prejudices, employ their sagacity to discover the latent wisdom which prevails in them. If they find what they seek, and they seldom fail, they think it more wise to continue the prejudice, with the reason involved, than to cast away the coat of prejudice, and to leave nothing but the naked reason; because prejudice, with its reason, has a motive to give action to that reason, and an affection which will give it permanence. Prejudice is of ready application in the emergency; it previously engages the mind in a steady course of wisdom and virtue, and does not leave the man hesitating in the moment of decision, sceptical, puzzled, and unresolved. Prejudice renders a man's virtue his habit; and not a series of unconnected acts. Through just prejudice, his duty becomes a part of his nature.

Your literary men, and your politicians, and so do the whole clan of the enlightened among us, essentially differ in these points. They have no respect for the wisdom of others; but they pay it off by a very full measure of confidence in their own. With them it is a sufficient motive to destroy an old scheme of things, because it is an old one. As to the new, they are in no sort of fear with regard to the duration of a building run up in haste; because duration is no object to those who think little or nothing has been done before their time, and who place all their hopes in discovery. They conceive, very systematically, that all things which give perpetuity are mischievous, and therefore they are at inexpiable war with all establishments. They think that government may vary like modes of dress, and with as little ill effect: that there need be no principle of attachment, except a sense of present conveniency, to any constitution of the state. They always speak as if they were of opinion that there is a singular species of compact between them and their magistrates, which binds the magistrate, but which has nothing reciprocal in it, but that the majesty of the people has a right to dissolve it without any reason, but its will. Their attachment to their country itself is only so far as it agrees with some of their fleeting projects; it begins and ends with that scheme of polity which falls in with their momentary opinion.

These doctrines, or rather sentiments, seem prevalent with your new statesmen. But they are wholly different from those on which we have always acted in this country.

Joseph de Maistre

Burke was writing from the safety of England. Another reaction to the French Revolution came from a man more closely touched by it. Joseph de Maistre (1753–1821) had to flee his home in Savoy because he refused to swear allegiance to the French Republic, which had conquered it from his master, the king of Sardinia. From 1803 to 1817 he served as Sardinia's envoy to the Russian court, where he composed the Saint Petersburg Dialogs, *published in 1821—a series of conversations about evil, suffering, and sin, but also government ("every society has the government it deserves") and the principles on which society should be based (monarchy should be absolute, papal authority supreme).*

Maistre dismissed as ridiculous rationalist claims that laws and constitutions can be established according to abstract rules, with no reference to concrete conditions and historical experience. Revolutionary constitutions, he said, are made for "man." But there is no man; there are only Frenchmen, Italians, Russians—all different. Universal dreams and abstractions should be replaced by reference to the providential wisdom incarnated in the Church and to the lessons of experience recorded in history. It also helps to take a good hard look at the way things really work in society. Hence the first of the Dialogs *contains a celebrated passage in defense of capital punishment. Without the executioner, said Maistre, order would give place to anarchy.*

Human Justice

. . . Wishing men to be governed by men at least in their external actions, God has given sovereigns the supreme prerogative of punishing crimes, in which above all they are his representatives. . . .

This formidable prerogative of which I have just spoken results in the necessary existence of a man destined to inflict on criminals the punishments awarded by human justice; and this man is in fact found everywhere, without there being any means of explaining how; for reason cannot discern in human nature any motive which could lead men to this calling. I am sure, gentlemen, that you are too accustomed to reflection not to have pondered often on the executioner. Who is then this inexplicable being who has preferred to all the pleasant, lucrative, honest, and even honorable jobs that present themselves in hundreds to human power and dexterity that of torturing and putting to death his fellow creatures? Are this head and this heart made like ours? Do they not hold something peculiar and foreign to our nature? For my own part, I do not doubt this. He is made like us externally; he is born like us but he is an extraordinary being, and for him to exist in the human family a particular decree, a FIAT of the creative power is necessary. He is a species to himself. Look at the place he holds in public opinion and see if you can understand how he can ignore or affront this opinion! Scarcely have the authorities fixed his dwelling-place, scarcely has he taken possession of it, than the other houses seem to shrink back until they no longer overlook his. In the midst of this solitude and this kind of vacuum that forms around him, he lives alone with his woman and his offspring who make the human voice known to him, for without them he would know only groans. A dismal signal is given; a minor judicial official comes to his house to warn him that he is needed; he leaves; he arrives at some public place packed with a dense and throbbing crowd. A poisoner, a parricide, or a blasphemer is thrown to him; he seizes him, he stretches him on the ground, he ties him to a horizontal cross, he raises it up: then a dreadful silence falls, and nothing can be heard except the crack of bones breaking under the crossbar and the howls of the victim. He unfastens him; he carries him to a wheel: the shattered limbs interweave with the spokes; the head falls; the hair stands on end, and the mouth, open like a furnace, gives out spasmodically only a few blood-splattered words calling for death to come. He is finished: his heart flutters, but it is with joy; he congratulates himself, he says sincerely, *No one can break men on the wheel better than I.* He steps down; he stretches out his blood-stained hand, and justice throws into it from a distance a few pieces of gold which he carries through a double row of men drawing back with horror. He sits down to a meal and eats; then to bed, where he sleeps. And next day, on waking, he thinks of anything other than what he did the day before. Is this a man? Yes: God receives him in his temples and permits him to pray. He is not a criminal, yet it is impossible to say, for example, that he *is virtuous, that he is an honest man, that he is estimable,* and so on. No moral praise can be appropriate for him, since this assumes relationships with men, and he has none.

And yet all grandeur, all power, all subordination rests on the executioner: he is the horror and the bond of human association. Remove this incomprehensible agent from the world, and at that very moment order gives way to chaos, thrones topple, and society disappears. God, who is the author of sovereignty, is the author also of chastisement: he has built our world on these two poles: *for Jehovah is the master of the two poles, and on these he makes the world turn.*

Thus there is in the temporal sphere a visible and divine law for the punishment of crime, and this law, as stable as the society it upholds, has been carried out invariably from the beginning of time. Evil exists on the earth and acts constantly, and by a necessary consequence it must be continually repressed by punishment; indeed, we see over the whole globe constant action by every government to prevent or punish criminal outrages. The sword of justice has no scabbard; it must always threaten or strike. What then do these complaints about the *impunity of crime* mean? For whom are the knout, the gallows, the wheels, and the stakes? Obviously for the criminal. The mistakes of courts are exceptions that do not shake the rule: I have, besides, several reflections to offer to you on this point. In the first place, these fatal errors are much less frequent than is imagined. If it is allowed to doubt, opinion is always contrary to authority, and the public ear listens avidly to the slightest suggestions of a judicial murder; a thousand individual passions can fortify this general inclination. . . .

That an innocent dies is a misfortune like any other; that is to say, it is common to all mankind. That a guilty man escapes is another exception of the same kind. But it always remains true, generally speaking, *that there is on the earth a universal and visible order for the temporal punishment of crimes;* and I must again draw your attention to the fact that criminals do not by any means cheat justice so often as might be ingenuously supposed in view of the infinite precautions they take to avoid it. There is often in the circumstances that betray the most cunning scoundrels something so unexpected, so surprising, so unforeseeable, that men who are called by their position or reflections to follow this kind of affair tend to believe that human justice is not entirely without a certain supernatural assistance in seeking out the guilty.

Allow me to add one more consideration to bring to an end this chronicle of punishments. Just as it is very possible for us to be wrong when we accuse human justice of sparing the guilty, since those we regard as being such are not really guilty, so it is equally possible on the other side that a man punished for a crime he has not committed has actually merited it by another completely unknown crime. Fortunately and unfortunately, there are several examples of this kind of thing shown by the confessions of criminals, and there are many more, I believe, of which we are ignorant. This last supposition deserves especially close attention, for, although in such a case the judges are extremely blameworthy or unfortunate, Providence, for whom everything, even an obstacle, is a means, makes full use of dishonesty or mistakes to execute the temporal justice we demand; and it is certain that these two suppositions restrict considerably the number of exceptions.

Reestablishing Peace in Europe

When Napoleon had been defeated for a second and final time, the tsar, the Austrian emperor, and the king of Prussia signed the famous treaty known as the Holy Alliance in September 1815. In time other European monarchs adhered to it; only the pope and the prince regent, the future George IV of England, steadfastly refused to sign. The alliance has been mistakenly regarded as the chief bond of unity among the conservative powers in their struggle against a revival of liberal ideas. In reality, it was signed chiefly in order to humor Alexander I of Russia, with whom the idea originated, and it functioned effectively only in terms of other, more concrete policies and interests, which may be followed in the memoranda of Metternich.

The Holy Alliance (1815)

In the Name of the very Holy and Indivisible Trinity.

Their majesties, the Emperor of Austria, the King of Prussia and the Emperor of Russia, in view of the great events which the last three years have brought to pass in Europe and in view especially of the benefits which it has pleased Divine Providence to confer upon those states whose governments have placed their confidence and their hope in Him alone, having reached the profound conviction that the policy of the powers, in their mutual relations, ought to be guided by the sublime truths taught by the eternal religion of God our Saviour, solemnly declare that the present act has no other aim than to manifest to the world their unchangeable determination to adopt no other rule of conduct, either in the government of their respective countries or in their holy religion, than the precepts of justice, charity and peace. These, far from being applicable exclusively to private life, ought on the contrary directly to control the resolutions of princes and to guide their steps as the sole means of establishing human institutions and of remedying their imperfections. Hence their majesties have agreed upon the following articles:

Article I. Conformably to the words of Holy Scripture which command all men to look upon each other as brothers, the three contracting monarchs will continue united by the bonds of a true and indissoluble fraternity, and regarding themselves as compatriots, they will lend aid and assistance to each other on all occasions and in all places; viewing themselves, in their relations to their subjects and to their armies, as fathers of families, they will direct them in that spirit of fraternity by which they are animated, for the protection of religion, peace and justice.

Article II. Hence the sole principle of conduct, be it between the said governments or their subjects, shall be that of rendering mutual service, and testifying by unceasing good-will, the mutual affection with which they should be animated. Considering themselves all as members of one great Christian nation, the three allied princes look upon themselves as delegates of Providence called upon to govern three branches of the same family, viz: Austria, Russia and Prussia. They thus confess that the Christian nation, of which they and their people form a part, has in reality no other sovereign than He alone to whom belongs by right the power, for in Him alone are to be found all the treasures of love, of knowledge and of infinite wisdom, that is to say God, our Divine Saviour, Jesus Christ, the word of the most High, the word of life. Their majesties recommend, therefore, to their peoples, as the sole means of enjoying that peace which springs from a good conscience and is alone enduring, to fortify themselves each day in the principles and practice of those duties which the Divine Saviour has taught to men.

Article III. All those powers who wish solemnly to make avowal of the sacred principles which have dictated the present act, and who would recognize how important it is to the happiness of nations, too long agitated, that these truths should hereafter

From *Translations and Reprints,* I, No. 3, J. H. Robinson, Ed.

exercise upon human destiny all the influence belonging to them, shall be received into this Holy Alliance with as much cordiality as affection.

Engrossed in three copies and signed at Paris, year of grace 1815, September 14–26.

Signed: Francis
Frederick William
Alexander

Metternich: From Memoirs

Clement-Wenceslas, Prince Metternich (1773–1859), was born at Coblenz, in the Rhineland, but entered the service of the house of Habsburg and married the daughter of Kaunitz, the trusted chancellor of Empress Maria Theresa. After Kaunitz's death, Metternich managed the destinies of the Austrian Empire through the Napoleonic period, until his own overthrow in the revolution of 1848. It was Metternich who arranged the marriage between Napoleon and the Austrian archduchess Marie Louise, but after Napoleon's fall he became the leading influence in the Austro-Prussian-Russian alliance that was to dominate Europe at least until 1830, and the chief supporter of reactionary policies designed to wipe out all traces of the revolutionary tide that had advanced over Europe only a short while before.

CONFESSION OF FAITH PRESENTED AS A SECRET MEMORANDUM
TO EMPEROR ALEXANDER I OF RUSSIA ON DECEMBER 15, 1820

Having now cast a rapid glance over the first causes of the present state of society, it is necessary to point out in a more particular manner the evil which threatens to deprive it, at one blow, of the real blessings, the fruits of genuine civilization, and to disturb it in the midst of its enjoyments. This evil may be described in one word: presumption; the natural effect of the rapid progression of the human mind towards the perfecting of so many things. This it is which at the present day leads so many individuals astray, for it has become an almost universal sentiment.

Religion, morality, legislation, economy, politics, administration, all have become common and accessible to everyone. Knowledge seems to come by inspiration; exception has no value for the presumptuous man; faith is nothing to him; he substitutes for it a pretended individual conviction, and to arrive at this conviction dispenses with all inquiry and with all study; for these means appear too trivial to a mind which believes itself strong enough to embrace at one glance all questions and facts. Laws have no value for him, because he has not contributed to make them. . . . Power resides in himself; why should he submit himself to that which was only useful for the man deprived of light and knowledge? . . . Presumption makes of every man the guide of his own belief, the arbiter of laws according to which he is pleased to govern himself,

From Metternich, *Memoirs*, 5 vol. (New York, 1880–1881), I, 458–475; III, 655.

or to allow some one else to govern him and his neighbors; it makes him, in short, the sole judge of his own faith, his own actions, and the principles according to which he guides them. . . .

We look upon it as a fundamental truth, that for every disease there is a remedy, and that the knowledge of the real nature of the one should lead to the discovery of the other. Few men, however, stop thoroughly to examine a disease which they intend to combat. There are hardly any who are not subject to the influence of passion, or held under the yoke of prejudice; there are a great many who err in a way more perilous still, on account of its flattering and often brilliant appearance; we speak of *l'esprit de système*,[1] that spirit always false but indefatigable, audacious and irrepressible, is satisfactory to men imbued with it (for they live and govern a world created by themselves), but it is so much the more dangerous for the inhabitants of the real world, so different from that created by *l'esprit de système*.

There is another class of men who, judging of a disease by its outward appearance, confound the accessory manifestations with the root of the disease, and, instead of directing their efforts to the source of the evil, content themselves with subduing some passing symptoms.

It is our duty to try and avoid both of these dangers.

The evil exists and it is enormous. We do not think we can better define it and its cause at all times and in all places than we have already done by the word "presumption," that inseparable companion of the half-educated, that spring of an unmeasured ambition, and yet easy to satisfy in times of trouble and confusion.

It is principally the middle classes of society which this moral gangrene has affected, and it is only among them that the real heads of the party are found.

Men in the higher classes of society who join the revolution are either falsely ambitious men, or, in the widest acceptation of the word, lost spirits. Their career, moreover, is generally short! They are the first victims of political reforms, and the part played by the small number among them who survive is mostly that of courtiers despised by upstarts, their inferiors, promoted to the first dignities of the State; and of this France, Germany, Italy, and Spain furnish a number of living examples. . . .

In all four countries the agitated classes are principally composed of wealthy men—real cosmopolitans, securing their personal advantage at the expense of any order of things whatever—paid State officials, men of letters, lawyers, and the individuals charged with the public education. To these classes may be added that of the falsely ambitious, whose number is never considerable among the lower orders, but is larger in the higher ranks of society.

There is besides scarcely any epoch which does not offer a rallying cry to some particular fashion. This cry, since 1815, has been *Constitution*. But do not let us deceive ourselves; this word, susceptible of great latitude of interpretation, would be but imperfectly understood if we supposed that the factions attached quite the same meaning to it under the different *regimes*. Such is certainly not the case. In pure monarchies it is qualified by the name of "national representation." In countries which have

---

[1] a systematic approach.

lately been brought under the representative *regime* it is called "development," and promises charters and fundamental laws. In the only State which possesses an ancient national representation it takes "reform" as its object. Everywhere it means change and trouble.

In pure monarchies it may be paraphrased thus: "The level of equality shall pass over your heads; your fortunes shall pass into other hands; your ambitions which have been satisfied for centuries, now shall give place to our ambitions, which have been hitherto repressed."

In the States under a new *regime* they say: "The ambitions satisfied yesterday must give place to those of the morrow, and this is the morrow for us."

Lastly, in England, the only place in the third class, the rallying cry—that of Reform—combines the two meanings.

The Governments having lost their balance, are frightened, intimidated, and thrown into confusion by the cries of the intermediary class of society, which, placed between the Kings and their subjects, breaks the sceptre of the monarch, and usurps the cry of the people—that class so often disowned by the people, and nevertheless too much listened to, caressed and feared by those who could with one word reduce it again to nothingness.

We see this intermediary class abandon itself with a blind fury and animosity which proves much more its own fears than any confidence in the success of its enterprises, to all the means which seem proper to assuage its thirst for power, applying itself to the task of persuading Kings that their rights are confined to sitting upon a throne, while those of the people are to govern, and to attack all that centuries have bequeathed as holy and worthy of man's respect—denying, in fact, the value of the past, and declaring themselves, the masters of the future. We see this class take all sorts of disguises, uniting and subdividing as occasion offers, helping each other in the hour of danger, and the next day depriving each other of all their conquests. It takes possession of the press, and employs it to promote impiety, disobedience to the laws of religions and the State, and goes so far as to preach murder as a duty of those who desire what is good.

We are convinced that society can no longer be saved without strong and vigorous resolutions on the part of the Governments still free in their opinions and actions. We are also convinced that this may yet be, if the Governments face the truth, if they free themselves from all illusion, if they join their ranks and take their stand on a line of correct, unambiguous, and frankly announced principles.

By this course the monarchs may fulfil the duties imposed upon them by Him, who by entrusting them with power, has charged them to watch over the maintenance of justice, and the rights of truth. Placed beyond the passions which agitate society, it is in days of trial chiefly that they are called upon to despoil realities of their false appearances, and to show themselves as they are, fathers invested with the authority belonging by right to the heads of families, to prove that, in days of mourning, they know how to be just, wise, and therefore strong, and that they will not abandon the people whom they ought to govern to be the sport of factions, to error and its consequences, which must involve the loss of society. The moment in which we are putting our thoughts on paper is one of these critical moments. The crisis is great; it will be decisive to the part we take or do not take.

There is a rule of conduct common to individuals and to States, established by the experience of centuries as by that of everyday life. This rule declares "that one must not dream of reformation while agitated by passion; wisdom directs that at such moments we should limit ourselves to maintaining."

Let the monarchs vigorously adopt this principle; let all their resolutions bear the impression of it. Let their actions, their measures, and even their words announce and prove to the world this determination—they will find allies everywhere. The Governments, in establishing the principle of *stability,* will in no wise exclude the development of what is good, for stability is not immobility. But it is for those who are burdened with the heavy task of government to augment the well-being of their people! It is for Governments to regulate it according to necessity and to suit the times. It is not by concessions, which the factious strive to force from legitimate power, and which they have neither the right to claim nor the faculty of keeping within just bounds, that wise reforms can be carried out. That all the good possible should be done is our most ardent wish; but that which is not good must never be confounded with that which is, and even real good should be done only by those who unite to the right of authority the means of enforcing it. Such should be also the sincere wish of the people, who know by sad experience the value of certain phrases and the nature of certain caresses. . . .

The first principle to be followed by the monarchs, united as they are by the coincidence of their desires and opinions, should be that of maintaining the stability of political institutions against the disorganized excitement which has taken possession of men's minds; the immutability of principles against the madness of their interpretation; and respect for laws actually in force against a desire for their destruction.

The hostile faction is divided into two very distinct parties. One is that of the Levellers; the other, that of the Doctrinaires. United in times of confusion, these men are divided in times of inaction. It is for Governments to understand and estimate them at their just value.

In the class of Levellers there are found men of strong will and determination. The Doctrinaires can count none such among their ranks. If the first are more to be feared in action, the second are more dangerous in that time of deceitful calm which precedes it; as with physical storms, so with those of social order. Given up to abstract ideas inapplicable to real wants, and generally in contradiction to those very wants, men of this class unceasingly agitate the people by their imaginary or simulated fears, and disturb Governments in order to make them deviate from the right path. The world desires to be governed by facts and according to justice, not by phrases and theories; the first need of society is to be maintained by strong authority (no authority without real strength deserves the name) and not to govern itself. In comparing the number of contests between parties in mixed Governments, and that of just complaints caused by aberrations of power in a Christian State, the comparison would not be in favor of the new doctrines. The first and greatest concern for the immense majority of every nation is the stability of the laws, and their uninterrupted action—never their change. Therefore let the Governments govern, let them maintain the groundwork of their institutions, both ancient and modern; for if it is at all times dangerous to touch them, it certainly would not now, in the general confusion, be wise to do so.

Let them announce this determination to their people, and demonstrate it by facts. Let them reduce the Doctrinaires to silence within their States, and show their contempt for them abroad. Let them not encourage by their attitude or actions the suspicion of being favorable or indifferent to error; let them not allow it to be believed that experience has lost all its rights to make way for experiments which at the least are dangerous. Let them be precise and clear in all their words, and not seek by concessions to gain over those parties who aim at the destruction of all power but their own, whom concessions will never gain over, but only further embolden in their pretensions to power.

Romantics and Romanticism

L ATE in the eighteenth century a reaction against the straitness and formalism of the dominant classical style encouraged the rise of a new attitude which we know as romantic. Romanticism is the antithesis of everything the eighteenth century appreciated in Pope and in Voltaire; it spurns order, reason, and impersonality in favor of impulse, dreams, mystery, and originality. Inspiration is found not in classical models of perfection but in varied, vital nature and in the observation of nature rather than its merely reasonable interpretation in the vast generalities dear to the heart of an earlier period.

The new fashion was popularized by the writings of Samuel Richardson (*Pamela*, 1740), Rousseau (*The New Héloïse*, 1761), and Goethe (*Werther*, 1774), but only became culturally dominant in the 1820s. During these years an older generation of romantic writers (Goethe, Wordsworth, Chateaubriand) coincided with a younger (Byron, Shelley, Hugo, Vigny), much more turbulent generation. However, the general characteristics of the romantic mood should be apparent in the following passages.

Goethe

Wolfgang von Goethe (1749–1832) is certainly the most accomplished man that Germany ever produced. Poet, scientist, dramatist, and statesman, he started his career in the 1770s with a verse play, Götz von Berlichingen, *and a novel presented as a series of letters,* The Sorrows of Young Werther, *which turned him into a symbol and leader of the angry and inspired young men of the German* Sturm und Drang *("storm and stress") movement. He never managed to outlive or equal his early fame, though he still had two-thirds of his life to live and his greatest work still to write in, for instance,* Faust *and* Wilhelm Meister. *He is more of a transitional figure than a pure romantic, and yet the remarks below well reflect a characteristic romantic attitude.*

From Poetry and Truth

... Voltaire, the wonder of his time, had grown old, along with the literature of which, for nearly a century, he had been the animating and ruling spirit. By his side there still existed many *littérateurs,* vegetating in a more or less active and happy old age, and then disappearing in their turn one by one. The influence of society upon authors

From Goethe, *Poetry and Truth,* tr. M. S. Smith (London: G. Bell & Sons, Ltd., 1908), II, 33–40, 301–303.

increased more and more; for the best society, consisting of persons of birth, rank, and property, chose literature as one of their chief recreations, making it entirely social and genteel in tone. Persons of rank and literary men mutually cultivated and of necessity mutually perverted one another; for the genteel is naturally exclusive; that is what French criticism became, negative, detracting, and fault-finding. The upper classes applied this kind of criticism to authors; the authors, with somewhat less decorum, used the same procedure towards each other, and even towards their patrons. If the public was not to be awed, they endeavoured to take it by surprise, or to persuade it by humility; and thus—apart from the movements which shook church and state to their inmost core—there arose such a literary ferment, that Voltaire himself had to strain to the utmost all the resources of his activity, and of his literary dictatorship, to keep himself afloat above the torrent of universal censure. As it was, he was openly called an old self-willed child; his indefatigable endeavours were regarded as the vain efforts of decrepit age; those principles, for which he had stood all his life, and to the spread of which he had devoted his days, were no longer held in honour or esteem: nay, that very Deity he acknowledged, and so continued to declare himself free from atheism, was discredited; and thus he himself, the venerable patriarch, was forced, like his youngest competitor, to watch the present moment, to sue for fresh favours—to show too much love to his friends, too much hate to his enemies; and under the appearance of a passionate striving after truth, to act deceitfully and falsely. Was it worth while to have led such a great and active life, if it was to end in greater dependence than it had begun? His high spirit, his delicate sensitiveness, felt only too keenly the galling nature of such a position. He often relieved himself by swift onslaughts, gave the reins to his humour, and exceeded all bounds,—at which both friends and enemies showed themselves indignant; for everyone thought himself capable of gauging him, though none could equal him. A public which hears only the judgment of old men, becomes over-wise too soon; and nothing is more unsatisfactory than a mature judgment adopted by an immature mind.

We young men, with our German love of truth and nature, considered honesty towards ourselves and others as the best guide in life and art; hence Voltaire's factious dishonesty and his constant perversion of noble subjects became more and more distasteful to us, and our aversion to him grew daily. He seemed never to have done with degrading religion and the Holy Scriptures on which it rests, for the sake of injuring priestcraft, as they called it, and had thereby awakened in me feelings of irritation. But when I now learned that, to weaken the tradition of a deluge, he had denied the existence of all fossilized shells, and admitted them only as *lusus naturae*,[1] he entirely lost my confidence; for my own eyes had shown me on the Bastberg, plainly enough, that I stood on what had been the floor of an ancient sea, among the *exuviae*[2] of its original inhabitants. These mountains had certainly been once covered with waves, whether before or during the deluge did not concern me; it was enough that the valley of the Rhine had been one vast lake, a bay extending further than eye could see; no amount

---

[1] Jokes or games played by nature.

[2] remnants, remains.

of talk could shake me in this conviction. I hoped, rather to extend my knowledge of lands and mountains, let the result be what it would. . . .

What I have here tried to state connectedly and in a few words was, at the time I speak of, the cry of the moment, a perpetual discord in our ears, unconnected and uninstructive. Nothing was heard but the praise of those who had gone before. The demand was continually for something good and new; yet the newest never found favour. . . .

If we heard the encyclopedists mentioned, or opened a volume of their colossal work, we felt as if we were moving amidst the innumerable whirling spools and looms of a great factory, where, what with the mere creaking and rattling—what with all the mechanism, bewildering both to eyes and brain—what with the mere impossibility of understanding how the various parts fit in and work with one another—what with the contemplation of all that is necessary to prepare a single piece of cloth, we felt disgusted with the very coat we wore upon our backs.

Diderot was sufficiently akin to us, as, indeed, in all the points for which the French blame him, he is a true German. But even his point of view was too lofty, his range of vision too wide for us to be able to rise to his height and place ourselves at his side. Yet the children of nature he continued to produce and to ennoble by his great rhetorical art delighted us: we were enchanted with his brave poachers and smugglers; and this rabble throve later only too well on the German Parnassus. He, too, like Rousseau, by diffusing a disgust of social life, unobtrusively paved the way for those monstrous world-wide changes, in which all that had hitherto existed seemed to be swallowed up.

However, we should now put aside these considerations, and observe what influence these two men have had upon art. Here, too, they pointed to nature and urged us to turn from art and follow her.

The highest problem of all art is to produce by illusion the semblance of a higher reality. But it is a false endeavour to push the realization of the illusion so far that at last only a commonplace reality remains. . . .

We had neither desire nor inclination to be enlightened or advanced by the aid of philosophy; on religious subjects we thought we had sufficiently enlightened ourselves, and therefore looked on with comparative indifference at the violent contest between the French philosophers and the priesthood. Prohibited books condemned to the flames, of which so much was heard at the time, produced no effect upon us. I mention as a typical instance, the *Système de la Nature* [of Holbach] which we looked into out of curiosity. We did not understand how such a book could be dangerous. It seemed to us so gloomy, so Cimmerian, so deathlike, that we found it difficult to endure its presence, and shuddered at it as at a spectre. The author fancies he is giving his book a great recommendation, when he declares in his preface, that as a decrepit old man, just sinking into the grave, he is anxious to announce the truth to his contemporaries and to posterity.

We laughed at him; for we thought we had observed that old people are incapable of appreciating whatever is good and loveable in the world. "Old churches have dark windows.—To know how cherries and berries taste, we must ask children and sparrows." These were our gibes and maxims; and so that book, as the very quintessence of senility, seemed to us insipid, or even offensive. "All had of necessity to be," so said the book, "and therefore there was no God." But could not God also exist of necessity? we asked. We did indeed admit, at the same time, that we could not escape from the necessities of day and night, the seasons, the influence of climate, and from physical and animal conditions; but nevertheless we felt within us something that seemed like perfect freedom of will, and again something which sought to counter-balance this freedom.

We could not give up the hope of becoming more and more rational, of making ourselves more and more independent of external things, and even of ourselves. The word freedom has so fair a sound, that we cannot dispense with it, even though it designates an error.

None of us had read the book through; for it had disappointed the expectation with which we opened it. It had announced a system of nature; and we had, therefore, hoped really to learn something of nature—of this idol of ours. Physics and chemistry, descriptions of heaven and earth, natural history and anatomy, with much besides, had now for years, and up to this very moment, constantly pointed us to the great world and its wealth of beauty; and we would fain have heard more, both in particular and in general, of suns and stars, planets and moons, mountains, valleys, rivers and seas, with all that live and move in them. That in the course of such an exposition much must occur which would appear to the common man as pernicious, to the clergy as dangerous, and to the state as inadmissible, we had no doubt; and we hoped that the small volume had not unworthily undergone the fiery ordeal. But how hollow and empty did we feel this melancholy, atheistic half-night to be, where earth vanished with all its creatures, heaven with all its stars. Matter was supposed to have existed and to have been in motion from all eternity, and to this motion, to right and to left and in every direction, were attributed the infinite phenomena of existence. We might have allowed even so much to pass, if the author, out of his matter in motion, had really built up the world before our eyes. But he seemed to know as little about nature as we did; for, after simply propounding some general ideas, he forthwith disregards them in order to change what seems above nature, or a higher nature within nature, into matter with weight and motion but without aim or shape—and by this he fancies he has gained much.

If this book did us any harm at all, it was in giving us a hearty and lasting dislike to all philosophy, and especially to metaphysics; while, on the other hand, we threw ourselves into living knowledge, experience, action, and poetry, with all the more zeal and ardour.

Thus, on the very borders of France, we had at one blow got rid of everything French about us. The French way of life was too definite and too genteel for us, their poetry cold, their criticism annihilating, their philosophy abstruse, and yet unsatisfying. . . .

In the course of this biography we have shown in detail how the child, the boy, the youth, sought by various ways to approach the supernatural; first, looking with strong inclination to a religion of nature; then, clinging with love to a positive one; and, finally, concentrating himself in the trial of his own powers and joyfully giving himself up to a general faith. Whilst he wandered to and fro, seeking and looking about him, in the intervals which lay between these several phases, he met with much that would not fit into any of them, and he seemed to realize more and more clearly the desirability of turning his thoughts away from the immense and incomprehensible.

He thought he could detect in nature—both animate and inanimate, with soul and without soul—something which manifested itself only in contradictions, and which, therefore, could not be comprehended under any idea, still less under one word. It was not godlike, for it seemed without reason; nor human, for it had no understanding; nor devilish, for it was beneficent; nor angelic, for it often betrayed a malicious pleasure. It resembled chance, for it evinced no succession; it was like Providence, for it hinted at connection. It seemed to penetrate all that limits us; it seemed to deal arbitrarily with the necessary elements of our existence; it contracted time and expanded space. In the impossible alone did it appear to find pleasure, while it rejected the possible with contempt.

To this principle, which seemed to come in between all other principles and separate them, and yet link them together, I gave the name of Daemonic, after the example of the ancients and others with similar experiences. I sought to escape from this terrible principle, by taking refuge, according to my wont, in a creation of the imagination.

Among the parts of history which I had particularly studied, were the events that made the countries which subsequently became the United Netherlands so famous. I had diligently examined the original sources, and had endeavoured, as far as possible, to get my facts at first hand, and to bring the whole period vividly before me. The situations it presented appeared to me to be in the highest degree dramatic, while Count Egmont, whose greatness as a man and a hero most captivated me, seemed to me a suitable central figure round whom the others might be grouped with happiest effect.

But for my purpose it was necessary to convert him into a character marked by such peculiarities as would grace a youth better than a man in years, and an unmarried man better than the father of a family; a man leading an independent life, rather than one, who, however free in thought, is nevertheless restrained by the various relations of life.

Having then, in my conception of Egmont's character, made him youthful, and freed him from all fettering restraints, I gave him unlimited love of life, boundless self-reliance, a gift of attracting all men, enabling him to win the favour of the people, the unspoken attachment of a princess, the avowed passion of a child of nature, the sympathy of a shrewd politician, and even the loving admiration of the son of his greatest adversary. The personal courage which distinguishes the hero is the foundation upon which his whole character rests, the ground whence it springs. He knows no danger, and is blind to the greatest peril when it confronts him.

When surrounded by enemies, we may, at need, cut our way through them; the meshes of state policy are harder to break. The Daemonic element, which plays a part on both sides, in conflict with which what is loveable falls while what is hated triumphs; further the prospect that out of this conflict will spring a third element, and fulfil the wishes of all men;—this perhaps is what has gained for the piece (not, indeed, on its first appearance, but later and in due time), the favour which it still enjoys. Here, therefore, for the sake of many dear readers, I will forestall myself, and as I do not know when I shall have another opportunity, will express a conviction, which did not become clear to me till a later date.

Although this Daemonic element manifests itself in all corporeal and incorporeal things, and even expresses itself most distinctly in animals, yet it is primarily in its relation to man that we observe its mysterious workings, which represent a force, if not antagonistic to the moral order, yet running counter to it, so that the one may be regarded as the warp, and the other as the woof.

For the phenomena which result there are innumerable names; for all philosophies and religions have sought in prose and poetry to solve this enigma and to read once for all the riddle; and may they still continue to seek.

But the most fearful manifestation of the Daemonic is when it is seen predominating in some individual character. During my life I have observed several instances, either closely or at a distance. Such persons are not always the most eminent men, either in intellect or special gifts, and they are seldom distinguished by goodness of heart; a tremendous energy seems to emanate from them, and they exercise a wonderful power over all creatures, and even over the elements; and, indeed, who shall say how much further such influence may extend? All the moral powers combined are of no avail against them; in vain does the more enlightened portion of mankind attempt to throw suspicion upon them as dupes or as deceivers—the masses are attracted by them. Seldom if ever do they find their equals among their contemporaries; nothing can vanquish them but the universe itself, with which they have begun the fray.

Friedrich Hölderlin

Though little known outside Germany, Johann Christian Friedrich Hölderlin (1770–1843) provides one of the major links between the classical and romantic schools of literature in that country. Influenced by the poetry of Schiller and of the ancient Greeks, his work was lyrical and highly subjective, and his themes often referred to classical times.

As a young man, Hölderlin earned his living as a private tutor. An unhappy love affair deranged his high-strung mind. He would live to the age of seventy-three, but the last forty years of his life were passed in an advanced state of schizophrenia, with brief recoveries during which his poetry was as magnificent as ever. Hyperion, written before this disaster, between 1797 and 1799, is a strange, elegiac novel about a Grecian hermit sage and his considerations on the ways of the world. The penultimate letter of the book, which follows, vents certain uncomplimentary views on his German countrymen.

From Hyperion

I do not know who once said that the virtues of the ancients are nothing but brilliant vices; but it is truer to say that their faults themselves are virtues, for a spirit of youth

---

From the *Letters of Hyperion to Bellarmin* (Leipzig, 1822), the penultimate letter, tr. Eugen Weber.

and beauty is still alive in them and, without this spirit, they would not have accomplished all that they have. The virtues of the Germans, on the other hand, are the brilliant reverse of a vice, and nothing more; for they are of necessity, forcibly drawn from the desert of the heart, in heavy slavery, by a fear born of cowardice. The pure soul, which would so wish to find its nourishment in beauty, they leave it without consolation. Alas! used as it is to the sacred harmony of all noble natures, it cannot endure the cacophony that breaks out everywhere throughout the dead order of these humans.

I tell you this: there is nothing sacred which is not profaned, in this people, not lowered to sordidly utilitarian ends; and even that which, most of the time, savages maintain pure and divine these barbarians, who are accountants above all, deal with as if it were a trade. What else could they do? Since, with them, hardly has a man grown up than he has to serve a useful purpose and earn money; no more enthusiasm, God save us! and no more dreams: settled, besotted, that is how he remains even in his rejoicings, his loves, his prayers. Even in the graces of spring, in the time of universal reconciliation and freedom from care, when even the guilty heart miraculously rediscovers its first innocence and when, under the caress of the sun's warm rays, the merry slave comes to forget his chains, when even misanthropists, disarmed by the divine breath of the breeze, become sweet as children—yea, when even caterpillars find wings and the hive swarms, the German, for his part, stays in his place, shut up, keeps to his specialty and gives not a hoot for the weather!

But you, Holy Nature, shall judge him! For this humanity could at least be modest enough not to impose its law on the best among it! It could at least avoid denouncing that which it is not and, at the very least, not blaspheme God in its denigrations.

For is it not the divine which you mock and hold to be without a soul? And the air on which you feed, is it not better than all your chatter? Has not the sunshine a greater price and a higher nobility than all your clever men? The springs of the earth and the dew refresh your meadows; can you do as much? Alas! to kill them, that you know how, but not to revivify them as love does, love which does not come from you, which you have not discovered. Your care and effort are to escape Destiny, when your childish arts—you will not understand it—are no use; and meanwhile, up there, the serene constellations accomplish their course. You degrade and ravage patient nature in the very places where it bears you; and yet its life continues in its endless youth, and you cannot abolish its spring or fall, nor soil its immaculate air.

O divine, how divine she must be for you to ravage her thus, yet without her ever growing old, and how splendid, despite you, remains her beauty!

It is a heartbreaking sight, also, to see your poets and artists and all those who still feel respect for Genius, still love and are devoted to Beauty. Poor miserable creatures! They are in the world like strangers in their own house, alike in every way to the patient Ulysses as he sat, in beggar's garb, before the gate of his own palace, the insolent suitors noisily asking: who brought us this tramp?

See them growing, filled with hope and love and intelligence, the young disciples of the Muse among this German people. But see them seven years later: they move like shadows, silent and frozen, and see them altogether like those arid lands which the enemy has sown with salt so that not the slightest blade of grass should ever grow on them again; or if they speak, woe to him who hears them! for he can only behold, in the unleashing of this titanic force, the changing and protean forms of the great and desperate struggle that a troubled spirit leads against the barbarians with whom he deals.

Nothing perfect here on earth, is the Germans' old song. But may someone come to tell these damned people, once for all, that if all is so imperfect with them it is because nothing pure exists which they do not soil, nothing sacred which they do not profane, with their big paws; and that nothing prospers with them because the root and providence of all success, which is divine nature, receives no respect from them; that life with them is altogether insipid, crushed down with cares, wholly the prey of cold and secret discord, because of the way in which they despise Genius—that Genius which introduces nobility and virtue into the human condition, serenity into suffering, communion and love into cities and homes.

And that is why they fear death so much, yes, that is why, in order to lead this life of molluscs, they suffer every infamy. They know nothing more sublime than the dreary shoddy works turned out by the hands of saboteurs.

Ah! Bellarmin, if only a people has the love of Beauty, if it may express, through its artists, devotion and reverence for Genius, then a spirit moves in it, the universal spirit, like a breath of life at whose touch heretofore intimidated personalities bloom, before which self-satisfied presumption retreats: and all hearts ripen to piety, to grandeur; enthusiasm flowers and heroes are born. Such a nation is the fatherland of all mankind and the stranger likes to draw out his stay there. But where, on the contrary, divine nature and its artists are so outraged, nothing of the best, nothing of joy of life remains, alas! and then my other planet is a better abode than this earth! Ever more desolate and arid become the men who yet are all born of equally noble origin; and one can see a servile mentality develop, a lackey-spirit, and with it the pride of the bully; drunkenness grows together with anxiety, and along with opulence hunger and fear of want increase; the benediction of every season turns to malediction, and all gods flee.

Indeed, woe to the stranger whom love of travel has brought as far as this nation, and woe, O! three times woe, to him who, like myself, moved by a great sorrow, has come to this people!

But enough! Knowing me, Bellarmin, you will not take this ill. I have spoken in your name too, as I have spoken for all those who are here, in this country, and who suffer in it as I have suffered myself.

August-Wilhelm Schlegel

August-Wilhelm Schlegel (1767–1845), the elder of two brothers who both left their mark on German letters, was responsible for introducing Madame de Staël to German literature and thus, perhaps, the French public to romanticism. More important, he naturalized Shakespeare in Germany with his great translation of the poet's works, and introduced German readers to Ariosto, Tasso, Petrarch, Camoens, the Ramayana, and the great plays of the Spanish theater. Quarrelling with his younger brother when the latter turned to

Catholicism, as other members of the romantic generation were doing, he spent the last years of his life publishing his works only in French.

Classic Art and Romantic Art

It is evident that the imperishable spirit of poesy acquires a different guise every time it reappears in the human race, and that in every age the habits and ideas of the different centuries provide it with a new and peculiar existence. The forms of poesy must change with the direction that the peoples' poetic imagination may take, and when one wants to apply the names of the old styles and their old rules to new compositions, to judge them according to these ideas, this is an ill-conceived usage of classical authority. None should be judged in a court under whose jurisdiction he does not come.

Ancient art and poetry never admitted the mixture of heterogeneous styles; the romantic spirit, on the contrary, enjoys a continual juxtaposition of the most diverse things. All the antinomies: nature and art, poetry and prose, seriousness and joking, memory and foreboding, abstract ideas and concrete sensations, the earthly and the divine, life and death, become one in the closest and most intimate union. . . . If ancient poesy, ancient art as a whole, are . . . a harmonious and regular revelation of the legislation forever fixed for an ideal world reflecting the eternal types of things, romantic poetry, on the contrary, is the expression of a mysterious secret aspiration towards the chaos that ever labors to conceive ever new and more wondrous things—that chaos which always subsists beneath the harmonious creation and hides even in its breast. Here the vivifying breath of the original love still floats above the waters.

The inspiration of the ancients was simple, clear, more alike to nature in its most isolated and most perfect works. The romantic genius, despite its fragmentary aspect and its apparent disorder, is yet nearer the mystery of the universe; for if *intelligence* can never grasp in every isolated thing more than a part of truth, *feeling* on the contrary, embracing everything, perceives and penetrates all in all.

To return to the dramatic style under discussion, one may compare ancient tragedy to the group in sculpture; in one and the other art equally, each figure corresponds to a character, and the action lies in the manner in which they are grouped: the characters and the action, it is solely on these two elements that attention is directed, since this alone is represented. As for romantic drama, one must present it as a painted scene, where there appear not only figures in the most varied attitudes and forming groups endowed with the richest, most diverse movements, but also objects surrounding the characters and even perspectives upon the distant horizon, so that the whole is bathed in a magic light which, precisely, determines and orients its singular effect.

Such a painting would be less circumscribed, less clearly framed than the plastic

---

From the thirteenth lesson of the Course on Dramatic Literature, delivered at Vienna, 1808; translated by Eugen Weber from the Collected Works of August-Wilhelm Schlegel, *Course on Dramatic Literature* (Leipzig, 1876).

group because it is, in effect, something like a fragment of the universal perspective. Nevertheless, by the framework within which he encloses his foreground, by the light which he focuses upon it, by still other means, the artist can attract and hold the beholder's gaze and avoid its being distracted or dissatisfied.

Painting cannot match sculpture in the reproduction of form, since it reproduces it only with the aid of an illusion and from only one point of view; but by means of color it gives this imitation more life, and its figures, by means of facial expression, express the most diverse feelings to their most delicate nuances. By the expression of a gaze, which sculpture can indicate only very imperfectly, painting can let us read far more profoundly in the heart and can reveal its most subtle movements. Above all, the peculiar charm of painting is to reveal those most immaterial aspects of material objects: light and air.

It is exactly this kind of beauty that is peculiar to romantic drama. To the contrary of ancient tragedy, the romantic play does not rigorously isolate the tragic element and the action of the elements of vital life: it resumes the whole show in its total variety and with its surroundings; and while it may seem to reproduce only fortuitously juxtaposed details, in fact it satisfies the unconscious rights of our imagination, and plunges us into a contemplative, meditative mood, by giving us the feeling of wonderful harmony and of the profound meaning connected with it, by the mixture and the bizarre appearance of its imitation of life. It lends, so to speak, a soul to the perspectives of appearance.

Letter to a French Friend[1]

At the time of my entry into the literary career, we carried on, my friends and I, an active campaign against the prosaic and negative tendencies of the time. We awakened the remembrance of the middle ages, of those centuries so vigorous and at the same time so full of faith. We brought back into poetry the Christian subjects which had gone so completely out of fashion. Protestantism does not lend itself at all to this sort of thing: witness Milton and Klopstock. Dante, whom I had studied thoroughly, and Calderon, whom I discovered later, are of quite a different nature. So one could not help drawing upon the traditions of the Roman Church. All the world admires the great painters who glorified the cosmogony and the patriarchal history of the Jews, ennobled the humble garments of the Scriptures, and veiled the absurdities of the legend. I retranslated, so to speak, into words some of the most beautiful picturesque subjects. It was an artist's predilection; and this connection is even more clearly marked in my poem: "The Alliance of the Church with the Fine Arts."

Among my friends, Novalis, audacious thinker, prophetic dreamer, visionary in the end, gave himself wholly over to the Christian faith, as a migratory bird, tired by its flight over an immense ocean, falls on to a small green island and there forgets the land whence it came and the vast spaces it had hoped to reach. However, he did not

---

[1] Written in French from Bonn, August 13, 1838.

change confession; his father had been a member of the Society of Moravian Brethren, and one could notice a hereditary tinge in the piety of his son. He died soon after.

I wanted to get to know the mystics, those exploring divers of consciousness and sensibility who sometimes bring back pearls from the bottom of the sea, and the theosophists, who discern the imprint of Christian doctrines throughout the whole of nature. And it is true that there are grains of gold in their writings, but in such strange company that, when they want to pass all this off as pure gold, it looks more like an alchemist's trick.

Returns to the old religion were becoming ever more frequent. Among painters, especially, abjuration at Rome had become almost an epidemic, One would be mistaken in thinking that I had any influence upon this.

For my part, I never seriously entertained the idea of contracting a solemn engagement, although I did not lack for solicitations. On the contrary, to the degree that my brother, Frédéric, was moving forward, I was drawing back. I can only blame myself for overmuch indulgence; but I expiated it by one of my life's bitterest sorrows. It was the divorce of the souls. Revolted by the role he played since 1819, as writer and as ally of the Jesuits, I ended by an open declaration of hostility, in the manner of the ancient Romans.

Let us admit that what we have seen in Europe since the peace [of 1815] does not encourage a new union with one of the two Christian communities. On one side, frightful reactions, efforts to submit mankind once more to the priestly yoke; on the other side, intolerance, separation, a pedantic morality which tries to pass itself off for holiness, finally all sorts of sects, one more extravagant than the other. It all surpasses belief, but the facts are there. I speak only of Germany.

Madame de Staël

The mother of Madame de Staël, Suzanne Curchod, daughter of a Swiss country parson, was reputed the most accomplished maiden of her province. Courted by Edward Gibbon, she eventually married a great Genevan banker, Jacques Necker, who soon took her to Paris, where she presided over his literary and philosophical salon while he presided over the finances of the monarchy. It was in that salon that little Germaine (1766–1817) first discovered the art of conversation and all the games that could be played with it. Words, she would explain on one occasion, are not just "a means to communicate ideas, feelings and needs, but an instrument one likes to play and which revives the spirit, just as does music in some nations, and strong liquors in others." Conversation, at its best, was "a certain way in which people act upon one another, a quick give-and-take of pleasure, a way of speaking as soon as one thinks, of rejoicing in oneself in the immediate present, of being applauded without making an effort, of displaying one's intelligence by every nuance of intonation, gesture and look— in short the ability to produce at will a kind of electricity which, emitting a shower of sparks, relieves the excess of liveliness in some and rouses others from their painful apathy."

Coming from a literary family, the young woman wrote—and she wrote well, all of her books having been talked before they were written. Talking a bit too much, she got on the wrong side of Napoleon, who exiled her from Paris. One sequel of this rather benign relegation was a trip to Germany that resulted in her book Concerning Germany, *published in 1810 and promptly banned by Napoleon. As a contemporary observed, there was more light in the book than there was clarity; but the chapters on literature and philosophy presented its readers (first in England, where it was published in 1813, and only later in France and elsewhere) with a loaded but suggestive picture of a romantic country and a romantic climate.*

Romanticism

The word *romantic* has been lately introduced in Germany, to designate that kind of poetry which is derived from the songs of the Troubadours; that which owes its birth to the union of chivalry and Christianity. It we do not admit that the empire of literature has been divided between paganism and Christianity, the north and the south, antiquity and the middle ages, chivalry and the institutions of Greece and Rome, we shall never succeed in forming a philosophical judgment of ancient and modern taste.

Some French critics have asserted that German literature is still in its infancy; this opinion is entirely false: men who are best skilled in the knowledge of languages, and the works of the ancients, are certainly not ignorant of the defects and advantages attached to the species of literature which they either adopt or reject; but their character, their habits, and their modes of reasoning have led them to prefer that which is founded on the recollection of chivalry, on the wonders of the middle ages, to that which has for its basis the mythology of the Greeks. The literature of romance is alone capable of further improvement, because, being rooted in our own soil, that alone can continue to grow and acquire fresh life: it expresses our religion; it recalls our history; its origin is ancient, although not of classical antiquity. Classic poetry, before it comes home to us, must pass through our recollections of paganism: that of the Germans is the Christian era of the fine arts; it employs our personal impressions to excite strong and vivid emotions; the genius by which it is inspired addresses itself immediately to our hearts, and seems to call forth the spirit of our own lives, of all phantoms at once the most powerful and the most terrible.

It is said there are persons who discover springs, hidden under the earth, by the nervous agitation which they cause in them: in German poetry, we often think we discover that miraculous sympathy between man and the elements. The German poet comprehends nature not only as a poet, but as a brother; and we might almost say that the bonds of family union connect him with the air, the water, flowers, trees—in short, all the primary beauties of the creation.

When I began the study of German literature, it seemed as if I was entering on a new sphere, where the most striking light was thrown on all that I had before perceived only in a confused manner. For some time past, little has been read in France except memoirs and novels, and it is not wholly from frivolity that we are become less capable

---

From *Concerning Germany* (London, 1814).

of more serious reading, but because the events of the revolution have accustomed us to value nothing but the knowledge of men and things: we find in German books, even on the most abstract subjects, that kind of interest which confers their value upon good novels, and which is excited by the knowledge which they teach us of our own hearts. The peculiar character of German literature, is to refer everything to an interior existence; and as that is the mystery of mysteries, it awakens an unbounded curiosity.

The new school maintains the same system in the fine arts as in literature, and affirms that Christianity is the source of all modern genius; the writers of this school also characterize, in a new manner, all that in Gothic architecture agrees with the religious sentiments of Christians. It does not follow however from this, that the moderns can and ought to construct Gothic churches; neither art nor nature admit of repetition; it is only of consequence to us, in the present silence of genius, to lay aside the contempt which has been thrown on all the conceptions of the middle ages; it certainly does not suit us to adopt them, but nothing is more injurious to the development of genius, than to consider as barbarous everything that is original.

William Blake

William Blake (1757–1827) was from the first a dreamer and a seer of visions. These he sought to reproduce in poems and plays of great simplicity and directness. His work, original and intense, was neglected and misunderstood by all but a few; but in the verses that follow, he reflects as well as anyone the anti-French, antirationalist reaction of the age.

"Mock on, Mock on, Voltaire, Rousseau" (1800–1810)

Mock on, mock on, Voltaire, Rousseau;
Mock on, mock on; 'tis all in vain!
You throw the sand against the wind,
And the wind blows it back again.

And every sand becomes a gem
Reflected in the beams divine;
Blown back they blind the mocking eye
But still in Israel's path they shine.

The Atoms of Democritus
And Newton's Particles of Light
Are sands upon the Red Sea shore
Where Israel's tents do shine so bright.

"The Tiger" (1794)

Tiger! Tiger! burning bright
In the forests of the night,
What immortal hand or eye
Could frame thy fearful symmetry?

In what distant deeps or skies
Burnt the fire of thine eyes?
On what wings dare he aspire?
What the hand dare seize the fire?

And what shoulder, and what art,
Could twist the sinews of thy heart?
And when thy heart began to beat,
What dread hand? and what dread feet?

What the hammer? what the chain?
In what furnace was thy brain?
What the anvil? what dread grasp
Dare its deadly terrors clasp?

When the stars threw down their spears,
And watered heaven with their tears,
Did he smile his work to see?
Did he who made the Lamb make thee?

Tiger! Tiger! burning bright
In the forests of the night,
What immortal hand or eye
Dare frame thy fearful symmetry?

"London" (1794)

I wander through each chartered street,
Near where the chartered Thames does flow,
And mark in every face I meet
Marks of weakness, marks of woe.

In every cry of every Man,
In every Infant's cry of fear,
In every voice, in every ban,
The mind-forged manacles I hear.

How the Chimney-sweeper's cry
Every blackening Church appalls;
And the hapless Soldier's sigh
Runs in blood down Palace walls.

But most through midnight streets I hear
How the youthful Harlot's curse
Blasts the new born Infant's tear,
And blights with plagues the Marriage hearse.

William Wordsworth

William Wordsworth (1770–1850) lived most of his life in the hills and dales of the English Lake District. His boyhood was rather poor and wild, and he says of himself at the time that he showed "a stiff, moody, and violent temper." A visit to France in 1790 filled him with enthusiastic sympathy for the revolution, but this ebbed away in a few years. His reputation as a poet grew with time, and he was mellowed by both pecuniary and critical recognition. Wordsworth settled at Grasmere, where he led a tranquil and fruitful life crowned by his appointment as poet laureate a few years before his death.

"The Tables Turned" (1798)

Up! up! my Friend, and quit your books;
Or surely you'll grow double:
Up! up! my Friend, and clear your looks;
Why all this toil and trouble?

The sun, above the mountain's head,
A freshening lustre mellow
Through all the long green fields has spread,
His first sweet evening yellow.

Books! 'tis a dull and endless strife:
Come, hear the woodland linnet,
How sweet his music! on my life,
There's more of wisdom in it.

And hark! how blithe the throstle sings!
He, too, is no mean preacher:
Come forth into the light of things,
Let Nature be your teacher.

She has a world of ready wealth,
Our minds and hearts to bless—

Spontaneous wisdom breathed by health,
Truth breathed by cheerfulness.

One impulse from a vernal wood
May teach you more of man,
Of moral evil and of good,
Than all the sages can.

Sweet is the lore which Nature brings;
Our meddling intellect
Mis-shapes the beauteous forms of things:
We murder to dissect.

Enough of Science and of Art;
Close up those barren leaves;
Come forth, and bring with you a heart
That watches and receives.

London, 1802

Milton! thou shouldst be living at this hour:
England hath need of thee: she is a fen
Of stagnant waters: altar, sword, and pen,
Fireside, the heroic wealth of hall and bower,
Have forfeited their ancient English dower
Of inward happiness. We are selfish men;

Oh! raise us up, return to us again;
And give us manners, virtue, freedom, power.
Thy soul was like a Star, and dwelt apart;
Thou hadst a voice whose sound was like the sea:
Pure as the naked heavens, majestic, free,
So didst thou travel on life's common way,
In cheerful godliness; and yet thy heart
The lowliest duties on herself did lay.

Lord Byron

George Gordon, sixth Lord Byron (1788–1824), appears as very much the type of volcanic romantic hero. The misery of lameness, a violent and capricious mother, and an extravagant youth (one of his escapades consisted of keeping a bear cub in his rooms at Trinity College, Cambridge) helped form the spirit of revolt which was his lifelong characteristic. The first two cantos of "Childe Harold," published in 1812, met with acclamation. In his own words, he awoke one morning and found himself famous. But, though lionized, his marital difficulties, his temper, and his refusal to conform kept him out of English society

and out of England for most of the rest of his life. It was in Italy that he wrote many of
his later poems and in Greece that he died, of malarial fever, having gone there to fight
for Hellenic independence against the Turks.

From "Childe Harold's Pilgrimage"

CANTO III (1816)

But quiet to quick bosoms is a hell,
And there hath been thy bane; there is a fire
And motion of the soul which will not dwell
In its own narrow being, but aspire
Beyond the fitting medium of desire;
And, but once kindled, quenchless evermore,
Preys upon high adventure, nor can tire
Of aught but rest; a fever at the core,
Fatal to him who bears, to all who ever bore.

This makes the madmen who have made men mad
By their contagion; Conquerors and Kings,
Founders of sects and systems, to whom add
Sophists, Bards, Statesmen, all unquiet things
Which stir too strongly the soul's secret springs,
And are themselves the fools to those they fool;
Envied, yet how unenviable! what stings
Are theirs! One breast laid open were a school

Which would unteach mankind the lust to shine or rule:
Their breath is agitation, and their life
A storm whereon they ride, to sink at last,
And yet so nursed and bigoted to strife,
That should their days, surviving perils past,
Melt to calm twilight, they feel overcast
With sorrow and supineness, and so die;
Even as a flame unfed, which runs to waste
With its own flickering, or a sword laid by,
Which eats into itself, and rusts ingloriously.

From "Lara, Canto I" (1814)

There was in him a vital scorn of all:
As if the worst had fall'n which befall,
He stood a stranger in this breathing world,

An erring spirit from another hurl'd;
A thing of dark imaginings, that shaped
By choice the perils he by chance escaped;
But 'scaped in vain, for in their memory yet
His mind would half exult and half regret:
With more capacity for love than earth
Bestows on most of mortal mould and birth,
His early dreams of good outstripp'd the truth,
And troubled manhood followed baffled youth;
With thought of years in phantom chase misspent,
And wasted powers for better purpose lent;
And fiery passions that had poured their wrath
In hurried desolation o'er his path,
And left the better feelings all at strife
In wild reflection o'er his stormy life;
But haughty still, and loth himself to blame,
He call'd on Nature's self to share the shame,
And charged all faults upon the fleshly form
She gave to clog the soul, and feast the worm;
Till he at last confounded good and ill,
And half mistook for fate the acts of will:
Too high for common selfishness, he could
At times resign his own for others' good,
But not in pity, not because he ought,
But in some strange perversity of thought,
That sway'd him onward with a secret pride
To do what few or none would do beside;
And this same impulse would, in tempting time,
Mislead his spirit equally to crime;
So much he soar'd beyond, or sunk beneath,
The men with whom he felt condemn'd to breathe,
And long'd by good or ill to separate
Himself from all who shared his mortal state;
His mind abhorring this, had fix'd her throne
Far from the world, in regions of her own:
Thus coldly passing all that pass'd below,
His blood in temperate seeming now would flow:
Ah! happier if it ne'er with guilt had glow'd,
But ever in that icy smoothness flow'd!
'Tis true, with other men their path he walk'd,
And like the rest in seeming did and talk'd,
Nor outraged Reason's rules by flaw nor start,
His madness was not of the head, but heart;
And rarely wander'd in his speech, or drew
His thoughts so forth as to offend the view.

Percy Bysshe Shelley

Percy Bysshe Shelley (1792–1822), the son of a Sussex country gentleman, was educated at Eton and expelled from Oxford for writing a pamphlet called "The Necessity of Atheism." At odds with his disapproving family, the ensuing years of wandering produced some beautiful verses, an unfortunate first marriage, and an elopement to Italy with Mary Wollstonecraft Godwin, the daughter of the radical philosopher William Godwin and famous in her own right for the novel Frankenstein *(1818). Shelley was able to wed Mary in 1816, when his former wife drowned herself. He too lived the last years of his life in Italy, where he made friends with Byron and where he was drowned in the course of a boating expedition.*

"England in 1819"

An old, mad, blind, despised, and dying king,—
Princes, the dregs of their dull race, who flow
Through public scorn,—mud from a muddy spring,—
Rulers who neither see, nor feel, nor know,
But leech-like to their fainting country cling,
Till they drop, blind in blood, without a blow,—
A people starved and stabbed in the untilled field,—
An army, which liberticide and prey
Makes as a two-edged sword to all who wield
Golden and sanguine laws which tempt and slay;
Religion Christless, Godless—a book sealed;
A Senate,—Time's worst statute unrepealed,—
Are graves, from which a glorious Phantom may
Burst, to illumine our tempestuous day.

"Final Chorus from Hellas" (1822)

The world's great age begins anew,
The golden years return,
The earth doth like a snake renew
Her winter weeds outworn:
Heaven smiles, and faiths and empires gleam,
Like wrecks of a dissolving dream.

A brighter Hellas rears its mountains
From waves serener far;
A new Peneus rolls his fountains
Against the morning star.

Where fairer Tempes bloom, there sleep
Young Cyclads on a sunnier deep.

A loftier Argo cleaves the main,
Fraught with a later prize;
Another Orpheus sings again,
And loves, and weeps, and dies.
A new Ulysses leaves once more
Calypso for his native shore.

Oh, write no more the tale of Troy,
If earth Death's scroll must be!
Nor mix with Laian rage the joy
Which dawns upon the free:
Although a subtler Sphinx renew
Riddles of death Thebes never knew.

Another Athens shall arise,
And to remoter time
Bequeath, like sunset to the skies,
The splendour of its prime;
And leave, if nought so bright may live,
All earth can take or Heaven can give.

Saturn and Love their long repose
Shall burst, more bright and good
Than all who fell, then One who rose,
Than many unsubdued:
Not gold, not blood, their altar dowers,
But votive tears and symbol flowers.

Oh, cease! must hate and death return?
Cease! must men kill and die?
Cease! drain not to its dregs the urn
Of bitter prophecy.
The world is weary of the past,
Oh, might it die or rest at last!

Economic Revolution

Iₙ political and economic matters the dominant doctrine of the nineteenth century was liberalism, which stood in general terms for constitutional government, private enterprise, and free trade. In England much of this liberal doctrine was based on ideas first formulated by Adam Smith and Jeremy Bentham (1748–1832), to the effect that individual self-interest intelligently pursued is bound to work to the good of society as a whole. In his *Inquiry into the Nature and Causes of the Wealth of Nations* (1776), the former analyzed the sources of society's economic well-being and concluded that specialization of labor on the one hand and free enterprise on the other were the most important of these. As he saw it, "Every individual is continually exerting himself to find out the most advantageous employment of whatever capital he can command. It is his own advantage, indeed, and not that of the society, which he has in view. But the study of his own advantage naturally, or rather necessarily, leads him to prefer that employment which is most advantageous to the society."

Bentham, for his part, expounded his ideas in a series of works sadly deficient in clarity or ease of reading that were saved from obscurity largely through the efforts of several talented and enthusiastic disciples, interpreters, and translators. Yet in the first chapter of his *Introduction to the Principles of Morals and Legislation,* privately printed in 1780 but first published only in 1789, we may find a working definition of the new creed:

> Nature has placed mankind under the governance of two sovereign masters, *pain* and *pleasure.* It is for them alone to point out what we ought to do, as well as to determine what we shall do. On the one hand the standard of right and wrong, on the other the chain of causes and effects, are fastened to their throne. They govern us in all we do, in all we say, in all we think: every effort we can make to throw off our subjection will serve but to demonstrate and confirm it. In words a man may pretend to abjure their empire: but in reality he will remain subject to it all the while. The *principle of utility* recognizes this subjection, and assumes it for the foundation of that system, the object of which is to rear the fabric of felicity by the hands of reason and law. Systems which attempt to question it, deal in caprice instead of reason, in darkness instead of light. . . . By the principle of utility is meant that principle which approves or disapproves of every action whatsoever, according to the tendency that it appears to have to augment or diminish the happiness of the party whose interest is in question: or, what is the same thing in other words, to promote or to oppose that happiness. I say of every action whatsoever; and therefore not only of every action of a private individual, but of every measure of government.

Based upon these views, the so-called utilitarian philosophy became tremendously influential in legislation, business, and economic thought.

Adam Smith

Born in the little village of Kirkaldy, near Edinburgh, Scotland, Adam Smith (1723–1790) was kidnapped when he was four years old by gypsies who soon abandoned him. He would have made a very poor gypsy because he later revealed himself to be a towering figure in social economics. Gentle and prodigiously absent-minded, Smith was impressed by what he called "the progress of opulence," that is, the increasing wealth he observed around him. He attributed this to the productive aspects of natural selfishness, observing that self-seeking individuals are often "led by an invisible hand . . . without knowing it, without intending it, [to] advance the interest of society." Let individual interest run free, and it would benefit the interest of all, he claimed. Government constraint hampered beneficent private enterprise. "Civil government, so far as it is instituted for the security of property [see Locke], is in reality instituted for the defence of the rich against the poor, or of those who have some property against those who have none at all." Only "the obvious and simple system of natural liberty" would allow rich and poor alike to compete on an even field.

Published in the same year as the Declaration of Independence, The Wealth of Nations *(1776) explained how the invisible hand of competition guided an economic system based on self-interest. On the national level as on the international, competition and the acquisitive drive set free would cause wealth to grow. But the essence of material success lay in the division of labor, which leads to rising production. Written in a preindustrial age,* The Wealth of Nations *opens with a famous passage describing a pin factory in which ten persons, by specializing in a variety of tasks, turn out 48,000 pins a day, much more than the few that each could have produced alone.*

From The Wealth of Nations

ON PINMAKING

To take an example, therefore, from a very trifling manufacture, but one in which the division of labour has been very often taken notice of, the trade of the pinmaker; a workman not educated to this business (which the division of labour has rendered a distinct trade), nor acquainted with the use of the machinery employed in it (to the invention of which the same division of labour has probably given occasion), could scarce, perhaps, with his utmost industry, make one pin in a day, and certainly could not make twenty. But in the way in which this business is now carried on, not only the whole work is a peculiar trade, but it is divided into a number of branches, of

From *An Inquiry into the Nature and Causes of the Wealth of Nations*, J. E. T. Rogers, ed. (Oxford: Clarendon Press, 1880).

which the greater part are likewise peculiar trades. One man draws out the wire, another straights it, a third cuts it, a fourth points it, a fifth grinds it at the top for receiving the head; to make the head requires two or three distinct operations; to put it on is a peculiar business, to whiten the pins is another; it is even a trade by itself to put them into the paper; and the important business of making a pin is, in this manner, divided into about eighteen distinct operations, which in some manufactories are all performed by distinct hands, though in others the same man will sometimes perform two or three of them. I have seen a small manufactory of this kind where ten men only were employed, and where some of them consequently performed two or three distinct operations. But though they were very poor, and therefore but indifferently accommodated with the necessary machinery, they could when they exerted themselves make among them about twelve pounds of pins in a day. There are in a pound upwards of four thousand pins of a middling size. Those ten persons, therefore, could make among them upwards of forty-eight thousand pins in a day. Each person, therefore, making a tenth part of forty-eight thousand pins, might be considered as making four thousand eight hundred pins in a day. But if they had all wrought separately and independently, and without any of them having been educated to this peculiar business, they certainly could not each of them have made twenty, perhaps not one in a day; that is, certainly, not the two hundred and fortieth, perhaps not the four thousand eight hundredth part of what they are at present capable of performing, in consequence of a proper division and combination of their different operations.

On Freedom of Trade

The unproductive class, that of merchants, artificers, and manufacturers, is maintained and employed altogether at the expense of the two other classes—of that of proprietors, and of that of cultivators. They furnish it both with the materials of its work and with the fund of its subsistence, with the corn and cattle which it consumes while it is employed about that work. The proprietors and cultivators finally pay both the wages of all the workmen of the unproductive class, and the profits of all their employers. Those workmen and their employers are properly the servants of the proprietors and cultivators. They are only servants who work without doors, as menial servants work within. Both the one and the other, however, are equally maintained at the expense of the same masters. The labour of both is equally unproductive. It adds nothing to the value of the sum total of the rude produce of the land. Instead of increasing the value of that sum total, it is a charge and expense which must be paid out of it.

The unproductive class, however, is not only useful, but greatly useful to the other two classes. By means of the industry of merchants, artificers, and manufacturers, the proprietors and cultivators can purchase both the foreign goods and the manufactured produce of their own country which they have occasion for, with the produce of a much smaller quantity of their own labour than what they would be obliged to employ if they were to attempt, in an awkward and unskilful manner, either to import the one or to make the other for their own use. By means of the unproductive class, the cultivators are delivered from many cares which would otherwise distract their attention from the cultivation of land. The superiority of produce, which, in consequence of this undivided attention, they are enabled to raise, is fully sufficient to pay the whole expense which the maintenance and employment of the unproductive class costs either the proprietors or themselves. The industry of merchants, artificers, and manufacturers, though in its own nature altogether unproductive, yet contributes in this manner indirectly to increase the produce of the land. It increases the productive powers of productive labour, by leaving it at liberty to confine itself to its proper employment, the cultivation of land; and the plough goes frequently the easier and the better by means of the labour of the man whose business is most remote from the plough.

It can never be the interest of the proprietors and cultivators to restrain or to discourage in any respect the industry of merchants, artificers, and manufacturers. The greater the liberty which this unproductive class enjoys, the greater will be the competition in all the different trades which compose it, and the cheaper will the other two classes be supplied, both with foreign goods and with the manufactured produce of their own country.

It can never be the interest of the unproductive class to oppress the other two classes. It is the surplus produce of the land, or what remains after deducting the maintenance, first, of the cultivators, and afterwards of the proprietors, that maintains and employs the unproductive class. The greater this surplus, the greater must likewise be the maintenance and employment of that class. The establishment of perfect justice, of liberty, and of perfect equality, is the very simple secret which most effectually secures the highest degree of prosperity to all the three classes.

The merchants, artificers, and manufacturers of those mercantile states which, like Holland and Hamburg, consist chiefly of this unproductive class, are in the same manner maintained and employed altogether at the expense of the proprietors and cultivators of land. The only difference is, that those proprietors and cultivators are, the greater part of them, placed at a most inconvenient distance from the merchants, artificers, and manufacturers whom they supply with the materials of their work and the fund of their subsistence, are the inhabitants of other countries, and the subjects of other governments.

Such mercantile states, however, are not only useful, but greatly useful to the inhabitants of those other countries. They fill up, in some measure, a very important void, and supply the place of the merchants, artificers, and manufacturers whom the inhabitants of those countries ought to find at home, but whom, from some defect in their policy, they do not find at home.

It can never be the interest of those landed nations, if I may call them so, to discourage or distress the industry of such mercantile states, by imposing high duties upon their trade, or upon the commodities which they furnish. Such duties, by rendering those commodities dearer, could serve only to sink the real value of the surplus produce of their own land, with which, or, what comes to the same thing, with the price of which those commodities are purchased. Such duties could serve only to discourage the increase of that surplus produce, and consequently the improvement and cultivation of their own land. The most effectual expedient, on the contrary, for raising the value of that surplus produce, for encouraging its increase, and consequently the improvement and cultivation of their own land, would be to allow the most perfect freedom to the trade of all such mercantile nations.

This perfect freedom of trade would even be the most effectual expedient for supplying them, in due time, with all the artificers, manufacturers, and merchants whom they wanted at home, and for filling up in the properest and most advantageous manner that very important void which they felt there.

The continual increase of the surplus produce of their land would, in due time, create a greater capital than what could be employed with the ordinary rate of profit in the improvement and cultivation of land; and the surplus part of it would naturally turn itself to the employment of artificers and manufacturers at home. But those artificers and manufacturers, finding at home both the materials of their work and the fund of their subsistence, might immediately, even with much less art and skill, be able to work as cheap as the like artificers and manufacturers of such mercantile states, who had both to bring from a great distance. Even though, from want of art and skill, they might not for some time be able to work as cheap, yet, finding a market at home, they might be able to sell their work there as cheap as that of the artificers and manufacturers of such mercantile states, which could not be brought to that market but from so great a distance; and as their art and skill improved, they would soon be able to sell it cheaper. The artificers and manufacturers of such mercantile states, therefore, would immediately be rivalled in the market of those landed nations, and soon after undersold and justled out of it altogether. The cheapness of the manufactures of those landed nations, in consequence of the gradual improvements of art and skill, would, in due time, extend their sale beyond the home market, and carry them to many foreign markets, from which they would in the same manner gradually justle out many of the manufactures of such mercantile nations.

This continual increase both of the rude and manufactured produce of those landed nations would in due time create a greater capital than could, with the ordinary rate of profit, be employed either in agriculture or in manufactures. The surplus of this capital would naturally turn itself to foreign trade, and be employed in exporting to foreign countries such parts of the rude and manufactured produce of its own country as exceeded the demand of the home market. In the exportation of the produce of their own country, the merchants of a landed nation would have an advantage of the same kind over those of mercantile nations, which its artificers and manufacturers had over the artificers and manufacturers of such nations: the advantage of finding at home that cargo, and those stores and provisions, which the others were obliged to seek for at a distance. With inferior art and skill in navigation, therefore, they would be able to sell that cargo as cheap in foreign markets as the merchants of such mercantile nations; and with equal art and skill they would be able to sell it cheaper. They would soon, therefore, rival those mercantile nations in this branch of foreign trade, and in due time would justle them out of it altogether.

According to this liberal and generous system, therefore, the most advantageous method in which a landed nation can raise up artificers, manufacturers, and merchants of its own, is to grant the most perfect freedom of trade to the artificers, manufacturers, and merchants of all other nations. It thereby raises the value of the surplus produce of its own land, of which the continual increase gradually establishes a fund which in due time necessarily raises up all the artificers, manufacturers, and merchants whom it has occasion for.

When a landed nation, on the contrary, oppresses either by high duties or by prohibitions the trade of foreign nations, it necessarily hurts its own interest in two different ways. First, by raising the price of all foreign goods and of all sorts of manufactures, it necessarily sinks the real value of the surplus produce of its own land, with which, or, what comes to the same thing, with the price of which, it purchases those foreign goods and manufactures. Secondly, by giving a sort of monopoly of the home market to its own merchants, artificers, and manufacturers, it raises the rate of mercantile and manufacturing profit in proportion to that of agricultural profit, and consequently either draws from agriculture a part of the capital which had before been employed in it, or hinders from going to it a part of what would otherwise have gone to it. . . .

David Ricardo

David Ricardo (1772–1823) was a stockbroker and a member of Parliament. His economic thinking, originally inspired by reading Adam Smith, treated labor like any other commodity in a laissez-faire economy. The iron law of wages that he developed argued that all attempts to improve the real income of workers were futile and that wages were bound to remain near the subsistence level—unless workers themselves limited their numbers by limiting their families (an unlikely supposition in those days). Far from aiding the workers, the Poor Laws, which kept the miserable portion of the workforce alive and breeding at subsistence levels, merely aggravated their uncompetitive position.

Karl Marx, who strongly disagreed with Ricardo's general philosophy, later drew heavily on Ricardo's economic analyses. Marx was to argue for radical changes in a society and a system that treated human beings as if they were simply goods in a self-regulating market.

On Wages

The Natural Rate of Wages

Labour, like all other things which are purchased and sold, and which may be increased or diminished in quantity, has its natural and its market price. The natural price of labour is that price which is necessary to enable the labourers, one with another, to subsist and to perpetuate their race, without either increase or diminuation.

The power of the labourer to support himself, and the family which may be necessary to keep up the number of labourers, does not depend on the quantity of money which he may receive for wages, but on the quantity of food, necessaries, and conveniences become essential to him from habit, which that money will purchase. The

From David Ricardo, *Principles of Political Economy and Taxation* (London: John Murray, 1817), Chapter V.

natural price of labour, therefore, depends on the price of the food, necessaries, and conveniences required for the support of the labourer and his family. With a rise in the price of food and necessaries, the natural price of labour will rise; with the fall in their price, the natural price of labour will fall.

With the progress of society the natural price of labour has always a tendency to rise, because of the principal commodities by which its natural price is regulated, has a tendency to become dearer, from the greater difficulty of producing it. As, however, the improvements in agriculture, the discovery of new markets, whence provisions may be imported, may for a time counteract the tendency to rise in the price of necessaries, and may even occasion their natural price to fall, so will the same causes produce a correspondent effect on the natural price of labour. . . .

The market price of labour is the price which is really paid for it, from the natural operation of the proportion of the supply to demand; labour is dear when it is scarce, and cheap when it is plentiful. However much the market price of labour may deviate from its natural price, it has, like commodities, a tendency to conform to it.

It is when the market price of labour exceeds its natural price, that the condition of the labourer is flourishing and happy, that he has it in his power to command a greater proportion of the necessaries and enjoyments of life, and therefore to rear a healthy and numerous family. When, however, by the encouragement which high wages give to the increase of population, the number of labourers is increased, wages again fall to their natural price, and indeed from a re-action sometimes fall below it.

When the market price of labour is below its natural price, the condition of the labourers is most wretched; then poverty deprives them of those comforts which custom renders absolute necessaries. It is only after their privations have reduced their number, or the demand for labour has increased, that the market price of labour will rise to its natural price, and that the labourer will have the moderate comforts which the natural rate of wages will afford.

It is a truth which admits not a doubt, that the comforts and well-being of the poor cannot be permanently secured without some regard on their part, or some effort on the part of the legislature, to regulate the increase of their numbers, and to render less frequent among them early and improvident marriages. The operation of the system of poor laws has been indirectly contrary to this. They have rendered restraint superfluous, and have invited imprudence, by offering it a portion of the wages of prudence and industry. . . .

John Stuart Mill

A good presentation of the new economic doctrines is furnished by John Stuart Mill (1806–1873), the son of one of Bentham's most devoted followers. The Essay on Utilitarianism *is made up of a series of articles that Mill had written in 1854 and refurbished into one volume in 1860. In it he attempted to reconcile the principle of individual self-regard with the greatest happiness of the greatest number. By the time Mill was through he had left little of Bentham's original ideas, but he had prepared the groundwork for what might be called liberal collectivism. As might be expected, Mill himself soon left the straight and narrow path of undiluted utilitarianism. He respected individual liberty and thought that this was threatened by majority rather than by minority pressures; this led him to write the famous* Essay on Liberty *(1859). But a growing feeling that individual liberty might be more in danger from the jungle laws of free enterprise than from some form of defensive organization drove him in his later years toward socialism. A man of tremendous intelligence and almost equal sensitiveness, Mill has left us a fascinating and rather frightening* Autobiography.

From Essay on Utilitarianism

WHAT UTILITARIANISM IS

A passing remark is all that needs be given to the ignorant blunder of supposing that those who stand up for utility as the test of right and wrong, use the term in that restricted and merely colloquial sense in which utility is opposed to pleasure. An apology is due to the philosophical opponents of utilitarianism, for even the momentary appearance of confounding them with any one capable of so absurd a misconception: which is the more extraordinary, inasmuch as the contrary accusation, of referring everything to pleasure, and that too in its grossest form, is another of the common charges against utilitarianism; and, as has been pointedly remarked by an able writer, the same sort of persons, and often the very same persons, denounce the theory "as impracticably dry when the word pleasure precedes the word utility." Those who know anything about the matter are aware that every writer, from Epicurus to Bentham, who maintained the theory of utility, meant by it, not something to be contradistinguished from pleasure, but pleasure itself, together with exemption from pain; and instead of opposing the useful to the agreeable or the ornamental, have always declared that the useful means these, among other things. Yet the common herd, including the herd of writers, not only in newspapers and periodicals, but in books of weight and pretension, are perpetually falling into this shallow mistake. Having caught up the word utilitarian, while knowing nothing whatever about it but its sound, they habitually express by it the rejection, or the neglect, of pleasure in some of its forms; of beauty, or ornament, or of amusement. Nor is the term thus ignorantly misapplied solely in disparagement, but occasionally in compliment; as though it implied superiority to frivolity and the mere pleasures of the moment. And this perverted use is the only one in which the word is popularly known, and the one from which the new generation are acquiring their sole notion of its meaning. Those who introduced the word, but who had for many years discontinued it as a distinctive appellation, may well feel themselves called upon to resume it, if by doing so they can hope to contribute anything towards rescuing it from this utter degradation.

The creed which accepts as the foundation of morals, Utility, or the Greatest Happiness Principle, holds that actions are right in proportion as they tend to promote happiness, wrong as they tend to produce the reverse of happiness. By happiness is intended pleasure, and the absence of pain; by unhappiness, pain, and the privation of pleasure. To give a clear view of the moral standard set up by the theory, much more requires to be said; in particular, what things it includes in the ideas of pain and pleasure; and to what extent this is left an open question. But these supplementary explanations do not affect the theory of life on which this theory of morality is grounded—namely, that pleasure, and freedom from pain, are the only things desirable as ends; and that all desirable things (which are as numerous in the utilitarian as in any other scheme) are desirable either for the pleasure inherent in themselves, or as means to the promotion of pleasure and the prevention of pain.

Now, such a theory of life excites in many minds, and among them in some of the most estimable in feeling and purpose, inveterate dislike. To suppose that life has (as they express it) no higher end than pleasure—no better and nobler object of desire and pursuit—they designate as utterly mean and grovelling; as a doctrine worthy only of swine, to whom the followers of Epicurus were, at a very early period, contemptuously likened; and modern holders of the doctrine are occasionally made the subject of equally polite comparisons by its German, French, and English assailants.

When thus attacked, the Epicureans have always answered, that it is not they, but their accusers, who represent human nature in degrading light; since the accusation supposes human begins to be capable of no pleasures except those of which swine are capable. If this supposition were true, the charge could not be gainsaid, but would then be no longer an imputation; for if the sources of pleasure were precisely the same to human beings and to swine, the rule of life which is good enough for the one would be good enough for the other. The comparison of the Epicurean life to that of beasts is felt as degrading, precisely because a beast's pleasures do not satisfy a human being's conceptions of happiness. Human beings have faculties more elevated than the animal appetites, and when once made conscious of them, do not regard anything as happiness which does not include their gratification. I do not, indeed, consider the Epicureans to have been by any means faultless in drawing out their scheme of consequences from the utilitarian principle. To do this in any sufficient manner, many Stoic as well as Christian elements require to be included. But there is no known Epicurean theory of life which does not assign to the pleasures of the intellect, of the feelings and imagination, and of the moral sentiments, a much higher value as pleasures than to those of mere sensation. It must be admitted, however, that utilitarian writers in general have placed the superiority of mental over bodily pleasures chiefly in the greater permanency, safety, uncostliness, etc., of the former—that is, in their circumstantial advantages rather than in their intrinsic nature. And on all these points utilitarians have fully proved their case; but they might have taken the other, and, as it may be called, higher ground, with entire consistency. It is quite compatible with the principle of utility to recognize the fact, that some kinds of pleasure are more desirable and more valuable than others. It would be absurd that while, in estimating all other things, quality is considered as well as quantity, the estimation of pleasures should be supposed to depend on quantity alone.

Now it is an unquestionable fact that those who are equally acquainted with, and equally capable of appreciating and enjoying, both, do give a most marked preference to the manner of existence which employs their higher faculties. Few human creatures would consent to be changed into any of the lower animals, for a promise of the fullest allowance of a beast's pleasures; no intelligent human being would consent to be a fool, no instructed person would be an ignoramus, no person of feeling and conscience would be selfish and base, even though they should be persuaded that the fool, the dunce, or the rascal is better satisfied with his lot than they are with theirs. They would not resign what they possess more than he for the most complete satisfaction of all the desires which they have in common with him. If they ever fancy they would, it is only in cases of unhappiness so extreme, that to escape from it they would exchange their lot for almost any other, however undesirable in their own eyes. A being of higher faculties requires more to make him happy, is capable probably of more acute suffering, and certainly accessible to it at more points, than one of an inferior type; but in spite of these liabilities, he can never really wish to sink into what he feels to be a lower grade of existence. We may give what explanation we please of this unwillingness; we may attribute it to pride, a name which is given indiscriminately to some of the most and to some of the least estimable feelings of which mankind are capable: we may refer it to the love of liberty and personal independence, an appeal to which was with the Stoics one of the most effective means for the inculcation of it; to the love of power or to the love of excitement, both of which do really enter into and contribute to it: but its most appropriate appellation is a sense of dignity, which all human beings possess in one form or other, and in some, though by no means in exact, proportion to their higher faculties, and which is so essential a part of the happiness of those in whom it is strong, that nothing which conflicts with it could be, otherwise than momentarily, an object of desire to them. Whoever supposed that this preference takes place at a sacrifice of happiness—that the superior being, in anything like equal circumstances, is not happier than the inferior—confounds the two very different ideas, of happiness, and content. It is indisputable that the being whose capacities of enjoyment are low, has the greatest chance of having them fully satisfied; and a highly endowed being will always feel that any happiness which he can look for, as the world is constituted, is imperfect. But he can learn to bear its imperfections, if they are at all bearable; and they will not make him envy the being who is indeed unconscious of the imperfections, but only because he feels not at all the good which those imperfections qualify. It is better to be a human being dissatisfied than a pig satisfied; better to be Socrates dissatisfied than a fool satisfied. And if the fool, or the pig, are of a different opinion, it is because they only know their own side of the question. The other party to the comparison knows both sides.

It may be objected, that many who are capable of the higher pleasures, occasionally, under the influence of temptation, postpone them to the lower. But this is quite compatible with full appreciation of the intrinsic superiority of the higher. Men often, from infirmity of character, make their election for the nearer good, though they know it to be the less valuable; and this no less when the choice is between two bodily pleasures, than when it is between bodily and mental. They pursue sensual indulgences to the injury of health, though perfectly aware that health is the greater good. It may be further objected, that many who begin with youthful enthusiasm for everything noble, as they advance in years sink into indolence and selfishness. But I do not believe that those who undergo this very common change, voluntarily choose the lower description of pleasures in preference to the higher. I believe that before they devote themselves exclusively to the one, they have already become incapable of the other. Capacity for the nobler feelings is in most natures a very tender plant, easily killed, not only by hostile influences, but by mere want of sustenance; and in the majority of young persons it speedily dies away if the occupations to which their position in life has devoted them, and the society into which it has thrown them, are not favorable to keeping that higher capacity in exercise. Men lose their high aspirations as they lose their intellectual tastes, because they have not time or opportunity for indulging them; and they addict themselves to inferior pleasures, not because they deliberately prefer them but because they are either the only ones to which they have access, or the only ones which they are any longer capable of enjoying. It may be questioned whether any one who has remained equally susceptible to both classes of pleasures, ever knowingly and calmly preferred the lower; though many, in all ages, have broken down in an ineffectual attempt to combine both.

From this verdict of the only competent judges, I apprehend there can be no appeal. On a question which is the best worth having of two pleasures, or which of two modes of existence is the most grateful to the feelings, apart from its moral attributes and from its consequences, the judgment of those who are qualified by knowledge of both, or, if they differ, that of the majority among them, must be admitted as final. And there needs be the less hesitation to accept this judgment respecting the quality of pleasures, since there is no other question of quantity. What means are there of determining which is the acutest of two pains, or the intensest of two pleasurable sensations, except the general suffrage of those who are familiar with both? Neither pains nor pleasures are homogeneous, and pain is always heterogeneous with pleasure. What is there to decide whether a particular pleasure is worth purchasing at the cost of a particular pain, except the feelings and judgment of the experienced? When, therefore, those feelings and judgments declare the pleasures derived from the higher faculties to be preferable *in kind,* apart from the question of intensity, to those of which the animal nature, disjoined from the higher faculties, is susceptible, they are entitled on this subject to the same regard.

I have dwelt on this point, as being a necessary part of a perfectly just conception of Utility or Happiness, considered as the directive rule of human conduct. But it is by no means an indispensable condition to the acceptance of the utilitarian standard; for that standard is not the agent's own greatest happiness, but the greatest amount of happiness altogether; and if it may possibly be doubted whether a noble character is always the happier for its nobleness, there can be no doubt that it makes other people happier, and that the world in general is immensely a gainer by it. Utilitarianism, therefore, could only attain its end by the general cultivation of nobleness of character, even if each individual were only benefited by the nobleness of others, and his own, so far as happiness is concerned, were a sheer deduction from the benefit. But the bare enunciation of such an absurdity as this last, renders refutation superfluous.

OF THE ULTIMATE SANCTION OF THE PRINCIPLE OF UTILITY

The question is often asked, and properly so, in regard to any supposed moral standard—What is its sanction? what are the motives to obey it? or more specifically, what is the source of its obligation? whence does it derive its binding force? It is a necessary part of moral philosophy to provide the answer to this question; which, though frequently assuming the shape of an objection to the utilitarian morality, as if it had some special applicability to that above others, really arises in regard to all standards. It arises, in fact, whenever a person is called on to adopt a standard, or refer morality to any basis on which he has not been accustomed to rest it. For the customary morality, that which education and opinion have consecrated, is the only one which presents itself to the mind with the feeling of being in itself obligatory; and when a person is asked to believe that this morality derives its obligation from some general principle round which custom has not thrown the same halo, the assertion is to him a paradox; the supposed corollaries seem to have a more binding force than the original theorem; the super-structure seems to stand better without, than with, what is represented as its foundation. He says to himself, I feel that I am bound not to rob or murder, betray or deceive; but why am I bound to promote the general happiness? If my own happiness lies in something else, why may I not give that the preference?

If the view adopted by the utilitarian philosophy of the nature of the moral sense be correct, this difficulty will always present itself, until the influences which form moral character have taken the same hold of the principle which they have taken of some of the consequences,—until, by the improvement of education, the feeling of unity with our fellow-creatures shall be (what it cannot be denied that Christ intended it to be) as deeply rooted in our character, and to our own consciousness as completely a part of our nature, as the horror of crime is in an ordinarily well brought up young person. In the meantime, however, the difficulty has no peculiar application to the doctrine of utility, but is inherent in every attempt to analyze morality and reduce it to principles; which, unless the principle is already in men's minds invested with as much sacredness as any of its applications, always seems to divest them of a part of their sanctity.

The principle of utility either has, or there is no reason why it might not have, all the sanctions which belong to any other system of morals. Those sanctions are either external or internal. Of the external sanctions it is not necessary to speak at any length. They are, the hope of favor and the fear of displeasure, from our fellow-creatures or from the Ruler of the Universe, along with whatever we may have of sympathy or affection for them, or of love and awe of Him, inclining us to do his will independently of selfish consequences. There is evidently no reason why all these motives for observance should not attach themselves to the utilitarian morality, as completely and as powerfully as to any other. Indeed, those of them which refer to our fellow-creatures are sure to do so, in proportion to the amount of general intelligence; for whether there be any other ground of moral obligation than the general happiness or not, men do desire happiness; and however imperfect may be their own practice, they desire and commend all conduct in others towards themselves, by which they think their happiness is promoted. With regard to the religious motive, if men believe, as most profess to do, in the goodness of God, those who think that conduciveness to the general happiness is the essence, or even only the criterion of good, must necessarily believe that it is also that which God approves. The whole force therefore of external reward and punishment, whether physical or moral, and whether proceeding from God or from our fellow men, together with all that the capacities of human nature admit of disinterested devotion to either, become available to enforce the utilitarian morality, in proportion as that morality is recognized; and the more powerfully, the more the appliances of education and general cultivation are bent to the purpose.

So far as to external sanctions. The internal sanction of duty, whatever our standard of duty may be, is one and the same—a feeling in our own mind; a pain, more or less intense, attendant on violation of duty, which in properly cultivated moral natures rises, in the more serious cases, into shrinking from it as an impossibility. This feeling, when disinterested, and connecting itself with the pure idea of duty, and not with some particular form of it, or with any of the merely accessory circumstances, is the essence of Conscience; though in that complex phenomenon as it actually exists, the simple fact is in general all encrusted over with collateral associations, derived from sympathy, from love, and still more from fear; from all the forms of religious feeling; from the recollections of childhood and of all our past life; from self-esteem, desire of the esteem of others, and occasionally even self-abasement. This extreme complication is, I apprehend, the origin of the sort of mystical character, which, by a tendency of the human mind of which there are many other examples, is apt to be attributed to the idea of moral obligation, and which leads people to believe that the idea cannot possibly attach itself to any other objects than those which, by a supposed mysterious law, are found in our present experience to excite it. Its binding force, however, consists in the existence of a mass of feeling which must be broken through in order to do what violates our standard of right, and which, if we do nevertheless violate that standard, will probably have to be encountered afterwards in the form of remorse. Whatever theory we have of the nature or origin of conscience, this is what essentially constitutes it.

The ultimate sanction, therefore, of all morality (external motives apart) being a subjective feeling in our own minds, I see nothing embarrassing to those whose standard is utility, in the question, what is the sanction of that particular standard? We may answer, the same as of all other moral standards—the conscientious feelings of mankind. Undoubtedly this sanction has no binding efficacy on those who do not possess the feelings it appeals to; but neither will these persons be more obedient to any other moral principle than to the utilitarian one. On them morality of any kind has no hold but through the external sanctions. Meanwhile the feelings exist, a fact in human nature, the reality of which, and the great power with which they are capable of acting on those in whom they have been duly cultivated, are proved by experience. No reason has ever been shown why they may not be cultivated to as great intensity in connection with the utilitarian, as with any other rule of morals.

There is, I am aware, a disposition to believe that a person who sees in moral obligation a transcendental fact, an objective reality belonging to the province of "Things in themselves," is likely to be more obedient to it than one who believes it to be entirely subjective, having its seat in human consciousness only. But whatever a person's opinion may be on this point of Ontology, the force he is really urged by is his own subjective feeling, and is exactly measured by its strength. No one's belief that duty is an objective reality is stronger than the belief that God is so; yet the belief in God, apart from the expectation of actual reward and punishment, only operates on conduct through, and in proportion to, the subjective religious feeling. The sanction, so far as it is disinterested, is always in the mind itself; and the notion therefore of the transcendental moralists must be, that this sanction will not exist in the mind unless it is believed to have its root out of the mind; and that if a person is able to say to himself, this which is restraining me, and which is called my conscience, is only a feeling in my own mind, he may possibly draw the conclusion that when the feeling ceases the obligation ceases, and that if he find the feeling inconvenient, he may disregard it, and endeavour to get rid of it. But is this danger confined to the utilitarian morality? Does the belief that moral obligation has its seat outside the mind make the feeling of it too strong to be got rid of? The fact is so far otherwise, that all moralists admit and lament the ease with which, in the generality of minds, conscience can be silenced or stifled. The question, Need I obey my conscience? is quite as often put to themselves by persons who never heard of the principle of utility, as by its adherents. Those whose conscientious feelings are so weak as to allow of their asking this question, if they answer it affirmatively, will not do so because they believe in the transcendental theory, but because of the external sanctions.

It is not necessary, for the present purpose, to decide whether the feeling of duty is innate or implanted. Assuming it to be innate, it is an open question to what objects it naturally attaches itself; for the philosophic supporters of that theory are now agreed that the intuitive perception is of principles of morality and not of the details. If there be anything innate in the matter, I see no reason why the feeling which is innate should not be that of regard to the pleasures and pains of others. If there is any principle of morals which is intuitively obligatory, I should say it must be that. If so, the intuitive ethics would coincide with the utilitarian, and there would be no further quarrel between them. Even as it is, the intuitive moralists, though they believe that there are other intuitive moral obligations, do already believe this to be one; for they unanimously hold that a large portion of morality turns upon the consideration due to the interests of our fellow-creatures. Therefore, if the belief in the transcendental origin of moral obligation gives any additional efficacy to the internal sanction, it appears to me that the utilitarian principle has already the benefit of it.

On the other hand if, as is my own belief, the moral feelings are not innate, but acquired, they are not for that reason the less natural. It is natural to man to speak, to reason, to build cities, to cultivate the ground, though these are acquired faculties. The moral feelings are not indeed a part of our nature, in the sense of being in any perceptible degree present in all of us; but this, unhappily, is a fact admitted by those who believe the most strenuously in their transcendental origin. Like the other acquired capacities above referred to, the moral faculty, if not a part of our nature, is a natural outgrowth from it; capable, like them, in a certain small degree, of springing up spontaneously; and susceptible of being brought by cultivation to a high degree of development. Unhappily it is also susceptible, by a sufficient use of the external sanctions and of the force of early impressions, of being cultivated in almost any direction: so that there is hardly anything so absurd or so mischievous that it may not, by means of these influences, be made to act on the human mind with all the authority of conscience. To doubt that the same potency might be given by the same means to the principle of utility, even if it had no foundation in human nature, would be flying in the face of all experience.

But moral associations which are wholly of artificial creation, when intellectual culture goes on, yield by degrees to the dissolving force of analysis: and if the feeling of duty, when associated with utility, would appear equally arbitrary; if there were no leading department of our nature, no powerful class of sentiments, with which that association would harmonize, which would make us feel it congenial, and incline us not only to foster it in others (for which we have abundant interested motives), but also to cherish it in ourselves; if there were not, in short, a natural basis of sentiment for utilitarian morality, it might well happen that this association also, even after it had been implanted by education, might be analyzed away.

But there is this basis of powerful natural sentiment; and this it is which, when once the general happiness is recognized as the ethical standard, will constitute the strength of the utilitarian morality. This firm foundation is that of the social feelings of mankind; the desire to be in unity with our fellow-creatures, which is already a powerful principle in human nature, and happily one of those which tend to become stronger even without express inculcation, from the influences of advancing civilization. The social state is at once so natural, so necessary, and so habitual to man, that, except in some unusual circumstances or by an effort of voluntary abstraction, he never conceives himself otherwise than as a member of a body; and this association is riveted more and more, as mankind are further removed from the state of savage independence. Any condition, therefore, which is essential to a state of society, becomes more and more an inseparable part of every person's conception of the state of things which he is born into, and which is the destiny of a human being. Now, society between human beings, except in the relation of master and slave, is manifestly impossible on any other footing than that the interests of all are to be consulted. Society between equals can only exist on the understanding that the interests of all are to be regarded equally. And since in all states of civilization, every person except an absolute monarch, has equals, everyone is obliged to live on these terms with somebody; and in every age some advance is made towards a state in which it will be impossible to live permanently on other terms with anybody. In this way people grow up unable to conceive as possible to them a state of total disregard of other people's interests. They are under a necessity of conceiving themselves as at least abstaining from all the grosser injuries, and (if only for their own protection) living in a state of constant protest against them. They are also familiar with the fact of co-operating with others; there is at least a temporary feeling that the interests of others are their own interests. Not only does all strengthening of social ties, and all healthy growth of society, give to each individual a stronger personal interest in practically consulting the welfare of others; it also leads him to identify his feelings more and more with their good, or at least with an even greater degree of practical consideration for it. He comes, as though instinctively, to be conscious of himself as a being who of course pays regard to others. The good of others becomes to him a thing naturally and necessarily to be attended to, like any of the physical conditions of our existence. Now, whatever amount of this feeling a person has, he is urged by the strongest motives both of interest and of sympathy to demonstrate it, and to the utmost of his power encourage it in others; and even if he has none of it himself, he is as greatly interested as any one else that others should have it. Consequently the smallest germs of the feeling are laid hold of and nourished by the contagion of sympathy and the influences of education; and a complete web of corroborative association is woven round it, by the powerful agency of the external sanctions. This mode of conceiving ourselves and human life, as civilization goes on, is felt to be more and more natural. Every step in political improvement renders it more so, by removing the sources of opposition of interest, and levelling those inequalities of legal privilege between individuals or classes, owing to which there are large portions of mankind whose happiness it is still practicable to disregard. In an improving state of the human mind, the influences are constantly on the increase, which tend to generate in each individual a feeling of unity with all the rest; which, if perfect, would make him never think of, or desire, any beneficial condition for himself, in the benefits of which they are not included. If we now suppose this feeling of unity to be taught as a religion, and the whole force of education, of institutions, and of opinion, directed, as it once was in the case of religion, to make every person grow up from infancy surrounded on all sides both by the profession and the practice of it, I think that no one, who can realize this conception, will feel any misgiving about the sufficiency of the ultimate sanction for the Happiness morality. To any ethical student who finds the realization difficult, I recommend, as a means of facilitating it, the second of M. Comte's two principal works, the Traité de Politique Positive. I entertain the strongest objections to the system of politics and morals set forth in that treatise; but I think it has superabundantly shown the possibility of giving to the service of humanity, even without the aid of belief in a Providence, both the psychological power and the social efficacy of a religion; making it take hold of human life, and colour all thought, feeling, and action, in a manner of which the greatest ascendancy ever exercised by any religion may be but a type and foretaste; and of which the danger is, not that it should be insufficient, but that it should be so excessive as to interfere unduly with human freedom and individuality.

Neither is it necessary to the feeling which constitutes the binding force of the utilitarian morality on those who recognize it, to wait for those social influences which would make its obligation felt by mankind at large. In the comparatively early state of human advancement in which we now live, a person cannot indeed feel that entireness of sympathy with all others, which would make any real discordance in the general direction of their conduct in life impossible; but already a person in whom the social feeling is at all developed, cannot bring himself to think of the rest of his fellow-creatures as struggling rivals with him for the means of happiness, whom he must desire to see defeated in their object in order that he may succeed in his. The deeply rooted conception which every individual even now has of himself as a social being, tends to make him feel it one of his natural wants that there should be harmony between his feelings and aims and those of his fellow-creatures. If differences of opinion and of mental culture make it impossible for him to share many of their actual feelings—perhaps make him denounce and defy those feelings—he still needs to be conscious that his real aim and theirs do not conflict; that he is not opposing himself to what they really wish for, namely their own good, but is, on the contrary, promoting it. This feeling in most individuals is much inferior in strength to their selfish feelings, and is often wanting altogether. But to those who have it, it possesses all the characters of a natural feeling. It does not present itself to their minds as a superstition of education, or a law despotically imposed by the power of society, but as an attribute which it would not be well for them to be without. This conviction is the ultimate sanction of the greatest happiness morality. This it is which makes any mind, of well-developed feelings, work with, and not against, the outward motives to care for others, afforded by what I have called the external sanctions; and when those sanctions are wanting, or act in an opposite direction, constitutes in itself a powerful internal binding force, in proportion to the sensitivities and thoughtfulness of the character; since few but those whose mind is a moral blank, could bear to lay out their course of life on the plan of paying no regard to others except so far as their own private interest compels.

From On Liberty

The subject of this Essay is not the so-called Liberty of the Will, so unfortunately opposed to the misnamed doctrine of Philosophical Necessity; but Civil, or Social Liberty: the nature and limits of the power which can be legitimately exercised by society over the individual. A question seldom stated, and hardly ever discussed, in general terms, but which profoundly influences the practical controversies of the age by its latent presence, and is likely soon to make itself recognized as the vital question of the future. It is so far from being new, that, in a certain sense, it has divided mankind, almost from the remotest ages; but in the stages of progress into which the more civilized portions of the species have now entered, it presents itself under new conditions, and requires a different and more fundamental treatment.

The struggle between Liberty and Authority is the most conspicuous feature in the portions of history with which we are earliest familiar, particularly in that of Greece, Rome, and England. But in old times this contest was between subjects, or some classes of subjects, and the Government. By liberty, was meant protection against the tyranny of the political rulers. The rulers were conceived (except in some of the popular governments of Greece) as in a necessarily antagonistic position to the people whom they ruled. They consisted of a governing One, or a governing tribe or caste, who derived their authority from inheritance or conquest, who, at all events, did not hold it at the pleasure of the governed, and whose supremacy men did not venture, perhaps did not desire, to contest, whatever precautions might be taken against its oppressive exercise. Their power was regarded as necessary, but also as highly dangerous; as a weapon which they would attempt to use against their subjects, no less than against external enemies. To prevent the weaker members of the community from being preyed upon by innumerable vultures, it was needful that there should be an animal of prey stronger than the rest, commissioned to keep them down. But as the king of the vultures would be no less bent upon preying on the flock than any of the minor harpies, it was indispensable to be in a perpetual attitude of defence against his beak and claws. The aim, therefore, of patriots was to set limits to the power which the ruler should be suffered to exercise over the community; and this limitation was what they meant by liberty.

From Mill, *On Liberty* (London, 1859), chap. 1.

It was attempted in two ways. First, by obtaining a recognition of certain immunities, called political liberties or rights, which it was to be regarded as a breach of duty in the ruler to infringe, and which, if he did infringe, specific resistance, or general rebellion, was held to be justifiable. A second, and generally a later expedient, was the establishment of constitutional checks, by which the consent of the community, or of a body of some sort, supposed to represent its interests, was made a necessary condition to some of the more important acts of the governing power. To the first of these modes of limitation, the ruling power, in most European countries, was compelled, more or less, to submit. It was not so with the second; and, to attain this, or when already in some degree possessed, to attain it more completely, became everywhere the principal object of the lovers of liberty. And so long as mankind were content to combat one enemy by another, and to be ruled by a master, on condition of being guaranteed more or less efficaciously against his tyranny, they did not carry their aspirations beyond this point.

A time, however, came, in the progress of human affairs, when men ceased to think it a necessity of nature that their governors should be an independent power, opposed in the interest to themselves. It appeared to them much better that the various magistrates of the State should be their tenants or delegates, revocable at their pleasure. In that way alone, it seemed, could they have complete security that the powers of government would never be abused to their disadvantage. By degrees this new demand for elective and temporary rulers became the prominent object of the exertions of the popular party, wherever any such party existed; and superseded, to a considerable extent, the previous efforts to limit the power of rulers. As the struggle proceeded for making the ruling power emanate from the periodical choice of the ruled, some persons began to think that too much importance had been attached to the limitation of the power itself. *That* (it might seem) was a resource against rulers whose interests were habitually opposed to those of the people. What was now wanted was, that the rulers should be identified with the people; that their interest and will should be the interest and the will of the nation. The nation did not need to be protected against its own will. There was no fear of its tyrannizing over itself. Let the rulers be effectually responsible to it, promptly removable by it, and it could afford to trust them with power of which it could itself dictate the use to be made. Their power was but the nation's own power, concentrated, and in form convenient for exercise. This mode of thought, or rather perhaps of feeling, was common among the last generation of European liberalism, in the continental section of which it still apparently predominates. Those who admit any limit to what a government may do, except in the case of such governments as they think ought not to exist, stand out as brilliant exceptions among the political thinkers of the continent. A similar tone of sentiment might by this time have been prevalent in our own country, if the circumstances which for a time encouraged it, had continued unaltered.

But, in political and philosophical theories, as well as in persons, success discloses faults and infirmities which failure might have concealed from observation. The notion, that the people have no need to limit their power over themselves, might seem axiomatic, when popular government was a thing only dreamed about, or read of as having existed at some distant period of the past. Neither was that notion necessarily disturbed by such temporary aberrations as those of the French Revolution, the worst of which were the work of an usurping few, and which, in any case, belonged not to the permanent working of popular institutions, but to a sudden and convulsive outbreak against monarchical and aristocratic despotism. In time, however, a democratic republic came to occupy a large portion of the earth's surface, and made itself felt as one of the most powerful members of the community of nations; and elective and responsible government became subject to the observations and criticisms which wait upon a great existing fact. It was now perceived that such phrases as "self-government," and "the power of the people over themselves," do not express the true state of the case. The "people" who exercise the power are not always the same people with those over whom it is exercised; and the "self-government" spoken of is not the government of each by himself, but of each by all the rest. The will of the people, moreover, practically means the will of the most numerous or the most active *part* of the people; the majority, or those who succeed in making themselves accepted as the majority; the people, consequently, *may* desire to oppress a part of their number; and precautions are as much needed against this as against any other abuse of power. The limitation, therefore, of the power of government over individuals loses none of its importance when the holders of power are regularly accountable to the community, that is, to the strongest party therein. This view of things, recommending itself equally to the intelligence of thinkers and to the inclination of those important classes in European society to whose real or supposed interests democracy is adverse, has had no difficulty in establishing itself; and in political speculations "the tyranny of the majority" is now generally included among the evils against which society requires to be on its guard.

Like other tyrannies, the tyranny of the majority was at first, and is still, vulgarly, held in dread, chiefly as operating through the acts of the public authorities. But reflecting persons perceive that when society is itself the tyrant—society collectively, over the separate individuals who compose it—its means of tyrannizing are not restricted to the acts which it may do by the hands of its political functionaries. Society can and does execute its own mandates: and if it issues wrong mandates instead of right, or any mandates at all in things with which it ought not to meddle, it practises a social tyranny more formidable than many kinds of political oppression, since, though not usually upheld by such extreme penalties, it leaves fewer means of escape, penetrating much more deeply into the details of life, and enslaving the soul itself. Protection, therefore, against the tyranny of the magistrate is not enough: there needs protection also against the tyranny of the prevailing opinion and feeling; against the tendency of society to impose, by other means than civil penalties, its own ideas and practices as rules of conduct on those who dissent from them; to fetter the development, and, if possible, prevent the formation, of any individuality not in harmony with its ways, and compel all characters to fashion themselves upon the model of its own. There is a limit to the legitimate interference of collective opinion with individual independence: and to find that limit, and maintain it against encroachment, is as indispensable to a good condition of human affairs, as protection against political despotism.

But though this proposition is not likely to be contested in general terms, the practical question, where to place the limit—how to make the fitting adjustment between individual independence and social control—is a subject on which nearly everything remains to be done. All that makes existence valuable to anyone, depends on the enforcement of restraints upon the actions of other people. Some rules of conduct, therefore, must be imposed, by law in the first place and by opinion on many things which are not fit subjects for the operation of law. What these rules should be, is the principal question in human affairs; but if we except a few of the most obvious cases, it is one of those which least progress has been made in resolving. No two ages, and scarcely any two countries, decided it alike; and the decision of one age or country is a wonder to another. Yet the people of any given age and country no more suspect any difficulty in it than if it were a subject on which mankind had always been agreed. The rules which obtain among themselves appear to them self-evident and self-justifying. This all but universal illusion is one of the examples of the magical influence of custom, which is not only, as the proverb says, a second nature, but is continually mistaken for the first. The effect of custom, in preventing any misgiving respecting the rules of conduct which mankind impose on one another, is all the more complete because the subject is one on which it is not generally considered necessary that reasons should be given, either by one person to others, or by each to himself. People are accustomed to believe, and have been encouraged in the belief by some who aspire to the character of philosophers, that their feelings, on subjects of this nature, are better than reasons, and render reasons unnecessary. The practical principle which guides them to their opinions on the regulation of human conduct, is the feeling in each person's mind that everybody should be required to act as he, and those with whom he sympathizes, would like them to act. No one, indeed, acknowledges to himself that his standard of judgment is his own liking; but an opinion on a point of conduct, not supported by reasons, can only count as one person's preference; and if the reasons, when given, are a mere appeal to a similar preference felt by other people it is still only many people's liking instead of one. To an ordinary man, however, his own preference, thus supported, is not only a perfectly satisfactory reason, but the only one he generally has for any of his notions of morality, taste, or propriety, which are not expressly written in his religious creed; and his chief guide in the interpretation even of that. Men's opinions, accordingly, on what is laudable or blameable, are affected by all the multifarious causes which influence their wishes in regard to the conduct of others, and which are as numerous as those which determine their wishes on any other subject. Sometimes their reason—at other times their prejudices or superstitions: often their social affections, not seldom their anti-social ones, their envy or jealousy, their arrogance or contemptuousness: but most commonly, their desires or fears for themselves—their legitimate or illegitimate self-interest. Wherever there is an ascendant class, a large portion of the morality of the country emanates from its class-interests, and its feelings of class superiority. The morality between Spartans and helots, between planters and negroes, between princes and subjects, between nobles and roturiers, between men and women, has been for the most part the creation of these class interests and feelings: and the sentiments thus generated, react in turn upon the moral feelings of the members of the ascendant class, in their relations among themselves. Where, on the other hand, a class, formerly ascendant, has lost its ascendancy, or where its ascendancy is unpopular, the prevailing moral sentiments frequently bear the impress of an impatient dislike of superiority. Another grand determining principle of the rules of conduct, both in act and forbearance, which have been enforced by law or opinion, has been the servility of mankind towards the supposed preferences of aversions of their temporal masters, or of their gods. This servility, though essentially selfish, is not hypocrisy; it gives rise to perfectly genuine sentiments of abhorence; it made men burn magicians and heretics. Among so many baser influences, the general and obvious interests of society have of course had a share, and large one, in the direction of the moral sentiments: less, however, as a matter of reason, and on their own account, than as a consequence of the sympathies and antipathies which grew out of them: and sympathies and antipathies which had little or nothing to do with the interests of society, have made themselves felt in the establishment of moralities with quite as great force.

The likings and dislikings of society, or of some powerful portion of it, are thus the main thing which has practically determined the rule laid down for general observance under the penalties of law or opinion. And in general, those who have been in advance of society in thought and feeling, have left this condition of things unassailed in principle, however they may have come into conflict with it in some of its details. They have occupied themselves rather in inquiring what things society ought to like or dislike, than in questioning whether its likings or dislikings should be a law to individuals. They prefer endeavouring to alter the feelings of mankind on the particular points on which they were themselves heretical, rather than make common cause in defence of freedom, with heretics generally. The only case in which the higher ground has been taken on principle and maintained with consistency, by any but an individual here and there, is that of religious belief: a case instructive in many ways, and not least so as forming a most striking instance of the fallibility of what is called the moral sense: for the *odium theologicum,*[1] in a sincere bigot, is one of the most unequivocal cases of moral feeling. Those who first broke the yoke of what called itself the Universal Church, were in general as little willing to permit difference of religious opinion as that church itself. But when the heat of the conflict was over, without giving a complete victory to any party, and each church or sect was reduced to limit its hopes to retaining possession of the ground it already occupied; minorities seeing that they had no chance of becoming majorities, were under the necessity of pleading to those whom they could not convert for permission to differ. It is accordingly on this battlefield, almost solely, that the rights of the individual against society have been asserted on broad grounds of principle, and the claim of society to exercise authority over dissentients, openly controverted. The great writers to whom the world owes what religious liberty it possesses, have mostly asserted freedom of conscience as an indefeasible right, and denied absolutely that a human being is accountable to others for his religious beliefs. Yet so natural to mankind is intolerance in whatever they really care about, that religious freedom has hardly anywhere been practically realised, except where religious indifference, which dislikes to have its peace disturbed by theological quarrels, has added its weight to the scale. In the minds of almost all religious persons, even in the most tolerant countries, the duty of toleration is admitted with tacit reserves. One person will bear with dissent in matters of church government, but not of dogma; another

---

[1] Hatred characterizing theological disputes.

can tolerate everybody, short of a Papist or a Unitarian; another, everyone who believes in revealed religion; a few extend their charity a little further, but stop at the belief in a God and in a future state. Wherever the sentiment of the majority is still genuine and intense, it is found to have abated little of its claim to be obeyed.

In England, from the peculiar circumstances of our political history, though the yoke of opinion is perhaps heavier, that of law is lighter than in most other countries of Europe; and there is considerable jealousy of direct interference, by the legislative or executive power, with private conduct; not so much from any just regard for the independence of the individual, as from the still subsisting habit of looking on the government as representing an opposite interest to the public. The majority have not yet learned to feel the power of the government their power, or its opinions their opinions. When they do so, individual liberty will probably be as much exposed to invasion from the government, as it already is from public opinion. But, as yet, there is a considerable amount of feeling ready to be called forth against any attempt of the law to control individuals in things in which they have not hitherto been accustomed to be controlled by it; and this with very little discrimination as to whether the matter is, or is not, within the legitimate sphere of legal control; insomuch that the feeling, highly salutary on the whole, is perhaps quite as often misplaced as well grounded in the particular instances of its application. There is, in fact, no recognized principle by which the propriety or impropriety of government interference is customarily tested. People decide according to their personal preferences. Some, whenever they see any good to be done, or evil to be remedied, would willingly instigate the government to undertake the business; while others prefer to bear almost any amount of social evil, rather than add one to the departments of human interests amenable to governmental control. And men range themselves on one or the other side in any particular case, according to this general direction of their sentiments; or according to the degree of interest which they feel in the particular thing which it is proposed that the government should do, or according to the belief they entertain that the government would, or would not, do it in the manner they prefer; but very rarely on account of any opinion to which they consistently adhere, as to what things are fit to be done by a government. And it seems to me that in consequence of this absence of rule or principle, one side is at present as often wrong as the other; the interference of government is, with about equal frequency, improperly invoked and improperly condemned.

The object of this Essay is to assert one very simple principle, as entitled to govern absolutely the dealings of society with the individual in the way of compulsion and control, whether the means used be physical force in the form of legal penalties, or the moral coercion of public opinion. That principle is, that the sole end for which mankind are warranted, individually or collectively, in interfering with the liberty of action of any of their number, is self-protection. That the only purpose for which power can be rightfully exercised over any member of a civilised community, against his will, is to prevent harm to others. His own good, either physical or moral, is not a sufficient warrant. He cannot rightfully be compelled to do or forbear because it will be better for him to do so, because it will make him happier, because, in the opinions of others, to do so would be wise, or even right. These are good reasons for remonstrating with him, or reasoning with him, or persuading him, or entreating him, but not for compelling him, or visiting him with any evil in case he do otherwise. To justify that, the conduct from which it is desired to deter him, must be calculated to produce evil to someone else. The only part of the conduct of anyone, for which he is amenable to society, is that which concerns others. In the part which merely concerns himself, his independence is, of right, absolute. Over himself, over his own body and mind, the individual is sovereign.

Conditions in Industry

Liberal economics seemed an integral part of the booming activity and prosperity of the times. But behind the façade of the industrial revolution were hundreds of thousands of people torn by economic and social dislocation. They were the displaced persons of the revolution: law, industry, and society seemed to operate without regard for them as human beings. And though opportunity gleamed golden above the grim and grimy mills, and though Samuel Smiles and others provided good advice on how a man could save and grow rich—hence respectable—the new industrial proletariat was too harassed and brutalized, too busy coping with the tremendous task of merely keeping alive from one day to another, to lift its eyes too high above the hopeless present. This task was undertaken instead by reformers—many of them manufacturers themselves, many of them Tories— who spoke, wrote, and fought on behalf of the victims of progress; by independent observers such as Dr. P. Gaskell, whose opinion as a medical man appears after the following excerpt, and by parliamentary commissions of inquiry such as those headed by Michael Sadler or by Anthony Ashley Cooper, the future seventh earl of Shaftesbury. The evidence these men produced shocked the public and led to measures regulating conditions of labor in factories and mines and restricting the number of hours that women and children could work.

Evidence Given Before the Sadler Committee

MR. MATTHEW CRABTREE, CALLED IN; AND EXAMINED

What age are you?—Twenty-two.
What is your occupation?—A blanket manufacturer.
Have you ever been employed in a factory?—Yes.
At what age did you first go to work in one?—Eight.
How long did you continue in that occupation?—Four years.
Will you state the hours of labor at the period when you first went to the factory, in ordinary times?—From 6 in the morning to 8 at night.
Fourteen hours?—Yes.
With what intervals for refreshment and rest?—An hour at noon.
When trade was brisk what were your hours?—From 5 in the morning to 9 in the evening.
Sixteen hours?—Yes.

From *Parliamentary Papers, 1831–1832* (London, 1832), XV.

With what intervals at dinner?—An hour.

How far did you live from the mill?—About two miles.

Was there any time allowed for you to get your breakfast in the mill?—No.

Did you take it before you left your home?—Generally.

During those long hours of labor could you be punctual; how did you awake?—I seldom did awake spontaneously; I was most generally awoke or lifted out of bed, sometimes asleep, by my parents.

Were you always in time?—No.

What was the consequence if you had been too late?—I was most commonly beaten.

Severely?—Very severely, I thought.

In those mills is chastisement towards the latter part of the day going on perpetually?—Perpetually.

So that you can hardly be in a mill without hearing constant crying?—Never an hour, I believe.

Do you think that if the overlooker were naturally a human person it would still be found necessary for him to beat the children, in order to keep up their attention and vigilance at the termination of those extraordinary days of labor?—Yes; the machine turns off a regular quantity of cardings, and of course they must keep as regularly to their work the whole of the day; they must keep with the machine, and therefore however human the slubber may be, as he must keep up with the machine or be found fault with, he spurs the children to keep up also by various means; but that which he commonly resorts to is to strap them when they become drowsy.

At the time when you were beaten for not keeping up with your work, were you anxious to have done it if you possibly could?—Yes; the dread of being beaten if we could not keep up with our work was a sufficient impulse to keep us to it if we could.

When you got home at night after this labor, did you feel much fatigued?—Very much so.

Had you any time to be with your parents, and to receive instructions from them?—No.

What did you do?—All that we did when we got home was to get the little bit of supper that was provided for us and to go to bed immediately. If the supper had not been ready directly, we should have gone to sleep while it was preparing.

Did you not, as a child, feel it a very grievous hardship to be roused so soon in the morning?—I did.

Were the rest of the children similarly circumstanced?—Yes, all of them; but they were not all of them so far from their work as I was.

And if you had been too late you were under the apprehension of being cruelly beaten?—I generally was beaten when I happened to be too late, and when I got up in the morning the apprehension of that was so great, that I used to run, and cry all the way as I went to the mill.

ELIZABETH BENTLEY, CALLED IN; AND EXAMINED

What age are you?—Twenty-three.

Where do you live?—At Leeds.

What time did you begin to work at a factory?—When I was six years old.

At whose factory did you work?—Mr. Busk's.

What kind of mill is it?—Flax-mill.

What was your business in that mill?—I was a little doffer.

What were your hours of labor in that mill?—From 5 in the morning till 9 at night, when they were thronged.

For how long a time together have you worked that excessive length of time?—For about half a year.

What were your usual hours of labor when you were not so thronged?—From 6 in the morning till 7 at night.

What time was allowed for your meals?—Forty minutes at noon.

Had you any time to get your breakfast or drinking?—No, we got it as we could.

And when your work was bad, you had hardly any time to eat it at all?—No; we were obliged to leave it or take it home, and when we did not take it, the overlooker took it, and gave it to his pigs.

Do you consider doffing a laborious employment?—Yes.

Explain what it is you had to do?—When the frames are full, they have to stop the frames, and take the flyers off, and take the full bobins off, and carry them to the roller; and then put empty ones on, and set the frame going again.

Does that keep you constantly on your feet?—Yes, there are so many frames, and they run so quick.

Your labor is very excessive?—Yes; you have not time for any thing.

Suppose you flagged a little, or were too late, what would they do?—Strap us.

Are they in the habit of strapping those who are last in doffing?—Yes.

Constantly?—Yes.

Girls as well as boys?—Yes.

Have you ever been strapped?—Yes.

Severely?—Yes.

Could you eat your food well in that factory?—No, indeed, I had not much to eat, and the little I had I could not eat it, my appetite was so poor, and being covered with dust; and it was no use to take it home, I could not eat it, and the overlooker took it, and gave it to the pigs.

You are speaking of the breakfast?—Yes.

How far had you to go for dinner?—We could not go home to dinner.

Where did you dine?—In the mill.

Did you live far from the mill?—Yes, two miles.

Had you a clock?—No, we had not.

Supposing you had not been in time enough in the morning at these mills, what would have been the consequence?—We should have been quartered.

What do you mean by that?—If we were a quarter of an hour too late, they would take off half an hour; we only got a penny an hour, and they would take a halfpenny more.

The fine was much more considerable than the loss of time?—Yes.

Were you also beaten for being too late?—No, I was never beaten myself, I have seen the boys beaten for being too late.

Were you generally there in time?—Yes, my mother has been up at 4 o'clock in the morning, and at 2 o'clock in the morning; the colliers used to go to their work about 3 or 4 o'clock, and when she heard them stirring she has got up out of her warm bed, and gone out and asked them the time, and I have sometimes been at Hunslet Car at 2 o'clock in the morning, when it was streaming down with rain, and we have had to stay till the mill was opened.

PETER SMART, CALLED IN;
AND EXAMINED

You say you were locked up night and day?—Yes.

Do the children ever attempt to run away?—Very often.

Were they pursued and brought back again?—Yes, the overseer pursued them and brought them back.

Did you ever attempt to run away?—Yes, I ran away twice.

And you were brought back?—Yes, and I was sent up to the master's loft, and thrashed with a whip for running away.

Were you bound to this man?—Yes, for six years.

By whom were you bound?—My mother got 15s. for the six years.

Do you know whether the children were, in point of fact, compelled to stop during the whole time for which they were engaged?—Yes, they were.

By law?—I cannot say by law; but they were compelled by the master; I never saw any law used there but the law of their own hands.

To what mill did you next go?—To Mr. Webster's, at Battus Den, within eleven miles of Dundee.

In what situation did you act there?—I acted as an overseer.

At 17 years of age?—Yes.

Did you inflict the same punishment that you yourself had experienced?—I went as an overseer; not as a slave, but as a slave-driver.

What were the hours of labor in that mill?—My master told me that I had to produce a certain quantity of yarn; the hours were at that time fourteen; I said that I was not able to produce the quantity of yarn that was required; I told him if he took the timepiece out of the mill I would produce that quantity, and after that time I found no difficulty in producing the quantity.

How long have you worked per day in order to produce the quantity your master required?—I have wrought nineteen hours.

Was this a water-mill?—Yes, water and steam both.

To what time have you worked?—I have seen the mill going till it was past 12 o'clock on the Saturday night.

So that the mill was still working on the Sabbath morning?—Yes.

Were the workmen paid by the piece, or by the day?—No, all had stated wages.

Did not that almost compel you to use great severity to the hands then under you?—Yes; I was compelled often to beat them, in order to get them to attend to their work, from their being overwrought.

Were not the children exceedingly fatigued at that time?—Yes, exceedingly fatigued.

Were the children bound in the same way in that mill?—No; they were bound from one year's end to another, for twelve months.

Did you keep the hands locked up in the same way in that mill?—Yes; we locked up the mill; but we did not lock the bothy.

Did you find that the children were unable to pursue their labor properly to that extent?—Yes; they have been brought to that condition, that I have gone and fetched up the doctor to them, to see what was the matter with them, and to know whether they were able to rise or not able to rise; they were not at all able to rise; we have had great difficulty in getting them up.

When that was the case, how long have they been in bed, generally speaking?—Perhaps not above four or five hours in their beds.

An Independent Observer

Any man who has stood at twelve o'clock at the single narrow doorway, which serves as the place of exit for the hands employed in the great cottonmills, must acknowledge that an uglier set of men and women, of boys and girls, taking them in the mass, it would be impossible to congregate in a smaller compass. Their complexion is sallow and pallid—with a peculiar flatness of feature, caused by the want of a proper quantity of adipose substance to cushion out the cheeks. Their stature low—the average height of four hundred men, measured at different times and different places, being five feet six inches. Their limbs, slender, and playing badly and ungracefully. A very general bowing of the legs. Great numbers of girls and women walking lamely or awkwardly, with raised chests and spinal flexures. Nearly all have flat feet, accompanied with a down-tread, differing very widely from the elasticity of action in the foot and ankle, attendant upon perfect formation. Hair thin and straight—many of the men having but little beard, and that in patches of a few hairs, much resembling its growth among the red men of America. A spiritless and dejected air, a sprawling and wide action of the legs, and an appearance, taken as a whole, giving the world but "little assurance of a man," or if so, "most sadly cheated of his fair proportions. . . ."

Factory labor is a species of work, in some respects singularly unfitted for children. Cooped up in a heated atmosphere, denied the necessary exercise, remaining in one position for a series of hours, one set or system of muscles alone called into activity, it cannot be wondered at that its effects are injurious to the physical growth of a child. Where the bony system is still imperfect, the vertical position it is compelled to retain, influences its direction; the spinal column bends beneath the weight of the head, bulges out laterally, or is dragged forward by the weight of the parts composing the chest, the pelvis yields beneath the opposing pressure downwards, and the resistance given by the thigh-bones; its capacity is lessened, sometimes more and sometimes less; the

From P. Gaskell, *The Manufacturing Population of England* (London, 1833).

legs curve, and the whole body loses height, in consequence of this general yielding and bending of its parts.

Evidence Given Before Lord Ashley's Mines Commission of 1842

SARAH GOODER, AGED 8 YEARS

I'm a trapper in the Gawber pit. It does not tire me, but I have to trap without a light and I'm scared. I go at four and sometimes half past three in the morning, and come out at five and half past. I never go to sleep. Sometimes I sing when I've light, but not in the dark; I dare not sing then. I don't like being in the pit. I am very sleepy when I go sometimes in the morning. I go to Sunday-schools and read *Reading made Easy.* She knows her letters and can read little words. They teach me to pray. She repeated the Lord's Prayer, not very perfectly, and ran on with the following addition:—"God bless my father and mother, and sister and brother, uncles and aunts and cousins, and everybody else, and God bless me and make me a good servant. Amen. I have heard tell of Jesus many a time. I don't know why he came on earth, I'm sure, and I don't know why he died, but he had stones for his head to rest on. I would like to be at school far better than in the pit."

THOMAS WILSON, ESQ.,
OF THE BANKS, SILKSTONE,
OWNER OF THREE COLLIERIES

The employment of females of any age in and about the mines is most objectionable, and I should rejoice to see it put an end to; but in the present feeling of the colliers, no individual would succeed in stopping it in a neighborhood where it prevailed, because the men would immediately go to those pits where their daughters would be employed. The only way effectually to put an end to this and other evils in the present colliery system is to elevate the minds of the men; and the only means to attain this is to combine sound moral and religious training and industrial habits with a system of intellectual culture much more perfect than can at present be obtained by them.

I object on general principles to government interference in the conduct of any trade, and I am satisfied that in mines it would be productive of the greatest injury and injustice. The art of mining is not so perfectly understood as to admit of the way in which a colliery shall be conducted being dictated by any person, however experienced, with such certainty as would warrant an interference with the management of private business. I should also most decidedly object to placing collieries under the present provisions of the Factory Act with respect to the education of children employed therein. First, because, if it is contended that coal-owners, as employers of chil-

From *Parliamentary Papers* (London, 1842), XV–XVII, Appendix 1; Appendix 2.

dren, are bound to attend to their education, this obligation extends equally to all other employers, and therefore it is unjust to single out one class only; secondly, because, if the legislature asserts a right to interfere to secure education, it is bound to make that interference general; and thirdly, because the mining population is in this neighborhood so intermixed with other classes, and is in such small bodies in any one place, that it would be impossible to provide separate schools for them.

ISABELLA READ, 12 YEARS OLD, COAL-BEARER

Works on mother's account, as father has been dead two years. Mother bides at home, she is troubled with bad breath, and is very weak in her body from early labor. I am wrought with sister and brother, it is very sore work; cannot say how many rakes or journeys I make from pit's bottom to wall face and back, thinks about 30 or 25 on the average; the distance varies from 100 to 250 fathom.

I carry about 1 cwt. and a quarter on my back; have to stoop much and creep through water, which is frequently up to the calves of my legs. When first down, fell frequently asleep while waiting for coal from heat and fatigue.

I do not like the work, nor do the lassies, but they are made to like it. When the weather is warm there is difficulty in breathing, and frequently the lights go out.

ISABEL WILSON, 38 YEARS OLD, COAL-PUTTER [HAULER]

When women have children thick [fast] they are compelled to take them down early, I have been married 19 years and have had 10 bairns; seven are in life. When on Sir John's work was a carrier of coals, which caused me to miscarry five times from the strains, and was ill after each. Putting is not so oppressive; last child was born on Saturday morning, and I was at work on the Friday night.

Once met with an accident; a coal brake my cheek-bone, which kept me idle some weeks.

I have wrought below 30 years, and so has the guid man; he is getting touched in the breath now.

None of the children read; as the work is not regular. I did read once, but not able to attend to it now; when I go below lassie 10 years of age keeps house and makes the broth or stir-about.

Nine sleep in two bedsteads; there did not appear to be any beds, and the whole of the other furniture consisted of two chairs, three stools, a table, a kail-pot and a few broken basins and cups. Upon asking if the furniture was all they had, the guid wife said, furniture was of no use, as it was so troublesome to flit with.

PATIENCE KERSHAW, AGED 17

My father has been dead about a year; my mother is living and has ten children, five lads and five lasses; the oldest is about thirty, the youngest is four; three lasses go to mill; all the lads are colliers, two getters and three hurriers; one lives at home and does nothing; mother does nought but look after home.

All my sisters have been hurriers, but three went to the mill. Alice went because her legs swelled from hurrying in cold water when she was hot. I never went to day-school; I go to Sunday-school, but I cannot read or write; I go to pit at five o'clock in the morning and come out at five in the evening; I get my breakfast of porridge and milk first; I take my dinner with me, a cake, and eat it as I go; I do not stop or rest any time for the purpose; I get nothing else until I get home, and then have potatoes and meat, not every day meat. I hurry in the clothes I have now got on, trousers and ragged jacket; the bald place upon my head is made by thrusting the corves [baskets]; my legs have never swelled, but sisters' did when they went to mill; I hurry the corves a mile and more under ground and back; they weigh 300 cwt.; I hurry 11 a day; I wear a belt and chain at the workings to get the corves out; the getters that I work for are naked except their caps; they pull off all their clothes; I see them at work when I go up; sometimes they beat me, if I am not quick enough, with their hands; they strike me upon my back; the boys take liberties with me; sometimes they pull me about; I am the only girl in the pit; there are about 20 boys and 15 men; all the men are naked; I would rather work in mill than in coal-pit.

(This girl is an ignorant, filthy, ragged, and deplorable-looking object, and such a one as the uncivilized natives of the prairies would be shocked to look upon.)

MARY BARRETT, AGED 14, JUNE 15

I have worked down in pit five years; father is working in next pit; I have 12 brothers and sisters—all of them but one live at home; they weave, and wind, and hurry, and one is a counter, one of them can read, none of the rest can, or write; they never went to day-school, but three of them go to Sunday-school; I hurry for my brother John, and come down at seven o'clock about; I go up at six, sometimes seven; I do not like working in pit, but I am obliged to get a living; I work always without stockings, or shoes, or trousers; I wear nothing but my chemise; I have to go up to the headings with the men; they are all naked there; I am got well used to that, and don't care now much about it; I was afraid at first, and did not like it; they never behave rudely to me; I cannot read or write.

Samuel Smiles

Samuel Smiles (1812–1904), whose real name was Samuel Smiles, studied medicine at Edinburgh, and took to journalism and then to biography and inspirational writings. Self Help, his most popular work, was published in 1859; it was tremendously successful and before long had been translated into seventeen languages. It was followed by books on Character (1871), Thrift (1875), and Duty (1880). He also wrote biographies of worthy men, mostly engineers; received an honorary degree (L.L.D.) from the University of Edinburgh in 1878; and died replete with honors and years, having reaped the rewards of the lifestyle he had proposed so enthusiastically to others.

From Self Help

"Heaven helps those who help themselves," is a well-worn maxim, embodying in a small compass the results of vast human experience. The spirit of self-help is the root of all genuine growth in the individual; and, exhibited in the lives of many, it constitutes the true source of national vigor and strength. Help from without is often enfeebling in its effects, but help from within invariably invigorates. Whatever is done for men or classes, to a certain extent takes away the stimulus and necessity of doing for themselves; and where men are subjected to over-guidance and over-government, the inevitable tendency is to render them comparatively helpless.

Even the best institutions can give a man no active aid. Perhaps the utmost they can do, is, to leave him free to develop himself and improve his individual condition. But in all times men have been prone to believe that their happiness and well-being were to be secured by means of institutions rather than by their own conduct. Hence the value of legislation as an agent in human advancement has always been greatly over-estimated. To constitute the millionth part of a legislature, by voting for one or two men once in three or five years, however conscientiously this duty may be performed, can exercise but little active influence upon any man's life and character. Moreover, it is every day becoming more clearly understood, that the function of government is negative and restrictive, rather than positive and active; being resolvable principally into protection—protection of life, liberty and property. Hence the chief "reforms" of the last fifty years have consisted mainly of abolitions and disenactments. But there is no power of law that can make the idle man industrious, the thriftless provident, or the drunken sober; though every individual can be each and all of these if he will, by the exercise of his own free powers of action and self-denial. Indeed, all experience serves to prove that the worth and strength of a state depend far less upon the form of its institutions than upon the character of its men. For the nation is only the aggregate of individual conditions, and civilization itself is but a question of personal improvement.

National progress is the sum of individual industry, energy, and uprightness, as national decay is of individual idleness, selfishness, and vice. What we are accustomed to decry as great social evils, will, for the most part, be found to be only the outgrowth of our own perverted life; and though we may endeavour to cut them down and extirpate them by means of law, they will only spring up again with fresh luxuriance in some other form, unless the individual conditions of human life and character are radically improved. If this view be correct, then it follows that the highest patriotism and philanthropy consist, not so much in altering laws and modifying institutions, as in helping and stimulating men to elevate and improve themselves by their own free and independent action as individuals.

Practical industry, wisely and vigorously applied, never fails of success. It carries a man onward and upward, brings out his individual character, and powerfully stimu-

---

From S. Smiles, *Self Help* (Boston, 1860).

lates the action of others. All may not rise equally, yet each, on the whole, very much according to his deserts. "Though all cannot live on the piazza," as the Tuscan proverb has it, "every one may feel the sun."

We have already referred to some illustrious Commoners raised from humble to elevated positions by the power of application and industry; and we might point to even the peerage itself as affording equally instructive examples. One reason why the peerage of England has succeeded so well in retaining its vigor and elasticity, arises from the fact that, unlike the peerages of other countries, it has been fed from time to time by the best industrial blood of the country—the very "liver, heart, and brain of Britain."

The great bulk of our peerage is comparatively modern, so far as the titles go; but it is not the less noble in that it has been recruited to so large an extent from the ranks of honorable industry. In olden times, the wealth and commerce of London, conducted as it was by energetic and enterprising men, was a prolific source of peerages. Thus, the earldom of Cornwallis was founded by Thomas Cornwallis, the Cheapside merchant; that of Essex by William Capel, the draper; and that of Craven by William Craven, the merchant tailor. The modern Earl of Warwick is not descended from "the Kingmaker," but from William Greville, the woolstapler; whilst the modern dukes of Northumberland find their head, not in the Percies, but in Hugh Smithson, a respectable London apothecary.

It is will, force of purpose, that enables a man to do or be whatever he sets his mind on being or doing. A holy man was accustomed to say, "Whatever you wish, that you are: for such is the force of our will, joined to the Divine, that whatever we wish to be, seriously, and with a true intention, that we become. No one ardently wishes to be submissive, patient, modest, or liberal, who does not become what he wishes." The story is told of a working carpenter, who was observed one day planing a magistrate's bench, which he was repairing, with more than usual carefulness, and when asked the reason, he replied, "Because I wish to make it easy against the time when I come to set upon it myself." And singularly enough, the man actually lived to sit upon that very bench as a magistrate.

Whatever theoretical conclusions logicians may have formed as to the freedom of the will, each individual feels that practically he is free to choose between good and evil—that he is not like a mere straw thrown upon the water to mark the direction of the current, but that he has within him the power of a strong swimmer, and is capable of striking out for himself, of buffeting with the waves, and directing to a great extent his own independent course. There is no absolute constraint upon our violations, and we feel and know that we are not bound, as by a spell, with reference to our actions. It would paralyze all desire of excellence were we to think otherwise. The entire business and conduct of life, with its domestic rules, its social arrangements, and its public institutions, proceed upon the practical conviction that the will is free. Without this where would be responsibility?—and what the advantage of teaching, advising, preaching, reproof, and correction? What were the use of laws, were it not the universal belief, as it is the universal fact, that men obey them or not, very much as they individually determine? In every moment of our life, conscience is proclaiming that our will is free. It is the only thing that is wholly ours, and it rests solely with ourselves individually, whether we give it the right or the wrong direction. Our habits or our temptations are not our masters, but we of them. Even in yielding, conscience tells us we might resist; and that were we determined to master them, there would not be required for that purpose a stronger resolution than we know ourselves to be capable of exercising.

Any class of men that lives from hand to mouth will ever be an inferior class. They will necessarily remain impotent and helpless, hanging on to the skirts of society, the sport of times and seasons. Having no respect for themselves, they will fail in securing the respect of others. In commercial crises, such men must inevitably go to the wall. Wanting that husbanded power which a store of savings, no matter how small, invariably gives them, they will be at every man's mercy, and, if possessed of right feelings, they cannot but regard with fear and trembling the future possible fate of their wives and children. "The world," once said Mr. Cobden to the working men of Huddersfield, "has always been divided into two classes,—those who saved, and those who have spent,—the thrifty and the extravagant. The building of all the houses, the mills, the bridges, and the ships, and the accomplishment of all other great works which have rendered man civilized and happy, has been done by the savers, the thrifty; and those who have wasted their resources have always been their slaves. It has been the law of nature and of Providence, that this should be so; and I were an imposter if I promised any class that they would advance themselves if they were improvident, thoughtless, and idle."

Equally sound was the advice given by Mr. Bright to an assembly of working men at Rochdale, in 1847, when, after expressing his belief that "so far as honesty was concerned, it was to be found in pretty equal amount among all classes," he used the following words: "There is only one way that is safe for any man, or any number of men, by which they can maintain their present position if it be a good one, or raise themselves above it if it be a bad one,—that is, by the practice of the virtues of industry, frugality, temperance, and honesty. There is no royal road by which men can raise themselves from a position which they feel to be uncomfortable and unsatisfactory, as regards their mental or physical condition, except by the practice of those virtues by which they find numbers amongst them are continually advancing and bettering themselves. What is it that has made, that has in fact created, the middle class in this country, but the virtues to which I have alluded? There was a time when there was hardly any class in England, except the highest, that was equal in condition to the poorest class at this moment. How is it that the hundreds of thousands of men, now existing in this our country, of the middle class, are educated, comfortable, and enjoying an amount of happiness and independence, to which our forefathers were wholly unaccustomed? Why, by the practice of those very virtues; for I maintain that there has never been in any former age as much of these virtues as is now to be found amongst the great middle class of our community. When I speak of the middle class, I mean that class which is between the privileged class, the richest, and the very poorest in the community; and I would recommend every man to pay no attention whatever to public writers or speakers, whoever they may be, who tell them that this class or that class, that this law or that law, that this government or that government, can do all these things for them. I assure you, after long reflection and much observation, that there is no way for the working classes of this country to improve their condition but that which so many of them have already availed themselves of,—that is, by the practice of those virtues, and by reliance upon themselves."

Many popular books have been written for the purpose of communicating to the public the grand secret of making money. But there is no secret whatever about it, as the proverbs of every nation abundantly testify. "Many a little makes a meikle."—"Take care of the pennies and the pounds will take care of themselves."—"A penny saved is a penny gained."—"Diligence is the mother of good-luck."—"No pains no gains."—"No sweat no sweet."—"Sloth, the key of poverty."—"Work, and thou shalt have."—"He who will not work, neither shall he eat."—"The world is his, who has patience and industry."—"It is too late to spare when all is spent."—"Better go to bed supperless than rise in debt."—"The morning hour has gold in its mouth."—"Credit keeps the crown of the causeway." Such are specimens of the proverbial philosophy, embodying the hoarded experience of many generations, as to the best means of thriving in the world. They were current in people's mouths long before books were invented; and like other popular proverbs, they were the first codes of popular morals. Moreover they have stood the test of time and the experience of every day still bears witness to their accuracy, force, and soundness.

But Life Goes On

In England

At a more pedestrian level than that of parliaments and banks, everyday life carried on with its petty concerns, its rationalizations and its cares. The brief selections that follow reflect some of the more commonplace attitudes and reactions to mid-nineteenth-century England: the first European country to enter the new industrial world and to try to adjust to the changes that implied.

A. W. Pugin: Chapels

[Chapels] are erected by men who ponder between a mortgage, a railroad or a chapel, as the best investment of their money, and who, when they have resolved on relying on the persuasive eloquence of a cushion-thumping, popular preacher, erect four walls with apertures for windows, cram the same full of seats, which they readily let; and so greedy after self are these chapel-raisers, that they form dry and spacious vaults underneath which are soon occupied at a good rent by some wine and brandy merchant.

Frederich Engels: Cheap Irish Labor

The rapid extension of English industry could not have taken place if England had not possessed in the numerous and impoverished population of Ireland a reserve at command. The Irish had nothing to lose at home, and much to gain in England; and from the time when it became known in Ireland that the East side of St. George's Channel offered steady work and good pay for strong arms, every year has brought armies of the Irish hither. It has been calculated (in 1840) that more than a million have already immigrated, and not far from 50,000 still come every year. . . . These people having grown up almost without civilization, accustomed from youth to every sort of privation, rough, intemperate and improvident, bring all their brutal habits with them among a class of the English population which has, in truth, little inducement to

---

From A. W. Pugin, *Contrasts,* Second Edition (London, 1841), p. 41.

From Fr. Engels, *The Condition of the Working Classes in England in 1844* (London, 1844).

cultivate education and morality. . . . These Irishmen who migrate for 4-pence, to England, on the deck of a steamship on which they are often packed like cattle, insinuate themselves everywhere. The worst dwellings are good enough for them; their clothing causes them little trouble, so long as it holds together by a single thread; shoes they know not; their food consists of potatoes and potatoes only; whatever they earn beyond these needs they spend on drink. What does such a race want with high wages?

Panaceas: An Advertisement

A Society for the Distribution
of Religious Prints
amongst the Middle Classes, the Poor
and Charity Schools
With Lord John Russell as a Patron.

Blair: A Catechism

Q. What are the classes of society?
A. Proprietors, money-dealers, farmers, manufacturers, traders, professions, servants and labourers. . . .
Q. What are money-dealers?
A. Persons who live on the interest of money, by lending it on some security.

The London Times: A Report on Charity

The anniversary of the [Ladies' Sanitary] association was held yesterday at the Hanover Square Rooms. The Bishop of Oxford, who presided, advocated the claims of the association upon the several grounds of religion, humanity and self-interest, showing the effect of its operations in making it possible for the poor to become religious and respectable, reducing the amount of disease and death, and lowering the taxation of the country. The association did this in the most direct manner by teaching the poor to help themselves, and the promotion of such objects had a tendency to lessen the separation which gradually grew up between the rich and the poor and between different classes of religionists, in proportion to the increase of wealth and of the intensity

---

From an advertisement in London *Athenaeum*, November 18, 1848, p. 1138.

From *Blair's First or Mother's Catechism*, 124th edition (London, 1856), p. 39.

From *The London Times*, April 24, 1861.

of Christian principle. Mr. Thomas Hughes, author of *Tom Brown's Schooldays,* proposed the first resolution, which was seconded by Dr. Lankester, who dwelt with considerable warmth upon the duty of lessening the mortality of the population by disseminating information as to the laws of life and health, a knowledge of which, he considered should not by a false delicacy be withheld from females, for it was their ignorance of the subject that caused a vast number of deaths, which could as easily be prevented as deaths from accidents upon railways. . . .

The Bishop of London said there was, no doubt, a great want of sanitary knowledge, but there was a greater want of sanitary belief; the poor needed the importance of cleanliness to be brought home to them; and if they were saved from an epidemic, for instance, by means of the brushes and whitewash which he was glad to find the missionaries of the association carried with them, they would see there was something practical in what was told them by the lecturer.

Charles Kingsley: The Trouble with the System

When any [Manchester manufacturer] boasts to me that the earnings of his workpeople average 16s. a week, woman, man, and child, I am inclined to answer so much the worse for them. It is a very great question whether such high wages are a benefit, without a corresponding high education. You must know well . . . that most of them do not know what to do with their money, and waste it on drink, on rich food, on finery, etc. God knows, I do not grudge it them; but the waste, and the temptation to coarse self-indulgence, is extreme. . . .

Another great evil of our system is, that the children earn wages too nearly equal to those of their parents. Hence the family is broken up, the children are independent too early, boys and girls go off and live in lodgings of their own, and so a great deal of fearful profligacy is engendered. . . .

Another great evil, by the masters' own account, is that mill labour effeminates the men and renders them unfit for any other sort of labour. . . . That large bodies of men should be employed in exclusively performing, day after day, the same minute mechanical operation till their whole intellect is concentrated on it, and their fingers kept delicate for the purpose, is to me shocking.

Letter from a Working Woman

12 May. While reading in the herald to Day on the subject on shorter houers of Labour I was Reminded of A cercomstance that came under my hone notis when the 10 hours

From *Ch. Kingsley; His Letters and Memories* (London, 1863), Volume II, p. 148.
Letter from a working woman, quoted in J. Ruskin, *Fors Clavigera* (London, 1873), XXVIII, 65.

sistom Began in the cotton mills in Lancashire. . . . I was Minding a masheen with 30 treds in it I was then maid to mind 2 of 30 treds each with one shilling Advance of wages wich was 5s. for one and 6s. for tow with an increes of speed and with improved mecheens in A few years I was minding tow mecheens with two 100 treds each and Dubel speed for 9s. perweek so that in our improved condation we had to turn out some 100 weght per day and we went as if the Devel was After us for 10 houers per day and with that comparetive small Advance in money and the feemals have often Been carred out fainting what with the heat and hard work and those that could not keep up must go and make room for another and all this is Done in Christian England and then we are tould to be content in the station of Life to wich the Lord as places us But I say the Lord never Did place us there so we have no Right to Be content. . . .

Coming to Terms with Hardship

The author recommends grey paper for the drawing-room, with inscriptions from the book of Job such as "Man is born unto travail, as the sparks fly upward" painted in black letters in diagonal lines.

Mrs. John Sandford: The Other Oppressed

The sentiment for woman has undergone a change. The romantic passion, which once almost deified her, is on the decline; and it is by intrinsic qualities that she must now inspire respect.

A woman may make a man's home delightful, and may thus increase his motives for virtuous exertion. She may refine and tranquilize his mind—may turn away his anger, or allay his grief. Where want of congeniality impairs domestic comfort, the fault is generally chargeable on the female side; for it is for woman, not for man, to make the sacrifice, especially in indifferent matters. She must, in a certain degree, be plastic herself, if she would mould others, and this is one reason why very good women are sometimes very uninfluential. They do a great deal, but they yield nothing. . . .

In everything that women attempt, they should show their consciousness of dependence. There is something so unpleasant in female self-sufficiency, that it not infrequently prejudices instead of persuading.

Their sex should ever teach them to be subordinate; and they should remember that, by them, influence is to be obtained, not by assumption, but by a delicate appeal to affection or principle. Women, in this respect, are something like children: the more they show their need of support, the more engaging they are.

From Anon., *A Plea for Art in the Home* (London, n.d.), p. 39.

From Mrs. John Sandford, *Woman in her Social and Domestic Character* (1837).

The *bas bleu* [bluestocking] is eager for notoriety, and avails herself of her requirement only to secure it. She does all she can to sustain her claims; she accumulates
around her the materials of learning, and her very boudoir breathes an academic air.
Its decorations are sufficient to proclaim her character; its shelves are filled with books
of every tongue; its tables are strewed with the apparatus of science; the casket of jewels
is displaced for the cabinet of stones, and the hammer and alembic occupy the stand
allotted for the work-box. One niche glooms with a quartered skull; another is enriched
by a classic statue; the easel stands in the background, and the harp is admitted to
complete the picturesque. And she herself is in accordance with all this paraphernalia;
and her conversation, dress and manner equally attest her eagerness to make good her
pretensions to literary notoriety.

Alfred, Lord Tennyson: Order Established

Man for the field and woman for the hearth;
Man for the sword and for the needle she;
Man with the head and woman with the heart;
Man to command and woman to obey;
All else confusion.

G. V. Cox: Order Threatened

November, 1859. In chronicling the striking incidents and varying shades of Oxford
life, it is but fair to mention the following notice, by the Vice-Chancellor and Proctors,
as a proof of a growing neglect of manners, the natural accompaniment of a rougher
bearing and a coarser *external:* "Whereas complaints have been made that some undergraduate members of the University are in the habit of smoking at *public entertainments*
and other wise creating annoyance, they are hereby cautioned against the repetition
of such ungentlemanlike conduct."

France Follows Suit

*When the England of the 1840s was already industrialized, continental countries such as
France were only beginning their industrial revolution. In 1846 the great historian Jules
Michelet (1798–1874), himself the son of a poor printer, interrupted his historical writings
to pen a pamphlet on the condition of the popular masses in France. Well aware that*

From Alfred, Lord Tennyson, *The Princess* (1847).
From G. V. Cox, *Recollections of Oxford* (1868), 428.

machines enslaved and demeaned their serfs, he noticed nevertheless that machine products improved the general condition of the laboring poor, among whom peasants and artisans were still much more numerous than industrial workers. This improvement in material conditions, he felt, could lead to a rise in self-respect and help to integrate into the nation classes heretofore politically irrelevant and socially dangerous.

Jules Michelet: The Revolution of Cheap Calico

There used to be in the past, admission tolls apart, another barrier that drove the peasant from the towns and kept him from turning workman. This barrier was the difficulty of entering a trade, the length of apprenticeship, the exclusive spirit of guilds and corporations. Industrial families took few apprentices, most often their own children whom they exchanged among themselves. Today, new trades have been created, which require no apprenticeship and accept any man. The true worker in these trades is the machine; man needs neither much strength nor skill; he is there only to survey and help that iron worker.

This miserable population enslaved to the machines includes four hundred thousand souls or a little more.[1] That is about one fifteenth of our workers. All who do not know how to do anything come to offer themselves to the machines, to serve the machines. The more they come, the lower the wages, the more miserable they are. On the other hand, the merchandise thus turned out at low cost falls within reach of the poor, so that the misery of the workman-machine slightly lessens the misery of the [other] workers and peasants who are probably seventy times more numerous.

This is what we saw in 1842. The spinning industry was in a desperate condition. It was choking; the warehouses were bursting; there were no sales. The manufacturer, terrified, dared neither work nor cease work with his devouring machines; usury knows no standstill; he worked half-time and crowded his crowded stores still further. Prices fell, in vain; new reductions followed, until cotton had fallen to six farthings. There, something unexpected happened. This word, *six farthings,* was an awakening. Millions of buyers, poor people who never bought anything, set themselves in motion. That was when one saw what an immense and powerful consumer the people is, when it takes a hand. The shops were emptied at one go. The machines went furiously back to work; the chimneys smoked again. It was a revolution in France, little noticed, but great; revolution in cleanliness, sudden improvement in the poor household; body linen, bed and table linen, curtains: whole classes came to have them that had never had them since the beginning of the world.

It is easy to understand, no other example is needed: the machine, which seems a wholly aristocratic force by the centralization of capital that it implies, is nevertheless, by the cheapness and the vulgarization of its products, a very powerful agent of demo-

---

From Jules Michelet, *The People* (Paris, 1946), part I, ch. 2. Translated by Eugen Weber.

[1] The census of 1846 found the French population to stand at 34,400,000.

cratic progress. It places within reach of the poorest a host of useful objects, and even of luxury goods and artifacts, to which they never before had access. Wool, thank God, has come down to the people, and warms it. Silk begins to adorn it. But the great and capital revolution has been calico. The combined efforts of science and art were needed to force a rebellious, uncomfortable fabric, cotton, to undergo every day so many brilliant transformations; then, thus transformed, to spread it everywhere, to place it within grasp of the poorest purse. Once upon a time, every woman wore a single blue or black gown that she kept ten years without washing, for fear that it would fall to shreds. Today, her husband, poor working man, for one day's wages, covers her with a garment of flowers. All this multitude of women that turns our street into a dazzling many-colored rainbow, was once in mourning.

These changes that one considered futile have an immense bearing. Here are no mere material improvements. This is a progress of the people in externals and appearance, upon which men judge each other; it is, so to speak, *visible equality*. From this, the people rises to new ideas which otherwise it would not reach; fashion and taste are for it an initiation to art. Add, more momentous still, that dress impresses even the wearer; he wants to be worthy of it, and seeks to live up to it by his moral bearing.

Liberalism, Nationalism, and 1848

O F the many political developments that sprang from the travail of the French Revolution, the most important were the ideas of popular sovereignty and national self-determination. After the French had sown these ideas and reaped a whirlwind in their own defeat, attempts were made to restore regimes based on different values, with no constitutional way to express the people's will, and sometimes, as in Italy, involving alien occupation of lands which wanted to determine their own future. But such regimes were given no peace by constitutionalist or nationalist liberals, and sooner or later they all either came to grief or learned to adapt themselves to the temper of the times.

Joseph Mazzini

Joseph Mazzini (1805–1872), the anticlerical son of a Genoese doctor, was a typical liberal nationalist of the mid-nineteenth century. A prophet of the risorgimento *(the movement for Italian political unity) and an admirer of Dante rather than Machiavelli, Mazzini spent his life preaching the doctrine of the Italian republic, one and indivisible. What he wanted was a regenerated republic, linked in perpetual and pacific bonds with free republics all over the world. This may have been a utopian dream; it certainly appeared so when the short-lived Roman Republic of 1848, which he had been elected to head, was crushed by—of all things—French troops on June 30, 1849. Thereafter he spent most of his life in exile, propagandizing the Italian masses and plotting the overthrow of Austrian rule in Italy. In spite of his apparent personal failure, the moral fervor of the Italian national movement was largely due to him and to his passionate preaching.*

Mazzini's Conversion to Nationalism

One Sunday in April 1821, while I was yet a boy, I was walking in the Strada Nuova of Genoa with my mother, and an old friend of our family named Andrea Gambini. The Piedmontese insurrection had just been crushed; partly by Austria, partly through treachery, and partly through the weakness of its leaders.

The revolutionists, seeking safety by sea, had flocked to Genoa, and, finding themselves distressed for means, they went about seeking help to enable them to cross into

---

From *Life and Writings of Joseph Mazzini*, 6 vol. (London, 1864–1870).

Spain, where the revolution was yet triumphant. The greater number of them were crowded in S. Pier d'Arena, waiting a chance to embark; but not a few had contrived to enter the city one by one, and I used to search them out from amongst our own people, detecting them either by their general appearance, by some peculiarity of dress, by their warlike air, or by the signs of a deep and silent sorrow on their faces.

The population were singularly moved. Some of the boldest had proposed to the leaders of the insurrection—Santarosa and Ansaldi, I think—to concentrate themselves in, and take possession of the city, and organize a new resistance; but Genoa was found to be deprived of all means of successful defense; the fortresses were without artillery, and the leaders rejected the proposition, telling them to preserve themselves for a better fate.

Presently we were stopped and addressed by a tall black-bearded man, with a severe and energetic countenance, and a fiery glance that I have never since forgotten. He held out a white handkerchief towards us, merely saying, for the refugees of Italy. My mother and friend dropped some money into the handkerchief, and he turned from us to put the same request to others. I afterwards learned his name. He was one Rini, a captain in the National Guard, which had been instituted at the commencement of the movement. He accompanied those for whom he had thus constituted himself collector, and, I believe, died—as so many of ours have perished—for the cause of liberty in Spain.

That day was the first in which a confused idea presented itself to my mind—I will not say of country, or of liberty—but an idea that we Italians could and therefore ought to struggle for the liberty of our country. I had already been unconsciously educated in the worship of equality by the democratic principles of my parents, whose bearing toward high or low was ever the same. Whatever the position of the individual, they simply regarded the man and sought only the honest man. And my own natural aspirations towards liberty were fostered by constantly hearing my father and the friend already mentioned speak of the recent republican era in France; by the study of the works of Livy and Tacitus, which my Latin master had given me to translate; and by certain old French newspapers, which I discovered half-hidden behind my father's medical books. Amongst these last were some numbers of the *Chronique du Mois*, a Girondist publication belonging to the first period of the French Revolution.

But the idea of an existing wrong in my own country, against which it was a duty to struggle, and the thought that I too must bear my part in that struggle, flashed before my mind on that day for the first time, never again to leave me. The remembrance of those refugees, many of whom became my friends in after life, pursued me wherever I went by day, and mingled with my dreams by night. I would have given I know not what to follow them. I began collecting names and facts, and studied, as best I might, the record of that heroic struggle, seeking to fathom the causes of its failure.

They had been betrayed and abandoned by those who had sworn to concentrate every effort in the movement; the new king [Carlo Felice] had invoked the aid of Austria; part of the Piedmontese troops had even preceded the Austrians at Novara; and the leaders had allowed themselves to be overwhelmed at the first encounter, without making an effort to resist. All the details I succeeded in collecting led me to think that they might have conquered, if all of them had done their duty; then why not renew the attempt?

This idea ever took stronger possession of my soul, and my spirit was crushed by the impossibility I then felt of even conceiving by what means to reduce it to action. Upon the benches of the University (in those days these existed a course of Belles Lettres, preparatory to the courses of law and medicine, to which even the very young were admitted,) in the midst of the noisy tumultuous life of the students around me, I was sombre and absorbed, and appeared like one suddenly grown old. I childishly determined to dress always in black, fancying myself in mourning for my country. Jacopo Ortis happened to fall into my hands at this time, and the reading of it became a passion with me. I learned it by heart. Matters went so far that my poor mother became terrified lest I should commit suicide.

On the Duties of Man

Your first duties—first as regards importance—are, as I have already told you, towards Humanity. You are men before you are either citizens or fathers. If you do not embrace the whole human family in your affection, if you do not bear witness to your belief in the Unity of that family, consequent upon the Unity of God, and in that fraternity among the peoples which is destined to reduce that unity to action; if, wheresoever a fellow-creature suffers, or the dignity of human nature is violated by falsehood or tyranny—you are not ready, if able, to aid the unhappy, and do not feel called upon to combat, if able, for the redemption of the betrayed or oppressed—you violate your law of life, you comprehend not that Religion which will be the guide and blessing of the future.

But, you tell me, you cannot attempt united action, distinct and divided as you are in language, customs, tendencies, and capacity. The individual is too insignificant, and Humanity too vast. The mariner of Brittany prays to God as he puts to sea: Help me, my God! my boat is so small and thy ocean so wide! And this prayer is the true expression of the condition of each one of you, until you find the means of infinitely multiplying your forces and powers of action.

This means was provided for you by God when he gave you a country; when, even as a wise overseer of labour distributes the various branches of employment according to the different capacities of the workmen, he divided Humanity into distinct groups or nuclei upon the face of the earth, thus creating the germ of Nationalities. Evil governments have disfigured the divine design. Nevertheless you may still trace it, distinctly marked out—at least as far as Europe is concerned—by the course of the great rivers, the direction of the higher mountains, and other geographical conditions. They have disfigured it by their conquests, their greed, and their jealousy even of the righteous

---

From Emilie A. Venturi, *Joseph Mazzini: A Memoir* (London, 1875).

power of others; disfigured it so far that, if we except England and France—there is not perhaps a single country whose present boundaries correspond to that design.

These governments did not, and do not, recognize any country save their own families or dynasty, the egotism of caste. But the Divine design will infallibly be realized. Natural divisions, and the spontaneous, innate tendencies of the peoples, will take the place of the arbitrary divisions sanctioned by evil governments. The map of Europe will be redrawn. The countries of the Peoples, defined by the vote of free men, will arise upon the ruins of the countries of kings and privileged castes, and between these countries harmony and fraternity will exist. And the common work of Humanity, of general amelioration and the gradual discovery and application of its Law of life, being distributed according to local and general capacities, will be wrought out in peaceful and progressive development and advance. Then may each one of you, fortified by the power and the affection of many millions, all speaking the same language, gifted with the same tendencies, and educated by the same historical tradition, hope, even by your own single effort, to be able to benefit all Humanity.

O my brothers, love your Country! Our country is our Home, the house that God has given us, placing therein a numerous family that loves us, and whom we love; a family with whom we sympathise more readily, and whom we understand more quickly than we do others; and which, from its being centred around a given spot, and from the homogeneous nature of its elements, is adapted to a special branch of activity. Our country is our common workshop, whence the products of our activity are sent forth for the benefit of the whole world; wherein the tools and implements of labour we can most usefully employ are gathered together: nor may we reject them without disobeying the plan of the Almighty, and diminishing our own strength.

In labouring for our own country on the right principle, we labour for Humanity. Our country is the fulcrum of the lever we have to wield for the common good. If we abandon that fulcrum, we run the risk of rendering ourselves useless not only to humanity but to our country itself. Before men can associate with the nations of which humanity is composed, they must have a National existence. There is no true association except among equals. It is only through our country that we can have a recognized collective existence.

Humanity is a vast army advancing to the conquest of lands unknown, against enemies both powerful and astute. The peoples are the different corps, the divisions of that army. Each of them has its post assigned to it, and its special operation to execute; and the common victory depends upon the exactitude with which those distinct operations shall be fulfilled. Disturb not the order of battle. Forsake not the banner given you by God. Wheresoever you may be, in the centre of whatsoever people circumstances may have placed you, be ever ready to combat for the liberty of that people should it be necessary, but combat in such wise that the blood you shed may reflect glory, not on yourselves alone, but on your country. Say not I, but we. Let each man among you strive to incarnate his country in himself. Let each man among you regard himself as a guarantee, responsible for his fellow-countrymen, and learn so to govern his actions as to cause his country to be loved and respected through him. Your country is the sign of the mission God has given you to fulfill towards Humanity. The faculties and forces of all her sons should be associated in the accomplishment of that mission.

The true country is a community of free men and equals, bound together in fraternal concord to labour towards a common aim. You are bound to make it and to maintain it such. The country is not an aggregation, but an association. There is therefore no true country without an uniform right. There is no true country where the uniformity of that right is violated by the existence of castes, privilege, and inequality. Where the activity of a portion of the powers and faculties of the individual is either cancelled or dormant; where there is not a common Principle, recognized, accepted, and developed by all, there is no true nation, no People; but only a multitude, a fortuitous agglomeration of men whom circumstances have called together, and whom circumstances may again divide. In the name of the love you bear your country you must peacefully but untiringly combat the existence of privilege and inequality in the land that gave you life.

There is but one sole legitimate privilege, the privilege of Genius when it reveals itself united with virtue. But this is a privilege given by God, and when you acknowledge it and follow its inspiration, you do so freely, exercising your own reason and your own choice. Every privilege which demands submission from you in virtue of power, inheritance, or any other right than the Right common to all, is a usurpation and a tyranny which you are bound to resist and destroy.

Be your country your Temple. God at the summit; a people of equals at the base.

Accept no other formula, no other moral law, if you would not dishonour alike your country and yourselves. Let all secondary laws be but the gradual regulation of your existence by the progressive application of this supreme law. And in order that they may be such, it is necessary that all of you should aid in framing them. Laws framed only by a single fraction of the citizens, can never, in the very nature of things, be other than the mere expression of the thoughts, aspirations, and desires of that fraction; the representation, not of the Country, but of a third or fourth part, of a class or zone of the country.

The laws should be the expression of the universal aspiration, and promote the universal good. They should be a pulsation of the heart of the nation. The entire nation should, either directly or indirectly, legislate.

By yielding up this mission into the hands of a few, you substitute the egotism of one class for the Country, which is the union of all classes.

Country is not a mere zone or territory. The true country is the Idea to which it gives birth; it is the Thought of love, the sense of communion which unites in one all the sons of that territory.

So long as a single one amongst your brothers has no vote to represent him in the development of the national life, so long as there is one left to vegetate in ignorance where others are educated, so long as a single man, able and willing to work, languishes in poverty through want of work to do, you have no country in the sense in which country ought to exist—the country of all and for all.

Education, labour, and the franchise, are the three main pillars of the nation. Rest not until you have built them strongly up with your own labour and exertions.

Never deny your sister nations. Be it yours to evolve the life of your country in loveliness and strength; free from all servile fears or sceptical doubts; maintaining as its basis the People; as its guide the consequences of the principles of its Religious

Faith, logically and energetically applied; its strength, the united strength of all; its aim, the fulfilment of the mission given to it by God.

And so long as you are ready to die for Humanity, the life of your country will be immortal.

The French Revolutions of 1848

The eighteenth century had demonstrated that the status quo *could be changed by force, and the nineteenth century proceeded to apply this lesson at every opportunity. But though each revolution might be successful in solving some of the problems that had caused it, each also revealed new ones. And, especially in 1848, the political and social claims that had been telescoped early in the year came to clash when those satisfied with purely political reforms were challenged by others who wanted more—work, food, and a redistribution of property. The two accounts of the French Revolutions of 1848 that follow are by one of the leaders of the Left, Louis Blanc, and by the foremost liberal thinker of the time, Alexis de Tocqueville.*

Louis Blanc: from Historical Revelations

Louis Blanc (1811–1882) was one of the leading writers of the French Left under the July monarchy of Louis Philippe. Blanc's popularity led to his designation as a member of the temporary government that was set up in February 1848 after the fall of the king. There Louis Blanc persuaded his colleagues to abolish the death penalty and to found national workshops which, he hoped, would help solve the problems of unemployed and hungry laborers. Soon, however, because his activities were hindered by official suspicion and his safety endangered by the counterrevolution in May, the radical leader had to seek refuge in England. He returned to France only after Napoleon III's fall in 1870, and he was immediately elected deputy of Paris to the new National Assembly. His account of the events of 1848 comes from his years of exile in England.

HOW THE PROVISIONAL GOVERNMENT WAS ESTABLISHED

Louis Philippe was a prince gifted with many good qualities. His domestic virtues were such as to command respect. He was by no means wanting in enlightened perceptions. Both from a disposition naturally merciful, and from a philosophical notion of the value of human life, he was so averse to shedding blood, that his ministers were sure to meet with an almost desperate resistance on his part, whenever they asked him to affix his signature to a sentence of death. Upon the whole, he was a man of remarkably sober character. Nor did Liberty, under his reign, receive any mortal wound. In times

---

From Louis Blanc, *1848* (London, 1858).

of foreign and internal difficulties, he succeeded in warding off imminent dangers, and the middle classes were indebted to him for the repose they so dearly prized.

Still, when the hour of his doom struck, no wish was expressed for his crown's preservation; no helping hand was held out to him; the moneyed classes kept aloof; the soldiers either refused to fight or fought reluctantly; for the first time, the shopkeepers seemed to have forgotten that revolutions are bad for trade; the most active part of the National Guard actually countenanced the insurrection; the old King, looking around him, and seeing nothing but a dreary solitude, became disheartened, and a government which had lasted no less than seventeen years was overthrown by a touch.

How is such a phenomenon to be accounted for? In my "History of Ten Years," the reader will find the causes explained and the result foretold. Of these causes, the most effective lay in Louis Philippe's utter inability to comprehend all that was chivalrous and elevated in the genius of France. To the meaner principles of action he applied for support. Bribery was his principal engine of government. He fostered the blind fears of the bourgeoisie, and took pleasure in nursing selfishness. His policy was systematically inimical to anything like a generous hope or a noble impulse. Not only did he struggle against all efforts originating in the spirit of improvement, but it was his constant endeavour to make the nation, if possible, after his own image; that is, greedy of gain, true only to the debasing worship of the cash-box, heedless of the past, and faithless in the future. Even what happened to be good in his policy was done through objectionable means, and everyone knows that it was only by wounding beyond measure in the heart of the French the feeling of national self-importance, that he succeeded in averting the calamities of war. So completely had he stifled around him all promptings of devotedness and disinterested attachment, that these supreme resources proved wanting when needed; so that he may verily be said to have been the sole artificer of his own ruin.

The fact is, that, two months before the downfall of Louis Philippe, it had become quite certain that the Democratic party was about to appear, in its turn, on the public stage, and to take possession of it exclusively.

This was made obvious by the "banquet de Dijon," whose news spread all over France with the rapidity of lightning. There, in an immense hall, decorated with flags and devices symbolic of liberty, in the presence of thirteen hundred guests—operatives, manufacturers, tradesmen, magistrates—words reverberated; which M. de Lamartine, seized with short-sighted terror, termed the "tocsin of opinion." At Lille, M. Ledru Rollin had previously said:

"Sometimes, the stagnant pools of the dried-up Nile, and the detritus in a state of decomposition on its banks, engender epidemics; but let the flood return, the river, in its impetuous course, will sweep away all these impurities, and will deposit on its borders germs of fecundity and reawakened life."

These audacious allusions were repeated by MM. Ledru Rollin and Flocon at the "banquet de Dijon" without exciting surprise, so thoroughly was the idea of an impending revolution present to every mind. And, for the same reason, no one took exception to this passage of my speech—prophecy and menace:

"The power which but yesterday seemed so vigorous, sinks under its own weight, without even being pushed. An invisible will goes on its way through the highest regions of society, sowing degrading catastrophes. Unexpected acts of insanity, shameful disasters, unaccountable suicides, crimes to make the hair stand on end, come, one after another, stunning public opinion into stupor. Then, that Society, apparently so prosperous, becomes agitated; it wonders at the mysterious virus which it feels running through its veins. 'Corruption' is the cry of the day; and everyone exclaims: 'That such things should last any longer, is impossible; what will tomorrow bring?' Gentlemen, when the fruit is rotten, it only needs a breath of wind to shake it from the tree."

This was said towards the end of December; and at the end of February, hardly two months after, the blast had come which blew down the monarchy.

The circumstances connected with the downfall of Louis Philippe being generally known, I will enter at once upon my subject by explaining how the Provisional Government was established.

At that period, the Republican party, numerically inferior in the provinces, was prevalent in Paris. Its accredited organs were the *National* and the *Réforme;* the latter paper being more acceptable to the workmen, on account of its social tendencies, whilst the other, merely political, had a stronger hold on the middle classes. . . .

The situation was one of extraordinary enthusiasm mingled with dangerous excitement. The passions let loose by the struggle were still burning. The aspect of Paris was terrible. Here and there infuriated groups were seen emerging from behind the barricades boastful of the blood which stained their dress, flourishing muskets, swords, hatchets, or pikes, and shouting fiercely: *"A bas les Bourbons!"* The palace of the Tuileries had just been invaded, amidst an unparalleled tempest formed by the threatening clamours of the combatants, the uproar of the rushing multitudes, the beating of drums, the shots incessantly fired, the fits of laughing and the loud jests in which, on any such occasion, the *gamins de Paris*[1] are wont to indulge. As to the particulars which marked the invasion of the royal abode, I know nothing more than what any one could, at the time, pick up from flying reports. But it is a matter of public notoriety that some sat down at card-tables and began in joke to bet the millions of the Civil list; that many a jolly fellow delighted in putting on the rich velvet dressing gowns which had been worn by princely personages; that two insurgents whose firelocks lay beside them on the ground, were noticed playing at chess with a fixed look and uninterrupted attention, despite the deafening turmoil. "Marquis," asked a facetious companion of a youth who held in his hands a plan of Neuilly, "What are you about?" "Viscount," replied the lad, "I am examining the plan of my estates." By superficial minds, these apparently trifling incidents may be deemed to have no other import than to show the levity so complacently ascribed to the French. But those who do not judge of the inside by the outside will easily perceive through all this the deep-rooted love of equality which is the true characteristic of the French nation.

Under such circumstances, M. Martin (of Strasbourg) and I concurred in thinking that this was not the proper time for handling the abstruse questions which the Revolu-

---

[1] Paris ragamuffins.

tion was likely to start. The main point was to insure the triumph of the Republic by baffling the intrigues of petty parliamentary coteries on one hand, and by preventing, on the other, the wild confusion into which the general rush towards the unknown could not fail to plunge everything, in the absence of all regular direction. Two great evils were to be averted: despotism and anarchy, for anarchy is nothing better than a tumultuous despotism. An immediate selection of united leaders was therefore required; and although the republicanism of M. de Lamartine, a new convert, seemed somewhat unsteady; although rumours had already become current about the support which M. Garnier Pagès might possibly be disposed to give to the Regency of the Duchess of Orleans, the influence of such men over the middle classes certainly deserved to be taken into serious consideration. Subsequent events have shown, indeed, that alliances of this kind are fraught with impediments and perils. But it must be borne in mind that the republican party, however strong in Paris, was far from being able to get the mastery in the provinces. The middle classes contained a considerable number of republicans, sincere though timid, whom it was impolitic to frighten out of our ranks. Moreover, the situation was dreadfully unsettled, and the morrow overcast with clouds. To bring a man like M. de Lamartine to commit himself irrevocably in the service of the Republic was considered a stroke of sound policy, and even now, I do not think the step we took would have proved a fatal one, had it not been made so by an astounding concurrence of unfavourable circumstances, which it was then impossible for any one to foresee.

So, it was determined that M. de Lamartine should rank with the republican leaders.

The exertions of M. Martin (of Strasbourg) and my own having been attended with full success, the two leading papers of the republican party came to an understanding, the result of which was the adoption in common of a list to be presented to the people.

It is singular—and this is one of the most peculiar features of the Parisians—how an intuitive perception of the necessity of order combines in their character with occasional outbursts of turbulence. One may think it wonderful, still, it is perfectly true, that Paris never witnessed a rising in which the insurgents did not preserve, all through, a sense of discipline, and an almost uneasy preoccupation of the immediate consequences. In June, for instance, in those formidable days of June, the fact was ascertained that the insurgents, while fighting desperately, were busy writing down, on the very stones of the barricades stained with their blood, the names of a Provisional Government.

So, on the 24th of February, scarcely was the light at an end, when the people flocked from every quarter to the offices of both Republican papers, in quest of a central direction.

An immense crowd surrounded the office of the *Réforme*, the smallest part of which was pent up to suffocation in the court of the *Hotel Buillon*, while the rest overflowed the neighbouring streets, and more especially the street of Jean Jacques Rousseau. A sort of considerate anxiety was visible in everyone's countenance. The only shout sent forth was *"Vive la République!"*—a shout which grew tremendous, but gradually dwindled into solemn silence, when I made my appearance at a window, holding a paper in my hand. Then it was that I read the following list, which had been agreed to be the *Réforme* and the *National:*

Dupont (de L'Eure)
François Arago
Ledru Rollin
Flocon
Marie
Armand Marrast
Crémieux
Garnier Pagès
Lamartine
Louis Blanc

The utterance of these names was hailed with loud acclamations, quickly succeeded by a general cry: *Albert! Albert!*

Albert had never been considered as a political leader. Still less had he ever entertained any hope or desire of being chosen as such. He was a mechanic. Amongst us, he was but little known personally. For my part, I had never seen him. But his uprightness, both of heart and mind, his unbounded devotion to the cause of the people, the disinterested fervour of his convictions, his unassuming manners, his courage, had endeared him to the workmen. To them the presence of a man of that stamp in the Provisional Government was a token that no measure would be taken without being anxiously scrutinised, and, if prejudicial to their interests, strenuously opposed. Moreover, what could be better calculated to mark the commencement of a new era—what could inaugurate in a more striking way the official acknowledgment of the rights of labour, than this previously unheard of rising of a workman to a post of the highest eminence? I took up a pen; I wrote down the name of Albert with a feeling of deep emotion, and, hastening to the office of the *National,* I had there no difficulty in getting the name added to the list, which was immediately circulated all over Paris, and happened, as regards the other names, to agree with those which emanated from every other popular centre of action, save that on some the name of M. Recurt, afterwards Minister of the Interior, and very popular then in the Faubourg St. Antoine, figured in the place of the names of Crémieux or Garnier Pagès.

THE INTELLECTUAL EFFERVESCENCE OF THE TIME

Home policy, foreign policy, taxation, emancipation of working men, the improvement of the condition of poor women, gratuitous national education, the union of peoples,—what questions were there not raised and discussed in these ardent laboratories of public opinion? [the clubs] Oh, how swift was the march of life then! How each man's heart beat quicker! and what swift wings the imagination lent to the mind's conceptions! So intense was the life of society, moved to its very depths, that in a few days the number of the clubs rose to 300; and though immense halls had been placed at the disposal of these popular meetings in various public buildings, yet, from these halls, crammed every night to suffocation, intellectual excitement overflowed into the streets, spread from man to man, and finally, penetrating into those miserable haunts, where the most noble faculties of man had been hitherto asleep, awakened a powerful and impassioned curiosity.

Add to this, the incessant action of a crowd of new journals, to which the abolition of the stamp-duty had largely contributed; and the combative character of literature, as represented by such writers as MM. Victor Hugo, Eugène Sue, Félix Pyat, and Madame George Sand.

I need hardly say, that in the midst of this vast mixture of aspirations and feelings, all of which were permitted, without exception, to express and justify themselves, the Provisional Government praised by some, was the object of vehement and repeated attacks from others; if allowance was made for the difficulty of its task in the club of Barbès, it was criticized with ever-increasing severity in the club of Blanqui. If the majority of the council was supported by the *National,* whose views had undergone no change, and if the minority found an advocate in the *Réforme,* edited by M. Ribeyrolles in the most brilliant manner, how many were the journals that indiscriminately attacked, and even flung their invectives at the whole Provisional Government? Not one of our acts escaped the bitterest scrutiny from M. Émile de Girardin, chief editor of the *Presse.* Not a single thing we did which was not cited by M. Proudhon, editor of the *Représentant du Peuple,* as a proof that all governments, be they what they might, ought to be suppressed, and that the only thing which should be left standing was *anarchy,* or to use the orthography of Proudhon, *an-archy.* M. de Lamennais, too, who a little later, came over to Socialism, opposed it at that time, from not having sufficiently studied it, and his journal, *Le Peuple Constituant,* waged active war against the Luxembourg.

Thus lashed by every wave of this agitated and roaring sea, what course did the Provisional Government take? Were they to be seen, doing what Louis Bonaparte and his supporters do at this very hour—interdicting discussion, reducing their adversaries to silence, trembling at the least appearance of criticism, growing pale before the mere shadow of an allusion, seeking their safety and force in darkness? No. The Provisional Government were so convinced of their moral strength, so bold from the consciousness of their good intentions, and so confiding in the spontaneous support of a free people, that far from fearing the light—a fear that should be left to malefactors—they spread their special protection over the liberty of their most violent enemies. The printing-house of M. Émile de Girardin having been menaced by a crowd of people exasperated at the excess to which he carried his systematic attacks upon the official agents of the Republic, M. Caussidière at once despatched his Montagnards to keep the crowd in order, and M. Ledru Rollin went himself to assist personally in preserving unscathed that liberty which M. de Girardin was so remorselessly using at our expense. A farce like this took place at the Luxembourg. Some delegates having come and told me that the people were irritated at our persistence in suffering the *Constitutionnel* to pour its venom every morning on the Luxembourg, and that a great number of workmen were assembled at that very moment in the court, intending to go and bring it to account for its calumnies, I instantly went out to them, and turned them from their purpose by words whose extreme vehemence disarmed them.

There survives, moreover, an official and decisive testimony to the confidence of the Provisional Government in the sympathies of the nation. I allude to the Proclamation they published on the 20th of April, concerning the Clubs. It begins with these words: "The Republic lives by discussion and liberty," and finishes thus: "The best safe-guard of liberty, is liberty."

Let the people of England compare the principles so openly professed by the Provisional Government, with those that are now directing the policy of Louis Bonaparte, and then let them say, if, for Great Britain, an alliance with the Republic would not have been more natural, more reasonable, more certain, than an alliance with the Empire?

After all, the license given to the Clubs and to the newspapers had, together with some of the drawbacks inseparable from all human things, advantages which will not be lost to the future. The question under discussion alarmed and irritated egotists of every kind, all who live by abuses; factitious agitation was encouraged; the tendency to innovation sometimes manifested itself under ridiculous forms; there was much declamation; and the allurements offered to public curiosity were not always wholesome or substantial. But problems of a high interest were proposed, and their solution matured; the attention of the people was keenly aroused on points on which the light of knowledge was cast for the first time; true working ideas sprang up amongst others that were vain and chimerical; in a word, the soil was ploughed in all directions, and seed was thrown into it, which nothing hereafter can destroy, which even at this moment is germinating silently, and which, when the winter shall have passed away, that is, on the morrow of the day when despotism shall have vanished, will yield a harvest whose rich abundance will be the astonishment of Europe.

THE JUNE DAYS

Out of doors, the people continued to cry: Du Pain ou du Plomb!—bread or lead.

But as if to stifle those words of woe, it was not enough to load guns with grape, to set infantry and cavalry in movement, to reinforce the National Guard with troops of the line, and the republican guard with the Garde Mobile—the aid of calumny was called to their support. In a circular addressed to the municipalities of the twelve arrondissements, M. Marrast dared to represent this insurgent army of hunger as a horde of brigands in foreign pay. He dared to write these words, speaking of the chiefs of the insurrection: "It is not only civil war that they would light up among us, it is PILLAGE that they prepare."

No doubt the parties that wore the legitimist and imperial liveries had, crowded into their ranks, men ready to instigate disorder in the hope of abetting the triumph of their conspiracies; and these men were in effect the active agents of disorder. But to confound the instigations of conspirators like these, who scarcely dared to show their faces or their objects, with the true cause which was then arming thousands of fellowmen; to pretend that the barricades were being reared against the Republic, and that PILLAGE was the object of men driven to despair, and hurrying to death,—a more audacious calumny, I say, was never published. Yet it had the success of audacious calumny. Sincere Republicans believed that the Republic was in peril; false Republicans affected to believe that it was attacked: there was an immense uncertainty, and an immense confusion. The insurgents continued crying, as they marched to the combat, BREAD OR LEAD!

Whether the insurrection might not have been prevented from the first—whether barricades need have been quietly left to boys to construct—whether, in short, General Cavaignac, by letting the insurrection pass, reserved to himself the sinister honour of suppressing it,—these are questions for History to solve. For the present, I will only state this fact, that, at four o'clock in the afternoon, on the 23rd of June, in the Faubourg St. Marceau, although it was in full insurrection, the circulation was still free, and that it would have been perfectly easy for either the civil or the military authorities to ascertain that many of the barricades were guarded by men incompletely armed, and utterly without ammunition of any kind. I have ample evidence in my possession to produce, when the proper time arrives for doing justice to all.

It is worthy of remark that this insurrection, so general in its causes and in its spirit, assumed at almost every point the character of a local protest. In many districts, the inhabitants reserved to themselves exclusively the guard of their own barricades, rejected the assistance of strangers, and after closing all access to their streets, refused to cooperate in the general attack. After the capture of the Eighth and Ninth Mairies, for instance, when preparations were making for storming the Hôtel de Ville—a very strong position, strongly defended—scarcely a few hundred combatants could be got together at the bottom of the Rue St. Antoine.

Reinforcements were demanded from the Faubourgs, where the barricades could easily have spared numbers of men, but in vain. Not but that among the combatants there were many who knew well that an insurrection which stands still, or does not go forward, is lost; but that there was a total want of unity of direction, and many of the insurgents were paralyzed by the sense of their inferiority in the use of their weapons. Fifty thousand men had taken up arms: how many in that number were utterly unable to use them! Some, who might have vigorously defended a barricade, were more than inefficient for any other purpose. And whilst in the rich quarters of the town there were thousands of isolated combatants, who were on the look out for a loophole to pass over to the insurgents, there was probably a reserve of twenty thousand men in the Faubourgs, whose strength might have changed the fate of the battle.

Another cause of the unwillingness of the combatants to venture far beyond their barricades was the want of ammunition. The gunpowder was manufactured by the insurgents, and from this fact we may determine their chances of success against regular troops, amply furnished with all the resources of war.

Yet, in spite of the inadequacy of the ammunition for offensive warfare, of the want of chiefs to concentrate their movements, of means to prolong the combat, the indomitable energy of the insurgents was astounding. The regular troops and National Guards fought well, as Frenchmen always fight; but those who were least liable to suspicion of sympathy with the insurgents, confessed that their prodigious resolution and audacity would have sufficed, under an able general, for the conquest of the world!

Besides, thanks to M. Marie, the Atéliers Nationaux had received a military organization, and had been divided into brigades, squadrons, and companies, comprising the men of the same arrondissement, of the same quarter, of the same street; and, in a war of barricades, in which every man resolved to fight and die at his own door, for the bread of his own household, such an organization lent a certain ensemble to the resistance, although the resistance was a local one.

The movement had continued to spread from point to point, until all Paris was in arms. It was not until Friday evening that the *Société des Droits de l'Homme* was enabled to hold a meeting; and the communications were already interrupted in so many places, that it was impossible to give the sections anything like uniformity of operation. Having at their head men of ardour and decision, the sectionaries of the eighth arrondissement took an active part in the attack of the Place des Vosges. In the offices of the Socialist journals, a poignant uncertainty prevailed amidst the contradictory rumours arriving every moment from the scene of conflict. A list of names for a new Government came from a barricade in the Faubourg St. Marceau, containing the name of M. de Lamartine, together with other names then more dear to the people.

Overwhelming as the forces of the Government appeared, the end was still doubtful. At some points, the desperation of the insurgents was incredibly triumphant. In the Faubourg du Temple, where General Cavaignac had reconnoitred the fortresses, the fight assumed gigantic proportions. At the attack of the barricade Saint Maure, the troops suffered terrible loss, and were repulsed. When the darkness of night enveloped the streets, the insurgents were completely masters of that portion of the city.

Terrible was that night—a night of expectation and grief! On the following morning, the heavy guns began to thunder once more against the Faubourg, without gaining the least advantage over the insurgents, while the troops advanced, retreated, and advanced again, with alternate wrath and discouragement. Until Sunday evening, the blood of countrymen and fellow-citizens was flowing in disastrous rivalry. What was most lamentable of all, was the inexorable fury of the fight between the working-men and the Garde Mobile—between fathers on one side, and sons on the other! Everybody knows now, that when insurrection began, the Garde Mobile was more disposed to join than to attack the insurgents. But it had been so pertinaciously asserted that the insurrection was against the Republic, that one more terrible misunderstanding was added to the history of civil conflicts. . . .

That night passed without any fresh attack by the troops; it was not until the following (Monday) morning, about eight or nine o'clock, that the Faubourg was completely invested. The insurgents beat a retreat, but did not cease to fire until they had expended their last cartridge. At five o'clock in the evening, La Villette was taken: that was the end of the bloody tragedy.

An eye-witness assured me that after that final struggle, a National Guard shot a man for the simple reason that he wore a red comforter round his throat.

I had myself a narrow escape from some of the party of order. Going home when the insurrection had just been put down, in company with several of my colleagues, I was set upon by a number of National Guards crying out: "Here is the contriver of the national workshops. Down with him!" Not satisfied with threatening to kill me, one of them clapped his pistol to my temple; but the weapon, being fortunately struck up by one of my companions, went off in the air. Others rushed upon me with their sabres; and I should have been killed in this cowardly way, had not my fellow-representatives on the spot, and some respectable National Guards come to my defense, and succeeded, after a desperate struggle, in rescuing me from my murderous assailants, by forcing me into the Café Frascati, which I soon after left under the protection of two worthy citizens, M. Bouillon, the lieutenant-colonel of the second legion, and one of my colleagues, M. Dutier. The latter gentleman's tilbury was waiting for him on the boulevard; he put me into it, and we drove to the Assembly. Two shots were fired at me, from behind!

After the victory the reprisals were terrible. Prisoners huddled together in the vaults beneath the terrace, in the garden of the Tuileries, which faces the Seine, were shot at random through the air-holes in the wall: others were shot in masses in the Plaine de Grenelle, in the cemetery of Mont Parnasse, in the quarries of Montmartre, in the cloister of Saint Benoît, in the court of the Hôtel de Cluny. Wretched men, whom General Cavaignac in his proclamation of the 23rd of June had addressed in these words—"Come to us, the Republic opens her arms to you"—were dragged before Councils of War to be judged by the men they had fought: and the vanquished, whom General Cavaignac had promised not to treat as victims, were despatched *en masse*, without trial. In short, a horrible and humiliating terror spread over the devastated city for many days. A single episode will complete the picture.

On the 3rd of July a considerable number of prisoners were taken out of the cellars of the École Militaire to be removed to the Prefecture of Police, and thence to the forts. They were bound four and four with cords very tightly drawn. As these poor wretches, exhausted by hunger, could hardly drag their limbs along, porringers filled with coarse soup were placed before them. Having their hands tied, they were obliged to lie down on their stomachs, and to drag themselves to the porringers like animals, amidst shouts of laughter from the officers of the escort, who called it "Socialism in practice."—I heard this from one of the unfortunate victims of this punishment, which no Indian savage could ever have invented.

Alexis de Tocqueville: from Recollections

Alexis de Tocqueville (1805–1859), trained as a lawyer and magistrate, made his name when, in 1835, he published his famous essay, Democracy in America. *The admired friend of men such as J. S. Mill, Tocqueville was elected to the Chamber of Deputies in 1839 and to the French Academy in 1841, and came to be regarded as an outstanding man, liberal but detached. Opposing the extremism of both Left and Right, Tocqueville, who in 1849 had served briefly as foreign minister of the Second Republic, retired from public life after Louis Napoleon's coup of 1851, and spent his remaining years in writing history and compiling his own* Recollections, *from which the following passages are taken.*

And so the Monarchy of July was fallen, fallen without a struggle, and before rather than beneath the blows of the victors, who were as astonished at their triumph as were

From Alexis de Tocqueville, *Recollections,* tr. Alexander Teixeira de Mattos (New York, 1896).

the vanquished at their defeat, I have often, since the Revolution of February, heard Mr. Guizot and even M. Molé and M. Thiers declare that this event should only be attributed to a surprise and regarded as a mere accident, a bold and lucky stroke and nothing more. I have always felt tempted to answer them in the words which Molière's *Misanthrope* used to Oronte: "To judge as you do, you have your own reasons"; for these three men had conducted the affairs of France, under the guidance of King Louis-Philippe, during eighteen years, and it was difficult for them to admit that it was the King's bad government which had prepared the catastrophe which hurled him from the Throne.

As for me, I have not the same motives for forming an opinion, and I could hardly persuade myself to be of theirs. I am not prepared to say that accidents played no part in the Revolution of February; on the contrary, they played a great one; but they were not the only thing.

I have come across men of letters, who have written history without taking part in public affairs, and politicians, who have only concerned themselves with producing events without thinking of describing them. I have observed that the first are always inclined to find general causes, whereas the others, living in the midst of disconnected daily facts, are prone to imagine that everything is attributable to particular incidents, and that the wires which they pull are the same that move the world. It is to be presumed that both are equally deceived.

For my part, I detest these absolute systems, which represent all the events of history as depending upon great first causes linked by the chain of fatality, and which, as it were, suppress men from the history of the human race. They seem narrow, to my mind, under their pretence of broadness, and false beneath their air of mathematical exactness. I believe (*pace* the writers who have invented these sublime theories in order to feed their vanity and facilitate their work) that many important historical facts can only be explained by accidental circumstances, and that many others remain totally inexplicable. Moreover, chance, or rather that tangle of secondary causes which we call chance, for want of the knowledge how to unravel it, plays a great part in all that happens on the world's stage; although I firmly believe that chance does nothing that has not been prepared beforehand. Antecedent facts, the nature of institutions, the cast of minds and the state of morals are the materials of which are composed those impromptus which astonish and alarm us.

The Revolution of February, in common with all other great events of this class, sprang from general causes, impregnated, if I am permitted the expression, by accidents; and it would be as superficial a judgment to ascribe it necessarily to the former or exclusively to the latter.

The industrial revolution which, during the past thirty years, had turned Paris into the principal manufacturing city of France and attracted within its walls an entire new population of workmen (to whom the works of the fortifications had added another population of laborers at present deprived of work) tended more and more to inflame this multitude. Add to this the democratic disease of envy, which was silently permeating it; the economical and political theories which were beginning to make their way and which strove to prove that human misery was the work of laws and not of Providence, and that poverty could be suppressed by changing the conditions of society; the contempt into which the governing class, and especially the men who led it, had fallen, a contempt so general and so profound that it paralyzed the resistance even of those who were most interested in maintaining the power that was being overthrown; the centralization which reduced the whole revolutionary movement to the overmastering of Paris and the seizing of the machinery of government, and lastly, the mobility of all things, institutions, ideas, men and customs, in a fluctuating state of society which had, in less than sixty years, undergone the shock of seven great revolutions, without numbering a multitude of smaller, secondary upheavals. These were the general causes without which the Revolution of February would have been impossible. The principal accidents which led to it were the passions of the dynastic Opposition, which brought about a riot in proposing a reform; the suppression of this riot, first over-violent, and then abandoned; the sudden disappearance of the old Ministry, unexpectedly snapping the threads of power, which the new ministers, in their confusion, were unable either to seize upon or to reunite; the mistakes and disorder of mind of these ministers, so powerless to re-establish that which they had been strong enough to overthrow; the vacillation of the generals; the absence of the only Princes who possessed either personal energy or popularity; and above all, the senile imbecility of King Louis-Philippe, his weakness, which no one could have foreseen, and which still remains almost incredible, after the event has proved it.

I have sometimes asked myself what could have produced this sudden and unprecedented depression in the King's mind. Louis-Philippe had spent his life in the midst of revolutions, and certainly lacked neither experience, courage, nor readiness of mind, although these qualities all failed him so completely on that day. In my opinion, his weakness was due to his excessive surprise; he was overwhelmed with consternation before he had grasped the meaning of things. The Revolution of February was unforeseen by all, but by him more than any other; he had been prepared for it by no warning from the outside, for since many years his mind had withdrawn into that sort of haughty solitude into which in the end the intellect almost always settles down of princes who have long lived happily, and who, mistaking luck for genius, refuse to listen to anything, because they think there is nothing left for them to learn from anybody. Besides, Louis-Philippe had been deceived, as I have already said that his ministers were, by the misleading light cast by antecedent facts upon present times. One might draw a strange picture of all the errors which have thus been begotten, one by the other, without resembling each other. We see Charles I driven to tyranny and violence at the sight of the progress which the spirit of opposition had made in England during the gentle reign of his father; Louis XVI determined to suffer everything because Charles I had perished by refusing to endure anything; Charles X provoking the Revolution, because he had with his own eyes beheld the weakness of Louis XVI; and lastly, Louis-Philippe, who had more perspicacity than any of them, imagining that, in order to remain on the Throne, all he had to do was to observe the letter of the law while violating its spirit, and that, provided he himself kept within the bounds of the Charter, the nation would never exceed them. To warp the spirit of the Constitution without changing the letter; to set the vices of the country in opposition to each other; gently to drown revolutionary passion in the love of material enjoyment; such was the idea of his whole life. Little by little, it had become, not his leading, but his sole idea. He had wrapped himself in it, he had lived in it; and when he suddenly saw that it was a false idea, he became like a man who is awakened in the night by an earthquake, and who, feeling his house crumbling in the darkness, and the very ground seeming to yawn beneath his feet, remains distracted amid this unforeseen and universal ruin.

I am arguing very much at my ease today concerning the causes that brought about the events of the 24th of February [1848]; but on the afternoon of that day I had many other things in my head: I was thinking of the events themselves, and sought less for what had produced them than for what was to follow.

I returned slowly home. I explained in a few words to Madame de Tocqueville what I had seen, and sat down in a corner to think. I cannot remember ever feeling my soul so full of sadness. It was the second revolution I had seen accomplish itself, before my eyes, within seventeen years!

On the 30th of July 1830, at daybreak, I met the carriages of King Charles X on the outer boulevards of Versailles, with damaged escutcheons, proceeding at a foot pace, in Indian file, like a funeral, and I was unable to restrain my tears at the sight. This time my impressions were of another kind, but even keener. Both revolutions had afflicted me; but how much more bitter were the impressions caused by the last! I had until the end felt a remnant of hereditary affection for Charles X; but that King fell for having violated rights that were dear to me, and I had every hope that my country's freedom would be revived rather than extinguished by his fall. But now this freedom seemed dead; the Princes who were fleeing were nothing to me, but I felt that the cause I had at heart was lost.

I had spent the best days of my youth amid a society which seemed to increase in greatness and prosperity as it increased in liberty; I had conceived the idea of a balanced, regulated liberty, held in check by religion, custom and law; the attractions of this liberty had touched me; it had become the passion of my life; I felt that I could never be consoled for its loss, and that I must renounce all hope of its recovery.

I had gained too much experience of mankind to be able to content myself with empty words; I knew that, if one great revolution is able to establish liberty in a country, a number of succeeding revolutions make all regular liberty impossible for very many years.

I could not yet know what would issue from this last revolution, but I was already convinced that it could give birth to nothing that would satisfy me; and I foresaw that, whatever might be the lot reserved for our prosperity, our own fate was to drag on our lives miserably amid alternate reactions of license and oppression.

I began to pass in review the history of our last sixty years, and I smiled bitterly when I thought of the illusions formed at the conclusion of each period in this long revolution; the theories on which these illusions had been fed; the sapient dreams of our historians, and all the ingenious and deceptive systems by the aid of which it had been endeavoured to explain a present which was still incorrectly seen, and a future which was not seen at all.

The Constitutional Monarchy had succeeded the Ancient Regime; the Republic, the Monarchy; the Empire, the Republic; the Restoration, the Empire; and then came the Monarchy of July. After each of these successive changes it was said that the French Revolution, having accomplished what was presumptuously called its work, was finished; this had been said and it had been believed. Alas! I myself had hoped it under the Restoration, and again after the fall of the Government of the Restoration; and here is the French Revolution beginning over again, for it is still the same one. As we go on, its end seems farther off and shrouded in greater darkness. Shall we ever—as we are assured by other prophets, perhaps as delusive as their predecessors—shall we ever attain a more complete and more far-reaching social transformation than our fathers foresaw and desired, and than we ourselves are able to foresee; or are we not destined simply to end in a condition of intermittent anarchy, the well-known chronic and incurable complaint of old races? As for me, I am unable to say; I do not know when this long voyage will be ended; I am weary of seeing the shore in each successive mirage, and I often ask myself whether the *terra firma* we are seeking does really exist, and whether we are not doomed to rove upon the seas forever.

I spent the rest of the day with Ampère, who was my colleague at the Institute, and one of my best friends. He came to discover what had become of me in the affray, and to ask himself to dinner. I wished at first to relieve myself by making him share my vexation; but I soon perceived that his impression was not the same as mine, and that he looked differently upon the revolution which was in progress. Ampère was a man of intelligence and, better still, a man full of heart, gentle in manner, and reliable. His good nature caused him to be liked; and he was popular because of his versatile, witty, amusing, good-humoured conversation, in which he made many remarks that were at once entertaining and agreeable to hear but too shallow to remember. Unfortunately, he was inclined to carry the spirit of the salons into literature and the spirit of literature into politics. What I call literary spirit in politics consists in seeking for what is novel and ingenious rather than for what is true; in preferring the showy to the useful; in showing one's self very sensible to the playing and elocution of the actors, without regard to the results of the play; and lastly, in judging by impressions rather than reasons. I need not say that this eccentricity exists among others besides Academicians. To tell the truth, the whole nation is a little inclined that way, and the French Public very often takes a man-of-letters' view of politics. Ampère held the fallen Government in great contempt, and its last actions had irritated him greatly. Moreover, he had witnessed many instances of courage, disinterestedness, and even generosity among the insurgents; and he had been bitten by the popular excitement.

I saw that he not only did not enter into my view, but that he was disposed to take quite an opposite one. Seeing this, I was suddenly impelled to turn against Ampère all the feelings of indignation, grief and anger that had been accumulating in my heart since the morning; and I spoke to him with a violence of language which I have often since recalled with a certain shame, and which none but a friendship so sincere as his could have excused. I remember saying to him, *inter alia:*

"You understand nothing of what is happening; you are judging like a poet or a Paris cockney. You call this the triumph of liberty, when it is its final defeat. I tell you that the people which you so artlessly admire has just succeeded in proving that it is unfit and unworthy to live a life of freedom. Show me what experience has taught it! Where are the new virtues it has gained, the old vices it has laid aside? No, I tell you, it is always the same, as impatient, as thoughtless, as contemptuous of law and order, as easily led and as cowardly in the presence of danger as its fathers were before it.

Time has altered it in no way, and has left it as frivolous in serious matters as it used to be in trifles."

After much vociferation we both ended by appealing to the future, that enlightened and upright judge who always, alas! arrives too late.

I come at last to the insurrection of June, the most extensive and the most singular that has occurred in our history, and perhaps in any other; the most extensive, because, during four days, more than a hundred thousand men were engaged in it; the most singular, because the insurgents fought without a war-cry, without leaders, without flags, and yet with a marvellous harmony and an amount of military experience that astonished the oldest officers.

What distinguished it also, among all the events of this kind which have succeeded one another in France for sixty years, is that it did not aim at changing the form of government, but at altering the order of society. It was not, strictly speaking, a political struggle, in the sense which until then we had given to the word, but a combat of class against class, a sort of Servile War. It represented the facts of the Revolution of February in the same manner as the theories of Socialism represented its ideas; or rather it issued naturally from these ideas, as a son does from his mother. We behold in it nothing more than a blind and rude, but powerful, effort on the part of the workmen to escape from the necessities of their condition, which had been depicted to them as one of unlawful oppression, and to open up by main force a road towards that imaginary comfort with which they had been deluded. It was this mixture of greed and false theory which first gave birth to the insurrection and then made it so formidable. These poor people had been told that the wealth of the rich was in some way the product of a theft practiced upon themselves. They had been assured that the inequality of fortunes was as opposed to morality and the welfare of society as it was to nature. Prompted by their needs and their passions, many had believed this obscure and erroneous notion of right, which, mingled with brute force, imparted to the latter an energy, a tenacity and a power which it would never have possessed unaided.

It must also be observed that this formidable insurrection was not the enterprise of a certain number of conspirators, but the revolt of one whole section of the population against another. Women took part in it as well as men. While the latter fought, the former prepared and carried ammunition; and when at last the time had come to surrender, the women were the last to yield. These women went to battle with, as it were, a housewifely ardour: they looked to victory for the comfort of their husbands and the education of their children. They took pleasure in this war as they might have taken pleasure in a lottery.

As to the strategic science displayed by this multitude, the warlike nature of the French, their long experience of insurrections, and particularly the military education which the majority of the men of the people have in turn received, suffice to explain it. Half of the Paris workmen have served in our armies, and they are always glad to take up arms again. Generally speaking, old soldiers abound in our riots. On the 24th of February when Lamoricière was surrounded by his foes, he twice owed his life to insurgents who had fought under him in Africa, men in whom the recollection of their military life had been stronger than the fury of civil war.

As we know, it was the closing of the national workshops that occasioned the rising. Dreading to disband this formidable soldiery at one stroke, the Government had tried to disperse it by sending part of the workmen into the country. They refused to leave. On the 22nd of June, they marched through Paris in troops, singing in cadence, in a monotonous chant, "We won't be sent away, we won't be sent away . . ." Their delegates waited upon the members of the Committee of the Executive Power with a series of arrogant demands, and on meeting with a refusal, withdrew with the announcement that next day they would have recourse to arms. Everything, indeed, tended to show that the long-expected crisis had come.

Thomas Carlyle: Afterthought

All Europe exploded, boundless, uncontrollable, and we had the year 1848, one of the most singular, disastrous, amazing and on the whole humiliating years the European world ever saw. Not since the irruption of the Northern Barbarians has there been the like. Everywhere immeasurable democracy rose monstrous, loud, blatant, inarticulate as the voice of chaos. . . . Universal *democracy*, whatever one may think of it, has declared itself as an inevitable fact of the days in which we live; and he who has any chance to instruct, or lead, in his days, must begin by admitting that: new street-barricades, and new anarchies, still more scandalous, if still less sanguinary, must return and again return, till governing persons everywhere know and admit that.

Thomas Carlyle, *Latter Day Pamphlets*, No. 1 (London, 1850).

A Time of Questioning

The Rise of Social-Revolutionary Doctrines
The Drift of Scientific Thought
Patterns of Change
Nationalism and Imperialism
War and Revolution
The Fallout of Slaughter
Russia

FTER 1848 THE CERTAINTY OF A BETTER WORLD WAITING at the end of the road began to pale, and the unity of method by which it was to have been reached disintegrated. The better world was no longer built according to a universal pattern of thought acceptable to all; henceforth we have several versions of the world: those of the bourgeoisie, the proletariat, the nationalist, and perhaps the scientist. Existing standards were questioned no longer in the name of one supreme value—that of Reason—but in the name of many different values, offered by contending churches and antichurches, classes and nations, whose interests failed to produce harmony in a shattered world.

The divisive tendency that we have followed since the Reformation now rose to a peak, with each interest and world view challenging every other, struggling to impose *its* values and *its* patterns. National revolutions stressed the piecemeal quality of a world whose rising barriers in turn were emphasized by ever more complicated hindrances to the free movement of people, money, and goods. Social revolution, or its doctrines, continued the pattern of fragmentation at the national level, and class rose up against class while nation

411

reared against nation. Successful scientific revolutions shook the prevailing conception of reality, creating doubt as to whether an understandable pattern of the world order existed. The great world war of 1914–1918 and the Russian Revolution simply completed this process. The inability of politicians to solve their problems without war, the carnage and lunacy of the hostilities, the prodigious lies of the contending propaganda machines, the collapse of tsarist rule and survival of the Bolshevik regime—these taken together sapped all remaining belief in the sanity or the rationality or the coherence of the Western world. The long years of questioning had done their work, but the distracted lack of self-confidence to which they testified did not seem exactly unfounded.

The Rise of Social-Revolutionary Doctrines

A FTER 1830, and even more after 1848, it seemed very clear that the erstwhile bourgeois allies of the lower classes were determined to keep the profits of reforms and revolutions for themselves, without serious thought for the interests of the propertyless and the poor. Revolution had not removed oppression; it had merely replaced one oppressor with a more vigorous and determined one, who would manipulate in its own interest the forces of organized society that it now controlled. This revelation was followed by two reactions. One, embodied in anarchism, hoped for the removal of coercive authority, which would leave people free to act and cooperate unconstrained. The other, most powerfully expressed by Karl Marx, relied on the organization of the oppressed classes to oppose and defeat the forces of their oppressors.

Anarchism

Prince Pietr Alexander Alexeyevitch Kropotkin—Russian anarchist, geographer, naturalist, and explorer—was born in Moscow in 1842 and died there in 1921. In between he served as an army officer in Siberia and as a convict in Russia and France, and came to be regarded as the intellectual head of anarchism. In July 1917, Kropotkin, who had endorsed the war against "German imperialism," returned to Russia. There he supported Kerensky and rejected the Communist dictatorship after the October Revolution, but stayed on in the country unmolested, probably because of his prestige and advanced age. In today's Moscow his name graces a fashionable street as well as the subway station near it.

Pietr Kropotkin: from Anarchism: Its Philosophy and Ideal

Educated men—"civilized," as Fourier used to say with disdain—tremble at the idea that society might some day be without judges, police, or gaolers.

But, frankly, do you need them as much as you have been told in musty books! Books written, be it noted, by scientists who generally know well what has been written

---

From Peter Kropotkin, *Anarchism: Its Philosophy and Ideal* (San Francisco, 1898).

before them, but, for the most part, absolutely ignore the people and their every-day life.

If we can wander, without fear, not only in the streets of Paris, which bristle with police, but especially in rustic walks where you rarely meet passers by, is it to the police that we owe this security? Or rather to the absence of people who care to rob or murder us? I am evidently not speaking of the one who carries millions about him. That one—a recent trial tells us—is soon robbed, by preference in places where there are as many policemen as lampposts. No, I speak of the man who fears for his life and not for his purse filled with ill-gotten sovereigns. Are his fears real?

Besides, has not experience demonstrated quite recently that Jack the Ripper performed his exploits under the eye of the London police—a most active force—and that he only left off killing when the population of Whitechapel itself began to give chase to him?

And in our every-day relations with our fellow-citizens, do you think that it is really judges, gaolers, and the police that hinder antisocial acts from multiplying? The judge, ever ferocious, because he is a maniac of law, the accuser, the informer, the police spy, all those interlopers that live from hand to mouth around the Law Courts, do they not scatter demoralization far and wide into society? Read the trials, glance behind the scenes, push your analysis further than the exterior facade of law courts, and you will come out sickened.

Have not prisons—which kill all will and force of character in man, which enclose within their walls more vices than are met with on any other spot of the globe—always been universities of crime? Is not the court of a tribunal a school of ferocity? And so on.

When we ask for the abolition of the State and its organs we are always told that we dream of a society composed of men better than they are in reality. But no; a thousand times, no. All we ask is that men should not be made worse than they are, by such institutions!

Once a German jurist of great renown, Lhering, wanted to sum up the scientific work of his life and write a treatise in which he proposed to analyze the factors that preserve social life in society. *Purpose in Law* (der Zweck im Rechte), such is the title of that book, which enjoys a well-deserved reputation.

He made an elaborate plan of his treatise, and, with much erudition, discussed both coercive factors which are used to maintain society: wagedom, and the different forms of coercion which are sanctioned by law. At the end of his work, he reserved two paragraphs only to mention the two noncoercive factors—the feeling of duty and the feeling of mutual sympathy—to which he attached very little importance, as might be expected from a writer in law.

But what happened? As he went on analyzing the coercive factors, he realized their insufficiency. He consecrated a whole volume to their analysis, and the result was to lessen their importance! When he began the last two paragraphs, when he began to reflect upon the noncoercive factors of society, he perceived, on the contrary, their immense, outweighing importance; and instead of two paragraphs, he found himself obliged to write a second volume, twice as large as the first, on these two factors: voluntary restraint and mutual help; and yet he analyzed but an infinitesimal part of these latter—those which result from social institutions.

Well, then, leave off repeating the formulae which you have learned at school; meditate on this subject; and the same thing that happened to Lhering will happen to you. You will recognize the infinitesimal importance of coercion, as compared to the voluntary assent, in society.

On the other hand, if by following the very old advice given by Bentham you begin to think of the fatal consequences—direct, and especially indirect—of legal coercion, like Tolstoy, like us, you will begin to hate the use of coercion, and you will begin to say that society possesses a thousand other means for preventing antisocial acts. If it neglects those means today, it is because, being educated by Church and State, our cowardice and apathy of spirit hinder us seeing clearly on this point. When a child has committed a fault, it is so easy to hang a man—especially when there is an executioner who is paid so much for each execution—and it dispenses us from thinking of the cause of crimes.

Marxian Communism

Karl Marx (1818–1883) was born in Prussia, the son of a Jewish lawyer. He himself studied law at Bonn and Berlin. By 1842 he had begun his long battle against the accepted ideas of society by publishing his radical views in a liberal journal of which he became editor. Within six months, the journal was suppressed by the Prussian government. Virtually a political exile, Marx lived in Paris and Brussels, finally settling in London, where his major life's work was done. Friedrich Engels (1820–1895) also was born in Prussia, the son of a wealthy manufacturer. From 1842 on, Engels worked in a commercial house in Manchester, at the same time studying British conditions. In 1844 he met Marx in Paris, and from then on the two were close friends, jointly developing the theories that afterward became known as Marxism.

Karl Marx and Friedrich Engels: The Communist Manifesto

PREFACE TO THE ENGLISH EDITION OF 1888

The *Manifesto* was published as the platform of the Communist League, a workingmen's association, first exclusively German, later on international, and, under the political conditions of the Continent before 1848, unavoidably a secret society. At a Congress of the League, held in London in November, 1847, Marx and Engels were commissioned to prepare for publication a complete theoretical and practical party programme. Drawn up in German, in January, 1848, the manuscript was sent to the printer in London a few weeks before the French revolution of February 24th. A French translation was brought out in Paris, shortly before the insurrection of June, 1848. The first English translation, by Miss Helen Macfarlane, appeared in George Julian Harney's *Red Republic,* London, 1850. A Danish and a Polish edition had also been published.

From Karl Marx and Frederick Engels, *The Communist Manifesto* (London, 1888).

The defeat of the Parisian insurrection of June, 1848,—the first great battle between proletariat and bourgeoisie—drove again into the background, for a time, the social and political aspirations of the European working class. Thenceforth, the struggle for supremacy was again, as it had been before the revolution of February, solely between different sections of the propertied class; the working class was reduced to a fight for political elbowroom, and to the position of extreme wing of the middle-class Radicals. Wherever independent proletarian movements continued to show signs of life, they were ruthlessly hunted down. Thus the Prussian police hunted out the Central Board of the Communist League then located in Cologne. The members were arrested, and, after eighteen months' imprisonment, they were tried in October, 1852. This celebrated "Cologne Communist Trial" lasted from October 4th till November 12th: seven of the prisoners were sentenced to terms of imprisonment in a fortress, varying from three to six years. Immediately after the sentence, the League was formally dissolved by the remaining members. As to the *Manifesto,* it seemed thenceforth to be doomed to oblivion.

When the European working class had recovered sufficient strength for another attack on the ruling classes, the International Workingmen's Association sprang up.[1] But this association, formed with the express aim of welding into one body the whole militant proletariat of Europe and America, could not at once proclaim the principles laid down in the *Manifesto.* The International was bound to have a programme broad enough to be acceptable to the English trades unions, to the followers of Proudhon in France,[2] Belgium, Italy and Spain, and to the Lassalleans[3] in Germany. Marx, who drew up this programme to the satisfaction of all parties, entirely trusted to the intellectual development of the working class, which was sure to result from combined action and mutual discussion. The very events and vicissitudes of the struggle against capital, the defeats even more than the victories, could not help bringing home to men's minds the insufficiency of their various favourite nostrums, and preparing the way for a more complete insight into the true conditions of working-class emancipation. And Marx was right. The International, on its breaking up in 1874, left the workers quite different men from what it had found them in 1864. Proudhonism in France, Lassalleanism in Germany were dying out, and even the conservative English trades unions, though most of them had long since severed their connection with the International, were gradually advancing towards that point at which, last year at Swansea, their president could say in their name "Continental Socialism has lost its terrors for us." In fact, the principles of the *Manifesto* had made considerable headway among the working men of all countries.

The *Manifesto* itself thus came to the front again. Since 1850 the German text had been reprinted several times in Switzerland, England and America. In 1872, it was translated into English in New York, where the translation was published in *Woodhull*

---

[1] Now known as the First International.

[2] P. J. Proudhon (1809–1865), French anarchist who disagreed with Marx.

[3] Lasalle personally, to us, always acknowledged himself to be a disciple of Marx, and, as such, stood on the ground of the Manifesto. But in his public agitation, 1862–64, he did not go beyond demanding cooperative workshops supported by State credit.—F. E. [Friedrich Engels]

and Calftin's Weekly. From this English version, a French one was made in *Le Socialiste* of New York. Since then at least two more English translations, more or less mutilated, have been brought out in America, and one of them has been reprinted in England. The first Russian translation, made by Bakunin,[4] was published at Herzen's *Kolokol* office in Geneva,[5] about 1863; a second one, by the heroic Vera Zasulich,[6] also in Geneva in 1882. A new Danish edition is to be found in *Socialdemokratisk Bibliothek,* Copenhagen, 1885; a fresh French translation in *Le Socialiste,* Paris, 1886. From this latter, a Spanish version was prepared and published in Madrid, in 1886. The German reprints are not to be counted; there have been twelve altogether at the least. An Armenian translation, which was to be published in Constantinople some months ago, did not see the light, I am told, because the publisher was afraid of bringing out a book with the name of Marx on it, while the translator declined to call it his own production. Of further translations into other languages I have heard, but have not seen them. Thus the history of the *Manifesto* reflects, to a great extent, the history of the modern working-class movement; at present it is undoubtedly the most widespread, the most international production of all Socialist literature, the common platform acknowledged by millions of working men from Siberia to California.

Yet, when it was written, we could not have called it a *Socialist* manifesto. By Socialists, in 1847, were understood, on the one hand, the adherents of the various Utopian systems; Owenites in England,[7] Fourierists in France,[8] both of them already reduced to the position of mere sects, and gradually dying out; on the other hand, the most multifarious social quacks, who by all manner of tinkering professed to redress, without any danger to capital and profit, all sorts of social grievances; in both cases men outside the working-class movement, and looking rather to the "educated" classes for support. Whatever portion of the working class had become convinced of the insufficiency of mere political revolutions, and had proclaimed the necessity of a total social change, called itself Communist. It was a crude, rough-hewn, purely instinctive sort of Communism; still it touched the cardinal point and was powerful enough amongst the working class to produce the Utopian Communism of Cabet in France, and of Weitling in Germany.[9] Thus, in 1847, Socialism was a middle-class movement, Communism a working-class movement. Socialism was, on the Continent at least, "respectable"; Communism was the very opposite. And as our notion, from the very beginning, was that "the emancipation of the working class must be the act of the working class itself," there could be no doubt as to which of the two names we must take. Moreover, we have, ever since, been far from repudiating it.

---

[4] Bakunin (1814–1876), Russian anarchist; at first a supporter, then an opponent of Marx.

[5] Herzen (1812–1870), Russian liberal and socialist. His newspaper, *Kolokol* ("The Bell"), published mostly in London, was smuggled regularly into tsarist Russia.

[6] Vera Zasulich (1849–1919) shot the governor of St. Petersburg in 1878; later a member of the first Russian Marxist organization.

[7] Owenites were followers of Robert Owen (1771–1858).

[8] Fourierists were followers of Charles Fourier (1772–1858).

[9] E. Cabet (1788–1856), French writer and lawyer with utopian ideas; Weitling (1808–1871), German tailor, who wrote the first German socialist work in 1842.

The *Manifesto* being our joint production, I consider myself bound to state that the fundamental proposition which forms its nucleus, belongs to Marx. That proposition is: That in every historical epoch, the prevailing mode of economic production and exchange, and the social organization necessarily following from it, form the basis upon which is built up, and from which alone can be explained, the political and intellectual history of that epoch; that consequently the whole history of mankind (since the dissolution of primitive tribal society, holding land in common ownership) has been a history of class struggles, contests between exploiting and exploited, ruling and oppressed classes; that the history of these class struggles forms a series of evolutions in which, nowadays, a stage has been reached where the exploited and oppressed class—the proletariat—cannot attain its emancipation from the sway of the exploiting and ruling class—the bourgeoisie—without, at the same time, and once and for all, emancipating society at large from all exploitation, oppression, class distinctions and class struggles.

This proposition, which, in my opinion, is destined to do for history what Darwin's theory has done for biology, we both of us had been gradually approaching for some years before 1845. How far I had independently progressed towards it is best shown by my *Condition of the Working Class in England in 1844*. But when I again met Marx at Brussels, in spring, 1845, he had it already worked out, and put it before me, in terms almost as clear as those in which I have stated it here.

From our joint preface to the German edition of 1872, I quote the following: "However much the state of things may have altered during the last 25 years, the general principles laid down in this *Manifesto* are, on the whole, as correct today as ever. Here and there some detail might be improved. The practical application of the principles will depend, as the *Manifesto* itself states, everywhere and at all times, on the historical conditions for the time being existing; and for that reason, no special stress is laid on the revolutionary measures proposed at the end of Section II. That passage would, in many respects, be very differently worded today. In view of the gigantic strides of modern industry since 1848, and of the accompanying improved and extended organization of the working class, in view of the practical experience gained, first in the February Revolution, and then, still more, in the Paris Commune, where the proletariat for the first time held political power for two whole months, this programme has in some details become antiquated. One thing especially was proved by the Commune, viz., that 'the working class cannot simply lay hold of the ready-made State machinery, and wield it for its own purposes.' (See *The Civil War in France; Address of the General Council of the International Workingmen's Association, 1871,* where this point is further developed.) Further, it is self-evident that the criticism of Socialist literature is deficient in relation to the present time, because it comes down only to 1847; also, that the remarks on the relation of the Communists to the various opposition parties (Section IV), although in principle still correct, yet in practice are antiquated, because the political situation has been entirely changed, and the progress of history has swept from off the earth the greater portion of the political parties there enumerated."

But then, the *Manifesto* has become a historical document which we have no longer any right to alter.

The present translation is by Mr. Samuel Moore, the translator of the greater portion of Marx's *Capital*. We have revised it in common, and I have added a few notes explanatory of historical allusions.

Frederick Engels

London, January 30th, 1888

INTRODUCTION

A spectre is haunting Europe—the spectre of Communism. All the powers of old Europe have entered into a holy alliance to exorcise this spectre: Pope and Czar, Metternich and Guizot,[10] French Radicals and German political police.

Where is the party in opposition that has not been decried as communistic by its opponents in power? Where is the Opposition that has not hurled back the branding reproach of Communism, against the more advanced opposition parties as well as against its reactionary adversaries?

Two things result from this fact:

1. Communism is already acknowledged by all European powers to be itself a power.

2. It is high time that Communists should openly, in the face of the whole world, publish their views, their aims, their tendencies, and meet this nursery tale of the spectre of Communism with a manifesto of the party itself.

To this end, Communists of various nationalities have assembled in London, and sketched the following manifesto, to be published in the English, French, German, Italian, Flemish and Danish languages.

CHAPTER I
BOURGEOIS AND PROLETARIANS[11]

The history of all hitherto existing society[12] is the history of class struggles.

Freeman and slave, patrician and plebeian, lord and serf, guild-master[13] and jour-

---

[10] Guizot (1787–1874), French premier under King Louis Philippe.

[11] By bourgeoisie is meant the class of modern capitalists, owners of the means of social production and employers of wage-labour. By proletariat, the class of modern wage-labourers who, having no means of production of their own, are reduced to selling their labour power in order to live.—F. E.

[12] That is, all *written* history. In 1847, the pre-history of society, the social organization existing previous to recorded history, was all but unknown. Since then Haxthausen [August von, 1792–1866] discovered common ownership of land in Russia, Maurer [Georg Ludwig von, 1790–1872] proved it to be the social foundation from which all Teutonic races started in history, and, by and by, village communities were found to be, or to have been, the primitive form of society everywhere from India to Ireland. The inner organization of this primitive communistic society was laid bare, in its typical form, by Morgan's [Henry, 1818–1881] crowning discovery of the true nature of the *gens* and its relation to the *tribe*. With the dissolution of these primeval communities, society begins to be differentiated into separate and finally antagonistic classes. I have attempted to retrace this process of dissolution in *Der Ursprung der Familie, des Privateigenthums und des Staats,* 2nd edition, Stuttgart, 1886 ["The Origin of the Family, Private Property and the State"].—F. E.

[13] Guild-master, that is a full member of a guild, a master within, not a head of a guild.—F. E.

neyman, in a word, oppressor and oppressed, stood in constant opposition to one another, carried on an uninterrupted, now hidden, now open fight, a fight that each time ended, either in a revolutionary reconstitution of society at large, or in the common ruin of the contending classes.

In the earlier epochs of history, we find almost everywhere a complicated arrangement of society into various orders, a manifold gradation of social rank. In ancient Rome we have patricians, knights, plebeians, slaves; in the Middle Ages, feudal lords, vassals, guild-masters, journeymen, apprentices, serfs; in almost all of these classes, again, subordinate gradations.

The modern bourgeois society that has sprouted from the ruins of feudal society has not done away with class antagonisms. It has but established new classes, new conditions of oppression, new forms of struggle in place of the old ones.

Our epoch, the epoch of the bourgeoisie, possesses, however, this distinctive feature: it has simplified the class antagonisms. Society as a whole is more and more splitting up into two great hostile camps, into two great classes directly facing each other—bourgeoisie and proletariat.

From the serfs of the Middle Ages sprang the chartered Burghers of the earliest towns. From these burgesses the first elements of the bourgeoisie were developed.

The discovery of America, the rounding of the Cape, opened up fresh ground for the rising bourgeoisie. The East-Indian and Chinese markets, the colonization of America, trade with the colonies, the increase in the means of exchange and in commodities generally, gave to commerce, to navigation, to industry, an impulse never before known, and thereby, to the revolutionary element in the tottering feudal society, a rapid development.

The feudal system of industry, in which industrial production was monopolized by closed guilds, now no longer sufficed for the growing wants of the new markets. The manufacturing system took its place. The guild-masters were pushed aside by the manufacturing middle class; division of labour between the different corporate guilds vanished in the face of division of labour in each single workshop.

Meantime the markets kept ever growing, the demand ever rising. Even manufacture no longer sufficed. Thereupon, steam and machinery revolutionized industrial production. The place of manufacture was taken by the giant, modern industry, the place of the industrial middle class by industrial millionaires, the leaders of whole industrial armies, the modern bourgeois.

Modern industry has established the world market, for which the discovery of America paved the way. This market has given an immense development to commerce, to navigation, to communication by land. This development has, in its turn, reacted on the extension of industry; and in proportion as industry, commerce, navigation, railways extended, in the same proportion the bourgeoisie developed, increased its capital, and pushed into the background every class handed down from the Middle Ages.

We see, therefore, how the modern bourgeoisie is itself the product of a long course of development, of a series of revolutions in the modes of production and of exchange.

Each step in the development of the bourgeoisie was accompanied by a corresponding political advance of that class. An oppressed class under the sway of the feudal nobility, an armed and self-governing association in the medieval commune;[14] here independent urban republic (as in Italy and Germany), there taxable "third estate" of the monarchy (as in France); afterwards, in the period of manufacture proper, serving either the semi-feudal or the absolute monarchy as a counterpoise against the nobility, and, in fact, corner-stone of the great monarchies in general, the bourgeoisie has at last, since the establishment of modern industry and of the world market, conquered for itself, in the modern parliamentary State, exclusive political sway. The executive of the modern State is but a committee for managing the common affairs of the whole bourgeoisie.

The bourgeoisie, historically, has played a most revolutionary part.

The bourgeoisie, wherever it has got the upper hand, has put an end to all feudal, patriarchal, idyllic relations. It has pitilessly torn asunder the motley feudal ties that bound man to his "natural superiors," and has left no other nexus between man and man than naked self-interest, than callous "cash payment." It has drowned the most heavenly ecstasies of religious fervour, of chivalrous enthusiasm, of Philistine sentimentalism, in the icy water of egotistic calculation. It has resolved personal worth in exchange value and in place of the numberless indefeasible chartered freedoms has set up that single, unconscionable freedom—Free Trade. In one word, for exploitation veiled by religious and political illusions it has substituted naked, shameless, direct, brutal exploitation.

The bourgeoisie has stripped of its halo every occupation hitherto honoured and looked up to with reverent awe. It has converted the physician, the lawyer, the priest, the poet, the man of science, into its paid wage-labourers.

The bourgeoisie has torn away from the family its sentimental veil, and has reduced the family relation to a mere money relation.

The bourgeoisie has disclosed how the brutal display of vigour in the Middle Ages, which reactionaries so much admire, found its fitting complement in the most slothful indolence. It has been the first to show what man's activity can bring about. It has accomplished wonders far surpassing Egyptian pyramids, Roman aqueducts, and Gothic cathedrals; it has conducted expeditions that put in the shade all former Exoduses of nations and crusades.

The bourgeoisie cannot exist without constantly revolutionising the instruments of production, and thereby the relations of production, and with them the whole relations of society. Conservation of the old modes of production in unaltered form, was, on the contrary, the first condition of existence for all earlier industrial classes. Constant revolutionising of production, uninterrupted disturbance of all social conditions, everlasting uncertainty and agitation distinguish the bourgeois epoch from all earlier ones. All fixed, fast-frozen relations, with their train of ancient and venerable prejudices and

---

[14] "Commune" was the name taken, in France, by the nascent towns even before they had conquered from their feudal lords and masters local self-government and political rights as "the Third Estate." Generally speaking, for the economical development of the bourgeoisie, England is here taken as the typical country, for its political development, France.—F. E.

opinions, are swept away, all new-formed ones become antiquated before they can ossify. All that is privileged and established melts into air, all that is holy is profaned, and man is at last compelled to face with sober senses his real conditions of life and his relations with his kind.

The need of a constantly-expanding market for its products chases the bourgeoisie over the whole surface of the globe. It must get a footing everywhere, settle everywhere, establish connections everywhere.

The bourgeoisie has through its exploitation of the world market given a cosmopolitan character to production and consumption in every country. To the great chagrin of reactionaries, it has drawn from under the feet of industry the national ground on which it stood. Old established national industries have been destroyed and are still being destroyed every day. They are dislodged by new industries, whose introduction becomes a life and death question for all civilized nations, by industries that no longer work up indigenous raw material, but raw material drawn from the remotest zones; industries whose products are consumed, not only at home, but in every quarter of the globe. In place of the old wants, satisfied by the production of the country, we find new wants, requiring for their satisfaction the products of distant lands and climes. In place of the old local and national seclusion and self-sufficiency, we have exchange in every direction, universal interdependence of nations. And as in material, so also in intellectual production. The intellectual creations of individual nations become common property. National onesidedness and narrowmindedness become more and more impossible, and from the numerous national and local literatures there arises a world literature.

The bourgeoisie, by the rapid improvement of all instruments of production, by the immensely facilitated means of communication, draws all, even the most barbarian, nations into civilization. The cheap prices of its commodities are the heavy artillery with which it batters down all Chinese walls, with which it forces the barbarians' intensely obstinate hatred of foreigners to capitulate. It compels all nations, on pain of extinction, to adopt the bourgeois mode of production; it compels them to introduce what it calls civilization into their midst, i.e., to become bourgeois themselves. In one word, it creates a world after its own image.

The bourgeoisie has subjected the country to the rule of the towns. It has created enormous cities, has greatly increased the urban population as compared with the rural, and has thus rescued a considerable part of the population from the idiocy of rural life. Just as it has made the country dependent on the towns, so it has made barbarian and semi-barbarian countries dependent on the civilized ones, nations of peasants on nations of bourgeois, the East on the West.

The bourgeoisie keeps more and more doing away with the scattered state of the population, of the means of production, and of property. It has agglomerated population, centralized means of production, and has concentrated property in a few hands. The necessary consequence of this was political centralization. Independent, or but loosely connected provinces, with separate interests, laws, governments and local dues, became lumped together into one nation, with one government, one code of laws, one national class interest, one frontier and one customs tariff.

The bourgeoisie, during its class rule of scarce one hundred years, has created more massive and more colossal productive forces than have all preceding generations together. Subjection of Nature's forces to man, machinery, application of chemistry to industry and agriculture, steam-navigation, railways, electric telegraphs, clearing of whole continents for cultivation, making rivers navigable, whole populations conjured out of the ground—what earlier century had even a presentiment that such productive forces slumbered in the lap of social labour?

We see then: the means of production and of exchange, on whose foundation the bourgeoisie built itself up, were generated in feudal society. At a certain stage in the development of these means of production and of exchange, the conditions under which feudal society produced and exchanged, the feudal organization of agriculture and manufacturing industry, in one word, the feudal relations of property, became no longer compatible with the already developed productive forces; they hindered production instead of promoting it; they became so many fetters. They had to be burst asunder; they were burst asunder.

Into their place stepped free competition, accompanied by a social and political constitution adapted to it, and by the economical and political sway of the bourgeois class.

A similar movement is going on before our own eyes. Modern bourgeois society with its relations of production, of exchange and of property, a society that has conjured up such gigantic means of production and of exchange, is like the sorcerer who is no longer able to control the powers of the nether world whom he has called up by his spells. For many a decade past the history of industry and commerce is but the history of the revolt of modern productive forces against modern conditions of production, against the property relations that are the conditions for the existence of the bourgeoisie and of its rule. It is enough to mention the commercial crises that by their periodical return put the existence of the entire bourgeois society on its trial, each time more threateningly. In these crises a great part, not only of the existing products, but also of the previously-created productive forces, are periodically destroyed. In these crises there breaks out an epidemic that, in all earlier epochs, would have seemed an absurdity—the epidemic of over-production. Society suddenly finds itself put back into a state of momentary barbarism; it appears as if a famine, a universal war of devastation, had cut off the supply of every means of subsistence; industry and commerce seem to be destroyed. And why? Because there is too much civilization, too much means of subsistence, too much industry, too much commerce. The productive forces at the disposal of society no longer tend to promote bourgeois civilization and bourgeois property; on the contrary, they have become too powerful for these relations, by which they are fettered, and so soon as they overcome these fetters, they bring disorder into the whole of bourgeois society, endanger the existence of bourgeois property. The conditions of bourgeois society are too narrow to contain the wealth created by them. And how does the bourgeoisie get over these crises? On the one hand by enforced destruction of a mass of productive forces; on the other, by the conquest of new markets, and by the more thorough exploitation of the old ones. That is to say, by paving the way for more extensive and more destructive crises, and by diminishing the means whereby crises are prevented.

The weapons with which the bourgeoisie felled feudalism to the ground are now turned against the bourgeoisie itself.

But not only has the bourgeoisie forged the weapons that bring death to itself; it has also called into existence the men who are to wield those weapons—the modern working class—the proletarians.

In proportion as the bourgeoisie, i.e., capital, is developed, in the same proportion is the proletariat developed—the modern class of workers, who live only so long as they find work, and who find work only so long as their labour increases capital. These workmen, who must sell themselves piecemeal, are a commodity, like every other article of commerce, and are consequently exposed to all the vicissitudes of competition, to all the fluctuations of the market.

Owing to the extensive use of machinery and to division of labour, the work of the proletarians has lost all independent character, and, consequently, all charm for the workman. He becomes a mere appendage of the machine, and it is only the most simple, most monotonous, and most easily acquired knack, that is required of him. Hence, the cost of production of a workman is restricted, almost entirely, to the means of subsistence that he requires for his maintenance, and for the propagation of his race. But the price of a commodity, and therefore also of labour, is equal to its cost of production.[15] In proportion, therefore, as the repulsiveness of the work increases, the wage decreases. Nay, more, in proportion as the use of machinery and division of labour increases, in the same proportion the burden of toil also increases, whether by prolongation of the working hours, by increase of the work exacted in a given time, or by increased speed of the machinery, etc.

Modern industry has converted the little workshop of the patriarchal master into the great factory of the industrial capitalist. Masses of labourers, crowded into the factory, are organized like soldiers. As privates of the industrial army they are placed under the command of a perfect hierarchy of officers and sergeants. Not only are they slaves of the bourgeois class, and of the bourgeois State; they are daily and hourly enslaved by the machine, by the overlooker, and, above all, by the individual bourgeois manufacturer himself. The more openly this despotism proclaims gain to be its end and aim, the more petty, the more hateful and the more embittering it is.

The less the skill and exertion of strength implied in manual labour, in other words, the more modern industry becomes developed, the more is the labour of men superseded by that of women. Differences of age and sex have no longer any distinctive social validity for the working class. All are instruments of labour, more or less expensive to use, according to their age and sex.

No sooner is the exploitation of the labourer by the manufacturer so far at an end that he receives his wages in cash, than he is set upon by the other portions of the bourgeoisie, the landlord, the shopkeeper, the pawnbroker, etc.

The former lower strata of the middle class—the small manufacturers, traders and persons living on small incomes, the handicraftsmen and peasants—all these sink gradually into the proletariat, partly because their diminutive capital does not suffice for the scale on which modern industry is carried on and is swamped in the competition with the large capitalists, partly because their specialized skill is rendered worthless by new methods of production. Thus the proletariat is recruited from all classes of the population.

---

[15] According to Marx and Engels, the worker sells to the capitalist not his labor, but his labor power.

The proletariat goes through various stages of development. With its birth begins its struggle with the bourgeoisie. At first the contest is carried on by individual labourers, then by the workpeople of a factory, then by the operatives of one trade, in one locality, against the individual bourgeois who directly exploits them. They direct their attacks not only against the bourgeois conditions of production, but against the instruments of production themselves; they destroy imported wares that compete with their labour, they smash to pieces machinery, they set factories ablaze, they seek to restore by force the vanished status of the workman of the Middle Ages.

At this stage the labourers still form an incoherent mass scattered over the whole country, and broken up by their mutual competition. If anywhere they unite in greater masses, this is not yet the consequence of their own active union, but of the union of the bourgeoisie, which class, in order to attain its own political ends, is compelled to set the whole proletariat in motion, and is moreover yet, for a time, able to do so. At this stage, therefore, the proletarians do not fight their enemies, but the enemies of their enemies, the remnants of absolute monarchy, the landowners, the non-industrial bourgeois, the petty bourgeoisie. Thus the whole historical movement is concentrated in the hands of the bourgeoisie; every victory so obtained is a victory for the bourgeoisie.

But with the development of industry the proletariat not only increases in number; it becomes concentrated in greater masses, its strength grows, and it feels that strength more. The various interests and conditions of life within the ranks of the proletariat are more and more equalized, in proportion as machinery obliterates all distinctions of labour, and nearly everywhere reduces wages to the same low level. The growing competition among the bourgeois, and the resulting commercial crises, make the wages of the workers ever more fluctuating. The unceasing improvement of machinery, ever more rapidly developing, makes their livelihood more and more precarious; the collisions between individual workmen and individual bourgeois take more and more the character of collisions between two classes. Thereupon the workers begin to form combinations against the bourgeois; they club together in order to keep up the rate of wages; they themselves found permanent associations in order to make provision beforehand for these occasional revolts. Here and there the contest breaks out into riots. Now and then the workers are victorious, but only for a time. The real fruit of their battles lies, not in the immediate result, but in the ever-expanding union of the workers. This union is helped on by the improved means of communication that are created by modern industry and that place the workers of different localities in contact with one another. It was just this contact that was needed to centralize the numerous local struggles, all of the same character, into one national struggle between classes. But every class struggle is a political struggle. And that union, to attain which the burghers of the Middle Ages, with their miserable highways, required centuries, the modern proletarians, thanks to railways, achieve in a few years.

This organization of the proletarians into a class, and consequently into a political party, is continually being upset again by the competition between the workers themselves. But it ever rises up again, stronger, firmer, mightier. It compels legislative recognition of particular interests of the workers, by taking advantage of the divisions among the bourgeoisie itself. Thus the ten-hours' bill in England was carried.

Altogether, collisions between the classes of the old society further in many ways the course of development of the proletariat. The bourgeoisie finds itself involved in a constant battle. At first with the aristocracy; later on, with those portions of the bourgeoisie itself, whose interests have become antagonistic to the progress of industry; at all times with the bourgeoisie of foreign countries. In all these battles it sees itself compelled to appeal to the proletariat, to ask for its help, and thus, to drag it into the political arena. The bourgeoisie itself, therefore, supplies the proletariat with its own elements of political and general education, in other words, it furnishes the proletariat with weapons for fighting the bourgeoisie.

Further, as we have already seen, entire sections of the ruling classes are, by the advance of industry, precipitated into the proletariat, or are at least threatened in their conditions of existence. These also supply the proletariat with fresh elements of enlightenment and progress.

Finally, in times when the class struggle nears the decisive hour, the process of dissolution going on within the ruling class, in fact within the whole range of old society, assumes such a violent, glaring character, that a small section of the ruling class cuts itself adrift, and joins the revolutionary class, the class that holds the future in its hands. Just as, therefore, at an earlier period, a section of the nobility went over to the bourgeoisie, so now a portion of the bourgeoisie goes over to the proletariat, and in particular, a portion of the bourgeois ideologists who have raised themselves to the level of comprehending theoretically the historical movement as a whole.

Of all the classes that stand face to face with the bourgeoisie today, the proletariat alone is a really revolutionary class. The other classes decay and finally disappear in the face of modern industry; the proletariat is its special and essential product.

The lower middle class, the small manufacturer, the shopkeeper, the artisan, the peasant, all these fight against the bourgeoisie, to save from extinction their existence as fractions of the middle class. They are therefore not revolutionary, but conservative. Nay, more, they are reactionary, for they try to roll back the wheel of history. If by chance they are revolutionary, they are so only in view of their impending transfer into the proletariat; they thus defend not their present, but their future interests; they desert their own standpoint to place themselves at that of the proletariat.

The "dangerous class," the social scum, that passively rotting mass thrown off by the lowest layers of old society, may, here and there, be swept into the movement by a proletarian revolution; its conditions of life, however, prepare it far more for the part of a bribed tool of reactionary intrigue.

In the conditions of the proletariat, those of old society at large are already virtually swamped. The proletarian is without property; his relation to his wife and children has no longer anything in common with the bourgeois family relations; modern industrial labour, modern subjection to capital, the same in England as in France, in America as in Germany, has stripped him of every trace of national character. Law, morality, religion, are to him so many bourgeois prejudices, behind which lurk in ambush just as many bourgeois interests.

All the preceding classes that got the upper hand sought to fortify their already-acquired status by subjecting society at large to their conditions of appropriation. The proletarians cannot become masters of the productive forces of society except by abolishing their own previous mode of appropriation, and thereby also every other previous mode of appropriation. They have nothing of their own to secure and to fortify; their mission is to destroy all previous securities for, and insurances of, individual property.

All previous historical movements were movements of minorities, or in the interest of minorities. The proletarian movement is the self-conscious, independent movement of the immense majority, in the interest of the immense majority. The proletariat, the lowest stratum of our present society, cannot stir, cannot raise itself up, without the whole superincumbent strata of official society being sprung into the air.

Though not in substance, yet in form, the struggle of the proletariat with the bourgeoisie is at first a national struggle. The proletariat of each country must, of course, first of all settle matters with its own bourgeoisie.

In depicting the most general phases of the development of the proletariat, we traced the more or less veiled civil war, raging within existing society, up to the point where that war breaks out into open revolution, and where the violent overthrow of the bourgeoisie lays the foundation for the sway of the proletariat.

Hitherto, every form of society has been based, as we have already seen, on the antagonism of oppressing and oppressed classes. But in order to oppress a class, certain conditions must be assured to it under which it can, at least, continue its slavish existence. The serf, in the period of serfdom, raised himself to membership in the commune, just as the petty bourgeois, under the yoke of feudal absolutism, managed to develop into a bourgeois. The modern labourer, on the contrary, instead of rising with the progress of industry, sinks deeper and deeper below the conditions of existence of his own class. He becomes a pauper, and pauperism develops more rapidly than population and wealth. And here it becomes evident that the bourgeoisie is unfit to rule because it is incompetent to assure an existence to its slave within his slavery, because it cannot help letting him sink into such a state that it has to feed him, instead of being fed by him. Society can no longer live under this bourgeoisie; in other words, its existence is no longer compatible with society.

The essential condition for the existence and for the sway of the bourgeois class is the accumulation of wealth in the hands of private individuals, the formation and augmentation of capital; the condition for capital is wage-labour. Wage-labour rests exclusively on competition between the labourers. The advance of industry, whose involuntary promoter is the bourgeoisie, replaces the isolation of the labourers, due to competition, by their revolutionary combination, due to association. The development of modern industry, therefore, cuts from under the feet of the bourgeoisie the very foundation on which it produces and appropriates products. What the bourgeoisie therefore produces, above all, are its own grave-diggers. Its fall and the victory of the proletariat are equally inevitable.

CHAPTER II
PROLETARIANS AND COMMUNISTS

In what relation do the Communists stand to the proletarians as a whole?

The Communists do not form a separate party opposed to other working-class parties.

They have no interests separate and apart from those of the proletariat as a whole.

They do not set up any sectarian principles of their own, by which to shape and mould the proletarian movement.

The Communists are distinguished from the other working-class parties by this only: 1. In the national struggles of the proletarians of the different countries, they point out and bring to the front the common interests of the entire proletariat, independently of all nationality. 2. In the various stages of development which the struggle of the working class against the bourgeoisie has to pass through, they always and everywhere represent the interests of the movement as a whole.

The Communists, therefore, are on the one hand, in their practice, the most advanced and resolute section of the working-class parties of every country, that section which pushes forward all others; on the other hand, theoretically, they have over the great mass of the proletariat the advantage of clearly understanding the line of march, the conditions, and the ultimate general results of the proletarian movement.

The immediate aim of the Communists is the same as that of all the other proletarian parties: formation of the proletariat into a class, overthrow of the bourgeois supremacy, conquest of political power by the proletariat.

The theoretical conclusions of the Communists are in no way based on ideas or principles that have been invented, or discovered, by this or that would-be universal reformer.

They merely express, in general terms, actual relations springing from an existing class struggle, from an historical movement going on under our very eyes. The abolition of existing property relations is not at all a distinctive feature of Communism.

All property relations in the past have continually been subject to historical change consequent upon the change in historical conditions.

The French revolution, for example, abolished feudal property in favour of bourgeois property.

The distinguishing feature of Communism is not the abolition of property generally, but the abolition of bourgeois property. But modern bourgeois private property is the final and most complete expression of the system of producing and appropriating products that is based on class antagonisms, on the exploitation of some by others.

In this sense, the theory of the Communists may be summed up in the single sentence: Abolition of private property.

We Communists have been reproached with the desire of abolishing the right of personally acquiring property as the fruit of a man's own labour, which property is alleged to be the groundwork of all personal freedom, activity and independence.

Hard-won, self-acquired, self-earned property! Do you mean the property of the petty artisan and of the small peasant, a form of property that preceded the bourgeois form? There is no need to abolish that; the development of industry has to a great extent already destroyed it, and is still destroying it daily.

Or do you mean modern bourgeois private property?

But does wage-labour create any property for the labourer? Not a bit. It creates capital, i.e., that kind of property which exploits wage-labour, and which cannot increase except upon condition of begetting a new supply of wage-labour for fresh exploitation. Property, in its present form, is based on the antagonism of capital and wage-labour. Let us examine both sides of this antagonism.

To be a capitalist is to have not only a purely personal, but a social, status in production. Capital is a collective product, and only by the united action of many members, nay, in the last resort, only by the united action of all members of society, can it be set in motion.

Capital is therefore not a personal, it is a social power.

When, therefore, capital is converted into common property, into the property of all members of society, personal property is not thereby transformed into social property. It is only the social character of the property that is changed. It loses its class character.

Let us now take wage-labour.

The average price of wage-labour is the minimum wage, i.e., that quantum of the means of subsistence which is absolutely requisite to keep the labourer in bare existence as a labourer. What, therefore, the wage-labourer appropriates by means of his labour, merely suffices to prolong and reproduce a bare existence. We by no means intend to abolish this personal appropriation of the products of labour, an appropriation that is made for the maintenance and reproduction of human life, and that leaves no surplus wherewith to command the labour of others. All that we want to do away with is the miserable character of this appropriation, under which the labourer lives merely to increase capital, and is allowed to live only in so far as the interest of the ruling class requires.

In bourgeois society, therefore, the past dominates the present; in Communist society, the present dominates the past. In bourgeois society capital is independent and has individuality, while the living person is dependent and has no individuality.

And the abolition of this state of things is called by the bourgeois, abolition of individuality and freedom! And rightly so. The abolition of bourgeois individuality, bourgeois independence, and bourgeois freedom is undoubtedly aimed at.

By freedom is meant, under the present bourgeois conditions of production, free trade, free selling and buying.

But if selling and buying disappear, free selling and buying disappear also. This talk about free selling and buying, and all the other "brave words" of our bourgeoisie about freedom in general, have a meaning, if any, only in contrast with restricted selling and buying, with the fettered traders of the Middle Ages, but have no meaning when opposed to the Communist abolition of buying and selling, of the bourgeois conditions of production, and of the bourgeoisie itself.

You are horrified at our intending to do away with private property. But in your existing society, private property is already done away with for nine-tenths of the population; its existence for the few is solely due to its non-existence in the hands of those nine-tenths. You reproach us, therefore, with intending to do away with a form of property, the necessary condition for whose existence is the non-existence of any property for the immense majority of society.

In one word, you reproach us with intending to do away with your property. Precisely so: that is just what we intend.

From the moment when labour can no longer be converted into capital, money, or rent, into a social power capable of being monopolized, i.e., from the moment when individual property can no longer be transformed into bourgeois property, into capital, from that moment, you say, individuality vanishes.

You are, therefore, confessing that by "individual" you mean no other person than the bourgeois, than the owner of bourgeois property. This person must, indeed, be swept out of the way, and made impossible.

Communism deprives no man of the power to appropriate the products of society; all that it does is to deprive him of the power to subjugate the labour of others by means of such appropriation. It has been objected, that upon the abolition of private property all work will cease, and universal laziness will overtake us.

According to this, bourgeois society ought long ago to have gone to the dogs through sheer idleness; for those of its members who work acquire nothing, and those who acquire anything do not work. The whole of this objection is but another expression of the tautology: There can no longer be any wage-labour when there is no longer any capital.

All objections urged against the Communistic mode of producing and appropriating material products, have, in the same way, been urged against the Communistic modes of producing and appropriating intellectual products. Just as to the bourgeois the disappearance of class property is the disappearance of production itself, so the disappearance of class culture is to him identical with the disappearance of all culture.

That culture, the loss of which he laments, is for the enormous majority, a mere training to act as a machine.

But don't wrangle with us so long as you apply, to our intended abolition of bourgeois property, the standard of your bourgeois notions of freedom, culture, law, etc. Your very ideas are but the outgrowth of the conditions of your bourgeois production and bourgeois property, just as your jurisprudence is but the will of your class elevated into a law, a will whose essential character and direction are determined by the material conditions of existence of your class.

The selfish conception that induces you to transform into eternal laws of nature and of reason the relations springing from your present mode of production and form of property—historical relations that rise and disappear in the progress of production—this conception you share with every ruling class that has preceded you. What you see clearly in the case of ancient property, what you admit in the case of feudal property, you are of course forbidden to admit in the case of your own bourgeois form of property.

Abolition of the family! Even the most radical flare up at this infamous proposal of the Communists.

On what foundation is the present family, the bourgeois family, based? On capital, on private gain. In its completely developed form this family exists only among the bourgeoisie. But this state of things finds its complement in the enforced absence of the family among the proletarians, and in public prostitution.

The bourgeois family will vanish as a matter of course when its complement vanishes, and both will vanish with the vanishing of capital.

Do you charge us with wanting to stop the exploitation of children by their parents? To this crime we plead guilty. But, you will say, we destroy the most hallowed of relations, when we replace home education by social.

And your education! Is not that also social, and determined by the social conditions under which you educate, by the intervention, direct or indirect, of society, by means of schools, etc.? The Communists have not invented the intervention of society in education; they do but seek to alter the character of that intervention, and to rescue education from the influence of the ruling class.

The bourgeois claptrap about the family and education, about the hallowed relation of parent and child, becomes all the more disgusting, the more, by the action of modern industry, all family ties among the proletarians are torn asunder, and their children transformed into simple articles of commerce and instruments of labour.

But you Communists would introduce community of women, screams the whole bourgeoisie in chorus.

The bourgeois sees in his wife a mere instrument of production. He hears that the instruments of production are to be exploited in common, and, naturally, can come to no other conclusion than that the lot of being common to all will likewise fall to the women.

He has not even a suspicion that the real point aimed at is to do away with the status of women as mere instruments of production.

For the rest, nothing is more ridiculous than the virtuous indignation of our bourgeois at the community of women which, they pretend, is to be openly and officially established by the Communists. The Communists have no need to introduce community of women; it has existed almost from time immemorial.

Our bourgeois, not content with having the wives and daughters of their proletarians at their disposal, not to speak of common prostitutes, take the greatest pleasure in seducing each other's wives.

Bourgeois marriage is in reality a system of wives in common, and thus, at the most, what the Communists might possibly be reproached with is that they desire to introduce, in substitution for a hypocritically concealed, an openly legalized community of women. For the rest, it is self-evident that the abolition of the present system of production must bring with it the abolition of the community of women springing from that system, i.e., of prostitution both official and unofficial.

The Communists are further reproached with supposedly desiring to abolish fatherland and nationality.

The working men have no country. We cannot take from them what they have not got. Since the proletariat must first of all acquire political supremacy, must rise to be the leading class of the nation, must constitute itself the nation, it is, so far, itself national, though not in the bourgeois sense of the word.

National differences and antagonisms between peoples are daily more and more vanishing, owing to the development of the bourgeoisie, to freedom of commerce, to the world market, to uniformity in the mode of production and in the conditions of life corresponding thereto.

The supremacy of the proletariat will cause them to vanish still faster. United action, of the leading civilized countries at least, is one of the first conditions for the emancipation of the proletariat.

In proportion as the exploitation of one individual by another is put an end to, the exploitation of one nation by another will also be put an end to. In proportion as the antagonism between classes within the nation vanishes, the hostility of one nation to another will come to an end.

The charges against Communism made from a religious, a philosophical and, generally, from an ideological standpoint, are not deserving of any more detailed examination.

Does it require deep intuition to comprehend that man's ideas, views, and conceptions, in one word, man's consciousness, change with every change in the conditions of his material existence, in his social relations and in his social life?

What else does the history of ideas prove, than that intellectual production changes its character in proportion as material production is changed? The ruling ideas of each age have been only the ideas of its ruling class.

When people speak of ideas that revolutionize society, they do but express the fact that, within the old society, the elements of a new one have been created, and that the dissolution of the old ideas keeps even pace with the dissolution of the old conditions of existence.

When the ancient world was in its last throes, the ancient religions were overcome by Christianity. When Christian ideas succumbed in the 18th century to rationalist ideas, feudal society fought its death battle with the then revolutionary bourgeoisie. The ideas of religious liberty and freedom of conscience merely gave expression to the sway of free competition within the domain of knowledge.

"Undoubtedly," it will be said, "religious, moral, philosophical, political and juridical ideas have been modified in the course of historical development. But religion, morality, philosophy, political science, and law, constantly survived this change."

"There are, besides, eternal truths, such as Freedom, Justice, etc., that are common to all states of society. But Communism abolishes eternal truths, it abolishes all religion and all morality, instead of constituting them on a new basis; it therefore acts in contradiction to all past historical experience."

What does this assertion reduce itself to? The history of all past society has developed through class antagonisms, antagonisms that assumed different forms at different epochs.

But whatever form they may have taken, one fact is common to all past ages, viz., the exploitation of one part of society by the other. No wonder, then, that the social consciousness of past ages, despite all the multiplicity and variety it displays, moves within certain common forms, or general ideas, which cannot completely vanish except with the total disappearance of class antagonisms.

The Communist revolution is the most radical rupture with traditional property relations; no wonder that its development involves the most radical rupture with traditional ideas.

But let us have done with the bourgeois objections to Communism.

We have seen above that the first step in the revolution by the working class is to raise the proletariat to the position of ruling class, to win the battle for democracy.

The proletariat will use its political supremacy to wrest, by degrees, all capital from the bourgeoisie, to centralize all instruments of production in the hands of the State, i.e., of the proletariat organized as the ruling class; and to increase the total of productive forces as rapidly as possible.

Of course, in the beginning, this cannot be effected except by means of despotic inroads on the rights of property, and on the conditions of bourgeois production; by means of measures, therefore, which appear economically insufficient and provisional, but which in the course of the movement, outstrip themselves, necessitate further inroads upon the old social order, and are unavoidable as a means of entirely revolutionizing the mode of production.

These measures will of course be different in different countries.

Nevertheless, in the most advanced countries, the following will be pretty generally applicable.

1. Abolition of property in land and application of all rents of land to public purposes.

2. A heavy progressive or graduated income tax.

3. Abolition of all right of inheritance.

4. Confiscation of the property of all emigrants and rebels.

5. Centralization of credit in the hands of the State, by means of a national bank with State capital and an exclusive monopoly.

6. Centralization of the means of communication and transport in the hands of the State.

7. Extension of the number of State factories and instruments of production: the bringing into cultivation of waste lands, and the improvement of the soil generally in accordance with a common plan.

8. Equal obligation of all to work. Establishment of industrial armies, especially for agriculture.

9. Combination of agriculture with manufacturing industries; gradual abolition of the distinction between town and country, by a more equable distribution of the population over the country.

10. Free education for all children in public schools. Abolition of children's factory labour in its present form. Combination of education with industrial production, etc.

When, in the course of development, class distinctions have disappeared, and all production has been concentrated in the hands of a vast association of the whole nation, the public power will lose its political character. Political power, properly so called, is merely the organized power of one class for oppressing another. If the proletariat during its contest with the bourgeoisie is compelled, by the force of circumstances, to organize itself as a class; if, by means of a revolution, it makes itself the ruling class, and as such sweeps away by force the old conditions of production, then it will, along with these conditions, have swept away the conditions for the existence of class antagonisms and of classes generally, and will thereby have abolished its own supremacy as a class.

In place of the old bourgeois society, with its classes and class antagonisms, we shall have an association, in which the free development of each is the condition for the free development of all. . . .

The Communists disdain to conceal their views and aims. They openly declare that their ends can be attained only by the forcible overthrow of all existing social conditions. Let the ruling classes tremble at a Communist revolution. In it the proletarians have nothing to lose but their chains. They have a world to win.

WORKING MEN OF ALL COUNTRIES, UNITE!

Social Issues and the Church

The social problem also came to the attention of the Church, which had every reason to intervene in questions involving Christian charity as well as justice. In 1864 Pope Pius IX, who had never recovered from his disillusion with liberalism in 1848, had published a Syllabus of Errors *that were to be avoided by Catholics, among them the following: "That every man is free to embrace and profess the religion he shall believe true, guided by the light of reason"; "That eternal salvation may be hoped for by those who are not in the true Church of Christ"; "That it is allowable to refuse obedience to legitimate princes or rise in insurrection against them." Socialism and Bible societies were lumped together as "pests." The idea of secular popular schools, open to children of all classes, merited the same condemnation as the idea "that, in the present day, it is no longer necessary that the Catholic religion be held as the only religion of the State, to the exclusion of all other modes of worship." Finally, the pope denied "that the Roman pontiff can and ought to, reconcile himself to, and agree with, progress, liberalism, and modern civilization."*

With this fine flourish, Pius IX had begun what many regarded as a retreat to the Middle Ages, a stance deplored even by many pious Catholics. On May 15, 1891, Pope Leo XIII reverted to a great and more progressive tradition when he published his encyclical letter, De Rerum Novarum *("Concerning New Issues"), which long remained the most important papal pronouncement on the social question.*

Leo XIII: from De Rerum Novarum

Once the passion for revolutionary change was aroused—a passion long disturbing governments—it was bound to follow sooner or later that eagerness for change would pass from the political sphere over into the related field of economics. In fact, new developments in industry, new techniques striking out on new paths, changed relations of employer and employee, abounding wealth among a very small number and destitution among the masses, increased self-reliance on the part of the workers as well as a closer bond of union with one another, and, in addition to all this, a decline in morals, have caused conflict to break forth.

The momentous nature of the questions involved in this conflict is evident from the fact that it keeps men's minds in anxious expectation, occupying the talents of the learned, the discussions of the wise and experienced, the assemblies of the people, the

---

The complete text of the Encyclical Letter may be found in the *American Catholic Review*, July 1891.

judgment of the lawmakers, and the deliberations of rulers, so that now no topic more strongly holds men's interests.

Therefore, Venerable Brethren, with the cause of the Church and the common welfare before Us, We have thought it advisable, following Our custom on other occasions when We issued to you the Encyclicals On Political Power, On Human Liberty, On the Christian Constitution of States, and others of similar nature, which seemed opportune to refute erroneous opinions, that We ought to do the same now, and for the same reasons, On the Condition of Workers. We have on occasion touched more than once upon this subject. In this Encyclical, however, consciousness of Our Apostolic office admonishes Us to treat the entire question thoroughly, in order that the principles may stand out in clear light, and the conflict may thereby be brought to an end as required by truth and equity.

The problem is difficult to resolve and is not free from dangers. It is hard indeed to fix the boundaries of the rights and duties within which the rich and the proletariat—those who furnish material things and those who furnish work—ought to be restricted in relation to each other. The controversy is truly dangerous, for in various places it is being twisted by turbulent and crafty men to pervert judgment as to truth and seditiously to incite the masses.

In any event, We see clearly, and all are agreed that the poor must be speedily and fittingly cared for, since the great majority of them live undeservedly in miserable and wretched conditions.

After the old trade guilds had been destroyed in the last century, and no protection was substituted in their place, and when public institutions and legislation had cast off traditional religious teaching, it gradually came about that the present age handed over the workers, each alone and defenseless, to the inhumanity of employers and the unbridled greed of competitors. A devouring usury, although often condemned by the Church, but practiced nevertheless under another form by avaricious and grasping men, has increased the evil; and in addition the whole process of production as well as trade in every kind of goods has been brought almost entirely under the power of a few, so that a very few rich and exceedingly rich men have laid a yoke almost of slavery on the unnumbered masses of non-owning workers.

To cure this evil, the Socialists, exciting the envy of the poor toward the rich, contend that it is necessary to do away with private possession of goods, and in its place to make the goods of individuals common to all, and that the men who preside over a municipality or who direct the entire State should act as administrators of these goods. They hold that, by such a transfer of private goods from private individuals to the community, they can cure the present evil through dividing wealth and benefits equally among the citizens.

But their program is so unsuited for terminating the conflict that it actually injures the workers themselves. Moreover, it is highly unjust, because it violates the rights of lawful owners, perverts the functions of the State, and throws governments into utter confusion.

Clearly the essential reason why those who engage in any gainful occupation undertake labor, and at the same time the end to which workers immediately look, is to procure property for themselves and to retain it by individual right as theirs and as their very own. When the worker places his energy and his labor at the disposal of another, he does so for the purpose of getting the means necessary for livelihood. He seeks in return for the work done, accordingly, a true and full right not only to demand his wage but to dispose of it as he sees fit. Therefore, if he saves something by restricting expenditures and invests his savings in a piece of land in order to keep the fruit of his thrift more safe, a holding of this kind is certainly nothing else than his wage under a different form; and on this account land which the worker thus buys is necessarily under his full control as much as the wage which he earned by his labor. But, as is obvious, it is clearly in this that the ownership of movable and immovable goods consists. Therefore, inasmuch as the Socialists seek to transfer the goods of private persons to the community at large, they make the lot of all wage earners worse, because in abolishing the freedom to dispose of wages they take away from them by this very act the hope and the opportunity of increasing their property and of securing advantages for themselves.

But, what is of more vital concern, they propose a remedy openly in conflict with justice, inasmuch as nature confers on man the right to possess things privately as his own. . . .

The fact that God gave the whole human race the earth to use and enjoy cannot indeed in any manner serve as an objection against private possessions. For God is said to have given the earth to mankind in common, not because He intended indiscriminate ownership of it by all, but because He assigned no part to anyone in ownership, leaving the limits of private possessions to be fixed by the industry of men and the institutions of peoples. Yet, however the earth may be apportioned among private owners, it does not cease to serve the common interest of all, inasmuch as no living being is sustained except by what the fields bring forth. Those who lack resources supply labor, so that it can be truly affirmed that the entire scheme of securing a livelihood consists in the labor which a person expends either on his own land or in some working occupation, the compensation for which is drawn ultimately from no other source than from the varied products of the earth and is exchanged for them.

For this reason it also follows that private possessions are clearly in accord with nature. The earth indeed produces in great abundance the things to preserve and, especially, to perfect life, but of itself it could not produce them without human cultivation and care. Moreover, since man expends his mental energy and his bodily strength in procuring the goods of nature, by this very act he appropriates that part of physical nature to himself which he has cultivated. On it he leaves impressed, as it were, a kind of image of his person, so that it must be altogether just that he should possess that part as his very own and that no one in any way should be permitted to violate his right. . . .

It is a most sacred law of nature that the father of a family see that his offspring are provided with all the necessities of life, and nature even prompts him to desire to provide and to furnish his children, who, in fact reflect and in a sense continue his person, with the means of decently protecting themselves against harsh fortune in the uncertainties of life. He can do this surely in no other way than by owning fruitful goods to transmit by inheritance to his children. As already noted, the family like the State is by the same token a society in the strictest sense of the term, and it is *governed* by its own proper authority, namely, by that of the father. Wherefore, assuming, of course, that those limits be observed which are fixed by its immediate purpose, the family assuredly possesses rights, at least equal with those of civil society, in respect to choosing and employing the things necessary for its protection and its just liberty. We say "at least equal" because, inasmuch as domestic living together is prior both in thought and in fact to uniting into a polity, it follows that its rights and duties are also prior and more in conformity with nature. But if citizens, if families, after becoming participants in common life and society, were to experience injury in a commonwealth instead of help, impairment of their rights instead of protection, society would be something to be repudiated rather than to be sought for.

To desire, therefore, that the civil power should enter arbitrarily into the privacy of homes is a great and pernicious error. If a family perchance is in such extreme difficulty and is so completely without plans that it is entirely unable to help itself, it is right that the distress be remedied by public aid, for each individual family is a part of the community. Similarly, if anywhere there is a grave violation of mutual rights within the family walls, public authority shall restore to each his right: for this is not usurping the rights of citizens, but protecting and confirming them with just and due care. Those in charge of public affairs, however, must stop here: nature does not permit them to go beyond these limits. Paternal authority is such that it can be neither abolished nor absorbed by the State, because it has the same origin in common with that of a man's own life. "Children are a part of their father," and, as it were, a kind of extension of the father's person; and, strictly speaking, not through themselves, but through the medium of the family society in which they are begotten, they enter into and participate in civil society. And for the very reason that children "are by nature part of their father . . . before they have the use of free will, they are kept under the care of their parents." Inasmuch as the Socialists, therefore, disregard care by parents and in its place introduce care by the State, they act against natural justice and dissolve the structure of the home.

And apart from the injustice involved, it is also only too evident what turmoil and disorder would obtain among all classes; and what a harsh and odious enslavement of citizens would result! The door would be open to mutual envy, detraction, and dissension. If incentives to ingenuity and skill in individual persons were to be abolished, the very fountains of wealth would necessarily dry up; and the equality conjured up by the Socialist imagination would, in reality, be nothing but uniform wretchedness and meanness for one and all, without distinction.

From all these considerations, it is perceived that the fundamental principle of Socialism which would make all possessions public property is to be utterly rejected because it injures the very ones whom it seeks to help, contravenes the natural rights of individual persons, and throws the functions of the State and public peace into confusion. Let it be regarded, therefore, as established that in seeking help for the masses this principle before all is to be considered as basic, namely that private ownership must be preserved inviolate.

It is a capital evil with respect to the question we are discussing to take for granted that the one class of society is of itself hostile to the other, as if nature had set rich and poor against each other to fight fiercely in implacable war. This is so abhorrent to reason and truth that the exact opposite is true; for just as in the human body the different members harmonize with one another, whence arises that disposition of parts and proportion in the human figure rightly called symmetry, so likewise nature has commanded in the case of the State that the two classes mentioned should agree harmoniously and should properly form equally balanced counterparts to each other. Each needs the other completely: neither capital can do without labor, nor labor without capital. Concord begets beauty and order in things. Conversely, from perpetual strife there must arise disorder accompanied by bestial cruelty. But for putting an end to conflict and for cutting away its very roots, there is wondrous and multiple power in Christian institutions.

And first and foremost, the entire body of religious teaching and practice, of which the Church is the interpreter and guardian, can pre-eminently bring together and unite the rich by recalling the two classes of society to their mutual duties, and in particular to those duties which derive from justice.

Among these duties the following concern the poor and the workers: To perform entirely and conscientiously whatever work has been voluntarily and equitably agreed upon; not in any way to injure the property or to harm the person of employers; in protecting their own interests, to refrain from violence and never to engage in rioting; not to associate with vicious men who craftily hold out exaggerated hopes and make huge promises, a course usually ending in vain regrets and in the destruction of wealth.

The following duties, on the other hand, concern rich men and employers: Workers are not to be treated as slaves; justice demands that the dignity of human personality be respected in them, ennobled as it has been through what we call the Christian character. If we hearken to natural reason and to Christian philosophy, gainful occupations are not a mark of shame to man, but rather of respect, as they provide him with an honorable means of supporting life. It is shameful and inhuman, however, to use men as things for gain and to put no more value on them than what they are worth in muscle and energy. Likewise it is enjoined that the religious interests and the spiritual well-being of the workers receive proper consideration. Wherefore, it is the duty of employers to see that the worker is free for adequate periods to attend to his religious obligations; not to expose anyone to corrupting influences or the enticements of sin, and in no way to alienate him from care for his family and the practice of thrift. Likewise, more work is not to be imposed than strength can endure, nor that kind of work which is unsuited to a worker's age or sex.

Among the most important duties of employers the principal one is to give every worker what is justly due him. Assuredly, to establish a rule of pay in accord with justice, many factors must be taken into account. But, in general, the rich and employers should remember that no laws, either human or divine, permit them for their own profit to oppress the needy and the wretched or to seek gain from another's want. To defraud anyone of the wage due him is a great crime that calls down avenging wrath from Heaven. "Behold, the wages of the laborers . . . which have been kept back by you unjustly, cry out: and their cry has entered into the ears of the Lord of Hosts." Finally, the rich must religiously avoid harming in any way the savings of the workers either by coercion, or by fraud, or by the arts of usury; and the more for this reason, that the workers are not sufficiently protected against injustices and violence, and their property, being so meagre, ought to be regarded as all the more sacred. Could not the observance alone of the foregoing laws remove the bitterness and the causes of conflict? . . .

Those who lack fortune's goods are taught by the Church that, before God as Judge, poverty is no disgrace, and that no one should be ashamed because he makes his living by toil. And Jesus Christ has confirmed this by fact and by deed, Who for the salvation of men, "being rich, became poor"; and although He was the Son of God and God Himself, yet He willed to seem and to be thought the son of a carpenter; nay, He even did not disdain to spend a great part of his life at the work of a carpenter. "Is not this the carpenter, the Son of Mary?" Those who contemplate this Divine example will more easily understand these truths: True dignity and excellence in men resides in moral living, that is, in virtue; virtue is the common inheritance of man, attainable equally by the humblest and the mightiest, by the rich and the poor; and the reward of eternal happiness will follow upon virtue and merit alone, regardless of the person in whom they may be found. Nay, rather the favor of God Himself seems to incline more toward the unfortunate as a class; for Jesus Christ calls the poor blessed, and He invites most lovingly all who are in labor or sorrow to come to Him for solace, embracing with special love the lowly and those harassed by injustice. At the realization of these things the proud spirit of the rich is easily brought down, and the downcast heart of the afflicted is lifted up; the former are moved toward kindness, the latter, toward reasonableness in their demands. Thus the distance between the classes which pride seeks is reduced, and it will easily be brought to pass that the two classes, with hands clasped in friendship, will be united in heart.

Such is the economy of duties and rights according to Christian philosophy. Would it not seem that all conflict would soon cease wherever this economy were to prevail in civil society?

Finally, the Church does not consider it enough to point out the way of finding the cure, but she administers the remedy herself. For she occupies herself fully in training and forming men according to discipline and doctrine; and through the agency of bishops and clergy, she causes the health-giving streams of this doctrine to be diffused as widely as possible. Furthermore, she strives to enter into men's minds and to bend their wills so that they may suffer themselves to be ruled and governed by the discipline of the divine precepts. And in this field, which is of first and greatest importance because in it the whole substance and matter of benefits consists, the Church indeed has a power that is especially unique. For the instruments which she used to move souls were given her for this very purpose by Jesus Christ, and they have an efficacy implanted in them by God. Such instruments alone can properly penetrate the inner recesses of the heart and lead man to obedience, to duty, to govern the activities of his self-seeking mind, to love God and his neighbors with a special and sovereign love, and to overcome courageously all things that impede the path of virtue. . . .

But it is now in order to inquire what portion of the remedy should be expected from the State. By State here We understand not the form of government which this or that people has, but rather that form which right reason in accordance with nature required and the teachings of Divine wisdom approve. . . .

Therefore those governing the State ought primarily to devote themselves to the service of individual groups and of the whole commonwealth, and through the entire scheme of laws and institutions to cause both public and individual well-being to develop spontaneously out of the very structure and administration of the State. For this is the duty of wise statesmanship and the essential office of those in charge of the State. Now, States are made prosperous especially by wholesome morality, properly ordered family life, protection of religion and justice, moderate imposition and equitable distribution of public burdens, progressive development of industry and trade, thriving agriculture, and by all other things of this nature, which the more actively they are promoted, the better and happier the life of the citizens is destined to be. Therefore, by virtue of these things, it is within the competence of the rulers of the State that, as they benefit other groups, they also improve in particular the condition of the workers. Furthermore, they do this with full right and without laying themselves open to any charge of unwarranted interference. For the State is bound by the very law of its office to serve the common interest. And the richer the benefits which come from this general providence on the part of the State, the less necessary it will be to experiment with other measures for the well-being of workers.

This ought to be considered, as it touches the question more deeply, namely, that the State has one basic purpose for existence, which embraces in common the highest and the lowest of its members. Non-owning workers are unquestionably citizens by nature in virtue of the same right as the rich, that is, true and vital parts whence, through the medium of families, the body of the State is constituted; and it hardly need be added that they are by far the greatest number in every urban area. Since it would be quite absurd to look out for one portion of the citizens and to neglect another, it follows that public authority ought to exercise due care in safeguarding the well-being and the interests of non-owning workers. Unless this is done, justice, which commands that everyone be given his own, will be violated. Wherefore St. Thomas says wisely: "Even as part and whole are in a certain way the same, so too that which pertains to the whole pertains in a certain way to the part also." Consequently, among the numerous and weighty duties of rulers who would serve their people well, this is first and foremost, namely, that they protect equitably each and every class of citizens, maintaining inviolate that justice especially which is called distributive.

Although all citizens, without exception, are obliged to contribute something to the sum-total of common goods, some share of which naturally goes back to each individual, yet all can by no means contribute the same amount and in equal degree. Whatever the vicissitudes that occur in the forms of government, there will always be those differences in the condition of citizens without which society could neither exist nor be conceived. It is altogether necessary that there be some who dedicate themselves to the service of the State, who make laws, who dispense justice, and finally, by whose counsel and authority civil and military affairs are administered. These men, as is clear, play the chief role in the State, and among every people are to be regarded as occupying first place, because they work for the common good most directly and preeminently. On the other hand, those engaged in some calling benefit the State, but not in the same way as the men just mentioned, nor by performing the same duties; yet they, too, in a high degree, although less directly, serve the public weal. Assuredly, since social good must be of such a character that men through its acquisition are made better, it must necessarily be founded chiefly on virtue.

Nevertheless, an abundance of corporeal and external goods is likewise a characteristic of a well constituted State, "the use of which goods is necessary for the practice of virtue." To produce these goods the labor of the workers, whether they expend their skill and strength on farms or in factories, is most efficacious and necessary. Nay, in this respect, their energy and effectiveness are so important that it is incontestable that the wealth of nations originates from no other source than from the labor of workers. Equity therefore commands that public authority show proper concern for the worker so that from what he contributes to the common good he may receive what will enable him, housed, clothed, and secure, to live his life without hardship. Whence, it follows that all those measures ought to be favored which seem in any way capable of benefiting the condition of workers. Such solicitude is so far from injuring anyone, that it is destined rather to benefit all, because it is of absolute interest to the State that those citizens should not be miserable in every respect from whom such necessary goods proceed.

It is not right, as We have said, for either the citizen or the family to be absorbed by the State; it is proper that the individual and the family should be permitted to retain their freedom of action, so far as this is possible without jeopardizing the common good and without injuring anyone. Nevertheless, those who govern must see to it that they protect the community and its constituent parts: the community, because nature has entrusted its safeguarding to the sovereign power in the State to such an extent that the protection of the public welfare is not only the supreme law, but is the entire cause and reason for sovereignty; and the constituent parts, because philosophy and Christian faith agree that the administration of the State has from nature as its purpose, not the benefit of those to whom it has been entrusted, but the benefit of those who have been entrusted to it. And since the power of governing comes from God and is a participation, as it were, in His supreme sovereignty, it ought to be administered according to the example of the Divine power, which looks with paternal care to the welfare of individual creatures as well as to that of all creation. If, therefore, any injury has been done to or threatens either the common good or the interests of individual groups, which injury cannot in any other way be repaired or prevented, it is necessary for public authority to intervene.

It is vitally important to public as well as to private welfare that there be peace and good order; likewise, that the whole regime of family life be directed according to the ordinances of God and the principles of nature, that religion be observed and cultivated, that sound morals flourish in private and public life, that justice be kept sacred and that no one be wronged with impunity by another, and that strong citizens grow up, capable of supporting, and if necessary, of protecting the State. Wherefore, if at any time disorder should threaten because of strikes or concerted stoppages of work, if the natural bonds of family life should be relaxed among the poor, if religion among the workers should be outraged by failure to provide sufficient opportunity for performing religious duties, if in factories danger should assail the integrity of morals through the mixing of the sexes or other pernicious incitements to sin, or if the em-

ployer class should oppress the working class with unjust burdens or should degrade
them with conditions inimical to human personality or to human dignity, if health
should be injured by immoderate work and such as is not suited to sex or age—in all
these cases, the power and authority of the law, but of course within certain limits,
manifestly ought to be employed. And these limits are determined by the same reason
which demands the aid of the law, that is, the law ought not undertake more, nor go
farther, than the remedy of evils or the removal of danger requires.

Rights indeed, by whomsoever possessed, must be religiously protected; and public
authority, in warding off injuries and punishing wrongs, ought to see to it that individuals may have and hold what belongs to them. In protecting the rights of private individuals, however, special consideration must be given to the weak and the poor. For
the nation, as it were, of the rich, is guarded by its own defenses and is in less need
of governmental protection, whereas the suffering multitude, without the means to
protect itself, relies especially on the protection of the State. Wherefore, since wage
workers are numbered among the great mass of the needy, the State must include them
under its special care and foresight.

But it will be well to touch here expressly on certain matters of special importance.
The capital point is this, that private property ought to be safeguarded by the sovereign
power of the State and through the bulwark of its laws. And especially, in view of such
a great flaming up of passion at the present time, the masses ought to be kept within
the bounds of their moral obligations. For while justice does not oppose our striving
for better things, on the other hand, it does forbid anyone to take from another what
is his and, in the name of a certain absurd equality, to seize forcibly the property of
others; nor does the interest of the common good itself permit this. Certainly, the great
majority of working people prefer to secure better conditions by honest toil, without
doing wrong to anyone. Nevertheless, not a few individuals are found who, imbued
with evil ideas and eager for revolution, use every means to stir up disorder and incite
to violence. The authority of the State, therefore, should intervene and, by putting
restraint upon such disturbers, protect the morals of workers from their corrupting
arts and lawful owners from the danger of spoliation.

Labor which is too long and too hard and the belief that pay is inadequate not
infrequently give workers cause to strike and become voluntarily idle. This evil, which
is frequent and serious, ought to be remedied by public authority, because such interruption of work inflicts damage not only upon employers and upon the workers themselves, but also injures trade and commerce and the general interest of the State; and,
since it is usually not far removed from violence and rioting, it very frequently jeopar-
dizes public peace. In this matter it is more effective and salutary that the authority
of the law anticipate and completely prevent the evil from breaking out by removing
early the causes from which it would seem that conflict between employers and workers
is bound to arise.

And in like manner, in the case of the worker, there are many things which the
power of the State should protect; and, first of all, the good of his soul. For however
good and desirable mortal life be, yet it is not the ultimate goal for which we are born,
but a road only and a means for perfecting, through knowledge of truth and love of
good, the life of the soul. The soul bears the express image and likeness of God, and

there resides in it that sovereignty through the medium of which man has been bidden to rule all created nature below him and to make all lands and all seas serve his interest. "Fill the earth and subdue it, and rule over the fishes of the sea and the fowls of the air and all living creatures that move upon the earth." In this respect all men are equal, and there is no difference between rich and poor, between masters and servants, between rulers and subjects: "For there is the same Lord of all." No one may with impunity outrage the dignity of man, which God Himself treats with great reverence, nor impede his course to that level of perfection which accords with eternal life in heaven. Nay, more, in this connection a man cannot even by his own free choice allow himself to be treated in a way inconsistent with his nature, and suffer his soul to be enslaved; for there is no question here of rights belonging to man, but of duties owed to God, which are to be religiously observed.

Hence follows necessary cessation from toil and work on Sundays and Holy Days of Obligation. Let no one, however, understand this in the sense of greater indulgence of idle leisure, and much less in the sense of that kind of cessation from work, such as many desire, which encourages vice and promotes wasteful spending of money, but solely in the sense of a repose from labor made sacred by religion. Rest combined with religion calls man away from toil and the business of daily life to admonish him to ponder on heavenly goods and to pay his just and due homage to the Eternal Deity. This is especially the nature and this the cause, of the rest to be taken on Sundays and Holy Days of Obligation, and God has sanctioned the same in the Old Testament by a special law: "Remember thou keep holy the Sabbath Day," and He Himself taught it by His own action: namely the mystical rest taken immediately after He had created man: "He rested on the seventh day from all His work which He had done."

Now as concerns the protection of corporeal and physical goods, the oppressed workers above all, ought to be liberated from the savagery of greedy men, who inordinately use human beings as things of gain. Assuredly, neither justice nor humanity can countenance the exaction of so much work that the spirit is dulled from excessive toil and that along with it the body sinks crushed from exhaustion. The working energy of a man, like his entire nature, is circumscribed by definite limits beyond which it cannot go. It is developed indeed by exercise and use, but only on condition that a man cease from work at regular intervals and rest. With respect to daily work, therefore, care ought to be taken not to extend it beyond the hours that human strength warrants. The length of rest intervals ought to be decided on the basis of the varying nature of the work, of the circumstances of time and place, and of the physical condition of the workers themselves. Since the labor of those who quarry stone from the earth, or who mine iron, copper, and other underground materials, is much more severe and harmful to health, the working period for such men ought to be correspondingly shortened. The seasons of the year also must be taken into account; for often a given kind of work is easy to endure in one season but cannot be endured at all in another, or not without the greatest difficulty.

Finally, it is not right to demand of a woman or a child what a strong adult man is capable of doing or would be willing to do. Nay, as regards children, special care ought to be taken that the factory does not get hold of them before age has sufficiently matured their physical, intellectual, and moral powers. For budding strength in childhood, like greening verdure in spring, is crushed by premature harsh treatment; and under such circumstances all education of the child must needs be foregone. Certain occupations likewise are less fitted for women, who are intended by nature for work of the home—work indeed which especially protects modesty in women and accords by nature with the education of children and the well-being of the family. Let it be the rule everywhere that workers be given as much leisure as will compensate for the energy consumed by toil, for rest from work is necessary to restore strength consumed by use. In every obligation which is mutually contracted between employers and workers, this condition, either written or tacit, is always present, that both kinds of rest be provided for; nor would it be equitable to make an agreement otherwise, because no one has the right to demand of, or to make an agreement with, anyone to neglect those duties which bind a man to God or to himself.

The Drift of Scientific Thought

THE political debate that went on in public was accompanied by another whose results would be just as far-reaching. Darwin's publication of *The Origin of Species* in 1859, and the scientific arguments that immediately sprang up around it, affected accepted ideas and fundamentally altered the pattern of reality. The new scientific revelations persuaded a great many people that all the secrets of a mechanically determined world awaited eventual discovery by scientific processes which were ultimately infallible. They also persuaded some more skeptical thinkers that, pending conclusive proof, doubt—even on religious questions—was at least as reasonable and worthy of respect as affirmation. As the philosopher Bertrand Russell was to put it, Darwinism was simply the extension of laissez-faire economics to the animal and vegetable world. Conversely, when vulgarized and (mis)interpreted, the findings of nineteenth-century scientists seemed to endorse the current doctrines of free enterprise and the idea that survival and success went to the fittest in human society, as, apparently, they did in nature.

Auguste Comte

It is not surprising that at a time when science seemed to challenge established religion and cast serious doubts on any divine sanction for morality, men and women should turn toward a religion of science: an attempt to explain the world (and hence lay down rules for behavior in it) in positive—scientific—terms. One of these scholars was Auguste Comte (1798–1857), the French mathematician, philosopher, and founder of positivism whose Course of Positive Philosophy *was one of the century's most influential works. His philosophical system was completed by a religion of humanity that would be inculcated, in part, by the use of a new and original calendar designed to express a "positive" hierarchy of values, a theory of historical progress culminating in the "positive" scientific achievements of the nineteenth century.*

Comte published the calendar that follows in his Positivistic Catechism *of 1852. The calendar purports to reflect the progress of humanity from a relatively primitive organization of society and stage of civilization, to the heights attained in Comte's time. It also divides the year into thirteen months, each broken down into four weeks of seven days each. Each month edifyingly symbolizes a stage in humanity's advance from the initial theocracy as incarnated in Moses, to the revelations of modern science as represented by Bichat (1771–1802), a French anatomist and physiologist of the eighteenth century who has long been forgotten, along with his once-much-admired magnum opus, the* Anatomie Générale.

From Positivistic Catechism

POSITIVISTIC CALENDAR

for any given year

or A CONCRETE TABLE OF HUMAN PREPARATION

		First Month MOSES THE INITIAL THEOCRACY		Second Month HOMER ANCIENT POETRY		Third Month ARISTOTLE ANCIENT PHILOSOPHY	
Mon.	1	Prometheus		Hesiod		Anaximander	
Tues.	2	Hercules	. . . *Theseus*	Tyrteus	. . . *Sappho*	Anaximenes	
Wed.	3	Orpheus		Anacreon		Heraclitus	
Thurs.	4	Ulysses		Pindarus		Anaxagoras	
Fri.	5	Lycurgus		Sophocles	. . . *Euripides*	Democritus	. . . *Leucippus*
Sat.	6	Romulus		Theocritus	. . . *Longus*	Herodotus	
Sun.	7	NUMA		ESCHYLUS		THALES	
	8	Belus	. . . *Semiramis*	Scopas		Solon	
	9	Sesostris		Zeuxis		Xenophanes	
	10	Manus		Ictinus		Empedocles	
	11	Cyrus		Praxiteles		Thucydides	
	12	Zoroaster		Lysippus		Archytas	. . . *Philolaus*
	13	The Druids	. . . *Ossian*	Apelles		Apollonius of Tyana	
	14	BUDDHA		PHIDIAS		PYTHAGORAS	
	15	Fo-Hi		Esopus		Aristippus	
	16	Lao-Tse		Plautus		Antisthenes	
	17	Meng-Tse		Terence	. . . *Menander*	Zeno	
	18	The theocrats of Tibet		Phedra		Cicero	. . . *Pliny the Younger*
	19	The theocrats of Japan		Juvenal		Epictetus	. . . *Arius*
	20	Manco-Capac		Lucian		Tacitus	
	21	CONFUCIUS		ARISTOPHANES		SOCRATES	
	22	Abraham	. . . *Joseph*	Ennius		Xenocrates	
	23	Samuel		Lucretius		Philo of Alexandria	
	24	Solomon	. . . *David*	Horace		St. John the Evangelist	
	25	Isaiah		Tibullus		St. Justin	. . . *St. Ireneus*
	26	St. John the Baptist		Ovid		St. Clement of Alexandria	
	27	Harun-al-Rashid		Lucan		Origen	. . . *Tertullian*
	28	MAHOMET		VIRGIL		PLATO	

Fourth Month ARCHIMEDES ANCIENT SCIENCE		Fifth Month CESAR MILITARY CIVILISATION		Sixth Month ST. PAUL CATHOLICISM	
Theophrastus		Miltiades		St. Luke	
Hierophilus		Leonidas		St. Cyprian	
Erasistratus		Aristides		St. Athanasius	
Celsius		Cimon		St. Jerome	
Galen		Xenophon		St. Ambrose	
Avicenna	. . . *Averrhoes*	Phocion	. . . *Epaminondas*	St. Monica	
HIPPOCRATES		THEMISTOCLES		ST. AUGUSTIN	
Euclid		Pericles		Constantine	
Aristeus		Philip		Theodosius	
Theodosius of Bythinia		Demosthenes		St. Chrysostom	. . . *St. Basil*
Hero	. . . *Clesibius*	Ptolemeus Lagus		St. Pulcheria	. . . *Marcian*
Pappus		Philopoemen		St. Genevieve of Paris	
Diophantes		Polybius		St. Gregory the Great	
APOLLONIUS		ALEXANDER		HILDEBRAND	
Eudoxius		Junius Brutus		St. Benedict	. . . *St. Anthony*
Pytheas	. . . *Nearchus*	Camillus	. . . *Cincinnatus*	St. Boniface	
Aristarchus	. . . *Berosius*	Fabricius	. . . *Regulus*	St. Isidore of Seville	. . . *St. Bruno*
Eratosthenes		Hannibal		Lanfranc	. . . *St. Anselm*
Ptolemeus		Paulus-Emilius		Heloïse	. . . *Beatrice*
Albategnius	. . . *Nasr-ed-Din*	Marius	. . . *The Gracchi*	The medieval architects	
HIPPARCHUS		SCIPIO		ST. BERNARD	
Varro		Augustus	. . . *Mecenas*	St. Francis Xavier	
					. . . *St. Ignatius Loyola*
Columella		Vespasian	. . . *Titus*	St. Charles Borromeus	
Vitruvius		Hadrian	. . . *Nerva*	St. Theresa	
					. . . *St. Catherine of Sienna*
Strabo		Antoninus	. . . *Marcus-Aurelius*	St. Vincent de Paul	
Frontinus		Papinian	. . . *Ulpian*	Bourdaloue	. . . *Claude Fleury*
Plutarch		Alexander Severus		W. Penn	. . . *G. Fox*
PLINIUS THE ELDER		TRAJAN		BOSSUET	

Seventh Month CHARLEMAGNE FEUDAL CIVILISATION		Eighth Month DANTE THE MODERN EPIC		Ninth Month GUTENBERG MODERN INDUSTRY	
Theodoric the Great		The Troubadours		Marco Polo	. . . *Chardin*
Pelagius		Boccacio	. . . *Chaucer*	Jacques Coeur	. . . *Gresham*
Otto the Great		Rabelais		Gama	. . . *Magellan*
	. . . *Henry the Fowler*				
St. Henry		Cervantes		Neper [Napier]	. . . *Briggs*
Villiers	. . . *La Valette*	La Fontaine		Lacaille	. . . *Delambre*
Don Juan of Lepanto		De Foe	. . . *Smith*	Cook	. . . *Tasman*
	. . . *Jan Sobieski*				
KING ALFRED		ARIOSTO		COLUMBUS	
Charles Martel		Leonardo	. . . *Titian*	Benvenuto Cellini	
Le Cid	. . . *Tancred*	Michelangelo	. . . *Veronese*	Amontons	. . . *Wheatstone*
Richard Lion Heart	. . . *Saladdin*	Holbein	. . . *Rembrandt*	Harrison	. . . *Pierre Leroy*
Joan of Arc		Poussin	. . . *Lesueur*	Dollond	. . . *Graham*
Albuquerque	. . . *Walter Raleigh*	Velasquez	. . . *Alonzo Cano*	Arkwright	. . . *Jacquart*
Bayard		Teniers	. . . *Rubens*	Conté	
GODEFROI DE BOUILLON		Raphael		VAUCANSON	
St. Leo the Great	. . . *Leo IV*	Froissart	. . . *Joinville*	Stevin	. . . *Torricelli*
Gerbert	. . . *Peter Damian*	Camoens		Mariotte	. . . *Robert Boyle*
Peter the Hermit		The Spanish Romanceros		Papin	. . . *Worcester*
Abbot Suger	. . . *St. Elöi*	Chateaubriand		Black	
Alexander III	. . . *Thomas Becket*	Walter Scott	. . . *Cooper*	Jouffroy	. . . *Fulton*
St. Francis of Assisi		Manzoni		Dalton	. . . *Thilorier*
	. . . *St. Dominic*				
INNOCENT III		TASSO		WATT	
St. Clotilda		Petrarch		Bernard Palissy	
St. Bathilda		Thomas à Kempis		Guglielmini	. . . *Riquet*
	. . . *St. Matthew of Tuscany*				
St. Stephen of Hungary		Mme. de Lafayette		Duhamel du Monceau	
	. . . *Matthias Corvinus*		. . . *Mme. de Staël*		
St. Elizabeth of Hungary		Fénelon	. . . *St. Francis of Sales*	Saussure	. . . *Bouguer*
Blanche of Castile		Klopstock	. . . *Gessner*	Coulomb	. . . *Borda*
St. Ferdinand III	. . . *Alphonse X*	Byron	. . . *Elisa Mercoeur*	Carnot	. . . *Vauban*
SAINT LOUIS		MILTON		MONTGOLFIER	

Tenth Month SHAKESPEARE MODERN DRAMA	Eleventh Month DESCARTES MODERN PHILOSOPHY	Twelfth Month FREDERIC MODERN POLITICS
Lope de Vega	Albert the Great *... John of Salisbury*	Molina
Moreto *... Guillen de Castro*	Roger Bacon *... Raimond Lulle*	Cosimo Medici the Older
Rojas *... Guevara*	St. Bonaventura *... Joachim*	Comines *... Guicciardini*
Otway	Ramus *... Card. of Cusa*	Isabel of Castile
Lessing	Montaigne *... Erasmus*	Charles V *... Sixtus V*
Goethe	Campanella *... Thomas More*	Henry IV
CALDERON	ST. THOMAS AQUINAS	LOUIS XI
Tirso	Hobbes *... Spinoza*	Coligny *... de l'Hôpital*
Vondel	Pascal *... Giordano Bruno*	Barneveldt
Racine	Locke *... Malebranche*	Gustavus-Adolphus
Voltaire	Vauvenargues *... Mme. de Lambert*	De Witt
Metastasio *... Alfieri*	Diderot *... Destutt de Tracy*	Ruyter
Schiller	Cabanis *... Georges Leroy*	William III of Orange
CORNEILLE	CHANCELLOR BACON	WILLIAM THE SILENT
Alarcon	Grotius *... Cujas*	Ximenes
Mme. de Motteville *... Mme. Roland*	Fontenelle *... Maupertuis*	Sully *... Oxenstierna*
Mme. de Sévigné *... Lady Montague*	Vico *... Herder*	Colbert *... Louis XIV*
Lesage *... Sterne*	Fréré *... Winckelmann*	Walpole *... Mazarin*
Mme. de Staël *... Miss Edgeworth*	Montesquieu *... d'Aguesseau*	d'Aranda *... Pombal*
Fielding *... Richardson*	Buffon *... Oken*	Turgot *... Campomanes*
MOLIÈRE	LEIBNITZ	RICHELIEU
Pergolese *... Palestrina*	Robertson *... Gibbon*	Sidney *... Lambert*
Sachini *... Grétry*	Adam Smith *... Dunoyer*	Franklin
Gluck *... Lully*	Kant *... Fichte*	Washington *... Kosciusko*
Beethoven *... Handel*	Condorcet *... Ferguson*	Jefferson
Rossini *... Weber*	Joseph de Maistre *... Bonald*	Bolivar *... Toussaint l'Ouverture*
Bellini *... Donizetti*	Hegel *... Sophie Germain*	Francia
MOZART	HUME	CROMWELL

Thirteenth Month BICHAT MODERN SCIENCE	
Copernicus . . . *Tycho Brahe* Kepler . . . *Halley* Huyghens . . . *Varignou* Jacques Bernoulli . . . *Jean Bernoulli* Bradley . . . *Roëmer* Volta . . . *Sauveur* GALILEO	One complementary day dedicated to a UNIVERSAL FESTIVAL OF THE DEAD.
Viète . . . *Harriott* Wallis . . . *Fermat* Clairaut . . . *Poinsot* Euler . . . *Monge* D'Alembert . . . *Daniel Bernoulli* Lagrange . . . *Joseph Fourier* NEWTON	On leap years, the extra day is to be devoted to the solemn reprobation of the two main regressive figures in the history of humanity—Julian the Apostate and Napoleon Bonaparte—but this only during the first half-generation. Thus, after the first four celebrations of this *festival of reprobates*, this exceptional day will be used for its normal purpose of celebrating the Cult of the Absolute.
Bergmann . . . *Scheele* Priestley . . . *Davy* Cavendish Guyton-Morveau . . . *Geoffroy* Berthollet Berzelius . . . *Ritter* LAVOISIER	
Harvey . . . *Charles Bell* Boërhaave . . . *Stahl* Linneus . . . *Bernard de Jussieu* Haller . . . *Vicq-d'Azyr* Lamarck . . . *Blainville* Broussais . . . *Morgagni* GALL	

Absurd though all this may seem today, it affords precious evidence on the values and ideas of an exceptional though eccentric man; and it remains, when all is said and done, no more ridiculous than any other schematic interpretation of history.

Alfred Russel Wallace

Alfred Russel Wallace (1823–1913), one of the founders of zoological geography, was a Scottish naturalist and interpreter of Darwin. While Darwin was still working on his theory, Wallace, thinking upon Malthus's Essay on Population, *hit upon the idea of the survival of the fittest and wrote to Darwin about it. The coincidence has caused him to be coupled with Darwin as one of the originators of the theory of natural selection. There is, however, no indication of this in the following extract, which provides a luminous account of Darwin's theory and its effect on current scientific thought.*

From Darwinism

THE CHANGE OF OPINION EFFECTED BY DARWIN

The point I wish especially to urge is this. Before Darwin's work appeared, the great majority of naturalists, and almost without exception the whole literary and scientific world, held firmly to the belief that species were realities, and had not been derived from other species by any process accessible to us; the different species of crow and of violet were believed to have been always as distinct and separate as they are now, and to have originated by some totally unknown process so far removed from ordinary reproduction that it was usually spoken of as "special creation." There was, then, no question of the origin of families, orders, and classes, because the very first step of all, the "origin of species," was believed to be an insoluble problem. But now this is all changed. The whole scientific and literary world, even the whole educated public, accepts, as a matter of common knowledge, the origin of species from other allied species by the ordinary process of natural birth. The idea of special creation or any altogether exceptional mode of production is absolutely extinct! Yet more: this is held also to apply to many higher groups as well as to the species of a genus, and not even Mr. Darwin's severest critics venture to suggest that the primeval bird, reptile, or fish must have been "specially created." And this vast, this totally unprecedented change in public opinion has been the result of the work of one man, and was brought about in the short space of twenty years! This is the answer to those who continue to maintain that the "origin of species" is not yet discovered; that there are still doubts and difficulties; that there are divergencies of structure so great that we cannot understand how they had their beginning. We may admit all this, just as we may admit that there are enormous difficulties in the way of a complete comprehension of the origin and nature of all the parts of the solar system and of the stellar universe. But we claim for Darwin

From Alfred Russel Wallace, *Darwinism* (London, 1889).

that he is the Newton of natural history, and that, just so surely as that the discovery and demonstration by Newton of the law of gravitation established order in place of chaos and laid a sure foundation for all future study of the starry heavens, so surely has Darwin, by his discovery of the law of natural selection and his demonstration of the great principle of the preservation of useful variations in the struggle for life, not only thrown a flood of light on the process of development of the whole organic world, but also established a firm foundation for all future study of nature.

In order to show the view Darwin took of his own work, and what it was that he alone claimed to have done, the concluding passage of the introduction to the *Origin of Species* should be carefully considered. It is as follows: "Although much remains obscure, and will long remain obscure, I can entertain no doubt, after the most deliberate and dispassionate judgment of which I am capable, that the view which most naturalists until recently entertained and which I formerly entertained—namely, that each species has been independently created—is erroneous. I am fully convinced that species are not immutable; but that those belonging to what are called the same genera are lineal descendants of some other and generally extinct species, in the same manner as the acknowledged varieties of any one species are the descendants of that species. Furthermore, I am convinced that Natural Selection has been the most important, but not the exclusive, means of modification."

It should be especially noted that all which is here claimed is now almost universally admitted, while the criticisms of Darwin's works refer almost exclusively to those numerous questions which, as he himself says, "will long remain obscure."

THE DARWINIAN THEORY

The theory of natural selection rests on two main classes of facts which apply to all organised beings without exception, and which thus take rank as fundamental principles or laws. The first is, the power of rapid multiplication in a geometrical progression; the second, that the offspring always vary slightly from the parents, though generally very loosely resembling them. From the first fact or law there follows, necessarily, a constant struggle for existence; because, while the offspring always exceed the parents in number, generally to an enormous extent, yet the total number of living organisms in the world does not, and cannot, increase year by year. Consequently every year, on the average, as many die as are born, plants as well as animals; and the majority die premature deaths. They kill each other in a thousand different ways; they starve each other by some consuming the food that others want; they are destroyed largely by the powers of nature—by cold and heat, by rain and storm, by flood and fire. There is thus a perpetual struggle among them which shall live and which shall die; and this struggle is tremendously severe, because so few can possibly remain alive—one in five, one in ten, often only one in a hundred or even one in a thousand.

Then comes the question, Why do some live rather than others? If all the individuals of each species were exactly alike in every respect, we could only say it is a matter of chance. But they are not alike. We find that they vary in many different ways. Some are stronger, some swifter, some hardier in constitution, some more cunning. An obscure colour may render concealment more easy for some, keener sight may enable others to discover prey or escape from an enemy better than their fellows. Among plants the smallest differences may be useful or the reverse. The earliest and strongest shoots may escape the slug; their greater vigour may enable them to flower and seed earlier in a wet autumn; plants best armed with spines or hairs may escape being devoured; those whose flowers are most conspicuous may be soonest fertilised by insects. We cannot doubt that, on the whole, any beneficial variations will give the possessors of it a greater probability of living through the tremendous ordeal they have to undergo. There may be something left to chance, but on the whole the fittest will survive.

THE ETHICAL ASPECT OF THE STRUGGLE FOR EXISTENCE

Our exposition of the phenomena presented by the struggle for existence may be fitly concluded by a few remarks on its ethical aspect. Now that the war of nature is better known, it has been dwelt upon by many writers as presenting so vast an amount of cruelty and pain as to be revolting to our instincts of humanity, while it has proved a stumbling-block in the way of those who would fain believe in an all-wise and benevolent ruler of the universe. Thus, a brilliant writer says: "Pain, grief, disease, and death, are these the inventions of a loving God? That no animal shall rise to excellence except by being fatal to the life of others, is this the law of a kind Creator? It is useless to say that pain has its benevolence, that massacre has its mercy. Why is it so ordained that bad should be the raw material of good? Pain is not the less pain because it is useful; murder is not less murder because it is conducive to development. Here is blood upon the hand still, and all the perfumes of Arabia will not sweeten it."

Even so thoughtful a writer as Professor Huxley adopts similar views. In a recent article on "The Struggle for Existence" he speaks of the myriads of generations of herbivorous animals which "have been tormented and devoured by carnivores"; of the carnivores and herbivores alike "subject to all the miseries incidental to old age, disease, and over-multiplication"; and of the "more or less enduring suffering," which is the meed of both vanquished and victor. And he concludes that, since thousands of times a minute, were our ears sharp enough, we should hear sighs and groans of pain like those heard by Dante at the gate of hell, the world cannot be governed by what we call benevolence.

Now there is, I think, good reason to believe that all this is greatly exaggerated; that the supposed "torments" and "miseries" of animals have little real existence, but are the reflection of the imagined sensations of cultivated men and women in similar circumstances; and that the amount of actual suffering caused by the struggle for existence among animals is altogether insignificant. . . .

We have a horror of all violent and sudden death, because we think of the life full of promise cut short, of hopes and expectations unfulfilled, and of the grief of mourning relatives. But all this is quite out of place in the case of animals, for whom a violent and a sudden death is in every way the best. Thus the poet's picture of "Nature red in tooth and claw/With ravine" is a picture the evil of which is read into it by our imaginations, the reality being made up of full and happy lives, usually terminated by the quickest and least painful of deaths.

On the whole, then, we conclude that the popular idea of the struggle for existence entailing misery and pain on the animal world is the very reverse of the truth. What it really brings about, is, the maximum of life and of the enjoyment of life with the minimum of suffering and pain. Given the necessity of death and reproduction—and without these there could have been no progressive development of the organic world,—it is difficult even to imagine a system by which a greater balance of happiness could have been secured. And this view was evidently that of Darwin himself, who thus concludes his chapter on the struggle for existence: "When we reflect on this struggle, we may console ourselves with the full belief that the war of nature is not incessant, that no fear is felt, that death is generally prompt, and that the vigorous, the healthy, and the happy survive and multiply."

The Great Evolution Debate

The kind of ruckus that surrounded the emergence of Darwinian ideas appears in the following excerpt from Leonard Huxley's account of the debate between his celebrated father, biologist Thomas Huxley, and Dr. Wilberforce, the bishop of Oxford. Such exchanges reflect the high feelings aroused by the controversy that surged around The Origin of Species *and that, incidentally, furnished it with further publicity.*

Leonard Huxley: The Debate Between Huxley and Wilberforce

The famous Oxford Meeting of 1860 was of no small importance in Huxley's career. It was not merely that he helped to save a great cause from being stifled under misrepresentation and ridicule—that he helped to extort for it a fair hearing; it was not that he first made himself known in popular estimation as a dangerous adversary in debate—a personal force in the world of science which could not be neglected. From this moment he entered the front fighting line in the most exposed quarter of the field.

Most unluckily, no contemporary account of his own exists of the encounter. Indeed, the same cause which prevented his writing home the story of the day's work nearly led to his absence from the scene. It was known that Bishop Wilberforce, whose first class in mathematics gave him, in popular estimation, a right to treat on scientific matters intended to "smash Darwin"; and Huxley, expecting that the promised debate would be merely an appeal to prejudice in a mixed audience, before which the scientific arguments of the Bishop's opponents would be at the utmost disadvantage, intended to leave Oxford that very morning and join his wife at Hardwicke, near Reading, where she was staying with her sister. But in a letter, quoted below, he tells how, on the Friday afternoon, he chanced to meet Robert Chambers, the reputed author of the *Vestiges of Creation,* who begged him "not to desert them." Accordingly he postponed his departure; but seeing his wife next morning, had no occasion to write a letter.

From Leonard Huxley, *Life and Letters of Thomas Henry Huxley,* 2 vol. (New York, 1900).

Several accounts of the scene are already in existence: one in the *Life of Darwin* (vol. ii, p. 320), another in the 1892 *Life,* p. 236 sq.; a third that of *Lyell* (vol. ii, p. 335), the slight difference between them representing the difference between individual recollections of eye-witnesses. In addition to these I have been fortunate enough to secure further reminiscences from several other eye-witnesses.

Two papers in Section D, of no great importance in themselves, became historical as affording the opponents of Darwin their opportunity of making an attack upon his theory which should tell with the public. The first was on Thursday, June 28. Dr. Daubeny of Oxford made a communication to the Section, "On the final causes of the sexuality of plants, with particular reference to Mr. Darwin's work on the *Origin of Species.*" Huxley was called upon to speak by the President, but tried to avoid a discussion, on the ground "that a general audience, in which sentiment would unduly interfere with intellect, was not the public before which such a discussion should be carried on."

This consideration, however, did not stop the discussion; it was continued by Owen. He said he "wished to approach the subject in the spirit of the philosopher," and declared his "conviction that there were facts by which the public could come to some conclusion with regard to the probabilities of the truth of Mr. Darwin's theory." As one of these facts, he stated that the brain of the gorilla "presented more differences, as compared with the brain of man, than it did when compared with the brain of the very lowest and most problematical of the Quadrumana."

Now this was the very point, as said above, upon which Huxley had made special investigations during the last two years, with precisely opposite results, such as, indeed, had been arrived at by previous investigators. Hereupon he replied, giving these assertions a "direct and unqualified contradiction," and pledging himself to "justify that unusual procedure elsewhere,"—a pledge which was amply fulfilled in the pages of the *Natural History Review* for 1861.

Accordingly it was to him, thus marked out as the champion of the most debatable thesis of evolution, that, two days later, the Bishop addressed his sarcasms, only to meet with a withering retort. For on the Friday there was peace; but on the Saturday came a yet fiercer battle over the "Origin," which loomed all the larger in the public eye, because it was not merely the contradiction of one anatomist by another, but the open clash between Science and the Church. It was, moreover, not a contest of bare fact or abstract assertion, but a combat of wit between two individuals, spiced with the personal element which appeals to one of the strongest instincts of every large audience.

It was the merest chance . . . that Huxley attended the meeting of the section that morning. Dr. Draper of New York was to read a paper on the "Intellectual Development of Europe considered with reference to the views of Mr. Darwin." "I can still hear," writes one who was present, "the American accents of Dr. Draper's opening address when he asked 'Are we a fortuitous concourse of atoms?'" However, it was not to hear him but the eloquence of the Bishop, that the members of the Association[1]

---

[1] The British Association for the Advancement of Science.

crowded in such numbers into the Lecture Room of the Museum, that this, the appointed meeting-place of the section, had to be abandoned for the long west room, since cut in two by a partition for the purposes of the library. It was not term time, nor were the general public admitted; nevertheless the room was crowded to suffocation long before the protagonists appeared on the scene, 700 persons or more managing to find places. The very windows by which the room was lighted down the length of its west side were packed with ladies, whose white handkerchiefs, waving and fluttering in the air at the end of the Bishop's speech, were an unforgettable factor in the acclamation of the crowd.

The clergy, who shouted lustily for the Bishop, were massed in the middle of the room; behind them in the north-west corner a knot of undergraduates (one of these was T. H. Green, who listened but took no part in the cheering) had gathered together beside Professor Brodie, ready to lift their voices, poor minority though they were, for the opposite party. Close to them stood one of the few men among the audience already in Holy Orders, who joined in—and indeed led—the cheers for the Darwinians.

So "Dr. Draper droned out his paper, turning first to the right hand and then to the left, of course bringing in a reference to the *Origin of Species* which set the ball rolling."

An hour or more that paper lasted, and then discussion began. The President "wisely announced *in limine* that none who had not valid arguments to bring forward on one side or the other would be allowed to address the meeting; a caution that proved necessary, for no fewer than four combatants had their utterances burked by him, because of their indulgence in vague declamation."

First spoke (writes Professor Farrar) a layman from Brompton, who gave his name as being one of the Committee of the (newly formed) Economic section of the Association. He, in a stentorian voice, let off his theological venom. Then jumped up Richard Greswell with a thin voice, saying much the same, but speaking as a scholar; but we did not merely want any theological discussion, so we shouted them down. Then a Mr. Dingle got up and tried to show that Darwin would have done much better if he had taken him into consultation. He used the blackboard and began a mathematical demonstration on the question—"let this point A be man, and let that point B be the mawnkey." He got no further; he was shouted down with cries of "mawnkey." None of these had spoken more than three minutes. It was when these were shouted down that Henslow said he must demand that the discussion should rest on scientific grounds only.

Then there were calls for the Bishop, but he rose and said he understood his friend Professor Beale had something to say first. Beale, who was an excellent histologist, spoke to the effect that the new theory ought to meet with fair discussion, but added, with great modesty, that he himself had not sufficient knowledge to discuss the subject adequately. Then the Bishop spoke the speech that you know, and the question about his mother being an ape, or his grandmother.

From the scientific point of view, the speech was of small value. It was evident from his mode of handling the subject that he had been "crammed up to the throat," and knew nothing at first hand; he used no argument beyond those to be found in his *Quarterly* article, which appeared a few days later, and is now admitted to have been inspired by Owen. "He ridiculed Darwin badly and Huxley savagely; but," confesses one of his strongest opponents, "all in such dulcet tones, so persuasive a manner, and in such well turned periods, that I who had been inclined to blame the President for allowing a discussion that could serve no scientific purpose, now forgave him from the bottom of my heart."

The Bishop spoke thus "for full half an hour with inimitable spirit, emptiness and unfairness." "In a light, scoffing tone, florid and fluent, he assured us there was nothing in the idea of evolution; rock-pigeons were what rock-pigeons had always been. Then, turning to his antagonist with a smiling insolence, he begged to know, was it through his grandfather or his grandmother that he claimed his descent from a monkey?"

This was the fatal mistake of his speech. Huxley instantly grasped the tactical advantage which the descent to personalities gave him. He turned to Sir Benjamin Brodie, who was sitting beside him, and emphatically striking his hand upon his knee, exclaimed, "The Lord hath delivered him into mine hands." The bearing of the exclamation did not dawn upon Sir Benjamin until after Huxley had completed his "forcible and eloquent" answer to the scientific part of the Bishop's argument, and proceeded to make his famous retort.

On this (continues the writer in *Macmillan's Magazine*) Mr. Huxley slowly and deliberately arose. A slight, tall figure, stern and pale, very quiet and very grave, he stood before us and spoke those tremendous words—words which no one seems sure of now, nor, I think, could remember just after they were spoken, for their meaning took away our breath, though it left us in no doubt as to what it was. He was not ashamed to have a monkey for his ancestor; but he would be ashamed to be connected with a man who used great gifts to obscure the truth. No one doubted his meaning, and the effect was tremendous. One lady fainted and had to be carried out; I, for one, jumped out of my seat.

The fullest and probably most accurate account of these concluding words is the following, from a letter of the late John Richard Green, then an undergraduate, to his friend, afterwards Professor Boyd Dawkins:

> I asserted—and I repeat—that a man has no reason to be ashamed of having an ape for his grandfather. If there were an ancestor whom I should feel shame in recalling it would rather be a man—a man of restless and versatile intellect—who, not content with an equivocal success in his own sphere of activity, plunges into scientific questions with which he has no real acquaintance, only to obscure them by an aimless rhetoric, and distract the attention of his hearers from the real point at issue by eloquent digressions and skilled appeals to religious prejudice.

Ernst Haeckel

Ernst Haeckel (1834–1919), a German biologist and one of Darwin's most devoted propagandists, was one of many who tried to apply the doctrine of evolution to philosophical and religious problems. His philosophy, called monism, sees organic and inorganic nature as one, and life as deriving from carbon. The conclusions that Haeckel drew from his scientific speculations were brutally revolutionary at the time.

From The Riddle of the Universe

In the philosophy of history—that is, in the general reflections which historians make on the destinies of nations and the complicated course of political evolution—there still prevails the notion of a "moral order of the universe." Historians seek in the vivid drama of history a leading design, an ideal purpose, which has ordained one or other race or state to a special triumph, and to dominion over the others. This teleological view of history has recently become more strongly contrasted with our monistic view in proportion as monism has proved to be the only possible interpretation of inorganic nature. Throughout the whole of astronomy, geology, physics, and chemistry there is no question to-day of a "moral order," or a personal God, whose "hand hath disposed all things in wisdom and understanding." And the same must be said of the entire field of biology, the whole constitution and history of organic nature, if we set aside the question of man for the moment. Darwin has not only proved by his theory of selection that the orderly processes in the life and structure of animals and plants have arisen by mechanical laws without any preconceived design, but he has shown us in the "struggle for life" the powerful natural force which has exerted supreme control over the entire course of organic evolution for millions of years. It may be said that the struggle for life is the "survival of the fittest" or the "victory of the best"; that is only correct when we regard the strongest as the best (in a moral sense). Moreover, the whole history of the organic world goes to prove that, besides the predominant advance towards perfection, there are at all times cases of retrogression to lower stages. Even Baer's notion of "design" has no moral feature whatever.

Do we find a different state of things in the history of peoples, which man, in his anthropocentric presumption, loves to call "the history of the world"? Do we find in every phase of it a lofty moral principle or a wise ruler, guiding the destinies of nations? There can be but one answer in the present advanced stage of natural and human history: No. The fate of those branches of the human family, those nations and races which have struggled for existence and progress for thousands of years, is determined by the same "eternal laws of iron" as the history of the whole organic world which has peopled the earth for millions of years.

Thomas Huxley

Thomas Henry Huxley (1825–1895) was recognized as the foremost English biologist of the 1860s and '70s and was elected president of the Royal Society in 1883. His insistence on a strictly scientific approach, as distinguished from one that was metaphysical or theo-logical, earned him many enemies and much opposition; but the ethical attitude reflected

From Ernst Haeckel, *The Riddle of the Universe*, tr. Joseph McCabe (New York, 1900).

in his lecture on Evolution and Ethics *seems far from the ruthlessness of contemporary materialists.*

From Evolution and Ethics

As no man fording a swift stream can dip his foot twice into the same water, so no man can, with exactness, affirm of anything in the sensible world that it is. As he utters the words, nay, as he thinks them, the predicate ceases to be applicable; the present has become the past; the "is" should be "was." And the more we learn of the nature of things, the more evident is it that what we call rest is only unperceived activity; that seeming peace is silent but strenuous battle. In every part, at every moment, the state of the cosmos is the expression of a transitory adjustment of contending forces; a scene of strife, in which all the combatants fall in turn. What is true of each part, is true of the whole. Natural knowledge tends more and more to the conclusion that "all the choir of heaven and furniture of the earth" are the transitory forms of parcels of cosmic substance wending along the road of evolution, from nebulous potentiality, through endless growths of sun and planet and satellite; through all varieties of matter; through infinite diversities of life and thought; possibly, through modes of being of which we neither have a conception, nor are competent to form any, back to the indefinable latency from which they arose. Thus the most obvious attribute of the cosmos is its impermanence. It assumes the aspect not so much of a permanent entity as of a changeful process, in which naught endures save the flow of energy and the rational order which pervades it.

We are more than sufficiently familiar with modern pessimism. . . . We also know modern speculative optimism, with its perfectibility of the species, reign of peace, and lion and lamb transformation scenes; but one does not hear so much of it as one did forty years ago; indeed, I imagine it is to be met with more commonly at the tables of the healthy and wealthy, than in the congregations of the wise. The majority of us, I apprehend, profess neither pessimism nor optimism. We hold that the world is neither so good, nor so bad, as it conceivably might be: and, as most of us have reason, now and again, to discover that it can be. Those who have failed to experience the joys that make life worth living are, probably, in as small a minority as those who have never known the griefs that rob existence of its savour and turn its richest fruits into mere dust and ashes.

Further, I think I do not err in assuming that, however diverse their views on philosophical and religious matters, most men are agreed that the proportion of good and evil in life may be very sensibly affected by human action. I never heard anybody doubt that the evil may be thus increased, or diminished; and it would seem to follow that good must be similarly susceptible of addition or subtraction. Finally, to my

From Thomas H. Huxley, *Evolution and Ethics*, The Romanes Lecture, London, 1893.

knowledge, nobody professes to doubt that, so far forth as we possess a power of bettering things, it is our paramount duty to use it and to train all our intellect and energy to this supreme service of our kind.

Hence the pressing interest of the question, to what extent modern progress in natural knowledge, and, more especially, the general outcome of that progress in the doctrine of evolution, is competent to help us in the great work of helping one another?

The propounders of what are called the "ethics of evolution," when the "evolution of ethics" would usually better express the object of their speculations, adduce a number of more or less interesting facts and more or less sound arguments, in favour of the origin of the moral sentiments, in the same way as other natural phenomena, by a process of evolution. I have little doubt, for my own part, that they are on the right track; but as the immoral sentiments have no less been evolved, there is, so far, as much natural sanction for the one as the other. The thief and the murderer follow nature just as much as the philanthropist. Cosmic evolution may teach us how the good and the evil tendencies of man may have come about; but, in itself, it is incompetent to furnish any better reason why what we call good is preferable to what we call evil than we had before. Some day, I doubt not, we shall arrive at an understanding of the evolution of the aesthetic faculty; but all the understanding in the world will neither increase nor diminish the force of the intuition that this is beautiful and that is ugly.

There is another fallacy which appears to me to pervade the so-called "ethics of evolution." It is the notion that because, on the whole, animals and plants have advanced in perfection of organization by means of the struggle for existence and the consequent "survival of the fittest"; therefore men in society, men as ethical beings, must look to the same process to help them towards perfection. I suspect that this fallacy has arisen out of the unfortunate ambiguity of the phrase "survival of the fittest." "Fittest" has a connotation of "best"; and about "best" there hangs a moral flavour. In cosmic nature, however, what is "fittest" depends upon the conditions. Long since, I ventured to point out that if our hemisphere were to cool again, the survival of the fittest might bring about, in the vegetable kingdom, a population of more and more stunted and humbler and humbler organisms, until the "fittest" that survived might be nothing but lichens, diatoms, and such microscopic organisms as those which give red snow its colour; while, if it became hotter, the pleasant valleys of the Thames and Isis might be uninhabitable by any animated beings save those that flourish in a tropical jungle. They, as the fittest, the best adapted to the changed conditions, would survive.

Men in society are undoubtedly subject to the cosmic process. As among other animals, multiplication goes on without cessation, and involves severe competition for the means of support. The struggle for existence tends to eliminate those less fitted to adapt themselves to the circumstances of their existence. The strongest, the most self-assertive, tend to tread down the weaker. But the influence of the cosmic processes on the evolution of society is the greater the more rudimentary its civilization. Social progress means a checking of the cosmic process at every step and the substitution for it of another, which may be called the ethical process; the end of which is not the survival of those who may happen to be the fittest, in respect of the whole of the conditions which obtain, but of those who are ethically the best.

As I have already urged, the practice of that which is ethically best—what we call goodness or virtue—involves a course of conduct which, in all respects, is opposed to that which leads to success in the cosmic struggle for existence. In place of ruthless self-assertion it demands self-restraint; in place of thrusting aside, or treading down, all competitors, it requires that the individual shall not merely respect, but shall help his fellows; its influence is directed, not so much to the survival of the fittest, as to the fitting of as many as possible to survive. It repudiates the gladiatorial theory of existence. It demands that each man who enters into the enjoyment of the advantages of a polity shall be mindful of his debt to those who have laboriously constructed it; and shall take heed that no act of his weakens the fabric in which he has been permitted to live. Laws and moral precepts are directed to the end of curbing the cosmic process and reminding the individual of his duty to the community, to the protection and influence of which he owes, if not existence itself, at least the life of something better than a brutal savage.

It is from neglect of these plain considerations that the fanatical individualism of our time attempts to apply the analogy of cosmic nature to society. Once more we have a misapplication of the stoical injunction to follow nature; the duties of the individual to the state are forgotten, and his tendencies to self-assertion are dignified by the name of rights. It is seriously debated whether the members of a community are justified in using their combined strength to constrain one of their number to contribute his share to the maintenance of it; or even to prevent him from doing his best to destroy it. The struggle for existence, which has done such admirable work in cosmic nature, must, it appears, be equally beneficent in the ethical sphere. Yet if that which I have insisted upon is true; if the cosmic process has no sort of relation to moral ends; if the imitation of it by man is inconsistent with the first principles of ethics; what becomes of this surprising theory?

Let us understand, once for all, that the ethical progress of society depends, not on imitating the cosmic process, still less in running away from it, but in combating it. It may seem an audacious proposal thus to pit the microcosm against the macrocosm and to set man to subdue nature to his higher ends; but I venture to think that the great intellectual difference between the ancient times with which we have been occupied and our day, lies in the solid foundation we have acquired for the hope that such an enterprise may meet with a certain measure of success.

Ethical nature may count upon having to reckon with a tenacious and powerful enemy as long as the world lasts. But, on the other hand, I see no limit to the extent to which intelligence and will, guided by sound principles of investigation, and organized in common effort, may modify the conditions of existence, for a period longer than that now covered by history. And much may be done to change the nature of man himself. The intelligence which has converted the brother of the wolf into the faithful guardian of the flock ought to be able to do something towards curbing the instincts of savagery in civilized men.

Leslie Stephen

The following extract from Leslie Stephen's "An Agnostic's Apology" explains the very moderate attitude of an earnest and thoughtful man who left holy orders and resigned his fellowship in Cambridge when he lost faith in Christianity. Stephen lived to marry one of novelist William Thackeray's daughters, edit the Dictionary of National Biography, *climb the Matterhorn, and be knighted; but he never saw any reason to change his mind or abandon the opposition to religious dogma expressed in this article.*

From "An Agnostic's Apology"

The name Agnostic, originally coined by Professor Huxley about 1869, has gained general acceptance. It is sometimes used to indicate the philosophical theory which Mr. Herbert Spencer, as he tells us, developed from the doctrine of Hamilton and Mansel. Upon that theory I express no opinion. I take the word in a vaguer sense, and am glad to believe that its use indicates an advance in the courtesies of controversy. The old theological phrase for an intellectual opponent was Atheist—a name which still retains a certain flavour as of the stake in this world and hell-fire in the next, and which, moreover, implies an inaccuracy of some importance. Dogmatic Atheism—the doctrine that there is no God, whatever may be meant by God—is, to say the least, a rare phase of opinion. The word Agnosticism, on the other hand, seems to imply a fairly accurate appreciation of a form of creed already common and daily spreading. The Agnostic is one who asserts—what no one denies—that there are limits to the sphere of human intelligence. He asserts, further, what many theologians have expressly maintained, that those limits are such as to exclude at least what Lewes called "metempirical" knowledge. But he goes further, and asserts, in opposition to theologians, that theology lies within this forbidden sphere. This last assertion raises the important issue; and, though I have no pretension to invent an opposition nickname, I may venture, for the purposes of this article, to describe the rival school as Gnostics.

The Gnostic holds that our reason can, in some sense, transcend the narrow limits of experience. He holds that we can attain truths not capable of verification, and not needing verification, by actual experiment or observation. He holds, further, that a knowledge of those truths is essential to the highest interests of mankind, and enables us in some sort to solve the dark riddle of the universe. A complete solution, as everyone admits, is beyond our power. But some answer may be given to the doubts which harass and perplex us when we try to frame any adequate conception of the vast order of which we form an insignificant portion. We cannot say why this or that arrangement is what it is; we can say, though obscurely, that some answer exists, and would be satisfactory, if we could only find it. Overpowered, as every honest and serious thinker

From Leslie Stephen, "An Agnostic's Apology," Fortnightly Review, London, 1876.

is at times overpowered, by the sight of pain, folly, and helplessness, by the jarring discords which run through the vast harmony of the universe, we are yet enabled to hear at times a whisper that all is well, to trust to it as coming from the most authentic source, and to know that only the temporary bars of sense prevent us from recognising with certainty that the harmony beneath the discords is a reality and not a dream. This knowledge is embodied in the central dogma of theology. God is the name of the harmony; and God is knowable. Who would not be happy in accepting this belief, if he could accept it honestly? Who would not be glad if he could say with confidence: "the evil is transitory, the good eternal: our doubts are due to limitations destined to be abolished, and the world is really an embodiment of love and wisdom, however dark it may appear to our faculties"? And yet, if the so-called knowledge be illusory, are we not bound by the most sacred obligations to recognise the facts? Our brief path is dark enough on any hypothesis. We cannot afford to turn aside after every *ignis fatuus* without asking whether it leads to sounder footing or to hopeless quagmires. Dreams may be pleasanter for the moment than realities; but happiness must be won by adapting our lives to the realities. And who, that has felt the burden of existence, and suffered under well-meant efforts to consolation, will deny that such consolations are the bitterest of mockeries? Pain is not an evil; death is not a separation; sickness is but a blessing in disguise. Have the gloomiest speculations of avowed pessimists ever tortured sufferers like those kindly platitudes? Is there a more cutting piece of satire in the language than the reference in our funeral service to the "sure and certain hope of a blessed resurrection"? To dispel genuine hopes might be painful, however salutary. To suppress these spasmodic efforts to fly in the face of facts would be some comfort, even in the distress which they are meant to alleviate.

Besides the important question whether the Gnostic can prove his dogmas, there is, therefore, the further question whether the dogmas, if granted, have any meaning. Do they answer our doubts, or mock us with the appearance of an answer? The Gnostics rejoice in their knowledge. Have they anything to tell us? They rebuke what they call the "pride of reason" in the name of a still more exalted pride. The scientific reasoner is arrogant because he sets limits to the faculty in which he trusts, and denies the existence of any other faculty. They are humble because they dare to tread in the regions which he declares to be inaccessible. But without bandying such accusations, or asking which pride is the greatest, the Gnostics are at least bound to show some ostensible justification for their complacency. Have they discovered a firm resting-place from which they are entitled to look down in compassion or contempt upon those who hold it to be a mere edifice of moonshine? If they have diminished by a scruple the weight of one passing doubt, we should be grateful: perhaps we should be converts. If not, why condemn Agnosticism?

Andrew Carnegie

The Darwinian theories and the speculations that followed them could also lead to other conclusions concerning the purpose of life and, hence, our attitude to life and to our fellows. The apparently stern inferences of the doctrine of the survival of the fittest were drawn by the English philosopher Herbert Spencer (1820–1903). To a generation that no longer sought its spiritual guidance from the churches, Spencer offered a confident creed grounded on natural knowledge. He saw society passing from a military and despotic phase to an industrial and democratic phase. He condemned state interference with the healthy struggle for survival, and preached a robust individualism that appealed especially to the middle class. Some of his basic ideas may be found in the following words of one of Spencer's most successful disciples, the Scottish-American steel magnate and philanthropist Andrew Carnegie (1835–1919).

From "The Gospel of Wealth"

The problem of our age is the proper administration of wealth, that the ties of brotherhood may still bind together the rich and poor in harmonious relationship. The conditions of human life have not only been changed, but revolutionized, within the past few hundred years. In former days there was little difference between the dwelling, dress, food, and environment of the chief and those of his retainers. . . . The contrast between the palace of the millionaire and the cottage of the laborer with us to-day measures the change which has come with civilization. This change, however, is not to be deplored, but welcomed as highly beneficial. It is well, nay, essential for the progress of the race that the houses of some should be homes for all that is highest and best in literature and the arts, and for all the refinements of civilization, rather than that none should be so. Much better this great irregularity than universal squalor. Without wealth there can be no Maecenas. The "good old times" were not good old times. Neither master nor servant was as well situated then as to-day. A relapse to old conditions would be disastrous to both—not the least so to him who serves—and would sweep away civilization with it. But whether the change be for good or ill, it is upon us, beyond our power to alter, and therefore, to be accepted and made the best of. It is a waste of time to criticize the inevitable. . . .

The price we pay for this salutary change is, no doubt, great. We assemble thousands of operatives in the factory, and in the mine, of whom the employer can know little or nothing, and to whom he is little better than a myth. All intercourse between them is at an end. Rigid castes are formed, and, as usual, mutual ignorance breeds mutual distrust. Each caste is without sympathy with the other, and ready to credit anything disparaging in regard to it. Under the law of competition, the employer of thousands is forced into the strictest economies, among which the rates paid to labor figure prominently, and often there is friction between the employer and the employed, between capital and labor, between rich and poor. Human society loses homogeneity.

The price which society pays for the law of competition, like the price it pays for cheap comforts and luxuries, is also great; but the advantages of this law are also greater still than its cost—for it is to this law that we owe our wonderful material development,

From Andrew Carnegie, *The Gospel of Wealth* (New York: *North American Review*, 1889).

which brings improved conditions in its train. But, whether the law be benign or not, we must say of it, as we say of the change in the conditions of men to which we have referred: It is here; we cannot evade it; no substitutes for it have been found; and while the law may be sometimes hard for the individual, it is best for the race, because it insures the survival of the fittest in every department. We accept and welcome, therefore, as conditions to which we must accommodate ourselves, great inequality of environment; the concentration of business, industrial and commercial, in the hands of a few; and the law of competition between these, as being not only beneficial, but essential to the future progress of the race. . . . Nor is there any middle ground which such men can occupy, because the great manufacturing or commercial concern which does not earn at least interest upon its capital soon becomes bankrupt. It must either go forward or fall behind; to stand still is impossible. It is a condition essential to its successful operation that it should be thus far profitable, and even that, in addition to interest on capital, it should make profit. It is a law, as certain as any of the others named, that men possessed of this peculiar talent for affairs, under the free play of economic forces must, of necessity, soon be in receipt of more revenue than can be judiciously expended upon themselves; and this law is as beneficial for the race as the others.

Objections to the foundations upon which society is based are not in order, because the condition of the race is better with these than it has been with any other which has been tried. Of the effect of any new substitutes proposed we cannot be sure. The Socialist or Anarchist who seeks to overturn present conditions is to be regarded as attacking the foundation upon which civilization itself rests, for civilization took its start from the day when the capable, industrious workman said to his incompetent and lazy fellow, "If thou dost not sow, thou shalt not reap," and thus ended primitive Communism by separating the drones from the bees. One who studies this subject will soon be brought face to face with the conclusion that upon the sacredness of property civilization itself depends—the right of the laborer to his hundred dollars in the savings-bank, and equally the legal right of the millionaire to his millions. . . . To those who propose to substitute Communism for this intense Individualism, the answer therefore is: The race has tried that. All progress from that barbarous day to the present time has resulted from its displacement. Not evil, but good, has come to the race from the accumulation of wealth by those who have had the ability and energy to produce it. But even if we admit for a moment that it might be better for the race to discard its present foundation, Individualism—that it is a nobler ideal that man should labor, not for himself alone, but in and for a brotherhood of his fellows, and share with them all in common, . . . even admit all this, and a sufficient answer is, This is not evolution, but revolution. It necessitates the changing of human nature itself—a work of eons, even if it were good to change it, which we cannot know.

It is not practicable in our day or in our age. Even if desirable theoretically, it belongs to another and long-succeeding sociological stratum. Our duty is with what is practicable now—with the next step possible in our day and generation. It is criminal to waste our energies in endeavoring to uproot, when all we can profitably accomplish is to bend the universal tree of humanity a little in the direction most favorable to the production of good fruit under existing circumstances. We might as well urge the destruction of the highest existing type of man because he failed to reach our ideal as to favor the destruction of Individualism, Private Property, the Law of Accumulation of Wealth, and the Law of Competition; for these are the highest result of human experience, the soil in which society, so far, has produced the best fruit. Unequally or unjustly, perhaps, as these laws sometimes operate, and imperfect as they appear to the Idealist, they are, nevertheless, like the highest type of man, the best and most valuable of all that humanity has yet accomplished. . . .

Poor and restricted are our opportunities in this life, narrow our horizon, our best work most imperfect; but rich men should be thankful for one inestimable boon. They have it in their power during their lives to busy themselves in organizing benefactions from which the masses of their fellows will derive lasting advantage, and thus dignify their own lives. The highest life is probably to be reached, not by such imitation of the life of Christ as Count Tolstoi gives us, but, while animated by Christ's spirit, by recognizing the changed conditions of this age, and adopting modes of expressing this spirit suitable to the changed conditions under which we live, still laboring for the good of our fellows, which was the essence of his life and teaching, but laboring in a different manner.

This, then, is held to be the duty of the man of wealth: To set an example of modest, unostentatious living, shunning display or extravagance; to provide moderately for the legitimate wants of those dependent upon him; and, after doing so, to consider all surplus revenues which come to him simply as trust funds, which he is called upon to administer, and strictly bound as a matter of duty to administer in the manner which, in his judgment, is best calculated to produce the most beneficial result for the community—the man of wealth thus becoming the mere trustee and agent for his poorer brethren, bringing to their service his superior wisdom, experience, and ability to administer, doing for them better than they would or could do for themselves. . . .

One of the serious obstacles to the improvement of our race is indiscriminate charity. It were better for mankind that the millions of the rich were thrown into the sea than so spent as to encourage the slothful, the drunken, the unworthy. Of every thousand dollars spent in so-called charity today, it is probable that nine hundred and fifty dollars is unwisely spent—so spent, indeed, as to produce the very evils which it hopes to mitigate or cure. A well-known writer of philosophic books admitted the other day that he had given a quarter of a dollar to a man who approached him as he was coming to visit the house of his friend. He knew nothing of the habits of this beggar, knew not the use that would be made of this money, although he had every reason to suspect that it would be spent improperly. This man professed to be a disciple of Herbert Spencer; yet the quarter-dollar given that night will probably work more injury than all the money will do good which its thoughtless donor will ever be able to give in true charity. He only gratified his own feelings, saved himself from annoyance—and this was probably one of the most selfish and very worst actions of his life, for in all respects he is most worthy.

In bestowing charity, the main consideration should be to help those who will help themselves; to provide part of the means by which those who desire to improve may do so; to give those who desire to rise the aids by which they may rise; to assist, but rarely or never to do all. Neither the individual nor the race is improved by almsgiving. Those worthy of assistance, except in rare cases, seldom require assistance. The really valuable men of the race never do, except in case of accident or sudden change. Every one has, of course, cases of individuals brought to his own knowledge where temporary assistance can do genuine good, and these he will not overlook. But the amount which can be wisely given by the individual for individuals is necessarily limited by his lack of knowledge of the circumstances connected with each. He is the only true reformer who is as careful and as anxious not to aid the unworthy as he is to aid the worthy, and, perhaps, even more so, for in almsgiving more injury is probably done by rewarding vice than by relieving virtue.

Thus is the problem of rich and poor to be solved. The laws of accumulation will be left free, the laws of distribution free. Individualism will continue, but the millionaire will be but a trustee for the poor, intrusted for a season with a great part of the increased wealth of the community, but administering it for the community far better than it could or would have done for itself. The best minds will thus have reached a stage in the development of the race in which it is clearly seen that there is no mode of disposing of surplus wealth creditable to thoughtful and earnest men into whose hands it flows, save by using it year by year for the general good. This day already dawns.

Eugenics

Yet one more conclusion was drawn from Darwin's theory of evolution, this one by his cousin, Francis Galton (1822–1911), a distinguished quantifier, explorer, and anthropologist. In 1883 Galton coined the term eugenics *to denote the effort to improve human beings by selective breeding. Insofar as it favored biological over social forces, and "nature" over "nurture," eugenics has been denounced as reactionary and has, indeed, operated in grim and ominous ways.*

The American Eugenics Society supported restrictions on immigration and argued for the sterilization of the insane, retarded, and epileptic. The following report, from 1930, which also called for contraception and the regulation of child labor, reflects these positions.

From the American Eugenics Society's 1930 Report

IMMIGRATION PROGRAM

Recognizing the vital importance to the health, prosperity and general physical and mental well-being of the American people of a rational, just, and eugenic immigration policy, the Committee on Selective Immigration of the American Eugenics Society recommends to the President and Congress of the United States, to the scientists of this country and to the American people generally, the following immigration program:

From *Organized Eugenics* (January 1931), pp. 19–22. (American Eugenics Society, Inc., 185 Church St., New Haven, Conn.)

1. The National Origins basis of immigration restriction, now in operation for countries of Europe, as the most scientific, soundest in principle and fairest to all elements in the population of any method of quota limitation which has yet been proposed. Only by this method can that large proportion of our population which is descended from the colonists and early settlers, as well as the members of the newer immigration, have fair and reasonable representation in the quotas.

2. In view of the general sentiment of the country for further limitation upon immigration, with which the committee is in full accord, it is recommended that all quotas now in force be reduced by one-half except that the present minimum quota of 100 be preserved. The Committee is of the opinion that while there is much to commend a policy of permanent exclusion of immigration, the problem of devising a reasonable method for controlling the admission of near relatives of recent immigrants renders the adoption of such a policy impracticable at the present time.

3. Establishment of the principle of numerical limitation upon immigration from all countries of the Western Hemisphere. The Committee believes that permanent numerical limitation is essential in order to ensure restriction upon admissions now being accomplished in large measure by industrial depression and by virtue of recent administrative action in strictly enforcing certain provisions in the law which are susceptible of broad interpretation.

4. Appropriation by Congress of adequate funds for the deportation of all deportable aliens in this country, and for an effective immigration service and border patrol which will prevent deportable aliens from entering the country, together with the general strengthening of the statutes regarding deportation.

5. Registration of the alien population in this country, both for the protection of the aliens legally here, and for the protection of the American people against the smuggling of aliens into the country.

6. Selection of immigrants so as to admit only those who are superior to the median American in mental endowment as far as this is shown by approved psychological tests, at the same time fulfilling the other qualifications established by existing law. . . .

EUGENICAL STERILIZATION

One of the chief aims of the Committee is to initiate conservative legislation pertaining to the eugenical sterilization of certain hereditary defectives. The types of sterilization now generally accepted as eugenically satisfactory are accomplished by the surgical operations known as *vasectomy* in the male and *salpingectomy* in the female. The operation in no way interferes with the normal sex life except to eliminate the power of procreation. In the majority of cases under observation, the operation is welcomed not only by the community which is called upon to support more and more defective children from such unions, but also by the sterilized persons themselves, to whom life itself is usually enough of a burden without the addition of children. A summary of the various phases and results of 6,000 eugenical sterilization operations in California may be found in *Sterilization for Human Betterment* (Macmillan, 1929), by E. S. Gosney and Paul Popenoe. California passed its first sterilization law in 1909, and today this state offers the largest single body of data on eugenical sterilization procedure and results. . . .

The first eugenical sterilization law in the United States was passed in Indiana in 1907. To May 1, 1930, 25 states had eugenical sterilization laws on their statute books. To January 1, 1930, the number of eugenical sterilization operations performed in state institutions under state laws was 10,833. Of these operations, 6,787 were performed under the California law.

Eugenical sterilization laws were in effect in these 25 states, May 1, 1930: Alabama, Arizona, California, Connecticut, Delaware, Idaho, Iowa, Indiana, Kansas, Maine, Michigan, Minnesota, Mississippi, Montana, Nebraska, New Hampshire, North Carolina, North Dakota, Oregon, South Dakota, Utah, Virginia, Washington, West Virginia, and Wisconsin.

A test case was brought from Virginia to the United States Supreme Court in 1925, testing the legality of eugenical sterilization, and a most favorable decision resulted in 1927. Chief Justice Holmes stated:

We have seen more than once that the public welfare may call upon the best citizens for their lives. It would be strange if it could not call upon those who already sap the strength of the state for these lesser sacrifices, often not felt to be such by those concerned, in order to prevent our being swamped with incompetence. It is better for all the world, if instead of waiting to execute degenerate offspring for crime, or to let them starve for their imbecility, society can prevent those who are manifestly unfit from continuing their kind. The principle that sustains compulsory vaccination is broad enough to cover cutting the Fallopian tubes. . . . Three generations of imbeciles are enough. . . .

IMAGES: THE WONDERS OF TECHNOLOGY

Technology has to do with the industrial arts: novel inventions abounding in the nineteenth century—fewer than in our own, of course, but the more striking then for being less familiar. Lithography, photography, picture posters, and moving pictures, iron rail, iron structures, steam engines, flying engines, skyscrapers, and machines for living were all talked about, introduced, and wondered over, well before 1914. Standardized products, interchangeable parts, prefabrication, and efficiency were opening the way to mass production and mass consumption—and encouraging mass aspirations and frustrations. The technological revolution made the bed on which the twentieth century lies, and it is a more comfortable bed than we enjoyed before. The question is whether, in technology's bed, there is enough room for all of us, or for other animals.

Photography Takes Off. Photography was invented in 1839 and then steadily improved. In an 1861 publicity photo, which is a cocktail of technological novelties, one of photography's showman-pioneers Gaspard-Felix Tournachon (known as Nadar [1820–1910]) pictured himself traveling through the clouds in a balloon. This image inspired lithographer Honoré Daumier (1808–1879) to dedicate this satirical cartoon to him, entitled "Nadar raising photography to the heights of art."
(Bibliothèque Nationale Paris, 74C, 66315)

470

Moving Toward Movies. Painter and decorator Jules Cherét (1836–1932) was one of the most famous poster designers of his day. The playbill shown here advertises one of the first projections of *dessins animés*—literally, animated drawings, the ancestors of our movie cartoons.

Posters advertising drinks, food products, and all kinds of entertainment were another offspring of color lithography, and one that helped very ordinary people to become used to the swift, stenographic style of avant-garde artists. The dances and pantomines advertised here, in 1892, are nothing new; but they're enhanced by optical tricks, lighting, and magic lantern projections. Within three years of this poster, the demands of contemporary theatre and music hall combined with public expectations of ever more novel illusions to spur the invention of moving pictures.

(*Pantomime lumineuses au Musée Grevin* by Jules Cherét, courtesy Musée Cherét, Nice)

La Gare St. Lazare, 1877 by Claude Monet
(Claude Monet, *La Gare St. Lazare*, Musée d'Orsay, RF2775, © Photo RMN)

Saint-Lazare Railway Station, Paris, 1877. A great shed of glass and steel frames, this station is a major expression of nineteenth-century technology: rails, trains, engines, and power. Claude Monet (1840–1926) focuses not on human figures, which he simply outlines, but on the station, quays, machines, and the clouds of steam that swathe them. "Our artists have to discover the poetry of railway stations," declared Emile Zola, the avant-garde novelist, that year, "as their fathers found the poetry of forests and of streams." A few years after this, Zola himself would turn a railway engine into an allegory of the modern world.

Pont del'Europe, Gare St. Lazare, 1877 by Claude Monet
(Musée Marmottan Paris, *Pont del'Europe, Gare St. Lazare, 1877* by Claude Monet)

The Crystal Palace, London, 1851. Joseph Paxton (1801–1865) was a gardener and builder of hothouses who turned architect to design the Crystal Palace for the London Exhibition of 1851. Put together of a prefabricated iron frame and sheet glass, his structure was a marvel of ingenious simplicity, and it provided the model for subsequent exhibition pavillions in France and elsewhere. Enclosing nineteen acres, four times the area of Saint Peter's in Rome, the Crystal Palace was built in six months and brought Paxton a knighthood.
(Archive Photos)

Engineering by Eiffel. Gustave Eiffel (1832–1923), a civil engineer, specialized in the metal construction characteristic of the new age. He designed the lofty, massive machine gallery for the Paris Exhibition of 1867; and then, in the early 1880s, the 540-foot span Garabit viaduct in southern France. Pictured here, it soared 400 feet over the stream it crossed. Within a few years of that revolutionary bridge, Eiffel startled the world with the 984 foot tower that he built as a centerpiece for the Paris Centennial Exposition of 1889, to commemorate the anniversary of the French Revolution. Twice as high as the dome of Saint Peter's in Rome or the Great Pyramid at Gizeh, the Eiffel Tower would remain the tallest building in the world until overtaken in 1930 by the Chrysler Building in Manhattan. Denounced as an American-inspired eyesore, the tower's glass cage elevators, which rose on a curve, were designed by the Otis Elevator Company. They helped to make the tower one of the world's great tourist attractions. The photograph used here shows the official party at the opening ceremony. Note how their cumbersome ceremonial dress clashes with the stark structure behind.

The Garabit Viaduct, 1880–1884
(Musée d'Orsay Archives Eiffel, courtesy Jean-Loup Charmet, Paris)

The Eiffel Tower on Opening Day, 1889
(Photoworld/Pix, © FPG International)

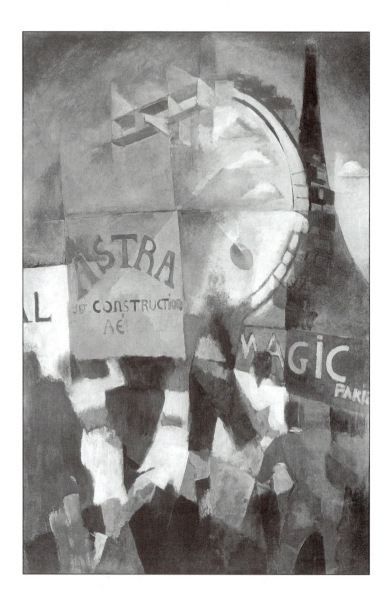

The Cardiff Team (1912) by Robert Delaunay. This painting brings together a number of turn-of-the-century novelties. Advancing from schoolboy shindigs to popular spectator sport, football and rugby football were to turn into mass entertainment within a decade. Above the Welsh rugby team at play one glimpses a flying machine (developed only a few years before) a giant ferris wheel, and the outline of the Eiffel Tower. Around the team, publicity panels remind us of yet another contemporary phenomenon: advertising.

(*The Cardiff Team* by Robert Delaunay, 1912, courtesy of Stedelijk van Abbemuseum, Eindhoven, NL)

(*New City* by Antonio Sant' Elia, 1914. Private collection, courtesy of Editions d'Art Albert Skira, Geneva)

Fascinated by the possibilities of steel, glass, and concrete, architects designed ever more adventurous structures—not least in the United States, where taller and taller buildings rose to provide work and living space. In 1914, the Italian socialist and futurist Antonio Sant' Elia (1888–1916) sketched a vast, lofty, highly-mechanized *New City,* complete with multilevel traffic ramps and designed as a "machine for dwelling." Sant' Elia died in the First World War, but in 1922 the Franco-Swiss architect Charles Edouard Jeanneret, who worked under the name of Le Corbusier (1887–1965), sketched his own ideal contemporary city. It is worth noting that neither design included a single living being. Machines for living had become more important than those for whom they were allegedly designed.

(*Contemporary City with Three Million Inhabitants* by Le Corbusier, 1922. Courtesy Editions d'Art Albert Skira, Geneva and SPADEM)

Patterns of Change

THE variety of views quoted in the following selections bears witness to the variety of the patterns of change at this time. A striking point they all have in common is the pragmatism they express. The more effective political thinkers of this new age thought in terms of what is possible and followed principle only when it led to practical ends. This is territory upon which Bismarck and Bernstein, Fabians and Lenin can all meet, and it seems to foreshadow the democratic politics of the twentieth century, for which a platform was made to run on, not to stand on.

Dostoyevsky and Nietzsche represent a different orientation: one that is no less clear-sighted, but that in a visionary way extrapolates from possibilities inherent in the present to predict the realities of a dire future.

Otto von Bismarck

Prince Otto von Bismarck (1815–1898), something of a stormy petrel in his youth, became minister president of Prussia in 1862 and forged German unity around and under Prussian rule. In 1864 he achieved the conquest of Schleswig from Denmark; in 1866 the defeat of Austria, which established Prussia's predominant place in Germany; and in 1870 his final aim, the proclamation of a German Empire under the rule of the Prussian king. Henceforth his policy as imperial chancellor was devoted to the maintenance of peace both at home and abroad. Until his dismissal from office in 1890 by the young William II, the old prince remained the dominant figure of European affairs—not only a great statesman but also a very smart operator. He found it useful to accept and use some of the progressive ideas of his time in order to strengthen the power of the monarchy he served. As he saw it, the end justified the means; as contemporaries saw it, success justified Bismarck.

From: A Speech to the Prussian Budget Commission

Germany is not looking to Prussia's liberalism, but to her power; Bavaria or Würtemberg or Baden may choose to be liberal, but no one is going to expect of them what they expect of Prussia. Prussia must gather up her strength and hold it ready for the moment of opportunity—an opportunity we have already missed several times. Prus-

From a speech delivered by Bismarck in the Budget Commission of the Prussian Lower Chamber, 30 Sept. 1862; in Hohlfeld, *Deutsche Reichsgeschichte in Dokumenten* (Berlin, 1927).

sia's borders since the Treaty of Vienna, have not been the sort that a healthy state needs; the great questions of the day are not decided by speeches and by the votes of the majority—that was the great mistake of 1848 and 1849. They are decided by blood and iron.

On State Interference

Herr Richter has called attention to the responsibility of the State for what it does. But it is my opinion that the State can also be responsible for what it does not do. I do not think that doctrines like those of "*Laissez-faire, laissez-aller*," "Pure Manchesterdom in politics,"[1] "He who is not strong enough to stand must be knocked down, and trodden to the ground," "To him that hath shall be given, and from him that hath not shall be taken away even that which he hath"—that doctrines like these should be applied in the State, and especially in a monarchically, paternally governed State. On the other hand, I believe that those who profess horror at the intervention of the State for the protection of the weak lay themselves open to the suspicion that they are desirous of using their strength—be it that of capital, that of rhetoric, or whatever it be—for the benefit of a section, for the oppression of the rest, for the introduction of party domination, and that they will be chagrined as soon as this design is disturbed by any action of the government.

I ask you what right had I to close the way to the throne against these people? The kings of Prussia have never been by preference kings of the rich. Frederick the Great said when Crown Prince: "*Quand je serai roi, je serai un vrai roi des gueux.*" He undertook to be the protector of the poor, and this principle has been followed by our later kings. At their throne suffering has always found a refuge and a hearing. . . .

Our kings have secured the emancipation of the serfs, they have created a thriving peasantry, and they may possibly be successful—the earnest endeavour exists, at any rate—in improving the condition of the working classes somewhat. To have refused access to the throne to the complaints of these operatives would not have been the right course to pursue, and it was, moreover, not my business to do it. The question would afterwards have been asked: "How rich must a deputation be in order to insure its reception by the King?" . . .

I am not antagonistic to the rightful claims of capital; I am far from wanting to flourish a hostile flag; but I am of opinion that the masses, too, have rights which should be considered.

I wish we could immediately create a few hundred millionaires. They would expend their money in the country, and this expenditure would act fruitfully on labour all round. They could not eat their money themselves; they would have to spend the

---

From William H. Dawson, *Bismarck and State Socialism* (London, 1891).

[1]"Let [them] do, let [them] go": In other words, don't interfere with the free operation of the market. This was the liberal, free-trade doctrine associated with the great manufacturing center of Manchester. Hence the reference to Manchesterdom.—William Dawson

interest on it. Be glad, then, when people become rich with us. The community at large, and not only the tax authority, is sure to benefit.

The large land-owner who lives in the country is not the worst evil; the worst is the large land-owner who lives in town, be it Paris, Rome, or Berlin, and who only requires money from his estates and agents, who does not represent his estates in the Reichstag or Land-tag, and does not even know how it fares with them. Therein lies the evil of large estates. Large estates whose owners live in the country are under certain circumstances a great blessing, and very useful. . . . I regard the large land-owners who are really farmers, and buy land from a predilection for this industry, as a blessing for our country, and especially for the provinces where I live. And if you succeed in destroying this race, you would see the result in the palsying of our entire economic and political life. . . . But so long as God is still minded to preserve the German Empire and the Kingdom of Prussia, this war of yours against landed proprietorship will not succeed, however many allies you may obtain.

Give the working-man the right to work as long as he is healthy; assure him care when he is sick; assure him maintenance when he is old. If you do that, and do not fear the sacrifice, or cry out at State Socialism directly the words "Provision for old age" are uttered,—if the State will show a little more Christian solicitude for the working-man, then I believe that the gentlemen of the Wyden (Social-Democratic) programme will sound their birdcall in vain, and that the thronging to them will cease as soon as workingmen see that the Government and legislative bodies are earnestly concerned for their welfare.

Yes, I acknowledge unconditionally a right to work, and I will stand up for it as long as I am in this place. But here I do not stand upon the ground of Socialism, which is said to have only begun with the Bismarck Ministry, but on that of the Prussian common law. . . . Was not the right to work openly proclaimed at the time of the publication of the common law? Is it not established in all our social arrangements that the man who comes before his fellow-citizens and says, "I am healthy, I desire to work, but can find no work," is entitled to say also, "Give me work," and that the State is bound to give him work?

I will further every endeavour which positively aims at improving the condition of the working classes. . . . As soon as a positive proposal comes from the Socialists for fashioning the future in a sensible way, in order that the lot of the working-man might be improved, I would not at any rate refuse to examine it favourably, and I would not even shrink from the idea of State help for the people who would help themselves.

The establishment of the freedom of the peasantry was Socialistic; Socialistic, too, is every expropriation in favour of railways: Socialistic to the utmost extent is the aggregation of estates—the law exists in many provinces—taking from one and giving to another, simply because this other can cultivate the land more conveniently; Socialistic is expropriation under the Water Legislation, on account of irrigation, etc., where a man's land is taken away from him because another can farm it better; Socialistic is our entire poor relief, compulsory school attendance, compulsory construction of roads, so that I am bound to maintain a road upon my lands for travellers. That is all

Socialistic, and I could extend the register further; but if you believe that you can frighten any one or call up spectres with the word "Socialism," you take a standpoint which I abandoned long ago, and the abandonment of which is absolutely necessary for our entire imperial legislation.

On Universal Suffrage

Looking to the necessity, in a fight against an overwhelming foreign Power, of being able, in extreme need, to use even revolutionary means, I had had no hesitation whatever in throwing into the frying-pan, by means of the circular dispatch of June 10, 1866, the most powerful ingredient known at that time to liberty-mongers, namely, universal suffrage, so as to frighten off foreign monarchies from trying to stick a finger into our national omelette. I never doubted that the German people would be strong and clever enough to free themselves from the existing suffrage as soon as they realized that it was a harmful institution. If it cannot, then my saying that Germany can ride when once she has got into the saddle was erroneous. The acceptance of universal suffrage was a weapon in the war against Austria and other foreign countries, in the war for German Unity, as well as a threat to use the last weapons in a struggle against coalitions. In a war of this sort, when it becomes a matter of life and death, one does not look at the weapons that one seizes; nor at the value of what one destroys in using them: one is guided at the moment by no other thought than the issue of the war, and the preservation of one's external independence; the settling of affairs and reparation of the damage has to take place after the peace. Moreover, I still hold that the principle of universal suffrage is a just one, not only in theory but also in practice, provided always that voting be not secret, for secrecy is a quality that is indeed incompatible with the best characteristics of German blood.

The influence and the dependence on others that the practical life of man brings in its train are God-given realities which we cannot and must not ignore. If we refuse to transfer them to political life, and base that life on a faith in the secret insight of everybody, we fall into a contradiction between public law and the realities of human life which practically leads to constant frictions, and finally to an explosion, and to which there is no theoretical solution except by the way of the insanities of social-democracy, the support given to which rests on the fact that the judgment of the masses is sufficiently stultified and undeveloped to allow them, with the assistance of their own greed, to be continually caught by the rhetoric of clever and ambitious leaders.

The counterpoise to this lies in the influence of the educated classes which would be greatly strengthened if voting were public, as for the Prussian Diet. It may be that the greater discretion of the more intelligent classes rests on the material basis of the preservation of their possessions. The other motive, the struggle for gain, is equally

---

From Bismarck, *His Reflections and Reminiscences*, tr. A. J. Butler, 2 vol. (London, 1898).

justifiable; but a preponderance of those who represent property is more serviceable for the security and development of the state. A state, the control of which lies in the hands of the greedy, of the new rich, and of orators who have in a higher degree than others the capacity for deceiving the unreasoning masses, will constantly be doomed to a restlessness of development, which so ponderous a mass as the commonwealth of the state cannot follow without injury to its organism. Ponderous masses, and among these the life and development of great nations must be reckoned, can only move with caution, since the road on which they travel to an unknown future has no smooth iron rails. Every great state-commonwealth that loses the prudent and restraining influence of the propertied class, whether that influence rests on material or moral grounds, will always end by being rushed along at a speed which must shatter the coach of state, as happened in the development of the French Revolution. The element of greed has the preponderance arising from large masses which in the long run must make its way. It is in the interests of the great mass itself to wish decision to take place without dangerous acceleration of the speed of the coach of state, and without its destruction. If this should happen, however, the wheel of history will revolve again, and always in a proportionately shorter time, to dictatorship, to despotism, to absolutism, because in the end the masses yield to the need of order; if they do not recognize this need *a priori*, they always realize it eventually after manifold arguments *ad hominem;* and in order to purchase order from a dictatorship and Caesarism they cheerfully sacrifice that justifiable amount of freedom which ought to be maintained, and which the political society of Europe can endure without ill-health.

I should regard it as a serious misfortune, and as an essential weakening of our security in the future, if we in Germany are driven into the vortex of this French cycle. Absolutism would be the ideal form of government for an European political structure were not the King and his officials ever as other men are to whom it is not given to reign with superhuman wisdom, insight and justice. The most experienced and well-meaning absolute rulers are subject to human imperfections, such as overestimation of their own wisdom, the influence and eloquence of favourites, not to mention petticoat influence, legitimate and illegitimate. Monarchy and the most ideal monarch, if in his idealism he is not to be a common danger, stand in need of criticism; the thorns of criticism set him right when he runs the risk of losing his way. Joseph II is a warning example of this.

Criticism can only be exercised through the medium of a free press and parliaments in the modern sense of the term. Both correctives may easily weaken and finally lose their efficacy if they abuse their powers. To avert this is one of the tasks of a conservative policy, which cannot be accomplished without a struggle with parliament and press. The measurement of the limits within which such a struggle must be confined, if the control of the government, which is indispensable to the country, is neither to be checked nor allowed to gain a complete power, is a question of political tact and judgment.

It is a piece of good fortune for his country if a monarch possess the judgment requisite for this—a good fortune that is temporary, it is true, like all human fortune. The possibility of establishing ministers in power who possess adequate qualifications must always be granted in the constitutional organism; but also the possibility of maintaining in office ministers who satisfy these requirements in face of occasional votes of an adverse majority and of the influence of courts and camarillas. This aim, so far as human imperfections in general allow its attainment, was approximately reached under the government of William I.

Constantin Pobyedonostsev

In his time, Constantin Pobyedonostsev, supreme procurator of the Holy Synod, was the highest Russian lay official in charge of religious and educational affairs; he was also the most influential adviser of Tsar Alexander III and, for a time, of his successor, Nicholas II. This very powerful man, who dominated so much of Russian policy in the 1880s and '90s, was "a thorough despiser of human nature who had turned reaction into a system of philosophy," who saw representative institutions as "the greatest falsehood of our time" and advised that "fear of, not love of God, and fear of, and devotion to the Tsar, are to be cultivated as aids to government." His remarks on democracy, which follow in the translation of R. C. Long, have frequently been repeated against it.

On the Democratic Myth

The philosophy of the school of Rousseau has done much evil to humanity. This philosophy took possession of many minds; but at the same time it was all based on one false idea of human perfectibility, and on the assumption in every individual of capacity to comprehend and appreciate those principles of social organisation which it proclaimed.

The prevalent doctrine of the perfection of Democracy and of democratic government, stands on the same delusive foundation. This doctrine presupposes the capacity of the people to understand subtleties of political science which have a clear and substantial existence in the minds of its apostles only. Precision of knowledge is attainable only by the few minds which constitute the aristocracy of intellect; the mass, always and everywhere, is *vulgus*, and its conceptions of necessity are vulgar.

Democracy is the most complicated and the most burdensome system of government recorded in the history of humanity. For this reason it has never appeared save as a transitory manifestation, with few exceptions giving place before long to other systems. This is in no way surprising. The duty of the State is to act and to ordain: its dispositions are manifestations of a single will; without this government is inconceivable. But how can a multitude of men, or a popular assembly, act with a single will? The upholder of Democracy takes little trouble over the decision of this question, but evades it by means of those favourite phrases and formulas:—"The will of the people," "public opinion," "the supreme decision of the nation," "the voice of the people is

---

From K. P. Pobyedonostsev, *Reflections of a Russian Statesman*, tr. R. C. Long (London, 1898).

the voice of God," and others of a like nature. All these phrases signify that a multitude of men on a multitude of questions may form a common conclusion, and, conformably with their conclusion, arrive at a common decision. This may be possible sometimes, but only on the simplest questions. Where questions present the slightest complexity their decision by a numerous assembly is possible only through the medium of men capable of judging them in all their details, and of persuading the people to accept their judgment. In the number of complex questions may be counted all political questions requiring great concentration of the intellectual forces of the most capable and experienced statesmen; on such questions it would be absurd to rely upon unanimity of thought and will in a numerous assembly; the decision of the people only could be ruinous to the State. The enthusiasts of Democracy contend that the people may manifest its will in affairs of State: this is a shallow theory. In reality, we find that popular assemblies are capable only of accepting—through enthusiasm—the opinion expressed by individuals or by a small minority—the opinion, for instance, of the recognised leader of their party, of some local worker of repute, of some organised association, or the impersonal opinion of an influential journal. Thus the discussions which precede decisions become an absurd comedy played on a vast stage by a multitude of heads and voices; the greater the multitude the more unintelligible is the comedy, and the more the *dénouement*[1] depends upon fortuitous and disorderly impulses.

To evade all these difficulties, the system of government by representation has been devised, a system first established and first justified by success, in England. Thence, through the influence of fashion, it spread to other European countries, but proved successful only in the United States of America, and there by tradition and by right. Yet even in England, the land of their origin, representative institutions are in a critical epoch of their history. The very essence of the idea of representation has submitted already to modifications which have changed its primitive significance. In the beginning, the assemblies of electors, on a strictly limited franchise, sent to Parliament a certain number of persons whose duty it was to represent the opinions of the country, but who were not bound by any definite instructions from the mass of their constituents. It was assumed that these elected representatives were men who understood the real needs of their country, and who were capable of justly controlling the politics of the State. The problem was resolved simply and plainly: it was required to lessen, as far as possible, the difficulties of government by the people, by limiting in number the members of the assemblies summoned for the decision of questions of State. These men appeared in the capacity of free representatives of the people, and not as instruments of the opinions of factions; they were bound by no instructions. But in the course of time this system changed under the influence of that fatal delusion about the great value of public opinion, as enlightened by the periodical Press which gave to the people the capacity to participate directly in the decision of political questions. The idea of representation altogether lost its form, and reappeared as the idea of a mandate; or of specific commission. From this point of view each representative is accounted a representative of the dominant opinions of his constituency, or of the party under the

---

[1] outcome.

banner of which his victory was gained. Thus he is no longer a representative of the country or of the people, but a delegate bound by the instructions of his party. This change in the very essence of the idea of representation was the germ of the disease which has since devoured the whole system of representative government. With the disintegration of parties, elections have taken the character of personal struggle restricted by local interests and opinions, but independent of their primary purpose of subserving the advantage of the State. With the great increase of the numbers in Parliament, most of the members, apart from the interests of party strife, are characterised by indifference to public affairs; they neglect their duty of attendance at all sessions, and of direct participation in the consideration of business. Thus the work of legislation, and the direction of the gravest political affairs, become a play composed of formality, compromise, and fiction. The system of representation has falsified itself in practice.

The Fabian Society

The Fabian Society was set up in 1883 to propagate a non-Marxian, evolutionary socialism. Its leading personalities were Sidney Webb, Beatrice Webb, George Bernard Shaw, and later, for a while, H. G. Wells. Their principle of cautious advance, which would leave its mark on the British Labour party, was implied in the society's name, derived from Quintus Fabius Cunctator, the circumspect Roman general whose tactics had worn down Hannibal's first victorious impetus.

George Bernard Shaw: from A Manifesto

The Fabians are associated for spreading the following opinions held by them and discussing their practical consequences.

That under existing circumstances wealth cannot be enjoyed without dishonor or foregone without misery.

That it is the duty of each member of the State to provide for his or her wants by his or her own Labor.

That a life interest in the Land and Capital of the nation is the birthright of every individual born within its confines and that access to this birthright should not depend upon the will of any private person other than the person seeking it.

That the most striking result of our present system of farming out the national Land and Capital to private persons has been the division of Society into hostile classes, with large appetites and no dinners at one extreme and large dinners and no appetites at the other.

That the practice of entrusting the Land of the nation to private persons in the hope that they will make the best of it has been discredited by the consistency with

From G. B. Shaw, *A Manifesto*, Fabian Tract No. 2 (London, 1884).

which they have made the worst of it; and that Nationalization of the Land in some form is a public duty.

That the pretensions of Capitalism to encourage Invention and to distribute its benefits in the fairest way attainable, have been discredited by the experience of the nineteenth century.

That, under the existing system of leaving the National Industry to organize itself Competition has the effect of rendering adulteration, dishonest dealing and inhumanity compulsory.

That since Competition amongst producers admittedly secures to the public the most satisfactory products, the State should compete with all its might in every department of production.

That such restraints upon Free Competition as the penalties for infringing the Postal monopoly, and the withdrawal of workhouse and prison labor from the markets, should be abolished.

That no branch of Industry should be carried on at a profit by the central administration.

That the Public Revenue should be levied by a direct Tax; and that the central administration should have no legal power to hold back for the replenishment of the Public Treasury any portion of the proceeds of Industries administered by them.

That the State should compete with private individuals—especially with parents—in providing happy homes for children, so that every child may have a refuge from the tyranny or neglect of its natural custodians.

That Men no longer need special political privileges to protect them against Women and that the sexes should henceforth enjoy equal political rights.

That no individual should enjoy any Privilege in consideration of services rendered to the State by his or her parents or other relation.

That the State should secure a liberal education and an equal share in the National Industry to each of its units.

That the established Government has no more right to call itself the State than the smoke of London has to call itself the weather.

That we had rather face a Civil War than such another century of suffering as the present one has been.

Eduard Bernstein

The economic changes of the late nineteenth century and the improvement in the condition of the proletariat persuaded socialist thinkers that some revision of Marxian theory and tactics was required. Eduard Bernstein was a prominent intellectual of the German Socialist party, who argued that socialists should now stress evolution and cooperation rather than revolution and class conflict. Bernstein's revisionism, or reformism, found favor with many socialist leaders in the West, but was bitterly criticized by men like Kautsky and Lenin who saw gradual reforms as drops in a bucket and compromise as only a dangerous corrupting force.

From Evolutionary Socialism

PREFACE

It has been maintained in a certain quarter that the practical deductions from my treatises would be the abandonment of the conquest of political power by the proletariat organised politically and economically. That is quite an arbitrary deduction, the accuracy of which I altogether deny.

I set myself against the notion that we have to expect shortly a collapse of the bourgeois economy, and that social democracy should be induced by the prospect of such an imminent, great, social catastrophe to adapt its tactics to that assumption. That I maintain most emphatically.

The adherents of this theory of a catastrophe, base it especially on the conclusions of the *Communist Manifesto*. This is a mistake in every respect.

The theory which the *Communist Manifesto* sets forth of the evolution of modern society was correct as far as it characterised the general tendencies of that evolution. But it was mistaken in several special deductions, above all in the estimate of the time the evolution would take. The last has been unreservedly acknowledged by Friedrich Engels, the joint author with Marx of the *Manifesto* in his preface to the *Class War in France*. But it is evident that if social evolution takes a much greater period of time than was assumed, it must also take upon itself forms and lead to forms that were not foreseen and could not be foreseen then.

Social conditions have not developed to such an acute opposition of things and classes as is depicted in the *Manifesto*. It is not only useless, it is the greatest folly to attempt to conceal this from ourselves. The number of members of the possessing classes is to-day not smaller but larger. The enormous increase of social wealth is not accompanied by a decreasing number of large capitalists but by an increasing number of capitalists of all degrees. The middle classes change their character but they do not disappear from the social scale.

The concentration in productive industry is not being accomplished even today in all its departments with equal thoroughness and at an equal rate. In a great many branches of production it certainly justifies the forecasts of the socialist critic of society; but in other branches it lags even to-day behind them. The process of concentration in agriculture proceeds still more slowly. Trade statistics show an extraordinarily elaborated graduation of enterprises in regard to size. No rung of the ladder is disappearing from it. The significant changes in the inner structure of these enterprises and their inter-relationship cannot do away with this fact.

In all advanced countries we see the privileges of the capitalist bourgeoisie yielding step by step to democratic organisations. Under the influence of this, and driven by the movement of the working classes which is daily becoming stronger, a social reaction has set in against the exploiting tendencies of capital, a counteraction which, although

From Eduard Bernstein, *Evolutionary Socialism*, tr. E. C. Harvey (London, Independent Labour Party, 1909).

it still proceeds timidly and feebly, yet does exist, and is always drawing more departments of economic life under its influence. Factory legislation, the democratising of local government, and the extension of its area of work, the freeing of trade unions and systems of co-operative trading from legal restrictions, the considerations of standard conditions of labour in the work undertaken by public authorities—all these characterise this phase of the evolution.

But the more the political organisations of modern nations are democratised the more the needs and opportunities of great political catastrophes are diminished. He who holds firmly to the catastrophic theory of evolution must, with all his power, withstand and hinder the evolution described above, which, indeed, the logical defenders of that theory formerly did. But is the conquest of political power by the proletariat simply to be by a political catastrophe? Is it to be the appropriation and utilisation of the power of the State by the proletariat exclusively against the whole non-proletarian world?

He who replies in the affirmative must be reminded of two things. In 1872 Marx and Engels announced in the preface to the new edition of the *Communist Manifesto* that the Paris Commune had exhibited a proof that "the working classes cannot simply take possession of the ready-made State machine and set it in motion for their own aims." And in 1895 Friedrich Engels stated in detail in the preface to *War of the Classes* that the time of political surprises, of the "revolutions of small conscious minorities at the head of unconscious masses" was to-day at an end, that a collision on a large scale with the military would be the means of checking the steady growth of social democracy and of even throwing it back for a time—in short, that social democracy would flourish far better by lawful than by unlawful means and by violent revolution. And he points out in conformity with this opinion that the next task of the party should be "to work for an uninterrupted increase of its votes" or to carry on a slow propaganda of parliamentary activity.

Thus Engels, who, nevertheless, as his numerical examples show, still somewhat over-estimated the rate of process of the evolution! Shall we be told that he abandoned the conquest of political power by the working classes, because he wished to avoid the steady growth of social democracy secured by lawful means being interrupted by a political revolution?

If not, and if one subscribes to his conclusions, one cannot reasonably take any offence if it is declared that for a long time yet the task of social democracy is, instead of speculating on a great economic crash, "to organise the working classes politically and develop them as a democracy and to fight for all reforms in the State which are adapted to raise the working classes and transform the State in the direction of democracy."

That is what I have said in my impugned article and what I still maintain in its full import. As far as concerns the question propounded above it is equivalent to Engels' dictum, for democracy is, at any given time, as much government by the working classes as these are capable of practising according to their intellectual ripeness and the degree of social development they have attained. Engels, indeed, refers at the place just mentioned to the fact that the *Communist Manifesto* has "proclaimed the conquest of the democracy as one of the first and most important tasks of the fighting proletariat."

In short, Engels is so thoroughly convinced that the tactics based on the presumption of a catastrophe have had their day, that he even considers a revision of them necessary in the Latin countries where tradition is much more favourable to them than in Germany. "If the conditions of war between nations have altered," he writes, "no less have those for the war between classes." Has this already been forgotten?

No one has questioned the necessity for the working classes to gain the control of government. The point at issue is between the theory of a social cataclysm and the question whether, with the given social development in Germany and the present advanced state of its working classes in the towns and the country, a sudden catastrophe would be desirable in the interest of the social democracy. I have denied it and deny it again, because in my judgment a greater security for lasting success lies in a steady advance than in the possibilities offered by a catastrophic crash.

And as I am firmly convinced that important periods in the development of nations cannot be leapt over I lay the greatest value on the next tasks of social democracy, on the struggle for the political rights of the working man, on the political activity of working men in town and country for the interests of their class, as well as on the work of the industrial organisation of the workers.

In this sense I wrote the sentence that the movement means everything for me and that what is usually called "the final aim of socialism" is nothing; and in this sense I write it down again to-day. Even if the word "usually" had not shown that the proposition was only to be understood conditionally, it was obvious that it could not express indifference concerning the final carrying out of socialist principles, but only indifference—or, as it would be better expressed, carelessness—as to the form of the final arrangement of things. I have at no time had an excessive interest in the future, beyond general principles; I have not been able to read to the end any picture of the future. My thoughts and efforts are concerned with the duties of the present and the nearest future, and I only busy myself with the perspectives beyond so far as they give me a line of conduct for suitable action now.

The conquest of political power by the working classes, the expropriation of capitalists, are no ends in themselves but only means for the accomplishment of certain aims and endeavours. As such they are demands in the programme of social democracy and are not attacked by me. Nothing can be said beforehand as to the circumstances of their accomplishment; we can only fight for their realisation. But the conquest of political power necessitates the possession of political rights; and the most important problem of tactics which German social democracy has at the present time to solve, appears to me to be to devise the best ways for the extension of the political and economic rights of the German working classes.

The following work has been composed in the sense of these conclusions. I am fully conscious that it differs in several important points from the ideas to be found in the theory of Karl Marx and Engels—men whose writings have exercised the greatest influence on my socialist line of thought, and one of whom—Engels—honoured me with his personal friendship not only till his death but who showed beyond the grave, in his testamentary arrangements, a proof of his confidence in me.

This deviation in the manner of looking at things certainly is not of recent date; it is the product of an inner struggle of years and I hold in my hand a proof that this was no secret to Friedrich Engels, and moreover I must guard Engels from the suspicion that he was so narrow-minded as to exact from his friends an unconditional adherence to his views. Nevertheless, it will be understood from the foregoing why I have till now avoided as much as possible giving to my deviating points of view the form of a systematic and detailed criticism of the Marx-Engels doctrine. This could the more easily be avoided up till now because as regards the practical questions with which we were concerned Marx and Engels in the course of time considerably modified their views.

All that is now altered. I have now a controversy with socialists who, like me, have sprung from the Marx-Engels school; and I am obliged, if I am to maintain my opinions, to show them the points where the Marx-Engels theory appears to me especially mistaken or to be self-contradictory.

EVOLUTIONARY SOCIALISM

Unfortunately for the scientific socialism of Plekhanov, the Marxist propositions on the hopelessness of the position of the worker have been upset in a book which bears the title, *Capital: A Criticism of Political Economy.* There we read of the "physical and moral regeneration" of the textile workers in Lancashire through the Factory Law of 1847, which "struck the feeblest eye." A bourgeois republic was not even necessary to bring about a certain improvement in the situation of a large section of workers! In the same book we read that the society of to-day is no firm crystal, but an organism capable of change and constantly engaged in a process of change, that also in the treatment of economic questions on the part of the official representatives of this society an "improvement was unmistakable." Further that the author had devoted so large a space in his book to the results of the English Factory Laws in order to spur the Continent to imitate them and thus to work so that the process of transforming society may be accomplished in ever more humane forms. All of which signifies not hopelessness but capability of improvement in the condition of the worker. And, as since 1866, when this was written, the legislation depicted has not grown weaker but has been improved, made more general, and has been supplemented by laws and organisations working in the same direction, there can be no more doubt to-day than formerly of the hopefulness of the position of the worker.

Now, it can be asserted against me that Marx certainly recognized those improvements, but that the chapter on the historical tendency of capitalist accumulation at the end of the first volume of *Capital* shows how little these details influenced his fundamental mode of viewing things. To which I answer that as far as that is correct it speaks against that chapter and not against me.

One can interpret this chapter in very different kinds of ways. I believe I was the first to point out, and indeed repeatedly, that it was a summary characterisation of the tendency of a development which is found in capitalist accumulation, but which in practice is not carried out completely and which therefore need not be driven to the critical point of the antagonism there depicted.

One can, however, understand this chapter differently. One can conceive it in this way, that all the improvements mentioned there, and some possibly ensuing, only create temporary remedies against the oppressive tendencies of capitalism, that they signify unimportant modifications which cannot in the long run effect anything substantially against the critical point of antagonisms laid down by Marx, that this will finally appear—if not literally yet substantially—in the manner depicted, and will lead to catastrophic change by violence. This interpretation can be founded on the categoric wording of the last sentences of the chapter, and receives a certain confirmation because at the end reference is again made to the *Communist Manifesto*.

According to my view, it is impossible simply to declare the one conception right and the other absolutely wrong. To me the chapter illustrates a dualism which runs through the whole monumental work of Marx, and which also finds expression in a less pregnant fashion in other passages—a dualism which consists in this, that the work aims at being a scientific inquiry and also at proving a theory laid down long before its drafting; a formula lies at the basis of it in which the result to which the exposition should lead is fixed beforehand. The return to the *Communist Manifesto* points here to a real residue of Utopianism in the Marxist system. Marx had accepted the solution of the Utopians in essentials, but had recognised their means and proofs as inadequate. He therefore undertook a revision of them, and this with the zeal, the critical acuteness, and love of truth of a scientific genius. He suppressed no important fact, he also forebore belittling artificially the importance of these facts as long as the object of the inquiry had no immediate reference to the final aim of the formula to be proved. To that point his work is free of every tendency necessarily interfering with the scientific method.

For the general sympathy with the strivings for emancipation of the working classes does not in itself stand in the way of the scientific method. But, as Marx approaches a point when that final aim enters seriously into the question, he becomes uncertain and unreliable. Such contradictions then appear as were shown in the book under consideration, for instance, in the section on the movement of incomes in modern society. It thus appears that this great scientific spirit was, in the end, a slave to a doctrine. To express it figuratively, he has raised a mighty building within the framework of a scaffolding he found existing, and in its erection he kept strictly to the laws of scientific architecture as long as they did not collide with the conditions with the construction of the scaffolding prescribed, but he neglected or evaded them when the scaffolding did not allow of their observance. Where the scaffolding put limits in the way of the building, instead of destroying the scaffolding, he changed the building itself at the cost of its right proportions and so made it all the more dependent on the scaffolding. Was it the consciousness of this irrational relation which caused him continually to pass from completing his work to amending special parts of it? However that may be, my conviction is that wherever that dualism shows itself the scaffolding must fall if the building is to grow in its right proportions. In the latter, and not in the former, is found what is worthy to live in Marx.

Lenin

Vladimir Ilyitch Ulianov, better known as Lenin, was born in 1870 in Simbirsk, the son of a local teacher and educational official of some talent; he died in Moscow in 1924, first head of the Union of Soviet Socialist Republics, which he had helped to create. Entering revolutionary activity after his brother had been executed by the tsar's government, Lenin spent several years of exile in Siberia, and far more in the usual wanderings of the political exile abroad. He soon became a leader of the left wing of the Russian Social-Democratic party, preaching the necessity of an independent Socialist party that would contain no "opportunists,"[1] make no opportunistic compromises, and maintain a clear revolutionary policy. Naturally, he attacked those who, like Bernstein, concentrated on the possibilities of gradual reform and failed to put revolutionary activity first. "Our Programme" was written in this connection, in 1899, but did not appear in print at the time (not, as a matter of fact, until after Lenin's death) because police interference prevented its publication while it was still relevant. But Lenin stuck tirelessly to the theme the essay announced, and this eventually led to the party's split, in 1903, between the Bolshevik (majority) faction, which followed Lenin, and the more moderate Menshevik (minority) faction under Martoff.

"Our Programme"

International social democracy is at present going through a period of theoretical vacillations. Up to the present the doctrines of Marx and Engels were regarded as a firm foundation of revolutionary theory—nowadays voices are raised everywhere declaring these doctrines to be inadequate and antiquated. Anyone calling himself a social-democrat and having the intention to publish a social-democratic organ, must take up a definite attitude as regards this question, which by no means concerns German social-democrats alone.

We base our faith entirely on Marx's theory; it was the first to transform socialism from a Utopia into a science, to give this science a firm foundation and to indicate the path which must be trodden in order further to develop this science and to elaborate it in all its details. It discovered the nature of present-day capitalist economy and explained the way in which the employment of workers—the purchase of labour power—the enslavement of millions of those possessing no property by a handful of capitalists, by the owners of the land, the factories, the mines, etc., is concealed. It has shown how the whole development of modern capitalism is advancing towards the large producer ousting the small one, and is creating the prerequisites which make a socialist order of society possible and necessary. It has taught us to see, under the disguise of ossified habits, political intrigues, intricate laws, cunning theories, the class struggle, the struggle between, on the one hand, the various species of the possessing classes, and, on the other hand, the mass possessing no property, the proletariat, which leads all those who possess nothing. It has made clear what is the real task of a revolutionary socialist party—not to set up projects for the transformation of society, not to preach sermons to the capitalists and their admirers about improving the position of the workers, not the instigation of conspiracies, but the organisation of the class struggle of the

---

[1] outcome.

From *The Communist* (Petrograd), July 1928.

proletariat, and the carrying on of this struggle, the final aim of which is the seizure of political power by the proletariat and the organisation of a socialist society.

We now ask: What new elements have the touting "renovators" introduced into this theory, they who have attracted so much notice in our day and have grouped themselves round the German socialist Bernstein? Nothing, nothing at all; they have not advanced by a single step the science which Marx and Engels adjured us to develop; they have not taught the proletariat any new methods of fighting; they are only marching backwards in that they adopt the fragments of antiquated theories and are preaching to the proletariat not the theory of struggle but the theory of submissive-ness—submissiveness to the bitterest enemies of the proletariat, to the governments and bourgeois parties who never tire of finding new methods of persecuting socialists. Plekhanov, one of the founders and leaders of Russian social-democracy, was perfectly right when he subjected to merciless criticism the latest "Criticism" of Bernstein, whose views have now been rejected even by the representatives of the German workers at the 1899 Party Congress in Hanover.

We know that on account of these words we shall be drenched with a flood of accusations; they will cry out that we want to turn the Socialist Party into a holy order of the "orthodox," who persecute the "heretics" for their aberrations from the "true dogma," for any independent opinion, etc. We know all these nonsensical phrases which have become the fashion nowadays. Yet there is no shadow of truth in them, no iota of sense. There can be no strong socialist party without a revolutionary theory which unites all socialists, from which the socialists draw their whole conviction, which they apply in their methods of fighting and working. To defend a theory of this kind, of the truth of which one is completely convinced, against unfounded attacks and against attempts to debase it, does not mean being an enemy of criticism in general. We by no means regard the theory of Marx as perfect and inviolable; on the contrary, we are convinced that this theory has only laid the foundation stones of that science on which the socialists must continue to build in every direction, unless they wish to be left behind by life. We believe that it is particularly necessary for Russian socialists to work out the Marxist theory independently, for this theory only gives general precepts, the details of which must be applied in England otherwise than in France, in France otherwise than in Germany, and in Germany otherwise than in Russia. For this reason we will willingly devote space in our paper to articles about theoretical questions, and we call upon all comrades openly to discuss the matters in dispute.

What are the main questions which arise in applying the common programme of all social-democrats to Russia?

We have already said that the essence of this programme consists in the organisa-tion of the class struggle of the proletariat and in carrying on this struggle, the final aim of which is the seizure of political power by the proletariat and the construction of a socialist society. The class struggle of the proletariat is divided into: The *economic* fight (the fight against individual capitalists, or against the individual groups of capital-ists by the improvement of the position of the workers), and the *political* fight (the fight against the Government for the extension of the rights of the people, i.e., for democracy, and for the expansion of the political power of the proletariat). Some Rus-sian social-democrats regard the economic fight as incomparably more important and almost go so far as to postpone that political fight to a more or less distant future. This standpoint is quite wrong. All social-democrats are unanimous in believing that it is necessary to carry on an agitation among the workers on this basis, i.e., to help the workers in their daily fight against the employers, to direct their attention to all kinds and all cases of chicanery, and in this way to make clear to them the necessity of unity. To forget the political for the economic fight would, however, mean a digression from the most important principle of international social-democracy; it would mean forgetting what the whole history of the Labour movement has taught us. Fanatical adherents of the bourgeoisie and of the Government which serves it, have indeed repeatedly tried to organise purely economic unions of workers and thus to deflect them from the "politics" of socialism. It is quite possible that the Russian Government will also be clever enough to do something of the kind, as it has always endeavoured to throw some largesse or other sham presents to the people in order to prevent them becoming conscious that they are oppressed and without rights.

No economic fight can give the workers a permanent improvement of their situation, it cannot, indeed, be carried on on a large scale unless the workers have the free right to call meetings, to join in unions, to have their own newspapers and to send their representatives to the National Assembly as do the workers in Germany and all European countries (with the exception of Turkey and Russia). In order, however, to obtain these rights, a political fight must be carried on. In Russia, not only the workers but all the citizens are deprived of political rights. Russia is an absolute monarchy. The Tsar alone promulgates laws, nominates officials and controls them. For this reason it seems as though in Russia the Tsar and the Tsarist Government were dependent on no class and cared for all equally. In reality, however, all the officials are chosen exclusively from the possessing class, and all are subject to the influence of the large capitalists who obtain whatever they want—the Ministers dance to the tune the large capitalists play. The Russian worker is bowed under a double yoke; he is robbed and plundered by the capitalists and the landowners, and, lest he should fight against them, he is bound hand and foot by the police, his mouth is gagged and any attempt to defend the rights of the people is followed by persecution. Any strike against a capitalist results in the military and police being let loose on the workers. Every economic fight of necessity turns into a political fight, and social-democracy must indissolubly combine the economic with the political fight into a united class struggle of the proletariat.

But political management, whether paternalistic, authoritarian, or reformist, did not answer the concerns of those for whom contemporary problems went deeper than politics. Dostoyevsky and Nietzsche, whose thoughts appear in the next two selections, do not exhaust the range of reactions against the rationalistic and scientific confidence of the nineteenth century. They do, however, suggest some discomfiting contemporary strains.

Fyodor Dostoyevsky

Fyodor Dostoyevsky (1821–1881) was born at the Moscow Foundling Hospital, where his father practiced medicine, and died being recognized as one of his country's greatest writers.

In between, he graduated as a military engineer but resigned his army commission to devote himself to writing; was sentenced to death for his participation in a radical discussion group, spent several years in Siberian exile when his death sentence was commuted to banishment, and built his reputation on a steady flow of psychological stories and novels.

The passage that follows is taken from the last of Dostoyevsky's novels, The Brothers Karamazov, *published in 1880. Here, one of the characters in the novel tells a parable of Christ returning to earth at the height of the Spanish Inquisition, to be arrested and harangued by the Grand Inquisitor. Visiting Christ in jail, the old man attacks him for overestimating human capacities. Men, says the Grand Inquisitor, cannot bear freedom, let alone handle it. Instead, the inquisitor offers them bread, miracles, and the authority that saves them the trouble of coping with freedom. And he will burn at the stake any "heretic" who upsets his system by trying to assert his individual freedom—including Christ himself.*

From The Brothers Karamazov

". . . My story is laid in Spain, in Seville, in the most terrible time of the Inquisition, when fires were lighted every day to the glory of God, and 'in the splendid *auto da fé*[1] the wicked heretics were burnt.' Oh, of course, this was not the coming in which He will appear according to His promise at the end of time in all His heavenly glory, and which will be sudden 'as lightning flashing from east to west.' No, He visited His children only for a moment, and there where the flames were crackling round the heretics. In His infinite mercy He came once more among men in that human shape in which He walked among men for three years fifteen centuries ago. He came down to the 'hot pavement' of the southern town in which on the day before almost a hundred heretics had, *ad majorem gloriam Dei,*[2] been burnt by the cardinal, the Grand Inquisitor, in a magnificent *auto da fé*, in the presence of the king, the court, the knights, the cardinals, the most charming ladies of the court, and the whole population of Seville.

"He came softly, unobserved, and yet, strange to say, every one recognised Him. . . . He stops at the steps of the Seville cathedral at the moment when the weeping mourners are bringing in a little open white coffin. In it lies a child of seven, the only daughter of a prominent citizen. The dead child lies hidden in flowers. 'He will raise your child,' the crowd shouts to the weeping mother. 'The priest, coming to meet the coffin, looks perplexed, and frowns, but the mother of the dead child throws herself at His feet with a wail. 'If it is Thou, raise my child!' she cries, holding out her hands to Him. The procession halts, the coffin is laid on the steps at His feet. He looks with

---

From *The Brothers Karamazov* by Fyodor Dostoyevsky, tr. Constance Garnett (New York: Random House, Inc., 1950), pp. 294–311.
[1]literally, act of faith; practically, burning a heretic at the stake.
[2]for the greater glory of God.

compassion, and His lips once more softly pronounce, 'Maiden, arise!' and the maiden arises. The little girl sits up in the coffin and looks round, smiling with wide-open wondering eyes, holding a bunch of white roses they had put in her hand.

"There are cries, sobs, confusion among the people, and at that moment the cardinal himself, the Grand Inquisitor, passes by the cathedral. He is an old man, almost ninety, tall and erect, with a withered face and sunken eyes, in which there is still a gleam of light. He is not dressed in his gorgeous cardinal's robes, as he was the day before, when he was burning the enemies of the Roman Church—at that moment he was wearing his coarse, old, monk's cassock. At a distance behind him come his gloomy assistants and slaves and the 'holy guard.' He stops at the sight of the crowd and watches it from a distance. He sees everything; he sees them set the coffin down at His feet, sees the child rise up, and his face darkens. He knits his thick grey brows and his eyes gleam with a sinister fire. He holds out his finger and bids the guards take Him. And such is his power, so completely are the people cowed into submission and trembling obedience to him, that the crowd immediately makes way for the guards, and in the midst of deathlike silence they lay hands on Him and lead Him away. The crowd instantly bows down to the earth, like one man, before the old inquisitor. He blesses the people in silence and passes on. The guards lead their prisoner to the close, gloomy vaulted prison in the ancient palace of the Holy Inquisition and shut Him in it. The day passes and is followed by the dark, burning 'breathless' night of Seville. The air is 'fragrant with laurel and lemon.' In the pitch darkness the iron door of the prison is suddenly opened and the Grand Inquisitor himself comes in with a light in his hand. He is alone; the door is closed at once behind him. He stands in the doorway and for a minute or two gazes into His face. At last he goes up slowly, sets the light on the table and speaks.

" 'Is it Thou? Thou?' but receiving no answer, he adds at once, 'Don't answer, be silent. What canst Thou say, indeed? I know too well what Thou wouldst say. And Thou hast no right to add anything to what Thou hadst said of old. Why, then, art Thou come to hinder us? For Thou hast come to hinder us, and Thou knowest that. But dost Thou know what will be tomorrow? I know not who Thou art and care not to know whether it is Thou or only a semblance of Him, but tomorrow I shall condemn Thee and burn Thee at the stake as the worst of heretics. And the very people who have today kissed Thy feet, tomorrow at the faintest sign from me will rush to heap up the embers of Thy fire. Knowest Thou that? Yes, maybe Thou knowest it,' he added with thoughtful penetration, never for a moment taking his eyes off the Prisoner." . . . 'For now' (he is speaking of the Inquisition, of course) 'for the first time it has become possible to think of the happiness of men. Man was created a rebel; and how can rebels be happy? Thou wast warned,' he says to Him. 'Thou hast had no lack of admonitions and warnings, but Thou didst not listen to those warnings; Thou didst reject the only way by which men might be made happy. But, fortunately, departing Thou didst hand on the work to us. Thou hast promised, Thou hast established by Thy word, Thou hast given to us the right to bind and to unbind, and now, of course, Thou canst not think of taking it away. Why, then, hast Thou come to hinder us? . . .

" 'The wise and dread spirit, the spirit of self-destruction and non-existence,' the old man goes on, 'the great spirit talked with Thee in the wilderness, and we are told in the books that he "tempted" Thee. Is that so? And could anything truer be said than what he revealed to Thee in three questions and what Thou didst reject, and what in the books is called "the temptation"? . . .

" 'Judge Thyself who was right—Thou or he who questioned Thee then? Remember the first question; its meaning, in other words, was this: "Thou wouldst go into the world, and art going with empty hands, with some promise of freedom which men in their simplicity and their natural unruliness cannot even understand, which they fear and dread—for nothing has ever been more insupportable for a man and human society than freedom. But seest Thou these stones in this parched and barren wilderness? Turn them into bread, and mankind will run after Thee like a flock of sheep, grateful and obedient, though for ever trembling, lest Thou withdraw Thy hand and deny them Thy bread." But Thou wouldst not deprive man of freedom and didst reject the offer, thinking, what is that freedom worth, if obedience is bought with bread? Thou didst reply that man lives not by bread alone. But dost Thou know that for the sake of that earthly bread the spirit of the earth will rise up against Thee and will strive with Thee and overcome Thee, and all will follow him, crying, "Who can compare with this beast? He has given us fire from heaven!" Dost Thou know that the ages will pass, and humanity will proclaim by the lips of their sages that there is no crime, and therefore no sin; there is only hunger? "Feed men, and then ask of them virtue!" . . . No science will give them bread so long as they remain free. In the end they will lay their freedom at our feet, and say to us, "Make us your slaves, but feed us." They will understand themselves, at last, that freedom and bread enough for all are inconceivable together, for never, never will they be able to share between them! They will be convinced, too, that they can never be free, for they are weak, vicious, worthless and rebellious. Thou didst promise them the bread of Heaven, but, I repeat again, can it compare with earthly bread in the eyes of the weak, ever sinful and ignoble race of man? . . . They are sinful and rebellious, but in the end they too will become obedient. They will marvel at us and look on us as gods, because we are ready to endure the freedom which they have found so dreadful and to rule over them—so awful it will seem to them to be free. . . . I tell Thee that man is tormented by no greater anxiety than to find some one quickly to whom he can hand over that gift of freedom with which the ill-fated creature is born. But only one who can appease their conscience can take over their freedom. . . . Instead of taking men's freedom from them, Thou didst make it greater than ever! Didst Thou forget that man prefers peace, and even death, to freedom of choice in the knowledge of good and evil? . . .

" 'There are three powers, three powers alone, able to conquer and to hold captive for ever the conscience of these impotent rebels for their happiness—those forces are miracle, mystery and authority. . . . Thou wouldst not enslave man by a miracle, and didst crave faith given freely, not based on miracle. Thou didst crave for free love and not the base raptures of the slave before the might that has overawed him for ever. But Thou didst think too highly of men therein, for they are slaves, of course, though rebellious by nature. . . . But they will see at last, the foolish children, that, though they are rebels, they are impotent rebels, unable to keep up their own rebellion. . . . Hadst Thou taken the world and Caesar's purple, Thou wouldst have founded the universal state and have given universal peace. For who can rule men if not he who holds their conscience and their bread in his hands? . . . Thou wouldst have accomplished all that man seeks on earth—that is, some one to worship, some one to keep his conscience, and some means of uniting all in one unanimous and harmonious antheap, for the craving for universal unity is the third and last anguish of men. . . .

" 'We have taken the sword of Caesar . . . with us all will be happy and will no more rebel nor destroy one another as under Thy freedom. Oh, we shall persuade them that they will only become free when they renounce their freedom to us and submit to us. And shall we be right or shall we be lying? They will be convinced that we are right, for they will remember the horrors of slavery and confusion to which Thy freedom brought them. Freedom, free thought and science, will lead them into such straits and will bring them face to face with such marvels and insoluble mysteries, that some of them, the fierce and rebellious, will destroy themselves, others, rebellious but weak, will destroy one another, while the rest, weak and unhappy, will crawl fawning to our feet and whine to us: "Yes, you were right, you alone possess His mystery, and we come back to you, save us from ourselves!"

" 'Receiving bread from us, they will see clearly that we take the bread made by their hands from them, to give it to them, without any miracle. They will see that we do not change the stones to bread, but in truth they will be more thankful for taking it from our hands than for the bread itself! . . .

" 'Then we shall give them the quiet humble happiness of weak creatures such as they are by nature. . . . We shall show them that they are weak, that they are only pitiful children, but that childlike happiness is the sweetest of all. They will become timid and will look to us and huddle close to us in fear, as chicks to the hen. They will marvel at us and will be awestricken before us, and will be proud at our being so powerful and clever, that we have been able to subdue such a turbulent flock of thousands of millions. They will tremble impotently before our wrath, their minds will grow fearful, they will be quick to shed tears like women and children, but they will be just as ready at a sign from us to pass to laughter and rejoicing, to happy mirth and childish song. Yes, we shall set them to work, but in their leisure hours we shall make their life like a child's game. . . . We shall allow them even sin, they are weak and helpless, and they will love us like children because we allow them to sin. We shall tell them that every sin will be expiated, if it is done with our permission, that we allow them to sin because we love them, and the punishment for these sins we take upon ourselves. And we shall take it upon ourselves, and they will adore us as their saviours who have taken on themselves their sins before God. And they will have no secrets from us. . . . The most painful secrets of their conscience, all, all they will bring to us, and we shall have an answer for all. And they will be glad to believe our answer, for it will save them from the great anxiety and terrible agony they endure at present in making a free decision for themselves. And all will be happy, all the millions of creatures except the hundred thousand who rule over them. For only we, we who guard the mystery, shall be unhappy. There will be thousands of millions of happy babes, and a hundred thousand sufferers who have taken upon themselves the curse of the knowledge of good and evil. . . .

" 'What I say to Thee will come to pass, and our dominion will be built up. I repeat, tomorrow Thou shalt see that obedient flock who at a sign from me will hasten to heap up the hot cinders about the pile on which I shall burn Thee for coming to hinder us. For if any one has ever deserved our fires, it is Thou. Tomorrow I shall burn Thee.' " . . .

"When the Inquisitor ceased speaking he waited some time for his Prisoner to answer him. His silence weighed down upon him. He saw that the Prisoner had listened intently all the time, looking gently in his face and evidently not wishing to reply. The old man longed for Him to say something, however bitter and terrible. But He suddenly approached the old man in silence and softly kissed him on his bloodless aged lips. That was all his answer. The old man shuddered. His lips moved. He went to the door, opened it, and said to Him: 'Go, and come no more. . . . Come not at all, never, never!' And he let Him out into the dark alleys of the town. The Prisoner went away."

Friedrich Nietzsche

Friedrich Nietzsche (1844–1900) was perhaps the most original thinker of his time. Professor of classical philology at the University of Basle at the age of twenty-four, admiring friend and then bitter critic of composer Richard Wagner, thinker and writer of tremendous power, he was to spend the last twelve years of his life in hopeless insanity.

More than that of most philosophers, Nietzche's work has suffered from misinterpretation and misrepresentation, and large chunks of it have been quoted out of context not only by Nazis who had an axe to grind but also by those from whom he might have expected better understanding. Certainly his ideas cannot be grasped from any brief or superficial reading and, to this extent, the passages that follow, compiled by Thomas Common (London, 1901), may merely accentuate the confusion. Even so, they will serve their purpose if they provide an idea of the impression they were to create when tossed, like bombs, into the self-satisfied intellectual world of the late nineteenth century.

In the last generation, Nietzsche was regarded as a prophet of totalitarianism and race hatred. Today, however, we can see him as a rebel against a society whose complacent mediocrity he abhorred, and against democratic conformity, which he despised. His "will to power" aspires to power over oneself. And his insistence on individualism, self-assertion, and self-transcendence reveals him rather as a forerunner of contemporary existentialist thought.

Our Outlook

The Greatest modern event—that God is dead, that the belief in the Christian God has become unworthy of belief—has now begun to cast its first shadows over Europe. To the few, at least, whose eye, whose suspecting glance is strong enough and subtle enough for a spectacle, a sun seems to have set to them, some old profound truth seems to have changed into doubt; our ancient world must every day seem to them "older", stranger, more unreliable, more vespertine. In the main, however, one may say that the event itself is far too great, too much beyond the power of apprehension of many people, for even the report of it to have reached them, to say nothing of their capacity for knowing what is really involved and what must all collapse, now that this belief has been undermined—by being built thereon, by being buttressed thereby, by being engrafted therein; for example, our entire European morality. The prolonged excess and continuation of demolition, ruin and overthrow which is now impending— who has yet understood it sufficiently to be obliged to stand up as the teacher and herald of such tremendously frightful logic, as the prophet of such an overshadowing, of such a solar eclipse as has probably never happened on earth before? Even we, the born riddle-readers, who, as it were, wait on the mountains, posted betwixt today and tomorrow, and engirt by the contradiction between today and tomorrow, we, the firstlings and premature births of the coming century, to whom especially the shadows which must forthwith envelop Europe *should* already have come to sight—how is it that even we, without genuine sympathy for this over-shadowing, contemplate its advent without personal solicitude or fear? Are we still perhaps too much under the *immediate effects* of the event—and are these effects, especially as regards *ourselves,* perhaps the reverse of what was to be expected—not at all sad and depressing, but rather like a new and difficultly describable variety of light, happiness, alleviation, enlivenment, encouragement and rosy dawn? In fact, we philosophers and "free spirits" feel ourselves irradiated as by a new rosy dawn by the report that "the old God is dead"; our hearts thereby overflow with gratitude, astonishment, presentiment and expectation. At last the horizon seems once more unobstructed, granting even that it is not bright; our ships can at last start on their voyages once more, in face of every danger; every risk is again permitted to the knowing ones; the sea, our sea, again lies open before us; perhaps there never was such an open sea.

The Wild Beast in Man

At the bottom of all distinguished races the beast of prey is not to be mistaken, the magnificent *blond beast,* roaming wantonly in search of prey and victory. It requires from time to time the discharge of this hidden source of its nature the animal must again show itself, it must again go back into the wilderness. Roman, Arabic, German and Japanese nobles, Homeric heroes, Scandinavian vikings—they are all alike in this requirement. . . . The same men who are held in such strict bonds by usage, reverence, custom, gratitude and, still more, by mutual watching and jealousy *inter pares*[1] (while, at the same time, they show themselves so ingenious in deference, self-command, delicacy, fidelity, pride and friendship in relation to one another), these same men are not

---

[1] among equals.

much better than wild beasts let loose towards the outside world, where what is unfamiliar, unfamiliar *people* commence. They there enjoy freedom from all social constraint; . . . like exulting monsters, they go back into the condition of innocent conscience of the beast of prey.

Life as Exploitation

Life itself is *essentially* appropriating, injuring and vanquishing of what is foreign and weak: it is suppression, severity, obtrusion of its own forms, incorporation and, at least, putting it most mildly, exploitation; but why should one for ever use precisely these words on which for ages a disreputable significance has been stamped? Even an organization within which individuals deal with one another on equal terms (it is so in every healthy aristocracy) must, if it is a living and not a dying organization, act hostilely towards other organizations in all matters wherein the several individuals restrain themselves in their dealings with one another; it must be the embodied Will to Power, it has to seek to grow, it has to endeavor to gain ground, obtain advantage and acquire ascendancy—not on account of any morality or immorality whatsoever, but because it *lives*, and because life itself *is* Will to Power.

There is nothing, however, on which the ordinary consciousness of Europeans is more unwilling to be corrected than on this matter; at present people rave everywhere, even under the guise of science, about coming conditions of society in which "the exploiting character" will be absent: that sounds to me as if they proposed to invent a mode of life which should not exercise organic functions. "Exploitation" does not belong to a depraved or an imperfect and primitive state of society; it belongs to the *essence* of living beings, as a fundamental organic function; it is a consequence of the intrinsic Will to Power, which is just the Will to Life. Granting that as a theory this is an innovation, as a reality it is the original fact of history.

Master-Morality and Slave-Morality

In strolling through the many finer and coarser forms of morality which have hitherto prevailed or yet prevail on the earth, I found certain characteristics recurring regularly in connection with one another, until at last two fundamental types betrayed themselves to me, and a fundamental distinction was brought to light. There is *Master-morality* and *Slave-morality*. I would at once add, however, that in all higher and compound civilizations one finds attempts at the reconciliation of the two systems, while still oftener one finds their confusion and mutual misunderstanding; in fact, sometimes their close juxtaposition—even in the same man, in the same soul. The distinctions of moral worth have arisen either in a ruling caste, agreeably conscious of being distinct from the ruled; or among the ruled themselves, the slaves and dependents of all classes. In the first case, when it is the ruling caste that determines the conception "good", it is the exalted, proud disposition which is regarded as distinguishing and decisive as to the degree of rank. The noble type of man separates from himself those in whom the opposite of this is exalted, proud disposition displays itself—he despises them. (Let it be noted that in this first kind of morality the antithesis "good" and "bad" signifies practically the same as "noble" and "contemptible"; the antithesis "good" and "evil" has a different origin.) The despised ones are the cowards, the timid, the insignificant, those thinking merely of narrow utility, and moreover the distrustful with their constrained glances, the self-abasing, the dog-species of men who allow themselves to be misused, the mendacious flatterers and, above all, the liars—it is a fundamental belief of all aristocrats that the common people are deceitful; "we true ones", the nobility of ancient Greece called themselves.

It is obvious that the designations of moral worth everywhere were at first applied to *men,* and were only derivatively and at a later period applied to actions. It is a bad mistake, therefore, when historical moralists start with questions such as—"Why have sympathetic actions been praised?" The noble type of man regards *himself* as the determiner of worth, it is not necessary for him to be approved of, he passes the judgment— "What is injurious to me is injurious in itself"; he recognizes that it is he himself only that confers honor on things—he is a *creator of worth,* of values. The type of man in question honors whatever qualities he recognizes in himself: his morality is selfglorification. In the foreground there is the feeling of plenitude and power which seeks to overflow, the happiness of high tension, the consciousness of riches which would fain give and bestow; the noble man also helps the unfortunate, not (or scarcely) out of sympathy, but rather out of an impulse produced by the super-abundance of power. The noble man honors the powerful one in himself, and also him who has self-command, who knows how to speak and keep silence, who joyfully exercises strictness and severity over himself and reverences all that is strict and severe. "Woman has put a hard heart in my breast" says the hero of an old Scandinavian saga: the idea is thus expressed right out of the heart of a proud viking. Such a type of man is in fact proud of *not* being made for sympathy; the hero of the saga therefore adds by way of warning: "He who has not had a hard heart when young, will never have a hard heart." The noble and brave who think thus are furthest removed from the morality which sees precisely in sympathy, in acting for the good of others, or in disinterestedness, the characteristic of morality; a belief in oneself, a pride in oneself, a fundamental hostility and irony with respect to "selflessness", belong as distinctly to the higher morality as do careless scorn and precaution in presence of sympathy and the "warm heart". It is the powerful who *know* how to honor: it is their art, their domain, their invention. The profound reverence for age and tradition—all law rests on this double reverence— the belief and prejudice in favor of ancestors and unfavorable to newcomers, is typical of the morality of the powerful; and if, reversely, men of "modern ideas" believe almost instinctively in "progress" and "the future", and are more and more lacking in respect for the old, the ignoble origin of these "ideas" complacently betrays itself thereby.

The morality of the ruling class, however, is more especially foreign and irritating to the taste of the present day, owing to the sternness of the principle that one has only obligations to one's equals, that one may act towards beings of a lower rank, and towards all that is foreign to one, according to discretion, or "as the heart desires", and in any case "beyond Good and Evil". It is here that sympathy and similar sentiments like to have a place. The capacity and obligation for prolonged gratitude and prolonged revenge—both only among equals—artfulness in retaliation, refinement of ideas in friendship, a certain necessity to have enemies (as outlets for the passions of envy, quarrelsomeness, arrogance—in fact, in order to be a good friend): these are all typical characteristics of the noble morality, which, as we have indicated, is not the morality of "modern ideas", and on that account is at present difficult to realise, and also difficult to unearth and disclose.

It is different with the second type of morality, Slave-morality. Supposing that the misused, the oppressed, the suffering, the enslaved, the weary and those uncertain of themselves should moralise, what will be the common element in their estimates of moral worth? Probably a pessimistic suspicion with regard to the whole situation of man will find expression, perhaps a condemnation of man together with his situation. The slave contemplates with disapproval the virtues of the powerful; he has a thorough skepticism and distrust, a *refinement* of distrust, of everything "good" that is there honored; he would like to persuade himself that the very happiness there is not genuine. On the other hand, *those* qualities are brought into prominence and into the light which tend to alleviate the existence of sufferers; it is here that the kind helping hand, the warm heart, along with sympathy, patience, diligence, submissiveness and friendliness attain to honor; for these are the most useful qualities here, and almost the only expedients for supporting the burden of existence. Slave-morality is essentially the morality of utility. This is the seat of the origin of the celebrated antithesis "good" and "evil"; the notion of power and dangerousness is introduced into the evil, the ideas of dreadfulness, subtlety and strength, which do not admit of being despised. According to slave-morality, the "evil" man also excites fear; according to master-morality, it is precisely the "good" man who excites fear and seeks to excite it, while the "bad" man is regarded as the contemptible being. The contrast attains its maximum when, according to the logical consequences involved, a tinge of depreciation attaches itself to the "good" man of slave-morality; because in any case he has to be the *safe* man: he is good-natured, easily-deceived, perhaps a little stupid, *un bonhomme.* Wherever slave-morality gets the upper hand, language shows a tendency to approximate the significations of the words "good" and "stupid".

A last fundamental distinction: the desire for *liberty,* the instinct for happiness, and the refinements of the feeling of freedom, belong as necessarily to the domain of slave-morals and slave morality, as enthusiasm and art in reverence and devotion are the regular symptoms of an aristocratic mode of thinking and valuing.

John Stuart Mill

Misogyny—hatred, or at any rate suspicion, of women—is at least as old as the Greeks who coined the term. Since history is written by the winners, lots of texts tell us why women should be mistrusted or scorned; few speak for them. We have encountered a few exceptions to this rule in earlier readings; but it was only in modern times that women and their supporters began to make their voices heard in public. The first truly influential personality to take sides for the emancipation of women was the liberal philosopher John Stuart Mill.

More a romantic than a utilitarian, Mill met Harriet Taylor, a married woman, in 1831 and loved her constantly for twenty years until, in 1851, her husband's death enabled them to marry. Their union lasted only seven years, for Harriet died in 1858; but Mill attributed to her the inspiration for his ideals about individuals and society. Not least of his works is the essay on The Subjection of Women, *which he wrote in 1861 and published in 1868. Mill was a founder of the first women's suffrage society, and his essay remains the classic nineteenth-century statement of the case for women's suffrage and equal rights.*

From The Subjection of Women

The social subordination of women thus stands out an isolated fact in modern social institutions; a solitary breach of what has become their fundamental law; a single relic of an old world of thought and practice exploded in everything else, but retained in the one thing of most universal interest. . . .

The least that can be demanded is, that the question should not be considered as prejudged by existing fact and existing opinion, but open to discussion on its merits, as a question of justice and expediency; the decision on this, as on any of the other social arrangements of mankind, depending on what an enlightened estimate of tendencies and consequences may show to be most advantageous to humanity in general, without distinction of sex.

Neither does it avail anything to say that the *nature* of the two sexes adapts them to their present functions and position, and renders these appropriate to them. Standing on the ground of common sense and the constitution of the human mind, I deny that anyone knows, or can know, the nature of the two sexes, as long as they have only been seen in their present relation to one another. If men had ever been found in society without women, or women without men, or if there had been a society of men and women in which the women were not under the control of the men, something might have been positively known about the mental and moral differences which may be inherent in the nature of each. What is now called the nature of women is an eminently artificial thing—the result of forced repression in some directions, unnatural stimulation in others. It may be asserted without scruple, that no other class of dependents have had their character so entirely distorted from its natural proportions by their relation with their masters; for, if conquered and slave races have been, in some respects, more forcibly repressed, whatever in them has not been crushed down by an iron heel has generally been let alone, and if left with any liberty of development it has developed itself according to its own laws; but in the case of women, a hot-house and stove cultivation has always been carried on of some of the capabilities of their nature, for the benefit and pleasure of their masters. Then, because certain products of the general vital force sprout luxuriantly and reach a great development in this heated atmosphere and under this active nurture and watering, while other shoots

---

From John Stuart Mill, *The Subjection of Women*, 1869 (New York: F. Stokes Co., 1911), pp. 42–51, 54.

from the same root, which are left outside in the wintry air, with ice purposely heaped all round them, have a stunted growth, and some are burnt off with fire and disappear; men, with that inability to recognize their own work which distinguishes the unanalytic mind, indolently believe that the tree grows of itself in the way they have made it grow, and that it would die if one-half of it were not kept in a vapor-bath and the other half in the snow.

Of all difficulties which impede the progress of thought, and the formation of well-grounded opinions on life and social arrangements, the greatest is now the unspeakable ignorance and inattention of mankind in respect to the influences which form human character. Whatever any portion of the human species now are, or seem to be, such, it is supposed, they have a natural tendency to be: even when the most elementary knowledge of the circumstances in which they have been placed, clearly points out the causes that made them what they are.

. . . Because women, as is often said, care nothing about politics except their personalities, it is supposed that the general good is naturally less interesting to women than to men. History, which is now so much better understood than formerly, teaches another lesson: if only by showing the extraordinary susceptibility of human nature to external influences, and the extreme variableness of those of its manifestations which are supposed to be most universal and uniform. But in history, as in traveling, men usually see only what they already had in their own minds; and few learn much from history, who do not bring much with them to its study.

Hence, in regard to that most difficult question, what are the natural differences between the two sexes—a subject on which it is impossible in the present state of society to obtain complete and correct knowledge—while almost everybody dogmatizes upon it, almost all neglect and make light of the only means by which any partial insight can be obtained into it. This is, an analytic study of the most important department of psychology, the laws of the influence of circumstances on character. For, however great and apparently ineradicable the moral and intellectual differences between men and women might be, the evidence of there being natural differences could only be negative. Those only could be inferred to be natural which could not possibly be artificial—the residuum, after deducting every characteristic of either sex which can admit of being explained from education or external circumstances. The profoundest knowledge of the laws of the formation of character is indispensable to entitle anyone to affirm even that there is any difference, much more what the difference is, between the two sexes considered as moral and rational beings; and since no one, as yet, has that knowledge (for there is hardly any subject which, in proportion to its importance, has been so little studied), no one is thus far entitled to any positive opinion on the subject. . . .

Even the preliminary knowledge, what the differences between the sexes now are, apart from all questions as to how they are made what they are, is still in the crudest and most incomplete state. Medical practitioners and physiologists have ascertained, to some extent, the differences in bodily constitution; and this is an important element to the psychologist; but hardly any medical practitioner is a psychologist. Respecting the mental characteristics of women, their observations are of no more worth than those of common men. It is a subject on which nothing final can be known, so long as those who alone can really know it, women themselves, have given but little testimony, and that little, mostly suborned. . . .

. . . We may safely assert that the knowledge which men can acquire of women, even as they have been and are, without reference to what they might be, is wretchedly imperfect and superficial, and always will be so, until women themselves have told all that they have to tell.

Suffragettes

The peaceful propaganda of suffrage advocates having proved ineffective, some English suffragists decided to try violence. Disorder and demonstrations incensed defenders of the status quo and crowds unsympathetic to "wild women." But propaganda by the deed continued until the outbreak of World War I in 1914. The war's much worse disorders were followed in 1918 by a law that enfranchised all English men over the age of twenty-one and English women over thirty.

The London Times: *"The Militant 'Suffragettes'"*

I. EXAMPLES OF SUFFRAGIST AND ANTI-SUFFRAGIST DISORDERS

Militant suffragists yesterday chose the two principal Roman Catholic places of worship for their acts of brawling. Several women were ejected from Brompton Oratory for interruptions at midday Mass. In the evening a woman ascended one of the pulpits at Westminster Cathedral and attempted to address the congregation.

A house at Tyler's-Green, near High Wycombe, was burned early on Saturday morning. The usual evidences of militant agency were found.

Disorderly demonstrations against the militants occurred at the usual open-air meetings in London.

A suffragist named Nancy Lightman, who was speaking in Hyde Park, was severely handled by a large and angry crowd. She was rescued by the police and taken along with a male sympathizer to the police station in the Park. Later in the day they were both released. A clergyman who was with her was also hustled by the crowd. Another militant suffragist who afterwards attempted to speak had to be rescued in the same manner.

The London Times (June 8, 27, 1914).

II. Lord Curzon on the Militant Suffragists

Lord Curzon, speaking at the annual meeting of the National League for Opposing Woman Suffrage yesterday afternoon, entered a strong protest against the criminal conduct of the militant suffragists.

He said that there could be no doubt that the anti-suffrage cause stood in a stronger position at present than it had done at any time during the past 20 years. That had been due perhaps in the main to the tactics and the errors of their opponents, but it had also been due in no small measure to their own activities. The phenomenon of the year had been the revival of militancy in its most outrageous and abominable forms. The efforts of these wild women had put back the cause which they advocated for at least a decade, if not longer, and they had shown how easily disturbed the mental balance of some women could be and how a perverted line of reasoning could render some women, at any rate, simultaneously indifferent to a sense both of honour and of shame.

The methods of the wild women suggested an evil possibility in the future, for they must not suppose for a moment that with the grant of the vote to one million or five or six million women militancy would necessarily cease. It would find fresh outlets of activity, perhaps even more sinister and more devastating than those with which they were now familiar. Anti-suffragists might be grateful for that warning of future danger, but there was not a thoughtful citizen in the country who did not deplore the continuance of those outrages. Little by little they were breaking down that sense of chivalry and respect which had hitherto existed like a shield to defend women from outrage and insult in the world.

Nationalism and Imperialism

THERE is no necessary connection between nationalism and imperialism: one is an ideological, almost mythological, phenomenon; the other is a policy that can be carried out by an individual such as Alexander the Great, by a dynasty such as that of the Habsburgs, by a city-state such as Athens or Rome, or even, figuratively, by a great business enterprise.

It is true, however, that the forty years preceding 1914 saw the conjunction of these two forces, with the great nations of the West engaging in economic and territorial enterprises of an imperialistic nature and using nationalistic arguments in their support—nationalism being the use or misuse of patriotism for political ends. There was a great deal of idealism mixed with the various national conceptions of manifest destiny which often sincere writers, politicians, and crackpots expressed in every country. It would appear, however, that in the long run the ideals either served to cover the interests of skillful pragmatists or else carried politicians and public alike into policies that had little to do with reason, logic, or the real interests of a nation.

The tale of this modern imperialism must be traced back at least to the policies of Bismarck, who achieved the unification of Germany as a Prussian-dominated realm by defeating three successive enemies—Danes, Austrians, and French—in three successive wars, each a put-up job. Having achieved his aim with the defeat of France in 1871, Bismarck devoted the rest of his career to securing the international stability without which he feared his new structure might be destroyed. But he had set in motion forces that he could not long control. His very success persuaded the Germans that they were destined to rule Europe . . . and the world; and "scientific" theories succeeded in proving the point. As we shall see, the Germans were not alone in their illusions of grandeur. The Anglo-Saxon peoples, too, had been advancing in great strides, and had come to believe that their achievements were only a promise of greater ones to come. It would be only a matter of time before such expansive tendencies, mystical in part but expressed in concrete economic and territorial interests, would clash on the international plane.

Otto von Bismarck

As we have seen already, for Bismarck the end justified the means, and these means might be either dubious or respectable provided they served the interests of Germany. His own account of the events preceding the outbreak of war with France in 1870 affords an instance of his readiness to claim responsibility even for acts of doubtful propriety provided they served the national cause. On a different tack, the Triple Alliance was also a part of his work—of his striving, once German unity had been achieved, to preserve European peace and a balance of power favorable to the newly created empire.

The Ems Telegram

On July 12 I decided to hurry off from Varzin to Ems to discuss with his Majesty about summoning the Reichstag for the purpose of the mobilization. As I passed through Wussow my friend Mulert, the old clergyman, stood before the parsonage door and warmly greeted me; my answer from the open carriage was a thrust in carte and tierce in the air, and he clearly understood that I believed I was going to war. As I entered the courtyard of my house at Berlin, and before leaving the carriage, I received telegrams from which it appeared that the King was continuing to treat with Benedetti,[1] even after the French threats and outrages in parliament and in the press, and not referring him with calm reserve to his ministers. During dinner, at which Moltke and Roon were present, the announcement arrived from the embassy in Paris that the Prince of Hohenzollern had renounced his candidature in order to prevent the war with which France threatened us. My first idea was to retire from the service, because, after all the insolent challenges which had gone before I perceived in this extorted submission a humiliation of Germany for which I did not desire to be responsible. This impression of a wound to our sense of national honour by the compulsory withdrawal so dominated me that I had already decided to announce my retirement at Ems. I considered this humiliation before France and her swaggering demonstrations as worse than that of Olmütz,[2] for which the previous history on both sides, and our want of preparation for war at the time, will always be a valid excuse. I took it for granted that France would lay the Prince's renunciation to her account as a satisfactory success, with the feeling that a threat of war, even though it had taken the form of international insult and mockery, and though the pretext for war against Prussia had been dragged in by the head and shoulders, was enough to compel her to draw back, even in a just cause; and that even the North German Confederation did not feel strong enough to protect the national honour and independence against French arrogance. I was very much depressed, for I saw no means of repairing the corroding injury I dreaded to our national position from a timorous policy, unless by picking quarrels clumsily and seeking them artificially. I saw by that time that war was a necessity, which we could no longer avoid with honour. I telegraphed to my people at Varzin not to pack up or start, for I should be back again in a few days. I now believed in peace; but as I would not represent the attitude by which this peace had been purchased, I gave up the journey to Ems and asked Count Eulenburg to go thither and represent my opinion to his Majesty. In the same sense I conversed with the Minister of War, von Roon: we had got our slap in the face from France, and had been reduced, by our complaisance, to look like seekers of a quarrel if we entered upon war, the only way in which we could wipe away the stain. My position was now untenable. . . .

From *Bismarck, The Man and the Statesman*, tr. A. J. Butler, 2 vol. (New York, 1899), II, Chaps. 22, 29.

[1] The French representative to Prussia.

[2] Agreement of 1850, in which Prussia accepted Austrian supremacy in the German Confederation.

Having decided to resign, in spite of the remonstrances which Roon made against it, I invited him and Moltke to dine with me alone on the 13th, and communicated to them at table my views and projects for doing so. Both were greatly depressed, and reproached me indirectly with selfishly availing myself of my greater facility for withdrawing from service. I maintained the position that I could not offer up my sense of honour to politics, that both of them, being professional soldiers and consequently without freedom of choice, need not take the same point of view as a responsible Foreign Minister. During our conversation I was informed that a telegram from Ems in cipher, was being deciphered. When the copy was handed to me it showed that Abeken had drawn up and signed the telegram at his Majesty's command, and I read it out to my guests, whose dejection was so great that they turned away from food and drink.

The telegram, handed in at Ems on July 13, 1870, at 3:50 P.M. and received in Berlin at 6:09, ran as deciphered:

"His Majesty writes to me: 'Count Benedetti spoke to me on the promenade, in order to demand from me, finally in a very importunate manner, that I should authorize him to telegraph at once that I bound myself for all future time never again to give my consent if the Hohenzollerns should renew their candidature. I refused at last somewhat sternly, as it is neither right nor possible to undertake engagements of this kind *à tout jamais*.[3] Naturally I told him that I had as yet received no news, and as he was earlier informed about Paris and Madrid than myself, he could clearly see that my government once more had no hand in the matter.' His Majesty has since received a letter from the Prince. His Majesty having told Count Benedetti that he was awaiting news from the Prince, has decided, with reference to the above demand, upon the representation of Count Eulenburg and myself, not to receive Count Benedetti again, but only to let him be informed through an aide-de-camp: That his Majesty had now received from the Prince confirmation of the news which Benedetti had already received from Paris, and had nothing further to say to the ambassador. His Majesty leaves it to your Excellency whether Benedetti's fresh demand and its rejection should not be at once communicated both to our ambassadors and to the press."

On a repeated examination of the document I lingered upon the authorization of his Majesty, which included a command, immediately to communicate Benedetti's fresh demand and its rejection both to our ambassadors and to the press. I put a few questions to Moltke as to the extent of his confidence in the state of our preparations, especially as to the time they would still require in order to meet this sudden risk of war. He answered that if there was to be war he expected no advantage to us by deferring its outbreak; and even if we should not be strong enough at first to protect all the territories on the left bank of the Rhine against French invasion, our preparation would nevertheless soon overtake those of the French, while at a later period this advantage would be diminished; he regarded a rapid outbreak as, on the whole, more favourable to us than delay.

In view of the attitude of France, our national sense of honour compelled us, in my opinion, to go to war; and if we did not act according to the demands of this

---

[3] forever.

feeling, we should lose, when on the way to its completion, the entire impetus towards our national development won in 1866, while the German national feeling south of the Main, aroused by our military successes in 1866, and shown by the readiness of the southern states to enter the alliances, would have to grow cold again. The German feeling, which in the southern states lived along with the individual and dynastic state feeling, had, up to 1866, silenced its political conscience to a certain degree with the fiction of a collective Germany under the leadership of Austria, partly from South German preference for the old imperial state, partly in the belief of her military superiority to Prussia. After events had shown the incorrectness of that calculation, the very helplessness in which the South German states had been left by Austria at the conclusion of peace was a motive for the political Damascus that lay between Varnbuler's *"Vae victis"* and the willing conclusion of the offensive and defensive alliance with Prussia. It was confidence in the Germanic power developed by means of Prussia, and the attraction which is inherent in a brave and resolute policy if it is successful, and then proceeds within reasonable and honourable limits. This nimbus had been won by Prussia; it would have been lost irrevocably, or at all events for a long time, if in a question of national honour the opinion gained ground among the people that the French insult, *La Prusse cane*,[4] had a foundation in fact.

In the same psychological train of thought in which during the Danish war in 1864 I desired, for political reasons, that precedence should be given not to the old Prussian, but to the Westphalian battalions, who so far had no opportunity of proving their courage under Prussian leadership, and regretted that Prince Frederick Charles had acted contrary to my wish, did I feel convinced that the gulf, which diverse dynastic and family influences and different habits of life had in the course of history created between the south and north of the Fatherland, could not be more effectually bridged over than by a joint national war against the neighbour who had been aggressive for many centuries. I remembered that even in the short period from 1813 to 1815, from Leipzig and Hanau to Belle-Alliance, the joint victorious struggle against France had rendered it possible to put an end to the opposition between a yielding Rhine-Confederation policy and the German national impetus of the days between the Vienna congress and the Mainz commission of enquiry, days marked by the names of Stein, Gorres, Jahn, Wartburg, up to the crime of Sand. The blood shed in common, from the day when the Saxons came over at Leipzig down to their participation at Waterloo under English command, had fostered a consciousness before which the recollections of the Rhine-Confederation were blotted out. The historical development in this direction was interrupted by the anxiety aroused by the over-haste of the national craving for the stability of state-institutions.

This retrospect strengthened me in my conviction, and the political considerations in respect to the South German states proved applicable likewise, *mutatis mutandis* [with the necessary changes], to our relations with the populations of Hanover, Hesse, and Schleswig-Holstein. That this view was correct is shown by the satisfaction with which, at the present day, after a lapse of twenty years, not only the Holsteiners, but

---

[4] Prussia's backing out (or Prussia's junking it).

likewise the people of the Hanse towns remember the heroic deeds of their sons in 1870. All these considerations, conscious and unconscious, strengthened my opinion that war could be avoided only at the cost of the honour of Prussia and of the national confidence in it. Under this conviction I made use of the royal authorization communicated to me through Abeken, to publish the contents of the telegram; and in the presence of my two guests I reduced the telegram by striking out words, but without adding or altering, to the following form: "After the news of the renunciation of the hereditary Prince of Hohenzollern had been officially communicated to the imperial government of France by the royal government of Spain, the French ambassador at Ems further demanded of his Majesty the King that he would authorize him to telegraph to Paris that his Majesty the King bound himself for all future time never again to give his consent if the Hohenzollerns should renew their candidature. His Majesty the King thereupon decided not to receive the French ambassador again, and sent to tell him through the aide-de-camp on duty that his Majesty had nothing further to communicate to the ambassador." The difference in the effect of the abbreviated text of the Ems telegram as compared with that produced by the original was not the result of stronger words but of the form, which made this announcement appear decisive, while Abeken's version only would have been regarded as a fragment of a negotiation still pending, and to be continued at Berlin.

After I had read out the concentrated edition to my two guests, Moltke remarked: "Now it has a different ring; it sounded before like a parley; now it is like a flourish in answer to a challenge." I went on to explain: "If in execution of his Majesty's order I at once communicate this text, which contains no alteration in or addition to the telegram, not only to the newspapers, but also by telegraph to all our embassies, it will be known in Paris before midnight, and not only on account of its contents, but also on account of the manner of its distribution, will have the effect of a red rag upon the Gallic bull. Fight we must if we do not want to act the part of the vanquished without a battle. Success, however, essentially depends upon the impression which the origination of the war makes upon us and others; it is important that we should be the party attacked, and this Gallic overweening and touchiness will make us, if we announce in the face of Europe, so far as we can without the speaking-trumpet of the Reichstag, that we fearlessly meet the public threats of France."

This explanation brought about in the two generals a revulsion to a more joyous mood, the liveliness of which surprised me. They had suddenly recovered their pleasure in eating and drinking and spoke in a more cheerful vein. Roon said: "Our God of old lives still and will not let us perish in disgrace." Moltke so far relinquished his passive equanimity that, glancing up joyously towards the ceiling and abandoning his usual punctiliousness of speech, he smote his hand upon his breast and said: "If I may but live to lead our armies in such a war, then the devil may come directly afterwards and fetch away the 'old carcass.'"

The Triple Alliance

The triple alliance which I originally sought to conclude after the peace of Frankfort, and about which I had already sounded Vienna and St. Petersburg, from Meaux, in

September 1870, was an alliance of the three Emperors with the further idea of bringing into it monarchical Italy. It was designed for the struggle which, as I feared, was before us; between the two European tendencies which Napoleon called Republican and Cossack, and which I, according to our present ideas, should designate on the one side as the system of order on a monarchical basis, and on the other as the social republic to the level of which the anti-monarchical development is wont to sink, either slowly or by leaps and bounds, until the conditions thus created become intolerable, and the disappointed populace are ready for a violent return to monarchical institutions in a Cesarean form. I consider that the task of escaping from this vicious circle, or, if possible, of sparing the present generation and their children an entrance into it, ought to be more closely incumbent upon the strong existing monarchies, those monarchies which still have a vigorous life, than any rivalry over the fragments of nations which people the Balkan peninsula. If the monarchical governments have no understanding of the necessity for holding together in the interests of political and social order, but make themselves subservient to the chauvinistic impulses of their subjects, I fear that the international revolutionary and social struggles which will have to be fought out will be all the more dangerous, and take such a form that the victory on the part of monarchical order will be more difficult. Since 1871 I have sought for the most certain assurance against these struggles in the alliance of the three Emperors, and also in the effort to impart to the monarchical principle in Italy a firm support in that alliance. I was not without hope of a lasting success when the meeting of the three Emperors took place at Berlin in September 1872, and this was followed by the visits of my Emperor to St. Petersburg in May, of the king of Italy to Berlin in September, and of the German Emperor to Vienna in October of the next year. The first clouding over of that hope was caused in 1875 by the provocations of Prince Gortchakoff, who spread the lie that we intended to fall upon France before she had recovered from her wounds. . . .

It is explicable that for the Russian policy there is a limit beyond which the importance of France in Europe must not be decreased. That limit was reached, as I believe, at the peace of Frankfort—a fact which in 1870 and 1871 was not so completely realized at St. Petersburg as five years later. I hardly think that during our war the Russian cabinet clearly foresaw that, when it was over, Russia would have as neighbour so strong and consolidated a Germany. In 1875 I had the impression that some doubt prevailed on the Neva as to whether it had been prudent to let things go so far without interfering in their development. The sincere esteem and friendship of Alexander II for his uncle concealed the uneasiness already felt in official circles. . . .

Count Suvaloff was perfectly right when he said that the idea of coalition gave me nightmares. We had waged victorious wars against two of the European Great Powers; everything depended on inducing at least one of the two mighty foes whom we had beaten in the field to renounce the anticipated designs of uniting with the other in a war of revenge. To all who know history and the character of the Gallic race, it was obvious that that Power could not be France, and if a secret treaty of Reichstadt was possible without consent, without our knowledge, so also was a renewal of the old coalition—Kaunitz's handiwork—of France, Austria, and Russia, whenever the elements which it represented, and which beneath the surface were still present in Austria, should gain the upper hand there. . . .

This situation demanded an effort to limit the range of the possible anti-German coalition by means of treaty arrangements which would place our relations with at least one of the Great Powers upon a firm footing. The choice could only lie between Austria and Russia, for the English constitution does not admit of alliances of assured permanence, and a union with Italy alone did not promise an adequate counterpoise to a hostile coalition. The choice could therefore be narrowed till only the alternative remained which I have indicated.

In point of material force I held a union with Russia to have the advantage. I had also been used to regard it as safer, because I have placed more reliance on traditional dynastic friendship, on community of conservative monarchical instincts, on the absence of indigenous political division, than on the fits and starts of public opinion among the Hungarian, Slav, and Catholic population of the Habsburg Monarchy. Complete reliance could be placed upon the lasting quality of neither union, whether one estimated the strength of the dynastic bond with Russia, or of the German sympathies of the Hungarian populace. If the balance of opinion in Hungary were always determined by sober political calculations, this brave and independent people, isolated in the broad ocean of Slav populations, and comparatively insignificant in numbers, would remain constant to the conviction that its position can only be secured by the support of the German element in Austria and Germany. But the Kossuth episode, and the suppression in Hungary itself of the German elements that remained local to the Empire, along with other symptoms, showed that among Hungarian hussars and lawyers self-confidence is apt at critical moments to get the better of political calculation and self-control. Even in quiet times many a Magyar will get the Gypsies to play him the song that goes "The German is a blackguard."

Houston Stewart Chamberlain

The ideas of Houston Stewart Chamberlain, an Englishman who was naturalized a German subject, reflect the nationalist thinking current at the turn of the century, and had a strong influence upon Hitler and the theory to which his National Socialists subscribed. Here are three short passages from Chamberlain's book, The Foundations of the Nineteenth Century, *first published in 1899. Notice the way in which the appeal to common sense is combined with assertions quite unsupported by fact. In this case the writer boosts the Teuton; but similar jumbles of mystical nonsense could be cited to glorify the national vanity and sense of manifest destiny of every other country in the world. Nevertheless, we have to admit that Mr. Chamberlain and his father-in-law, Richard Wagner, did particularly well in this line.*

From The Foundations of the Nineteenth Century

Seldom have the consciousness of race, national feeling, and suspicious safeguarding of the rights of personality been so active and vigorous as in our time; a phase of

From H. S. Chamberlain, *The Foundations of the Nineteenth Century,* tr. John Lees, 2 vol. (London: John Lane The Bodley Head Limited, 1912), II, 180–181, 196–197, 222–223.

feeling is passing over the nations at the close of the nineteenth century which reminds one of the dull cry of the hunted animal, when the noble creature at bay suddenly turns, determined to fight for its life. And in our case resolution means victory. For the great attractiveness of every Universalist idea is due to the weakness of men; the strong man turns from it and finds in his own breast, in his own family, in his own people, the Limitless, which we would not surrender for the whole cosmos with its countless stars. Now from the nation-building Teutons of former generations we can learn that there is a higher enjoyment than to surrender, and that is to assert ourselves. . . . Our Teutonic culture is a result of toil and pain and faith—not ecclesiastical but religious faith. If we go lovingly through those annals of our ancient forbears, which tell us so little and yet so much, what will strike us most is the almost incredible strength of the developed sense of duty; for the worst cause, as for the best, every one yields up his life unquestioningly. Did these men know what they wanted? I scarcely think so. But they knew what they did not want, and that is the beginning of all practical wisdom.

Wherever the reader casts his eyes, he will find examples to prove the fact that the present civilization and culture of Europe are specifically Teutonic, fundamentally distinct from all the un-Aryan ones and very essentially different from the Indian, the Hellenic and the Roman, directly antagonistic to the halfbreed ideal of the anti-national Imperium and the so-called "Roman" system of Christianity. The matter is so perfectly clear that further discussion would surely be superfluous. . . . This one fact had first to be laid down. For our world of today is absolutely new, and in order to comprehend it and form an estimate of its rise and present condition, the first fundamental question is: Who has created it? The new world was created by the same Teuton who after such an obstinate struggle discarded the old. He alone possessed that "wild willing" of which I spoke at the end of the last chapter, the determination not to surrender, but to remain true to self. . . . Will this be censured as empty pride? Surely it is only recognition of a manifest fact. Will the objection be offered that no mathematical proof is possible? Surely from all sides this fact is borne in upon us with the same certainty as that twice two makes four.

Nothing is more instructive in this connection than a reference to the manifest significance of purity of race. How feebly throbs today the heart of the Slav, who had entered history with such boldness and freedom: though highly gifted, he is losing his real informing power and the constancy to carry through whatever he undertakes. Anthropology solves the riddle, for it shows us that by far the greater number of Slavs today have, by mingling with another human race, lost the physical—and naturally also the moral—characteristics of their ancestors, who were identical with the ancient Teutons. And yet there is still in these nations so much Teutonic blood that they form one of the greatest civilizing forces in the continuous subjection of the world by Europe.

If we then free ourselves from the delusion of there being such a thing as a human-ity, and content ourselves with the realization of the fact that our culture is specifically North European, i.e. Teutonic, we shall at once gain a sure standard by which to judge our own past and our present, and at the same time a very useful standard to a future which has yet to come. For nothing Individual is limitless. So long as we regard our-selves as the responsible representatives of all humanity, the more clearsighted among us must be driven to despair by our poverty and obvious incapacity to pave the way for a golden age; at the same time, however, all shallow-brained phrase-makers turn us from those earnest aims which we might attain, and undermine what I should like to call historical morality, in that, shutting their eyes, blind to our universal limitations, and totally failing to realize the value of our specific talents, they dangle before our eyes the Impossible, the Absolute: natural rights, eternal peace, universal brotherhood, mutual fusion, etc. But if we know that we Northern Europeans are a definite individuality, responsible not for humanity but certainly for our own personality, we shall love and value our work as something individual, we shall recognize the fact that is by no means complete, but still very defective, and, above all, far from being sufficiently independent; no vision of an "absolute" perfection will mislead us but we shall, as Shakespeare wished, remain true to ourselves and be satisfied with doing our very best within the limits of the Teuton's power of achievement; we shall deliberately defend ourselves against the un-Teutonic, and seek not only to extend our empire farther and farther over the surface of the globe and over the powers of nature, but, above all, unconditionally to subject the inner world to ourselves by mercilessly overthrowing and excluding those who are alien to us, and who, nevertheless, would fain gain mastery over our thought. It is often said that politics can know no scruples: nothing at all can know scruples; scruples are a crime against self. Scruple is the soldier who in battle takes to his heels, presenting his behind as a target to the enemy. The most sacred duty of the Teuton is to serve the Teutonic cause. This fact supplies us with an historical standard of measurement. In all spheres that man and that deed will be glorified as great and most important which most successfully advance specific Teutonism or have most vigorously supported its supremacy. Thus and thus only do we acquire a limiting, organising, absolutely positive principle of judgment.

German Attitudes

Prior to 1914, a strong German imperialist movement arose, its aims to unite all German-speaking people in a common empire and to promote German expansion abroad. Its program included the conquest of territories in eastern Europe, colonial expansion, and a big navy for Germany. The pan-Germans also evolved racial and antisemitic doctrines; these doctrines and demands foreshadowed those of Nazism.

Living Space

A people needs land for its activities, land for its nourishment. No people needs it as much as the German people which is increasing so rapidly and whose old boundaries have become dangerously narrow. If we do not soon acquire new territories, we are moving towards a frightful catastrophe. It matters little whether it be in Brazil, in

---

From A. Wirth, *The Race and World Power in History* (Berlin, 1904); quoted in C. Andler, *Le Pangermanisme philosophique* (Paris, 1917), p. 178.

Siberia, in Anatolia or in South Africa, as long as we can once again move full of freedom and fresh energy, as long as we can once more offer our children wholesome light and air in plenty. Once more, as 2000 years ago when the Cimbri and the Teutons were hammering at the gates of Rome, sounds the cry, now full of anguish and unappeased desires, now arrogant and full of confidence—sounds more and more strongly the cry "We must have lands, new lands!"

How the New Germany Will Be Built

The manner in which Germany will realize the aggrandizement of its territory poses a problem difficult to solve, because it is a practical one. (*sic*) This problem is closely bound to the necessities which the peculiar characteristics of the germanic race impose. Where the idea of racial unity is concerned, the division of the germanic race into different peoples and different states can raise an obstacle. And outside difficulties become more important for the Germans because they incline them towards particularism. However, these difficulties are easier to overcome than one might think at first. In effect, the moment the belief should appear in the dominant German states that a closer political union of certain germanic elements in Europe is both necessary and possible, the situation appears at once to be similar to that at the time when the (Holy Roman) Empire was founded. The most powerful state of Germany must seize the hegemony, and the little states must sacrifice that part of their autonomy that is needed to establish a lasting unity for the new Empire.

It is unimportant whether armed force can or cannot be done without. The essential thing is that the state which aspires to the hegemony should dispose of sufficient moral, economic and military power to reach the end which must be attained and never forgotten. What could this state be if not the (present) German Empire engaged on a quest for fresh territories? No one can doubt it, seeing what we have said about the other great powers. All will depend on the submission of France. Germany must rule in Central and Western Europe. She must annex simultaneously, or shortly afterwards, the German provinces of Austria, in conformity with the purposes of the germanic race. The pressure exerted by the new Empire will be so great that, willy-nilly, the little germanic states will be forced to join us on terms that we shall have to lay down.[1]

Germany's Manifest Destiny

There is no need to state concerning the German idea, as of the Roman idea, that it can only be mistress of the world or not be at all. But we can press the comparison

---

Condensed from J. L. Reimer, *A Pangerman Germany* (Berlin, 1905), pp. 121–122.

[1] Remember that countries such as Holland, Luxemburg, and Switzerland were considered "germanic" by the Pangermans.

Condensed from P. Rohrbach, *The German Idea in the World* (Berlin, 1912), p. 6.

further and say: she will only conquer and dominate as the auxiliary of universal civilization, or not at all. It is easy to state the reasons for this. The Anglo-American element has today grown to such an extraordinary extent that, based on those countries belonging to it, on its means of action and on its internal power, it seems on the way to establish its dominion over the world's civilization. Russia, the greatest and most numerous of political communities after the Anglo-Americans, appears to us stripped of its old hopes of a world policy because of its internal barbarism and its fragile structure. France has of its own accord renounced competition in the future with the other world powers. By the side of the Anglo-Americans, only the German nation has developed in such a fashion that she now appears sufficiently numerous and strong internally for its national thought to claim its formal right of a share in the shaping of the future. How can we understand this? We must know that we can only preserve our energy and our strength by an endless increase of the German idea. For us there can be no halt, no immobility. We cannot give up, even for a moment, the widening of our living space. We have only the choice between the alternative of relapsing into the ranks of the territorial peoples (bound by narrow boundaries) and that of conquering by force a place beside the Anglo-Americans (on the world scale).

Anglo-Saxon Attitudes

Many things affected imperialists and colonialists, of which a feeling of manifest destiny was only one. Economic enterprise, missionary activity, the selfish but natural pursuit of private interest—all entered into the colonial attitude. The following extracts illuminate some of these motives and the extent to which such aims were fulfilled.

Letters and Diaries from The Sahibs

LETTERS FROM MADRAS, 1836

Every horse has a man and a maid to himself—the maid cuts grass for him; and every dog has a boy. I inquired whether the cat had any servants, but I found that she was allowed to wait upon herself; and, as she seemed the only person in the establishment capable of so doing, I respected her accordingly. . . .

Notwithstanding their numbers, they are dreadfully slow. I often tire myself with doing things for myself rather than wait for their dawdling; but Mrs. Staunton laughs at me, and calls me a "griffin" [green, or new], and says that I must learn to have patience and save my strength. The real Indian ladies lie on a sofa and, if they drop their handkerchief, they just lower their voices and say "Boy!" in a very gentle tone, and then creeps in, perhaps, some old wizen, skinny brownie, looking like a superannuated threadpaper, who twiddles after them for a little while, and then creeps out again as

From *The Sahibs*, ed. Hilton Brown (London: William Hodge & Company Limited, 1948), pp. 68–69, 96, 212, 224, 228. By permission of the publishers.

softly as a black cat, and sits down cross-legged in the verandah till "Mistress please to call again."

LETTERS OF MISS EDEN, 1836–1840

I wish you could see my passage sometimes. The other day when I set off to pay George a visit I could not help thinking how strange it would have seemed at home. It was a rainy day, so all the servants were at home. The two tailors were sitting in one window, making a new gown for me, and Rosina by them chopping up her betel-nut; at the opposite window were my two Dacca embroiderers working at a large frame, and the sentry, in an ecstasy of admiration mounting guard over them. There was the bearer standing upright, in a sweet sleep, pulling away at my punkah.[1] My own five servants were sitting in a circle, with an English spelling-book, which they were learning by heart; and my iemadar,[2] who, out of compliment to me, has taken to draw, was sketching a bird. Chance's (Miss Eden's dog) servant was waiting at the end of the passage for his "little excellency" to go out walking, and a Chinese was waiting with some rolls of satin that he had brought to show.

RUSSELL, MY DIARY OF INDIA, 1857–1858

"Who is that in the smart gharry, with servants in livery?" "That is the chaplain of the station, who marries and baptises, and performs services for the Europeans." "Does he go among the natives?" "Not he; he leaves that to the missionaries, of whom there are lots here." . . .

"Well: and who comes next along the drive, in that very smart buggy with the grey mare?" "That is the doctor of the station. He attends the sick Europeans. He also gets, under certain circumstances, head-money for every native soldier in garrison." "Does he attend them?" "I should think not! Why, how on earth could he attend a lot of niggers?" "But why is he paid for them?" "Ah, that is another matter. You must understand our system a little better before you can comprehend things of this sort."

LETTERS FROM MADRAS, 1838

We had heard that two Missionaries were established there (in Narsapoor), and we wanted to see them, and learn how they went on, and whether there was anything we could do to make them more comfortable. They were English shoemakers, Mr. Bowden and Mr. Beer, dissenters of Mr. Grove's class, but good, innocent, zealous creatures, and in the way to be very useful. They have two pretty, young English wives, as simple as themselves. They are living completely among the natives, teaching and talking to them, and distributing books. One of them is a man of great natural talent, strong-headed, and clear and sensible in his arguments; if he had been educated, he would

---

[1] A ceiling fan moved by a rope.

[2] head servant.

probably have turned out a very superior person. They complained much of the difficulties of the language; but A—says that the two men spoke it really much better than the general run of Missionaries. One of the wives said to me very innocently, "It is pertickly difficult to us, ma'am, on account of our never having learnt any language at all. I don't know what to make of the grammar." I advised her not to trouble herself with the grammar but just to try and learn to speak the language so as to converse with the natives—to learn it, in short, as a child learns to talk. At her age, and without any education, it was next to impossible for her to learn the grammar of an Oriental language; but I do not suppose she will follow my advice, as she had a great notion of studying, Moonshees, and so on. They live almost like the natives, without either bread or meat, but they have rice, fish, fowls, and vegetables, and they say, "The Lord has brought down our appetites to what he gives us to feed them on."

LADY FALKLAND, CHOW CHOW, 1848

Shortly before we left India, the railroad at Bombay was completed to a short distance beyond Tannah.

This was the first railroad opened in India. It can well be imagined what astonishment and excitement it caused among the natives, as well as what surprise it occasioned to many Europeans; for there were Anglo-Indians at Bombay, who had not been in Europe for many years, and who, therefore, had not seen a railroad.

A very handsome new temple had been commenced before the railroad was contemplated, and was on the verge of completion when the latter was opened. A railway station and a Hindoo temple in juxtaposition—the work of the rulers and the ruled. Could one possibly imagine buildings more opposite in their purposes, or more indicative of the character of the races? The last triumphs of science side by side with the superstitions of thousands of years ago.

THE CIVILIAN'S SOUTH INDIA, 1915

What in the name of all that is wonderful are we doing in India at all? What indeed? The Civilian cannot tell you, for he does not know, but he does think we are doing something. He thinks this because of a letter he saw the other day in the papers. It was a letter signed by a number of Indian gentlemen, and they asked that their District which had had an Indian Collector for some years past might be given a European Collector for a change. Now, if there is anything in Self-Government for India at all, an Indian Collector ought to be its finest product, and the raising of Indians to be Collectors should be India's noblest aim. The Civilian is, moreover, competent to state that the Indian Collector in question was a first-class man and an able. But they wanted a European. There you are, and the Civilian leaves you to make of it what you can. He himself, frankly, is beaten.

Rudyard Kipling

The concept of manifest destiny in another guise appears with the idea of the white man's burden, which may be simply the idea of "noblesse oblige" translated into modern terms—

but no less typically presumptuous for all that. Its classic expression appears in the following poem by Rudyard Kipling, which Kipling wrote—while the United States was engaged in the Spanish-American War—as an invitation to the Americans to help shoulder the burden. These lines appeared in the London Times *on February 4, 1899, and in the New York* Sun *and* Tribune *on the following day. On February 6, the United States Senate voted to take over the administration of the Philippines.*

From "The White Man's Burden"

Take up the White Man's burden—
Send forth the best ye breed—
Go bind your sons to exile
To serve your captives' need;
To wait in heavy harness,
On fluttered folk and wild—
Your new-caught, sullen peoples,
Half-devil and half-child.

Take up the White Man's burden—
In patience to abide,
To veil the threat of terror
And check the show of pride;
By open speech and simple,
An hundred times made plain
To seek another's profit,
And work another's gain.

Take up the White Man's burden—
The savage wars of peace—
Fill full the mouth of Famine
And bid the sickness cease;
And when your goal is nearest
The end for others sought,
Watch sloth and heathen Folly
Bring all your hopes to nought.

Take up the White Man's burden—
No tawdry rule of kings,
But toil of serf and sweeper—
The tale of common things.
The ports ye shall not enter,
The roads ye shall not tread,
Go make them with your living,
And mark them with your dead.

Take up the White Man's burden—
And reap his old reward:
The blame of those ye better,
The hate of those ye guard—
The cry of hosts ye humour
(Ah, slowly!) toward the light:—
"Why brought he us from bondage,
Our loved Egyptian night?"

Take up the White Man's burden—
Ye dare not stoop to less—
Nor call too loud on Freedom
To cloke your weariness;
By all ye cry or whisper,
By all ye leave or do,
The silent, sullen peoples
Shall weigh your Gods and you.

Take up the White Man's burden—
Have done with childish days—
The lightly proffered laurel,
The easy, ungrudged praise.
Comes now, to search your manhood
Through all the thankless years,
Cold, edged with dear-bought wisdom,
The judgment of your peers!

Arminius Vambery

A modified version of the white man's burden may be found in the works of contemporary explorers and world travelers, of whom there were many. Phineas Fogg, hero of Jules Verne's Around the World in Eighty Days, *testifies not only to the opportunities made available by modern means of transport, but to the excitement and delight open to those who could take advantage of them.*

Arminius Vambery was an anglicized Hungarian who traveled widely in Asia and published a great many accounts of his journeys. The preface that follows, from one of his less autobiographical works, reflects a widespread contemporary point of view.

Western Influence in the East

In the regions where some decades ago the travellers' life was in constant danger, and where the struggle with the elements and with the natives made his progress necessarily

---

Arminius Vambery, *Western Culture in Eastern Lands* (London, 1906), pp. 1–5.

slow and tedious, we now find a well-organised railway system, and in the place of the grunting camel the fiery steam-horse ploughs its way through endless vistas of sandy steppes. When, comfortably seated in our well-upholstered railway-carriage, we gaze upon the Hyrkanian Steppe, upon the terrible deserts of Karakum and Kisilkum, we can scarcely realise the terrors, the sufferings, and the privations, to which travellers formerly were exposed. Truly, *Tempora mutantur, nos et mutamur in illis.*[1] And great changes similar to those which have taken place in Central Asia may also be noticed in greater or less degree in other parts and regions of the Eastern world: in Siberia, West and North China, Mongolia, Manchuria, and Japan, which were in the first half of the nineteenth century scarcely known to us, and where the early martyrs of geo-graphical research, such as Schlagintweit, Hayward, Wyburd, Conolly, Margary, and others, fell victims to barbarism, we now find that the supreme power of the Western world is gradually making itself felt. The walls of seclusion are ruthlessly pulled down, and the resistance caused by the favoured superstitions, prejudices, and the ignorance of the sleepy and apathetic man in the East, is slowly being overcome. If the English poet Matthew Arnold is right when he sang,

> The East bowed down before the blast
> > In patient, deep disdain;
> She let the legions thunder past,
> > And plunged in thought again,

our present-day Europe, in its restless, bustling activity will take good care not to let the East relapse again into its former indolence. We forcibly tear its eyes open; we push, jolt, toss, and shake it, and we compel it to exchange its world-worn, hereditary ideas and customs for our modern views of life; nay, we have even succeeded to some extent in convincing our Eastern neighbours that our civilisation, our faith, our cus-toms, our philosophy, are the only means whereby the well-being, the progress, and the happiness, of the human race can be secured.

For well-nigh 300 years we have been carrying on this struggle with the Eastern world, and persist in our unsolicited interference, following in the wake of ancient Rome, which began the work with marked perseverance, but naturally never met with much success because of the inadequate means at its disposal. When we read the words of patriotic enthusiasm and inspiration with which Virgil addresses Caesar, we naturally begin to think that the Roman legions not only conquered the Asiatic world, but also exercised a civilising and beneficial influence over the whole East. This, however, was not the case. We may admire the splendour, the might, and the glory of Ancient Rome, we may allow that the glitter of its arms struck terror and alarm into the furthest corners of Asia; but in spite of all that, it would be difficult to admit that the civilising influence of Rome was ever more than an external varnish, a transitory glamour. Com-pared with the real earnest work done in our days by Western Powers, the efforts of Rome are as the flickering of an oil-lamp in comparison with the radiance of the sun in its full glory. It may be said without exaggeration that never in the world's history

---

[1] Times change, and we change with them.

has any one continent exercised such influence over another as has the Europe of our days over Asia: never were two such diametrically opposed elements engaged in so deadly a strife as is now to be seen in all parts of the Old World. This being so, it appears to me most important that we should realise what is the extent and the purpose of our civilising influence over Asia. We have to consider not only its historical growth and the means employed in its development, but also the results so far obtained, and the ultimate ends to be accomplished. And we are the more anxious to do so as our investigations into the remotest nooks and corners of the Old World have become fairly familiar ground to us all. We are in constant communication with those nations, we are familiar with their thoughts and their aspirations, we know what they think of our civilisation and the value they attach to the innovations which we are proposing to introduce into their lives. Our inquiries will in the first place make us acquainted with the means and the resources employed by the promoters of civilisation in the East. The advantages and disadvantages of our interference in the destiny of Eastern nations will stand out in bold relief, and the purely objective and unprejudiced estimate of the changes already effected may perchance have a beneficial influence upon future political relations all over the world. In the first place, then, we must ask ourselves the question: Have we a right thus to interfere in the concerns of the ancient world; and in the second place, What do the Asiatics think of it?

If we start with the assumption that every man has a right to his own opinion and to the views which best correspond with his ideas of morality and material comfort, our pretended crusade in the name of civilisation must look like an unwarrantable interference. But the correctness of this assumption has so far been contradicted by historical events, for no community can remain in absolute isolation. Even China, the prototype of a seclusion extending over thousands of years, has before now migrated far into neighbouring lands. If Rome and Greece had remained within the narrow precincts of their native lands humanity would not have reached the present height of culture, and if Western nations had checked their passion for migration the aspect of things in Asia would now be even worse than it actually is. Of course the Asiatics themselves do not view the matter in this light. Many of them look upon our enforced reforms as hostile attacks upon their liberty, and as means to bring their people under our yoke. But the better-informed amongst them, who know what the East now is and what it used to be, will hardly share this view. Humanity in Asia has never known culture and liberty in the sense in which we understand it, and has therefore never known true happiness, which is unavoidably dependent upon these two chief factors of mental and physical well-being.

During the much-extolled golden era of the history of Asia, tyranny and despotism were the ruling elements, justice a vain chimera, everything depended on the arbitrary will of the Sovereign, and a prolonged period of rest and peace was quite the exception. Asiatics, from motives of vanity or inborn laziness, may condone these abnormal conditions, but still it remains our duty to recognize the true state of affairs, and to take pity upon our oppressed fellow-men. Without our help Asia will never rise above its low level, and even granted that the politics of European Powers are not purely unselfish, we must nevertheless, keeping the ultimate object in view, approve of the interference of Europe in the affairs of the East, and give the undertaking our hearty support.

American Attitudes

The last third of the nineteenth century saw a steady increase in the material and potential political power of the United States. The country's expanding economy tempted it into overseas imperialism in the Pacific, South America, and Central America. The high point of this policy came in 1898, when the United States intervened in Spain's Cuban difficulties; shortly thereafter war broke out between the two countries. The Spanish-American War ended in a few months with the defeated Spain leaving its Caribbean and Philippine possessions in American hands.

Americans did not feel entirely easy in this matter because the expansionist policy sponsored by men such as Theodore Roosevelt clashed with the traditional anticolonialism of the Founding Fathers. This ambivalent American attitude is well illustrated by the following passages. The first reports an interview in which President William McKinley explained his attitude toward the Philippines. The second is from instructions that the president gave the American peace commissioners who went to Paris in 1898.

William McKinley: Attitude Toward the Philippines

I have been criticized a good deal about the Philippines, but I don't deserve it. The truth is, I didn't want the Philippines, and when they came to us, as a gift from the gods, I did not know what to do with them. When the Spanish war broke out, Dewey was at Hongkong, and I ordered him to go to Manila, and he had to; because, if defeated, he had no place to refit on that side of the globe, and if the Dons were victorious they would likely cross the Pacific and ravage our Oregon and California coasts. And so he had to destroy the Spanish fleet, and did it. But that was as far as I thought then. When next I realized that the Philippines had dropped into our lap, I confess that I did not know what to do with them. I sought counsel from all sides— Democrats as well as Republicans—but got little help. I thought first we would take only Manila; then Luzon; then other islands, perhaps all. I walked the floor of the White House night after night until midnight; and I am not ashamed to tell you, gentlemen, that I went down on my knees and prayed Almighty God for light and guidance more than one night.

And one night late it came to me this way—I don't know how it was, but it came: (1) That we could not give them back to Spain—that would be cowardly and dishonorable; (2) that we could not turn them over to France or Germany—that would be bad business and discreditable; (3) that we could not leave them to themselves— they were unfit for self-government—and they would soon have anarchy and misrule over there worse than Spain's was; and (4) that there was nothing left for us to do but to take them all, and to educate the Filipinos, and uplift and civilize and Christianize them, and, by God's grace, do the very best we could by them, as our fellowmen for whom Christ also died. And then I went to bed, and went to sleep, and slept soundly,

From G. A. Malcolm and M. M. Kalaw, *Philippine Government* (Boston, 1932), p. 63.

and next morning I sent for the chief engineer of the War Department (our map-maker), and told him to put the Philippines on the map of the United States (pointing to a large map on the wall of his office); "and there they are, and there they will stay while I am president!"

William McKinley: Instructions to Peace Commissioners

Without any original thought of complete or even partial acquisition the presence and success of our arms at Manila imposes upon us obligations which we cannot disregard. The march of events rules and overrules human action. Avowing unreservedly the purpose which has animated all our effort, and still solicitous to adhere to it, we cannot be unmindful that, without any desire or design on our part, the war has brought us new duties and responsibilities which we must meet and discharge as becomes a great nation on whose growth and career from the beginning the Ruler of Nations has plainly written the high command and pledge of civilization. Incidental to our tenure in the Philippines is the commercial opportunity to which American statesmanship cannot be indifferent. It is just to use every legitimate means for the enlargement of American trade; but we seek no advantages in the Orient which are not common to all. Asking only the open door for ourselves, we are ready to accord the open door to others. The commercial opportunity which is naturally and inevitably associated with this new opening depends less on large territorial possession than upon an adequate commercial basis and upon broad and equal privileges. . . . The United States cannot accept less than the cession in full right and sovereignty of the Island of Luzon.

Jacques Ellul

Particularly since the mid-twentieth century, the West's colonization and exploitation of other parts of the world have been denounced widely and eloquently. One reaction to these condemnations came from a progressive-minded French sociologist and political scientist called Jacques Ellul (1912–1985). A professor at the University of Bordeaux, Ellul had fought in the Resistance. His readable writings have consistently criticized all conformisms, conventions, and clichés, whether Left or Right. In the passages that follow, Ellul raises a cheer for the positive contributions of Western civilization.

From The Betrayal of the West

. . . I am not criticizing or rejecting other civilizations and societies; I have deep admiration for the institutions of the Bantu and other peoples (the Chinese among them)

From *Foreign Relations of the United States, 1898* (Washington, Department of State), G. P. O., p. 907, 16 Sept. 1898.

From *Betrayal of the West*, tr. Matthew J. O'Connell. English translation © 1978 by the Continuum Publishing Corporation. Reprinted by permission of the publisher.

and for the inventions and poetry and architecture of the Arabs. I do not claim at all that the West is superior. In fact, I think it absurd to lay claim to superiority of any kind in these matters. What criterion would you apply? What scale of values would you use? I would add that the greatest fault of the West since the seventeenth century has been precisely its belief in its own unqualified superiority in all areas.

The thing, then, that I am protesting against is the silly attitude of western intellectuals in hating their own world and then illogically exalting all other civilizations. Ask yourself this question: If the Chinese have done away with binding the feet of women, and if the Moroccans, Turks, and Algerians have begun to liberate their women, whence did the impulse to these moves come from? From the West, and nowhere else! Who invented the "rights of man"? The same holds for the elimination of exploitation. Where did the move to socialism originate? In Europe, and in Europe alone. The Chinese, like the Algerians, are inspired by western thinking as they move toward socialism. Marx was not Chinese, nor was Robespierre an Arab. How easily the intellectuals forget this! The whole of the modern world, for better or for worse, is following a western model; no one imposed it on others, they have adopted it themselves, and enthusiastically.

I shall not wax lyrical about the greatness and benefactions of the West. Above all, I shall not offer a defense of the material goods Europe brought to the colonies. We've heard that kind of defense too often: "We built roads, hospitals, schools, and dams; we dug the oil wells. . . ." And the reason I shall say nothing of this invasion by the technological society is that I think it to be the West's greatest crime, as I have said at length elsewhere. The worst thing of all is that we exported our rationalist approach to things, our "science," our conception of the state, our bureaucracy, our nationalist ideology. It is this, far more surely than anything else, that has destroyed the other cultures of the world and shunted the history of the entire world onto a single track.

But is that all we can say of the West? No, the essential, central, undeniable fact is that the West was the first civilization in history to focus attention on the individual and on freedom. Nothing can rob us of the praise due us for that. We have been guilty of denials and betrayals (of these we shall be saying something more), we have committed crimes, but we have also caused the whole of mankind to take a gigantic step forward and to leave its childhood behind.

This is a point we must be quite clear on. If the world is everywhere rising up and accusing the West, if movements of liberation are everywhere under way, what accounts for this? Its sole source is the proclamation of freedom that the West has broadcast to the world. The West, and the West alone, is responsible for the movement that has led to the desire for freedom and to the accusations now turned back upon the West.

Today men point the finger of outrage at slavery and torture. Where did that kind of indignation originate? What civilization or culture cried out that slavery was unacceptable and torture scandalous? Not Islam, or Buddhism, or Confucius, or Zen, or the religions and moral codes of Africa and India! The West alone has defended the inalienable rights of the human person, the dignity of the individual, the man who is alone with everyone against him. But the West did not practice what it preached?

The extent of the West's fidelity is indeed debatable: the whole European world has certainly not lived up to its own ideal all the time, but to say that it has never lived up to it would be completely false.

In any case, that is not the point. The point is that the West originated values and goals that spread throughout the world (partly through conquest) and inspired man to demand his freedom, to take his stand in the face of society and affirm his value as an individual. I shall not be presumptuous enough to try to "define" the freedom of the individual. . . .

. . . The West gave expression to what man—every man—was seeking. The West turned the whole human project into a conscious, deliberate business. It set the goal and called it freedom, or, at later date, individual freedom. It gave direction to all the forces that were working in obscure ways, and brought to light the value that gave history its meaning. Thereby, man became man.

The West attempted to apply in a conscious, methodical way the implications of freedom. The Jews were the first to make freedom the key to history and to the whole created order. From the very beginning their God was the God who liberates; his great deeds flowed from a will to give freedom to his people and thereby to all mankind. This God himself, moreover, was understood to be sovereignly free (freedom here was often confused with arbitrariness or with omnipotence). This was something radically new, a discovery with explosive possibilities. The God who was utterly free had nothing in common with the gods of eastern and western religions; he was different precisely because of his autonomy.

The next step in the same movement saw the Greeks affirming both intellectual and political liberty. They consciously formulated the rules for a genuinely free kind of thinking, the conditions for human freedom, and the forms a free society could take. Other peoples were already living in cities, but none of them had fought so zealously for the freedom of the city in relation to other cities, and for the freedom of the citizen within the city.

The Romans took the third step by inventing civil and institutional liberty and making political freedom the key to their entire politics. Even the conquests of the Romans were truly an unhypocritical expression of their intention of freeing peoples who were subject to dictatorships and tyrannies the Romans judged degrading. It is in the light of that basic thrust that we must continue to read Roman history. Economic motives undoubtedly also played a role, but a secondary one; to make economic causes the sole norm for interpreting history is in the proper sense superficial and inadequate. You can not write history on the basis of your suspicions! If you do, you only project your own fantasies.

I am well aware, of course, that in each concrete case there was darkness as well as light, that liberty led to wars and conquests, that it rested on a base of slavery. I am not concerned here, however, with the excellence or defects of the concrete forms freedom took; I am simply trying to say (as others have before me) that at the beginning of western history we find the awareness, the explanation, the proclamation of freedom as the meaning and goal of history.

No one has ever set his sights as intensely on freedom as did the Jews and Greeks and Romans, the peoples who represented the entire West and furthered its progress.

In so doing, they gave expression to what the whole of mankind was confusedly seeking. In the process we can see a progressive approach to the ever more concrete: from the Jews to the Greeks, and from the Greeks to the Romans there is no growth in consciousness, but there is the ongoing search for more concrete answers to the question of how freedom can be brought from the realm of ideas and incarnated in institutions, behavior, thinking, and so on.

Today the whole world has become the heir of the West, and we Westerners now have a twofold heritage: we are heirs to the evil the West has done to the rest of the world, but at the same time we are heirs to our forefathers' consciousness of freedom and to the goals of freedom they set for themselves. Other peoples, too, are heirs to the evil that has been inflicted on them, but now they have also inherited the consciousness of and desire for freedom. Everything they do today and everything they seek is an expression of what the western world has taught them. . . .

. . . Everything used to be so organized that wealth and poverty were stable states, determined (for example) by the traditional, accepted hierarchy, and that this arrangement was regarded as due to destiny or an unchangeable divine will. The West did two things: it destroyed the hierarchic structures and it did away with the idea of destiny. It thus showed the poor that their state was not something inevitable. This is something Marx is often credited with having done, but only because people are ignorant. It was Christianity that did away with the idea of destiny and fate. . . .

Once Christianity had destroyed the idea of destiny or fate, the poor realized that they were poor, and they realized that their condition was not inevitable. Then the social organisms that had made it possible to gloss over this fact were challenged and undermined from within.

Against all this background we can see why the whole idea of revolution is a western idea. Before the development of western thought, and apart from it, no revolution ever took place. Without the individual and freedom and the contradictory extremes to which freedom leads, a society cannot engender a revolution. Nowhere in the world—and I speak as one with a knowledge of history—has there ever been a revolution, not even in China, until the western message penetrated that part of the world. Present-day revolutions, whether in China or among the American Indians, are the direct, immediate, unmistakable fruit of the western genius. The entire world has been pupil to the West that it now rejects. . . .

. . . I wish only to remind the reader that the West has given the world a certain number of values, movements, and orientations that no one else has provided. No one else has done quite what the West has done. I wish also to remind the reader that the whole world is living, and living almost exclusively, by these values, ideas, and stimuli. There is nothing original about the "new" thing that is coming into existence in China or Latin America or Africa: it is all the fruit and direct consequence of what the West has given the world.

In the fifties it was fashionable to say that "the third world is now entering upon the stage of history." The point was not, of course, to deny that Africa or Japan had a history. What the cliché was saying, and rightly saying, was that these peoples were now participating in the creative freedom of history and the dialectic of the historical process. Another way of putting it is that the West had now set the whole world in motion. It had released a tidal wave that would perhaps eventually drown it. There had been great changes in the past and vast migrations of peoples; there had been planless quests for power and the building of gigantic empires that collapsed overnight. The West represented something entirely new because it set the world in movement in every area and at every level; it represented, that is, a coherent approach to reality. Everything—ideas, armies, the state, philosophy, rational methods, and social organization—conspired in the global change the West had initiated.

It is not for me to judge whether all this was a good thing or bad. I simply observe that the entire initiative came from the West, that everything began there. I simply observe that the peoples of the world had abided in relative ignorance and [religious] repose until the encounter with the West set them on their journey.

Please, then, don't deafen us with talk about the greatness of Chinese or Japanese civilization. These civilizations existed indeed, but in a larval or embryonic state; they were approximations, essays. They always related to only one sector of the human or social totality and tended to be static and immobile. Because the West was motivated by the ideal of freedom and had discovered the individual, it alone launched society in its entirety on its present course.

Again, don't misunderstand me. I am not saying that European science was superior to Chinese science, nor European armies to Japanese armies; I am not saying that the Christian religion was superior to Buddhism or Confucianism; I am not saying that the French or English political system was superior to that of the Han dynasty. I am saying only that the West discovered what no one else had discovered; freedom and the individual, and that this discovery later set everything else in motion. Even the most solidly established religions could not help changing under the influence. . . .

It was not economic power or sudden technological advances that made the West what it is. These played a role, no doubt, but a negligible one in comparison with the great change—the discovery of freedom and the individual—that represents the goal and desire implicit in the history of all civilizations. That is why, in speaking of the West, I unhesitatingly single out freedom from the whole range of values. After all, we find justice, equality, and peace everywhere. Every civilization that has attained a certain level has claimed to be a civilization of justice or peace. But which of them has ever spoken of the individual? Which of them has been reflectively conscious of freedom as a value?

The decisive role of the West's discovery of freedom and the individual is beyond question, but the discovery has brought with it . . . tragic consequences. First, the very works of the West now pass judgment on it. For, having proclaimed freedom and the individual, the West played false in dealing with other peoples. It subjected, conquered, and exploited them, even while it went on talking about freedom. It made the other peoples conscious of their enslavement by intensifying that enslavement and calling it freedom. It destroyed the social structures of tribes and clans, turned men into isolated atoms, and shaped them into a worldwide proletariat, and all the time kept on talking of the great dignity of the individual: his autonomy, his power to decide for himself, his capacity for choice, his complex and many-sided reality. . . .

. . . Reason makes it possible for the individual to master impulse, to choose the ways in which he will exercise his freedom, to calculate the chances for success and the manner in which a particular action will impinge upon the group, to understand human relations, and to communicate. Communication is the highest expression of freedom, but it has little meaning unless there is a content which, in the last analysis, is supplied by reason. . . . Here precisely we have the magnificent discovery made by the West: that the individual's whole life can be, and even is, the subtle, infinitely delicate interplay of reason and freedom.

This interplay achieved its highest form in both the Renaissance and classical literature since the Enlightenment. No other culture made this discovery. We of the West have the most rounded and self-conscious type of man. For, the development of reason necessarily implied reason's critique of its own being and action as well as a critique of both liberty and reason, through a return of reason upon itself and a continuous reflection which gave rise to new possibilities for the use of freedom as controlled by new developments of reason. . . .

Let me return to my main argument. It was the West that established the splendid interplay of freedom, reason, self-control, and coherent behavior. It thus produced a type of human being that is unique in history: true western man. (I repeat: the type belongs neither to nature nor to the animal world; it is a deliberate construct achieved through effort.) I am bound to say that I regard this type as superior to anything I have seen or known elsewhere. A value judgment, a personal and subjective preference? Of course. But I am not ready on that account to turn my back on the construction and on the victory and affirmation it represents. Why? Because the issue is freedom itself, and because I see no other satisfactory model that can replace what the West has produced.

War and Revolution

THE growing friction between the world powers eventually led to war—a war which was accepted not as a solution to their problems but as an excuse for not finding one. In any event, war had been threatening for so long that its coming seemed almost a relief. Though the British appear to have entered it only half-heartedly, even they soon succumbed to the general enthusiasm that led each side to feel that it was fighting for the triumph of justice and civilization over the powers of evil. The conflict dragged on, sucking more countries into its vortex, consuming ever more of the world's energy, material, and blood. Those who could stand the strain longest came out on top; those who could not, collapsed not only militarily but economically and politically, too (indeed, usually, first). All four eastern empires—Germany, Austria, Russia, and Turkey—disintegrated, and in every one of them revolution went along with peace.

The Logic of Ententes

As Britain found itself thrust rather suddenly, and not very willingly, into a great European war that would develop into a conflict on a world scale, Punch, *the humorous and influential English weekly magazine, produced its own comment on events.*

Punch: *Satirical Verses*

To Serbia
You have won whatever of fame it brings
To have murdered a king and the heir of kings,
And it well may be that your sovereign pride
Chafes at a touch of its tender hide;
But why should I follow your fighting line,
For a matter that's no concern of mine?

From *Punch* (August 5, 1914).

To Austria
You may, if you like, elect to curb
The dark designs of the dubious Serb
And to close your Emperor's days in strife,
A tragic end to a tragic life,
By your bellicose taste for Balkan coups,
But why in the world should I stand to lose?

To Russia
No doubt the natural course for you
Is to bid the Austrian bird "Go to!"
He can't be suffered to spoil your dream
Of a beautiful pan-Slavonic scheme:
But Britons can never be Slave, you see,
So what has your case to do with me?
But since another if you insist
Will be cutting in with his mailed fist
I shall be asked to a general scrap
All over the European map,
Dragged into somebody else's war
For that's what a double Entente is for.

Well, if I must, I shall have to fight
For the love of a bounding Balkanite,
But O what a tactless choice of time
When the bathing season is at its prime,
And how I should hate to lose my chance
Of wallowing off the coast of France.

The Internationalist Left and the War

The great majority of Europeans, whatever their view on politics, class conflict, or international amity, responded to the news like old war horses to a cavalry bugle. Though socialists and their leaders had long affirmed that workers had no country and threatened, if mobilized, to turn their guns first against their own officers and capitalist oppressors, they, too, like their fellow citizens, were swept forward in a great wave of patriotic fervor. "My country right or wrong" still sounded sweeter than the International, *though naturally no one suspected that his or her own country could be other than right. This letter from a Russian socialist appeared in the* London Times *on September 18, 1914.*

A Russian Socialist: Letter to The London Times

Sir—May I be allowed to say a few words in connection with the excellent letter by my compatriot, Professor Vinogradov, which appeared in your paper today, September 14? Professor Vinogradov is absolutely right when he says that not only is it desirable that complete unity of feeling should exist in Russian political circles, but that this unity is already an accomplished fact.

The representatives of all political parties and of all nationalities in Russia are now at one with the Government, and this war with Germany and Austria, both guided by the Kaiser, has already become a national war for Russia.

Even we, the adherents of the parties of the Extreme Left, and hitherto ardent antimilitarists and pacifists, even we believe in the necessity of *this* war. This war is a war to protect justice and civilization. It will, we hope, be a decisive factor in our united *war against war,* and we hope that after it, it will at last be possible to consider seriously the question of disarmament and universal peace. There can be no doubt that victory, and decisive victory at that (personally I await this in the immediate future), will be on the side of the Allied nations—England, France, Belgium, Serbia, and Russia.

The German peril, the curse which has hung over the whole world for so many decades, will be crushed, and crushed so that it will never again become a danger to the peace of the world. The peoples of the world desire peace.

To Russia this war will bring regeneration.

We are convinced that after this war there will no longer be any room for political reaction, and Russia will be associated with the existing group of cultured and civilized countries.

Yours truly,
V. Bourtzeff

Allied War Aims

In an address to Congress delivered on January 8, 1918, President Woodrow Wilson produced a statement of Allied war aims that was to be known as the Fourteen Points. Britain, France, and the other powers in the Allied camp were not enthusiastic about all the points but were ready to regard them as a basis for discussion and negotiation. They also realized that the Americans were the dominant partner in the alliance and that they could not afford to anger Wilson by refusing to go along with his statement. The Germans, on the other hand, who were winning at the time, ignored the Fourteen Points completely. In the treaties of peace that they imposed on Rumania and Russia during the spring of 1918, the only apparent principle we can find is that might makes right. By October, however, the Germans realized that defeat was upon them, and they very wisely decided that the

From *Documents of Russian History, 1914–1917,* ed. F. A. Golder, tr. E. Aronsberg (New York: Appleton-Century-Crofts, Inc. 1927).

offers which they once had ignored could be accepted as the basis of an honorable peace in the hour of defeat. By then the Allied interpretation of the points had changed somewhat; but because this was not publicly known, in later years the Germans claimed that they had been tricked into signing the armistice, when in fact the German military situation had left no alternative between armistice and invasion. The following text is a passage from Wilson's speech, and it contains the much-debated suggestions.

Woodrow Wilson: The Fourteen Points

We entered this war because violations of right had occurred which touched us to the quick and made the life of our own people impossible unless they were corrected and the world secure once and for all against their recurrence. What we demand in this war, therefore, is nothing peculiar to ourselves. It is that the world be made fit and safe to live in; and particularly that it be made safe for every peace-loving nation which, like our own, wishes to live its own life, determine its own institutions, be assured of justice and fair dealing by the other peoples of the world as against force and selfish aggression. All the peoples of the world are in effect partners in this interest, and for our own part we see very clearly that unless justice be done to others it will not be done to us. The programme of the world's peace, therefore, is our programme: and as we see it, is this:

I. Open covenants of peace, openly arrived at, after which there shall be no private international understandings of any kind, but diplomacy shall proceed always frankly and in the public view.

II. Absolute freedom of navigation upon the seas, outside territorial waters, alike in peace and in war, except as the seas may be closed in whole or in part by international action for the enforcement of international covenants.

III. The removal, so far as possible, of all economic barriers and the establishment of an equality of trade conditions among all the nations consenting to the peace and associating themselves for its maintenance.

IV. Adequate guarantees given and taken that national armaments will be reduced to the lowest point consistent with domestic safety.

V. A free, open-minded, and absolutely impartial adjustment of all colonial claims, based upon a strict observance of the principle that in determining all such questions of sovereignty the interests of the populations concerned must have equal weight with the equitable claims of the government whose title is to be determined.

VI. The evacuation of all Russian territory and such a settlement of all questions affecting Russia as will secure the best and freest cooperation of the other nations of the world in obtaining for her an unhampered and unembarrassed opportunity for the independent determination of her own political development and national policy,

From *Foreign Relations of the United States, 1918* (Washington, Department of State), Sup. 1, Vol. 1, pp. 13–17.

and assure her of a sincere welcome into the society of free nations under institutions of her own choosing; and, more than a welcome, assistance also of every kind that she may need and may herself desire. The treatment accorded Russia by her sister nations in the months to come will be the acid test of their good will, of their comprehension of her needs as distinguished from their own interests, and of their intelligent and unselfish sympathy.

VII. Belgium, the whole world will agree, must be evacuated and restored, without any attempt to limit the sovereignty which she enjoys in common with all other free nations. No other single act will serve to restore confidence among the nations in the laws which they have themselves set and determined for the government of their relations with one another. Without this healing act, the whole structure and validity of international law is forever impaired.

VIII. All French territory should be freed and the invaded portions restored, and the wrong done to France by Prussia in 1871 in the matter of Alsace-Lorraine, which has unsettled the peace of the world for nearly fifty years, should be righted, in order that peace may once more be made secure in the interest of all.

IX. A readjustment of the frontiers of Italy should be effected along clearly recognizable lines of nationality.

X. The peoples of Austria-Hungary, whose place among the nations we wish to see safeguarded and assured, should be accorded the freest opportunity of autonomous development.

XI. Rumania, Serbia, and Montenegro should be evacuated; occupied territories restored; Serbia accorded free access to the sea; and the relations of the several Balkan states to one another determined by friendly counsel along historically established lines of allegiance and nationality; and international guarantees of the political and economic independence and territorial integrity of the several Balkan states should be entered into.

XII. The Turkish portions of the present Ottoman Empire should be assured a secure sovereignty, but the other nationalities which are now under Turkish rule should be assured an undoubted security of life and an absolutely unmolested opportunity of autonomous development, and the Dardanelles should be permanently opened as a free passage to the ships and commerce of all nations under international guarantees.

XIII. An independent Polish state should be erected which should include the territories inhabited by indisputably Polish populations, which should be assured a free and secure access to the sea, and whose political and economic independence and territorial integrity should be guaranteed by international covenant.

XIV. A general association of nations must be formed under specific covenants for the purpose of affording mutual guarantees of political independence and territorial integrity to great and small states alike.

We have spoken now, surely, in terms too concrete to admit of any further doubt or question. An evident principle runs through the whole programme I have outlined.

It is the principle of justice to all peoples and nationalities, and their right to live on equal terms of liberty and safety with one another, whether they be strong or weak. Unless this principle be made its foundation, no part of the structure of international justice can stand. . . .

From The Treaty of Versailles

The Treaty of Versailles, which Germany and her victorious enemies signed on June 28, 1919, is an extremely long and verbose document. The clauses cited here contain its most significant provisions.

Article 42 Germany is forbidden to maintain or construct any fortifications either on the left bank of the Rhine or on the right bank to the west of a line drawn 50 kilometres to the East of the Rhine.

Article 45 As compensation for the destruction of the coal mines in the north of France and as part payment towards the total reparation due from Germany for the damage resulting from the war, Germany cedes to France in full and absolute possession, with exclusive right of exploitation, unencumbered and free from all debts and charges of any kind, the coal mines situated in the Saar Basin. . . .

Article 49 Germany renounces in favor of the League of Nations, in the capacity of trustee, the government of the territory defined above.

At the end of fifteen years from the coming into force of the present Treaty the inhabitants of the said territory shall be called upon to indicate the sovereignty under which they desire to be placed.

Alsace-Lorraine The High Contracting Parties, recognizing the moral obligation to redress the wrong done by Germany in 1871 both to the rights of France and to the wishes of the population of Alsace and Lorraine, which were separated from their country in spite of the solemn protest of their representatives at the Assembly of Bordeaux, agree upon the following. . . .

Article 51 The territories which were ceded to Germany in accordance with the Preliminaries of peace signed at Versailles on February 26, 1871, and the Treaty of Frankfort of May 10, 1871, are restored to French sovereignty as from the date of the Armistice of November 11, 1918.

The provisions of the Treaties establishing the delimitation of the frontiers before 1871 shall be restored. . . .

Article 80 Germany acknowledges and will respect strictly the independence of Austria, within the frontiers which may be fixed in a Treaty between that State and the Principal Allied and Associated Powers; she agrees that this independence shall be inalienable, except with the consent of the Council of the League of Nations.

Article 81 Germany, in conformity with the action already taken by the Allied and Associated Powers, recognizes the complete independence of the Czecho-Slovak State which will include the autonomous territory of the Ruthenians to the south of the Carpathians. Germany hereby recognizes the frontiers of this State as determined by the Principal Allied and Associated Powers and the other interested States. . . .

Article 87 Germany, in conformity with the action already taken by the Allied and Associated Powers, recognizes the complete independence of Poland. . . .

Article 89 Poland undertakes to accord freedom of transit to persons, goods, vessels, carriages, wagons and mails in transit between East Prussia and the rest of Germany over Polish territory, including territorial waters, and to treat them at least as favorably as the persons, goods, vessels, carriages, etc., of Polish or of any other more favored nationality, origin, importation, starting-point, or ownership, as regards facilities, restrictions, and all other matters. . . .

Article 102 The Principal Allied and Associated Powers undertake to establish the town of Danzig, together with the rest of the territory described in Article 100, as a Free City. It will be placed under the protection of the League of Nations. . . .

Article 116 Germany acknowledges and agrees to respect as permanent and inalienable the independence of all the territories which were part of the former Russian Empire on August 1, 1914.

Germany accepts definitely the abrogation of the Brest-Litovsk Treaties and of all other treaties, conventions and agreements entered into by her with the Maximalist (Bolshevik) Government in Russia.

The Allied and Associated Powers formally reserve the rights of Russia to obtain from Germany restitution and reparation based on the principles of the present Treaty. . . .

Article 119 Germany renounces in favor of the Principal Allied and Associated Powers all her rights and titles over her overseas possessions. . . .

Article 159 The German military forces shall be demobilised and reduced as prescribed hereinafter.

Article 160 By a date which must not be later than March 31, 1920, the German Army must not comprise more than seven divisions of infantry and three divisions of cavalry.

After that date the total number of effectives in the Army of the States constituting Germany must not exceed 100,000 men, including officers and establishments of depots. The Army shall be devoted exclusively to the maintenance of order within the territory and to the control of the frontiers.

The total effective strength of officers, including the personnel of staffs, whatever their composition, must not exceed four thousand. . . .

Article 198 The armed forces of Germany must not include any military or naval air forces. . . .

Article 231 The Allied and Associated Governments affirm and Germany accepts the responsibility of Germany and her allies for causing all the loss and damage to which the Allied and Associated Governments and their nationals have been subjected as a consequence of the war imposed upon them by the aggression of Germany and her allies.

Article 232 The Allied and Associated Governments recognize that the resources of Germany are not adequate, after taking into account permanent diminutions of such resources which will result from other provisions of the present Treaty, to make complete reparation for all such loss and damage.

The Allied and Associated Governments, however, require, and Germany undertakes, that she will make compensation for all damage done to the civilian population of the Allied and Associated Powers and to their property during the period of the belligerency of each as an Allied or Associated Power against Germany. . . .

Article 233 The amount of the above damage for which compensation is to be made by Germany shall be determined by an Inter-Allied Commission. . . . This Commission shall consider the claims and give to the German Government a just opportunity to be heard.

The findings of the Commission as to the amount of damage defined as above shall be concluded and notified to the German Government on or before May 1, 1921, as representing the extent of that Government's obligations. . . .

Article 234 The Reparation Commission shall after May 1, 1921, from time to time, consider that resources and capacity of Germany and, after giving her representatives a just opportunity to be heard, shall have discretion to extend the date, and to modify the form of payments, such as are to be provided in accordance with Article 233; but not to cancel any part, except with the specific authority of the several Governments represented upon the Commission. . . .

Article 428 As a guarantee for the execution of the present Treaty by Germany, the German territory situated to the west of the Rhine, together with the bridge-heads, will be occupied by Allied and Associated troops for a period of fifteen years from the coming into force of the present Treaty. . . .

Article 431 If before the expiration of the period of fifteen years Germany complies with all the undertakings resulting from the present Treaty, the occupying forces will be withdrawn immediately.

The Fallout of Slaughter

BEYOND the disintegration of existing regimes and of the international order, four years of war left their mark on the spirit of those who lived—or eventually died—in those bloody times. Young men who cheerfully had marched off to battle returned torn and mangled, if not in body then in mind. War had been glorified as splendid and ennobling, and civilians and propagandists behind the lines continued to talk of it that way. But those who experienced combat developed a different view: they were alienated, rebellious, bitter, and determined that the butchery in which they took part should not ever be repeated. This perspective would play a major role in postwar society—in the pacifism that colored the politics of postwar societies where pacifism was free to express itself; in the iconoclasm and deliberate incoherence characteristic of art and literature between the wars; and in the ebb of the confidence that marked previous centuries in which social progress had seemed inevitable.

Rupert Brooke

Rupert Brooke (1887–1915), who was a naval officer, died of blood poisoning in the Mediterranean.

Poem Fragments

The change of heart that fighting men, many of whom went to war straight from university or from school, experienced can be followed in the changing tone of the poetry some of them wrote. Typical of their first reactions was Rupert Brooke's invocation:

> Now God be thanked Who matched us with His hour,
> And caught our youth, and wakened us from sleeping,
> With hand made sure, clear eye, and sharpened power,
> To turn as swimmers into cleanness leaping,
> Glad from a world grown old and cold and weary . . .

From Rupert Brooke, *The Complete Poems* (London: Sidgwick & Jackson Ltd., 1943), pp. 146, 150.

and his well-known lines from "The Soldier":

> If I should die, think only this of me:
> That there's some corner of a foreign field
> That is forever England.

Julian Grenfell

Julian Grenfell (1888–1915) was killed at the battle of Ypres shortly after the London
Times *published his poem, "Into Battle."*

"Into Battle"

The naked earth is warm with spring,
   And with green grass and bursting trees
Leans to the sun's gaze glorying,
   And quivers in the sunny breeze;
And life is colour and warmth and light,
   And a striving evermore for these;
And he is dead who will not fight;
   And who dies fighting has increase.

The fighting man shall from the sun
   Take warmth, and life from the glowing earth;
Speed with the light-foot winds to run,
   And with the trees to newer birth;
And find, when fighting shall be done,
   Great rest, and fullness after dearth.

Siegfried Sassoon

*Siegfried Sassoon (1886–1967), who survived several years of fighting, wounds, and decora-
tions, began in the same vein as Brooke and Grenfell, but changed his tune. We can follow
Sassoon's evolution through "The Kiss," with its heroic metaphors, to the realism of
"Counter-Attack," to "'They'," with its sarcastic rejection of the high-flown nonsense
spouted by home-front authorities.*

From Julian Grenfell, The Oxford Book of English Verse (Oxford: Clarendon Press, 1939), p. 1135 (C. Lord
and Lady Desborough).

"The Kiss"

To these I turn, in these I trust;
Brother Lead and Sister Steel.
To his blind power I make appeal;
I guard her beauty clean from rust.

He spins and burns and loves the air,
And splits a skull to win my praise;
But up the nobly marching days
She glitters naked, cold and fair.

Sweet Sister, grant your soldier this;
That in good fury he may feel
The body where he sets his heel
Quail from your downward darting kiss.

"Counter-Attack"

We'd gained our first objective hours before
While dawn broke like a face with blinking eyes,
Pallid, unshaved and thirsty, blind with smoke.
Things seemed all right at first. We held their line,
With bombers posted, Lewis guns well placed,
And clink of shovels deepening the shallow trench.
The place was rotten with dead; green clumsy legs
High-booted, sprawled and grovelled along the saps
And trunks, face downward in the sucking mud,
Wallowed like trodden sand-bags loosely filled;
And naked sodden buttocks, mats of hair,
Bulged, clotted heads, slept in the plastering slime.
And then the rain began,—the jolly old rain!

A yawning soldier knelt against the bank,
Staring across the morning blear with fog;
He wondered when the Allemands would get busy;
And then, of course, they started with five-nines
Traversing, sure as fate, and never a dud.
Mute in the clamour of shells he watched them burst
Spouting dark earth and wire with gusts from hell,

From Siegfried Sassoon, *Collected Poems 1908–1956* (London: Faber & Faber, 1947, 1961, 1971), pp. 15, 68,
23, 188.

While posturing giants dissolved in drifts of smoke.
He crouched and flinched, dizzy with galloping fear,
Sick for escape,—loathing the strangled horror
And butchered, frantic gestures of the dead.

An officer came blundering down the trench:
"Stand-to and man the fire-step!" On he went . . .
Gasping and bawling, "Fire-step . . counter-attack!"
Then the haze lifted. Bombing on the right
Down the old sap: machine-guns on the left;
And stumbling figures looming out in front.
"O Christ, they're coming at us!" Bullets spat,
And he remembered his rifle . . . rapid fire . . .
And started blazing wildly . . . then a bang
Crumbled and spun him sideways, knocked him out
To grunt and wriggle: none heeded him; he choked
And fought the flapping veils of smothering gloom,
Lost in a blurred confusion of yells and groans . . .
Down, and down, and down, he sank and drowned,
Bleeding to death. The counter-attack had failed.

" 'They' "

The Bishop tells us: "When the boys come back
They will not be the same; for they'll have fought
In a just cause: they lead the last attack
On Anti-Christ; their comrade's blood has bought
New right to breed an honourable race.
They have challenged Death and dared him face to face."

"We're none of us the same!" the boys reply.
"For George lost both his legs; and Bill's stone blind;
Poor Jim's shot through the lungs and like to die;
And Bert's gone syphilitic: you'll not find
A chap who's served that hasn't found *some* change."
And the Bishop said: "The ways of God are strange!"

For those who died, as for survivors, Flanders proved a graveyard of illusions. As Wilfrid
Owen (1893–1918) cried in his "Anthem for Doomed Youth":
  What passing-bells for those who die as cattle?
  Only the monstrous anger of the guns.
  Only the stuttering rifles' rapid rattle
  Can patter out their hasty orisons.

Ypres

Owen died a week before the armistice, but those who lived on never lost their scars. One of the most murderous battles of the war had been fought in rain and mud during the high summer and autumn of 1917, as British troops sought to advance on German-held Ypres. When, after the war, Siegfried Sassoon visited the Belgian city rising from its ruins, he reacted to the new city gate on the road to nearby Menin, where so many perished.

Siegfried Sassoon: "On Passing the New Menin Gate"

Who will remember, passing through this Gate,
The unheroic Dead who fed the guns?
Who shall absolve the foulness of their fate,—
Those doomed, conscripted, unvictorious ones?
   Crudely renewed, the Salient holds its own.
   Paid are its dim defenders by this pomp;
   Paid, with a pile of peace-complacent stone,
   The armies who endured that sullen swamp.

Here was the world's worst wound. And here with pride
'Their name liveth for ever,' the Gateway claims.
Was ever an immolation so belied
As these intolerably nameless names?
Well might the Dead who struggled in the slime
Rise and deride this sepulchre of crime.

Paul Valéry

A French poet and essayist drew more far-ranging conclusions. Too old to fight, Paul Valéry (1871–1945) watched the war from a privileged position, at the secretariat of the national news agency Havas. For Valéry, soon to be elected to the Académie Française, the war brought an end to the long world supremacy of Europe, and its spirit and values. In a 1919 essay he reminded his readers that progress was not a necessary aspect of human history. In fact, he said, history is just as strongly marked by periods of regression, and civilizations are mortal. The suggestion that the twentieth century, with all its scientific and artistic triumphs, might be an age of regression, is still a question well worth facing.

   Valéry raised other questions, too. Was creeping mass society—the "perfect and final ant-hill"—a serious threat? Was Europe fated to return to relative insignificance commensurate with its puny size? Is it true that history is myth, and that "in the beginning was the Fable"? Such fears and suggestions were to affect the rest of the century and politics, ideological debates, and literary and historical criticism. We might consider whether Valéry was right when he asserted the "absolute law that everywhere, in every place, in every period of civilization, in every form of belief . . . the false supports the true; truth has falsehood for an ancestor, as its cause, its author, and its point of origin. . . . All antiquity, all causality, every human principle, are fabulous inventions and obey the simple laws of invention."

From The Intellectual Crisis *(1919)*

Today, on an immense platform which might be that of Elsinore, but runs instead from Basle to Cologne, touching the sands of Nieuport, the marshes of the Somme, the granites of Alsace, and the chalky plateaus of Champagne—the European Hamlet stares at millions of ghosts.

But he is an intellectual Hamlet. He meditates on the life and death of truths. For phantoms he has all the subjects of our controversies; for regrets he has all our titles to glory; he bows under the weight of discoveries and learning, unable to renounce and unable to resume this limitless activity. He reflects on the boredom of recommencing the past, on the folly of always striving to be original. He wavers between one abyss and the other, for two dangers still threaten the world: order and disorder.

It he takes a skull in his hands, the skull is illustrious.—"Whose was it?"—That was *Leonardo.* He invented the flying man, but the flying man has hardly fulfilled the purpose of the inventor; we know that the flying man mounted on his great swan (*il grande uccello sopra del dosso del suo magno cecero*) has other uses in our days than to go fetch snow from the mountain-tops and sprinkle it over city streets in the heat of summer. . . . And this other skull is that of *Leibnitz,* who dreamed of universal peace. And this was *Kant, Kant who begat Hegel, who begat Marx, who begat . . .*

Hamlet hardly knows what to do with all these skulls. But if he throws them away! . . . Will he then cease to be himself? His fearfully lucid mind surveys the passage from war to peace. This transition is more dangerous, more obscure than the passage from peace to war; all nations are convulsed by it. "And I, the European intellect, what will become of me? . . . And what is peace?" he asks. *"Peace is perhaps the state of things in which the natural hostility of man toward man is manifested by creation, in place of the destruction which marks a war.* It is the period of creative competition and the struggle of inventions. But as for me, am I not weary of inventing? Have I not exhausted the desire for extreme attempts and made a vice of my skillful fabrications? Must I abandon my difficult duties and my transcendent ambitions? Should I follow the movement like Polonius, who has become the editor of a great newspaper? like Laertes, who is somewhere in the aviation? like Rosenkrantz, who does I don't know what under a Russian name?

"Phantoms, farwell! The world has no more need of you. Nor of me. The world, which has given the name of 'progress' to its tendency toward a fatal precision, is seeking to unite the blessings of life with the advantages of death. A certain confusion still reigns, but yet a little while and all will be made clear; at last we shall behold the miracle of a strictly animal society, a perfect and final ant-hill."

II

Now, the present situation permits of this capital question: Will Europe retain its leadership in all activities?

Will Europe become *what she is in reality:* that is, a little cape of the Asiatic continent?

Or will Europe remain *what she seems to be:* that is, the most precious part of the terrestrial universe, the pearl of the globe, the brain of a vast body?

In order to set forth this alternative in all its rigor, I will take the liberty of developing a sort of fundamental theorem.

Consider a map which shows the whole of the habitable world. This whole is divided into regions, and in each of these regions there is a certain density of population, a certain quality of men. To each of these regions also corresponds a natural wealth—a more or less fertile soil, a more or less precious subsoil, a more or less watered territory, more or less adapted to transportation, etc. These characteristics enable us to classify these regions at any epoch, in such a way that at any epoch *the state of the living world can be defined by a system of inequalities between the inhabited regions of its surface.*

At any moment the *history* of the following moment depends on this given inequality.

Let us now examine, not this theoretical classification, but the classification which existed in reality, and still existed yesterday. We perceive a fact which is both remarkable in itself and extremely familiar to us: The little region of Europe stands at the head of the classification, and so has stood for centuries. In spite of its small area, and although the wealth of the soil is not extraordinary, it dominates the picture. By what miracle? Certainly the miracle must reside in the quality of its population. This quality must compensate for the smaller number of men, square miles, and tons of ore assigned to Europe. Put the Empire of India in one scale of a balance; put the United Kingdom in the other. See: the balance inclines toward the scale with the lighter weight!

Here is an extraordinary upset of equilibrium. But its consequences are more extraordinary still: *they lead us to foresee a progressive change in the opposite direction.*

We suggested a moment ago that the quality of its men must determine the preeminence of Europe. I cannot analyze this quality in detail, but I find by rapid examination that burning desire, ardent and disinterested curiosity, a happy blend of imagination and logical precision, a scepticism that is not pessimistic and a mysticism that is not resigned . . . are the more specifically active qualities of the European psyche.

A single example of this European spirit—it is an example of the first rank and of paramount importance. Greece—for all the shores of the Mediterranean belong in Europe, Smyrna and Alexandria being as European as Athens or Marseilles—Greece invented geometry. It was a foolhardy enterprise; we are still disputing over the *possibility* of such folly.

In order to achieve this fantastic creation, what had to be done? Remember that neither the Egyptians nor the Chinese, the Chaldeans nor the Hindus ventured so far. Reflect that it was an enthralling adventure, a conquest a thousand times more precious and positively more poetic than that of the Golden Fleece. No mere sheepskin is worth the proposition of Pythagoras.

Geometry was an enterprise demanding gifts which are generally incompatible. It required Argonauts of the mind, hardy pilots who would let themselves neither be lost in their thoughts, nor distracted by their impressions. Neither the fragility of the premises which bore them on, nor the sublety or infinity of the inferences which they were exploring, could divert them from their course. They were equidistant from the variable Negroes and the indefinite yogis. They adjusted common speech to precise reasoning, an extraordinary delicate and improbable achievement. They analyzed motor and visual operations of great complexity. They made these operations correspond to grammatical and linguistic properties. Blind seers, they trusted in speech to guide them through space. . . . And space itself, as the centuries passed, became an always richer and more surprising creation; it developed along with thought, which was acquiring more mastery over itself and placing more confidence both in the power of reason and in the initial subtlety which had provided it with such incomparable tools: definitions, axioms, lemmata, theorems, problems, porisms, and the rest.

I should need a whole book to discuss the subject. I only wished to specify, in a few words, one of the characteristic acts of the European genius. This very example carries me back to my original thesis.

I was arguing that the inequality which has so long been observed to favor Europe might, *by its own effects,* be changed progressively into an opposite sort of inequality. This is what I called by the ambitious name of a fundamental theorem.

How can we demonstrate this proposition?—I will take the same example, that of Greek geometry, and ask the reader to consider the effects of this discipline through the ages. Little by little, very slowly but very surely, one can see it assuming such authority that all researches and all acquired experience tend irresistibly to borrow its rigorous manner, its scrupulous economy of 'matter,' its automatic generalization, its subtle methods, and that infinite prudence which permits it the wildest daring. . . . Modern science was born from this education in the grand style.

But once it was born, once tried and rewarded by its practical applications, our science, becoming a means of power, a means of concrete domination, a stimulant of wealth, a device for exploiting the capital of the planet, ceased to be an artistic activity, and an end in itself; instead it has become an exchange value. The utility of knowledge makes it a *commodity,* desired no longer by a few distinguished enthusiasts, but by Everyman.

This commodity, as a result, will be prepared in more and more convenient or comestible forms; it will be distributed to a larger and larger circle of buyers; it will be transformed into something commercial, something which is imitated and produced almost everywhere.

Result: the inequality which used to exist between the different regions of the world, in respect to the mechanical arts, applied sciences, and scientific methods of war or peace—the inequality on which European predominance was based—tends gradually to disappear.

Hence, *the classification of the habitable regions of the world tends to become such that brute size, numbers, and statistical elements—population, area, raw materials—will at last exclusively determine this classification of the compartments of the world.*

And hence, the balance which inclined to our side, although we *seemed* lighter, is slowly beginning to change its direction—as if we had stupidly taken the invisible weight which bore us down and cast it into the other scale. *We have been fools enough to make forces proportional to masses.*

This phenomenon of our times might be compared with another, which can be observed in the heart of every nation; it consists in the diffusion of culture, and in the accession to culture of larger and larger categories of individuals.

To predict the consequences of this diffusion, and determine whether it will necessarily produce a degradation, would be attempting a delightfully complicated problem of intellectual physics.

For the speculative mind the charm of this problem arises first from its resemblance to the physical fact of diffusion, and thence from the sudden change of this resemblance into a profound difference, as soon as the thinker returns to his first subject, which was *men* and not *molecules.*

A drop of wine will fall into water and hardly color it; after a rosy mist the wine tends to disappear. This is the physical fact. But now suppose that some time after this disappearance and this return to limpidity, we saw drops of *pure wine* being formed here and there in this vessel which seemed once more to contain only *pure water—* our wonder would have no bounds. . . .

This miracle of Cana is not impossible in the field of intellectual and social physics. We then speak of *genius* and oppose it to diffusion.

A short time ago we were considering a curious balance, which moved contrary to weight. Now we are watching a liquid system which passes, as if spontaneously, from homogeneous to heterogeneous, from a thorough mixture to complete separation. . . . These paradoxical images give the simplest and most practical representation of the rôle played in the world by what has been called—for five or ten thousand years—the Mind.

"But can the European mind, or at least its most precious elements, be totally diffused? The exploitation of the globe, the equalization of techniques, democracy— these phenomena point to a *deminutio capitis,* a loss of rights, by Europe; should they be taken as irrevocable decisions of destiny? Or have we some liberty *against* this menacing conspiracy of things?"

It is perhaps by seeking this liberty that one creates it. However, for such a research, we must temporarily abandon the consideration of groups, and study the struggle of personal life against social life in the thinking individual.

Extraneous Remarks *(1927)*

In modern times, not one great power, not one empire in Europe has been able to remain at the top, to extend its influence, or even to hold on to its conquests for longer than fifty years. The greatest men have failed in that direction; even the most successful have led their countries to ruin. Charles V, Louis XIV, Napoleon, Metternich, Bismarck—average duration: forty years. No exceptions.

Europe had the ability to submit, to govern and to regulate the rest of the world to European ends. It had invincible means and the men who had created them. Far inferior to these were the men who disposed of her fortunes. They fed on the past: they only knew how to recreate the past. Also the opportunity has gone. European history and political traditions; its petty, short-sighted, shop-worn quarrels; its jealousies and envy of its neighbors; and in short the lack of insight, the narrow-mindedness inherited from the period when Europe was as ignorant and as weak as other parts of the globe, made it miss this great opportunity, the existence of which it did not even suspect at the right time. Napoleon seems to be the only man who had any inkling of what could happen and of what should be undertaken. He thought on the scale of the world as it was, was not understood, and admitted it. But he came too soon; the time was not ripe; his means were far less than ours. After him people again started surveying their neighbors' acres and thinking in terms of the immediate present.

The wretched Europeans preferred to play at being Normans or Burgundians to taking over, throughout the world, the great role that the Romans had known how to play, and to maintain for centuries, in the world of their time. Their numbers and their means were nothing in comparison to ours; but they found in the entrails of their chickens more correct and consequential ideas than all our political science contains. . . .

Europe visibly aspires to be governed by an American commission. Its entire policy is directed to that end.

Not knowing how to rid ourselves of our history, we will be relieved of it by a fortunate people who have almost none. They are a happy people and they will force their happiness on us. . . .

History is the most dangerous product that the chemistry of the intellect has invented. Its properties are well known. It engenders dreams, it intoxicates the people, it begets false memories, it exaggerates their reactions, keeps their old wounds open, disturbs their sleep, leads them to delusions of grandeur or of persecution, and makes nations bitter, arrogant, insufferable and vain.

History can justify anything. It can teach nothing with restraint, for it contains everything and gives examples of everything.

How many books have been written called: *Lessons in This, Instructions in That!* . . . And there is nothing more ridiculous to reread after the events which followed the events that these books attempt to interpret in the light of the future.

In the present state of the world, the danger of allowing oneself to be seduced by history is greater than ever it was.

The political phenomena of our time are accompanied and complicated by a change in scale without parallel, or rather by a change in the *order of things*. The world to which we are beginning to belong, both as men and as nations, is not a *replica* of the world with which we were familiar. The system of causes which governs the fate of us all, extending from now on over the whole globe, makes all of it resound with each concussion: there are no more local problems, no more finite questions to be dealt with on the spot.

History, as it was formerly understood, was presented as a series of parallel chronological tables with accidental transversals indicated here and there between them. A few attempts at synchronization gave no results other than a sort of demonstration of their futility. What was going on in Peking in Caesar's time, or in Zambesi in Napoleon's, was going on on another planet. But *melodic* history is no longer possible. All political themes are entangled and every event that takes place immediately assumes a multitude of simultaneous and inseparable meanings.

The politics of a Richelieu or a Bismarck are lost and lose their meaning in this new environment. The ideas that they made use of in their schemes, the aims that they could advance to satisfy the ambitions of their people, the forces which figured in their calculations, all become of no import. The main object of politics was, and still is for some, *to acquire territory*. Coercion was used, this coveted territory was taken from someone, and all was over. But who cannot see that those enterprises which consisted of a conference, followed by a duel, followed by a pact, will have such inevitable general consequences in the future that *nothing is more likely to happen than that the whole world becomes involved,* and that one can never foresee nor limit the *almost immediate results* of what one has begun.

All the genius of the great governments of the past is exhausted, made impotent and even *worthless* by the enlargement and increase in the interdependence of political phenomena; for it is certainly not genius, not strength of character or intellect, not tradition (even British) which can now boast of being able to counteract or modify at will the conditions and the reactions of a human world to which the old *political geometry* and the old *political mechanics* are not at all suited.

Europe makes me think of an object that finds itself suddenly transplanted into a more complex sphere, where its known characteristics remain the same in appearance but are subject to quite different *interpretations*. In particular the predictions and the traditional forecasts that once could be made become more futile than ever.

The consequences of the war demonstrate that events which, formerly, would have determined for a long time to come, and *in the sense of their results,* the aspect and the trend of politics in general, have in a few years and in consequence of the number of participants, of the enlargement of the stage, and of the complication of divergent interests, been as though drained of their energy, amortized or contradicted by their immediate consequences.

One must wait until such transformations become the rule. The further we go, the less simple and the less predictable will be the results, and the less will political undertakings and even interventions by force, in other words direct and obvious actions, be what one expected them to be. Their extent, their superficialities, their aggregate effect, their interconnections, the impossibility of localizing them, the promptitude of their repercussions will increasingly impose a very different kind of politics than that of the present.

With effects so rapidly becoming independent of their causes, and even antagonistic to their causes, perhaps it will now be considered puerile, dangerous and insane to *seek out events*—a habit essentially due to history and sustained by it. It is not that, in the meanwhile, there will no longer be events and *monumental moments;* there will be prodigious ones! But those whose function it is to await them, or prepare them, or to ward them off, will of necessity learn more and more to beware of their results. It will no longer suffice to combine the will with the ability in order to undertake some enterprise. Nothing has been more destroyed by the last war than the pretention to foresight. But it seems to me that historical knowledge was not lacking?

Russia

Of all the great powers involved in the First World War, Russia was the least able to cope with the needs of a modern conflict in which production and supply counted at least as much as martial valor. Though it was becoming industrialized, the country and its government were still a hundred years behind the West, politically as well as economically. And when the unwieldy machinery of tsarist autocracy collapsed under the strains of three years of war, this evidence of failure was quick to bring the political revolution that had been brewing since 1905. During the spring and summer of 1917, power passed from one political group or personality to another, each under fire from more radical adversaries, each in turn succumbing to an appeal from further left. The final debate was held between the moderate Social Democrats and the Bolsheviks. The former refused to go too far in the direction of a radical revolutionary program; they favored a Constituent Assembly that would define the country's new regime and laws, and in the meantime proposed to continue the war on the side of the Allies. The Bolsheviks, at least after Lenin's appearance in Petersburg in April 1917, called for all power to the Soviets (councils) of Soldiers', Workers', and Peasants' Deputies, for distribution of the land, and for an immediate peace. Assured of the support of the Petrograd Soviet, the Bolsheviks seized power on November 7, 1917; organized a Soviet Republic; ended the war with the peace of Brest-Litovsk; and succeeded in maintaining their power through four years of bloody civil and foreign war.

Two Impotent Governments

From the beginning of the hostilities, the tsar's ministers had little influence against the will of the military authorities. Much of the chaos and corruption that had overtaken Russia by 1917 must be attributed to its attempt to wage a twentieth-century war with the administrative and political structure of an eighteenth-century country.

Meetings of the Council of Ministers (1915)

AUGUST 24, 1915

Scherbatov: The Council of Ministers knows that there were disturbances in Moscow which ended in bloodshed. . . . There were even more serious disorders at Ivanovo-Voznesensk when it was necessary to fire on the crowd with the result that sixteen were killed and thirty wounded. There was a critical moment when it was uncertain what the garrison would do. . . .

Shakhovskoi: I have information . . . that the workmen are quite aroused. Any kind of spark may start a fire. . . .

Goremykin: . . . I should like to ask the Minister of the Interior what measures he is taking to put an end to the lawlessness . . . going on everywhere. His principal function is to protect the State from disorder and danger.

Scherbatov: The Minister of the Interior is taking all the measures which his duty and present circumstances permit. I have more than once called your attention to the abnormal position of the Minister. Half of European Russia is out of his jurisdiction. Elsewhere in the rear the real government is in the hands of lieutenants who have despotic inclinations and little understanding. I have brought to your notice the fact that even in Petrograd, which gives the tone to the whole of Russia, the Minister of the Interior is a mere resident. He has only as much power as the war lords will grant him. . . . How can you expect me to fight the growing revolutionary movement when I am refused the support of the troops on the ground that they are unreliable, that one can not be certain that they will fire on the mob? You can not quiet the whole of Russia by the police alone, especially now when the ranks of the police are being thinned out hourly, and the population is growing daily more excited by the speeches in the Duma, by newspaper stories, by continuous defeats, and rumors of disorders in the rear. The demonstrations and disorders come about from most unforeseen causes. At Moscow patriotic reasons were responsible. Newspapers gave out that the Dardanelles had been taken and that our troops had recaptured Kovno. One silver-tongued orator was arrested and trouble started. . . . I agree that something ought to be done. But how can you do anything when you have no support, when those in responsible places (ministers) can not get a hearing (from the Emperor) on questions on which the fate of the State may depend? . . . I have in my portfolio several telegrams from governors. They inform me that the flow of refugees, German colonists and Jews driven out by the military authorities is ever rising and that the local population is so aroused against the newcomers that they receive them with clubs. . . . The governors ask for instructions and help. What can the Minister of the Interior reply? . . . Among the workmen, as among the population in general, there are terrible reports of graft in connection with war orders. . . .

Formation and Program of Provisional Government (1917)

Citizens, the Provisional Executive Committee of the members of the Duma, with the aid and support of the garrison of the capital and its inhabitants, has triumphed over the dark forces of the Old Regime to such an extent as to enable it to organize a more stable executive power.

From *Documents of Russian History,* 1914–1917 ed. F. A. Golder, tr. E. Aronsberg (New York: Appleton-Century-Crofts, Inc., 1927).

The cabinet will be guided in its actions by the following principles:

1. An immediate general amnesty for all political and religious offenses, including terrorist acts, military revolts, agrarian offenses, etc.

2. Freedom of speech and press; freedom to form labor unions and to strike. These political liberties should be extended to the army in so far as war conditions permit.

3. The abolition of all social, religious and national restrictions.

4. Immediate preparation for the calling of a Constituent Assembly, elected by universal and secret vote, which shall determine the form of government and draw up the Constitution for the country.

5. In place of the police, to organize a national militia with elective officers, and subject to the local self-governing body.

6. Elections to be carried out on the basis of universal, direct, equal, and secret suffrage.

7. The troops that have taken part in the revolutionary movement shall not be disarmed or removed from Petrograd.

8. On duty and in war service, strict military discipline should be maintained, but when off duty, soldiers should have the same public rights as are enjoyed by other citizens.

The Provisional Government wishes to add that it has no intention of taking advantage of the existence of war conditions to delay the realization of the above-mentioned measures of reform.

President of the Duma,
M. Rodzianko
President of the Council of Ministers,
Prince Lvov
Ministers Miliukov, Nekrasov,
Manuilov, Konovalov, Tereschenko,
Vl. Lvov, Shingarev, Kerenski.
March 16, 1917

The All-Russian Congress of Soviets

During the summer of 1917 the Petrograd Soviet tended to act as if it were the representative or head of all the other Soviets that had sprung up throughout Russia. This was a position contested both by the moderate government to which it stood in opposition and by various other groups. The critics of the Soviet argued that Petrograd was not Russia, and that the Petrograd Soviet, which was entitled to speak for the soldiers and workers in that city, had no right to speak for anyone else. To meet this criticism, the Petrograd Soviet decided to call an All-Russian Congress of Soviets of Workers and Soldiers' Deputies to meet in its city in June. It was here (as we can see in the following selections) that the moderate socialists and the more extreme radicals clashed in an attempt to secure the support of the Congress—with Tseretselli speaking for the Mensheviks, Kerenski for the Social Revolutionists, and Lenin for the extreme Left. After days of debate, the resolutions of the Mensheviks and Social Revolutionists, who stood together, won a clear majority by a vote of 543 to 126.

Invitation to the Congress

To all Soviets of Workers' and Soldiers' Deputies and Army Committees:

The Executive Committee of the Petrograd Soviet . . . has resolved to call, June 14, an All-Russian Congress of Soviets of Workers' and Soldiers' Deputies and army organizations at the front.

To this Congress, all the existing Soviets . . . and army organs are asked. Selections should be made according to the regulations laid down by the All-Russian Conference of Soviets of Workers' and Soldiers' Deputies:

Soviets numbering from

   25.000 to   50.000 have 2 delegates
   50.000 to   75.000   ″   3   ″
   75.000 to 100.000   ″   4   ″
100.000 to 150.000   ″   5   ″
150.000 to 200.000   ″   6   ″
Over 200.000   ″   8   ″

Delegates from the front should represent armies and not regiments, etc. It would be best if the delegates were selected at the army congresses. . . . Each army is entitled to no more than 8 delegates. . . .

Soviets having less than 25.000 members should combine. . . .

The Executive Committee of the Petrograd Soviet of Workers' and Soldiers' Deputies

Clash Between Moderates and Bolsheviks (June 1917)

TSERETSELLI'S SPEECH

In taking upon itself the fight for universal peace, the Russian revolution has also to take over the war, begun by other governments, the end of which does not depend on the efforts of the Russian revolution alone. . . .

In order that it may succeed in its object, the Provisional Government must say clearly and emphatically . . . that it has broken with the old imperialist policy, and must propose to the Allies that the first question in order of importance is to reexamine

From *Documents of Russian History.*
From *Documents of Russian History.*

on a new basis all agreements made until now . . . so that this general platform of war and peace may be given out, not only in the name of the Russian revolution, but in the name of all those who are allied with us. . . . We are moving in that direction. . . . We should do nothing which would break our ties with the Allies. . . . The worst thing that could happen to us would be a separate peace. It would be ruinous for the Russian revolution, ruinous for international democracy. . . . A separate peace is both undesirable and impossible. Should we bring about a situation that would break relations with the Allies and necessitate a separate peace, the Russian revolution would be obliged, immediately afterwards, to take up arms on the side of the German coalition. Even if we brush aside the talk of a possible attack by Japan . . . picture to yourself the condition of the Russian revolution after the conclusion of a separate peace, while the rest of the world goes on fighting. Her economic and financial ties with the powers with which she is now united would be severed. . . . Under the circumstances, can there be any doubt that the German coalition, continuing with the war, would force the weaker side to give military support? . . . He who talks about a separate peace, talks about Utopia. . . .

We come to the question of taking the offensive, the actions of the Minister of War, Comrade Kerenski, and the whole Provisional Government, in their efforts to strengthen the front and the army. It is said that due to pressure from imperialist circles, the Provisional Government, and the Minister of War in particular, are taking steps to bring about immediate action at the front, in order thereby to put an end to the political campaign for universal peace, which this same Provisional Government is carrying on. . . . We believe that the measures taken by Comrade Kerenski tend to strengthen the cause of the revolution and prepare the way for the success of our object in the field of international relations and universal peace. It is clear to us that now, when our country is threatened from the outside, the Russian revolutionary army should be strong, able to take the offensive. . . . Comrades, this inactivity which has been going on at the front does not strengthen, but weakens and disorganizes our revolution and army. . . .

I should like to paint in a few strokes the picture of our internal situation. . . . The Russian revolution has taken over the burdensome inheritance of the last three years' war and the last three years' reaction. The economic disorganization, the crushing financial difficulties, the food chaos which threatens to bring the country into a state of famine—all these are the inheritance of the old regime. We firmly believe that we can solve these problems, but we know that they can be solved only if the Russian democracy will make unheard-of sacrifices and self-denials. The most radical and extreme fiscal measures could not at the present moment liquidate altogether the financial crisis, and bring the finances of the country into a normal condition. A country that spends sixteen billion and has a net income of not more than half that amount cannot be saved by mere financial reforms, by fundamental reorganization. Only great self-sacrifice and mighty efforts can help at this moment. . . .

All classes of the population should be called upon to make these sacrifices and self-denials. . . . We are charged with not having done this so far in economic regulation, but laws alone will not benefit Russia. . . . Even that revolutionary organization [the Bolsheviks] which criticizes the acts of the Government and demands a speeding up, has nothing better to offer than declarations and principles. Time is necessary to put these into acts. . . .

As to the land question—we regard it as our duty at the present time to prepare the ground for a just solution of that problem by the Constituent Assembly. We believe that the question of the passing of the land into the hands of the laboring class can be, and should be, definitely settled by the Constituent Assembly. . . .

At the present moment, there is not a political party in Russia which would say: Hand the power over to us, resign, and we will take your place. Such a party does not exist in Russia (*Lenin:* "It does exist."). . . . The Bolsheviks say: When we have a majority, or when the majority comes over to our point of view, then the power should be seized. Comrade Lenin, you said that. At least the Bolsheviks, and you with them, say it in their official statements.

Gentlemen, until now there has not been a single party in Russia which has come out openly for getting for itself all power at once, although there have been such cries by irresponsible groups on the Right and the Left. . . . The Right says, let the Left run the Government, and we and the country will draw our conclusions; and the Left says, let the Right take hold, and we and the country will draw our conclusions. . . . Each side hopes that the other will make such a failure, that the country will turn to it for leadership.

But, gentlemen, this is not the time for that kind of a play. . . . In order to solve the problems of the country, we must unite our strength and must have a strong Government . . . strong enough to put an end to experiments dangerous for the fate of the revolution, . . . experiments that may lead to civil war. . . .

This, gentlemen, is our policy. . . .

LENIN'S SPEECH

The first and fundamental question which we have to answer is: What are these Soviets which are meeting in this All-Russian Congress? What is this revolutionary democracy about which so much is said? To speak of revolutionary democracy before the All-Russian Congress of Soviets, and to keep silent about its formation, its class character, its role in the revolution, is a strange state of affairs. We had presented to us a program of a bourgeois parliamentary republic, a program of reform, which is accepted by all bourgeois governments, including our own; and at the same time we are told of a revolutionary democracy. To whom do they say this? To the Soviets. I ask you, is there any bourgeois, democratic, republican country in Europe where an institution similar to the Soviet exists? Of course, you will say no. It does not exist, and cannot exist, because it is either a bourgeois government, with these "plans" of reform which are presented to us, and which have been presented numerous times, and have remained on paper; or this institution—this new type of "government" which the revolution has created, and which has appeared before in history, at a time of great revolutionary enthusiasm, for example in France in 1792 and 1871, in Russia in 1905. The Soviet is an institution that does not exist in any bourgeois parliamentary government, and cannot exist alongside a bourgeois government. The Soviet is that new, more democratic type of government which we called, in our party resolutions, peasant-proletarian, democratic republic, and in which the whole authority belongs to the Soviet of Workers' and Soldiers' Deputies. It is vain to think that it is a theoretic question, vain to imagine that it can be passed over, vain to pretend that some other kind of institution can exist together with the Soviet. Yes, they exist together. But it gives rise to numerous misunderstandings, conflicts, and divisions. . . . One of the two: either the ordinary bourgeois government or the Soviet. A bourgeois government would make the Soviets unnecessary. They would either be dispersed by the generals, the counterrevolutionary generals who hold the army in hand, who pay no attention to our eloquent Minister of War, or they would die an inglorious death. There is no other alternative. We cannot stand still. We must either go forward or backward.

The Soviet is the form of government . . . which the revolution itself brought forth. Without it the revolution cannot conquer . . . the Soviets cannot go on as they are now. . . . We are told that the first Provisional Government was bad. At that time, when the Bolsheviks said: "Do not support, do not have any confidence in that Government," we were overwhelmed with charges of anarchism. Now everybody admits that the Government was bad. In what respect is this coalition government of almost-socialistic ministers better than its predecessor? Let us stop discussing programs, projects, and let's do something. . . . We are asked, is it possible to establish Socialism in Russia immediately, to reorganize the State from top to bottom? . . . Nowhere in the world in time of war can you go from pure capitalism to pure Socialism, but there should be something between, something new, unheard-of, because hundreds of millions are dying in the criminal war of the capitalists. It is not a question of reforms in the future—these are empty words—but of doing something which needs to be done now. If you wish to appeal to the "revolutionary" democracy, then differentiate between it and the "reform" democracy in a capitalist ministry. . . . That which is proposed is a transition to reform-democracy in a capitalistic government. It may be excellent, and looks well from the point of view of western Europe. But just now a whole series of countries are on the brink of ruin, and those practical measures which are, seemingly, so complicated that it is necessary to work them out, as we were told by the previous speaker . . . can be put into force now. These measures are very clear. Tseretselli said that there is not a political party in Russia which would say that it is ready to take all the power into its hands. I say there is. Our party is ready at any minute to do that. (*Applause and laughter.*) Laugh all you want to. . . . Our program in relation to the economic crisis is this—to demand the publication of all those unheard-of profits, reaching to 500%, to 800%, which the capitalists make on war orders; to arrest 50 or 100 of the more important capitalists and, in this way, break all the threads of intrigue. Without such a step, all this talk of peace without annexation and indemnity is worthless. Our next step would be to announce to all the nations, separate from their Governments, that we regard all capitalists—French, English, all—as robbers.

Your own *Izvestia* has become confused. In place of peace without annexation and indemnity, it proposes the *status quo*.[1] We believe that the Russian Republic should not oppress a single nation—neither the Finns, nor the Ukrainians, with whom the Minister of War is now quarreling. . . . We cannot make a peace without annexation

---

[1] existing order.

and indemnity until we are willing to give up our own annexations. It is really funny, this play! Every workman in Europe is laughing at it. He says: They are calling on the people to overthrow their bankers, while they, themselves, send their bankers into the Ministry. Arrest them; lay bare their schemes; find out their intrigues. But you will not do this, although you have the power. . . . You have lived through 1905 and 1917. You know that revolution is not made to order; that in other countries it was brought about through bloody uprisings, but in Russia there is no group or class that could oppose the power of the Soviets. Today or tomorrow, let us propose peace to all the peoples by breaking with all the capitalistic classes, and in a short time the peoples of France and Germany will agree to it, because their countries are perishing. . . .

If Russia were a revolutionary democracy, not merely in words, but in deeds, she would lead the revolutionary movement and not make peace with the capitalists; she would not talk so much of peace without annexation and indemnity, but would put an end to all forms of annexation in Russia itself, and would announce that she considers every annexation as robbery. If she were to do that, an imperialistic military offensive would not be necessary. . . .

You can write on paper what you please. But as long as the capitalists are in majority in the Government, it makes no difference what you say, and how well you say it; the fact is that the war remains an imperialistic one. . . . It is easy to write, peace without annexations, but see what has happened in Albania, Greece, and Persia since the coalition government was formed. . . . The only way to end the war is by going on with the revolution. . . . If you were to take power into your own hands, if it were used against the Russian capitalists, then the laborers of other countries would believe you, and you could offer them peace. . . . The question is: Shall we advance or retreat? In revolutionary times, you cannot stand still. A military offensive now is a setback for the revolution; it means the continuation of the imperialistic butchery of millions. . . . The taking over of the power by the revolutionary proletariat, with the help of the poorest peasants, is the taking over of the revolutionary fight for peace . . . and gives assurance that power and victory will be given to the revolutionary workmen in Russia, and in the whole world.

KERENSKI'S SPEECH

Comrades:

You have been told of 1792 and 1905. How did 1792 end in France? It ended by the fall of the republic and the rise of a dictator. How did 1905 end? With the triumph of reaction. And now, in 1917, we are doing that which we could have done earlier. The problem of the Russian Socialist parties and the Russian democracy is to prevent such an end as was in France—to hold on to the revolutionary conquests already made; to see to it that our comrades who have been let out from prison do not return there; that Comrade Lenin, who has been abroad, may have the opportunity to speak here again, and not be obliged to fly back to Switzerland. (*Applause.*) We must see to it that the historic mistakes do not repeat themselves; that we do not bring on a situation that would make possible the return of reaction, the victory of force over democracy.

Certain methods of fighting have been indicated to us. We have been told that we should not fight with words, nor talk of annexation, but should show by deeds that we are fighting against capitalism. What means are recommended for this fight? To arrest Russian capitalists. (*Laughter.*) Comrades, I am not a Social-Democrat. I am not a Marxist, but I have the highest respect for Marx, his teaching, and his disciples. But Marxism has never taught such childlike and primitive means. I dare say that it is likely that Citizen Lenin has forgotten what Marxism is. He cannot call himself a Socialist, because Socialism nowhere recommends the settling of questions of economic war, of the war of classes in their economic relations, the question of the economic reorganization of the State, by arresting people, as is done by Asiatic despots. . . . Every Marxist who knows his Socialism would say that capitalism is of an international character, that the arrest of a few capitalists in a certain State would not affect the iron law of the economic development of a given period. . . . You [Bolsheviks] recommend childish prescriptions—"arrest, kill, destroy." What are you—Socialists or the police of the old regime? (*Uproar. Lenin:* "You should call him to order.")

This gathering of the flower of the Russian democracy understands its problems. Such prescriptions do not excite it, but among the masses such words will be taken seriously. We do not cater to the mob; we are not demagogues. What we say now, we said ten years ago. We are warm defenders of the autonomy of Finland and the Ukraine. We say this: Members of the Provisional Government have not and do not desire to have absolute power, and until the meeting of the Constituent Assembly, they have no right to declare the independence of this or that part of Russian territory. . . .

As to fraternization—why is it that while German officers fraternize in our trenches, they do not fraternize on the French front? Why is it that while our front is inactive, the German forces attack the English? . . . Why is it that this policy of fraternization falls in so well with the plan of the German General Staff on the Russian front? . . .

I can understand that there are people who are naive enough to believe that an exchange of a piece of bread for a glass of vodka by a Russian soldier brings the kingdom of Socialism nearer, but we, who have borne the brunt of the old regime on our shoulders, cannot afford the luxury of such a naiveté. . . .

You [Bolsheviks] recommend that we follow the road of the French revolution of 1792. You recommend the way of further disorganization of the country. . . . When you, in alliance with reaction, shall destroy our power, then you will have a real dictator. It is our duty, the duty of the Russian democracy, to say: Don't repeat the historic mistakes. You are asked to follow the road that was once followed by France, and which will lead Russia to a new reaction, to a new shedding of democratic blood.

The November Revolution, 1917

The paper Izvestia *"The News" had been started in the early days of the revolution by a body calling itself the Committee of Petrograd Journalists. Soon it was taken over by the Petrograd Soviet and published by the Central Executive Committee of the Soviet. The issue of November 8, 1917, excerpts from which follow, was the last published by the Central Executive Committee. On the following day the paper was taken over by the Bol-*

sheviks and henceforward toed the party line. But in these, its last free reports, we can follow the swift unfolding of the November Revolution, in which a handful of determined Bolsheviks grasped the power that the Kerenski government could not longer defend.

From Izvestia

THE COUP

Kerenski remained at the office of the Staff from 2 until 7 A.M. . . . . At 7 he set out for the front. . . . He is expected back any minute. . . . At 8:30 P.M. the Provisional Government at the Winter Palace received an ultimatum signed by the Petrograd Soviet. Members of the government were given 20 minutes in which to surrender and, in case of refusal, they were threatened with having the guns of the Peter and Paul fortress and the cruiser Aurora turned on the Winter Palace. The Government refused to discuss matters and to accept the ultimatum. . . .

News reached us at 2 A.M. that the Winter Palace was taken, that the members of the Government were arrested . . . and locked up at the Peter and Paul fortress.

THE PETROGRAD SOVIET MEETS

The meeting opened at 2:35 P.M. with Trotski in the chair. He said: "In the name of the War-Revolutionary Committee, I announce that the Provisional Government no longer exists. (*Applause.*) Some of the Ministers are already under arrest. (*Bravo.*) Others soon will be. (*Applause.*) The revolutionary garrison, under the control of the War-Revolutionary Committee, has dismissed the Assembly of the Pre-Parliament. (*Loud applause.* "Long live the War-Revolutionary Committee.") . . . The railway stations, post and telegraph offices, the Petrograd Telegraph Agency, and State Bank are occupied." . . .

Trotski continued by saying: "In our midst is Vladimir Ilyich Lenin, who, by force of circumstances, has not been able to be with us all the time. . . . Hail the return of Lenin!" The audience gave him a noisy ovation. . . .

LENIN'S SPEECH

Comrades, the workmen's and peasants' revolution, the need of which the Bolsheviks have emphasized many times, has come to pass. What is the significance of this revolution? Its significance is, in the first place, that we shall have a soviet government, without the participation of bourgeoisie of any kind. The oppressed masses will of themselves form a government. The old state machinery will be smashed into bits and in its place will be created a new machinery of government by the soviet organizations. From now on there is a new page in the history of Russia, and the present, third Russian revolution, shall in its final result lead to the victory of Socialism.

All four excerpts on the November Revolution are from *Documents of Russian History.*

One of our immediate tasks is to put an end to the war at once. But in order to end the war, which is closely bound up with the present capitalistic system, it is necessary to overthrow capitalism itself. In this work we shall have the aid of the world labor movement, which has already begun to develop in Italy, England, and Germany.

A just and immediate offer of peace by us to the international democracy will find everywhere a warm response among the international proletarian masses. In order to secure the confidence of the proletariat, it is necessary to publish at once all secret treaties.

In the interior of Russia a very large part of the peasantry has said: Enough playing with the capitalists; we will go with the workers. We shall secure the confidence of the peasants by one decree, which will wipe out the private property of the landowners. The peasants will understand that their only salvation is in union with the workers.

We will establish a real labor control over production.

We have now learned to work together in a friendly manner, as is evident from the revolution. We have the force of mass organization which has conquered all, and which will lead the proletariat to world revolution. We should now busy ourselves in Russia in building up a proletarian socialist state. Long live the world-wide socialistic revolution.

EDITORIAL COMMENT

Yesterday we said that the Bolshevik uprising is a mad adventure and today, when their attempt is crowned with success, we are of the same mind. We repeat: that which is before us is not a transfer of power to the Soviets, but a seizure of power by one party—the Bolsheviks. Yesterday we said that a successful attempt meant the breaking up of the greatest conquest of the revolution—the Constituent Assembly. Today we add that it means, also, the breaking up of the Congress of Soviets, and perhaps the whole Soviet organization. These are the facts: the Social-Revolutionists and the Social-Democrat Mensheviks have found it impossible under present circumstances to take part in the Congress. This is also the point of view of the men from the front. With the departure of these groups from the Congress, there are left . . . the Bolsheviks. They can call themselves what they please; the fact remains that the Bolsheviks alone took part in the uprising. All the other socialistic and democratic parties protest against it.

How the situation may develop, we do not know, but little good is to be expected. We are quite confident that the Bolsheviks cannot organize a state government. As yesterday, so today, we repeat that what is happening will react worst of all on the question of peace. . . . Today the Pre-Parliament was to vote a special resolution on the question of peace. But the Mariinski Palace was occupied by the Revolutionary Committee, and the Pre-Parliament did not meet.

Peace

The western Allies have often been blamed for the peace which they imposed upon their defeated enemies at Versailles, especially after President Wilson had laid down Fourteen Points upon which a just peace might be based. It is worth remembering that for a good while after Wilson's speech of January 1918 the Germans refused to give his suggestions any serious attention and that, when they had a chance to impose peace upon their defeated enemies to the east, the resulting terms bore no trace of the Wilsonian principles to which Germany itself would appeal before long.

In the spring of 1918 the Treaty of Bucarest turned Rumania into a German colony. The Treaty of Brest-Litovsk imposed conditions disastrous to Russia: the Ukraine, Poland, Finland, and the Baltic states received their independence, and became, in effect, German satellites. Three Transcaucasian provinces were ceded to Turkey. Russia lost 26 percent of its population, 27 percent of its arable land, 26 percent of its railroads, 33 percent of its textile and consumer-goods industries, 73 percent of its iron industries, 75 percent of its coal fields; in addition, it agreed to pay a large war indemnity. The documents that follow illustrate the Communists' attempts to secure a peace "without annexations or indemnities"—and their failure.

Brest-Litovsk: Accounts of the Conference

After securing power in November 1917, the new Russian leaders set out to get the peace they had promised. An armistice was negotiated with Russia's enemies—Germany, Bulgaria, Austria-Hungary, and Turkey—and hostilities ceased on all fronts on December 2 while peace delegations met at Brest-Litovsk. Discussions dragged on when the Central Powers put forward demands that the Soviet delegation felt were contrary to the principles they had laid down. A Russian attempt to break the stalemate by withdrawing from the conference merely led to a resumption of the German advance on a front that had been practically deserted by Russian troops. As the Germans surged forward, the Soviet leaders realized that unless they concluded a peace the Germans would soon be in Petersburg and they out of office. So negotiations were renewed and peace agreed to on Germany's terms.

NOTE TO THE EMBASSIES AT PETROGRAD

Monsieur l'Ambassadeur.

I have the honour to announce that the Congress of Councils of Workmen's, Soldiers', and Peasants' Delegates of All the Russias instituted on 8 November a new Government of the Republic of all the Russias.

Having been appointed Commissary of Foreign Affairs in this Government, I beg to call to the attention of your Excellency the following words, which have been approved by the Congress of the Delegates of the Councils, and contain proposals for a truce and for a democratic peace without annexation and without indemnities, based

---

From the (British) *Daily Review of the Foreign Press*, 26 November 1917.

on the principle of the independence of nations, and of their right to determine the nature of their own development themselves. I have the honour to suggest that you should consider this document in the light of an official proposal for an immediate truce upon all the fronts, and to take immediate steps to set on foot negotiations for peace. The Government, in the name of the Republic of All the Russias, is addressing the same proposal to all the nations and their Governments. Pray accept the assurance of the most perfect respect on the part of the Government of the Councils towards the people of France, which still keeps aloof from peace aspirations, as well as to all other nations who are drained of their blood and exhausted by the prolonged carnage.

(Signed) L. Trotsky
Petrograd, Nov. 22

BREST CONFERENCE SESSION OF FEBRUARY 9, 1918

Trotsky: We considered it necessary *to sum up all our preceding work.* The peace negotiations began with our declaration of Dec. 23 and the declaration of Dec. 25, by which the Quadruple Alliance replied to our declaration. These two declarations formulated the object of the negotiations as being based upon the principle of self-determination of peoples. During a short interval, which could be measured by hours, it appeared that this principle, accepted by both sides, would serve as a means for the solution of these national and territorial questions as arising out of the war. But after an exchange of views on Dec. 27, it became clear that the appeal to this principle was of a character calculated only to complicate all other questions. The points of view of one side, namely, our side, as applied by the other side were a direct negation of the very principle itself. Afterwards all the discussions took an entirely academic character, without any prospect of a practical settlement, because the opposite side was striving, with the aid of complicated logical maneuvers, to draw from the principle of self-determination what, in their opinion, was in accordance with the true situation as disclosed by the military maps.

The question concerning the occupied regions, which was the principal theme of all the discussions, was reduced, after a number of sessions, to the question of the evacuation of these regions by the troops in occupation. . . . So far as we understood it—and we honestly tried to understand it—the situation was as follows: Until the end of the war, so far as Germany was concerned and so far as Austria-Hungary was concerned, there could be no question of the evacuation of occupied territory on any front, owing to military considerations. Our Delegation later understood that the opposite side now had the intention of evacuating these occupied regions on the conclusion of a general peace, when the above-mentioned strategical considerations would have been put on one side. This conclusion, however, also appeared to be wrong. The German and Austro-Hungarian Delegations have refused categorically to make a declaration which could force them to withdraw their troops from the occupied regions, with the exception of the small belt of territory which they proposed to return to Russia. The situation only then became clear. This clarity became, if possible, greater when General Hoffmann, in the name of both Delegations, proposed to us the frontier line which would in future separate Russia from its western neighbors, namely, from Germany and Austria-Hungary, because the separated regions were to be occupied by their troops for an indefinite period, unrestricted by any treaty.

We have already realized during the past discussions that if we were to trace the new frontier of Russia in accordance with the principle of self-determination, then we should have the best guarantee, under present conditions, against military aggression, because all the peoples on both sides of this frontier would be interested in maintaining it. The German conditions and the policy which dictates them, entirely exclude any such kind of guarantees for peaceful relations between Russia on the one side and Germany and Austria-Hungary on the other. The new frontier proposed by the other side is dictated by military and strategical considerations, and from this point of view must be estimated not only the separation from Russia of Poland and Lithuania, but even the separation of the Lettish countries. If such had been the desire of the peoples of those regions, then no danger would arise for the safety of the Russian Republic. Friendly relations with these States, which had freely formed for themselves an independent existence, would follow as a natural consequence of their origin and of their conditions. In such circumstances questions concerning the strategical character of the new frontiers would have for us no important significance. But these new frontiers which the opposite side propose appear to us in a very different light. Germany and Austria-Hungary, while maintaining their troops in the occupied regions, are linking these regions to their States by railways and by other means, and for us the new frontier must thus be considered not as a frontier with Poland, Lithuania, and Courland, and so on, but as a frontier with Germany and Austria-Hungary. Both these States are seeking military expansion, as is clearly shown by their attitude toward the occupied regions. A new question arises for us, therefore, as to what these independent States mean for the Russian Republic in the future. The dependence of these peoples upon these two States will place very near to Russia the new frontier within their territories proposed by Germany and Austria-Hungary. What are really the military conceptions of the other side when they ask for such a frontier? For the purpose of examining this new question from the point of view of the leading military institutions of the Republic, I shall ask for the views of our military advisers. We have here to meet a fresh difficulty.

We have heard nothing of that part of the new frontier which is to run to the south from Brest-Litovsk. The opposite side was of the opinion that this part of the frontier had to be established in discussion with the Delegation of the Kiev Rada.[1] We have decided that, irrespective of the unestablished political state of Ukrainia, there can be no question of a one-sided tracing of the frontier, based upon an agreement with the Rada alone; we declared that the consent of the Delegation of the Council of the People's Commissaries was also necessary. Subsequently the political situation of Ukrainia was defined by its entrance into the Federal Russian Republic. The Delegation of the Central Powers, in spite of their declaration that they would examine the international position of the Ukraine after the conclusion of peace, has hurriedly recognized the independence of Ukrainia, and, to wit, at the very moment when Ukrainia entered

---

[1] The Ukrainian National Assembly.

the Russian Federation. After this date events took place which should have had a decisive influence upon these separate negotiations of the other side with the Kiev Rada. The latter fell under the blow of the Ukrainian Council. The fate of the Rada, inviolable in itself, was accelerated by the fact that the Rada, in its struggle for authority, made attempts, with the help of the Central Powers, to draw the Ukrainian people away from the Russian Federal Republic. We officially informed the opposite side that the Ukrainian Rada was deposed, but, nevertheless, the negotiations with a nonexistent Government have been continued. We proposed to the Austro-Hungarian Delegation, in a private conversation, it is true, but formally, nevertheless, that they should send their representative to Ukrainia with the object of seeing for himself that the Ukrainian Rada no longer existed, and that the negotiations with its Delegation could not have any practical value. We understood that, so far as the Delegations of the Central Powers needed confirmation of facts, they would postpone the signature of the Peace Treaty until the return of their representative from Ukrainia. We have been informed that the signature to the Peace Treaty could not be postponed any longer. Whilst negotiating with the Government of the Federal Russian Republic the Governments of the Central Empires not only, in spite of their former declaration, hurried to recognize the independence of the Ukrainian Republic on Feb. 1, at the very moment when it declared itself to be a part of the Russian Federation; but it is signing a treaty with a Government which, as we have categorically declared to the opposite side, does not exist any longer.

Such conduct is creating doubts if there is any sincerity of purpose on the side of the Central Powers for the establishment of peaceful relations with the Russian Federation. We are striving for peace now as in the beginning of the negotiations. The whole conduct of the opposite side, as far as this question is concerned, is creating the impression that the Central Powers were striving to [message defective] for the representatives of the Russian Republic. Only such a peace treaty will be binding for the Russian Federal Republic and its countries as will be signed by our Delegation.

SESSION OF 10 FEBRUARY, 1918

German Account: The W.T.B. wires give the following conclusion:

On February 10, the Sub-Committee mentioned above held two sittings under the chairmanship of the Austrian Sectional President, Dr. Gratz, when the respective military experts were the principal speakers. The Russian delegates attempted to demonstrate the strategical disadvantages to which Russia would be exposed by the proposed new frontier line, whilst the Germans denied this contention, adding that it was not a matter of the Russo-German frontier, but of the frontier between Russia and the new border States. Agreement, however, could not be reached on this point.

At a plenary sitting held on the same day M. Trotsky, replying to Baron von Kühlmann, denied any knowledge of an alleged order by the Russian Supreme Command urging Russian soldiers to incite German troops against their Generals and officers.

From the (British) *Daily Review of the Foreign Press,* 18 February 1918. The *Deutscher Reichsanzeiger* of 15 February 1918 has an account substantially identical with this.

Dr. Gratz having reported that an agreement could not be reached in the sub-committee over which he had presided, Baron von Kühlmann asked M. Trotsky whether he had any communication to make which might contribute to a satisfactory solution.

M. Trotsky, replying, said his Delegation considered that the decisive hour had arrived. After a bitter attack on Imperialism, M. Trotsky declared that Russia would no longer participate in the war, as she was unwilling to shed the blood of her soldiers in the interests of one party against another. Russia, therefore, had decided to withdraw her army and people from the war. She had notified all peoples and their Governments of her decision, and had ordered the complete demobilization of all the Russian Armies now confronting the armies of Germany, Austria-Hungary, Bulgaria, and Turkey. His Government, however, refused to sanction the conditions of Germany and Austria-Hungary. Russia had abandoned the war, but she was obliged to forego the signing of a peace treaty.

Then follows the declaration of the ending of the state of war, and the demobiliza-tion order, which have already been published.

To this statement of M. Trotsky, Baron von Kühlmann rejoined that, if he analyzed the present position correctly, he found that the Quadruple Alliance was still at war with the Russian Government. Warlike operations were suspended for the time being by the armistice treaty, but on the lapse of this treaty these would automatically revive. If his memory did not deceive him, the real purpose of the armistice was the conclusion of peace. If, therefore, peace were not concluded, and the essential object of the armi-stice should thus vanish, Baron von Kühlmann concluded that warlike operations would revive again after the termination of the prescribed period. The fact that one of the two contracting parties had demobilized its armies would in nowise alter this, either in fact or in law. The existence of the customary international relations between States, and of legal and commercial relations, was the mark of a state of peace. He therefore requested M. Trotsky to state whether the Russian Government intended, in addition to making its declaration regarding the termination of the state of war, to say where the frontiers of Russia ran, as this would be a necessary requisite before the resumption of diplomatic, consular, legal, and commercial relations, and also to say whether the Government of People's Commissioners was willing to resume legal and commercial relations to precisely the same extent as would naturally result from the termination of the state of war.

These questions, he said, it was essential to determine in order to judge whether the Quadruple Alliance was still at war or not.

Baron von Kühlmann then proposed a sitting for the next day, at which the atti-tude of the Central Powers to the latest statement of the Russian Delegation might be made known.

To this proposal M. Trotsky replied that his Delegation had now exhausted all its power, and considered it necessary to return to Petrograd. All communications, he added, which the allied Delegations might make would be deliberated upon, by the Federal Russian Government, and a reply would be given in due course.

On being asked through what channel this exchange of views was to take place, M. Trotsky said that the Russian Delegation had had direct telegraphic communication with Petrograd from Brest-Litovsk. Furthermore, before the inauguration of the armistice negotiations, an understanding had been reached by wireless, and, moreover, there would be presently representatives of the four allied Powers in Petrograd who might communicate with their respective governments. Communication might, therefore, suggested M. Trotsky, be restored in this way.

The sitting then closed.

NEGOTIATIONS RENEWED

According to Russian wireless (Feb. 23) it is notified that, in reply to the proposal dated Feb. 19, 1918, of the Russian Government, Germany will renew peace negotiations with Russia, and will conclude peace upon the following conditions:

1. Germany and Russia to declare the state of war to end. Both nations believe that in the future they will live in peace and friendship.

2. Regions which are to the west of a line as indicated at Brest-Litovsk to the Russian Delegation, and which formerly belonged to the Russian State, are no more under the territorial protection of Russia. In the region of Dvinsk this line must be advanced to the eastern frontier of Courland. The former attachment of these regions to the Russian State must in no case involve for them an obligation toward Russia. Russia renounces every claim to intervene in the internal affairs of those regions. Germany and Austria-Hungary have the intention to define the further fate of these regions in agreement with their populations. Germany is ready, after the completion of the Russian demobilization, to evacuate regions which are to the east of the above-named line so far as it is not stated otherwise in Clause 3.

3. Livonia and Esthonia must be immediately cleared of Russian troops and Red Guards, and will be occupied by German police until the date when the constitution of the respective countries will guarantee their social security and political order. All inhabitants who were arrested for political reasons must be released immediately.

4. Russia will conclude peace with the Ukrainian People's Republic. Ukraine and Finland will be immediately evacuated by Russian troops and Red Guards.

5. Russia will do all in its power to secure for Turkey an orderly return of its eastern Anatolian frontiers. Russia recognizes the annulation of the Turkish Capitulation.

6. Complete demobilization of the Russian Army, inclusive of detachments newly formed by the present Government, must be carried out immediately.

7. Russian warships in the Black Sea, Baltic Sea, and Arctic Ocean must immediately either be sent to Russian harbors and kept there till the conclusion of a general peace or be disarmed. Warships of the Entente which are in the sphere of the Russian authority must be regarded as Russian ships. Merchant navigation on the

Black and Baltic Seas must be renewed as stated in the Armistice Treaty. The clearing away of mines to begin immediately. The blockade of the Arctic Ocean to remain in force till the conclusion of a general peace.

8. The Russo-German commercial treaty of 1904 comes into force, as stated in paragraph 11, clause 2, of the peace treaty with the Ukraine, with the exceptions as foreseen in paragraph 11, clause 3, of the Commercial Treaty concerning special privileges in the Arctic countries. Further, the whole of the first part of the final limits is reestablished. In addition, there must be a guarantee for the free, untariffed export of ores; the immediate commencement of negotiations for the conclusion of a new commercial treaty; the guarantee of the most-favored-nation treatment at least until 1925, even in the case of the termination of the provisorium; and, finally, the sanctioning of clauses corresponding to paragraph 11 of the clauses 3, 4a, and 15 of the Peace Treaty with Ukraine.

9. The legal-political relations to be regulated in accordance with the decision of the first version of the German-Russian Convention. So far as action on that decision has not been taken, especially in respect to indemnities for civil damages, this must be in accordance with the German proposal, and there must be indemnification with expenses for war prisoners in accordance with the Russian proposal. Russia will permit and support as far as it can German commissioners for war prisoners, civil prisoners, and war refugees.

10. Russia promises to put an end to every propaganda and agitation either on the part of the Government or on the part of persons supported by the Government against the members of the Quadruple Alliance and their political and military institutions, even in localities occupied by the Central Powers.

11. The above-named conditions must be accepted within 48 hours. Russian plenipotentiaries must start immediately for Brest-Litovsk and sign there within three days the Peace Treaty, which must be ratified within two weeks.

Minister for Foreign Affairs,
Von Kühlmann.
Berlin, Feb. 21, 1918.

THE DECLARATION OF
THE PEACE DELEGATION

Russian Government wireless [Mar. 9] issues the following:
To all

To Paris, Vienna, Berlin, Sebastopol, Odessa, Kharkov, Nikolaiev, Tashkent, Arkhangelsk, Kazan, Irkutsk

The Russian Peace Delegation made the following Declaration before signing the Peace Treaty at the Session of the Conference at Brest-Litovsk on Mar. 3:

The Workmen's and Peasants' Government of the Russian Republic was forced, after the offensive of the German troops against Russia, when the latter had declared the war to be at an end and had commenced the demobilization of its armies, to accept an ultimatum presented by Germany on Feb. 24. We have been delegated to sign these conditions, which have been forced upon us by violence.

The negotiations which have been carried out so far at Brest-Litovsk between us, on the one part, and Germany and her allies, on the other, have shown strongly and clearly enough that the "peace by agreement," as it is termed by the German representatives, is really and definitely an annexationist and imperialistic peace. The Brest-Litovsk conditions at the moment are considerably worse than this. The peace which is being concluded here at Brest-Litovsk is not a peace based upon a free agreement of the peoples of Russia, Germany, Austria-Hungary, and Turkey, but a peace dictated by force of arms. This is the peace which Russia, grinding its teeth, is compelled to accept. This is a peace which, whilst pretending to free Russian border provinces, really transforms them into German provinces and deprives them of the right of free self-determination, such as was recognized by the Workmen's and Peasants' Government of Revolutionary Russia, as due to them. This is a peace which, whilst pretending to reestablish order, gives armed support in these regions to exploiting classes against the working classes, and is helping again to put upon them the yoke of oppression which was removed by the Russian Revolution. This is a peace which gives back the land to the landlords, and again drives the workers into the serfdom of the factory owners. This is a peace which for a long time to come imposes upon the workers of Russia in a still more aggravated form the old commercial treaty which was concluded in 1904 in the interests of German agrarians, and which is at the same time guaranteeing to German and Austro-Hungarian capitalists interest on the debts of the Tsarist Government, which have been repudiated by Revolutionary Russia. Finally, as if it was the purpose explicitly to emphasize the character of the German armed offensive, the German ultimatum is attempting to muzzle the Russian Revolution by forbidding all agitation directed against the Governments of the Quadruple Alliance and their military authorities. But even this does not suffice. Under the same pretense of reestablishing order, Germany is also occupying by arms regions in which the population is purely Russian and is establishing there a regime of military occupation in disregard of revolutionary institutions. For the Ukraine and Finland Germany is requesting the nonintervention of Revolutionary Russia, and at the same time is intervening actively with the object of supporting the counter-revolutionary forces against the workmen and peasants.

In the Caucasus, in direct contradiction to the conditions of the ultimatum of Feb. 21, as formulated by the German Government itself, Germany is breaking away for the benefit of Turkey regions of Ardahan, Kars, and Batum, which never have been taken by Turkish troops during this war, and with complete disregard of the real wishes of the populations of these regions. The most cynical and violent territorial seizures, the occupation of the most important strategical points, can have but one purpose—to prepare a new offensive against Russia and to defend capitalistic interests against the Workmen's and Peasants' Revolution. Such is the real object of the offensive undertaken by the German troops on Feb. 18 without the seven days' notice which was agreed upon in the armistice treaty concluded between Russia and the Central Powers. This advance was not stopped, in spite of the Declaration of the Council of the People's Commissioners that they accepted the German ultimatum of February 21. This advance was not stopped in spite of the fact that the conference of Brest-Litovsk was resumed and in spite of an official protest by the Russian Delegation. Through this, all the conditions of peace presented by Germany and by her allies are transformed into an ultimatum presented by them to Russia and supported in the interests of such a peace treaty, with the threat of immediate armed violence. Nevertheless, in the present situation Russia has no alternative choice. After having demobilized her armies, the Russian Revolution has by the same act given its fate into the hands of the German people. The Russian Delegation has already declared openly at Brest-Litovsk that no honest man can believe that the war against Russia can now be termed a defensive war. Germany has taken the offensive under the pretense of reestablishing order, but in reality with the purpose of strangling the Russian Workmen's and Peasants' Revolution. For the benefit of world imperialism German militarism has succeeded at the present time in moving its troops against the masses of the workmen and peasants of the Russian Republic. The German proletariat has not as yet shown itself powerful enough to stop this offensive movement. We do not doubt for one moment that this triumph of the imperialist and the militarist over the international proletarian Revolution is only a temporary and passing one. Under the present conditions the Soviet Government of the Russian Republic, being left to its own forces, is unable to withstand the armed onrush of German imperialism, and is compelled, for the sake of saving Revolutionary Russia, to accept the conditions put before it. We, being empowered by our Government to sign the treaty of peace, are compelled, in spite of our protest, to negotiate under the absolutely exceptional conditions of continued hostilities against non-resisting Russia. We can not submit to any further shooting of Russian workmen and peasants who have refused to continue the war. We declare openly before the workmen, peasants and soldiers of Russia and Germany, and before the laboring and exploited masses of the whole world, that we are forced to accept the peace dictated by those who, at the moment, are the more powerful, and that we are going to sign immediately the treaty presented to us as an ultimatum, but that at the same time we refuse to enter into any discussion of these terms.

Lenin's Writings and Speeches

The years after Brest-Litovsk were full of terrible strain and conflict; though for a while the tide of revolution seemed to flow westward, there were few moments before 1921–1922 when the Bolsheviks could feel secure in their power. Nevertheless, while fighting their lives the Bolshevik leaders had to keep rethinking their political doctrine in order to provide their followers in Russia and abroad with both dogma and practical advice. After Lenin's death in 1924, The Communist International *published certain extracts from his speeches and writings. These works, which follow, throw a useful light on the drift of Lenin's thoughts during his final years.*

Speech at the Third International

THE NECESSITY TO SEVER CONNECTION WITH
OPPORTUNIST-MENSHEVIKS

It is not enough to know by heart Communist resolutions and to use revolutionary forms of speech at every opportunity. This is not enough, and we are decidedly against all Communists who know by heart this or that resolution. The prerequisite of sincere Communism is—severance from opportunism. We shall talk freely and openly to all Communists who subscribe to this, and we shall be entitled to say to them boldly: "Do not commit foolish acts, be wise and clever." But such language will only be addressed to Communists who have severed all connection with opportunism, and this does not as yet apply to you. Therefore, I reiterate, I hope that the Congress will endorse the resolution of the Executive Committee. Comrade Lazzari said: "We are in a preparatory period." Nothing could be truer. You are in a preparatory period. The first phase of this period is—severance from the Mensheviks, similar to the severance between us and our Mensheviks in 1903. And it is due to the fact that the German Party has not broken off all connection with the Mensheviks, that the entire German working class is undergoing great hardship and suffering during the prolonged and wearisome post-war period in the history of the German revolution.

From "'Left Wing' Communism"

REVOLUTIONARY TACTICS OF THE COMMUNIST PARTY
AFTER CAPTURING POWER

After the first Socialist revolution of the proletariat, upon the overthrow of the bourgeoisie in a country, the proletariat remains for a time weaker than the bourgeoisie, simply by virtue of the latter's far-reaching international connections, and also on account of the ceaseless and spontaneous re-birth of capitalism and the bourgeoisie, through the small producers of commodities in the country which has overthrown them. To overcome so potent an enemy is possible only through the greatest effort and by dint of the obligatory, thorough, careful, attentive and skillful utilisation of every breach, however small, between the enemies; of every clash of interests between the bourgeoisie of all countries, between various groups and species of bourgeoisie within individual countries; of every possibility, however small, of gaining an ally, even though he be temporary, shaky, unstable, unreliable and conditional. Who has not grasped this has failed to grasp one iota of Marxism and of scientific modern Socialism in general. Whoever has failed to prove in practice, during a considerable period of time and in sufficiently varied political situations, his ability to apply this truth, has not yet learned to aid the revolutionary class in its struggle for the liberation of all

From *The Communist International, Petrograd, May 1924.*

From *a Speech Delivered at the Third Congress of the Communist International, 28/11/21.*

From *Pamphlet, "Left Wing" Communism, Chap. 8.*

toiling humanity from its exploiters. All this applies equally to the period before and after the conquest of political power by the proletariat. . . .

THE TASKS OF THE REVOLUTIONARY CLASS

History in general, the history of revolutions in particular, has always been richer, more varied and variform, more vital and "cunning" than is conceived of by the best parties, by the most conscious vanguards of the most advanced classes. This is natural, for the best vanguards express the consciousness, will, passions and fancies of but tens of thousands, whereas the revolution is effected at the moment of the exceptional uplift and exertion of *all* the human faculties—consciousness, will, passion, phantasy—of tens of millions, spurred on by the bitterest class war. From this there follow two very important practical conclusions; first, the revolutionary class, for the realisation of its object, must be able to master *all* forms or aspects of social activity, without the slightest exception (completing, after the conquest of political power, sometimes with great risk and tremendous danger, what had been left undone before this conquest); secondly, that the revolutionary classes must be ready for the most rapid and unexpected substitution of one form or another. . . .

REVOLUTIONARY TACTICS AND COMPROMISES

Naive and quite inexperienced persons imagine that it is sufficient to recognise the permissibility of compromise in general, and all differences between opportunism on the one hand (with which we do and must wage uncompromising war) and revolutionary Marxism or Communism on the other will be obliterated. But for those people who do not yet know that all distinctions in nature and in society are unstable (and, to a certain extent, arbitrary), nothing will do but a long process of training, education, enlightenment, political and everyday experience. In practical questions of the policy appropriate to each separate or specific historic moment, it is important to be able to distinguish those in which are manifested the main species of inadmissible treacherous compromises, which embody opportunism detrimental to the revolutionary class, and to direct all possible efforts towards elucidating and fighting them. During the imperialist war, 1914–1918, between two groups of equally ruffianly and rapacious countries, such a main fundamental species of opportunism was social-chauvinism, that is, upholding "defence of Fatherland," which, in such a war, was really equivalent to a defence of the plundering interests of one's own bourgeoisie. Since the war, the defence of the robber "League of Nations," the defence of direct or indirect alliance with the bourgeoisie of one's country against the revolutionary proletariat and the "soviet" movement; the defence of the bourgeois democracy and bourgeois parliamentarism against "Soviet power," such are the chief manifestations of those inadmissible and treacherous compromises, which taken in all, have given rise to an opportunism fatal to the revolutionary proletariat and its cause.

From *Pamphlet "Left Wing" Communism, Chap. 10.*
From *Pamphlet "Left Wing" Communism, Chap. 8.*

PRINCIPLES OF REVOLUTIONARY TACTICS
OF COMMUNIST PARTIES UNDER GIVEN CONDITIONS

The main thing now is that the Communists of each country should, in full conscious-ness, study both the fundamental problems of the struggle with opportunism and "Left" doctrinairism, and specific peculiarities which this struggle inevitably assumes in each separate country, according to the idiosyncrasies of its politics, economics, culture, national composition (e.g., Ireland), its colonies, religious divisions, etc. Every-where is felt an ever-widening and increasing dissatisfaction with the Second (Socialist) International, dissatisfaction due to its opportunism and its incapacity of creating a real leading centre, able to direct the international tactics of the revolutionary proletariat in the struggle for the world Soviet Republic. One must clearly realise that such a leading centre can, under no circumstances, be built after a single model, by a mechanical adjustment and equalisation of the tactical rules of the struggle. The national and State differences, now existing between peoples and countries, will continue to exist for a very long time yet, even after the realisation of the proletarian dictatorship on a world scale. Unity of international tactics in the Communist Labour movement everywhere demands, not the elimination of variety, not the abolition of national peculiarities (this at the present moment is a foolish dream), but such application of the fundamental principles of Communism—Soviet power and the dictatorship of the proletariat—as will admit of the right modification of these principles, in their adaptation and applica-tion to national and national-State differences. The principal problem of the historical moment in which all advanced (and not only the advanced) countries now find them-selves, lies here; that special national peculiarities must be studied, ascertained and grasped before concrete attempts are made in any country to solve the aspects of the single international problem, to overcome opportunism and Left doctrinairism within the working-class movement, to overthrow the bourgeoisie, and to institute a Soviet Republic and proletarian dictatorship. . . .

THE FUNDAMENTAL CONDITIONS FOR THE VICTORY
OF THE PROLETARIAN REVOLUTION

The fundamental law of revolution confirmed by all revolutions, and particularly by all three Russian revolutions of the twentieth-century, is as follows: It is not sufficient for the revolution that the exploited and oppressed masses understand the impossibility of living in the old way and demand changes: for the revolution it is necessary that the exploiters should not be able to live and rule as of old. Only when the masses *do not want* the old regime, and when the rulers are *unable* to govern them as of old, then only can the revolution succeed. This truth may be expressed in other words, revolution is impossible without an all-national crisis, affecting both the exploited and the exploiters. It follows that for the revolution it is essential, first, that a majority of the workers (or at least a majority of the conscious, thinking, politically active workers) should fully understand the necessity for a revolution, and be ready to sacrifice their lives for it; second, that the ruling class be in a state of governmental crisis which attracts even

From *Pamphlet "Left Wing" Communism, Chap. 10.*
From *Pamphlet "Left Wing" Communism, Chap. 9.*

the most backward masses into politics. It is a sign of every real revolution, this rapid tenfold, or even hundredfold increase in the number of representatives of the toiling and oppressed masses, heretofore apathetic, who are able to carry on a political fight which weakens the government and facilitates its overthrow by the revolutionaries. . . .

PLIABLE REVOLUTIONARY TACTICS—NO RIGHT OR LEFT DOCTRINAIRISM

That which has happened to Kautsky, Otto Bauer and other highly erudite Marxists, devoted to Socialism, and leaders of the Second International, could and ought to serve as a useful lesson. They fully appreciated the necessity of pliable tactics, they learned and taught to others the Marxist dialectics—and much of what they have done in that respect will remain for ever a valuable acquisition to Socialist literature. But in the application of these dialectics they made a great mistake; they showed themselves in practice to be so *un*dialectic, and so incapable of reckoning with the rapid changes of forms and the rapid filling of old forms with new contents, that their fate is not much more enviable than that of Hyndman, Guesde and Plekhanov. The main reason for their bankruptcy was that their eyes were "fastened" upon one fixed form of the growth of the working class movement and of socialism. They forgot all about its one-sidedness, and were afraid to perceive the sharp break which, by virtue of objective conditions, became unavoidable; so they continue to repeat the simple, at first glance, self-evident truth, once learned by rote: "Three are more than two." But politics resembles algebra more than arithmetic, and it is more like higher than lower mathematics. In reality all the old forms of the Socialist movement have been filled with new contents; there appears before the figures, consequently, a new sign, a "minus," and our wiseacres stubbornly continue to persuade themselves and others that "minus three" is more than "minus two!"

Communists must endeavour not to repeat the same mistake; or to speak more precisely the same mistake—committed the other way round by the Left Communists—must be corrected sooner and more quickly in order to get rid of it with less pain to the organism. Not only Right but Left doctrinairism is a mistake. Of course, the mistake of the latter in Communism is at the present moment, a thousand times less dangerous and less significant than the mistake of Right doctrinairism (i.e., Social-Chauvinism and Kautskianism); but, after all, this is due to the fact that Left Communism is quite a young current, just coming into being. For this reason the disease under certain conditions can be easily cured, and it is necessary to begin its treatment with the utmost energy.

The old forms have burst; for the contents (antiproletarian and reactionary) obtained an inordinate development. We now have, from the standpoint of the development of international Communism, strong, powerful contents at work for Soviet power and the proletarian dictatorship, and these can and must manifest themselves in any form, new as well as old; the new spirit can and must regenerate, conquer and subjugate all forms, not only the new but the old, not for the purpose of reconciling the new with the old forms, but to enable us to forge all forms, new and old, into a weapon for the final decisive and unswerving victory of Communism.

From *Pamphlet "Left Wing" Communism, Chap. 10.*

The Communists must strain every effort to direct the movement of the working class, and the development of society generally, along the straightest and quickest way to the universal victory of Soviet Power and the proletarian dictatorship. This truth is incontestable. But it is enough to take one little step farther—a step it would seem in the same direction—and truth is transformed into error! It is enough to say, as do the German and British "Left" Communists, that we acknowledge only one straight road, that we do not admit manoeuvres, co-operation, compromises—and this will already be a mistake, which is capable of bringing, and, in fact, has brought and is bringing, the most serious harm to Communism. Right doctrinairism has foundered on the recognition of only the old forms, and has become totally bankrupt, not having perceived the new contents. Left doctrinairism unconditionally repudiates certain old forms, failing to see that the new content is breaking its way through all and every form, that it is our duty as Communists to master them all, to learn how to supplement with the maximum rapidity, one form by another, and to adapt our tactics to all such changes, caused not by our class nor by our endeavours.

World revolution has been given a powerful impetus by the horrors, atrocities and villainies of the world imperialist war, and by the hopelessness of the position created by it. This revolution is spreading more widely and deeply with such supreme rapidity, with such splendid richness of varying forms, with such an instructive, practical refutation of all doctrinairism, that there is every hope of a speedy and thorough recovery of the international Communist movement from the infantile disorder of "Left" Communism.

Speech at the Fourth International

LEARN FROM THE EXPERIENCE OF THE RUSSIAN REVOLUTION

At the Third Congress of 1921, we adopted a resolution concerning the organisatory upbuilding of the Communist Parties and concerning the method and the substance of their work. It was a good resolution. But the resolution is almost exclusively Russian; it was wholly derived from a study of Russian developments. That is the good side of the resolution, but it is also the bad side. It is the bad side of the resolution because hardly any foreigner (I have read the resolution over again before expressing my conviction) is able to read it. In the first place, it is too long, for it contains fifty or more paragraphs. Foreigners are apt to find it impossible to read anything of this sort. In the next place, even if a foreigner should manage to read it through, it is too Russian. I do not mean because it was written in the Russian language, for there are excellent translations in the various tongues, but because it is permeated with the Russian spirit. Thirdly, if by a rare chance a foreigner could understand it, he could not possibly carry it out. That is the third defect.

I have talked matters over with some of the delegates, and I hope that in the later

---

From *Speech Delivered at Fourth Congress of the Communist International.*

course of the Congress I shall find it possible (not in the Congress itself, for in that I am unfortunately not able to participate), to talk matters over in full detail with a large number of delegates from various lands. My impression is that we made a great mistake in the matter of this resolution, thereby blocking our own advance.

Let me repeat, it is an excellent resolution, I myself endorse every one of its fifty or more paragraphs; but we did not really know what we were about when we turned to foreigners with our Russian experience. Everything in the resolution has remained a dead letter. If we fail to understand why, we shall make no progress.

I think the most important thing for us all, Russians and foreigners alike, is that after five years of the Russian Revolution, we should set ourselves to school. Now for the first time we have the possibility of learning. I do not know how long this possibility will last. I do not know how long the capitalist powers will give us the opportunity of learning in peace and quietude; but we must utilise every moment in which we are free from war that we may learn, and learn from the bottom up.

The whole Party, and Russia at large, show by their hunger for culture that they are aware of this. The aspiration for culture proves that our most important task consists in this, to learn and to go on learning. But foreigners, too, must learn, though not in the sense in which we have to learn, namely, to read, to write, and to understand what is read. This is our lack. There is much dispute as to whether such things belong to proletarian culture or to bourgeois culture. I leave the question open. This much is certain, that our first task must be to learn reading and writing and to understand what is read. In foreign lands, this is no longer necessary.

Foreigners need something different. They need some things higher. First of all, they have to learn how to understand all that we have written about the organisation and upbuilding of the Communist Parties, which they have subscribed to without reading and without understanding it. You foreign comrades must make this your first duty. This resolution must be carried into effect. These things cannot be done between one day and the next. That is absolutely impossible. The resolution is too Russian. It is a reflection of Russian experience. That is why it cannot be understood by foreigners, and why foreigners are not content to treat this resolution as a miraculous picture which they are to hang on the wall and pray to. That sort of attitude will not help us forward. You will have to make a portion of Russian experience your own. How can it be done? I do not know. Perhaps the Fascists in Italy will do us a good turn by showing the Italians how. After all, they are not so highly cultured that the development of Black Hundreds in Italy has become impossible. This may have a good effect. We Russians must look for means of explaining to foreigners the elements of this reason. Otherwise it will be absolutely impossible for them to carry it out.

I am confident that in this sense (we have to say, not only for the Russians, but for foreigners as well) that the most important thing for us all in the period now opening is to learn. We Russians have to learn in the general sense. You have to learn in the special sense that you may gain a genuine understanding of the organisation, structure, method and substance of revolutionary work. If you do this I am confident that the prospects for the world revolution are not merely favourable, but splendid.

A Time of Fear

Mussolini and Italian Fascism
National Socialism
Appeasement
The Second World War

SEVERAL WRITERS HAVE OFFERED NAMES TO FIT THE YEARS that ran from one world war to the next (and their more recent fallout): *An Age of Anxiety* (Professor F. Le Van Baumer); *An Age of Longing* (Arthur Koestler); in 1917 Oswald Spengler published his widely read volumes, *The Decline of the West;* thirty years later George Orwell closed the span with his most successful and depressing novel, *1984.*

The titles and the mood of such works are representative: the whole between-wars period was characterized by a marked loss of confidence. Politically this trait was very obvious among the supporters of democracy and limited liberalism, who watched with growing fear a busy search for alternative patterns upon which the good society might be built. These alternative patterns—Fascist, Nazi, Communist, or other—all tended to be authoritarian, violent, and ruthless; and, because another characteristic of our century is its tremendous technological advances, these new regimes possessed bigger and better means of imposing their will than the most absolute rulers of the past ever dreamed of in their most ambitious visions. They claimed absolute power not only over the public activities of their subjects but also over their private lives and, finally and ideally, over their thoughts. There is not much reason to suppose that our technical ingenuity is unable to accomplish the most totalitarian ambitions.

But these new totalitarian systems did not limit their claims to a given area. Founded on exclusive interpretations of history, equipped with the vast potential of modern industry, each of them wanted to order the world. The leaders of these totalitarian governments believed that any elements that withstood or refused to fit their pattern—classes, nations, or races—must be eliminated—which may mean exterminated. This tendency to discuss and transact national and international affairs in terms of irreconcilable and ultimate points of view added a new and terrifying dimension to commonplace, everyday conflicts, at every level. Ultimate philosophies equipped with ultimate weapons make the world a nervous place to live in—and our century very much a time of fear.

Mussolini and Italian Fascism

THE First World War left behind it a long trail of discredited governments, collapsed or collapsing economies, and broken illusions of a better world—or at least a profitable victory—to justify the immense efforts of the preceding few years. Nowhere were these aftereffects more obvious than in Italy, the least favored power of the Allied camp. Embittered by a peace that had failed to give the country what it had hoped for and shaken by the revolutionary epidemic that had spread from Russia, by 1922 Italy had drifted into the arms of a national revolutionary dictatorship that promised the firm leadership, social reforms, internal order, and national self-assertion that most Italians seemed to want.

Fascism: For and Against

The new Fascist regime, with its ex-Socialist leader and picturesque methods such as doping political opponents with castor oil, fascinated the more sedate countries of the West and caused a good deal of discussion—abroad, that is, for in Italy itself controversial discussions were soon to be forbidden. The two selections that follow, both of which appeared in American publications of the 1920s, present the arguments of Mussolini's liberal opponent (Nitti) and the classic reasons for supporting the successful and efficient dictator (Cippico).

Francesco Nitti: The Case for the Prosecution

Bolshevism and Fascism are the two menaces to the future prosperity of Europe. Both are similar phenomena in that they deny human liberty and involve the exercise of power on the part of an armed minority. Bolshevism sets about establishing the dictatorship of the proletariat—in other words, putting all resources in the hands of the workers and peasants. It attains this end by force. Fascism suppresses all political liberty and all free manifestations, saying that this is necessary to make Italy a great nation and to found an empire. Mussolini has made numerous speeches insulting the decaying corpse of democracy and asserting that liberty is a prejudice of the past. He has announced that Fascism will found an Italian Empire. To found an empire would mean taking some piece of foreign territory—which in this case would be either a French

---

From Francesco Nitti, "Probabilities of War in Europe," *Atlantic Monthly,* September 1928. By permission of the Atlantic Monthly Press.

or a British possession, since it would be out of the question to despoil Switzerland, Austria, or Yugoslavia, which lie along the Italian frontiers.

Italy lacks economic resources, and Italian finance is so wretched that public credit has been profoundly shaken. Italy lacks the prime necessities for war—coal, steel, and oil. She also lacks food and cotton. In her present situation, she could not wage war without the support of Great Britain or the United States. Is it possible that these two countries would encourage such absurd, such grotesque, proposals?

Bolshevism has cut down Russia's productive capacity; and her foreign business, which the Government controls, has been utterly disastrous. The truth is that Russia is producing much less than she did before the war—in other words, much less than she did under the deplorable Tsarist regime. Economic production demands above all else order, liberty, and individual initiative—three things that no dictatorship can bring about.

Fascism has seriously weakened Italian production. In spite of appearances Italy has fallen into a state of the greatest economic disorder in the course of the last six years. Fascism has not bent its efforts to obtaining results, but to producing manifestations. All over the country there are celebrations, parades, and processions of Black Shirts. Wheat and rice production has declined; yet great festivals are held in honor of wheat and rice, and there is a special celebration in behalf of bread. Expressed in gold pounds,—in other words, without statistical manipulation,—the deficit of Italian business has risen from 643 million gold pounds in 1924 to 1259 million gold pounds in 1927. In short, it has almost doubled. Mr. MacLean, the American commercial attaché at Rome, has calculated that domestic business has dropped 40 per cent in the last two years. This is a terrible figure. Nevertheless, Mr. MacLean is a little too optimistic, for the real decline is nearly 50 per cent. The loans negotiated in America have been used to maintain the lira, though no one knows how long this will last, and to stabilize it at its present level.

This extravagant stabilization, however, has ruined all industrial exporters. Italy now suffers more bankruptcies than any other country in Europe. In actual figures she has suffered twice as many as any other country, and, relatively to her industrial power, nine or ten times as many as any other country. Because of this absurd lira stabilization at a false level, undertaken not as a part of any economic programme, but merely as a piece of political bluff, the Italians are obliged to pay almost the same taxes as the French, whose country is at least three times as rich. In short, Italian taxes are heavier than those of any other country.

Since the Government bases itself on violence, it needs an even greater number of special militia to maintain it than Bolshevism does. These groups include militia to maintain general order, the voluntary Fascist militia, the railway militia, the post and telegraph militia, the harbor militia, the forest militia, and, most recently of all, the highway militia. About 200,000 people thus make their living off the Fascist Government, and it is like maintaining an army to support them. The industrialists and farmers have to pay for these militias. Besides this, all producers, both employers and employees, are grouped into corporations which involve still another enormous expense. There are fourteen ministries, but Mussolini scoffs at the rest of the world and occupies seven of them, comprising the office of Prime Minister, of Minister of the Interior, of Foreign

Affairs, War, Marine, Aviation, and Corporations—in other words, Minister of Labor. Under these conditions he is able to involve the country in a war before anyone knows what is happening and before the people can manifest their desires in any way.

All free journals in Italy have been suppressed, and the press is suffering. The amount of paper used for the various daily journals has fallen off about one half or three fifths during the last two years. The ablest Italians are in exile, having either been deported or retired from public life. Poverty is increasing, and the Government has refused to meet its obligations on the treasury and has forced them to be transformed into a consolidated debt. No criticism is allowed, even the most cordial. The press cannot discuss the economic crisis except to say that everything is going smoothly. Elections have disappeared. Even the Chamber of Deputies is going to be transformed into an assembly named by the Government. The administrators of local government and even the representatives of the chambers of commerce are no longer elected. They are appointed by the Government.

The economic situation is bad, but the financial situation is worse. On the day when Fascism feels itself lost, will it not attempt to distract attention by some international adventure? Is not this what all dictatorships have done in the past?

Fascism and Bolshevism, although apparently direct opposites, act in the same manner. Several centuries before Jesus, Plato, the greatest of Greek philosophers, wrote that dictatorship always ended in war, saying that when the dictator felt himself lost he made war. There is no example in modern history of a dictatorship that has not ended in war, revolution, or both.

Antonio Cippico: The Case for the Defense

In the last months of 1919 and the early ones of 1920, a good third of Italy was red. Over two thousand of the most flourishing communes were in the hands of the Communists. Their administration was characterized by violence and waste of public money. The government was incapable of protecting the public against the outrages of the reds, who imposed themselves more and more on the life of the people by means of assaults, strikes, blackmail, usurpation and occupation of factories and land. It was, therefore, necessary for those who still kept their belief in the nation, in order and in the sanctity of civil rights, to protect themselves by force of arms, i.e., by answering destructive violence with reconstructive violence.

At the beginning the number of these brave defenders of the nation and of order was small. At the end of March, 1919, about forty spirited young men of the proletariat and middle classes gathered in Milan—in red Milan—around Mussolini, and founded the famous original new Fascismo. This rapidly found adherents, apostles, and willing fighters, from all classes of the nation, in every city and every village, especially in the populous industrial districts of northern and central Italy, where the tyranny was the

From A. Cippico, *Italy, the Central Problem of the Mediterranean,* (New Haven: Yale University Press, 1926). By permission of the Yale University Press.

strongest of the Socialist Syndicates and of the Red Councils of workmen founded on the example of Moscow. There was scarcely a factory of a municipality of the rich industrial towns that did not fly a red or black flag, symbol of social war and destruction.

We then witnessed a whole series of just reprisals, which silently and systematically organized the defense of the nation. Here a Communist Cooperative, there a Socialist Chamber of Labor, in another place the offices and printing works of a Bolshevik newspaper, supported by rubles from Moscow, were attacked, besieged, and burnt. Workmen and peasants, who were inscribed in the red leagues and who lorded it over the country, were, rightly, put *hors de combat* by just measures of reprisal. The authors of these assaults were, in turn, attacked and stabbed, often treacherously, by means of ambuscades and mass attacks. War was declared. But it was not civil war in the real meaning of the word: it was the necessary and legitimate individual defense of the trampled-on rights of all the citizens, above all in defense of the vital interests of the country.

It thus comes about that in Romagna, Tuscany, Lombardy, and Piedmont, risings and encounters between armed bands, looting, and killing increased enormously. The struggle seems unequal—as the Chambers of Labor and the Red Syndicates, in addition to a vast organization and the authority which has accrued to them from the power-lessness of the liberal organs of the state against their criminal arrogance, and their systematic coercion and intimidation both of the working and middle classes, seem determined to undermine the state itself and make themselves masters of it.

The attacks and counterattacks became every day more frequent and violent. The Fascisti were determined to give no quarter. The mass of the workers, misled by their leaders and organizers, who had promised them shortly the earthly paradise of a communist revolution, rapidly realized the emptiness of such promises, and realized that their leaders were the false and timid prophets of an Asiatic social religion, foreign to Italian civilization and temperament. The workers at last perceived that the Second and Third International were merely organs of disruption, incapable of reconstruction; that internationalism was a lie; that their own interests were identical with those of the nation, till then forgotten and combated.

Incidents of brutal violence occurred, such as the murder at a meeting of the Communal Council of a member of the red municipality of Bologna, Dr. Giordani, who had fought bravely in the Great War; such as the bomb thrown in the Diana Theatre at Milan, which killed at least forty harmless work-people; such as the man-hunts carried out by the reds of Empoli against sailors of the Royal Navy; like the sentence executed on the workmen Scimula and Sonzini, who, because they did not agree with their companions, were condemned by the latter to be thrown alive into the blast furnaces of the factory where they worked at Turin. Such incidents necessarily brought the Italian people, so essentially just and moral, to a rebellion against the tyranny of these brutal social-communist organizers.

In the end, the Fascisti got the upper hand in the bloody fight. They were by now an admirably organized and disciplined army composed of ex-soldiers, well-educated youths, peasants, and workmen, representatives of the best classes of the Italian people, who had seen through the communist propaganda, who had given everything to their country during the war, and who expected no recompense except the prosperity and moral greatness of their nation. They were men of thought and action who were determined to mould by their sacrifices a new Italy, no longer to be a museum of dead things, a vast and useless political and literary academy, nor a dreamy scientific Arcadia, dealing more in words than in deeds.

Italy, even in her periods of blindest anarchy, desired vaguely to be a state, led and governed by a firm hand, with an economic structure worthy of its capacity of industrial initiative and work. This aspiration, at present incarnated in Fascism, has become her will. In order to reach this goal over three thousand Fascisti, generous, disinterested youths, from all classes of the nation, have laid down their lives.

The Fascist program of national reconstruction was synthetized by Mussolini in June, 1921, when he proposed in Parliament to "define some historical and political positions." He then asked that the functions of the state should be limited to the creation of conditions suitable for individual activity, and of advantage to the consumer, in science, art, economic life, agriculture, industry, and commerce. The state must not confer privileges on one class to the detriment of others. It must resign monopolies: it must be neither banker, manufacturer, dealer, co-operative society, nor newspaper owner. It must not encourage unemployment by the palliative of "doles," nor enrich a favored few and impoverish the rest of the people by means of state contracts granted because of political protection or as gifts disguised under the name of cooperation. It is the state's business to do away with all that is superfluous and useless in the great bureaucratic machine. Only thus can true liberty—not license—and the equality of the citizens before the state be assured; only thus can the state be in condition to assure rapid justice and protection for life and property, and to safeguard the dignity and interests of its subjects in foreign countries.

In those years the prestige of Italy had dwindled miserably. There was no faith in the public finances. It will be opportune to compare some figures of today with those of yesterday. The consolidated war funds in October, 1922, had fallen [disastrously]; later on in January, 1924, they were again at par. During 1920 there took place in Italy 1,881 industrial strikes and 189 agricultural strikes, which cost over 30,000,000 working days to the country. During 1923, the first year of the Fascist regime, industrial strikes were reduced to 200 and there was only one agricultural strike, involving the country in a loss of little more than 265,000 working days. In December, 1921, there were 541,000 unemployed; in October, 1924, they had fallen to 117,000, which number is today sensibly decreased.

In those troubled years almost all the industries dragged out a precarious existence. Today the activity of the then existing and since established industries has multiplied enormously; the workers work feverishly, forgetful of the unhealthy laziness of that time; they earn good wages; orders for goods are constantly increasing. In 1921 goods were exported to the value of 8,275,000,000 lire. For the first four months alone of this year exports have reached 5,350,000,000; for the corresponding period of 1923 the figures were 800,000,000. Importations of foreign goods amounted in 1921 to 17,266,000,000; in 1924 to 19,387,000,000. In 1921 the railways carried 20,181,000 tons of goods; in 1924, 31,689,000. In 1921 the consumption of electric energy amounted to 4,300,000,000 kilowatts; in 1924 to 6,500,000,000.

The Doctrines of Fascism

Benito Mussolini (1883–1945), the leader of Italian fascism, was the son of a blacksmith and a schoolteacher in "Red" Emilia. By 1914 he had become one of the leaders of the radical wing of the Socialist party and editor of the party paper, Avanti. *Expelled from the party for advocating intervention in the First World War, he founded his own newspaper to continue urging this policy, went to the front in 1915, and returned after being wounded. In Milan, in 1919, he founded the first* fascio di combattimento *(combat group), with only forty members. Three years later the "March on Rome" won him the premiership, which he held until 1943.*

Fascism arose in opposition to left-wing radicalism and was an expression of national-ist resentment at the poor deal Italy had got after the war. It proclaimed itself a movement of national rebirth, and, lacking any clear doctrine, was free to appeal to all classes and political persuasions. However, after reaching power, the movement's leaders felt the need for a theoretical doctrine; this was outlined in an article contributed by Mussolini to the Enciclopaedia Italiana *in 1932.*

Mussolini: "The Political and Social Doctrine of Fascism"

When, in the now distant March of 1919, I summoned a meeting at Milan through the columns of the *Popolo d'Italia* of the surviving members of the Interventionist Party who had themselves been in action, and who had followed me since the creation of the Fascist Revolutionary Party (which took place in the January of 1915), I had no specific doctrinal attitude in mind. I had a living experience of one doctrine only— that of Socialism, from 1903–4 to the winter of 1914—that is to say, about a decade: and from Socialism itself, even though I had taken part in the movement first as a member of the rank and file and then later as a leader, yet I had no experience of its doctrine in practice. My own doctrine, even in this period, had always been a doctrine of action. A unanimous, universally accepted theory of Socialism did not exist after 1905, when the revisionist movement began in Germany under the leadership of Bern-stein, while under pressure of the tendencies of the time, a Left Revolutionary move-ment also appeared, which though never getting further than talk in Italy, in Russian Socialistic circles laid the foundations of Bolshevism. Reformation, Revolution, Cen-tralization—already the echoes of these terms are spent—while in the great stream of Fascism are to be found ideas which began with Sorel, Péguy, with Lagardelle in the "Mouvement Socialiste," and with the Italian trade union movement which through-out the period of 1904–14 was sounding a new note in Italian Socialist circles (already weakened by the betrayal of Giolitti) through Olivetti's *Pagine Libre*, Orano's *La Lupa*, and Enrico Leone's *Divenire Sociale*.

After the War, in 1919, Socialism was already dead as a doctrine: it existed only as hatred. There remained to it only one possibility of action, especially in Italy, repri-

From Benito Mussolini, "The Political and Social Doctrine of Fascism," in *International Conciliation*, No. 306 (January 1935), pp. 5–17. Reprinted by permission of the Carnegie Endowment for International Peace.

sals against those who had desired the War and who must now be made to "expiate" its results. The *Popolo d'Italia* was then given the subtitle of "The newspaper of ex-servicemen and producers," and the word "producers" was already the expression of a mental attitude. Fascism was not the nursling of a doctrine worked out beforehand with detailed elaboration; it was born of the need for action and it was itself from the beginning practical rather than theoretical; it was not merely another political party but, even in the first two years, in opposition to all political parties as such, and itself a living movement. The name which I then gave to the organization fixed its character. And yet, if one were to re-read, in the now dusty columns of that date, the report of the meeting in which the *Fasci Italiani di combattimento* were constituted, one would there find no ordered expression of doctrine, but a series of aphorisms, anticipations, and aspirations which, when refined by time from the original ore, were destined after some years to develop into an ordered series of doctrinal concepts, forming the Fascists' political doctrine—different from all others either of the past or the present day.

"If the bourgeoisie," I said then, "think that they will find lightning-conductors in us, they are the more deceived; we must start work at once. . . . We want to accustom the working-class to real and effectual leadership, and also to convince them that it is no easy thing to direct an industry or a commercial enterprise successfully. . . . We shall combat every retrograde idea, technical or spiritual. . . . When the succession to the seat of government is open, we must not be unwilling to fight for it. We must make haste; when the present regime breaks down, we must be ready at once to take its place. It is we who have the right to the succession, because it was we who forced the country into the War, and led her to victory. The present method of political representation cannot suffice, we must have a representation direct from the individuals concerned. It may be objected against this program that it is a return to the conception of the corporation,[1] but that is no matter. . . . Therefore, I desire that this assembly shall accept the revendication of national trades-unionism from the economic point of view. . . ."

Now is it not a singular thing that even on this first day in the Piazza San Sepolcro that word "corporation" arose, which later, in the course of the Revolution, came to express one of the creations of social legislation at the very foundation of the regime?

The years which preceded the March to Rome were years of great difficulty, during which the necessity for action did not permit of research or any complete elaboration of doctrine. The battle had to be fought in the towns and villages. There was much discussion, but—what was more important and more sacred—men died. They knew how to die. Doctrine, beautifully defined and carefully elucidated, with headlines and paragraphs, might be lacking; but there was to take its place something more decisive—Faith. Even so, anyone who can recall the events of the time through the aid of books, articles, votes of congresses, and speeches of great and minor importance—anyone who knows how to research and weigh evidence—will find that the fundamentals of

---

[1] Facists advocated the "corporate" state, governed not by representatives of electoral districts but by delegates of trade and professional corporations joining employers and employees in every industry and profession.

doctrine were cast during the years of conflict. It was precisely in those years that Fascist thought armed itself, was refined, and began the great task of organization. The problem of the relation between the individual citizen and the State; the allied problems of authority and liberty; political and social problems as well as those specifically national—a solution was being sought for all these while at the same time the struggle against Liberalism, Democracy, Socialism, and the Masonic bodies was being carried on, contemporaneously with the "punitive expedition." But, since there was inevitably some lack of system, the adversaries of Fascism have disingenuously denied that it had any capacity to produce a doctrine of its own, though that doctrine was growing and taking shape under their very eyes, even though tumultuously; first, as happens to all ideas in their beginnings, in the aspect of a violent and dogmatic negation, and then in the aspect of positive construction which has found its realization in the laws and institutions of the regime as enacted successively in the years 1926, 1927 and 1928.

Fascism is now a completely individual thing, not only as a regime, but as a doctrine. And this means that today Fascism, exercising its critical sense upon itself and upon others, has formed its own distinct and peculiar point of view, to which it can refer and upon which, therefore, it can act in the face of all problems, practical or intellectual, which confront the world.

And above all, Fascism, the more it considers and observes the future and the development of humanity quite apart from political considerations of the moment, believes neither in the possibility nor the utility of perpetual peace. It thus repudiates the doctrine of Pacifism—born of a renunciation of the struggle and an act of cowardice in the face of sacrifice. War alone brings up to its highest tension all human energy and puts the stamp of nobility upon the peoples who have the courage to meet it. All other trials are substitutes, which never really put men into the position where they have to make the great decision—the alternative of life or death. Thus a doctrine which is founded upon this harmful postulate of peace is hostile to Fascism. And thus hostile to the spirit of Fascism, though accepted for what use they can be dealing with particular political situations, are all the international leagues and societies which, as history will show, can be scattered to the winds when once strong national feeling is aroused by any motive—sentimental, ideal, or practical. This anti-pacifist spirit is carried by Fascism even into the life of the individual; the proud motto of the Squadrista, "*Me ne frego*" (I do not fear), written on the bandage of the wound, is an act of philosophy not only stoic, the summary of a doctrine not only political—it is the education to combat, the acceptance of the risks which combat implies, and a new way of life for Italy. Thus the Fascist accepts life and loves it, knowing nothing of and despising suicide: he rather conceives of life as duty and struggle and conquest, life which should be high and full, lived for oneself, but above all for others—those who are at hand and those who are far distant, contemporaries, and those who will come after.

This "demographic" policy of the regime is the result of the above premise. Thus the Fascist loves in actual fact his neighbor, but this "neighbor" is not merely a vague and undefined concept, this love for one's neighbor puts no obstacle in the way of necessary educational severity, and still less to differentiation of status and to physical distance. Fascism repudiates any universal embrace, and in order to live worthily in the community of civilized peoples watches its contemporaries with vigilant eyes, takes good note of their state of mind and, in the changing trend of their interests, does not allow itself to be deceived by temporary and fallacious appearances.

Such a conception of life makes Fascism the complete opposite of that doctrine, the base of the so-called scientific and Marxian Socialism, the materialist conception of history; according to which the history of human civilization can be explained simply through the conflict of interests among the various social groups and by the change and development in the means and instruments of production. That the changes in the economic field—new discoveries of raw materials, new methods of working them, and the inventions of science—have their importance no one can deny; but that these factors are sufficient to explain the history of humanity excluding all others is an absurd delusion. Fascism, now and always, believes in holiness and in heroism; that is to say, in actions influenced by no economic motive, direct or indirect. And if the economic conception of history be denied, according to which theory men are no more than puppets, carried to and fro by the waves of chance, while the real directing forces are quite out of their control, it follows that the existence of an unchangeable and unchanging class war is also denied—the natural progeny of the economic conception of history. And above all Fascism denies that class war can be the preponderant force in the transformation of society. These two fundamental concepts of Socialism being thus refuted, nothing is left of it but the sentimental aspiration—as old as humanity itself—towards a social convention in which the sorrows and sufferings of the humblest shall be alleviated. But here again Fascism repudiates the conception of "economic" happiness, to be realized by Socialism and, as it were, at a given moment in economic evolution to assure to everyone the maximum of well-being. Fascism denies the materialist conception of happiness as a possibility, and abandons it to its inventors, the economists of the first half of the nineteenth century: that is to say, Fascism denies the validity of the equation, well-being = happiness, which would reduce men to the level of animals, caring for one thing only—to be fat and well-fed—and would thus degrade humanity to a purely physical existence.

After Socialism, Fascism combats the whole complex system of democratic ideology, and repudiates it, whether in its theoretical premises or in its practical application. Fascism denies that the majority, by the simple fact that it is a majority, can direct human society; it denies that numbers alone can govern by means of a periodical consultation, and it affirms the immutable, beneficial, and fruitful inequality of mankind, which can never be permanently leveled through the mere operation of a mechanical process such as universal suffrage. The democratic regime may be defined as from time to time giving the people the illusion of sovereignty, while the real effective sovereignty lies in the hands of other concealed and irresponsible forces. Democracy is a regime nominally without a king, but it is ruled by many kings—more absolute, tyrannical, and ruinous than one sole king, even though a tyrant. This explains why Fascism, having first in 1922 (for reasons of expediency) assumed an attitude tending towards republicanism, renounced this point of view before the March to Rome; being convinced that the question of political form is not today of prime importance, and after having studied the examples of monarchies and republics past and present reached the conclusion that monarchy or republicanism are not to be judged, as it were, by an absolute standard; but that they represent forms in which the evolution—political, historical, traditional, or psychological—of a particular country has expressed itself.

Fascism has taken up an attitude of complete opposition to the doctrines of Liberalism, both in the political field and the field of economics. There should be no undue exaggeration (simply with the object of immediate success in controversy) of the importance of Liberalism in the last century, nor should what was but one among many theories which appeared in that period be put forward as a religion for humanity for all time, present and to come. Liberalism only flourished for half a century. It was born in 1830 in reaction against the Holy Alliance, which had been formed with the object of diverting the destinies of Europe back to the period before 1789, and the highest point of its success was the year 1848, when even Pius IX was a Liberal. Immediately after that date it began to decay, for if the year 1848 was a year of light and hope, the following year, 1849, was a year of darkness and tragedy. The Republic of Rome was dealt a mortal blow by a sister republic—that of France—and in the same year Marx launched the gospel of the Socialist religion, the famous *Communist Manifesto.* In 1851 Napoleon III carried out his far from liberal *coup d'état* and reigned in France until 1870, when he was deposed by a popular movement as the consequence of a military defeat which must be counted as one of the most decisive in history. The victor was Bismarck, who knew nothing of the religion of liberty, or the prophets by which that faith was revealed. And it is symptomatic that such a highly civilized people as the Germans were completely ignorant of the religion of liberty during the whole of the nineteenth century. It was nothing but a parenthesis, represented by that body which has been called "The ridiculous Parliament of Frankfort," which lasted only for a short period. Germany attained her national unity quite outside the doctrines of Liberalism—a doctrine which seems entirely foreign to the German mind, a mind essentially monarchic—while Liberalism is the logical and, indeed, historical forerunner of anarchy. The stages in the achievement of German unity are the three wars of '64, '66, and '70, which were guided by such "Liberals" as Von Moltke and Bismarck. As for Italian unity, its debt to Liberalism is completely inferior in contrast to that which it owes to the work of Mazzini and Garibaldi, who were not Liberals. Had it not been for the intervention of the anti-Liberal Bismarck at Sadowa and Sedan it is very probable that we should never have gained the province of Venice in '66, or been able to enter Rome in '70. From 1870 to 1914 a period began during which even the very high priests of the religion themselves had to recognize the gathering twilight of their faith—defeated as it was by the decadence of literature and atavism in practice—that is to say, Nationalism, Futurism, Fascism. The era of Liberalism, after having accumulated an infinity of Gordian knots, tried to untie them in the slaughter of the World War—and never has any religion demanded of its votaries such a monstrous sacrifice. Perhaps the Liberal Gods were athirst for Blood? But now, today, the Liberal faith must shut the doors of its deserted temples, deserted because the peoples of the world realize that its worship—agnostic in the field of economics and indifferent in the field of politics and morals—will lead, as it has already led, to certain ruin. In addition to this, let it be pointed out that all the political hopes of the present day are anti-Liberal, and it is therefore supremely ridiculous to try to classify this sole creed as outside the judgment of history, as though history were a hunting ground reserved for the professors of Liberalism alone—as though Liberalism were the final unalterable verdict of civilization.

But the Fascist negation of Socialism, Democracy, and Liberalism must not be taken to mean that Fascism desires to lead the world back to the state of affairs before 1789, the date which seems to be indicated as the opening year of the succeeding semi-

Liberal century: we do not desire to turn back; Fascism has not chosen De Maistre[2] for its high-priest. Absolute monarchy has been and can never return, any more than blind acceptance of ecclesiastical authority.

So, too, the privileges of the feudal system "have been," and the division of society into castes impenetrable from outside, and with no intercommunication among themselves: the Fascist conception of authority has nothing to do with such a polity. A party which entirely governs a nation is a fact entirely new to history, there are no possible references or parallels. Fascism uses in its construction whatever elements in the Liberal, Social, or Democratic doctrines still have a living value; it maintains what may be called the certainties which we owe to history, but it rejects all the rest—that is to say, the conception that there can be any doctrine of unquestioned efficacy for all times and all peoples. Given that the nineteenth century was the century of Socialism, Liberalism, and Democracy: political doctrines pass, but humanity remains; and it may rather be expected that this will be a century of Fascism. For if the nineteenth century was the century of individualism (Liberalism always signifying individualism) it may be expected that this will be the century of collectivism, and hence the century of the State. It is a perfectly logical deduction that a new doctrine can utilize all the still vital elements of previous doctrines.

No doctrine has ever been born completely new, completely defined and owing nothing to the past; no doctrine can boast a character of complete originality; it must always derive, if only historically, from the doctrines which have preceded it and develop into further doctrines which will follow. Thus the scientific Socialism of Marx is the heir of the Utopian Socialism of Fourier, of the Owens and of Saint-Simon; thus again the Liberalism of the eighteenth century is linked with all the advanced thought of the seventeenth century, and thus the doctrines of Democracy are the heirs of the Encyclopedists. Every doctrine tends to direct human activity towards a determined objective; but the action of men also reacts upon the doctrine, transforms it, adapts it to new needs, or supersedes it with something else. A doctrine then must be no mere exercise in words, but a living act; and thus the value of Fascism lies in the fact that it is veined with pragmatism, but at the same time has a will to exist and a will to power, a firm front in face of the reality of "violence."

The foundation of Fascism is the conception of the State, its character, its duty, and its aim. Fascism conceives of the State as an absolute, in comparison with which all individuals or groups are relative, only to be conceived of in their relation to the State. The conception of the Liberal State is not that of a directing force, guiding the play and development, both material and spiritual, of a collective body, but merely a force limited to the function of recording results: on the other hand, the Fascist State is itself conscious, and has itself a will and a personality—thus it may be called the "ethic" State. In 1929, at the first five-yearly assembly of the Fascist regime, I said:

"For us Fascists, the State is not merely a guardian, preoccupied solely with the duty of assuring the personal safety of the citizens; nor is it an organization with purely material aims, such as to guarantee a certain level of well-being and peaceful conditions

---

[2]See p. 317.

of life; for a mere council of administration would be sufficient to realize such objects. Nor is it a purely political creation, divorced from all contact with the complex material reality which makes up the life of the individual and the life of the people as a whole. The State, as conceived of and as created by Fascism, is a spiritual and moral fact in itself, since its political, juridical, and economic organization of the nation is a concrete thing: and such an organization must be in its origins and development a manifestation of the spirit. The State is the guarantor of security both internal and external, but it is also the custodian and transmitter of the spirit of the people, as it has grown up; through the centuries in language, in customs, and in faith. And the State is not only a living reality of the present, it is also linked with the past and above all with the future, and thus transcending the brief limits of individual life, it represents the immanent spirit of the nation. The forms in which States express themselves may change, but the necessity for such forms is eternal. It is the State which educates its citizens in civic virtue, gives them a consciousness of their mission and welds them into unity; harmonizing their various interests through justice, and transmitting to future generations the mental conquests of science, of art, of law and the solidarity of humanity. It leads men from primitive tribal life to that highest expression of human power which is Empire; it links up; through the centuries the names of those of its members who have died for its existence and in obedience to its laws, it holds up the memory of the leaders who have increased its territory and the geniuses who have illumined it with glory as an example to be followed by future generations. When the conception of the State declines, and disunifying and centrifugal tendencies prevail, whether of individuals or of particular groups, the nations where such phenomena appear are in their decline."

From 1929 until today, evolution, both political and economic, has everywhere gone to prove the validity of these doctrinal premises. Of such gigantic importance is the State. It is the force which alone can provide a solution to the dramatic contradictions of capitalism, and that state of affairs which we call the crisis can only be dealt with by the State, as between other States. . . . Fascism desires the State to be a strong and organic body, at the same time reposing upon broad and popular support. The Fascist State has drawn into itself even the economic activities of the nation, and, through the corporative social and educational institutions created by it, its influence reaches every aspect of the national life and includes, framed in their respective organizations, all the political, economic and spiritual forces of the nation. A State which reposes upon the support of millions of individuals who recognize its authority, are continually conscious of its power and are ready at once to serve it, is not the old tyrannical State of the medieval lord nor has it anything in common with the absolute governments either before or after 1789. The individual in the Fascist State is not annulled but rather multiplied, just in the same way that a soldier in a regiment is not diminished but rather increased by the number of his comrades. The Fascist State organizes the nation, but leaves a sufficient margin of liberty to the individual; the latter is deprived of all useless and possibly harmful freedom, but retains what is essential; the deciding power in this question cannot be the individual, but the State alone.

The Fascist State is not indifferent to the fact of religion in general, or to that particular and positive faith which is Italian Catholicism. The State professes no theology, but a morality, and in the Fascist State religion is considered as one of the deepest manifestations of the spirit of man; thus it is not only respected but defended and protected. The Fascist State has never tried to create its own God, as at one moment Robespierre and the wildest extremists of the Convention tried to do; nor does it vainly seek to obliterate religion from the hearts of men as does Bolshevism; Fascism respects the God of the ascetics, the saints and heroes, and equally, God, as He is perceived and worshipped by simple people.

The Fascist State is an embodied will to power and government; the Roman tradition is here an ideal of force in action. According to Fascism, government is not so much a thing to be expressed in territorial or military terms as in terms of morality and the spirit. It must be thought of as an empire—that is to say, a nation which directly or indirectly rules other nations, without the need for conquering a single square yard of territory. For Fascism, the growth of empire, that is to say the expansion of the nation, is an essential manifestation of vitality, and its opposite a sign of decadence. Peoples which are rising, or rising again after a period of decadence, are always imperialist: any renunciation is a sign of decay and of death.

Fascism is the doctrine best adapted to represent the tendencies and the aspirations of a people, like the people of Italy, who are rising again after many centuries of abasement and foreign servitude. But empire demands discipline, the co-ordination of all forces and a deeply felt sense of duty and sacrifice: this fact explains many aspects of the practical working of the regime, the character of many forces in the State, and the necessarily severe measures which must be taken against those who would oppose this spontaneous and inevitable movement of Italy in the twentieth century, and would oppose it by recalling the outworn ideology of the nineteenth century—repudiated wheresoever there has been the courage to undertake great experiments of social and political transformation: for never before has the nation stood more in need of authority, of direction, and of order. If every age has its own characteristic doctrine, there are a thousand signs which point to Fascism as the characteristic docrine of our time. For if a doctrine must be a living thing, this is proved by the fact that Fascism has created a living faith; and that this faith is very powerful in the minds of men, is demonstrated by those who have suffered and died for it.

Fascism has henceforth in the world the universality of all those doctrines which, in realizing themselves, have represented a stage in the history of the human spirit.

National Socialism

THERE is no logical necessity to connect socialism and internationalism. The traditional connection between the two reflects a feeling that the oppressed of this world have more in common with one another than with their masters, that common economic interests are more real than spurious bonds of nationality. This seemed reasonable enough in the relatively free late nineteenth-century world, where people, money, and goods passed with little hindrance from one country to another—at any rate, west of the unenlightened territories of the sultan and the tsar. But with the beginning of the twentieth century, one country after another began to use tariffs and regulations to control imports and immigration. National interests would henceforth be furthered by deliberate economic policies, and this economic nationalism seemed to league employers and workers of a given country together, profits for the former meaning benefits for the latter, even if those benefits came at the expense of fellow workers across the border.

Internationalist arguments grew less convincing in a world cut up by a multitude of economic and political barriers. The First World War exacerbated nationalistic and chauvinistic feelings, and its aftermath persuaded many who until then had hesitated that they must look after number one and the devil take the hindmost. This could well be done by reconciling the two most popular creeds of the time, nationalism and socialism; the idea was hardly new, and in the twenties much of Mussolini's appeal was based on it. But its fullest and most effective expression was to appear in the party of Hitler—the National Socialist movement—that conquered Germany in the thirties.

The Program of the National Socialists

German Workers' Party: The Twenty-Five Points

The National Socialist German Workers' Party at a great mass meeting on February 25th, 1920, in the Hofbrauhaus-Festsaal in Munich announced their Programme to the world.

In section 2 of the Constitution of Our Party this Programme is declared to be inalterable.

The Programme of the German Workers' Party is limited as to period. The leaders have no intention, once the aims announced in it have been achieved, of setting up fresh ones, merely in order to increase the discontent of the masses artificially, and so ensure the continued existence of the party.

1. We demand the union of Germans to form a Great Germany on the basis of the right of the self-determination enjoyed by nations.

2. We demand equality of rights for the German People in its dealings with other nations, and abolition of the Peace Treaties of Versailles and St. Germain.

3. We demand land and territory (colonies) for the nourishment of our people and for settling our superfluous population.

4. None but members of the nation may be citizens of the State. None but those of German blood, whatever their creed, may be members of the nation. No Jew, therefore, may be a member of the nation.

5. Anyone who is not a citizen of the State may live in Germany only as a guest and must be regarded as being subject to foreign laws.

6. The right of voting on the State's government and legislation is to be enjoyed by the citizen of the State alone. We demand therefore that all official appointments, of whatever kind, whether in the Reich, in the country, or in the smaller localities, shall be granted to citizens of the State alone.

   We oppose the corrupting custom of Parliament of filling posts merely with a view to party considerations, and without reference to character or capability.

7. We demand that the State shall make it its first duty to promote the industry and livelihood of citizens of the State. If it is not possible to nourish the entire population of the State, foreign nationals (non-citizens of the State) must be excluded from the Reich.

8. All non-German immigration must be prevented. We demand that all non-Germans, who entered Germany subsequent to August 2nd, 1914, shall be required forthwith to depart from the Reich.

9. All citizens of the State shall be equal as regards rights and duties.

10. It must be the first duty of each citizen of the State to work with his mind or with his body. The activities of the individual may not clash with the interests of the whole, but must proceed within the frame of the community and be for the general good.

    We demand therefore:

11. Abolition of incomes unearned by work.

12. In view of the enormous sacrifice of life and property demanded of a nation by every war, personal enrichment due to a war must be regarded as a crime against the nation. We demand therefore ruthless confiscation of all war gains.

13. We demand nationalisation of all businesses which have been up to the present formed into companies (Trusts).

14. We demand that the profits from wholesale trade shall be shared out.

15. We demand extensive development of provision for old age.

16. We demand creation and maintenance of a healthy middle class, immediate communalisation of wholesale business premises, and their lease at a cheap rate to small traders, and that extreme consideration shall be shown to all small purveyors to the State, district authorities and smaller localities.

17. We demand land-reform suitable to our national requirements, passing of a law for confiscation without compensation of land for communal purposes; abolition of interest on land loans, and prevention of all speculation in land.

18. We demand ruthless prosecution of those whose activities are injurious to the common interest. Sordid criminals against the nation, usurers, profiteers, etc. must be punished with death, whatever their creed or race.

19. We demand that the Roman Law, which serves the materialistic world order, shall be replaced by a legal system for all Germany.

20. With the aim of opening to every capable and industrious German the possibility of higher education and of thus obtaining advancement, the State must consider a thorough re-construction of our national system of education. The curriculum of all educational establishments must be brought into line with the requirements of practical life. Comprehension of the State idea (State sociology) must be the school objective, beginning with the first dawn of intelligence in the pupil. We demand development of the gifted children of poor parents, whatever their class or occupation, at the expense of the State.

21. The State must see to raising the standard of health in the nation by protecting mothers and infants, prohibiting child labour, increasing bodily efficiency by obligatory gymnastics and sports laid down by law, and by extensive support of clubs engaged in the bodily development of the young.

22. We demand abolition of a paid army and formation of a national army.

23. We demand legal warfare against conscious political lying and its dissemination in the Press. In order to facilitate creation of a German national Press we demand:
    (a) that all editors of newspapers and their assistants, employing the German language, must be members of the nation;
    (b) that special permission from the State shall be necessary before non-German newspapers may appear. These are not necessarily printed in the German language;
    (c) that non-Germans shall be prohibited by law from participating financially in or influencing German newspapers, and that the penalty for contravention of the law shall be suppression of any such newspaper, and immediate deportation of the non-German concerned in it.

    It must be forbidden to publish papers which do not conduce to the national welfare. We demand legal prosecution of all tendencies in art and literature of a kind likely to disintegrate our life as a nation, and the suppression of institutions which militate against the requirements above-mentioned.

24. We demand liberty for all religious denominations in the State, so far as they are not a danger to it and do not militate against the moral feelings of the German race.

    The Party, as such, stands for positive Christianity, but does not bind itself in the matter of creed to any particular confession. It combats the Jewish-materialist spirit within us and without us, and is convinced that our nation can only achieve permanent health from within on the principle: THE COMMON INTEREST BEFORE SELF.

25. That all the foregoing may be realized we demand the creation of a strong central power of the State. Unquestioned authority of the politically centralised Parliament over the entire Reich and its organisations; and formation of Chambers for classes and occupations for the purpose of carrying out the general laws promulgated by the Reich in the various States of the confederation.

    The leaders of the party swear to go straight forward—if necessary to sacrifice their lives—in securing fulfilment of the foregoing Points.

Munich, February 24th, 1920.

Mein Kampf

Adolf Hitler (1889–1945), the son of an Austrian customs official, was influenced by two currents in his youth: the pan-Germanism rife in his hometown and the antisemitism of Vienna. He served through the war in the German army and after 1918 continued to serve the army by spying on minor political groups. In this capacity he got in touch with the German Workers' Party and quickly made himself its leader. In November 1923, after the failure of a putsch, or uprising, that he and General Ludendorff had attempted in Munich, Hitler was sentenced to a term of imprisonment. During this time he wrote the first volume of Mein Kampf *"My Struggle," which was completed by a second volume in 1927. After his accession to power in 1933,* Mein Kampf *served as the Nazi movement's bible. It was widely distributed, a copy being presented to every German bride. If the book ever did come to the attention of Western leaders, their policies unfortunately showed little sign of it.*

Adolf Hitler: from Mein Kampf

RULES OF ACTION

I wish, moreover, to state the following general premises:

If by foreign policy we understand the regulation of the relations of a people to the rest of the world, then the nature of this regulation will be determined by very definite facts. As National Socialists, we can further set forth the following principle with regard to the nature of the foreign policy of a folk-state:

It is the task of the foreign policy of a folk-state to secure the existence on this planet of the race which is encompassed by the state and at the same time to establish a healthy, viable, natural relation between the number and growth of the folk on the one hand and the size and quality of its soil and territory on the other hand.

In this connection only that condition may be regarded as a healthy relation which insures the nourishment of the people from its own soil and territory. Any other condition, even though it may endure for hundreds or even thousands of years, is none the less unhealthy and will lead sooner or later to the damaging, if not to the destruction, of the people in question.

We National Socialists must never at any time join in the distasteful hurrah-patriotism of the present-day bourgeois world. It would be particularly deadly to regard the last developments before the war as in any way binding upon our present course. Not a single obligation from the whole historical period of the nineteenth century can be followed up by us. In contrast to the representatives of that period we have again proclaimed ourselves the representatives of the supreme historical viewpoint of all foreign policy, namely: to bring the territory into harmony with the size of the population. Yes, we can only learn from the past that we must undertake the setting of aims for our political activity in two directions: Soil and territory as the goal of our foreign policy, and a new, philosophically firm and uniform foundation as the goal of our domestic political activity.

Our task, the mission of the National Socialist movement, however, is to lead our folk to such political insight that it will see its future goal fulfilled not in the intoxicating impression of a new Alexandrian campaign but rather in the industrious work of the German plow, which waits only to be given land by the sword.

If the National Socialist movement, in view of this greatest and most important task, frees itself of all illusions and lets reason prevail as its sole guide, then the catastrophe of the year 1918 can one day turn into an infinite blessing for the future of our folk. As a result of this collapse our people can achieve a complete reorientation of its foreign political activity, and, furthermore, inwardly strengthened by its new philosophy, it can arrive externally at a final stabilization of its foreign policy. It can then, at last, attain that which England has, which even Russia used to have, and which enabled France always to make uniform decisions which were in the last analysis best for her interests, namely: a political testament.

But the political testament of the German nation for its outwardly directed activity should and must always have the following import:

Never tolerate the establishment of two continental powers in Europe. See an attack against Germany in every attempt to organize a second military power on the German borders, even if it is only in the form of the establishment of a state which is a potential military power, and see therein not only the right but also the duty to prevent the formation of such a state with all means, even to the use of force, or if it has already been established, to destroy it again. See to it that the strength of our folk has its foundations not in colonies but in the soil of the European homeland. Never regard the foundations of the Reich as secure, if it is not able to give every off-shoot of our folk its own bit of soil and territory for centuries to come. Never forget that the most sacred right in the world is the right to the soil which a man wishes to till himself, and the most sacred sacrifice is the blood which he spills for this soil.

The basic racial elements are differently situated, not only territorially but also in individual cases within the same territory. Nordic men exist side by side with Eastern types; Easterners, with Dinarics; both of these types, with Westerners; and everywhere among them are mixed types. On the one hand this is a great disadvantage: The German folk lacks that sure instinct of the herd which has its roots in the unity of blood and, especially in moments when great danger threatens, preserves the nation from collapse, in as much as with such a folk all small internal distinctions will then immediately disappear and the common enemy will be faced with the closed front of the uniform herd. In the existence side by side of our most varied component racial elements, which have remained unmixed, lies the foundation of that which we designate with the word superindividualism. In peaceful times it may sometimes perform good services for us, but, considered all in all, it has deprived us of world supremacy. If the German folk, in its historical development, had possessed that herdlike unity which other peoples have enjoyed, the German Reich would today be mistress of the globe. World history would have taken another course, and no one can tell whether in this way that might not have been attained which so many deluded pacifists are hoping today to wheedle by moaning and whining: A peace supported not by the palm branches of tearful pacifistic female mourners but founded by the victorious sword of a master race (Herrenvolk) which places the world in the service of a higher culture. . . .

PROPAGANDA

In this regard one proceeded from the very correct principle that the size of the lie always involves a certain factor of credibility, since the great mass of a people will be more spoiled in the innermost depths of its heart, rather than consciously and deliberately bad. Consequently, in view of the primitive simplicity of its mind it is more readily captivated by a big lie than by a small one, since it itself often uses small lies but would be, nevertheless, too ashamed to make use of big lies. Such an untruth will not even occur to it, and it will not even believe that others are capable of the enormous insolence of the most vile distortions. Why, even when enlightened, it will still vacillate and be in doubt about the matter and will nevertheless accept as true at least some cause or other. Consequently, even from the most impudent lie something will always stick.

To whom must propaganda appeal? To the scientific mind or to the less educated masses?

The task of propaganda does not lie in a scientific education of the individual but in pointing out to the masses definite facts, processes, necessities, etc., the significance of which in this way is first to be brought within the masses' range of vision.

The art lies exclusively therein, to do this in such an excellent way that a universal conviction arises of the reality of a fact, of the necessity of a process, of the correctness of something necessary, etc. Since it is not and cannot be necessary in itself, since its task, just as in the case of a placard, consists of bringing something before the attention of the crowd and not in the instruction of those who are scientifically trained or are seeking education and insight, its efficacy must always be oriented more to the emotions and only in a very restricted way to the so-called "intellect."

All propaganda has to appeal to the people and its intellectual level has to be set in accordance with the receptive capacities of the most-limited persons among those to whom it intends to address itself. The larger the mass of men to be reached, the lower its purely intellectual level will have to be set.

The more modest, then, its scientific balast, and the more it exclusively takes account of the emotions of the masses, the more decisive will be its success. This, however, is the best proof of the accuracy or non-accuracy of propaganda and not the successful satisfaction of a few scholars or youthful esthetes.

The art of propaganda lies precisely therein, that, comprehending the great masses' world of emotions and imagination, it finds the way, in a psychologically correct form, to the attention and, further, to the hearts of the great masses.

The receptive capacity of the great masses is very restricted, its understanding small. On the other hand, however, its forgetfulness is great. On account of these facts all effective propaganda must restrict itself to very few points and impress these by slogans, until even the last person is able to bring to mind what is meant by such a word.

The task of propaganda is, for instance, not to evaluate diverse rights but to emphasize exclusively the single right of that which it is representing. It does not have to investigate objectively the truth, so far as this is favorable to the others, in order then to present it to the masses in strict honesty, but rather to serve its own side ceaselessly.

If one's own propaganda even once accords just the shimmer of right to the other side, then the basis is therewith laid for doubt regarding one's own cause. The masses are not able to distinguish where the error of the other side ends and the error of one's own side begins.

But all talent in presentation of propaganda will lead to no success if a fundamental principle is not always strictly followed. Propaganda has to restrict itself to a few matters and to repeat these eternally. Persistence is here, as with so many other things in the world, the first and most important presupposition for success.

Propaganda is, however, not designed to furnish jaded gentlemen currently with interesting diversions but rather to convince, and, indeed, to convince the masses. In view of their slowness of mind, they require always, however, a certain period before they are ready even to take cognizance of a matter, and only after a thousandfold repetition of the most simple concept will they finally retain it.

Any variation ought never to affect the content of that which the propaganda seeks to present, rather the same thing must always be said at the end. Thus the catchword must be elucidated from various sides, but the end of every consideration must always reiterate anew the catchword itself. Only in this way can and will the propaganda have a unified and concentrated effect.

In general the art of all truly great popular leaders at all times consists primarily in not scattering the attention of a people but rather in concentrating it always on one single opponent. The more unified this use of the fighting will of a people, the greater will be the magnetic attractive force of a movement and the more powerful the force of its push. It is a part of the genius of a great leader to make even quite different opponents appear as if they belonged only to one category, because the recognition of different enemies leads weak and unsure persons only too readily to begin doubting their own cause.

When the vacillating masses see themselves fighting against too many enemies, objectivity at once sets in and raises the question whether really all the others are wrong and only one's own people or one's own movement is right.

Therewith, however, appears already the first weakening of one's own force. Consequently, a number of intrinsically different opponents must always be comprehended together, so that in the view of the masses of one's own adherents the fight is only being carried on against one enemy alone. This strengthens the faith in one's own cause and increases the bitterness toward the aggressor against this cause.

In all cases in which there is a question of the fulfillment of apparently impossible demands or tasks, the entire attention of a people must be concentrated only on this one question, in such a way as if being or non-being actually depends on its solution. Only in this way will one make a people willing and capable of really great accomplishments and exertions.

This principle is also true for the individual man, if he wants to attain high goals. He also will be able to accomplish this only in steplike stages. He also will have to concentrate his entire exertions toward the attainment of a definitely restricted task until this one appears to be fulfilled, and the determination of a new segment can be undertaken. If he does not undertake to divide in separate stages the path to be mastered and does not seek to accomplish these one by one, systematically, by means of the greatest concentration of all energies, he will never be able to arrive at the final goal but rather will remain somewhere on the way, perhaps indeed somewhere off on a tangent. This slow approach to the goal is an art and always requires the use of all energies in order thus to accomplish the way step by step.

The most primary prerequisite, accordingly, which is necessary for the attack on a very difficult partial segment of the human path is this, that the leadership succeeds in presenting to the mass of the people precisely that partial goal, which is now to be attained, better, to be fought for, as the only goal worthy of attention, on whose attainment everything depends. The great mass of the people can never see the entire way before them, without tiring and doubting the task. It will to a certain extent keep the goal in mind; in general, however, it is only able to survey the path in small partial segments, just as the hiker, who likewise knows the destination of his journey but who proceeds better along the endless road if he divides it up for himself in segments and marches in each single one as if it were the desired goal itself. Only in this way does he get ahead without despairing.

Elements of Nazi Ideology

As National Socialist ideas of race, state, and the cult of the leader developed, they became more than mere inanities to be bandied about beer halls; they were now the law of the German state, a state bent on spreading them throughout the world. A number of learned works drew the legal and constitutional implications of Nazi doctrines. Of these, one of the best is Ernst Rudolf Huber's Constitutional Law of the Greater German Reich, *published in 1939. The passages that follow are taken from the U.S. State Department's compilation on* National Socialism, *and the commentaries with which they are interspersed are those of the chief editor, Raymond E. Murphy, and his fellow editors.*

U.S. State Department: *from* National Socialism

THE VOLK

Ernst Rudolf Huber, in his basic work *Verfassungsrecht des grossdeutschen Reiches (Constitutional Law of the Greater German Reich),* published in 1939, states:

"The new constitution of the German Reich . . . is not a constitution in the formal sense such as was typical of the nineteenth century. The new Reich has no written constitutional declaration, but its constitution exists in the unwritten basic political order of the Reich. One recognizes it in the spiritual powers which fill our people, in the real authority in which our political life is grounded, and in the basic laws regarding the structure of the state which have been proclaimed so far. The advantage of such an unwritten constitution over the formal constitution is that the basic principles do not become rigid but remain in a constant, living movement. Not dead institutions but living principles determine the nature of the new constitutional order."

In developing his thesis Huber points out that the National Socialist state rests on three basic concepts, the Volk or people, the Führer,[1] and the movement or party. With reference to the first element, the Volk, he argues that the democracies develop their concept of the people from the wrong approach: They start with the concept of the state and its functions and consider the people as being made up of all the elements which fall within the borders or under the jurisdiction of the state. National Socialism, on the other hand, starts with the concept of the people, which forms a political unity, and builds the state upon this foundation.

"There is no people without an objective unity, but there is also none without a common consciousness of unity. A people is determined by a number of different factors: by racial derivation and by the character of its land, by language and other forms of life, by religion and history, but also by the common consciousness of its solidarity and by its common will to unity. For the concrete concept of a people, as represented by the various peoples of the earth, it is of decisive significance which of these various factors they regard as determinants for the nature of the people. The new German Reich proceeds from the concept of the political people, determined by the natural characteristics and by the historical idea of a closed community. The political people is formed through the uniformity of its natural characteristics. Race is the natural basis of the people. . . . As a political people the natural community becomes conscious of its solidarity and strives to form itself, to develop itself, to defend itself, to

---

[1] leader.

realize itself. 'Nationalism' is essentially this striving of a people which has become conscious of itself toward self-direction and self-realization, toward a deepening and renewing of its natural qualities.

"This consciousness of self, springing from the consciousness of a historical idea, awakens in a people its will to historical formation: the will to action. The political people is no passive, sluggish mass, no mere object for the efforts of the state at government or protective welfare work. . . . The great misconception of the democracies is that they can see the active participation of the people only in the form of plebiscites according to the principle of majority. In a democracy the people does not act as a unit but as a complex of unrelated individuals who form themselves into parties. . . . The new Reich is based on the principle that real action of a self-determining people is only possible according to the principle of leadership and following."

THE FÜHRER

The second pillar of the Nazi state is the Führer, the infallible leader, to whom his followers owe absolute obedience. The Führer principle envisages government of the state by a hierarchy of leaders, each of whom owes unconditional allegiance to his immediate superior and at the same time is the absolute leader in his own particular sphere of jurisdiction.

One of the best expositions of Nazi concept of the Führer principle is given by Huber in his *Constitutional Law of the Greater German Reich*:

"The Führer-Reich of the (German) people is founded on the recognition that the true will of the people cannot be disclosed through parliamentary votes and plebiscites but that the will of the people in its pure and uncorrupted form can only be expressed through the Führer. Thus a distinction must be drawn between the supposed will of the people in a parliamentary democracy, which merely reflects the conflict of the various social interests, and the true will of the people in the Führer-state, in which the collective will of the real political unit is manifested. . . .

"The Führer is the bearer of the people's will; he is independent of all groups, associations, and interests, but he is bound by laws which are inherent in the nature of his people. In this twofold condition: independence of all factional interests but unconditional dependence on the people, is reflected the true nature of the Führer principle. Thus the Führer has nothing in common with the functionary, the agent, or the exponent who exercises a mandate delegated to him and who is bound to the will of those who appoint him. The Führer is no 'representative' of a particular group whose wishes he must carry out. He is no 'organ' of the state in the sense of a mere executive agent. He is rather himself the bearer of the collective will of the people. In his will the will of the people is realized. He transforms the mere feelings of the people into a conscious will. . . . Thus it is possible for him, in the name of the true will of the people which he serves, to go against the subjective opinions and convictions of single individuals within the people if these are not in accord with the objective destiny of the people. . . . He shapes the collective will of the people within himself and he embodies the political unity and entirety of the people in opposition to individual interests. . . .

"But the Führer, even as the bearer of the people's will, is not arbitrary and free of all responsibility. His will is not the subjective, individual will of a single man, but the collective national will is embodied within him in all its objective, historical greatness. . . . Such a collective will is not a fiction, as is the collective will of the democracies, but it is a political reality which finds its expression in the Führer. The people's collective will has its foundation in the political idea which is given to a people. It is present in the people, but the Führer raises it to consciousness and discloses it. . . .

"In the Führer are manifested also the natural laws inherent in the people: It is he who makes them into a code governing all national activity. In disclosing these natural laws he sets up the great ends which are to be attained and draws up the plans for the utilization of all national powers in the achievement of the common goals. Through his planning and directing he gives the national life its true purpose and value. This directing and planning activity is especially manifested in the lawgiving power which lies in the Führer's hand. The great change in significance which the law has undergone is characterized therein that it no longer sets up the limits of social life, as in liberalistic times, but that it drafts the plans and the aims of the nation's actions. . . .

"The Führer principle rests upon unlimited authority but not upon mere outward force. It has often been said, but it must constantly be repeated, that the Führer principle has nothing in common with arbitrary bureaucracy and represents no system of brutal force, but that it can only be maintained by mutual loyalty which must find its expression in a free relation. The Führer-order depends upon the responsibility of the following, just as it counts on the responsibility and loyalty of the Führer to his mission and to his following. . . ."

The nature of the plebiscites which are held from time to time in a National Socialist state, Huber points out, cannot be understood from a democratic standpoint. Their purpose is not to give the people an opportunity to decide some issue but rather to express their unity behind a decision which the Führer, in his capacity as the bearer of the people's will, has already made:

"That the will of the people is embodied in the Führer does not exclude the possibility that the Führer can summon all members of the people to a plebiscite on a certain question. In this 'asking of the people' the Führer does not, of course, surrender his decisive power to the voters. The purpose of the plebiscite is not to let the people act in the Führer's place or to replace the Führer's decision with the result of the plebiscite. Its purpose is rather to give the whole people an opportunity to demonstrate and proclaim its support of an aim announced by the Führer. It is intended to solidify the unity and agreement between the objective people's will embodied in the Führer and the living, subjective conviction of the people as it exists in the individual members. . . . This approval of the Führer's decision is even more clear and effective if the plebiscite is concerned with an aim which has already been realized rather than with a mere intention."

Huber states that the Reichstag elections in the Third Reich have the same character as the plebiscites. The list of delegates is made up by the Führer and its approval by the people represents an expression of renewed and continued faith in him. The

Reichstag no longer has any governing or lawgiving powers but acts merely as a sounding board for the Führer:

"It would be impossible for a law to be introduced and acted upon in the Reichstag which had not originated with the Führer or, at least, received his approval. The procedure is similar to that of the plebiscite: The lawgiving power does not rest in the Reichstag; it merely proclaims through its decision its agreement with the will of the Führer, who is the lawgiver of the German people."

Huber also shows how the position of the Führer developed from the Nazi Party movement:

"The office of the Führer developed out of the National Socialist movement. It was originally not a state office; this fact can never be disregarded if one is to understand the present legal and political position of the Führer. The office of the Führer first took root in the structure of the Reich when the Führer took over the powers of the Chancelor, and then when he assumed the position of the Chief of State. But his primary significance is always as leader of the movement; he has absorbed within himself the two highest offices of the political leadership of the Reich and has created thereby the new office of 'Führer of the people and the Reich.' That is not a superficial grouping together of various offices, functions, and powers. . . . It is not a union of offices but a unity of office. The Führer does not unite the old offices of Chancelor and President side by side within himself, but he fills a new, unified office.

"The Führer unites in himself all the sovereign authority of the Reich; all public authority in the state as well as in the movement is derived from the authority of the Führer. We must speak not of the state's authority but of the Führer's authority if we wish to designate the character of the political authority within the Reich correctly. The state does not hold political authority as an impersonal unit but receives it from the Führer as the executor of the national will. The authority of the Führer is complete and all-embracing; it unites in itself all the means of political direction; it extends into all fields of national life; it embraces the entire people, which is bound to the Führer in loyalty and obedience. The authority of the Führer is not limited by checks and controls, by special autonomous bodies or individual rights, but it is free and independent, all-inclusive and unlimited. It is not, however, self-seeking or arbitrary and its ties are within itself. It is derived from the people; that is, it is entrusted to the Führer by the people. It exists for the people and has its justification in the people; it is free of all outward ties because it is in its innermost nature firmly bound up with the fate, the welfare, the mission, and the honor of the people."

THE PARTY

The third pillar of the Nazi state, the link between Volk and Führer, is the Nazi Party. According to Nazi ideology, all authority within the nation is derived ultimately from the people, but it is the party through which the people expresses itself. In *Rechtseinrichtungen und Rechtsaufgaben der Bewegung* (Legal Organisation and Legal Functions of the Movement) published in 1939, Otto Gauweiler states:

"The will of the German people finds its expression in the party as the political organization of the people. It represents the political conception, the political conscience, and the political will. It is the expression and the organ of the people's creative will to life. It comprises a select part of the German people for 'only the best Germans should be party members.' . . . The inner organization of the party must therefore bring the national life which is concentrated within itself to manifestation and development in all the fields of national endeavor in which the party is represented."

The party derives its legal basis from the law inherent in the living organism of the German Volk:

"The inner law of the NSDAP is none other than the inner law of the German people. The party arises from the people; it has formed an organization which crystallizes about itself the feelings of the people, which seemed buried, and the strength of the people, which seemed lost."

The Party has two great tasks—to insure the continuity of national leadership and to preserve the unity of the Volk:

"The first main task of the party, which is in keeping with its organic nature, is to protect the National Socialist idea and to constantly renew it by drawing from the depths of the German soul, to keep it pure and clear, and to pass it on thus to coming generations: this is predominantly a matter of education of the people."

PROPERTY

In the Third Reich the holder of property is considered merely as a manager responsible to the Volk for the use of the property in the common interest. Huber sets forth the Nazi view in the following words:

" 'Private property' as conceived under the liberalistic economic order was a reversal of the true concept of property. This 'private property' represented the right of the individual to manage and to speculate with inherited or acquired property as he pleased, without regard for the general interests. . . . German socialism had to overcome this 'private,' that is, unrestrained and irresponsible view of property. All property is common property. The owner is bound by the people and the Reich to the responsible management of his goods. His legal position is only justified when he satisfies this responsibility to the community."

Appeasement

To the challenge of the dictators, the Western powers adopted a policy of weakness and uncertainty that came to be known as appeasement. Most English and French citizens wanted to live in peace and thought that wanting peace was enough to maintain it. Unwilling to prepare for war or pay for arms that would discourage aggression, they preferred to negotiate with the dictators, hoping to satisfy them—preferably at the expense of someone else. This flaccid policy explains why the Western powers did not go beyond mere protests when Hitler reoccupied the demilitarized zone of the Rhineland in 1936 and annexed Austria in 1938; it helps account for their extraordinary pusillanimity in the Czech crisis shortly thereafter. Other factors also entered in: the fear of communism and of Russian ambitions, which since 1918 had stood the Germans in good stead, had brought Hitler and Mussolini a certain amount of sympathy as the most active opponents of Bolshevism, and had made for the policy of nonintervention in Spain (meaning no intervention on the democratic side); the long-standing mess in French internal affairs; and the American withdrawal from effective international activity, which encouraged European statesmen to underrate the significance of American power and to regard international issues only in terms of European power. But the essence of the debate in the West is reflected in the speeches made in the British House of Commons during the Munich crisis of 1938.

Debate on the German Crisis

The development of the Munich crisis during the late summer of 1938 is outlined in the following account, which the British prime minister, Neville Chamberlain, presented to the House of Commons. Germany demanded the Sudeten-German territories of Czechoslovakia, whose territorial integrity was guaranteed by France, who, in turn, was the ally of Britain. Had war broken out over the Sudetenland, the Germans would have had to fight the Czechs in their strongly fortified Bohemian positions, their French allies on the Rhine, and probably the British as well. Hitler wanted to avoid this by persuading Czechoslovakia's Western allies that the Sudetenland was not worth a war; and in his efforts he was unwittingly but mightily helped by the somewhat confused but sincere ideas held by Chamberlain and his friends as to the possibilities of a just settlement followed by a lasting peace.

British Parliament: Debate of September 28, 1938

The Prime Minister, Mr. Chamberlain: Shortly before the House adjourned at the end of July 1 remember that some questions were addressed to me as to the possibility of summoning the House before the time arranged, and during the Recess, in certain eventualities. Those eventualities referred to possible developments in Spain. But the matter which has brought us together today is one which even at that time was already threatening but which, I think, we all hoped would find a peaceful solution before we met again. Unhappily those hopes have not been fulfilled. Today we are faced with a situation which has had no parallel since 1914.

To find the origins of the present controversy it would be necessary to go back to the constitution of the state of Czechoslovakia with its heterogeneous population. No doubt at the time when it was constituted it seemed to those then responsible that it was the best arrangement that could be made in the light of conditions as they then supposed them to exist. I cannot help reflecting that if Article 19 of the Covenant providing for the revision of the Treaties by agreement had been put into operation, as was contemplated by the framers of the Covenant, instead of waiting until passions became so exasperated that revision by agreement became impossible, we might have avoided the crisis. For that omission all Members of the League must bear their responsibility. I am not here to apportion blame among them.

The position that we had to face in July was that a deadlock had arisen in the negotiations which had been going on between the Czechoslovak Government and the Sudeten Germans and that fears were already entertained that if it were not readily broken the German Government might presently intervene in the dispute. For His Majesty's Government there were three alternative courses that we might have adopted. Either we could have threatened to go to war with Germany if she attacked Czechoslovakia, or we could have stood aside and allowed matters to take their course, or, finally, we could attempt to find a peaceful settlement by way of mediation. The first of those courses we rejected. We had no treaty liabilities to Czechoslovakia. We always refused to accept any such obligation. Indeed, this country, which does not readily resort to war, would not have followed us if we had tried to lead it into war to prevent a minority from obtaining autonomy, or even from choosing to pass under some other Government.

The second alternative was also repugnant to us. However remote this territory may be, we knew, of course, that a spark once lighted there might give rise to a general conflagration, and we felt it our duty to do anything in our power to help the contending parties to find agreement. We addressed ourselves to the third course, the task of mediation. We knew that the task would be difficult, perhaps even perilous, but we felt that the object was good enough to justify the risk, and when Lord Runciman had expressed his willingness to undertake our mission, we were happy to think that we had secured a mediator whose long experience, and well-known qualities . . . gave us

---

the best hope of success. That in the end Lord Runciman did not succeed was no fault of his. . . .

On 21st September Lord Runciman addressed a letter to me reporting the results of his mission. . . . Perhaps I may conveniently mention some of the salient points of his story. On 7th June the Sudeten German party had put forward certain proposals. . . . The Czechoslovak Government on their side had embodied their proposals in a draft Nationality Statute, a Language Bill, and an Administrative Reform Bill. By the middle of August it had become clear to Lord Runciman that the gap between these two proposals was too wide to permit of negotiations between the parties on that basis. In his capacity as mediator, he was successful in preventing the Sudeten German party from closing the door upon further negotiations, and he was largely instrumental in inducing Dr. Benes to put forward new proposals on 21st August, which appear to have been regarded by the Sudeten party leaders as a suitable basis for the continuance of negotiations. The prospects of negotiations being carried through to a successful conclusion were, however, handicapped by the recurrence of incidents in Czechoslovakia, involving casualties both on the Czech and on the Sudeten German side.

On 1st and 2nd September Herr Henlein went to Berchtesgaden to consult with Herr Hitler about the situation. [Henlein returns "convinced of Herr Hitler's desire for a peaceful solution" but calling once more for the maximum programme from which he had started.] . . .

In the meantime, however, developments in Germany itself had been causing considerable anxiety to His Majesty's Government. On 28th July the Secretary of State for Foreign Affairs had written a personal letter to the German Minister of Foreign Affairs, Herr von Ribbentrop, expressing his regret at the latter's statement to Sir Neville Henderson, our Ambassador in Berlin, that the German Government must reserve its attitude towards Lord Runciman's mission and regard the matter as one of purely British concern. The Secretary of State had gone on to express the hope that the German Government would collaborate with His Majesty's Government in facilitating a peaceful solution of the Sudeten question and so opening the way to establishing relations between Great Britain and Germany on a basis of mutual confidence and cooperation.

But early in August we received reports of military preparations in Germany on an extensive scale. . . . These measures, which involved a widespread dislocation of civilian life, could not fail to be regarded abroad as equivalent to partial mobilisation, and they suggested that the German Government were determined to find a settlement of the Sudeten question by the autumn. In these circumstances H.M. Ambassador in Berlin was instructed, in the middle of August, to point out to the German Government that these abnormal measures could not fail to be interpreted abroad as a threatening gesture towards Czechoslovakia, that they must therefore increase the feeling of tension throughout Europe, and that they might compel the Czechoslovak Government to take precautionary measures on their side. The almost certain consequence would be to destroy all chance of successful mediation by Lord Runciman's mission and perhaps endanger the peace of every one of the great Powers of Europe. This, the Ambassador added, might also destroy the prospects of the resumption of Anglo-German conversations. In these circumstances it was hoped that the German Government might be able to modify their military measures in order to avoid these dangers.

To these representations Herr von Ribbentrop replied in a letter in which he re-fused to discuss the military measures referred to and expressed the opinion that the British efforts in Prague had only served to increase Czech intransigence. In face of this attitude H.M. Government, through the Chancellor of the Exchequer, who happened to be speaking at Lanark on 27th August, drew attention again to some words which I had used on 24th March in this House. . . .

> Where peace and war are concerned, legal obligations are not alone involved, and, if war broke out, it would be unlikely to be confined to those who have assumed such obligations. It would be quite impossible to say where it would end and what governments might become involved. The inexorable pressure of facts might well prove more powerful than formal pronouncements, and in that event it would be well within the bounds of probability that other countries, besides those which were parties to the original dispute, would almost immediately become involved. This is especially true in the case of two countries like Great Britain and France, with long associations of friendship, with interests closely interwoven, devoted to the same ideals of democratic liberty, and determined to uphold them. (Official Report, 24 March, 1938)

Towards the end of August further events occurred which marked the increasing seriousness of the situation. The French Government, in consequence of information which had reached them about the moving of several German divisions towards their frontier, took certain precautionary measures themselves, including the calling up of reserves to man the Maginot Line. On 28th August Sir Neville Henderson had been recalled to London for consultation and a special meeting of Ministers was held on 30th August to consider his report and the general situation. On the 31st he returned to Berlin and he gave Baron von Weizsäcker, the State Secretary at the Wilhelmstrasse, a strong personal warning regarding the probable attitude of H.M. Government in the event of German aggression against Czechoslovakia, particularly if France were compelled to intervene. On 1st September the Ambassador saw Herr von Ribbentrop and repeated to him, as a personal and most urgent message, the warning he had already given to the State Secretary on the previous day.

In addressing these personal warnings . . . and in making the reference to Czecho-slovakia contained in the Chancellor of the Exchequer's speech on 27th August, H.M. Government desired to impress the seriousness of the situation upon the German Gov-ernment without risking a further aggravation of the situation by any formal represen-tations, which might have been interpreted by the German Government as a public rebuff, as had been the case (before). . . . H.M. Government also had to bear in mind the close approach of the Nazi Party Conference at Nuremberg, which was to open on 5th September and to last until the 12th. It was to be anticipated that the German Chancellor would feel himself compelled to make some public statement regarding the Sudeten question, and it therefore appeared necessary, in addition to warning the Ger-man Government . . . to make every effort in Prague to secure a resumption of negotia-tions between the Czechoslovak Government and the Sudeten representatives. . . .

Accordingly, H.M. Minister at Prague saw Dr. Benes on 3rd September and emphasized to him that it was vital in the interests of Czechoslovakia to offer immediately and without reservation those concessions without which the Sudeten question could not be immediately settled. H.M. Government were not in a position to say whether anything less than the full Carlsbad programme (Henlein's original demands) would suffice. They certainly felt that the Czechoslovak Government should go forthwith and unreservedly to the limit of concessions. . . . Dr. Benes responded to these representations, which were made in the best interests of Czechoslovakia, by putting forward proposals afterwards known as the Fourth Plan, which were communicated to the Sudeten German representatives on 6th September. In Lord Runciman's opinion this plan embodied almost all the requirements of the eight Carlsbad points and formed a very favourable basis for the resumption of negotiations. In forming this opinion he was guided partly by his own examination . . . and partly by the favourable reception that was accorded to it by the Sudeten negotiators. . . . The prospects of a satisfactory solution of the Sudeten question on the basis of autonomy within the Czechoslovak State appeared not unpromising. . . . The publication of the Fourth Plan (September 7th) was, unfortunately, however, immediately followed by a serious incident. . . . It would appear from the investigations of the British observer that the importance of this incident was very much exaggerated. The immediate result was a decision on the part of the Sudeten leaders not to resume negotiations until this incident had been liquidated. Immediately measures were taken by the Czechoslovak government to liquidate it, but further incidents took place on 11th September near Eger, and, in spite of Lord Runciman's efforts to bring both parties together, negotiations could not be resumed before Herr Hitler's speech winding up the Nuremberg Congress on 12th September. . . .

In his speech on 12th September Herr Hitler laid great stress upon the defensive military measures taken on Germany's western frontier. In his references to Czechoslovakia he reminded the world that on 22nd February he had said that the Reich would no longer tolerate further oppression or persecution of the Sudeten Germans. They demanded the right of self-determination, he said, and they were supported in their demand by the Reich. Therefore, for the first time this speech promised the support of the Reich to the Sudeten Germans if they could not obtain satisfaction for themselves, and for the first time it publicly raised the issue of self-determination. He did not, however, close the door upon further negotiations in Prague, nor did he demand a plebiscite. As the speech was also accompanied by pacifying references to Germany's frontiers with Poland and France, its general effect was to leave the situation unchanged, with a slight diminution of tension.

The speech, however, and in particular Herr Hitler's reference to German support for the cause of the Sudeten Germans, had an immediate and unfortunate effect among those people. Demonstrations took place throughout the Sudetenland, resulting in an immediate extension of the incidents which had already begun on 11th September. Serious rioting occurred, accompanied by attacks upon Czech police and officials, and by 14th September . . . there had been 21 killed and 75 wounded, the majority of whom were Czechs. Martial law was immediately proclaimed in the affected districts. On the evening of 13th September Herr Henlein and other Sudeten leaders assembled at Eger and sent a telegram to the Czechoslovak Government, declaring that they could not be responsible for the consequences of martial law and the special Czech emergency measures if they were not immediately withdrawn. Attempts by Lord Runciman's Mission to bring the Sudeten leaders into discussion with the Czechoslovak Government failed, and on 14th September Herr Henlein issued a proclamation stating that the Carlsbad points were no longer enough and that the situation called for self-determination. Thereupon, Herr Henlein fled to Germany. . . . The House will recall that by the evening of the 14th September a highly critical situation had developed in which there was immediate danger of the German troops now concentrated upon the frontier entering Czechoslovakia to prevent further incidents occurring in Sudetenland, and fighting between the Czech forces and the Sudeten Germans, although reliable reports indicated that order had been completely restored in those districts by 14th September. On the other hand, the Czechoslovak Government might have felt compelled to mobilise at once and so risk provoking a German invasion. In either event German invasion might have been expected to bring into operation French obligations to come to the assistance of Czechoslovakia, and so lead to a European war in which this country might well have been involved in support of France.

In those circumstances I decided that the time had come to put into operation a plan which I had had in my mind for a considerable period as a last resort. One of the principal difficulties in dealing with totalitarian Governments is the lack of any means of establishing contact with the personalities in whose hands lie the final decisions of the country. So I resolved to go to Germany myself to interview Herr Hitler and find out in personal conversation whether there was yet any hope of saving the peace. I knew very well that in taking such an unprecedented course I was laying myself open to criticism on the ground that I was detracting from the dignity of a British Prime Minister, and to disappointment and perhaps even resentment, if I failed to bring back a satisfactory agreement. But I felt that in such a crisis, where the issues at stake were so vital for millions of human beings, such considerations could not be allowed to count.

Herr Hitler responded to my suggestion with cordiality, and on 15th September I made my first flight to Munich. Thence I travelled by train to Herr Hitler's mountain home at Berchtesgaden. I confess I was astonished at the warmth of the approval with which this adventure was everywhere received, but the relief which it brought for the moment was an indication of the gravity with which the situation had been viewed. At this first conversation . . . I very soon became aware that the position was much more acute and much more urgent than I had realised. . . . Herr Hitler made it plain that he had made up his mind that the Sudeten Germans must have the right of self-determination, and of returning, if they wished, to the Reich. If they could not achieve this by their own efforts, he said, he would assist them to do so, and he declared categorically that rather than wait he would be prepared to risk a world war. . . .

So strongly did I get the impression that the Chancellor was contemplating an immediate invasion of Czechoslovakia that I asked him why he had allowed me to travel all that way, since I was evidently wasting my time. On that he said that if I could give him there and then an assurance that the British Government accepted the principle of self-determination, he would be quite ready to discuss ways and means of carrying it out; but, if, on the contrary, I told him that such a principle could not be considered by the British Government, then he agreed it was of no use to continue our conversations. I of course was not in a position to give there and then such an assurance, but I undertook to return at once to consult with my colleagues if he would refrain from active hostilities until I had had time to obtain a reply. That assurance he gave me. . . . I have no doubt whatever now, looking back, that my visit alone prevented an invasion, for which everything was ready. It was clear to me that with the German troops in the positions they then occupied there was nothing that anybody could do to prevent that invasion unless the right of self-determination were granted to the Sudeten Germans, and that quickly. That was the sole hope of a peaceful solution.

I came back to London next day, and that evening the Cabinet met and it was attended by Lord Runciman who, at my request, had also travelled from Prague on the same day. Lord Runciman informed us that although, in his view, the responsibility for the final breach in the negotiations at Prague rested with the Sudeten extremists, nevertheless, in view of recent developments, the frontier districts between Czechoslovakia and Germany where the Sudeten population was in such an important majority, should be given the full right of self-determination at once. He considered the cession of territory to be inevitable and thought it should be done promptly. . . . Moreover, he considered that the integrity and security of Czechoslovakia could only be maintained if her policy, internal and external, was directed to enabling her to live at peace with all her neighbours. For this purpose, in his opinion, her policy should be entirely neutral, as in the case of Switzerland. This would involve assurances from Czechoslovakia that in no circumstances would she attack any of her neighbours, and it would also mean guarantees from the principal powers of Europe against aggression. . . .

Naturally, H.M. Government felt it necessary to consult the French Government before they replied to Herr Hitler, and, accordingly, M. Daladier and M. Bonnet were invited to fly to London for conversations with British Ministers on 18th September. . . . During these conversations the representatives of the two Governments were guided by a desire to find a solution which would not bring about a European War, and, therefore, a solution which would not automatically compel France to take action in accordance with her obligations. It was agreed that the only means of achieving this object was to accept the principle of self-determination, and, accordingly, the British and French Ministers in Prague were instructed to inform the Czech Government that the further maintenance within the boundaries of the Czechoslovak State of the districts mainly inhabited by Sudeten Germans could not continue any longer without imperilling the interests of Czechoslovakia herself and of European peace. The Czechoslovak Government were, therefore, urged to agree immediately to the direct transfer to the Reich of all areas with over 50% Sudeten inhabitants. An international body was to be set up to deal with questions like the adjustment of frontiers and the possible exchange of populations. . . .

The Czechoslovak Government were informed that, to meet their natural desire for security for their future, H.M. Government would be prepared, as a contribution to the pacification of Europe, to join in an international guarantee of the new boundaries of the Czechoslovak State against unprovoked aggression. Such a guarantee would safeguard the independence of Czechoslovakia by substituting a general guarantee against unprovoked aggression in place of the existing treaties with France and Soviet

Russia, which involve reciprocal obligations of a military character. In urging this solution upon the Czechoslovak Government, the British and French Governments took account of the probability that the Czechoslovak Government would find it preferable to deal with the problem by the method of direct transfer rather than by means of a plebiscite, which would involve serious difficulties as regards other nationalities in Czechoslovakia.

In agreeing to guarantee the future boundaries of Czechoslovakia against unprovoked aggression, H.M. Government were accepting a completely new commitment as we were not previously bound by any obligations towards Czechoslovakia, other than those involved in the League of Nations.

The Czechoslovak Government replied on 20th September to these representations by suggesting that the Sudeten dispute should be submitted to arbitration under the terms of the German-Czechoslovak Arbitration Treaty of 1926. The British and French Ministers in Prague were, however, instructed to point out to the Czechoslovak Government that there was no hope of a peaceful solution on this basis, and, in the interests of Czechoslovakia and of European peace, the Czechoslovak Government was urged to accept the Anglo-French proposals immediately. This they did immediately and unconditionally on 21st September. H.M. Minister in Prague was instructed on 22nd September to inform Dr. Benes that H.M. Government were profoundly conscious of the immense sacrifices to which the Czechoslovak Government had agreed, and the great public spirit they had shown. These proposals had naturally been put forward in the hope of averting a general disaster and saving Czechoslovakia from invasion. The Czechoslovak Government's readiness to go to such extreme limits of concession had assured her of a measure of sympathy which nothing else could have aroused.

That Government resigned on 22nd September, but it was immediately succeeded by a Government of National Concentration under General Syrovy. . . . We had hoped that the immediate problem of the Sudeten Germans would not be further complicated at this particular juncture by the pressing of the claims of the Hungarian and Polish minorities. These minorities have, however, consistently demanded similar treatment to that accorded to the Sudeten minority, and the acceptance of the Anglo-French proposals, involving the cession of the predominantly Sudeten German territories, has led to a similar demand for cession of the territory predominantly inhabited by Polish and Hungarian minorities being advanced by the Hungarian and Polish Governments. . . . Troop movements have taken place in the direction of Teschen and considerable popular feeling has been aroused in Poland. The Hungarian Government has been encouraged by the visits of the Regent to Field Marshal Goering at Rominten on 20th September, and of the Prime Minister, Foreign Minister, and Chief of the General Staff to Berchtesgaden on 21st September. Mobilisation measures have been taken to double the strength of the Hungarian Army.

In view of these developments, the task of finding a solution of the Sudeten German problem was still further complicated. However, on the 22nd, I went back to Germany to Godesberg on the Rhine. . . . Once again I had a very warm welcome in the streets and villages through which I passed, demonstrating to me the desire of the German people for peace, and on the afternoon of my arrival I had my second meeting with the Chancellor. . . . (After some preliminary discussion) Herr Hitler said he could not accept the . . . proposals I had described to him, on the ground that they were too dilatory and offered too many opportunities for further evasion on the part of the Czechs. He insisted that a speedy solution was essential, on account of the oppression and terrorism to which the Sudeten Germans were being subjected, and he proceeded to give me the main outlines of the proposal which he subsequently embodied in a memorandum—except that he did not in this conversation actually name any time limit.

Hon. Members will realise the perplexity in which I found myself, faced with this totally unexpected situation. I had been told at Berchtesgaden that if the principle of self-determination were accepted Herr Hitler would discuss with me the ways and means of carrying it out. He told me afterwards that he never for one moment supposed that I should be able to come back and say that the principle was accepted. I do not want Hon. Members to think that he was deliberately deceiving me—I do not think so for one moment—but, for me, I expected that when I got back to Godesberg I had only to discuss quietly with him the proposals that I had brought with me; and it was a profound shock to me when I was told at the beginning of the conversation that these proposals were not acceptable, and that they were to be replaced by other proposals of a kind which I had not contemplated at all.

I felt that I must have a little time to consider what I was to do. Consequently, I withdrew, my mind full of foreboding as to the success of my mission. [After this, the two statesmen exchanged some written communications, met for a last conversation during which Hitler handed Chamberlain a Memorandum containing his proposals and fixing a time limit for their acceptance, and Chamberlain declared that the manner and the language of the document was "more that of an ultimatum than that of a memorandum."] . . . I think I should add that before saying farewell to Herr Hitler I had a few words with him in private, which I do not think are without importance. In the first place, he repeated to me with great earnestness what he had said already at Berchtesgaden, namely, that this was the last of his territorial ambitions in Europe and that he had no wish to include in the Reich people of other races than Germans. In the second place he said, again very earnestly, that he wanted to be friends with England and that if only this Sudeten question could be got out of the way in peace he would gladly resume conversations. It is true he said, "there is one awkward question, The Colonies." [*Hon. Members:* "Spain." (*Laughter.*)] I really think that at a time like this these are not subjects for idle laughter. They are words which count in the long run and ought to be fully weighed. He said, "There is one awkward question, The Colonies, but that is not a matter for war," and, alluding to the mobilisation of the Czechoslovakian army, which had been announced to us in the middle of our conversations and had given rise to some disturbance, he said, about the colonies, "There will be no mobilisation about that."

I may now briefly recapitulate the contents of the Memorandum. He proposed immediate separation from Czechoslovakia on the areas shaded on the map (which went with the Memorandum). These areas included all areas in which Sudeten Germans constituted more than 50 per cent of the population, and some additional areas. These were to be completely evacuated by Czech soldiers and officials and occupied by German troops by 1st October. A plebiscite was to be held in November, and according to the results a definitive frontier was to be settled. . . . In addition, certain other areas, marked in green, were to be the subject of a plebiscite but these were to remain in occupation of Czech troops. . . . I returned to London on 24th September, and arrangements were made for the German Memorandum and map to be communicated directly to the Czech Government, who received them that evening. On Sunday, the 25th, we received from Mr. Masaryk, the Czech Minister here, the reply of the Czech Government, which stated that they considered Herr Hitler's demands in their present form to be absolutely and unconditionally unacceptable. This reply was communicated to the French Ministers, M. Daladier and M. Bonnet, who arrived that same evening and exchanged views with us on the situation. Conversations were resumed the next morning, when the French Ministers informed us that if Czechoslovakia were attacked France would fulfil her treaty obligations, and in reply we told them that if as a result of these obligations French forces became actively engaged in hostilities against Germany, we should feel obliged to support them.

Meanwhile, as a last effort to preserve peace, I sent Sir Horace Wilson to Berlin on the 26th, with a personal message to Herr Hitler to be delivered before the speech that Herr Hitler was to make in Berlin at 8 o'clock that night. The French Ministers entirely approved this initiative, and issued a communiqué to that effect at midday. Sir Horace Wilson took with him a letter from me . . . pointing out that the reception of the German Memorandum by the Czechoslovak Government and public opinion in the world generally had confirmed the expectations which I had expressed to him at Godesberg. I, therefore, made a further proposal with a view to rendering it possible to get a settlement by negotiation rather than by military force, namely, that there should be immediate discussions between German and Czechoslovak representatives in the presence of British representatives. Sir Horace Wilson arrived in Berlin on the afternoon of the 26th and he presented his letter to Herr Hitler, who listened to him, but expressed the view that he could not depart from the procedure of the Memorandum, as he felt conferences would lead to further intolerable procrastinations.

I should tell the House how deeply impressed on my mind by my conversations with Herr Hitler and by every speech he has made, is his rooted distrust and disbelief in the sincerity of the Czech Government. That has been one of the governing factors in all this difficult story of negotiation.

In the meantime, after reading Herr Hitler's speech in Berlin, in which he, as I say, expressed his disbelief in the intention of the Czech Government to carry out their promises, I issued a statement in which I offered, on behalf of the British Government, to guarantee that the promises they had made to us and the French Government should be carried out. But yesterday morning Sir Horace Wilson resumed his conversations with Herr Hitler, and finding his views apparently still unchanged, he by my instructions repeated to him in precise terms what I said a few minutes ago was the upshot of our conversations with the French, namely, that if the Czechs reject the German Memorandum and Germany attacks Czechoslovakia, we had been informed by the French Government that they would fulfil their obligations to Czechoslovakia, and that should the forces of France in consequence become actively engaged in hostilities against Germany the British Government would feel obliged to support them.

. . . Now the story which I have told the House brings us up to last night. About 10.30 I received from Herr Hitler a reply to my letter sent by Sir Horace Wilson. . . . There is, for example, a definite statement that troops are not to move beyond the red line (on the map), that they are only to preserve order, that the plebiscite will be carried out by a free vote under no outside influence, and that Herr Hitler will abide by the result, and, finally, that he will join the international guarantee of the remainder of Czechoslovakia once the minorities questions are settled. Those are all reassuring statements as far as they go, and I have no hesitation in saying, after the personal contact I had established with Herr Hitler, that I believe he means what he says when he states that. But the reflection which was uppermost in my mind when I read his letter to me was that once more the differences and the obscurities had been narrowed down still further to a point where, really, it was inconceivable that they could not be settled by negotiations. So strongly did I feel this, that I felt impelled to send one more last letter—the last to the Chancellor. I sent him the following personal message:

> After reading your letter I feel certain that you can get all essentials without war and without delay. I am ready to come to Berlin myself at once to discuss arrangements for transfer with you and representatives of Czech Government, together with representatives of France and Italy if you desire. I feel convinced that we could reach agreement in a week. However much you distrust the Prague Government's intentions, you cannot doubt the power of the British and French Governments to see that the promises are carried out fairly and fully and forthwith. As you know, I have stated publicly that we are prepared to undertake that they shall be so carried out. I cannot believe that you will take the responsibility of starting a world war which may end civilization, for the sake of a few days' delay in settling this long-standing problem.

At the same time I sent the following personal message to Signor Mussolini:

> I have today addressed last appeal to Herr Hitler to abstain from force to settle Sudeten problem, which, I feel sure, can be settled by a short discussion and will give him the essential territory, population and protection for both Sudetens and Czechs during transfer. I have offered myself to go at once to Berlin to discuss arrangements with German and Czech representatives, and if the Chancellor desires, representatives also of Italy and France. Trust your Excellency will inform the German Chancellor that you are willing to be represented and ask him to agree to my proposal which will keep all our peoples out of war. I have already guaranteed that Czech promises shall be carried out and feel confident full agreement could be reached in a week.

In reply to my message to Signor Mussolini, I was informed that instructions had been sent by the Duce to the Italian Ambassador in Berlin to see Herr von Ribbentrop at once and to say that whilst Italy would fulfil completely her pledges to stand by Germany, yet, in view of the great importance of the request made by H.M. Government to Signor Mussolini, the latter hoped Herr Hitler would see his way to postpone action which the Chancellor had told Sir Horace Wilson was to be taken at 2 P.M. today for at least 24 hours so as to allow Signor Mussolini time to reexamine the situation and endeavor to find a peaceful settlement. In response, Herr Hitler has agreed to postpone mobilization for 24 hours.

Whatever view Hon. Members may have had about Signor Mussolini in the past, I believe that everyone will welcome his gesture of being willing to work with us for peace in Europe. That is not all. I have something further to say to the House yet. I have now been informed by Herr Hitler that he invites me to meet him at Munich tomorrow morning. He has also invited Signor Mussolini and M. Daladier. Signor Mussolini has accepted and I have no doubt M. Daladier will also accept. I need not say what my answer will be. [*Hon. Member:* "Thank God for the Prime Minister!"] We are all patriots, and there can be no Hon. Member of this House who did not feel his heart leap that the crisis has been once more postponed to give us once more an opportunity to try what reason and good will and discussion will do to settle a problem which is already within sight of settlement. Mr. Speaker, I cannot say any more. I am sure that the House will be ready to release me now to go and see what I can make of this last effort. Perhaps they may think it will be well, in view of this new development, that this debate shall stand adjourned for a few days, when perhaps we may meet in happier circumstances.

The Chamberlain-Hitler Agreement

So the statesmen met at Munich, and Czechoslovakia had to foot the bill. And from Munich Chamberlain returned to the cheers of a relieved and slightly ashamed London crowd, flourishing his private agreement with Hitler which, he claimed, promised "Peace in our time."

We, the German Führer and Chancellor and the British Prime Minister have had a further meeting today and are agreed in recognizing that the question of Anglo-German relations is of the first importance for the two countries and for Europe.

We regard the agreement signed last night and the Anglo-German Naval Agreement as symbolic of the desire of our two peoples never to go to war with one another again.

We are resolved that the method of consultation shall be the method adopted to deal with any other questions that may concern our two countries, and we are determined to continue our efforts to remove possible sources of differences and thus to contribute to assure the peace of Europe.

British Parliament: Debate of October 3, 1938

The debate, which had been adjourned on Wednesday, September 28, reopened the following Monday, October 3, with the resignation speech of Mr. Duff Cooper, who had been first lord of the Admiralty in the Chamberlain government.

Mr. Duff Cooper: The House will, I am sure, appreciate the peculiarly difficult circumstances in which I am speaking this afternoon. It is always a painful and delicate task for a Minister who has resigned to explain his reasons to the House of Commons, and my difficulties are increased this afternoon by the fact, of which I am well aware, that the majority of the House are most anxious to hear the Prime Minister and that I am standing between them and him. But I shall have, I am afraid, to ask for the patience of the House, because I have taken a very important, for me, and difficult decision, and I feel that I shall have to demand a certain amount of time in which to make plain to the House the reasons for which I have taken it.

At the last Cabinet meeting that I attended, last Friday evening, before I succeeded in finding my way to No. 10, Downing Street, I was caught up in a large crowd that were demonstrating their enthusiasm and were cheering, laughing and singing; and there is no greater feeling of loneliness than to be in a crowd of happy, cheerful people and to feel that there is no occasion for oneself for gaiety or for cheering. That there was every cause for relief I was deeply aware, as much as anybody in this country, but that there was great cause for self-congratulation I was uncertain. Later, when I stood in the hall at Downing Street, again among enthusiastic throngs of friends and colleagues who were all as cheerful, happy, glad, and enthusiastic as the crowd in the street, and when I heard the Prime Minister from the window above, saying that he had returned, like Lord Beaconsfield, with "Peace with Honor," claiming that it was Peace for our time, once again I felt lonely and isolated; and when later, in the Cabinet room, all his other colleagues were able to present him with bouquets, it was an extremely painful and bitter moment that all that I could offer him was my resignation.

Before taking such a step as I have taken, on a question of international policy, a Minister must ask himself many questions, not the least important of which is this: Can my resignation at the present time do any material harm to H.M. Government; can it weaken our position; can it suggest to our critics that there is not a united front in Great Britain? Now I would not have flattered myself that my resignation was of great importance, and I did feel confident that so small a blow could easily be borne at the present time, when I think that the Prime Minister is more popular than he has ever been at any period; but had I had any doubts with regard to that facet of the problem, they would have been set at rest, I must say, by the way in which my resignation was accepted, not, I think, with reluctance, but really with relief.

I have always been a student of foreign politics. I have served ten years in the Foreign Office, and I have studied the history of this and of other countries, and I have always believed that one of the most important principles in foreign policy and the conduct of foreign policy should be to make your policy plain to other countries, to let them know where you stand and what, in certain circumstances, you are prepared to do. I remember so well in 1914 meeting a friend, just after the declaration of war, who had come back from the British Embassy in Berlin, and asking him whether it was the case as I had seen it reported in the papers, that the Berlin crowd had behaved very badly and had smashed all the windows of the Embassy, and that the military had had to be called out in order to protect them. I remember my friend telling me that, in his opinion and in that of the majority of the staff, the Berlin crowds were not to blame, that the members of the British Embassy staff had great sympathy with the feelings of the populace, because, they said, "these people have never thought that there was a chance of our coming into the war." They were assured by their Government—and the Government themselves perhaps believed it—that Britain would remain neutral, and therefore it came to them as a shock when, having already been engaged with other enemies, as they were, they found that Great Britain had turned against them.

I thought then, and I have always felt, that in any other international crisis that should occur our first duty was to make it plain exactly where we stood and what we would do. I believe that the great defect in our foreign policy during recent months and recent weeks has been that we have failed to do so. During the last four weeks we have been drifting, day by day, nearer into war with Germany, and we have never said, until the last moment, and then in most uncertain terms, that we were prepared to fight. We knew that information to the opposite effect was being poured into the ears of the head of the State. He had been assured, reassured, and fortified in the opinion that in no case would Great Britain fight.

When Ministers met at the end of August on their return from a holiday there was an enormous accumulation of information from all parts of the world, the ordinary information from our Diplomatic representatives, also secret, and less reliable information from other sources, information from members of Parliament who had been traveling on the Continent and who had felt it their duty to write to their friends in the Cabinet and give them first-hand information which they had received from good sources. I myself had been travelling in Scandinavia and in the Baltic States, and with regard to all this information—Europe was very full of rumors at that time—it was quite extraordinary the unanimity with which it pointed to one conclusion and with which all sources suggested that there was one remedy. All information pointed to the fact that Germany was preparing for war at the end of September, and all recommendations agreed that the one way in which it could be prevented was by Great Britain making a firm stand and stating that she would be in that war, and would be upon the other side.

I had urged even earlier, after the rape of Austria, that Great Britain should make a firm declaration of what her foreign policy was, and then and later I was met with this, that the people of this country are not prepared to fight for Czechoslovakia. That is perfectly true, but I tried to represent another aspect of the situation, that it was not for Czechoslovakia that we should have to fight, that it was not for Czechoslovakia that we should have been fighting if we had gone to war last week. God knows how thankful we all are to have avoided it, but we also know that the people of this country were prepared for it—resolute, prepared, and grimly determined. It was not for Serbia that we fought in 1914. It was not even for Belgium, although it occasionally suited some people to say so. We were fighting then, as we should have been fighting last week, in order that one great Power should not be allowed, in disregard of treaty obligations, of the laws of nations and the decrees of morality to dominate by brutal force the Continent of Europe. For that principle we fought against Napoleon Bonaparte, and against Louis XIV of France and Philip II of Spain. For that principle we must ever be prepared to fight, for on the day when we are not prepared to fight for it we forfeit our Empire, our liberties, and our independence.

I besought my colleagues not to see this problem, always in terms of Czechoslovakia, not to review it always from the difficult strategic position of that small country, but rather to say to themselves, "A moment may come when, owing to the invasion of Czechoslovakia a European war will begin, and when that moment comes we must take part in that war, we cannot keep out of it, and there is no doubt upon which side we shall fight. Let the world know that and it will give those who are prepared to disturb the peace reason to hold their hand." It is perfectly true that after the assault on Austria the Prime Minister made a speech in this House—an excellent speech with every word of which I was in complete agreement—and what he said then was repeated and supported by the Chancellor of the Exchequer at Lanark. It was, however, a guarded statement. It was a statement to the effect that if there were such a war it would be unwise for anybody to count upon the possibility of our staying out.

That is not the language which the dictators understand. Together with new methods and a new morality they have introduced also a new vocabulary into Europe. They have discarded the old diplomatic methods of correspondence. Is it not significant that during the whole of this crisis there has not been a German Ambassador in London and, so far as I am aware, the German Chargé d'Affaires has hardly visited the Foreign Office? They talk a new language, the language of the headlines of the tabloid Press, and such guarded diplomatic and reserved utterances as were made by the Prime Minister and the Chancellor of the Exchequer mean nothing to the mentality of Herr Hitler or Signor Mussolini. I had hoped that it might be possible to make a statement to Herr Hitler before he made his speech at Nuremberg. On all sides we were being urged to do so by people in this country, by Members in this House, by Leaders of the Opposition, by the Press, by the heads of foreign States, even by Germans who were supporters of the regime and did not wish to see it plunged into a war which might destroy it. But we were always told that on no account must we irritate Herr Hitler; it was particularly dangerous to irritate him before he made a public speech, because if he were so irritated he might say some terrible things from which afterwards there would be no retreat. It seems to me that Herr Hitler never makes a speech save under the influence of considerable irritation, and the addition of one more irritant would not, I should have thought, have made a great difference, whereas the communication of a solemn fact would have produced a sobering effect.

After the chance of Nuremberg was missed I had hoped that the Prime Minister at his first interview with Herr Hitler at Berchtesgaden would make the position plain, but he did not do so. Again, at Godesberg I had hoped that that statement would be made in unequivocal language. Again I was disappointed. Hitler had another speech to make in Berlin. Again an opportunity occurred of telling him exactly where we stood before he made that speech, but again the opportunity was missed, and it was only after the speech that he was informed. He was informed through the mouth of a distinguished English civil servant that in certain conditions we were prepared to fight. We know what the mentality, or something of the mentality, of that great dictator is. We know that a message delivered strictly according to instructions with at least three qualifying clauses was not likely to produce upon him on the morning after his great oration the effect that was desired. Honestly, I did not believe that he thought there was anything of importance in that message. It certainly produced no effect whatever upon him and we can hardly blame him. Then came the last appeal from the Prime Minister on Wednesday morning. For the first time from the beginning to the end of the four weeks of negotiations Herr Hitler was prepared to yield an inch, an ell perhaps, but to yield some measure to the representations of Great Britain. But I would remind the House that the message from the Prime Minister was not the first news that he had received that morning. At dawn he had learned of the mobilisation of the British Fleet. It is impossible to know what are the motives of man and we shall probably never be satisfied as to which of these two sources of inspiration moved him most when he agreed to go to Munich, but we do know that never before had he given in, and that then he did. I had been urging the mobilisation of the Fleet for many days. I had thought that this was the kind of language which would be easier for Herr Hitler to understand than the guarded language of diplomacy or the conditional clauses of the Civil Service. I had urged that something in that direction might be done at the end of August and before the Prime Minister went to Berchtesgaden. I had suggested that it should accompany the mission of Sir Horace Wilson. I remember the Prime Minister stating it was the one thing that would ruin that mission, and I said it was the one thing that would lead it to success.

That is the deep difference between the Prime Minister and myself throughout these days. The Prime Minister has believed in addressing Herr Hitler through the language of sweet reasonableness. I have believed that he was more open to the language of the mailed fist. I am glad so many people think that sweet reasonableness has prevailed, but what actually did it accomplish? The Prime Minister went to Berchtesgaden with many excellent and reasonable proposals and alternatives to put before the Führer, prepared to argue and negotiate, as anybody would have gone to such a meeting. He was met by an ultimatum. So far as I am aware no suggestion of an alternative was ever put forward. Once the Prime Minister found himself in the atmosphere of Berchtesgaden and face to face with the personality of Hitler he knew perfectly well, being a good judge of men, that it would be a waste of time to put forward any alternative suggestion. So he returned to us with those proposals, wrapped up in a cloak called "Self-determination," and laid them before the Cabinet. They meant partition of a country, the cession of territory, they meant what, when it was suggested by a newspaper some weeks or days before, had been indignantly repudiated throughout the country. After long deliberation the Cabinet decided to accept that ultimatum, and I was one of those who agreed in that decision. I felt all the difficulty of it; but I foresaw also the danger of refusal. I saw that if we were obliged to go to war it would be hard to have it said against us that we were fighting against the principle of self-determination, and I hoped that if a postponement could be reached by this compromise there was a possibility that the final disaster might be permanently avoided. It was not a pleasant task to impose upon the Government of Czechoslovakia so grievous a hurt to their country, no pleasant or easy task for those upon whose support the Government of Czechoslovakia had relied to have to come to her and say "You have got to give up all for which you were prepared to fight"; but, still, she accepted those terms. The Government of Czechoslovakia, filled with deep misgiving, and with great regret, accepted the harsh terms that were proposed to her. That was all that we had got by sweet reasonableness at Berchtesgaden. Well, I did think that when a country had agreed to be partitioned, when a Government of a country had agreed to split up the ancient Kingdom of Bohemia, which has existed behind its original frontier for more than 1000 years, that was the ultimate demand that would be made upon it, and that after everything which Herr Hitler had asked for in the first instance had been conceded he would be willing, and we should insist, that the method of transfer of those territories should be conducted in a normal, in a civilised, manner, as such transfers have always been conducted in the past.

The Prime Minister made a second visit to Germany, and at Godesberg he was received with flags, bands, trumpets, and all the panoply of Nazi parade; but he returned again with nothing but an ultimatum. Sweet reasonableness had won nothing except terms which a cruel and revengeful enemy would have dictated to a beaten foe after a long war. Crueller terms could hardly be devised than those of the Godesberg ultimatum. The moment I saw them I said to myself, "if these are accepted, it will be the end of all decency in the conduct of public affairs in the world." We had a long and anxious discussion in the Cabinet with regard to the acceptance or rejection of those terms. It was decided to reject them, and that information, also, was conveyed to the German government. Then we were face to face with an impossible position, and at the last moment—not quite the last moment, but what seemed the last moment—another effort was made, by the despatch of an emissary to Herr Hitler with suggestions for a last appeal. That emissary's effort was in vain and it was only, as the House knows, on that fateful Wednesday morning that the final change of policy was adopted. I believe that change of policy, as I have said, was due not to any argument that had been addressed to Herr Hitler—it has never been suggested that it was—but due to the fact that for the first moment he realised, when the Fleet was mobilized, that what his advisers had been assuring him of for weeks, months, was untrue and that the British people were prepared to fight in a great cause.

So, last of all, he came to Munich and terms, of which the House is now aware, were devised at Munich, and those were the terms upon which this transfer of territory is to be carried out. The Prime Minister will shortly be explaining to the House the particulars in which the Munich terms differ from the Godesberg ultimatum. There are great and important differences, and it is a great triumph for the Prime Minister that he was able to acquire them. I spent the greater part of Friday trying to persuade myself that those terms were good enough for me. I tried to swallow them—I did not want to do what I have done—but they stuck in my throat, because it seemed to me that although the modifications which the Prime Minister obtained were important and of great value (the House will realise how great the value is when the Prime Minister has developed them) that still there remained the fact that that country was to be invaded, and I had thought that after accepting the humiliation of partition she should have been spared the ignominy and the horror of invasion. If anybody doubts that she is now suffering from the full horror of invasion they have only to read an article published in the *Daily Telegraph* of this morning which will convince them. After all, when Naboth had agreed to give up his vineyard he should have been allowed to pack up his goods in peace and depart, but the German Government, having got their man down, were not to be deprived of the pleasure of kicking him. Invasion remained; even the date of invasion remained unaltered. The date laid down by Herr Hitler was not to be changed. There are five stages, but those stages are almost as rapid as an army can move. Invasion and the date remained the same. Therefore, the works, fortifications, and guns of emplacements upon which that poor country had spent an enormous amount of its wealth were to be handed over intact. Just as the German was not to be deprived of the pleasure of kicking a man when he was down, so the army was not to be robbed of its loot. That was another term in the ultimatum which I found it impossible to accept. That was why I failed to bring myself to swallow the terms that were proposed—although I recognize the great service that the Prime Minister has performed in obtaining very material changes in them which will result in great benefit and a great lessening of the sufferings of the people of Czechoslovakia.

Then he brought home also from Munich something more than the terms to which we had agreed. At the last moment, at the farewell meeting, he signed with the Führer a joint declaration [*Hon. Member:* "Secret."]. I do not think there was anything secret about the declaration. The joint declaration has been published to the world. I saw no harm, no great harm, and no very obvious harm, in the terms of that declaration, but I would suggest that for the Prime Minister of England to sign, without consulting with his colleagues, and without, so far as I am aware, any reference to his allies, obviously without any communication with the Dominions and without the assistance of any expert diplomatic advisers, such a declaration with the Dictator of a great State, is not the way in which the foreign affairs of the British Empire should be conducted.

There is another aspect of this joint declaration. After all, what does it say? That Great Britain and Germany will not go to war in future and that everything will be settled by negotiation. Was it ever our intention to go to war? Was it ever not to settle things by communication and counsel? There is a danger. We must remember that this is not all that we are left with as the result of what has happened during the last few weeks. We are left, and we must all acknowledge it, with a loss of esteem on the part of countries that trusted us. We are left also with a tremendous commitment. For the first time in our history we have committed ourselves to defend a frontier in Central Europe. [*Brigadier General Sir Henry Croft:* "It is what you have been asking for."] We are left with the additional serious commitment that we are guaranteeing a frontier that we have at the same time destroyed. We have taken away the defences of Czechoslovakia in the same breath as we have guaranteed them, as though you were to deal a man a mortal blow and at the same time insure his life. I was in favor of giving this commitment. I felt that as we had taken so much away we must, in honor, give something in return, but realised what the commitment meant. It meant giving a commitment to defend a frontier in Central Europe, a difficult frontier to defend because it is surrounded on all sides by enemies. I realised that giving this commitment must mean for ourselves a tremendous quickening up of our rearmament schemes on an entirely new basis, a far broader basis upon which they must be carried out in future.

I had always been in favor of maintaining an army that would take a serious part in Continental war. I am afraid that I differed from the Prime Minister when I was at the War Office and he was at the Treasury, two years ago or more, on this point, but if we are now committed to defend a frontier in Central Europe, it is, in my opinion, absolutely imperative that we should maintain an army upon something like a Continental basis. It is no secret that the attitude maintained by this Government during recent weeks would have been far stiffer had our defences been far stronger. It has been said that we shall necessarily now increase both the speed at which they are reconditioned and the scale upon which they are reconditioned, but how are we to justify the extra burden laid upon the people of Great Britain if we are told at the same time that there is no fear of war with Germany and that, in the opinion of the Prime Minister, this settlement means peace in our time? That is one of the most profoundly disquieting aspects of the situation.

The Prime Minister has confidence in the good will and in the word of Herr Hitler, although when Herr Hitler broke the Treaty of Versailles he undertook to keep the Treaty of Locarno, and when he broke the Treaty of Locarno he undertook not to interfere further, or to have further territorial aims in Europe. When he entered Austria by force he authorized his henchmen to give an authoritative assurance that he would not interfere with Czechoslovakia. That was less than six months ago. Still, the Prime Minister believes that he can rely on the good faith of Hitler; he believes that Hitler is interested only in Germany, as the Prime Minister was assured. Well, there are Germans in other countries. There are Germans in Switzerland, in Denmark, and in Alsace; I think that one of the only countries in Europe in which there are no Germans is Spain. And yet there are rumors that Germany has taken an interest in that country. But the Prime Minister believes (and he has the advantage over us, or over most of us, that he has met the man) that he can come to a reasonable settlement of all outstanding questions between us. Herr Hitler said that he has got to have some settlement about colonies, but he said that this will never be a question of war. The Prime Minister attaches considerable importance to those words, but what do they mean? Do they mean that Herr Hitler will take "No" for an answer? He has never taken it yet. Or do they mean that he believes that he will get away with this, as he has got away with everything else without fighting, by well-timed bluff, bluster and blackmail? Otherwise it means very little.

The Prime Minister may be right. I can assure you, Mr. Speaker, with the deepest sincerity, that I hope and pray that he is right, but I cannot believe what he believes. I wish I could. Therefore I can be of no assistance to him in his Government. I should be only a hindrance, and it is much better that I should go. I remember when we were discussing the Godesberg ultimatum that I said that if I were a party to persuading, or even to suggesting to, the Czechoslovak Government that they should accept that ultimatum, I should never be able to hold up my head again. I have forfeited a great deal. I have given up an office that I love, work in which I was deeply interested and a staff of which any man might be proud. I have given up associations in that work with my colleagues with whom I had maintained for many years the most harmonious relations, not only as colleagues but as friends. I have given up the privilege of serving as lieutenant to a leader whom I still regard with the deepest admiration and affection. I have ruined, perhaps, my political career. But that is a little matter; I have retained something which is to me of great value—I can still walk about the world with my head erect.

The Prime Minister (Mr. Chamberlain): When the House met last Wednesday, we were all under the shadow of a great and imminent menace. War, in a form more stark and terrible than ever before, seemed to be staring us in the face. Before I sat down, a message had come which gave us new hope that peace might yet be saved, and today, only a few days after, we all meet in joy and thankfulness that the prayers of millions have been answered, a cloud of anxiety has been lifted from our hearts. . . .

Ever since I assumed my present office my main purpose has been to work for the pacification of Europe, for the removal of those suspicions and those animosities which have so long poisoned the air. The path which leads to appeasement is long and bristles with obstacles. The question of Czechoslovakia is the latest and perhaps the most dangerous. Now that we have got past it, I feel that it may be possible to make further progress along the road to sanity.

My Right Hon. Friend has alluded in somewhat bitter terms to my conversation last Friday morning with Herr Hitler. I do not know why that conversation should give rise to suspicion, still less to criticism. I entered into no pact. I made no new commitments. There is no secret understanding. Our conversation was hostile to no other nation. The object of that conversation, for which I asked, was to try to extend a little further the personal contact which I had established with Herr Hitler and which I believe to be essential in modern diplomacy. We had a friendly and entirely non-committal conversation, carried on, on my part, largely with a view to seeing whether there could be points in common between the head of a democratic Government and the ruler of a totalitarian State. We see the result in the declaration which has been published, in which my Right Hon. Friend finds so much ground for suspicion. What does it say?

There are three paragraphs. The first says that we agree "in recognising that the question of Anglo-German relations is of the first importance for the two countries and for Europe." Does anyone deny that? The second is an expression of opinion only. It says that: "We regard the agreement signed last night and the Anglo-German Naval Agreement as symbolic of the desire of the two peoples never to go to war with one another again." Once more I ask, does anyone doubt that that is the desire of the two peoples? What is the last paragraph? "We are resolved that the method of consultation shall be the method adopted to deal with any other questions that may concern our two countries, and we are determined to continue our efforts to remove possible sources of difference and thus to contribute to assure the peace of Europe." Who will stand up and condemn that sentence?

I believe there are many who will feel with me that such a declaration, signed by the German Chancellor and myself, is something more than a pious expression of opinion. In our relations with other countries everything depends upon there being sincerity and good will on both sides. I believe that there is sincerity and good will on both sides in this declaration. That is why to me its significance goes far beyond its actual words. If there is one lesson which we should learn from the events of these last weeks it is this, that lasting peace is not to be obtained by sitting still and waiting for it to come. It requires active, positive efforts to achieve it. No doubt I shall have plenty of critics who will say that I am guilty of facile optimism, and that I should disbelieve every word that is uttered by rulers of other great states in Europe. I am too much of a realist to believe that we are going to achieve our paradise in a day. We have only laid the foundations of peace. The superstructure is not even begun.

For a long period now we have been engaged in this country in a great programme of rearmament, which is daily increasing in pace and in volume. Let no one think that because we have signed this agreement between these four Powers at Munich we can afford to relax our efforts in regard to that programme at this moment. Disarmament on the part of this country can never be unilateral again. We have tried that once, and we very nearly brought ourselves to disaster. If disarmament is to come it must come by steps, and it must come by the agreement and the active cooperation of other countries. Until we know that we have obtained that cooperation and until we have agreed upon the actual steps to be taken, we here must remain on guard. . . .

While we must renew our determination to fill up the deficiencies that yet remain in our armaments and in our defensive precautions, so that we may be ready to defend ourselves and make our diplomacy effective . . . (*Interruption.*) Yes, I am a realist— nevertheless, I say with an equal sense of reality that I do see fresh opportunities of approaching this subject of disarmament opening up before us, and I believe that they are at least as hopeful today as they have been at any previous time. It is to such tasks (the winning back of confidence, the gradual removal of hostility between nations until they feel that they can safely discard their weapons, one by one) that I would wish to devote what energy and time may be left to me before I hand over my office to younger men.

British Parliament: Debate of October 5, 1938

The debate continued, and it was only two days later, on Wednesday, October 5, that a somewhat unpopular Conservative backbencher was able to have his say.

Mr. Churchill: If I do not begin this afternoon by paying the usual, and indeed almost invariable, tributes to the Prime Minister for his handling of this crisis, it is certainly not from lack of any personal regard. We have always, over a great many years, had very pleasant relations, and I have deeply understood from personal experiences of my own in a similar crisis the stress and strain he has had to bear; but I am sure it is much better to say exactly what we think about public affairs, and this is certainly not the time when it is worth anyone's while to court political popularity. We had a shining example of firmness of character from the late First Lord of the Admiralty two days ago. He showed that firmness of character which is utterly unmoved by currents of opinion, however swift and violent they may be. My hon. Friend the Member for South West Hull . . . was quite right in reminding us that the Prime Minister has himself throughout his conduct of these matters shown a robust indifference to cheers or boos and to the alternations of criticism and applause. If that be so, such qualities and elevation of mind should make it possible for the most severe expressions of honest opinion to be interchanged in this House without rupturing personal relations, and for all points of view to receive the fullest possible expression.

Having thus fortified myself by the example of others, I will proceed to emulate them. I will, therefore, begin by saying the most unpopular and most unwelcome thing. I will begin by saying what everybody would like to ignore or forget but which must nevertheless be stated, namely, that we have sustained a total and unmitigated defeat, and that France has suffered even more than we have. [*Viscountess Astor:* "Nonsense!"] When the noble Lady cries "Nonsense," she could not have heard the Chancellor of the Exchequer admit in his illuminating and comprehensive speech just now that Herr Hitler had gained in this particular leap forward in substance all he set out to gain. The utmost my right hon. Friend, the Prime Minister, has been able to secure by all his immense exertions, by all the great efforts and mobilization which took place in this country, and by all the anguish and strain through which we have passed in this country, the utmost he has been able to gain . . . [*Hon. Members:* "Is Peace"] I thought I might be allowed to make that point in its due place, and I propose to deal with it. The utmost he has been able to gain for Czechoslovakia and in the matters which were in dispute has been that the German Dictator, instead of snatching his victuals from the table has been content to have them served to him course by course.

The Chancellor of the Exchequer said it was the first time Herr Hitler has been made to retract (I think that was the word) in any degree. We really must not waste time, after all this long Debate, upon the difference between the positions reached at Berchtesgaden, at Godesberg and at Munich. They can be very simply epitomized, if the House will permit me to vary the metaphor. One pound was demanded at the pistol's point. When it was given, two pounds were demanded at the pistol's point. Finally, the Dictator consented to take one pound, seventeen shillings and six pence, and the rest in promises of good will for the future.

Now I come to the point, which was mentioned to me just now from some quarters of the House, about the saving of peace. No one has been a more resolute and uncompromising struggler for peace than the Prime Minister. Everyone knows that. Never has there been such intense and undaunted determination to maintain and to secure peace. That is quite true. Nevertheless, I am not quite clear why there was so much danger of Great Britain or France being involved in a war with Germany at this juncture if, in fact, they were ready all along to sacrifice Czechoslovakia. The terms which the Prime Minister brought back with him (I quite agree, at the last moment; everything had got off the rails and nothing but his intervention could have saved the peace, but I am talking of the events of the summer) could easily have been agreed, I believe, through the ordinary diplomatic channels at any time during the summer. And I will say this, that I believe the Czechs, left to themselves, and told they were going to get no help from the western Powers, would have been able to make better terms than they have got—they could hardly have worse—after all this tremendous perturbation.

There never can be any absolute certainty that there will be a fight if one side is determined that it will give way completely. When one reads the Munich terms, when one sees what is happening in Czechoslovakia from hour to hour, when one is sure, I will not say of parliamentary approval, but of parliamentary acquiescence, when the Chancellor of the Exchequer makes a speech which at any rate tries to put in a very powerful and persuasive manner the fact that, after all, it was inevitable and indeed righteous; when we say all this, and every one on this side of the House, including many members of the Conservative Party who are supposed to be vigilant and careful guardians of the national interest, it is quite clear that nothing vitally affecting us was at stake, it seems to me that one must ask, What was all the trouble and fuss about?

The resolve was taken by the British and the French Governments. Let me say that it is very important to realise that it is by no means a question which the British Government only have had to decide. I very much admire the manner in which, in the House, all references of a recriminatory nature have been repressed, but it must be realised that this resolve did not emanate particularly from one or other of the Governments, but was a resolve for which both must share in common the responsibility. When this resolve was taken, and the course was followed (you may say it was wise or unwise, prudent or short sighted), once it had been decided not to make the defence of Czechoslovakia a matter of war, then there was really no reason, if the matter had been handled during the summer in the ordinary way, to call into being all this formidable apparatus of crisis. I think that point should be considered. . . .

I have always held the view that the maintenance of peace depends upon the accumulation of deterrents against the aggressor, coupled with a sincere effort to redress grievances. Herr Hitler's victory, like so many of the famous struggles that have governed the fate of the world, was won upon the narrowest of margins. After the seizure of Austria in March, we faced this problem in our debates. I ventured to appeal to the Government to go a little further than the Prime Minister went, and to give a pledge that in conjunction with France and other powers they will guarantee the security of Czechoslovakia, while the Sudeten Deutsch question was being examined either by a League of Nations commission, or some other impartial body, and I still believe that if that course had been followed events would not have fallen into this disastrous state. I agree very much with . . . [Mr. Amery] when he said on that occasion (I cannot remember his actual words) "Do one thing or the other; either say you will disinterest yourself in the matter altogether, or take the step of giving a guarantee which will have the greatest chance of securing protection for that country."

France and Great Britain together, especially if they had maintained a close contact with Russia, which certainly was not done, would have been able in those days in the summer, when they had the prestige, to influence many of the smaller States of Europe, and I believe they could have determined the attitude of Poland. Such a combination, prepared at the time when the German Dictator was not deeply and irrevocably committed to his new adventure, would, I believe, have given strength to all those forces in Germany which resisted this departure, this new design. . . .

All these forces, added to the other deterrents which combinations of powers great and small, ready to stand firm upon the front of law and for the ordered remedy of grievances, would have formed, might well have been effective. . . . Between submission and immediate war there was this third alternative, which gave a hope not only of peace but of justice. It is quite true that such a policy in order to succeed demanded that Britain should declare straight out and a long time beforehand that she would, with others, join to defend Czechoslovakia against an unprovoked aggression. H.M. Government refused to give this guarantee when it would have saved the situation, yet in the end they gave it when it was too late, and now, for the future, they renew it when they have not the slightest power to make it good.

All is over. Silent, mournful, abandoned, broken, Czechoslovakia recedes into the darkness. She has suffered in every respect by her association with the Western democracies and with the League of Nations, of which she has always been an obedient servant. She has suffered in particular from her association with France, under whose guidance and policy she has been actuated for so long. The very measures taken by H.M. Government in the Anglo-French Agreement to give her the best chance possible, namely the 50% clean cut in certain districts instead of a plebiscite, have turned to her detriment, because there is to be a plebiscite too in wide areas, and those other Powers who had claims have also come down upon the helpless victim. . . . No one has a right to say that the plebiscite which is to be taken in certain areas under Saar conditions, and the clean cut of the 50% areas—that those two operations together amount in the slightest degree to a verdict of self-determination. It is a fraud and a farce to invoke that name. We in this country, as in other Liberal and democratic countries, have a perfect right to exalt the principle of self-determination, but it comes ill out of the mouths of those in totalitarian States who deny even the smallest element of toleration to every section and creed within their bounds. But, however you put it, this particular block of land, this mass of human beings to be handed over, has never expressed the desire to go into the Nazi rule. I do not believe that even now—if their opinion could be asked, they would exercise such an option. . . .

I venture to think that in future the Czechoslovak State cannot be maintained as an independent entity. You will find that in a period of time which may be measured by years, but may be measured only by months, Czechoslovakia will be engulfed in the Nazi regime. Perhaps they may join it in despair or in revenge. At any rate, that story is over and told. But we cannot consider the abandonment and ruin of Czechoslovakia in the light only of what happened last month. It is the most grievous consequence which we have yet experienced of what we have done and of what we have left undone in the last five years: five years of futile good intention, five years of eager search for the line of least resistance, five years of uninterrupted retreat of British power, five years of neglect of our air defences. Those are the features that I stand here to declare and which marked an improvident stewardship for which Great Britain and France have dearly to pay. We have been reduced in those five years from a position of security so overwhelming and so unchallengeable that we never cared to think about it. We have been reduced from a position where the very word "war" was considered one which would be used only by persons qualifying for a lunatic asylum. We have been reduced from a position of safety and power—power to do good, power to be generous to a beaten foe, power to make terms with Germany, power to give her proper redress for her grievances, power to stop her arming if we chose, power to take any step in strength or mercy or justice which we thought right—reduced in five years from a position safe and unchallenged, to where we stand now.

When I think of the fair hopes of a long peace which still lay before Europe at the beginning of 1933 when Herr Hitler first obtained power, and of all the opportunities of arresting the growth of the Nazi power which have been thrown away, when I think of the immense combinations and resources which have been neglected or squandered, I cannot believe that a parallel exists in the whole course of history. So far as this country is concerned the responsibility must rest with those who have the undisputed control of our political affairs. They neither prevented Germany from rearming, nor did they rearm ourselves in time. They quarrelled with Italy without saving Ethiopia. They exploited and discredited the vast institution of the League of Nations and they neglected to make alliances and combinations which might have repaired previous errors, and thus they left us in the hour of trial without adequate national defence or effective international security.

In my holiday I thought it was a chance to study the reign of King Ethelred the Unready. The House will remember that that was a period of great misfortune, in which, from a strong position, which we had gained under the descendants of King Alfred, we fell very swiftly into chaos. It was the period of the Danegeld and of foreign pressure. I must say that the rugged words of the Anglo-Saxon Chronicle, written 1000 years ago, seem to me apposite, at least as apposite as those quotations from Shakespeare with which we have been regaled. . . . Here is what the Anglo-Saxon Chronicle said, and I think the words apply very much to our treatment of Germany and our relations with her:

> All these calamities fell upon us because of evil counsel, because tribute was not offered to them at the right time nor yet were they resisted; but when they had done the most evil, then was peace made with them.

That is the wisdom of the past, for all wisdom is not new wisdom. . . .

We are in the presence of a disaster of the first magnitude which has befallen Great Britain and France. Do not let us blind ourselves to that. It must now be accepted that all the countries of Central and Eastern Europe will make the best terms they can with the triumphant Nazi Power. The system of alliances in Central Europe upon which France has relied for her safety has been swept away, and I can see no means by which it can be reconstituted. The road down the Danube Valley to the Black Sea, the resources of corn and oil, the road which leads as far as Turkey, has been opened. In fact, if not in form, it seems to me that all those countries of Middle Europe, all those Danubian countries, will, one after another, be drawn into this vast system of power politics (not only power military politics but power economic politics) radiating from Berlin, and I believe this can be achieved quite smoothly and swiftly and will not necessarily entail the firing of a single shot. [To prove his point, he then cites the success of the pro-German policy of Stoyadinovitch in Yugoslavia, and the dismay of the pro-Allied Opposition] . . .

Again, what happened in Warsaw? The British and French Ambassadors visited

Colonel Beck, or sought to visit him, the Foreign Minister, in order to ask for some mitigation in the harsh measures being pursued against Czechoslovakia about Teschen. The door was shut in their faces. The French Ambassador was not even granted an audience, and the British Ambassador was given a most curt reply by a political director. The whole matter is described in the Polish Press as a political indiscretion committed by those two Powers, and we are today reading of the success of Colonel Beck's blow. I am not forgetting, I must say, that it is less than 20 years ago since British and French bayonets rescued Poland from the bondage of a century and a half. I think it is indeed a sorry episode in the history of that country, for whose freedom and rights so many of us have had warm and long sympathy.

Those illustrations are typical. You will see, day after day, week after week, the entire alienation of those regions. Many of those countries, in fear of the rise of the Nazi Power, have already got politicians, ministers, governments, who were pro-German, but there was always an enormous popular movement in Poland, Romania, Bulgaria and Yugoslavia, which looked to the Western democracies and loathed the idea of having this arbitrary rule of the totalitarian system thrust upon them, and hoped that a stand would be made. All that has gone by the board. We are talking about countries which are a long way off and of which, as the Prime Minister might say, we know nothing. (*Interruption.*) The noble Lady says that that very harmless allusion is . . . [*Viscountess Astor:* "Rude."] She must very recently have been receiving her finishing course in manners. What will be the position, I want to know, of France and England this year and the year afterwards? What will be the position of that Western front of which we are in full authority the guarantors? . . . Relieved from all anxiety in the East, and having secured resources which will greatly diminish, if not entirely remove, the deterrent of a naval blockade, the rulers of Nazi Germany will have a free choice open to them in what direction they will turn their eyes. If the Nazi Dictator should choose to look westward, as he may, bitterly will France and England regret the loss of that fine army of ancient Bohemia which was estimated last week to require not fewer than thirty German divisions for its destruction. . . . Many people, no doubt, honestly believe that they are only giving away the interests of Czechoslovakia, whereas I fear we shall find that we have deeply compromised, and perhaps fatally endangered, the safety and even the independence of Great Britain and France. This is not merely a question of giving up the German colonies, as I am sure we shall be asked to do. Nor is it a question only of losing influence in Europe. It goes far deeper than that. You have to consider the character of the Nazi movement and the rule which it implies. The Prime Minister desires to see cordial relations between this country and Germany. There is no difficulty at all in having cordial relations with the German people. Our hearts go out to them. But they have no power. You must have diplomatic and correct relations, but there can never be friendship between the British democracy and the Nazi Power, that power which spurns Christian ethics, which cheers its onward course by a barbarous paganism, which vaunts the spirit of aggression and conquest, which derives strength and perverted pleasure from persecution, and uses, as we have seen, with pityless brutality, the threat of murderous force. That power cannot ever be the trusted friend of the British democracy.

What I find unendurable is the sense of our country falling into the power, into the orbit and influence of Nazi Germany, and of our existence becoming dependent upon their good will or pleasure. It is to prevent that, that I have tried my best to urge the maintenance of every bulwark of defence—first the timely creation of an Air Force superior to anything within striking distance of our shores; secondly, the gathering together of the collective strength of many nations; and thirdly, the making of alliances and military conventions, all within the Covenant, in order to gather together forces, at any rate to restrain the onward movement of this Power. It has all been in vain. Every position has been successively undermined and abandoned on specious and plausible excuses. We do not want to be led upon the high road to becoming a satellite of the German Nazi system of European domination. In a very few years, perhaps in a very few months, we shall be confronted with demands with which we shall no doubt be invited to comply. Those demands may affect the surrender of territory or the surrender of liberty. I foresee and foretell that the policy of submission will carry with it restrictions upon the freedom of speech and debate in Parliament, on public platforms, and discussions in the Press, for it will be said (indeed, I hear it said sometimes now) that we cannot allow the Nazi system of dictatorship to be criticized by ordinary, common English politicians. Then, with a Press under control, in part direct but more potently indirect, with every organ of public opinion doped and chloroformed into acquiescence, we shall be conducted along further stages of our journey. . . .

I do not grudge our loyal, brave people, who were ready to do their duty no matter what the cost, who never flinched under the strain of last week—I do not grudge them the natural, spontaneous outburst of joy and relief when they learnt that the hard ordeal would no longer be required of them at the moment; but they should know the truth. They should know that there has been gross neglect and deficiency in our defences; they should know that we have sustained a defeat without a war, the consequences of which will travel far with us along our road; they should know that we have passed an awful milestone in our history, when the whole equilibrium of Europe has been deranged, and that the terrible words have for the time being been pronounced against the Western democracies:

"Thou art weighed in the balance and found wanting."

And do not suppose that this is the end. This is only the beginning of the reckoning. This is only the first sip, the foretaste of a bitter cup which will be proffered to us year by year unless by a supreme recovery of moral health and martial vigor, we arise again and take our stand for freedom as in the olden times.

The Second World War

P ERHAPS the most frightful peculiarity of the Second World War was the extent to which it developed methods of mass extermination. Both sides indulged in bombings designed to flatten large areas, and civilians became targets for enemy action to a greater degree and with more destructive results than any time since the Hunnish or Viking invasions. But while these patterns of destruction were new only in terms of their unusual scale and were common to both sides, genocide was an innovation of the Germans alone—or, at least, of the Nazis, whom the Germans welcomed. Through genocide, people considered harmful to Germany and to its new order were sentenced to mass destruction, a plan that remained uncompleted only because time or opportunity did not suffice to carry the project through. Little was known abroad about the extermination policies that decimated Jews, Slavs, gypsies, and others who might seriously displease the German masters. Some Germans and newly vocal neo-Nazis today deny that such policies ever existed, apart from isolated acts of sadism, and see in the West's present efforts to hush up discussion of the subject an admission that here are merely stories, invented by enemies out to discredit Germany and indiscriminately used by Allied propaganda to encompass and hasten its defeat.

Yet well-attested evidence is not lacking, particularly in the vast files of the Allied War Crimes Tribunal and in the personal accounts of survivors. The whole matter of the Holocaust (as well as the inclination to deny or forget its existence) poses problems that are difficult, but important to us all: the problem of responsibility, both personal and collective; the question of whether such a phenomenon might have developed elsewhere—"there, but for the grace of God, go I"; and above all, perhaps, the problem of the reality and meaning of evil and of good in a world where values tend increasingly to be relative, pragmatic, and ultimately amoral.

Harvest of Hate

Though genocide may now be seen as a logical implication of their racial doctrines, the German leaders were unprepared for the tremendous opportunities opened by their conquests of 1939–1943. This meant that much of their extermination policy had to be improvised ad hoc: special killer commandos, mass shootings, and clumsy mobile gas chambers preceded the final perfection achieved at Auschwitz and elsewhere toward the end of the war. But all this time their exterminatory genius never lagged. The campaign was carried forward on all fronts. And, while the SS performed the killings, bureaucrats in Berlin legislated to prevent birth and survival. All this is summarized, in gruesome detail, in Leon Poliakov's remarkable study, Harvest of Hate.

Leon Poliakov: from Harvest of Hate

EXTERMINATION POLICY

Shooting was not the only method the commandos used. On the shores of the Black Sea there were mass drownings; at Backtchissarai, that pearl of the Crimea which Pushkin sang about, the drowning of 1,029 Jews during the period July 1–15, 1942, was reported. There were cases of Jews being burned alive, especially at Minsk in White Russia. Finally in the spring of 1942, mobile gas chambers, designed and manufactured in Berlin and disguised as gas trucks, made their appearance all over Russia.

As we shall see, these death chambers were still very rudimentary machines which the homicide or "euthanasia" section of the Führer's chancellery had devised in Berlin. By a very simple arrangement, the exhaust gases of the Diesel motor, essentially carbon monoxide, were piped into the hermetically sealed interior of the truck instead of out into open air. Such trucks were put at the disposal of all commandos. We have a great number of documents, veritable manuals on the use of the trucks, describing their operation:

> The gas is generally not used in the right way. To get things over with as soon as possible, the driver presses the accelerator to the floor. This kills the people by suffocation instead of making them gradually doze off. My directives have proved that, with the correct adjustment of the levers, death comes quicker and the prisoners sleep peacefully. There are no more of the contorted faces or defecations there used to be.

This was written by SS Lieutenant Becker on May 16, 1942; his job was to check on the functioning of the trucks. He added,

> I had ordered the trucks of Group D to be camouflaged as houses on wheels by hanging a pair of shutters on each side, a sight that is frequently seen on our farms in the country. But these vehicles got to be so well known that not only the authorities but the civil population called them "death trucks" as soon as they appeared. In my opinion, these vehicles, even when camouflaged, cannot long be kept a secret.

The commando men stated during their trial that they disliked using these trucks. Besides, they gave mediocre results, at best fifty to sixty people per execution. Shooting continued to be the chief mode of execution during one period of the chaotic exterminations in Russia. Here is a clear and exact description of what they were like, by the witness Hermann Graebe:

> I, the undersigned, Hermann Friedrich Graebe, make the following declaration under oath:

From Leon Poliakov, *Harvest of Hate* (Syracuse University Press, 1954). By permission of The American Jewish Committee.

From September 1941 to January 1944 I was director and chief engineer of the Sdolbunow branch of the Josef Jung Construction Company of Solingen. In this capacity I had, among my other duties, to visit the firm's projects. Under the terms of a contract with the army construction services, the company was to build grain warehouses on the old Dubno airfield in the Ukraine.

On October 5, 1942, at the time of my visit to the construction offices in Dubno, my foreman, Hubert Moennikes, living at 21 Aussenmühlenweg, Hamburg-Haarburg, told me that some Dubno Jews had been shot near the building in three huge ditches about 30 metres long and 3 metres deep. The number of people killed daily was about 1,500. The 5,000 Jews who had lived in Dubno before the Pogrom were all marked for liquidation. Since the executions took place in the presence of my employee, he was painfully impressed by them.

Accompanied by Moennikes, I then went to the work area. I saw great mounds of earth about 30 metres long and 2 high. Several trucks were parked nearby. Armed Ukrainian militia were making people get out, under the surveillance of SS soldiers. The same militia men were responsible for guard duty and driving the trucks. The people in the trucks wore the regulation yellow pieces of cloth that identified them as Jews on the front and back of their clothing.

Moennikes and I went straight toward the ditches without being stopped. When we neared the mound, I heard a series of rifle shots close by. The people from the trucks—men, women and children—were forced to undress under the supervision of an SS soldier with a whip in his hand. They were obliged to put their effects in certain spots: shoes, clothing, and underwear separately. I saw a pile of shoes, about 800–1,000 pairs, great heaps of underwear and clothing. Without weeping or crying out, these people undressed and stood together in family groups, embracing each other and saying goodbye while waiting for a sign from the SS soldier, who stood on the edge of the ditch, a whip in his hand, too. During the fifteen minutes I stayed there, I did not hear a single complaint, or plea for mercy. I watched a family of about eight: a man and woman about fifty years old, surrounded by their children of about one, eight, and ten, and two big girls about twenty and twenty-four. An old lady, her hair completely white, held the baby in her arms, rocking it, and singing it a song. The infant was crying aloud with delight. The parents watched the groups with tears in their eyes. The father held the ten-year-old boy by the hand, speaking softly to him: the child struggled to hold back his tears. Then the father pointed a finger to the sky, and, stroking the child's head, seemed to be explaining something. At this moment, the SS near the ditch called something to his comrade. The latter counted off some twenty people and ordered them behind the mound. The family of which I have just spoken was in the group. I still remember the young girl, slender and dark, who, passing near me, pointed at herself, saying, "Twenty-three." I walked around the mound and faced a frightful common grave. Tightly packed corpses were heaped so close together that only the heads showed. Most were wounded in the head and the blood flowed over their shoulders. Some still moved. Others raised their hands and turned their heads to show that they were still alive. The ditch was two-thirds full. I estimate that it held a thousand bodies. I turned my eyes toward the man who had carried out the execution. He was an SS man; he was seated, legs swinging, on the narrow edge of the ditch; an automatic rifle rested on his knees and he was smoking a cigarette. The people, completely naked, climbed down a few steps cut in the clay wall and stopped at the spot indicated by the SS man. Facing the dead and wounded, they spoke softly to them. Then I heard a series of rifle shots. I looked in the ditch and saw their bodies contorting, their heads, already inert, sinking on the corpses beneath. The blood flowed from the nape of their necks. I was astonished not to be ordered away, but I noticed two or three uniformed postmen nearby. A new batch of victims approached the place. They climbed down into the ditch, lined up in front of the previous victims, and were shot.

On the way back, while rounding the mound, I saw another full truck which had just arrived. This truck contained only the sick and crippled. Women already naked were undressing an old woman with an emaciated body; her legs frightfully thin. She was held up by two people and seemed paralyzed. The naked people led her behind the mound. I left the place with Moennikes and went back to Dubno in a car.

The next morning, returning to the construction, I saw some thirty naked bodies lying thirty to fifty yards from the ditch. Some were still alive; they stared into space with a set look, seeming not to feel the coolness of the morning air; nor to see the workers standing around. A young girl of about twenty spoke to me, asking me to bring her clothes and to help her escape. At that moment we heard the sound of a car approaching at top speed; I saw that it was an SS detachment. I went back to my work. Ten minutes later rifle shots sounded from the ditch. The Jews who were still alive had been ordered to throw the bodies in the ditch; then they had to lie down themselves to receive a bullet in the back of the neck.

Whose Responsibility?

A great deal of debate has surrounded the question of who was actually involved in these crimes, who was aware of what went on, and who might be termed responsible for them to some degree. Another issue of more immediate concern during the war itself was the effect of these practices on the technicians, soldiers, and officials involved in them. The following passages furnish a few brief glimpses into the consciences and concerns of these men. The first is an abstract from the diary of one who worked in a Polish death camp, a professional man, Dr. Kremer.

The Death Camps

"1. IX. 1942. I wrote to Berlin for a leather belt and suspenders. During the afternoon I was present at the disinfection of a cell block with Cyclone B, to kill the lice.

2. IX. 1942. This morning at three o'clock I attended a special action for the first time. Dante's hell seemed like a comedy in comparison. Not for nothing is Auschwitz called an extermination camp.

5. IX. 1942. I was present this afternoon at a special action applied to prisoners in the female camp (Moslems), the worst I have ever seen. Dr. Thilo was right this morning in telling me that we are in the *anus mundi*. Tonight, about eight, I was present at a special action on the Dutch. All the men are anxious to take part in these actions because of the special rations they get on such occasions, consisting of ⅕ of a liter of schnapps, 5 cigarettes, 100 grams of sausage and bread.

6–7. IX. 1942. Today, Sunday, an excellent lunch: tomato soup, half a chicken with potatoes and red cabbage, petits fours, a marvelous vanilla ice cream. After lunch I was introduced to . . . (illegible word). Left at eight in the evening for a special action, for the fourth time.

23. IX. 1942. Present last night at the sixth and seventh special actions. In the morning, Obergruppenführer Pohl arrived with his staff at the Waffen SS house. The sentinel at the door was the first to salute me. In the evening, at eight o'clock, dinner in the commanding officer's house, with General Pohl, a real banquet. We had apple pie, as much as we wanted, good coffee, excellent beer, and cakes.

7. X. 1942. Present at the ninth special action. Foreigners and women.

11. X. 1942. Today, Sunday, rabbit, a good leg, for lunch, with red cabbage and pudding, all for 1.25 RM.

12. X. 1942. Inoculation for typhus. Following this, feverish in the evening; still, went to a special action that night (1,600 Dutch). Terrible scenes near the last bunker. The tenth special action."

Dr. Kremer's diary goes on in this way to the end of the year, alternating between noting the menus he particularly enjoyed and the carefully numbered special actions he attended, on which he commented with growing indifference.

If a few dozen Germans, some hundreds at the most, actually observed the last agony of the Jews in the gas chambers, those who witnessed their long Calvary were numbered in the hundreds of thousands. The SS formations stationed in the camps; the German workers, Army units, and officials at the numerous yards and factories where the Jewish slaves were used, whom they passed by daily; the railway men handling the innumerable transports of deportees all over Germany, which they saw coming back empty, if they were not loaded with the used clothing which was distributed to the needy by all the welfare offices in the country. This is a very incomplete list of those who can properly be called eyewitnesses. As for the rest of the Germans, the press and radio of the Reich undertook to inform them more and more openly of what was going on. The time for vague and prophetic imprecations by Hitler had passed. The language now sharpens and it is the past tense that is employed. "The Jewish population of Poland has been neutralized and the same may be said right now for Hungary. By this action five million Jews have been eliminated in these two countries," a Danzig newspaper wrote in May 1944. And the next day Goebbels' *Der Angriff* published under the byline of Ley: "Judea must perish that mankind may be saved." The fate of the Jews was an example and a warning: "Whosoever imitates the Jew deserves the same end: extermination, death," threatened *Der Stürmer*. The extermination policy thus became a matter of common knowledge and enough information filtered through a thousand channels for the location of the murder camps and the methods of execution to become notorious. A witness states that in the trains passing near Auschwitz (where, we will recall, four rail lines crossed) "the passengers stood up and leaned out the windows to see as much as they could." Another witness, none other than Rudolf Diels, the first director of the Prussian Gestapo in 1933–34, later police prefect of Cologne and administrator of the Hermann Goering Works during the war, stated that as far as he knew, the expression, "You will go up the chimney," had become proverbial in Germany toward the end of the war. Only those who did not wish to know might continue to pretend ignorance. During a dramatic session at one of the Nuremberg trials, a highly qualified witness, SS General Bach-Zelewsky, who was "head of the anti-partisan campaign" of the German armies during the war, insisted on clarifying the matter.

"For me it is a question. Though imprisoned for years, I see that people are still saying: Who knew? Nobody wants to be in the position of having known anything. I want to establish the truth here, regardless of whether it hurts or helps me. . . . Of all the German generals, I am perhaps the one who traveled most all over Europe during the war, since it was my job to manage the entire fight against the guerrillas. I talked to hundreds of generals and thousands of officers of all categories, and it is a fact that exterminations began on the first day of the war. This is the truth; anything else is a lie and a euphemism. . . . And anyone who traveled knew from the beginning that the Jews were being exterminated in a way that at first was not systematic. Later, when the Russian campaign began, the extermination of Judaism was an explicit part of the aim."

We have already quoted many personal accounts. Let us quote still another, the fact that it is not of SS provenance, and is uttered so casually, lends it a particular significance. It is dated October 23, 1941. Its author was a Wehrmacht officer, reporting his observations during a trip to the "Eastern zone of operations." Notice the similar construction of the two paragraphs quoted, both of which end on the same note of self-solicitude. The first paragraph concerns Russian prisoners of war:

"The columns of prisoners marching along the roads resemble a senseless flock of sheep. . . . Because of the physical exertion of the marches, the poor food and the bad conditions in the camps, the prisoners often collapse and have to be dragged along by their comrades or left where they are. The 6th Army ordered all stragglers shot. This was done on the road and even in the villages, with the unfortunate result that German employees returning home at night had to pass by the bodies of prisoners who were shot."

The second paragraph of the report concerns Jews: "In accordance with orders, the Jews are transferred. This is done in the following way: They receive an order to report the next night, in their best clothes and with all their jewels or valuables, at a designated assembly point. . . . They are then taken to a place already got ready for them, outside the particular locality. Under the pretext of fulfilling certain formalities, they are required to deposit all their clothing, jewels, and ornaments. They are then led off the road and liquidated. The resulting situations are so agonizing that they cannot be described. The consequences this has for the German Commandos are inevitable. In general, the executions can be carried out only in an alcoholic stupor. According to what an SS officer who had been detailed for this duty told me, he had to endure (*durchstehen*) the most terrifying nightmares the next night." (NOKW 3147)

Other Methods of Genocide

"LOWERING THE FERTILITY OF THE PEOPLE"

Next to pure and simple homicide, this was the most direct method. Instead of physically suppressing the present generation, it was seen to it that there would be no future generations. The mass sterilization plans which have already been mentioned never got beyond the planning stage, but other large-scale measures did. The minutes of a meeting of experts charged with drawing up these plans list the following measures:

a) Raising the marriage age to twenty-five (after completion of labor service or some such required service for a period of three to four years).
b) Authorization of marriage only in cases where the economic position (of the people concerned) is assured.
c) Requiring financial restitution to the public welfare funds in every case of illegitimate birth. If the mother is without funds, she will have to furnish her labor.
d) If the same mother has burdened the public funds with several illegitimate children, her sterilization can be ordered.
e) Deliberate lowering of the standard of living of large families (no monetary relief, no allocations for children, no premium during the nursing period, etc.).
f) Official authorization for abortion at the mother's request (when desirable from the social point of view).

These measures were prepared by the experts of the Reich Ministry of the Interior and primarily had the Polish population in mind. They were introduced into the Government General by a decree of October 19, 1941. One year later, the Führer ordered their extension to all populations under the control of the "Ministry of the Occupied Territories of the East." Bormann sent the following instructions to Rosenberg:

July 23, 1942

My dear Party Comrade Rosenberg:
    "The Führer wishes you to see to it that the following principles are applied and observed in the Occupied Territories of the East, and I am entrusting you with this task.

1) When girls and women in the Occupied Territories of the East have abortions, we can only be in favor of it; in any case, German jurists should not oppose. The

Führer believes that we should authorize the development of a thriving trade in contraceptives. We are not interested in seeing the non-German population multiply.

2) The danger that the non-German population in the Eastern territories may increase more than before is very great. Their living conditions have improved considerably. For this very reason we must take the necessary precautionary measures to prevent an expansion of the non-German population.

3) German medical relief must therefore not be set up for the non-German population in the Eastern territories in any way. Vaccination, for example, and other such health measures, are out of the question.

4) The population must in no way benefit from higher education. If we let ourselves be pushed into committing this error, we shall ourselves be cultivating the elements of a future resistance against us. According to the Führer, then, it will be enough for the non-German populations—even the so-called Ukrainians—to learn to read and write.

5) We must on no condition by any measure whatsoever cultivate any sort of feeling of superiority in the population! The contrary is necessary!"

In the recommendations in his memorandum for the practical execution of these measures, Wetzel gave proof of a fertile imagination.

"Every propaganda means, especially the press, radio, and movies, as well as pamphlets, booklets, and lectures, must be used to instill in the Russian population the idea that it is harmful to have several children. We must emphasize the expenses that children cause, the good things people could have had with the money spent on them. We could also hint at the dangerous effect of child-bearing on a woman's health. Paralleling such propaganda, a large-scale campaign should be launched in favor of contraceptive devices. A contraceptive industry must be established. Neither the circulation and sale of contraceptives nor abortions must be prosecuted. It will even be necessary to open special institutions for abortion, and to train midwives and nurses for this purpose. The population will practice abortion all the more willingly if these institutions are competently operated. The doctors must be able to help out without there being any question of this being a breach of their professional ethics. Voluntary sterilization must also be recommended by propaganda. Infant mortality must not be combatted. Mothers must be kept in ignorance of child care and of everything that has to do with children's diseases. We must try to reduce as much as possible the training and knowledge of Russian doctors in this field. Such institutions as day nurseries and children's homes must be abolished as far as it is possible."

THE KIDNAPPING OF CHILDREN

This method was generally applied after intervention by a "racial inspector." It was mostly the children of foreign workers who were affected. As future janissaries of the Third Reich, children of recognized Nordic descent were placed in nurseries for SS children, while a network of homes was provided for children and babies of foreigners who did not pass the "racial test." A few establishments of this kind were already functioning in 1944. An inspector's report sent to Himmler gives a few details on their functioning:

"During my visit, I noticed that all the babies in that home were undernourished. As the director of the home, SS Oberführer Langoth, told me, the home receives only a pint of milk and a piece and a half of sugar per day per baby. With these rations the babies are sure to die of malnutrition in a few months.

I asked SS Oberführer Langoth to inform Gauleiter Eigruber of this state of affairs, and to ask him to assure sufficient supplies for these babies while waiting for your opinion on the subject. I consider the manner in which this business is now being managed to be impossible. There are only two solutions. Either we do not want these children alive, in which case we should not let them die slowly of hunger while they use up so much milk from the general supply; there are ways to achieve this without torture or pain. Or, on the other hand, we intend to bring up these children for later use as labor. In this case they must be nourished in such a way that it will be possible to make full use of them as workers."

Kidnappings of children from the occupied territories were particularly frequent during the time of the German retreat in the East. The Wehrmacht services were the principal perpetrators. A memorandum from the Political Section at headquarters in June 1944 envisaged the following huge operation under the characteristic code name of "Operation Hay" (Heuaktion):

"1. The Center Army group intends to assemble and send to the Reich 40,000 to 50,000 children between ten and fourteen from the territories now under its control. This measure is taken at the suggestion of the 9th Army. It will have to be strongly backed up by propaganda and have as its slogan: Reich Aid to White Russian Children, Protection Against the Partisans. This operation has already been commenced in a five-kilometer zone. . . . The operation is planned not only to reduce the direct growth of enemy strength, but also to impair its biological strength in the distant future. This point of view has been expressed by both the SS Reichführer and the Führer. Appropriate orders to this effect were consequently given in the Southern Sector at the time of last year's retreat.

"2. A similar action is now under way in the region controlled by the North Ukraine Army group (General Field Marshal Model). In the Galician sector, which enjoys special privileges from the political point of view, measures have been taken to collect 135,000 workers in labor battalions, while young men over seventeen will be incorporated into SS divisions and youngsters under seventeen will be placed in charge of the SS Aid. This operation, which was begun a few weeks ago, has led to no political unrest up to now."

Slaves as Guinea Pigs

The treatment of human beings as objects was not confined to the prison camps. When workers and materials began to fall short, German industry learned to dip into the pool of human resources represented by the regime's slaves. In some cases this provided useful—and expendable—slave labor; in other instances, such as the brief glimpse that follows, they served as guinea pigs.

The Herald Tribune: *Nuremberg Trials*

Nuremberg, November 14, 1947 (A.P.) A French witness testified today that the I.G. Farben combine purchased 150 women from the Oswiecim concentration camp, after complaining about a price of 200 marks (then $80.00) each, and killed all of them in experiments with a soporific drug.

The witness was Gregoire M. Afrine. He told the American military tribunal trying 23 Farben directors on war crimes charges that he was employed as an interpreter by the Russians after they overran the Oswiecim camp in January 1945 and found a number of letters there. Among the letters, he said, were some addressed from Farben's "Bayer" plant to the Nazi commandant of the camp.

These excerpts were offered in evidence:

1. In contemplation of experiments with a new soporific drug, we would appreciate your procuring for us a number of women.

2. We received your answer but consider the price of 200 marks a woman excessive. We propose to pay not more than 170 marks a head. If agreeable, we will take possession of the women. We need approximately 150.

3. We acknowledge your accord. Prepare for us 150 women in the best possible condition, and as soon as you advise us you are ready we will take charge of them.

4. Received the order of 150 women. Despite their emaciated condition, they were found satisfactory. We shall keep you posted on developments concerning the experiment.

5. The tests were made. All subjects died. We shall contact you shortly on the subject of a new load.

Forgive? Perhaps. Forget? Never.

The essay that follows is not included as a rehash of European suffering in the last German war but as a reminder that forgiveness and forgetfulness are not one and the same. Forgiveness is a positive and generous attitude that helps people—frequently clumsy, brutal, or thoughtless—to live together in a difficult world. Forgetfulness is an attempt to escape reality and responsibility, and it is generally prompted by motives that are foolish or cowardly or both. When one insists on forgetting the past, there can be no historical perspective

From New York *Herald Tribune*, 15 November 1947.

and hence no way of appreciating the problems and circumstances of the day in terms of their origins and background. Forgiveness brings peace; forgetfulness brings myths. The two do not, should not, go together.

Michel François: "Against Oblivion"

Soon, eleven years will have passed since the death chambers went out of business. One feels almost ashamed to mention it, petty to spoil the satisfaction of a good conscience so quickly recovered. And I am not thinking, at this point, about the good conscience of the torturers, of their friends, of their immediate accomplices, of all their spiritual family; there is nothing more legitimate than to see them wish for oblivion: have we not done our best these last few years to convince them that after all they were not so very wrong? But it is striking to observe in others—the nonaccomplices, the surviving victims, the witnesses—a strange inhibition, a sort of fashion of "don't let's speak of it any more." And this behavior is not due to a wish to forgive: it shows the need to wipe out a memory which, if allowed to survive, would affect us every moment of our lives. The blood of the martyrs can only be effective if the society which survives them allows it to be.

People will say that it is necessary to forgive. And that is true, if only because we have no valid way of deciding the degree of guilt, or of complicity. We cannot fight against forgetfulness by protesting against the liberation of war criminals. But the very notion of forgiveness becomes ambiguous when, under the cover of a magnanimity which accepts the suffering and the death of others, we encourage and we practice the deliberate oblivion of Nazi crimes. Because, when we do this, we are trying to escape the bitter reproach of an act of treason that we are about to commit, of a denial which has already been committed. We hold our tranquility by paying this price: Could we live the way we live if we had made an honest effort to understand what was done to men by men from 1939 (and even from 1933) to 1945? The real scandal is that we are able, without giving it a thought, to speak and to write about other things. The image of the early martyrs dominated Christian thought during a number of centuries; the great plague of mid-14th century weighed, by the apocalyptic and macabre elements which it introduced, over the art and the thought of the late Middle Ages. But Nazism, which was both persecution and terrible plague, does not seem to have affected people, does not seemed to have shocked people in any such way.

Perhaps we might be tempted to believe that we have a thinner skin than our ancestors, and that a sense of decency, an instinctive horror of cruelty prevents our mentioning the gassed or crushed babies, the mass shootings of prisoners, the hangings, the innumerable horrors of the camps. There is no truth in that, and the very people who seem determined on spreading eternal silence over Nazi crimes, who hardly care to touch, let alone believe, the Jews of the Warsaw Ghetto, do not hesitate to furnish

Adapted and translated by Eugen Weber from Michel François, "Contre l'Oubli," in the Catholic Monthly *Esprit* (Paris, 1956). Reprinted by permission of the author and *Esprit*.

us with detailed descriptions of persecutions in China or Bulgaria, high-pitched descriptions, with all the accompaniment of torn-out nails, burned flesh, raped women. Our decent respectable friend who covers his eyes when there is talk of Auschwitz, is hypnotized by the sight of blood, as soon as this blood has been shed by Communists. And certain good Christians who, for purely Christian reasons, preach that we should forgive and forget "because 10 years have passed," find it very easy to skip back over whole centuries and evoke with indignation the death of Christian martyrs and stigmatize their murderers. The readiness to forgive and forget varies according to the quality (and sometimes according to the color) of the killer and the killed.

As a cause and as a factor of this oblivion, anti-Communism has played a tremendous role. Among other things, there was a utilitarian reason why this should be so; one could not, without forgetting the past, think of mobilizing the Germans for the defense of Western Civilization. "The subject with which you deal and, more particularly, the photographs that you propose to publish, are of a nature likely to revive the feelings of hatred towards the German people and, consequently, to furnish arguments to those who oppose the policy which tends to give the Germans the possibility, through re-armament or any other means, to reestablish their influence in world affairs," wrote in August, 1954, the Lord Chancellor of the United Kingdom to Lord Russell of Liverpool who was preparing to publish in his book, *The Scourge of the Svastica*, an account of German war crimes, based wholly on uncontested official evidence. Having refused to take part in the conspiracy of silence, Lord Russell had to resign from his post as legal counselor of the British Army. In all Western countries, the governments which were trying (sometimes in rather underhanded ways) to get German re-armament accepted, used all the means that served their purpose to make sure that war crimes should be forgotten. They did not always avoid making themselves ridiculous. On March 1, 1955, a court in Alexandria, Italy, acquitted two members of the local trade union who had used in a wall-newspaper, photographs from Lord Russell's book, and who had as a result been charged with a "crime against decency." And it is true that some of the prisoners shown in the photograph were naked. "It is the Court which has committed a crime against decency," the defense counsel remarked, "and also a crime against the memory of the victims." There have been other similar cases.

I was just thinking about the connection between the capacity to imagine and the will to forget, when I received a work entitled *Martyrdom and Heroism of the Women of East Germany,* published by the Federal German Ministry for Refugees and Deportees. It deals with the calvary of the German women of Silesia, raped or killed by the soldiers of the Soviet and the Polish armies in the spring of 1945. It is a calvary that I have no intention of denying or minimizing, even though it is well not to forget (as Mr. Khrushchev pointed out in Moscow to Dr. Adenauer) that it was not the Soviet Union which invaded Germany, and that the road from the River Bug to the Volga, both going and coming, was marked by innumerable massacres and by indescribable sufferings for the Russian people. But in any case, even just one raped woman, whether she is German or whether she is Russian, is too much.

The Preface to the work in question was written by Monsignor Joseph Ferche, Auxiliary Bishop of Cologne, ex-Auxiliary of Breslau. This prelate, at least, means to make the most of other people's atrocities. "This book" he writes, "must fix for history the heroism of these women attacked by the Bolshevik hordes; it must become for Western Christendom a warning and a memorial." And further: "For Western men . . . these documents, with their pathetic truths, may seem unbelievable because they have not lived face to face with Bolshevism. Human imagination can hardly understand these facts; personal experience alone can give the necessary intelligence."

Does Monsignor Ferche really believe that, after five years of German domination in Europe, there can still be any horrors left that we cannot imagine? I begin to understand why "while we have not had the consolation of hearing the successor of the Galilean Simon Peter condemn clearly and definitely the crucifixion of so many Jews, brothers of our Lord," certain among the highest dignitaries of the Church have reacted much more promptly and spontaneously when after the war they had to denounce the rape of German women or the expulsion of Germans from the territories that went to Poland. The silence of 1940–1945 was certainly not the silence of accomplices; it was not even imposed by fear. It was the silence of men who lacked precisely, as far as German crimes were concerned, the very imagination that Monsignor Ferche seems to think we lack.

And so it seems that a partial explanation of our present forgetfulness is a lack of sensitiveness to Nazi crimes due to over-sensitiveness to Communism. But the capacity to forget, the confused desire to forget, have other causes. The deportations and exterminations carried out by the Nazis have been a phenomenon of such dimensions that we could not begin to classify them within ready-made categories, or to simplify them so as to make them more accessible, more understandable, more conceivable. We cannot, for instance, consider such immense horrors as mere multiplications of individual murders or hardships, or as collections of arbitrary police acts or judicial errors. We are told that at Lidice or at Oradour the S.S. murderers got the wrong village; we are told that in a certain camp gas chambers were set up as a result of the individual initiative of the local S.S. leader; we shall never manage to sum up the totality of these acts within a familiar and therefore reassuring pattern. It has been tried. People have tried to rationalize the tragedy of deportation and extermination in some fashion that would allow for traditional explanation; they have tried with perseverance to invoke some kind of blindness, of intermittent folly, of intermittent madness. It is being explained that Germany is struggling against its peculiar demons, against its evil spirits; sometimes these evil spirits get the better of it in the struggle, and then there is Hitler, and then there are all the abominations that we have known. Now, in the first place, this business of evil spirits tends to class Hitlerism among other phenomena such as Prussian Militarism, German Nationalism, etc., and to do away with its undeniable originality. It also allows every sort of trick: the very people who, in order to get German rearmament accepted, were arguing that these familiar demons had been driven out for good, are now busily engaged in explaining their obvious revival by the delay that the enemies of E.D.C. have imposed on this aforementioned rearmament. Which produces a strange reversal of causes and effects! And lastly, the explanation of the Concentration Camps and the policy of genocide in terms of evil spirits or a passing fit of collective insanity is a lazy solution; and it tends, above all perhaps, to prevent our recognizing ourselves and our civilization (even though as seen in a distorting mirror) in the murderers of the S.S.

As a matter of fact the organization of oblivion had begun at the very moment when the crimes were carried out. Gradually, as the archives and memoirs give us access to the great and little secrets of the war, we discover the responsibilities which are still little known and which oblivion alone can maintain in a propitious shadow. The great trial of those who sinned by omission, the trial of those who failed to give assistance to people in peril of their lives, has never come up. We know now that in London, in Washington, in Moscow, even at the Holy See, it was no longer possible to ignore in 1942 the projects of mass extermination of the Jews. More was known sometimes in such places than among the future victims. What was done to save several million human beings, several million Jews? Nothing, or nearly nothing. The underground organizations were bombarding London with their supplications. "Here are the plans, organize some massive retaliation, bomb their communications, destroy the camps of death." But the conscience of the Allies was completely inhibited by the blackmail of the Nazis. Nothing was done because nothing should be done that would furnish material to enemy propaganda, create the impression that, as Hitler affirmed, this war was a war desired and ordered by the Jews. It was the supreme inanity. Again and again we find the same insensitivity to concrete horrors, the same will to take refuge in easy abstractions. If at that moment we had declared that we should fight quite simply to prevent the murder of six million Jews (and many more non-Jews), we should have given its real dimension to the war against Nazism—a more real dimension, in any case, a more authentic war-aim, than the phraseology of the Atlantic Charter. But, between gentlemen, it was impossible to fight for Jews!! Oblivion wipes out everything: no more crime, no more criminals, no more accomplices, no more indifferent onlookers. An easy conscience is well worth a little effort.

And yet the deportations, the exterminations, the massacres and the killings of the Second World War have become the object of serious studies. It may seem inhuman to probe and sear wounds that are still so fresh, according to the strict methods of historical research. This work is nevertheless necessary; and perhaps this kind of work alone may be able to oppose any kind of barrier to the invasion of wilful oblivion.

The direct testimonies on the life of the Concentration Camps, testimonies which appeared in great numbers in the immediate aftermath of war, have sometimes served as a pretext for those who wanted to bury such memories. This kind of literature did not always reach a very high standard, and some of the stories were not always true. People take advantage of it first to discredit certain men, then to group all the victims under a common disapproval, and lastly, to deny the very existence of the concentration camp world. Some want to diminish or abolish the guilt of the Germans, and, hence, of their accomplices in the occupied lands; others want to show that the miseries of the prisoners were mostly due to their own companions, and that everything was really much less terrible than people pretended. . . . What a gift for the craftsmen of oblivion!

Nor has it been so difficult to find, in the millions of published stories, errors, omissions, lapses of memory, and (why not?) some fables and lies. Because a story has mentioned gas chambers in a camp where apparently there were no gas chambers, it is suggested that gas chambers in general were perhaps nothing but the figment of an overheated imagination. And if there were no gas chambers, then it is all right. They have lied; we can sleep in peace.

The right-thinking man is so quickly reassured only because he is never really worried; naturally he will never think to ask himself what would remain of the History of Christianity if, taking advantage of the lies, the inventions, the omissions and the fables of which the *Lives of the Martyrs* are full, we decided to deny both the reality of the persecutions and the value of the evidence of the persecuted.

We should be grateful to the Commission for the History of Deportations for having quickly undertaken the scientific study of deportations, beginning with as large as possible a collection of documents checked in the most rigorous possible way. . . . There could be no more illuminating reading for those who continue to grasp the illusion according to which the immense majority of the German people ignored the existence of the camps. At a given moment the "integration" of the inmates of the camps into the German war industry, through a great number of enterprises and in every part of the German Reich, had grown to proportions which were far too large to remain hidden. The movement of forced labor produced a wealth of constant exchange and contact between the concentration camp world and the outside world. . . . To German industry the camps furnished an ideal labor force; "it could be endlessly renewed, it could be exterminated at will." From all this . . . "we get the impression of a frightful sort of tacit consent of a whole nation (doubtlessly powerless in its great majority) to the extermination of millions of beings who were put to work, in rags or in prison clothes; and all in order to enable the nation itself to be exterminated in uniform on all the battlefields of the 2nd World War, in the hypothetical hope of enlarging its dominion."

As the policies of the allied powers towards Germany have evolved, the principle of collective guilt has given place . . . to that of collective innocence or, at least, of the untroubled conscience of the nation; but the right-thinking man is not going to be completely at ease until we shall also have proclaimed the innocence of the elites, of the ruling class, and of the administration. It is not possible, it cannot be conceived, that such a great people, in which we can see ourselves reflected so clearly, should be criminalized. It is touching to see the arguments which are brought up to prove that the German administration could not know what was going on in the camps. The naive and anodyne correspondence by which the offices in Berlin tried to regulate the rations and the hygiene of the camps is supposed to be a proof of this. If future historians are sufficiently uncritical to rely on the fictions and the formulas that the Germans used, our grandchildren are going to be presented with a queer version of the facts. . . . For instance, they will be intrigued to find in the official German correspondence frequent mention of "*Häftlingszahnstationen*" (dental stations for prisoners): and they will praise the sanitary arrangements of the camps without realizing that these are the offices of an organization whose purpose it was to remove the gold teeth of the murdered prisoners. Yet even the most credulous historian, the most inclined to believe in the innocence and the thoughtlessness of the German administration, might nevertheless experience some surprise if he came across a certain list of "Objects Found" in the railroad station of Radogoscz (Poland), which lists under the date of 28 May, 1942, 300 pants, brassieres and garters, 150 woolen rugs, 170 towels, 160 men's shirts, etc., etc. Even our well-intentioned friend might ask himself if the German official who drew up this list, the one who passed it on, the one who filed it (without counting all the others who might have known about it), really believed that the women of Poland, as careless as you like to imagine them, had lost 300 brassieres, etc., in one day alone in the railroad station of Radogoscz, tiny little hamlet that it is. Everything becomes much clearer when one knows that this station was used as a selection center of the victims destined for the gas chambers. . . . Yet, however many and valuable might be the studies, monographs and anthologies dealing with the German crimes of the 2nd World War, we shall never be able to build up a documentation without gaps. Our knowledge of the subject must necessarily remain a partial one. There was, for instance, a camp in Poland where 600,000 persons were exterminated and on which we have only the evidence of one lonely survivor. Beyond this, even the concentration camp world, about which we know most, reflects after all only a part of the immense abjection. We shall never know the whole truth about the killings and the massacres which, from Crete to Letonia, from the Black Sea to the Pyrenees, accompanied the German occupation. When we have made allowances for certain operations explained as reprisals, and for the fear which turned military leaders into executioners, there still remains an infinite number of quite gratuitous hecatombs, which we might be able to list, but the circumstances of which could never be reconstituted. For these crimes, oblivion is almost inevitable. The human sacrifice has taken place without any ceremony, the martyrdom has lost its value as witness; it is just as if it had never been.

And so, to prevent oblivion, we shall have on our library shelves, statistics, evidence, historical interpretations: they are not enough. But perhaps, if only we could resist the insistent advances of oblivion, if only we could remember what has been done, we might make some use of these sufferings, of these martyrdoms, of these deaths. Through the evidence on our bookshelves, through the witnesses still living among us, the concentration camp world *is* to a certain extent, *could be* in a really constructive fashion, integrated in our reality and in our ways of feeling and thinking. It is because he was dead and came back to life that Lazarus lives in a world which cannot be the world of before his death. And, in the long run, Lazarus must affect also the world of those around him.

The Atom Bomb

It might be well to remember that, in many parts of the world, the American bomb attacks on Hiroshima and Nagasaki are also regarded as crimes akin to genocide. Certainly, these attacks were not undertaken in a spirit of revenge or murderous principle, but rather as a matter of military convenience. Nevertheless, their shadow has loomed large over the conscience of the West, which long lived with the thought that the fate of these ports could await its own cities and countries.

From The United States Strategic Bombing Survey

To appreciate the effects of the atomic bombs on Hiroshima and Nagasaki, one must realize something of the character and extent of medical institutions in the two cities. In addition,

---

From "The Effects of Atomic Bombs on Health and Medical Services in Hiroshima and Nagasaki," in *The United States Strategic Bombing Survey* (Washington, 1948).

it is important to realize the magnitude of the destructive forces, which completely surpassed all previous concepts of destruction in terms of ordinary incendiary or high-explosive bombing.

STATUS OF MEDICAL CARE PRIOR TO BOMBING

Generally speaking, the Japanese are not accustomed to good medical care as one uses the term in light of practice in the Western world. Hospitals are usually available to only those who are able to pay and the average Japanese citizen has never been educated to the value and use of hospitals. Though the number of physicians per unit of population compares favorably with that in the United States, the average physician is poorly trained and the character of medicine which he practices is far below Western standards. Even the licensed physicians resort to unconventional and unscientific methods which have their origin in Far Eastern religion and superstition. In addition, the government licenses a group of "persons engaged in the traditional methods of treatment," such as acupuncture, massage, and moxa. There are also a large number of unlicensed cultists who treat persons by means of faith healing. Both the licensed and unlicensed cultists have fairly large followings, particularly in the rural population and the lower classes.

The average Japanese hospital is a small private hospital which consists of 10 to 50 beds. Actually, the term "beds" is used loosely in this respect since few of them have Western-style beds. The rooms in such hospitals are very much like rooms in Japanese homes with tatami floors and beds made by spreading bedding upon the floor. It is thus impossible to give an accurate bed capacity, this figure actually representing the number that can be crowded into the available space. On the other hand, the larger city institutions and university hospitals are usually well equipped, of modern construction, and use Western beds throughout. Despite this fact, there are in every city large numbers of these small Japanese-style hospitals. Too, a large percentage of the population never go to hospitals, but they are born, have their illnesses and babies, and die in their own homes. Most of the births in Japan are attended by midwives.

Hiroshima and Nagasaki did not differ from the usual medium-sized Japanese city. Hiroshima had two Army hospitals and an Army-Navy relief hospital in addition to the civilian institutions. The Red Cross Hospital and the Communications Hospital were modern structures and were the better institutions of the city. In addition there were many small Japanese hospitals scattered over the city. In the spring of 1945 a medical college was started in Hiroshima and the first class had matriculated. Though no school building was available they were being taught in one of the local hospitals at the time of the bombing. The supply of doctors and nurses seemed up to Japanese standards and it was thought that the city was well provided with medical care.

The situation in Nagasaki differed from Hiroshima in that it possessed one of the finest medical centers in Japan. The University Hospital was the pride of the city and was reputed to be second to none in Japan except the Imperial University Hospital in Tokyo. It was a large modern unit consisting of many buildings and contained about 500 beds. This number represented more than three-quarters of the hospital facilities in the city. The Medical College was located near the hospital and had a large staff of well-trained teachers. There were in addition a tuberculosis sanatorium and many small private and industrial hospitals. Here too, the number of physicians and nurses seemed to be adequate in comparison to other Japanese cities.

Since most of the other large cities of Japan had been subjected to demolition and incendiary raids during late 1944 and 1945 it was natural for Nagasaki and Hiroshima to expect similar treatment. Hiroshima contained no large war industries and had been bombed on one previous occasion only. At that time a single B-29 had dropped several demolition bombs on a suburban district, but there was little damage done. Nagasaki had experienced demolition bombing on several occasions but these raids were directed at key industrial plants. On 1 August 1945, 6 bombs were dropped on the University Hospital hitting the operating room and laboratories and resulting in the death of 3 students and 30–40 other casualties. Many patients were then evacuated as an air-raid precaution. The fact that Hiroshima had been so completely spared of bombing apparently gave rise to some rumors that the city was being saved for some "fantastic" weapon. Several survivors relate having heard such rumors. There was, however, no real reason to suspect that any fate other than that experienced by other cities was in store for it. Accordingly, the officials proceeded with the creation of large firebreaks. This work was started in March 1945 and continued until the time of the atomic bombing. Thousands of homes were thus destroyed and their occupants were required to leave the city. It was estimated by the Prefectural Health Officer that 150,000 people were evacuated from Hiroshima from March to August 1945, of whom probably 10,000 had returned. Similar preparations were being carried out in Nagasaki but they appear to have been on a somewhat smaller scale.

THE ATOMIC BOMBING

It was upon the previously described conditions that the atomic bombs were dropped on Hiroshima on 6 August and on Nagasaki three days later. In order to appreciate the conditions at the time of the blast and immediately thereafter it will be well to reconstruct the scene in Hiroshima as best it can be determined from talking with survivors.

The morning of 6 August 1945 began bright and clear. At about 0700 there was an air-raid alarm and a few planes appeared over the city. Many people within the city went to prepared air-raid shelters, but since alarms were heard almost every day the general population did not seem to have been greatly concerned. About 0800 an all-clear was sounded after the planes had disappeared. At this hour of the morning many people were preparing breakfast. This fact is probably important since there were fires in charcoal braziers in many of the homes at this time. Some of the laboring class were at work but most of the downtown business people had not gone to work. Consequently, a large percentage of the population was in their homes and relatively few were in the more strongly constructed business buildings.

After the all-clear sounded, persons began emerging from air-raid shelters and within the next few minutes the city began to resume its usual mode of life for that time of day. It is related by some survivors that they had watched planes fly over the city. At about 0815 there was a blinding flash. Some described it as brighter than the sun, others likened it to a magnesium flash. Following the flash there was a blast of heat and wind. The large majority of people within 3,000 feet of ground zero were killed immediately. Within a radius of about 7,000 feet almost every Japanese house collapsed. Beyond this range and up to 15,000–20,000 feet many of them collapsed and others received serious structural damage. Persons in the open were burned on exposed surfaces, and within 3,000–5,000 feet many were burned to death while others received severe burns through their clothes. In many instances clothing burst into spontaneous flame and had to be beaten out. Thousands of people were pinned beneath collapsed buildings or injured by flying debris. Flying glass particularly produced many non-lethal injuries and the distances at which they occurred are discussed in the following chapter, but the foregoing presentation was necessary for one to appreciate the state of the population immediately after the bomb exploded.

Shortly after the blast fires began to spring up over the city. Those who were able made a mass exodus from the city into the outlying hills. There was no organized activity. The people appeared stunned by the catastrophe and rushed about as jungle animals suddenly released from a cage. Some few apparently attempted to help others from the wreckage, particularly members of their family or friends. Others assisted those who were unable to walk alone. However, many of the injured were left trapped beneath collapsed buildings as people fled by them in the streets. Pandemonium reigned as the uninjured and slightly injured fled the city in fearful panic. Teams which had been previously organized to render first aid failed to form and function. Those closer to ground zero were largely demobilized due to injuries and death. However, there were physically intact teams on the outskirts of the city which did not function. Panic drove these people from the city just as it did the injured who could walk or be helped along. Much of the city's fire-fighting equipment was damaged beyond use so that soon the conflagrations were beyond control.

In Nagasaki a similar but slightly less catastrophic picture occurred. The blast was not centered over the main business section of the city but was up the valley about 2 miles. There were large industrial plants, hospitals, the medical school and partially built-up residential areas near the ground zero. The terrain in this area was uneven with large hills which shielded certain areas. Due to the shielding factor and the distance of the explosion from the center of the city, Nagasaki was less completely destroyed than Hiroshima and the panic was apparently less.

THE FATE OF MEDICAL FACILITIES

The fate of the hospitals in Hiroshima is particularly interesting in the light of this chaos and destruction. Many of the smaller hospitals and clinics were located in the center of the city and were of typical Japanese construction. For instance, the Shima Surgical Hospital was only 1000 feet from ground zero. It was partly brick but largely wooden construction. The blast blew it flat and it is believed that all of the occupants were killed immediately. The remains of the building burned, and the spot is now a mass of flattened rubble. The Tada Hospital was partly reinforced concrete and partly wooden construction. Located at 2,600 feet from ground zero it was completely demolished, and the only remnants were the concrete foundation and the gutted and broken concrete portions of the building. The exact fate of its occupants could not be definitely determined but it is believed that they were all killed by the blast and succeeding fire. Another building of medical nature which was located near the center of the blast was the Japan Red Cross Office Building. It was only 740 feet from ground zero and was almost completely demolished. The windows, window casements, and doors were blown out and even the concrete structure was broken by the downward thrust of the blast. The building was then gutted by fire and all occupants perished. The Hiroshima Army Hospitals No. 1 and No. 2 were located within 1,500–2,000 feet of ground zero. It is reported that 80 percent of the personnel and all of the patients (500 in No. 1 and 650 in No. 2) were killed. The ultimate fate of the surviving 20 percent of the personnel is not known, but on the basis of other experiences at this distance it is probable that a large percentage of them died of injuries or radiation effects. The hospital buildings collapsed and burned. The Red Cross Hospital, which was the city's largest and best hospital, was located 4,860 feet from ground zero. The basic structure of the building, which is reinforced concrete, remained virtually intact. However, steel window casements were blown out or twisted and torn on the side near the blast and the interior was seriously damaged by falling plaster, broken partitions, and falling ceilings. There were 90 percent casualties of the occupants of this building and the damage was so great that the hospital ceased operations for several weeks after the bombing. It did, however, serve as a first-aid station and out-patient clinic in the interim. Practically all instruments and supplies in this hospital were completely destroyed or damaged beyond repair. The Hiroshima Communications Hospital was located at a similar distance from the ground zero, 4,900 feet. It, too, was of reinforced concrete construction. Though the concrete framework of the building remained intact it suffered even more severe damage than did the Red Cross Hospital. Steel window casements were blown out, partitions blown down, and all of the contents were damaged beyond repair. It was later reoccupied as were most of the buildings which were left standing. An example of a hospital located at greater distance from ground zero is the Army-Navy Relief Hospital. It was 10,400 feet from the ground zero and sustained considerable damage. The building was stucco and two floors in height. Though it did not collapse, it was seriously damaged. Most of the tile roof was broken and blown off, window frames were broken and blown out, and in a few places walls were crushed. The principal injuries to the occupants of this hospital were due to flying glass and other missiles. Many smaller hospitals and clinics were destroyed in a similar manner, depending upon their distance from the center of the blast. Since practically all of these buildings were of wooden construction they were either blown down and/or burned shortly thereafter. There was little evidence of their existence to one who came into the area later. It has been impossible to trace the fate of their occupants but it is felt that it coincided to some extent with the fate of other persons in Japanese-type homes at similar distances from ground zero. Actually the incidence of flash burns was probably lower, since few of them would have been outdoors, but the secondary injuries were probably higher. Inasmuch as they were already ill and many no doubt were helpless, the mortality rate surely exceeded that of the general population at comparable distances.

Thus it may be said of Hiroshima that essentially all of the civilian hospitals and

2 large Army hospitals were located within 5,000 feet of ground zero and were functionally completely destroyed. Those within 3,000 feet were totally destroyed and the mortality rate of the occupants was practically 100 percent. Two large hospitals of reinforced concrete construction were located 4,860 and 4,900 feet from the ground zero. The basic structures remained erect but there was such severe interior damage that neither was able to continue operation as a hospital. The casualty rate in these 2 hospitals was approximately 90 percent. Hospitals and clinics beyond 7,000–10,000 feet often remained standing but were badly damaged and there were many casualties due to flying glass and other missiles.

The destruction of hospitals in Nagasaki was even more outstanding than that in Hiroshima. Since the Nagasaki University Hospital contained over three-quarters of the hospital beds in the city it represented the bulk of the city's hospital facilities. The center of the hospital grounds was only 2,400 feet from ground zero and from a functional standpoint the hospital was completely obliterated. Most of the buildings were of reinforced-concrete construction but a great deal of wood was used in interior construction and fittings. The basic structure of all these buildings remained essentially intact but there was severe damage otherwise. The blast effects were very severe and almost every building was gutted by fire. The mortality rate of occupants of this hospital was at least 80 percent, two-thirds being killed outright. The Nagasaki Medical College was located even closer to ground zero, being only 1,700 feet distant. A large portion of the buildings were of inflammable nature but a few small buildings were constructed of reinforced concrete. The wooden buildings were blown down and subsequently consumed by flames. The concrete structures remained erect but were completely gutted by fire. Of the 850 medical students present 600 were killed and 12 out of the 16 professors were also lost. The third- and fourth-year medical students escaped by virtue of the fact that they were elsewhere at the time of the bomb blast. Almost all of the other occupants of the buildings were killed outright. All medical equipment and supplies in the medical college buildings were completely destroyed by blast and fire. The Nagasaki Tuberculosis Sanatorium was located across the valley from the college and the hospital but was only 2,600 feet from ground zero. Since the buildings were all of wooden construction they were completely destroyed by blast and fire. It was reported that all of the patients and other occupants of the sanatorium were killed. Except the 2 hospitals mentioned above there were no others of any size located within Nagasaki, although there were many small private hospitals and clinics of typical Japanese construction, scattered throughout the city. The fate of these buildings and their occupants corresponded in general to that of buildings of similar construction at comparable distances from the bomb in Hiroshima. However, there was an additional factor of the hills shielding some structures in Nagasaki. In Hiroshima the effective zone was entirely flat and hills on the outskirts of the city were so distant that they did not interefere with the effects of the bomb to any appreciable extent. On the other hand, in Nagasaki many structures that would otherwise have suffered much more severe damage were partially or completely protected from the bomb effects by hills.

In summary, it may be said of the hospital facilities in Nagasaki that over 80 percent of the hospital beds and the Medical College were located within 3,000 feet of ground zero and were completely destroyed. Reinforced-concrete buildings within this range remained standing but were completely gutted by fire; buildings of wooden construction were completely destroyed by fire and blast; the mortality rate of occupants of this group of buildings was about 75–80 percent.

RESTORATION OF HOSPITALS AFTER BOMBING

An amazing feature of the Atomic bombings to one going into the areas later was the poor recuperative powers of the population towards the restoration of all types of facilities. Though this was probably less so in the medical field than in others it was still alarmingly apparent. The panic of the people immediately after the bombing was so great that Hiroshima was literally deserted. It was apparently less true of Nagasaki and this was probably due to the fact that the city was less completely destroyed, but the same apathy was there. The colossal effects of the bombs and the surrender following shortly thereafter seemed to have completely stunned the people. The effects of the typhoons of September and early October may have contributed to this psychological reaction.

Since the most outstanding feature of the atomic bombs was the high rate of human casualties, it was natural that this was the greatest problem in the areas following the bombing. But even in this regard the progress was astoundingly slow and haphazard. Other evidences of restoration were almost completely absent. For instance, at the time the Medical Division visited Hiroshima, 3 months after the bombing, the first street car was beginning operation, people wandered aimlessly about the ruins, and only a few shacks had been built as evidence of reoccupation of the city. No system for collection of night soil or garbage had been instituted. Leaking water pipes were seen all over the city with no evidence of any attention. It was reported that following the bombing several days were required for disposal of the dead and they were simply piled into heaps and burned without attempts at identification or enumeration. Street cars were burned as a method of cremating the bodies within. All in all, there appeared to be no organization and no initiative.

The care of the wounded immediately after the bombing was essentially nil in Hiroshima. Beyond the sphere of family ties there seemed to be little concern for their fellow man. It is true that essentially all of the medical supplies were destroyed by the bombing and that there were no hospitals and little with which to work. For the first 3 days there was no organized medical care. At the end of this time the Prefectural Health Department was successful in getting a portion of the surviving physicians together and to begin ministering to the wounded who remained in the city. Up until this time all nursing and medical care had been on an individual basis. The more seriously injured were placed in the few remaining public buildings on the outskirts of the city. Many of them died but many seriously burned cases remained. Small stocks of medical supplies which had been stored in caves outside the city were brought out but were soon exhausted. With all medical supplies gone and practically none being brought in, the treatment of the injured seems to have consisted largely of offering a place of refuge. There is no doubt that many died who might have been saved by modern, competent medical care. As time elapsed many of the small hospitals and clinics were able to reopen and offer some help. Japanese medical authorities and other scientists visited the city in order to appraise the nature and extent of the damage but they did not contribute materially to the care of the sick and injured. Finally, medical teams consisting of medical students and physicians were sent into the area from the larger cities such as Tokyo, Osaka and Kyoto. They assisted materially in administering medical care but were handicapped by the overwhelming size of the task and the lack of supplies. The Red Cross Hospital was cleared of wreckage and finally reopened without any repair of the building. In many respects it was fortunate that such a large proportion of the injured fled to nearby towns and villages. Except for Kure which had been largely destroyed by incendiary bombing, the facilities in these areas were relatively intact.

Most of the fatalities due to flash burns and secondary injuries occurred within a few days after the bombing. The peak of deaths due to radiation effects was not reached until late August or the early part of September. Very few cases suffering from radiation died after 1 October and deaths due to other causes had practically ceased by this time. Thus during October the essential medical care was directed almost exclusively toward burn cases, most of which were flash burns. A large number were still in hospitals but the vast majority of these patients could be treated as outpatients. By 1 November adequate hospital space was available but it was still of emergency nature and medical supplies were inadequate. Many of the burns remained unhealed. Inadequate medical care, poor nutrition, and secondary infection were important factors in this delayed healing.

The effects of the atomic bombing of Nagasaki were very similar to those in Hiroshima. Even though it followed the bombing of Hiroshima by 3 days, wartime secrecy, general confusion and the short lapse of time did not allow the population of Nagasaki any particular advantage from the previous experience. The psychological reaction of the people was essentially the same and the chaos in the city seems to have been almost as great. A very important difference between the two cities was that Nagasaki was not so completely destroyed. Further, the bomb blast was centered over a more industrial area and the character of the buildings resulted in less extensive fires. But from the medical standpoint the bombing was particularly catastrophic because the bulk of the city's hospital facilities were located within a radius of 3,000 feet of the center of the explosion. The destruction of the University Hospital and the Medical College was so great that the buildings left standing could not be reoccupied even for emergency medical care. Other hopsitals and clinics, including the Tuberculosis Sanatorium, had burned to a heap of ashes. The only remaining facilities were small, private clinics and hopsitals and many of them were seriously damaged. Essentially no organized medical care was carried out for several days after the bombing. The Shinkosen Hospital was established in an old school building for the care of bomb victims, but it was woefully inadequate. At one time it harbored over 500 victims. Fortunately, there was a large medical depot at Omura, 20 miles away. Such large stocks of supplies were on hand here that Nagasaki did not suffer in this respect as did Hiroshima. Another school building was converted into an infectious disease hospital.

At the time the Allied Military Government entered Nagasaki, about 1 October, the population was found to be apathetic and profoundly lethargic. Even at this time the collection of garbage and night soil had not been re-established, restoration of other public utilities was lacking, and the hospital facilities were inadequate. Through the initiative of the military Government, a system of reporting infectious diseases was instituted, the collection of garbage and night soil was re-established, and attempts were made to increase the supply of safe water. A survey of the remaining hospitals and clinics at this time by Captain Horne of American Military Government revealed such obvious inadequacies that the survey was not even completed. A perusal of the incomplete report reveals that there were many small private hospitals remaining, most of which were damaged and without satisfactory potential value even if they were re-paired. In the face of the inadequacy of the Shinkosen Hospital, and the absence of other facilities in Nagasaki, bomb victims were transferred to the Omura Naval Hospi-tal where the conditions were much better. The Shinkosen Hospital has now been evacuated and abandoned.

When Nagasaki was visited by the Medical Division, about three months after the bombing, conditions were still very primitive. A visit to the Infectious Disease Hospital revealed that the school building in which it was located had been seriously damaged by bombing and no repairs had been made. The roof was partially destroyed, there were no window-panes, and the building was filthy. All the patients, both male and female, were in adjacent beds in the same ward. Members of their families were present and were going in and out at will. The hospital had a capacity of 35 beds and contained 21 patients; 18 cases of dysentery and 3 cases of typhoid fever, at the time of the visit. There were no isolation precautions in practice. The only medicine and supplies were those furnished by the Military Government. Because of these conditions the Military Government had taken over a Japanese Army Hospital of 103 beds and 12 bassinets and was converting it for use as a Japanese civilian hospital. It was expected to be available very shortly thereafter. The Omura General Hospital (formerly a Naval hospi-tal) was in excellent condition and was being used for the care of atomic bomb victims. Thus, it may be seen that by 1 November some semblance of medical care and sanitary procedures had been re-established in Nagasaki but the facilities were still inadequate. The entire program had to be directed and forced by the Americans though they did not enter the area until nearly 2 months after the bombing.

The devastating effects of the atomic bombs upon medical facilities can be appreci-ated in the light of the foregoing presentation. Not only were the existing facilities almost completely destroyed but there was extreme apathy toward the restoration of hospitals and the care of the injured.

EFFECTS ON MEDICAL PERSONNEL

It was almost impossible to get any accurate information relative to the number of doctors, nurses and other medical personnel in the area prior to bombing, the number injured and killed, or even the number actually present at the time of the visit by the Medical Division. Data obtained from various sources showed extreme variation and were often unreliable. Naturally, the medical personnel in general met the same fate as others located at the same distances from the bomb. The number of casualties also probably bore a direct relationship to the fate of hospitals since medical personnel would be concentrated at those institutions and roughly in proportion to the size of the hospital or clinic.

The number of physicians in Hiroshima prior to the bombing has been variously estimated from 200 to 298. The former figure was supplied to the Medical Division by the Prefectural Health Officer and the latter figure was included in an address by the Prefectural Governor on 9 September 1945. The actual figures probably fall between these two extremes. Regardless of the total number it is known that the casualty rate among this group was very high. About 90 percent were casualties, and 60 of these physicians were killed. One month later only 30 physicians were able to perform their usual duties.

The Hiroshima Prefectural Medical College was started in the spring of 1945 and the first class had matriculated. As a result of the bombing the hospital was demolished and one member of the faculty was killed and another injured. The number of students killed and injured could not be determined.

Prior to the bombing there were 1,780 nurses in Hiroshima. Of these, 1,654 were killed or injured on 6 August. Consequently, the city suffered greatly because of the lack of nurses and many untrained volunteers had to be pressed into service in caring for the injured.

The experience in Nagasaki was very similar to that in Hiroshima. The exact number of physicians in the city prior to the bombing could not be determined but there were probably about 200–250 in 1944. This number may have decreased slightly in 1945 as a result of actual bombing and the effects of partial evacuation of the city in preparation for raids. Due to the different character of the two cities it would at first appear that the loss of medical personnel would have been proportionately less in Nagasaki. However, a factor which counterbalanced this fact to some extent was that the largest number and best of the medical personnel were concentrated in the medical school and the University Hospital, both of which were completely destroyed with a large percentage of their occupants. Actual investigation as of 1 November revealed that there were about 120 physicians in Nagasaki. So apparently the city did fare better than Hiroshima which had less than half that many physicians at about the same time.

The damage to the Nagasaki Medical College and University Hospital has already been described. Reports reveal that 650 of the 850 medical students were killed and some others may have died later. Of the survivors practically every one was injured and at least half had radiation sickness later. There were 16 of the 20 faculty members present at the time of the bombing and 12 of them were killed and the others injured.

The casualty rate among nurses in Nagasaki could not be accurately determined. There were 683 nurses in the city on 1 November but it is not known how many of these had come in after the bombing. The percentage of fatalities and injuries probably closely paralleled that of the physicians but no accurate figures are available to support this supposition. . . .

Another Postwar World

The Cold War
Population: Overpopulation?
Education: Failure or Success?
Political Correctness
Crime
Epilogue

THE CLOSER ONE DRAWS TO THE PRESENT, THE HARDER IT is to determine what is historically significant and what is not. Matters of moment have a way of proving only momentarily momentous. Public memory is short. The Battle of Waterloo becomes the name of a London railway station, then a film named after the bridge nearby, then not even that. Once-dreaded revolutions are tamed by association with alleged "revolutions" in detergents or breakfast food. Revered religious symbols such as the crescent of Islam turn into crunchy *croissants*, and Watergate becomes a hotel again, and a building complex. Even *Memory* is just another perfume.

Knowing this makes it doubly hard to select among the issues that concern us now those that are worth serious discussion—at least until now turns into yesterday.

A host of contending topics clamored for attention, but their justified inclusion would have turned this selection of texts into an unwieldy Yellow Pages. In the end, I settled on one story that has a beginning and an end: the cold war and its concomitants, the making of a European Union and the unmaking of Soviet despotism. Begun in 1945 or 1946, the cold war petered out only in the 1980s, searing the substance of half a century—for we are still living through its sequels. The same is true of Soviet despotism, longer lived and overshadowing the cold-war world with its ambitions, its rivalry with freer countries, and the military and ideological challenges that forced a certain unity upon the West.

The section on the cold war is followed by glimpses of current issues that spark discussion and debate: population (meaning the rising tide of overpopulation), education, and political correctness. None of these are contemporary only, but all are actual, and all evoke a diversity of responses.

The Cold War

THE feeling of hope that briefly survived the end of the First World War was not duplicated after the Second. At best, people felt, as did Sieyès, that survival was an achievement. They were relieved that the struggle was over, but even their relief was tainted by qualms that more struggles lay ahead. To most people war had brought destruction and defeat, and the poverty of victory was only slightly better than the poverty of defeat.

Very soon after the hostilities ended, the rivalry between the Soviet Union and that Atlantic powers, led by the United States, became the central theme of international affairs. Liberal democracy, which had not done too well in the struggle against the totalitarian populism of fascism, now had to face another totalitarian challenge in communism. In 1947 Bernard Baruch, an American financier and presidential adviser, first used the term *cold war* to describe the political, economic, and propaganda struggle that was to dominate the next four decades. It was a war waged with only limited recourse to weapons due to the fear of a nuclear holocaust. It was also a war between two doctrines, in which the ideal of a planned and regulated society challenged that of an individualistic society that was a little less planned and regulated. It is difficult to say how much ideas counted in this contest. At any rate, the West, challenged to put its house in order or else lose it, and faced with the arguments and power of an aggressive rival, was forced into an "agonizing reappraisal" of policies and values.

The Iron Curtain

In February 1945, while Allied forces were invading Germany from the east and the west, Roosevelt, Stalin, and Churchill met at Yalta, in [then] Russian Crimea, to decide the fate of postwar Europe. The declaration at the conclusion of the conference proclaimed:
> *The establishment of order in Europe and the rebuilding of national economic life must be achieved by processes which will enable the liberated peoples to destroy the last vestiges of Nazism and Fascism and to create democratic institutions of their own choice. This is a principle of the Atlantic Charter—the right of all peoples to choose the form of government under which they will live—the restoration of sovereign rights and self-government to those peoples who have been forcibly deprived of them by the aggressor nations.*

In fact, the right of people to choose the form of government under which they live became an open-ended opportunity for Stalin's Russia to organize "free elections" in all the countries occupied by its troops; by the end of the decade, they had all become Soviet satellites. In March 1946, Winston Churchill, who had been replaced as prime minister of England by a Labor government, analyzed Soviet encroachments in a speech delivered—in President Truman's presence—at Westminster College in Fulton, Missouri.

Winston Churchill: from the "Iron Curtain" Speech

. . . A shadow has fallen upon the scenes so lately lightened, lighted by the Allied victory. Nobody knows what Soviet Russia and its Communist international organization intends to do in the immediate future, or what are the limits, if any, to their expansive and proselytizing tendencies. . . .

From Stettin in the Baltic to Trieste in the Adriatic, an iron curtain has descended across the Continent. Behind that line lie all the capitals of the ancient states of central and eastern Europe . . . all these famous cities and the populations around them lie in what I might call the Soviet sphere. . . . Police governments are pervading from Moscow. . . . The Russian-dominated Polish government has been encouraged to make enormous and wrongful inroads upon Germany. . . . The Communist parties, which were very small in all these eastern states of Europe, have been raised to preeminence and power far beyond their numbers and are seeking everywhere to obtain totalitarian control. Police governments are prevailing in nearly every case, and so far, except in Czechoslovakia, there is no true democracy. . . .

An attempt is being made by the Russians, in Berlin, to build up a quasi-Communist party in their zone of occupied Germany. . . . At the end of the fighting last June the American and British armies withdrew westward, in accordance with an earlier agreement . . . in order to allow our Russian allies to occupy this vast expanse of territory which the western democracies had conquered.

. . . Whatever conclusions may be drawn from these facts . . . this is certainly not the liberated Europe we fought to build up. Nor is it one which contains the essentials of permanent peace.

The safety of the world, ladies and gentlemen, requires a unity in Europe from which no nation should be permanently outcast. It is from the strong parent races in Europe that world wars . . . have sprung. . . . Surely we should work with conscious purpose for a grand pacification of Europe within the structure of the United Nations and in accordance with our charter. . . .

In front of the iron curtain which lies across Europe are other causes for anxiety. In Italy the Communist party is seriously hampered by having to support the Communist-trained Marshal Tito's claims to former Italian territory at the head of the Adriatic. Nevertheless the future of Italy hangs in the balance. Again one cannot imagine a regenerated Europe without a strong France. . . .

However, in a great number of countries, far from the Russian frontiers and throughout the world, Communist fifth columns are established and work in complete unity and absolute obedience to directions they receive from the Communist center. Except in the British Commonwealth and in the United States, where communism is in its infancy, the Communist parties or fifth columns constitute a growing challenge

From The *New York Times*, March 6, 1946, p. 4.

and peril to Christian civilization. These are somber facts for anyone to have to recite on the morrow of a victory gained by so much splendid comradeship in arms and in the cause of freedom and democracy, but we should be most unwise not to face them squarely while time remains.

The outlook is also anxious in the Far East and especially in Manchuria. The agreement which was made at Yalta, to which I was party, was extremely favorable to Soviet Russia, but it was made at a time when no one could say that the German war might not extend all through the summer and autumn of 1945 and when the Japanese war was expected by the best judges to last for a further eighteen months from the end of the German war. . . .

I was a Minister at the time of the Versailles treaty. . . . In those days there were high hopes and unbounded confidence that the wars were over, and that the League of Nations would become all-powerful. I do not see or feel that same confidence or even the same hopes in the haggard world at the present time.

On the other hand, ladies and gentlemen, I repulse the idea that a new war is inevitable; still more that it is imminent. It is because I am sure that our fortunes are still in our hands, in our own hands, and that we hold the power to save the future, that I feel the duty to speak out now that I have the occasion and opportunity to do so.

I do not believe that Soviet Russia desires war. What they desire is the fruits of war and the indefinite expansion of their power and doctrines. . . .

From what I have seen of our Russian friends and allies during the war, I am convinced that there is nothing they admire so much as strength, and there is nothing for which they have less respect than for weakness, especially military weakness. . . .

If the Western democracies stand together in strict adherence to the principles of the United Nations Charter, their influence for furthering those principles will be immense and no one is likely to molest them. If, however, they become divided or falter in their duty, and if these all-important years are allowed to slip away, then indeed catastrophe may overwhelm us all.

Last time I saw it all coming and cried aloud to my own fellow-countrymen and to the world, but no one paid any attention. Up to the year 1933 or even 1935, Germany might have been saved from the awful fate which has overtaken her. . . . There never was a war easier to prevent by timely action than the one which has just desolated such great areas of the globe. It could have been prevented, in my belief, without the firing of a single shot, and Germany might be powerful, prosperous and honored today. . . .

We surely, ladies and gentlemen, I put it to you, but surely we must not let that happen again. This can only be achieved by reaching now, in 1946 . . . a good understanding on all points with Russia under the general authority of the United Nations Organization and by the maintenance of that good understanding through many peaceful years, by the world instrument, supported by the whole strength of the English-speaking world and all its connections. . . .

. . . If the population of the English-speaking Commonwealth be added to that of the United States . . . there will be no quivering, precarious balance of power to offer its temptation to ambition and adventure. On the contrary there would be an overwhelming assurance of security. . . .

Economic and Military Renewal

Not all of Europe's problems were external. The war had left the continent not only in ruins, but poorer and more disorganized than it had been in centuries. Fifteen months after Churchill's speech, Secretary of State George Marshall, in his 1947 commencement address at Harvard University, suggested the plan for economic recovery that would earn him a Nobel Prize in 1953 and a permanent place in history.

George Marshall: The Marshall Plan

I need not tell you, gentlemen, that the world situation is very serious. . . . I think one difficulty is that the problem is one of such enormous complexity and that the very mass of facts . . . make it exceedingly difficult for the man in the street to reach a clear appraisement of the situation. Furthermore, the people in this country are distant from the troubled areas . . . and it is hard for them to comprehend the plight and consequent reactions of the long-suffering peoples, and the effect of those reactions on their governments in connection with our efforts to promote peace in the world.

In considering the requirements for the rehabilitation of Europe the physical loss . . . was correctly estimated, but it has become obvious during recent months that this visible destruction was probably less serious than the dislocation of the entire fabric of European economy. . . . The breakdown of the business structure of Europe during the war was complete. . . . [T]he rehabilitation of the economic structure of Europe quite evidently will require a much longer time and greater effort than had been foreseen.

There is a phase of this matter which is both interesting and serious. The farmer has always produced the foodstuffs to exchange with the city dweller for the other necessities of life. This division of labor is the basis of modern civilization. At the present time it is threatened with breakdown. The town and city industries are not producing adequate goods to exchange with the food producing farmers. . . . The farmer or peasant cannot find the goods for sale which he desires to purchase. So the sale of his farm produce for the money which he cannot use seems to him an unprofitable transaction. He, therefore, has withdrawn many fields from crop cultivation and is using them for grazing. He feeds more grain to stock. . . . Meanwhile people in the cities are short of food and fuel. So the governments are forced to use their foreign money and credits to procure these necessities abroad. This process exhausts funds which are urgently needed for reconstruction. Thus a very serious situation is rapidly developing which bodes no good for the world. The modern system of the division of labor upon which the exchange of products is based is in danger of breaking down.

The truth of the matter is that Europe's requirements for the next three or four years of foreign food and other essential products—principally from America—are so

From The *New York Times,* June 6, 1947, p. 2.

much greater than her present ability to pay that she must have substantial additional help, or face economic, social and political deterioration of a very grave character.

The remedy lies in breaking the vicious circle and restoring the confidence of the European people in the economic future of their own countries and of Europe as a whole. The manufacturer and the farmer throughout wide areas must be able and willing to exchange their products for currencies, the continuing value of which is not open to question.

Aside from the demoralizing effect on the world at large and the possibilities of disturbances arising as a result of the desperation of the people concerned, the consequences to the economy of the United States should be apparent to all. It is logical that the United States should do whatever it is able to do to assist in the return of normal economic health in the world, without which there can be no political stability and no assured peace.

Our policy is directed not against any country or doctrine but against hunger, poverty, desperation and chaos. Its purpose should be the revival of a working economy in the world so as to permit the emergence of political and social conditions in which free institutions can exist. Such assistance, I am convinced, must not be on a piecemeal basis as various crises develop. Any assistance that this government may render in the future should provide a cure rather than a mere palliative.

Any government which is willing to assist in the work of recovery will find full cooperation, I am sure, on the part of the United States Government. Any government which maneuvers to block the recovery of other countries cannot expect help from us. Furthermore, governments, political parties and groups which seek to perpetuate human misery in order to profit therefrom politically or otherwise will encounter the opposition of the United States.

It is already evident that before the United States Government can proceed much further in its efforts to alleviate the situation . . . there must be some agreement among the countries of Europe as to the requirements of the situation and the part those countries themselves will take in order to give proper effect to whatever action might be undertaken by this Government. It would be neither fitting nor efficacious for this Government to undertake to draw up unilaterally a program designed to place Europe on its feet economically. This is the business of the Europeans. The initiative, I think, must come from Europe. The role of this country should consist of friendly aid in the drafting of a European program and of later support of such a program so far as it may be practical for us to do so. The program should be a joint one, agreed to by a number, if not all European nations. . . .

Dean Acheson: *The North Atlantic Pact* (1949)

Marshall aid, which cost the United States over ten billion dollars, laid the foundations for European revival. One of its unexpected effects, however, was Soviet pressure on Czecho-

From the U.S. Department of State *Bulletin*, Vol. XX, No. 508 (March 27, 1949) pp. 385–386.

slovakia not to avail itself of American aid. This culminated in 1948 in a Communist takeover in Prague. That same year it became clear that joint Allied occupation of defeated Germany had broken down. The Soviets set up a blockade to Allied access to Berlin, which ended only after a year-long American airlift had demonstrated U.S. technological and air power. The Berlin blockade forced the fumbling West to face the reality of a divided Europe—and a divided Germany, too, whose western portion would become a new state, rearmed and integrated in a formal new defense structure. The North Atlantic Pact was signed in April 1949; what follows is Secretary of State Dean Acheson's explanation of it.

. . . It is important to keep in mind that the really successful national and international institutions are those that recognize and express underlying realities. The North Atlantic community of nations is such a reality. It is based on the affinity and natural identity of interests of the North Atlantic powers.

The North Atlantic treaty, which now formally unites them, is the product of at least three hundred and fifty years of history, perhaps more. There developed on our Atlantic coast a community, which has spread across the continent, connected with Western Europe by common institutions and moral and ethical beliefs. Similarities of this kind are not superficial, but fundamental. They are the strongest kind of ties, because they are based on moral conviction, on acceptance of the same values in life.

The very basis of western civilization, which we share with the other nations bordering the North Atlantic, and which all of us share with many other nations, is the ingrained spirit of restraint and tolerance. This is the opposite of the Communist belief that coercion by force is a proper method of hastening the inevitable. Western civilization has lived by mutual restraint and tolerance. This civilization permits and stimulates free inquiry and bold experimentation. It creates the environment of freedom, from which flows the greatest amount of ingenuity, enterprise, and accomplishment.

These principles of democracy, individual liberty, and the rule of law have flourished in this Atlantic community. They have universal validity. They are shared by other free nations and find expression on a universal basis in the Charter of the United Nations; they are the standards by which its members have solemnly agreed to be judged. They are the elements out of which are forged the peace and welfare of mankind.

Added to this profoundly important basis of understanding is another unifying influence—the effect of living on the sea. The sea does not separate people as much as it joins them, through trade, travel, mutual understanding, and common interests.

For this second reason, as well as the first, North America and Western Europe have formed the two halves of what is in reality one community, and have maintained an abiding interest in each other.

It is clear that the North Atlantic pact is not an improvisation. It is the statement of the facts and lessons of history. We have learned our history lesson from two world wars in less than half a century. That experience has taught us that the control of Europe by a single aggressive, unfriendly power would constitute an intolerable threat to the national security of the United States. We participated in those two great wars to preserve the integrity and independence of the European half of the Atlantic community in order to preserve the integrity and independence of the American half. It is a simple fact, proved by experience, that an outside attack on one member of this community is an attack upon all members.

We have also learned that if the free nations do not stand together, they will fall one by one. The stratagem of the aggressor is to keep his intended victims divided, or, better still, set them to quarreling among themselves. Then they can be picked off one by one without arousing unified resistance. We and the free nations of Europe are determined that history shall not repeat itself in that melancholy particular. . . .

The Treaty of Paris (1951)

Military and economic cooperation went hand in hand: a European economic community paralleled the European military alliance. It began with just six countries—Belgium, Holland, Luxembourg, France, West Germany, and Italy—that pooled their coal and steel resources in the Treaty of Paris.

THE HIGH CONTRACTING PARTIES

Considering that world peace may be safeguarded only by creative efforts which measure up to the dangers which menace it;

Convinced that the contribution which an organized and vital Europe can bring to civilization is indispensable to the maintenance of peaceful relations;

Conscious of the fact that Europe can be built only by concrete actions which create a real solidarity and by the establishment of common bases of economic development;

Desirous of assisting through the expansion of their basic production in raising the standard of living and in furthering the works of peace;

Resolved to substitute for historic rivalries a fusion of their essential interests; to establish, by creating an economic community, the foundation of a broad and independent community among peoples long divided by bloody conflicts; and to lay the bases of institutions capable of giving direction to their future common destiny;

Have decided to create a European Coal and Steel Community and have agreed to the following provisions. . . .

Six years later, in 1957, the Treaty of Rome joined the six countries in a common market that would, in 1992, become a full-fledged European Union: a coalition of 360 million people in the nations of Western, Southern, and Central Europe. With growing economic and political unity, Europe could become a major player in world affairs.

Draft Treaty Constituting the European Coal and Steel Community (Washington, D.C., 1951), p. 7.

The Situation in the Soviet Union

The Soviet Union, meanwhile, faced problems of its own. In 1956, three years after Stalin's death, the new secretary general of the Communist party, Nikita Khrushchev, speaking in a secret session of the party's congress, made a sensational attack on the dead dictator. Stalin, Khrushchev explained, had turned himself "into a superman . . . akin to a god. Such a man supposedly knows everything, sees everything, thinks for everyone, can do anything, is infallible. . . ."

Nikita Khrushchev: from Speech to the Twentieth Congress of the Communist Party

At the present we are concerned with a question which has immense importance for the party now and for the future—[we are concerned] with how the cult of the person of Stalin has been gradually growing, the cult which became at a certain specific stage the source of a whole series of exceedingly serious and grave perversions of party principles, of party democracy, of revolutionary legality. . . .

Allow me first of all to remind you how severely the classics of Marxism-Leninism denounced every manifestation of the cult of the individual. . . .

While ascribing great importance to the role of the leaders and organizers of the masses, Lenin at the same time mercilessly stigmatized every manifestation of the cult of the individual, inexorably combated the foreign-to-Marxism views about a "hero" and a "crowd" and countered all efforts to oppose a "hero" to the masses and to the people. . . .

[Yet] in December, 1922, in a letter to the party congress Vladimir Ilyich [Lenin] wrote: "After taking over the position of Secretary General, Comrade Stalin accumulated in his hands immeasurable power and I am not certain whether he will be always able to use this power with the required care." . . .

Vladimir Ilyich said: "Stalin is excessively rude, and this defect, which can be freely tolerated in our midst and in contacts among us Communists, becomes a defect which cannot be tolerated in one holding the position of the Secretary General. Because of this, I propose that the comrades consider the method by which Stalin would be removed from this position and by which another man would be selected for it; a man who, above all, would differ from Stalin in only one quality, namely, greater tolerance, greater loyalty, greater kindness and more considerate attitude towards the comrades, a less capricious temper, etc." . . .

When we analyze the practice of Stalin in regard to the direction of the party and of the country, when we pause to consider everything which Stalin perpetrated, we must be convinced that Lenin's fears were justified. The negative characteristics of Stalin, which, in Lenin's time, were only incipient, transformed themselves during the

---

last years into a grave abuse of power by Stalin, which caused untold harm to our party. . . .

Stalin acted not through persuasion, explanation, and patient cooperation with people, but by imposing his concepts and demanding absolute submission to his opinion. Whoever opposed this concept or tried to prove his viewpoint and the correctness of his position was doomed to removal from the leading collective and to subsequent moral and physical annihilation. This was especially true during the period following the seventeenth party congress, when many prominent party leaders and rank-and-file party workers, honest and dedicated to the cause of communism, fell victim to Stalin's despotism. . . .

It was precisely during this period (1935–1937–1938) that the practice of mass repression through the Government apparatus was born, first against the enemies of Leninism—Trotskyites, Zinovievites, Bukharinites, long since politically defeated by the party, and subsequently also against many honest Communists, against those party cadres who had borne the heavy load of the Civil War and the first and most difficult years of industrialization and collectivization, who actively fought against the Trotskyites and the rightists for the Leninist party line.

Stalin originated the concept "enemy of the people." This term automatically rendered it unnecessary that the ideological errors of a man or men engaged in a controversy be proven; this term made possible the usage of the most cruel repression, violating all norms of revolutionary legality, against anyone who in any way disagreed with Stalin, against those who were only suspected of hostile intent, against those who had bad reputations.

. . . In the main, and in actuality, the only proof of guilt used, against all norms of current legal science, was the "confession" of the accused himself; and, as subsequent probing proved, "confessions" were acquired through physical pressures against the accused. . . .

Lenin used severe methods only in the most necessary cases, when the exploiting classes were still in existence and were vigorously opposing the revolution, when the struggle for survival was decidedly assuming the sharpest forms, even including a civil war.

Stalin, on the other hand, used extreme methods and mass repressions at a time when the revolution was already victorious, when the Soviet state was strengthened, when the exploiting classes were already liquidated and Socialist relations were rooted solidly in all phases of national economy, when our party was politically consolidated and had strengthened itself both numerically and ideologically. It is clear that here Stalin showed in a whole series of cases his intolerance, his brutality and his abuse of power. Instead of proving his political correctness and mobilizing the masses, he often chose the path of repression and physical annihilation, not only against actual enemies, but also against individuals who had not committed any crimes against the party and the Soviet Government. Here we see no wisdom but only a demonstration of the brutal force which had once so alarmed V. I. Lenin. . . .

. . . It became apparent that many party, Government and economic activists who were branded in 1937–38 as "enemies," were actually never enemies, spies, wreckers, etc., but were always honest Communists.

They were only so stigmatized and often, no longer able to bear barbaric tortures, they charged themselves (at the order of the investigative judges—falsifiers) with all kinds of grave and unlikely crimes. . . .

The same fate met not only the Central Committee members but also the majority of the delegates to the seventeenth party congress. Of 1,966 delegates with either voting or advisory rights, 1,108 persons were arrested on charges of anti-revolutionary crimes, i.e., decidedly more than a majority. This very fact shows how absurd, wild and contrary to common sense were the charges of counter-revolutionary crimes made, as we now see, against a majority of participants at the seventeenth party congress. (*Indignation in the hall.*) . . .

Facts prove that many abuses were made on Stalin's orders without reckoning with any norms of party and Soviet legality. Stalin was a very distrustful man, sickly suspicious; we knew this from our work with him. He could look at a man and say: "Why are your eyes so shifty today," or "Why are you turning so much today and avoiding to look me directly in the eyes?" The sickly suspicion created in him a general distrust even toward eminent party workers whom he had known for years. Everywhere and in everything he saw "enemies," "two-facers" and "spies."

Possessing unlimited power, he indulged in great willfulness and choked a person morally and physically. A situation was created where one could not express one's own will.

When Stalin said that one or another should be arrested, it was necessary to accept on faith that he was an "enemy of the people." Meanwhile, Beria's gang, which ran the organs of state security, outdid itself in proving the guilt of the arrested and the truth of materials which it falsified.

And what proofs were offered? The confessions of the arrested, and the investigative judges accepted these "confessions." And how is it possible that a person confesses to crimes which he has not committed? Only in one way—because of application of physical methods of pressuring him, tortures, bringing him to a state of unconsciousness, deprivation of his judgment, taking away of his human dignity. In this manner were "confessions" acquired. . . .

Stalin's reluctance to consider life's realities and the fact that he was not aware of the real state of affairs in the provinces can be illustrated by his direction of agriculture.

All those who interested themselves even a little in the national situation saw the difficult situation in agriculture, but Stalin never even noted it. Did we tell Stalin about this? Yes, we told him, but he did not support us. Why? Because Stalin never traveled anywhere, did not meet city and collective workers; he did not know the actual situation in the provinces.

He knew the country and agriculture only from films. And these films had dressed up and beautified the existing situation in agriculture. . . .

Some comrades may ask us: Where were the members of the Political Bureau of the Central Committee? Why did they not assert themselves against the cult of the individual in time? And why is this being done only now? . . .

Stalin evidently had plans to finish off the old members of the Political Bureau. He often stated that Political Bureau members should be replaced by new ones. . . .

Comrades! In order not to repeat errors of the past, the Central Committee has declared itself resolutely against the cult of the individual. We consider that Stalin was excessively extolled. However, in the past Stalin doubtlessly performed great services to the party, to the working class and to the international workers' movement.

This question is complicated by the fact that all this that we have just discussed was done during Stalin's life under his leadership and with his concurrence; here Stalin was convinced that this was necessary for the defense of the interests of the working classes against the plotters of the enemies and against the attack of the imperialist camp.

He saw this from the position of the interest of the working class, of the interest of the laboring people, of the interest of the victory of socialism and communism. We cannot say that these were the deeds of a giddy despot. He considered that this should be done in the interest of the party; of the working masses, in the name of the defense of the revolution's gains. In this lies the whole tragedy! . . .

The End of the Cold War

Writing about the reforms attempted by Louis XVI's monarchy at the end of its tether, Alexis de Tocqueville reflected that "the most dangerous time for a bad government is when it starts to reform itself." In 1985 Mikhail Gorbachev, last in a succession of Commu-nist party secretaries, admitted that the Soviet system of centralized planning and control was as obsolete and counterproductive on the economic as on the human plane. He launched perestroika—*a program of radical reform—and* glasnost—*openness and open discussion—as a way to energize the nation and stimulate innovation. Within a few years, however, these reforms had led not to renewal but to disintegration, of both the Russian Empire and the Soviet state.*

Timothy Garton Ash: from "Eastern Europe: The Year of Truth"

Last year communism in Eastern Europe died. 1949–1989 RIP. And the epitaph might be:

> *Nothing in his life*
> *Became him like the leaving it.*

The thing that was comprehensively installed in the newly defined territories of Poland, Czechoslovakia, Hungary, Romania, and Bulgaria, and in the newly created German Democratic Republic after 1949, the thing called, according to one's point of view, "socialism," "totalitarianism," "Stalinism," "politbureaucratic dictatorship," "real ex-isting socialism," "state capitalism," "dictatorship over needs," or, most neutrally, "the

---

From *The New York Review of Books* (1990).

Soviet-type system"—that thing will never walk again. And arguably, if we can no longer talk of communism we should no longer talk of Eastern Europe, at least with a capital "E" for Eastern. Instead, we shall have central Europe again, east central Europe, southeastern Europe, eastern Europe with a small "e," and, above all, individual peoples, nations, and states.

To be sure, even without a political-military reversal inside the Soviet Union there will be many further conflicts, injustices, and miseries in these lands. But they will be different conflicts, injustices, and miseries—new and old, post-communist but also pre-communist. In the worst case, there might yet be new dictators; but they would be different dictators. We shall not see again that particular system, characterized by the concentration of political and economic power and the instruments of coercion in the hands of one Leninist party, manifested sociologically as a privileged new class, and initially aspiring to total control, in states with arbitrarily limited sovereignty.

Of course, if we walk the streets of any Eastern European city we can still find the gray, familiar traces: the flattened neoclassical Stalinist facades on all the Victory Squares, the Lenin Boulevards, Steelworks, Shipyards, the balding middle-aged officials with their prefabricated lies, the cheap paper forms for completion in quadruplicate, the queues, the attitude of "we pretend to work and you pretend to pay us." Yet even the physical evidences are being removed at a speed that must cause some anxiety to conservationists. (In Poland there is a scheme for preserving all the old props in an entertainment park. The proposed name is Stalinland.) . . .

Z: from "To the Stalin Mausoleum"

As 1989 draws to a close, it is clear that it will enter history as the beginning of communism's terminal crisis, the year of the Second Great Break, but in the descending, not the ascending, phase of utopia in power; and this not just in Russia, but from the Baltic to the China Sea, and from Berlin to Beijing. It is also clear that perestroika and glasnost, welcome as they are in their intention, have in their application only aggravated the systemic crisis they were intended to alleviate. And they have done so because like all forms of soft communism, they go against the logic of the system they are trying to save. The internal contradiction of perestroika is that Gorbachev has been trying to promote soft communism through structures and a population programmed for hard communism. But the latter is the only variety of Sovietism that is the genuine article, for the essence of all varieties of Sovietism is Party supremacy. Thus, the instrument of Gorbachev's reform—the Party—is at the same time the basic cause of Sovietism's troubles. To adapt a diagnosis of Alexander Herzen regarding earlier revolutionaries, the Party is not the doctor; it is the disease.

And the way out of this contradiction then? As one Soviet reformer put it after the June Congress, "The country now stands at a crossroads. From here we either go

From *Daedalus*, Journal of the American Academy of Arts and Sciences, Vol. 119, No. 1 (Winter 1990), Cambridge, Mass.

the Chinese way or the Polish-Hungarian way." Although the speaker obviously wished for the latter course, the alternative he posed may well be a Hobson's choice. The Chinese way since June 1989 means relative, though now declining, market prosperity under a regime of political and military repression. Repression is certainly a possibility in Russia, but market prosperity is quite out of the question for the indefinite future. Conversely, the Polish-Hungarian way means genuine democracy, but this is being attempted in the midst of economic ruin so severe as to threaten the survival of the new constitutional order. In Russia the economic ruin is even worse than in Poland and Hungary, but real democracy, as opposed to mere democratization, is not even on the agenda. Thus, the Russian way could well combine the worst of the Chinese and the Central European scenarios: economic failure in conjunction with an inexpungeable leading role for the Party.

Indeed, all three paths of communist reform (we may leave out of consideration the frozen Albanias such as Romania, Cuba, and North Korea) seem to end in one or another type of impasse. In this way Leninist totalitarianism shows another facet of its difference from ordinary authoritarianism. As Polish radicals discovered in the early 1980s in looking for possible models of liberation, post-Franco Spain and post-Pinochet Chile could not serve as examples. For those countries were able to make the transition to democracy because they had only been political authoritarianisms, not economic, social, and ideological monoliths. And, of course, they possessed market economies, so when political tyranny was ended, civil society, which had never been destroyed, could emerge fully into the light of day. But Leninist regimes, when they enter their final decline, seem able only either to implode, as in Poland, Hungary, and East Germany, or to dig in their heels militarily to stave off implosion, . . .

Yet whether they implode or hang on for a last desperate stand, all that they leave behind is economic and social rubble—hardly the foundation for building a "normal" society, . . .

Ernest Gellner: from "Nationalisms and the New World Order"

The collapse of totalitarian dictatorship in the East brought both explosions and implosions. The most threatening examples of either could be found in armed conflicts related to national and ethnic rivalries, aspirations, and claims. In the Caucasus, the areas around the Black Sea, and the Balkans, nationalist mayhem followed hot on the heels of communist disintegration. In the following passage, a distinguished Cambridge sociologist places these problems in historical perspective, only to reach an implausibly optimistic conclusion.

We are living in a new world order following events of 1989 and 1991. . . . This world is preoccupied with the problem of military intervention and with the criteria that do,

---

"Nationalisms and the New World Order" an Address by Ernest Gellner as found in *Bulletin of the American Academy of Arts and Sciences,* XLVII, February 1994, no. 5, pp. 29–36. Reprinted with permission of Professor Ernest Gellner.

or should, govern it. The enemy (or disturbance to the order) is nationalism, along with fundamentalism. The two share similar roots: Europe expresses certain impulses through nationalism, the Middle East through fundamentalism.

What is nationalism? The theory that nationalism is self-evident or inherent in human nature (like gender) is mistaken. There are two other main theories: (1) nationalism is the expression of dark, atavistic forces, and (2) nationalism is a reflection of the basic social organization of industrial and industrializing people. (The former theory is, in my view, mistaken; the latter correct.) Industrial society, because it lives by economic growth, is made legitimate by such growth (i.e., bribery by economic improvement). It is therefore committed to a mobile occupational structure and powerful technology, whereby work becomes semantic (the manipulation of people and symbols) and ceases to be physical (the manipulation of things). At work people must interact constantly with economic, political, educational, and other bureaucracies. It follows that people's most important investment, which alone grants them dignity, employability, and acceptability (and even their humanity), is control over the idioms in which the bureaucracies that surround them generally operate. Without such control, life is a long series of humiliations. If someone lacks such rapport with the bureaucracy and its idioms, the only strategies left open to him or her are either to change his or her own culture (i.e., assimilate), to migrate to a place where he or she is accepted, or to change the political boundaries so as to ensure that the social and institutional milieu is that of his or her own culture. Human beings, therefore, must become assimilationists or nationalists, unless they are so fortunate as to be in a situation in which there is congruence between their speech and the idioms of the bureaucracies that surround them.

Industrial society is the first culture ever in which high culture (based on literacy and formal education) is the pervasive culture of the entire society, for the reasons stated. This fact is linked intimately to the importance of nationalism in modern society. In agrarian societies, culture is not endowed with the function it has in industrial societies (namely, that of defining the limits of political units). On the contrary, in agrarian societies, the main function of culture is to express people's status. Hence, there is a premium on cultural differentiation, so cultural boundaries seldom coincide with political ones (which in any case are much more plural and complex and overlapping than they are in an industrial society).

In national states, high or literate culture makes a marriage with the state. In Europe the general transition from a nonnationalist, agrarian society to an industrial, culturally homogeneous, and therefore national state/society passes through five stages: (1) The era leading up to the Congress of Vienna—nationalism was already on the move, thanks to Joseph II and other enlightened despots and their pervasive, expanding bureaucracies (i.e., the snake was in the garden but unnoticed, so the 1815 peacemakers ignored nationalist principles entirely, without provoking any protest). (2) The century between the Congress of Vienna and World War I—the age of nationalist irredentism, in the course of which nationalism became the accepted norm, even though it was not overly successful, particularly in Eastern Europe. The three empires that carved up Eastern Europe in 1815 still controlled Eastern Europe in 1914. (3) The triumph and subsequent self-defeat of nationalism, implemented in 1918. New states, created through fragmentation, had all the weaknesses of the empires they replaced (they were riddled with minorities and were smaller, more inexperienced, and weaker; the new minorities included groups that were used to being dominant and were endowed with allies abroad). This created a very fragile system that collapsed with little resistance to Hitler and Stalin. (4) The result of the frustration in the course of stages (2) and (3)— ethnic genocide during the 1940s, including the victors' retaliation after World War II; and (5) perhaps half reality and half wish fulfillment on my part—the diminution of the political saliency of ethnicity under the impact of the partial truth of the convergence thesis: advanced industrial societies do in fact resemble one another culturally, and, moreover, the intensity of economic jealousy lessens as the gap between the rich and poor diminishes.

The way these five stages have played themselves out varies greatly in diverse parts of Europe. The essence of nationalism is the marriage of state and culture. The legitimate state expresses and protects a culture, and cultures need a state if they are to express themselves properly. Examining Europe from west to east, we find that in the most western region, nationalism has been the least disruptive, because in those countries the de facto marriage of state and culture occurred before the age of nationalism, by sheer historical accident. The couple had been cohabiting anyway. (This was true in Britain, Spain, Portugal, and France.) All that had to be done was to turn peasants into proper members of the high culture. The only major change in a political boundary in this region was that arising from the creation of the Republic of Ireland.

Farther east (in the next time zone), the bride was waiting ready at the altar, but the bridegroom was missing. The cultural bride was available; the Italians and Germans each had a well-developed high culture, ready to provide the basis for a modern, culturally homogeneous state; but the bridegroom was missing. Prussia and Piedmont obliged in due course, and the nation-states were created without excessive disturbance or disruption—at least no more than had accompanied dynastic, as opposed to national, politics in the preceding century.

The trouble starts once we move east. In both of the easternmost time zones, neither the bride nor the groom was available; neither of them was ready. (Here one had only seen large empires, which were nonethnic, religious, and dynastic in nature.) Unification nationalisms of the Italians and Germans, occurring where the bride was ready, could at least be liberal and not too horrible. But in the third zone of Europe, east of Trieste, things became much more unpleasant. The complexity of the ethnic map east of Trieste is such than one cannot achieve cultural political homogeneity without what is now called "ethnic cleansing." The relatively humane method of assimilation is generally not sufficient. Cultural engineering is needed as well as political engineering; the mere political, diplomatic, and military activity of a Bismarck or a Cavour is not enough. The difference between the two easternmost time zones arises from the fact that two of the three empires that carved up eastern Europe in Vienna went on to the dust heap of history, but one of them was rapidly revived under new management and in the name of a new ideology implemented with incredible ruthlessness, determination, and effectiveness. (This regime was even more effective in restraining nationalism than had been the Ancien Régime.) This fourth zone of Europe, which became the USSR, expanded after 1945 into portions of the third zone, with the advance of the Red Army and the imposition of the Iron Curtain.

The crucial question for those looking at the new world order is what will happen in that fourth zone, that of the former Soviet Union. With the other zones, it has gone through the first two stages specified above: the stage of the unobserved snake in the garden and the stage of morally victorious but politically feeble irredentism. But the third, fourth, and fifth stages were artificially suppressed by the Soviets. Which of these stages will now commence? Nobody knows. One sees signs of each of the three—the creation of new small and weak states, ethnic cleansing, and even the diminution of ethnic ferocity. . . .

Let me discuss events of this century. Humankind in general is dominated by three types of motivations: honor, interest, and salvation. Honor is the characteristic value system of agrarian societies, defined by a stable, unchanging technology. In such societies people are aggressively protective of their own status; this is how they define honor. They are contemptuous of work (and people who work) and consider economic specialization to be morally suspect. The second motivation, interest, is connected with a shift to a high valuation of work and productivity, and can operate only in conditions of economic growth, made possible by a scientific revolution. The main trend of recent history is the shift from honor to interest. The third motivation, salvation, enters capriciously at various times.

The basic events of this century are connected with two dates—1945 and 1989. Pre-1945 virulent nationalism was an attempt to run an industrial society by using the idiom of honor to promote the values of aggressiveness and control of land. This pathological exaggeration of nationalism occurred at precisely the appropriate time, when economic jealousies were still quite strong, and there was an ideological fusion of romantic communalism with the Darwinian notions of aggression and competitiveness as preconditions to excellence. The attempt to run an industrial society along these lines characterized parts of Europe before World War II. After 1945 the economic successes of the defeated states demonstrated that the old values of aggressiveness, honor, and territoriality did not really hold; what really mattered was the rate of economic growth. So the prewar option of honor was eliminated by events of and following 1945.

One further option, also eliminated in due course, was that of salvation—the idea of running an industrial society through the establishment of righteousness on earth. That option was eliminated even more conclusively in 1989 and 1991 than the honor option had been in and after 1945. It is fascinating to observe events in the states of the former Soviet Union; it was comprised of areas wildly different from one another (some industrial, some agrarian; some Catholic, Protestant, Orthodox, Moslem, Buddhist, Shamanist; some colonial, some imperial; some homogeneous, some fluid; most of them authoritarian, but some democratic). The salvationist system in place prior to 1989 failed to work and was repudiated over a large and astonishingly varied region. The experiment ranged over all variables and had the same end result everywhere, and so is conclusive.

Marxism, because it unites the political, ideological, and economic hierarchies, inevitably leads to totalitarianism. Conversely, any modern industrial totalitarianism must be Marxist. This doesn't mean that all the specific features of Marxism, accidentally assembled by Marx and Engels in the nineteenth century from current intellectual fashions, must all be present. But the central traits of messianic infallibilism and subjection of the whole of society to one united hierarchy are inevitable. In a modern society, in which the economy is so very powerful—unless the three hierarchies are unified, unless the economy is totally subjected to the polity—a quietly independent civil society, at the very least, will inevitably emerge. Totalitarianism demands the fusion of the three hierarchies, which is the essence of Marxism—and which, as we now know, does not work. So the option of making virtue the business of the state, or organizing society around salvation, has been eliminated very conclusively. Honor and territoriality (the old agrarian values) are also out.

What remains? We now have not only the need but also the possibility of progress toward world government. In general I'm not necessarily in favor of that happening, for with a multistate system there is a kind of guarantee that not all societies will make the exact same mistakes at the exact same time, and so the way forward is not blocked. Through political unification, this insurance-through-pluralism is at the very least diminished. Nonetheless, world government is now inherently desirable because of the need to combat ecological threats and those posed by terrorism. A central authority seems almost inevitable; it may emerge by a kind of case law, for which a precedent was set by the Persian Gulf War. That war demonstrated that states such as Iraq, possessing the potential for blackmail through weapons or control of resources, will probably provoke intervention from the developed consumerist powers.

With the demise of government organization based on honor and territoriality or on secular salvationism (read: Marxism), what remains? A kind of International of Consumerist Unbelievers, committed to the view that salvation is an individual concern and not the business of the state. We may therefore create a central authority based on this tacit consensus, combined with a maximum of cultural pluralism. The centralization would enforce economic and ecological discipline, and stop the trade of drugs and arms as well as the terrorist use of weapons, while simultaneously encouraging cantonalization. Where it doesn't do any harm, small is beautiful. Some small units, such as Estonia, possess a remarkable cultural vitality. So, for instance, the cantonalization of Europe, combined with a central authority now emerging through case law, is a desirable slope down which one slides joyfully. The central state would protect against ecological catastrophe, blackmail, and conspicuous tyranny while maintaining cultural pluralism—a combination most acceptable to today's consumerist unbelievers.

Vaclav Havel: Thriller

Another view of a world situation that extends well beyond Eastern Europe may be found in the following essay by Vaclav Havel, once a prisoner of Czechoslovakia's communist rulers, then the president of the Czech Republic. He wrote these lines while still a lonely dissenter within a regime gradually loosening its restrictions.

Before me lies the famous *Occult Philosophy* of Heinrich Cornelius Agrippa von Nettesheim, where I read that the ingestion of the living (and if possible still beating) heart of a hoopoe, a swallow, a weasel, or a mole will bestow upon one the gift of prophecy. It is nine o'clock in the evening and I turn on the radio. The announcer, a woman, is reading the news in a dry, matter-of-fact voice: Mrs. Indira Gandhi has been shot by two Sikhs in her personal bodyguard. The corpse of Father Popiełuszko, kidnapped by officers of the Polish police, has been fished out of the Vistula River. International aid is being organized for Ethiopia, where a famine is threatening the lives of millions, while the Ethiopian regime is spending almost a quarter of a billion dollars to celebrate its tenth anniversary. American scientists have developed plans for a permanent observatory on the Moon and for a manned expedition to Mars. In California, a little girl has received a heart transplanted from a baboon; various animal welfare societies have protested.

Ancient myths are certainly not just a manifestation of archetypal images from man's collective unconsciousness. But they are undoubtedly that as well. Much of the mystery of being and of man, many of his dark visions, obsessions, longings, forebodings, much of his murky "pre-scientific" knowledge and many important metaphysical certainties are obviously encoded in old myths. Such myths, of course, transcend their creators: something higher spoke through them, something beyond their creators, something that not even they were fully able to understand and give a name to. The authority invested in old myths by people of ancient cultures indicates that this higher power, whatever it is, was once generally felt and acknowledged. If we go no further than Jung's interpretation of myths, it is obvious that they introduced a partial or temporary "order" into the complex world of those unconscious forebodings, unprovable certainties, hidden instincts, passions, and longings that are an intrinsic part of the human spirit. And they obviously exercised something like a "check" or "supervisory power" over those forces of the human unconscious.

The civilization of the new age has robbed old myths of their authority. It has put its full weight behind cold, descriptive Cartesian reason and recognizes only thinking in concepts.

I am unwilling to believe that this whole civilization is no more than a blind alley of history and a fatal error of the human spirit. More probably it represents a necessary phase that man and humanity must go through, one that man—if he survives—will ultimately, and on some higher level (unthinkable, of course, without the present phase), transcend.

Whatever the case may be, it is certain that the whole rationalistic bent of the new age, having given up on the authority of myths, has succumbed to a large and dangerous illusion: it believes that no higher and darker powers—which these myths in some ways touched, bore witness to, and whose relative "control" they guaranteed—ever existed, either in the human unconscious or in the mysterious universe. Today, the opinion prevails that everything can be "rationally explained," as they say, by alert reason. Nothing is obscure—and if it is, then we need only cast a ray of scientific light on it and it will cease to be so.

This, of course, is only a grand self-delusion of the modern spirit. For though it make that claim a thousand times, though it deny a thousand times the "averted face" of the world and the human spirit, it can never eliminate that face, but merely push it further into the shadows. At the most, it will drive this entire complex world of hidden things to find surrogate, counterfeit, and increasingly confusing manifestations; it will compel the "order" that myth once brought into this world to vanish along with the myth, and the "forces of the night" to go on acting, chaotically and uncontrollably, shocking man again and again by their, for him, inexplicable presence, which glimmers through the modern shroud that conceals them. But more than that: the good powers—because they were considered irrational as well—were buried along with the dark powers. Olympus was completely abolished, leaving no one to punish evil and drive the evil spirits away. Goodness, being well mannered, has a tendency to treat these grand obsequies seriously and withdraw ; evil, on the contrary, senses that its time has come, for people have stopped believing in it altogether.

To this day, we cannot understand how a great, civilized nation—or at least a considerable part of it—could, in the twentieth century, succumb to its fascination for a single, ridiculous, complex-ridden *petit bourgeois,* could fall for his pseudo-scientific theories and in their name exterminate nations, conquer continents, and commit unbelievable cruelties. Positivistic science, Marxism included, offers a variety of scientific explanations for this mysterious phenomenon, but instead of eliminating the mystery, they tend rather to deepen it. For the cold, "objective" reason that speaks to us from these explanations in fact only underlines the disproportion between itself—a power that claims to be the decisive one in this civilization—and the mass insanity that has nothing in common with any form of rationality.

Yes, when traditional myth was laid to rest, a kind of "order" in the dark region of our being was buried along with it. And what modern reason has attempted to substitute for this order has consistently proved erroneous, false, and disastrous, because it is always in some way deceitful, artificial, rootless, lacking in both ontology[1] and morality. It may even border on the ludicrous, like the cult of the "Supreme Being" during the French Revolution, the collectivist folklore of totalitarian systems, or their "realist," self-celebrating art. It seems to me that with the burial of myth, the barn in which the mysterious animals of the human unconscious were housed over thousands of years has been abandoned and the animals turned loose—on the tragically mistaken assumption that they were phantoms—and that now they are devastating the countryside. They devastate it, and at the same time they make themselves at home where we least expect them to—in the secretariats of modern political parties, for example. These sanctuaries of modern reason lend them their tools and their authority so that ultimately the plunder is sanctioned by the most scientific of world views.

Generally, people do not begin to grasp the horror of their situation until too late: that is, until they realize that thousands of their fellow humans have been murdered for reasons that are utterly irrational. Irrationality, hiding behind sober reason and a belief that the inexorable march of history demands the sacrifice of millions to assure a happy future for billions, seems essentially more irrational and dangerous than the kind of irrationality that, in and through myth, admits to its own existence, comes to terms with the "positive powers," and, at most, sacrifices animals. The demons simply do what they want while the gods take diffident refuge in the final asylum to which they have been driven, called "human conscience." And so at last bloodlust, disguised as the most scientific of the world's views (which teaches, by the way, that conscience must submit to historical necessity) throws a twentieth-century John of Nepomuk into the Vistula. And the nation immediately canonizes its martyr in spirit.

---

[1] Science (study) of being or the essence of being.

In the events which chance tossed together in a single newscast, and juxtaposed with Agrippa's *Occult Philosophy,* I begin to see a sophisticated collage that takes on the dimensions of a symbol, an emblem, a code. I do not know what message is hidden in that unintentional artifact, which might be called "Thriller," after Michael Jackson's famous song. I only feel that chance—that great poet—is stammering an indistinct message about the desperate state of the modern world.

First, Marxist demonologists in the Polish papers label Popiełuszko a practitioner of black magic who, with the assistance of the Devil, serves the black mass of anticommunism in the church of St. Stanisław Kostka; then, other scientific Marxists waylay him at night, beat him to death, and throw him into the Vistula; and finally, still other "scientists" on one sixth of the earth's surface claim that the Devil in disguise—the CIA, in other words—is behind it. It is all pure medieval history. Except that the actors are scientists, people shielded by science, possessing an allegedly scientific world view. Of course that makes the whole thing so much more powerful. The demons have been turned loose and go about, grotesquely pretending to be honorable twentieth-century men who do not believe in evil spirits.

The Sikhs do not even need to masquerade as men of science. Confronting this modern world with modern machine guns in their hands, they believe themselves to be instruments of providence: after all, they are merely meting out punishment in accordance with the ancient prophecy about the desecrator of their Golden Temple. The Hindus then turn around and murder Sikhs, burning them alive, as though all Sikhs, to the last man, had taken part in Mrs. Gandhi's murder. How can this happen in the century of science and reason? How can science and reason explain it? How does it relate to colonizing the Moon and making ready an expedition to Mars? How does it relate to an age capable of transplanting the heart of a baboon into a person? Could we be getting ready to go to Mars in the secret hope of leaving our demons behind on the earth and so disposing of them? And who, in fact, has a baboon heart: that little girl in California—or the Marxist government of Ethiopia, building its mausoleums in a time of famine; or the Polish police; or the Sikhs in the personal bodyguard of the Indian prime minister who died—thanks to their belief in ancient prophecies— like an antique emperor at the hands of his own servants?

It seems to me that man has what we call a human heart, but that he also has something of the baboon within him. The modern age treats the heart as a pump and denies the presence of the baboon within us. And so again and again, this officially nonexistent baboon, unobserved, goes on the rampage, either as the personal bodyguard of a politician, or wearing the uniform of the most scientific police force in the world.

Modern man, that methodical civil servant in the great bureaucracy of the world, mildly frustrated by the collapse of his "scientific" world view, finally switches on his video recorder to watch Michael Jackson playing a vampire in "Thriller," the bestselling video cassette in the history of the world, then goes into the kitchen to remove from a thermos flask—behind the backs of all animal welfare societies—the still warm heart of a hoopoe. And he swallows it, hoping to have the gift of prophecy conferred upon him.

November 1984

Population: Overpopulation?

THE Reverend Thomas Malthus (1766–1834) was a mathematician and Christian whose *Essay on the Principle of Population as it affects the future Improvement of Society* (1798) suggested that population and "improvement"—meaning progress— went together only up to a point. The industrial revolution was changing the face of England, and of its demography, too. But, argued Malthus, since population tends to increase faster than the food supply, higher wages or charity could only encourage fertility and breed poverty and distress.

In some respects Malthus was right. The second half of the eighteenth century had seen English population grow by 40 percent. By the time of Malthus's death three decades later, in 1834, it had grown another 50 percent. All this time English birthrates remained high but steady; what changed were mortality rates, which fell steeply with the impacts of more and better food, housing, hygiene, and medical attention. That is how, for two centuries at least, Malthus was proved wrong. Population progressed hand in hand with technological and medical advances. *World* population in the days of Malthus numbered less than 800 million. In 1950, it was 2,500 million, by 1990 it stood around 5,300 million. At the growth rate of 1750, it would take more than a thousand years to double the population of the world; by 1990, it would take thirty-eight years. Though slowing, the present momentum should carry world population to about 8 billion in 2020.

Population Prophet

Malthus's conclusion—that humanity's choice lay between starvation and restraint—pro-moted him to that small elite whose names soon became nouns. Like his near-contempo-raries, Captain Charles Boycott (boycott), Private Nicolas Chauvin (chauvinism), Charles Macintosh (the mackintosh), and the Marquis de Sade (sadism), the country vicar who fathered three children gave his name to malthusianism.

Thomas Malthus: from Essay on the Principle of Population

I have read some of the speculations on the perfectibility of man and of society with great pleasure. I have been warmed and delighted with the enchanting picture which

From T. H. Malthus, *Parallel Chapters from the First and Second Editions of an Essay on the Principle of Population* (New York: The Macmillan Company, 1906), pp. 4, 6–8.

they hold forth. I ardently wish for such happy improvements. But I see great, and, to my understanding, unconquerable difficulties in the way to them. . . .

I think I may fairly make two postulata.

First, That food is necessary to the existence of man.

Secondly, That the passion between the sexes is necessary, and will remain nearly in its present state.

These two laws ever since we have had any knowledge of mankind, appear to have been fixed laws of our nature; and, as we have not hitherto seen any alteration in them, we have no right to conclude that they will ever cease to be what they are now, without an immediate act of power in that Being who first arranged the system of the universe; and for the advantage of his creatures, still executes, according to fixed laws, all its various operations. . . .

Assuming, then, my postulata as granted, I say, that the power of population is indefinitely greater than the power in the earth to produce subsistence for man.

Population, when unchecked, increases in a geometrical ratio. Subsistence only increases in an arithmetical ratio. A slight acquaintance with numbers will show the immensity of the first power in comparison of the second.

By that law of our nature which makes food necessary to the life of man, the effects of these two unequal powers must be kept equal.

This implies a strong and constantly operating check on population from the difficulty of subsistence. This difficulty must fall some where; and must necessarily be severely felt by a large portion of mankind.

Through the animal and vegetable kingdoms, nature has scattered the seeds of life abroad with the most profuse and liberal hand. She has been comparatively sparing in the room, and the nourishment necessary to rear them. The germs of existence contained in this spot of earth, with ample food, and ample room to expand it, would fill millions of worlds in the course of a few thousand years. Necessity, that imperious, all-pervading law of nature, restrains them within the prescribed bounds. The race of plants, and the race of animals shrink under this great restrictive law. And the race of man cannot, by any efforts of reason, escape from it. Among plants and animals its effects are waste of seed, sickness, and premature death. Among mankind, misery and vice. The former, misery, is an absolutely necessary consequence of it. Vice is a highly probable consequence, and we therefore see it abundantly prevail; but it ought not, perhaps, to be called an absolutely necessary consequence. The ordeal of virtue is to resist all temptation to evil.

This natural inequality of the two powers of population, and of production in the earth, and that great law of our nature which must constantly keep their effects equal, form the great difficulty that to me appears insurmountable in the way to perfectibility of society. . . .

Population Trends Since Malthus

It is not clear how long this growth trend in world population can go on, but the effects are clear enough: pressure on natural and social resources, levels of water and energy consumption that create shortages and inflate costs for all, pollution, crowding, crime, not to mention in- and out-migration and their concomitant, xenophobia. The selections that follow speak for themselves. The first represents the conclusions of a distinguished statistician and demographer, Massimo Livi-Bacci, professor at the University of Florence. The second reflects the concerns of Virginia D. Abnernethy, an American trained in anthropology and economics.

Massimo Livi-Bacci: from A Concise History of World Population

Two centuries ago, in the process of achieving greater demographic order and efficiency, human population embarked upon an unprecedented cycle of growth. And while this cycle is now coming to an end in the rich countries, it is still in full swing in the poor. World population hit the one billion mark as steam engines began to revolutionize transportation; the second billion was reached after the First World War, as airplanes became an ever more common means of transportation; the third billion was achieved at the beginning of the aerospace era. The fourth and fifth billion marks did not wait for similar revolutionary epochs and were reached in 1973 and 1987. Many demographers, sure of winning, would be willing to bet that the sixth billion will be reached before the year 2000 and the seventh before 2010. The combination of current young age structures and high fertility ensures that these levels will be easily reached within this time frame. . . .

Many view this growth process like a spring that is ever more tightly compressed, ready at the first jolt to unload an accumulation of devastating force. From an economic point of view diminishing returns must sooner or later lower living standards, since land, water, air, and minerals are all fixed and limited resources, allowing only partial substitution and so bound to place a limit on growth. The link between demographic growth and environmental deterioration also seems clear, judging from the pollution caused by industrial expansion and the general ecological degradation associated with the increase of agricultural, industrial, residential, and other human activity. And demographic growth is also a threat to health and social order, given the impossibility of indefinitely expanding food production and the inevitability of competition and conflict between individuals, groups, and peoples in search of a higher standard of living.

Another camp, instead, has complete faith in the ability of populations to adjust to larger numbers. Technological progress, they point out, allows for the substitution of primary resources and leads to increasing agricultural production. In addition, the relative prices of energy, primary resources, and food are at historically low levels and, in any case, the market would react to scarcity by increasing prices and so stimulating technological progress, guaranteeing increased productivity and the possibility of re-

From *A Concise History of World Population* by Massimo Livi-Bacci, translated by Carl Ipsen, pp. 197–199, 210–211. Reprinted by permission of Blackwell Publishers.

source substitution. With regard to the costs of unregulated production, currently paid for by humanity at large in the form of environmental deterioration, population optimists maintain that these costs can be "internalized"—that is, paid for by those responsible. Their final argument is that the physical and economic well-being of world population is constantly improving as a result of scientific and economic progress and there is no reason to fear that this situation might change.

It is difficult, if not impossible, to choose between these two modes of foreseeing the future. Once again we return to the Malthusian model and, with regard to the more radical versions of the above arguments, what seems to be a revival of the catastrophist versus optimist debate. However, perhaps the debate itself misses the point and the problem can be better understood by employing an alternative approach, . . . I have presented the history of population as a continual compromise between the forces of constraint and the forces of choice. Constraints have been imposed by a hostile environment, by disease, by the limitations of available food and energy, and now by an environment in danger. Choices have included flexible strategies of marriage and reproduction, of mobility, migration, and settlement, and of defense from disease. This interaction between the forces of constraint and choice has continually altered the point of population equilibrium and generated long cycles of growth as well as phases of stagnation and regression. The repeated reestablishment of equilibrium should not be seen as the product of spontaneous self-regulating mechanisms which minimize suffering and loss, but rather as a difficult process of adaptation which rewards more flexible populations while penalizing those more fragile and rigid. Many populations have succeeded at self-regulation, while others either have not or have done so too late, paying a hard price in the form of increased mortality, demographic regression, or in some cases disappearance. In the case of still other populations, mistaken decisions have impaired defensive ability in the face of catastrophe, increasing demographic vulnerability. . . .

While modern society may be better equipped with regard to the regulation of mortality and fertility than societies of the past, the same cannot be said with regard to another mechanism of choice, namely migration. The peopling of the world has been accomplished by means of migration and settlement which has distributed population according to existing or potential resources. This "freedom" of settlement, which in modern times has led to the Europeanization of temperate America and Australia, is today much impaired. In response to primarily political considerations, nations generally regard immigration as a marginal fact, acceptable only within a fairly rigid framework and in small numbers. Given the enormous national differences in wages and assets and the relative ease of mobility, perhaps it could not have been otherwise. Nonetheless, it is also the case that there exists no open and available territory to act as an outlet for demographic excess and to colonize with human population, plants, and animals. In addition, greater economic integration (for example, the increased value of international trade in relation to production) is accompanied by greater separation of peoples and ethnic groups; the creation of new national states, often bounded by unnatural borders, has led to the redistribution of ethnic groups, previously mixed, within well-defined political units; and a tendency toward segregation between groups is also frequent within national borders. So the effectiveness of an important tool of "choice," migration, has declined as compared to the past.

Our balance sheet, then, has both credit and debit entries, and it is not easy to calculate the bottom line, though the ability to control fertility, when it becomes universal, will constitute the decisive factor for controlling growth.

Let me close with a final consideration. More and more one hears that the control of population growth has been accepted as a positive value and so does not require demonstration or confirmation. All things considered, this is a fortunate development for demographers who will no longer be obliged to demonstrate the advantages of this or that trend. Our environment is certainly finite, even if its limits can be repeatedly expanded, and unlimited growth cannot continue without increasing risks. This observation should be sufficient to support the conviction that the human race must prepare itself for a long phase of demographic moderation, and in some cases reversal.

Another factor should be kept in mind: beyond certain limits, demographic growth creates diseconomies of scale, reversing a trend which seems to have dominated much of human history. Consider the unrestrained growth of urban agglomerations in poor countries: in 1970 only two exceeded a population of 10 million, in 1985 their number was seven, and in the year 2000 they should be 18 (with a total population of 242 million as opposed to 98 million in 1970). Citing one example per continent: Mexico City had 17 million inhabitants in 1985 and should have 24 million in the year 2000; in the same period Calcutta will grow from 10 to 16 million and Lagos from 6 to 12. Social, sanitary, and environmental problems associated with this growth will involve management difficulties which increase at a greater rate than the aggregate they concern. Other diseconomies of scale will be encountered in the areas of poverty, nutrition, and illiteracy: even in the context of general economic progress, rapid demographic growth brings with it—in spite of a decrease in the overall frequency of these social blights (expressed as a percentage of total population)—an increase in the absolute numbers of the poor, malnourished, and illiterate. For example, the World Bank estimates that the frequency of poverty in sub-Saharan Africa will decline from 47 to 43 percent between 1985 and 2000, but the absolute number of the poor will increase from 180 to 265 million. Relief programs forced to cope with a poor population that has increased by one-third will probably run into greater than proportional problems. The situation for malnutrition and education is analogous, given a large increase in the number of the hungry and illiterate. In many cases the elimination of a problem becomes proportionately more difficult as its dimensions grow; this is a diseconomy of scale. . . .

Virginia D. Abernethy: from Population Politics

The humanitarian cause is perennially popular. Compassion is a call to action. An urge to do good prompts us to take more and more of the world's homeless and destitute. And if taking the world's poor really helped, the opportunity to do good would be nearly limitless. The United States could take 100 million people a year, every year for

From Virginia D. Abernethy, *Population Politics* (Insight Books, 1993). Reprinted by permission of Plenum Publishing Corporation and the author.

many decades, without easing population pressure abroad from its present excruciating pitch.

The perceived moral imperative to take in the needy arises in the context of an exploding world population: 2.5 billion in 1950, 5 billion in 1987, and a sixth billion to be added perhaps as early as 1996. Worldwide population growth is accelerating because of the increasing number of reproductive-age women and the frustratingly slow decline in their average fertility.

As recently as five years ago, 90 million people were said to be added annually but, by 1990, the more generally accepted number for annual increase to world population was 93 million. By 1992, the U.N. Population Fund estimated that it was 97 million.

The ever-larger base (i.e., total world population) contributes to the mathematical result that the *rate* of growth appears to be slowing. It may have declined over the past fifteen years from 1.8 to 1.7 percent per year. Thus, rates and absolute numbers are moving in opposite directions. This has to temper somewhat a conclusion—heard in some quarters—that progress is being made. Celebration is premature.

Close to home, Mexico's population is expected to reach 109 million by the year 2000, and 154 million by 2025. Over 900,000 young adults will enter the labor pool each year during the 1990s. In Central America the population growth rate is somewhat higher, so that, write demographers Leon Bouvier and David Simcox (1989), "These nations face the staggering task of creating productive employment for their estimated 2.8 million citizens already unemployed or underemployed and for more than 300,000 new job seekers who will reach working age each year between now and 2000." Counting Mexico and Central America together, 1.25 million young people are entering the labor market annually.

With such need, say self-styled humanitarians, how can the United States shut the door even a bit? Indeed, why not let it be shoved wide open? The answer is that one must think through the consequences. Otherwise, the claim to beneficence and goodwill is simply vacuous.

The possibility of unintended and counterproductive effects exists in almost any course of action. As some sectors press for open borders and more international aid, it is time to make sure that the minimum humanitarian criterion (that our policy do no harm) is met. To find that past efforts to help have possibly done harm is disconcerting. Nevertheless, all evidence points that way. Fertility has remained stubbornly high and, with modernization, foreign aid, and other signals of better times ahead, may even at times have risen. . . .

. . . At the least, one concludes that the humanitarian case is flawed. Belief in abundance somewhere neutralizes local signs of limits. Perceiving poverty as a distributional problem that can be resolved by emigrating or by appeals to equity, people may not be motivated to plan realistically.

A further important political consequence of a liberal immigration and refugee policy should also concern us. The possiblity of simply leaving a bad situation undercuts pressure for internal reform. The most energetic people, who are most likely to initiate change, may choose emigration if that option is easy; whereas they might otherwise engage constructively with conditions in their country of birth. Thus, emigration is a safety valve for excess population and retards change both because it fosters belief in expanding opportunity and because it lets a nation's dissident elements *out*. . . .

Insightful governments which seek stability, including dictatorships, often try to rid themselves of population. When President Jimmy Carter pressed China on human-rights violations and demanded that emigration policy be liberalized, he got the answer he deserved: "Will you take 10 million?" From Cuba, Carter did get the Mariel boatload, a "boat" which held 120,000 people. . . .

It cannot be denied that most immigrants benefit from settling in a country richer than the one they leave. But when those remaining behind also raise their expectations, the consequences for birth control are poor. Moreover, populations in countries to which immigrants come suffer a loss—often substantial—in their standard of living. . . .

Immigration in a too-crowded world is a zero-sum game.

A reasoned humanitarian position must weigh multiple interests: the wishes of those who would come, the effect on those left behind, and the well-being of earlier immigrants and citizens at the destination. These are competing claims—claims which vary in legitimacy. All told, a strong case exists that liberal immigration policies help relatively few but harm many. In the long run, the destination countries will close their doors out of a sense of responsibility for their own citizens and in recognition of environmental limits. In the meantime, the number admitted will never be more than a tiny fraction of the world's poor. Those who can never come are, nevertheless, likely to be tragically misled. . . .

Much is wrong . . . with an apologist climate of public opinion which puts Americans on the defensive, obligating us to justify that which should be learned at home, in school, and in church and absorbed with the air we breathe. Charity begins at home. Why so great an outcry over abuses and want abroad when destitution visits our own streets? Believing it a matter of morality to take in the needy, start by taking a few deserving poor into one's own household. Those who want to do good should start at home. Save the poor? Start at home. Set an example? The rural and urban poor of America need you. Save the children? One-fifth of America's own live in poverty. Conditions here worsen, driving out hope. *God save America.*

The environment also sickens. Many communities are as polluted as a decade ago despite public and private efforts. Los Angeles spends millions on air quality, but the air is little better today than it was when cleanup efforts started. The Chesapeake Bay, three hundred miles of once-thriving coastland and estuary, may be dying as a life-support system. Assaults on the environment do not stop. Despite remedial efforts, how much net gain do *you* know about? Why is America going backward?

The President's Commission on Population Growth and the American Future (1972) had the answer. Although stabilizing population size would not in itself solve the nation's problems, the Commission stated that all would become harder to solve if the population grew. They were on the money. Take the environment, everyone's life-support system, and begin with pollution.

The nineties are forecast to be a decade of fighting nonpoint sources of pollution and garbage flows. The term *nonpoint source* describes the average American's contribution to the well-publicized environmental witches' broth. Our automobile emissions,

our waste water, our refigerator's chlorofluorocarbons, the agricultural runoff of fertil-
izer and pesticides, the fossil-fuel-based production and distribution of our food supply, toxics and CO_2 emitted by furniture makers and bakers and dry-cleaners, our
packaging and "disposables"—the list goes on—are sources of such pollution. Nonpoint sources are us. The more of us there are, the more pointlets: not points of light,
but pointlets of pollution.

This observation is not a criticism of character. At worst, Americans are guilty of
innocence, generosity, belief in abundance and renewable wealth, and blithe denial
that Earth's resources and capacity to absorb waste are finite. Americans also "pay"
for their high consumption by limiting fertility to below replacement level. American
women do not have four children each.

Third-world countries would mimic Americans' standard of living if they could.
All struggle to reach a higher average level of consumption, which is to say pollution
generation, and those of their citizens who can afford it are as consumption-oriented
as any. The World Bank, the International Monetary Fund, various U.N. agencies, and
national governments share the explicit goal of increasing consumption worldwide.
Thereby they would enable all to become more like the industrial world in per capita
emissions of atmosphere-altering gases and pollutants.

Immigration, also, has the principal objective of raising the migrants' standard of
living. The average immigrant or refugee to Europe or the United States has no fonder
hope than to adopt the host country's level of per capita consumption, that is, level
of emission and garbage production. With 5 percent of the world's people, the United
States consumes 25 percent of the world's energy, and many people understandably
covet this standard of living.

The irony is that America will change. Despite ourselves, modesty in consumption
seems about to be added to modesty in reproduction. In virtually no case will price-
driven, voluntary, or compulsory measures to limit consumption and pollution be
costless. Our grandchildren, if not our children and ourselves, will relearn Ben Franklin's admonition (from *Poor Richard's Almanac*):

> Use it up,
> Wear it out,
> Make it do
> Or do without.

One hopes for apt pupils because Americans' time, energy, and money are all
about to be engaged in the struggle to prevent further downgrading of our standard
of living and the environment. . . .

If population growth can be stopped, we may . . . be spared some very tragic
choices. The new trend in energy conservation (recall that in the whole time since 1970
Americans increased per capita energy use by less than 1 percent) means that without
population growth we would have a much lower demand for oil today. Indeed, energy
specialist John Holdren (1991) writes that "If the United States still had the population
with which it fought World War II—135 million people—the 1990 level of per capita
energy use for this country could be met from its 1990 array of energy sources *minus*
all the imported oil and all the coal." Think of that. Maybe no Gulf War. And without

population growth to spur higher demand for oil, debate about test drilling in the Arctic National Wildlife Refuge (ANWR) might be postponed indefinitely.

Think also of wetlands and diversity of species. Wetlands in the United States are disappearing at a rate of 300,000 acres a year. Former Housing and Urban Development Secretary Jack Kemp thinks they should go faster. In 1991, he said that we should set aside provisions of state wetlands protection legislation so that builders could add to the nation's stock of low-cost housing.

Examples of clashing environmental and people-oriented values put environmentalists on the defensive because of the widespread presumption in favor of people. Thus, loggers need jobs? Shrink the old forest reserve, home to the spotted owl. People need oil? Explore ANWR. People need water? Drain the Sacramento River dry and let the delta smelt and salmon adapt to gravel. . . .

Environmental battles are perennially refought because the needs of people for jobs and housing grow in proportion to the number of people. How long will the cycle go on? How long do Americans intend to watch while population growth adds both to poverty and to justification for taking more from Nature? Why fuel Jack Kemp's use of "poor people" to front for the developers' lobby?

With overpopulation, the clash of values grows both more bitter and more illogical. Does Kemp support open borders *and* housing the poor *and* preserving wetlands? Not possible. These are mutually exclusive goals; clumping them together reminds us that every environmental cause is a lost cause if population growth continues. . . .

Annual increases in the U.S. population mean that conservation and pollution-control measures become an accommodation to growth rather than a solution. All efforts at lasting environmental protection will be defeated by the claims of needy people. People need jobs, need water, need oil—and there goes the environment. Add enough people, and any potential gain from per capita conservation is overwhelmed. . . .

Apply this concept to America's population growth. Over 3 million more consumers and polluters each year means that each American must reduce emissions and garbage flow just to keep total waste production from growing. With continuing increase in population, the environment can recover only with difficulty and temporarily. Each American who debates location of the next community landfill and the costs of a new (added-capacity) town incinerator, who faces higher utility bills, who pays extra for pollution-control devices on a motor vehicle, or is told when and where that vehicle may not be driven experiences a cost of growth. Further degradation is a distinct possibility in the near term and inevitable in the long term.

Demographer B. Meredith Burke . . . recalls a 1970 National Academy of Science study which

> urged Americans to consider explicitly how they wanted their future society to look and what this would necessitate in reconciling mutually exclusive goals. We were not ready to do this, then were appalled at the paving over of Southern California and the threatened collapse of Florida's fragile ecology. [Now] above all, we must announce that curtailed immigration and population policy are not taboo subjects for public debate. Otherwise, we cannot object if our politicians deliver us to a future we deplore.

Some Americans see only what cheap immigrant labor can do for them. David Rieff . . . in *Los Angeles: Capital of the Third World* describes the oblivious Anglo to whom immigrants appear mainly as maids and gardeners. Writes reviewer Samuel Taylor . . . , "Mr. Rieff has stumbled onto one of the most appalling mysteries of late-twentieth century America: that people who live face to face with the imminent dispossession of European America have scarcely given the future a thought."

Not everyone is surprised by the ongoing reconquest of the Southwest. Hispanic activists have renamed parts of Texas and the area of the Gadsden Purchase. The new name, Aztlàn, means the "bronze continent." Self-appointed Mexican-American spokespersons perennially call for tearing down the statues of white explorers and conquerors. Appealing to history ("This was Mexican land anyway"), others assert that California is a part of Mexico which will be reclaimed in due course by sheer weight of numbers. . . .

In this climate of opinion, the Immigration and Naturalization Service (INS) agents removing illegal aliens from residential complexes and job sites are likened to "storm troopers," and Anglos are called "racist." The same slur is aimed at California Gov. Pete Wilson for saying that immigration imposes financial burdens on state and local government. . . . A bomb was mailed to him at the state capitol, accompanied by a note which "denounced Wilson for linking the state's mounting budget problems to an influx of new Californians, who have increased demands for expensive government services such as welfare and Medi-Cal." . . .

So far, Americans have been largely silent while state and federal governments try to accommodate growing and conflicting entitlement claims. Congress makes immigration policy and mandates most social, health-care, and education benefits; but costs are often borne locally so that the states and Congress have different incentives. The negatives associated with population growth have less immediacy for Congress. Congress dances to the tune of the shortsighted cheap-labor lobby and to immigrant-advocacy lobbies which see their political power increasing as constituencies grow. Other members of Congress respond to self-styled humanitarian arguments and to who knows what else.

It is certain that Congress was not responding to the American people when, with the 1990 Immigration Reform Act, it raised legal immigration by 40 percent. A May 1990, national Roper poll showed that 77 percent of Americans, including 78 percent of blacks and 74 percent of Hispanics, believed the United States should not increase immigration. Two Gallup polls in 1992 confirmed the breadth of sentiment. Dallas columnist Richard Estrada . . . makes no bones about the interests of the average American: "Labor economists . . . testified [before Congress] that there is not a labor shortage in the country. [But] Congress pretended not to hear and proceeded to pass a bill expanding legal immigration."

The Rev. Calvin Butts, pastor of New York's Abyssinian Baptist Church, is another who does not mince words. During television interviews in spring, 1991, he stated that the nation must limit immigration if New York City is to prosper or even survive (U.S. Cities, 1991). Butts observed that, "We have huge numbers from Eastern Europe, Asia, Africa, [and] the Caribbean. A city with dwindling resources and crumbling infrastructure will never recover if we don't get a grip on this. . . . Either you deal with this practically or you have chaos in the streets."

All Americans are *not* well-off, and all of us know it. Moreover, immigration hurts most those who can least afford it. Some Americans may feel guilty because of their own high consumption, but it is irresponsible for them to salve their consciences by bringing in more people who compete with our own least advantaged citizens. America *first* means, among other things, that Americans should take care of their own. Resources are limited. The Earth is finite. More for one is less for another. So it is not trivial to step over one's own working poor and middle class in order to accommodate new arrivals.

A decent standard of living for all is slipping away. America's growing population is the root cause of some troubles and an aggravating cause of many more. A fighting chance to solve our problems—instead of temporizing by treating symptoms—depends on stabilizing population size.

America's population cannot stop growing if immigration continues at a rate above replacement level. About 160,000 persons voluntarily leave each year. So, rounding out the numbers, an all-inclusive target of 200,000 immigrants a year would get America where it needs to be. *All-inclusive* means just that: regular legal immigrants, illegal would-be immigrants, refugees, and asylees. . . .

Americans' capacity for independent thought, as revealed in the polls, is the more remarkable considering how often they get "human interest" news. The plight of would-be immigrants and refugees is touchingly reported. The implicit instruction to Americans is that we should make all welcome. Immigration is almost never linked to damage we deplore. Yet, coverage of endangered species, jobless Americans, overcrowded schools, and overburdened systems of all kinds could alert people to the costs of population growth and its sources. Americans, given information, can decide for themselves if opposition to immigration is racist, if immigration hurts our own poor, if the middle class is undercut by population growth, if taxpayers end up holding the bag, and if all may someday suffer because of resource scarcity and environmental degradation. More Americans know each day that this debate is their business.

Jobs no less than environmental values are at stake. During the 1980s, the U.S. economy created 19 million net new jobs. But 8 million immigrants came in that decade, seeking jobs or benefits. . . . [Y]oung Americans entering the labor market in the same period were the principal losers.

With present liberal immigration policy, the future holds still less opportunity for the young. Immigration in the decade of the 1990s is projected to reach 12 million. . . . At the same time, young Americans entering the labor market will outnumber their elders who leave it by at least 15 million. New job creation will have to be more rapid than ever before seen if severe unemployment is to be averted.

However, impediments to job creation will include the stricter conservation and pollution-control measures needed to mitigate the effect of more and more people: Pollution abatement is costly and thus works against business expansion. Nevertheless, Congress—which has just about exhausted local governments' capacities to pay for programs mandated at the federal level—is eyeing the business sector as the next sugar daddy. The burden of the Clean Air Act has been put on industry; health-care insurance for the poor is likely to follow. Whatever the goal, population growth and increasing poverty make its attainment more costly. If costs are socialized to the individual tax-payer or business, this itself makes it difficult to create high-quality, well-capitalized jobs. Thus, the 1990s and the twenty-first century promise endless conflict among incompatible goals; the dilemmas will worsen in proportion to population size. . . .

Education: Failure or Success?

SOME issues never go away. Plato and Socrates talked about schooling; Robespierre insisted on it, and so does Bill Clinton. Is history a race between education and catastrophe, or is schooling just a way of misleading the young into repeating the errors of their elders? And, if we ever agree on just what should be taught, how is that to be done: what is the best way of teaching? Against this immemorial background, today's debates repeat and innovate. Are schoolchildren really growing brighter, but just being taught with methods designed for another age or according to standards ill-suited to contemporary experience? Is education about literacy or relevancy? Is its main purpose to teach people how to think, or merely to read simple instructions and fill in unavoidable forms and checks? If school is about conveying useful knowledge and "communication skills," how limited are such concepts . . . and how extensive? If education doesn't leave one generation's intellectual, imaginative, moral, and emotional inheritance to the next, can we maintain even the present semblance of civilized society?

In any case, is universal literacy itself so crucial? The world has managed quite well without it for thousands of years. Why should our society, chock-full of signs and images, worry because some of its members have only limited opportunities to join the communications revolution or reject the opportunities offered? Could it be that a little learning is more dangerous than no learning, and that a superficially literate public is more vulnerable to confusing and delusive appeals? Answers to questions of this sort are not evident; but the questions are raised often, as evidenced in the last two passages of this chapter.

The Medium Is the Message

Marshall McLuhan (1911–1980), a Canadian, served for a long time as professor of English literature at the University of Toronto. But he is better known as the communications theorist whose aphorism "the medium is the message" summarized his point of view: that disseminators of information—whether by voice, print, television, or computer—shape styles of thinking and perception. In short, the communicators shape our culture. In the age of electronics, he argued, printed books are fated to disappear, along with the culture associated with them. One wonders if all McLuhan's historical references are warranted: the romantic movement was the product of a mechanical age? Did railways and factories exist when Goethe, Wordsworth, and Byron wrote? The gist of his argument, however, remains impressive, and not irrelevant to those concerned with the issue of children and schools today. The passage that follows is taken from a McLuhan lecture of 1965, delivered when he was beginning to write one of his most influential books, The Medium Is the Message *(1967).*

Marshall McLuhan from "Address at Vision 65"

. . . The world of humour, as a system of communications, is one that has occasionally interested people, and we live in a time when joke styles have changed very rapidly. I am told by my own children that the latest form of joke concerns the "Poles," and they gave me as an example: "Alexander Graham Kowalski—the first 'telephone Pole.'" This kind of humour is like the slightly older form of the elephant joke and the kind that the computer programmers enjoy—"What is purple and hums?" Of course, the answer is: "An electric grape." "And, why does it hum?" "It doesn't know the words." This kind of joke appeals enormously to youngsters today.

If you notice, the tendency in these kinds of jokes, or gags, is for the story line to be stripped off. They tend to be deprived of the old story line, and in its place you have a capsule, a compressed overlay, of stories. In fact, there are usually two stories in these little jokes, simultaneously. The older-fashioned jokes had a straight story line. . . .

The new stories tend to be much more compressed and on two levels at once, like the sort of *Finnegans Wake* phrase: "though he might have been more humble, there's no police like Holmes." That kind of compressed double-plot story is a very interesting development; and, if you notice, great successes like *My Fair Lady* usually have two plots. One of them is explicit. One is perfectly obvious, like the story of Liza Doolittle acquiring the King's English and becoming a great social success. But there is a subplot in *My Fair Lady* that is much more potent and much concealed. The subplot would seem to be "how to succeed in business without really trying."

The subplot is an environmental one—it included everybody. The main plot, the little story about Liza Doolittle, appeals to a relatively small group and is not a new story. It is a Cinderella story. But the story of "how to succeed in business without really trying," or, in other words, how to become a huge success by sheer gimmickry, would seem to be the life story, the inside life story, of a very large proportion of the top executives of our world. In other words, *My Fair Lady* had this environmental subplot that is implicit and unverbalized, and that includes the audience. With the subplot, the audience goes right into action. With the main plot, they simply sit outside looking on. . . .

There is a new book by Jacques Ellul, the Frenchman. The book has recently been published in English. It is called *Propaganda*. Ellul's book has as a theme that propaganda is not ideology. . . . It is rather the hidden, but complete, image of a social way of life that is embedded in the social technologies and social patterns, as it is embedded in, say, the English language. Ellul would say the action of the English language, the action of the French language—*that* is propaganda. That presents a total environmental image to men, whereas the ideologies, the explicit verbalized messages, are relatively insignificant compared to this overall image. Ellul's theme in a word is this: Propaganda consists in using all the available means of one's society to create a way of life. Whatever

---

"Address at Vision 65" by Herbert Marshall McLuhan with omissions from *The American Scholar*, Spring 1966.

that way may be, is propaganda—that is action that is total and invisible, and invincible.

This is another mysterious feature about the new and potent environment we now live in. The really total and saturating environments are invisible. The ones we notice are quite fragmentary and insignificant compared to the ones we don't see. The English language, for example, as it shapes our perceptions and all our habits of thought and feeling, is quite unperceived by the users of the English language. It becomes much more perceptible if we switch suddenly to French. But in the case of environments that are created by new technologies, while they are quite invisible in themselves, they do make visible the old environments. We can always see the Emperor's old clothes, but not his new ones. . . . If the new environment is invisible, it does serve to make very visible the preceding environment. The obvious and simple illustration of that is the late show. On the late show on television we see old movies. They are very visible; they are very noticeable. Since television, the movie form has been reprocessed. The form of movie that once was environmental and invisible has been reprocessed into an art form, and, indeed, a highly valued art form. Indirectly, the new art films of our time have received an enormous amount of encouragement and impact from the television form. The television form has remained quite invisible—and will only become visible at the moment that television itself becomes the content of a new medium. . . .

As we move into the world of integral, computerized knowledge, mere classification becomes secondary and inadequate to the speeds with which data can now be processed. As data can be processed very rapidly we move literally into the world of pattern recognition, out of the world of mere data classification. One way of putting this is to say that our children today live in a world in which the environment itself is made of electric information. The environment of the young person today is typically and principally electrically fashioned information. The young person today is a data processor on a very large scale. Some people have estimated that the young person, the infant and the small child, growing up in our world today works harder than any child ever did in any previous human environment—only the work he has to perform is that of data processing. The small child in twentieth-century America does more data processing—more work—than any child in any previous culture in the history of the world, according to Jacques Ellul, among others. We haven't really cottoned on to the fact that our children work furiously, processing data in an electrically structured information world; and when these children enter a classroom—elementary school—they encounter a situation that is very bewildering to them. The youngster today, stepping out of his nursery or TV environment, goes to school and enters a world where the information is scarce but is ordered and structured by fragmented, classified patterns, subjects, schedules. He is utterly bewildered because he comes out of this intricate and complex integral world of electric information and goes into this nineteenth-century world of classified information that still characterizes the educational establishment. The educational establishment is a nineteenth-century world of classified data much like any factory set up with its inventories and assembly lines. The young today are baffled because of this extraordinary gap between these two worlds.

Paul Goodman has a book recording one aspect of the situation. It is titled *Growing*

Up Absurd. To grow up today is to be absurd, because we live in two worlds, and neither one of them inclines us to grow up. . . . Our youngsters today are mainly confronted with the problem of just growing up—that is our new work—and it is total. That is why it is not a job; it is a role. Growing up has become, in the age of electrically processed information, the major task of mankind. We still have our eyes fixed on the rearview mirror looking firmly and squarely at the job that is receding into the nineteenth-century past. The job that we feel we should have by rights belongs to the old mechanical technology of classified data and of fragmented tasks. Yet we are now surrounded by a new environment, of integrated tasks, integrated knowledge, and it demands pattern recognition. The kind of contrast between those two situations creates an absurdity that has launched the theater of the absurd. The theater of the absurd itself is postulated on this kind of dichotomy between these two cultures that never seem to get any closer together.

I have started then with the theme of the imperceptibility of new environments, and that what is perceptible in typical human situations is the old environment. It is plain that the content of Plato's work, of his new written form, was the old oral dialogue. The content of the print technology of the Renaissance was medieval writing. For two hundred years after printing there was hardly anything printed except medieval texts—think of poor Don Quixote! Don Quixote was the victim of the current Renaissance craze for medieval comic books or medieval romances. This went on for another century. What got printed in the main, for two centuries and more after the printing press, was the medieval tale, medieval Books of Hours, medieval liturgies and medieval philosophy. Shakespeare lived in the Renaissance world, and the content of Shakespeare's plays, as everybody knows, is medieval. His politics, and his world picture—the Elizabethan world picture—present a medieval world picture. They too looked back firmly and squarely at the receding medieval forms. But the Middle Ages were the late show for the Renaissance. By the nineteenth century the Renaissance had come into full view. As the industrial environment formed, this progressive time firmly and squarely confronted the Renaissance. The content of the nineteenth-century mind was the Renaissance; the content of the twentieth-century mind is the nineteenth century. We are obsessed with it. It is not as easy to banish that mirage as one might wish. But one of the most bizarre growths in this development occurred when railways and factories came in. The content of this new industrial, mechanical environment was the old agrarian world, and there was this upsurge of awareness and delight in the old agrarian environment of arts and crafts—the pastoral world. This discovery of the receding age was called the "romantic movement."

The sudden discovery of nature was made possible by the railway and the factories that were so very different from nature. The romantic movement was a product of the mechanical age by way of a contrapuntal environment. It was not a repeat of the mechanical age; rather it was the content of the mechanical age, and the artists and poets turned to processing the old agrarian world into delightful landscapes and delightful pastoral poems. This was in turn altered by the rise of electric technology that went around the old mechanical world of a few decades ago. When the electric technology jacketed the machine world, when circuitry took over from the wheel, and the circuit went around the old factory, the machine became an art form. Abstract art, for example, is very much a result of the electric age going around the mechanical one.

In our time we can see that pop art consists in taking the outer environment and putting it in the art gallery, or indoors somewhere, suggesting that we have reached the stage where we have begun to process the environment itself as an art form. . . . Even as the Romantics began to deal with the old pastoral, agrarian world as an art form when machinery was new, so we will now begin to deal with the planet itself as a work of art.

I think the computer is admirably suited to the artistic programming of such an environment, of taking over the task of programming the environment itself as a work of art, instead of programming the content as a work of art. This situation suggests some considerable changes in the human state. It suggests that the role of art in the past has been not so much the making of environments as making of counterenvironments, or antienvironments. Flaubert, a hundred years ago, said: "Style is a way of seeing." Ever since that time the painters and artists have been quite conscious of their jobs as teaching people how to perceive the world they live in. . . ." The training of perception upon the otherwise unheeded environment became the basis of experimentation in what is called modern art and poetry. The artist, instead of expressing himself in various patterns and packages of message, turned his senses and the work of art to the business of probing the environment. The symbolists, for example, broke up the old romantic landscape into fragments that they used as probes to explore the urban and metropolitan environments. Then they turned to probing the inner life of man with the same verbal instruments in hand. Instead of using the verbal as a way of expression, they turned it inward for the purpose of exploring and discovering the contours of the inner life.

The psychiatrist took over in the same pattern and began to erode the unconscious. If the unconscious has an important and irreplaceable function in human affairs, we had best look to it—it is being eroded at a furious pace; it is being invaded by dazzling investigations and insights; and we could quickly reach a stage in which we had no unconscious. This would be like dreaming awake. . . . This possibility that we are actively engaged in liquidating the unconscious, for the first time in history, behooves us to pay some attention to how it is structured, and to that function it serves in human affairs. It may prove to be indispensable to sanity.

One overall consideration for our time . . . is to consider how, in the past, the environment was invisible in its operation upon us. Environments are not just containers, but are processes that change the content totally. New media are new environments. That is why the media are the message. One related consideration is that antienvironments, or counterenvironments created by the artist, are indispensable means of becoming aware of the environment in which we live and of the environments we create for ourselves technically. John Cage has a book called *Silence* in which, very early in the book, he explains that silence consists of all of the unintended noises of the environment. All the things that are going on all the time in any environment, but things that were never programmed or intended—that is silence. The unheeded world is silence. . . . If the environment or process of change gets going at a clip consistent with electronic information movement, it becomes very easy to perceive social patterns for the first time in human history. In the pre-Electric Age patterns were imperceptible because change occurred just slowly enough to be visible. Was it Betrand Russell who asked, if we were in a bath whose temperature rose half a degree an hour, how would we know when to scream? The pattern recognition that is quite impossible during processes of slow change, becomes quite easy when the same changes are speeded up even to movie or cinematic levels. So, the artist, as a creator of antienvironments, or counterenvironments, created to permit perception of environments, has a very peculiar role in our society.

We have, in the Electric Age, come suddenly to the end of the Neolithic Age. After a good many thousands of years of specialized habits and technology and fragmentary toolmaking, we discovered the electric circuits. It is the circuit that has ended the Neolithic Age. The Neolithic Age, just like its ultimate phase, the factory age in the nineteenth century, was dedicated to specialism, fragmentation, and extensions of this or that limb of man. With circuitry we have, instead of extensions of hand, or foot, or back, or arm, a kind of involvement of the whole nervous system, an extension of the nervous system itself, a most profoundly involving operation. The form and function of the telegraph press can help our observations here. One of the mysterious things about newspapers is that the items in them have no connection except the dateline that enables us to enter the world of the news, as it were, by going through the looking glass. Just as Alice in Wonderland went through the looking glass, when you enter the world of the telegraph or of the circuit, you really become involved in the information process. When you enter through the dateline, when you enter your newspaper, you begin to put together the news—you are producer. And this is a most important fact to understand about the electric time, for it is an age of decentralism. It is hard to face this. We still like to look in the rearview mirror. We still tend to think of the Electric Age as a mechanical age. It is in effect organic and totally decentralist. But the reader of the news, when he goes through his dateline appertures, enters the news world as a maker. There is no "meaning" in the news except what we make—there is no connection between any of the items except the instant dimension of electric circuitry. News items are like the parts of the symbolist structure. The reader is the co-creator, in a newspaper as in a detective story, in which the reader has to make the plot as he goes. The detective story was one of the very first anticipations of electric technology. Edgar Allan Poe was a considerable innovator in the matter of antienvironments for the Electric Age. . . .

Perhaps the most startling and most upsetting electric innovation is coming in the matter of Xerox and Xerography. Xerography is bringing a reign of terror into the world of publishing because it means that every reader can become both author and publisher. It totally decentralizes the long centralized publishing process. . . . There is no possible protection from technology except by technology. When you create a new environment with one phase of a technology, you have to create an antienvironment with the next. But Xerography is electricity invading the world of typography, and it means a total revolution in this old sphere, or this old technology, a revolution that is being felt in the classroom itself.

I invite you to consider that perhaps the best way of estimating the impact of any new environmental technology is to notice what happens to the older technologies. You can never perceive the impact of any new technology directly, but it can be done in the manner of Perseus looking in the mirror at Medusa. It has to be done indirectly. You have to perceive the consequences of the new environment on the old environment before you know what the new environment is. You cannot tell what it is until you have seen it do things to the old one. The need, however, to understand the processes and changes brought about by new technology gets stronger as the technology does. . . .

On this continent the sensory levels have changed drastically since television. The visual component in our lives has been dropped dramatically and the visceral, the kinetic, the auditory modes of response have shot up to compensate for the drop in the visual component of our culture. This sensory shift has changed the taste in design, in packing, in every form of entertainment, as well as in every form of vehicle, food and in clothing.

To repeat, and to make toward a conclusion, the effect of any new environment— every new technology creates a new environment just as the motor car does, as the railway did, or as radio and airplanes do—any new technology changes the whole human environment, and envelops and includes the old environments. It turns these old environments into "art forms"—old Model T's become precious art objects, as do old coach lamps, old anything. The world of Camp, for example, is the world of the nursery of thirty years ago being turned into a conscious art form. By simply taking into the shopwindow old toys, old ornaments, and the things Mom used to wear thirty years ago, you turn them into art forms and you have C-A-M-P, this mysterious new archetype.

As the audience becomes participant, involved in the total electric drama, it can become a major work force; and the classroom, as much as any other place, can become a scene in which the audience can perform an enormous amount of work.

. . . There are enormous possibilities for using an audience as work force in scientific research, or any other type of research. It is simply that we insist on beaming instruction at them instead of allowing them to participate in the action of discovery.

For example, when printing was new, it created what was known as the Public. In the sixteenth century and after, Montaigne's phrase, *"la publique,"* came into use. The sixteenth century created the public as a new environment. This completely altered politics and altered all social arrangements in education, in work and in every other area. Electric circuitry did not create the public, it created the mass, meaning an environment of information that involved everybody in everybody. Now, to a man brought up in the environment of the public, the mass audience is a horror—it is a mess. In the same way, the public was a many-headed monster to a feudal aristocrat. He never bothered to study its structure any more than we study the mass. Circuitry brings people into relation with each other in total involvement which creates the possibility of dialogue and discovery on an enormous scale. The structure of the public had less of such possibility. The public consisted of fragmented separate individuals with separate points of view. The public was an additive structure. The mass audience is a quite different structure, enormously richer—enormously more capable of integrated creative activity than the old public was. All the old public could do was to enunciate private points of view which . . . clashed into each other furiously. . . .

Let me suggest that it may be possible to write programs for changes, not only in consciousness but in unconsciousness in the future. . . . The future of consciousness is already assuming a very different pattern, a very different character. The future of the child is changing beneath our gaze. The small child was an invention of the seventeenth century . . . ; historically, the child came out of the seventeenth century, did not exist, so to speak, in Shakespeare's day. The child had, up until that time, been so completely merged in the adult world that there was nothing that could be called childhood in our sense at all. And so it is with the family, another seventeenth-century discovery. Suddenly today the child is merging with the total adult environment under electric information processing, and is disappearing from the scene as child.

The future of child may resemble the future of city. The city under conditions of very rapid movement takes on a totally new meaning. The motor car has served to destroy the city as it existed under the railway conditions. The future of city may be very much like a world's fair—a place to show off new technology—not a place of work or residence whatever.

It is also fascinating to consider the future of language. We know right now some very important structural things about language that are new. The future of language will not be as a system of classified data or meanings. The future of language as a complex structure which can be learned without learning the words at all is a possibility that the computer presents increasingly. A child does not learn language as a series of meanings of words. He learns language as he learns to walk, or to hear, or to see. He learns language as a way of feeling and exploring his environment. Therefore, he is totally involved. He learns very fast because of this enormous sensuous involvement and the resulting motivation. It will be possible in this generation, I hope, to program the environment in such a way that we can learn a second language as we learned our mother tongue, rapidly and totally, as a means of perception and of discovery. The future of language presents the possibility of a world without words, a wordless, intuitive world, like a technological extension of the action of consciousness. . . .

A Nation at Risk

The state and the results of teaching in American schools and colleges provided one major subject of debate for the 1980s. In 1983, an urgent report entitled A Nation at Risk *warned on the "rising tide of mediocrity" overwhelming the nation's schools. Five years later, another report by U.S. Secretary of Education William Bennett found that modest gains had been made in student achievement but complained that teaching performance continued to be "unacceptably low." Educational experts who reacted to this last report found its views unduly pessimistic and attributed shortcomings largely to insufficient funds. Little mention was made of the difficulty of teaching (or learning) in schools where work discipline is lax, homework exceptional, and metal detectors against student weaponry increasingly frequent. But even critics of Bennett's report admitted that few seventeen-year-olds—*

especially in blighted urban areas—could write an organized job-application letter, read a bus schedule, or arrange six common fractions in order of size.

In colleges and universities, meanwhile, large minorities of incoming students continue to need remedial courses in elementary math or the proper use of English. Many students in American universities do not know how to write an essay or read a map, let alone handle a foreign language.

U.S. Department of Education: from A Nation At Risk

Our Nation is at risk. Our once unchallenged preeminence in commerce, industry, science, and technological innovation is being overtaken by competitors throughout the world. This report is concerned with only one of the many causes and dimensions of the problem, but it is the one that undergirds American property, security, and civility. We report to the American people that while we can take justifiable pride in what our schools and colleges have historically accomplished and contributed to the United States and the well-being of its people, the educational foundations of our society are presently being eroded by a rising tide of mediocrity that threatens our very future as a Nation and a people. What was unimaginable a generation ago has begun to occur—others are matching and surpassing our educational attainments.

If an unfriendly foreign power had attempted to impose on America the mediocre educational performance that exists today, we might well have viewed it as an act of war. As it stands, we have allowed this to happen to ourselves. We have even squandered the gains in student achievement made in the wake of the Sputnik challenge. Moreover, we have dismantled essential support systems which helped make those gains possible. We have, in effect, been committing an act of unthinking, unilateral educational disarmament.

Our society and its educational institutions seem to have lost sight of the basic purposes of schooling, and of the high expectations and disciplined effort needed to attain them. This report, the result of 18 months of study, seeks to generate reform of our educational system in fundamental ways and to renew the Nation's commitment to schools and colleges of high quality throughout the length and breadth of our land.

That we have compromised this commitment is, upon reflection, hardly surprising, given the multitude of often conflicting demands we have placed on our Nation's schools and colleges. They are routinely called on to provide solutions to personal, social, and political problems that the home and other institutions either will not or cannot resolve. We must understand that these demands on our schools and colleges often exact an educational cost as well as a financial one. . . .

THE RISK

History is not kind to idlers. The time is long past when America's destiny was assured simply by an abundance of natural resources and inexhaustible human enthusiasm,

From *An Open Letter to the American People: A Nation At Risk* (Washington, D.C., 1983), pp. 5–23.

and by our relative isolation from the malignant problems of older civilizations. The world is indeed one global village. We live among determined, well-educated, and strongly motivated competitors. We compete with them for international standing and markets, not only with products but also with the ideas of our laboratories and neighborhood workshops. America's position in the world may once have been reasonably secure with only a few exceptionally well-trained men and women. It is no longer.

The risk is not only that the Japanese make automobiles more efficiently than Americans and have government subsidies for development and export. It is not just that the South Koreans recently built the world's most efficient steel mill, or that American machine tools, once the pride of the world, are being displaced by German products. It is also that these developments signify a redistribution of trained capability throughout the globe. Knowledge, learning, information, and skilled intelligence are the new raw materials of international commerce and are today spreading throughout the world as vigorously as miracle drugs, synthetic fertilizers, and blue jeans did earlier. If only to keep and improve on the slim competitive edge we still retain in world markets, we must dedicate ourselves to the reform of our educational system for the benefit of all—old and young alike, affluent and poor, majority and minority. Learning is the indispensable investment required for success in the "information age" we are entering.

Our concern, however, goes well beyond matters such as industry and commerce. It also includes the intellectual, moral, and spiritual strengths of our people which knit together the very fabric of our society. The people of the United States need to know that individuals in our society who do not possess the levels of skill, literacy, and training essential to this new era will be effectively disenfranchised, not simply from the material rewards that accompany competent performance, but also from the chance to participate fully in our national life. A high level of shared education is essential to a free, democratic society and to the fostering of a common culture, especially in a country that prides itself on pluralism and individual freedom.

For our country to function, citizens must be able to reach some common understandings on complex issues, often on short notice and on the basis of conflicting or incomplete evidence. Education helps form these common understandings, . . .

INDICATORS OF THE RISK

The educational dimensions of the risk before us have been amply documented in testimony received by the Commission. For example:

- International comparisons of student achievement, completed a decade ago, reveal that on 19 academic tests American students were never first or second and, in comparison with other industrialized nations, were last seven times.

- Some 23 million American adults are functionally illiterate by the simplest tests of everyday reading, writing, and comprehension.

- About 13 percent of all 17-year-olds in the United States can be considered functionally illiterate. Functional illiteracy among minority youth may run as high as 40 percent.

- Average achievement of high school students on most standardized tests is now lower than 26 years ago when Sputnik was launched.
- Over half the population of gifted students do not match their tested ability with comparable achievement in school.
- The College Board's Scholastic Aptitude Tests (SAT) demonstrate a virtually unbroken decline from 1963 to 1980. Average verbal scores fell over 50 points and average mathematics scores dropped nearly 40 points.
- College Board achievement tests also reveal consistent declines in recent years in such subjects as physics and English.
- Both the number and proportion of students demonstrating superior achievement on the SATs (i.e., those with scores of 650 or higher) have also dramatically declined.
- Many 17-year-olds do not possess the "higher order" intellectual skills we should expect of them. Nearly 40 percent cannot draw inferences from written material; only one-fifth can write a persuasive essay; and only one-third can solve a mathematics problem requiring several steps.
- There was a steady decline in science achievement scores of U.S. 17-year-olds as measured by national assessments of science in 1969, 1973, and 1977.
- Between 1975 and 1980, remedial mathematics courses in public 4-year colleges increased by 72 percent and now constitute one-quarter of all mathematics courses taught in those institutions.
- Average tested achievement of students graduating from college is also lower.
- Business and military leaders complain that they are required to spend millions of dollars on costly remedial education and training programs in such basic skills as reading, writing, spelling, and computation. The Department of the Navy, for example, reported to the Commission that one-quarter of its recent recruits cannot read at the ninth grade level, the minimum needed simply to understand written safety instructions. Without remedial work they cannot even begin, much less complete, the sophisticated training essential in much of the modern military.

These deficiencies come at a time when the demand for highly skilled workers in new fields is accelerating rapidly. For example:

- Computers and computer-controlled equipment are penetrating every aspect of our lives—homes, factories, and offices.
- One estimate indicates that by the turn of the century millions of jobs will involve laser technology and robotics.
- Technology is radically transforming a host of other occupations. They include health care, medical science, energy production, food processing, construction, and the building, repair, and maintenance of sophisticated scientific, educational, military and industrial equipment.

Analysts examining these indicators of student performance and the demands for new skills have made some chilling observations. Educational researcher Paul Hurd concluded at the end of a thorough national survey of student achievement that within the context of the modern scientific revolution, "We are raising a new generation of Americans that is scientifically and technologically illiterate." In a similar vein, John Slaughter, a former Director of the National Science Foundation, warned of "a growing chasm between a small scientific and technological elite and citizenry ill-informed, indeed uninformed, on issues with a science component."

But the problem does not stop there, nor do all observers see it the same way. Some worry that schools may emphasize such rudiments as reading and computation at the expense of other essential skills such as comprehension, analysis, solving problems, and drawing conclusions. Still others are concerned that an over-emphasis on technical and occupational skills will leave little time for studying the arts and humanities that so enrich daily life, help maintain civility, and develop a sense of community. Knowledge of the humanities, they maintain, must be harnessed to science and technology if the latter are to remain creative and humane, just as the humanities need to be informed by science and technology if they are to remain relevant to the human condition. Another analyst, Paul Copperman, has drawn a sobering conclusion. Until now, he has noted:

> Each generation of Americans has outstripped its parents in education, in literacy, and in economic attainment. For the first time in the history of our country, the educational skills of one generation will not surpass, will not equal, will not even approach, those of their parents.

It is important, of course, to recognize that *the average citizen* today is better educated and more knowledgeable than the average citizen of a generation ago—more literate, and exposed to more mathematics, literature, and science. The positive impact of this fact on the well-being of our country and the lives of our people cannot be overstated. Nevertheless, *the average graduate* of our schools and colleges today is not as well-educated as the average graduate of 25 or 35 years ago, when a much smaller proportion of our population completed high school and college. The negative impact of this fact likewise cannot be overstated.

HOPE AND FRUSTRATION

Statistics and their interpretation by experts show only the surface dimension of the difficulties we face. Beneath them lies a tension between hope and frustration that characterizes current attitudes about education at every level.

We have heard the voices of high school and college students, school board members, and teachers; of leaders of industry, minority groups, and higher education; of parents and State officials. We could hear the hope evident in their commitment to quality education and in their descriptions of outstanding programs and schools. We could also hear the intensity of their frustration, a growing impatience with shoddiness in many walks of American life, and the complaint that this shoddiness is too often reflected in our schools and colleges. Their frustration threatens to overwhelm their hope.

What lies behind this emerging national sense of frustration can be described as both a dimming of personal expectations and the fear of losing a shared vision for America.

On the personal level the student, the parent, and the caring teacher all perceive that a basic promise is not being kept. More and more young people emerge from high school ready neither for college nor for work. This predicament becomes more acute as the knowledge base continues its rapid expansion, the number of traditional jobs shrinks, and new jobs demand greater sophistication and preparation.

On a broader scale, we sense that this undertone of frustration has significant political implications, for it cuts across ages, generations, races, and political and economic groups. We have come to understand that the public will demand that educational and political leaders act forcefully and effectively on these issues. Indeed, such demands have already appeared and could well become a unifying national preoccupation. This unity, however, can be achieved only if we avoid the unproductive tendency of some to search for scapegoats among the victims, such as the beleaguered teachers.

On the positive side is the significant movement by political and educational leaders to search for solutions—so far centering largely on the nearly desperate need for increased support for the teaching of mathematics and science. This movement is but a start on what we believe is a larger and more educationally encompassing need to improve teaching and learning in fields such as English, history, geography, economics, and foreign languages. We believe this movement must be broadened and directed toward reform and excellence throughout education.

EXCELLENCE IN EDUCATION

We define "excellence" to mean several related things. At the level of the *individual learner,* it means performing on the boundary of individual ability in ways that test and push back personal limits, in school and in the workplace. Excellence characterizes a *school or college* that sets high expectations and goals for all learners, then tries in every way possible to help students reach them. Excellence characterizes a *society* that has adopted these policies, for it will then be prepared through the education and skill of its people to respond to the challenges of a rapidly changing world. Our Nation's people and its schools and colleges must be committed to achieving excellence in all these senses.

We do not believe that a public commitment to excellence and educational reform must be made at the expense of a strong public commitment to the equitable treatment of our diverse population. The twin goals of equity and high-quality schooling have profound and practical meaning for our economy and society, and we cannot permit one to yield to the other either in principle or in practice. To do so would deny young people their chance to learn and live according to their aspirations and abilities. It also would lead to a generalized accommodation to mediocrity in our society on the one hand or the creation of an undemocratic elitism on the other.

Our goal must be to develop the talents of all to their fullest. Attaining that goal requires that we expect and assist all students to work to the limits of their capabilities. We should expect schools to have genuinely high standards rather than minimum ones, and parents to support and encourage their children to make the most of their talents and abilities.

The search for solutions to our educational problems must also include a commitment to life-long learning. The task of rebuilding our system of learning is enormous and must be properly understood and taken seriously: Although a million and a half new workers enter the economy each year from our schools and colleges, the adults working today will still make up about 75 percent of the workforce in the year 2000. These workers, and new entrants into the workforce, will need further education and retraining if they—and we as a Nation—are to thrive and prosper.

THE LEARNING SOCIETY

In a world of ever-accelerating competition and change in the conditions of the workplace, of ever-greater danger, and of ever-larger opportunities for those prepared to meet them, educational reform should focus on the goal of creating a Learning Society. At the heart of such a society is the commitment to a set of values and to a system of education that affords all members the opportunity to stretch their minds to full capacity, from early childhood through adulthood, learning more as the world itself changes. Such a society has as a basic foundation the idea that education is important not only because of what it contributes to one's career goals but also because of the value it adds to the general quality of one's life. Also at the heart of the Learning Society are educational opportunities extending far beyond the traditional institutions of learning, our schools and colleges. They extend into homes and workplaces; into libraries, art galleries, museums, and science centers; indeed, into every place where the individual can develop and mature in work and life. In our view, formal schooling in youth is the essential foundation for learning throughout one's life. But without life-long learning, one's skills will become rapidly dated.

In contrast to the ideal of the Learning Society, however, we find that for too many people education means doing the minimum work necessary for the moment, then coasting through life on what may have been learned in its first quarter. But this should not surprise us because we tend to express our educational standards and expectations largely in terms of "minimum requirements." And where there should be a coherent continuum of learning, we have none, but instead an often incoherent, outdated patchwork quilt. Many individual, sometimes heroic, examples of schools and colleges of great merit do exist. Our findings and testimony confirm the vitality of a number of notable schools and programs, but their very distinction stands out against a vast mass shaped by tensions and pressures that inhibit systematic academic and vocational achievement for the majority of students. In some metropolitan areas basic literacy has become the goal rather than the starting point. In some colleges maintaining enrollments is of greater day-to-day concern than maintaining rigorous academic standards. And the ideal of academic excellence as the primary goal of schooling seems to be fading across the board in American education.

Thus, we issue this call to all who care about America and its future: . . . America is at risk.

. . . [It has to] reverse the current declining trend—a trend that stems more from weakness of purpose, confusion of vision, underuse of talent, and lack of leadership, than from conditions beyond our control.

THE TOOLS AT HAND

It is our conviction that the essential raw materials needed to reform our educational system are waiting to be mobilized through effective leadership:

- the natural abilities of the young that cry out to be developed and the undiminished concern of parents for the well-being of their children;
- the commitment of the Nation to high retention rates in schools and colleges and to full access to education for all;
- the persistent and authentic American dream that superior performance can raise one's state in life and shape one's own future;
- the dedication, against all odds, that keeps teachers serving in schools and colleges, even as the rewards diminish;
- our better understanding of learning and teaching and the implications of this knowledge for school practice, and the numerous examples of local success as a result of superior effort and effective dissemination;
- the ingenuity of our policymakers, scientists, State and local educators, and scholars in formulating solutions once problems are better understood;
- the traditional belief that pay for education is an investment in ever-renewable human resources that are more durable and flexible than capital plant and equipment, and the availability in this country of sufficient financial means to invest in education;
- the equally sound tradition, from the Northwest Ordinance of 1787 until today, that the Federal Government should supplement State, local, and other resources to foster key national educational goals; and
- the voluntary efforts of individuals, businesses, and parent and civic groups to cooperate in strengthening educational programs.

These raw materials, combined with the unparalleled array of educational organizations in America, offer us the possibility to create a Learning Society, in which public, private, and parochial schools; colleges and universities, vocational and technical schools and institutes; libraries; science centers, museums, and other cultural institutions; and corporate training and retraining programs offer opportunities and choices for all to learn throughout life.

THE PUBLIC'S COMMITMENT

Of all the tools at hand, the public's support for education is the most powerful. . . . People are steadfast in their belief that education is the major foundation for the future strength of this country. . . .

Another dimension of the public's support offers the prospect of constructive reform. The best term to characterize it may simply be the honorable word "patriotism." Citizens know intuitively what some of the best economists have shown in their research, that education is one of the chief engines of a society's material well-being. They know, too, that education is the common bond of a pluralistic society and helps tie us to other cultures around the globe. Citizens also know in their bones that the safety of the United States depends principally on the wit, skill, and spirit of a self-confident people, today and tomorrow. . . .

. . . perhaps most important, citizens know and believe that the meaning of America to the rest of the world must be something better than it seems to many today. Americans like to think of this Nation as the preeminent country for generating the great ideas and material benefits for all mankind. The citizen is dismayed at a steady 15-year decline in industrial productivity, as one great American industry after another falls to world competition. The citizen wants the country to act on the belief, . . . that education should be at the top of the Nation's agenda.

FINDINGS

We conclude that declines in educational performance are in large part the result of disturbing inadequacies in the way the educational process itself is often conducted. The findings that follow, culled from a much more extensive list, reflect four important aspects of the educational process: content, expectations, time, and teaching.

. . . REGARDING CONTENT

By content we mean the very "stuff" of education, the curriculum. Because of our concern about the curriculum, the Commission examined patterns of courses high school students took in 1964–69 compared with course patterns in 1976–81. On the basis of these analyses we conclude:

- Secondary school curricula have been homogenized, diluted, and diffused to the point that they no longer have a central purpose. In effect, we have a cafeteria-style curriculum in which the appetizers and desserts can easily be mistaken for the main courses. . . .

- This curricular smorgasbord, combined with extensive student choice, explains a great deal about where we find ourselves today. We offer intermediate algebra, but only 31 percent of our recent high school graduates complete it; we offer French I, but only 13 percent complete it; and we offer geography, but only 16 percent complete it. Calculus is available in schools enrolling about 60 percent of all students, but only 6 percent of all students complete it.

- Twenty-five percent of the credits earned by general track high school students are in physical and health education, work experience outside the school, remedial English and mathematics, and personal service and development courses, such as training for adulthood and marriage.

... REGARDING EXPECTATIONS

We define expectations in terms of the level of knowledge, abilities, and skills school and college graduates should possess. They also refer to the time, hard work, behavior, self-discipline, and motivation that are essential for high student achievement. Such expectations are expressed to students in several different ways:

- by grades, which reflect the degree to which students demonstrate their mastery of subject matter;
- through high school and college graduation requirements, which tell students which subjects are most important;
- by the presence or absence of rigorous examinations requiring students to demonstrate their mastery of content and skill before receiving a diploma or a degree;
- by college admissions requirements, which reinforce high school standards; and
- by the difficulty of the subject matter students confront in their texts and assigned readings.

Our analyses in each of these areas indicate notable deficiencies:

- The amount of homework for high school seniors has decreased (two-thirds report less than 1 hour a night) and grades have risen as average student achievement has been declining.
- In many other industrialized nations, courses in mathematics (other than arithmetic or general mathematics), biology, chemistry, physics, and geography start in grade 6 and are required of *all* students. The time spent on these subjects, based on class hours, is about three times that spent by even the most science-oriented U.S. students, i.e., those who select 4 years of science and mathematics in secondary school.
- A 1980 State-by-State survey of high school diploma requirements reveals that only 8 States require high schools to offer foreign language instruction, but none requires students to take the courses. Thirty-five States require only 1 year of mathematics, and 36 require only 1 year of science for a diploma.
- In 13 States, 50 percent or more of the units required for high school graduation may be electives chosen by the student. Given this freedom to choose the substance of half or more of their education, many students opt for less demanding personal service courses, such as bachelor living.
- "Minimum competency" examinations (now required in 37 States) fall short of what is needed, as the "minimum" tends to become the "maximum," thus lowering educational standards for all.
- One-fifth of all 4-year public colleges in the United States must accept every high school graduate within the State regardless of program followed or grades, thereby serving notice to high school students that they can expect to attend college even if they do not follow a demanding course of study in high school or perform well.
- About 23 percent of our more selective colleges and universities reported that their general level of selectivity declined during the 1970s, and 29 percent reported reduc-

ing the number of specific high school courses required for admission (usually by dropping foreign language requirements, which are now specified as a condition for admission by only one-fifth of our institutions of higher education).

- Two few experienced teachers and scholars are involved in writing textbooks. During the past decade or so a large number of texts have been "written down" by their publishers to ever-lower reading levels in response to perceived market demands.

- A recent study by Education Products Information Exchange revealed that a majority of students were able to master 80 percent of the material in some of their subject-matter texts before they had even opened the books. Many books do not challenge the students to whom they are assigned.

- Expenditures for textbooks and other instructional materials have declined by 50 percent over the past 17 years. While some recommend a level of spending on texts of between 5 and 10 percent of the operating costs of schools, the budgets for basal texts and related materials have been dropping during the past decade and a half to only 0.7 percent today.

. . . REGARDING TIME

Evidence presented to the Commission demonstrates three disturbing facts about the use that American schools and students make of time: (1) compared to other nations, American students spend much less time on school work; (2) time spent in the classroom and on homework is often used ineffectively; and (3) schools are not doing enough to help students develop either the study skills required to use time well or the willingness to spend more time on school work.

- In England and other industrialized countries, it is not unusual for academic high school students to spend 8 hours a day at school, 220 days per year. In the United States, by contrast, the typical school day lasts 6 hours and the school year is 180 days.

- In many schools, the time spent learning how to cook and drive counts as much toward a high school diploma as the time spent studying mathematics, English, chemistry, U.S. history, or biology.

- A study of the school week in the United States found that some schools provided students only 17 hours of academic instruction during the week, and the average school provided about 22.

- A California study of individual classrooms found that because of poor management of classroom time, some elementary students received only one-fifth of the instruction others received in reading comprehension.

- In most schools, the teaching of study skills is haphazard and unplanned. Consequently, many students complete high school and enter college without disciplined and systematic study habits.

... REGARDING TEACHING

The Commission found that not enough of the academically able students are being attracted to teaching; that teacher preparation programs need substantial improvement; that the professional working life of teachers is on the whole unacceptable; and that a serious shortage of teachers exists in key fields.

- Too many teachers are being drawn from the bottom quarter of graduating high school and college students.

- The teacher preparation curriculum is weighted heavily with courses in "educational methods" at the expense of courses in subjects to be taught. A survey of 1,350 institutions training teachers indicated that 41 percent of the time of elementary school teacher candidates is spent in education courses, which reduces the amount of time available for subject matter courses.

- The average salary after 12 years of teaching is only $17,000 per year, and many teachers are required to supplement their income with part-time and summer employment. In addition, individual teachers have little influence in such critical professional decisions as, for example, textbook selection.

- Despite widespread publicity about an overpopulation of teachers, severe shortages of certain kinds of teachers exist: in the fields of mathematics, science, and foreign languages; and among specialists in education for gifted and talented, language minority, and handicapped students.

- The shortage of teachers in mathematics and science is particularly severe. A 1981 survey of 45 States revealed shortages of mathematics teachers in 43 States, critical shortages of earth sciences teachers in 33 States, and of physics teachers everywhere.

- Half of the newly employed mathematics, science, and English teachers are not qualified to teach these subjects; fewer than one-third of U.S. high schools offer physics taught by qualified teachers.

The Debate Continues

Few seem to note that literate societies are a recent phenomenon; that most humans since the beginning of time spent their lives in cultures where literacy was reserved for very few, if any; that mass schooling and mass literacy date back only to the day before yesterday.

What if the imperfect literacy that we bewail reflects our aspirations rather than our failures, and the dismal performance of the schools looks worse for our impatience to achieve in one or two generations what might take a good deal longer? Alternatively, what if the age of mass literacy in the West, which began in the late nineteenth century and is flagging a hundred years later, proves to be only an interlude in the apparent historical norm of mass illiteracy?

The selection that follows, abstracted from a longer essay, tries to place our circumstances in a different perspective.

Eugen Weber: from Schooling for Whom?

> Young people today love luxury, they are badly brought up, despise authority, have no respect for their elders, and prattle instead of working. They contradict their parents, hurry to swallow the desserts when they sit at table, cross their legs [hold themselves badly], and torment their teachers.

That is Socrates, speaking in Athens of the fifth century before Christ. Any dedicated graduate student would be capable of producing an interminable list of similar statements, which would prove that over the past twenty-five centuries (at least) education has gone from bad to worse. This poses a problem. The young have been deteriorating down the ages so consistently that one wonders what was left to deteriorate still further in 1983, when the future President of my University heading a prestigious commission declared the Nation at Risk, and "the educational foundations of our society eroded by a rising tide of mediocrity."

Standards must have been tremendously high in the stone age for so much erosion to leave anything standing at all. Especially when, in 1993 as in 1983, the average citizen of our nation-at-risk appears better educated, more literate, more knowledgeable, than average citizens ever were before. I'm embarrassed to stand here before you and paint a picture, or rather a perspective, that fits neither current fashion nor our own rather dismal perceptions. But, if we hear so much about illiteracy, it isn't because illiteracy is higher today than it was a hundred years ago. Illiteracy is lower. It's our standards that are higher. Or, at least, broader.

In the nineteenth century, schooling, for those who got any, offered two tracks: elementary, which could be very elementary indeed; and higher, which was reserved for very few, most of whom went on as far as they wanted which, for the majority of that small minority, was not very far. As late as the 1940s and 50s, when I was a student, access to university was the privilege of a few. Four times as many people fill colleges today as they did in the 50s, and they press their studies farther; there are five times as many master's degrees, six times as many doctoral degrees. And women account for more than half of students, and of degrees (except PhD), when they accounted for only one third in the 50s.

Furthermore, many of the women who were in college in the 50s were there because college offered a good place to find a husband. And a lot of the boys were there for not much better reasons. When it didn't function as a marriage market, college quite often remained what it had been for centuries: the provider of relatively narrow training, or an opportunity for conspicuous consumption. I have been associated with universities in several countries for more than forty years, and I would hazard the impression that the overall quality of students is not radically different, but the quality of teaching has improved, and overall standards are higher today, even if the dropout rate is higher too.

Arguments and some data were drawn from or confirmed by, Mike Rose, *Lives on the Boundary* (New York, 1989) and Christian Baudelot and Roger Establet, *Le Niveau monte* (Paris, 1989).

Not that it feels that way. The way I feel is closer to Socrates than to Polyanna: things ain't what they used to be. But when I look hard at the way they used to be, I begin to wonder whether falling standards are not a foundation myth invented in every generation by the old trying to reassure (and reinsure) themselves against the rise of the young.

Could the conjunction of higher standards and a higher dropout rate provide a key to the paradox? The fact is that, in historical perspective, the dropout rate we hear so much about is lower than it ever was. In 1910, less than 9% of seventeen-year-olds graduated high school, in 1950, 59%, today it's 75%. So, when you read about a dropout rate of 25% (which is horrendous enough), remember that it represents a graduation rate of 75%, compared to 8.8% in 1910: two and a half million a year compared to about a hundred thousand. Remember also that schools are taking an ever greater proportion of the population, and a vastly greater proportion of the under-privileged population. Around the First World War, less than 15% of students continued beyond elementary school; around the Second World War about one fourth of them went on to high school. Many of these have to be taught a new culture as well as new skills, and a greater proportion of them expect to go on to college and be prepared for that— ten times more than in 1914.

Take another angle: in the 1930s, when the Civilian Conservation Corps defined "functional literacy," it made it equivalent to three or more years of schooling. During the Second World War the army set Fourth Grade as standard. In 1947, the Census Bureau defines functional illiterates as those with less than five years of schooling. By 1960, the Office of Education sets the benchmark at Eighth Grade. By the late 70s, some authors suggest that functional literacy be equated with completion of high school.

We keep raising the level of expectations, we keep raising the bar of the high jump, we keep inviting more people to jump higher. Once upon a time, the like of most people who get to go to college today wouldn't have dreamed about it, and a lot of the students who got there got through doing very little work and learning very little. Once upon a time the university was a barrier to social mobility: its fees and requirements served to limit access to the elite. Now, unconsciously or deliberately, college and university are expected to encourage and accelerate socio-economic mobility, in a society where intellectual demands and operating standards are a good deal higher than they used to be—whether in theology or in manufacturing.

In absolute terms, contemporary society counts more intellectuals and highly trained professionals than any previous society. In relative terms, their proportion of the active population has grown significantly. Between 1890 and 1990 the proportion of adults with access to university degrees has exploded. In 1940, 11% of the 18–21 age group were enrolled in degree credit programs in higher education; in 1950, 15%, in 1970, 34%, in 1990, 52%.

Less than half of these actually graduate within five years, but a lot more graduate in the longer term, because they have to earn a living or run a household. And this growing body of nontraditional students may just as easily reflect less interest in academic achievement as such, or rising recognition of what Higher Education has to offer.

Does all this mean that standards have fallen? We certainly offer a lot of remedial courses, and I sometimes think that college serves as a reform school, trying to remedy the failures of previous education. But that feeling was strong a hundred years ago. In 1896, *The Nation* ran an article on "The Growing Illiteracy of American Boys" who, at Harvard and in other prestige institutions, had to be taught "what they ought to have learnt already." Two years after this, in 1898, the University of California instituted the Subject A exam in basic English, for the students it admitted; and ever since a steady 30 to 40% of our freshmen have been forced to take remedial English classes.

The fact is that more people get to university, which means that more badly-trained people get in, and less able people, and more able ones too. A couple of articles published in the journal, *Nature,* in 1987 suggest that, if anything, something may be getting better. Tests conducted on schoolchildren and army recruits show massive rises in scores achieved on Intelligence Tests between the 1950s and the 1980s: as much as twenty points per generation. These young people do not necessarily make a better showing in school, but many are brighter, smarter, quicker on the uptake, more sophisticated. And it's some of these people with apparently higher IQ who get into universities and contribute to declining college test scores.

So, it is not that these people perform better in schools. It is rather that more people get more schooling, and take more and higher degrees. But what if the higher degrees reflect lower academic standards? That brings us back to the question of standards, of whether standards represent some objective criteria or mere current prejudice. And, on this, you pays your money and you picks your standards.

Do more people read, for example? Between 1950 and 1980, yearly publishing totals in the United States increased more than fourfold. But that does not satisfy some critics, because lots of people do not read very much, and some do not read books at all. Only six in ten Americans over eighteen read a work of fiction or poetry every year.

A French survey made a few years ago identified a category of what it called "weak readers": people who read between one and four books a year, sometimes as many as nine; and it found that between 1973 and 1981 that category had risen from 23% to nearly 28% of the French reading public. The Ministry of Culture deplored this as reflecting the fragile state of current literacy. But it is equally possible to rejoice that, in the eight years between 1973 and 1981, a million more readers read a few more books than they (or their like) had read before. "Weak" readers are better than no readers!

A less equivocal index is provided by the fact that, everywhere throughout the Western world, more people visit museums and engage in other cultural activities. In the United States, for example, eleven million visited art museums in 1952, while by 1980 visitors were five times as numerous. In 1962, five and a half million people went to hear symphony concerts, by 1987 they were over twenty-five million. In 1970 four and a half million went to the opera, by 1987 nearly seventeen million attended. In France also, between 1980 and 1987, the number of visitors in thirty-three major national museums rose by one third, from nine to twelve million. In 1980, the Impressionists in the Jeu de Paume were admired by 139,000 visitors. In 1986 the pictures were moved to the new Musée d'Orsay and, in the two years that followed, two and a half million people went to see them. Educational development makes for higher levels of cultural consumption.

So where does our educational development stand? The good news is that all Americans between eighteen and twenty-four command reading, writing and reckoning skills around Fifth Year level. The bad news is that very few can go beyond that level. I shall return to this. But, first, let me put that in perspective too.

Over the past eighty years, the number of years spent in school has more than doubled. The day before yesterday, not everyone went to school and relatively few went to high school. Today everyone goes to school, everyone goes to high school until they graduate or drop out. This poses novel kinds of pedagogical problems—not only in terms of numbers, but in terms of study matter. It isn't that eleven or twelve-year-olds read and write worse than their ancestors, it's that their ancestors often didn't read or write at all, and that high schools, even junior high schools, accept today children who never came near them yesterday. But even in school, what happened during most of the nineteenth century? We talk about the three R's, we think about the three R's as if they have been joined in a *ménage à trois* for ever and ever, when in fact they were only distantly related. In many countries, well into the middle of the nineteenth century, school teachers taught reading. If they were capable of teaching writing too, they were paid more; and more still if they taught you how to count or to decipher Latin. So, subjects that we regard as basic were for a long time taught separately, and learned separately and at different levels of adequacy, if they were learnt at all. Lots of people could make out the Almanac who couldn't sign their names, and lots of people managed to sign their name who couldn't write a letter.

Remember that, when you weep over the information that 13% of Americans, like 15% of French, are functional illiterates. In the best of times there is an irreducible kernel of men and women who cannot or will not learn certain skills. Even driving. Yet they function, and society functions as it functioned in the days when illiterates made up a far higher proportion of its members. The Athens of Pericles, the Italy of Raphael, the France of Racine, the extraordinarily creative Europe of the nineteenth century, were all basically illiterate societies; but what we remember is the thin layer of cream at the top of the milk. The gap between the leaders and the rest is narrower today, but what strikes us is the extent of the gap. We don't notice that some of the cream has been diluted, and the milk below is a smidgin richer. What we notice is that, as the top rises, it doesn't carry the rest with it, not all the rest, certainly. And Scholastic Aptitude Tests make this embarrassingly clear. As more students, and more poor and disadvantaged students, take SATs and the like, SAT scores fall. The authorities blame the schools and blame the tests: the ones don't teach the basics, the others are culturally biased. If our school system is sick with failure, the cure is to break the thermometer. And, of course, to teach not substance but self-esteem. Doctor the schools, doctor the tests, and the decline will halt. What if the decline, such as it is, is the result of progress, such as it may be?

Can the decline be halted? King Canute didn't persuade the tide to turn back. Political pressures have manipulated both schools and tests. The only result I see is that, by the mid-1980s, a quarter of all Math and English courses taught in four-year colleges were remedial courses. Perhaps education can only adjust to democratization up to a point. Schools that used to be narrow, rigid and coercive have given way to schools that are broad, flexible and lax. Standards have been denounced as repressive, so they've become permissive; demands for excellence have been denounced as aggressive, and discrimination as prejudice. Now we regard talent as a form of maladjustment and condemn selection as undemocratic. But the rising tide of mediocrity will not be halted and, who knows, perhaps it should not be, because mediocrity is quite simply the middling/average level, and that is rising with the tide.

Yes, illiteracy will be an increasing problem, but we shall find ways of adjusting to it, especially when illiterates manage to function, and functional illiteracy actually works in other than a pejorative sense. We hear a lot about our need for a skilled work force. The fact is that there will continue to be a mass of openings for truck and train drivers, sanitation workers, security guards, nurses' aids, fast food producers and domestic help—not to mention certain kinds of skilled artisans, all of whom manage quite well with limited reading skills. Yes, literacy correlates with wealth and power, absence of literacy with less power and wealth, or with none. But *some* literacy, enough for your needs, may go with moderate success. Yes, it would be nice if everybody could read more than brief notices, but most of them can operate with color codes and a few easily-deciphered indications. Mass literacy may translate to mitigated illiteracy, but the masses possess sufficient skills to survive with little pain. They will manage, as the majority have always managed, by decoding signs and messages, by reacting to simple or complex signals. You don't have to read to understand a stop sign, or to find a rest room. All around us simplification and standardization diminish the practical importance of traditional literacy. Even the oral tradition of a not-so distant past is making a comeback.

But, surely, the post-industrial economy calls for more skills, not less? In the first place, it's not clear to me that many specific skills call for more than minimal literacy. In the second place, the skilled labor pool once supplied by way of high and junior high school is increasingly irrigated by colleges and junior colleges. It should be fed by Vocational Schools, but I'm not addressing what should be, only what I see around. And there, it seems to me, the number of those entering the job market from college makes up for the imperfect preparation of those who approach it from high school.

A comparison with some popular sports might clarify the situation, because certain sports that used to be reserved for the few have also opened up to many more in recent decades. There are vastly more skiers today, and tennis players and swimmers, than a generation ago, let alone in the 1930s. As a result there are proportionately more bad and simply mediocre swimmers, skiers and tennis players. But there is also a greater pool of skill and talent from which to recruit excellent ones.

We don't go around complaining about the lackadaisical way people play tennis nowadays, and we don't insist on excellence for all and cry failure if it isn't achieved. We don't, first, because we know and accept that competence and achievement are unequal, but also because the effort involved to raise standards significantly would maximize costs. We are glad that almost all who want to have access to the practice of one sport or more, and we're glad when they practice it with the kind of competency that prevents them from drowning or breaking a leg. In the same way, in the world of employment and unemployment, we welcome success, but don't deplore mediocrity, and we make provision for failure: a minimum wage, social security, unemployment insurance, recognize and preserve the rights of the weak in a world where the strong do better. An LCD (Lowest Common Denominator) is not altogether bad, provided there is access to the HCF (Highest Common Factor) too—and to excellence beyond. . . .

The problem illiterates and their society face lies in another direction than the one on which most critics focus. Minimal literacy equips you to function in many jobs, but not in the political marketplace. This suits those politicians who have a vested interest in functioning as interpreters for a particular group, but leaves those affected partly crippled, partly disenfranchised, dysfunctional or less than functional in this respect. Literacy is not a necessity but a relative advantage, and this is something that neither school, nor society, nor many families, make sufficiently clear. . . .

Is Truth Possible?

What has been denounced as drive-in education seems to have spawned a kind of drive-by journalism, both in print and on the air, in which the commentary comes closer to drive-by shooting than to rational discourse. This is not surprising when—for some, at least—rational discourse has been demoted to elitist self-indulgence. But serious minds find it hard to cope with frail attention spans or to provide twenty-second sound bites. A 1994 review of these symptoms, by Michiko Kakutani, raises the question of whether relativism has gone too far. Valéry may have been right in asserting that objective truth is an illusion ("in the beginning was the Fable"); but people still need to build bridges that stay up, planes that fly, and computers that don't go down too often. Just as we need to trust objects, we need to trust our judgment, and that of others, whether in building structures, making promises, or interpreting history. Every game has rules. It is absurd to declare such rules irrelevant while we are still playing the game. Relativism usefully counterbalances dogmatic assertion; but relativism as dogma goes just one bridge too far.

Michiko Kakutani: "Opinion vs. Reality in an Age of Pundits and Spin Doctors"

It's been 18 years since Tom Wolfe heralded the arrival of the "Me Generation," and 15 years since Christopher Lasch anatomized "the culture of narcissism"; in those intervening years the self has become, in Robert Hughes's words, "the sacred cow of American culture." In literature, in philosophy, even in the writing of history, subjectivity has gained a new ascendency.

Post-modernists now place quotation marks around words like "reality," insisting that the old notion of objective knowledge has become obsolete. Multiculturalists argue for new curriculums not on the basis of factual accuracy, but on the basis of "self-esteem." And politicians and their spin doctors use pseudo-events and photo-ops to market virtual-reality versions of themselves to the public.

Throughout our culture, the old notions of "truth" and "knowledge" are in danger of being replaced by the new ones of "opinion," "perception" and "credibility."

On television, on radio, in the pages of newspapers and magazines, on the sidewalks and in taxicabs, we are pelted with opinions. There are reviews of books, movies and plays; and there are reviews of hamburgers, spas and cosmetics. Waiters editorialize about the menu selections in restaurants. And polls are conducted daily, weekly, annually on everything from the state of the nation to the state of one's marriage. Never mind that respondents sometimes offer opinions on matters they know nothing about: in one famous poll, students cheerfully dispensed opinions on three completely fictional nationalities (the Pireneans, the Danireans and the Wallonians).

At the same time, critics, columnists and opinion-makers seem to have acquired a new visibility on the public stage. In a bizarre news conference last week, Bobby Ray Inman largely blamed newspaper columns for his abrupt decision to withdraw his name from nomination as Secretary of Defense. Two radio-show loudmouths, Rush Limbaugh and Howard Stern, recently shared a cover of Time magazine titled "Voice of America?" And two new series featuring fictional pundits recently made their debut on television: Fox has begun broadcasting a sit-com called "Monty," starring Henry Winkler as a right-wing talk show host, while this week ABC introduced a new cartoon series called "The Critic," which comes from the creators of "The Simpsons" and features a pudgy, balding movie critic who reviews pictures like "Home Alone 5," "Rabbi P.I." and "The Bad News Mets."

On Oprah and Geraldo's public confessionals, on Larry King and C-Span and Court TV, people stand up or call in to volunteer their thoughts on Michael Jackson and the Buffalo Bills, the future of NATO and the existence of U.F.O.'s. This week, President Clinton's State of the Union Address was not only followed, on assorted networks, by spin sessions from Democrats and Republicans, but also by commentary from journalists and think-tank observers, and instant polls of the American public. A handful of selected citizens offered their personal reactions to the speech on CBS, while hundreds of others called the White House public comment line.

People who prefer to consume passively the opinions of professional pundits have also sent new books by Mr. Stern ("Private Parts") and Mr. Limbaugh ("See, I Told You So") to the top of the best-seller lists. The virtue of each man, their mutual book editor, Judith Regan, recently told Time magazine, is that he "says what's on his mind." Their fans don't necessarily agree with their views; rather Mr. Stern and Mr. Limbaugh are celebrated for their outrageousness, their vitriol, their ability to combine show business with social aperçus.

BULLY TALK SHOWS

Similar dynamics are at work on some of those roundtable talk shows that pit journalists (and the occasional politician) against one another in rancorous debate. Reason and knowledge aren't the deciding factors in these shows; aggressiveness, sarcasm and élan often are. John McLaughlin, the bullying host of "The McLaughlin Group," goads his fellow panel members to make snap predictions about recent political developments on a scale of 0 to 10 ("Ten being metaphysical confidence; zero being metaphysical doubt"), while members of "The Capital Gang" cockily present their picks for "Outrage of the Week."

In "Sound and Fury: The Washington Punditocracy and the Collapse of American Politics," Eric Alterman, a senior fellow of the World Policy Institute in New York City, argues that the sound bites offered on such shows are "designed to trigger the emotions without disturbing the mind."

"Unlike print journalism," Mr. Alterman writes in an essay, "television does not hold itself to recognized journalistic standards of truth-telling and fact-checking. Name calling, wimp-baiting and liberal-bashing prove more exciting to viewers. The result of the rise of this punditocracy has been an increase in invective, oversimplification and militarization of the Washington political dialogue."

Accompanying this development has been the proliferation of a phenomenon Daniel J. Boorstin identified in his 1961 book "The Image: A Guide to Pseudo-Events in America": that is, nonspontaneous, carefully planned happenings "planted primarily (not always exclusively) for the immediate purpose of being reported or reproduced." Since the publication of "The Image," the pseudo-event—in the form of news conferences, photo-ops, ceremonial appearances—has permeated political culture, as has the art of the spin. In fact, in the current media environment, a lot of politics takes place along a Möbius strip of perception: focus groups (carefully interviewed sets of voters) are used to hone a politician's image, which is further polished—and assaulted—by spin doctors on either side who, along with commentators, reinterpret a candidate back to the voter.

The net effect of all this spinning and sculpturing can be an air of unreality: in Mr. Boorstin's words, the displacement of "the language of ideals" by "the language of images." Interpretation comes to overshadow facts.

IMPROVING HISTORY

It's a phenomenon visible throughout our culture today. Film makers like Oliver Stone feel the license to refashion historical events, even recent ones, into stories of their own making, while more and more biographers choose to put their own spin on their subjects' lives, in some cases turning the story they've supposedly researched into a parable meant to illustrate feminist or other ideological points; in some cases, interpolating their own thoughts, feelings and musings into the narrative itself. The trend culminated, most distressingly, last summer with the publication of "The Last Brother," Joe McGinniss's highly speculative portrait of Senator Edward M. Kennedy, which was filled with phrases like "it must have seemed" and "it was entirely possible."

What's more, as reality comes to seem increasingly artificial; complex and manipulable, people tend to grow increasingly cynical, increasingly convinced of the authenticity of their own emotions and increasingly inclined to trust their ideological reflexes, a development reflected by polarized public reaction to recent controversies in the news.

During the Anita Hill–Clarence Thomas hearings, for instance, completely contradictory portraits of Ms. Hill emerged. While some witnesses depicted her as demure and passive, others portrayed her as ambitious and calculating; her supporters and detractors outside the courtroom similarly clung to highly contradictory views. The recent Bobbitt and Menendez trials have also elicited passionate and sharply divided perceptions, which often have more to do with innate sympathies and instincts than actual testimony and facts.

REALISM, R.I.P.

Over the last few decades, literature, too, has turned toward the knowable world of the self. In a much-talked-about 1989 essay, Tom Wolfe lamented the demise of the realistic novel, the sort of novel once written by the likes of Balzac, Zola, Dickens and Thackeray and played out against the big, noisy public world of society at large. "Young writers," Mr. Wolfe observed, "are constantly told, 'Write what you know.' There is nothing wrong with that rule as a starting point, but it seems to get quickly magnified into an unspoken maxim: The only valid experience is personal experience."

Not only has there been an efflorescence of fiction centered on the private realm of domestic difficulties and existential woes, but there are also more and more stories that focus on characters' inability to connect, what the critic Benjamin DeMott has called their "interpersonal blankness."

Earlier generations of writers, Mr. DeMott noted in an essay, "were not yet tyrannized by the notion, spawned by the sexual revolution, that the claims of public reality and long-term human connection were less significant than those of private ego and merely personal will."

As the ambition to depict a larger social world has eroded, the old-fashioned omniscient narrative has begun to lose ground to stories delivered by a single first-person narrator, or a series of first-person narrators. The latter technique, pioneered by William Faulkner in "As I Lay Dying," has become highly popular in recent years, used by novelists as varied as Louise Erdrich, Michael Dorris, Francis King and Julian Barnes to emphasize the relativity of perception and the fragmentary nature of truth.

Other writers, like Alice Hoffman and Fay Weldon, have appropriated the techniques of magical realism—pioneered by writers in places like Latin America and Eastern Europe to grapple with those regions' surreal political realities—for purely personal ends. In their hands, techniques that once conveyed the absurdities and disjunctions of the world at large have devolved into charming bits of whimsy, meant to add sparkle to their characters' domestic dilemmas.

TOO MUCH TO KNOW

Why, in this age of the "information highway," have people rushed to embrace the principle of subjectivity? No doubt the exponential growth of information is partly to blame. As the world grows more complicated and knowledge becomes more specialized, it becomes difficult for anyone to have a genuinely comprehensive overview of the world. On many subjects, people either volunteer a largely uninformed opinion of their own, or rely upon the opinions of advisers, specialists or so-called experts.

Meanwhile, the new accessibility of facts made possible by computer networks and 24-hour television news has been matched by an awareness of how easily those facts can be manipulated.

In her forthcoming book, "Tainted Truth: The Manipulation of Fact in America," the Wall Street Journal reporter Cynthia Crossen argues that biased polls and questionable statistics are routinely used by lobbyists, advertisers and special-interest groups for their own ends.

"The proposition that there is no such thing as objective reality is easier on researchers than on consumers of information," she writes. "For researchers, it means the standard of proof is whatever can be defended, and absent outright fraud, there is no real way for anyone to disprove any particular set of findings. For the rest of us, it means that we, who lack the tools, expertise and confidence to judge most information, must delicately weigh results against motives before we believe anything. We are left adrift in doubt, losing our grip on one of our most potent tools: numbers."

ON CAMPUS

At the same time, in academia, the rise of post-modernism and deconstruction has further galvanized the assault on objectivity. As far as postmodernists are concerned, it's the critic, not the author, who counts. As they see it, all texts (that is, all novels, all pronouncements, all historical events, etc.) are indeterminate, subject to endless interpretation and reinterpretation. In terms of history, the historian Gertrude Himmelfarb writes in her new book, "On Looking Into the Abyss: Untimely Thoughts on Culture and Society," this view suggests "a denial of the fixity of the past, of the reality of the past apart from what the historian chooses to make of it, and thus of any objective truth about the past."

Post-modernist history, she adds, "recognizes no reality principle, only the pleasure principle—history at the pleasure of the historian."

To complicate matters further, the idea of objective knowledge has also come under assault from radical multiculturalists, who see history as an ideological battleground for control of a nation's memory. As the historians Joyce Appleby, Lynn Hunt and Margaret Jacob observe in their new book, "Telling the Truth About History": "The more extreme multiculturalists celebrate the virtues of fragmentation. History for them has become an adjunct to 'identity politics,' which seeks to realign political forces according to voters' ethnic, social, and sexual identities. Some insist that since all history has a political—often a propaganda—function, it is time for each group to rewrite history from its own perspective and thereby reaffirm its own past."

THE IMPLICATIONS

Few would deny that all historical studies are, to some degree, tentative and fragmentary. Nor is subjectivity, in and of itself, a bad thing. As the basis for a philosophical outlook, it was a product of the Romantic movement, evolving as an antidote to the arrogant rationality of the Enlightenment. In recent years, however, the virtual enshrinement of subjectivity in both academia and popular culture has serious implications.

The post-modernists' celebration of discontinuity and contradiction, combined with their willful determination to view everything through an ideological lens, suggests that the very search for truth (or truths) is an absurd and irrelevant end. It suggests that the democratic idea of consensus is futile. And it suggests that everyone, in Tocqueville's words, is confined "entirely within the solitude of his own heart."

It also postulates a completely relativistic universe in which all theories—however reprehensible or preposterous—must be accorded respect, a universe in which truths are replaced by opinions. As the literary theorist and law professor Stanley Fish once ominously declared, the death of objectivity "relieves me of the obligation to be right"; it "demands only that I be interesting."

Political Correctness

BORN in the ideological debates of the last quarter-century and generated by well-intentioned hopes that public behavior, hence thinking and attitudes, might be changed by changing speech, "PC" has become a catch-all—and a football. Demands for political correctness, complaints against its restrictions, mutual accusations, and mutual claims of victimization have all become common.

The first three selections in this chapter are excerpts from longer articles that address the PC issue. The fourth is a *New York Times* account that illustrates the possibilities of unfettered political expression.

Freedom and Political Correctness

C. Vann Woodward: from "Freedom and the Universities"

The most critical issue raised by the current academic upheaval is the denial of freedom—freedom of thought, speech, and teaching—academic freedom. It is critical because freedom is the very lifeline of universities, the indispensable condition of their being and mission. That issue has been at the center of every major attack on the academy of the last half century and more. To recall briefly only two recent ones, both beyond memory of the present generation, might supply a historical perspective missing in the account of the attack currently addressed and also indicate its distinctiveness.

The assault on academic freedom called McCarthyism began in the 1940s, before the senator from Wisconsin surfaced to become its symbol in the 1950s. The attack was nationwide and, while not confined to the academy, was extensively felt there in all respects. Careers were wrecked, scholars fled, institutes folded, journals collapsed, and books were censored, while the standards, values, and principles of higher education were subversively politicized. The most shameful thing was the frequency with which scholars under fire for their views and assertions were deserted by colleagues, administrators, and even the American Association of University Professors, their own defense organization. The oppression came from outside the university, had few active supporters within its walls, and was supported by Cold War activists in the government—federal, state, and local.

Unlike the assault on freedom in the fifties, that in the sixties came from within the academy, was led by students, supported by many professors, and justified on moral

From C. Van Woodward, "Freedom and the Universities," *New York Review of Books* (July 18, 1991).

grounds to silence defenders of unpopular government policies, notably the Vietnam War. For some years speakers favoring disapproved views risked being shouted down, insulted, or even physically abused at some universities. Yale was not the worst, but on its campus a Nobel Laureate scholar, a governor, a U.S. secretary of state, and the U.S. commanding general were prevented from speaking. All of them took the unpopular side. That continued until the trustees, on the recommendation of the president and faculty, adopted a code of university rules declaring a policy of "unfettered freedom" defined as "the right to think the unthinkable, discuss the unmentionable, and challenge the unchallengeable." And as cherished as civility and good fellowship are, the right of free speech, offensive as it might become, must be assured priority. Violations still occur at Yale, but miscreants face severe penalties and victims penalized for expressed opinions can appeal such decisions successfully.

In the present crisis the attack on freedom comes from outside as well as inside and is led by minorities, that is, people who speak or claim to speak for groups of students and faculty. Their cause is minority rights and sensitivities within the academy, instead of change in national policies. In behalf of their cause and to protect feelings from offensive speech they have, as we shall see, proved themselves willing to silence speakers and professors, abuse standards of scholarship, curriculum, and admissions, and impose conformity or silent submission on the campus. In these strivings they have often received support from university administrations. Their greatest asset, however, is a moral one: the demand for justice in behalf of groups that have long suffered injustice, discrimination, and deprivation. Some groups are larger than others and some have suffered more than others, but all have some claim on these grounds. Few would deny this. Another important asset is an ideological one: the very first of those truths in the Declaration of Independence said "to be self-evident, that all men are created equal"— to which Lincoln later said this nation from the moment it was conceived was "dedicated."

A perverse reading of the equality doctrine is frequently used to justify the revolution in university recruitment and admission of students. At Berkeley the new policy, in the name of "diversity," takes the form of seeking a student body that approximates the proportions of blacks, Hispanics, whites, Asian Americans, and other groups in California's population. Proportional admission was impossible to reconcile with old policies (not always faithfully followed, to be sure) of acceptance according to merit and achievement, which would admit a disproportionately large percentage of high-scoring and rapidly increasing Asians and a very disproportionately low percentage of the black and Hispanic population. Chancellor Ira M. Heyman of Berkeley therefore resorted to what he called "a little social engineering." Merit criteria would be applied only *within* groups, accepting stronger over weaker blacks *and* Asians, but admitting much weaker black over superior Asian and white students. Thus some minorities gained by affirmative action and some lost. Some were treated as more equal than others. Whites, now a minority, were underrepresented in the entering class of 1989. Quotas intended to include also exclude. Speaking of achievement in social engineering, Vice Chancellor Roderic Parks boasted that "Berkeley has a bellwether role." Surely he did not intend one of the dictionary definitions of bellwether: "leader of a thought-less crowd." But followers Berkeley did have.

The social engineers seem to have produced more problems than solutions. For one thing, they thrust affirmative action students, many of whom had not been given adequate preparation in elementary and high school, into situations in which they find it impossible to compete effectively at Berkeley. Thus fewer than 40 percent of blacks and fewer than 50 percent of Hispanics graduate. More than half drop out, about 30 percent of them before the end of their freshman year.

Highly selective as well as unselective universities continue to compete desperately in an ever-diminishing pool of talent for recruits of the proper skin color to fulfill some ideal of equality. There were indeed minority applicants with high qualifications and scores. Black scores in the Scholastic Aptitude Test for admission have improved slightly of late, but the overall white-black differential is still a huge 198 points in the aggregate, with only 116 out of 100,000 blacks who took the test in 1988 scoring over 699 out of 800 in the verbal section. As competition for qualified applicants sharpens, universities resort to inducements of high financial aid. An increasing number of universities restore subjective criteria and wave aside test scores.

As demand grew and supply diminished, more ill-equipped students were admitted and among them frustration, failures, and unhappiness multiplied. So did racial tensions, suspicions, slurs, and stereotypes. Defensive withdrawal and self-segregation were growing minority reactions, often with the encouragement and aid of university administrators eager to advance "pluralism" and "diversity." Minority dormitories, Third World clubs, African centers, and "ethnic theme houses" line some campuses to provide minority students havens from distress and anxieties bred in part by failures attributed to white bigotry and, in some cases, to incomprehensible reading assignments or lectures. Increasingly they have thought of themselves as groups rather than as individuals, and their culture as determined by their race.

One form separatism has taken is an attack upon the curriculum as an expression of white racial arrogance and propaganda, an attack accompanied by demands for a curriculum of their own. Compliant universities responded in the name of "multicultural" enrichment, diversity, and pluralism. Valid reasons did exist for complaint of outrageous curricular neglect and distortion in university curricula of minority contributions to Western civilization. But these reasons for complaint were used at times to denigrate and reject the whole heritage of Western civilization, the common culture to which they owed their very right to protest. . . .

Katharine T. Bartlett: Surplus Visibility

Criticizing campus "radicals" for browbeating the majority into some "politically correct" ideological conformity has become more fashionable than the practice it con-

From Katharine T. Bartlett, "Some Factual Corrections about Political Correctness," *Wall Street Journal*, (June 6, 1991). Copyright Katharine T. Bartlett.

demns. But the PC rap is a bum one. PC critics mischaracterize the enemy, exaggerate its presence, and fail to debate or even acknowledge the important substantive issues underlying the controversy. In doing so, they not only obscure, but also help to prove, the insights they themselves do not appear to understand.

The pejorative label "political correctness" represents an effort by PC critics to seize the moral high ground of the First Amendment. They claim that those protesting the continuation of racism and sexism on college campuses are moral ideologues, intolerant censors. Vietnam-protesters-turned-fascists. They also claim that these ideologues have taken over the universities, and that from this place of power they are threatening the quality of academic standards and the integrity of free intellectual inquiry.

Where is this ideological coercion? Where is this threat to open dialogue? I see little evidence of it, even at Duke University, which has been cited as a hotbed of PC. At Duke, courses on Shakespeare, Milton, and other "traditional" liberal arts subjects are not under siege; courses on such subjects as Marxism, women's studies, and Afro-American literature are. The average female Duke student shuns the label "feminist." In contrast, no shame appears to attach to association with conservative causes. Outspoken conservative students have their own newspaper, the *Duke Review,* and an active chapter of the National Association of Scholars speaks freely. At Duke, academic traditionalists head almost all departments and hold almost all chaired professorships. Duke has only one female dean; all other top leadership positions are held by white men.

If Duke is typical, what accounts for the perception that university radicals have taken over? "Surplus visibility," answers Daphne Patai of the University of Massachusetts at Amherst. Certain voices are being heard in the university more often, more loudly, and more insistently than in the past. Given what we are accustomed to hearing from these voices—silence—the noise is deafening. As Ms. Patai observes, when members of groups we do not expect to hear from begin to speak, their voices appear too loud, out of place, inappropriate, excessive.

Surplus visibility exemplifies a larger phenomenon PC critics have been unwilling to understand: the privilege of those who have power to say what needs defending and what does not. In any social organization, the views of the dominant tend to be taken for granted as objective and neutral. Challenges to these views—like those we are now hearing in the universities—appear to seek special favors for the "less qualified," or some compromising of academic standards.

This phenomenon helps to explain why some demands pressed at universities are viewed as "political" or "special pleadings," while others are not. Some PC critics dismiss as interest-group politics requests that authors such as Toni Morrison or Mary Wollstonecraft be included in the curriculum; others malign courses in feminist theory or black studies as a "Balkanization" of the curriculum.

In contrast, assignments of writings by Nathaniel Hawthorne or T.S. Eliot draw no notice and require no defense; neither does the "basic" political philosophy course that begins with Aristotle and ends with John Rawls. The difference is *not* that the standard "Western civilization" courses are apolitical. In fact, it is precisely the alignment of these courses with particular points of view—the dominant ones in our society—that makes them appear neutral. This is not to argue that such courses should be abolished, but nobody should pretend that only feminist and minority-studies courses have political content.

PC critics attack as ideologically coercive, condescending, and petty the insistence by some "blacks" and "Indians" that they be called "African Americans" or "native Americans." Yet they take for granted their own titles of "Professor," "Doctor," or "Judge" as a matter of simple civility.

Most, perhaps all, titles and labels convey substantive political messages about power and self-definition. But those that conform to existing lines of authority are taken as neutral signs of respect, while those that implicitly encroach upon that authority stand out as shamelessly political and arrogant.

It is clear that some PC critics are using a double standard to judge those who do not respect their authority. These critics invoke important principles of academic freedom to shield themselves from criticism of classroom remarks that some students find racist or sexist. Yet they appear to acknowledge no reciprocal freedom on the part of students to resist classroom humiliation; and it is that resistance that is now labeled a "politically correct" effort at censorship.

Most of us who have been labeled PC are not seeking special favors. We are not trying to stifle debate. We are trying to begin one—a difficult one that challenges perspectives that are taken for granted in the university and in society. If our critics were true to the free-speech principles they profess, they would be engaging in that debate. All too often, they have chosen personal denunciation and caricature instead.

There is room, and a great need, for a genuine debate in our universities about academic quality and diversity. PC critics have diverted the debate by the distracting assertion, backed by only a few isolated anecdotes, that traditional voices are being silenced.

The one-sidedness of the PC critique mocks this assertion. It also demonstrates a central paradox of the whole PC problem: The more established the status quo, the less defense it requires, and the more easily challenges to it can be made to appear self-serving and tyrannical. The PC charge is a smoke-screen. The fact that it packs rhetorical punch demonstrates that there has been far less change in who controls the university, and in what we take for granted there, than many would have us believe.

Elizabeth Fox-Genovese: from "The Self-Interest of Multiculturalism"

Few would contest the obvious truth that we live in a multicultural world and that the more we know about it, the more productive citizens we are likely to be. But in most instances, the defense of multiculturalism does not propose to prepare us with any rigor to be citizens of that world. It does not, for instance, usually take the form

From Elizabeth Fox-Genovese, "The Self-Interest of Multiculturalism," *Tikkun* (1991).

of impassioned requests for more and stiffer language requirements. Rarely does it take the form of demands for greater exposure to the elite texts of other cultures. Even more rarely does it take the form of pleas for substantive training in economics or geography. Clearly, multiculturalism in its most pervasive form is not viewed as a skill. Multiculturalism primarily consists in exposure to English language texts that testify to and affirm the diversity of the personal experience of those who have reason to believe that their kind has been oppressed and excluded by dead white men.

At the core of the multicultural agenda lies a commitment to education—and, indeed, culture itself—as primarily the quest for an acceptable autobiography. Multiculturalists, building upon the demands for "relevance," assume that education must, above all, strengthen the student's positive sense of identity. Racial and ethnic pride, in this perspective, serve to strengthen individual self-confidence. Multiculturalism of this kind does not even, or necessarily, promote toleration for the diversity of others. If members of different racial and ethnic groups may unite in an initial demand for multicultural education, they may also rapidly divide over the respective claims of different ethnicities on the assumption that no one who is not of one's own kind can understand one's specific experience.

In real terms, however, the battle over multiculturalism is a battle over scarce resources and shrinking opportunities. To recognize this much does not deny the related battle over national identity, but does caution us to take the more extreme pronouncements pro and con with a grain of salt.

Campus Fallout

Jon Nordheimer: "College Diatribe Ignites Furor on Race and Speech"

A student-sponsored speech by a Nation of Islam minister that attacked whites, homosexuals and Jews in mocking and often cruel ways has ignited a bitter debate at Kean College, a state school struggling to achieve racial diversity and multicultural scholarship.

The speech on campus last month has led to deepening tensions between black and Jewish faculty members and an exchange of recriminations between the college president, Dr. Elsa Gomez, and the New Jersey Chancellor for Higher Education, Dr. Edward D. Goldberg.

Some of the antagonists say the event has stripped away veneers of cordiality and exposed jealousies, resentments and the clashing perspectives inherent in higher education's search for multicultural harmony.

From The *New York Times* (December 29, 1993).

"Not Our Problem Alone"

"What is going on at Kean is not our problem alone and eventually must be faced by other colleges across America," said Dr. Gomez, who has denounced the speech but defended the speaker's right to express odious views. "We are paying the painful price of our commitment to diversity and the challenge to empower students, who often come from a disadvantaged background, to achieve their full potential."

The campus debate was deflected by the holiday recess, and some on campus say they hope tempers will cool by the time the college reconvenes.

Originally a state teachers college in Newark, Kean moved to its present campus in 1958 and became a liberal arts school attracting day students from declining cities like Elizabeth, Jersey City and New Brunswick. Black and Hispanic students each make up 14 percent of its student body of 12,000. Though the student body is only 1 percent Jewish, about 130 of 650 full-time or part-time teachers are Jews.

The row was ignited by the Nov. 29 appearance of Khalid Abdul Muhammad, a spokesman for Louis Farrakhan, leader of the Nation of Islam. Mr. Muhammad was paid $2,650 from student funds for his talk.

While Mr. Farrakhan's own fiery speech on Dec. 18 in New York made no reference to his 1985 remark that Judaism was a "gutter religion," Mr. Muhammad at Kean was unsparing in attacking Jews and other whites.

Often affecting a Jewish accent or effeminate mannerisms, he sprinkled phrases like "Columbia Jew-niversity" and "Jew York City" through a rambling three-hour talk billed as "The Secret Relationship between Blacks and Jews."

Before the speech, the Jewish Faculty and Staff Association handed out leaflets to people entering the theater, urging the "critical thinking and evaluation that would normally be expected in a college community." In his speech, Mr. Muhammad rebuked Jewish faculty members, saying, "The students chose this subject because they're catching so much hell here under you on the Kean College campus and in the surrounding Union area—a Jew stronghold."

With a handful of exceptions, the audience of about 140 consisted of black students or black followers of the Nation of Islam. In response to a question, Mr. Muhammad said that when blacks gain political control in South Africa, they should give whites 24 hours to leave and then kill all those who remained.

"We kill the women. We kill the babies, we kill the blind. We kill the cripples. We kill them all. We kill the faggot. We kill the lesbian . . . When you get through killing them all, go to the goddamn graveyard and dig up the grave and kill them a-goddamn-gain because they didn't die hard enough."

In a tape of his remarks, laughter and applause are heard after these exhortations.

Dr. Jay L. Spaulding, a history professor and an African specialist, was one of the few whites in the audience.

A week later, after the college administration had made no statement on the speaker or his remarks, Professor Spaulding wrote a letter of protest to the board of trustees. He said he had attended because black students had assured him he would hear from "a true authentic source" the Afrocentric perspective of Kean's black studies program.

"Cultist Garbage"

Instead, he wrote, what he beheld was "as competent a display of racist and sectarian stupidity as any other cultist garbage I have run across over the years." He also objected that "the leading Kean College faculty and student exponents of Afrocentricity sat in the front row cheering."

The administration's silence also reached Chancellor Goldberg in Trenton, where as chief administrator of the Department of Higher Education, he helps run the state's university and college system.

In a Dec. 10 letter to the Kean board, the chancellor faulted the trustees and Dr. Gomez for failing to set "a moral framework" for "patently racist ideas and opinions delivered in a campus setting."

Dr. Gomez, president of Kean College since 1989, said it took her and the trustees until Dec. 9 to respond to the speech because no tape was available sooner. At that point, she condemned Mr. Muhammad's remarks as "reprehensible" and "filled with verbal abuse and expressions of hate," and Kean trustees were similarly critical.

Dr. Gomez made it clear, however, she believed Mr. Muhammad had a right to free speech, however odious.

"Too Much Silence"

For his part, Chancellor Goldberg considered 10 days too slow in reacting to hate-mongering. "Our strong support for free speech on our campuses carries with it the obligation to surround hate speech with educational dialogue," he said this week. "Unfortunately, there was too little planning before the speech and too much silence after it."

Dr. Gomez on Tuesday replied angrily that the chancellor "has been anything but constructive."

The challenge at a multicultural campus that seeks "a balanced learning," she later explained, was to insure that "young students thirsty for knowledge—both minority and majority—are able to discern between ideological rhetoric and genuine scholarship."

The president of the Jewish Faculty and Staff Association, Dr. Henry Kaplowitz, was sharply critical of how "multiculturalism" had evolved at Kean, however. In his view, "the Kean campus has become a hotbed of anti-Semitism in recent years."

As he saw it, some black faculty members "were brought in for diversity and once here eschewed diversity. In their eyes everything is predicated on race and racism, but they deny they are racists because they say an oppressed minority cannot be racists."

Black faculty members scoffed at that criticism. James Conyers, assistant director of the Africana Studies Program, asserted that Jewish faculty members "will punish anyone who has a valid criticism of Jews."

In an interview, he said Jews were part of "a white power structure on campus that operates in a covert fashion covered up by the jargon of academia." To his eye, promotions, grants and research leaves were routinely given to white faculty but denied to black professors, and blacks were inhibited from freely expressing themselves in classrooms while whites suffered no similar restriction.

Dr. Kaplowitz expressed surprise at the notion of a white power structure. He noted that Dr. Gomez is Hispanic and two of five deans are black and two are Hispanic. The president of the board of trustees, Lawrence J. Lochart, is black, as is one of the six other trustees, Patricia Weston Rivera. Both condemned Mr. Muhammad's remarks.

"IT WOULD BE WRONG"

Dr. Kaplowitz and other white faculty members, non-Jews as well as Jews, this week expressed concern that Mr. Conyers and other black faculty who attended Mr. Muhammad's speech seemed unwilling to disassociate themselves unequivocally from his remarks.

Indeed they were. Eleanor McKnight, head of the Black Personnel Association on campus, said she sat through the speech and found only Mr. Muhammad's "use of profanity" objectionable. And Joel Ferris, a black junior who writes for the campus newspaper, said he was untroubled by Mr. Muhammad's assertions. "It would be wrong for me to tell him to change his thoughts because someone else might be offended by what he says," he said. "His remarks were not directed at me."

The faculty senate passed a resolution declaring that Dr. Gomez and the trustees had failed to exert leadership on issues "that have polarized this campus." But Dawood Farahi, the senate president, also said that "99 percent" of blacks at Kean found Mr. Muhammad's "expressions of hate repugnant and intolerable."

The "Business" of Political Correctness

The Economist: *"An All-American Industry"*

Something odd is happening to political correctness. On the one hand, it is thriving, right up to the highest levels of government (witness the equally-sized Christmas tree and Chanukkah menorah outside the White House). On the other hand, its opponents are thriving too (look at the best-seller lists, headed by Rush Limbaugh and Howard Stern).

Seemingly irreconcilable arguments surround it. Some dismiss political correctness (PC) as an irrelevance hyped up by the right; others see it as a leftist danger to the very

From The Economist (December 25, 1993–January 7, 1994).

fabric of American life; still others argue that it is plain passé. Is America in the throes of neo-PC, anti-PC or post-PC? It is hard to tell.

So much the better for the PC industry. For that is what political correctness has become. It is no longer a matter of who wins or loses the arguments. The arguments themselves are what sustain the industry. Competition in the PC business is not only healthy, it is essential.

Few industries can boast such rapid growth as this one. A computer search by the *New York Times* found 103 newspaper references to "political correctness" in 1988. In 1993 the number was roughly 10,000.

Such extraordinary growth would quickly slacken if the driving force behind it—the language of political correctness—were to go out of fashion. But there seems little prospect of that happening. The current controversy over style at the *Los Angeles Times* shows that there is still plenty of fuel for the PC industry.

The *Los Angeles Times*'s 19-page "Guidelines on Ethnic and Racial Identification", drafted by a committee, was sent to the paper's staff on November 10th. Journalists are told never to use the word "Jewess", but to remember to call a Latino woman a "Latina". They are urged to avoid referring to African "tribes", because this offends many blacks (who are more often "African-Americans"). "Eskimos" disappear (they are "not a homogeneous group and may view the term Eskimo negatively"). "Dutch treat" and "Dutch courage" are offensive (to the Dutch?), as are "French letters" (to condom-makers?).

There is more. The term "deaf and dumb" is, apparently, pejorative, much as "birth defects" are best replaced by "congenital disabilities". Because many women do the job, "letter carrier" is preferable to "mailman". "Mankind" is frowned upon. "Gringo", "savages" and "redskin" are among the words to be used only in quotes with the approval of the editor, managing editor, associate editor or senior editor.

Not surprisingly, the guidelines provoked a reaction, and the controversy has become public. A memo signed by journalists at the *Los Angeles Times*'s Washington bureau gives warning that it is a short step from "shunning offensive words to shying away from painful facts and subjects". All this is splendid for the PC industry (language fuss, for example, does wonders for the dictionary business).

In schools, the industry is ticking over nicely. For example, big grants are awarded to developers of "Afrocentric curriculums" for schools. That in turn boosts the fund-raising power of conservative organisations set up to lobby against such manifestations of "multiculturalism".

University campuses are even more fertile ground for the PC enterprise. Antioch College in Ohio drew attention to itself in 1993 for its innovations in sexual correctness, a PC subsidiary. At Antioch, a new code of practice requires verbal consent at each stage of students' sexual relationships. At Penn State University, a reproduction of Goya's "The Naked Maja" was removed from a classroom on the ground that it created a "climate of sexual harassment". An English professor at the University of New Hampshire recently felt compelled to explain to a female student who gasped at his use of the phrase "more bang for your buck" that this was a military metaphor, not a sexual one. Teachers are hounded from classrooms or sentenced to "sensitivity training" for giving unwitting offence.

THE CONSERVATION OF NONSENSE

But by the Newtonian law of PC, a (more or less) equal and opposite reaction is guaranteed. Campus conservatives cry foul, appeal to the First Amendment, pass resolutions against censorship. Articles appear in the press, documentaries (such as the recent "Campus Culture Wars") appear on television. And the industry expands.

PC is naturally diversifying into the museum business. It gives an excuse for activity, and publicity, on a grand scale. History museums are the most obvious candidates. . . . At the Museum of American History in Washington, a notice tells visitors that reconstruction is under way: "We are rethinking the way in which we present the National Collections to the American people in exhibitions, and striving to extend the reach of American history to include all Americans."

Yes, all Americans can get into the PC business. No minority is too small (or too big), no lobby or counter-lobby need be ignored. The opportunities are endless.

Does the industry do any harm? If either side were allowed to win, it might. Unchecked, political correctness could stifle the universities, murder the language and set one interest group against another. Unchecked, anti-PC could breed intolerance and repress minorities.

So it is probably for the best that competition is continuous and the industry thrives. To be sure, perpetual antagonism can give a shrill tone to arguments, and serious treatment of issues can give way to PC point-scoring. This is bad for serious discussion, but good for the entertainment business. Listen to a recent debate on PC at the University of Pennsylvania between Robert Bork, a former federal judge, and Linda Greene, who teaches law at the University of Wisconsin:

> Greene: Would you agree with me that what we need to do is talk about the real issues and stop hurling our charges at each other?

> Bork: Oh, the charges are much more fun.

Crime

Iᶠ politics is about public affairs (the word comes from the Greek *politikos,* meaning the business of society or of the city), then the most politically incorrect activity is crime. Robbery, rape, murder, and mayhem destabilize society and impair its functioning and the security it promises its members. But crime is whatever a society says is criminal: infanticide was not criminal in the Greece of Oedipus, and public or private combat for profit or honor was licit in most societies until not long ago (dueling, sometimes to the death, went on in France, Germany, and Italy into the twentieth century). War, of course, authorizes all kinds of violence, and not against enemies only. Criminal blasphemy in one society (that of Socrates, for example, or even of Voltaire) is permissible opinion in another: the sinful usury of Thomas Aquinas's day is the profitable investment of David Ricardo's; the intrusive playfulness of one generation becomes the sexual harrassment of the next. Social drinking was a crime in the United States of the 1920s, as was abortion; they are not so today. But back then racial or sexual discrimination was a matter of opinion, and hardly criminal. Both forms became illegal when legislation so declared them. Political correctness reflects opinion that is dominant or assertive; nonconformity becomes dangerous to the nonconformist when legislation defines that behavior as illicit deviance.

Though some of its conclusions have passed into law or local regulations, discussion of what is politically correct and what is not still revolves around opinions. Certain forms of deviance, such as manslaughter, are condemned by most people, yet they may receive more or less notice and be more lightly or more heavily penalized according to changing opinions that alter with circumstances, and changing laws as well.

Normal Crime

In an essay published in 1993, Senator Daniel Patrick Moynihan suggested that the way we regard, tolerate, or adjust to deviance varies with our experience of it. Today, overwhelmed by poverty, vagrancy, maladjustment, and crime, American society is de-fining down *some of the norms that it would have found unacceptable a short time-ago.*

Moynihan, the senior U.S. senator from New York, has published important studies on poverty, crime, and their pathology.

Daniel Patrick Moynihan: *"Defining Deviancy Down"*

In one of the founding texts of sociology, *The Rules of Sociological Method* (1895), Emile Durkheim set it down that "crime is normal." "It is," he wrote, "completely impossible for any society entirely free of it to exist." By defining what is deviant, we are enabled to know what is not, and hence to live by shared standards. This aperçu appears in the chapter entitled "Rules for the Distinction of the Normal from the Pathological." Durkheim writes:

> From this viewpoint the fundamental facts of criminology appear to us in an entirely new light. . . . [T]he criminal no longer appears as an utterly unsociable creature, a sort of parasitic element, a foreign, inassimilable body introduced into the bosom of society. He plays a normal role in social life. For its part, crime must no longer be conceived of as an evil which cannot be circumscribed closely enough. Far from there being cause for congratulation when it drops too noticeably below the normal level, this apparent progress assuredly coincides with and is linked to some social disturbance.

Durkheim suggests, for example, that "in times of scarcity" crimes of assault drop off. He does not imply that we ought to approve of crime—"[p]ain has likewise nothing desirable about it"—but we need to understand its function. He saw religion, in the sociologist Randall Collins's terms, as "fundamentally a set of ceremonial actions, assembling the group, heightening its emotions, and focusing its members on symbols of their common belongingness." In this context "a punishment ceremony creates social solidarity."

The matter was pretty much left at that until seventy years later when, in 1965, Kai T. Erikson published *Wayward Puritans,* a study of "crime rates" in the Massachusetts Bay Colony. The plan behind the book, as Erikson put it, was "to test [Durkheim's] notion that the number of deviant offenders a community can afford to recognize is likely to remain stable over time." The notion proved out very well indeed. Despite occasional crime waves, as when itinerant Quakers refused to take off their hats in the presence of magistrates, the amount of deviance in this corner of seventeenth-century New England fitted nicely with the supply of stocks and whipping posts. Erikson remarks:

> It is one of the arguments of the . . . study that the amount of deviation a community encounters is apt to remain fairly constant over time. To start at the beginning, it is a simple logistic fact that the number of deviancies which come to a community's attention are limited by the kinds of equipment it uses to detect and handle them, and to that extent the rate of deviation found in a community is at least in part a function of the size and complexity of its social control apparatus. A community's capacity for handling deviance, let us say, can be roughly

From Daniel Patrick Moynihan, "Defining Deviancy Down," *The American Scholar*, Vol. 62 (Winter 1993), pp. 17–30.

estimated by counting its prison cells and hospital beds, its policemen and psychiatrists, its courts and clinics. Most communities, it would seem, operate with the expectation that a relatively constant number of control agents is necessary to cope with a relatively constant number of offenders. The amount of men, money, and material assigned by society to "do something" about deviant behavior does not vary appreciably over time, and the implicit logic which governs the community's efforts to man a police force or maintain suitable facilities for the mentally ill seems to be that there is a fairly stable quota of trouble which should be anticipated.

In this sense, the agencies of control often seem to define their job as that of keeping deviance within bounds rather than that of obliterating it altogether. Many judges, for example, assume that severe punishments are a greater deterrent to crime than moderate ones, and so it is important to note that many of them are apt to impose harder penalties when crime seems to be on the increase and more lenient ones when it does not, almost as if the power of the bench were being used to keep the crime rate from getting out of hand.

Erikson was taking issue with what he described as "a dominant strain in sociological thinking" that took for granted that a well-structured society "is somehow designed to prevent deviant behavior from occurring." In both authors, Durkheim and Erikson, there is an undertone that suggests that, with deviancy, as with most social goods, there is the continuing problem of demand exceeding supply. Durkheim invites us to

imagine a society of saints, a perfect cloister of exemplary individuals. Crimes, properly so called, will there be unknown; but faults which appear venial to the layman will create there the same scandal that the ordinary offense does in ordinary consciousness. If, then, this society has the power to judge and punish, it will define these acts as criminal and will treat them as such.

Recall Durkheim's comment that there need be no cause for congratulations should the amount of crime drop "too noticeably below the normal level." It would not appear that Durkheim anywhere contemplates the possibility of too much crime. Clearly his theory would have required him to deplore such a development, but the possibility seems never to have occurred to him.

Erikson, writing much later in the twentieth century, contemplates both possibilities. "Deviant persons can be said to supply needed services to society." There is no doubt a tendency for the supply of any needed thing to run short. But he is consistent. There can, he believes, be *too much* of a good thing. Hence "the number of deviant offenders a community *can afford* to recognize is likely to remain stable over time." [My emphasis]

Social scientists are said to be on the lookout for poor fellows getting a bum rap. But here is a theory that clearly implies that there are circumstances in which society will choose *not* to notice behavior that would be otherwise controlled, or disapproved, or even punished.

It appears to me that this is in fact what we in the United States have been doing of late. I proffer the thesis that, over the past generation, since the time Erikson wrote, the amount of deviant behavior in American society has increased beyond the levels the community can "afford to recognize" and that, accordingly, we have been redefining deviancy so as to exempt much conduct previously stigmatized, and also quietly raising the "normal" level in categories where behavior is now abnormal by any earlier standard. This redefining has evoked fierce resistance from defenders of "old" standards, and accounts for much of the present "cultural war" such as proclaimed by many at the 1992 Republican National Convention.

Let me, then, offer three categories of redefinition in these regards: the *altruistic,* the *opportunistic,* and the *normalizing.*

The first category, the *altruistic,* may be illustrated by the deinstitutionalization movement within the mental health profession that appeared in the 1950s. The second category, the opportunistic, is seen in the interest group rewards derived from the acceptance of "alternative" family structures. The third category, the normalizing, is to be observed in the growing acceptance of unprecedented levels of violent crime.

II

It happens that I was present at the beginning of the deinstitutionalization movement. Early in 1955 Averell Harriman, then the new governor of New York, met with his new commissioner of mental hygiene, Dr. Paul Hoch, who described the development, at one of the state mental hospitals, of a tranquilizer derived from rauwolfia. The medication had been clinically tested and appeared to be an effective treatment for many severely psychotic patients, thus increasing the percentage of patients discharged. Dr. Hoch recommended that it be used systemwide; Harriman found the money. That same year Congress created a Joint Commission on Mental Health and Illness whose mission was to formulate "comprehensive and realistic recommendations" in this area, which was then a matter of considerable public concern. Year after year, the population of mental institutions grew. Year after year, new facilities had to be built. Never mind the complexities: population growth and such like matters. There was a general unease. Durkheim's constant continued to be exceeded. (In *Spanning the Century: The Life of W. Averell Harriman,* Rudy Abramson writes: "New York's mental hospitals in 1955 were overflowing warehouses, and new patients were being admitted faster than space could be found for them. When he was inaugurated, 94,000 New Yorkers were confined to state hospitals. Admissions were running at more than 2,500 a year and rising, making the Department of Mental Hygiene the fastest-growing, most-expensive, mosthopeless department of state government.")

The discovery of tranquilizers was adventitious. Physicians were seeking cures for disorders that were just beginning to be understood. Even a limited success made it possible to believe that the incidence of this particular range of disorders, which had seemingly required persons to be confined against their will or even awareness, could be greatly reduced. The Congressional Commission submitted its report in 1961; it proposed a nationwide program of deinstitutionalization.

Late in 1961, President Kennedy appointed an interagency committee to prepare legislative recommendations based upon the report. I represented Secretary of Labor Arthur J. Goldberg on this committee and drafted its final submission. This included the recommendation of the National Institute of Mental Health that 2,000 community mental health centers (one per 100,000 of population) be built by 1980. A buoyant Presidential Message to Congress followed early in 1963. "If we apply our medical knowledge and social insights fully," President Kennedy pronounced, "all but a small portion of the mentally ill can eventually achieve a wholesome and a constructive social adjustment." A "concerted national attack on mental disorders [was] now possible and practical." The President signed the Community Mental Health Centers Construction Act on October 31, 1963, his last public bill-signing ceremony. He gave me a pen.

The mental hospitals emptied out. At the time Governor Harriman met with Dr. Hoch in 1955, there were 93,314 adult residents of mental institutions maintained by New York State. As of August 1992, there were 11,363. This occurred across the nation. However, the number of community mental health centers never came near the goal of the 2,000 proposed community centers. Only some 482 received federal construction funds between 1963 and 1980. The next year, 1981, the program was folded into the Alcohol and Other Drug Abuse block grant and disappeared from view. Even when centers were built, the results were hardly as hoped for. David F. Musto of Yale writes that the planners had bet on improving national mental health "by improving the quality of general community life through expert knowledge, not merely by more effective treatment of the already ill." There was no such knowledge.

However, worse luck, the belief that there *was* such knowledge took hold within sectors of the profession that saw institutionalization as an unacceptable mode of social control. These activists subscribed to a re-defining mode of their own. Mental patients were said to have been "labeled," and were not to be drugged. Musto says of the battles that followed that they were "so intense and dramatic precisely because both sides shared the fantasy of an omnipotent and omniscient mental health technology which could thoroughly reform society; the prize seemed eminently worth fighting for."

But even as the federal government turned to other matters, the mental institutions continued to release inmates. Professor Fred Siegel of Cooper Union observes: "In the great wave of moral deregulation that began in the mid-1960s, the poor and the insane were freed from the fetters of middle-class mores." They might henceforth sleep in doorways as often as they chose. The problem of the homeless appeared, characteristically defined as persons who lacked "affordable housing."

The *altruistic* mode of redefinition is just that. There is no reason to believe that there was any real increase in mental illness at the time deinstitutionalization began. Yet there was such a perception, and this enabled good people to try to do good, however unavailing in the end.

III

Our second, or *opportunistic* mode of re-definition, reveals at most a nominal intent to do good. The true object is to do well, a long-established motivation among mortals. In this pattern, a growth in deviancy makes possible a transfer of resources, including prestige, to those who control the deviant population. This control would be jeopardized if any serious effort were made to reduce the deviancy in question. This leads to assorted strategies for re-defining the behavior in question as not all that deviant, really.

In the years from 1963 to 1965, the Policy Planning Staff of the U.S. Department of Labor picked up the first tremors of what Samuel H. Preston, in the 1984 Presidential Address to the Population Association of America, would call "the earthquake that shuddered through the American family in the past twenty years." *The New York Times* recently provided a succinct accounting of Preston's point:

> Thirty years ago, 1 in every 40 white children was born to an unmarried mother; today it is 1 in 5, according to Federal data. Among blacks, 2 of 3 children are born to an unmarried mother; 30 years ago the figure was 1 in 5.

In 1991, Paul Offner and I published longitudinal data showing that, of children born in the years 1967–69, some 22.1 percent were dependent on welfare—that is to say, Aid to Families with Dependent Children—before reaching age 18. This broke down as 15.7 percent for white children, 72.3 percent for black children. Projections for children born in 1980 gave rates of 22.2 percent and 82.9 percent respectively. A year later, a *New York Times* series on welfare and poverty called this a "startling finding . . . a symptom of vast social calamity."

And yet there is little evidence that these facts are regarded as a calamity in municipal government. To the contrary, there is general acceptance of the situation as normal. Political candidates raise the subject, often to the point of dwelling on it. But while there is a good deal of demand for symbolic change, there is none of the marshaling of resources that is associated with significant social action. Nor is there any lack of evidence that there is a serious social problem here.

Richard T. Gill writes of "an accumulation of data showing that intact biological parent families offer children very large advantages compared to any other family or non-family structure one can imagine." Correspondingly, the disadvantages associated with single-parent families spill over into other areas of social policy that now attract great public concern. Leroy L. Schwartz, M.D., and Mark W. Stanton argue that the real quest regarding a government-run health system such as that of Canada or Germany is whether it would work "in a country that has social problems that countries like Canada and Germany don't share to the same extent." Health problems reflect ways of living. The way of life associated with "such social pathologies as the breakdown of the family structure" lead to medical pathologies. Schwartz and Stanton conclude: "The United States is paying dearly for its social and behavioral problems," for they have now become medical problems as well.

To cite another example, there is at present no more vexing problem of social policy in the United States than that posed by education. A generation of ever-more ambitious statutes and reforms have produced weak responses at best and a fair amount of what could more simply be called dishonesty. ("Everyone knows that Head Start works." By the year 2000, American students will "be first in the world in science and mathematics.") None of this should surprise us. The 1966 report *Equality of Educational Opportunity* by James S. Coleman and his associates established that the family background of students played a much stronger role in student achievement relative to variations in the ten (and still standard) measures of school quality.

In a 1992 study entitled *America's Smallest School: The Family*, Paul Barton came up with the elegant and persuasive concept of the parent-pupil ratio as a measure of school quality. Barton, who was on the policy planning staff in the Department of Labor in 1965, noted the great increase in the proportion of children living in single-parent families since then. He further noted that the proportion "varies widely among the states" and is related to "variation in achievement" among them. The correlation between the percentage of eighth graders living in two-parent families and average mathematics proficiency is a solid .74. North Dakota, highest on the math test, is second highest on the family compositions scale—that is, it is second in the percentage of kids coming from two-parent homes. The District of Columbia, lowest on the family scale, is second lowest in the test score.

A few months before Barton's study appeared, I published an article showing that the correlation between eighth-grade math scores and distance of state capitals from the Canadian border was .522, a respectable showing. By contrast, the correlation with per pupil expenditure was a derisory .203. I offered the policy proposal that states wishing to improve their schools should move closer to Canada. This would be difficult, of course, but so would it be to change the parent-pupil ratio. Indeed, the 1990 Census found that for the District of Columbia, apart from Ward 3 west of Rock Creek Park, the percentage of children living in single-parent families in the seven remaining wards ranged from a low of 63.6 percent to a high of 75.7. This being a one-time measurement, over time the proportions become asymptotic. And this in the nation's capital. No demand for change comes from that community—or as near to no demand as makes no matter. *For there is good money to be made out of bad schools.* This is a statement that will no doubt please many a hard heart, and displease many genuinely concerned to bring about change. To the latter, a group in which I would like to include myself, I would only say that we are obliged to ask why things do not change.

For a period there was some speculation that, if family structure got bad enough, this mode of deviancy would have less punishing effects on children. In 1991 Deborah A. Dawson, of the National Institutes of Health, examined the thesis that "the psychological effects of divorce and single parenthood on children were strongly influenced by a sense of shame in being 'different' from the norm." If this were so, the effect should have fallen off in the 1980s, when being from a single-parent home became much more common. It did not. "The problems associated with task overload among single parents are more constant in nature," Dawson wrote, adding that since the adverse effects had not diminished, they were "not based on stigmatization but rather on inherent problems in alternative family structures"—*alternative* here meaning other than two-parent families. We should take note of such candor. Writing in the *Journal of Marriage and the Family* in 1989, Sara McLanahan and Karen Booth noted: "Whereas a decade ago the prevailing view was that single motherhood had no harmful effects on children, recent research is less optimistic."

The year 1990 saw more of this lesson. In a paper prepared for the Progressive Policy Institute, Elaine Ciulla Kamarck and William A. Galston wrote that "if the economic effects of family breakdown are clear, the psychological effects are just now coming into focus." They cite Karl Zinsmeister:

> There is a mountain of scientific evidence showing that when families disintegrate children often end up with intellectual, physical, and emotional scars that persist for life. . . . We talk about the drug crisis, the education crisis, and the problems of teen pregnancy and juvenile crime. But all these ills trace back predominantly to one source: broken families.

As for juvenile crime, they cite Douglas Smith and G. Roger Jarjoura: "Neighborhoods with larger percentages of youth (those aged 12 to 20) and areas with higher percentages of single-parent households also have higher rates of violent crime." They add: "The relationship is so strong that controlling for family configuration erases the relationship between race and crime and between low income and crime. This conclusion shows up time and time again in the literature; poverty is far from the sole determinant of crime." But the large point is avoided. In a 1992 essay "The Expert's Story of Marriage," Barbara Dafoe Whitehead examined "the story of marriage as it is conveyed in today's high school and college textbooks." Nothing amiss in this tale.

It goes like this:

The life course is full of exciting options. The lifestyle options available to individuals seeking a fulfilling personal relationship include living a heterosexual, homosexual, or bisexual single lifestyle; living in a commune; having a group marriage; being a single parent; or living together. Marriage is yet another lifestyle choice. However, before choosing marriage, individuals should weigh its costs and benefits against other lifestyle options and should consider what they want to get out of their intimate relationships. Even within marriage, different people want different things. For example, some people marry for companionship, some marry in order to have children, some marry for emotional and financial security. Though marriage can offer a rewarding path to personal growth, it is important to remember that it cannot provide a secure or permanent status. Many people will make the decision between marriage and singlehood many times throughout their life.

Divorce represents part of the normal family life cycle. It should not be viewed as either deviant or tragic, as it has been in the past. Rather, it establishes a process for "uncoupling" and thereby serves as the foundation for individual renewal and "new beginnings."

History commences to be rewritten. In 1992, the Select Committee on Children, Youth, and Families of the U.S. House of Representatives held a hearing on "Investing in Families: A Historical Perspective." A fact sheet prepared by committee staff began:

"INVESTING IN FAMILIES: A HISTORICAL PERSPECTIVE"

FACT SHEET

HISTORICAL SHIFTS IN FAMILY COMPOSITION
CHALLENGING CONVENTIONAL WISDOM

While in modern times the percentage of children living with one parent has increased, more children lived with just one parent in Colonial America.

The fact sheet proceeded to list program on program for which federal funds were allegedly reduced in the 1980s. We then come to a summary.

Between 1970 and 1991, the value of AFDC [Aid to Families with Dependent Children] benefits decreased by 41%. In spite of proven success of Head Start, only 28% of eligible children are being served. As of 1990, more than $18 billion in child support went uncollected. At the same time, the poverty rate among single-parent families with children under 18 was 44%. Between 1980 and 1990, the rate of growth in the total Federal budget was four times greater than the rate of growth in children's programs.

In other words, benefits paid to mothers and children have gone down steadily, as indeed they have done. But no proposal is made to restore benefits to an earlier level, or even to maintain their value, as is the case with other "indexed" Social Security programs. Instead we go directly to the subject of education spending.

Nothing new. In 1969, President Nixon proposed a guaranteed income, the Family Assistance Plan. This was described as an "income strategy" as against a "services strategy." It may or may not have been a good idea, but it was a clear one, and the resistance of service providers to it was equally clear. In the end it was defeated, to the huzzahs of the advocates of "welfare rights." What is going on here is simply that a large increase in what once was seen as deviancy has provided opportunity to a wide spectrum of interest groups that benefit from re-defining the problem as essentially normal and doing little to reduce it.

IV

Our *normalizing* category most directly corresponds to Erikson's proposition that "the number of deviant offenders a community can afford to recognize is likely to remain stable over time." Here we are dealing with the popular psychological notion of "denial." In 1965, having reached the conclusion that there would be a dramatic increase in single-parent families, I reached the further conclusion that this would in turn lead to a dramatic increase in crime. In an article in *America,* I wrote:

> From the wild Irish slums of the 19th century Eastern seaboard to the riot-torn suburbs of Los Angeles, there is one unmistakable lesson in American history: a community that allows a large number of young men to grow up in broken families, dominated by women, never acquiring any stable relationship to male authority, never acquiring any set of rational expectations about the future—that community asks for and gets chaos. Crime, violence, unrest, unrestrained lashing out at the whole social structure—that is not only to be expected; it is very near to inevitable.

The inevitable, as we now know, has come to pass, but here again our response is curiously passive. Crime is a more or less continuous subject of political pronouncement, and from time to time it will be at or near the top of opinion polls as a matter of public concern. But it never gets much further than that. In words spoken from the bench, Judge Edwin Torres of the New York State Supreme Court, Twelfth Judicial District, described how "the slaughter of the innocent marches unabated: subway riders, bodega owners, cab drivers, babies; in laundromats, at cash machines, on elevators, in hallways." In personal communication, he writes: "This numbness, this near narco-leptic state can diminish the human condition to the level of combat infantrymen, who, in protracted campaigns, can eat their battlefield rations seated on the bodies of the fallen, friend and foe alike. A society that loses its sense of outrage is doomed to extinction." There is no expectation that this will change, nor any efficacious public insistence that it do so. The crime level has been *normalized.*

Consider the St. Valentine's Day Massacre. In 1929 in Chicago during Prohibition, four gangsters killed seven gangsters on February 14. The nation was shocked. The event became legend. It merits not one but two entries in the *World Book Encyclopedia.* I leave it to others to judge, but it would appear that the society in the 1920s was simply not willing to put up with this degree of deviancy. In the end, the Constitution was amended, and Prohibition, which lay behind so much gangster violence, ended.

In recent years, again in the context of illegal traffic in controlled substances, this form of murder has returned. But it has done so at a level that induces denial. James Q. Wilson comments that Los Angeles has the equivalent of a St. Valentine's Day Massacre every weekend. Even the most ghastly re-enactments of such human slaughter produce only moderate responses. On the morning after the close of the Democratic National Convention in New York City in July, there was such an account in the second section of the *New York Times.* It was not a big story; bottom of the page, but with a headline that got your attention. "3 Slain in Bronx Apartment, but a Baby is Saved." A subhead continued: "A mother's last act was to hide her little girl under the bed." The article described a drug execution; the now-routine blindfolds made from duct tape; a man and a woman and a teenager involved. "Each had been shot once in the head." The police had found them a day later. They also found, under a bed, a three-month-old baby, dehydrated but alive. A lieutenant remarked of the mother, "In her last dying act she protected her baby. She probably knew she was going to die, so she stuffed the baby where she knew it would be safe." But the matter was left there. The police would do their best. But the event passed quickly; forgotten by the next day, it will never make *World Book.*

Nor is it likely that any great heed will be paid to an uncanny reenactment of the Prohibition drama a few months later, also in the Bronx. The *Times* story, page B3, reported:

9 Men Posing as Police

Are Indicted in 3 Murders

Drug Dealers Were Kidnapped for Ransom

The *Daily News* story, same day, page 17, made it *four* murders, adding nice details about torture techniques. The gang members posed as federal Drug Enforcement Administration agents, real badges and all. The victims were drug dealers, whose families were uneasy about calling the police. Ransom seems generally to have been set in the $650,000 range. Some paid. Some got it in the back of the head. So it goes.

Yet, violent killings, often random, go on unabated. Peaks continue to attract some notice. But these are peaks above "average" levels that thirty years ago would have been thought epidemic.

LOS ANGELES, AUG. 24 (Reuters) Twenty-two people were killed in Los Angeles over the weekend, the worst period of violence in the city since it was ravaged by riots earlier this year, the police said today.

Twenty-four others were wounded by gunfire or stabbings, including a 19-year old woman in a wheelchair who was shot in the back when she failed to respond to a motorist who asked for directions in south Los Angeles.

["The guy stuck a gun out of the window and just fired at her," said a police spokesman, Lieut. David Rock. The woman was later described as being in stable condition.

Among those who died was an off-duty officer, shot while investigating reports of a prowler in a neighbor's yard, and a Little League baseball coach who had argued with the father of a boy he was coaching.]

The police said at least nine of the deaths were gang-related, including that of a 14-year old girl killed in a fight between rival gangs.

Fifty-one people were killed in three days of rioting that started April 29 after the acquittal of four police officers in the beating of Rodney G. King.

Los Angeles usually has above-average violence during August, but the police were at a loss to explain the sudden rise. On an average weekend in August, 14 fatalities occur.

Not to be outdone, two days later the poor Bronx came up with a near record, as reported in *New York Newsday:*

Armed with 9-mm. pistols, shotguns and M-16 rifles, a group of masked men and women poured out of two vehicles in the South Bronx early yesterday and sprayed a stretch of Longwood Avenue with a fusillade of bullets, injuring 12 people.

A Kai Erikson of the future will surely need to know that the Department of Justice in 1990 found that Americans reported only about 38 percent of all crimes and 48 percent of violent crimes. This, too, can be seen as a means of *normalizing* crime. In much the same way, the vocabulary of crime reporting can be seen to move toward the normal-seeming. A teacher is shot on her way to class. The *Times* subhead reads: "Struck in the Shoulder in the Year's First Shooting Inside a School." First of the season.

It is too early, however, to know how to regard the arrival of the doctors on the scene declaring crime a "public health emergency." The June 10, 1992, issue of the *Journal of the American Medical Association* was devoted entirely to papers on the subject of violence, principally violence associated with firearms. An editorial in the issue signed by former Surgeon General C. Everett Koop and Dr. George D. Lundberg is entitled: "Violence in America: A Public Health Emergency." Their proposition is admirably succinct.

Regarding violence in our society as purely a sociological matter, or one of law enforcement, has led to unmitigated failure. It is time to test further whether violence can be amenable to medical/public health interventions.

We believe violence in America to be a public health emergency, largely unresponsive to methods thus far used in its control. The solutions are very complex, but possible.

The authors cited the relative success of epidemiologists in gaining some jurisdiction in the area of motor vehicle casualties by re-defining what had been seen as a law enforcement issue into a public health issue. Again, this process began during the Harriman administration in New York in the 1950s. In the 1960s the morbidity and mortality associated with automobile crashes was, it could be argued, a major public health problem; the public health strategy, it could also be argued, brought the problem under a measure of control. Not in "the 1970s and 1980s," as the *Journal of the American Medical Association* would have us think: the federal legislation involved was signed in 1965. Such a strategy would surely produce insights into the control of violence that elude law enforcement professionals, but whether it would change anything is another question.

For some years now I have had legislation in the Senate that would prohibit the manufacture of .25 and .32 caliber bullets. These are the two calibers most typically used with the guns known as Saturday Night Specials. "Guns don't kill people," I argue, "bullets do."

Moreover, we have a two-century supply of handguns but only a four-year supply of ammunition. A public health official would immediately see the logic of trying to control the supply of bullets rather than of guns.

Even so, now that the doctor has come, it is important that criminal violence not be defined down by epidemiologists. Doctors Koop and Lundberg note that in 1990 in the state of Texas "deaths from firearms, for the first time in many decades, surpassed deaths from motor vehicles, by 3,443 to 3,309." A good comparison. And yet keep in mind that the number of motor vehicle deaths, having leveled off since the 1960s, is now pretty well accepted as normal at somewhat less than 50,000 a year, which is somewhat less than the level of the 1960s—the "carnage," as it once was thought to be, is now accepted as normal. This is the price we pay for high-speed transportation: there is a benefit associated with it. But there is no benefit associated with homicide, and no good in getting used to it. Epidemiologists have powerful insights that can contribute to lessening the medical trauma, but they must be wary of normalizing the social pathology that leads to such trauma.

V

The hope—if there be such—of this essay has been twofold. It is, first, to suggest that the Durkheim constant, as I put it, is maintained by a dynamic process which adjusts upwards and *downwards*. Liberals have traditionally been alert for upward redefining that does injustice to individuals. Conservatives have been correspondingly sensitive to downward redefining that weakens societal standards. Might it not help if we could all agree that there is a dynamic at work here? It is not revealed truth, nor yet a scientifically derived formula. It is simply a pattern we observe in ourselves. Nor is it rigid. There may once have been an unchanging supply of jail cells which more or less determined the number of prisoners. No longer. We are building new prisons at a prodigious rate. Similarly, the executioner is back. There is something of a competition in Congress to think up new offenses for which the death penalty is seemed the only available deterrent. Possibly also modes of execution, as in "fry the kingpins." Even so, we are getting used to a lot of behavior that is not good for us.

As noted earlier, Durkheim states that there is "nothing desirable" about pain. Surely what he meant was that there is nothing pleasurable. Pain, even so, is an indispensable warning signal. But societies under stress, much like individuals, will turn to pain killers of various kinds that end up concealing real damage. There is surely nothing desirable about *this*. If our analysis wins general acceptance, if, for example, more of us came to share Judge Torres's genuine alarm at "the trivialization of the lunatic crime rate" in his city (and mine), we might surprise ourselves how well we respond to the manifest decline of the American civic order. Might.

PC and Rape

If police, judges, legislators, and portions of the general public work hard to adjust to the rising tide of crime and make it easier to live with, certain transgressions which not so long ago were dismissed or swept under the carpet are now less easily accepted or ignored. Rape, for example, is now denounced and condemned, as it should be. But cases of rape not only raise difficult questions of proof, with the verdict hanging on one person's word against another's; they also intersect with the ongoing debate concerning women's rights in a (Western) world where male domination has been whittled down by hard struggle and bad conscience but where legal equality raises new problems. Affirmative action has bred affirmative reaction; aggression on all sides has become more aggressive.

It is not insignificant that much of the ongoing argument on rape involves women debating women: not only reactionaries against radicals, but emancipated women warning other women that emancipation involves risks and that even the fullest life has to be lived with caution. This advice is sometimes described as being politically incorrect, indifferent to the rights of victims. Camille Paglia's essay gives the issue a fresh perspective. Prankish and aggressive, Paglia is full of verve and of an uncommon quality: common sense. Her reflections on rape have implications that go beyond brutal outrage to suggest that the world and one's self-interest call for foresight and caution, whatever one's gender.

Camille Paglia: "Rape and Modern Sex War"

Rape is an outrage that cannot be tolerated in civilized society. Yet feminism, which has waged a crusade for rape to be taken more seriously, has put young women in danger by hiding the truth about sex from them.

––––––––––
From Camille Paglia, "Rape and Modern Sex War," *New York Newsday* (January 27, 1991).

In dramatizing the pervasiveness of rape, feminists have told young women that before they have sex with a man, they must give consent as explicit as a legal contract's. In this way, young women have been convinced that they have been the victims of rape. On elite campuses in the Northeast and on the West Coast, they have held consciousness-raising sessions, petitioned administrations, demanded inquests. At Brown University, outraged, panicky "victims" have scrawled the names of alleged attackers on the walls of women's rest rooms. What marital rape was to the Seventies, "date rape" is to the Nineties.

The incidence and seriousness of rape do not require this kind of exaggeration. Real acquaintance rape is nothing new. It has been a horrible problem for women for all of recorded history. Once fathers and brothers protected women from rape. Once the penalty for rape was death. I come from a fierce Italian tradition where, not so long ago in the motherland, a rapist would end up knifed, castrated, and hung out to dry.

But the old clans and small rural communities have broken down. In our cities, on our campuses far from home, young women are vulnerable and defenseless. Feminism has not prepared them for this. Feminism keeps saying the sexes are the same. It keeps telling women they can do anything, go anywhere, say anything, wear anything. No, they can't. Women will always be in sexual danger.

One of my male students recently slept overnight with a friend in a passageway of the Great Pyramid in Egypt. He described the moon and sand, the ancient silence and eerie echoes. I will never experience that. I am a woman. I am not stupid enough to believe I could ever be safe there. There is a world of solitary adventure I will never have. Women have always known these somber truths. But feminism, with its pie-in-the-sky fantasies about the perfect world, keeps young women from seeing life as it is.

We must remedy social injustice whenever we can. But there are some things we cannot change. There are sexual differences that are based in biology. Academic feminism is lost in a fog of social constructionism. It believes we are totally the product of our environment. This idea was invented by Rousseau. He was wrong. Emboldened by dumb French language theory, academic feminists repeat the same hollow slogans over and over to each other. Their view of sex is naïve and prudish. Leaving sex to the feminists is like letting your dog vacation at the taxidermist's.

The sexes are at war. Men must struggle for identity against the overwhelming power of their mothers. Women have menstruation to tell them they are women. Men must do or risk something to be men. Men become masculine only when other men say they are. Having sex with a woman is one way a boy becomes a man.

College men are at their hormonal peak. They have just left their mothers and are questing for their male identity. In groups, they are dangerous. A woman going to a fraternity party is walking into Testosterone Flats, full of prickly cacti and blazing guns. If she goes, she should be armed with resolute alertness. She should arrive with girl-friends and leave with them. A girl who lets herself get dead drunk at a fraternity party is a fool. A girl who goes upstairs alone with a brother at a fraternity party is an idiot. Feminists call this "blaming the victim." I call it common sense.

For a decade, feminists have drilled their disciples to say, "Rape is a crime of violence but not of sex." This sugar-coated Shirley Temple nonsense has exposed young women to disaster. Misled by feminism, they do not expect rape from the nice boys from good homes who sit next to them in class.

Aggression and eroticism are deeply intertwined. Hunt, pursuit, and capture are biologically programmed into male sexuality. Generation after generation, men must be educated, refined, and ethically persuaded away from their tendency toward anarchy and brutishness. Society is not the enemy, as feminism ignorantly claims. Society is woman's protection against rape. Feminism, with its solemn Carry Nation repressiveness, does not see what is for men the eroticism or fun element in rape, especially the wild, infectious delirium of gang rape. Women who do not understand rape cannot defend themselves against it.

The date-rape controversy shows feminism hitting the wall of its own broken promises. The women of my Sixties generation were the first respectable girls in history to swear like sailors, get drunk, stay out all night—in short, to act like men. We sought total sexual freedom and equality. But as time passed, we woke up to cold reality. The old double standard protected women. When anything goes, it's women who lose.

Today's young women don't know what they want. They see that feminism has not brought sexual happiness. The theatrics of public rage over date rape are their way of restoring the old sexual rules that were shattered by my generation. Because nothing about the sexes has really changed. The comic film *Where the Boys Are* (1960), the ultimate expression of Fifties man-chasing, still speaks directly to our time. It shows smart, lively women skillfully anticipating and fending off the dozens of strategies with which horny men try to get them into bed. The agonizing date-rape subplot and climax are brilliantly done. The victim, Yvette Mimieux, makes mistake after mistake, obvious to the other girls. She allows herself to be lured away from her girlfriends and into isolation with boys whose character and intentions she misreads. *Where the Boys Are* tells the truth. It shows courtship as a dangerous game in which the signals are not verbal but subliminal.

Neither militant feminism, which is obsessed with politically correct language, nor academic feminism, which believes that knowledge and experience are "constituted by" language, can understand preverbal or nonverbal communication. Feminism, focusing on sexual politics, cannot see that sex exists in and through the body. Sexual desire and arousal cannot be fully translated into verbal terms. This is why men and women misunderstand each other.

Trying to remake the future, feminism cut itself off from sexual history. It discarded and suppressed the sexual myths of literature, art, and religion. Those myths show us the turbulence, the mysteries and passions of sex. In mythology we see men's sexual anxiety, their fear of woman's dominance. Much sexual violence is rooted in men's sense of psychological weakness toward women. It takes many men to deal with one woman. Woman's voracity is a persistent motif. Clara Bow, it was rumored, took on the USC football team on weekends. Marilyn Monroe, singing "Diamonds Are a Girl's Best Friend," rules a conga line of men in tuxes. Half-clad Cher, in the video for "If I Could Turn Back Time," deranges a battleship of screaming sailors and straddles a pink-lit cannon. Feminism, coveting social power, is blind to a woman's cosmic sexual power.

To understand rape, you must study the past. There never was and never will be sexual harmony. Every woman must take personal responsibility for her sexuality, which is nature's red flame. She must be prudent and cautious about where she goes and with whom. When she makes a mistake, she must accept the consequences and, through self-criticism, resolve never to make that mistake again. Running to Mommy and Daddy on the campus grievance committee is unworthy of strong women. Posting lists of guilty men in the toilet is cowardly, infantile stuff.

The Italian philosophy of life espouses high-energy confrontation. A male student makes a vulgar remark about your breasts? Don't slink off to whimper and simper with the campus shrinking violets. Deal with it. On the spot. Say, "Shut up, you jerk! And crawl back to the barnyard where you belong!" In general, women who project this take-charge attitude toward life get harassed less often. I see too many dopey, immature, self-pitying women walking around like melting sticks of butter. It's the Yvette Mimieux syndrome: make me happy. And listen to me weep when I'm not.

The date-rape debate is already smothering in propaganda churned out by the expensive Northeastern colleges and universities, with their overconcentration of boring, uptight academic feminists and spoiled, affluent students. Beware of the deep manipulativeness of rich students who were neglected by their parents. They love to turn the campus into hysterical psychodramas of sexual transgression, followed by assertions of parental authority and concern. And don't look for sexual enlightenment from academe, which spews out mountains of books but never looks at life directly.

As a fan of football and rock music, I see in the simple, swaggering masculinity of the jock and in the noisy posturing of the heavy-metal guitarist certain fundamental, unchanging truths about sex. Masculinity is aggressive, unstable, combustible. It is also the most creative cultural force in history. Women must reorient themselves toward the elemental powers of sex, which can strengthen or destroy.

The only solution to date rape is female self-awareness and self-control. A woman's number one line of defense is herself. When a real rape occurs, she should report it to the police. Complaining to college committees because the courts "take too long" is ridiculous. College administrations are not a branch of the judiciary. They are not equipped or trained for legal inquiry. Colleges must alert incoming students to the problems and dangers of adulthood. Then colleges must stand back and get out of the sex game.

Epilogue

A copybook is a primer containing models for learners to imitate. Copybook maxims, copybook morality, represent the basic values that society once sought to inculcate into its members.

Written in 1919, Rudyard Kipling's poem suggests that most generations face similar problems and that most sooner or later revert to traditional values when they try to cope; but few learn the lessons of the past. Kipling did not mean that the problems of his time could actually be solved, but that experience seems to teach that it's hard to learn from experience.

Rudyard Kipling: "The Gods of the Copybook Headings"

As I pass through my incarnations in every age and race,
I make my proper prostrations to the Gods of the Market-Place.
Peering through reverent fingers I watch them flourish and fall,
And the Gods of the Copybook Headings, I notice, outlast them all.

We were living in trees when they met us. They showed us each in turn
That Water would certainly wet us, as Fire would certainly burn:
But we found them lacking in Uplift, Vision and Breadth of Mind,
So we left them to teach the Gorillas while we followed the March of Mankind.

We moved as the Spirit listed. *They* never altered their pace,
Being neither cloud nor wind-borne like the Gods of the Market-Place;
But they always caught up with our progress, and presently word would come
That a tribe had been wiped off its icefield, or the lights had gone out in Rome.

With the Hopes that our World is built on they were utterly out of touch.
They denied that the Moon was Stilton; they denied she was even Dutch.
They denied that Wishes were Horses; they denied that a Pig had Wings.
So we worshipped the Gods of the Market Who promised these beautiful things.

When the Cambrian measures were forming, They promised perpetual peace.
They swore, if we gave them our weapons, that the wars of the tribes would cease.
But when we disarmed They sold us and delivered us bound to our foe,
And the Gods of the Copybook Headings said: *"Stick to the Devil you know."*

On the first Feminian Sandstones we were promised the Fuller Life
(Which started by loving our neighbour and ended by loving his wife)
Till our women had no more children and the men lost reason and faith,
And the Gods of the Copybook Headings said: *"The Wages of Sin is Death."*

In the Carboniferous Epoch we were promised abundance for all,
By robbing selected Peter to pay for collective Paul;
But, though we had plenty of money, there was nothing our money could buy,
And the Gods of the Copybook Headings said: *"If you don't work you die."*

Then the Gods of the Market tumbled, and their smooth-tongued wizards
    withdrew,
And the hearts of the meanest were humbled and began to believe it was true
That All is not Gold that Glitters, and Two and Two make Four—
And the Gods of the Copybook Headings limped up to explain it once more

       .   .   .   .

As it will be in the future, it was at the birth of Man—
There are only four things certain since Social Progress began:
That the Dog returns to his Vomit and the Sow returns to her Mire,
And the burnt Fool's bandaged finger goes wabbling back to the Fire;
And that after this is accomplished, and the brave new world begins
When all men are paid for existing and no man must pay for his sins,
As surely as Water will wet us, as surely as Fire will burn,
The Gods of the Copybook Headings with terror and slaughter return!